Toyota Supra Automotive Repair Manual

by Mike Stubblefield, Olaf Wolff, and John H Haynes

Member of the Guild of Motoring Writers

Models covered:

All Toyota Supra models

1979 through 1992

ABCD

(12A5 - 92025)

(1139)

Haynes Publishing Group

Sparkford Nr Yeovil

Somerset BA22 7JJ England

Haynes North America, Inc

861 Lawrence Drive

Newbury Park

California 91320 USA

Acknowledgements
We are grateful for the help and cooperation of the Toyota Motor Corporation for their assistance with technical information, certain illustrations and vehicle photos. Technical writers who contributed to this project include Robert Maddox.

A book in the Haynes Automotive Repair Manual Series

Printed in the U.S.A.

ISBN 1 56392 043 3

Library of Congress Catalog Card Number 92-73862

92-400

Contents

Haynes mechanic, author and photographer with Toyota Supra

About this manual

Its purpose

The purpose of this manual is to help you get the best value from your vehicle. It can do so in several ways. It can help you decide what work must be done, even if you choose to have it done by a dealer service department or a repair shop; it provides information and procedures for routine maintenance and servicing; and it offers diagnostic and repair procedures to follow when trouble occurs.

We hope you use the manual to tackle the work yourself. For many simpler jobs, doing it yourself may be quicker than arranging an appointment to get the vehicle into a shop and making the trips to leave it and pick it up. More importantly, a lot of money can be saved by avoiding the expense the shop must pass on to you to cover its labor and overhead costs. An added benefit is the sense of satisfaction and accomplishment that you feel after doing the job yourself.

Using the manual

The manual is divided into Chapters. Each Chapter is divided into numbered Sections, which are headed in bold type between horizontal lines. Each Section consists of consecutively numbered paragraphs.

At the beginning of each numbered Section you will be referred to any illustrations which apply to the procedures in that Section. The reference numbers used in illustration captions pinpoint the pertinent Section and the Step within that Section. That is, illustration 3.2 means the illustration refers to Section 3 and Step (or paragraph) 2 within that Section.

Procedures, once described in the text, are not normally repeated. When it's necessary to refer to another Chapter, the reference will be given as Chapter and Section number. Cross references given without use of the word "Chapter" apply to Sections and/or paragraphs in the same Chapter. For example, "see Section 8" means in the same Chapter.

References to the left or right side of the vehicle assume you are sitting in the driver's seat, facing forward.

Even though we have prepared this manual with extreme care, neither the publisher nor the author can accept responsibility for any errors in, or omissions from, the information given.

NOTE

A **Note** provides information necessary to properly complete a procedure or information which will make the procedure easier to understand.

CAUTION

A **Caution** provides a special procedure or special steps which must be taken while completing the procedure where the Caution is found. Not heeding a Caution can result in damage to the assembly being worked on.

WARNING

A Warning provides a special procedure or special steps which must be taken while completing the procedure where the Warning is found. Not heeding a Warning can result in personal injury.

Introduction to the Toyota Supra

The Toyota Supra features a front engine/rear-wheel drive layout.

The inline six-cylinder engines used in these vehicles are equipped with electronic port-type fuel injection. Some later models are turbocharged.

The engine drives the rear wheels through either a four or five-speed manual or automatic transmission via a driveshaft. A solid rear axle is used on earlier models while most later models have independent rear suspension.

Front suspension is independent, featuring coil spring/strut units. Coil springs and separate shock absorbers are used at the rear. Steering is rack-and-pinion type with power assist available on most models.

Brakes are power assisted discs at the front and self-adjusting drums at the rear (some later models have disc rear brakes).

Vehicle and engine identification numbers

Modifications are a continuing and unpublicized part of vehicle manufacturing. Since spare parts manuals and lists are compiled on a numerical basis, the individual vehicle numbers are essential to correctly identify the component required.

Vehicle Identification Number (VIN)

The VIN is very important because it's used for title and registration purposes. The VIN is stamped into a metal plate fastened to the dashboard, close to the windshield on the driver's side of the vehicle. It is also on the driver's door jamb and on the firewall in the engine compartment **(see illustration)**. It contains valuable information such as where and when the vehicle was manufactured, the model year and the body style.

Engine identification number

The engine identification number is stamped on a pad on the lower right side of the engine block, towards the front **(see illustration)**.

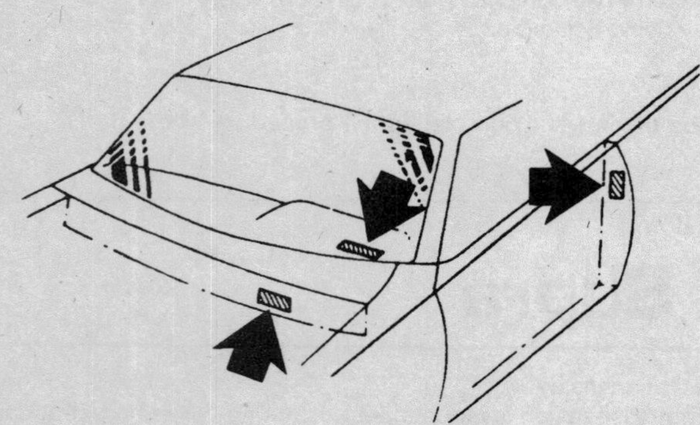

The Vehicle Identification Number (VIN) is located on the cowl in the engine compartment, on the driver's side door post and on a plate on the top of the dash (visible through the windshield)

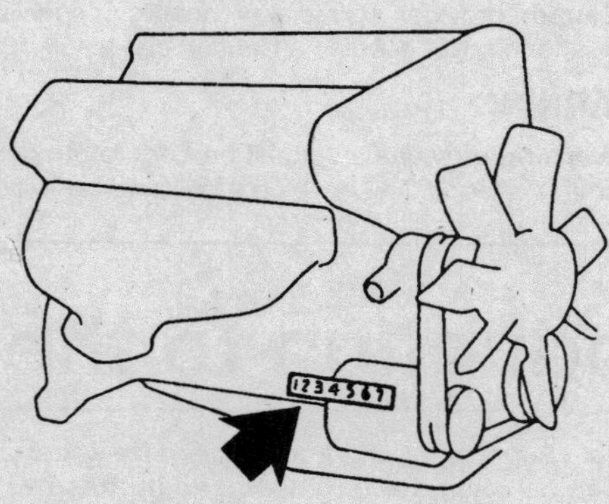

The engine identification number is located on the lower right side of the engine block, towards the front

Buying parts

Replacement parts are available from many sources, which generally fall into one of two categories - authorized dealer parts departments and independent retail auto parts stores. Our advice concerning these parts is as follows:

Retail auto parts stores: Good auto parts stores will stock frequently needed components which wear out relatively fast, such as clutch components, exhaust systems, brake parts, tune-up parts, etc. These stores often supply new or reconditioned parts on an exchange basis, which can save a considerable amount of money. Discount auto parts stores are often very good places to buy materials and parts needed for general vehicle maintenance such as oil, grease, filters, spark plugs, belts, touch-up paint, bulbs, etc. They also usually sell tools and general accessories, have convenient hours, charge lower prices and can often be found not far from home.

Authorized dealer parts department: This is the best source for parts which are unique to the vehicle and not generally available elsewhere (such as major engine parts, transmission parts, trim pieces, etc.).

Warranty information: If the vehicle is still covered under warranty, be sure that any replacement parts purchased - regardless of the source - do not invalidate the warranty!

To be sure of obtaining the correct parts, have engine and chassis numbers available and, if possible, take the old parts along for positive identification.

Maintenance techniques, tools and working facilities

Maintenance techniques

There are a number of techniques involved in maintenance and repair that will be referred to throughout this manual. Application of these techniques will enable the home mechanic to be more efficient, better organized and capable of performing the various tasks properly, which will ensure that the repair job is thorough and complete.

Fasteners

Fasteners are nuts, bolts, studs and screws used to hold two or more parts together. There are a few things to keep in mind when working with fasteners. Almost all of them use a locking device of some type, either a lockwasher, locknut, locking tab or thread adhesive. All threaded fasteners should be clean and straight, with undamaged threads and undamaged corners on the hex head where the wrench fits. Develop the habit of replacing all damaged nuts and bolts with new ones. Special locknuts with nylon or fiber inserts can only be used once. If they are removed, they lose their locking ability and must be replaced with new ones.

Rusted nuts and bolts should be treated with a penetrating fluid to ease removal and prevent breakage. Some mechanics use turpentine in a spout-type oil can, which works quite well. After applying the rust penetrant, let it work for a few minutes before trying to loosen the nut or bolt. Badly rusted fasteners may have to be chiseled or sawed off or removed with a special nut breaker, available at tool stores.

If a bolt or stud breaks off in an assembly, it can be drilled and removed with a special tool commonly available for this purpose. Most automotive machine shops can perform this task, as well as other repair procedures, such as the repair of threaded holes that have been stripped out.

Flat washers and lockwashers, when removed from an assembly, should always be replaced exactly as removed. Replace any damaged washers with new ones. Never use a lockwasher on any soft metal surface (such as aluminum), thin sheet metal or plastic.

Fastener sizes

For a number of reasons, automobile manufacturers are making wider and wider use of metric fasteners. Therefore, it is important to be able to tell the difference between standard (sometimes called U.S. or SAE) and metric hardware, since they cannot be interchanged.

All bolts, whether standard or metric, are sized according to diameter, thread pitch and length. For example, a standard 1/2 - 13 x 1 bolt is 1/2 inch in diameter, has 13 threads per inch and is 1 inch long. An M12 - 1.75 x 25 metric bolt is 12 mm in diameter, has a thread pitch of 1.75 mm (the distance between threads) and is 25 mm long. The two bolts are nearly identical, and easily confused, but they are not interchangeable.

In addition to the differences in diameter, thread pitch and length, metric and standard bolts can also be distinguished by examining the bolt heads. To begin with, the distance across the flats on a standard bolt head is measured in inches, while the same dimension on a metric bolt is sized in millimeters (the same is true for nuts). As a result, a standard wrench should not be used on a metric bolt and a metric wrench should not be used on a standard bolt. Also, most standard bolts have slashes radiating out from the center of the head to denote the grade or strength of the bolt, which is an indication of the amount of torque that can be applied to it. The greater the number of slashes, the greater the strength of the bolt. Grades 0 through 5 are commonly used on automobiles. Metric bolts have a property class (grade) number, rather than a slash, molded into their heads to indicate bolt strength. In this case, the higher the number, the stronger the bolt. Property class numbers 8.8, 9.8 and 10.9 are commonly used on automobiles.

Strength markings can also be used to distinguish standard hex nuts from metric hex nuts. Many standard nuts have dots stamped into one side, while metric nuts are marked with a number. The greater the number of dots, or the higher the number, the greater the strength of the nut.

Metric studs are also marked on their ends according to property class (grade). Larger studs are numbered (the same as metric bolts), while smaller studs carry a geometric code to denote grade.

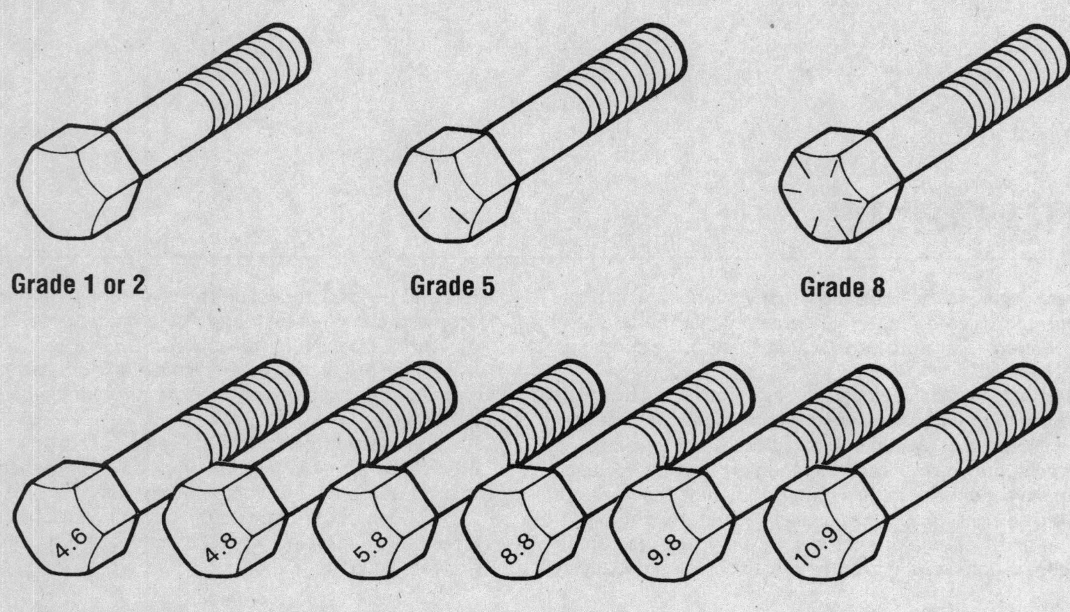

Bolt strength markings (top - standard/SAE/USS; bottom - metric)

Grade	Identification
Hex Nut Grade 5	3 Dots
Hex Nut Grade 8	6 Dots

Standard hex nut strength markings

Class	Identification
Hex Nut Property Class 9	Arabic 9
Hex Nut Property Class 10	Arabic10

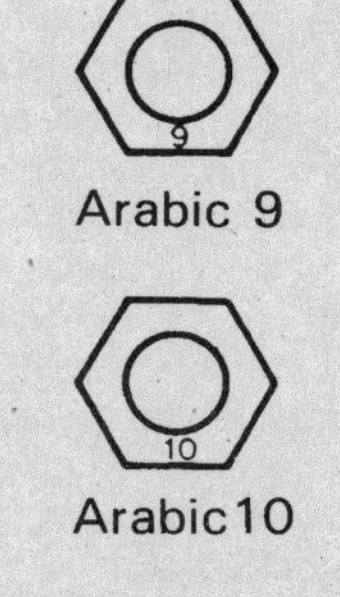

Metric hex nut strength markings

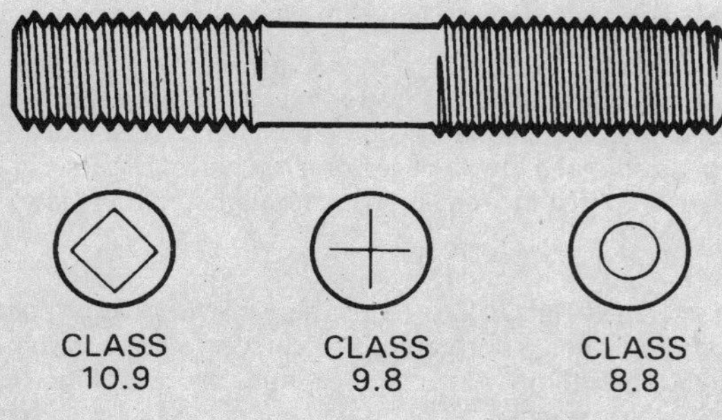

Metric stud length markings

It should be noted that many fasteners, especially Grades 0 through 2, have no distinguishing marks on them. When such is the case, the only way to determine whether it is standard or metric is to measure the thread pitch or compare it to a known fastener of the same size.

Standard fasteners are often referred to as SAE, as opposed to metric. However, it should be noted that SAE technically refers to a non-metric fine thread fastener only. Coarse thread non-metric fasteners are referred to as USS sizes.

Since fasteners of the same size (both standard and metric) may have different strength ratings, be sure to reinstall any bolts, studs or nuts removed from your vehicle in their original locations. Also, when replacing a fastener with a new one, make sure that the new one has a strength rating equal to or greater than the original.

Tightening sequences and procedures

Most threaded fasteners should be tightened to a specific torque value (torque is the twisting force applied to a threaded component such as a nut or bolt). Overtightening the fastener can weaken it and cause it to break, while undertightening can cause it to eventually come loose. Bolts, screws and studs, depending on the material they are made of and their thread diameters, have specific torque values, many of which are noted in the Specifications at the beginning of each Chapter. Be sure to follow the torque recommendations closely. For fasteners not assigned a specific torque, a general torque value chart is presented here as a guide. These torque values are for dry (unlubricated) fasteners threaded into steel or cast iron (not aluminum). As was previously mentioned, the size and grade of a fastener determine

Metric thread sizes	**Ft-lbs**	**Nm**
M-6	6 to 9	9 to 12
M-8	14 to 21	19 to 28
M-10	28 to 40	38 to 54
M-12	50 to 71	68 to 96
M-14	80 to 140	109 to 154
Pipe thread sizes		
1/8	5 to 8	7 to 10
1/4	12 to 18	17 to 24
3/8	22 to 33	30 to 44
1/2	25 to 35	34 to 47
U.S. thread sizes		
1/4 - 20	6 to 9	9 to 12
5/16 - 18	12 to 18	17 to 24
5/16 - 24	14 to 20	19 to 27
3/8 - 16	22 to 32	30 to 43
3/8 - 24	27 to 38	37 to 51
7/16 - 14	40 to 55	55 to 74
7/16 - 20	40 to 60	55 to 81
1/2 - 13	55 to 80	75 to 108

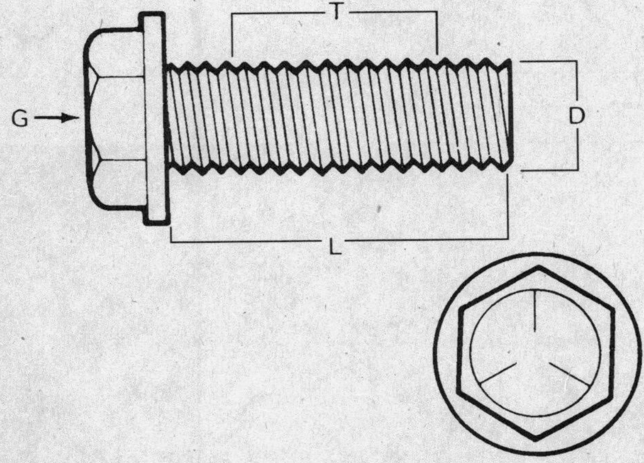

Standard (SAE and USS) bolt dimensions/grade marks

G *Grade marks (bolt length)*
L *Length (in inches)*
T *Thread pitch (number of threads per inch)*
D *Nominal diameter (in inches)*

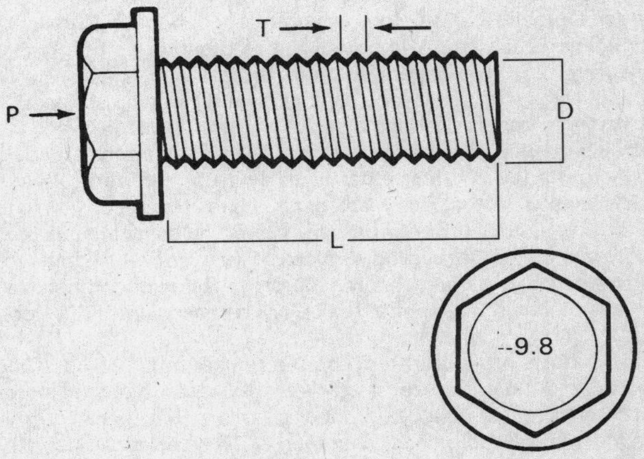

Metric bolt dimensions/grade marks

P *Property class (bolt strength)*
L *Length (in millimeters)*
T *Thread pitch (distance between threads in millimeters)*
D *Diameter*

the amount of torque that can safely be applied to it. The figures listed here are approximate for Grade 2 and Grade 3 fasteners. Higher grades can tolerate higher torque values.

Fasteners laid out in a pattern, such as cylinder head bolts, oil pan bolts, differential cover bolts, etc., must be loosened or tightened in sequence to avoid warping the component. This sequence will normally be shown in the appropriate Chapter. If a specific pattern is not given, the following procedures can be used to prevent warping.

Initially, the bolts or nuts should be assembled finger-tight only. Next, they should be tightened one full turn each, in a criss-cross or diagonal pattern. After each one has been tightened one full turn, return to the first one and tighten them all one-half turn, following the same pattern. Finally, tighten each of them one-quarter turn at a time until each fastener has been tightened to the proper torque. To loosen and remove the fasteners, the procedure would be reversed.

Component disassembly

Component disassembly should be done with care and purpose to help ensure that the parts go back together properly. Always keep track of the sequence in which parts are removed. Make note of special characteristics or marks on parts that can be installed more than one way, such as a grooved thrust washer on a shaft. It is a good idea to lay the disassembled parts out on a clean surface in the order that they were removed. It may also be helpful to make sketches or take instant photos of components before removal.

When removing fasteners from a component, keep track of their locations. Sometimes threading a bolt back in a part, or putting the washers and nut back on a stud, can prevent mix-ups later. If nuts and bolts cannot be returned to their original locations, they should be kept in a compartmented box or a series of small boxes. A cupcake or muffin tin is ideal for this purpose, since each cavity can hold the bolts and nuts from a particular area (i.e. oil pan bolts, valve cover bolts, engine mount bolts, etc.). A pan of this type is especially helpful when working on assemblies with very small parts, such as the carburetor, alternator, valve train or interior dash and trim pieces. The cavities can be marked with paint or tape to identify the contents.

Whenever wiring looms, harnesses or connectors are separated, it is a good idea to identify the two halves with numbered pieces of masking tape so they can be easily reconnected.

Gasket sealing surfaces

Throughout any vehicle, gaskets are used to seal the mating surfaces between two parts and keep lubricants, fluids, vacuum or pressure contained in an assembly.

Many times these gaskets are coated with a liquid or paste-type gasket sealing compound before assembly. Age, heat and pressure can sometimes cause the two parts to stick together so tightly that they are very difficult to separate. Often, the assembly can be loosened by striking it with a soft-face hammer near the mating surfaces. A regular hammer can be used if a block of wood is placed between the hammer and the part. Do not hammer on cast parts or parts that could be easily damaged. With any particularly stubborn part, always recheck to make sure that every fastener has been removed.

Avoid using a screwdriver or bar to pry apart an assembly, as they can easily mar the gasket sealing surfaces of the parts, which must remain smooth. If prying is absolutely necessary, use an old broom handle, but keep in mind that extra clean up will be necessary if the wood splinters.

After the parts are separated, the old gasket must be carefully scraped off and the gasket surfaces cleaned. Stubborn gasket material can be soaked with rust penetrant or treated with a special chemical to soften it so it can be easily scraped off. A scraper can be fashioned from a piece of copper tubing by flattening and sharpening one end. Copper is recommended because it is usually softer than the surfaces to be scraped, which reduces the chance of gouging the part. Some gaskets can be removed with a wire brush, but regardless of the method used, the mating surfaces must be left clean and smooth. If for some reason the gasket surface is gouged, then a gasket sealer thick enough to fill scratches will have to be used during reassembly of the components. For most applications, a non-drying (or semi-drying) gasket sealer should be used.

Hose removal tips

Warning: *If the vehicle is equipped with air conditioning, do not disconnect any of the A/C hoses without first having the system depressurized by a dealer service department or a service station.*

Hose removal precautions closely parallel gasket removal precautions. Avoid scratching or gouging the surface that the hose mates against or the connection may leak. This is especially true for radiator hoses. Because of various chemical reactions, the rubber in hoses can bond itself to the metal spigot that the hose fits over. To remove a hose, first loosen the hose clamps that secure it to the spigot. Then, with slip-joint pliers, grab the hose at the clamp and rotate it around the spigot. Work it back and forth until it is completely free, then pull it off. Silicone or other lubricants will ease removal if they can be applied between the hose and the outside of the spigot. Apply the same lubricant to the inside of the hose and the outside of the spigot to simplify installation.

As a last resort (and if the hose is to be replaced with a new one anyway), the rubber can be slit with a knife and the hose peeled from the spigot. If this must be done, be careful that the metal connection is not damaged.

If a hose clamp is broken or damaged, do not reuse it. Wire-type clamps usually weaken with age, so it is a good idea to replace them with screw-type clamps whenever a hose is removed.

Tools

A selection of good tools is a basic requirement for anyone who plans to maintain and repair his or her own vehicle. For the owner who has few tools, the initial investment might seem high, but when compared to the spiraling costs of professional auto maintenance and repair, it is a wise one.

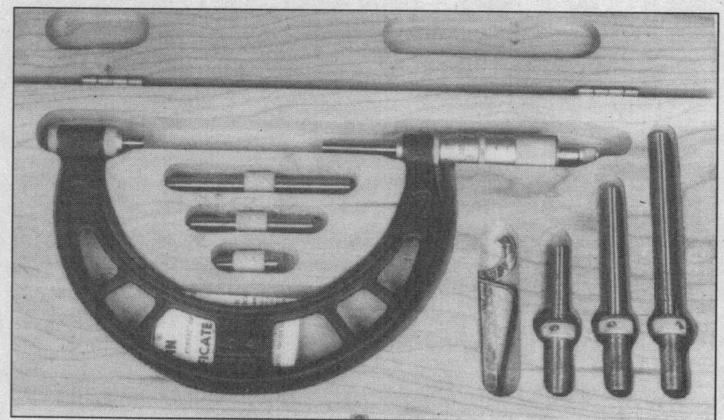

Micrometer set

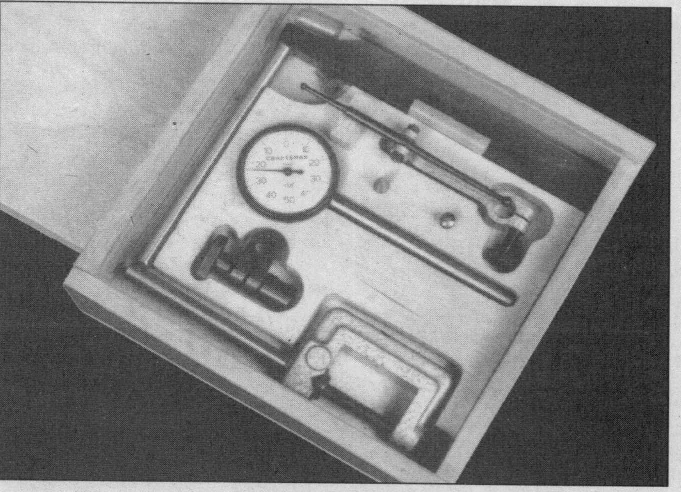

Dial indicator set

Dial caliper

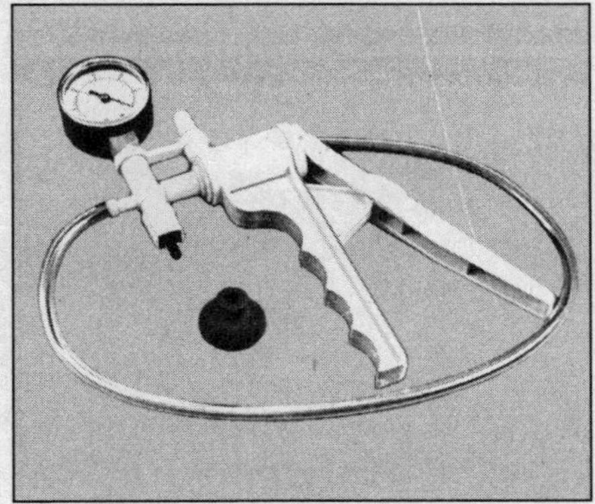
Hand-operated vacuum pump

Timing light

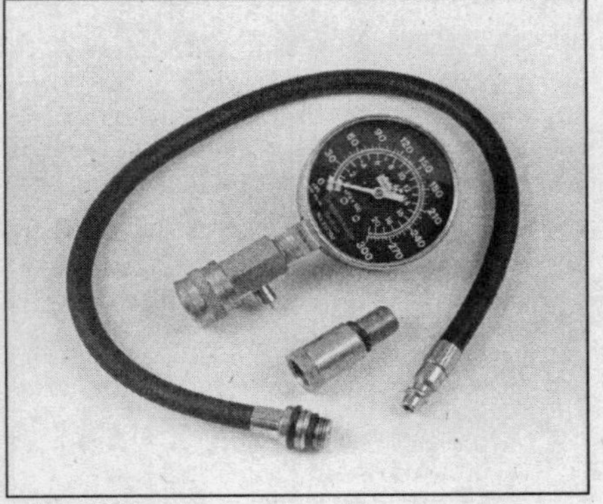
Compression gauge with spark plug hole adapter

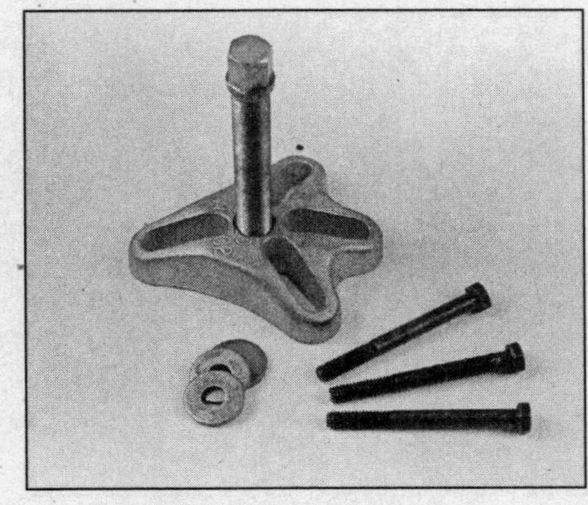
Damper/steering wheel puller

General purpose puller

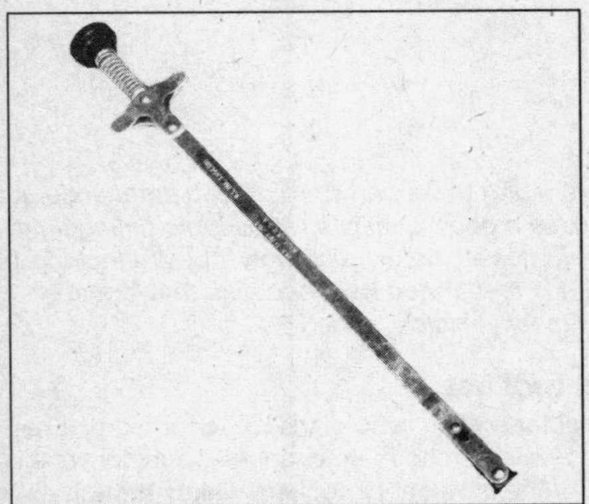
Hydraulic lifter removal tool

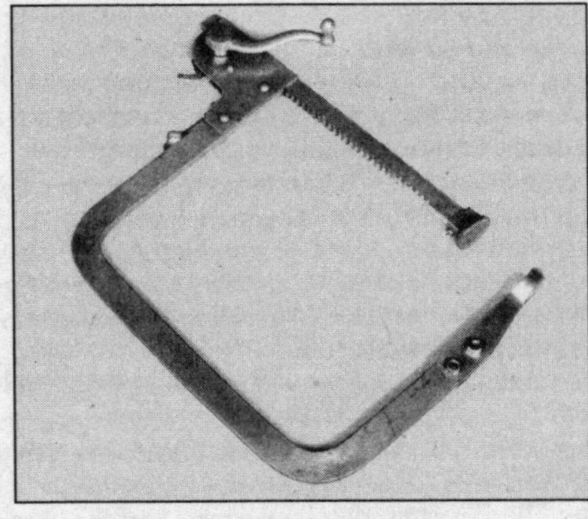
Valve spring compressor

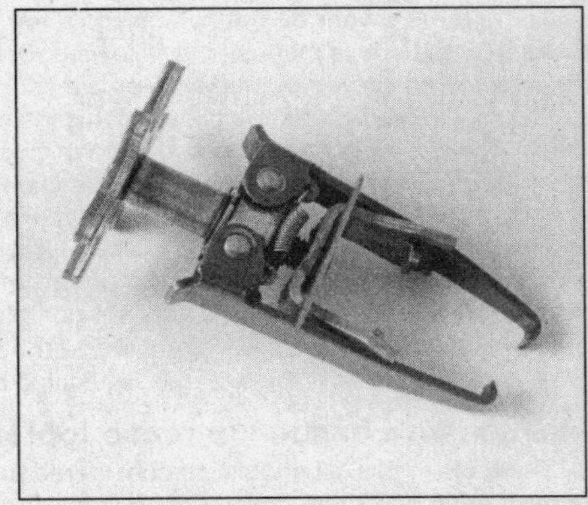
Valve spring compressor

Ridge reamer

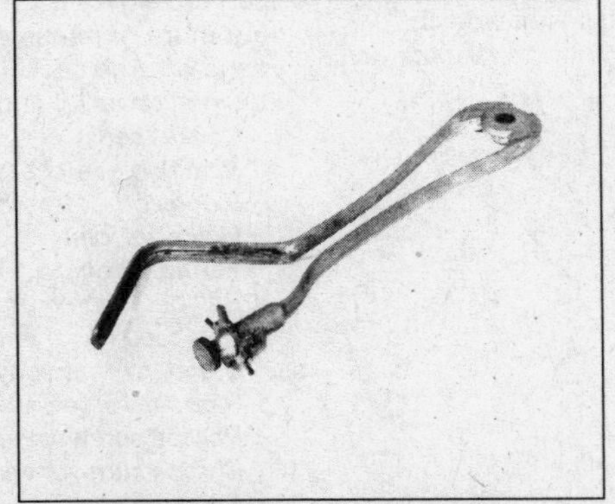
Piston ring groove cleaning tool

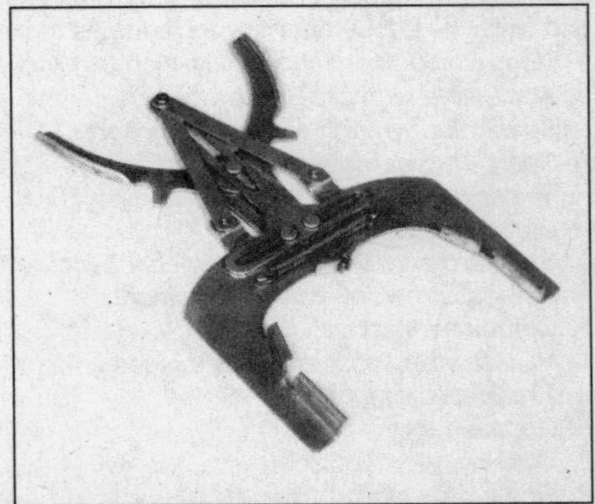
Ring removal/installation tool

Ring compressor

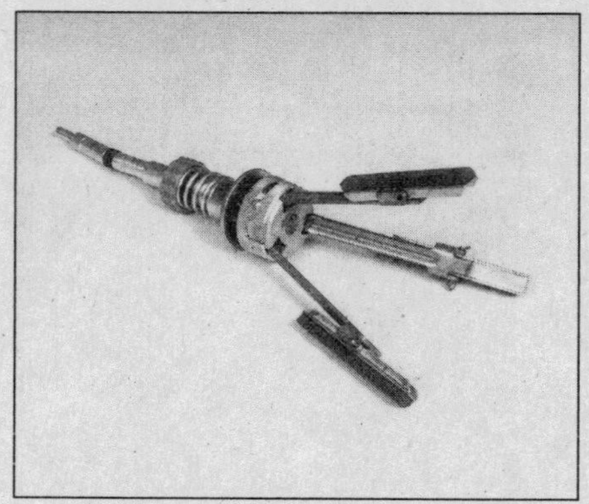
Cylinder hone

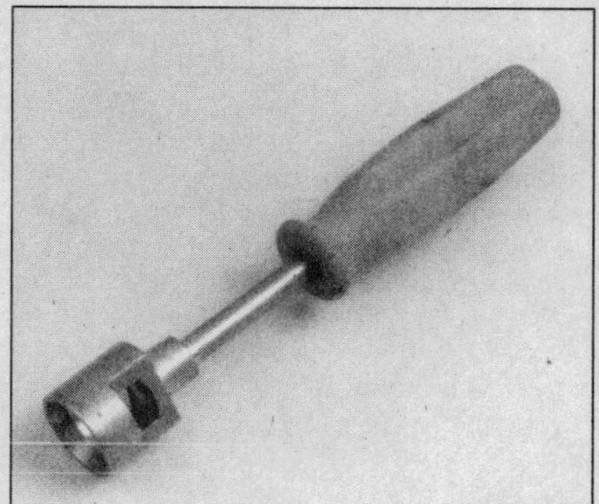
Brake hold-down spring tool

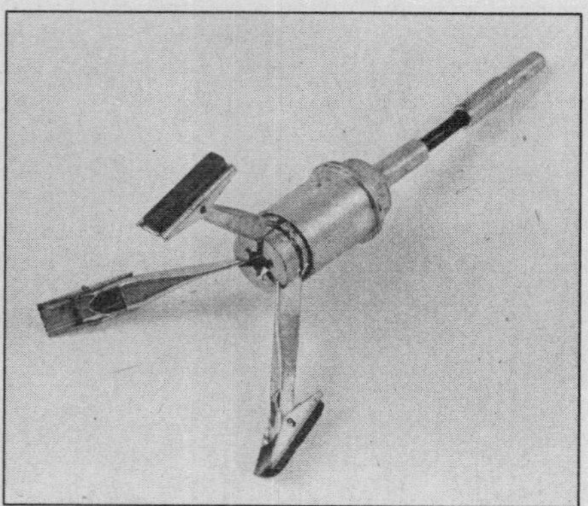
Brake cylinder hone

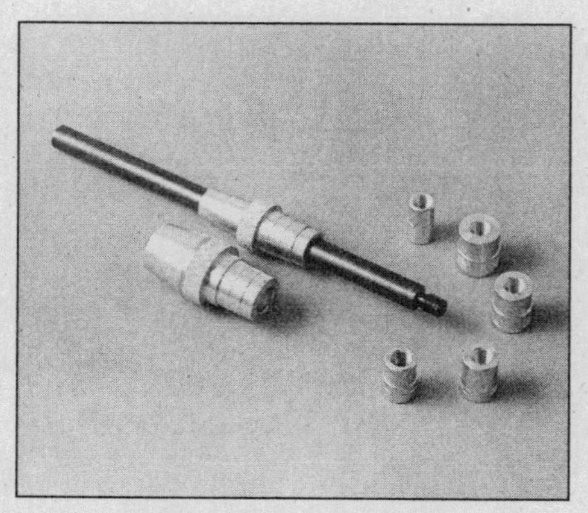
Clutch plate alignment tool

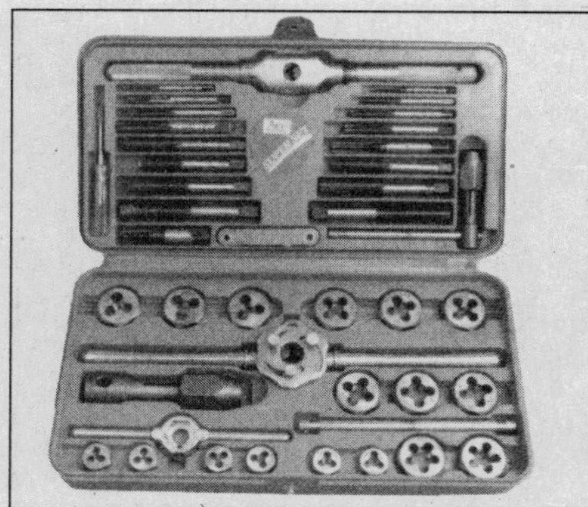
Tap and die set

To help the owner decide which tools are needed to perform the tasks detailed in this manual, the following tool lists are offered: *Maintenance and minor repair, Repair/overhaul* and *Special.*

The newcomer to practical mechanics should start off with the *maintenance and minor repair* tool kit, which is adequate for the simpler jobs performed on a vehicle. Then, as confidence and experience grow, the owner can tackle more difficult tasks, buying additional tools as they are needed. Eventually the basic kit will be expanded into the *repair and overhaul* tool set. Over a period of time, the experienced do-it-yourselfer will assemble a tool set complete enough for most repair and overhaul procedures and will add tools from the special category when it is felt that the expense is justified by the frequency of use.

Maintenance and minor repair tool kit

The tools in this list should be considered the minimum required for performance of routine maintenance, servicing and minor repair work. We recommend the purchase of combination wrenches (box-end and open-end combined in one wrench). While more expensive than open end wrenches, they offer the advantages of both types of wrench.

Combination wrench set (1/4-inch to 1 inch or 6 mm to 19 mm)
Adjustable wrench, 8 inch
Spark plug wrench with rubber insert
Spark plug gap adjusting tool
Feeler gauge set
Brake bleeder wrench
Standard screwdriver (5/16-inch x 6 inch)
Phillips screwdriver (No. 2 x 6 inch)
Combination pliers - 6 inch
Hacksaw and assortment of blades
Tire pressure gauge
Grease gun
Oil can
Fine emery cloth
Wire brush
Battery post and cable cleaning tool
Oil filter wrench
Funnel (medium size)
Safety goggles
Jackstands (2)
Drain pan

Note: *If basic tune-ups are going to be part of routine maintenance, it will be necessary to purchase a good quality stroboscopic timing light and combination tachometer/dwell meter. Although they are included in the list of special tools, it is mentioned here because they are absolutely necessary for tuning most vehicles properly.*

Repair and overhaul tool set

These tools are essential for anyone who plans to perform major repairs and are in addition to those in the maintenance and minor repair tool kit. Included is a comprehensive set of sockets which, though expensive, are invaluable because of their versatility, especially when various extensions and drives are available. We recommend the 1/2-inch drive over the 3/8-inch drive. Although the larger drive is bulky and more expensive, it has the capacity of accepting a very wide range of large sockets. Ideally, however, the mechanic should have a 3/8-inch drive set and a 1/2-inch drive set.

Socket set(s)
Reversible ratchet
Extension - 10 inch
Universal joint
Torque wrench (same size drive as sockets)
Ball peen hammer - 8 ounce
Soft-face hammer (plastic/rubber)
Standard screwdriver (1/4-inch x 6 inch)
Standard screwdriver (stubby - 5/16-inch)
Phillips screwdriver (No. 3 x 8 inch)
Phillips screwdriver (stubby - No. 2)
Pliers - vise grip
Pliers - lineman's
Pliers - needle nose

Pliers - snap-ring (internal and external)
Cold chisel - 1/2-inch
Scribe
Scraper (made from flattened copper tubing)
Centerpunch
Pin punches (1/16, 1/8, 3/16-inch)
Steel rule/straightedge - 12 inch
Allen wrench set (1/8 to 3/8-inch or 4 mm to 10 mm)
A selection of files
Wire brush (large)
Jackstands (second set)
Jack (scissor or hydraulic type)

Note: *Another tool which is often useful is an electric drill with a chuck capacity of 3/8-inch and a set of good quality drill bits*

Special tools

The tools in this list include those which are not used regularly, are expensive to buy, or which need to be used in accordance with their manufacturer's instructions. Unless these tools will be used frequently, it is not very economical to purchase many of them. A consideration would be to split the cost and use between yourself and a friend or friends. In addition, most of these tools can be obtained from a tool rental shop on a temporary basis.

This list primarily contains only those tools and instruments widely available to the public, and not those special tools produced by the vehicle manufacturer for distribution to dealer service departments. Occasionally, references to the manufacturer's special tools are included in the text of this manual. Generally, an alternative method of doing the job without the special tool is offered. However, sometimes there is no alternative to their use. Where this is the case, and the tool cannot be purchased or borrowed, the work should be turned over to the dealer service department or an automotive repair shop.

Valve spring compressor
Piston ring groove cleaning tool
Piston ring compressor
Piston ring installation tool
Cylinder compression gauge
Cylinder ridge reamer
Cylinder surfacing hone
Cylinder bore gauge
Micrometers and/or dial calipers
Hydraulic lifter removal tool
Balljoint separator
Universal-type puller
Impact screwdriver
Dial indicator set
Stroboscopic timing light (inductive pick-up)
Hand operated vacuum/pressure pump
Tachometer/dwell meter
Universal electrical multimeter
Cable hoist
Brake spring removal and installation tools
Floor jack

Buying tools

For the do-it-yourselfer who is just starting to get involved in vehicle maintenance and repair, there are a number of options available when purchasing tools. If maintenance and minor repair is the extent of the work to be done, the purchase of individual tools is satisfactory. If, on the other hand, extensive work is planned, it would be a good idea to purchase a modest tool set from one of the large retail chain stores. A set can usually be bought at a substantial savings over the individual tool prices, and they often come with a tool box. As additional tools are needed, add-on sets, individual tools and a larger tool box can be purchased to expand the tool selection. Building a tool set gradually allows the cost of the tools to be spread over a longer period of time and gives the mechanic the freedom to choose only those tools that will actually be used.

Tool stores will often be the only source of some of the special tools that are needed, but regardless of where tools are bought, try to avoid cheap ones, especially when buying screwdrivers and sockets, because they won't last very long. The expense involved in replacing cheap tools will eventually be greater than the initial cost of quality tools.

Care and maintenance of tools

Good tools are expensive, so it makes sense to treat them with respect. Keep them clean and in usable condition and store them properly when not in use. Always wipe off any dirt, grease or metal chips before putting them away. Never leave tools lying around in the work area. Upon completion of a job, always check closely under the hood for tools that may have been left there so they won't get lost during a test drive.

Some tools, such as screwdrivers, pliers, wrenches and sockets, can be hung on a panel mounted on the garage or workshop wall, while others should be kept in a tool box or tray. Measuring instruments, gauges, meters, etc. must be carefully stored where they cannot be damaged by weather or impact from other tools.

When tools are used with care and stored properly, they will last a very long time. Even with the best of care, though, tools will wear out if used frequently. When a tool is damaged or worn out, replace it. Subsequent jobs will be safer and more enjoyable if you do.

Working facilities

Not to be overlooked when discussing tools is the workshop. If anything more than routine maintenance is to be carried out, some sort of suitable work area is essential.

It is understood, and appreciated, that many home mechanics do not have a good workshop or garage available, and end up removing an engine or doing major repairs outside. It is recommended, however, that the overhaul or repair be completed under the cover of a roof.

A clean, flat workbench or table of comfortable working height is an absolute necessity. The workbench should be equipped with a vise that has a jaw opening of at least four inches.

As mentioned previously, some clean, dry storage space is also required for tools, as well as the lubricants, fluids, cleaning solvents, etc. which soon become necessary.

Sometimes waste oil and fluids, drained from the engine or cooling system during normal maintenance or repairs, present a disposal problem. To avoid pouring them on the ground or into a sewage system, pour the used fluids into large containers, seal them with caps and take them to an authorized disposal site or recycling center. Plastic jugs, such as old antifreeze containers, are ideal for this purpose.

Always keep a supply of old newspapers and clean rags available. Old towels are excellent for mopping up spills. Many mechanics use rolls of paper towels for most work because they are readily available and disposable. To help keep the area under the vehicle clean, a large cardboard box can be cut open and flattened to protect the garage or shop floor.

Whenever working over a painted surface, such as when leaning over a fender to service something under the hood, always cover it with an old blanket or bedspread to protect the finish. Vinyl covered pads, made especially for this purpose, are available at auto parts stores.

Jacking and towing

Jacking

The jack supplied with the vehicle should only be used for raising the vehicle for changing a tire or placing jackstands under the frame. **Warning:** *Never crawl under the vehicle or start the engine when the jack is being used as the only means of support.*

All vehicles are supplied with a scissors-type jack. When jacking the vehicle, it should be engaged with the seam notch, between the two dimples (see illustration).

The vehicle should be on level ground with the wheels blocked and the transmission in Park (automatic) or Reverse (manual). Pry off the hub cap (if equipped) using the tapered end of the lug wrench. Loosen the lug nuts one-half turn and leave them in place until the wheel is raised off the ground.

Place the jack under the side of the vehicle in the indicated position. Use the supplied wrench to turn the jackscrew clockwise until the wheel is raised off the ground. Remove the lug nuts, pull off the wheel and replace it with the spare.

With the beveled side in, replace the lug nuts and tighten them until snug. Lower the vehicle by turning the jackscrew counterclockwise. Remove the jack and tighten the nuts in a diagonal pattern to the torque listed in the Chapter 1 Specifications. If a torque wrench is not available, have the torque checked by a service station as soon as possible. Replace the hubcap by placing it in position and using the heel of your hand or a rubber mallet to seat it.

Towing

Manual transmission-equipped vehicles can be towed with all four wheels on the ground. Automatic transmission-equipped models should only be towed with all four wheels on the ground if speeds do not exceed 35 mph and the distance is not over 50 miles, otherwise transmission damage can result.

Towing equipment specifically designed for this purpose should be used and should be attached to the main structural members of the vehicle, not the bumper or brackets.

Safety is a major consideration when towing and all applicable state and local laws must be obeyed. A safety chain system must be used for all towing.

While towing, the parking brake should be released and the transmission and transfer case should be in Neutral. The steering must be unlocked (ignition switch in the Off position). Remember that power steering and power brakes will not work with the engine off.

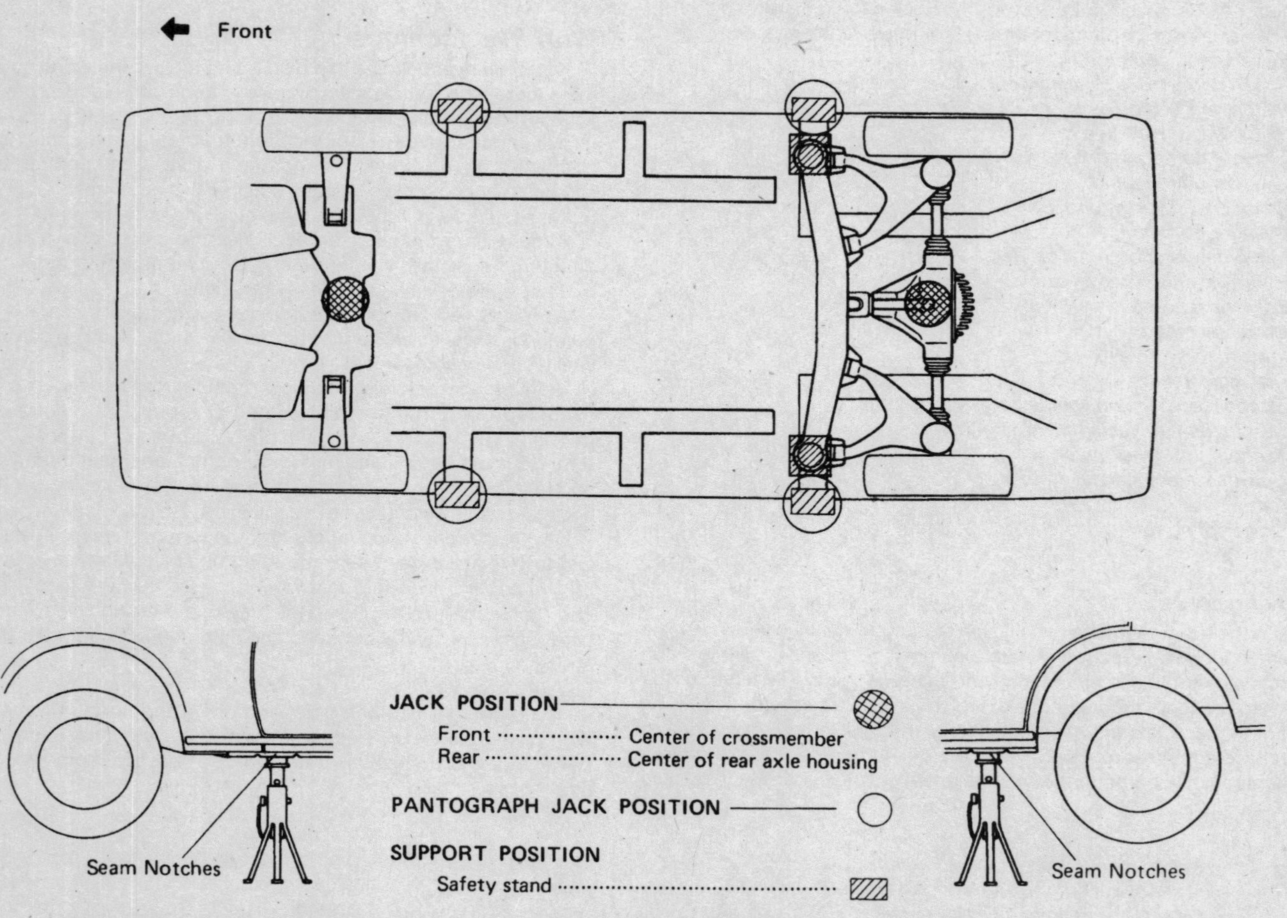

Support locations for a hoist, scissors-type (pantograph) jack, floorjack and safety stands (or jackstands)

Booster battery (jump) starting

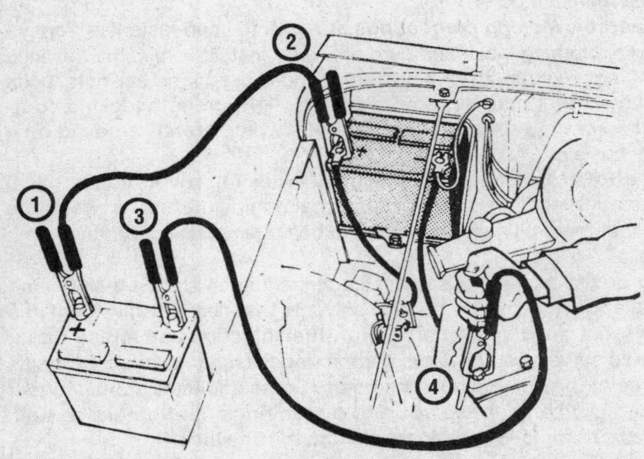

Make the booster battery cable connections in the numerical order shown (note that the negative cable of the booster battery is NOT attached to the negative terminal of the dead battery)

Observe these precautions when using a booster battery to start a vehicle:

a) Before connecting the booster battery, make sure the ignition switch is in the Off position.
b) Turn off the lights, heater and other electrical loads.
c) Your eyes should be shielded. Safety goggles are a good idea.
d) Make sure the booster battery is the same voltage as the dead one in the vehicle.
e) The two vehicles MUST NOT TOUCH each other!
f) Make sure the transaxle is in Neutral (manual) or Park (automatic).
g) If the booster battery is not a maintenance-free type, remove the vent caps and lay a cloth over the vent holes.

Connect the red jumper cable to the positive (+) terminals of each battery **(see illustration)**.

Connect one end of the black jumper cable to the negative (-) terminal of the booster battery. The other end of this cable should be connected to a good ground on the vehicle to be started, such as a bolt or bracket on the body.

Start the engine using the booster battery, then, with the engine running at idle speed, disconnect the jumper cables in the reverse order of connection.

Stereo anti-theft system precaution

Stereo systems displaying "ANTI-THEFT SYSTEM" on the cassette tape slot cover have a built-in theft deterrent system designed to render the stereo inoperative should the stereo be stolen. If the power source to the stereo is cut the anti-theft system will activate, so even if the power source is immediately reconnected the stereo will not function. If your vehicle is equipped with this anti-theft system, do not disconnect the cable from the negative terminal of the battery, remove the stereo or disconnect related components unless you have the individual ID (code) number for the stereo.

If you discover that the system is inoperative after disconnecting and reconnecting the power source, enter the ID number. If the wrong number is entered "Err" will appear on the display. You may make up to nine errors - a tenth error will activate the system and "HELP" will appear on the display. If this occurs, contact your local Toyota dealer service department.

Automotive chemicals and lubricants

A number of automotive chemicals and lubricants are available for use during vehicle maintenance and repair. They include a wide variety of products ranging from cleaning solvents and degreasers to lubricants and protective sprays for rubber, plastic and vinyl.

Cleaners

Carburetor cleaner and choke cleaner is a strong solvent for gum, varnish and carbon. Most carburetor cleaners leave a dry-type lubricant film which will not harden or gum up. Because of this film it is not recommended for use on electrical components

Brake system cleaner is used to remove grease and brake fluid from the brake system, where clean surfaces are absolutely necessary. It leaves no residue and often eliminates brake squeal caused by contaminants.

Electrical cleaner removes oxidation, corrosion and carbon deposits from electrical contacts, restoring full current flow. It can also be used to clean spark plugs, carburetor jets, voltage regulators and other parts where an oil-free surface is desired.

Demoisturants remove water and moisture from electrical components such as alternators, voltage regulators, electrical connectors and fuse blocks. They are non-conductive, non-corrosive and non-flammable.

Degreasers are heavy-duty solvents used to remove grease from the outside of the engine and from chassis components. They can be sprayed or brushed on and, depending on the type, are rinsed off either with water or solvent.

Lubricants

Motor oil is the lubricant formulated for use in engines. It normally contains a wide variety of additives to prevent corrosion and reduce foaming and wear. Motor oil comes in various weights (viscosity ratings) from 5 to 80. The recommended weight of the oil depends on the season, temperature and the demands on the engine. Light oil is used in cold climates and under light load conditions. Heavy oil is used in hot climates and where high loads are encountered. Multi-viscosity oils are designed to have characteristics of both light and heavy oils and are available in a number of weights from 5W-20 to 20W-50.

Gear oil is designed to be used in differentials, manual transmissions and other areas where high-temperature lubrication is required.

Chassis and wheel bearing grease is a heavy grease used where increased loads and friction are encountered, such as for wheel bearings, balljoints, tie-rod ends and universal joints.

High-temperature wheel bearing grease is designed to withstand the extreme temperatures encountered by wheel bearings in disc brake equipped vehicles. It usually contains molybdenum disulfide (moly), which is a dry-type lubricant.

White grease is a heavy grease for metal-to-metal applications where water is a problem. White grease stays soft under both low and high temperatures (usually from -100 to +190-degrees F), and will not wash off or dilute in the presence of water.

Assembly lube is a special extreme pressure lubricant, usually containing moly, used to lubricate high-load parts (such as main and rod bearings and cam lobes) for initial start-up of a new engine. The assembly lube lubricates the parts without being squeezed out or washed away until the engine oiling system begins to function.

Silicone lubricants are used to protect rubber, plastic, vinyl and nylon parts.

Graphite lubricants are used where oils cannot be used due to contamination problems, such as in locks. The dry graphite will lubricate metal parts while remaining uncontaminated by dirt, water, oil or acids. It is electrically conductive and will not foul electrical contacts in locks such as the ignition switch.

Moly penetrants loosen and lubricate frozen, rusted and corroded fasteners and prevent future rusting or freezing.

Heat-sink grease is a special electrically non-conductive grease that is used for mounting electronic ignition modules where it is essential that heat is transferred away from the module.

Sealants

RTV sealant is one of the most widely used gasket compounds. Made from silicone, RTV is air curing, it seals, bonds, waterproofs, fills surface irregularities, remains flexible, doesn't shrink, is relatively easy to remove, and is used as a supplementary sealer with almost all low and medium temperature gaskets.

Anaerobic sealant is much like RTV in that it can be used either to seal gaskets or to form gaskets by itself. It remains flexible, is solvent resistant and fills surface imperfections. The difference between an anaerobic sealant and an RTV-type sealant is in the curing. RTV cures when exposed to air, while an anaerobic sealant cures only in the absence of air. This means that an anaerobic sealant cures only after the assembly of parts, sealing them together.

Thread and pipe sealant is used for sealing hydraulic and pneumatic fittings and vacuum lines. It is usually made from a Teflon compound, and comes in a spray, a paint-on liquid and as a wrap-around tape.

Chemicals

Anti-seize compound prevents seizing, galling, cold welding, rust and corrosion in fasteners. High-temperature ant-seize, usually made with copper and graphite lubricants, is used for exhaust system and exhaust manifold bolts.

Anaerobic locking compounds are used to keep fasteners from vibrating or working loose and cure only after installation, in the absence of air. Medium strength locking compound is used for small nuts, bolts and screws that may be removed later. High-strength locking compound is for large nuts, bolts and studs which aren't removed on a regular basis.

Oil additives range from viscosity index improvers to chemical treatments that claim to reduce internal engine friction. It should be noted that most oil manufacturers caution against using additives with their oils.

Gas additives perform several functions, depending on their chemical makeup. They usually contain solvents that help dissolve gum and varnish that build up on carburetor, fuel injection and intake parts. They also serve to break down carbon deposits that form on the inside surfaces of the combustion chambers. Some additives contain upper cylinder lubricants for valves and piston rings, and others contain chemicals to remove condensation from the gas tank.

Miscellaneous

Brake fluid is specially formulated hydraulic fluid that can withstand the heat and pressure encountered in brake systems. Care must be taken so this fluid does not come in contact with painted surfaces or plastics. An opened container should always be resealed to prevent contamination by water or dirt.

Weatherstrip adhesive is used to bond weatherstripping around doors, windows and trunk lids. It is sometimes used to attach trim pieces.

Undercoating is a petroleum-based, tar-like substance that is designed to protect metal surfaces on the underside of the vehicle from corrosion. It also acts as a sound-deadening agent by insulating the bottom of the vehicle.

Waxes and polishes are used to help protect painted and plated surfaces from the weather. Different types of paint may require the use of different types of wax and polish. Some polishes utilize a chemical or abrasive cleaner to help remove the top layer of oxidized (dull) paint on older vehicles. In recent years many non-wax polishes that contain a wide variety of chemicals such as polymers and silicones have been introduced. These non-wax polishes are usually easier to apply and last longer than conventional waxes and polishes.

Safety first

Regardless of how enthusiastic you may be about getting on with the job at hand, take the time to ensure that your safety is not jeopardized. A moment's lack of attention can result in an accident, as can failure to observe certain simple safety precautions. The possibility of an accident will always exist, and the following points should not be considered a comprehensive list of all dangers. Rather, they are intended to make you aware of the risks and to encourage a safety conscious approach to all work you carry out on your vehicle.

Essential DOs and DON'Ts

DON'T rely on a jack when working under the vehicle. Always use approved jackstands to support the weight of the vehicle and place them under the recommended lift or support points.
DON'T attempt to loosen extremely tight fasteners (i.e. wheel lug nuts) while the vehicle is on a jack - it may fall.
DON'T start the engine without first making sure that the transmission is in Neutral (or Park where applicable) and the parking brake is set.
DON'T remove the radiator cap from a hot cooling system - let it cool or cover it with a cloth and release the pressure gradually.
DON'T attempt to drain the engine oil until you are sure it has cooled to the point that it will not burn you.
DON'T touch any part of the engine or exhaust system until it has cooled sufficiently to avoid burns.
DON'T siphon toxic liquids such as gasoline, antifreeze and brake fluid by mouth, or allow them to remain on your skin.
DON'T inhale brake lining dust - it is potentially hazardous (see Asbestos below)
DON'T allow spilled oil or grease to remain on the floor - wipe it up before someone slips on it.
DON'T use loose fitting wrenches or other tools which may slip and cause injury.
DON'T push on wrenches when loosening or tightening nuts or bolts. Always try to pull the wrench toward you. If the situation calls for pushing the wrench away, push with an open hand to avoid scraped knuckles if the wrench should slip.
DON'T attempt to lift a heavy component alone - get someone to help you.
DON'T rush or take unsafe shortcuts to finish a job.
DON'T allow children or animals in or around the vehicle while you are working on it.
DO wear eye protection when using power tools such as a drill, sander, bench grinder, etc. and when working under a vehicle.
DO keep loose clothing and long hair well out of the way of moving parts.
DO make sure that any hoist used has a safe working load rating adequate for the job.
DO get someone to check on you periodically when working alone on a vehicle.
DO carry out work in a logical sequence and make sure that everything is correctly assembled and tightened.
DO keep chemicals and fluids tightly capped and out of the reach of children and pets.
DO remember that your vehicle's safety affects that of yourself and others. If in doubt on any point, get professional advice.

Asbestos

Certain friction, insulating, sealing, and other products - such as brake linings, brake bands, clutch linings, torque converters, gaskets, etc. - contain asbestos. Extreme care must be taken to avoid inhalation of dust from such products, since it is hazardous to health. If in doubt, assume that they do contain asbestos.

Fire

Remember at all times that gasoline is highly flammable. Never smoke or have any kind of open flame around when working on a vehicle. But the risk does not end there. A spark caused by an electrical short circuit, by two metal surfaces contacting each other, or even by static electricity built up in your body under certain conditions, can ignite gasoline vapors, which in a confined space are highly explosive. Do not, under any circumstances, use gasoline for cleaning parts. Use an approved safety solvent.

Always disconnect the battery ground (-) cable at the battery before working on any part of the fuel system or electrical system. Never risk spilling fuel on a hot engine or exhaust component.It is strongly recommended that a fire extinguisher suitable for use on fuel and electrical fires be kept handy in the garage or workshop at all times. Never try to extinguish a fuel or electrical fire with water.

Fumes

Certain fumes are highly toxic and can quickly cause unconsciousness and even death if inhaled to any extent. Gasoline vapor falls into this category, as do the vapors from some cleaning solvents. Any draining or pouring of such volatile fluids should be done in a well ventilated area.

When using cleaning fluids and solvents, read the instructions on the container carefully. Never use materials from unmarked containers.

Never run the engine in an enclosed space, such as a garage. Exhaust fumes contain carbon monoxide, which is extremely poisonous. If you need to run the engine, always do so in the open air, or at least have the rear of the vehicle outside the work area.

If you are fortunate enough to have the use of an inspection pit, never drain or pour gasoline and never run the engine while the vehicle is over the pit. The fumes, being heavier than air, will concentrate in the pit with possibly lethal results.

The battery

Never create a spark or allow a bare light bulb near a battery. They normally give off a certain amount of hydrogen gas, which is highly explosive.

Always disconnect the battery ground (-) cable at the battery before working on the fuel or electrical systems.

If possible, loosen the filler caps or cover when charging the battery from an external source (this does not apply to sealed or maintenance-free batteries). Do not charge at an excessive rate or the battery may burst.

Take care when adding water to a non maintenance-free battery and when carrying a battery. The electrolyte, even when diluted, is very corrosive and should not be allowed to contact clothing or skin.

Always wear eye protection when cleaning the battery to prevent the caustic deposits from entering your eyes.

Household current

When using an electric power tool, inspection light, etc., which operates on household current, always make sure that the tool is correctly connected to its plug and that, where necessary, it is properly grounded. Do not use such items in damp conditions and, again, do not create a spark or apply excessive heat in the vicinity of fuel or fuel vapor.

Secondary ignition system voltage

A severe electric shock can result from touching certain parts of the ignition system (such as the spark plug wires) when the engine is running or being cranked, particularly if components are damp or the insulation is defective. In the case of an electronic ignition system, the secondary system voltage is much higher and could prove fatal.

Conversion factors

Length (distance)

Inches (in)	X	25.4	= Millimetres (mm)	X	0.0394	= Inches (in)
Feet (ft)	X	0.305	= Metres (m)	X	3.281	= Feet (ft)
Miles	X	1.609	= Kilometres (km)	X	0.621	= Miles

Volume (capacity)

Cubic inches (cu in; in^3)	X	16.387	= Cubic centimetres (cc; cm^3)	X	0.061	= Cubic inches (cu in; in^3)
Imperial pints (Imp pt)	X	0.568	= Litres (l)	X	1.76	= Imperial pints (Imp pt)
Imperial quarts (Imp qt)	X	1.137	= Litres (l)	X	0.88	= Imperial quarts (Imp qt)
Imperial quarts (Imp qt)	X	1.201	= US quarts (US qt)	X	0.833	= Imperial quarts (Imp qt)
US quarts (US qt)	X	0.946	= Litres (l)	X	1.057	= US quarts (US qt)
Imperial gallons (Imp gal)	X	4.546	= Litres (l)	X	0.22	= Imperial gallons (Imp gal)
Imperial gallons (Imp gal)	X	1.201	= US gallons (US gal)	X	0.833	= Imperial gallons (Imp gal)
US gallons (US gal)	X	3.785	= Litres (l)	X	0.264	= US gallons (US gal)

Mass (weight)

Ounces (oz)	X	28.35	= Grams (g)	X	0.035	Ounces (oz)
Pounds (lb)	X	0.454	= Kilograms (kg)	X	2.205	= Pounds (lb)

Force

Ounces-force (ozf; oz)	X	0.278	= Newtons (N)	X	3.6	= Ounces-force (ozf; oz)
Pounds-force (lbf; lb)	X	4.448	= Newtons (N)	X	0.225	= Pounds-force (lbf; lb)
Newtons (N)	X	0.1	= Kilograms-force (kgf; kg)	X	9.81	= Newtons (N)

Pressure

Pounds-force per square inch (psi; lbf/in^2; lb/in^2)	X	0.070	= Kilograms-force per square centimetre (kgf/cm^2; kg/cm^2)	X	14.223	= Pounds-force per square inch (psi; lbf/in^2; lb/in^2)
Pounds-force per square inch (psi; lbf/in^2; lb/in^2)	X	0.068	= Atmospheres (atm)	X	14.696	= Pounds-force per square inch (psi; lbf/in^2; lb/in^2)
Pounds-force per square inch (psi; lbf/in^2; lb/in^2)	X	0.069	= Bars	X	14.5	= Pounds-force per square inch (psi; lbf/in^2; lb/in^2)
Pounds-force per square inch (psi; lbf/in^2; lb/in^2)	X	6.895	= Kilopascals (kPa)	X	0.145	= Pounds-force per square inch (psi; lbf/in^2; lb/in^2)
Kilopascals (kPa)	X	0.01	= Kilograms-force per square centimetre (kgf/cm^2; kg/cm^2)	X	98.1	= Kilopascals (kPa)

Torque (moment of force)

Pounds-force inches (lbf in; lb in)	X	1.152	= Kilograms-force centimetre (kgf cm; kg cm)	X	0.868	= Pounds-force inches (lbf in; lb in)
Pounds-force inches (lbf in; lb in)	X	0.113	= Newton metres (Nm)	X	8.85	= Pounds-force inches (lbf in; lb in)
Pounds-force inches (lbf in; lb in)	X	0.083	= Pounds-force feet (lbf ft; lb ft)	X	12	= Pounds-force inches (lbf in; lb in)
Pounds-force feet (lbf ft; lb ft)	X	0.138	= Kilograms-force metres (kgf m; kg m)	X	7.233	= Pounds-force feet (lbf ft; lb ft)
Pounds-force feet (lbf ft; lb ft)	X	1.356	= Newton metres (Nm)	X	0.738	= Pounds-force feet (lbf ft; lb ft)
Newton metres (Nm)	X	0.102	= Kilograms-force metres (kgf m; kg m)	X	9.804	= Newton metres (Nm)

Power

Horsepower (hp)	X	745.7	= Watts (W)	X	0.0013	= Horsepower (hp)

Velocity (speed)

Miles per hour (miles/hr; mph)	X	1.609	= Kilometres per hour (km/hr; kph)	X	0.621	= Miles per hour (miles/hr; mph)

*Fuel consumption**

Miles per gallon, Imperial (mpg)	X	0.354	= Kilometres per litre (km/l)	X	2.825	= Miles per gallon, Imperial (mpg)
Miles per gallon, US (mpg)	X	0.425	= Kilometres per litre (km/l)	X	2.352	= Miles per gallon, US (mpg)

Temperature

Degrees Fahrenheit = (°C x 1.8) + 32

Degrees Celsius (Degrees Centigrade; °C) = (°F - 32) x 0.56

**It is common practice to convert from miles per gallon (mpg) to litres/100 kilometres (l/100km), where mpg (Imperial) x l/100 km = 282 and mpg (US) x l/100 km = 235*

Troubleshooting

Contents

This Section provides an easy reference guide to the more common problems that may occur during the operation of your vehicle. Various symptoms and their probable causes are grouped under headings denoting components or systems, such as Engine, Cooling system, etc. They also refer to the Chapter and/or Section that deals with the problem.

Remember that successful troubleshooting isn't a mysterious 'black art' practiced only by professional mechanics, it's simply the result of knowledge combined with an intelligent, systematic approach to a problem. Always use a process of elimination starting with the simplest solution and working through to the most complex - and never overlook the obvious. Anyone can run the gas tank dry or leave the lights on overnight, so don't assume that you're exempt from such oversights.

Finally, always establish a clear idea why a problem has occurred and take steps to ensure that it doesn't happen again. If the electrical system fails because of a poor connection, check all other connections in the system to make sure they don't fail as well. If a particular fuse continues to blow, find out why - don't just go on replacing fuses. Remember, failure of a small component can often be indicative of potential failure or incorrect functioning of a more important component or system.

Engine and performance

1 Engine will not rotate when attempting to start

1 Battery terminal connections loose or corroded. Check the cable terminals at the battery; tighten cable clamp and/or clean off corrosion as necessary (see Chapter 1).

2 Battery discharged or faulty. If the cable ends are clean and tight on the battery posts, turn the key to the On position and switch on the headlights or windshield wipers. If they won't run, the battery is discharged.

3 Automatic transmission not engaged in park (P) or Neutral (N).

4 Broken, loose or disconnected wires in the starting circuit. Inspect all wires and connectors at the battery, starter solenoid and ignition switch (on steering column).

5 Starter motor pinion jammed in flywheel ring gear. If manual transmission, place transmission in gear and rock the vehicle to manually turn the engine. Remove starter (Chapter 5) and inspect pinion and flywheel (Chapter 2) at earliest convenience.

6 Starter solenoid faulty (Chapter 5).

7 Starter motor faulty (Chapter 5).

8 Ignition switch faulty (Chapter 13).

9 Engine seized. Try to turn the crankshaft with a large socket and breaker bar on the pulley bolt.

2 Engine rotates but will not start

1 Fuel tank empty.

2 Battery discharged (engine rotates slowly). Check the operation of electrical components as described in previous Section.

3 Battery terminal connections loose or corroded. See previous Section.

4 Fuel not reaching fuel injector. Check for clogged fuel filter or lines and defective fuel pump. Also make sure the tank vent lines aren't clogged (Chapter 4).

5 Faulty distributor (if equipped) components. Check the cap and rotor (Chapter 1).

6 Low cylinder compression. Check as described in Chapter 2.

7 Valve clearances not properly adjusted (Chapter 1).

8 Water in fuel. Drain tank and fill with new fuel.

9 Dirty or clogged fuel injectors.

10 Wet or damaged ignition components (Chapters 1 and 5).

11 Worn, faulty or incorrectly gapped spark plugs (Chapter 1).

12 Broken, loose or disconnected wires in the starting circuit (see previous Section).

13 Loose distributor - if equipped - (changing ignition timing). Turn the distributor body as necessary to start the engine, then adjust the ignition timing as soon as possible (Chapter 1).

14 Broken, loose or disconnected wires at the ignition coil(s) or faulty coil(s) (Chapter 5).

15 Timing chain or belt failure or wear affecting valve timing (Chapter 2).

3 Starter motor operates without turning engine

1 Starter pinion sticking. Remove the starter (Chapter 5) and inspect.

2 Starter pinion or flywheel/driveplate teeth worn or broken. Remove the inspection cover on the left side of the engine and inspect.

4 Engine hard to start when cold

1 Battery discharged or low. Check as described in Chapter 1.

2 Fuel not reaching the fuel injectors. Check the fuel filter and lines (Chapters 1 and 4).

3 Defective spark plugs (Chapter 1).

4 Intake manifold vacuum leaks. Make sure all mounting bolts/nuts are tight and all vacuum hoses connected to the manifold are attached properly and in good condition.

5 Faulty cold-start injector system (see Chapter 4).

5 Engine hard to start when hot

1 Air filter dirty (Chapter 1).

2 Bad engine ground connection.

3 Fuel not reaching the injectors (Chapter 4).

4 Defective pick-up coil in distributor - if equipped - or dirty or loose connection in the ignition system (Chapter 5).

6 Starter motor noisy or engages roughly

1 Pinion or flywheel/driveplate teeth worn or broken. Remove the inspection cover on the left side of the engine and inspect.

2 Starter motor mounting bolts loose or missing.

7 Engine starts but stops immediately

1 Loose or damaged wiring in the ignition system.

2 Intake manifold vacuum leaks. Make sure all mounting bolts/nuts are tight and all vacuum hoses connected to the manifold are attached properly and in good condition.

8 Engine 'lopes' while idling or idles erratically

1 Vacuum leaks. Check mounting bolts at the intake manifold for tightness. Make sure that all vacuum hoses are connected and in good condition. Use a stethoscope or a length of fuel hose held against your ear to listen for vacuum leaks while the engine is running. A hissing sound will be heard. A soapy water solution will also detect leaks. Check the intake manifold gasket surfaces.

2 Leaking EGR valve or plugged PCV valve (see Chapters 1 and 6).

3 Air filter clogged (Chapter 1).

4 Leaking head gasket. Perform a cylinder compression check (Chapter 2).

5 Timing chain or belt worn (Chapter 2).

6 Camshaft lobes worn (Chapter 2).
7 Valve clearance out of adjustment (Chapter 1). Valves burned or otherwise leaking (Chapter 2).
8 Ignition timing out of adjustment (Chapter 1).
9 Ignition system not operating properly (Chapters 1 and 5).
10 Dirty or clogged injectors (Chapter 4).
11 Idle speed out of adjustment (Chapters 1 and 4).
12 Throttle body bore dirty. With the engine off, remove the intake air duct from the throttle body and open the throttle plate by hand. Clean the bore with carburetor cleaner and a toothbrush (be sure the cleaner is safe for use with catalytic converters and oxygen sensors).

9 Engine misses at idle speed

1 Spark plugs faulty or not gapped properly (Chapter 1).
2 Faulty spark plug wires (Chapter 1).
3 Wet or damaged distributor components (Chapter 1).
4 Short circuits in ignition, coil(s) or spark plug wires.
5 Sticking or faulty emissions systems (see Chapter 6).
6 Clogged fuel filter and/or foreign matter in fuel. Remove the fuel filter (Chapter 1) and inspect.
7 Vacuum leaks at intake manifold or hose connections. Check as described in Section 8.
8 Incorrect idle speed (Chapter 1) or idle mixture.
9 Incorrect ignition timing (Chapter 1).
10 Low or uneven cylinder compression. Check as described in Chapter 2.
11 Clogged or dirty fuel injectors (Chapter 4).
12 Throttle body bore dirty. With the engine off, remove the intake air duct from the throttle body and open the throttle plate by hand. Clean the bore with carburetor cleaner and a toothbrush (be sure the cleaner is safe for use with catalytic converters and oxygen sensors).

10 Excessively high idle speed

1 Sticking throttle linkage (Chapter 4).
2 Idle speed incorrectly adjusted (Chapter 4).
3 Valve clearances incorrectly adjusted (Chapter 1).
4 Dash pot out of adjustment (Chapter 6).

11 Battery will not hold a charge

1 Alternator drivebelt defective or not adjusted properly (Chapter 1).
2 Battery cables loose or corroded (Chapter 1).
3 Alternator not charging properly (Chapter 5).
4 Loose, broken or faulty wires in the charging circuit (Chapter 5).
5 Short circuit causing a continuous drain on the battery (Chapter 12).
6 Battery defective internally.
7 Faulty regulator (Chapter 5).

12 Alternator light stays on

1 Fault in alternator or charging circuit (Chapter 5).
2 Alternator drivebelt defective or not properly adjusted (Chapter 1).

13 Alternator light fails to come on when key is turned on

1 Faulty bulb (Chapter 12).
2 Defective alternator (Chapter 5).
3 Fault in the printed circuit, dash wiring or bulb holder (Chapter 12).

14 Engine misses throughout driving speed range

1 Fuel filter clogged and/or impurities in the fuel system. Check fuel filter (Chapter 1) or clean system (Chapter 4).
2 Faulty or incorrectly gapped spark plugs (Chapter 1).
3 Incorrect ignition timing (Chapter 1).
4 Cracked distributor cap - if equipped - or disconnected ignition system wires or damaged ignition system components (Chapter 1).
5 Defective spark plug wires (Chapter 1).
6 Emissions system components faulty (Chapter 6).
7 Low or uneven cylinder compression pressures. Check as described in Chapter 2.
8 Weak or faulty ignition coil(s) (Chapter 5).
9 Weak or faulty ignition system (Chapter 5).
10 Vacuum leaks at intake manifold or vacuum hoses (see Section 8).
11 Dirty or clogged fuel injector (Chapter 4).
12 Leaky EGR valve (Chapter 6).

15 Hesitation or stumble during acceleration

1 Ignition timing incorrect (Chapter 1).
2 Ignition system not operating properly (Chapter 5).
3 Dirty or clogged fuel injectors (Chapter 4).
4 Low fuel pressure. Check for proper operation of the fuel pump and for restrictions in the fuel filter and lines (Chapter 4).
5 Throttle body bore dirty. With the engine off, remove the intake air duct from the throttle body and open the throttle plate by hand. Clean the bore with carburetor cleaner and a toothbrush (be sure the cleaner is safe for use with catalytic converters and oxygen sensors).

16 Engine stalls

1 Idle speed incorrect (Chapter 1).
2 Fuel filter clogged and/or water and impurities in the fuel system (Chapter 1).
3 Damaged or wet ignition system wires or components.
4 Emissions system components faulty (Chapter 6).
5 Faulty or incorrectly gapped spark plugs (Chapter 1). Also check the spark plug wires (Chapter 1).
6 Vacuum leak at the intake manifold or vacuum hoses. Check as described in Section 8.
8 Valve clearances incorrect (Chapter 1).
9 Throttle body bore dirty. With the engine off, remove the intake air duct from the throttle body and open the throttle plate by hand. Clean the bore with carburetor cleaner and a toothbrush (be sure the cleaner is safe for use with catalytic converters and oxygen sensors).

17 Engine lacks power

1 Incorrect ignition timing (Chapter 1).
2 Excessive play in distributor (if equipped) shaft. At the same time check for faulty distributor cap, wires, etc. (Chapter 1).
3 Faulty or incorrectly gapped spark plugs (Chapter 1).
4 Air filter dirty (Chapter 1).
5 Spark timing control system not operating properly (Chapter 6).
6 Faulty ignition coil(s) (Chapter 5).
7 Brakes binding (Chapters 1 and 9).
8 Automatic transmission fluid level incorrect, causing slippage (Chapter 1).
9 Clutch slipping (Chapter 8).
10 Fuel filter clogged and/or impurities in the fuel system (Chapters 1 and 4).
11 EGR system not functioning properly (Chapter 6).
12 Use of sub-standard fuel. Fill tank with proper octane fuel.
13 Low or uneven cylinder compression pressures. Check as de-

scribed in Chapter 2.
14 Air (vacuum) leak at intake manifold (check as described in Section 8).

18 Engine backfires

1 EGR system not functioning properly (Chapter 6).
2 Ignition timing incorrect (Chapter 1).
3 Vacuum leak (refer to Section 8).
4 Valve clearances incorrect (Chapter 1).
5 Damaged valve springs or sticking valves (Chapter 2).
6 Intake air (vacuum) leak (see Section 8).

19 Engine surges while holding accelerator steady

1 Intake air (vacuum) leak (see Section 8).
2 Fuel pump not working properly.

20 Pinging or knocking engine sounds when engine is under load

1 Incorrect grade of fuel. Fill tank with fuel of the proper octane rating.
2 Ignition timing incorrect (Chapter 1) or problem in the ignition system (Chapter 5).
3 Carbon build-up in combustion chambers. Remove cylinder head and clean combustion chambers (Chapter 2).
4 Incorrect spark plugs (Chapter 1).

21 Engine diesels (continues to run) after being turned off

1 Idle speed too high (Chapter 1).
2 Ignition timing incorrect (Chapter 1).
3 Incorrect spark plug heat range (Chapter 1).
4 Intake air (vacuum) leak (see Section 8).
5 Carbon build-up in combustion chambers. Remove the cylinder head and clean the combustion chambers (Chapter 2).
6 Valves sticking (Chapter 2).
7 Valve clearance incorrect (Chapter 1).
8 EGR system not operating properly (Chapter 6).
9 Leaking fuel injector(s) (Chapter 4).
10 Check for causes of overheating (Section 27).

22 Low oil pressure

1 Improper grade of oil.
2 Oil pump regulator valve not operating properly (Chapter 2).
3 Oil pump worn or damaged (Chapter 2).
4 Engine overheating (refer to Section 27).
5 Clogged oil filter (Chapter 1).
6 Clogged oil strainer (Chapter 2).
7 Oil pressure gauge not working properly (Chapter 2).

23 Excessive oil consumption

1 Loose oil drain plug.
2 Loose bolts or damaged oil pan gasket (Chapter 2).
3 Loose bolts or damaged front cover gasket (Chapter 2).
4 Front or rear crankshaft oil seal leaking (Chapter 2).
5 Loose bolts or damaged valve cover gasket (Chapter 2).
6 Loose oil filter (Chapter 1).
7 Loose or damaged oil pressure switch (Chapter 2).
8 Pistons and cylinders excessively worn (Chapter 2).
9 Piston rings not installed correctly on pistons (Chapter 2).
10 Worn or damaged piston rings (Chapter 2).
11 Intake and/or exhaust valve oil seals worn or damaged (Chapter 2).
12 Worn valve stems.
13 Worn or damaged valves/guides (Chapter 2).

24 Excessive fuel consumption

1 Dirty or clogged air filter element (Chapter 1).
2 Incorrect ignition timing (Chapter 1).
3 Incorrect idle speed (Chapter 1).
4 Low tire pressure or incorrect tire size (Chapter 10).
5 Fuel leakage. Check all connections, lines and components in the fuel system (Chapter 4).
6 Dirty or clogged fuel injectors (Chapter 4).
7 Problem in the fuel injection system (Chapter 4).

25 Fuel odor

1 Fuel leakage. Check all connections, lines and components in the fuel system (Chapter 4).
2 Fuel tank overfilled. Fill only to automatic shut-off.
3 Charcoal canister filter in Evaporative Emissions Control system clogged (Chapter 1).
4 Vapor leaks from Evaporative Emissions Control system lines (Chapter 6).

26 Miscellaneous engine noises

1 A strong dull noise that becomes more rapid as the engine accelerates indicates worn or damaged crankshaft bearings or an unevenly worn crankshaft. To pinpoint the trouble spot, remove the spark plug wire from one plug at a time and crank the engine over. If the noise stops, the cylinder with the removed plug wire indicates the problem area. Replace the bearing and/or service or replace the crankshaft (Chapter 2).
2 A similar (yet slightly higher pitched) noise to the crankshaft knocking described in the previous paragraph, that becomes more rapid as the engine accelerates, indicates worn or damaged connecting rod bearings (Chapter 2). The procedure for locating the problem cylinder is the same as described in Paragraph 1.
3 An overlapping metallic noise that increases in intensity as the engine speed increases, yet diminishes as the engine warms up indicates abnormal piston and cylinder wear (Chapter 2).To locate the problem cylinder, use the procedure described in Paragraph 1.
4 A rapid clicking noise that becomes faster as the engine accelerates indicates a worn piston pin or piston pin hole. This sound will happen each time the piston hits the highest and lowest points in the stroke (Chapter 2). The procedure for locating the problem piston is described in Paragraph 1.
5 A metallic clicking noise coming from the water pump indicates worn or damaged water pump bearings or pump. Replace the water pump with a new one (Chapter 3).
6 A rapid tapping sound or clicking sound that becomes faster as the engine speed increases indicates "valve tapping" or improperly adjusted valve clearances. This can be identified by holding one end of a section of hose to your ear and placing the other end at different spots along the rocker arm cover. The point where the sound is loudest indicates the problem valve. Adjust the valve clearance (Chapter 1).
7 A steady metallic rattling or rapping sound coming from the area of the timing chain cover indicates a worn, damaged or out-of-adjustment timing chain. Service or replace the chain and related components (Chapter 2).

Cooling system

27 Overheating

1 Insufficient coolant in system (Chapter 1).
2 Drivebelt defective or not adjusted properly (Chapter 1).
3 Radiator core blocked or radiator grille dirty and restricted (Chapter 3).
4 Thermostat faulty (Chapter 3).
5 Fan not functioning properly (Chapter 3).
6 Radiator cap not maintaining proper pressure. Have cap pressure tested by gas station or repair shop.
7 Ignition timing incorrect (Chapter 1).
8 Defective water pump (Chapter 3).
9 Improper grade of engine oil.
10 Inaccurate temperature gauge (Chapter 12).

28 Overcooling

1 Thermostat faulty (Chapter 3).
2 Inaccurate temperature gauge (Chapter 12).

29 External coolant leakage

1 Deteriorated or damaged hoses. Loose clamps at hose connections (Chapter 1).
2 Water pump seals defective. If this is the case, water will drip from the weep hole in the water pump body (Chapter 3).
3 Leakage from radiator core or header tank. This will require the radiator to be professionally repaired (see Chapter 3 for removal procedures).
4 Engine drain plugs or water jacket freeze plugs leaking (see Chapters 1 and 2).
5 Leak from coolant temperature switch (Chapter 3).
6 Leak from damaged gaskets or small cracks (Chapter 2).
7 Damaged head gasket. This can be verified by checking the condition of the engine oil as noted in Section 30.

30 Internal coolant leakage

Note: *Internal coolant leaks can usually be detected by examining the oil. Check the dipstick and inside the valve cover for water deposits and an oil consistency like that of a milkshake.*
1 Leaking cylinder head gasket. Have the system pressure tested or remove the cylinder head (Chapter 2) and inspect.
2 Cracked cylinder bore or cylinder head. Dismantle engine and inspect (Chapter 2).
3 Loose cylinder head bolts (tighten as described in Chapter 2).

31 Abnormal coolant loss

1 Overfilling system (Chapter 1).
2 Coolant boiling away due to overheating (see causes in Section 27).
3 Internal or external leakage (see Sections 29 and 30).
4 Faulty radiator cap. Have the cap pressure tested.
5 Cooling system being pressurized by engine compression. This could be due to a cracked head or block or leaking head gasket(s).

32 Poor coolant circulation

1 Inoperative water pump. A quick test is to pinch the top radiator hose closed with your hand while the engine is idling, then release it. You should feel a surge of coolant if the pump is working properly (Chapter 3).
2 Restriction in cooling system. Drain, flush and refill the system (Chapter 1). If necessary, remove the radiator (Chapter 3) and have it reverse flushed or professionally cleaned.
3 Loose water pump drivebelt (Chapter 1).
4 Thermostat sticking (Chapter 3).
5 Insufficient coolant (Chapter 1).

33 Corrosion

1 Excessive impurities in the water. Soft, clean water is recommended. Distilled or rainwater is satisfactory.
2 Insufficient antifreeze solution (refer to Chapter 1 for the proper ratio of water to antifreeze).
3 Infrequent flushing and draining of system. Regular flushing of the cooling system should be carried out at the specified intervals as described in Chapter 1.

Clutch

Note: *All clutch related service information is located in Chapter 8, unless otherwise noted.*

34 Fails to release (pedal pressed to the floor - shift lever does not move freely in and out of Reverse)

1 Clutch contaminated with oil. Remove clutch plate and inspect.
2 Clutch plate warped, distorted or otherwise damaged.
3 Diaphragm spring fatigued. Remove clutch cover/pressure plate assembly and inspect.
4 Leakage of fluid from clutch hydraulic system. Inspect master cylinder, operating (release) cylinder and connecting lines.
5 Air in clutch hydraulic system. Bleed the system.
6 Insufficient pedal stroke. Check and adjust as necessary.
7 Piston seal in operating (release) cylinder deformed or damaged.
8 Lack of grease on pilot bushing.
9 Damaged transmission input shaft splines.

35 Clutch slips (engine speed increases with no increase in vehicle speed)

1 Worn or oil soaked clutch plate.
2 Clutch plate not broken in. It may take 30 or 40 normal starts for a new clutch to seat.
3 Diaphragm spring weak or damaged. Remove clutch cover/pressure plate assembly and inspect.
4 Flywheel warped or scored (Chapter 2).
5 Debris in master cylinder preventing the piston from returning to its normal position.
6 Clutch hydraulic line damaged.

36 Grabbing (chattering) as clutch is engaged

1 Oil on clutch plate. Remove and inspect. Repair any leaks.
2 Worn or loose engine or transmission mounts. They may move slightly when clutch is released. Inspect mounts and bolts.
3 Worn splines on transmission input shaft. Remove clutch components and inspect.
4 Warped pressure plate or flywheel. Remove clutch components and inspect.
5 Diaphragm spring fatigued. Remove clutch cover/pressure plate assembly and inspect.
6 Clutch linings hardened or warped.
7 Clutch lining rivets loose.

8 Engine and transmission not in alignment. Check for foreign object between bellhousing and engine block. Check for loose bellhousing bolts.

37 Squeal or rumble with clutch engaged (pedal released)

1 Improper pedal adjustment. Adjust pedal free play.
2 Release bearing binding on transmission shaft. Remove clutch components and check bearing. Remove any burrs or nicks, clean and relubricate before reinstallation.
3 Clutch rivets loose.
4 Clutch plate cracked.
5 Fatigued clutch plate torsion springs. Replace clutch plate.

38 Squeal or rumble with clutch disengaged (pedal depressed)

1 Worn or damaged release bearing.
2 Worn or broken pressure plate diaphragm fingers.
3 Worn or damaged pilot bearing.

39 Clutch pedal stays on floor when disengaged

1 Binding linkage or release bearing. Inspect linkage or remove clutch components as necessary.
2 Linkage springs being over extended. Adjust linkage for proper freeplay. Make sure proper pedal stop (bumper) is installed.

Manual transmission

Note: *All manual transmission service information is located in Chapter 7, unless otherwise noted.*

40 Noisy in Neutral with engine running

1 Input shaft bearing worn.
2 Damaged main drive gear bearing.
3 Insufficient transmission oil (Chapter 1).
4 Transmission lubricant in poor condition. Drain and fill with proper grade oil. Check old lubricant for water and debris (Chapter 1).
5 Noise can be caused by variations in engine torque. Change the idle speed and see if noise disappears.

41 Noisy in all gears

1 Any of the above causes, and/or:
2 Worn or damaged output gear bearings or shaft.

42 Noisy in one particular gear

1 Worn, damaged or chipped gear teeth.
2 Worn or damaged synchronizer.

43 Slips out of gear

1 Transmission loose on clutch housing.
2 Stiff shift lever seal.
3 Shift linkage binding.
4 Broken or loose input gear bearing retainer.
5 Dirt between clutch lever and engine housing.
6 Worn linkage.
7 Damaged or worn check balls, fork rod ball grooves or check springs.
8 Worn mainshaft or countershaft bearings.
9 Loose engine mounts (Chapter 2).
10 Excessive gear end play.
11 Worn synchronizers.

44 Oil leaks

1 Excessive amount of lubricant in transmission (see Chapter 1 for correct checking procedures). Drain lubricant as required.
2 Side cover loose or gasket damaged.
3 Rear oil seal or speedometer oil seal damaged.
4 To pinpoint a leak, first remove all built-up dirt and grime from the transmission. Degreasing agents and/or steam cleaning will achieve this. With the underside clean, drive the vehicle at low speeds so the air flow will not blow the leak far from its source. Raise the vehicle and determine where the leak is located.

45 Difficulty engaging gears

1 Clutch not releasing completely.
2 Loose or damaged shift linkage. Make a thorough inspection, replacing parts as necessary.
3 Insufficient transmission oil (Chapter 1).
4 Transmission oil in poor condition. Drain and fill with proper grade oil. Check oil for water and debris (Chapter 1).
5 Worn or damaged striking rod.
6 Sticking or jamming gears.

46 Noise occurs while shifting gears

1 Check for proper operation of the clutch (Chapter 8).
2 Faulty synchronizer assemblies. Measure baulk ring-to-gear clearance. Also, check for wear or damage to baulk rings or any parts of the synchromesh assemblies.

Automatic transmission

Note: *Due to the complexity of the automatic transmission, it's difficult for the home mechanic to properly diagnose and service. For problems other than the following, the vehicle should be taken to a reputable mechanic.*

47 Fluid leakage

1 Automatic transmission fluid is a deep red color, and fluid leaks should not be confused with engine oil which can easily be blown by air flow to the transmission.
2 To pinpoint a leak, first remove all built-up dirt and grime from the transmission. Degreasing agents and/or steam cleaning will achieve this. With the underside clean, drive the vehicle at low speeds so the air flow will not blow the leak far from its source. Raise the vehicle and determine where the leak is located. Common areas of leakage are:

a) **Fluid pan:** tighten mounting bolts and/or replace pan gasket as necessary (Chapter 1).
b) **Rear extension:** tighten bolts and/or replace oil seal as necessary.
c) **Filler pipe:** replace the rubber oil seal where pipe enters transmission case.
d) **Transmission oil lines:** tighten fittings where lines enter transmission case and/or replace lines.
e) **Vent pipe:** transmission overfilled and/or water in fluid (see checking procedures, Chapter 1).
f) **Speedometer connector:** replace the O-ring where speedometer cable enters transmission case.

48 General shift mechanism problems

Chapter 7 deals with checking and adjusting the shift linkage on automatic transmissions. Common problems which may be caused by out of adjustment linkage are:

a) Engine starting in gears other than P (Park) or N (Neutral).
b) Indicator pointing to a gear other than the one actually engaged.
c) Vehicle moves with transmission in P (Park) position.

49 Transmission will not downshift with the accelerator pedal pressed to the floor

Chapter 7 deals with adjusting the kickdown switch to enable the transmission to downshift properly.

50 Engine will start in gears other than Park or Neutral

Chapter 7 deals with adjusting the Neutral start switch installed on automatic transmissions.

51 Transmission slips, shifts rough, is noisy or has no drive in forward or Reverse gears

1 There are many probable causes for the above problems, but the home mechanic should concern himself only with one possibility; fluid level.

2 Before taking the vehicle to a shop, check the fluid level and condition as described in Chapter 1. Add fluid, if necessary, or change the fluid and filter if needed. If problems persist, have a professional diagnose the transmission.

Driveshaft

52 Leaks at front of driveshaft

Defective transmission rear seal. See Chapter 7 for replacement procedure. As this is done, check the splined yoke for burrs or roughness that could damage the new seal. Remove burrs with a fine file or whetstone.

53 Knock or clunk when transmission is under initial load (just after transmission is put into gear)

1 Loose or disconnected rear suspension components. Check all mounting bolts and bushings (Chapters 1 and 11).

2 Loose driveshaft bolts. Inspect all bolts and nuts and tighten them securely.

3 Worn or damaged universal joint bearings. Replace driveshaft (Chapter 8).

4 Worn sleeve yoke and mainshaft spline.

5 Defective center bearing or insulator.

54 Metallic grating sound consistent with vehicle speed

Pronounced wear in the universal joint bearings. Replace U-joints or driveshafts, as necessary.

55 Vibration

Note: *Before blaming the driveshaft, make sure the tires are perfectly balanced and perform the following test.*

1 Install a tachometer inside the vehicle to monitor engine speed as the vehicle is driven. Drive the vehicle and note the engine speed at which the vibration (roughness) is most pronounced. Now shift the transmission to a different gear and bring the engine speed to the same point.

2 If the vibration occurs at the same engine speed (rpm) regardless of which gear the transmission is in, the driveshaft is NOT at fault since the driveshaft speed varies.

3 If the vibration decreases or is eliminated when the transmission is in a different gear at the same engine speed, refer to the following probable causes.

4 Bent or dented driveshaft. Inspect and replace as necessary.

5 Undercoating or built-up dirt, etc. on the driveshaft. Clean the shaft thoroughly.

6 Worn universal joint bearings. Replace the U-joints or driveshaft as necessary.

7 Driveshaft and/or companion flange out of balance. Check for missing weights on the shaft. Remove driveshaft and reinstall 180-degrees from original position, then recheck. Have the driveshaft balanced if problem persists.

8 Loose driveshaft mounting bolts/nuts.

9 Defective center bearing, if so equipped.

10 Worn transmission rear bushing (Chapter 7).

56 Scraping noise

Make sure the dust cover on the sleeve yoke isn't rubbing on the transmission extension housing.

57 Whining or whistling noise

Defective center bearing, if so equipped.

Rear axle and differential

Note: *For differential servicing information, refer to Chapter 8, unless otherwise specified.*

58 Noise - same when in drive as when vehicle is coasting

1 Road noise. No corrective action available.

2 Tire noise. Inspect tires and check tire pressures (Chapter 1).

3 Front wheel bearings loose, worn or damaged (Chapter 1).

4 Insufficient differential oil (Chapter 1).

5 Defective differential.

6 On models with independent rear suspension, worn or damaged CV joints (see Chapter 8).

59 Knocking sound when starting or shifting gears

1 Defective or incorrectly adjusted differential.

2 On models with independent rear suspension, worn or damaged CV joints (see Chapter 8).

60 Noise when turning

Defective differential.

61 Vibration

See probable causes under Driveshaft. Proceed under the guidelines listed for the driveshaft. If the problem persists, check the rear wheel bearings by raising the rear of the vehicle and spinning the wheels by hand. Listen for evidence of rough (noisy) bearings. Remove and inspect (Chapter 8).

62 Oil leaks

1 Pinion oil seal damaged (Chapter 8).
2 Axleshaft or driveaxle oil seals damaged (Chapter 8).
3 Differential cover leaking. Tighten mounting bolts or replace the gasket as required.
4 Loose filler or drain plug on differential (Chapter 1).
5 Clogged or damaged breather on differential.

Brakes

Note: *Before assuming a brake problem exists, make sure the tires are in good condition and inflated properly, the front end alignment is correct and the vehicle is not loaded with weight in an unequal manner. All service procedures for the brakes are included in Chapter 9, unless otherwise noted.*

63 Vehicle pulls to one side during braking

1 Defective, damaged or oil contaminated brake pad on one side. Inspect as described in Chapter 1. Refer to Chapter 9 if replacement is required.
2 Excessive wear of brake pad material or disc on one side. Inspect and repair as necessary.
3 Loose or disconnected front suspension components. Inspect and tighten all bolts securely (Chapters 1 and 11).
4 Defective caliper assembly. Remove caliper and inspect for stuck piston or damage.
5 Brake pad-to-disc adjustment needed. Inspect automatic adjusting mechanism for proper operation.
6 Scored or out of round disc.
7 Loose caliper mounting bolts.
8 Incorrect wheel bearing adjustment.

64 Noise (high-pitched squeal)

1 Front brake pads worn out. This noise comes from the wear sensor rubbing against the disc. Replace pads with new ones immediately!
2 Glazed or contaminated pads.
3 Dirty or scored disc.
4 Bent support plate.

65 Excessive brake pedal travel

1 Partial brake system failure. Inspect entire system (Chapter 1) and correct as required.
2 Insufficient fluid in master cylinder. Check (Chapter 1) and add fluid - bleed system if necessary.
3 Air in system. Bleed system.
4 Excessive lateral disc play.
5 Brakes out of adjustment. Check the operation of the automatic adjusters.
6 Defective check valve. Replace valve and bleed system.

66 Brake pedal feels spongy when depressed

1 Air in brake lines. Bleed the brake system.
2 Deteriorated rubber brake hoses. Inspect all system hoses and lines. Replace parts as necessary.
3 Master cylinder mounting nuts loose. Inspect master cylinder bolts (nuts) and tighten them securely.
4 Master cylinder faulty.
5 Incorrect shoe or pad clearance.
6 Defective check valve. Replace valve and bleed system.
7 Clogged reservoir cap vent hole.
8 Deformed rubber brake lines.
9 Soft or swollen caliper seals.
10 Poor quality brake fluid. Bleed entire system and fill with new approved fluid.

67 Excessive effort required to stop vehicle

1 Power brake booster not operating properly.
2 Excessively worn pads. Check and replace if necessary.
3 One or more caliper pistons seized or sticking. Inspect and rebuild as required.
4 Brake pads contaminated with oil or grease. Inspect and replace as required.
5 New pads installed and not yet seated. It'll take a while for the new material to seat against the disc.
6 Worn or damaged master cylinder or caliper assemblies. Check particularly for frozen pistons.
7 Also see causes listed under Section 66.

68 Pedal travels to the floor with little resistance

Little or no fluid in the master cylinder reservoir caused by leaking caliper piston(s) or loose, damaged or disconnected brake lines. Inspect entire system and repair as necessary.

69 Brake pedal pulsates during brake application

1 Wheel bearings damaged, worn or out of adjustment (Chapter 1).
2 Caliper not sliding properly due to improper installation or obstructions. Remove and inspect.
3 Disc not within specifications. Remove the disc and check for excessive lateral runout and parallelism. Have the discs resurfaced or replace them with new ones. Also make sure that all discs are the same thickness.

70 Brakes drag (indicated by sluggish engine performance or wheels being very hot after driving)

1 Output rod adjustment incorrect at the brake pedal.
2 Obstructed master cylinder compensator. Disassemble master cylinder and clean.
3 Master cylinder piston seized in bore. Overhaul master cylinder.
4 Caliper assembly in need of overhaul.
5 Brake pads or shoes worn out.
6 Piston cups in master cylinder or caliper assembly deformed. Overhaul master cylinder.
7 Disc not within specifications (Section 69).
8 Parking brake assembly will not release.
9 Clogged brake lines.
10 Wheel bearings out of adjustment (Chapter 1).
11 Brake pedal height improperly adjusted.

71 Rear brakes lock up under light brake application

1 Tire pressures too high.
2 Tires excessively worn (Chapter 1).

72 Rear brakes lock up under heavy brake application

1 Tire pressures too high.
2 Tires excessively worn (Chapter 1).
3 Front brake pads contaminated with oil, mud or water. Clean or replace the pads.
4 Front brake pads excessively worn.
5 Defective master cylinder or caliper assembly.

Suspension and steering

Note: *All service procedures for the suspension and steering systems are included in Chapter 10, unless otherwise noted.*

73 Vehicle pulls to one side

1 Tire pressures uneven (Chapter 1).
2 Defective tire (Chapter 1).
3 Excessive wear in suspension or steering components (Chapter 1).
4 Front end alignment incorrect.
5 Front brakes dragging. Inspect as described in Section 70.
6 Wheel bearings improperly adjusted (Chapter 1).
7 Wheel lug nuts loose.
8 Worn upper or lower link or strut rod bushings.

74 Shimmy, shake or vibration

1 Tire or wheel out of balance or out of round. Have them balanced on the vehicle.
2 Loose, worn or out of adjustment wheel bearings (Chapter 1).
3 Shock absorbers and/or suspension components worn or damaged. Check for worn bushings in the upper and lower links.
4 Wheel lug nuts loose.
5 Incorrect tire pressures.
6 Excessively worn or damaged tire.
7 Loosely mounted steering gear housing.
8 Steering gear improperly adjusted.
9 Loose, worn or damaged steering components.
10 Damaged idler arm.
11 Worn balljoint.

75 Excessive pitching and/or rolling around corners or during braking

1 Defective shock absorbers. Replace as a set.
2 Broken or weak springs and/or suspension components.
3 Worn or damaged stabilizer bar or bushings.
4 Worn or damaged upper or lower links or bushings.

76 Wandering or general instability

1 Improper tire pressures.
2 Worn or damaged upper and lower link or strut bar bushings.
3 Incorrect front end alignment.
4 Worn or damaged steering linkage or upper or lower link.
5 Improperly adjusted steering gear.
6 Out of balance wheels.
7 Loose wheel lug nuts.
8 Worn rear shock absorbers.
9 Fatigued or damaged rear springs.

77 Excessively stiff steering

1 Lack of lubricant in power steering fluid reservoir, where appropriate (Chapter 1).
2 Incorrect tire pressures (Chapter 1).
3 Lack of lubrication at balljoints (Chapter 1).
4 Front end out of alignment.
5 Steering gear out of adjustment or lacking lubrication.
6 Improperly adjusted wheel bearings.
7 Worn or damaged steering gear.
8 Interference of steering column with turn signal switch.
9 Low tire pressures.
10 Worn or damaged balljoints.
11 Worn or damaged steering linkage.
12 See also Section 76.

78 Excessive play in steering

1 Loose wheel bearings (Chapter 1).
2 Excessive wear in upper or lower link or strut bar bushings (Chapter 1).
3 Steering gear improperly adjusted.
4 Incorrect front end alignment.
5 Steering gear mounting bolts loose.
6 Worn steering linkage.

79 Lack of power assistance

1 Steering pump drivebelt faulty or not adjusted properly (Chapter 1).
2 Fluid level low (Chapter 1).
3 Hoses or pipes restricting the flow. Inspect and replace parts as necessary.
4 Air in power steering system. Bleed system.
5 Defective power steering pump.

80 Steering wheel fails to return to straight-ahead position

1 Incorrect front end alignment.
2 Tire pressures low.
3 Steering gears improperly engaged.
4 Steering column out of alignment.
5 Worn or damaged balljoint.
6 Worn or damaged steering linkage.
7 Improperly lubricated idler arm.
8 Insufficient oil in steering gear.
9 Lack of fluid in power steering pump.

81 Steering effort not the same in both directions (power sytem)

1 Leaks in steering gear.
2 Clogged fluid passage in steering gear.

82 Noisy power steering pump

1 Insufficient oil in pump.
2 Clogged hoses or oil filter in pump.
3 Loose pulley.
4 Improperly adjusted drivebelt (Chapter 1).
5 Defective pump.

83 Miscellaneous noises

1 Improper tire pressures.
2 Insufficiently lubricated balljoint or steering linkage.
3 Loose or worn steering gear, steering linkage or suspension components.
4 Defective shock absorber.
5 Defective wheel bearing.
6 Worn or damaged upper or lower link or strut bar bushing.
7 Damaged spring.
8 Loose wheel lug nuts.
9 Worn or damaged rear axleshaft spline.
10 Worn or damaged rear shock absorber mounting bushing.
11 Incorrect rear axle end play.
12 See also causes of noises at the rear axle and driveshaft.

84 Excessive tire wear (not specific to one area)

1 Incorrect tire pressures.
2 Tires out of balance. Have them balanced on the vehicle.
3 Wheels damaged. Inspect and replace as necessary.
4 Suspension or steering components worn (Chapter 1).

85 Excessive tire wear on outside edge

1 Incorrect tire pressure
2 Excessive speed in turns.
3 Wheel alignment incorrect (excessive toe-in and/or camber).

86 Excessive tire wear on inside edge

1 Incorrect tire pressure.
2 Wheel alignment incorrect (toe-out and/or negative camber).
3 Loose or damaged steering components (Chapter 1).

87 Tire tread worn in one place

1 Tires out of balance. Have them balanced on the vehicle.
2 Damaged or buckled wheel. Inspect and replace if necessary.
3 Defective tire.

Chapter 1 Tune-up and routine maintenance

Contents

Specifications

Recommended lubricants and fluids

Note: *Listed here are manufacturer recommendations at the time this manual was written. Manufacturers occasionally upgrade their fluid and lubricant specifications, so check with your local auto parts store for current recommendations.*

Engine oil type	API grade SG
Engine oil viscosity	See accompanying chart
Automatic transmission fluid	
1979 through 1983	Type F automatic transmission fluid
1984 on	Dexron II automatic transmission fluid
Manual transmission lubricant	80W-90 GL-4 or GL-5 gear oil
Differential lubricant	
Standard	90W GL-5 hypoid gear oil
Limited slip differential	90W GL-5 limited slip hypoid gear oil
Power steering fluid	Dexron II automatic transmission fluid
Brake fluid	DOT 3 brake fluid
Engine coolant	50/50 mixture of ethylene glycol-base antifreeze and water
Wheel bearings and balljoints	NLGI No. 2 MP grease

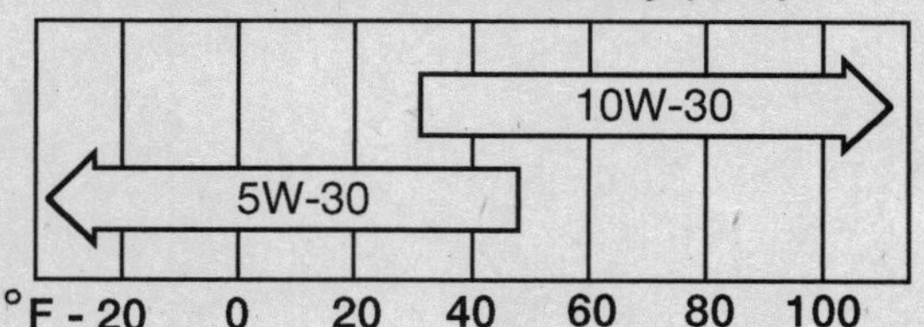

For best fuel economy and cold starting, select the lowest SAE viscosity grade for the expected temperature range

Capacities (approximate)

Engine oil	
1979 (with oil filter change)	5.5 qts
1980 and 1981 (with oil filter change)	4.9 qts
1982 through 1986	
Without oil filter change	4.9 qts
With oil filter change	5.4 qts
1987 through 1989	
Without oil filter change	4.1 qts
With oil filter change	5.0 qts
1990	
Without oil filter change	4.3 qts
With oil filter change	4.7 qts
1991 on	
7M-GE engine	
Without oil filter change	4.3 qts
With oil filter change	4.7 qts
7M-GTE engine	
Without oil filter change	4.7 qts
With oil filter change	5.0 qts
Automatic transmission (when draining pan only)	
1979 through 1986	2.5 qts
1987 on	1.7 qts
Manual transmission	
1979 through 1981	2.7 qts
1982 through 1986	2.6 qts
1987 on	
7M-GE	2.5 qts
7M-GTE	3.2 qts

Capacities (approximate) continued

Differential	
1979	1.4 qts
1980 and 1981	1.6 qts
1982 through 1986	1.3 qts
1987 on	1.4 qts
Cooling system	
1979 and 1980	11.6 qts
1981	9.5 qts
1982 through 1986	
Manual transmission	8.5 qts
Automatic transmission	8.3 qts
1987 on	
7M-GE	
Manual transmission	8.6 qts
Automatic transmission	8.5 qts
7M-GTE	
Manual transmission	8.7 qts
Automatic transmission	8.6 qts

General

Maximum steering wheel freeplay	1.18 in (30 mm)
Maximum balljoint vertical play	
1979 through 1986	0.098 in (2.5 mm)
1987 on	0.098 in (2.5 mm)
Upper	0
Lower	0.012 in
Clutch pedal freeplay	0.20 to 0.59 in (5.0 to 15.0 mm)
Idle speed	Refer to the VECI label under the hood or the ignition timing specifications
Drivebelt deflection (1979 through 1981)	
Power steering pump belt	5/16 to 3/8 inch (measured between the pump and the fan)
Alternator belt	3/8 to 9/16 inch (measured between the alternator and fan)
Air conditioner compressor belt	3/8 to 1/2 inch (measured between the crankshaft and compressor)
Drivebelt tension (using Borroughs tension gauge No. BT-33-73-F)	
1982 through 1986	
Alternator	
New	170 ± 10 lb
Used*	135 ± 20 lb
Power steering pump	
New	125 ± 25 lb
Used*	80 ± 20 lb
Air conditioning compressor	
New	125 ± 25 lb
Used*	80 ± 20 lb
1987 and later	
Alternator	
New	175 ± 5 lb
Used*	115 ± 20 lb
Power steering pump	
New	160 ± 20 lb
Used*	100 ± 20 lb
Air conditioning compressor	
1987 only	
New	132 ± 10 lb
Used*	88 ± 10 lb
1988 on	
New	160 ± 20 lb
Used*	105 ± 10 lb

* *A used belt is one that's been in use for five minutes or more.*

Ignition system

Spark plug type	
1979	ND W16EXR-U or NGK BPR5EA-L
1980 through 1982	ND W16EXR-U or NGK BPR5EY
1983 through 1986	ND P16R or NGK BPR 5E-P11

Ignition system (continued)

Spark plug type (continued)	
1987 on	
7M-GE	ND PQ16R or NGK BCPR5EP11
7M-GTE	ND PQ20R-P8 or NGK BCPR6EP-N8
Spark plug gap	
1979 through 1982	0.031 in (0.8 mm)
1983 through 1986	0.043 in (1.1 mm)
1987 on	
7M-GE	0.043 in (1.1 mm)
7M-GTE	0.031 in (0.8 mm)
Ignition timing and idle speed*	
1979 and 1980	12 degrees BTDC at 800 rpm with the vacuum lines connected
1981	8 degrees BTDC at 800 rpm with the vacuum lines disconnected and plugged
1982	8 degrees BTDC at 650 rpm with the vacuum lines disconnected and plugged
1983 through 1986	10 degrees BTDC at 650 rpm
1987 on	
Non turbo engine	10 degrees BTDC at 700 rpm
Turbo engine	
1987 and 1988	10 degrees BTDC at 650 rpm
1989 on	12 degrees BTDC at 650 rpm

* *Refer to information printed on the Vehicle Emissions Control Information label in the engine compartment. It supercedes information printed here.*

Firing order	1-5-3-6-2-4
Cylinder numbers (front-to-rear)	1-2-3-4-5-6

Valve clearances

Note: *1982 through 1986 engines are equipped with hydraulic lash adjusters; no adjustment is required.*

1979 through 1981 (hot engine)	
Intake	0.011 in (0.28 mm)
Exhaust	0.014 in (0.35 mm)
1987 on (cold engine)	
Intake	0.008 in (0.20 mm)
Exhaust	0.010 in (0.25 mm)

FRONT
1 2 3 4 5 6
1979 through 1981

FRONT
1 2 3 4 5 6
1982 through 1985

FRONT
1 2 3 4 5 6
1986 and later

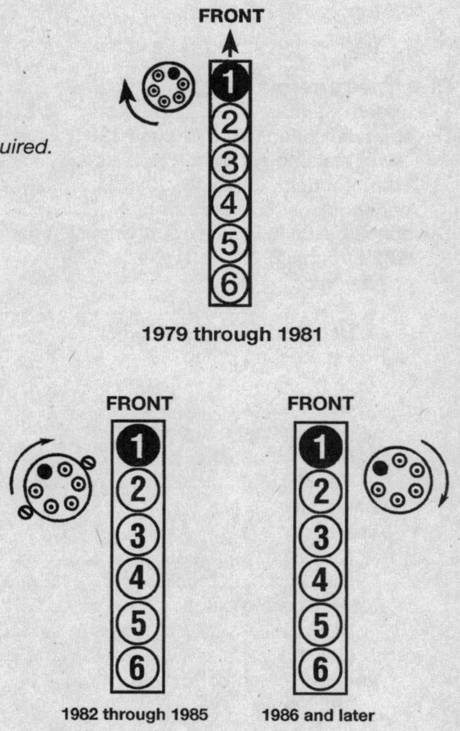

The blackened terminal shown on the distributor cap indicates the Number One spark plug wire position

Cylinder location and distributor rotation

Brakes

Minimum pad thickness	
1979 and 1980	0.040 in
1981 and 1982	
Front	0.120 in
Rear	0.040 in
1983 through 1986	0.118 in
1987 on	0.039 in

Torque specifications

	Ft-lbs
Automatic transmission drain plug	15
Rear axle	
Filler plug	30
Drain plug	15
Manual transmission drain and filler plugs	30
Oxygen sensor nuts	15
Spark plugs	15
Front hub nut (initial torque)	22
Valve cover bolts	5
Front seat mounting bolts	37
Front suspension member-to-body bolts and nuts	78
Rear suspension member-to-body bolts and nuts	118
Strut bar bracket-to-body bolts (1979 through 1986)	42
Wheel lug nuts	75

1 Toyota Supra maintenance schedule

The following recommendations are given with the assumption that the vehicle owner will be doing the maintenance or service work, as opposed to having a dealer service department do the work. The following are factory maintenance recommendations. However, the owner, interested in keeping his or her vehicle in peak condition at all times and with the vehicle's ultimate resale in mind, may want to perform many of these operations more often. Specifically, we would encourage the shortening of fluid and filter replacement intervals.

When the vehicle is new it may be wise to have the vehicle serviced initially by a factory authorized dealer service department to protect the factory warranty. In many cases the initial maintenance check is done at no cost to the owner. Check with your local dealer for additional information.

Every 250 miles or weekly, whichever comes first

Check the engine oil level (Section 4)
Check the engine coolant level (Section 4)
Check the windshield washer fluid level (Section 4)
Check the brake fluid and clutch fluid levels (Section 4)
Check the tires and tire pressures (Section 5)

Every 3000 miles or 3 months, whichever comes first

All items listed above plus:

Check the power steering fluid level (Section 6)
Check the automatic transmission fluid level (Section 7)
Change the engine oil and the oil filter (Section 8)

Every 6000 miles or 6 months, whichever comes first

All items listed above plus:

Inspect and, if necessary, replace the windshield wiper blades (Section 9)
Check the clutch pedal for proper freeplay (Section 10)
Check and, if necessary, service the battery (Section 11)
Check and, if necessary, adjust the engine drivebelts (Section 12)
Inspect and, if necessary, replace the underhood hoses (Section 13)
Check the cooling system (Section 14)
Rotate the tires (Section 15)
Inspect the brake system (Section 16)

Every 15,000 miles or 12 months, whichever comes first

All items listed above plus:

Replace the air filter (Section 17)
Inspect the PCV system (Section 18)
Inspect the fuel system (Section 19)
Replace the fuel filter (Section 20)
Adjust the valve clearances (1979 through 1981 models only) (Section 24)
Check and, if necessary, replace the spark plugs (non-platinum type) (Section 21)
Inspect the spark plug wires, distributor cap and rotor (Section 22)
Check the ignition timing (1979 through 1981 models only) (Section 25)
Check and, if necessary, adjust the engine idle speed (1979 through 1982 models only) (Section 23)
Check the differential lubricant level (Section 26)
Check the manual transmission lubricant level (Section 27)
Inspect the suspension and steering components (Section 28)
Drain and refill the limited slip differential (1979 through 1983 models only) (Section 37)
Replace the manual transmission and differential lubricant on vehicles operated in severe conditions such as low speed in-town driving, towing, cold weather, dusty or muddy roads etc. (Section 37)

Every 30,000 miles or 24 months, whichever comes first

All items listed above plus:

Inspect and, if necessary, replace the fuel filler cap gasket (Section 30)
Inspect the evaporative emissions control (EVAP) system (Section 31)
Inspect the exhaust pipes and mounts (Section 32)
Change the automatic transmission fluid (Section 33)
Lubricate the balljoints (Section 34)
Repack the front wheel bearings (1979 through 1986 models only) (Section 35)
Check the bolts and nuts on the chassis and body to make sure they are tight (Section 36)
Replace the oxygen sensor (1979 through 1981) with a new one (Section 38)
Check the condition of the timing belt (1982 and later) (Chapter 2)
Replace the engine coolant (1979 through 1982 models only) (Section 29)
Replace the manual transmission lubricant (Section 37)

Every 40,000 miles or 30 months, whichever comes first

Drain and refill the limited slip differential (LSD) lubricant (1984 and later models) (Section 37)

Every 60,000 miles or 48 months, whichever comes first

Replace the timing belt (1982 and later models only) on vehicles operated in severe conditions such as low speed in-town driving, towing, cold weather, dusty or muddy roads etc. (see Chapter 2)
Adjust the valve clearances (1987 and later models only) (see Section 24)
Replace the engine coolant (Section 29)
Replace spark plugs (platinum-tipped type)

In 10 years, then each succeeding 2 years

Check the airbag system (1990 and later models only) (see Section 39)

Engine compartment components (1981 model shown)

1. Battery
2. Battery positive post rubber protector
3. Idle speed screw
4. Upper radiator hose
5. Radiator cap
6. Engine oil filler
7. Air intake duct
8. Power steering pump drivebelt
9. Power steering fluid dipstick
10. Air filter housing
11. Windshield washer reservoir
12. Evaporative emission system canister
13. PCV hose
14. Clutch master cylinder reservoir
15. Brake fluid reservoir

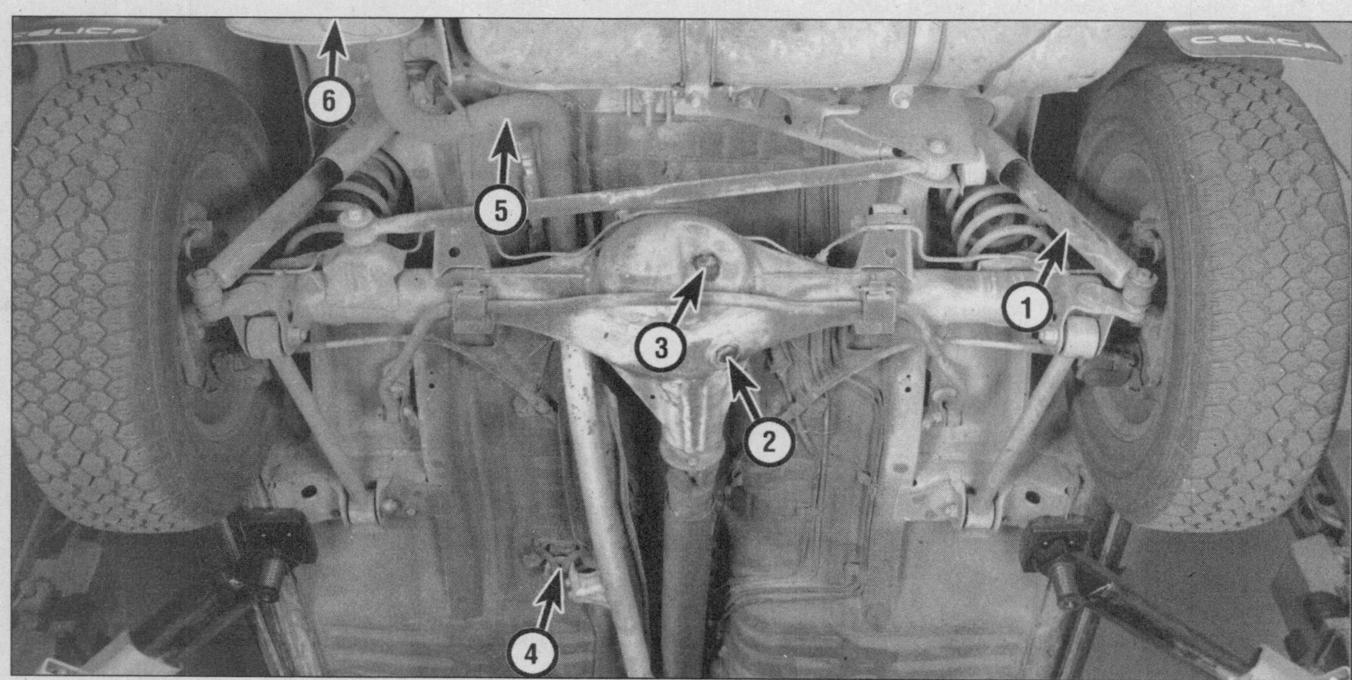

Several of the components located at the rear of the vehicle require maintenance at regular intervals (1981 model shown)

1. Shock absorber
2. Differential drain plug
3. Differential check/fill plug
4. Exhaust system rubber hanger
5. Exhaust pipe
6. Muffler

Engine compartment components (right side) (1983 model shown)

1. *Power steering pump drivebelt*
2. *Air filter housing*
3. *Power steering fluid dipstick*
4. *Engine oil dipstick*
5. *Air intake duct*
6. *Evaporative emission system hose*
7. *Windshield washer reservoir*
8. *PCV hose*
9. *Idle speed screws*
10. *Oil filler cap*
11. *Battery*
12. *Battery positive post rubber protector*
13. *Radiator cap*
14. *Upper radiator hose*

Engine compartment components (left side) (1983 model shown)

1. *Coil wire (high tension lead)*
2. *Battery hold-down clamp*
3. *Distributor cap*
4. *Spark plug wires*
5. *Air filter housing pop fasteners*
6. *Heater hose*
7. *Brake fluid reservoir*

Engine compartment underside components (1983 model shown)

1 *Exhaust pipe*
2 *Evaporative emission system canister*
3 *Steering gear boots*
4 *Brake hose*
5 *Balljoint grease fitting plug*
6 *Brake caliper*
7 *Lower radiator hose*
8 *Engine oil drain plug*
9 *Drivebelts*
10 *Radiator drain fitting*
11 *Power steering hoses*

Several of the components located at the rear of the vehicle require maintenance at regular intervals (1983 model shown)

1 *Exhaust system rubber hanger*
2 *Exhaust pipe*
3 *Shock absorber*
4 *Axleshaft rubber boot*
5 *Differential drain plug*
6 *Differential check/fill plug*
7 *Fuel hose*

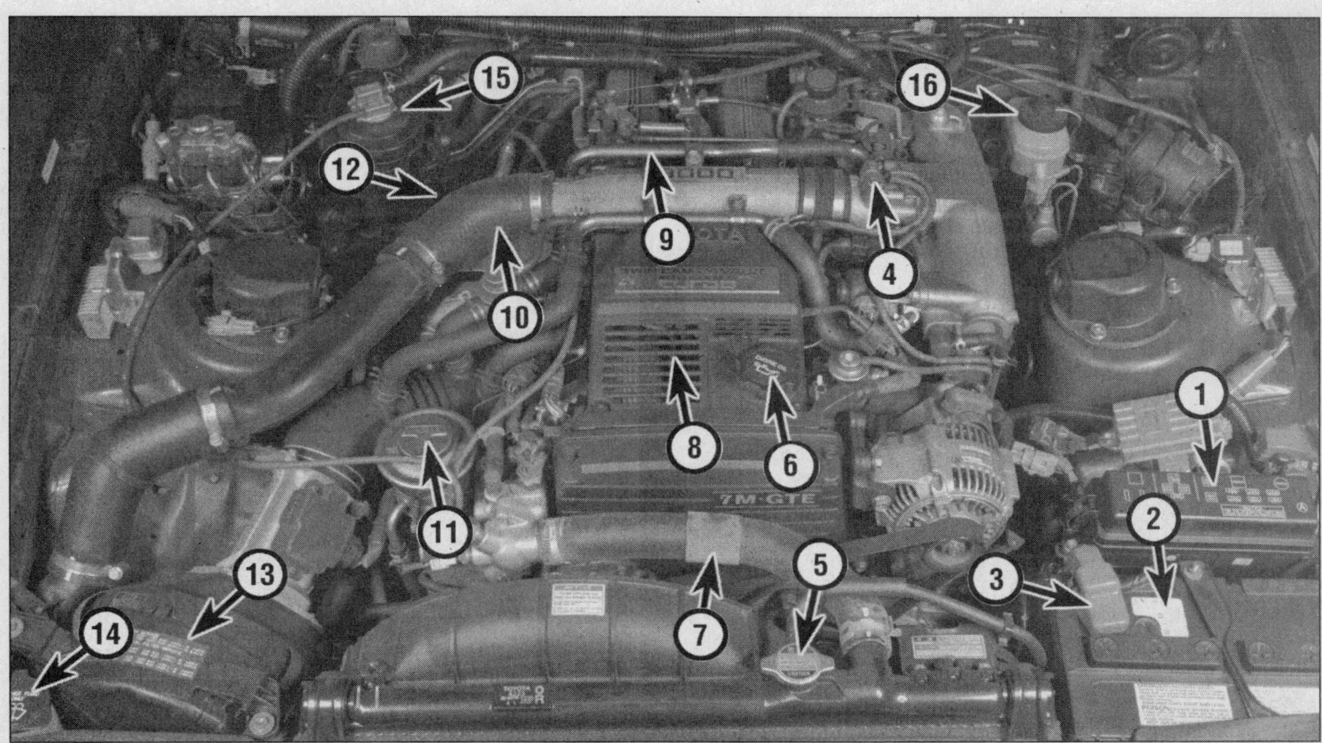

Engine compartment components (1992 Turbo model shown)

1. Fuses and relays
2. Battery
3. Battery positive post rubber protector
4. Idle speed screw (plugged)
5. Radiator cap
6. Engine oil filler cap
7. Upper radiator hose
8. Spark plug wires (under cover)
9. Crankcase vent tube
10. Air intake duct
11. Power steering fluid reservor
12. Engine oil dipstick
13. Air filter housing
14. Windshield washer reservoir
15. Evaporative emission system canister
16. Brake fluid reservoir

Engine compartment underside components (1992 Turbo model shown)

1. Brake hose
2. Steering gear boots
3. Radiator drain fitting
4. Power steering hoses
5. Drivebelts
6. Engine oil drain plug
7. Exhaust pipe
8. Lower radiator hose
9. Shock absorber
10. Brake caliper

Several of the components located at the rear of the vehicle require maintenance at regular intervals (1992 Turbo model shown)

1 *Axleshaft rubber boot*
2 *Shock absorber*
3 *Differential check/fill plug*
4 *Differential drain plug*
5 *Exhaust pipe*
6 *Brake hose*

2 Introduction

This Chapter is designed to help the home mechanic maintain his or her vehicle with the goals of maximum performance, economy, safety and reliability in mind.

On the following pages you will find a maintenance schedule, along with procedures which deal specifically with each item on the schedule. Included are visual checks, adjustments and item replacements.

Servicing your vehicle following the time/mileage maintenance schedule and the step-by-step procedures will result in a planned maintenance program. Keep in mind that it is an all-inclusive plan; maintaining only a few items at the specified intervals will not produce the desired results.

You will find as you service your vehicle that many of the procedures can and should be grouped together. Examples of this are:

If the vehicle is raised for chassis lubrication, check the exhaust system, suspension, steering and fuel system.

If the tires and wheels are removed, as during a routine tire rotation, check the brakes and wheel bearings at the same time.

If you must borrow or rent a torque wrench, replace the spark plugs and check the fastener torque.

The first step in this, or any, maintenance plan is to prepare yourself before the actual work begins. Read through the appropriate Sections for all work that is to be performed before you begin. Gather together all the necessary parts and tools. If it appears that you could have a problem during a particular job, don't hesitate to seek advice from your local parts man or dealer service department.

3 Tune-up general information

The term tune-up is used in this manual to represent a combination of individual operations rather then one specific procedure.

If, from the time the vehicle is new, the routine maintenance schedule is followed closely and frequent checks are made of fluid levels and high wear items, as suggested throughout this manual, the engine will be kept in relatively good running condition and the need for additional work will be minimized.

More likely then not, however, there will be times when the engine is running poorly due to lack of regular maintenance. This is even more likely if a used vehicle, which has not received regular and frequent maintenance checks, is purchased. In such cases, an engine tune-up will be needed outside of the regular routine maintenance intervals.

The first step in any tune-up or engine diagnosis to help correct a poor running engine would be a cylinder compression check. A check of the engine compression will give valuable information regarding the overall performance of many internal components and should be used as a basis for tune-up and repair procedures. If, for instance, a compression check indicates serious internal engine wear, a conventional tune-up will not help the running condition of the engine and would be a waste of time and money. Due to its importance, compression checking should be performed by someone who has the proper compression testing gauge and who is knowledgeable with its use. Further information on compression testing can be found in Chapter 2 of this manual.

The following series of operations are those most often needed to bring a generally poor running engine back into a proper state of tune.

4.2 Location of the engine oil dipstick on a 1992 turbo

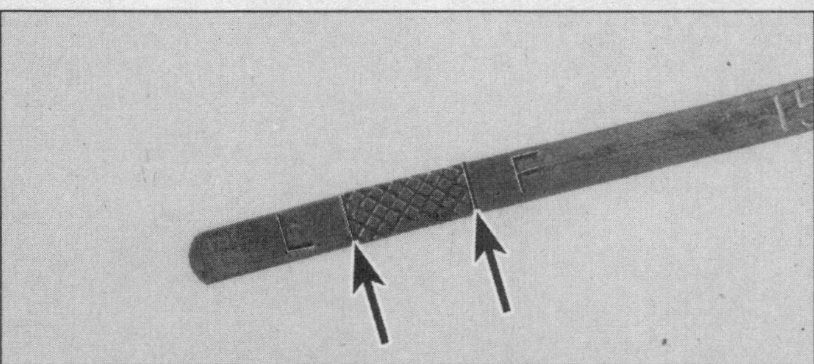

4.4 Engine oil dipstick level marks (the "safe" area is indicated by the crosshatch lines between the marks)

4.8 The coolant reservoir is usually located near the radiator

Minor tune-up

Clean, inspect and test the battery
Check all engine related fluids
Check and adjust the drivebelts
Check and if necessary replace the spark plugs
Inspect the distributor cap and rotor (if equipped)
Inspect the spark plug and coil wires
Check and adjust the idle speed (1979 through 1982 models only)
Check and adjust the ignition timing
Check the PCV system
Check the air filter
Check the cooling system
Check all underhood hoses

Major tune-up

All operations listed under Minor tune-up, plus:
Check the EGR system
Check the ignition system
Check the charging system
Check the fuel system
Install a new air filter
Install a new distributor cap and rotor
Install new spark plug wires

4 Fluid level checks (every 250 miles or weekly)

Refer to illustrations 4.2, 4.4, 4.8, 4.15, 4.17, 4.18a and 4.18b

Note: *The following are fluid level checks to be done on a 250 mile or weekly basis. Additional fluid level checks can be found in specific maintenance intervals which follow. Regardless of intervals, be alert for puddles under the vehicle, which would indicate fluid loss. Repair all leaks as soon as possible and keep a close eye on fluid levels in the meantime.*

1 There are a number of components on a vehicle which rely on the use of fluids to perform their job. During normal operation of the vehicle, these fluids are used up and must be replenished before damage occurs. See Recommended lubricants and fluids at the front of this Chapter for the specific fluid to be used when addition is required. When checking fluid levels, it is important to have the vehicle on a level surface.

Engine oil

2 The engine oil level is checked with a dipstick. The dipstick travels through a tube and into the oil pan to the bottom of the engine **(see illustration)**.

3 The oil level should be checked before the vehicle has been driven, or about 15 minutes after the engine has been shut off. If the oil is checked immediately after driving the vehicle, some of the oil will remain in the upper engine components, producing an inaccurate reading on the dipstick.

4 Pull the dipstick from the tube and wipe all the oil from the end with a clean rag or paper towel. Insert the clean dipstick all the way back into the tube and pull it out again. Note the oil at the end of the dipstick. At its highest point, the level should be between the L and F marks **(see illustration)**.

5 It takes one quart of oil to raise the level from the L mark to the F mark on the dipstick. Do not allow the level to drop below the L mark as engine damage due to oil starvation may occur. On the other hand, do not overfill the engine by adding oil above the F mark, since it may result in oil fouled spark plugs, oil leaks or oil seal failures.

6 Oil is added to the engine after removing a twist off cap located on the cam cover. An oil can spout or funnel will reduce spills.

7 Checking the oil level can be an important preventive maintenance step. If you find the oil level dropping abnormally, it is an indication of oil leakage or internal engine wear which should be corrected. If there are water droplets in the oil, or if it is milky looking, component failure is indicated and the engine should be checked immediately. The condition of the oil can also be checked along with the level. Wipe the oil up the dipstick with your thumb and index finger. Look for small dirt or metal particles clinging to the dipstick. If any are seen, the oil should be drained and fresh oil added.

Engine coolant

8 All vehicles covered by this manual are equipped with a pressurized coolant recovery system. A coolant reservoir attached to the inner fender panel is connected by a hose to the base of the radiator cap **(see illustration)**. As the engine heats up during operation, coolant is forced from the radiator, through the connecting tube and into the reservoir. As the engine cools, the coolant is automatically drawn back into the radiator to keep the level correct.

9 The coolant level should be checked when the engine is hot. Note the level of fluid in the reservoir, which should be at or near the FULL

4.15 The windshield washer reservoir is tucked up front near the air filter on the turbo

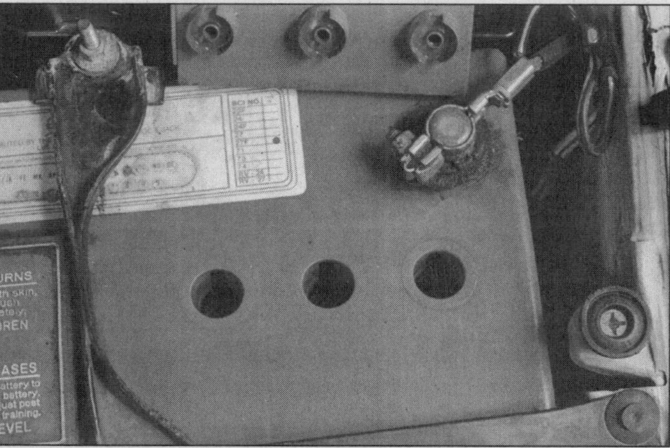

4.17 The battery electrolyte level can be checked after the caps have been removed - DO NOT overfill the cells

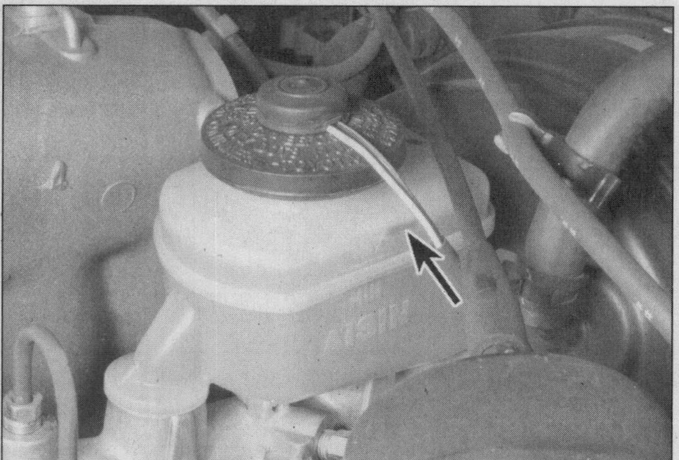

4.18a Visually check the brake fluid level in the master cylinder reservoir

4.18b Check the clutch master cylinder fluid level as well

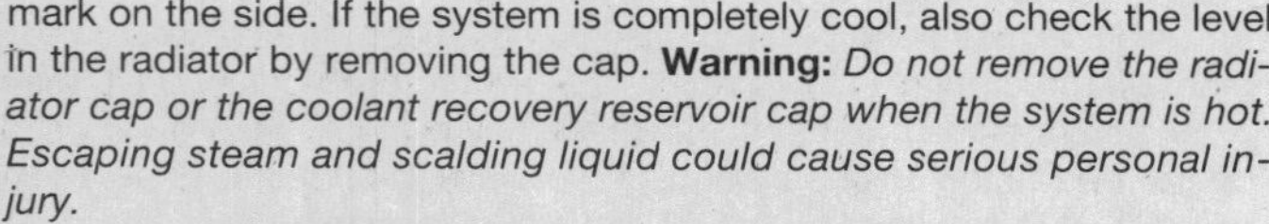

mark on the side. If the system is completely cool, also check the level in the radiator by removing the cap. **Warning:** *Do not remove the radiator cap or the coolant recovery reservoir cap when the system is hot. Escaping steam and scalding liquid could cause serious personal injury.*

10 In the case of the radiator, wait until the system has cooled completely, then wrap a thick cloth around the cap and turn it to the first stop. If any steam escapes, wait until the system has cooled further, then remove the cap. The coolant reservoir cap may be removed carefully after it is apparent that no further boiling is occurring in the reservoir.

11 If only a small amount of coolant is required to bring the system up to the proper level, regular water can be used. However, to maintain the proper antifreeze/water mixture in the system, both should be mixed together to replenish a low level. High quality antifreeze offering protection to -20-degrees F should be mixed with water in the proportion specified on the container. Do not allow antifreeze to come in contact with your skin or painted surfaces of the vehicle. Flush contacted areas immediately with plenty of water.

12 Coolant should be added to the reservoir until it reaches the FULL mark.

13 As the coolant level is checked, note the condition of the coolant. It should be relatively clear. If it is brown or a rust color, the system should be drained, flushed and refilled (Section 29).

14 If the cooling system requires repeated additions to maintain the proper level, have the radiator cap checked for proper sealing ability. Also check for leaks in the system from cracked hoses, loose hose connections, leaking gaskets, etc. (Section 14).

Windshield washer fluid

15 Fluid for the windshield washer system is located in a plastic reservoir located at the right rear corner of the engine compartment on non-turbos at the right front on turbos **(see illustration)**. Water can be used in this system, but commercially available windshield washer solvent is preferred, especially in colder climates where water could freeze. **Caution:** *Do not use cooling system antifreeze - it will damage the vehicle's paint.*

16 To help prevent icing in cold weather, warm the windshield with the defroster before using the washer.

Battery electrolyte

17 Vehicles equipped with maintenance-free batteries require no maintenance because the battery case is sealed and has no removable caps for adding water. If a maintenance-type battery is installed, the caps on the top of the should be removed periodically to check for a low electrolyte level **(see illustration)**. This check will be more critical during the warm summer months. If the electrolyte level is low, add distilled water until the level is above the cell plates. There is an indicator in each cell to help you judge when enough water has been added. Do not overfill.

Brake and clutch fluid

18 The brake master cylinder is mounted on the front of the power booster unit in the engine compartment. The clutch cylinder used with manual transmissions is mounted adjacent to the master cylinder **(see illustrations)**.

5.2 Use a tire tread depth indicator to monitor tire wear - they are available at auto parts stores and service stations and cost very little

19 If a low level is indicated, before removing the cover be sure to wipe the top of the reservoir with a clean rag to prevent contamination of the brake and/or clutch hydraulic system.

20 When adding fluid, pour it carefully into the reservoir, taking care not to spill any onto surrounding painted surfaces. Be sure the specified fluid is used, since mixing different types of brake fluid can cause damage to the system. See *Recommended lubricants and fluids* near the front of this Chapter or your owner's manual.

21 At this time the fluid and cylinder can be inspected for contamination. The system should be drained and refilled if deposits, dirt particles or water droplets are seen in the fluid.

22 After filling the reservoir to the proper level, make sure the cover is properly seated to prevent fluid leakage.

23 The brake fluid in the master cylinder will drop slightly as the brake pads at each wheel wear down during normal operation. If the master cylinder requires repeated replenishing to keep it at the proper level it is an indication of leakage in the brake system, which should be corrected immediately. Check all brake lines and connections, along with the wheel cylinders and booster (see Section 16 for more information).

24 If, upon checking the master cylinder fluid level, you discover the reservoir empty or nearly empty, the brake system should be bled (Chapter 9).

5 Tire and tire pressure checks (every 250 miles or weekly)

1

Refer to illustrations 5.2, 5.3, 5.4a, 5.4b and 5.8

1 Periodic inspection of the tires may spare you from the inconvenience of being stranded with a flat tire. It can also provide you with vital information regarding possible problems in the steering and suspension systems before major damage occurs.

2 Normal tread wear can be monitored with a simple, inexpensive device known as a tread depth indicator **(see illustration)**. When the tread depth reaches the specified minimum, replace the tire(s).

3 Note any abnormal tread wear **(see illustration)**. Tread pattern irregularities such as cupping, flat spots and more wear on one side than the other are indications of front end alignment and/or balance problems. If any of these conditions are noted, take the vehicle to a tire shop or service station to correct the problem.

4 Look closely for cuts, punctures and embedded nails or tacks. Sometimes a tire will hold its air pressure for a short time or leak down very slowly even after a nail has embedded itself into the tread. If a slow leak persists, check the valve stem core to make sure it is tight

Condition	Probable cause	Corrective action	Condition	Probable cause	Corrective action
Shoulder wear	• Underinflation (both sides wear) • Incorrect wheel camber (one side wear) • Hard cornering • Lack of rotation	• Measure and adjust pressure. • Repair or replace axle and suspension parts. • Reduce speed. • Rotate tires.	Feathered edge Toe wear	• Incorrect toe	• Adjust toe-in.
Center wear	• Overinflation • Lack of rotation	• Measure and adjust pressure. • Rotate tires.	Uneven wear	• Incorrect camber or caster • Malfunctioning suspension • Unbalanced wheel • Out-of-round brake drum • Lack of rotation	• Repair or replace axle and suspension parts. • Repair or replace suspension parts. • Balance or replace. • Turn or replace. • Rotate tires.

5.3 This chart will help you determine the condition of the tires, the probable cause(s) of abnormal wear and the corrective action necessary

5.4a If a tire loses air on a steady basis, check the valve core first to make sure it's snug (special inexpensive wrenches are commonly available at auto parts stores)

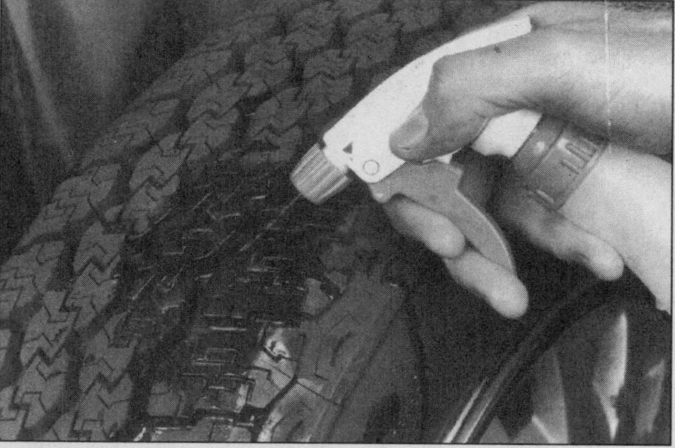

5.4b If the valve core is tight, raise the corner of the vehicle with the low tire and spray a soapy water solution onto the tread as the tire is turned slowly - leaks will cause small bubbles to appear

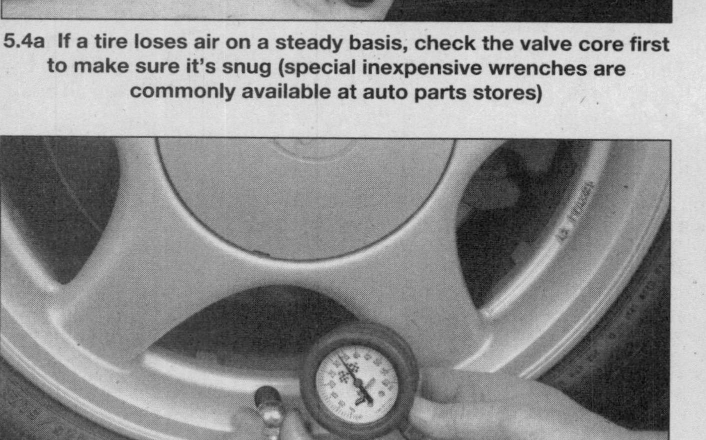

5.8 To extend the life of the tires, check the air pressure at least once a week with an accurate gauge (don't forget the spare!)

6.6 Checking the power steering fluid level

(see illustration). Examine the tread for an object that may have embedded itself into the tire or for a "plug" that may have begun to leak (radial tire punctures are repaired with a plug that is installed in a puncture). If a puncture is suspected, it can be easily verified by spraying a solution of soapy water onto the puncture area **(see illustration)**. The soapy solution will bubble if there is a leak. Unless the puncture is inordinately large, a tire shop or gas station can usually repair the punctured tire.

5 Carefully inspect the inner sidewall of each tire for evidence of brake fluid leakage. If you see any, inspect the brakes immediately.

6 Correct tire air pressure adds miles to the life span of the tires, improves mileage and enhances overall ride quality. Tire pressure cannot be accurately estimated by looking at a tire, particularly if it is a radial. A tire pressure gauge is therefore essential. Keep an accurate gauge in the glovebox. The pressure gauges fitted to the nozzles of air hoses at gas stations are often inaccurate.

7 Always check tire pressure when the tires are cold. "Cold," in this case, means the vehicle has not been driven over a mile in the three hours preceding a tire pressure check. A pressure rise of four to eight pounds is not uncommon once the tires are warm.

8 Unscrew the valve cap protruding from the wheel or hubcap and push the gauge firmly onto the valve **(see illustration)**. Note the reading on the gauge and compare this figure to the recommended tire pressure shown on the tire pressure chart in the owner's manual. Be sure to reinstall the valve cap to keep dirt and moisture out of the valve stem mechanism. Check all four tires and, if necessary, add enough air to bring them up to the recommended pressure levels.

9 Don't forget to keep the spare tire inflated to the specified pressure (consult your owner's manual). Note that the air pressure specified for the compact spare is significantly higher than the pressure of the regular tires.

6 Power steering fluid level check (every 3,000 miles or 3 months)

Refer to illustration 6.6

1 Unlike manual steering, the power steering system relies on fluid which may, over a period of time, require replenishing.

2 The fluid reservoir for the power steering pump is located behind the radiator near the front of the engine.

3 For the check, the front wheels should be pointed straight ahead and the engine should be off.

4 Use a clean rag to wipe off the reservoir cap and the area around the cap. This will help prevent any foreign matter from entering the reservoir during the check.

5 Run the engine until it is at normal operating temperature.

6 Remove the dipstick, wipe it off with a clean rag, reinsert it, then withdraw it and note the fluid level **(see illustration)**.

7 If additional fluid is required, pour the specified type directly into the reservoir, using a funnel to prevent spills.

8 If the reservoir requires frequent fluid additions, all power steering hoses, hose connections, the power steering pump and the rack and pinion assembly should be carefully checked for leaks.

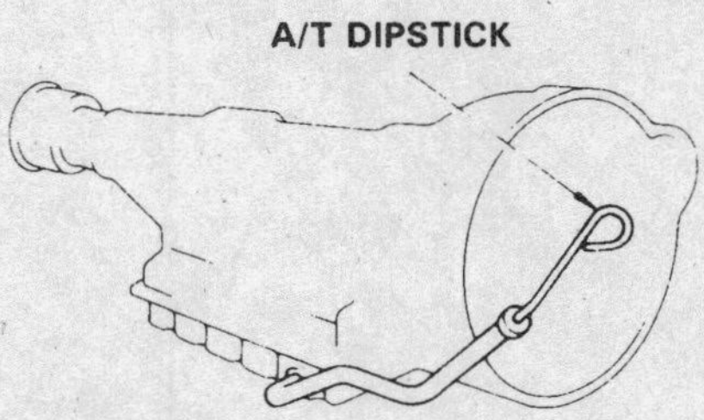

7.3 The automatic transmission fluid dipstick is located on the right-hand (passenger) side of the engine, near the firewall

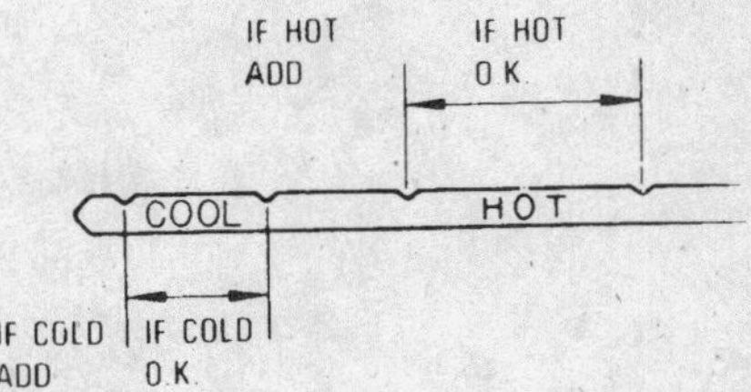

7.6 Although it can be checked cold, the transmission fluid level check will be more accurate if the vehicle is driven first to warm up the transmission - the level must be between the marks in the HOT range

7 Automatic transmission fluid level check (every 3,000 miles or 3 months)

Refer to illustrations 7.3 and 7.6

1 The level of the automatic transmission fluid should be carefully maintained. Low fluid level can lead to slipping or loss of drive, while overfilling can cause foaming and loss of fluid.

2 With the parking brake set, start the engine, then move the shift lever through all the gear ranges, ending in Park. The fluid level must be checked with the vehicle level and the engine running at idle. **Note:** *Incorrect fluid level readings will result if the vehicle has just been driven at high speeds for an extended period, in hot weather in city traffic, or if it has been pulling a trailer. If any of these conditions apply, wait until the fluid has cooled (about 30 minutes).*

3 With the transmission at normal operating temperature, remove the dipstick from the filler tube **(see illustration)**.

4 Wipe the fluid from the dipstick with a clean rag and push it back into the filler tube until the cap seats.

5 Pull the dipstick out again and note the fluid level.

6 If the transmission is hot as directed in Step 3 above, the level should be between the marks in the HOT range **(see illustration)**.

7 Add just enough of the recommended fluid to fill the transmission to the proper level. It takes about one pint to raise the level from the lower mark to the upper mark, so add the fluid a little at a time and keep checking the level until it is correct.

8 The condition of the fluid should also be checked along with the level. If the fluid is a dark reddish-brown color, or if the fluid has a burned smell, the fluid should be changed. If you are in doubt about the condition of the fluid, purchase some new fluid and compare the two for color and smell.

8 Engine oil and filter change (every 3,000 miles or 3 months)

Refer to illustrations 8.3, 8.9, 8.14, 8.19 and 8.23

1 Frequent oil changes may be the best form of preventive maintenance available to the home mechanic. When engine oil ages, it becomes diluted and contaminated, which leads to premature engine wear.

2 Although some sources recommend oil filter changes every other oil change, we feel that the minimal cost of an oil filter and the relative ease with which it is installed dictate that a new filter be used whenever the oil is changed.

3 Gather together all necessary tools and materials before beginning the procedure **(see illustration)**.

4 In addition, you should have plenty of clean rags and newspapers handy to mop up any spills. Access to the underside of the vehicle is greatly improved if the vehicle can be lifted on a hoist, driven onto ramps or supported by jackstands. **Warning:** *Do not work under a vehicle which is supported only by a bumper, hydraulic or scissors-type jack.*

5 If this is your first oil change, get under the vehicle and familiarize yourself with the locations of the oil drain plug and the oil filter. The engine and exhaust components will be warm during the actual work, so

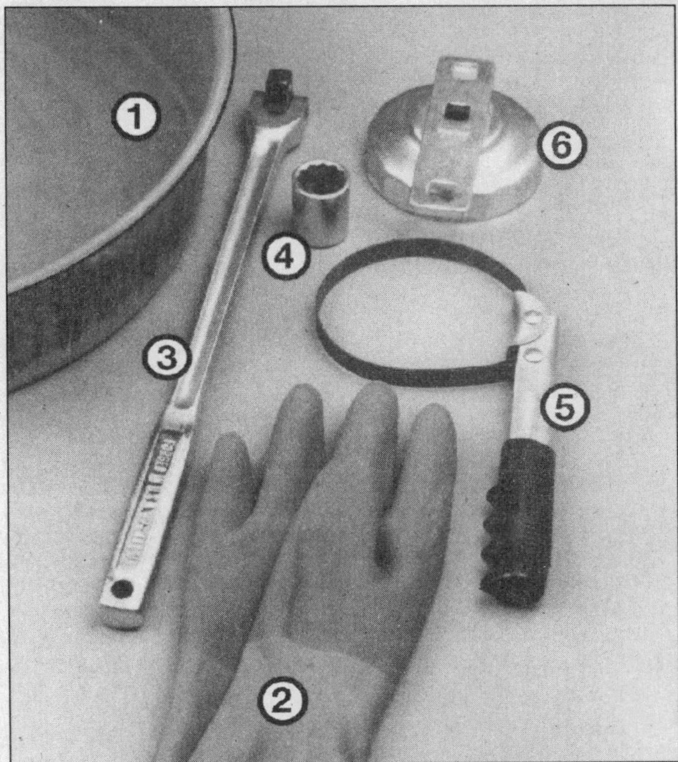

8.3 These tools are required when changing the engine oil and filter

1 ***Drain pan*** - *It should be fairly shallow in depth, but wide to prevent spills*
2 ***Rubber gloves*** - *When removing the drain plug and filter, you will get oil on your hands (the gloves will prevent burns)*
3 ***Breaker bar*** - *Sometimes the oil drain plug is tight, and a long breaker bar is needed to loosen it*
4 ***Socket*** - *To be used with the breaker bar or a ratchet (must be the correct size to fit the drain plug - six-point preferred)*
5 ***Filter wrench*** - *This is a metal band-type wrench, which requires clearance around the filter to be effective*
6 ***Filter wrench*** - *This type fits on the bottom of the filter and can be turned with a ratchet or breaker bar (different-size wrenches are available for different types of filters)*

figure out any potential problems before the engine and accessories are hot.

6 Warm the engine to normal operating temperature. If the new oil or any tools are needed, use this warm-up time to gather everything necessary for the job.

7 With the engine oil warm (warm engine oil will drain better and more built-up sludge will be removed with the oil), raise and support

8.9 Location of the engine oil drain plug (1983 model shown)

8.14 The engine oil filter is located near the engine mount (1992 turbo)

8.19 Lubricate the oil filter gasket with clean engine oil before installing the filter on the engine

8.23 Engine oil addition is made easier and less messy by using a funnel

the vehicle on jackstands.

8 Move all necessary tools, rags and newspapers under the vehicle. Place the drain pan under the drain plug. Keep in mind that the oil will initially flow from the pan with some force, so position the pan accordingly.

9 Being careful not to touch any of the hot exhaust components, use the wrench to remove the drain plug near the bottom of the oil pan **(see illustration)**. Depending on how hot the oil has become, you may want to wear gloves while unscrewing the plug the final few turns.

10 Allow the old oil to drain into the pan. It may be necessary to move the pan farther under the engine as the oil flow slows to a trickle.

11 After all the oil has drained, wipe off the drain plug with a clean rag. Small metal particles may cling to the plug and would immediately contaminate the new oil.

12 Clean the area around the drain plug opening and reinstall the plug.

13 Move the drain pan into position under the oil filter.

14 Use the filter wrench to loosen the oil filter **(see illustration)**. Chain or metal band filter wrenches may distort the filter canister, but this is of no concern as the filter will be discarded anyway.

15 Sometimes the oil filter is on so tight it cannot be loosened, or it is positioned in an area which is inaccessible with a filter wrench. As a last resort, you can punch a metal bar or long screwdriver directly through the side of the canister and use it as a T-bar to turn the filter. If so, be prepared for oil to spurt out of the canister as it is punctured.

16 Completely unscrew the old filter. Be careful, it is full of oil. Empty the oil inside the filter into the drain pan.

17 Compare the old filter with the new one to make sure they are the same type.

18 Use a clean rag to remove all oil, dirt and sludge from the area where the oil filter mounts to the engine. Check the old filter to make sure the rubber gasket is not stuck to the engine mounting surface. If the gasket is stuck to the engine (use a flashlight if necessary), remove it.

19 Apply a light coat of oil around the full circumference of the rubber gasket of the new oil filter **(see illustration)**.

20 Attach the new filter to the engine, following the tightening directions printed on the filter canister or packing box. Most filter manufacturers recommend against using a filter wrench due to the possibility of overtightening and damage to the seal.

21 Remove all tools, rags, etc. from under the vehicle, being careful not to spill the oil in the drain pan, then lower the vehicle.

22 Move to the engine compartment and locate the oil filler cap.

23 If an oil can spout is used, push the spout into the top of the oil can and pour the fresh oil through the filler opening. A funnel may also be used **(see illustration)**.

24 Pour three quarts of fresh oil into the engine. Wait a few minutes to allow the oil to drain into the pan, then check the level on the oil dipstick (see Section 4 if necessary). If the oil level is at or near the F mark, start the engine and allow the new oil to circulate.

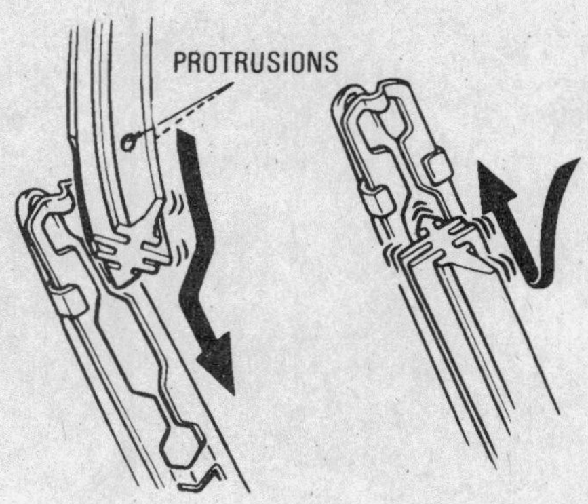

9.5a To install a new blade on the front wiper, insert the end with the small protrusion into the replacement hole and work the rubber along the slot in the blade frame. Finally, pull it back through the end slot

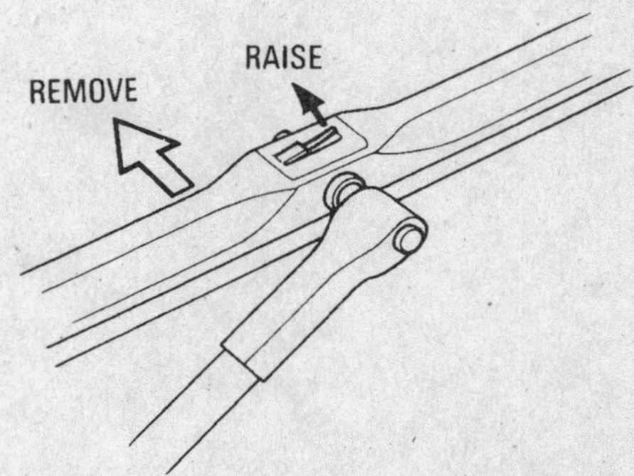

9.5b On rear wipers, raise the catch and remove the entire arm assembly.

25 Run the engine for only about a minute and then shut it off. Immediately look under the vehicle and check for leaks at the oil pan drain plug and around the oil filter. If either is leaking, tighten with a bit more force.
26 With the new oil circulated and the filter now completely full, recheck the level on the dipstick and add enough oil to bring the level to the F mark on the dipstick.
27 During the first few trips after an oil change, make it a point to check frequently for leaks and proper oil level.
28 The old oil drained from the engine cannot be reused in its present state and should be disposed of. Oil reclamation centers, auto repair shops and gas stations will normally accept the oil, which can be refined and used again. After the oil has cooled, it can be drained into a suitable container (capped plastic jugs, topped bottles, milk cartons, etc.) for transport to one of these disposal sites.

9 Wiper blade inspection and replacement (every 6,000 miles or 6 months)

Refer to illustrations 9.5a and 9.5b

1 The windshield wiper and blade assembly should be inspected periodically for damage, loose components and cracked or worn blade elements.
2 Road film can build up on the wiper blades and affect their efficiency, so they should be washed regularly with a mild detergent solution.
3 The action of the wiping mechanism can loosen the bolts, nuts and fasteners, so they should be checked and tightened, as necessary, at the same time the wiper blades are checked.
4 If the wiper blade elements are cracked, worn or warped, they should be replaced with new ones.
5 Lift the arm assembly away from the glass for clearance and remove the blade. Most rubber wiper blade elements can be replaced without replacing the entire wiper blade assembly **(see illustrations)**. Due to the differences in various manufacturer's models and retaining techniques, you will have to refer to the specific instructions provided with the new blade element.

10 Clutch pedal freeplay check and adjustment (every 6,000 miles or 6 months)

Refer to illustration 10.4

1 Proper clutch pedal freeplay is very important for proper clutch operation and to ensure normal clutch service life.

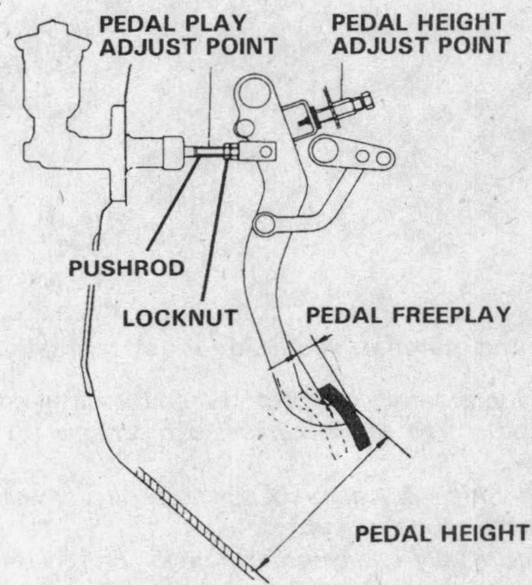

10.4 Checking clutch pedal freeplay

2 Clutch pedal freeplay is the distance the clutch pedal moves before the linkage actually begins to disengage the clutch plate from the flywheel and pressure plate.
3 To check the freeplay, slowly depress the clutch pedal until the resistance offered by the clutch release mechanism is felt (the pedal will suddenly become more difficult to move).
4 Measure the distance the clutch pedal has traveled and compare it to the specifications listed in this Chapter **(see illustration)**.
5 If adjustment is required, loosen the locknut and turn the pushrod until the freeplay is correct.
6 Retighten the locknut.

11 Battery check, maintenance and charging (every 6,000 miles or 6 months)

Check and maintenance

Refer to illustrations 11.1, 11.4, 11.8a, 11.8b, 11.8c and 11.8d

Warning: *Certain precautions must be followed when checking and servicing the battery. Hydrogen gas, which is highly flammable, is always present in the battery cells, so keep lighted tobacco and all other flames and sparks away from it. The electrolyte inside the battery is actually dilute sulfuric acid, which will cause injury if splashed on your skin or in your eyes. It will also ruin clothes and painted surfaces. When removing the battery cables, always detach the negative cable first and hook it up last!*

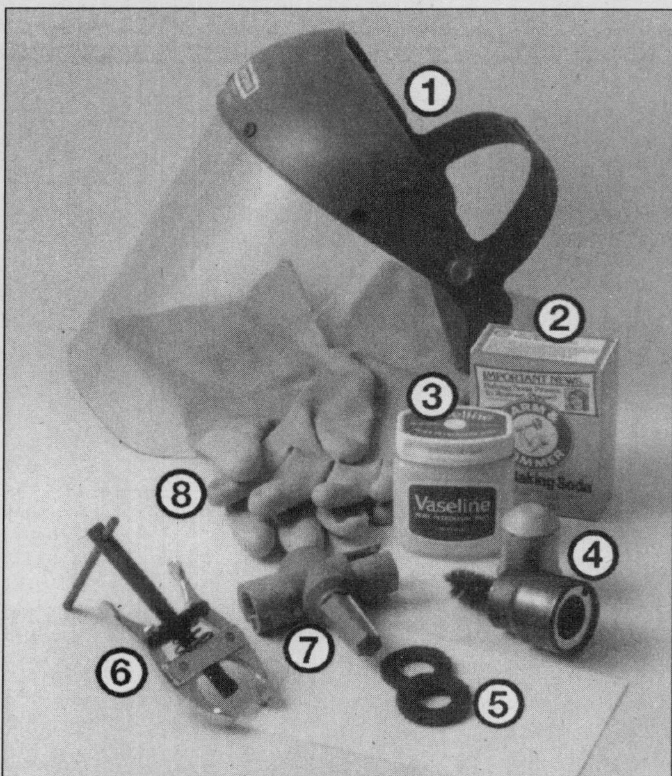

11.1 Tools and materials required for battery maintenance

1. ***Face shield/safety goggles*** *- When removing corrosion with a brush, the acidic particles can easily fly up into your eyes*
2. ***Baking soda*** *- A solution of baking soda and water can be used to neutralize corrosion*
3. ***Petroleum jelly*** *- A layer of this on the battery posts will help prevent corrosion*
4. ***Battery post/cable cleaner*** *- This wire brush cleaning tool will remove all traces of corrosion from the battery posts and cable clamps*
5. ***Treated felt washers*** *- Placing one of these on each post, directly under the cable clamps, will help prevent corrosion*
6. ***Puller*** *- Sometimes the cable clamps are very difficult to pull off the posts, even after the nut/bolt has been completely loosened. This tool pulls the clamp straight up and off the post without damage*
7. ***Battery post/cable cleaner*** *- Here is another cleaning tool which is a slightly different version of number 4 above, but it does the same thing*
8. ***Rubber gloves*** *- Another safety item to consider when servicing the battery; remember that's acid inside the battery*

11.4 Remove the cell caps to check the water level in the battery - if the level is low, add distilled water only

11.8a Battery terminal corrosion usually appears as light, fluffy powder

Caution: *If the stereo in your vehicle is equipped with an anti-theft system, refer to the information on page 0-15 at the front of this manual before detaching the cable.*

1 Battery maintenance is an important procedure which will help ensure that you are not stranded because of a dead battery. Several tools are required for this procedure **(see illustration)**.

2 Before servicing the battery, always turn the engine and all accessories off and disconnect the cable from the negative terminal of the battery.

3 A sealed (sometimes called maintenance free) battery is standard equipment. The cell caps cannot be removed, no electrolyte checks are required and water cannot be added to the cells. However, if an aftermarket battery has been installed and it is a type that requires regular maintenance, the following procedures can be used.

4 Check the electrolyte level in each of the battery cells **(see illustration)**. It must be above the plates. There's usually a split-ring indicator in each cell to indicate the correct level. If the level is low, add distilled water only, then install the cell caps. **Caution:** *Overfilling the cells may cause electrolyte to spill over during periods of heavy charging, causing corrosion and damage to nearby components.*

5 If the positive terminal and cable clamp on your vehicle's battery is equipped with a rubber protector, make sure that it's not torn or damaged. It should completely cover the terminal.

6 The external condition of the battery should be checked periodically. Look for damage such as a cracked case.

7 Check the tightness of the battery cable clamps to ensure good electrical connections and inspect the entire length of each cable, looking for cracked or abraded insulation and frayed conductors.

8 If corrosion (visible as white, fluffy deposits) is evident, remove the cables from the terminals, clean them with a battery brush and reinstall them **(see illustrations)**. Corrosion can be kept to a minimum by installing specially treated washers available at auto parts stores or by applying a layer of petroleum jelly or grease to the terminals and cable clamps after they are assembled.

9 Make sure that the battery carrier is in good condition and that the hold-down clamp bolt is tight. If the battery is removed (see Chapter 5 for the removal and installation procedure), make sure that no parts remain in the bottom of the carrier when it's reinstalled. When reinstalling the hold-down clamp, don't overtighten the bolt.

10 Corrosion on the carrier, battery case and surrounding areas can be removed with a solution of water and baking soda. Apply the mix-

11.8b Removing the cable from a battery post with a wrench - sometimes a special pliers is required for this procedure if corrosion has caused deterioration of the nut hex (always remove the ground cable first and hook it up last!)

11.8c Regardless of the type of tool used on the battery posts, a clean, shiny surface should be the result

11.8d When cleaning the cable clamps, all corrosion must be removed (the inside of the clamp is tapered to match the taper on the post, so don't remove too much material)

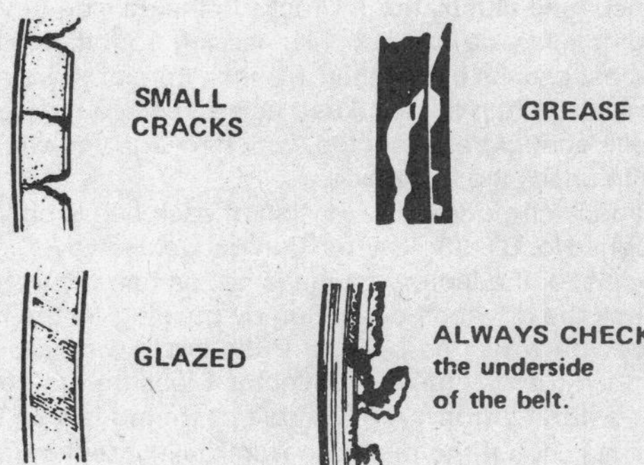

12.3 Here are some of the more common problems associated with drivebelts (check the belts very carefully to prevent an untimely breakdown)

ture with a small brush, let it work, then rinse it off with plenty of clean water.

11 Any metal parts of the vehicle damaged by corrosion should be coated with a zinc-based primer, then painted.

12 Additional information on the battery, charging and jump starting can be found in Chapter 5 and the front of this manual.

Charging

13 Remove all of the cell caps (if equipped) and cover the holes with a clean cloth to prevent spattering electrolyte. Disconnect the negative battery cable and hook the battery charger leads to the battery posts (positive to positive, negative to negative), then plug in the charger. Make sure it is set at 12 volts if it has a selector switch.

14 If you're using a charger with a rate higher than two amps, check the battery regularly during charging to make sure it doesn't overheat. If you're using a trickle charger, you can safely let the battery charge overnight after you've checked it regularly for the first couple of hours.

15 If the battery has removable cell caps, measure the specific gravity with a hydrometer every hour during the last few hours of the charging cycle. Hydrometers are available inexpensively from auto parts stores - follow the instructions that come with the hydrometer. Consider the battery charged when there's no change in the specific gravity reading for two hours and the electrolyte in the cells is gassing (bubbling) freely. The specific gravity reading from each cell should be very close to the others. If not, the battery probably has a bad cell(s).

16 Some batteries with sealed tops have built-in hydrometers on the top that indicate the state of charge by the color displayed in the hydrometer window. Normally, a bright-colored hydrometer indicates a full charge and a dark hydrometer indicates the battery still needs charging. Check the battery manufacturer's instructions to be sure you know what the colors mean.

17 If the battery has a sealed top and no built-in hydrometer, you can hook up a digital voltmeter across the battery terminals to check the charge. A fully charged battery should read 12.6 volts or higher.

18 Further information on the battery and jump starting can be found in Chapter 5 and at the front of this manual.

12 Drivebelt check, adjustment and replacement (every 6,000 miles or 6 months)

Check

Refer to illustrations 12.3 and 12.4

1 The drivebelts, sometimes called V-belts or simply "fan" belts, are located at the front of the engine and play an important role in the overall operation of the vehicle and its components. Due to their function and material make up, the belts are prone to failure after a period of time and should be inspected and adjusted periodically to prevent major engine damage.

2 The number of belts used on a particular vehicle depends on the accessories installed. Drivebelts are used to turn the alternator, power steering pump, water pump and air conditioning compressor. Depending on the pulley arrangement, a single belt may be used to drive more then one of these components.

3 With the engine off, open the hood and locate the various belts at the front of the engine. Using your fingers (and a flashlight, if necessary), move along the belts checking for cracks and separation of the belt plies. Also check for fraying and glazing, which gives the belt a

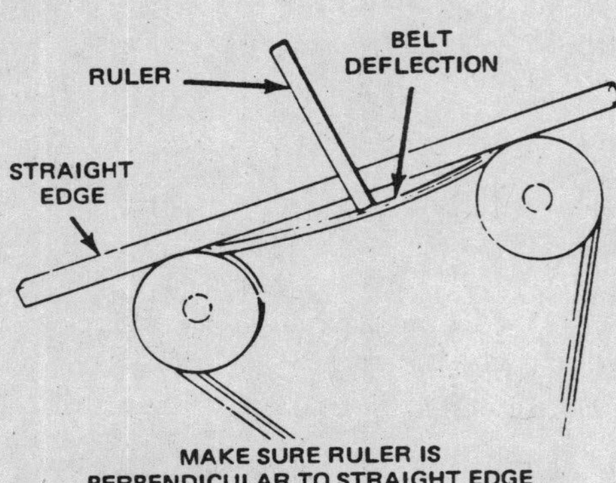

12.4 Measuring drivebelt deflection with a straightedge and ruler

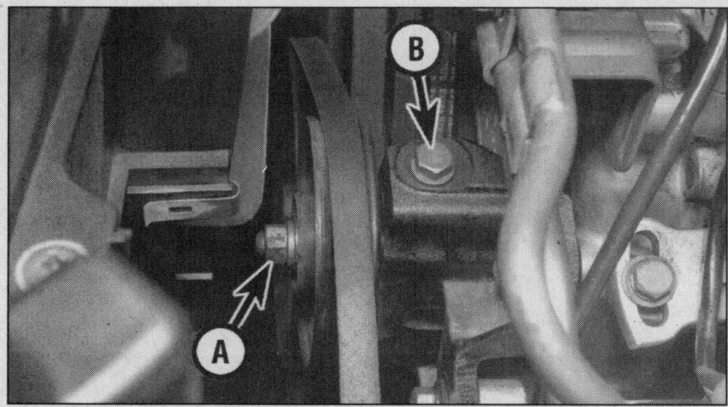

12.7 To adjust the drivebelt on models equipped with an adjustable idler pulley, loosen the pulley nut (A) and turn the adjuster bolt (B) to raise (tighten) or lower (loosen) the drivebelt

shiny appearance **(see illustration)**. Cracks in the rib side of V-ribbed belts are acceptable, as are small chunks missing from the ribs. If a V-ribbed belt has lost chunks bigger than 1/2-inch from any two adjacent ribs, or if the missing chunks cause belt noise, replace the belt. Both sides of the belts should be inspected, which means you will have to twist each belt to check the underside.

4 On 1982 and later models, the tension of each belt is checked by using a Borroughs No. BT-33-73-F tension gauge. However, on 1981 and earlier models, or if a factory gauge is not on hand, a good alternative is to check the drivebelt deflection by pushing on the belt at a distance halfway between the pulleys. Push firmly with your thumb and see how much the belt moves (deflects). Measure the deflection with a ruler **(see illustration)**. A good rule of thumb is that the belt should deflect 1/4-inch if the distance from pulley center-to-pulley center is between 7 and 11 inches. The belt should deflect 1/2-inch if the distance from pulley center-to-pulley center is between 12 and 16 inches.

Adjustment

Refer to illustration 12.7

5 If it is necessary to adjust the belt tension, either to make the belt tighter or looser, it is done by moving the belt driven accessory on the bracket.

6 For each component there will be an adjusting bolt and a pivot bolt. Both bolts must be loosened slightly to enable you to move the component.

7 After the two bolts have been loosened, move the component away from the engine to tighten the belt or toward the engine to loosen the belt. Hold the accessory in position and check the belt tension. If it is correct, tighten the two bolts until just snug, then recheck the tension. If the tension is correct, tighten the bolts. **Note:** *Some belts are equipped with an adjustable idler pulley* **(see illustration)**.

8 It will often be necessary to use some sort of pry bar to move the accessory while the belt is adjusted. If this must be done to gain the proper leverage, be very careful not to damage the component being moved or the part being pried against.

Replacement

Refer to illustration 12.11

9 To replace a belt, follow the instructions above for adjustment, however completely remove the belt from the pulleys.

10 In some cases you will have to remove more then one belt because of their arrangement on the front of the engine. Due to this and the fact that belts will tend to fail at the same time, it is wise to replace all belts together. Mark each belt and its appropriate pulley groove so all replacement belts can be installed in their proper positions.

11 It is a good idea to take the old belts with you when buying new ones in order to make a direct comparison for length, width and design. On V-ribbed belts, be sure the belt ribs engage the pulley correctly **(see illustration)**.

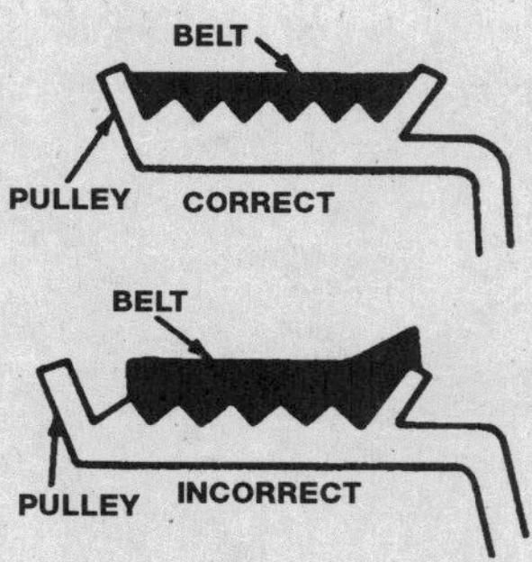

12.11 V-ribbed belts should be centered on the pulleys

13 Underhood hose check and replacement (every 6,000 miles or 6 months)

Warning: *Replacement of air conditioning hoses must be left to a dealer service department or air conditioning shop that has the proper equipment to depressurize the system safely. Never remove air conditioning components or hoses until the system has been depressurized.*

General

1 High temperatures under the hood can cause the deterioration of the rubber and plastic hoses used for engine, accessory and emission systems operation. Periodic inspection should be made for cracks, loose clamps, material hardening and leaks.

2 Information specific to the cooling system hoses can be found in Section 14.

3 Some, but not all, hoses use clamps to secure the hoses to fittings. Where clamps are used, check to be sure they haven't lost their tension, allowing the hose to leak. Where clamps are not used, make sure the hose has not expanded and/or hardened where it slips over the fitting, allowing it to leak.

Vacuum hoses

4 It is quite common for vacuum hoses, especially those in the emissions system, to be color coded or identified by colored stripes molded into the hose. Various systems require hoses with different wall thicknesses, collapse resistance and temperature resistance. When replacing hoses, be sure to use the same hose material on the new hose.

5 Often the only effective way to check a hose is to remove it completely from the vehicle. Where more then one hose is removed, be sure to label the hoses and their attaching points to insure proper reattachment.

6 When checking vacuum hoses, be sure to include any plastic T-fittings in the check. Check the fittings for cracks and the hose where

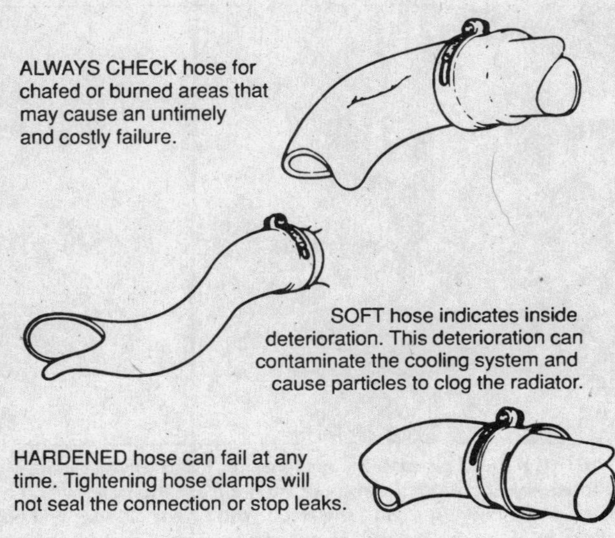

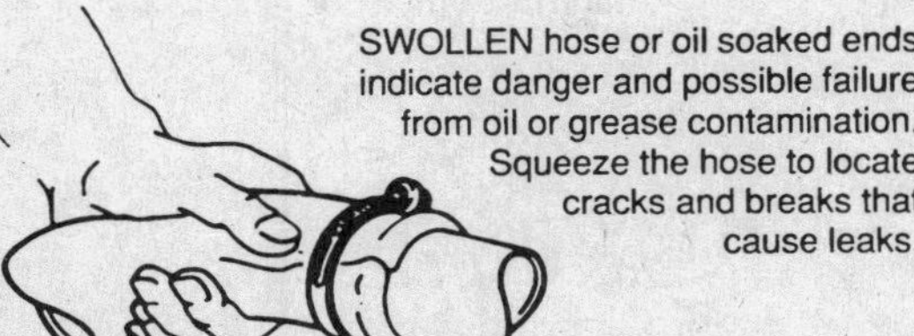

14.4 Hoses, like drivebelts, have a habit of failing at the worst possible time - to prevent the inconvenience of a blown radiator or heater hose, inspect them carefully as shown here

it fits over the fitting for enlargement, which could cause leakage.

7 A small piece of vacuum hose (1/4-inch inside diameter) can be used as a stethoscope to detect vacuum leaks. Hold one end of the hose to your ear and probe around vacuum hoses and fittings, listening for the hissing sound characteristic of a vacuum leak. **Warning:** *When probing with the vacuum hose stethoscope, be careful not to allow your body or the hose to come into contact with moving engine components such as drivebelts, the cooling fan, etc.*

Fuel hose

Warning: *Gasoline is extremely flammable, so take extra precautions when you work on any part of the fuel system. Don't smoke or allow open flames or bare light bulbs near the work area, and don't work in a garage where a natural gas-type appliance (such as a water heater or clothes dryer) with a pilot light is present. If you spill any fuel on your skin, rinse it off immediately with soap and water. When you perform any kind of work on the fuel system, wear safety glasses and have a Class B type fire extinguisher on hand.*

8 On models such as these, equipped with fuel injection, the fuel system pressure must be relieved (see Chapter 4) before disconnecting any fuel lines.

9 Check all rubber fuel lines for deterioration and chafing. Check especially for cracking in areas where the hose bends and just before clamping points, such as where a hose attaches to the fuel filter or fuel injection unit.

10 High quality fuel line, usually identified by the word Fluroelastomer printed on the hose, should be used for fuel line replacement. Under no circumstances should unreinforced vacuum line, clear plastic tubing or water hose be used for fuel line replacement.

11 Spring-type clamps are commonly used on fuel lines. These clamps often lose their tension over a period of time, and can be "sprung" during the removal process. Therefore it is recommended that all spring-type clamps be replaced with screw clamps whenever a hose is replaced.

Metal lines

12 Sections of metal line are often used for fuel line between the fuel pump and fuel injection unit. Check carefully to be sure the line has not been bent and crimped and that cracks have not started in the line, particularly in the area of bends.

13 If a section of metal fuel line must be replaced, only seamless steel tubing should be used, since copper and aluminum tubing do not have the strength necessary to withstand normal engine operating vibration.

14 Check the metal brake lines where they enter the master cylinder for cracks in the lines or loose fittings. Any sign of brake fluid leakage calls for an immediate thorough inspection of the brake system.

14 Cooling system check (every 6,000 miles or 6 months)

Refer to illustration 14.4

1 Many major engine failures can be attributed to a faulty cooling system. If the vehicle is equipped with an automatic transmission, the cooling system also cools the transmission fluid and thus plays an important role in prolonging transmission life.

2 The cooling system should be checked with the engine cold. Do this before the vehicle is driven for the day or after it has been shut off for at least three hours.

3 Remove the radiator cap and thoroughly clean the cap, inside and out, with clean water. Also, clean the filler neck on the radiator. All traces of corrosion should be removed. The coolant inside the radiator should be relatively transparent. If it is rust colored, the system should be drained and refilled (Section 29).

4 Carefully check the large upper and lower radiator hoses along with the smaller diameter heater hoses which run from the engine to the firewall. Inspect each hose along its entire length, replacing any hose which is cracked, swollen or shows signs of deterioration. Cracks may become more apparent if the hose is squeezed **(see illustration)**.

5 Make sure that all hose connections are tight. A leak in the cooling system will usually show up as white or rust colored deposits on the areas adjoining the leak. If wire-type clamps are used at the ends of the hoses, it may be wise to replace them with more secure screw-type clamps.

6 Use compressed air or a soft brush to remove bugs, leaves, etc. from the front of the radiator or air conditioning condenser. Be careful not to damage the delicate cooling fins or cut yourself on them.

7 Every other inspection, or at the first indications of a fault in the cooling system, have the cap and system pressure tested. If you do not have a pressure tester, most gas stations and repair shops will do this for a minimal charge.

15 Tire rotation (every 6,000 miles or 6 months)

Refer to illustration 15.1

1 The tires should be rotated at the specified intervals and whenever uneven wear is noticed **(see illustration)**. Since the vehicle will be raised and the tires removed anyway, check the brakes (Section 16) and the wheel bearings (Section 35) at this time.

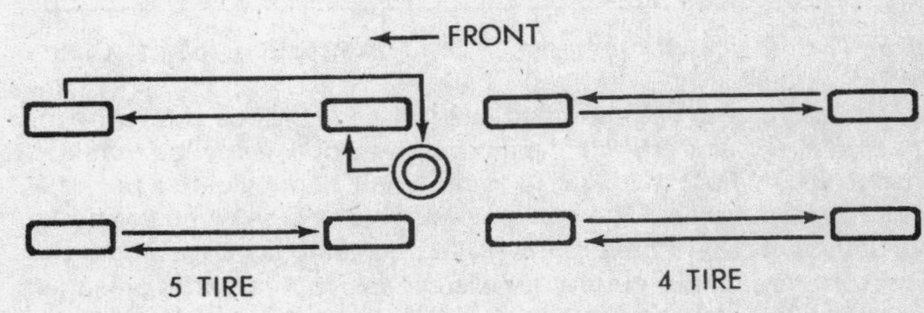

15.1 Tire rotation diagram

16.6 The pad lining material (arrow) is visible through the inspection hole in the caliper

16.9 If a more precise measurement of pad thickness is necessary, the pads must be removed from the caliper and measured like this - spraying the pads with brake cleaner will help you determine where the pad material ends and the steel backing material begins

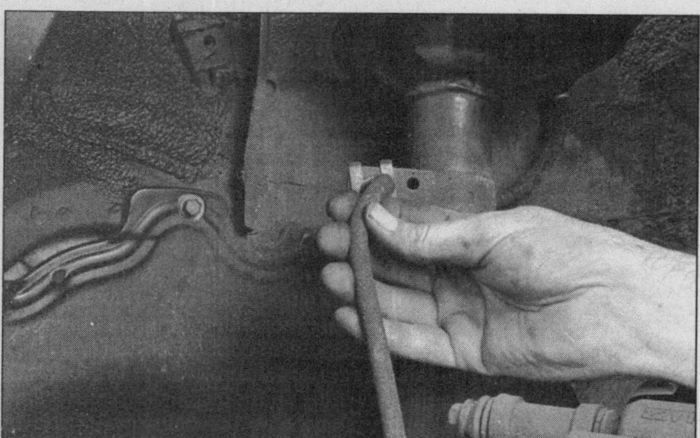

16.11a Always inspect the brake hoses before installing the wheels - look for cracks, leaks and damage of any kind

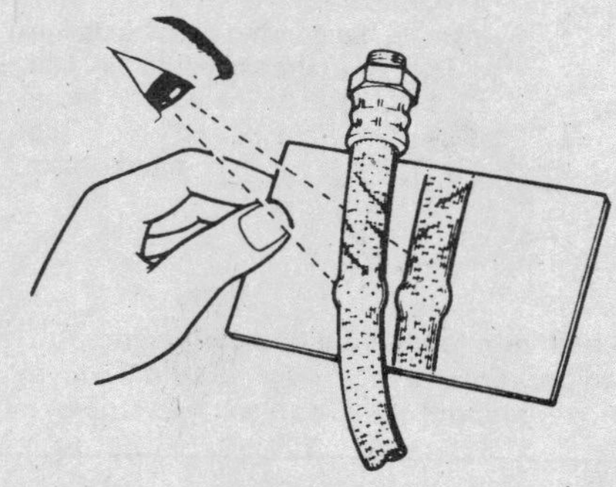

16.11b A mirror may help when checking the backside of the hose - any hose with cracks or swollen areas (shown here) should be replaced

2 Refer to the information in *Jacking and towing* at the front of this manual for the proper procedures to follow when raising the vehicle and changing a tire. If the brakes are to be checked, do not apply the parking brake as stated. Make sure the tires are blocked to prevent the vehicle from rolling.

3 Preferably, the entire vehicle should be raised at the same time. This can be done on a hoist or by jacking up each corner and then lowering the vehicle onto jackstands placed under the frame rails. Always use four jackstands and make sure the vehicle is safely supported.

4 After rotation, check and adjust the tire pressures as necessary and be sure to check the lug nut tightness.

5 For further information on the wheels and tires, refer to Chapter 10.

16 Brake check (every 6,000 miles or 6 months)

Note: *For detailed photographs of the brake system, refer to Chapter 9.*

1 In addition to the specified intervals, the brakes should be inspected every time the wheels are removed or whenever a defect is suspected. Any of the following symptoms could indicate a potential brake system defect: The vehicle pulls to one side when the brake pedal is depressed; the brakes make squealing or dragging noises when applied; brake pedal travel is excessive; the pedal pulsates; brake fluid leaks, usually onto the inside of the tire or wheel.

2 The disc brake pads have built-in wear indicators which should make a high pitched squealing or scraping noise when they are worn to the replacement point. When you hear this noise, replace the pads immediately or expensive damage to the rotors can result.

3 Loosen the wheel lug nuts.

4 Raise the vehicle and place it securely on jackstands.

5 Remove the wheels (see *Jacking and towing* at the front of this book, or your owner's manual, if necessary).

Disc brakes

Refer to illustrations 16.6, 16.9, 16.11a and 16.11b

6 There are two pads - an outer and an inner - in each caliper. The pads are visible through small inspection holes in each caliper **(see illustration)**.

7 Check the pad thickness by looking at each end of the caliper and through the inspection hole in the caliper body. If the lining material is less than the specified thickness, replace the pads. **Note:** *Keep in mind that the lining material is riveted or bonded to a metal backing plate and the metal portion is not included in this measurement.*

8 If it is difficult to determine the exact thickness of the remaining pad material by the above method, or if you are at all concerned about the condition of the pads, remove the caliper(s), then remove the pads from the calipers for further inspection (refer to Chapter 9).

9 Once the pads are removed from the calipers, clean them with brake cleaner and remeasure them with a small steel pocket ruler **(see illustration)** or a vernier caliper.

10 Check the condition of the brake discs (rotors). Look for scoring, gouging and burned spots. If these conditions exist, remove the disc and have it resurfaced (refer to Chapter 9).

11 Before installing the wheels, check all brake lines and hoses for damage, wear, deformation, cracks, corrosion, leakage, bends and twists, particularly in the vicinity of the rubber hoses at the calipers

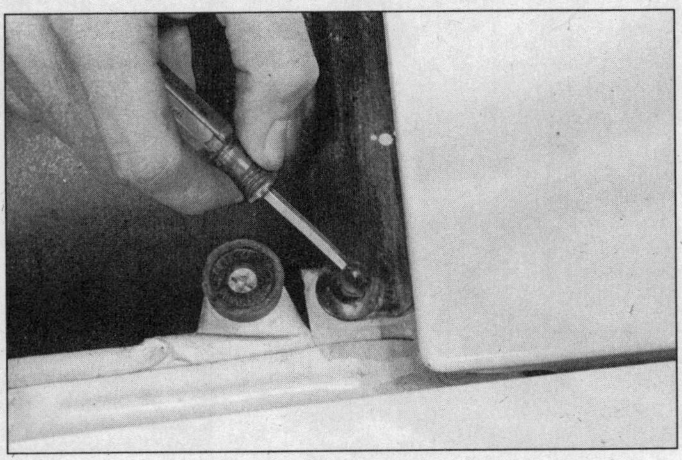

17.2a On 1982 through 1986 models, remove the plastic pop fasteners . . .

17.2b . . . then release the filter housing retaining ring

17.2c On 1981 models, first remove the air duct bolts (arrows) and the duct . . .

17.2d . . . then unfasten the clips and lift the air filter out

(see illustrations). Check the clamps for tightness and the connections for leakage. Make sure that all hoses and lines are clear of sharp edges, moving parts and the exhaust system. If any of the above conditions are noted, repair, reroute or replace the lines and/or fittings as necessary (refer to Chapter 9).

12 Later models are equipped with disc brakes on the rear wheels which incorporate drum-type parking brakes into the rear discs. See Chapter 9 for information on inspecting the parking brake shoes.

Brake booster check

13 Sit in the driver's seat and perform the following sequence of tests.

14 With the engine stopped, depress the brake pedal several times-the travel distance should not change.

15 With the brake fully depressed, start the engine - the pedal should move down a little when the engine starts.

16 Depress the brake, stop the engine and hold the pedal in for about 30 seconds - the pedal should neither sink nor rise.

17 Restart the engine, run it for about a minute and turn it off. Then firmly depress the brake several times - the pedal travel should decrease with each application.

18 If your brakes do not operate as described above when the preceding tests are performed, the brake booster is either in need of repair or has failed. Refer to Chapter 9 for the removal procedure.

Parking brake

19 Slowly pull up on the parking brake and count the number of clicks you hear until the handle is up as far as it will go. The adjustment is correct if you hear the specified number of clicks. If you hear more or fewer clicks, it's time to adjust the parking brake (refer to Chapter 9).

20 An alternative method of checking the parking brake is to park the vehicle on a steep hill with the parking brake set and the transmission in Neutral. If the parking brake cannot prevent the vehicle from rolling, it is in need of adjustment (see Chapter 9).

17 Air filter replacement (every 15,000 miles or 12 months)

Refer to illustrations 17.2a through 17.2h

1 At the specified intervals, the air filter should be replaced with a new one. A thorough program of preventive maintenance would require the filter to be inspected between changes.

2 The air filter is located inside the air filter housing on the right front side of the engine compartment. On 1983 models, the filter is replaced by first pulling up the two plastic pop fasteners then removing the filter housing retaining ring **(see illustrations)**. Other models are similar **(see illustrations)**.

3 Lift the air filter housing and the element out of the engine compartment.

4 Wipe out the inside of the air filter housing with a clean rag.

5 Place the new filter into the air filter housing. Make sure it seats properly.

6 To install, reverse the removal procedure. **Note:** *On 1983 models, be sure to align the tab on the housing with the notch in the cover before installing the retaining ring.*

17.2e On later turbo models, first remove the air intake tube . . .

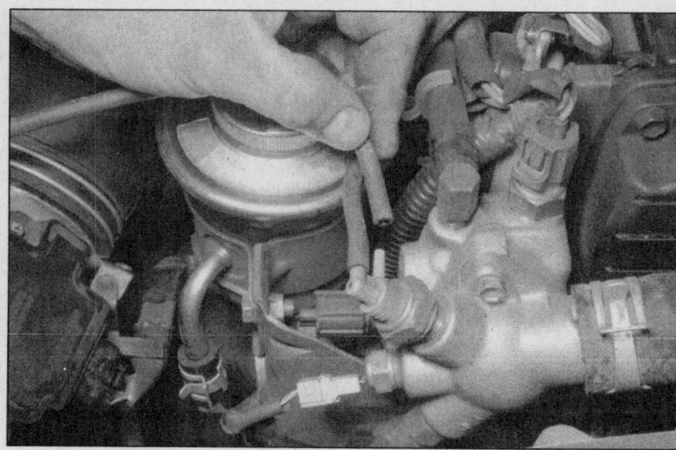

17.2f . . . label then disconnect the vacuum lines from the VSV located in the thermostat housing, . . .

17.2g . . . carefully pull the filter housing cover back . . .

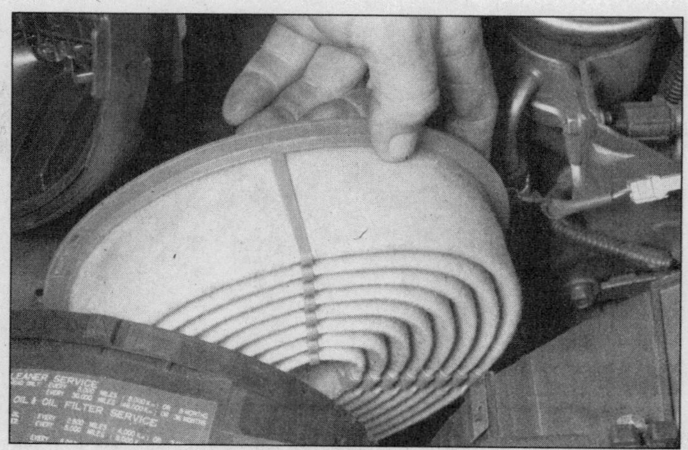

17.2h . . . and lift the air filter from the assembly

18.2a Remove the PCV hose from the fitting (1983 model shown)

18.2b Use carburetor cleaner to clean out the sludge deposits

18 PCV system check (every 15,000 miles or 12 months)

Refer to illustrations 18.2a, 18.2b, 18.3a and 18.3b

1 In order to reduce hydrocarbon emissions, crankcase blow-by gas is routed from the rear camshaft cover through a rubber hose to the intake manifold, where it mixes with incoming air before being burned in the combustion chamber.

2 Check the hose for cracks, leaks and other damage. Disconnect it from the cam cover and the intake manifold and inspect the inside for blockage. If it's clogged, clean the hose and the orifice with carburetor cleaner **(see illustrations)**.

3 The PCV system hose can cause a buildup of residue in the throttle bore area immediately behind the throttle plate, hindering free movement of the plate and causing low-speed driveability problems. Therefore, it is a good idea to periodically remove the intake ducting

18.3a Remove the air intake duct and check for residue that might prevent free movement of the throttle plate and cause rough running

18.3b Use carburetor cleaner to remove sludge deposits from behind the throttle plate

20.1a The lines are attached to the fuel filter with banjo bolts (arrow) - be sure to install new copper washers (1983 model shown)

20.1b On late models, the fuel filter is located at the rear of the vehicle next to the fuel tank (1992 model shown)

from the throttle body, rotate the throttle plate until it's wide open and inspect the throttle bore for residue **(see illustration)**. Carefully remove the residue with carburetor cleaner and a toothbrush **(see illustration)**. **Caution:** *Be sure the carburetor cleaner is safe for use with oxygen sensors and catalytic converters.*

19 Fuel system check (every 15,000 miles or 12 months)

Warning: *Gasoline is extremely flammable, so take extra precautions when you work on any part of the fuel system. Don't smoke or allow open flames or bare light bulbs near the work area, and don't work in a garage where a natural gas-type appliance (such as a water heater or clothes dryer) with a pilot light is present. If you spill any fuel on your skin, rinse it off immediately with soap and water. When you perform any kind of work on the fuel system, wear safety glasses and have a Class B type fire extinguisher on hand.*

1 Vehicles equipped with fuel injection maintain a higher pressure in the fuel system even when the engine is shut off, and this pressure must be relieved before any work is done on the fuel system. See Chapter 4 for the fuel pressure relief procedure. Plug all disconnected fuel lines immediately after disconnection to prevent the tank from emptying itself.

2 The fuel system is most easily checked with the vehicle raised on a hoist so the components underneath the vehicle are readily visible and accessible.

3 If the smell of gasoline is noticed while driving or after the vehicle has been in the sun, the system should be thoroughly inspected immediately.

4 Remove the gas filler cap and check for damage, corrosion and an unbroken sealing imprint on the gasket. Replace the gasket with a new one if necessary (Section 30).

5 With the vehicle raised, inspect the gas tank and filler neck for punctures, cracks and other damage. The connection between the filler neck and the tank is especially critical. Sometimes a rubber filler neck will leak due to loose clamps or deteriorated rubber, problems a home mechanic can usually rectify. **Warning:** *Do not, under any circumstances, try to repair a fuel tank yourself (except rubber components).*

6 Carefully check all rubber hoses and metal lines leading away from the fuel tank. Check for loose connections, deteriorated hoses, crimped lines and other damage. Follow the lines to the front of the vehicle, carefully inspecting them all the way. Repair or replace damaged sections as necessary.

7 If a fuel odor is still evident after the inspection, refer to Section 31.

20 Fuel filter replacement (every 15,000 miles or 12 months)

Refer to illustration 20.1a and 20.1b

Warning: *Gasoline is extremely flammable, so take extra precautions when you work on any part of the fuel system. Don't smoke or allow open flames or bare light bulbs near the work area, and don't work in a garage where a natural gas-type appliance (such as a water heater or clothes dryer) with a pilot light is present. If you spill any fuel on your skin, rinse it off immediately with soap and water. When you perform any kind of work on the fuel system, wear safety glasses and have a Class B type fire extinguisher on hand.*

1 The fuel filter is located near the starter motor (early models) or near the fuel tank (late models) and is most easily accessible with the vehicle raised on a hoist or supported on jackstands **(see illustrations)**.

2 Since the vehicle is equipped with fuel injection, refer to Chapter 4 for the fuel pressure relief procedure. DO NOT disconnect any fuel lines until after the pressure is relieved.

3 Place a pan under the fuel filter to catch any spilled gasoline, then remove the banjo fitting bolts and/or flare-nut(s) (use a flare-nut wrench on flare-nuts) from both ends of the filter. Discard the copper washers - new ones are packaged with the new fuel filter.

4 Remove the mounting bolts and detach the filter.

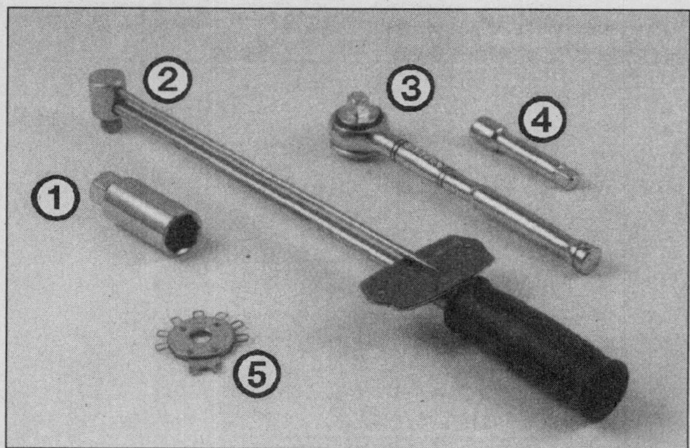

21.1 Tools required for changing spark plugs

1 **Spark plug socket** - *This will have special padding inside to protect the spark plug's porcelain insulator*
2 **Torque wrench** - *Although not mandatory, using this tool is the best way to ensure the plugs are tightened properly*
3 **Ratchet** - *Standard hand tool to fit the spark plug socket*
4 **Extension** - *Depending on model and accessories, you may need special extensions and universal joints to reach one or more of the plugs*
5 **Spark plug gap gauge** - *This gauge for checking the gap comes in a variety of styles. Make sure the gap for your engine is included*

5 Hold the new filter in position and install the bolts. Be sure the filter is correctly oriented; the end marked IN must face toward the fuel tank.

6 Make sure the lines are positioned between the tangs, then install the bolts and NEW washers or thread in the flare-nuts. Tighten the bolts/nuts securely, then start the engine and check carefully for leaks at the fuel line connections. If the connections are leaking, tighten the bolts/nuts slightly to eliminate the problem.

21 Spark plug check and replacement (see maintenance schedule)

Refer to illustrations 21.1, 21.4a, 21.4b, 21.5 and 21.9

1 Before beginning, obtain the necessary tools, which will include a spark plug socket and a gap gauge **(see illustration)**.

2 The best procedure to follow when replacing the spark plugs is to purchase the new spark plugs beforehand, adjust them to the proper gap, and then replace each plug one at a time. When buying the new spark plugs it is important to obtain the correct plugs for your specific engine. This information can be found on the Vehicle Emissions Control Information label located under the hood, in the Specifications section in the front of this Chapter or in the owner's manual. If differences exist between these sources, purchase the spark plug type specified on the Emissions Control label, because the information was printed for your specific engine.

3 With the new spark plugs at hand, allow the engine to cool completely before attempting plug removal. During this time, each of the new spark plugs can be inspected for defects and the gaps can be checked.

4 The gap is checked by inserting the proper thickness gauge between the electrodes at the tip of the plug **(see illustration)**. The gap between the electrodes should be the same as that given in the Specifications or on the Emissions Control label. The wire should just touch each of the electrodes. If the gap is incorrect, use the notched adjuster to bend the curved side of the electrode slightly until the proper gap is achieved **(see illustration)**. **Note:** *When adjusting the gap of a new plug, bend only the base of the ground electrode, do not touch the tip. Also, never attempt to adjust the gap on a used platinum tipped plug. If the side electrode is not exactly over the center electrode, use the notched adjuster to align the two. Check for cracks in the porcelain insulator, indicating the spark plug should not be used.*

21.4a Spark plug manufacturers recommend using a wire-type gauge when checking the gap - if the wire does not slide between the electrodes with a slight drag, adjustment is required

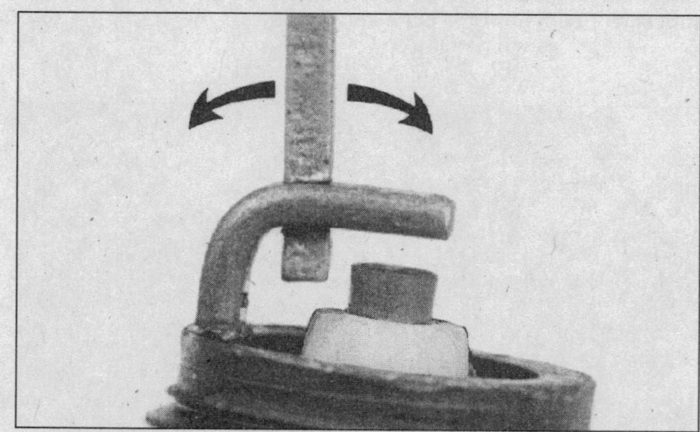

21.4b To change the gap, bend the side electrode only, as indicated by the arrows, and be very careful not to crack or chip the porcelain insulator surrounding the center electrode

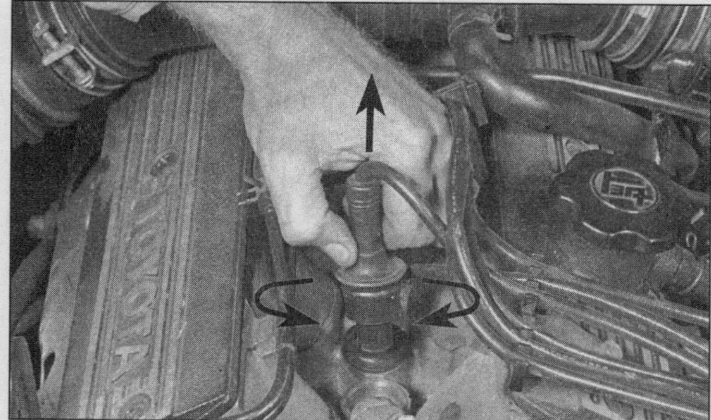

21.5 When removing the spark plug wires, pull only on the boot and use a twisting/pulling motion

5 With the engine cool, remove the spark plug wire from one spark plug. Do this by grabbing the boot at the end of the wire, not the wire itself **(see illustration)**. Sometimes it is necessary to use a twisting motion while the boot and plug wire are pulled free. On 1982 and later DOHC models, it will be necessary to remove the air intake duct and the throttle bellcrank (see Chapter 4) to gain access to the rear spark plug wires and spark plugs.

Common spark plug conditions

NORMAL

Symptoms: Brown to grayish-tan color and slight electrode wear. Correct heat range for engine and operating conditions.
Recommendation: When new spark plugs are installed, replace with plugs of the same heat range.

WORN

Symptoms: Rounded electrodes with a small amount of deposits on the firing end. Normal color. Causes hard starting in damp or cold weather and poor fuel economy.
Recommendation: Plugs have been left in the engine too long. Replace with new plugs of the same heat range. Follow the recommended maintenance schedule.

CARBON DEPOSITS

Symptoms: Dry sooty deposits indicate a rich mixture or weak ignition. Causes misfiring, hard starting and hesitation.
Recommendation: Make sure the plug has the correct heat range. Check for a clogged air filter or problem in the fuel system or engine management system. Also check for ignition system problems.

ASH DEPOSITS

Symptoms: Light brown deposits encrusted on the side or center electrodes or both. Derived from oil and/or fuel additives. Excessive amounts may mask the spark, causing misfiring and hesitation during acceleration.
Recommendation: If excessive deposits accumulate over a short time or low mileage, install new valve guide seals to prevent seepage of oil into the combustion chambers. Also try changing gasoline brands.

OIL DEPOSITS

Symptoms: Oily coating caused by poor oil control. Oil is leaking past worn valve guides or piston rings into the combustion chamber. Causes hard starting, misfiring and hesitation.
Recommendation: Correct the mechanical condition with necessary repairs and install new plugs.

GAP BRIDGING

Symptoms: Combustion deposits lodge between the electrodes. Heavy deposits accumulate and bridge the electrode gap. The plug ceases to fire, resulting in a dead cylinder.
Recommendation: Locate the faulty plug and remove the deposits from between the electrodes.

TOO HOT

Symptoms: Blistered, white insulator, eroded electrode and absence of deposits. Results in shortened plug life.
Recommendation: Check for the correct plug heat range, over-advanced ignition timing, lean fuel mixture, intake manifold vacuum leaks, sticking valves and insufficient engine cooling.

PREIGNITION

Symptoms: Melted electrodes. Insulators are white, but may be dirty due to misfiring or flying debris in the combustion chamber. Can lead to engine damage.
Recommendation: Check for the correct plug heat range, over-advanced ignition timing, lean fuel mixture, insufficient engine cooling and lack of lubrication.

HIGH SPEED GLAZING

Symptoms: Insulator has yellowish, glazed appearance. Indicates that combustion chamber temperatures have risen suddenly during hard acceleration. Normal deposits melt to form a conductive coating. Causes misfiring at high speeds.
Recommendation: Install new plugs. Consider using a colder plug if driving habits warrant.

DETONATION

Symptoms: Insulators may be cracked or chipped. Improper gap setting techniques can also result in a fractured insulator tip. Can lead to piston damage.
Recommendation: Make sure the fuel anti-knock values meet engine requirements. Use care when setting the gaps on new plugs. Avoid lugging the engine.

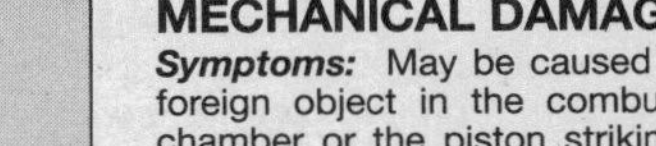

MECHANICAL DAMAGE

Symptoms: May be caused by a foreign object in the combustion chamber or the piston striking an incorrect reach (too long) plug. Causes a dead cylinder and could result in piston damage.
Recommendation: Repair the mechanical damage. Remove the foreign object from the engine and/or install the correct reach plug.

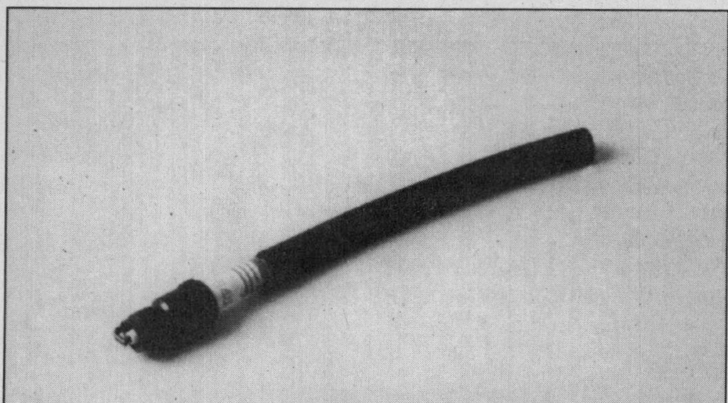

21.9 A length of 3/16-inch ID rubber hose will save time and prevent damaged threads when installing the spark plugs

6 If compressed air is available, use it to blow any dirt or foreign material away from the spark plug area. A common bicycle pump will also work. The idea here is to eliminate the possibility of debris falling into the cylinder as the spark plug is removed.

7 Place the spark plug socket over the plug and remove it from the engine by turning in a counterclockwise direction.

8 Compare the spark plug with those shown in the accompanying photos to get an indication of the overall running condition of the engine. The platinum tipped plugs recommended for this vehicle may not require replacement upon the first periodic checks and can simply be reinstalled.

9 Thread the plug into the head until you can no longer turn it with your fingers, then tighten it with the socket. Where there might be difficulty in inserting the spark plugs into the spark plug holes, or the possibility of cross threading them into the head, a short piece of 3/16-inch rubber tubing can be fitted over the end of the spark plug **(see illustration)**. The flexible tubing will act as a universal joint to help align the plug with the plug hole, and should the plug begin to cross thread, the hose will slip on the spark plug, preventing thread damage. If one is available, use a torque wrench to tighten the plug to ensure that it is seated correctly. The correct torque figure is included in the Specifications.

10 Before pushing the spark plug wire onto the end of the plug, inspect it following the procedures outlined in Section 22.

11 Attach the plug wire to the new spark plug, again using a twisting motion on the boot until it is firmly seated on the spark plug.

12 Follow the above procedure for the remaining spark plugs, replacing them one at a time to prevent mixing up the spark plug wires.

22 Spark plug wire, distributor cap and rotor check and replacement (every 15,000 miles or 12 months)

Refer to illustrations 22.11a and 22.11b

Note: *In the event of an accidental mix-up of the ignition wires, consult the firing order diagrams pictured in Chapter 2A for the proper sequence.*

1 The spark plug wires should be checked at the recommended intervals and whenever new spark plugs are installed in the engine.

2 Begin this procedure by making a visual check of the spark plug wires while the engine is running. In a darkened garage (make sure there is ventilation) start the engine and observe each plug wire. Be careful not to come into contact with any moving engine parts. If there is a break in the wire, you will see arcing or a small spark at the damaged area. If arcing is noticed, make a note to obtain new wires, then allow the engine to cool.

3 Disconnect the negative cable from the battery. **Caution:** *If the stereo in your vehicle is equipped with an anti-theft system, refer to the information on page 0-15 at the front of this manual before detaching the cable.*

4 The wires should be inspected one at a time to prevent mixing up the order, which is essential for proper engine operation.

5 Disconnect the plug wire from the spark plug. A removal tool can be used for this purpose or you can grab the plastic boot, twist slightly and pull the wire free. Do not pull on the wire itself, only on the boot.

6 Inspect inside the boot for corrosion, which will look like a white crusty powder. Push the wire and boot back onto the end of the spark plug. It should be a tight fit on the plug end. If it is not, remove the wire and use pliers to carefully crimp the metal connector inside the boot until it fits securely on the end of the spark plug.

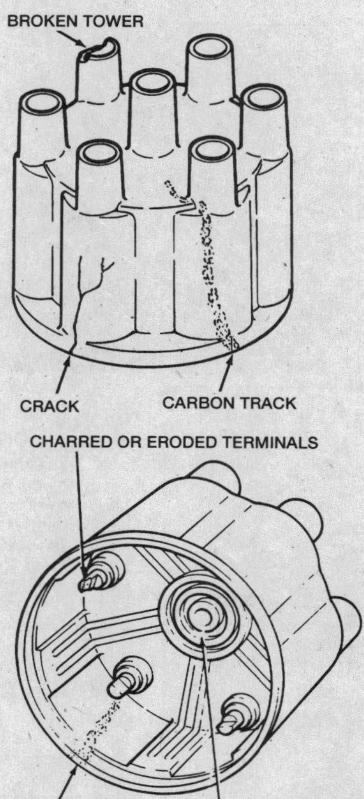

22.11a Shown here are some of the common defects to look for when inspecting the distributor cap (if in doubt about its condition, install a new one)

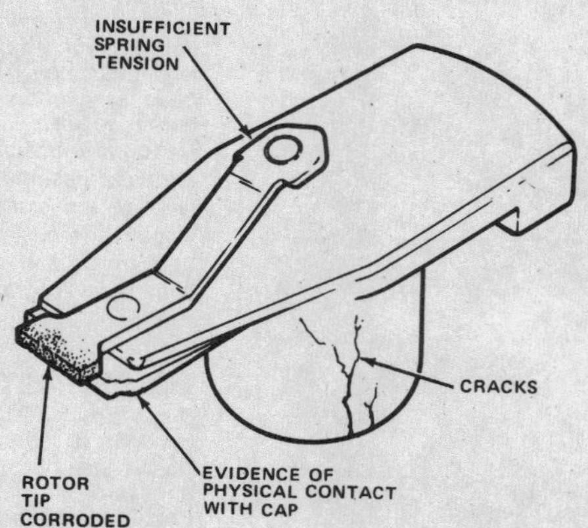

22.11b The ignition rotor should be checked for wear and corrosion as indicated here (if in doubt about its condition, buy a new one)

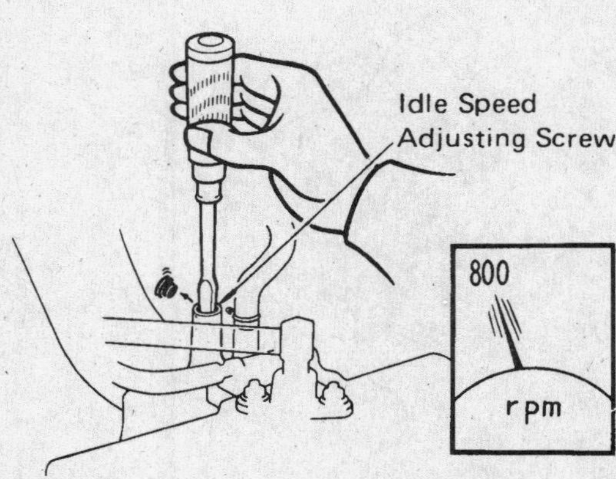

23.6a Typical idle speed adjusting screw on the early models (1979 through 1981)

23.6b Set the idle speed by turning the adjusting screw in or out as required (1982 model shown)

7 Using a clean rag, wipe the entire length of the wire to remove any built-up dirt and grease. Once the wire is clean, check for burns, cracks and other damage. Do not bend the wire excessively, since the conductor might break.

8 Disconnect the wire from the distributor or coil pack. Again, pull only on the boot. Check for corrosion and a tight fit in the same manner as the spark plug end. Replace the wire in the distributor or coil pack.

9 Check the remaining spark plug wires, making sure they are securely fastened at the distributor (or coil pack) and spark plug when the check is complete.

10 If new spark plug wires are required, purchase a set for your specific engine model. Wire sets are available pre-cut, with the boots already installed. Remove and replace the wires one at a time to avoid mix-ups in the firing order.

11 Check the distributor cap and rotor (if equipped) for wear. Look for cracks, carbon tracks and worn, burned or loose contacts **(see illustrations)**. Replace the cap and rotor with new parts if defects are found. It is common practice to install a new cap and rotor whenever new spark plug wires are installed. When installing a new cap, remove the wires from the old cap one at a time and attach them to the new cap in the exact same location - do not simultaneously remove all the wires or firing order mix-ups may occur.

23 Engine idle speed check and adjustment (every 15,000 miles or 12 months on 1979 through 1982 models only)

Refer to illustration 23.6a and 23.6b

Note: *On 1983 and later models, the idle speed is controlled by the ECU and requires no adjustment.*

1 Engine idle speed is the speed at which the engine operates when no accelerator pedal pressure is applied. This speed is critical to the performance of the engine itself, as well as many engine sub-systems.

2 A hand held tachometer must be used when adjusting idle speed to get an accurate reading. The exact hook-up for these meters varies with the manufacturer, so follow the particular directions included.

3 Since special test equipment is required to properly adjust the fuel/air mixture on these vehicles, the procedure should be left to a dealer service department or a reputable repair shop. The idle speed, however can be temporarily adjusted if a suitable tachometer is available.

4 Connect the tachometer to the engine by following the instructions supplied by the tachometer manufacturer. Keep in mind that some tachometers are not compatible with electronic ignition systems and remember that these vehicles are equipped with electronic ignition.

5 Before the idle speed is checked and adjusted, make sure that the air cleaner, the air intake system hoses, the vacuum lines and the EFI system wiring connectors are all properly installed. In addition, the engine must be at normal operating temperature, all accessories must be OFF and the transmission must be in NEUTRAL. Apply the parking brake and block the wheels to prevent accidental movement of the vehicle.

6 Raise the rpm's to 2500 for approximately two minutes, then adjust the idle speed to the proper rpm **(see illustrations)** by turning the idle speed adjusting screw.

7 Once the procedure is complete, be sure to disconnect the tachometer. Have the idle speed and mixture checked by a dealer service department.

24 Valve clearance adjustment (refer to maintenance schedule)

SOHC engines (1979 through 1981)

Refer to illustrations 24.6, 24.9 and 24.12

1 Before checking and adjusting the valve clearances, start and run the engine until it reaches normal operating temperature. **Caution:** *Since the engine will be hot as this procedure is done, extra care must be taken to avoid burns.*

2 Shut off the engine and remove the valve cover from the engine. The intake air connector will have to be removed in order to lift off the cover. Loosen the hose clamps, slide them out of the way and separate the intake air connector from the rubber joints and hoses.

3 Before removing the spark plug wires from the plugs, and the PCV hoses and vacuum hoses from the valve cover, tag them to ensure proper installation later.

4 The next step is to position the number one (front) piston at Top Dead Center (TDC) on the compression stroke. Remove all of the spark plugs from the engine, then locate the number one cylinder spark plug wire (it should have been tagged earlier) and trace it back to the distributor. Make a mark on the distributor body directly below the terminal where the number one spark plug wire attaches to the distributor cap, then remove the cap and wires from the distributor.

5 Slip a wrench or socket over the large bolt at the front of the crankshaft and slowly turn it in a clockwise direction until the notch on the crankshaft pulley is aligned with the O on the timing mark tag. At this point the rotor should be pointing directly at the mark you made on the distributor body. If it is not, turn the crankshaft one more complete revolution (360 degrees) in a clockwise direction. If the rotor is now pointing at the mark on the distributor body, then the number one piston is at TDC on the compression stroke and the valve clearances can be checked and adjusted.

1

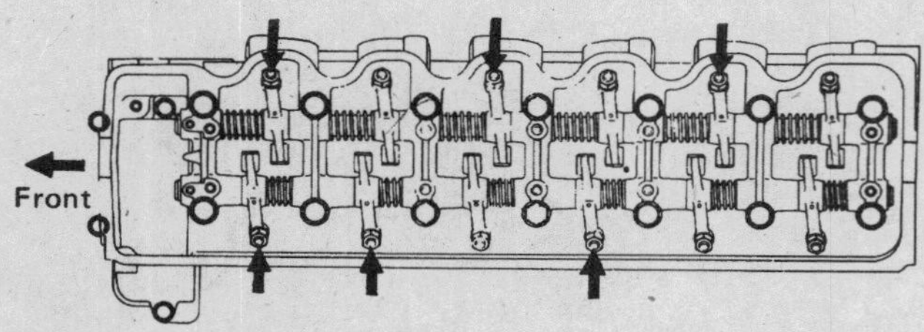

24.6 With the number 1 piston at TDC on the compression stroke, adjust the valves indicated by the arrows

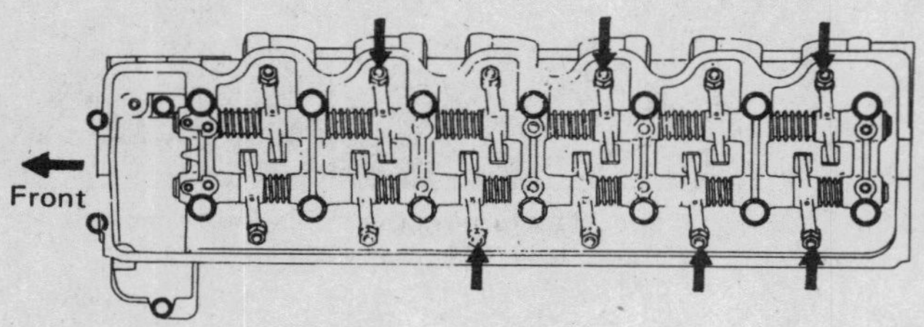

24.12 After the crankshaft is rotated 360 degrees, adjust the remaining valves

6 Check and adjust *only* the valves indicated by arrows **(see illustration)**.

7 Insert an appropriate size feeler gauge between the valve stem and the rocker arm adjusting screw. If the feeler gauge fits between the valve and adjuster with a slight drag, then the clearance is correct and no adjustment is required.

8 If the feeler gauge will not fit between the valve and adjuster, or if it is loose, loosen the adjusting screw locknut and carefully tighten or loosen the adjusting screw until you can feel a slight drag on the feeler gauge as it is withdrawn from between the valve stem and adjusting screw.

9 Hold the adjusting screw with a screwdriver **(see illustration)**, to keep it from turning, and tighten the locknut securely. Recheck the clearance to make sure it hasn't changed.

10 Repeat the procedure for the remaining valves indicted in illustration 24.6. Be sure to use correct feeler gauge; intake and exhaust valves require different clearances for proper engine operation.

11 Turn the crankshaft one complete revolution (360 degrees) in a clockwise direction and align the notch on the crankshaft pulley with the O on the timing mark tag.

12 Check and adjust the clearances for the remaining valves **(see illustration)**.

13 Install the valve cover (use a new gasket) and tighten the mounting nuts evenly and securely.

14 Install the distributor cap and spark plugs, then hook up the spark plug wires and the various hoses and vacuum lines.

15 Install the air intake connector and attach the hoses and vacuum lines as required. Be sure to install and tighten any hose clamps that may have been removed.

16 Start the engine and check for oil leakage between the valve cover and the cylinder head.

DOHC engines (1987 and later models only)

Refer to illustrations 24.22a, 24.22b, 24.23, 24.24, 24.26a, 24.26b and 24.27

Note: *The following procedure requires the use of a special valve lifter tool. It is impossible to perform this task without it.*

17 Disconnect the negative cable from the battery. **Caution:** *If the stereo in your vehicle is equipped with an anti-theft system, refer to the information on page 0-15 at the front of this manual before detaching the cable.*

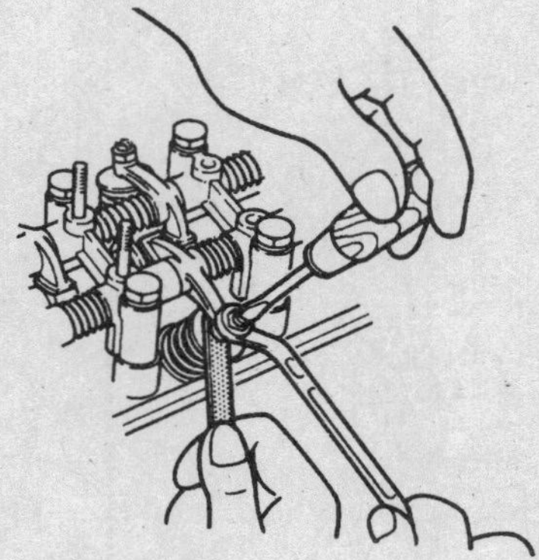

24.9 Adjusting valve clearance with the feeler gauge

24.22a Measure the clearance for each valve with a feeler gauge of the specified thickness - if the clearance is correct, you should feel a slight drag on the gauge as you pull it out

18 Disconnect the cruise control cable, air cleaner duct or other components which will interfere with valve cover removal.

19 Remove the valve cover(s) (refer to Chapter 2).

20 Blow out the recessed area between the camshafts with compressed air, if available, to remove any debris that might fall into the cylinders, then remove the spark plugs (Section 21).

21 Refer to Chapter 2 and position the number 1 piston at TDC on the compression stroke.

22 Measure the clearances of the indicated valves with a feeler gauge of the specified thickness **(see illustrations)**. Record the measurements which are out of specification. They will be used later to determine the required replacement shims.

23 Turn the crankshaft 2/3-turn (240 degrees), align the timing marks and measure the valve clearances shown **(see illustration)**. **Note:** *A good way to doublecheck for the correct position of the camshaft is to make sure the lobes of the valves about to be adjusted are pointing up and away from contacting the shim surface.*

24 Turn the crankshaft a further 2/3-turn and measure the remaining valves **(see illustration)**.

25 After all the valve clearances have been measured, turn the crankshaft pulley until the camshaft lobe above the first valve which you intend to adjust is pointing up, away from the shim.

26 Position the notch in the valve lifter toward the spark plug. Then press down the valve lifter with the special valve lifter tool **(see illustration)**. Place the special valve lifter tool in position as shown, with the longer jaw of the tool gripping the lower edge of the cast lifter boss and the upper, shorter jaw gripping the upper edge of the lifter itself. Press down the valve lifter by squeezing the handles of the valve lifter tool together and remove the adjusting shim with a small screwdriver

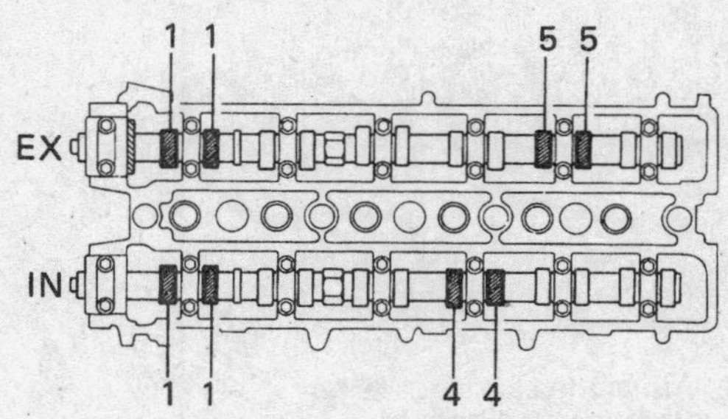

24.22b Measure only the valves indicated on the first step

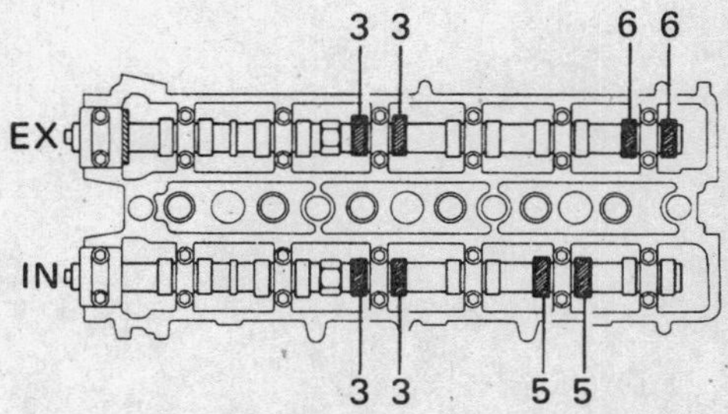

24.23 After rotating the engine 240 degrees, measure only the valves that are indicated

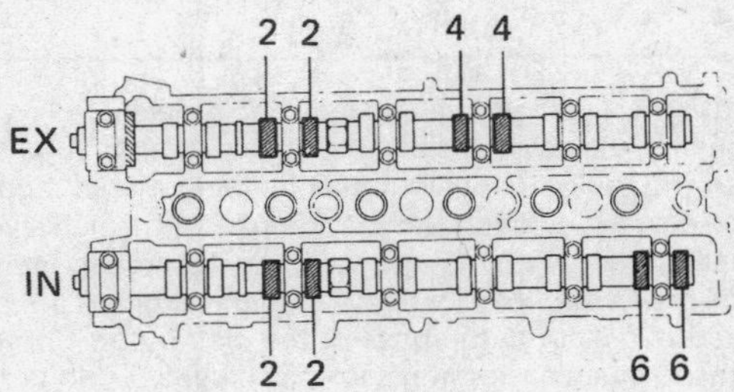

24.24 Finally, rotate the engine another 240 degrees and measure the valves that are indicated

24.26a Install the valve lifter tool as shown and squeeze the handles together to lower the valve lifter so the shim can be removed

24.26b Remove the shim with a small screwdriver, a pair of tweezers or a magnet

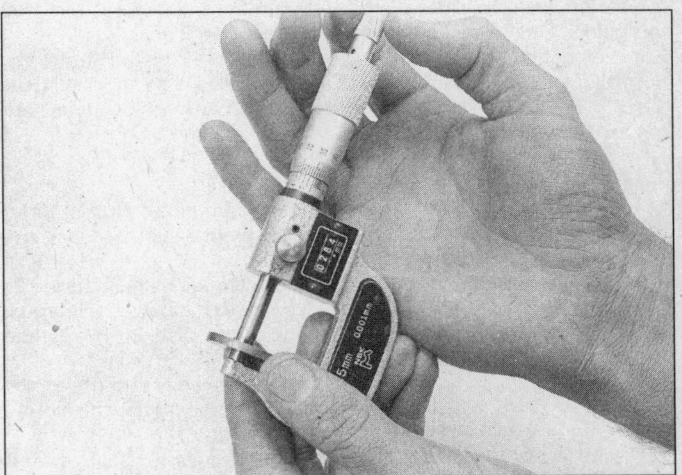

24.27 Measure the shim thickness with a micrometer

(see illustration) or a pair of tweezers. Note that the wire hook on the end of one valve lifter tool handle can be used to clamp both handles together to keep the lifter depressed while the shim is removed.

27 Measure the thickness of the shim with a micrometer **(see illustration)**. To calculate the correct thickness of a replacement shim that will place the valve clearance within the specified value, use the following formula:

Intake side: N = T + (A - 0.20 mm [0.0079 in])
Exhaust side: N = T + (A - 0.25 mm [0.0098 in])
T = thickness of the shim used
A = valve clearance measured
N = thickness of the new shim

28 Select a shim with a thickness as close as possible to the valve clearance calculated. Shims, which are available in 17 sizes in increments of 0.050 mm (0.0020 in), range in size from 2.500 mm (0.0984 in) to 3.300 mm (0.1299 in). **Note:** *Through careful analysis of the shim sizes needed to bring all the out-of-specification valve clearances within specification, it is often possible to simply move a shim that has to come out anyway to another valve lifter requiring a shim of that particular size, thereby reducing the number of new shims that must be purchased.*

29 Place the special valve lifter tool in position as shown in illustration 24.26a, with the longer jaw of the tool gripping the lower edge of the cast lifter boss and the upper, shorter jaw gripping the upper edge of the lifter itself, press down the valve lifter by squeezing the handles of the valve lifter tool together and install the new adjusting shim (note that the wire hook on the end of one valve lifter tool hand can be used to clamp the handles together to keep the lifter depressed while the

25.7 The timing marks on early models are slightly off to the left on the timing cover (1981 model shown)

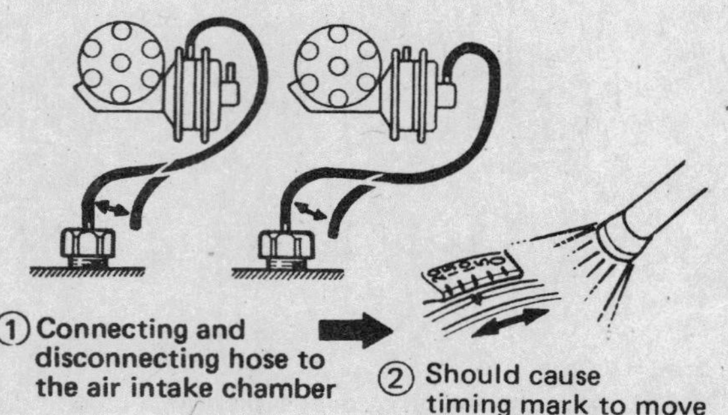

25.15 Checking vacuum advance operation

shim is inserted). Measure the clearance with a feeler gauge to make sure that your calculations are correct.

30 Repeat this procedure until all the valves which are out of clearance have been corrected.

31 Installation of the spark plugs, valve cover(s), center cover, spark plug wires and boots, accelerator cable bracket, etc. is the reverse of removal.

25 Ignition timing check and adjustment (refer to maintenance schedule)

Refer to illustrations 25.7, 25.15 and 25.17

1 All vehicles are equipped with an Emission Control Information label inside the engine compartment. This label gives important ignition timing settings and procedures to be followed specific to that vehicle. If information on the label is different than the information given in this Section, the label should be followed.

2 At the specified intervals or whenever the distributor is removed, the ignition timing must be checked and adjusted if necessary.

3 Before attempting to check the timing, make sure the engine is at normal operating temperature and the idle speed is as specified (Section 23). Set the parking brake and place the transmission in Park (automatic) or Neutral (manual).

1979 through 1981 models

4 On 1981 models, disconnect the hoses from both distributor diaphragms and plug the hose ends. Make sure the idle speed remains correct; adjust as necessary.

5 Connect a timing light in accordance with the manufacturer's instructions. Generally, the light will be connected to power and ground sources and the number one spark plug in some fashion. The number one spark plug is the very front one.

6 Locate the numbered timing tag on the front cover of the engine. It is just behind the lower crankshaft pulley. Clean it off with solvent if necessary to read the printing and small grooves.

7 Locate the notched groove across the crankshaft pulley **(see illustration)**. It may be necessary to have an assistant temporarily turn the ignition off and on in short bursts without starting the engine to bring this groove into a position where it can easily be cleaned and marked. Stay clear of all moving engine components if the engine is turned over in this manner.

8 Use white paint to mark the groove on the crankshaft pulley. Also put a mark on the timing tab in accordance with the number of degrees called for in the specifications or on the Emission Control Information label inside the engine compartment. Each notch on the timing tab represents five degrees. The O indicates Top Dead Center (TDC). If your vehicle specifications call for 12 degrees BTDC (Before Top Dead Center), you will make a mark on the timing tab between the second and third notches.

9 Check that the wiring for the timing light is clear of all moving engine components, then start the engine.

10 Point the flashing timing light at the timing marks, again being careful not to come in contact with moving parts. The marks you made should appear stationary. If the marks are in alignment, the timing is correct. If the marks are not aligned, turn off the engine.

11 Loosen the locknut at the base of the distributor. On most cars this task is made much easier with a special curved distributor wrench. Loosen the locknut only slightly, just enough to turn the distributor.

12 Now restart the engine and turn the distributor until the timing marks coincide.

13 Shut off the engine and tighten the distributor locknut, being careful not to move the distributor.

14 Start the engine and recheck the timing to make sure the marks are still in alignment.

15 Check the operation of the vacuum and mechanical advance (1979 models only) as follows:

Mechanical advance - Disconnect and plug the distributor vacuum hoses, then open and close the throttle so that engine speed rises and falls. As engine speed changes, the timing mark on the pulley should change position.

Vacuum advance - Hook a separate section of vacuum hose to the vacuum connection on the air intake chamber and one of the distributor diaphragm ports. Disconnect and connect the hose while aiming the timing light at the marks. As the hose is disconnected and reconnected, the timing should change **(see illustration)**. Move the hose to the remaining diaphragm port, repeat the check and look for the same results. When finished, be sure to hook up the original vacuum hoses to the proper ports.

16 Disconnect the timing light.

17 The Spark control system should be checked as follows:

a) The coolant temperature must be below 122 degrees F (50 degrees C).
b) Connect a vacuum gauge to the vacuum hose attached to the distributor sub-diaphragm (use a T-fitting) **(see illustration)**. On 1979 models only, remove the hose from the sub-diaphragm and attach the vacuum gauge to the hose.
c) Start the engine and run it at idle.
d) The gauge should indicate a relatively high vacuum. If not, check the BVSV, the check valve and the distributor diaphragm (see Chapter 6).
e) Allow the engine to reach normal operating temperature, then check the gauge again. It should indicate zero or very low vacuum at idle. If it does not, check the BVSV and the vacuum hoses.
f) Disconnect the vacuum gauge and reconnect the hose to the sub-diaphragm. **Note:** *On 1979 models only, disconnect the hose leading to the main diaphragm and attach it to the vacuum gauge. The gauge should indicate a low vacuum (if it is high, check the VCV). Increase the engine speed to approximately 2000 rpm. The gauge should now indicate a high vacuum (if it is low, check the distributor diaphragm and the VCV). Disconnect the vacuum gauge and reconnect the hose to the main diaphragm.*

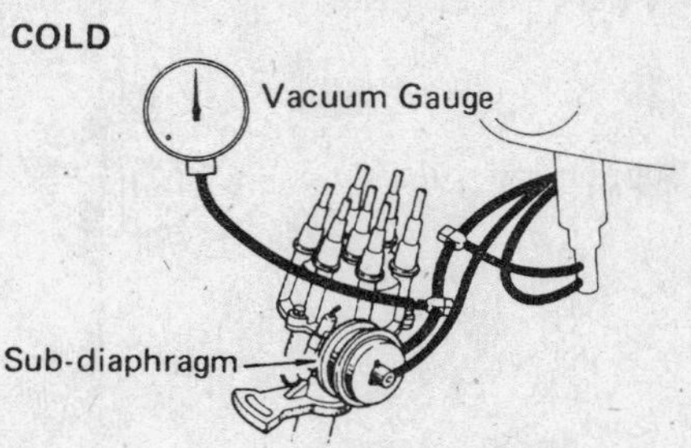

25.17 Distributor sub-diaphragm location (Spark Control system vacuum gauge hook-up is for 1980 and 1981 models)

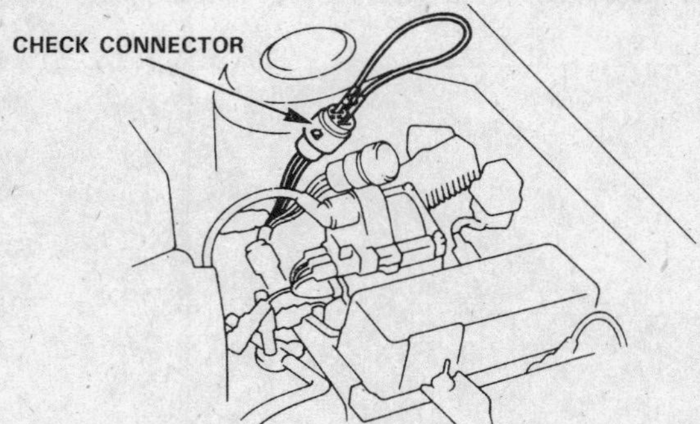

25.19 Jumper between the terminals of the check connector (1983 through 1986 models)

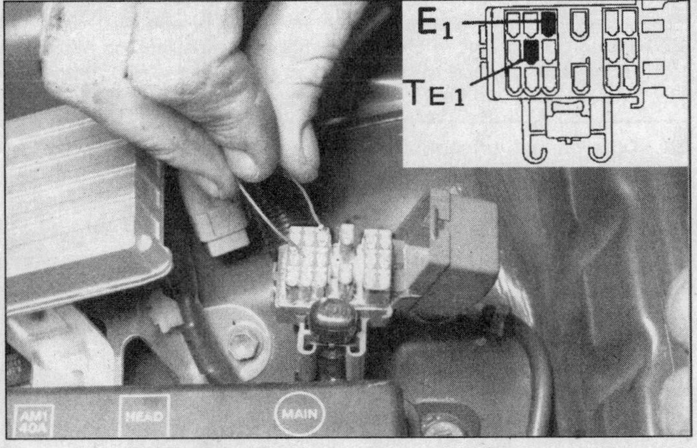

25.21 Use a jumper wire or a paper clip to connect the E1 and TE1 terminals on the diagnostic connector (1987 and later models)

1982 through 1986 models

Refer to illustrations 25.18, 25.19 and 25.20

18 On 1982 models, disconnect and plug the vacuum lines **(see illustration)**.

19 On 1983 through 1986 models, connect a jumper wire between the terminals on the check connector **(see illustration)**.

20 Follow steps 5 through 14 and set the timing according to the VECI label under the hood or the specifications listed in this Chapter **(see illustration)**.

1987 and later models

Refer to illustrations 25.21, 5.22 and 25.24

21 Connect a jumper wire between the terminals E1 and TE1 on the diagnostic terminal **(see illustration)**.

22 On turbo models, remove the engine cover from the forward section **(see illustration)** to gain access to the number 1 plug wire.

25.18 On 1982 models, disconnect and plug the vacuum lines (a bolt or a golf tee will make a good plug)

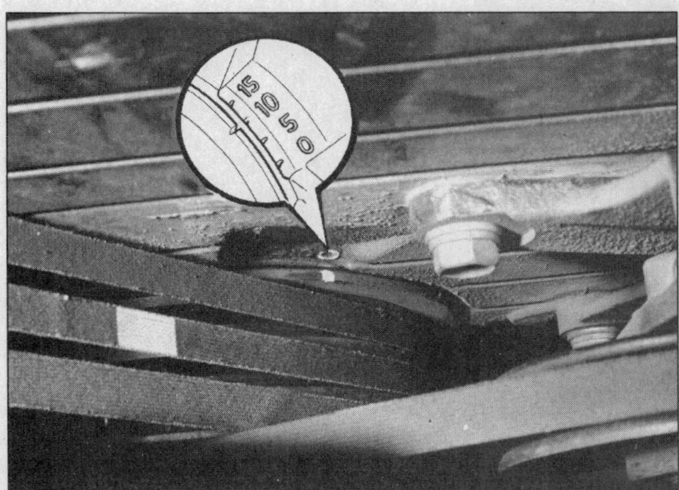

25.20 Each notch on the timing tab represents 5 degrees, with the 0-degree mark being TDC (1982 through 1986 models)

25.22 Remove the cap nuts (arrows) and lift the engine cover to expose the spark plug wires

1

25.24 Timing mark location on 1987 and later models (arrow)

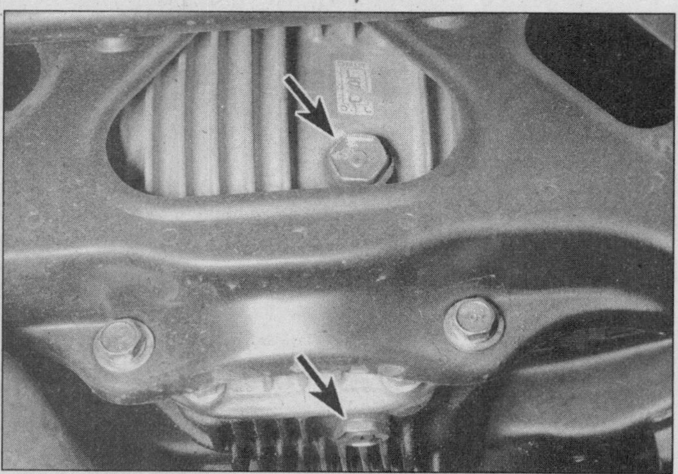

26.2b The upper arrow points to the check/plug and the lower arrow points to the drain plug (1992 model shown)

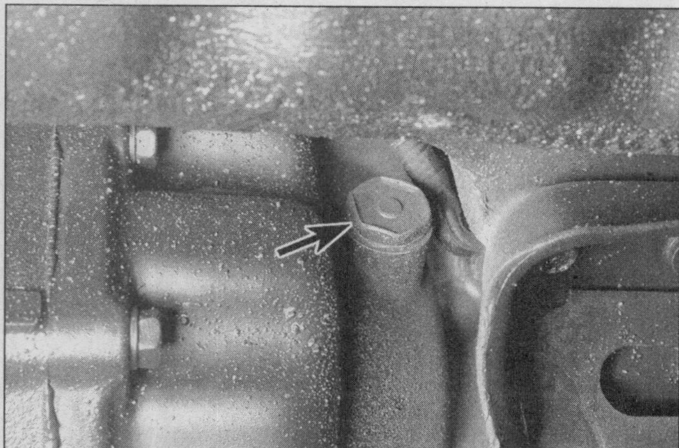

27.1b The fill plug (arrow) on the 1992 R154 manual 5 speed transmission is located near the back transmission mount

23 Follow the previous steps 5 through 14.

24 Set the timing according to the VECI label under the hood or the specifications listed in this Chapter **(see illustration)**. **Note:** *On turbo models, loosen the clamp and rotate the camshaft sensor to change the ignition timing (refer to Chapter 5).*

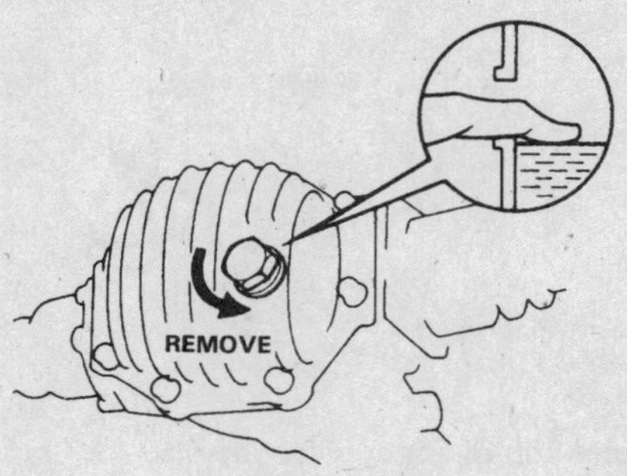

26.2a The differential lubricant level must be maintained at or below the bottom of the plug hole (1979 through 1986 models)

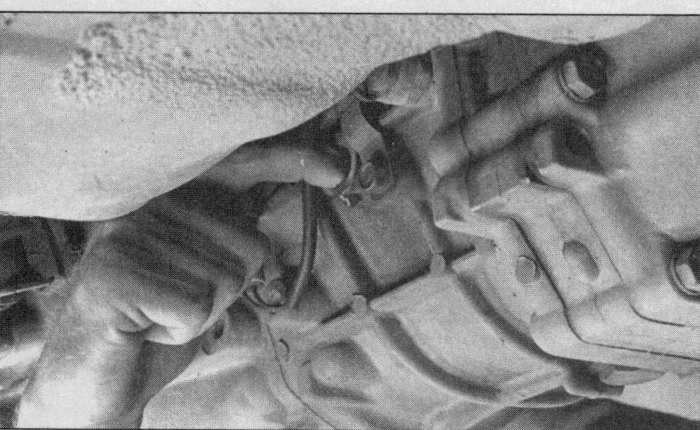

27.1a Use your finger to check the manual transmission lubricant level - it should be at or near the bottom of the filler hole

26 Differential lubricant level check (every 15,000 miles or 12 months)

Refer to illustration 26.2a and 26.2b

1 The differential is equipped with a check/fill plug which must be removed to check the lubricant level in the differential housing. If the vehicle is raised to gain access to the plug, be sure to support it securely on jackstands - DO NOT crawl under a vehicle supported only by a jack! If the vehicle has recently been driven for any distance at highway speeds, the lubricant in the differential will be hot - wait for a couple of hours before checking the lubricant level.

2 Remove the check/fill plug from the rear cover on the housing **(see illustrations)**. Reach inside the hole with your finger to make sure the lubricant level is even with the bottom of the plug hole (if lubricant begins to run out of the hole, the level is correct).

3 If it isn't, add the recommended lubricant through the hole with a syringe or squeeze bottle until the level is correct.

4 Install and tighten the plug. Check for leaks after the first few miles of driving.

27 Manual transmission lubricant level check (every 15,000 miles or 12 months)

Refer to illustration 27.1a and 27.1b

1 Manual transmissions do not have a dipstick. The lubricant level is checked by removing the filler plug from the side of the transmission case. Feel inside the hole with your finger **(see illustrations)**. The lubricant level should be within 5 mm (0.200-inch) of the bottom edge of the hole.

2 If the transmission needs more lubricant, use a syringe to squeeze the appropriate lubricant into the opening until it just begins

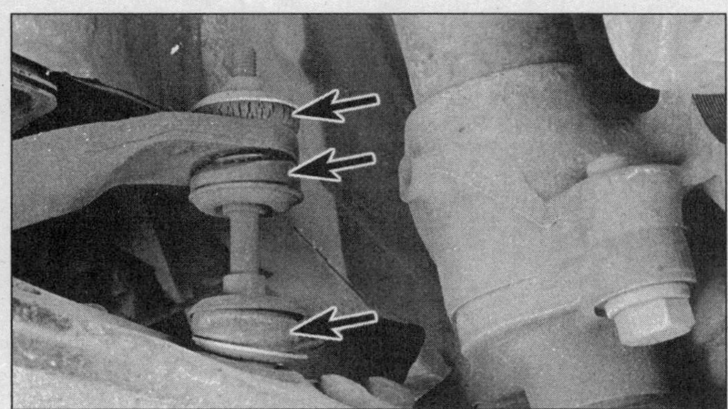

28.5a Check all suspension and steering components for deteriorated rubber bushings

28.5b Check the rubber boots for cracks and loose clamps

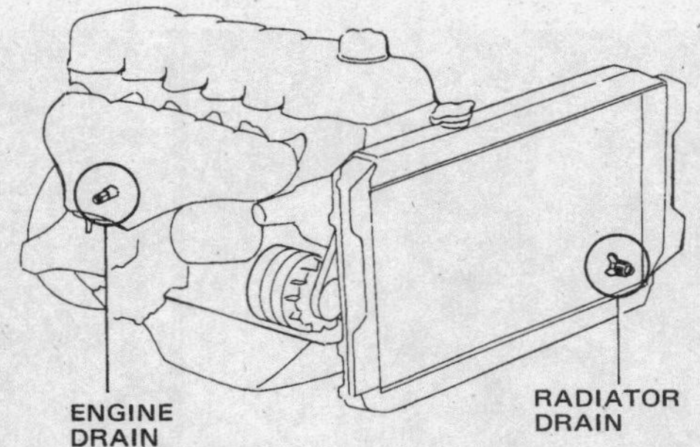

29.6a Engine and radiator coolant drain locations on SOHC engines

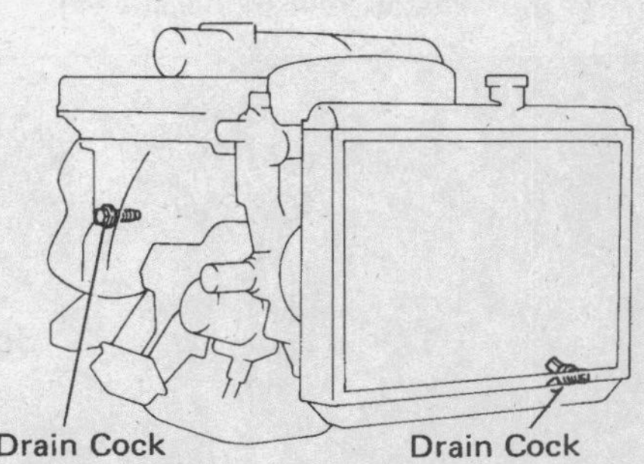

29.6b Engine and radiator coolant drain locations on DOHC engines

to run out of the filler hole.

3 Install the plug and tighten it securely. Drive the vehicle a short distance, then check for leaks.

28 Suspension and steering checks (every 15,000 miles or 12 months)

Refer to illustrations 28.5a and 28.5b

1 Raise the vehicle periodically and visually check the suspension and steering components for wear.

2 Indications of a fault in these systems are excessive play in the steering wheel before the front wheels react, excessive sway around corners, body movement over rough roads or binding at some point as the steering wheel is turned.

3 Before the vehicle is raised for inspection, test the shock absorbers by pushing down to rock the vehicle at each corner. If you push down and the vehicle does not come back to a level position within one or two bounces, the shocks are worn and must be replaced. As this is done, listen for noises coming from the suspension components. Additional information on suspension components can be found in Chapter 10.

4 Raise the front end of the vehicle and support it securely on jackstands placed under the frame rails. Because of the work to be done, make sure the vehicle cannot fall from the stands.

5 Working under the vehicle, check for loose bolts, broken or disconnected parts and deteriorated rubber bushings and boots on all suspension and steering components **(see illustrations)**. Look for grease or fluid leaking from the steering assembly. Check the power steering hoses and connections for leaks. Check the balljoints for wear.

6 Have an assistant turn the steering wheel from side-to-side and check the steering components for free movement, chafing and binding. If the wheels do not respond to movement of the steering wheel, try to determine where the slack is located.

29 Cooling system service (draining, flushing and refilling) (every 30,000 miles or 24 months)

Refer to illustration 29.6a, 29.6b and 29.6c

Warning: *Don't allow antifreeze to come in contact with your skin or painted surfaces of the vehicle. Rinse off spills immediately with plenty of water. Antifreeze is highly toxic if ingested. Never leave antifreeze lying around in an open container or in puddles on the floor; children and pets are attracted by its sweet smell and may drink it. Check with local authorities about disposing of used antifreeze. Many communities have collection centers which will see that antifreeze is disposed of safely. Antifreeze is also combustible, so don't store or use it near open flames.*

1 Periodically, the cooling system should be drained, flushed and refilled to replenish the antifreeze mixture and prevent formation of rust and corrosion, which can impair the performance of the cooling system and cause engine damage.

2 At the same time the cooling system is serviced, all hoses and the radiator cap should be inspected and replaced if defective.

3 Since antifreeze is a corrosive and poisonous solution, be careful not to spill any of the coolant mixture on the vehicle's paint or your skin. If this happens, rinse immediately with plenty of clean water. Consult local authorities about the dumping of antifreeze before draining the cooling system. In many areas, reclamation centers have been set up to collect automobile oil and drained antifreeze/water mixtures, rather then allowing them to be added to the sewage system.

4 With the engine cold, remove the radiator cap.

5 Move a large container under the radiator to catch the coolant as it is drained.

6 Drain the radiator by opening the drain plug at the bottom **(see illustrations)**. If this drain has excessive corrosion and cannot be turned easily, disconnect the lower radiator hose to allow the coolant to drain. Be careful that none of the solution is splashed on your skin or into your eyes.

29.6c The radiator drain plug is located at the lower left side of the radiator (1983 model shown)

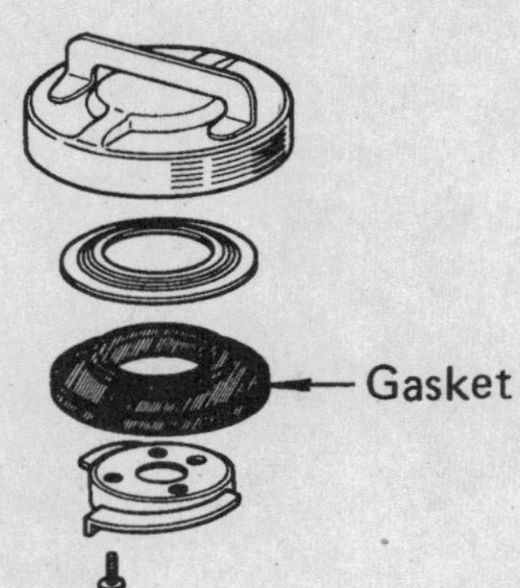

30.3 On earlier models, remove the four screws and detach the retaining plate to replace the filler cap gasket

31.3a Disconnect the hoses from the charcoal canister to test the system (1983 model shown)

31.3b Location of the charcoal canister on a 1992 turbo model

7 Disconnect the hose from the coolant reservoir and remove the reservoir. Flush it out with clean water.

8 Place a garden hose in the radiator filler neck and flush the system until the water runs clear at all drain points.

9 In severe cases of contamination or clogging of the radiator, remove it (see Chapter 3) and reverse flush it. This involves inserting the hose in the bottom radiator outlet to allow the water to run against the normal flow, draining through the top. A radiator repair shop should be consulted if further cleaning or repair is necessary.

10 When the coolant is regularly drained and the system refilled with the correct antifreeze/water mixture, there should be no need to use chemical cleaners or descalers.

11 To refill the system, reconnect the radiator hoses and install the reservoir and the overflow hose.

12 Fill the radiator to the base of the filler neck and then add more coolant to the reservoir until it reaches the lower mark.

13 Run the engine until normal operating temperature is reached and, with the engine idling, add coolant up to the Full level. Install the radiator and reservoir caps.

14 Keep a close watch on the coolant level and the cooling system hoses during the first few miles of driving. Tighten the hose clamps and/or add more coolant as necessary.

30 Fuel filler cap gasket check and replacement (every 30,000 miles or 24 months)

Refer to illustration 30.3

1 The loss of fuel or vapor out of the filler neck is prevented by a pressure/vacuum filler cap. Relief valves within the cap will release only under significant pressure or vacuum. This cap must be replaced by a similar unit if replacement is necessary, in order for the system to remain effective. Under normal conditions periodic gasket replacement will suffice.

2 Remove the filler cap and check for corrosion and damage to the cap, such as cracks.

3 Take out the old gasket (O-ring) from the fuel filler cap. On earlier models, four screws and a locking plate must first be removed **(see illustration)**. Be careful not to damage the cap.

4 Seat a new gasket on the cap and reinstall the cap on the filler neck.

31 Evaporative Emissions Control (EVAP) system check (every 30,000 miles or 24 months)

Refer to illustrations 31.3a, 31.3b and 31.4

1 The function of the Evaporative Emissions Control system is to draw fuel vapors from the tank and carburetor, store them in a charcoal canister and then burn them during normal engine operation.

2 The most common symptom of a fault in the evaporative emissions system is a strong fuel odor in the engine compartment. If a fuel odor is detected, inspect the charcoal canister, located near the rear exhaust manifold, and the system hoses.

3 A simple check of the system operation can be done by disconnecting the hoses from the charcoal canister **(see illustrations)**. Label the hoses to aid in correct installation.

4 Plug pipe A with your finger and blow compressed air through pipe B (fuel tank side) **(see illustration)**.

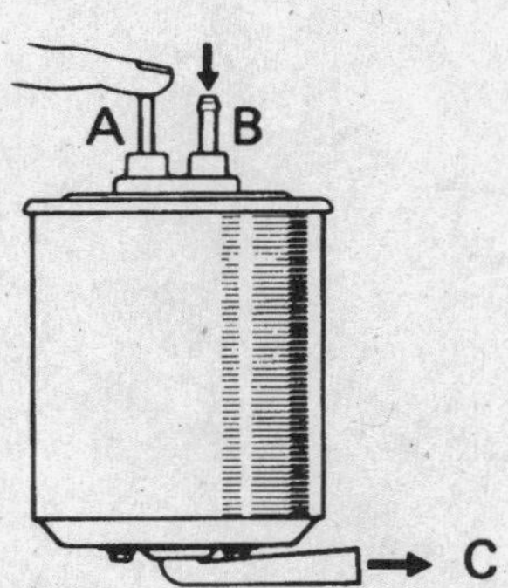

31.4 Air should flow through freely and no charcoal should escape

32.4 Make sure that all brackets and hangers are tight and in good condition

5 Check that air comes out of the bottom of pipe C without resistance. Also check that no activated charcoal comes out.

6 If necessary replace the charcoal canister and reconnect the hoses. Do not attempt to wash the charcoal.

32 Exhaust system check (every 30,000 miles or 24 months)

Refer to illustrations 32.2 and 32.4

1 With the engine cold (at least three hours after the vehicle has been driven), check the complete exhaust system from the engine to the end of the tailpipe. This should be done on a hoist where unrestricted access is available.

2 Check the pipes and connections for signs of leakage and/or corrosion indicating a potential failure **(see illustration)**. Make sure that all brackets and hangers are in good condition and tight.

3 At the same time, inspect the underside of the body for holes, corrosion, open seams, etc. which may allow exhaust gases to enter the passenger compartment. Seal all body openings with silicone or body putty.

4 Rattles and other noises can often be traced to the exhaust system, especially the mounts and hangers **(see illustration)**. Try to move the pipes, muffler and catalytic converter. If the components can come in contact with the body or suspension parts, secure the exhaust system with new mounts.

5 Check the running condition of the engine by inspecting inside the end of the tailpipe. The exhaust deposits here are an indication of engine state-of-tune. If the pipe is black and sooty or coated with white deposits, the engine is in need of a tune-up, including a thorough fuel system inspection and adjustment.

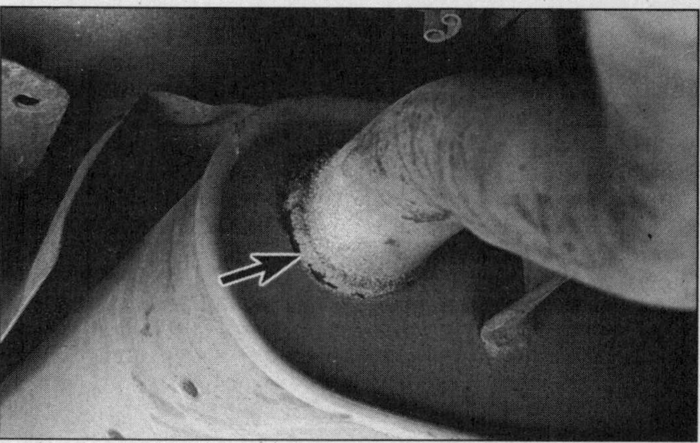

32.2 Check the welds around the muffler (arrow) for corrosion and leakage

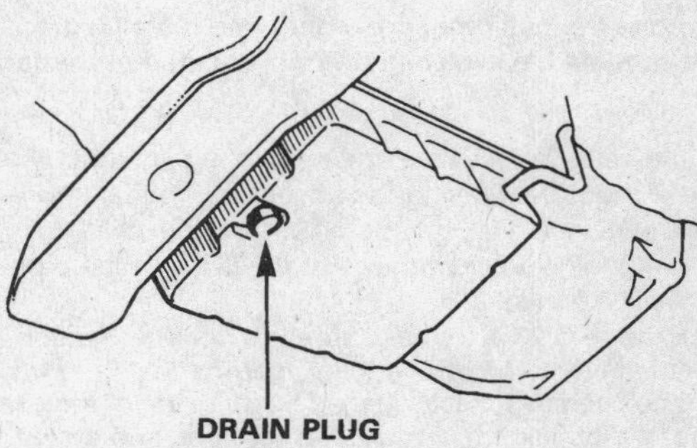

33.7 Typical location of the drain plug on the automatic transmission

33 Automatic transmission fluid change (every 30,000 miles or 24 months)

Refer to illustration 33.7

Note: *Replacement of the transmission fluid strainer is not specified by the manufacturer as a recommended maintenanc item. However, if you feel replacement of the strainer is necessary, see Chapter 7B for the procedure.*

1 At the specified time intervals, the transmission fluid should be drained and replaced.

2 Before beginning work, purchase the specified transmission fluid (see *Recommended lubricants and fluids* at the front of this Chapter).

3 Other tools necessary for this job include jackstands to support the vehicle in a raised position, a drain pan capable of holding at least 5 quarts, newspapers and clean rags.

4 The fluid should be drained immediately after the vehicle has been driven. This will remove any built up sediment better then if the fluid were cold. Because of this, it may be wise to wear protective gloves. Fluid temperature can exceed 350 degrees in a hot transmission.

5 After the vehicle has been driven to warm up the fluid, raise it and place it on the jackstands for access underneath.

6 Move the necessary equipment under the vehicle, being careful not to touch any of the hot exhaust components.

7 Place the drain pan under the transmission and remove the drain plug **(see illustration)**, allowing the hot fluid time to drain into the pan. Check the fluid for metal particles, which may be an indication of internal transmission problems.

8 Reinstall the drain plug securely and lower the vehicle.

9 Open the hood and remove the transmission fluid dipstick.

10 Add the specified amount and type of fluid through the filler tube (use a funnel to prevent spills). It is best to add a little fluid at a time, continually checking the level with the dipstick.

34.2 Remove the balljoint screw plug and install a grease fitting (some models have grease fittings installed at the factory)

11 With the selector lever in Park, apply the parking brake and start the engine without depressing the accelerator pedal (if possible). Do not race the engine at high speed; run at slow idle only.
12 With the engine still idling, check the level on the dipstick. Look under the vehicle for leaks.
13 Check the fluid level to make sure it is correct (Section 7). Do not allow the fluid level to go above the upper mark, as the transmission would then be overfilled, necessitating the draining of the excess fluid.
14 Push the dipstick firmly back into the tube and drive the vehicle far enough to reach normal operating temperature. Park the vehicle on a level surface and check the fluid level on the dipstick with the engine idling and the transmission in Park. The level should now be at the upper mark in the HOT range. If not, add more fluid to bring the level up to this point. Again, do not overfill.

34 Balljoint lubrication (every 30,000 miles or 24 months)

Refer to illustration 34.2

Note: *This procedure applies to 1979 through 1986 models only.*

1 Refer to *Recommended lubricants and fluids* near the front of this Chapter to obtain the necessary grease, etc. You will also need a grease gun and if your vehicle has plugs in the grease fitting holes, fittings will have to be purchased and installed.
2 Look under the vehicle and locate the balljoint grease fittings or screw plugs **(see illustration)**. Remove the plugs with a wrench and thread in the grease fittings. A dealer or auto parts store will be able to supply the correct fittings. Straight, as well as angled, fittings are available.
3 For easier access under the vehicle, raise it with a jack and place jackstands under the frame. Make sure it is securely supported by the stands. If the wheels are to be removed at this interval for rotation or brake inspection, loosen the lug nuts slightly while the vehicle is still on the ground.
4 Before beginning, force a little grease out of the nozzle to remove any dirt from the end of the gun. Wipe the nozzle clean with a rag.
5 With the grease gun and plenty of clean rags, crawl under the vehicle and begin lubricating the fittings.
6 Wipe the balljoint grease fitting nipple clean and push the nozzle firmly over it. Squeeze the trigger on the grease gun to force grease into the component. The balljoints should be lubricated until the rubber seal is firm to the touch. Do not pump too much grease into the fittings as it could rupture the seal. If grease escapes around the grease gun nozzle, the nipple is clogged or the nozzle is not completely seated on the fitting. Resecure the gun nozzle to the fitting and try again. If necessary, replace the fitting with a new one.

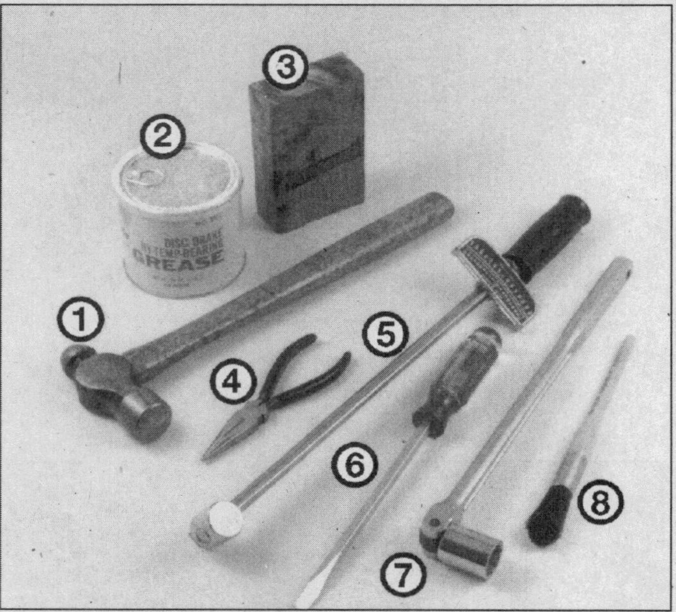

35.1 Tools and materials needed for front wheel bearing maintenance

1 **Hammer** - *A common hammer will do just fine*
2 **Grease** - *High-temperature grease that is formulated specially for front wheel bearings should be used*
3 **Wood block** - *If you have a scrap piece of 2x4, it can be used to drive the new seal into the hub*
4 **Needle-nose pliers** - *Used to straighten and remove the cotter pin in the spindle*
5 **Torque wrench** - *This is very important in this procedure; if the bearing is too tight, the wheel won't turn freely - if it's too loose, the wheel will "wobble" on the spindle. Either way, it could mean extensive damage*
6 **Screwdriver** - *Used to remove the seal from the hub (a long screwdriver is preferred)*
7 **Socket/breaker bar** - *Needed to loosen the nut on the spindle if it's extremely tight*
8 **Brush** - *Together with some clean solvent, this will be used to remove old grease from the hub and spindle*

35 Wheel bearing - check, repack and adjustment (every 30,000 miles or 24 months)

Refer to illustrations 35.1, 35.6a, 35.6b, 35.7, 35.8, 35.9, 35.11, 35.15, 35.16 and 35.19

Note: *This procedure applies to 1979 through 1986 models only. The bearings on 1987 and later models are not serviceable.*

1 In most cases the front wheel bearings will not need servicing until the brake pads are changed. However, the bearings should be checked whenever the front of the vehicle is raised for any reason. Several items, including a torque wrench and special grease, are required for this procedure **(see illustration)**.
2 With the vehicle securely supported on jackstands, spin each wheel and check for noise, rolling resistance and freeplay.
3 Grasp the top of each tire with one hand and the bottom with the other. Move the wheel in-and-out on the spindle. If there's any noticeable movement, the bearings should be checked and then repacked with grease or replaced if necessary.
4 Remove the wheel(s).
5 Fabricate a wood block to slide between the brake pads to keep them separated. Remove the brake caliper (Chapter 9) and hang it out of the way on a piece of wire.
6 Pry the grease cap out of the hub using a screwdriver or hammer and chisel **(see illustrations)**.

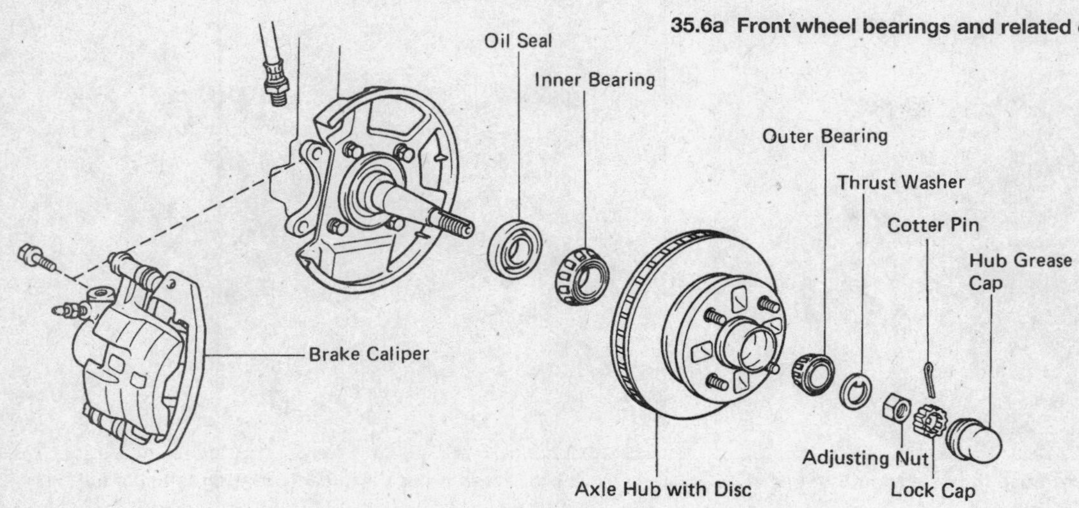

35.6a Front wheel bearings and related components - exploded view

35.6b The hub grease cap can be pried off with a screwdriver or chisel

35.7 Remove the cotter pin and lock cap . . .

35.8 . . . followed by the adjusting nut

35.9 Push the hub back onto the spindle and remove the thrust washer and bearing

7 Straighten the bent ends of the cotter pin, then pull the cotter pin out of the adjusting nut cap **(see illustration)**. Discard the cotter pin and use a new one during reassembly.

8 Remove the adjusting nut and washer from the end of the spindle **(see illustration)**.

9 Pull the hub out slightly, then push it back into its original position **(see illustration)**. This should force the outer wheel bearing off the spindle enough so it can be removed.

10 Pull the hub off the spindle.

35.11 Use a screwdriver to remove the seal from the rear of the hub

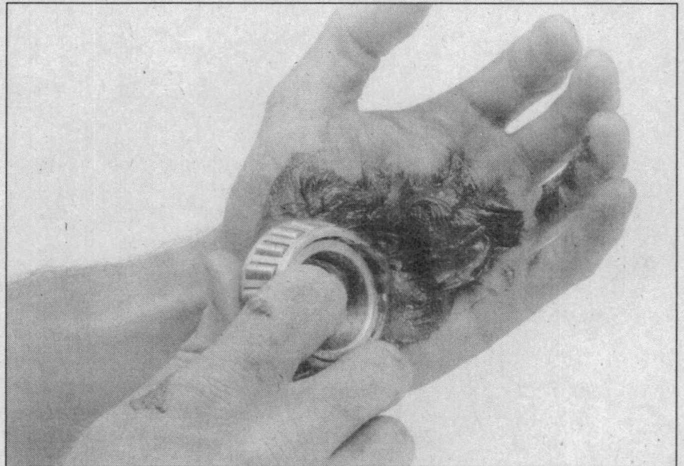

35.15 Press grease into each bearing until it's full

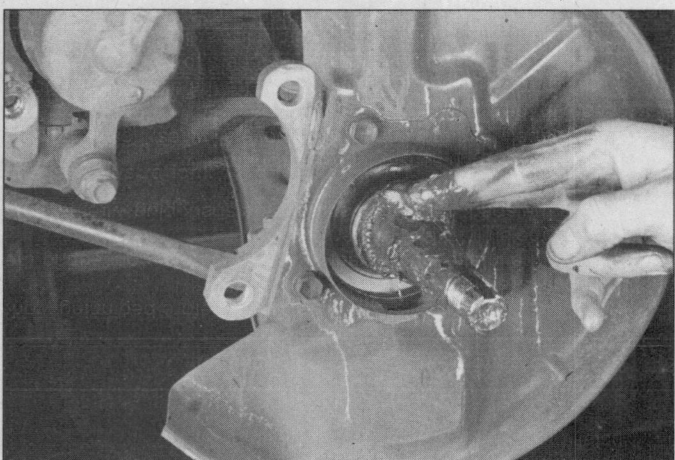

35.16 Apply a coat of grease to the spindle

35.19 Tap the seal into place with a piece of wood and a hammer

11 Use a screwdriver to pry the grease seal out of the rear of the hub **(see illustration)**. As this is done, note how the seal is installed.

12 Remove the inner wheel bearing from the hub.

13 Use solvent to remove all traces of the old grease from the bearings, hub and spindle. A small brush may prove helpful; however make sure no bristles from the brush embed themselves inside the bearing rollers. Allow the parts to air dry.

14 Carefully inspect the bearings for cracks, heat discoloration, worn rollers, etc. Check the bearing races inside the hub for wear and damage. If the bearing races are defective, the hubs should be taken to a machine shop with the facilities to remove the old races and press new ones in. Note that the bearings and races come as matched sets and old bearings should never be installed on new races.

15 Use high-temperature front wheel bearing grease to pack the bearings. Work the grease completely into the bearings, forcing it between the rollers, cone and cage from the back side **(see illustration)**.

16 Apply a thin coat of grease to the spindle at the outer bearing seat, inner bearing seat, shoulder and seal seat **(see illustration)**.

17 Put a small quantity of grease behind each bearing race inside the hub. Using your finger, form a dam at these points to provide for extra grease and to keep thinned grease from flowing out of the bearing.

18 Place the grease-packed inner bearing into the rear of the hub and put a little more grease outside of the bearing.

19 Place a new seal over the inner bearing and tap the seal evenly into place with a hammer and block of wood until it's flush with the hub **(see illustration)**.

20 Carefully place the hub assembly onto the spindle and push the grease-packed outer bearing into position.

21 Install the washer and adjusting nut. Tighten the nut slightly (only 20 ft-lbs of torque).

22 Spin the hub in a forward direction to seat the bearings and remove any grease or burrs which could cause excessive bearing play later.

23 Check to see that the tightness of the nut is still approximately 20 ft-lbs. Spin the hub in both directions several turns, then recheck the torque again (it must be 20 ft-lbs.).

24 Loosen the nut until it's just loose, no more.

25 Tighten the nut using a deep socket held in your hand. Tighten it as tight as possible by hand, but do not use a ratchet or breaker bar on the socket. Install the adjusting nut cap and see if the hole in the spindle is aligned with the slot in the cap. If the nut must be turned to align them, turn it clockwise only! Install a new cotter pin.

26 Bend the ends of the cotter pin until they're flat against the nut. Cut off any extra length which could interfere with the dust cap.

27 Install the dust cap, tapping it into place with a hammer.

28 Place the brake caliper near the rotor and carefully remove the wood spacer. Install the caliper (Chapter 9).

29 Install the tire/wheel assembly on the hub and tighten the lug nuts.

30 Grasp the top and bottom of the tire and check the bearings in the manner described earlier in this Section.

31 Lower the vehicle.

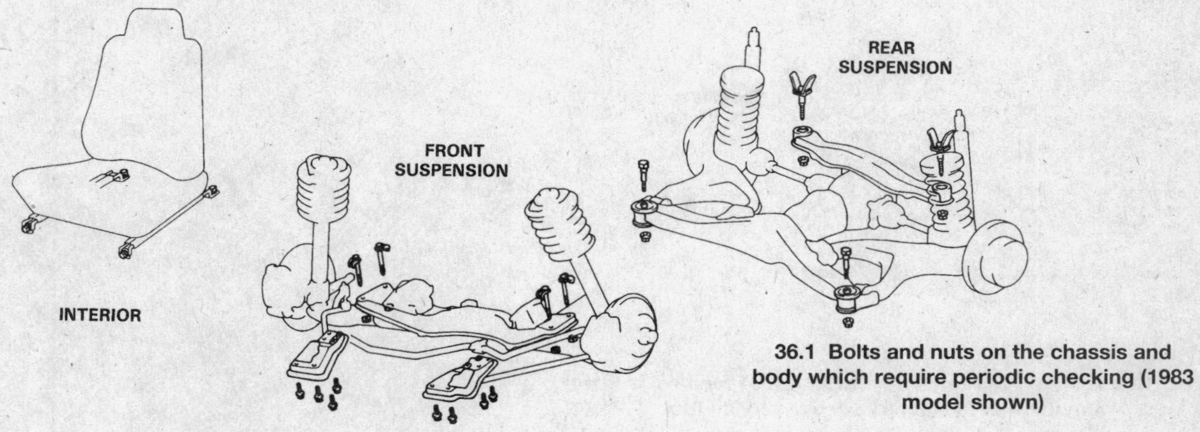

36.1 Bolts and nuts on the chassis and body which require periodic checking (1983 model shown)

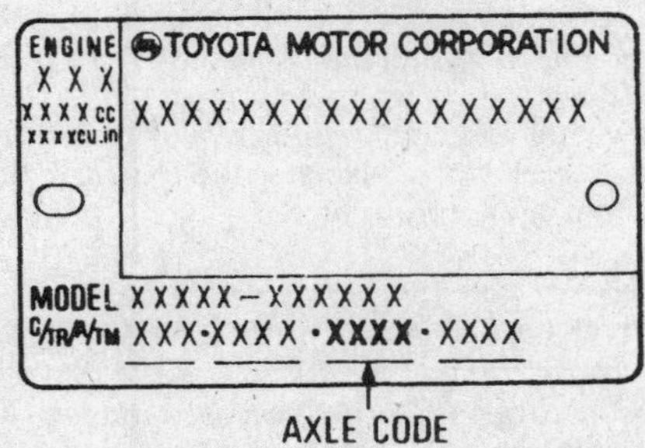

37.1 The axle code on the manufacturer's plate (located in the engine compartment) will indicate if the vehicle is equipped with the limited slip differential

36 Chassis and body fastener check (every 30,000 miles or 24 months)

Refer to illustration 36.1

Tighten the following parts to the specified torque: front seat mounting bolts, front suspension member-to-body mounting bolts and nuts and strut bar bracket-to-body mounting bolts (left and right hand sides) **(see illustration)**.

37 Manual transmission and differential lubricant change (see maintenance schedule)

Refer to illustrations 37.1, 37.6a and 37.6b

1 At the specified time intervals the transmission and differential lubricants should be changed to ensure trouble free operation. Before proceeding, purchase the specified type of lubricant. **Note:** *If your vehicle has a limited slip differential, a label bearing the letters "LSD" will be attached to the differential gear housing. If the label has been removed or is illegible, check the manufacturer's plate in the engine compartment* **(see illustration)***. If the last digit in the axle code is a 3 or a 5, your vehicle has a limited slip differential and will require a special lubricant (see the Specifications at the beginning of this Chapter).*

2 Tools necessary for this job include jackstands to support the vehicle in a raised position, a wrench to remove the drain plugs, a drain pan capable of holding at least four quarts, newspapers and clean rags.

3 The lubricant should be drained immediately after the vehicle has been driven. This will remove any contaminants better than if the lubricant were cold. Because of this, it may be wise to wear rubber gloves while removing the drain plug.

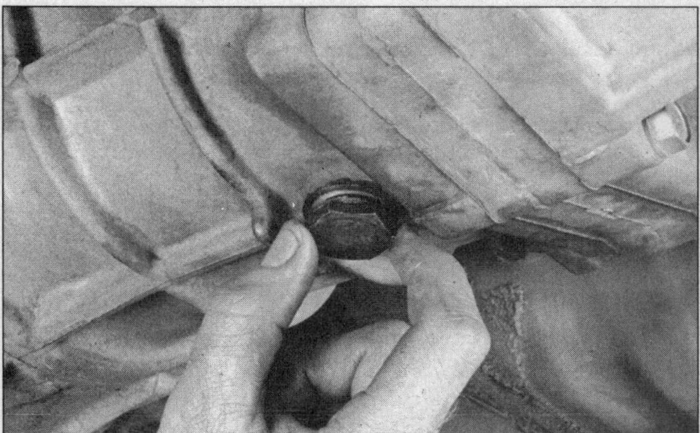

37.6a The manual transmission drain plug is usually very tight - use a six point socket when loosening it to avoid rounding off the points on the hex, then unscrew it by hand to avoid dropping it in the pan

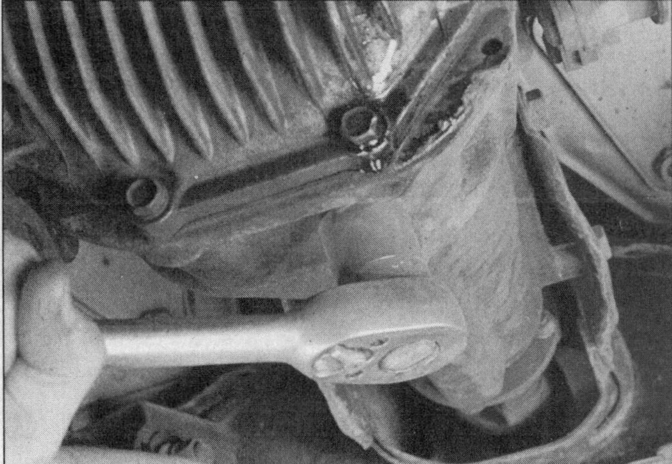

37.6b Removing the differential drain plug (1983 model shown)

4 After the vehicle has been driven to warm up the lubricant, raise it and place it on jackstands. Make sure it is safely supported and as level as possible.

5 Move the necessary equipment under the vehicle, being careful not to touch any of the hot exhaust components.

6 Place the drain pan under the transmission or differential and remove the drain plug **(see illustrations)**. Be careful not to burn yourself on the lubricant.

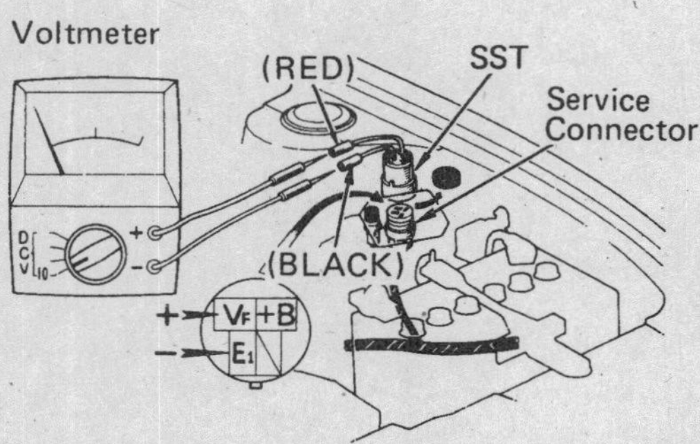

38.3 Checking oxygen sensor operation (1981 models) with a voltmeter and the factory special service tool

7 Allow the lubricant to drain completely, then reinstall the plug and tighten it securely.

8 Refer to Section 26 or 27 and fill the component to the correct level with new lubricant.

9 Pour the old lubricant into capped jugs (old antifreeze containers, milk cartons, etc.) and dispose of it at a service station or reclamation center.

38 Oxygen sensor check and replacement (every 30,000 miles or 24 months)

Refer to illustrations 38.3 and 38.9

Note: *This procedure applies to 1979 through 1981 models only.*

1 The oxygen sensor on 1979 and 1980 models should be replaced with a new one at the recommended intervals. On 1981 models, the oxygen sensor can be checked with a voltmeter, but special tool (No. 09842-14010) is required to make the connections. If the sensor on these models does not check out as specified, it must be replaced with a new one.

Checking (1981 models)

2 Remove the rubber cap from the four terminal service connector located on the left fender apron near the front shock tower. Attach the special tool (No. 09842-14010) to the service connector.

3 Connect the positive (+) probe of the voltmeter to the red wire of the special tool. Connect the negative (-) probe of the voltmeter to the black wire **(see illustration)**.

4 Connect a tachometer to the engine (by following the directions supplied with the tachometer), then start the engine and allow it to reach normal operating temperature.

5 Increase the engine speed to 2500 rpm and hold it there for 90 seconds.

6 After 90 seconds have elapsed, maintain the engine speed at 2500 rpm and observe the voltmeter. The needle should fluctuate or jump a minimum of eight times in ten seconds. If it does not, the oxygen sensor is probably faulty.

7 Stop the engine, disconnect the tachometer and voltmeter, unplug the special tool and cap the service connector.

Removal and installation

8 The oxygen sensor is located at the front side of the exhaust manifold outlet pipe and is attached to it with two nuts.

9 To remove the sensor, unplug the wiring connectors, remove the nuts **(see illustration)** and pull the sensor out of the manifold and clamps.

10 Remove all traces of the old gasket from the manifold.

11 When installing the new sensor, use a new gasket and be very careful not to bend, twist or kink the tube as you slip the sensor into the manifold and fender clamps. **Note:** *The sensor tube should not be touching any components and the connector at the front of the tube must be facing down.*

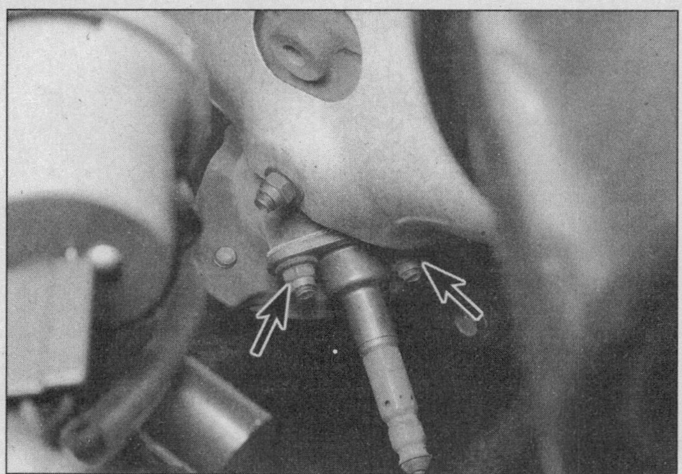

38.9 Remove the oxygen sensor mounting nuts (arrows)

12 Install new nuts and tighten them evenly to the torque listed in this Chapter's Specifications. Also, be sure to plug in the wiring connectors at the front of the sensor tube.

39 Airbag check (In 10 years, then each succeeding 2 years)

Note: *This procedure applies to 1990 and later models only.*

1 At the specified intervals, the airbag system should be checked.

2 Turn the ignition switch to the ON position and make sure the airbag warning light goes on, then after 6 seconds goes off. If the light does not go on or it stays on indefinitely, take the vehicle to a dealership service department and have the airbag system checked.

3 Refer to Chapter 12 for more information concerning the airbag system.

40 Warning lights - general information

Refer to illustrations 40.8, 40.10, 40.11, 40.13 and 40.14

1 The Supras are equipped with warning lights for the purpose of drawing attention to the driver the need for service or displaying diagnostic coded messages. Some of the warning lights have a dual purpose; for example, the BRAKE warning light indicates either a problem in a brake hydraulic system circuit or simply that the parking brake is applied.

Seat belt warning light

2 This light is pictured as a passenger with a seat belt crossed over their lap and is located in the combination meter. It is activated for 4 to 8 seconds with the ignition key turned to ON or ACC. The buzzer will only operate if the driver's seatbelt is not fastened.

Discharge warning light

3 This light is pictured as a battery with positive and negative terminals. This light indicates that the battery is being discharged. Check the alternator belt or the charging system for broken belts, loose wires or a defective alternator (see Chapter 5).

Oil pressure warning light

4 This light is pictured as a small can of oil with a drop of oil falling off the spout. This light indicates that the oil pressure is low due to a loss of oil or a defective oil pump. Pull the vehicle over immediately for a thorough check to determine the exact cause of the problem before proceeding.

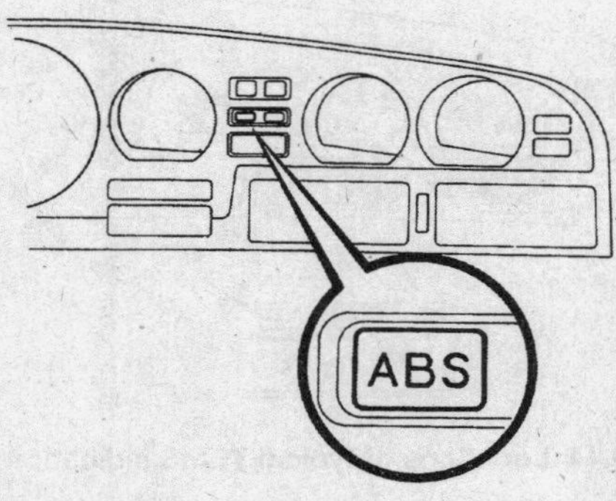

40.8 Location of the ABS warning light

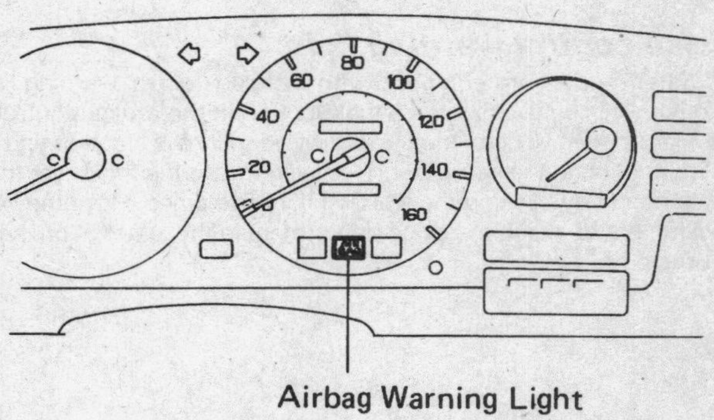

40.10 Location of the Airbag warning light

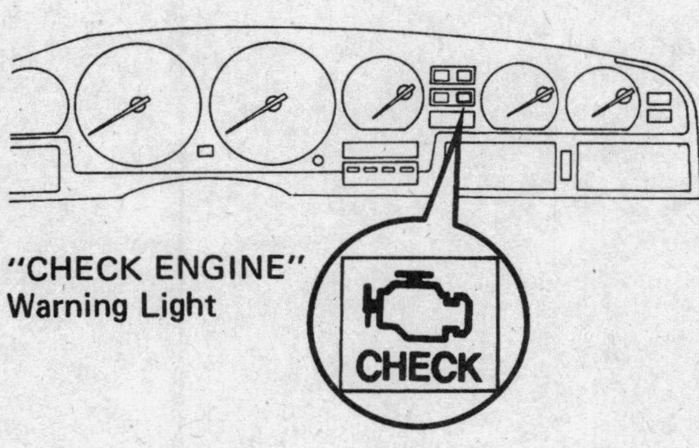

40.11 Location of the CHECK ENGINE warning light

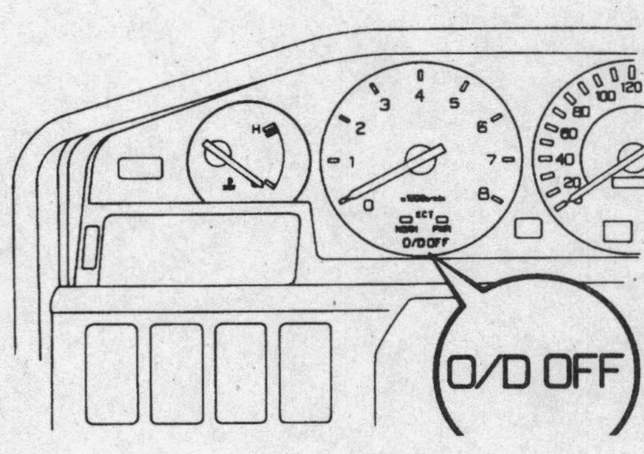

40.13 Location of the O/D OFF warning light

Brake warning light

5 The BRAKE warning light indicates one of two things:

a) The parking brake lever is applied, or
b) There is a problem in one of the brake hydraulic circuits. If this light comes on when the parking brake is released, fix the problem immediately (see Chapter 9).

Fuel tank warning light

6 This light is pictured as a small gasoline pump with a hose. This light indicates that the fuel tank is nearly empty.

Open door warning light

7 This light remains on until all the doors are completely closed.

ABS warning light

8 The ABS warning light (only on ABS-equipped vehicles) indicates a malfunction in the Anti Lock Braking system. If a problem occurs, the system will identify the location and store the information in the computer. At the same time the system informs the driver there is a malfunction by turning ON the ABS light **(see illustration)**.

9 Refer to Chapter 9 for more information on the ABS system.

Airbag warning light

10 The Airbag warning light (only on Airbag-equipped vehicles) indicates a malfunction in the Airbag system. If a problem occurs, the system will identify the location and store the information in the computer. At the same time the system informs the driver there is a malfunction by turning ON the Airbag light **(see illustration)**. Refer to Chapter 12 for more information on the Airbag system.

CHECK ENGINE warning light

11 The CHECK ENGINE warning light indicates a malfunction in the electronic engine management system **(see illustration)**.

12 Depending upon the year, the CHECK ENGINE light also serves as a warning light for engine malfunction. Consult your owner's manual for the exact details.

O/D OFF warning light

13 Later models are equipped with an O/D OFF indicator light(s) in the tachometer **(see illustration)**. These lights indicate a malfunction in the automatic transmission system. If a problem occurs, the system will identify the location and store the information in the computer. At the same time, the system informs the driver there is a malfunction by blinking the O/D OFF light. Refer to Chapter 7B for more information on this system.

TEMS (Toyota Electronic Modulated Suspension) system warning light

14 Later models are equipped with TEMS warning lights in the dash **(see illustration)**. These lights indicate a malfunction in the electronic suspension system. If a problem occurs, the system will identify the lo-

cation and store the information in the computer. Refer to Chapter 10 for more information on the electronic suspension system.

Cruise control warning light

15 Later models are equipped with a cruise control warning light in the dash. This light indicates a malfunction in the cruise control system. If a problem occurs, the system will identify the location and store the information in the computer. This system informs the driver there is a malfunction by blinking the warning light five times. Have the vehicle checked at a dealership service department in the event of cruise control problems.

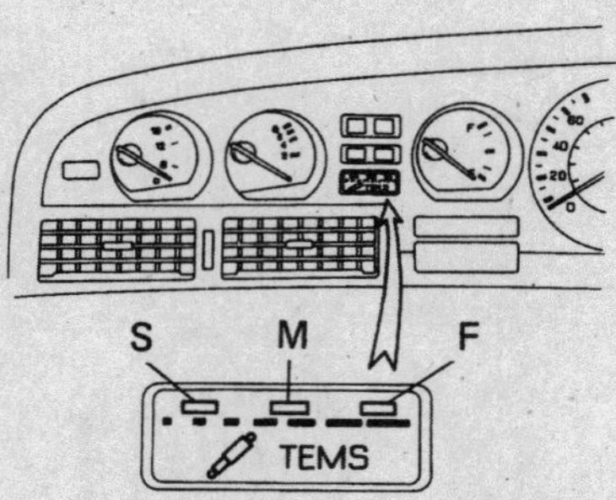

40.14 Locations of typical TEMS indication lights

Chapter 2 Part A
SOHC engines (1979 through 1981 models)

Contents

Specifications

General

Displacement
- 1979 and 1980 ..... 156.4 cu inches (2563 cc)
- 1981 ..... 168.4 cu inches (2759 cc)

Bore/stroke
- 1979 and 1980 ..... 3.15 x 3.35 inches (80.0 x 85.0 mm)
- 1981 ..... 3.27 x 3.35 inches (83.0 x 85.0 mm)

Firing order 1-5-3-6-2-4

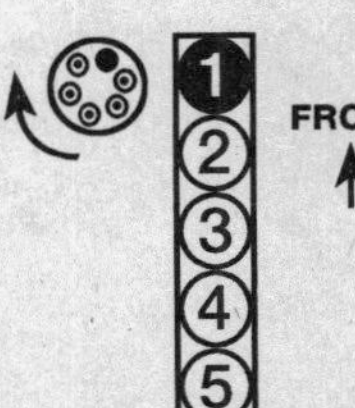

The blackened terminal shown on the distributor cap indicates the Number One spark plug wire position

Cylinder location and distributor rotation

Camshaft

Lobe height
- Standard
  - Intake ..... 1.7121 inches
  - Exhaust ..... 1.7146 inches

Camshaft (continued)

Lobe height (continued)	
Service limit	
Intake	1.6961 inches
Exhaust	1.6988 inches
Runout limit	0.0024 inch
Endplay	
Standard	0.003 to 0.007 inch
Service limit	0.012 inch
Journal diameter	
Standard	1.3378 to 1.3384 inches
Service limit	1.334 inches
Oil clearance	
Standard	0.0007 to 0.0022 inch
Service limit	0.004 inch

Rocker arm oil clearance

Standard	0.0005 to 0.0013 inch
Service limit	0.0024 inch

Timing chain and sprockets

Timing chain length (17 links)	5.787 inches max
Minimum sprocket diameters (chain meshed in teeth)	
Crankshaft	2.555 inches
Oil pump driveshaft	3.776 inches
Timing chain vibration damper thickness limit	
No. 1	0.157 inch
No. 2	0.197 inch

Manifold warpage limits

Intake manifold	0.004 inch
Exhaust manifold	0.020 inch

Oil pump

Side clearance	
Standard	0.0012 to 0.0035 inch
Service limit	0.006 inch
Gear-to-body clearance	
Standard	0.0012 to 0.0024 inch
Service limit	0.008 inch
Gear backlash	
Standard	0.020 to 0.024 inch
Service limit	0.035 inch

Torque specifications

	Ft-lbs
Cylinder head bolts	
Large	55 to 61
Small	11 to 15
Intake manifold bolts/nuts	10 to 15
Exhaust manifold bolts/nuts	13 to 16
Crankshaft pulley bolt	98 to 11
Driveplate/flywheel bolts	51 to 57
Camshaft sprocket bolt	47 to 54
Oil pump driveshaft sprocket bolt	
Class 4	8 to 11
Class 6	13 to 18
Camshaft bearing cap bolts	13 to 16
Oil pan bolts	5 to 6

1 General information

This part of Chapter 2 is devoted to in-vehicle repair procedures for single-overhead-camshaft (SOHC) engines. All information concerning engine removal and installation and engine block and cylinder head overhaul can be found in Chapter 2C.

The following repair procedures are based on the assumption that the engine is installed in the vehicle. If the engine has been removed from the vehicle and mounted on a stand, many of the steps outlined in this part of Chapter 2 will not apply.

The Specifications included in this Part of Chapter 2 apply only to the procedures contained in this Part. Chapter 2C contains the Specifications necessary for cylinder head and engine block rebuilding.

Two different SOHC engines were installed in the Supra during the years covered by this manual. The engine used in 1979 and 1980 models, designated the 4M-E, displaces 2563cc. The engine used in 1981 models, designated the 5M-E, has a three-millimeter-larger bore, increasing displacement to 2759cc.

Both engines have a cross-flow type aluminum cylinder head, a cast-iron block and a seven-bearing crankshaft. The camshaft is driven by the crankshaft via a double-row roller chain; the chain also drives the oil pump driveshaft.

2 Repair operations possible with the engine in the vehicle

Many major repair operations can be accomplished without removing the engine from the vehicle.

Clean the engine compartment and the exterior of the engine with some type of degreaser before any work is done. It will make the job easier and help keep dirt out of the internal areas of the engine.

Depending on the components involved, it may be helpful to remove the hood to improve access to the engine as repairs are performed (see Chapter 11 if necessary). Cover the fenders to prevent damage to the paint. Special pads are available, but an old bedspread or blanket will also work.

If vacuum, exhaust, oil or coolant leaks develop, indicating a need for gasket or seal replacement, the repairs can generally be made with the engine in the vehicle. The intake and exhaust manifold gaskets, oil pan gasket, crankshaft oil seals and cylinder head gasket are all accessible with the engine in place.

Exterior engine components, such as the intake and exhaust manifolds, the oil pan, the oil pump, the water pump, the starter motor, the alternator, the distributor and the fuel system components can be removed for repair with the engine in place.

Since the cylinder head can be removed without pulling the engine, camshaft and valve component servicing can also be accomplished with the engine in the vehicle. Replacement of the timing chain and sprockets is also possible with the engine in the vehicle.

In extreme cases caused by a lack of necessary equipment, repair or replacement of piston rings, pistons, connecting rods and rod bearings is possible with the engine in the vehicle. However, this practice is not recommended because of the cleaning and preparation work that must be done to the components involved.

3 Top Dead Center (TDC) for number one piston - locating

Refer to illustration 3.8

Note: *The following procedure is based on the assumption that the distributor is correctly installed. If you are trying to locate TDC to install the distributor correctly, piston position must be determined by feeling for compression at the number one spark plug hole, then aligning the ignition timing marks as described in step 8.*

1 Top Dead Center (TDC) is the highest point in the cylinder that each piston reaches as it travels up-and-down when the crankshaft turns. Each piston reaches TDC on the compression stroke and again on the exhaust stroke, but TDC generally refers to piston position on the compression stroke.

2 Positioning the piston(s) at TDC is an essential part of many procedures such as camshaft and timing belt/pulley removal and distributor removal.

3 Before beginning this procedure, be sure to place the transmission in Neutral and apply the parking brake or block the rear wheels. Also, disable the ignition system by detaching the coil wire from the center terminal of the distributor cap and grounding it on the block with a jumper wire. Remove the spark plugs (see Chapter 1).

4 In order to bring any piston to TDC, the crankshaft must be turned using one of the methods outlined below. When looking at the front of the engine, normal crankshaft rotation is clockwise.

a) The preferred method is to turn the crankshaft with a socket and ratchet attached to the bolt threaded into the front of the crankshaft.

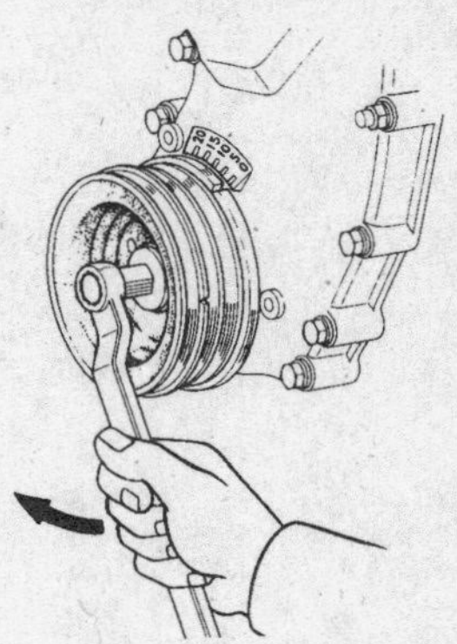

3.8 Turn the crankshaft in a clockwise direction until the notch in the crankshaft pulley is aligned with the 0 mark on the timing plate

b) A remote starter switch, which may save some time, can also be used. Follow the instructions included with the switch. Once the piston is close to TDC, use a socket and ratchet as described in the previous paragraph.

c) If an assistant is available to turn the ignition switch to the Start position in short bursts, you can get the piston close to TDC without a remote starter switch. Make sure your assistant is out of the vehicle, away from the ignition switch, then use a socket and ratchet as described in Paragraph a) to complete the procedure.

5 Note the position of the terminal for the number one spark plug wire on the distributor cap. If the terminal isn't marked, follow the plug wire from the number one cylinder spark plug to the cap.

6 Use a felt-tip pen or chalk to make a mark on the distributor body directly under the terminal.

7 Detach the cap from the distributor and set it aside (see Chapter 1 if necessary).

8 Turn the crankshaft (see Step 3 above) until the notch in the crankshaft pulley is aligned with the 0 on the timing plate (located at the front of the engine) **(see illustration)**.

9 Look at the distributor rotor - it should be pointing directly at the mark you made on the distributor body.

10 If the rotor is 180 degrees off, the number one piston is at TDC on the exhaust stroke.

11 To get the piston to TDC on the compression stroke, turn the crankshaft one complete turn (360-degrees) clockwise. The rotor should now be pointing at the mark on the distributor. When the rotor is pointing at the number one spark plug wire terminal in the distributor cap and the ignition timing marks are aligned, the number one piston is at TDC on the compression stroke. **Note:** *If it's impossible to align the ignition timing marks when the rotor is pointing at the mark on the distributor body, the timing chain may have jumped the teeth on the sprockets or may have been installed incorrectly.*

12 After the number one piston has been positioned at TDC on the compression stroke, TDC for any of the remaining pistons can be located by turning the crankshaft and following the firing order. Mark the remaining spark plug wire terminal locations on the distributor body just like you did for the number one terminal, then number the marks to correspond with the cylinder numbers. As you turn the crankshaft, the rotor will also turn. When it's pointing directly at one of the marks on the distributor, the piston for that particular cylinder is at TDC on the compression stroke.

4 Valve cover - removal and installation

Removal

Refer to illustrations 4.6 and 4.7

1 Disconnect the cable from the negative battery terminal. **Caution:** *If the stereo in your vehicle is equipped with an anti-theft system, refer*

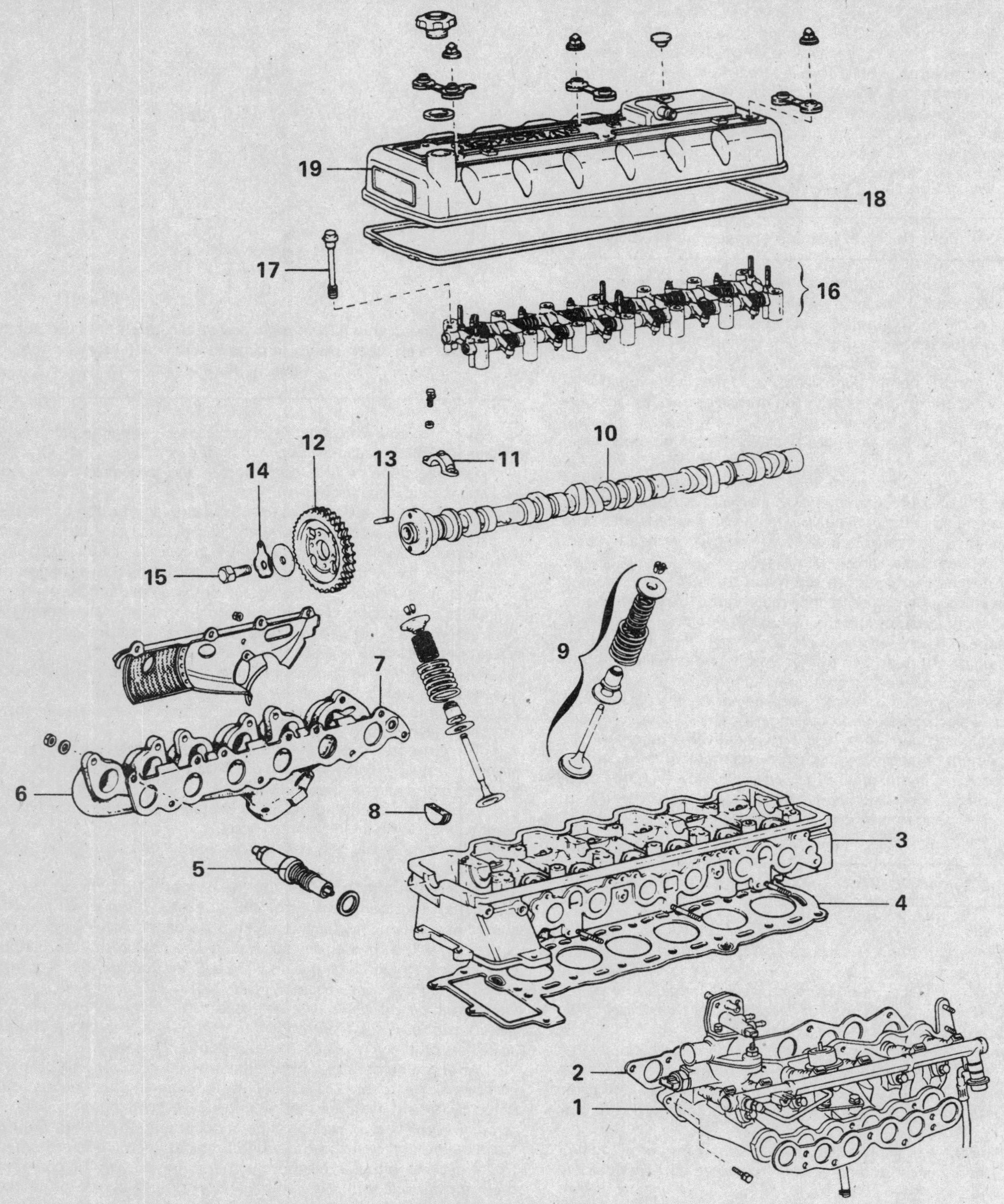

4.6 An exploded view of the valve cover, manifolds and cylinder head

1 *Intake manifold*
2 *Gasket*
3 *Cylinder head*
4 *Cylinder head gasket*
5 *Timing chain tensioner*
6 *Exhaust manifold*
7 *Gasket*
8 *Semi-circular seal*
9 *Valve components*
10 *Camshaft*
11 *Camshaft bearing cap*
12 *Camshaft sprocket*
13 *Dowel*
14 *Locking tab*
15 *Bolt*
16 *Rocker arm assembly*
17 *Cylinder head bolt*
18 *Gasket*
19 *Valve cover*

4.7 Remove the valve cover and gasket - discard the old gasket.

to the information on page 0-15 at the front of this manual before detaching the cable.

2 Unplug the spark plug wires and detach the spark plug wire harness from the valve cover.

3 Detach the breather hose from the valve cover.

4 Clearly label the smaller hoses attached to the intake air connector (the large hose connecting the air cleaner to the air intake chamber) and detach them from the intake air connector.

5 Remove the intake air connector.

6 Remove the valve cover retaining nuts and washers **(see illustration)**.

7 Remove the valve cover and gasket. Discard the old gasket **(see illustration)**.

8 Remove and discard the semi-circular rubber seal from the front of the cylinder head.

Installation

9 Place a new semi-circular rubber seal in the cutout at the front of the cylinder head, then apply RTV-type gasket sealant to the joints between the seal and the mating surface for the valve cover gasket.

10 Install the valve cover and a new gasket. Install the washers and nuts and tighten the nuts evenly and securely. Don't overtighten these nuts - they should be tight enough to prevent oil from leaking past the gasket, but not so tight that they warp the valve cover.

11 The remainder of installation is the reverse of removal.

5 Intake manifold - removal and installation

1 Remove the air intake chamber (see Chapter 4).

2 Remove the EGR valve and line (see Chapter 6).

3 Remove the bolts and nuts that attach the manifold to the head. Start at the ends and work toward the middle, loosening each one a little at a time until they can be removed. **Note:** *You can remove the manifold without removing the injectors and the fuel pressure regulator. If you're replacing the manifold, transfer the injectors, fuel pressure regulator, vacuum/thermo valves (see Chapter 4) and lines to the new manifold before it is bolted to the cylinder head.*

4 Move the manifold up and down to break the gasket seal, then lift it away from the head.

5 Remove the old gasket, then carefully scrape all traces of sealant off of the head and the manifold. Be very careful not to nick or scratch the gasket sealing surfaces.

6 Check the manifold-to-cylinder head gasket surface for warpage. Lay a straightedge along the manifold and try to slip a feeler gauge between the manifold and the straightedge at each runner. If the manifold is warped beyond the limit listed in this Chapter's Specifications, it must be resurfaced or replaced with a new one.

7 Check the manifold for corrosion (at the coolant passages), cracks and other damage. If defects are found, have the manifold repaired or replaced as necessary.

8 When installing the manifold, use a new gasket and apply a thin uniform layer of RTV-type gasket sealant to both sides.

9 Install the nuts and bolts and tighten them gradually, working from the center out to the ends, to the torque listed in this Chapter's Specifications.

10 Install the air intake chamber (see Chapter 4).

11 Install the EGR valve and line (see Chapter 6).

6 Exhaust manifold - removal and installation

1 Make sure the engine is completely cool before beginning work on the exhaust system.

2 Remove the intake air connector (the large hose connecting the air cleaner to the air intake chamber).

3 Unplug the spark plug wires and set the spark plug wire harness aside (see Chapter 1).

4 Unplug the oxygen sensor lead (see Chapter 6).

5 Clearly label, then disconnect or remove all wires, hoses, fittings, etc. that are in the way.

6 Working from under the vehicle, separate the exhaust pipe from the manifold. Use penetrating oil on the fasteners to ease removal.

7 Working from the ends of the manifold toward the center, loosen the retaining nuts gradually until they can be removed. Again, penetrating oil may prove helpful.

8 Pull the manifold off of the head, then remove the old gasket. **Note:** *Be very careful not to damage the oxygen sensor.*

9 Clean the gasket mating surfaces of the head and manifold and make sure the threads on the exhaust manifold studs are in good condition.

10 Using a straightedge and feeler gauge, check the manifold-to-cylinder head mating surface for warpage. If it is warped beyond the service limit, the manifold must be resurfaced or replaced with a new one.

11 Check for corrosion, cracks and other damage. Repair or replace the manifold as necessary.

12 When installing the manifold, use a new gasket and tighten the retaining nuts gradually, starting at the center and working out to the ends, to the torque listed in this Chapter's Specifications.

13 The remaining steps are simply a reversal of the removal procedure.

7 Cylinder head - removal and installation

Removal

Refer to illustrations 7.21, 7.22 and 7.23

1 Remove the battery (see Chapter 5). **Caution:** *If the stereo in your vehicle is equipped with an anti-theft system, refer to the information on page 0-15 at the front of this manual before detaching the cable.*

2 Drain the cooling system (see Chapter 1).

3 Remove the air cleaner assembly (see Chapter 4).

4 Disconnect the primary lead from the distributor and the high tension lead from the coil (see Chapter 5).

5 Disconnect the lead from the coolant temperature sending unit (see Chapter 3) and the thermo sensor (see Chapter 6).

6 Disconnect the fuel inlet hose (see Chapter 4).

7 Clearly label, then disconnect, all other hoses from the throttle body, intake manifold and/or cylinder head.

8 Disconnect the throttle cable from the throttle linkage (see Chapter 4).

9 Disconnect the exhaust pipe from the manifold flange (see Chapter 4).

10 Remove the engine oil dipstick and cover the hole to prevent the entry of dirt.

11 Remove the exhaust manifold and gaskets from the head (see Section 6).

7.21 Mark the relationship of the timing chain to the camshaft sprocket before disassembly

7.22 The camshaft sprocket bolt has left-hand threads - to loosen it, turn it clockwise

12 Remove and disconnect any remaining hoses or lines from the intake manifold, including the ignition advance vacuum line(s), and the coolant and heater hoses.
13 Remove the intake manifold and gaskets (see Section 5). Do not disassemble any EFI components unless it is absolutely necessary.
14 Remove the alternator and its mounting bracket (see Chapter 5).
15 Remove the fan belt and fan (see Chapter 3).
16 Remove the water pump assembly and bypass hose (see Chapter 3).
17 Unscrew the valve cover retaining nuts and remove the cover and sealing gasket. Remove the semi-circular rubber seal from the front of the cylinder head.
18 Rotate the engine (with a wrench on the large bolt at the front of the crankshaft) until the number one piston is at Top Dead Center on the compression stroke (see Section 3).
19 Before proceeding, determine whether the timing chain has stretched (see Step 3 in Section 16). If the chain has stretched, replace it (see Section 16); if it hasn't stretched, disconnect the chain and camshaft sprocket from the cam as follows:
20 Unscrew and remove the timing chain tensioner from the right side of the cylinder head. Set it aside for inspection.
21 Place a punch mark or small dab of white paint on one of the chain link side plates and a matching mark on the sprocket, adjacent to the marked link **(see illustration)**.
22 Bend back the locking tab, then remove the large bolt that attaches the camshaft sprocket to the camshaft **(see illustration)**. It has left-hand threads, so it must be turned in a clockwise direction to loosen it. If the camshaft begins to rotate as the bolt is loosened, insert a bar through one of the holes in the camshaft sprocket and allow it to rest on the cylinder head surface. Pull forward on the sprocket to free it from the camshaft, then separate it from the chain. Let the chain roll itself up and rest on the vibration dampers attached to the front of the engine block. Don't rotate the crankshaft while the cam sprocket is removed.
23 Loosen the cylinder head bolts 1/4-turn at a time each, in the sequence shown **(see illustration)**, then lift off the rocker arm assembly and head bolts as a unit. Do not dismantle the rocker arm assembly at this time.
24 Remove the cylinder head by lifting it straight up and off the engine block. Do not pry between the cylinder head and the engine block as damage to the gasket sealing surfaces may result. Instead, use a soft-faced hammer to tap the cylinder head up and break the gasket seal. Lift off the old head gasket.
25 Remove any remaining external components from the head to allow for thorough cleaning and inspection. See Chapter 2C, for cylinder head servicing procedures.

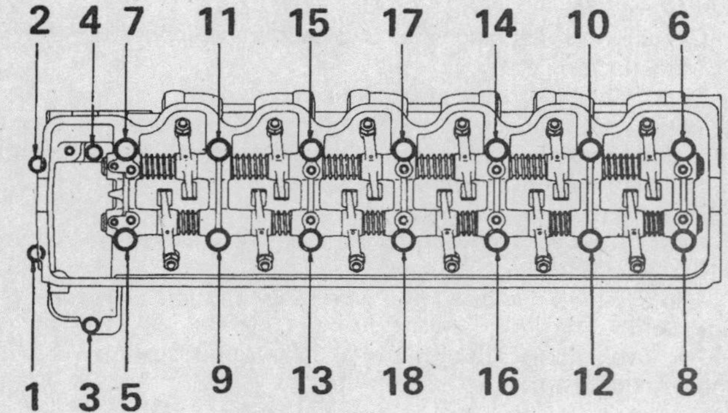

7.23 Cylinder head bolt *loosening* sequence

Installation

Refer to illustrations 7.31, 7.32, 7.34, 7.37 and 7.40

26 The mating surfaces of the cylinder head and block must be perfectly clean when the head is installed.
27 Use a gasket scraper to remove all traces of carbon and old gasket material, then clean the mating surfaces with lacquer thinner or acetone. If there's oil on the mating surfaces when the head is installed, the gasket may not seal correctly and leaks could develop. When working on the block, stuff the cylinders with clean shop rags to keep out debris. Use a vacuum cleaner to remove material that falls into the cylinders.
28 Check the block and head mating surfaces for nicks, deep scratches and other damage. If damage is slight, it can be removed with a file; if it's excessive, machining may be the only alternative.
29 Use a tap of the correct size to chase the threads in the head bolt holes, then clean the holes with compressed air - make sure that nothing remains in the holes.
30 Mount each bolt in a vise and run a die down the threads to remove corrosion and restore the threads. Dirt, corrosion, sealant and damaged threads will affect torque readings.
31 Install any components removed from the head prior to cleaning and inspection. The camshaft, timing chain and sprockets and the timing chain cover must also be in place on the engine (see Sections 9, 14 and 16, respectively) before the head is installed. Make sure the camshaft is positioned with the dowel pin at the 12 o'clock position - it should be aligned with the mark in the front rocker arm shaft support **(see illustration)**.

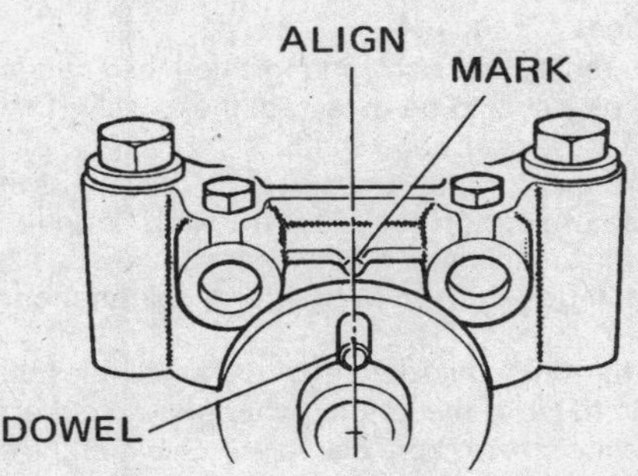

7.31 The locating dowel must be aligned with the mark before the cylinder head is installed

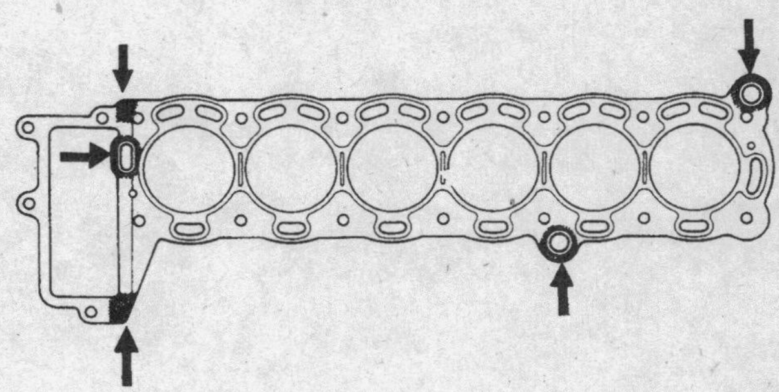

7.32 Apply RTV sealant to the indicated areas (arrows) on both sides of the cylinder head gasket before installing the head

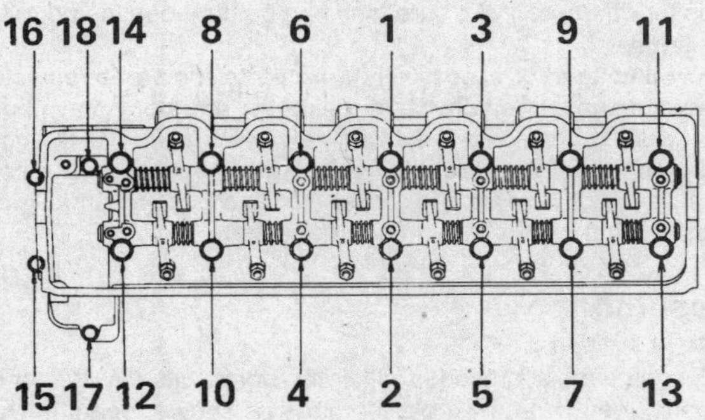

7.34 Cylinder head bolt *tightening* sequence

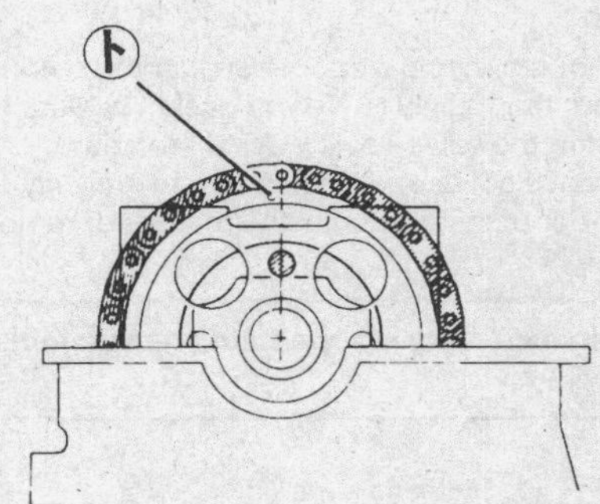

7.37 When installing a new chain and sprocket, position the timing mark as shown, and align the leading pin of the bright link on the chain with it

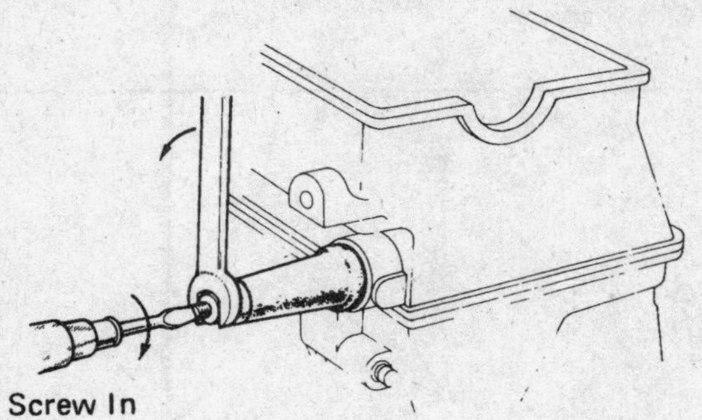

7.40 To adjust the timing chain tensioner, loosen the tensioner locknut and turn the adjusting screw clockwise until you feel resistance, then loosen the screw two full turns and tighten the locknut

32 Apply RTV-type gasket sealant to both sides of the new head gasket at the points shown **(see illustration)**. Make sure the gasket sealing surfaces of the engine block and cylinder head are clean and oil-free, then lay the head gasket in place on the block with the manufacturer's stamped mark facing up. Use the dowel pins in the top of the block to properly locate the gasket.

33 Carefully set the cylinder head in place on the block. Use the dowel pins to properly align it.

34 Install the rocker arm assembly (make sure the valve adjusting screws are backed-off as far as possible) and the head bolts. Tighten the bolts gradually and evenly, in the sequence shown **(see illustration)**, to 1/3, then 2/3, then all of the torque listed in this Chapter's Specifications.

35 Install the timing chain as follows:

36 Double check to be sure the locating dowel in the camshaft flange is aligned with the mark embossed in the front rocker arm shaft support **(see illustration 7.31)**. Make sure the mark on the crankshaft pulley is directly opposite the O on the timing chain cover. If it is not, turn the crankshaft a small amount, as required, to bring them into alignment.

37 Lift up on the timing chain, mesh the camshaft sprocket teeth with the chain and attach the sprocket to the camshaft. The marks made during disassembly should be aligned or, if a new chain/sprocket is being used, locate the small embossed mark on the sprocket and align the leading pin of the bright chain link with it **(see illustration). Note:** *Do not, under any circumstances, rotate the camshaft or crankshaft to get the sprocket to fit. Instead, move the sprocket in relation to the chain until the sprocket can be slipped over the camshaft locating dowel and the bolt can be installed.*

38 Install the bolt and locking tab in the end of the camshaft and tighten it to the torque listed in this Chapter's Specifications. Remember, the bolt has left-hand threads so it must be turned counterclockwise to tighten it. Insert a bar through one of the sprocket holes and wedge it against the top of the number one rocker arm shaft support to prevent the camshaft from turning as the bolt is tightened.

39 Bend the tab up against the bolt head to lock it in place.

40 Install the timing chain tensioner, then loosen the tensioner locknut and turn the adjusting screw clockwise until resistance is felt **(see illustration)**. From this point loosen the screw two full turns and tighten the locknut.

41 Adjust the valve clearances (see Chapter 1). After the valves are adjusted, coat the camshaft lobes with camshaft installation grease or engine assembly lube (we recommend using one containing molybdenum disulfide).

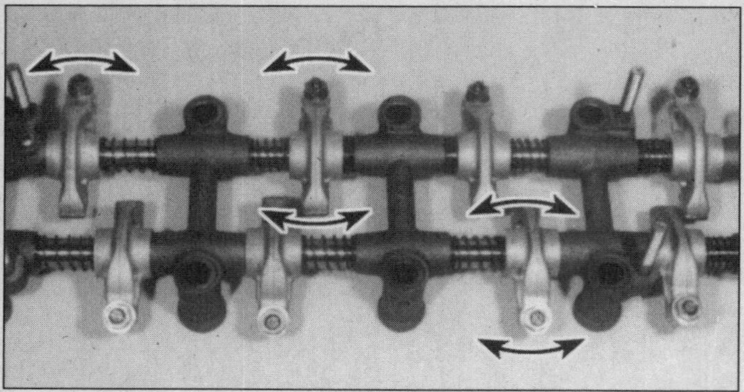

8.3 To check the rocker arm bushings and shafts, move each rocker arm back and forth on its shaft; you should notice very little play - if excessive play is evident, disassemble the rocker arms and shafts for further inspection

42 Position the semi-circular rubber seal in the cutout at the front of the cylinder head, then apply RTV-type gasket sealant to the joints between the seal and the valve cover gasket surface.
43 Install the valve cover and tighten the nuts evenly and securely.
44 The remainder of installation is the reverse of removal.

8 Rocker arm assembly - inspection, disassembly and reassembly

Removal

1 Remove the cylinder head (see Section 7). **Note:** *The rocker arm assembly is held in place by the cylinder head bolts - rocker arm removal is an integral part of cylinder head removal.*
2 Separate the cylinder head bolts from the rocker arm assembly. Keep them in order so they can be returned to their original locations during reassembly.

Inspection and disassembly

Refer to illustrations 8.3 and 8.4

3 Move each rocker arm back and forth on the shaft **(see illustration)**. Very little play should be detected. If excessive play is evident, disassemble the rocker arms and shafts.
4 Remove the spring clips from the rear of the shafts and the bolts from the front shaft support **(see illustration)**. Slide the shaft supports, rocker arms and springs off the shafts, but keep all the parts in order so they can be returned to their original locations during reassembly.
5 Using a 0-to-1 inch micrometer and a small telescoping gauge, measure the diameter of the shafts (where each rocker arm makes contact) and the rocker arm bore diameters. Subtract the shaft diameter from the corresponding rocker arm bore diameter to obtain the rocker arm oil clearance. Repeat the procedure for each rocker arm and compare the results to this Chapter's Specifications.
6 Check the rocker arm faces (that contact the camshaft lobes) and the ends of the adjusting screws (that contact the valve stems) for pitting, excessive wear and roughness. Check the adjusting screw threads for damage. Make sure they can be threaded in and out of the rocker arms.
7 Any damaged or excessively worn parts should be replaced with new ones. It should be noted that the rocker arm bores have bushings in them which can be replaced with new ones (a job which should be done by an automotive machine shop). If the bushings are replaced, make sure the oil holes in the rocker arm and bushing are aligned before assembling the rocker arm components.

Reassembly

Refer to illustration 8.8

8 Lubricate the shafts and rocker arm bores with clean oil or engine assembly lube, then assemble the parts as shown **(see illustration)**. Begin with the front shaft support and make sure that all parts are returned to their original locations. **Note:** *The shaft supports have different configurations and must not be interchanged.*
9 Install the bolts in the front shaft support and the spring clips in the rear of the shafts.

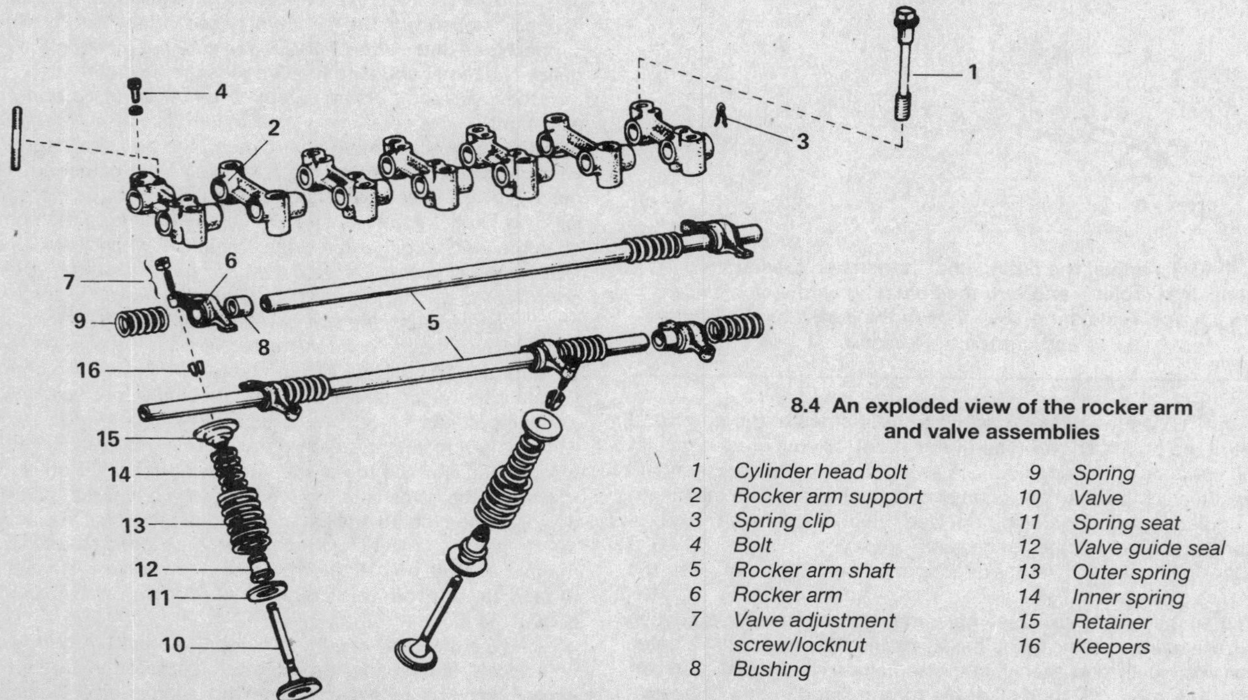

8.4 An exploded view of the rocker arm and valve assemblies

1 *Cylinder head bolt*
2 *Rocker arm support*
3 *Spring clip*
4 *Bolt*
5 *Rocker arm shaft*
6 *Rocker arm*
7 *Valve adjustment screw/locknut*
8 *Bushing*
9 *Spring*
10 *Valve*
11 *Spring seat*
12 *Valve guide seal*
13 *Outer spring*
14 *Inner spring*
15 *Retainer*
16 *Keepers*

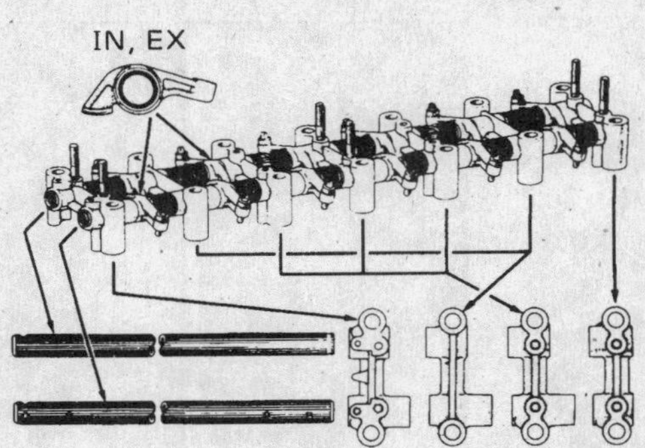

8.8 Make sure the rocker arm supports are positioned as shown during reassembly

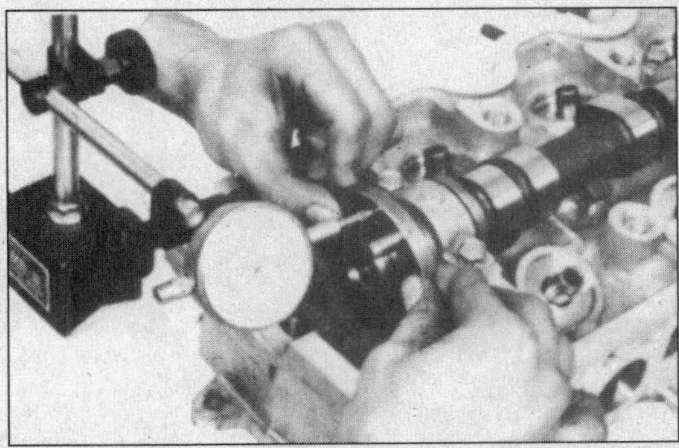
9.2 To check camshaft endplay, mount a dial indicator so that its stem is in-line with the camshaft and just touching the flange at the front

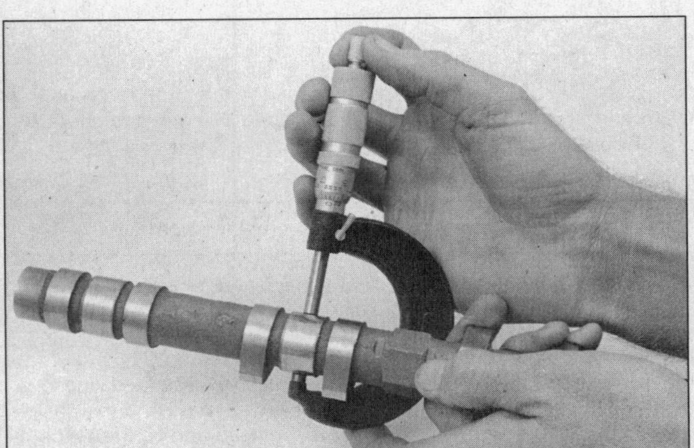
9.7 Measure the camshaft bearing journals with a 2-inch micrometer

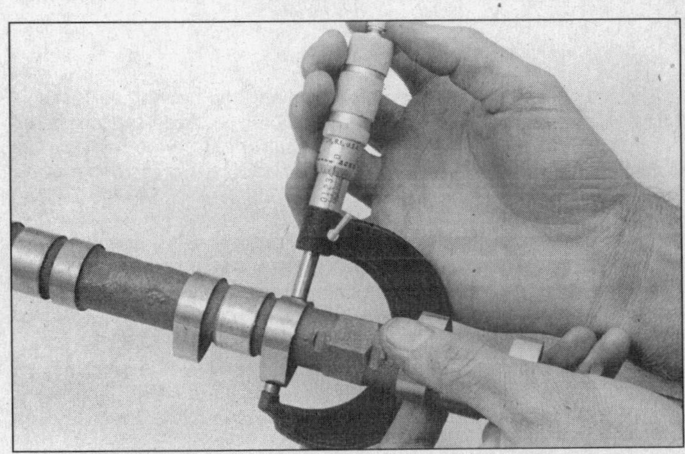
9.9 Measure the height of each camshaft lobe with a 2-inch micrometer

10 Make sure the rocker arms pivot freely on the shafts, then loosen the locknuts and back off the valve adjusting screws as far as possible.

Installation

11 The rocker arm assembly is installed with the cylinder head (see Section 7).

9 Camshaft and bearings - removal, inspection and installation

Removal and inspection

Refer to illustrations 9.2, 9.7, 9.9, 9.16 and 9.18

1 Remove the cylinder head (see Section 7) and set it on a workbench. Support the head on two hardwood blocks to avoid gouging or otherwise damaging the head gasket sealing surface.

2 Before removing the camshaft from the head, check the endplay as follows. Mount a dial indicator so that its stem is in-line with the camshaft and just touching the flange at the front **(see illustration)**.

3 Push the camshaft all the way to the rear and zero the dial indicator. Next, pull the camshaft forward, as far as possible, and check the reading on the indicator. The distance that the camshaft moves is the endplay. Compare your measurement to the endplay listed in this Chapter's Specifications.

4 To remove the camshaft from the head, unbolt the four bearing caps. Loosen the bolts in each cap very gradually (about 1/4-turn at a time), alternating between the two to avoid distortion of the caps.

5 Lift off the caps, then remove the camshaft. The caps should be numbered one through four, front-to-back, but if they're not, keep them in order to avoid problems during installation. They must be installed in their original locations.

6 Inspect the camshaft bearing journals for excessive wear and evidence of seizure. If the journals are damaged, the bearing surfaces in the head and bearing caps are probably damaged as well, Both the camshaft and cylinder head (as well as the bearing caps) will have to be replaced.

7 Using a 2-inch micrometer, measure the diameter of each of the cam bearing journals **(see illustration)**. Take the measurement at two locations on each journal (90-degrees apart). If the journal diameters are less than the service limit, the camshaft must be replaced.

8 The camshaft runout should also be checked to determine if the shaft is bent. This measurement requires a dial indicator and a special jig or V-blocks, so it should be done by an automotive machine shop.

9 Check the cam lobes for pitting, grooves, scoring or flaking. Measure the cam lobe height **(see illustration)** and compare it to the height listed in this Chapter's Specifications. If the lobe height is less than the specified minimum or the lobes are damaged, replace the camshaft.

10 Examine the bearing surfaces in the head and the bearing caps. Look for scoring, galling and burned areas. If damage is evident, the cylinder head, bearing caps and camshaft must be replaced.

11 If the previous inspection steps reveal no excessive wear or damage, the cam bearing oil clearance must be checked before you can decide whether to use the original camshaft. **Note:** *The cylinder head should be thoroughly cleaned before checking the bearing oil clearance (see Chapter 2C).*

12 Clean the camshaft and bearing caps with solvent and dry them thoroughly.

13 The bearing oil clearances is checked with Plastigage, which is available at auto parts stores. Use Type HPG-1 (green) for this procedure.

9.16 Lay a Plastigage strip across the camshaft bearing journal as shown, parallel to the centerline of the cam

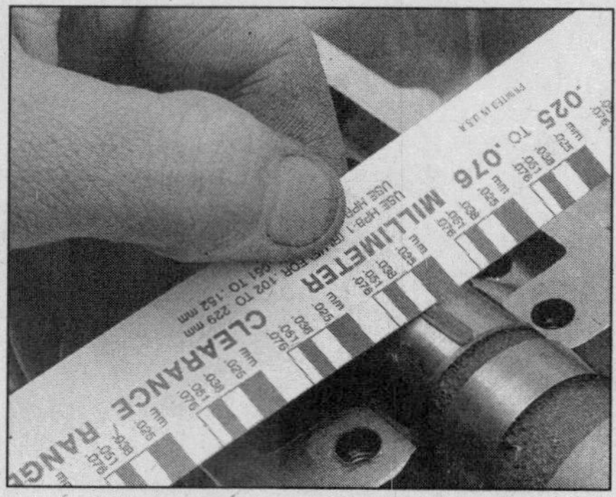

9.18 Measure the width of the crushed Plastigage strip by comparing it with the scale printed on the Plastigage envelope

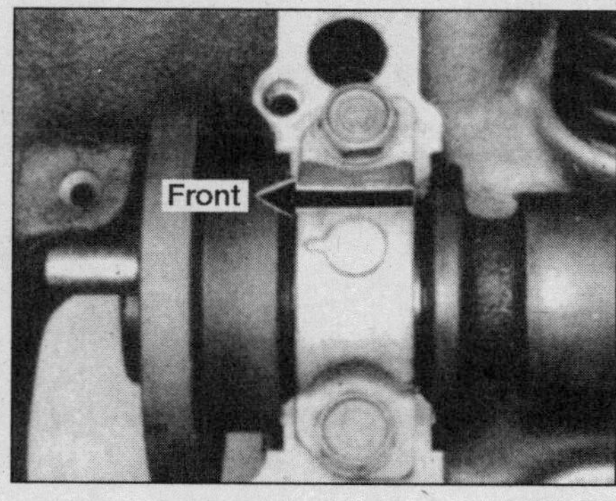

9.23 Make sure the marks on the camshaft bearing caps point toward the front of the engine

14 Make sure the cam bearing journals and the bearing surfaces in the caps and cylinder head are clean and oil-free. If the cylinder head has not been cleaned as described in Chapter 2C, wipe the bearing surfaces with a lint-free rag. **Note:** *Do not apply oil or any other lubricant to the cylinder head, camshaft or bearing caps during this procedure.*

15 Carefully lay the camshaft in position in the cylinder head.

16 Cut four pieces of Plastigage the same length as the bearing journal width. Lay a piece of Plastigage on each bearing journal, parallel to the camshaft centerline **(see illustration)**.

17 Install the bearing caps in their original locations with the marks facing forward. Tighten the bolts in each cap evenly and gradually, a 1/4-turn at a time, until you reach the torque listed in this Chapter's Specifications. **Caution:** *Do not turn the camshaft at any time during this procedure.*

18 Loosen the bolts gradually, to avoid distortion of the caps, remove them and lift off the caps. Compare the widest portion of the crushed Plastigage on each bearing journal to the scale printed on the Plastigage container. Locate the line in the scale that is the same width as the Plastigage, then read the number opposite the line **(see illustration)**. This number, in thousandths of an inch, is the bearing oil clearance.

19 If the oil clearance is greater than the service limit, the bearing surfaces in the head and caps are excessively worn. Since the cylinder head must be replaced restore the oil clearances, check with a dealer service department or an automotive machine shop for advice before proceeding.

20 Once the procedure is complete, remove all traces of the Plastigage material from the cam journals and the bearing caps. Use a soft, blunt instrument such as a piece of hardwood or your fingernail to avoid scratching the bearings. Wipe the journals and the bearing caps with a solvent-soaked cloth to complete the clean-up.

Installation

Refer to illustration 9.23

21 Before installing the camshaft, the cylinder head must be cleaned, all valve service work must be completed and the camshaft and bearings must be inspected and replacement parts obtained. If a new cylinder head, or a new camshaft, is being installed, check the cam bearing oil clearances (see above).

22 Lubricate the bearing surfaces in the cylinder head with clean oil or engine assembly lube (we recommend one containing molybdenum disulfide), then carefully lay the camshaft in position.

23 Make sure the bearing surfaces in the caps are clean, then lubricate them and lay them in position. The caps are numbered one through four, front-to-back, and the marks must face forward **(see illustration)**.

24 Install the cap bolts. Tighten the bolts in each cap evenly and gradually, a 1/4-turn at a time), to the torque listed in this Chapter's Specifications.

25 After the cap bolts have been tightened to the torque listed in this Chapter's Specifications, rotate the camshaft by hand and check for any obvious binding.

10 Valve springs, retainers and seals - replacement

On many engines, broken valve springs and defective valve stem seals can be replaced with the cylinder head still installed. However, on this engine, the cylinder head is already detached from the block by the time you have removed the rocker arm assembly because the rocker arm assembly bolts also retain the cylinder head (and whenever these bolts are loosened the head must be removed and the gasket replaced). So you might as well remove the head and perform a complete top end inspection and overhaul. For a guide to these procedures, refer to Chapter 2, Part C.

11 Oil pan - removal and installation

1 Drain the engine oil (see Chapter 1).

2 Raise the front of the vehicle and place it securely on jackstands.

3 Detach the steering relay rod and both tie-rods from the idler arm, pitman arm and steering knuckles (see Chapter 10).

4 Unbolt and remove both engine stiffener plates.

5 Remove the splash shields from under the engine.

6 Support the front of the engine with a floor jack.

7 Remove the front engine mount bolts.

8 Raise the front of the engine slightly.

9 Remove the bolts securing the oil pan to the engine block and the timing chain cover.

10 Tap on the pan with a soft-faced hammer, to break the gasket seal, and lower the oil pan from the engine.

11 Using a gasket scraper, scrape off all traces of the old gasket from the engine block, the timing chain cover, the rear main oil seal housing and the oil pan. Be especially careful not to nick or gouge the gasket sealing surfaces of the timing chain cover and the oil seal housing (they are made of aluminum and are quite soft).

12 Clean the oil pan with solvent and dry it thoroughly. Check the gasket sealing surfaces for distortion.

13 Before installing the oil pan, apply a thin coat of RTV-type gasket sealant to the engine block gasket sealing surfaces. Lay a new oil pan gasket in place and carefully apply a coat of gasket sealant to the exposed side of the gasket.

14 Gently lay the oil pan in place (do not disturb the gasket) and install the bolts. Start with the bolts closest to the center of the pan and tighten them to the torque listed in this Chapter's Specifications using a criss-cross pattern. Do not overtighten them or leakage may occur.

15 The remainder of installation is the reverse of removal.

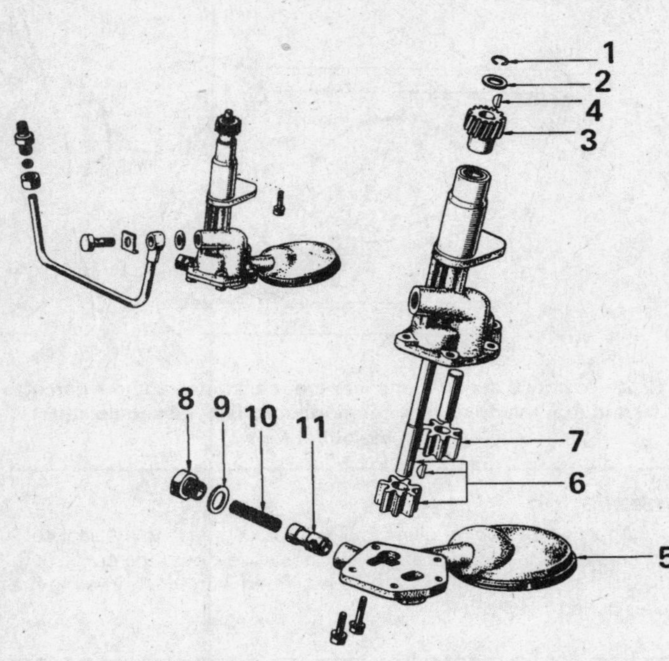

12.4 An exploded view of the oil pump assembly

1 *Snap-ring*
2 *Shim*
3 *Gear*
4 *Woodruff key*
5 *Pump cover*
6 *Shaft/gear*
7 *Driven gear*
8 *Relief valve plug*
9 *Sealing washer*
10 *Spring*
11 *Relief valve*

12 Oil pump - removal, inspection and installation

Removal

1 Remove the oil pan (see Section 11).
2 Remove the oil pump outlet tube. It's attached to the pump by a banjo fitting and hollow bolt, and to the block by a compression fitting. The banjo fitting bolt may have a locking tab which should be bent back before loosening the bolt.
3 Remove the mounting bolts and carefully slide the pump out of the engine block.

Inspection

Refer to illustrations 12.4, 12.10, 12.11 and 12.12

4 Remove the relief valve plug and slide the spring and valve out of the pump cover **(see illustration)**.
5 Remove the pump cover mounting bolts and separate the cover from the pump body. Do not disassemble the gears and shafts. Clean the pump components with solvent and dry them with compressed air.
6 Check the driveshaft gear for excessive wear, cracks, chipped teeth and other damage.
7 Check the pump body and cover for cracks and wear (especially in the gear contact areas).
8 Check the strainer to make sure it is not clogged or damaged.
9 Check the relief valve and bore for wear and damage. The valve should move freely in the bore with very little side play. Check the springs for cracks.
10 Using a straightedge and feeler gauges, measure the side clearance between the gears and the pump cover mounting surface **(see illustration)**. Compare your measurement with the side clearance listed in this Chapter's Specifications.
11 Measure the gear-to-body clearance with a feeler gauge **(see illustration)**. Compare your measurement to the gear-to-body clearance listed in this Chapter's Specifications.

12.10 Measure the oil pump gear side clearance with a straightedge and feeler gauge

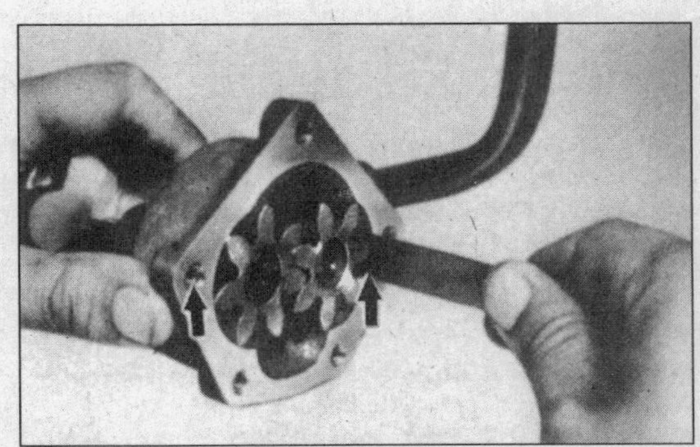

12.11 Measure the oil pump gear-to-body clearance with a feeler gauge

12.12 Measure the oil pump gear backlash with a feeler gauge

12 Measure the gear backlash with a feeler gauge **(see illustration)**. Compare your measurement to the gear backlash listed in this Chapter's Specifications.
13 If the clearances are not as specified, replace the pump with a new or rebuilt unit.
14 Lubricate the gears with clean engine oil, then attach the pump cover to the body and tighten the bolts evenly and securely.
15 Insert the relief valve and spring into the cover bore, then install the plug and washer and tighten the plug securely.

Installation

Refer to illustration 12.17

16 Before installing the pump - new, rebuilt or original - on the engine, check it for proper operation. Fill a clean drain pan to a depth of one inch with new, clean engine oil of the recommended viscosity.

17 Immerse the oil pump inlet in the oil and turn the driveshaft counterclockwise by hand. As the shaft is turned, oil should be discharged from the pump outlet **(see illustration)**.

18 Make sure the mounting surfaces are clean, then insert the pump into the engine block recess. Install the bolts and tighten them securely.

19 Install the oil line and tighten the fitting securely. Bend the locking tab on the banjo fitting bolt back into position.

20 Install the oil pan (see Section 11).

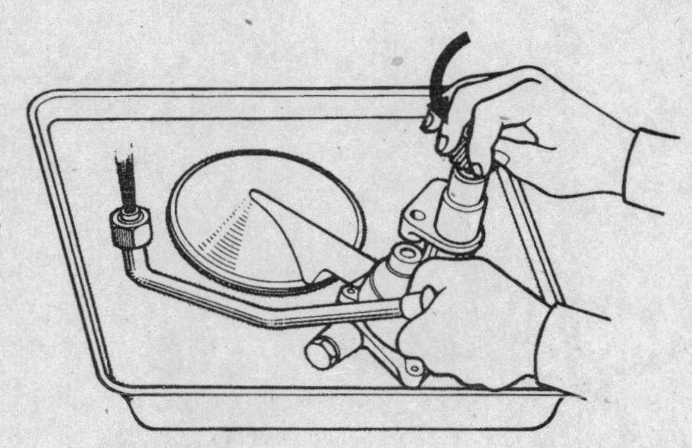

12.17 To check the oil pump's operation, immerse it in a pan of oil and turn the driveshaft counterclockwise - oil should squirt from the outlet tube

13 Crankshaft pulley - removal and installation

Removal

Refer to illustration 13.4

1 Remove the accessory drivebelts (see Chapter 1).

2 Raise the front of the vehicle and place it securely on jackstands.

3 Remove the radiator (see Chapter 3).

4 Remove the flywheel/driveplate access cover (see Chapter 7A or Chapter 7B). Immobilize the crankshaft by jamming a large screwdriver between the ring gear teeth, then remove the large bolt from the center of the pulley **(see illustration)**.

5 Use a puller to extract the pulley from the nose of the crankshaft. Do not use a puller with jaws that must grip the outside of the pulley, or you'll damage the pulley. Use a bolt-type puller.

Installation

6 Apply a thin layer of clean, multi-purpose grease to the seal contact surface of the crankshaft pulley, then slide it onto the crankshaft. Note that the Woodruff key must be aligned with the keyway in the pulley during installation.

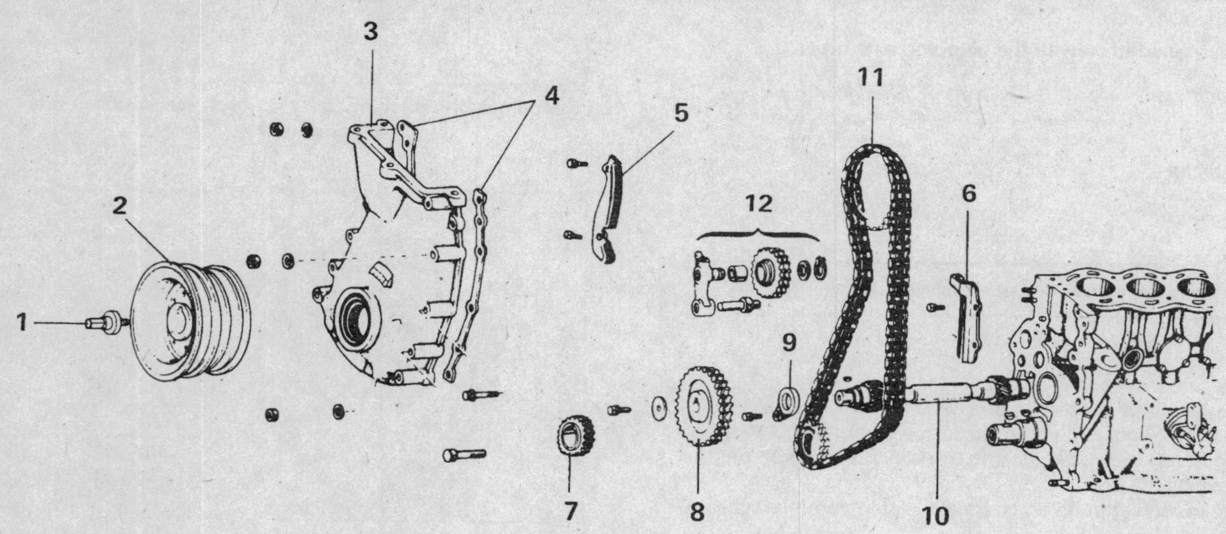

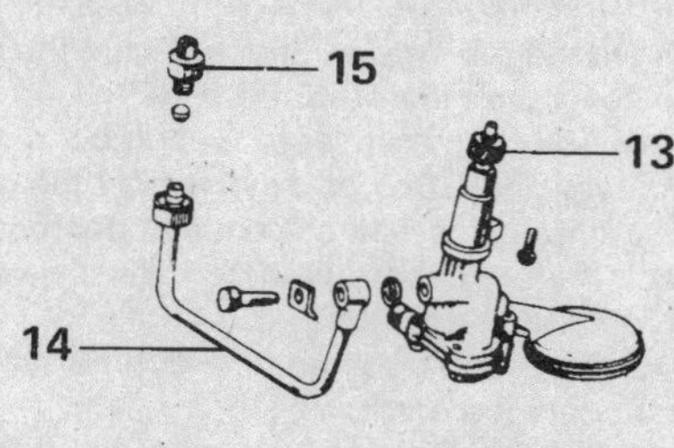

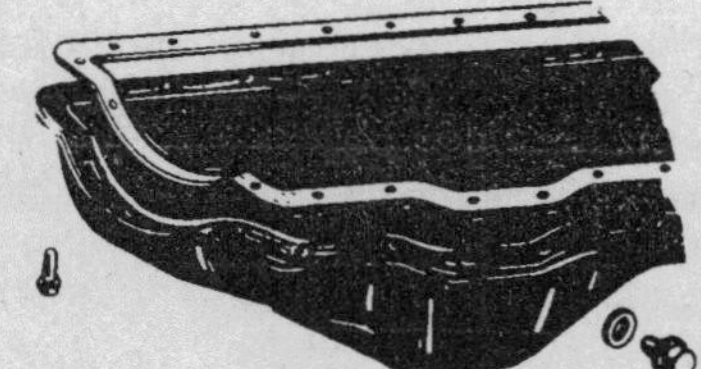

13.4 An exploded view of the crankshaft pulley, timing chain cover and timing chain assembly

1 *Bolt*
2 *Pulley*
3 *Timing chain cover*
4 *Gaskets*
5 *No. 2 chain vibration damper*
6 *No. 1 chain vibration damper*
7 *Crankshaft sprocket*
8 *Oil pump driveshaft sprocket*
9 *Retainer*
10 *Oil pump driveshaft*
11 *Timing chain*
12 *Tensioner sprocket assembly*
13 *Oil pump*
14 *Oil line*
15 *Fitting*

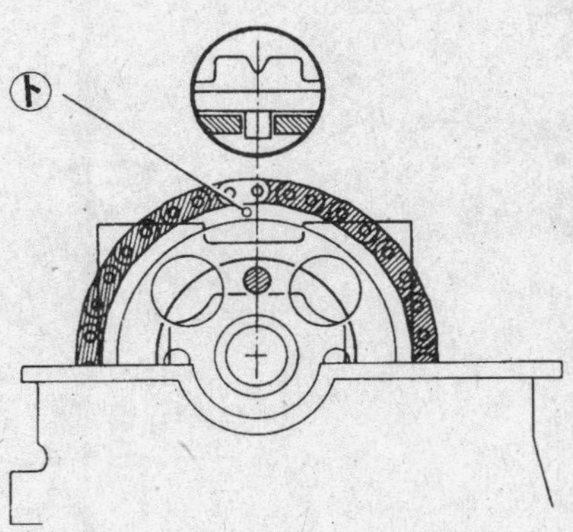

16.3a Turn the crankshaft until the dowel pin in the camshaft sprocket is aligned with the mark on the front rocker arm shaft support . . .

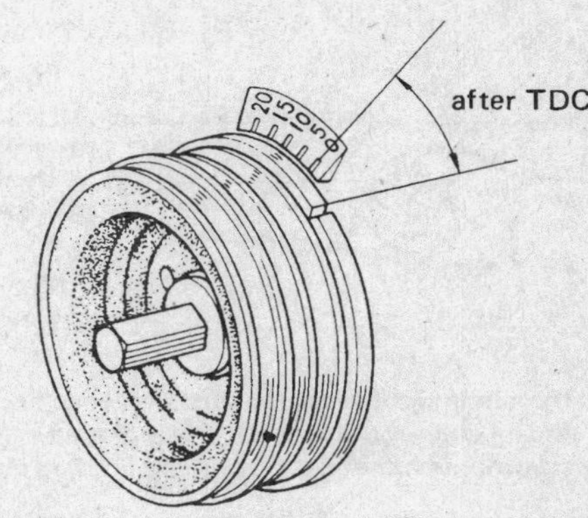

16.3b . . . then check the position of the timing mark on the crankshaft pulley - if the pulley mark is more than four degrees beyond Top Dead Center, the timing chain is stretched

7 Use a large socket or a section of pipe and a hammer to tap the pulley onto the crankshaft until it is seated properly.
8 Tighten the pulley bolt to the torque listed in this Chapter's Specifications. Use the method described in Step 4 to prevent the crankshaft from rotating.
9 The remainder of installation is otherwise the reverse of removal.

14 Timing chain cover - removal and installation

Removal

1 Drain the engine oil (see Chapter 1).
2 Remove the cylinder head (see Section 7).
3 Remove the radiator (see Chapter 3).
4 Remove the alternator (see Chapter 5).
5 Remove the fan/clutch and the water pump assemblies (see Chapter 3).
6 Remove the crankshaft pulley (see Section 13).
7 Remove the bolts which attach the front of the oil pan to the timing chain cover and separate the front of the oil pan from the cover.
8 Remove the bolts and nuts attaching the timing chain cover to the engine block **(see illustration 13.4)**. Draw a simple diagram showing the location of the bolts so they can be returned to the same holes from which they're removed.
9 Break the gasket seal by tapping the cover with a soft-faced hammer and remove it from the engine block. Do not pry between the cover and the engine block, as damage to the gasket sealing surfaces will result.
10 Remove all traces of old gasket material from the timing chain cover and the engine block. Be very careful not to damage the gasket sealing surfaces of the cover.

Installation

11 Using new gaskets and RTV-type gasket sealant, attach the timing chain cover to the front of the engine.
12 Install the bolts and tighten them evenly and securely following a criss-cross pattern. If the gaskets protrude beyond the top or bottom of the cover and the engine block, trim off the excess with a razor blade.
13 Installation is otherwise the reverse of removal.

15 Crankshaft front oil seal - replacement

1 Remove the crankshaft pulley (see Section 13).
2 Carefully pry the old seal out of the cover with a large screwdriver. Be very careful not to damage the seal bore or the crankshaft with the tool.
3 Clean the bore in the cover and coat the outer edge of the new seal with engine oil or multi-purpose grease. Also lubricate the lips of the seal with multi-purpose grease. Using a socket with an outside diameter slightly smaller than the outside diameter of the seal, carefully drive the new seal into place with a hammer. If a socket isn't available, a short section of large diameter pipe will work. Check the seal after installation to be sure the spring around the inside of the seal lip didn't pop out of place.
4 Reinstall the crankshaft pulley (see Section 13).

16 Timing chain and sprockets - inspection, removal and installation

Checking timing chain slack

Refer to illustrations 16.3a and 16.3b

1 Rotate the crankshaft until the piston is at Top Dead Center on the compression stroke (see Section 3).
2 Remove the valve cover (see Section 4).
3 Check the position of the locating dowel **(see illustration)** in the camshaft flange. It should be exactly in-line with the mark embossed in the front rocker arm shaft support. If the marks are not aligned, turn the crankshaft very slowly in a clockwise direction until they are. Next, look very closely at the timing marks on the crankshaft pulley and timing chain cover. If the pulley mark is 0 to 4-degrees after Top Dead Center **(see illustration)**, the timing chain is not stretched excessively (each line on the timing scale equals 5 degrees; O is Top Dead Center). If the pulley mark is more than 4 degrees after Top Dead Center, the timing chain has stretched excessively and must be replaced.

Removal

4 Remove the crankshaft pulley (see Section 13).
5 Remove the timing chain cover (see Section 14).
6 Remove the chain vibration dampers from the block.
7 Slide the tensioner sprocket and arm off of the engine block stud, then separate the timing chain from the sprockets.
8 Using a two or three-jaw puller, pull the crankshaft sprocket off the shaft. Remove the Woodruff keys from the shaft so they do not get lost.
9 If you want to remove the oil pump driveshaft for inspection, refer to Chapter 2C.
10 Clean all of the parts with solvent and dry them with compressed air.
11 Remove all traces of old gasket material from the timing chain cover and the engine block. Be very careful not to damage the gasket sealing surfaces of the cover.

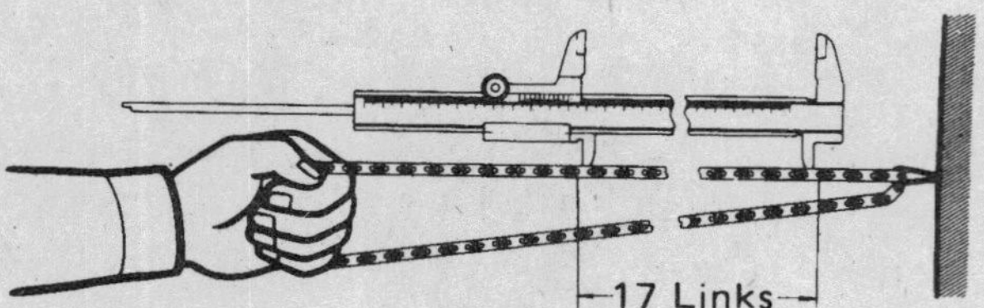

16.12 Pull the chain tight and measure the length of 17 links with a vernier or dial caliper at three different places - if even one of these measurements exceeds the service limit, replace the chain

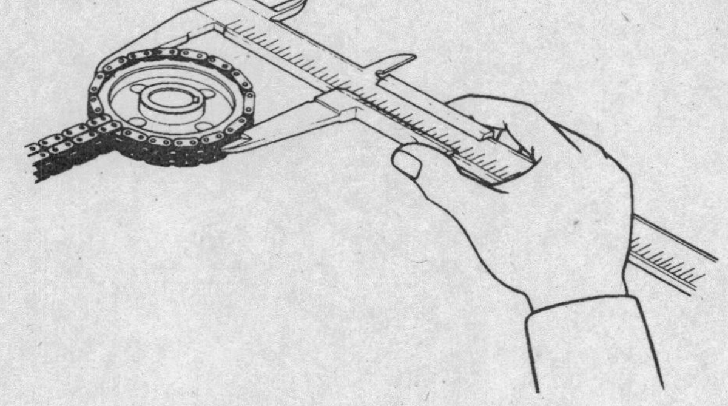

16.13 To check a sprocket for wear, measure its outside diameter with the chain wrapped around it (measure to the outside of the rollers)

Inspection

Timing chain and sprockets

Refer to illustrations 16.12 and 16.13

12 Check the chain for cracked plates and pitted or worn rollers. Stretch the chain tight by hand and measure the length of 17 links with a vernier or dial caliper **(see illustration)**. Repeat the measurement at two additional places, then compare your measurements with the acceptable length listed in this Chapter's Specifications. If the measurement exceeds the service limit at any one place, replace the chain.

13 Inspect the sprocket teeth for wear (they'll have a "hooked" appearance), cracks and other damage. Wrap the chain around the camshaft sprocket and measure the outside diameter **(see illustration)**. Repeat the procedure for the crankshaft sprocket and the oil pump driveshaft sprocket. If the measurements are less than the limits listed in this Chapter's Specifications, replace the sprockets.

Tensioner sprocket and arm

14 Separate the sprocket from the tensioner arm by removing the snap-ring from the shaft. Check the tensioner arm and sprocket for cracks and other damage. Inspect the sprocket bushing and shaft. Look for evidence of overheating and seizure.

15 Using a 1-inch micrometer and a small telescoping gauge, measure the outside diameter of the shaft and the inside diameter of the sprocket bushing. Subtract the shaft diameter from the bushing diameter to obtain the oil clearance. Compare your measurement to the clearance listed in this Chapter's Specifications. If it's excessive, remove the bushing from the sprocket and install a new one.

Chain tensioner

16 Check the movement of the chain tensioner plunger. It should slide smoothly into the tensioner body and return smoothly under spring pressure. If it doesn't, replace the tensioner. Don't try to disassemble and repair the tensioner.

Chain vibration dampers

Refer to illustration 16.18

17 Check the dampers for deterioration and flaking of the surfaces that contact the chain.

18 Measure the wall thickness of each damper **(see illustration)** and compare your measurements to the thickness listed in this Chapter's Specifications. If they're less than specified, replace the dampers.

Oil pump driveshaft and bearings

19 If you wish to inspect the oil pump driveshaft and bearings, refer to Chapter 2, Part C.

Installation

Refer to illustrations 16.20, 16.22 and 16.25

20 Place the Woodruff keys in position, then install the crankshaft sprocket. Make sure the timing mark on the sprocket faces out **(see illustration)**. Note that the Woodruff key must be aligned with the key-

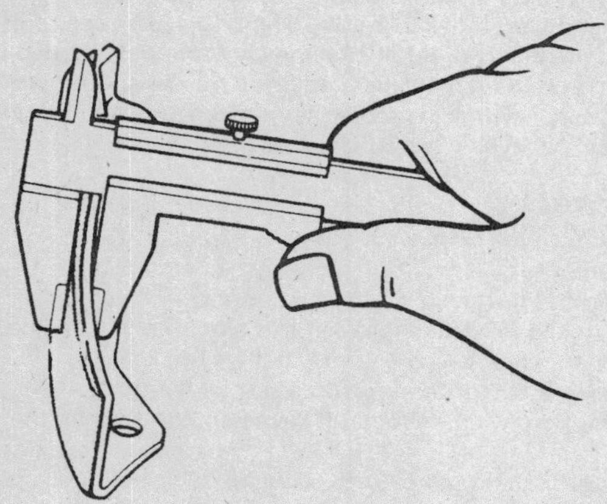

16.18 Measure the thickness of the wall of the chain vibration damper - if it's less than the specified thickness, replace the damper

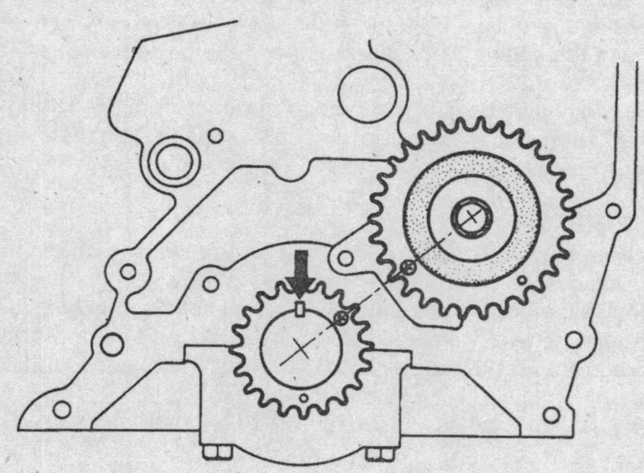

16.20 Before you install the timing chain, position the sprockets on the crankshaft and oil pump driveshaft so that the marks are aligned - note that the Woodruff key (arrow) points straight up

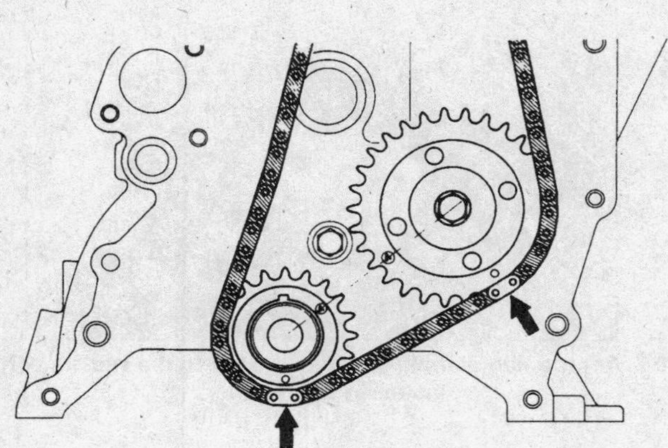

16.22 The bright links (arrows) on the chain must line up with the marks on the sprockets

way in the sprocket during installation. Use a large socket or section of pipe and a hammer to tap the sprocket onto the crankshaft until it is properly seated.
21 If you removed the oil pump driveshaft, install it (see Chapter 2C).
22 Align the timing marks on the oil pump driveshaft and crankshaft sprockets **(see illustration)**, then drape the timing chain over the sprockets with the bright links next to the punch marks on the sprockets. **Caution:** *If the chain is not installed exactly as described, serious engine damage could result when it is run.*
23 If it has not already been done, lubricate the bushing and slip the tensioner sprocket onto the tensioner arm shaft. Install the washer and snap-ring, then lubricate the pivot and attach the tensioner to the engine block. Engage the tensioner sprocket teeth with the timing chain.
24 Lubricate the chain contact surface of the No. 1 vibration damper with multi-purpose grease, then attach it to the engine block and tighten the bolts. Repeat the procedure for the No. 2 vibration damper. **Note:** *On some 4M-E models a collar is installed on the No. 2 vibration damper bolt that is nearest the crankshaft; make sure the collar is in place before proceeding.*
25 On 4-ME models only, apply RTV sealant to the areas shown **(see illustration)**.
26 Install the timing chain cover (see Section 14).
27 Install the crankshaft pulley (see Section 13).

17 Oil pump driveshaft - removal, inspection and installation

1 Remove the crankshaft pulley (see Section 13).
2 Remove the timing chain cover (see Section 14).
3 Remove the timing chain (see Section 16).
4 Remove the distributor (see Chapter 5).
5 Remove the oil pan (see Section 11).
6 Remove the oil pump (see Section 12).
7 Remove and inspect the oil pump driveshaft (see Chapter 2C).
8 Installation is the reverse of removal.

18 Flywheel/driveplate - removal and installation

1 Remove the transmission (on vehicles with a manual transmission, see Chapter 7A; on vehicles with an automatic transmission, see Chapter 7B).
2 On vehicles with a manual transmission, remove the clutch (see Chapter 8).
3 The flywheel/driveplate is attached to the rear of the crankshaft with six bolts. Loosen and remove the bolts, then separate it from the crankshaft flange. Be careful - the flywheel is heavy.

16.25 On 4M-E engines only, apply RTV sealant to the areas indicated by arrows

4 To install the flywheel/driveplate on the crankshaft, use a liquid thread locking compound on the bolts and tighten them gradually, using a criss-cross pattern, to the torque listed in this Chapter's Specifications.
5 The remainder of installation is the reverse of removal.

2A

19 Rear main oil seal - replacement

Refer to illustrations 19.7 and 19.9

1 Remove the transmission (on vehicles with a manual transmission, see Chapter 7A; on vehicles with an automatic transmission, see Chapter 7B).
2 On vehicles with a manual transmission, remove the clutch (see Chapter 8).
3 Remove the flywheel/driveplate (see Section 18).
4 Remove the bolts from the oil seal retainer and detach the retainer from the engine block.
5 If the retainer is difficult to remove, tap it with a soft-faced hammer to break the gasket seal. Don't pry between the block and the retainer - you'll damage the gasket sealing surface.
6 Using a gasket scraper, remove all traces of the old gasket from the retainer and the engine block. Be very careful not to nick or gouge the sealing surfaces of the aluminum retainer.
7 Note how the seal is installed, then drive it out from the backside of the retainer by positioning a punch or screwdriver in the slot provided **(see illustration)**.
8 Clean the bore in the retainer and the outer edge of the new seal, then lay the seal in place on the retainer. Make sure the correct side is facing out. Using a hammer and block of wood, tap the seal around its entire circumference until it is seated in the retainer. The seal must be square with the bore.

19.7 To remove the rear main oil seal, place the retainer on a clean workbench and prop it up with a block of wood, then place a screwdriver or punch in the slot provided and carefully tap out the old seal - make sure you don't gouge or nick the bore of the retainer

9 Lubricate the seal lip with multi-purpose grease **(see illustration)**, then attach the retainer to the engine block. Use a new gasket and RTV sealant. Install the bolts and tighten them evenly and securely.
10 Install the flywheel/driveplate (see Section 18).
11 Install the transmission (on vehicles with a manual transmission, see Chapter 7A; on vehicles with an automatic transmission, see Chapter 7B).

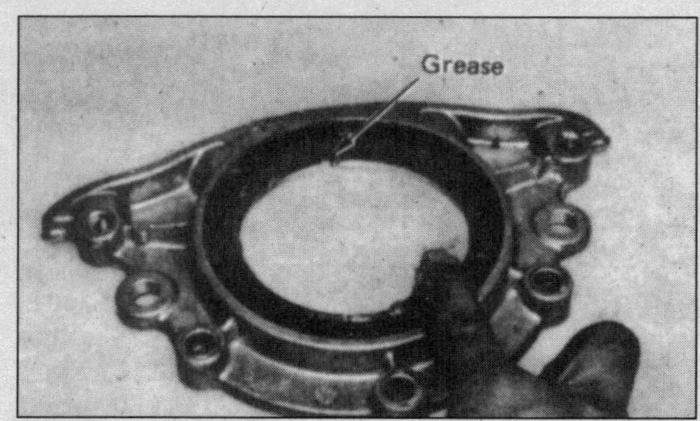

19.9 Apply a film of multi-purpose grease to the seal lip before installing the retainer

20 Engine mounts - check and replacement

Note: *See Chapter 7A or 7B for transaxle mount replacement.*
1 Engine mounts seldom require attention, but broken or deteriorated mounts should be replaced immediately or the added strain placed on the driveline components may cause damage or wear.

Check

2 During the check, the engine must be raised slightly to remove the weight from the mounts.
3 Raise the vehicle and support it securely on jackstands, then position a jack under the engine oil pan. Place a large block of wood between the jack head and the oil pan, then carefully raise the engine just enough to take the weight off the mounts. **Warning:** *DO NOT place any part of your body under the engine when it's supported only by a jack!*
4 Check the mounts to see if the rubber is cracked, hardened or separated from the metal plates. Sometimes the rubber will split right down the center.
5 Check for relative movement between the mount plates and the engine or frame (use a large screwdriver or pry bar to attempt to move the mounts). If movement is noted, lower the engine and tighten the mount fasteners.
6 Rubber preservative should be applied to the mounts to slow deterioration.

Replacement

7 Disconnect the negative battery cable from the battery, then raise the vehicle and support it securely on jackstands if you haven't already done so. Support the engine as described in Step 3. **Caution:** *If the stereo in your vehicle is equipped with an anti-theft system, refer to the information on page 0-15 at the front of this manual before detaching the cable.*
8 Remove the large bracket-to-mount nut. Raise the engine slightly, then remove the two mount-to-frame bolts and nuts from either side of the mount and detach the mount.
9 Installation is the reverse of removal. Use thread locking compound on the mount bolts/nuts and be sure to tighten them securely.

Chapter 2 Part B
DOHC engines (1982 and later models)

Contents

Specifications

General

Cylinder numbers (front-to-rear)	1-2-3-4-5-6
Firing order	1-5-3-6-2-4

FRONT

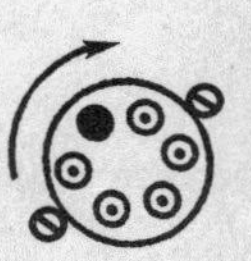

FRONT

The blackened terminal shown on the distributor cap indicates the Number One spark plug wire position

Cylinder location and distributor rotation

1982 through 1985

1986 and later

Camshaft

Bearing journal diameter (standard)	
1982 through 1986	
No. 1	1.4944 to 1.4951 inches
No. 2	1.6913 to 1.6919 inches
No. 3	1.7110 to 1.7116 inches
No. 4	1.7303 to 1.7313 inches
No. 5	1.7504 to 1.7510 inches
No. 6	1.7700 to 1.7707 inches
No. 7	1.7897 to 1.7904 inches
1987 on	
No. 1	1.0610 to 1.0616 inches
No. 2 through No. 7	1.0586 to 1.0620 inches
Minimum lobe height	
1982 through 1986	
Intake	1.3963 inches
Exhaust	1.3963 inches
1987 on	1.4961 inches
Endplay	
1982 through 1986	
Standard	0.002 to 0.0098 inch
Maximum	0.012 inch
1987 on	
Standard	0.0031 to 0.0075 inch
Maximum	0.0118 inch
Bearing oil clearance	
1982 through 1986	
Standard	0.001 to 0.0026 inch
Maximum	0.004 inch
1987 on	
Standard	
No. 1	0.0014 to 0.0028 inch
No. 2 through No. 7	0.0010 to 0.0037 inch
Maximum	0.0051 inch

Warpage limits

Camshaft housing (1982 through 1986)	0.0039 inch
Intake manifold	0.0039 inch
Exhaust manifold	
1982 through 1986	0.0039 inch
1987 on	
Non-turbo models	0.0295 inch
Turbo models	0.0197 inch

Valve lifters (1987 on)

Lifter diameter	1.1014 to 1.1018 in
Lifter bore oil clearance	
Standard	0.0006 to 0.0018 inch
Maximum	0.0039 inch

Timing belt

Idler pulley tension spring free length	
1982	2.776 inches
1983	2.669 inches
1984 on	2.720 inches

Torque specifications

	Ft-lbs (unless otherwise indicated)
Camshaft bearing cap bolts (1987 on)	14
Camshaft housing bolts (1982 through 1986)	16
Camshaft sprocket bolts	
1982 through 1986	51
1987 on	36
Crankshaft pulley bolt	
1982 and 1983	97 to 111
1984 and 1985	145 to 173
1986	159
1987 on	195
Cylinder head bolts	58

Torque specifications (continued)

	Ft-lbs (unless otherwise indicated)
Exhaust manifold bolts	
1982 through 1986	25 to 32
1987 on	29
Flywheel/driveplate bolts	54
Intake manifold bolts/nuts	
1982 through 1985	15 to 17
1986 on	13
Oil pan bolts	
1982 through 1984	55 to 81 in-lbs
1985	84 to 132 in-lbs
1986	68 in-lbs
1987 on	108 in-lbs
Oil pump drive sprocket bolt	
1982 through 1986	14 to 18
1987 on	16
Oil pump	
Mounting bolts	16
Nut	25
Rear main oil seal retainer bolts	108 in-lbs
Timing belt idler pulley bolt	
1982 through 1986	32 to 39
1987 on	36

1 General information

This Part of Chapter 2 is devoted to in-vehicle repair procedures for the engine. All information concerning engine removal and installation and engine block and cylinder head overhaul can be found in Part C of this Chapter.

Since the repair procedures included in this Part are based on the assumption that the engine is still installed in the vehicle, if they are being used during a complete engine overhaul (with the engine already out of the vehicle and on a stand) many of the steps included here will not apply.

The Specifications included in this Part of Chapter 2 apply only to the procedures found here. The Specifications necessary for rebuilding the block and cylinder head are included in Part C.

2 Repair operations possible with the engine in the vehicle

Many major repair operations can be accomplished without removing the engine from the vehicle.

Clean the engine compartment and the exterior of the engine with some type of pressure washer before any work is done. A clean engine will make the job easier and will help keep dirt out of the internal areas of the engine.

Depending on the components involved, it may be a good idea to remove the hood to improve access to the engine as repairs are performed (see Chapter 11).

If oil or coolant leaks develop, indicating a need for gasket or seal replacement, the repairs can generally be made with the engine in the vehicle. The oil pan gasket, the cylinder head gasket, intake and exhaust manifold gaskets, camshaft housing gaskets and oil seals and the crankshaft oil seals are accessible with the engine in place.

Exterior engine components, such as the water pump, the starter motor, the alternator, the distributor and the EFI components, as well as the intake and exhaust manifolds, can be removed for repair with the engine in place.

Since the cylinder head can be removed without removing the engine, valve component servicing can also be accomplished with the engine in the vehicle.

Replacement of, repairs to or inspection of the timing belt and sprockets and the oil pump are all possible with the engine in place.

In extreme cases caused by a lack of necessary equipment, repair or replacement of piston rings, pistons, connecting rods and rod bearings is possible with the engine in the vehicle. However, this practice is not recommended because of the cleaning and preparation work that must be done to the components involved.

3 Top Dead Center (TDC) for number 1 piston - locating

Refer to illustrations 3.3, 3.4 and 3.6

1 Top Dead Center (TDC) is the highest point in the cylinder that each piston reaches as it travels up and down when the crankshaft turns. Each piston reaches TDC on the compression stroke and again on the exhaust stroke, but TDC generally refers to piston position on the compression stroke.

2 Positioning the piston at TDC is an essential part of many procedures such as camshaft removal, timing belt and sprocket replacement and distributor removal.

3 In order to bring any piston to TDC, the crankshaft must be turned using one of the methods outlined below. When looking at the front of the engine, normal crankshaft rotation is clockwise. **Warning:** *Before beginning this procedure, be sure to place the transmission in Neutral and disconnect the electrical connector at the coil pack - see Chapter 5 - (1987 and later Turbos) or the coil wire at the distributor cap (all other models) to disable the ignition system.*

a) The preferred method is to turn the crankshaft with a large socket and breaker bar attached to the vibration damper bolt that is threaded into the front of the crankshaft **(see illustration)**.

3.3 Use a large socket and breaker bar to turn the crankshaft

3.4 Place a mark on the distributor housing directly in line with the number one spark plug wire terminal on the distributor

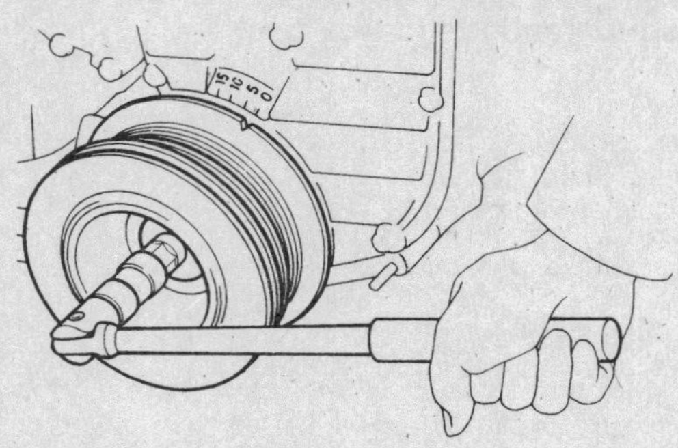

3.6 Turn the crankshaft and align the notch with the zero timing mark on the timing belt cover

b) A remote starter switch, which may save some time, can also be used. Attach the switch leads to the S (switch) and B (battery) terminals on the starter motor. Once the piston is close to TDC, use a socket and breaker bar as described in the previous paragraph.
c) If an assistant is available to turn the ignition switch to the Start position in short bursts, you can get the piston close to TDC without a remote starter switch. Use a socket and breaker bar as described in Paragraph a) to complete the procedure.

4 On all except 1987 and later Turbos, make a mark on the distributor housing directly below the number one spark plug wire terminal on the distributor **(see illustration)**. On 1987 and later Turbos, remove the number one cylinder spark plug, place your thumb over the spark plug hole and have an assistant turn the crankshaft until you begin to feel compression pressure at the hole.

5 On all except 1987 and later Turbos, remove the distributor cap as described in Chapter 1.

6 On all models, turn the crankshaft until the notch on the vibration damper is aligned with the zero mark on the timing plate **(see illustration)**.

7 On 1987 and later Turbos, the piston should now be at TDC. On all other models, the rotor should now be pointing directly at the mark on the distributor housing. If it isn't, the piston is at TDC on the exhaust stroke.

8 To get the piston to TDC on the compression stroke, turn the crankshaft one complete turn (360-degrees) clockwise. The rotor should now be pointing at the mark. When the rotor is pointing at the number one spark plug wire terminal in the distributor cap (which is indicated by the mark on the housing) and the timing marks are aligned, the number one piston is at TDC on the compression stroke.

9 After the number one piston has been positioned at TDC on the compression stroke, TDC for any of the remaining cylinders can be located by turning the crankshaft 120-degrees at a time and following the firing order (refer to the Specifications).

4 Valve covers - removal and installation

Refer to illustration 4.6

Note: *There are two valve covers - one for the intake camshaft housing*

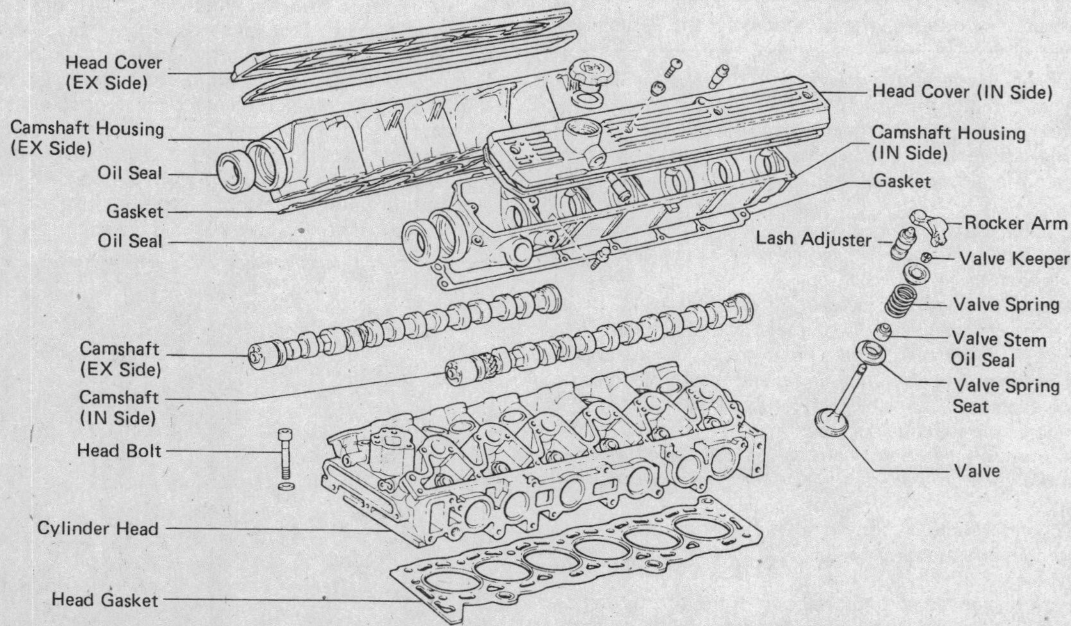

4.6 Cylinder head and related components - exploded view (1982 through 1986 model shown, later models similar except for rocker arms)

and one for the exhaust cam housing. The following procedure applies to either cover.

1 Disconnect the cable from the negative battery terminal. **Caution:** *If the stereo in your vehicle is equipped with an anti-theft system, refer to the information on page 0-15 at the front of this manual before detaching the cable.*

2 Disconnect the hose from the air intake duct (the large plastic tube between the air cleaner housing and the throttle body) and remove the duct.

3 If you're removing the intake cover, disconnect the spark plug wires from the spark plugs and set them aside (see Chapter 1).

4 If you're removing the intake cover, disconnect the PCV hose from the pipe at the oil filler neck.

5 If you're removing the intake cover, detach the throttle cable bracket.

6 Remove the valve cover screws and washers and remove the valve cover **(see illustration)**.l

7 Inspect the rubber O-ring type valve cover gasket. If it's broken, cracked, distorted, pinched or ragged, replace it.

8 Installation is the reverse of removal. Use new sealing washers on the screws if necessary, and be sure to tighten the screws securely.

5 Intake manifold - removal and installation

Removal

Refer to illustrations 5.8a and 5.8b

1 Disconnect the negative cable from the battery. **Caution:** *If the stereo in your vehicle is equipped with an anti-theft system, refer to the information on page 0-15 at the front of this manual before detaching the cable.*

2 Remove the air intake chamber from the engine (see Chapter 4).

3 Remove the distributor (see Chapter 5).

4 Remove the EGR cooler (see Chapter 6).

5 Label and disconnect all electrical connectors in the way and set the harnesses aside.

6 Detach the pulsation damper and the No. 1 fuel line (see Chapter 4).

7 Loosen the clamp and disconnect the radiator hose, then remove the bolts and detach the thermostat housing (see Chapter 3).

8 Remove the eight bolts and two nuts, then detach the intake manifold from the head **(see illustrations)**. The manifold will probably

2B

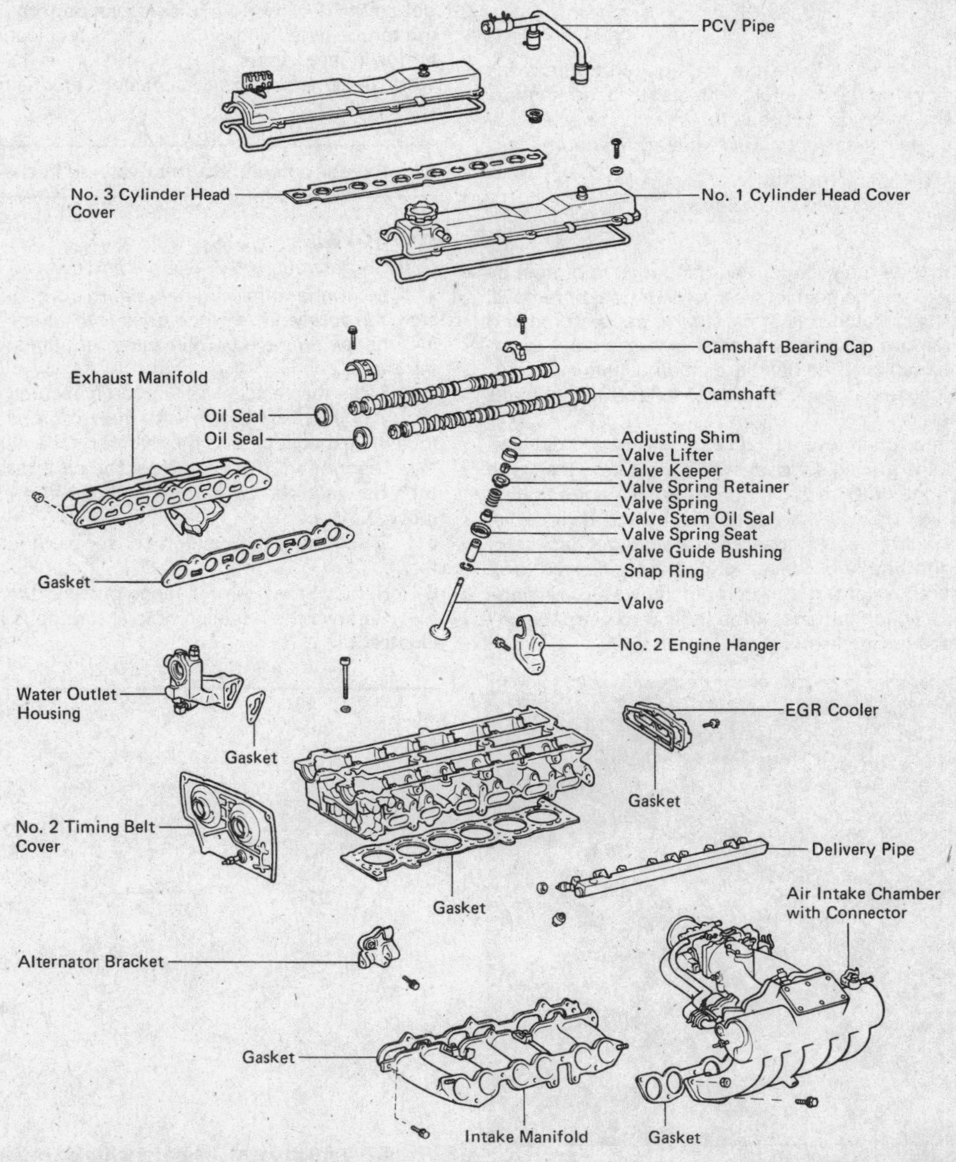

5.8a Exploded view of the cylinder head assembly on 1987 through 1992 non-turbo models (turbo models similar)

5.8b Remove the eight bolts and two nuts to separate the intake manifold from the head - visible here are six of the eight fasteners (arrows) (1982 through 1986 model shown)

be stuck to the cylinder head and force may be required to break the gasket seal. If necessary, tap the manifold with a soft-faced hammer to jar it loose. **Caution:** *Do not pry between the head and manifold or damage to the gasket sealing surfaces will result and vacuum leaks could develop.*

Installation

Refer to illustration 5.11

9 The mating surfaces of the cylinder head and manifold must be perfectly clean and flat when the manifold is installed. Gasket removal solvents in aerosol cans are available at most auto parts stores and may be helpful when removing old gasket material that is stuck to the components (since the manifold and head are made of aluminum, aggressive scraping can cause damage). Be sure to follow the directions printed on the container.

10 Use a gasket scraper to remove all traces of sealant and old gasket material, then wipe the mating surfaces with a cloth saturated with lacquer thinner or acetone. If there is old sealant or oil on the mating surfaces when the manifold is installed, vacuum leaks may develop.

11 After you've thoroughly cleaned the intake manifold, check it for warpage with a straightedge and a feeler gauge **(see illustration)**. Compare your measurements to the maximum allowable warpage listed in this Chapter's Specifications. If the indicated warpage exceeds this figure, replace the intake manifold.

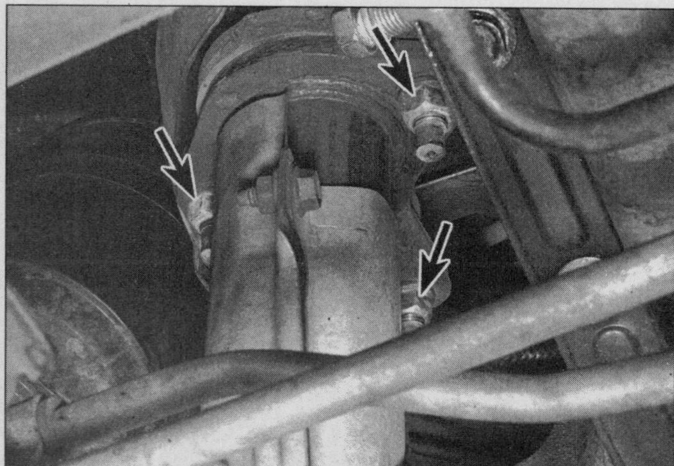

6.3 Remove the nuts (arrows) which connect the exhaust pipe to the manifold

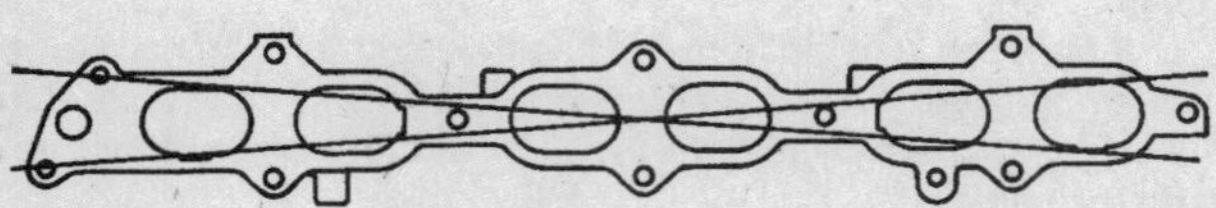

5.11 Using a straightedge and a feeler gauge, measure the warpage of the manifold - make your measurements lengthwise and diagonally

12 Use a tap of the correct size to chase the threads in the bolt holes, then use compressed air (if available) to remove the debris from the holes. **Warning:** *Wear safety glasses or a face shield to protect your eyes when using compressed air.*

13 Position the intake manifold gasket on the cylinder head. Make sure all intake port openings, coolant passage holes and bolt holes are aligned correctly.

14 Carefully place the manifold over the gasket, then install the bolts/nuts. Following a criss-cross pattern, tighten the bolts/nuts to the torque listed in this Chapter's Specifications. Work up to the final torque in three steps.

15 The remaining installation steps are the reverse of removal.

6 Exhaust manifold - removal and installation

Removal

Refer to illustrations 6.3, 6.7, 6.8 and 6.9

1 Disconnect the negative cable from the battery. **Caution:** *If the stereo in your vehicle is equipped with an anti-theft system, refer to the information on page 0-15 at the front of this manual before detaching the cable.*

2 Raise the vehicle and support it securely on jackstands.

3 Working from underneath the vehicle, remove the nuts which attach the exhaust pipe to the manifold **(see illustration)**.

4 Disconnect the hose from the air intake duct (the large plastic tube between the air cleaner housing and the throttle body) and remove the duct.

5 Disconnect the oxygen sensor electrical connector (see Chapter 6).

6 Remove the power steering pump brace.

7 Remove the retaining nuts and remove the heat insulator(s) **(see illustration)**.

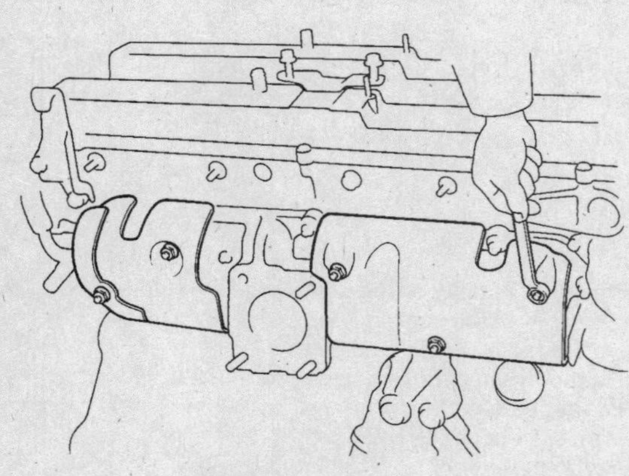

6.7 Typical heat insulators (turbo model shown) have five mounting nuts

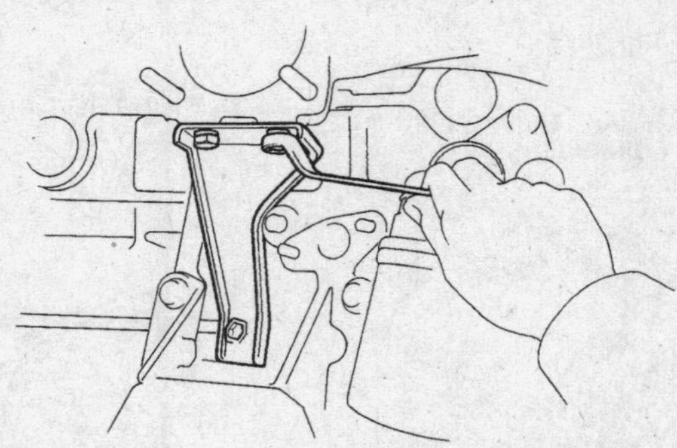

6.8 On turbo models, remove the three exhaust manifold stay bolts and the stay

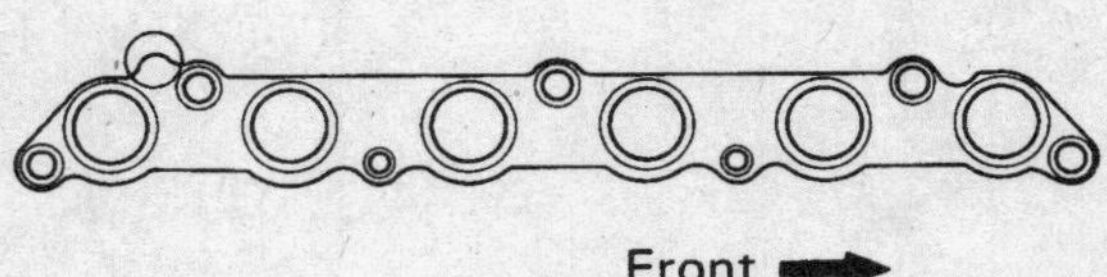

6.12 On 1987 and later models, make sure the protrusion on the exhaust manifold gasket (circled area) faces toward the rear of the engine

8 On turbo models, remove the three bolts from the exhaust manifold stay and remove the stay **(see illustration)**.
9 Take out the seven exhaust manifold-to-cylinder head nuts and detach the manifold **(see illustrations)**.

Installation

Refer to illustration 6.12

10 The manifold and cylinder head mating surfaces must be clean before the manifold is reinstalled. Use a gasket scraper to remove all traces of old gasket material and carbon deposits before installing a new gasket.
11 After you've thoroughly cleaned the exhaust manifold, check it for warpage with a straightedge and a feeler gauge **(see illustration 5.11)**. Compare your measurements to the maximum allowable warpage listed in this Chapter's Specifications. If the indicated warpage exceeds this figure, replace the exhaust manifold.
12 Place a new gasket on the head. On 1987 and later models, make sure the protrusion on the gasket faces the rear **(see illustration)**.
13 Install the exhaust manifold and the seven mounting nuts. Work from the center to the ends, tightening the nuts evenly and gradually, in three equal steps, to the torque listed in this Chapter's Specifications.
14 The remaining installation steps are the reverse of removal.

7 Crankshaft pulley - removal and installation

Removal

Refer to illustrations 7.4 and 7.5

1 Remove the accessory drivebelts (see Chapter 1).
2 Raise the front of the vehicle and place it securely on jackstands.
3 Remove the radiator (see Chapter 3).
4 Remove the flywheel/driveplate access cover (see Chapter 7A or Chapter 7B, respectively). Immobilize the crankshaft by jamming a large screwdriver between the ring gear teeth **(see illustration)**, then remove the large bolt from the center of the pulley.
5 Use a puller to extract the pulley from the nose of the crankshaft **(see illustration)**. Do not use a puller with jaws that grip the outside of the pulley, or you'll damage the pulley.

6.9 To detach the exhaust manifold, remove the seven retaining nuts (arrows) (1982 through 1986 model shown)

7.4 To prevent the crankshaft from turning as you loosen the bolt in the crankshaft pulley, lock the flywheel in place by wedging the tip of a screwdriver between the teeth on the ring gear

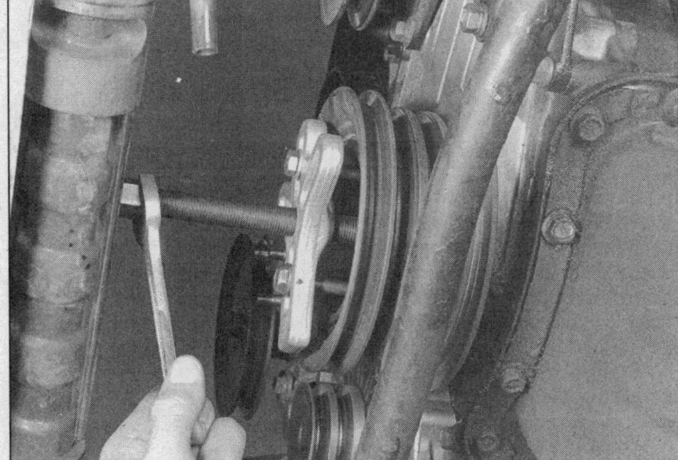

7.5 Remove the crankshaft pulley with a puller that attaches to the hub of the pulley

Installation

6 Apply a thin layer of clean, multi-purpose grease to the seal contact surface of the crankshaft pulley, then slide it onto the crankshaft. Note that the Woodruff key must be aligned with the keyway in the pulley during installation.

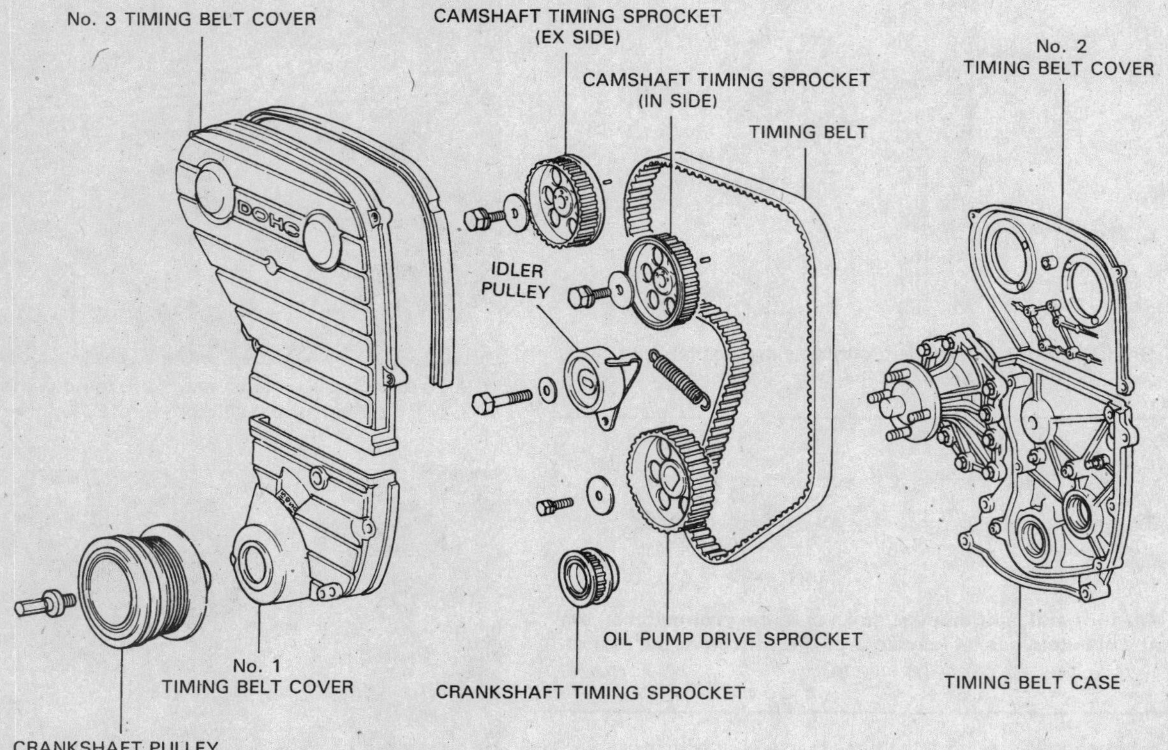

8.5 An exploded view of the timing belt covers, timing belt and sprockets on 1982 through 1986 models (1987 and later models similar)

7 Use a large socket or a section of pipe and a hammer to tap the pulley onto the crankshaft until it is seated properly.
8 Install the bolt and tighten it to the torque listed in this Chapter's Specifications.
9 The remainder of installation is the reverse of removal.

8 Timing belt covers - removal and installation

Refer to illustration 8.5
1 Disconnect the cable from the negative battery terminal. **Caution:** *If the stereo in your vehicle is equipped with an anti-theft system, refer to the information on page 0-15 at the front of this manual before detaching the cable.*
2 Remove the crankshaft pulley (see Section 7).
3 Remove the fan clutch and fan shroud (see Chapter 3).
4 On 1987 and later models, remove the air conditioner compressor, but *don't* disconnect the refrigerant hoses (see Chapter 3). Support the compressor with a piece of wire and hang it out of the way. Also remove the idler pulley bracket and the compressor bracket.
5 Remove all fasteners and remove the No. 1 and No. 3 timing belt covers and gaskets **(see illustration)**.
6 Installation is the reverse of removal.

9 Timing belt and sprockets - removal, inspection and installation

Removal

Refer to illustrations 9.12a, 9.12b, 9.13, 9.14a, 9.14b, 9.16 and 9.17
1 Disconnect the negative cable from the battery. **Caution:** *If the stereo in your vehicle is equipped with an anti-theft system, refer to the information on page 0-15 at the front of this manual before detaching the cable.*
2 Though it's not absolutely necessary, removing the radiator makes the following procedure easier. Drain the coolant (see Chapter 1) and remove the radiator (see Chapter 3).
3 Remove the air filter housing (see Chapter 4).
4 If the radiator is to remain in place, remove the upper radiator hose (see Chapter 3).
5 Loosen the drivebelts (see Chapter 1).
6 Remove the fan clutch and fan shroud (see Chapter 3).
7 Remove the drivebelts (see Chapter 1).
8 Detach the air intake duct (see Chapter 4).
9 Set the number one piston at TDC (see Section 3). **Caution:** *Once this has been done, do not turn the crankshaft until the timing belt and sprockets have been reinstalled.*
10 Remove the crankshaft pulley (see Section 7).
11 Remove the No. 1 and No. 3 timing belt covers and gaskets (see Section 8).
12 Loosen the idler pulley retaining bolt a little and push the idler pulley toward the water pump **(see illustration)**. With the timing belt tension relieved, retighten the retaining bolt and remove the belt. If the same belt is to be reinstalled, mark it with an arrow indicating direction of rotation **(see illustration)**. Also, mark the belt in line with the match marks on the sprockets and timing belt cover No. 2.
13 Remove the camshaft sprocket retaining bolt(s) **(see illustration)**.
14 With the bolts removed, place a mark on each camshaft sprocket in line with the camshaft match pin **(see illustration)**. Remove the sprocket with a puller, if necessary. Before removing the match pin, place a mark on the camshaft just above the hole in which it's installed **(see illustration)**. These marks ensure proper alignment during installation. **Note:** *It may be a good idea to use a permanent felt tip marker or punch marks if the parts are going to be cleaned with solvent. Other methods may result in marks that won't be legible later.*
15 Remove the bolt from the idler pulley and pull off the pulley along with the tension spring.

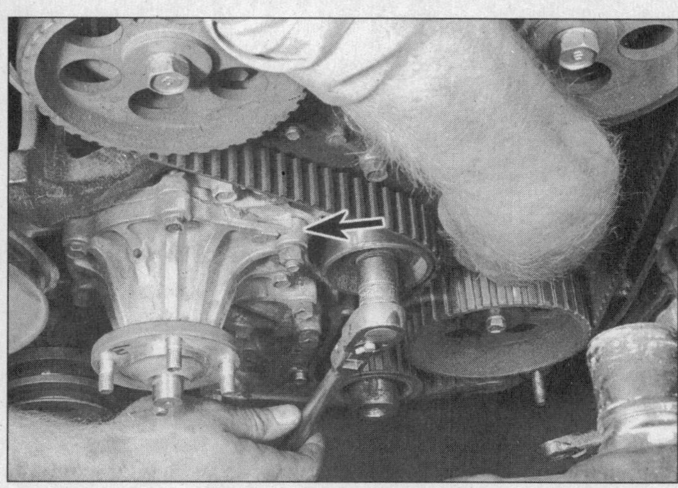

9.12a Loosen the idler pulley retaining bolt slightly and push the pulley towards the water pump, then temporarily tighten the bolt

9.12b If the same timing belt is to be reinstalled, make a directional mark on the belt to ensure proper installation

9.13 The camshaft/sprocket must be kept from turning as the bolt is removed - a two-jaw puller and a large screwdriver or prybar can be used to prevent movement

9.14a Make a mark on the camshaft sprocket just above the camshaft match pin

9.14b Make a mark on the camshaft, just above the match pin, then remove the pin

9.16 Use a punch or other tool to hold the oil pump sprocket in place, then remove the bolt and the sprocket

16 Place a punch, or other appropriate tool, through an opening in the oil pump drive sprocket and hold it in place against the case **(see illustration)**. Remove the retaining bolt and the sprocket.

9.17 The crankshaft timing sprocket can be pulled off by hand - it can only be installed one way

17 To remove the crankshaft timing sprocket, simply pull it off the shaft **(see illustration)**.

18 It's not necessary to remove the No. 2 timing belt cover (see Section 10) unless you're going to replace camshaft seals, or pull off the camshaft housings and/or the cylinder head for further service.

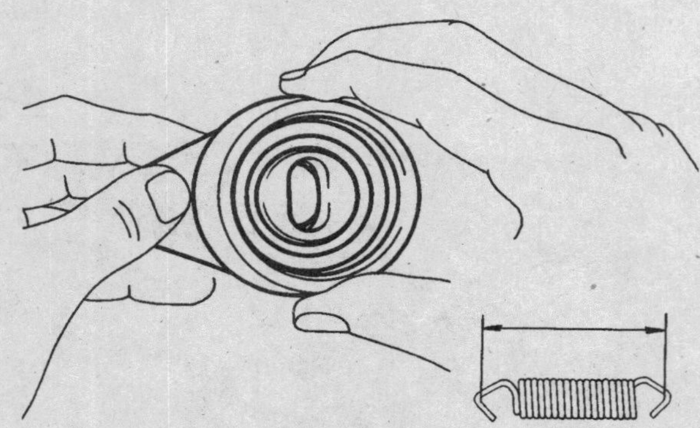

9.19 Check the idler pulley bearing for smooth operation and measure the free length of the tension spring for comparison to the Specifications

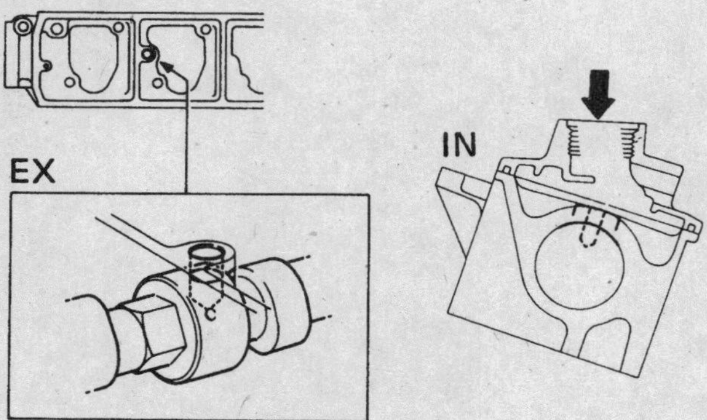

9.28a Removing the exhaust cam housing cover and the oil filler cap from the intake cam housing will allow you to check the alignment holes in the journals and the cam bearings

9.28b By looking into the oil filler opening you will be able to check the alignment of the holes in the journal and the bearing on the intake camshaft

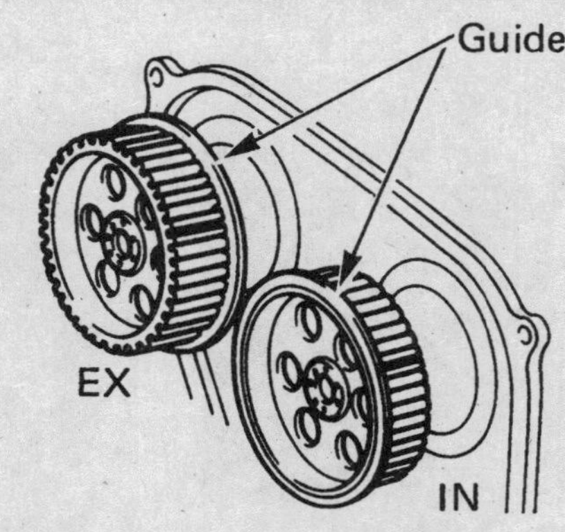

9.30 When installing the camshaft sprockets, the flange on the exhaust cam sprocket must face IN (against the inner timing cover) and the flange on the intake camshaft must face OUT (toward the fan)

Installation

Refer to illustrations 9.19, 9.28a, 9.28b, 9.30, 9.35, 9.40a and 9.40b

19 Inspect the idler pulley and tension spring. The pulley should turn freely and the free length of the tension spring should be within the limits listed in this Chapter's Specifications **(see illustration)**. If the spring has stretched, it should be replaced.

20 Install the oil pump drive sprocket and tighten the bolt to the torque listed in this Chapter's Specifications. A pin-type spanner wrench should be used to hold the sprocket as the bolt is tightened, but the method shown in illustration 9.16 can also be used.

21 Using a large socket or a piece of pipe, drive the timing belt sprocket onto the end of the crankshaft until it seats.

22 Install the idler pulley and spring, pushing the pulley towards the alternator side as far as it will go before tightening the bolt.

23 Install the timing belt on the crankshaft sprocket. If you are reinstalling the old belt, check to make sure the mark made to indicate belt direction of rotation is pointing the right way (the belt should rotate in a clockwise direction as you face the front of the engine).

24 Install the No. 1 timing belt cover (see Section 8).

25 Install the crankshaft pulley (see Section 7). Assuming the crankshaft hasn't been turned, the No. 1 cylinder should still be at Top Dead Center on the compression stroke (see Section 3).

26 On 1982 through 1986 models, remove the oil filler cap from the intake side valve cover.

27 On 1982 through 1986 models, remove the valve cover from the exhaust side camshaft housing (see Section 4).

28 Verify that the match hole over the No. 2 journal in each cam housing on 1982 through 1986 models is aligned with the hole in the camshaft journal; look through the oil filler hole in the intake side **(see illustrations)**. If it isn't, temporarily install the camshaft timing sprockets and match pins and turn the cams slightly until the holes are aligned.

29 If you removed it for any reason, install the No. 2 timing belt cover (see Section 8).

30 Each camshaft timing sprocket on 1982 through 1986 models has a single flange which prevents the belt from slipping off. The cam sprockets must be installed with the flange on the exhaust sprocket facing IN and the flange on the intake sprocket facing OUT **(see illustration)**.

Original timing belt

31 If the old timing belt is being reinstalled, the match pins between the camshafts and camshaft sprockets can probably be reinstalled in their original holes (align the marks you made in Step 14), and the sprockets installed over them. Install the timing belt over the sprockets, making sure the match marks made earlier are lined up, then adjust the belt tension (see below). After the belt is tensioned, check to make sure the holes in the No. 2 cam journals and the cam housings are still aligned. Also, the ignition timing mark on the crankshaft pulley should be aligned with the zero on the timing plate, indicating that the No. 1 piston is at TDC on the compression stroke. If the holes in the cam journals and housings are not aligned, the match pins will have to be removed and the belt installed in the same way as a new belt (see below).

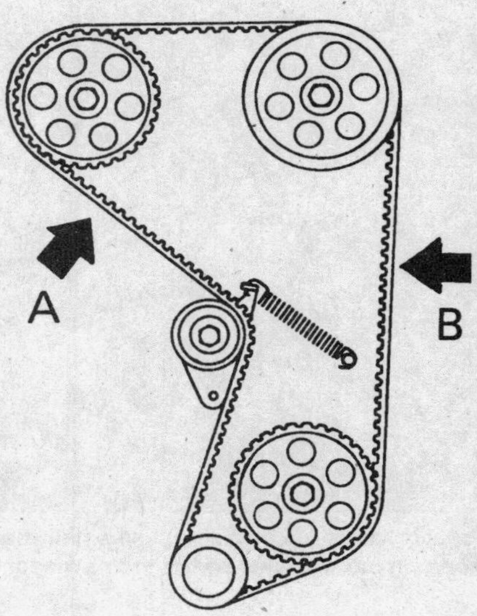

9.35 After the timing belt idler pulley has been tightened, the tension on the belt should be the same at points A and B.

New timing belt

32 Install the camshaft timing sprockets, aligning the marks made on the sprockets with the proper match pin hole, but without installing the match pins or the sprocket bolts.

33 Install the timing belt. When the belt is installed the tension should be between the crankshaft sprocket and the intake camshaft, and the slack portion of the belt should go over the idler pulley.

34 Check to make sure the number one piston is still at top dead center on the compression stroke.

35 Release the idler pulley bolt and stretch the timing belt until the tension is equal at A and B **(see illustration)**, then tighten the idler bolt to the torque listed in this Chapter's Specifications.

36 On 1982 and 1983 models, there are five match pin holes in each camshaft sprocket and in the end of each camshaft; on 1984 and later models, there are three holes. One hole in the sprocket should match a hole in the camshaft. If so, insert the match pin.

37 If none of the match pin holes align exactly, select the holes most closely in alignment and turn the crankshaft just enough to bring the holes into exact alignment, then install the pins.

38 Install the camshaft sprocket bolts and tighten them to the torque listed in this Chapter's Specifications. **Caution:** *Do not use the belt tension to hold the sprockets while tightening the bolts. A pin-type spanner wrench should be used to hold the sprocket while tightening the bolt.*

39 Loosen the idler pulley bolt, turn the crankshaft clockwise through two complete revolutions, then tighten the idler pulley bolt to the torque listed in this Chapter's Specifications.

40 Rotate the crankshaft clockwise through two complete revolutions, ending with the timing marks on the drivebelt pulley and the No. 1 timing belt cover indicating that the number one piston is at top dead center on the compression stroke. Verify that the marks on the camshaft sprockets match the marks on the No. 2 timing belt cover **(see illustrations)** and (on 1982 through 1986 models) that the holes in the cam journals and cam bearings are aligned (see Step 28). If there is a mismatch between the cam sprocket mark and the mark on the timing cover of less than one tooth, the alignment is satisfactory. If there is an alignment difference on either sprocket of more than one tooth, the belt will have to be removed and the camshaft turned sufficiently to bring the marks into alignment.

41 Install the exhaust camshaft housing cover and the oil filler cap in the intake camshaft housing.

42 Install the No. 3 timing belt cover and gasket.

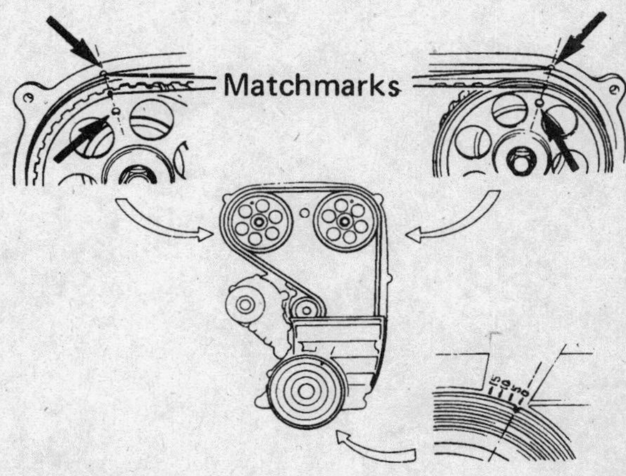

9.40a On 1982 through 1986 models, the marks on the camshaft timing sprockets must be aligned with the marks on timing belt cover no. 2 when the no. 1 piston is at TDC on the compression stroke - the match holes in the camshafts and housings should also be aligned

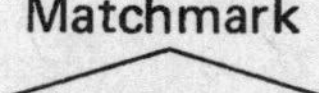

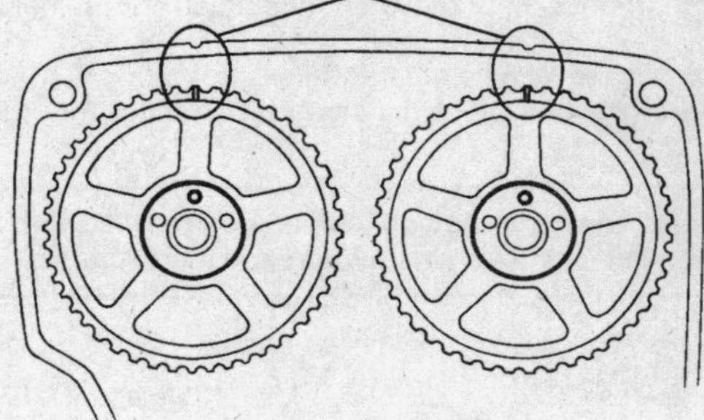

9.40b On 1987 and later models, the marks on the camshaft timing sprockets must be aligned with the marks on the no. 2 timing belt cover when the no. 1 piston is at TDC on the compression stroke

43 Install the fan clutch and fan shroud (see Chapter 3).

44 Install the upper radiator hose and fill the cooling system (see Chapter 1).

45 Install the drivebelts and adjust the tension (see Chapter 1).

46 Install the air intake duct and air filter housing (see Chapter 4).

47 Install the flywheel inspection cover (see Chapter 7A).

48 Connect the negative cable to the battery.

10 Camshaft oil seals - replacement

Refer to illustrations 10.3 and 10.4

Note: *Although it's certainly easier to replace the camshaft oil seals with the camshafts removed from their housings (on 1982 through 1986 models) or from the cylinder head (on 1987 and later models), the seals can be replaced with the camshafts installed in the cylinder head.*

1 Remove the crankshaft pulley (see Section 7), the timing belt covers (see Section 8), the timing belt and the camshaft sprockets (see Section 9).

2 Remove the No. 2 timing belt cover (the stamped metal plate behind the camshaft sprockets).

3 Using a pick or screwdriver, carefully pry the oil seal out of the camshaft housing (on 1982 through 1986 models) or the cylinder head

10.3 Using a screwdriver, pry the camshaft oil seal out of the housing - be careful not to scratch or gouge the camshaft!

10.4 If a seal driver is not available, use a hammer and a section of pipe or a large socket to tap the new seal into place

(on 1987 and later models) **(see illustration)**. Be careful not to scratch the camshaft or the seal bore.

4 To install the new seal, first apply multi-purpose grease to the entire outer edge and the lip of the seal, then use a seal driver, a short section of pipe or a large socket and a hammer to tap the new seal into the camshaft housing or the head **(see illustration)**. Make sure it is seated.

5 Installation is the reverse of removal.

6 Start the engine and check the camshaft housings for oil leaks.

11 Camshafts, rocker arms and lash adjusters (1982 through 1986 models) - removal, inspection and installation

Removal

Refer to illustrations 11.7a, 11.7b, 11.8, 11.9, 11.10a and 11.10b

1 Remove the negative cable from the battery. **Caution:** *If the stereo in your vehicle is equipped with an anti-theft system, refer to the information on page 0-15 at the front of this manual before detaching the cable.*

2 Take off the air intake duct and the air intake chamber (Chapter 4). Set the number one piston at TDC on the compression stroke (see Section 3) and remove the distributor (see Chapter 5).

3 Remove the retaining bolts from the throttle linkage bracket and detach the bracket.

4 Remove the bolt from the engine removal hook and, just below that, remove the power steering pipe bracket bolt. There is one additional power steering pipe bracket and bolt located on the top edge of the cylinder head cover which must also be removed.

5 Remove the timing belt covers, the timing belt and the camshaft sprockets (see Sections 8 and 9).

6 Remove the valve covers (see Section 3).

7 Remove both camshaft housings by loosening each nut/bolt a little at a time in the sequence shown **(see illustration)**. With the camshaft still in the housing, use a dial indicator to check camshaft endplay. Attach the gauge to the end of the housing and move the camshaft all the way to the rear. Next, use a screwdriver to pry it all the way forward. If the endplay exceeds the Specifications, replace the camshaft and/or the housing **(see illustration)**.

8 Separate the camshaft from the housing after removing the camshaft housing rear cover **(see illustration)**.

9 Use a small screwdriver and pry out the O-ring from the end of the camshaft. Then, while turning the camshaft, slowly pull it out, being careful not to damage the bearings in the housing **(see illustration)**.

10 Remove the rocker arms by lifting them off the lash adjusters **(see illustration)**. The lash adjusters can then be withdrawn by pulling

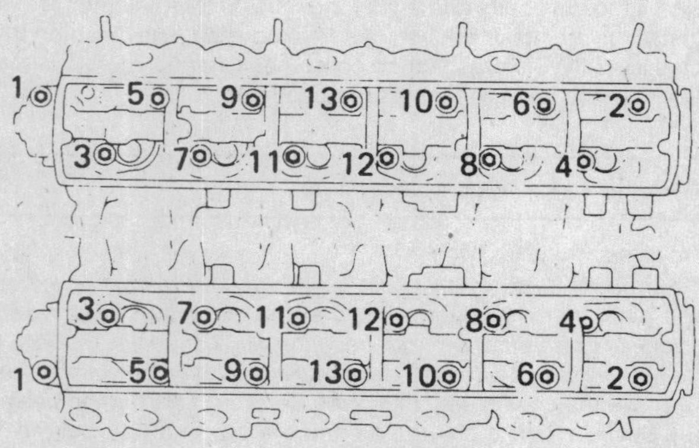

11.7a Loosen the camshaft housing nuts/bolts a little at a time in the sequence shown here to avoid warping the housings

11.7b Position the dial indicator on the end of the camshaft housing and use a screwdriver to pry the cam all the way forward - if the endplay exceeds the allowable maximum listed in this Chapter's Specifications, replace the camshaft and/or the housing

11.8 Take out the three retaining bolts and remove the camshaft housing rear cover - DO NOT pry the cover off as damage to the sealing surfaces may result and oil leaks could develop

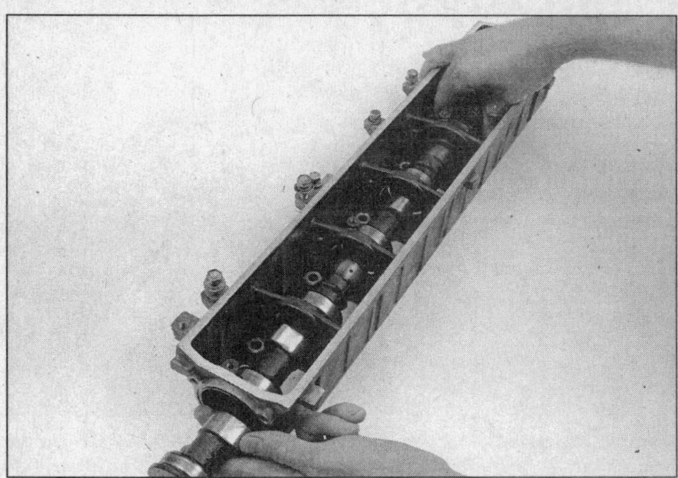
11.9 Turn the camshaft while pulling it from the camshaft housing - be careful not to nick or scratch the bearing surfaces in the housing!

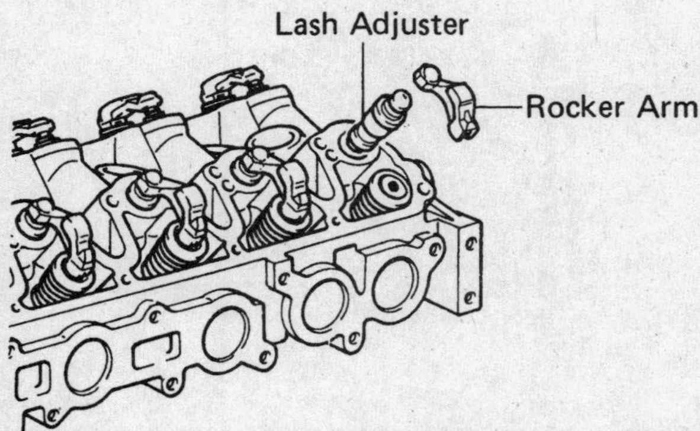

11.10a After you've removed the camshaft housings, remove the rocker arms . . .

11.10b . . . and remove the lash adjusters; make sure you keep each rocker arm and its respective lash adjuster together - they're a matched pair - and make sure you keep the rocker arm/lash adjuster pairs in order so they can be returned to their original locations

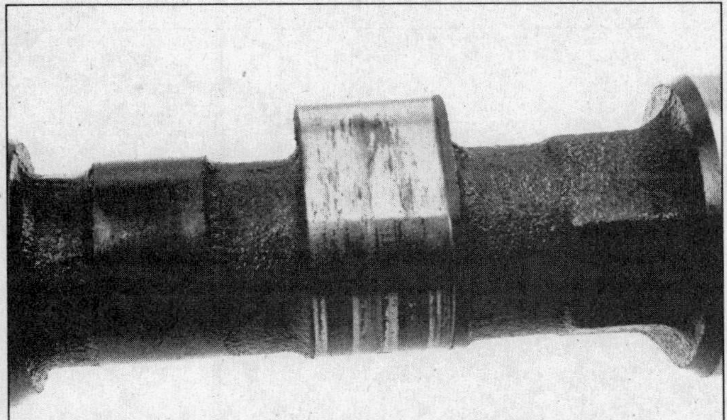
11.11a Check the cam lobes for pitting, wear and score marks - if scoring is excessive, as is the case here, replace the camshaft

11.11b Check the rocker arm pads for wear and damage as well

them out of the cylinder head **(see illustration)**. Keep the rocker arms and lash adjusters in order during removal to ensure that they are installed in their original locations.

Inspection

Refer to illustrations 11.11a, 11.11b, 11.12, 11.13, 11.14a, 11.14b, 11.15 and 11.17

11 Visually examine the camshaft and rocker arms. Check for score marks, pitting and evidence of overheating (blue, discolored areas) **(see illustrations)**. If wear is excessive, the component will have to be replaced.

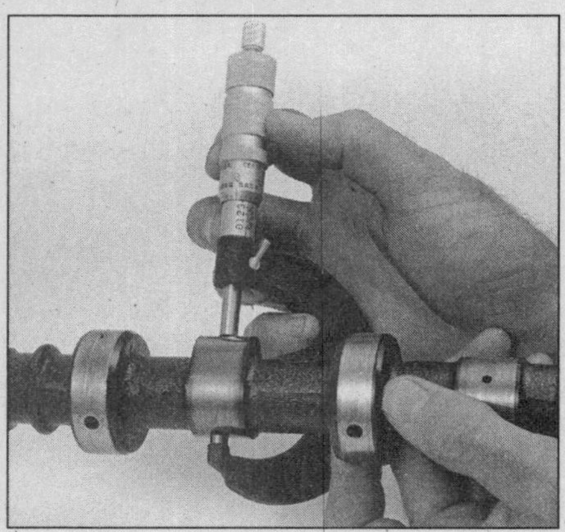

11.12 Measure the lobe heights on each camshaft - if any lobe height is less than the allowable minimum listed in this Chapter's Specifications, replace that camshaft

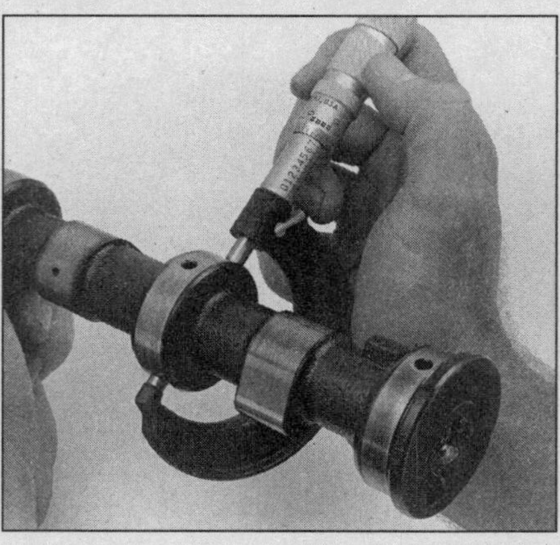

11.13 Measure each journal diameter with a micrometer (if any journal measures less than the dimension listed in this Chapter's Specifications, replace the camshaft)

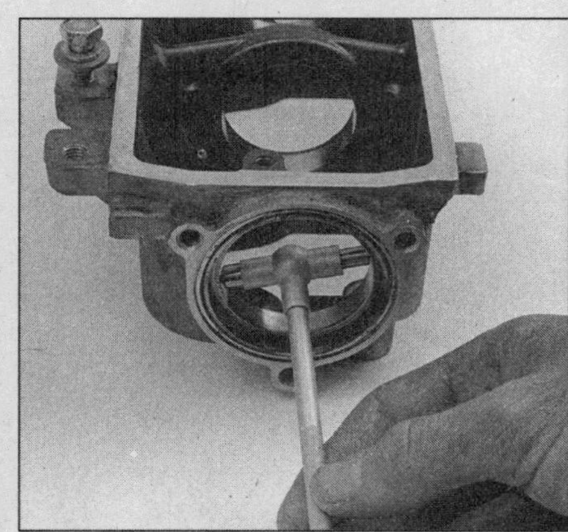

11.14a The ability to feel when the telescoping gauge is at the correct point will be developed over time, so work slowly and repeat the check until you are satisfied that the bore measurement is accurate

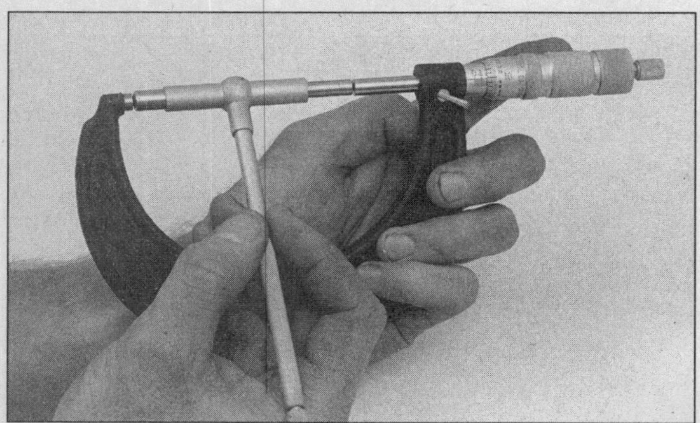

11.14b The gauge is measured with a micrometer to determine the bore size

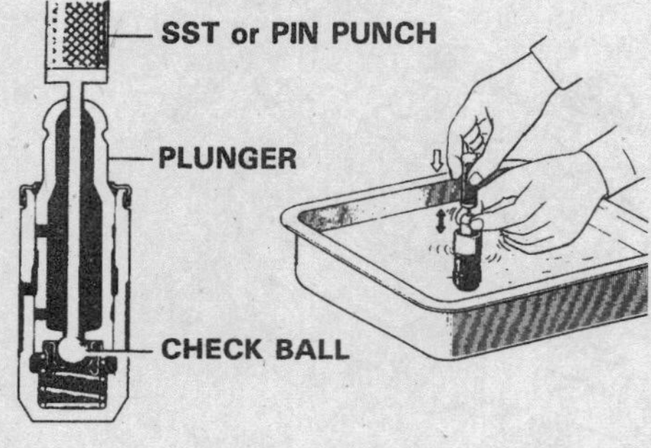

11.15 Place each lash adjuster in a container of light oil, insert an appropriately sized tool into the plunger hole and slide the plunger up-and-down several times

12 Using a micrometer, measure the cam lobe height and compare it to the lobe height listed in this Chapter's Specifications. If the lobe height is less than the minimum allowable, the camshaft is worn and must be replaced **(see illustration)**.

13 Using a micrometer, measure each journal diameter and compare it to the journal diameter listed in this Chapter's Specifications **(see illustration)**. If the journals measure less than the standard journal diameter, replace the camshaft.

14 Using an inside micrometer or a telescoping gauge, measure each housing bore **(see illustrations)**. Subtract the journal diameter measurements from the housing bore measurements to determine the bearing oil clearance. Compare it to the bearing oil clearance listed in this Chapter's Specifications. If the clearance is greater than the maximum, replace the camshaft and, if necessary, the housing.

15 Before being reinstalled, the lash adjusters must be bled. Immerse them, one at a time, in a container of light oil **(see illustration)**. Insert a pin punch into the plunger hole to depress the check valve and slide the plunger up-and-down several times while pushing down lightly on the check ball.

16 Replace the lash adjuster with a new one if the plunger stroke exceeds 0.5 mm (0.020-inch) after bleeding. Do not disassemble the lash adjuster.

17 Check each camshaft housing for warpage. Using a precision straightedge and feeler gauge, check the surface which contacts the cylinder head for warpage and compare it to the allowable warpage listed in this Chapter's Specifications **(see illustration)**. If the warpage is greater than the maximum listed in this Chapter's Specifications, replace the housing.

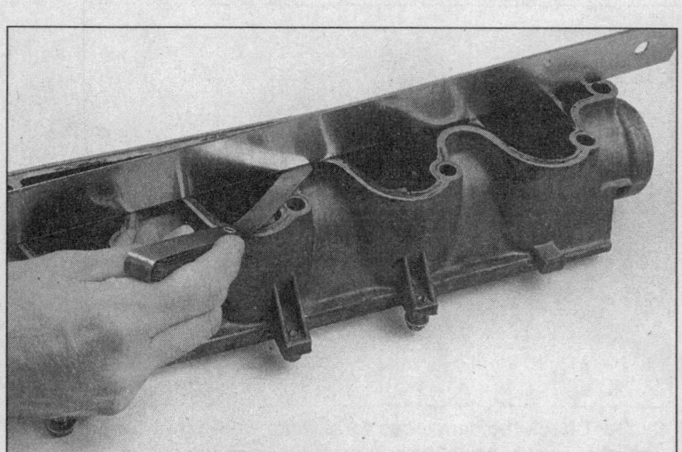

11.17 Using a straightedge and feeler gauge, check the camshaft housing surfaces for warpage and compare the results to the Specifications

Installation

Refer to illustrations 11.19, 11.20 and 11.22

18 Installation is basically the reverse of the removal procedures. However, keep these points in mind.

11.19 Generously apply engine assembly lube or moly-base grease to the cam lobes and journals before installing the camshafts in the housings

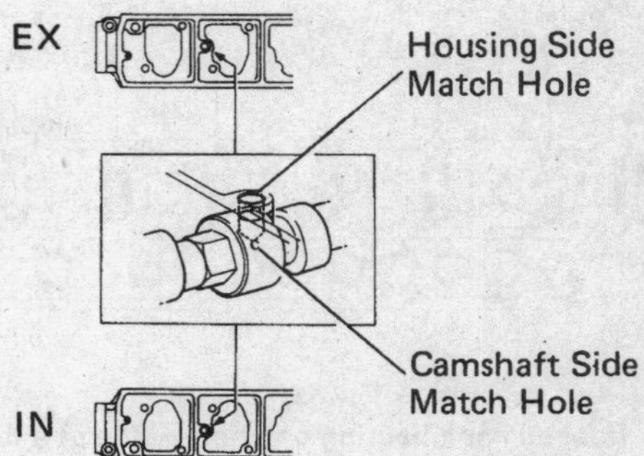

11.20 When installing the camshafts, be certain the match hole in each cam is aligned with the hole in the cam housing

19 Apply camshaft installation grease or engine assembly lube to the camshaft lobes and journals **(see illustration)**. Also apply the same lubricant to the rocker arms and lash adjusters.

20 Insert the camshafts into the housings, then install new O-rings and the rear end covers. When installing the camshafts, make sure that the match hole on the journal of the camshaft housing is aligned with the hole in the camshaft **(see illustration)**.

21 Before replacing the camshaft housing on the cylinder head, scrape any remaining gasket material off both mating surfaces, then install a new gasket.

22 Install the housing nuts and bolts and tighten them gradually in three passes in the sequence shown **(see illustration)**. Tighten the nuts and bolts to the torque listed in this Chapter's Specifications on the final pass.

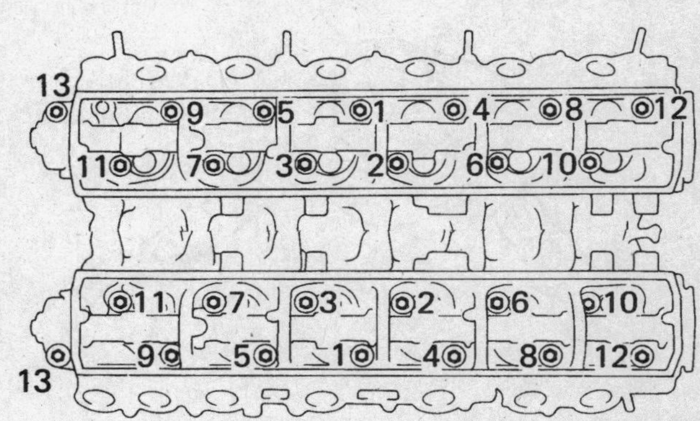

11.22 Tighten the camshaft housing fasteners in the sequence shown here - work up to the final torque in three steps

12 Camshafts, valve lifters and shims (1987 and later models) - removal, inspection and installation

Removal

Refer to illustrations 12.6a, 12.6b, 12.10 and 12.11

1 Detach the cable from the negative battery terminal. **Caution:** *If the stereo in your vehicle is equipped with an anti-theft system, refer to the information on page 0-15 at the front of this manual before detaching the cable.*

2 Detach the brackets for the accelerator cable and TV cable (if the vehicle is equipped with an automatic transmission) from the valve covers. Set the number one piston at TDC on the compression stroke (see Section 3) and remove the distributor or camshaft position sensor (see Chapter 5).

3 On non-turbo models, remove the No. 1 air cleaner hose and intake connector pipe (see Chapter 4); on turbo models, remove the No. 4 air cleaner pipe and the No. 1 and No. 2 air cleaner hoses (see Chapter 4).

4 Clearly label, detach and remove all coolant, fuel and vacuum hoses in the way. Do the same thing with all electrical wiring harnesses. Label the connectors, unplug them and lay the harnesses aside.

5 Remove the valve covers (see Section 4).

6 Remove the heater hose bracket **(see illustration)**. Using special tool SST 09923-00010 (or its equivalent), remove the No. 3 cylinder head cover **(see illustration)**.

7 Remove the spark plugs (see Chapter 1).

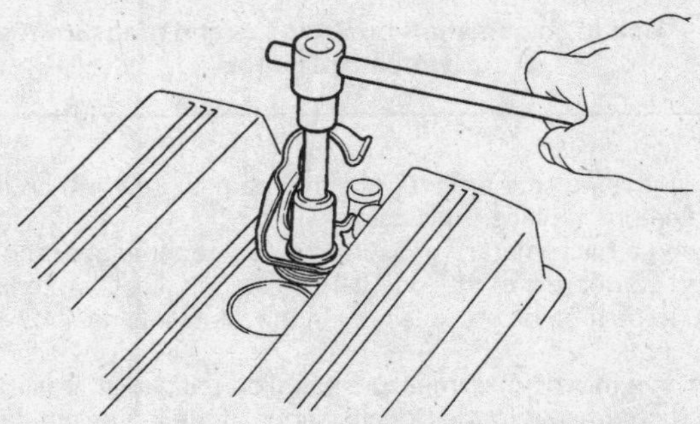

12.6a Remove the heater hose bracket

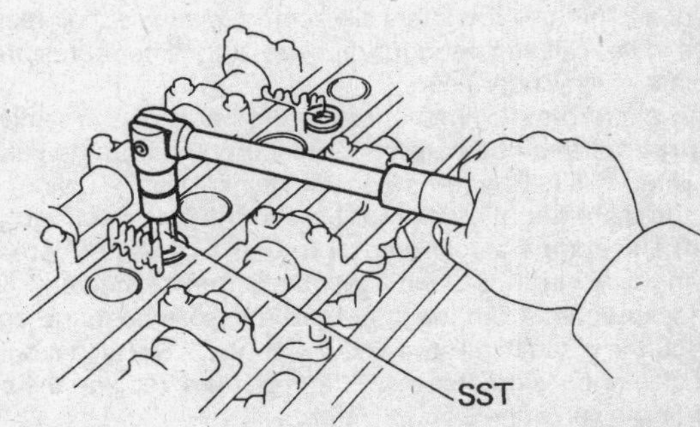

12.6b Using special tool SST 09923-00010 (or its equivalent), remove the No. 3 cylinder head cover

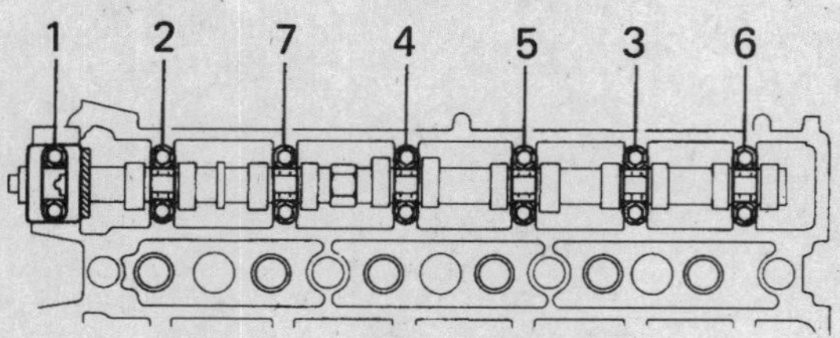

12.10 Loosen each bearing cap bolt a little at a time in the sequence shown

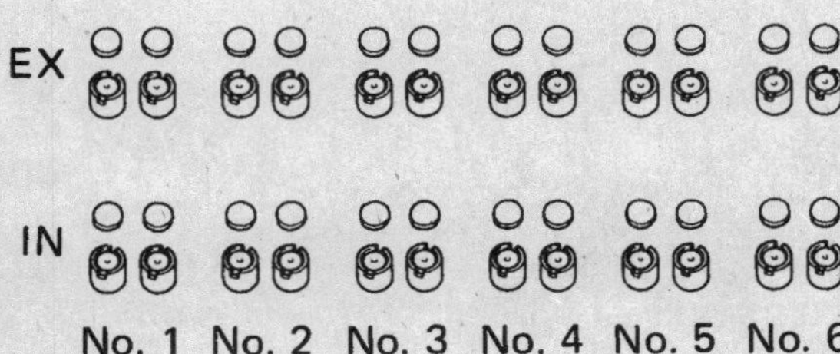

12.11 As you remove the shims and valve lifters, organize them so you won't accidentally install them in the wrong lifter bore or mix up lifters and their respective shims

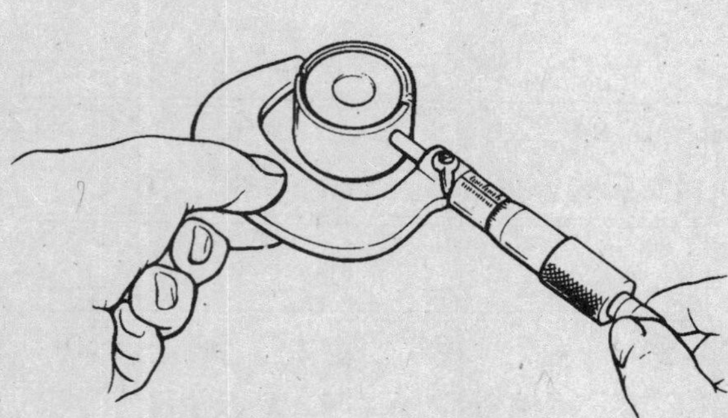

12.13a Using a micrometer, measure the diameter of each valve lifter and compare your measurements to the valve lifter diameter listed in this Chapter's Specifications, . . .

12.13b . . . measure the diameter of each lifter bore with a caliper gauge, subtract the valve lifter diameter measurement from the lifter bore measurement and compare this figure to the clearance listed in this Chapter's Specifications

8 Remove the crankshaft pulley (see Section 7), timing belt cover (see Section 8) and the timing belt (see Section 9).

9 Remove the No. 2 timing belt cover **(see illustration 8.6a)**.

10 Loosen each bearing cap bolt a little at a time in the sequence shown **(see illustration)**. Remove the camshaft bearing caps, oil seals and camshafts. Place the bearing caps in order.

11 Remove the shims and valve lifters. Keep them in order **(see illustration)**.

Inspection

Refer to illustrations 12.13a, 12.13b, 12.14, 12.15, 12.16, 12.17, 12.18 and 12.19

12 Visually examine the camshaft, shims and valve lifters. Check for score marks, pitting and evidence of overheating (blue, discolored areas). If wear is excessive, the component will have to be replaced. If the walls of any of the valve lifters are scored, examine their respective lifter bores in the cylinder head for damage. If the lifter bores are damaged, replace the cylinder head.

13 Using a micrometer, measure the diameter of each valve lifter **(see illustration)** and compare your measurements to the valve lifter diameter listed in this Chapter's Specifications. Using a caliper gauge, measure the diameter of each lifter bore in the cylinder head **(see illustration)** and compare your measurements to the lifter bore diameter listed in this Chapter's Specifications. Subtract the valve lifter diameter measurement from the lifter bore measurement and compare this figure to the clearance listed in this Chapter's Specifications. If the indicated clearance is greater than the maximum, replace the cylinder head and/or the valve lifter.

14 Place each camshaft on V-blocks and, using a dial gauge, measure the circle runout at the center journal **(see illustration)**. Compare your measurements to the circle runout listed in this Chapter's Specifications. If the indicated runout of either cam is greater than the allowable maximum, replace the cam(s).

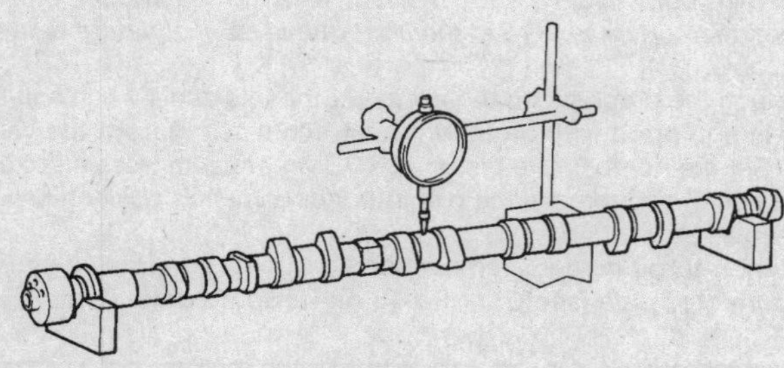

12.14 Place each camshaft on V-blocks and measure the runout with a dial gauge

15 Using a micrometer, measure the cam lobe height **(see illustration)** and compare it to the lobe height listed in this Chapter's Specifications. If the lobe height is less than the allowable minimum, replace the camshaft.

16 Using a micrometer, measure each journal diameter **(see illustration)** and compare it to the Specifications. If the journals measure less than the standard journal diameter, replace the camshaft.

17 Clean the camshaft bearing caps and the camshaft journals, place the camshafts in the head, lay a strip of Plastigage across each

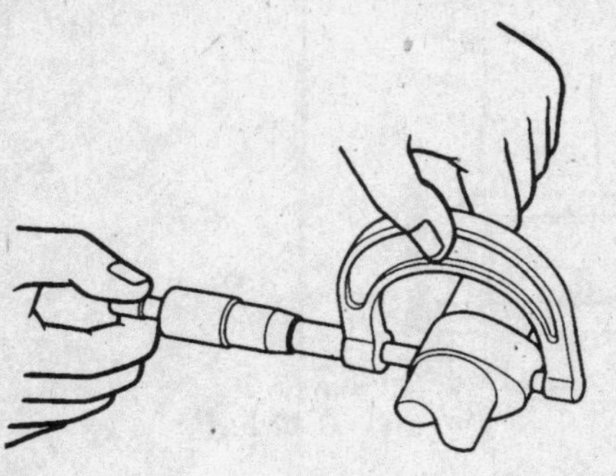

12.15 Measure the cam lobe height with a micrometer and compare it to the lobe height listed in this Chapter's Specifications

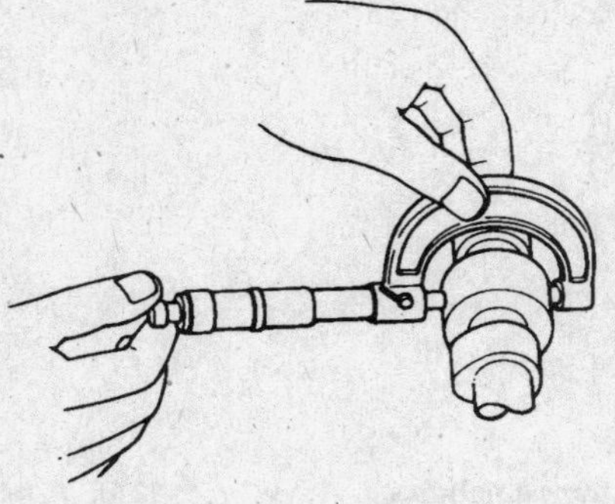

12.16 Using a micrometer, measure each journal diameter and compare it to the Specifications

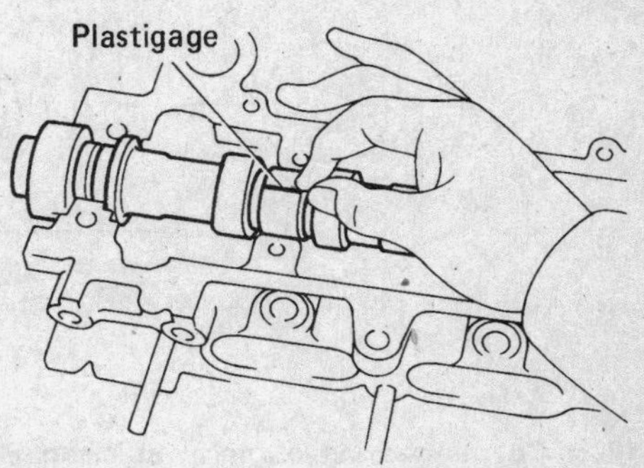

12.17 Lay a strip of Plastigage across each journal, place the caps in position with the number on top of each cap pointing toward the front of the engine and tighten the bearing cap bolts gradually and evenly to the torque listed in this Chapter's Specifications.

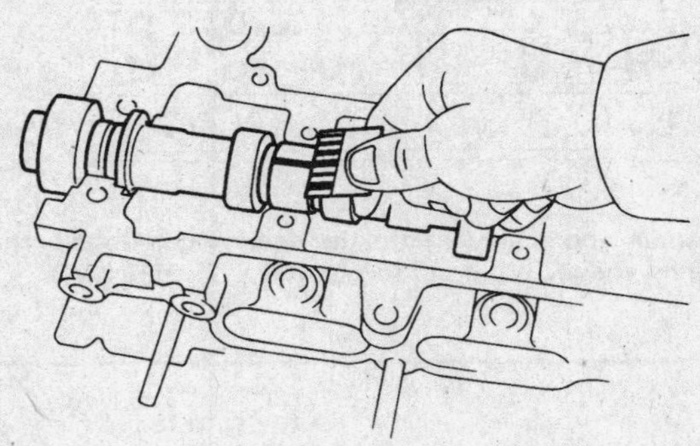

12.18 Remove the caps and measure the Plastigage on each cam journal by comparing its width at its widest point to the corresponding mark on the scale of the Plastigage package

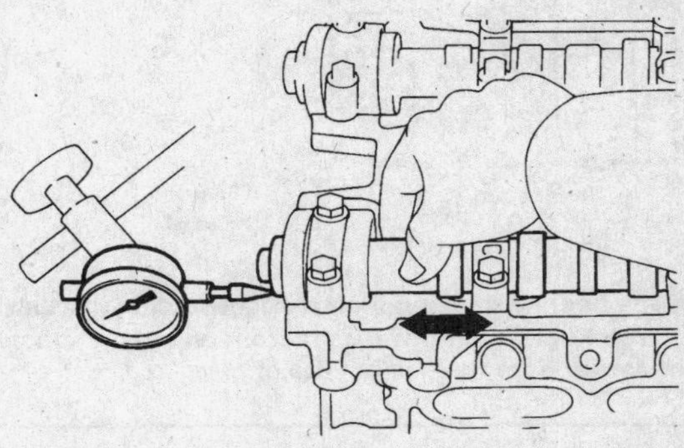

12.19 Install a dial gauge on the cylinder head as shown, zero the gauge probe and measure the camshaft endplay by moving the camshaft back and forth

journal **(see illustration)**, place the caps in position with the number on top of each cap pointing toward the front of the engine and tighten the bearing cap bolts gradually and evenly to the torque listed in this Chapter's Specifications. **Caution:** *DO NOT turn the camshafts during this procedure.*

18 Remove the caps and measure the Plastigage on each cam journal by comparing its width at its widest point to the corresponding mark on the scale of the Plastigage package **(see illustration)**. If the clearance at any journal is greater than the allowable maximum clearance, replace the cylinder head and/or the camshaft (depending on the amount).

19 Clean off all Plastigage material from the cam journals and bearing caps and install the camshaft and bearing caps. Install a dial gauge on the cylinder head as shown **(see illustration)**, zero the gauge probe and measure the camshaft endplay by moving the camshaft back and forth. Compare your endplay measurement for each cam to the endplay listed in this Chapter's Specifications. If the indicated endplay is greater than the allowable maximum, replace the camshaft and/or cylinder head.

20 If you want to replace the valve guide seals with the cylinder head installed on the block, refer to Section 12. If you want to overhaul the head, refer to Chapter 2C.

Installation

Refer to illustrations 12.23, 12.24, 12.25, 12.26, 12.27, 12.28, 12.29 and 12.30

21 Thoroughly clean the camshafts, shims and lifters and coat all sliding and rotating surfaces with fresh engine oil. Replace all gaskets and seals. Install the valves, springs, retainers and keepers, if you haven't already done so (see Chapter 2, Part C).

22 Install the lifters and shims. Unless you're using a complete new set of lifters, make sure you put the shims back in the same lifter bores from which they were removed.

23 Apply clean engine oil or multi-purpose grease to the lip of the new camshaft oil seals and install the seals on the cams **(see illustration)**.

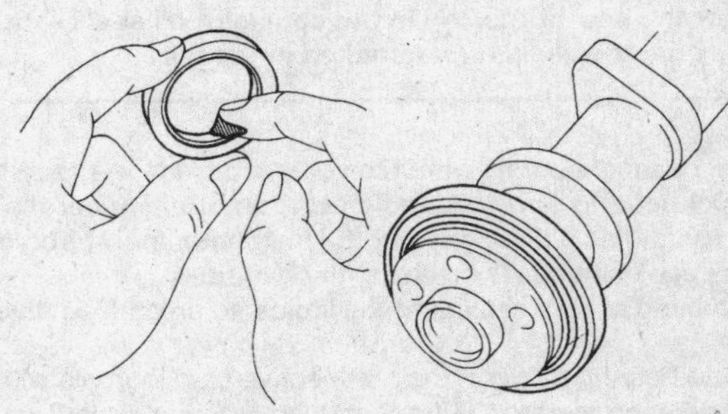

12.23 Apply clean engine oil or multi purpose grease to the lip of the new camshaft oil seals and install the seals on the cams as shown

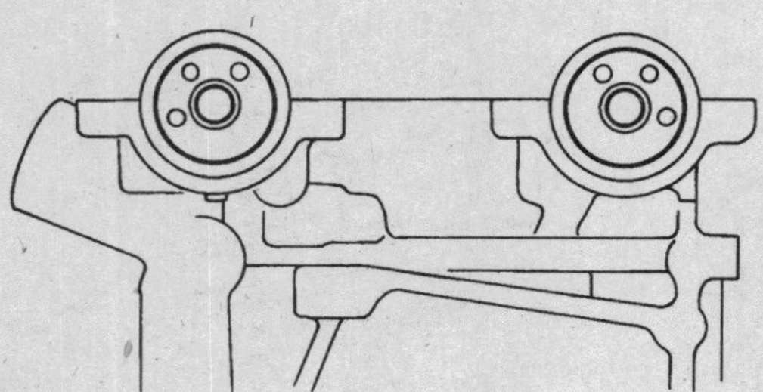

12.24 Coat all bearing journals with clean oil, place the camshafts in the cylinder head as shown; remember that the exhaust camshaft has a drive gear for the distributor (non-turbo models) or for the camshaft position sensor (turbo models)

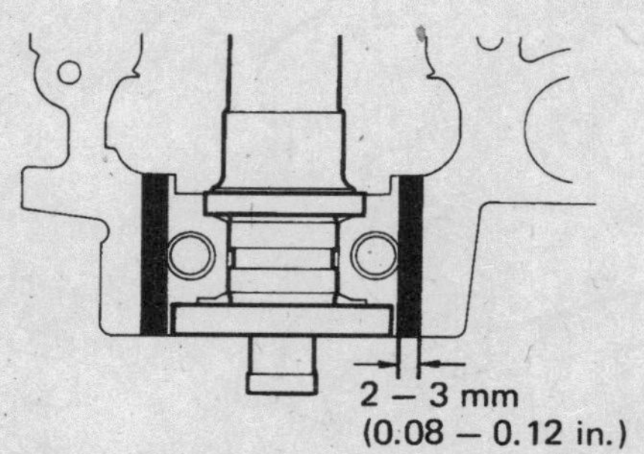

12.25 Apply RTV sealant to the indicated areas

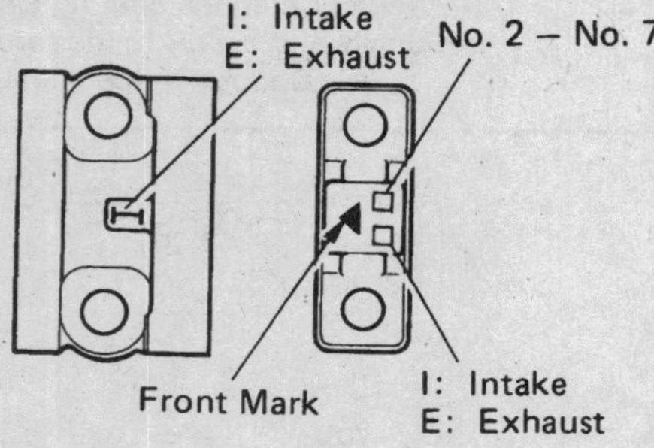

12.26 Place the bearing caps on their respective cam journals with the front marks pointing toward the front and in numerical order from the front of the engine

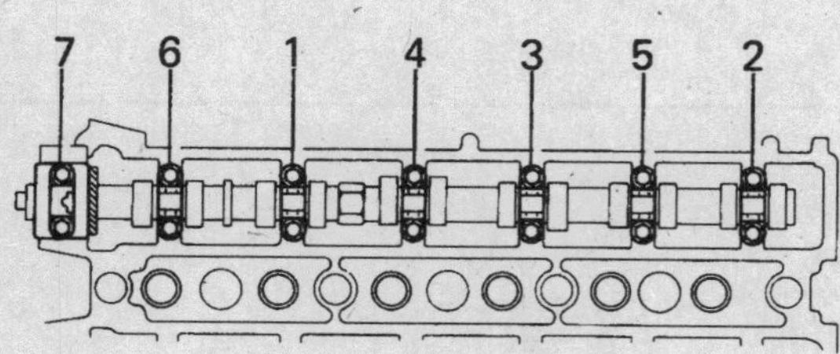

12.27 Gradually and evenly tighten the bearing cap bolts in the sequence shown, but don't torque them down just yet

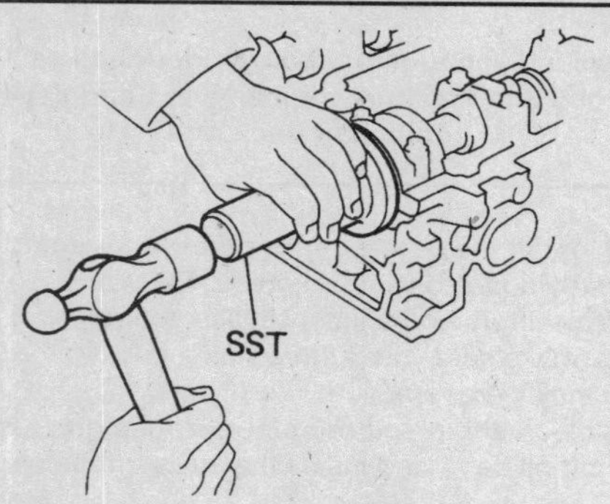

12.28 Using a Toyota special service tool, or a short section of pipe with an outside diameter slightly smaller than the inside diameter of the seal bores, tap in the camshaft oil seals - make sure the seals aren't cocked in the bores.

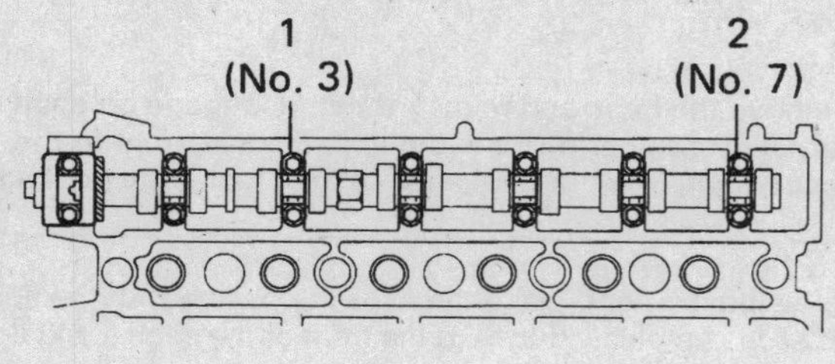

12.29 Gradually and evenly tighten the No. 3 and No. 7 bearing cap bolts in several passes, in the sequence shown

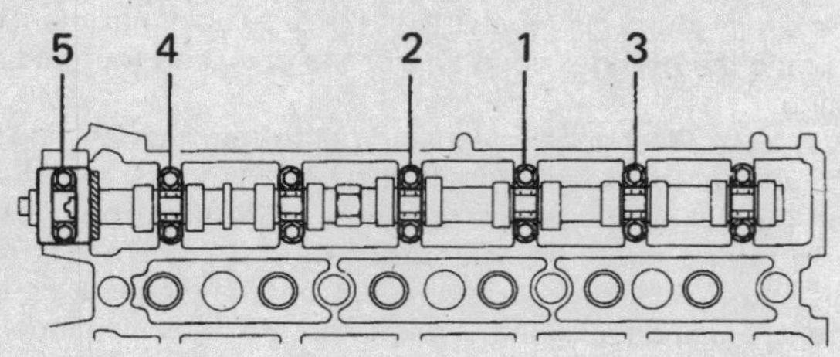

12.30 Gradually and evenly tighten the other bearing cap bolts in the sequence shown

24 Coat all bearing journals with fresh oil, then place the camshafts in the cylinder head as shown **(see illustration)**. Remember that the exhaust camshaft has a drive gear for the distributor (non-turbo models) or for the camshaft position sensor (turbo models).

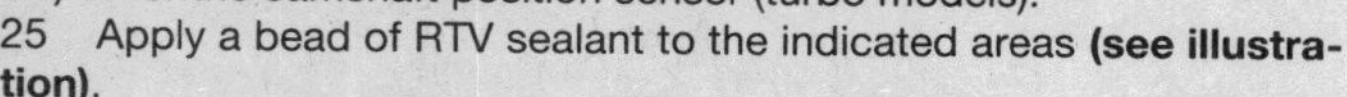

25 Apply a bead of RTV sealant to the indicated areas **(see illustration)**.

26 Place the bearing caps on their respective cam journals with the front marks pointing toward the front and in numerical order from the front of the engine **(see illustration)**.

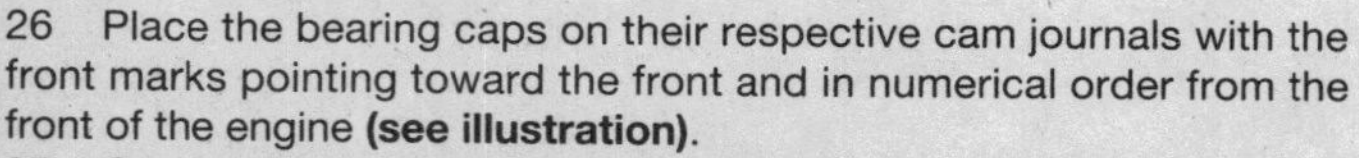

27 Gradually and evenly tighten the bearing cap bolts in the sequence shown **(see illustration)**, but don't torque them down yet.

28 Lubricate the lips of the camshaft seals with clean engine oil or multi-purpose grease. Using a Toyota special service tool, or a short section of pipe with an outside diameter slightly smaller than the inside diameter of the seal bores, tap in the camshaft oil seals **(see illustration)**. Make sure the cam seals aren't cocked in the bores.

29 Gradually and evenly tighten the No. 3 and No. 7 bearing cap bolts in several passes, in the sequence shown **(see illustration)**.

13.4 Thread an adapter into the spark plug opening, then connect an air hose - the compressed air should hold the valves in place

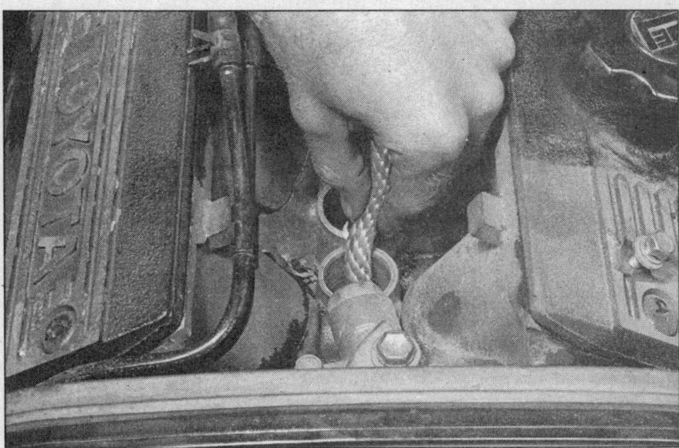

13.6 If compressed air is not available, after positioning the piston approximately 45-degrees before TDC, feed a long piece of nylon rope through the spark plug opening until it fills the combustion chamber

13.7a With this type of spring compressor, turning the knob compresses the spring coils against the retainer

13.7b Once the valve spring has been compressed, use tweezers, needle-nose pliers or a magnet to remove the keepers

30 Gradually and evenly tighten the other bearing cap bolts in the sequence shown **(see illustration)**.

31 Recheck the camshaft endplay (see Step 19).

32 The remainder of installation is the reverse of removal.

13 Valve springs, retainers and seals - replacement

Refer to illustrations 13.4, 13.6, 13.7a, 13.7b and 13.15

Note: *Broken valve springs and defective valve stem seals can be replaced without removing the cylinder head. Special tools and a compressed air source are normally required to perform this operation, so read through this Section carefully and rent or buy the tools before beginning the job. If compressed air is not available, a length of nylon rope can be used to keep the valves from falling into the cylinder during this procedure.*

1 Remove the timing belt cover (see Section 8) and the timing belt (see Section 9). On 1982 through 1986 models, remove the camshafts, housings and rocker arms (see Section 11); on 1987 through 1992 models, remove the camshafts, shims and lifters (see Section 12).

2 Remove the spark plug from the cylinder which has the defective component. If all of the valve stem seals are being replaced, all of the spark plugs should be removed.

3 Turn the crankshaft until the piston in the affected cylinder is at Top Dead Center on the compression stroke (see Section 3). If you are replacing all of the valve stem seals, begin with cylinder number one and work on the valves for one cylinder at a time. Move from cylinder to cylinder following the firing order sequence (1-5-3-6-2-4).

4 Thread an adapter into the spark plug hole and connect an air hose **(see illustration)**. Most auto parts stores can supply the air hose adapter. **Note:** *Many cylinder compression gauges utilize a screw-in fitting that may work with your air hose quick disconnect fitting.*

5 Apply compressed air to the cylinder. The valves should be held in place by the air pressure. If the valve faces or seats are in poor condition, leaks may prevent the air pressure from retaining the valves - refer to the alternative procedure below.

6 If you do not have access to compressed air, an alternative method can be used. Position the piston at a point approximately 45-degrees before TDC on the compression stroke, then feed a long piece of nylon rope through the spark plug hole until it fills the combustion chamber **(see illustration)**. Be sure to leave the end of the rope hanging out of the engine so it can be removed easily. Use a large breaker bar and socket to rotate the crankshaft in the normal direction of rotation until a slight resistance is felt.

7 Use a valve spring compressor to compress the spring **(see illustration)**. Remove the keepers **(see illustration)**. **Note:** *A couple of different types of tools are available for compressing the valve springs with the head in place. One type grips the lower spring coils and presses on the retainer as the knob is turned* **(see illustration)**. *The*

13.15 Apply a small dab of grease to each keeper before installation to hold them in place on the valve stem until the spring is released

lever type utilizes a bolt threaded into the head for leverage. Both types work very well, although the lever type is usually less expensive.

8 Remove the spring retainer and valve spring, then remove the valve stem oil seal. **Note:** *If air pressure fails to hold the valve in the closed position during this operation, the valve face or seat is probably damaged. If so, the cylinder head will have to be removed for additional repair operations.*

9 Wrap a rubber band or tape around the top of the valve stem so the valve will not fall into the combustion chamber, then release the air pressure. **Note:** *If a rope was used instead of air pressure, turn the crankshaft slightly in the direction opposite normal rotation.*

10 Inspect the valve stem for damage. Rotate the valve in the guide and check the end for eccentric movement, which would indicate that the valve is bent.

11 Move the valve up-and-down in the guide and make sure it doesn't bind. If the valve stem binds, either the valve is bent or the guide is damaged. In either case, the head will have to be removed for repair.

12 Apply air pressure to the cylinder to retain the valve in the closed position, then remove the tape or rubber band from the valve stem. If a rope was used instead of air pressure, rotate the crankshaft in the normal direction of rotation until slight resistance is felt.

13 Lubricate the valve stem with engine oil and install a new oil seal. Make sure it is seated on the valve guide.

14 Install the spring over the valve.

15 Install the valve spring retainer. Compress the valve spring and position the keepers in the groove. Apply a small dab of grease to the inside of each keeper to hold it in place if necessary **(see illustration)**. Remove the pressure from the spring compressor and make sure the keepers are seated.

16 Disconnect the air hose and remove the adapter from the spark plug hole. If a rope was used in place of air pressure, pull it out of the cylinder.

17 On 1982 through 1986 models, install the rocker arms, housings and camshafts (see Section 11); on 1987 through 1992 models, install the lifters, shim and camshafts (see Section 12). Reinstall the timing belt (see Section 9) and the timing belt cover (see Section 8).

18 Install the spark plugs and hook up the wires.

19 Start and run the engine, then check for oil leaks and unusual sounds coming from the camshaft housings.

14 Oil pump driveshaft and bearings - removal, inspection and installation

1 Remove the crankshaft pulley (see Section 7).

2 Remove the timing belt cover (see Section 8).

3 Remove the timing belt (see Section 9).

4 Remove the distributor (see Chapter 5).

5 Remove the oil pan (see Section 17).

6 Remove the oil pump (see Section 18).

7 Remove and inspect the oil pump driveshaft (see Chapter 2, Part C).

8 Installation is the reverse of removal.

15.10 Remove the two retaining bolts, loosen the hose clamp to pull off the bypass hose and detach the thermostat housing

15 Cylinder head - removal and installation

1 Disconnect the negative cable from the battery. **Caution:** *If the stereo in your vehicle is equipped with an anti-theft system, refer to the information on page 0-15 at the front of this manual before detaching the cable.*

2 Drain the coolant (Chapter 1).

1982 through 1986 models

Removal

Refer to illustrations 15.10, 15.11 and 15.12

3 Remove the upper radiator hose from the thermostat housing (see Chapter 3).

4 Remove the exhaust manifold (see Section 6).

5 Take off the timing belt (see Section 9).

6 Remove the air intake chamber along with the fuel rail (see Chapter 4).

7 Remove the distributor along with the cap and wires (see Chapter 5).

8 Remove the throttle linkage bracket from the cylinder head cover.

9 Label and disconnect the high tension lead from the ignition coil, the thermo switch wire (models with automatic transmissions), the solenoid resistor wire connector and the knock sensor wire connector (see the Wiring Diagrams at the end of Chapter 12). Then disconnect the brake booster vacuum hose, the actuator vacuum hose (models with a cruise control system), the fuel hose from the intake manifold, the EGR valve vacuum hose and the heater hose from the rear of the cylinder head.

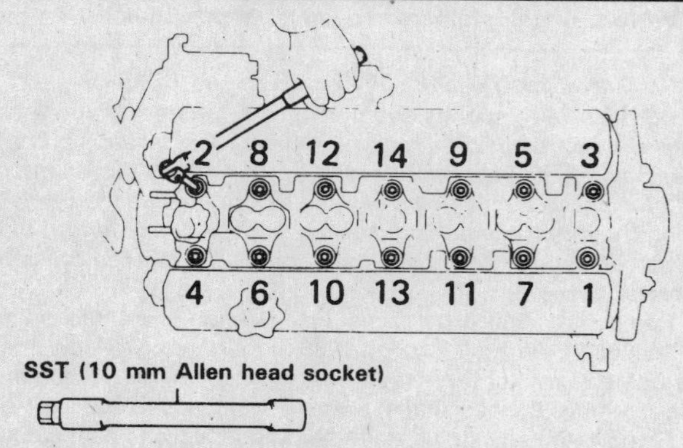

15.11 Cylinder head bolt LOOSENING sequence - note that the bolts require a 10 mm Allen wrench for removal and installation

15.12 If the head won't release from the block, pry it loose with a large screwdriver or pry bar, but DO NOT damage the gasket sealing surfaces!

15.14 Carefully scrape any remaining gasket material off the engine block - stuff rags into the cylinders to keep gasket material and dirt out

10 Remove the two retaining bolts and the bypass hose from the thermostat housing, then separate the housing from the cylinder head **(see illustration)**.

11 Loosen the fourteen head bolts in 1/4-turn increments, following the order shown **(see illustration)**. Mark the bolts to ensure that they can be reinstalled in their original locations.

12 Carefully lift the cylinder head straight up from the engine block dowel pins and remove it from the vehicle. If the head is difficult to remove from the block, pry it up with a large screwdriver or pry bar positioned between the head and water pump **(see illustration)**. Store the head on blocks of wood to prevent damage to the gasket sealing surface. Cylinder head disassembly and inspection procedures are covered in detail in Chapter 2, Part C.

Installation

Refer to illustrations 15.14, 15.17 and 15.19

13 The mating surfaces of the cylinder head and block must be perfectly clean when the head is installed.

14 Use a gasket scraper to remove all traces of carbon and old gasket material, then wipe the mating surfaces with a cloth saturated with lacquer thinner or acetone. If there is oil on the mating surfaces when the head is installed, the gasket may not seal correctly and leaks may develop. When working on the block, stuff the cylinders with shop rags to keep debris out of the engine **(see illustration)**. **Note:** *Since the head is made of aluminum, aggressive scraping can cause damage. Be extra careful not to nick or gouge the mating surface with the scraper. Use a vacuum cleaner to remove any debris that falls into the cylinders.*

15 Check the block and head mating surfaces for nicks, deep scratches and other damage. If damage is slight, it can be removed with a file; if it is excessive, machining may be the only alternative.

16 Use a tap of the correct size to clean up the threads in the head bolt holes. Mount each bolt in a vise and run a die down the threads to remove corrosion and restore the threads. Dirt, corrosion, sealant and damaged threads will affect torque readings.

17 Apply a bead of RTV sealant to the timing belt case-to-engine block joints **(see illustration)**, then position the new head gasket over the dowel pins in the block. Some head gaskets can only be installed one way, so look for a TOP or THIS SIDE UP mark.

18 Carefully position the head on the block without disturbing the gasket.

19 Install the bolts in their original locations and tighten them finger tight. Following the recommended sequence **(see illustration)**, tighten the bolts in several steps to the torque listed in this Chapter's Specifications.

20 The remaining installation steps are the reverse of removal.

1987 and later models

Removal

Refer to illustrations 15.58, 15.60, 15.65 and 15.66

21 Disconnect the exhaust pipe from the exhaust manifold (see Section 6).

2B

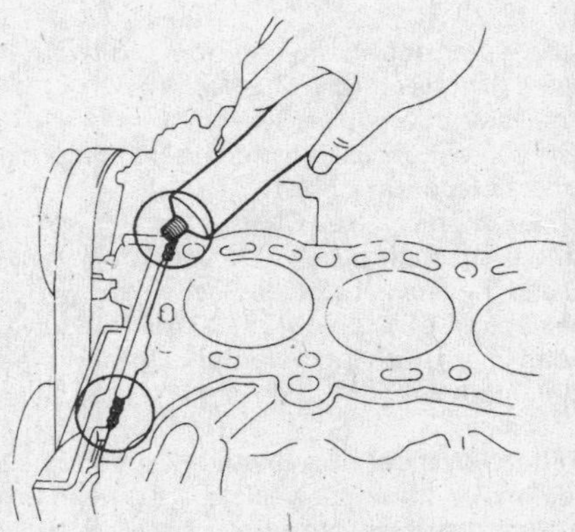

15.17 Apply a bead of RTV sealant to the areas shown here before laying the head gasket in place

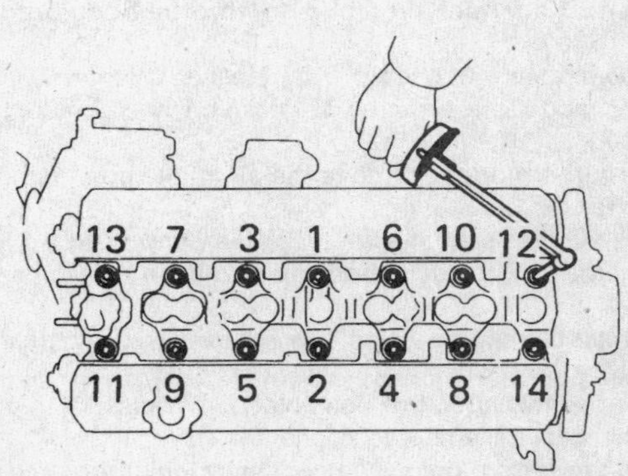

15.19 Tighten the cylinder head bolts to the torque listed in this Chapter's Specifications in the order shown - work up to the final torque in three steps

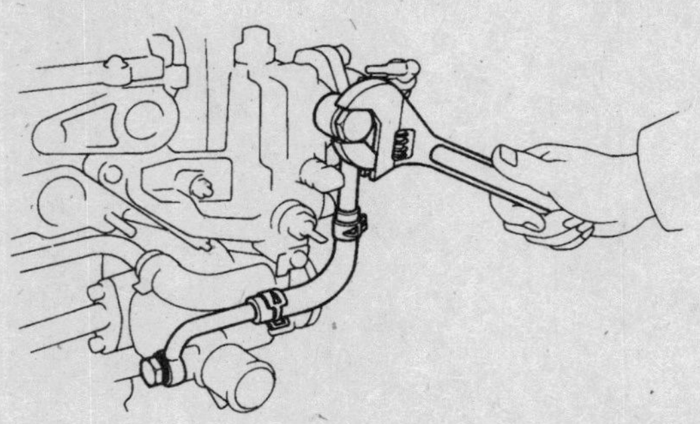

15.58 On non-turbo models, remove the banjo bolts and crush washers and disconnect the No. 4 water bypass hose

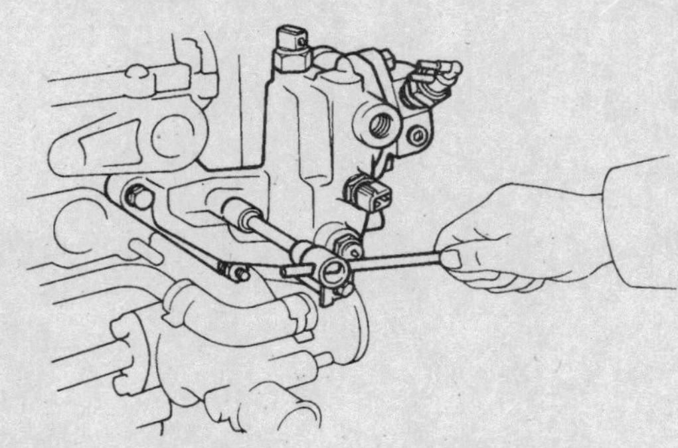

15.60 To remove the water outlet housing, remove the single retaining bolt and both nuts, then separate the housing and its gasket from the cylinder head

22 Detach the brackets for the accelerator cable and TV cable (if the vehicle is equipped with an automatic transmission) from the valve covers.

23 Disconnect the ground strap from the cylinder head.

24 On non-turbo models, remove the No. 1 air cleaner hose and intake connector pipe (see Chapter 4); on turbo models, remove the No. 4 air cleaner pipe and the No. 1 and No. 2 air cleaner hoses (see Chapter 4).

25 Disconnect the cruise control hose, charcoal canister hose and brake booster hose.

26 Remove the radiator inlet hose.

27 Disconnect the heater inlet hose.

28 Remove the alternator (see Chapter 5).

29 On turbo models, remove the power steering reservoir (see Chapter 10).

30 On turbo models, remove the cam position sensor (see Chapter 6).

31 Detach the PCV pipe.

32 Unplug the throttle position sensor and the ISC valve connectors. On non-turbo models, unplug the cold start injector connector.

33 Detach the BVSV and the EGR hoses from the throttle body. Detach the vacuum transmitting pipe hoses from the intake chamber. Detach the pressure regulator hose. Detach the power steering air hose. On turbo models, detach the VSV hoses for the FPU. On non-turbo models, detach the diaphragm hose. On turbo models, detach the auxiliary air pipe hose from the vacuum transmitting pipe hose. Detach the No. 1 coolant bypass hose from the ISC valve. On non-turbo models, detach the No. 3 coolant bypass hose from the throttle body. On turbo models, detach the No. 3 coolant bypass hose from the coolant bypass pipe.

34 Remove the EGR pipe mounting bolts (see Chapter 6).

35 Remove the manifold stay mounting bolts.

36 On non-turbo models, remove the throttle body bracket (see Chapter 4).

37 On turbo models, remove the ISC pipe (see Chapter 4).

38 On turbo models, remove the air intake connector mounting bolts (see Chapter 4).

39 On non-turbo models, remove the air intake connector bracket mounting bolts (see Chapter 4).

40 Remove the cold start injector tube (see Chapter 4).

41 Remove the EGR vacuum modulator from the bracket (see Chapter 6).

42 Disconnect the engine wiring harness from the clamps on the intake chamber.

43 Remove the two nuts, five bolts, vacuum transmitting pipes and remove the air intake chamber (see Chapter 4).

44 On turbo models, unplug the cold start injector connector (see Chapter 4).

45 On turbo models, remove the ignition coil and bracket (see Chapter 5).

46 Unplug or disconnect the connectors for the oxygen sensor, the oil pressure sender gauge, the water temperature sensor, the water temperature sender gauge, the cold start injector time switch, the distributor (non-turbo models only), the injectors, the two VSVs, the knock sensor (two connectors on some models), the ground strap from the intake manifold, the diagnostic check connector, the solenoid resistor (turbo models only), the ignition coil (non-turbos only), the igniter (turbos only), the noise filter, the main relay, the starter (terminal 50) and the transmission (see Wiring Diagrams at the end of Chapter 12).

47 Remove the engine wiring harness from all four clamps.

48 On 1987 and 1988 models, remove the fuel pulsation damper (see Chapter 4), the VSV (see Chapter 6) and the No. 1 fuel pipe. On 1989 and later models, remove the banjo bolt (non-turbo models) or the pulsation damper (turbo models) and both crush washers from the delivery pipe (see Chapter 4).

49 On 1989 and later models, remove the banjo bolt and both crush washers from the fuel support.

50 On 1989 and later models, remove the clamp bolt and the No. 1 fuel rail with the VSV (see Chapters 4 and 6).

51 Disconnect the fuel hose from the fuel support (see Chapter 4).

52 Remove the bolt, the banjo bolt, the No. 2 fuel pipe and the crush washers (see Chapter 4).

53 On turbo models, remove the auxiliary air pipe.

54 On non-turbo models, remove the spark plug wires and the distributor (see Chapter 5).

55 On non-turbo models, remove the oil dipstick.

56 On turbo models, remove the turbocharger (see Chapter 4).

57 Remove the exhaust manifold (see Section 6).

58 On non-turbo models, remove the banjo bolts, remove the crush washers and disconnect the No. 4 water bypass hose **(see illustration)**.

59 Disconnect the No. 6 water bypass hose from the water bypass pipe.

60 Remove the water outlet housing bolt and two nuts, the water outlet housing and the gasket **(see illustration)**.

61 Remove the valve covers (see Section 4).

62 Remove the heater hose clamp and the No. 3 cylinder head cover **(see illustrations 12.6a and 12.6b).**

63 Remove the spark plugs (see Chapter 1).

64 Remove the crankshaft pulley (see Section 7), timing belt cover (see Section 8) and the timing belt (see Section 9).

65 Using special tool SST 09043-38100 (or its equivalent), loosen the 14 head bolts in 1/4-turn increments, following the order shown **(see illustration)**. Mark the bolts to ensure that they can be reinstalled in their original locations.

66 Carefully lift the cylinder head straight up from the engine block dowel pins and remove it from the vehicle. If the head is difficult to remove from the block, pry it up with a large screwdriver or pry bar positioned between the head and the water pump **(see illustration)**. Store the head on blocks of wood to prevent damage to the gasket sealing surface. If you're simply switching head gaskets, no further disassem-

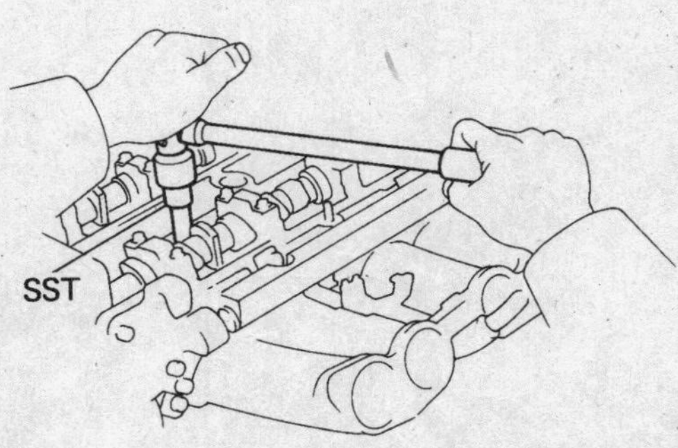

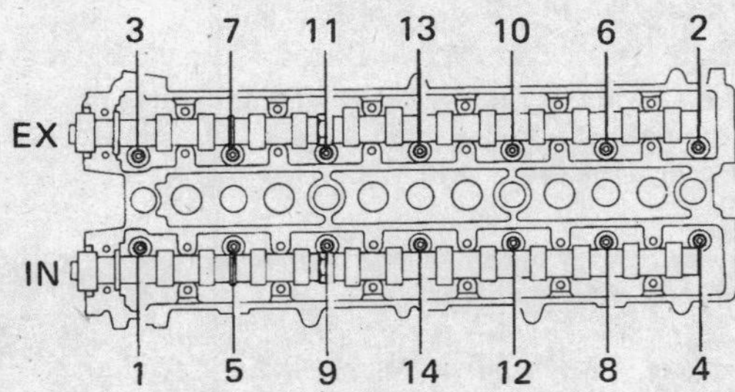

15.65 Using special tool SST 09043-38100 (or its equivalent), Loosen the 14 head bolts in 1/4-turn increments, in the order shown (mark the bolts to ensure that they can be reinstalled in their original locations)

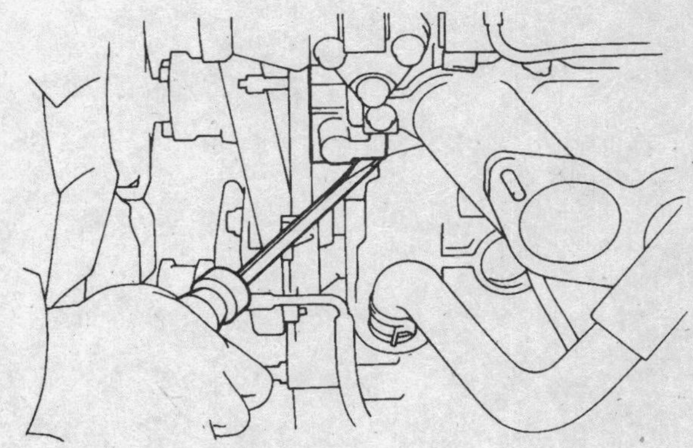

15.66 If the cylinder head is stuck, pry it up with a large screwdriver or prybar positioned between the head and the water pump

bly of the head is necessary.

67 If you're replacing or overhauling the head, remove the No. 2 timing belt cover (see Section 8), the fuel rail (see Chapter 4), the intake manifold (see Section 5), the EGR cooler (see Chapter 6), the camshafts, shims and valve lifters (see Section 12) and the valve train (see Chapter 2, Part C). You'll find head cleaning and inspection procedures and valve service procedures in Chapter 2C.

Installation

68 Refer to Steps 13 through 20.

16 Crankshaft front oil seal - replacement

Refer to illustrations 16.4 and 16.6

1 Disconnect the negative cable from the battery. **Caution:** *If the stereo in your vehicle is equipped with an anti-theft system, refer to the information on page 0-15 at the front of this manual before detaching the cable.*

2 Drain the coolant (Chapter 1) and remove the timing belt covers (see Section 8).

3 Remove the timing belt and the crankshaft sprocket (see Section 9).

4 Use a screwdriver or seal removal tool to pry the crankshaft front oil seal from the timing belt cover. Be careful not to scratch or gouge the crankshaft or the seal bore **(see illustration)**.

5 Apply multi-purpose grease to the entire outer edge and the lip of the new seal before installing it.

6 Drive the new seal into the case bore with a seal driver or a large socket and hammer until it is completely seated **(see illustration)**. If a socket is used, select one with an outside diameter slightly smaller than the outside diameter of the seal. A section of pipe can be used if a socket is not available.

7 Installation is the reverse of removal.

16.4 Pry out the front seal with a screwdriver - be careful not to scratch or gouge the crankshaft!

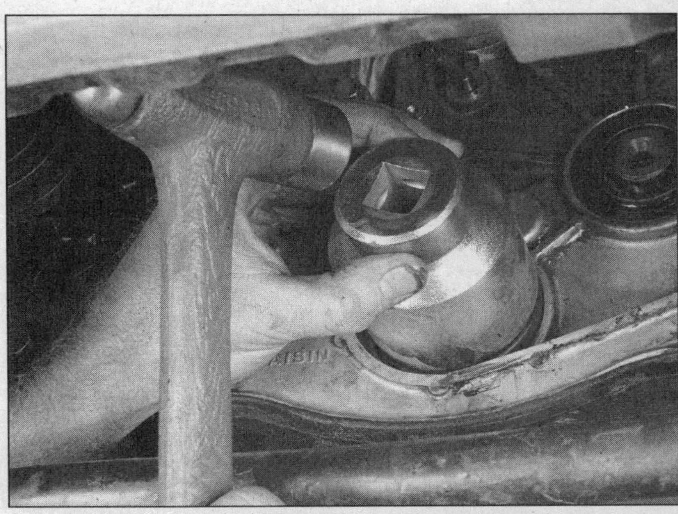

16.6 Drive the new seal into the opening with a large socket and hammer - DO NOT damage the seal in the process!

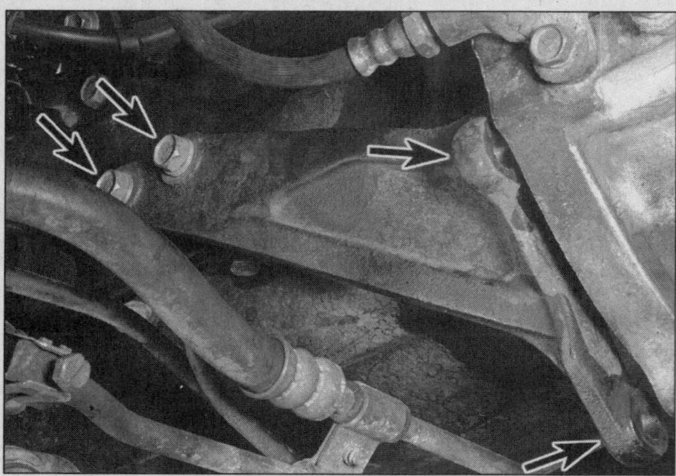

17.5 The two stiffener plates, one on each side of the engine, are held in place with four retaining bolts - two on the block and two on the bellhousing (arrows)

17 Oil pan - removal and installation

Removal

Refer to illustrations 17.5 and 17.7

1 Disconnect the negative cable from the battery, then refer to Chapter 1 and drain the engine oil. **Caution:** *If the stereo in your vehicle is equipped with an anti-theft system, refer to the information on page 0-15 at the front of this manual before detaching the cable.*
2 Raise the vehicle and support it on jackstands for better access to the pan.
3 Take out the bolts and remove the engine undercover.
4 Remove the exhaust pipe clamp bolt from the pipe bracket (see Chapter 4).
5 Take out the four retaining bolts from the stiffener plates and remove them **(see illustration)**. Along with the stiffener plates, slide out the flywheel inspection cover.
6 Attach an engine hoist to the engine removal hooks (see Chapter 2C). Working underneath the vehicle, remove the two bolts which secure the engine mounts to the vehicle and slightly raise the engine.
7 Remove the oil pan retaining bolts. Chances are the pan will remain stuck even after the retaining bolts have been removed. Use a knife blade and hammer to cut around the gasket and break the seal **(see illustration)**.

Installation

8 Use a gasket scraper to remove all traces of old gasket material and sealant from the pan and block.
9 Wipe the sealing surfaces with a cloth saturated with lacquer thinner or acetone. Make sure the bolt holes in the block are clean.
10 Check the oil pan flange for distortion, particularly around the bolt holes. If necessary, place the pan on a block of wood and use a hammer to flatten and restore the gasket surface in the areas of the bolt holes.
11 Install a new gasket on the pan flange, carefully position the pan against the block, install the bolts and tighten them in three steps to the torque listed in this Chapter's Specifications. Start at the center of the pan and work out toward the ends in a spiral pattern.
12 The remaining steps are the reverse of removal.
13 Start the engine and check carefully for oil leaks at the oil pan.

18 Oil pump - removal and installation

Refer to illustration 18.2

1 Remove the oil pan (see Section 17).

17.7 Using a hammer, tap the blade of a knife around the pan, cutting the gasket and breaking the seal - be careful not to damage the block and oil pan mating surfaces

18.2 Use two wrenches to disconnect the oil pump outlet pipe - one to hold the fitting bolt and the other to loosen the tube nut

2 Disconnect the oil pump outlet pipe. Hold the bottom fitting with a wrench, then with a second wrench loosen the tube nut **(see illustration)**.
3 Remove the oil pump mounting bolt, lower the pump and remove it along with the pump driveshaft.
4 Install the pump in the reverse order. Slowly insert the pump while turning the driveshaft so as not to damage the shaft bearing. Tighten the oil pump bolt to the torque listed in this Chapter's Specifications.
5 Install the oil pan.

19 Flywheel/driveplate - removal and installation

1 Remove the transmission (on vehicles with a manual transmission, see Chapter 7A; on vehicles with an automatic transmission, see Chapter 7B).
2 On vehicles with a manual transmission, remove the clutch (see Chapter 8).
3 The flywheel/driveplate is attached to the rear of the crankshaft with six bolts. Loosen and remove the bolts, then separate it from the crankshaft flange.
4 To install the flywheel/driveplate on the crankshaft, use a liquid

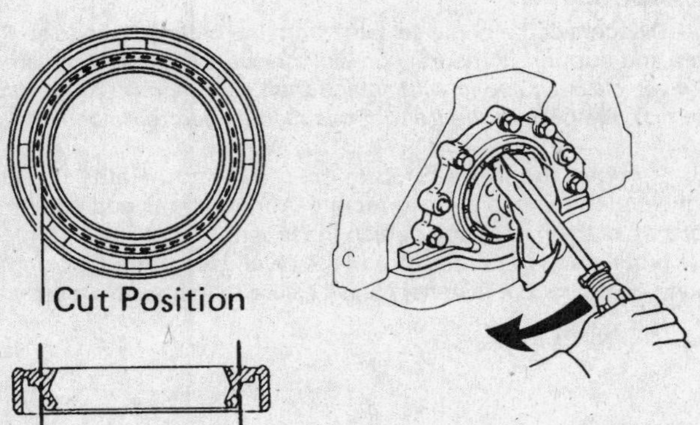

20.4 To remove the rear main oil seal with the retainer installed, use a knife to cut the lip of the old oil seal, then pry it out of the retainer with a screwdriver (tape the tip of the screwdriver to prevent damage to the seal bore)

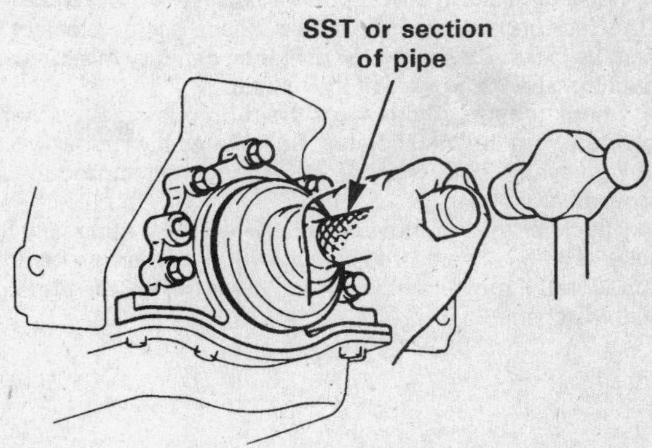

20.7 To install a new seal into a retainer bolted onto the block, you'll need Toyota's special seal installer or a short section of large diameter pipe with an outside diameter slightly smaller than the inside diameter of the seal bore

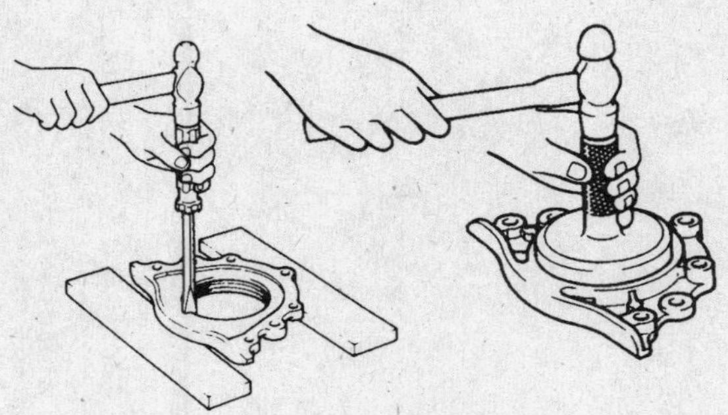

20.11 To remove the old seal from a retainer that's off the block, prop up the retainer on a workbench with a block of wood and tap out the seal with a screwdriver and hammer (use the groove in the bore as a guide for the screwdriver tip - it prevents the tip from slipping and gouging the retainer bore); drive the new seal into place with Toyota's special tool, a large diameter pipe or a block of wood

thread locking compound on the bolts and tighten them gradually, using a criss-cross pattern, to the torque listed in this Chapter's Specifications.

5 Installation is otherwise the reverse of removal.

20 Rear main oil seal - replacement

Note: *If the rear main oil seal is leaking, you can replace it without removing the engine from the vehicle. However, you'll have to remove the transmission and flywheel/driveplate to gain access to the seal, which can be replaced with the seal retainer installed or removed. Although it's quicker, we don't recommend replacing the seal with the retainer installed, because it increases the risk of damaging the seal bore or the new seal.*

1 Remove the transmission (on vehicles with a manual transmission, see Chapter 7A ; on vehicles with an automatic transmission, see Chapter 7B).

2 On vehicles with a manual transmission, remove the clutch (see Chapter 8).

3 Remove the driveplate/flywheel (see Section 19).

Retainer installed

Refer to illustrations 20.4 and 20.7

4 Use a knife to cut the oil seal lip **(see illustration)**.

5 Tape the top of a screwdriver to protect the crankshaft, then pry out the old oil seal.

6 Coat the outside diameter and the seal lips of the new seal with multi-purpose grease.

7 Using a seal driver, a piece of large diameter pipe or a special service tool, install the new oil seal in the retainer **(see illustration)**. The remainder of installation is the reverse of removal.

Retainer removed

Refer to illustration 20.11

8 Remove the bolts that attach the oil pan flange to the bottom of the rear main oil seal retainer.

9 Remove the retainer bolts and detach the retainer from the block. If it's stuck, tap it gently with a soft-face hammer to break the gasket seal. Do not pry it off or the sealing surfaces may be damaged and oil leaks could develop.

10 Use a gasket scraper or putty knife to remove all traces of the old gasket from the block and retainer, then wipe the sealing surfaces with a cloth saturated with acetone or lacquer thinner. Check the retainer and block for nicks and other damage that could allow oil to leak past the gasket. Replace the retainer if it is damaged or distorted.

11 Support the retainer between two blocks of wood and use a screwdriver to knock the old seal out of the retainer **(see illustration)**.

12 Coat the outside diameter of the new oil seal with multi-purpose grease, then use a piece of large diameter pipe, a block of wood or a factory installation tool to drive the new seal into the retainer.

13 Before you install the retainer on the block, apply a thin layer of RTV sealant to the block side of the gasket and to the sealing surface of the retainer. Position the gasket on the block, then install the retainer. Be sure it's correctly positioned over the dowel pins.

14 Install the bolts and, following a criss-cross pattern, tighten them in three steps, to the torque listed in this Chapter's Specifications.

15 The remainder of installation is the reverse of removal.

21 Engine mounts - check and replacement

1 Engine mounts seldom require attention, but broken or deteriorated mounts should be replaced immediately or the added strain placed on the driveline components may cause damage.

Check

2 During the check, the engine must be raised slightly to remove the weight from the mounts.

2B

3 Raise the vehicle and support it securely on jackstands, then position a jack under the engine oil pan. Place a large block of wood between the jack head and the oil pan, then carefully raise the engine just enough to take the weight off the mounts.

4 Check the mounts to see if the rubber is cracked, hardened or separated from the metal plates. Sometimes the rubber will split right down the center. Rubber preservative should be applied to the mounts to slow deterioration.

5 Check for relative movement between the mounts and the engine bracket or frame (use a large screwdriver or prybar to attempt to move the mounts). If movement is noted, lower the engine and tighten the mount fasteners.

Replacement

6 Disconnect the negative cable from the battery, then raise the vehicle and support it securely on jackstands. **Caution:** *If the stereo in your vehicle is equipped with an anti-theft system, refer to the information on page 0-15 at the front of this manual before detaching the cable.*

7 Remove the large bracket-to-mount nut. Raise the engine slightly, then remove the two mount-to-frame bolts and nuts from either side of the mount and detach the mount.

8 Installation is the reverse of removal. Use thread locking compound on the mount fasteners and be sure to tighten them securely.

2C

Chapter 2 Part C
General engine overhaul procedures

Contents

Specifications

General

Displacement

4M-E (1979 and 1980)	156.4 cubic inches
5M-E (1981)	168.4 cubic inches
5M-GE (1982 through 1986)	168.4 cubic inches
7M-GE (1987 on)	180.3 cubic inches
7M-GTE (turbo) (1987 on)	180.3 cubic inches

Cylinder compression pressure

Standard	
1979 through 1981	156 psi
1982 through 1986	164 psi
1987 through 1990	156 psi
1991 and 1992	171 psi
Turbo (1987 on)	142 psi
Minimum	128 psi
Maximum difference between cylinders	14 psi

Oil pressure

1979 and 1980	
At idle	Not available
At 2500 rpm	71 to 85 psi
1981	
At idle	Not available
At 2500 rpm	71 to 85 psi
1982 through 1992	
At idle	
1982 and 1983	3.6 psi
1984 on	4.3 psi
At 3000 rpm	36 to 71 psi

Cylinder head

Warpage limits	
1979 through 1981	
Block surface	0.0020 inch
Intake manifold surface	0.0031 inch
Exhaust manifold surface	0.0039 inch
1982 on	
Cam housing (1982 through 1986)	0.0040 inch
Block and manifold surfaces	0.0039 inch
Rocker arm oil clearance (1979 through 1981)	
Standard	0.0005 to 0.0013 inch
Service limit	0.0024 inch

Valve lifters (1987 on)

Lifter diameter	1.1014 to 1.1018 in
Lifter bore oil clearance	
Standard	0.0006 to 0.0018 inch
Maximum	0.0039 inch

Valves

Minimum valve margin width	
1979 through 1981	
Intake	0.024 inch
Exhaust	0.039 inch
1982 through 1986	
Intake	0.020 inch
Exhaust	0.039 inch
1987 on (intake and exhaust)	0.0020 inch
Valve stem diameter	
1979 through 1981	
Intake	0.3138 to 0.3144 inch
Exhaust	0.3134 to 0.3140 inch
1982 through 1986	
Intake	0.3138 to 0.3144 inch
Exhaust	0.3136 to 0.3142 inch
1987 on	
Intake	0.2350 to 0.2356 inch
Exhaust	0.2348 to 0.2354 inch
Valve stem-to-guide clearance	
1979 through 1981	
Standard	
Intake	0.001 to 0.0024 inch
Exhaust	0.0014 to 0.0028 inch

Service limit	
Intake	0.0039 inch
Exhaust	0.0051 inch
1982 through 1986	
Standard	
Intake	0.0010 to 0.0024 inch
Exhaust	
1982 through 1984	0.0012 to 0.0026 inch
1985	0.0015 to 0.0027 inch
1986	0.0012 to 0.0026 inch
Maximum	
Intake	0.0031 inch
Exhaust	0.0039 inch
1987 on	
Standard	
Intake	0.0010 to 0.0024 inch
Exhaust	0.0012 to 0.0026 inch
Maximum	
Intake	0.0031 inch
Exhaust	0.0039 inch
Valve length	
1979 through 1981	
Standard	
Intake	4.579 inches
Exhaust	4.441 inches
Minimum	
Intake	4.559 inches
Exhaust	4.421 inches
1982 through 1986	
Standard	
Intake	4.232 inches
Exhaust	4.319 inches
Minimum	
Intake	4.212 inches
Exhaust	4.299 inches
1987 on	
Standard	3.8642 inches
Minimum	3.8484 inches
Valve face angle	
1979 through 1981	44.5 degrees
1982	45 degrees
1983 and 1984	45.5 degrees
1985 on	44.5 degrees
Valve seat resurfacing angles	
1979 through 1981	
Intake	25, 45 and 60 degrees
Exhaust	30, 45 and 60 degrees
1982 through 1986	
Intake	30, 45 and 60 degrees
Exhaust	30, 45 and 67.5 degrees
1987 on	30, 45 and 60 degrees
Valve seat width	
1979 through 1986	0.047 to 0.063 inch
1987 on	0.039 to 0.055 inch

Valve springs

Out-of-square limit	
1979 through 1981	0.063 inch
1982 through 1986	0.079 inch
1987 on	0.059 inch
Free length	
1979 through 1981	
Inner	1.768 inches
Outer	1.846 inches
1982 through 1986	
1982	1.886 inches
1983 through 1986	
Intake	1.933 inches
Exhaust	2.067 inches
1987 on	1.6394 inches

Valve springs (continued)

Pressure/length	
1979 through 1981	
Outer	33.1 lbs at 1.630 inches
Inner	13.2 lbs at 1.492 inches
1982 through 1986	
Intake	76.5 to 84.4 lbs @ 1.575 inches
Exhaust	73.4 to 80.9 lbs @ 1.693 inches
1987 on	35 lbs @ 1.378 inches
Installed height	
1979 through 1981	1.630 inches
1982 through 1986	
Intake	1.575 inches
Exhaust	
1982	1.575 inches
1983 through 1986	1.693 inches
1987 on	1.378 inches

Oil pump driveshaft

Endplay	
Standard	0.0024 to 0.0051 inch
Service limit	0.0118 inch
Bearing journal diameter	
Front	1.6126 to 1.6132 inches
Rear	1.2976 to 1.2982 inches
Bearing oil clearance	
Standard	0.0010 to 0.0026 inch
Service limit	0.0031 inch
Engine block deck warpage limit	0.0020 inch

Crankshaft

Endplay	
1979 through 1981	
Standard	0.002 to 0.010 inch
Maximum	0.012 inch
1982 through 1986	
Standard	0.0020 to 0.0098 inch
Maximum	0.012 inch
1987 on	
Standard	0.0020 to 0.0098 inch
Maximum	0.0118 inch
Main journal diameter	
1979 through 1981	2.3617 to 2.3627 inches
1982 through 1986	2.3617 to 2.3627 inches
1987 on	2.3625 to 2.3627 inches
Main journal oil clearance	
1979 through 1981	
Standard	0.0013 to 0.0023 inch
Maximum	0.0031 inch
1982 through 1986	
Standard	0.0013 to 0.0023 inch
Maximum	0.0031 inch
1987	
Standard	0.0012 to 0.0022 inch
Maximum	0.0028 inch
1988 on	
Standard	0.0012 to 0.0019 inch
Maximum	0.0028 inch
Main journal taper and out-of-round limit	
1979 through 1981	0.001 inch
1982 on	0.0008 inch
Thrust washer thickness	
Standard	0.1152 to 0.1171 inch
Oversize type 0.125	0.1176 to 0.1196 inch
Oversize type 0.250 (through 1986)	0.1201 to 0.1220 inch
Runout limit	0.0024 inch

Connecting rods

Journal diameter	
1979 through 1986	2.0463 to 2.0472 inches
1987 on	
No. 0	2.0470 to 2.0472 inches
No. 1	2.0466 to 2.0469 inches
No. 2	2.0463 to 2.0466 inches
Journal taper and out-of-round limit	
1979 through 1981	0.001 inch
1982 on	0.0008 inch
Bearing oil clearance	
1979 through 1986	
Standard	0.0008 to 0.0021 inch
Maximum	0.0031 inch
1987	
Standard	0.0012 to 0.0019 inch
Maximum	0.0028 inch
1988 on	
Standard	0.0008 to 0.0021 inch
Maximum	0.0028 inch
Endplay	
1979 through 1986	
Standard	0.0063 to 0.0117 inch
Maximum	0.0118 inch

Cylinder bore

Diameter	
1979 and 1980	
Standard	3.1492 inches
Maximum	3.1592 inches
1981 through 1988	
Standard	3.2673 inches
Maximum	3.2776 inches
1989 on	
Standard	3.2673 inches
Maximum	3.2772 inches
Taper/out-of-round (maximum)	0.0008 inch

2C

Pistons and rings

Piston diameter (standard)	
1979 and 1980	3.1468 to 3.1488 inches
1981 through 1986	3.2650 to 3.2669 inches
1987	
Non-turbo	3.2646 to 3.2665 inches
Turbo	3.2642 to 3.2661 inches
1988	
Non-turbo	3.2638 to 3.2658 inches
Turbo	3.2642 to 3.2661 inches
1989 on	
Non-turbo	3.2638 to 3.2642 inches
Turbo	3.2642 to 3.2646 inches
Piston-to-bore clearance	
1979 through 1985	0.0020 to 0.0028 inch
1986	0.0024 to 0.0031 inch
1987	
Non-turbo	0.0024 to 0.0031 inch
Turbo	0.0028 to 0.0031 inch
1988	
Non-turbo	0.0020 to 0,0028 inch
Turbo	0.0028 to 0.0035 inch
1989 on	
Non-turbo	0.0031 to 0.0039 inch
Turbo	0.0028 to 0.0035 inch
Piston ring end gap	
1979 through 1981	
No. 1 (top)	0.0039 to 0.0110 inch
No. 2 (middle)	0.0060 to 0.0118 inch

Pistons and rings (continued)

1979 through 1981 (continued)	
Oil	
With wire	0.0079 to 0.0276 inch
Without wire	0.0039 to 0.0236 inch
1982 and 1983	
No. 1 (top)	0.0083 to 0.0146 inch
No. 2 (middle)	0.0067 to 0.0209 inch
Oil ring	0.0079 to 0.0276 inch
1984	
No. 1 (top)	0.0114 to 0.0185 inch
No. 2 (middle)	0.0098 to 0.0217 inch
Oil ring	0.0067 to 0.0335 inch
1985	
No. 1 (top)	0.0091 to 0.0161 inch
No. 2 (middle)	0.0098 to 0.0217 inch
Oil ring	0.0067 to 0.0335 inch
1986	
No. 1 (top)	0.0114 to 0.0185 inch
No. 2 (middle)	0.0098 to 0.0217 inch
Oil ring	0.0571 inch
1987	
No. 1 (top)	
Non-turbo	0.0091 to 0.0150 inch
Turbo	0.0114 to 0.0173 inch
No. 2	0.0098 to 0.0209 inch
Oil ring	
Non-turbo	0.0039 to 0.0201 inch
Turbo	0.0039 to 0.0220 inch
1988	
No. 1 (top)	
Non-turbo	0.0091 to 0.0150 inch
Turbo	0.0114 to 0.0173 inch
No. 2	0.0098 to 0.0209 inch
Oil ring	
Non-turbo	0.0039 to 0.0157 inch
Turbo	0.0039 to 0.0173 inch
Piston ring side clearance	
No. 1 (top)	0.0012 to 0.0028 inch
No. 2 (middle)	0.0008 to 0.0024 inch
Piston pin diameter	
1979 through 1981	Not available
1982 through 1987	0.8660 to 0.8665 inch
1988 through 1992	Not available

Torque specifications

	Ft-lbs
Connecting rod cap nuts	
1979 through 1981	31 to 34
1982 through 1986	33
1987 on	47
Main bearing cap bolts	
1979 through 1981	72 to 78
1982 on	75
Oil pump driveshaft bolt	13 to 18
Timing belt case	
8 mm bolt/nut	11 to 16
10 mm bolt	22 to 32

1 General information

Included in this portion of Chapter 2 are the general overhaul procedures for the cylinder head(s) and internal engine components.

The information ranges from advice concerning preparation for an overhaul and the purchase of replacement parts to detailed, step-by-step procedures covering removal and installation of internal engine components and the inspection of parts.

The following Sections have been written based on the assumption that the engine has been removed from the vehicle. For information concerning in-vehicle engine repair, as well as removal and installation of the external components necessary for the overhaul, see Chapter 2A or 2B and Section 7 of this Part.

The Specifications included in this Part are only those necessary for the inspection and overhaul procedures which follow. Refer to Parts A and B for additional Specifications.

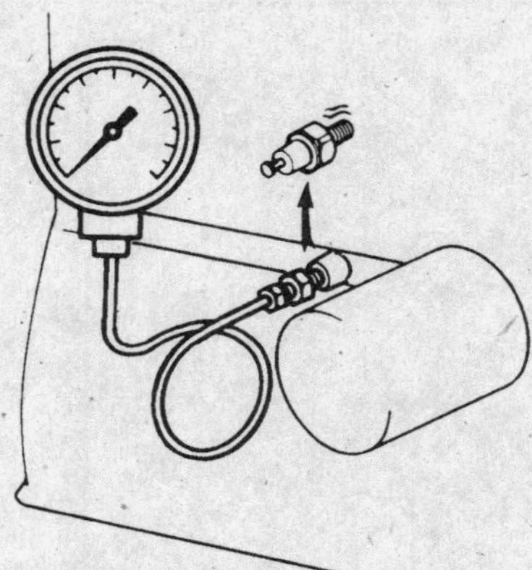

2.4a On 1986 and earlier models, the oil pressure sending unit is located behind the oil filter on the right side of the block

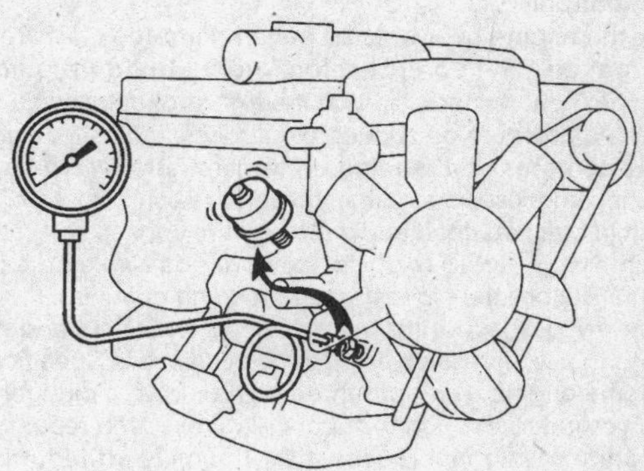

2.4b On 1987 and later models, the oil pressure sending unit is located in front of the oil filter on the right side of the block

2 Engine overhaul - general information

Refer to illustrations 2.4a and 2.4b

It's not always easy to determine when, or if, an engine should be completely overhauled, as a number of factors must be considered.

High mileage is not necessarily an indication that an overhaul is needed, while low mileage doesn't preclude the need for an overhaul. Frequency of servicing is probably the most important consideration. An engine that's had regular and frequent oil and filter changes, as well as other required maintenance, will most likely give many thousands of miles of reliable service. Conversely, a neglected engine may require an overhaul very early in its life.

Excessive oil consumption is an indication that piston rings, valve seals and/or valve guides are in need of attention. Make sure that oil leaks aren't responsible before deciding that the rings and/or guides are bad. Perform a cylinder compression check to determine the extent of the work required (see Section 3).

Check the oil pressure: Unscrew the oil pressure sending unit **(see illustrations)** and hook up an oil pressure gauge in its place. Measure the oil pressure with the engine at its normal operating temperature. Compare your measurements to the oil pressure listed in this Chapter's Specifications. If it's extremely low, the bearings and/or oil pump are probably worn out.

Loss of power, rough running, knocking or metallic engine noises, excessive valve train noise and high fuel consumption rates may also point to the need for an overhaul, especially if they're all present at the same time. If a complete tune-up doesn't remedy the situation, major mechanical work is the only solution.

An engine overhaul involves restoring the internal parts to the specifications of a new engine. During an overhaul, the piston rings are replaced and the cylinder walls are reconditioned (rebored and/or honed). If a rebore is done by an automotive machine shop, new oversize pistons will also be installed. The main bearings, connecting rod bearings and camshaft bearings are generally replaced with new ones and, if necessary, the crankshaft may be reground to restore the journals. Generally, the valves are serviced as well, since they're usually in less-than-perfect condition at this point. While the engine is being overhauled, other components, such as the distributor, starter and alternator, can be rebuilt as well. The end result should be a like-new engine that will give many trouble-free miles. **Note:** *Critical cooling system components such as the hoses, drivebelts, thermostat and water pump MUST be replaced with new parts when an engine is overhauled. The radiator should be checked carefully to ensure that it isn't clogged or leaking (see Chapter 1). Also, we don't recommend overhauling the oil pump - always install a new one when an engine is rebuilt.*

Before beginning the engine overhaul, read through the entire procedure to familiarize yourself with the scope and requirements of the job. Overhauling an engine isn't difficult if you follow all of the instructions carefully, have the necessary tools and equipment and pay close attention to all specifications; however, it is time consuming. Plan on the vehicle being tied up for a minimum of two weeks, especially if parts must be taken to an automotive machine shop for repair or reconditioning. Check on availability of parts and make sure that any necessary special tools and equipment are obtained in advance. Most work can be done with typical hand tools, although a number of precision measuring tools are required for inspecting parts to determine if they must be replaced. Often an automotive machine shop will handle the inspection of parts and offer advice concerning reconditioning and replacement. **Note:** *Always wait until the engine has been completely disassembled and all components, especially the engine block, have been inspected before deciding what service and repair operations must be performed by an automotive machine shop. Since the block's condition will be the major factor to consider when determining whether to overhaul the original engine or buy a rebuilt one, never purchase parts or have machine work done on other components until the block has been thoroughly inspected. As a general rule, time is the primary cost of an overhaul, so it doesn't pay to install worn or substandard parts.*

As a final note, to ensure maximum life and minimum trouble from a rebuilt engine, everything must be assembled with care in a spotlessly clean environment.

3 Compression check

Refer to illustration 3.6

1 A compression check will tell you what mechanical condition the upper end (pistons, rings, valves, head gaskets) of your engine is in. Specifically, it can tell you if the compression is down due to leakage caused by worn piston rings, defective valves and seats or a blown head gasket. **Note:** *The engine must be at normal operating temperature and the battery must be fully charged for this check. Also, if the engine is equipped with a carburetor, the choke valve must be all the way open to get an accurate compression reading (if the engine's warm, the choke should be open).*

2 Begin by cleaning the area around the spark plugs before you remove them (compressed air should be used, if available, otherwise a small brush or even a bicycle tire pump will work). The idea is to prevent dirt from getting into the cylinders as the compression check is being done.

3 Remove all of the spark plugs from the engine (see Chapter 1).

4 Block the throttle wide open.

5 Detach the coil wire from the center of the distributor cap and ground it on the engine block. Use a jumper wire with alligator clips on each end to ensure a good ground. The fuel pump circuit should also be disabled (see Chapter 4).

6 Install the compression gauge in the number one spark plug hole **(see illustration)**.

7 Crank the engine over at least seven compression strokes and watch the gauge. The compression should build up quickly in a healthy engine. Low compression on the first stroke, followed by gradually increasing pressure on successive strokes, indicates worn piston rings. A low compression reading on the first stroke, which doesn't build up during successive strokes, indicates leaking valves or a blown head gasket (a cracked head could also be the cause).
Deposits on the undersides of the valve heads can also cause low compression. Record the highest gauge reading obtained.

8 Repeat the procedure for the remaining cylinders and compare the results to the compression listed in this Chapter's Specifications.

9 Add some engine oil (about three squirts from a plunger-type oil can) to each cylinder, through the spark plug hole, and repeat the test.

10 If the compression increases after the oil is added, the piston rings are definitely worn. If the compression doesn't increase significantly, the leakage is occurring at the valves or head gasket. Leakage past the valves may be caused by burned valve seats and/or faces or warped, cracked or bent valves.

11 If two adjacent cylinders have equally low compression, there's a strong possibility that the head gasket between them is blown. The appearance of coolant in the combustion chambers or the crankcase would verify this condition.

12 If one cylinder is 20 percent lower than the others, and the engine has a slightly rough idle, a worn exhaust lobe on the camshaft could be the cause.

13 If the compression is unusually high, the combustion chambers are probably coated with carbon deposits. If that's the case, the cylinder head(s) should be removed and decarbonized.

14 If compression is way down or varies greatly between cylinders, it would be a good idea to have a leak-down test performed by an automotive repair shop. This test will pinpoint exactly where the leakage is occurring and how severe it is.

3.6 To ensure accurate readings, use a compression gauge with a threaded fitting which screws into the spark plug holes;

4 Engine removal - methods and precautions

If you've decided that an engine must be removed for overhaul or major repair work, several preliminary steps should be taken.

Locating a suitable place to work is extremely important. Adequate work space, along with storage space for the vehicle, will be needed. If a shop or garage isn't available, at the very least a flat, level, clean work surface made of concrete or asphalt is required.

Cleaning the engine compartment and engine before beginning the removal procedure will help keep tools clean and organized.

An engine hoist or A-frame will also be necessary. Make sure the equipment is rated in excess of the combined weight of the engine and accessories. Safety is of primary importance, considering the potential hazards involved in lifting the engine out of the vehicle.

If the engine is being removed by a novice, a helper should be available. Advice and aid from someone more experienced would also be helpful. There are many instances when one person cannot simultaneously perform all of the operations required when lifting the engine out of the vehicle.

Plan the operation ahead of time. Arrange for or obtain all of the tools and equipment you'll need prior to beginning the job. Some of the equipment necessary to perform engine removal and installation safely and with relative ease are (in addition to an engine hoist) a heavy duty floor jack, complete sets of wrenches and sockets as described in the front of this manual, wooden blocks and plenty of rags and cleaning solvent for mopping up spilled oil,
coolant and gasoline. If the hoist must be rented, make sure that you arrange for it in advance and perform all of the operations possible without it beforehand. This will save you money and time.

Plan for the vehicle to be out of use for quite a while. A machine shop will be required to perform some of the work which the do-it-yourselfer can't accomplish without special equipment. These shops often have a busy schedule, so it would be a good idea to consult them before removing the engine in order to accurately estimate the amount of time required to rebuild or repair components that may need work.

Always be extremely careful when removing and installing the engine. Serious injury can result from careless actions. Plan ahead, take your time and a job of this nature, although major, can be accomplished successfully. **Warning:** *The air conditioning system is under high pressure. Do not loosen any fittings or remove any components until after the system has been discharged. Air conditioning refrigerant should be properly discharged into an EPA-approved container at a dealer service department or an automotive air conditioning repair facility. Always wear eye protection when disconnecting air conditioning system fittings.*

5 Engine - removal and installation

Removal

Refer to illustrations 5.5, 5.19a, 5.19b and 5.24

1 Relieve the fuel system pressure (see Chapter 4), then disconnect the negative cable from the battery. **Caution:** *If the stereo in your vehicle is equipped with an anti-theft system, refer to the information on page 0-15 at the front of this manual before detaching the cable.*

2 Cover the fenders and cowl and remove the hood (see Chapter 11). Special pads are available to protect the fenders, but an old bedspread or blanket will also work.

3 Remove the air cleaner housing and intake ducts (see Chapter 4).

4 Drain the cooling system (see Chapter 1).

5 Label the vacuum lines, emissions system hoses, wiring connectors, ground straps and fuel lines, to ensure correct reinstallation, then detach them. Pieces of masking tape with numbers or letters written on them work well **(see illustration)**. If there's any possibility of confusion, make a sketch of the engine compartment and clearly label the lines, hoses and wires.

6 Label and detach all coolant hoses from the engine (see Chapter 3).

7 Remove the cooling fan, shroud and radiator (see Chapter 3).

8 Remove the drivebelts (see Chapter 1).

9 **Warning:** *Gasoline is extremely flammable, so take extra precautions when you work on any part of the fuel system. Don't smoke or allow open flames or bare light bulbs near the work area, and don't work in a garage where a natural gas-type appliance (such as a water heater or clothes dryer) with a pilot light is present. If you spill any fuel on your skin, rinse it off immediately with soap and water. When you perform any kind of work on the fuel system, wear safety glasses and have a Class B type fire extinguisher on hand.*

10 Disconnect the accelerator cable (see Chapter 4) and TV linkage/speed control cable (see Chapter 7), if equipped, from the engine.

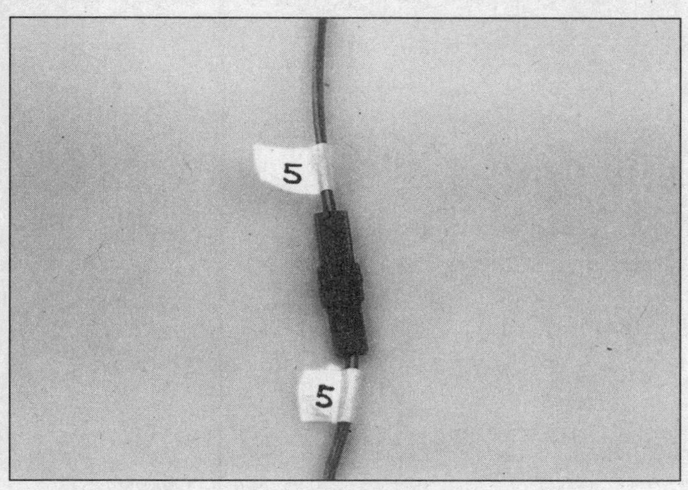

5.5 Label each wire before unplugging the connector

5.19a Typical front lifting hook

5.19b Typical rear lifting hook

5.24 Slowly raise the engine and slide it forward to separate it from the transmission - make sure everything clears and all components have been disconnected

11 Unbolt the power steering pump (see Chapter 10). Leave the lines/hoses attached and make sure the pump is kept in an upright position in the engine compartment (use wire or rope to restrain it out of the way).
12 On air-conditioned models, unbolt the compressor (see Chapter 3) and set it aside. Do not disconnect the hoses.
13 Drain the engine oil (see Chapter 1) and remove the filter.
14 Remove the starter motor (see Chapter 5).
15 Remove the alternator (see Chapter 5).
16 Unbolt the exhaust system from the engine (see Chapter 4).
17 If you're working on a vehicle with an automatic transmission, remove the torque converter-to-driveplate fasteners (see Chapter 7B).
18 Support the transmission with a jack. Position a block of wood between them to prevent damage to the transmission. Special transmission jacks with safety chains are available - use one if possible.
19 Attach an engine sling or a length of chain to the lifting brackets on the engine **(see illustrations)**.
20 Roll the hoist into position and connect the sling to it. Take up the slack in the sling or chain, but don't lift the engine. **Warning:** *DO NOT place any part of your body under the engine when it's supported only by a hoist or other lifting device.*
21 Remove the transmission-to-engine block bolts.
22 Remove the engine mount-to-frame bolts.
23 Recheck to be sure nothing is still connecting the engine to the transmission or vehicle. Disconnect anything still remaining.
24 Raise the engine slightly. Carefully work it forward to separate it from the transmission. If you're working on a vehicle with an automatic transmission, be sure the torque converter stays in the transmission (clamp a pair of vise-grips to the housing to keep the converter from sliding out). If you're working on a vehicle with a manual transmission, the input shaft must be completely disengaged from the clutch. Slowly raise the engine out of the engine compartment **(see illustration)**. Check carefully to make sure nothing is hanging up.
25 Remove the flywheel/driveplate and mount the engine on an engine stand.

Installation

26 Check the engine and transmission mounts. If they're worn or damaged, replace them.
27 If you're working on a manual transmission equipped vehicle, install the clutch and pressure plate (see Chapter 7A). Now is a good time to install a new clutch.
28 Carefully lower the engine into the engine compartment - make sure the engine mounts line up.
29 If you're working on an automatic transmission equipped vehicle, guide the torque converter into the crankshaft following the procedure outlined in Chapter 7B.
30 If you're working on a manual transmission equipped vehicle, apply a dab of high-temperature grease to the input shaft and guide it into the crankshaft pilot bearing until the bellhousing is flush with the engine block.
31 Install the transmission-to-engine bolts and tighten them securely. **Caution:** *DO NOT use the bolts to force the transmission and engine together!*

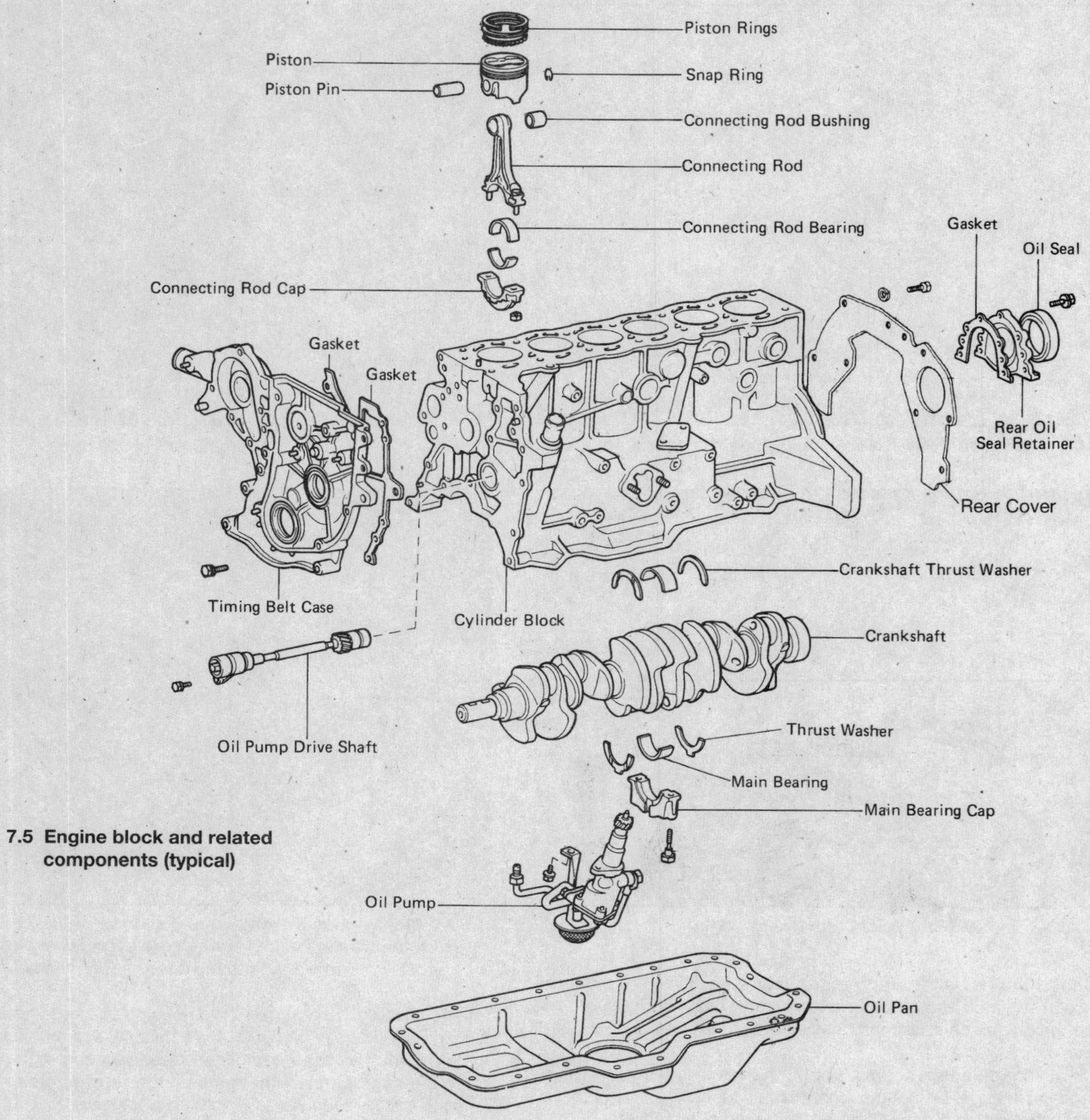

7.5 Engine block and related components (typical)

32 Reinstall the remaining components in the reverse order of removal.

33 Add coolant, oil, power steering and transmission fluid as needed.

34 Run the engine and check for leaks and proper operation of all accessories, then install the hood and test drive the vehicle.

35 Have the air conditioning system recharged and leak tested.

6 Engine rebuilding alternatives

The do-it-yourselfer is faced with a number of options when performing an engine overhaul. The decision to replace the engine block, piston/connecting rod assemblies and crankshaft depends on a number of factors, with the number one consideration being the condition of the block. Other considerations are cost, access to machine shop facilities, parts availability, time required to complete the project and the extent of prior mechanical experience on the part of the do-it-yourselfer.

Some of the rebuilding alternatives include:

Individual parts - If the inspection procedures reveal that the engine block and most engine components are in reusable condition, purchasing individual parts may be the most economical alternative. The block, crankshaft and piston/connecting rod assemblies should all be inspected carefully. Even if the block shows little wear, the cylinder bores should be surface honed.

Short block - A short block consists of an engine block with a crankshaft and piston/connecting rod assemblies already installed. All new bearings are incorporated and all clearances will be correct. The existing camshaft, valve train components, cylinder head(s) and external parts can be bolted to the short block with little or no machine shop work necessary.

Long block - A long block consists of a short block plus an oil pump, oil pan, cylinder head, valve cover(s), camshaft(s) and valve train components, timing sprockets and chain or gears and timing cover. All components are installed with new bearings, seals and gaskets incorporated throughout. The installation of manifolds and external parts is all that's necessary.

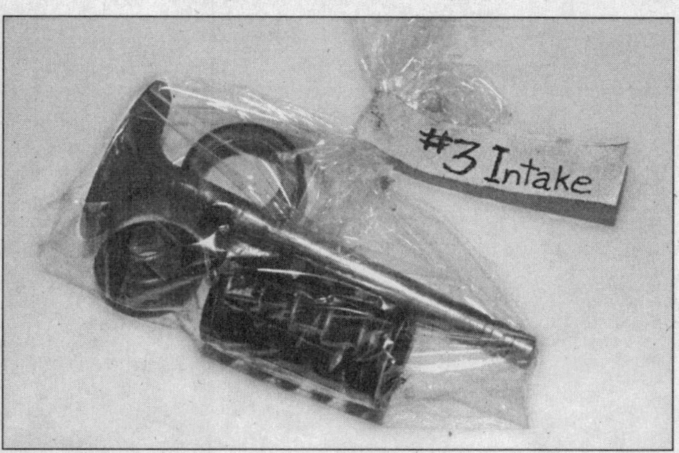

8.2 A small plastic bag, with an appropriate label, can be used to store the valve train components so they can be kept together and reinstalled in the original position

8.3 Compress the valve spring, then remove the keepers with a pair of needle nose pliers, a pair of tweezers or a magnet

Give careful thought to which alternative is best for you and discuss the situation with local automotive machine shops, auto parts dealers and experienced rebuilders before ordering or purchasing replacement parts.

7 Engine overhaul - disassembly sequence

Refer to illustration 7.5

1 It's much easier to disassemble and work on the engine if it's mounted on a portable engine stand. A stand can often be rented quite cheaply from an equipment rental yard. Before the engine is mounted on a stand, the flywheel/driveplate should be removed from the engine.

2 If a stand isn't available, it's possible to disassemble the engine with it blocked up on the floor. Be extra careful not to tip or drop the engine when working without a stand.

3 If you're going to obtain a rebuilt engine, all external components must come off first, to be transferred to the replacement engine, just as they will if you're doing a complete engine overhaul yourself. These include:

Alternator and brackets
Emissions control components
Distributor, spark plug wires and spark plugs
Thermostat and housing cover
Water pump
EFI components
Intake and exhaust manifolds
Oil filter and oil pressure sending unit
Engine mounts
Clutch and flywheel/driveplate
Engine rear plate

Note: *When removing the external components from the engine, pay close attention to details that may be helpful or important during installation. Note the installed position of gaskets, seals, spacers, pins, brackets, washers, bolts and other small items.*

4 If you're obtaining a short block, which consists of the engine block, crankshaft, pistons and connecting rods all assembled, then the cylinder head, oil pan and oil pump will have to be removed as well. See Engine rebuilding alternatives for additional information regarding the different possibilities to be considered.

5 If you're planning a complete overhaul, the engine must be disassembled and the internal components removed in the following order:

Valve cover(s)
Intake and exhaust manifolds
Rocker arms (1979 through 1986 models)
Valve lifters and shims (1987 and later models)
Cylinder head
Timing cover
Timing chain, or belt, and sprockets
Camshaft(s)
Oil pan
Oil pump
Piston/connecting rod assemblies
Crankshaft and main bearings

The accompanying exploded view shows a typical bottom end **(see illustration)**. Exploded views of the cylinder heads are in Chapters 2A and 2B.

6 Before beginning the disassembly and overhaul procedures, make sure the following items are available. Also, refer to Engine overhaul - reassembly sequence for a list of tools and materials needed for engine reassembly.

Common hand tools
Small cardboard boxes or plastic bags for storing parts
Gasket scraper
Ridge reamer
Vibration damper puller
Micrometers
Telescoping gauges
Dial indicator set
Valve spring compressor
Cylinder surfacing hone
Piston ring groove cleaning tool
Electric drill motor
Tap and die set
Wire brushes
Oil gallery brushes
Cleaning solvent

8 Cylinder head - disassembly

Refer to illustrations 8.2, 8.3 and 8.4

1 Remove the cylinder head (for 1979 through 1981 models, see Chapter 2A; for 1982 and later models, see Chapter 2B). On 1982 through 1986 models, remove the camshaft housings, rocker arms and lash adjusters (see Chapter 2B); on 1987 and later models, remove the camshafts, valve lifters and shims (see Chapter 2B).

2 Before the valves are removed, arrange to label and store them, along with their related components, so they can be kept separate and reinstalled in the same valve guides from which they're removed **(see illustration)**.

3 Compress the springs on the first valve with a spring compressor and remove the keepers **(see illustration)**. Carefully release the valve spring compressor and remove the retainer, the spring and the spring seat (if used).

2C

8.4 If the valve won't pull through the guide, deburr the edge of the stem end and the area around the top of the keeper groove with a file or whetstone

9.12 A dial indicator can be used to determine the valve stem-to-guide clearance (move the valve stem as indicated by the arrows)

4 Pull the valve out of the head, then remove the oil seal from the guide. If the valve binds in the guide (won't pull through), push it back into the head and deburr the area around the keeper groove with a fine file or whetstone **(see illustration)**.

5 Repeat the procedure for the remaining valves. Remember to keep all the parts for each valve together so they can be reinstalled in the same locations.

6 Once the valves and related components have been removed and stored in an organized manner, the head should be thoroughly cleaned and inspected. If a complete engine overhaul is being done, finish the engine disassembly procedures before beginning the cylinder head cleaning and inspection process.

9 Cylinder head - cleaning and inspection

1 Thorough cleaning of the cylinder head(s) and related valve train components, followed by a detailed inspection, will enable you to decide how much valve service work must be done during the engine overhaul. **Note:** *If the engine was severely overheated, the cylinder head is probably warped (see Step 12).*

Cleaning

2 Scrape all traces of old gasket material and sealing compound off the head gasket, intake manifold and exhaust manifold sealing surfaces. Be very careful not to gouge the cylinder head. Special gasket removal solvents that soften gaskets and make removal much easier are available at auto parts stores.

9.10 Check the cylinder head gasket surface for warpage by trying to slip a feeler gauge under the straightedge (to determine what size feeler gauge to use, see the maximum allowable warpage listed in this Chapter's Specifications)

3 Remove all built up scale from the coolant passages.

4 Run a stiff wire brush through the various holes to remove deposits that may have formed in them.

5 Run an appropriate size tap into each of the threaded holes to remove corrosion and thread sealant that may be present. If compressed air is available, use it to clear the holes of debris produced by this operation. **Warning:** *Wear eye protection when using compressed air!*

6 Clean the cylinder head with solvent and dry it thoroughly. Compressed air will speed the drying process and ensure that all holes and recessed areas are clean. **Note:** *Decarbonizing chemicals are available and may prove very useful when cleaning cylinder heads and valve train components. They are very caustic and should be used with caution. Be sure to follow the instructions on the container.*

7 Clean all the valve springs, spring seats, keepers and retainers with solvent and dry them thoroughly. Do the components from one valve at a time to avoid mixing up the parts.

8 Scrape off any heavy deposits that may have formed on the valves, then use a motorized wire brush to remove deposits from the valve heads and stems. Again, make sure the valves don't get mixed up.

Inspection

Note: *Be sure to perform all of the following inspection procedures before concluding that machine shop work is required. Make a list of the items that need attention.*

Cylinder head

Refer to illustrations 9.10 and 9.12

9 Inspect the head very carefully for cracks, evidence of coolant leakage and other damage. If cracks are found, check with an automotive machine shop concerning repair. If repair isn't possible, a new cylinder head should be obtained.

10 Using a straightedge and feeler gauge, check the head gasket mating surface for warpage **(see illustration)**. If the warpage exceeds the limit listed in this Chapter's Specifications, it can be resurfaced at an automotive machine shop.

11 Examine the valve seats in each of the combustion chambers. If they're pitted, cracked or burned, the head will require valve service that's beyond the scope of the home mechanic.

12 Check the valve stem-to-guide clearance by measuring the lateral movement of the valve stem with a dial indicator attached securely to the head **(see illustration)**. The valve must be in the guide and approximately 1/16-inch off the seat. The total valve stem movement in-

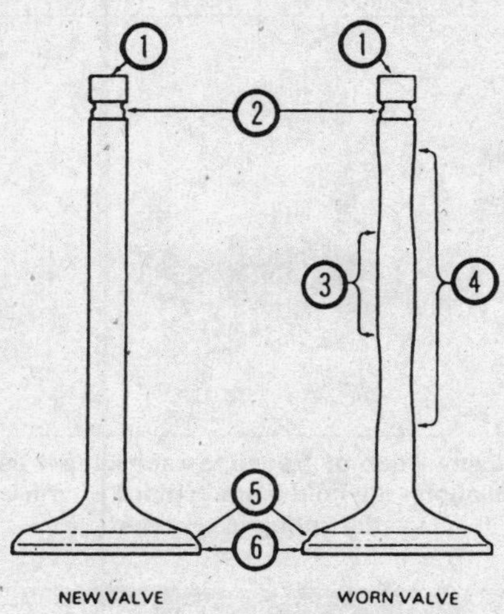

9.13 Check for valve wear at the points shown here

1 *Valve tip*
2 *Keeper groove*
3 *Stem (least worn area)*
4 *Stem (most worn area)*
5 *Valve face*
6 *Margin*

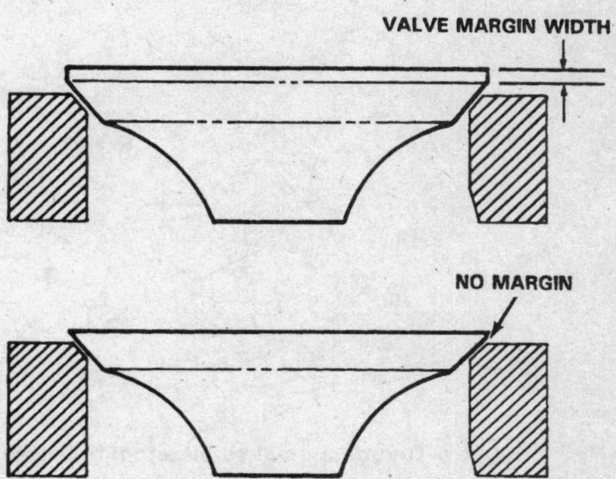

9.14 The margin width on each valve must be as specified (if no margin exists, the valve cannot be reused)

dicated by the gauge needle must be divided by two to obtain the actual clearance. After this is done, if there's still some doubt regarding the condition of the valve guides they should be checked by an automotive machine shop (the cost should be minimal).

Valves

Refer to illustrations 9.13 and 9.14

13 Carefully inspect each valve face for uneven wear, deformation, cracks, pits and burned areas **(see illustration)**. Check the valve stem for scuffing and galling and the neck for cracks. Rotate the valve and check for any obvious indication that it's bent. Look for pits and excessive wear on the end of the stem. The presence of any of these conditions indicates the need for valve service by an automotive machine shop.

14 Measure the margin width on each valve **(see illustration)**. Any valve with a margin narrower than specified will have to be replaced with a new one.

Valve components

Refer to illustrations 9.15 and 9.16

15 Check each valve spring for wear (on the ends) and pits. Measure the free length and compare it to the Specifications **(see illustration)**. Any springs that are shorter than specified have sagged and should not be reused. The tension of all springs should be checked with a special fixture before deciding that they're suitable for use in a rebuilt engine (take the springs to an automotive machine shop for this check).

16 Stand each spring on a flat surface and check it for squareness **(see illustration)**. If any of the springs are distorted or sagged, replace all of them with new parts.

17 Check the spring retainers and keepers for obvious wear and cracks. Any questionable parts should be replaced with new ones, as extensive damage will occur if they fail during engine operation.

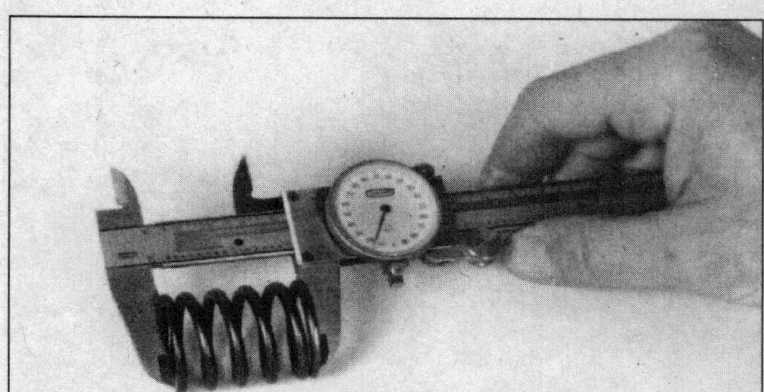

9.15 Measure the free length of each valve spring with a dial or vernier caliper

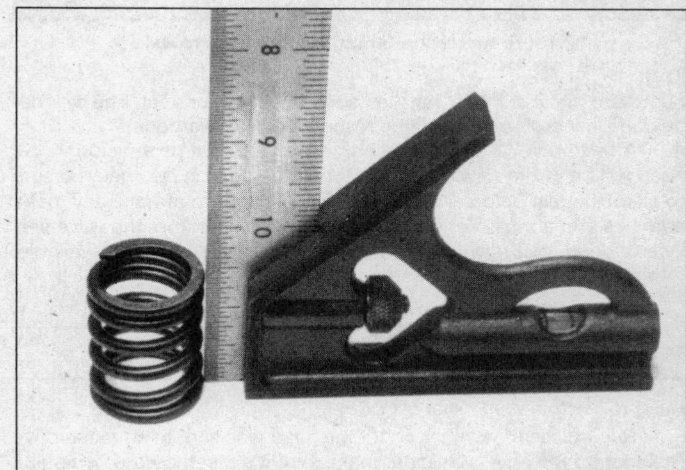

9.16 Check each valve spring for squareness

10 Valves - servicing

1 Because of the complex nature of the job and the special tools and equipment needed, servicing of the valves, the valve seats and the valve guides, commonly known as a valve job, should be done by a professional.

2 The home mechanic can remove and disassemble the head, do the initial cleaning and inspection, then reassemble and deliver it to a dealer service department or an automotive machine shop for the actual service work. Doing the inspection will enable you to see what condition the head and valvetrain components are in and will ensure that you know what work and new parts are required when dealing with an automotive machine shop.

3 The dealer service department, or automotive machine shop, will remove the valves and springs, recondition or replace the valves and valve seats, recondition the valve guides, check and replace the valve springs, spring retainers or rotators and keepers (as necessary), replace the valve seals with new ones, reassemble the valve compo-

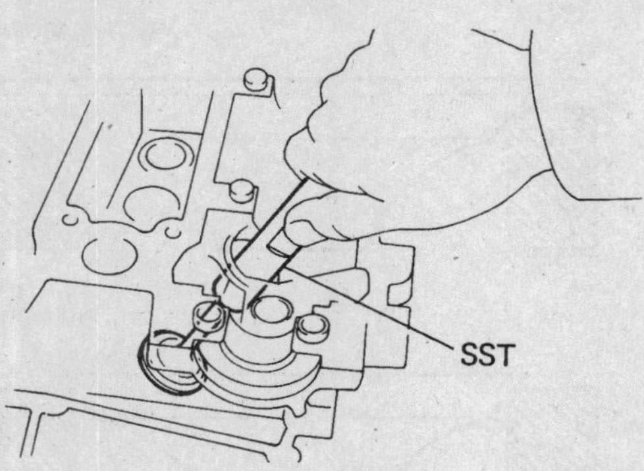

11.4 You can use a Toyota special service tool to install the valve guide seals over the valve guide, or you can use a small deep socket as long as it's long enough to clear the valve stem but small enough in diameter to push the seal down over the guide

12.1a Remove the timing belt case (arrows) . . .

nents and make sure the installed spring height is correct. The cylinder head gasket surface will also be resurfaced if it's warped.

4 After the valve job has been performed by a professional, the head will be in like-new condition. When the head is returned, be sure to clean it again before installation on the engine to remove any metal particles and abrasive grit that may still be present from the valve service or head resurfacing operations. Use compressed air, if available, to blow out all the oil holes and passages.

11 Cylinder head - reassembly

Refer to illustrations 11.4 and 11.6

1 Regardless of whether or not the head was sent to an automotive repair shop for valve servicing, make sure it's clean before beginning reassembly.

2 If the head was sent out for valve servicing, the valves and related components will already be in place. Begin the reassembly procedure with Step 8.

3 Starting at one end of the head, apply moly-base grease or clean engine oil to each valve stem and install the valve.

4 Lubricate the lip of each valve guide seal, carefully slide it over the tip of the valve, then slide it all the way down the stem to the guide. Using a hammer and a deep socket or seal installation tool, gently tap the seal into place until it's completely seated on the guide **(see illustration)**. Don't twist or cock a seal during installation or it won't seal properly against the valve stem. **Note:** *The seals for intake and exhaust valves are different - don't mix them up.*

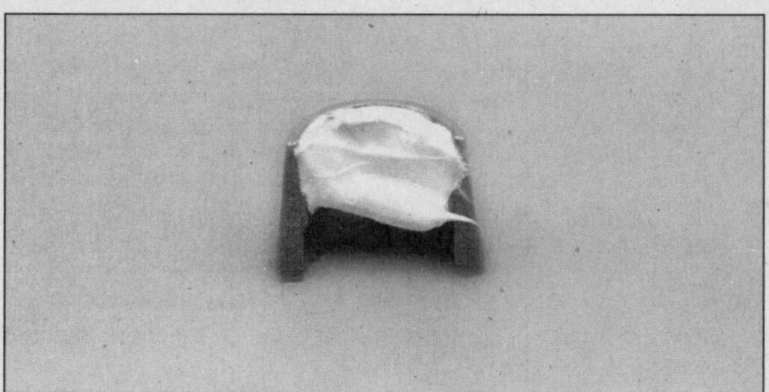

11.6 Apply a small dab of grease to each keeper as shown here before installation - it'll hold them in place on the valve stem as the spring is released

12.1b . . . and lightly tap the case to free it from the block - DO NOT attempt to pry it off or damage to the sealing surfaces and oil leaks may develop

5 Drop the spring seat or shim(s) over the valve guide and set the valve spring and retainer in place.

6 Compress the spring with a valve spring compressor and carefully install the keepers in the upper groove, then slowly release the compressor and make sure the keepers seat properly. Apply a small dab of grease to each keeper to hold it in place if necessary **(see illustration)**.

7 Repeat Steps 3 through 6 for each of the valves. Be sure to return the components to their original locations - don't mix them up!

8 Check the installed valve spring height with a ruler graduated in 1/32-inch increments or a dial caliper. If the head was sent out for service work, the installed height should be correct (but don't automatically assume that it is). The measurement is taken from the top of each spring seat or shim(s) to the bottom of the retainer. If the height is greater than the figure listed in this Chapter's Specifications, shims can be added under the springs to correct it. **Caution:** *Don't, under any circumstances, shim the springs to the point where the installed height is less than specified.*

9 For 1979 through 1981 models, the remainder of cylinder head assembly is in Chapter 2A. For 1982 and later models, it's in Chapter 2B.

12 Oil pump driveshaft - removal and inspection

Refer to illustrations 12.1a, 12.1b, 12.2a, 12.2b, 12.3, 12.4a, 12.4b and 12.4c

1 Remove the bolts holding the timing belt case to the block **(see illustration)**. It may be necessary to tap the cover lightly with a soft-faced hammer to break the gasket seal **(see illustration)**.

12.2a Remove the bolt holding the oil pump driveshaft retainer to the block, then ...

12.2b ... turn the oil pump driveshaft slightly while pulling it from the block

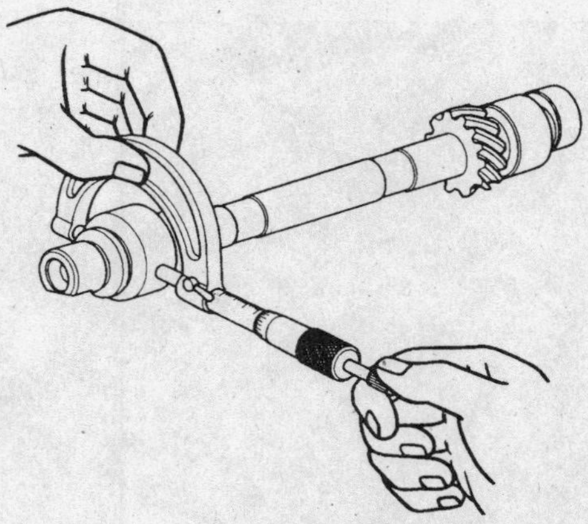
12.3 Use a micrometer to measure the diameter of the oil pump driveshaft journals and compare the measurement to the journal dimensions listed in this Chapter's Specifications

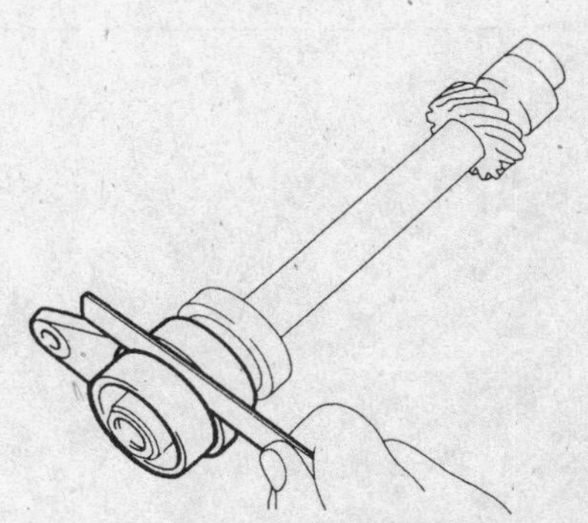
12.4a Use feeler gauges to determine the amount of endplay between the thrust plate and the shaft retainer

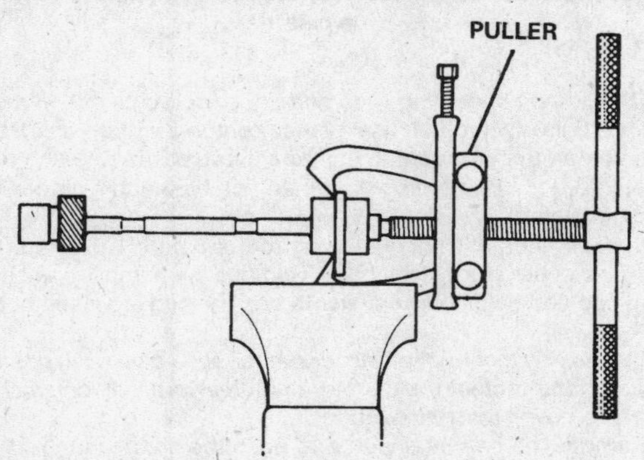

12.4b If the oil pump driveshaft endplay is excessive, the retainer and thrust plate can be removed with a puller mounted in a vise

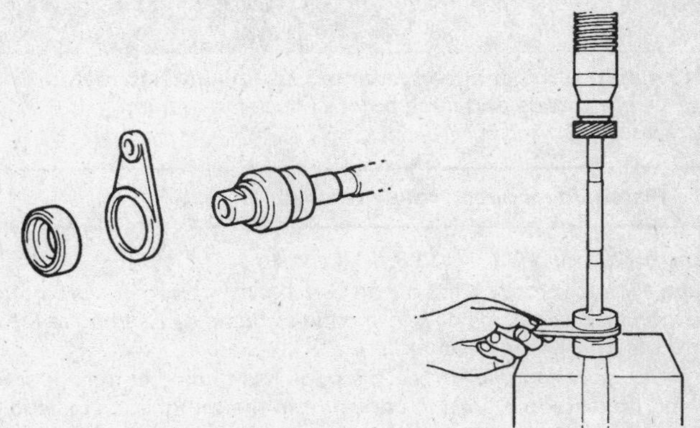
12.4c A press is used to install the new thrust plate and retainer, although the shaft can be tapped into the thrust plate and retainer with a hammer if extreme care is exercised

2 Remove the bolt holding the oil pump driveshaft retainer to the block **(see illustration)**. While turning the oil pump driveshaft, slowly pull it out of the block **(see illustration)**.

3 Measure the oil pump driveshaft bearing journals and compare the diameter to this Chapter's Specifications **(see illustration)**. Visually inspect the bearings in the block, using a flashlight if necessary. If the bearings appear excessively worn they can be measured using an inside micrometer. Most automotive machine shops will perform this measurement for a small fee. If the bearings must be replaced, a special tool is required, placing the job beyond the scope of the home mechanic. If the driveshaft journals are worn below the lower limit given in the Specifications, replace the shaft.

4 Use a feeler gauge to measure the endplay between the thrust plate and the oil pump driveshaft retainer **(see illustration)**. If the endplay is greater than that given in the Specifications, use a puller to remove the thrust plate and retainer **(see illustration)**, install a new thrust plate and replace the retainer **(see illustration)**.

13.1 A ridge reamer is required to remove the ridge from the top of the cylinder - do this *before* removing the piston

13.3 Check the connecting rod side clearance with a feeler gauge as shown

13.4 If they're not already marked, use a punch to identify the rods and caps before you remove them

13.6 To prevent damage to the crankshaft journals and cylinder walls, slip sections of hose over the rod bolts before removing the pistons

13 Pistons/connecting rods - removal

Refer to illustrations 13.1, 13.3, 13.4 and 13.6

Note: *Prior to removing the piston/connecting rod assemblies, remove the cylinder head(s), the oil pan and the oil pump by referring to the appropriate Sections in Chapter 2.*

1 Use your fingernail to feel if a ridge has formed at the upper limit of ring travel (about 1/4-inch down from the top of each cylinder). If carbon deposits or cylinder wear have produced ridges, they must be completely removed with a special tool **(see illustration)**. Follow the manufacturer's instructions provided with the tool. Failure to remove the ridges before attempting to remove the piston/connecting rod assemblies may result in piston breakage.

2 After the cylinder ridges have been removed, turn the engine upside-down so the crankshaft is facing up.

3 Before the connecting rods are removed, check the endplay with feeler gauges. Slide them between the first connecting rod and the crankshaft throw until the play is removed **(see illustration)**. The endplay is equal to the thickness of the feeler gauge(s). If the endplay exceeds the service limit, new connecting rods will be required. If new rods (or a new crankshaft) are installed, the endplay may fall under the specified minimum (if it does, the rods will have to be machined to restore it - consult an automotive machine shop for advice if necessary). Repeat the procedure for the remaining connecting rods.

4 Check the connecting rods and caps for identification marks. If they aren't plainly marked, use a small center-punch to make the appropriate number of indentations **(see illustration)** on each rod and cap (1, 2, 3, etc., depending on the engine type and cylinder they're associated with).

5 Loosen each of the connecting rod cap nuts 1/2-turn at a time until they can be removed by hand. Remove the number one connecting rod cap and bearing insert. Don't drop the bearing insert out of the cap.

6 Slip a short length of plastic or rubber hose over each connecting rod cap bolt to protect the crankshaft journal and cylinder wall as the piston is removed **(see illustration)**.

7 Remove the bearing insert and push the connecting rod/piston assembly out through the top of the engine. Use a wooden hammer handle to push on the upper bearing surface in the connecting rod. If resistance is felt, double-check to make sure that all of the ridge was removed from the cylinder.

8 Repeat the procedure for the remaining cylinders.

9 After removal, reassemble the connecting rod caps and bearing inserts in their respective connecting rods and install the cap nuts finger tight. Leaving the old bearing inserts in place until reassembly will help prevent the connecting rod bearing surfaces from being accidentally nicked or gouged.

10 Don't separate the pistons from the connecting rods (see Section 18).

14.1 To check crankshaft endplay, mount a dial indicator on the front of the block with the probe touching the nose of the crank

14.4a Use a center-punch or number stamping dies to mark the main bearing caps to ensure that they're reinstalled in their original locations on the block (make the punch marks near one of the bolt heads)

14.4b The arrow on the main bearing cap indicates the front of the engine

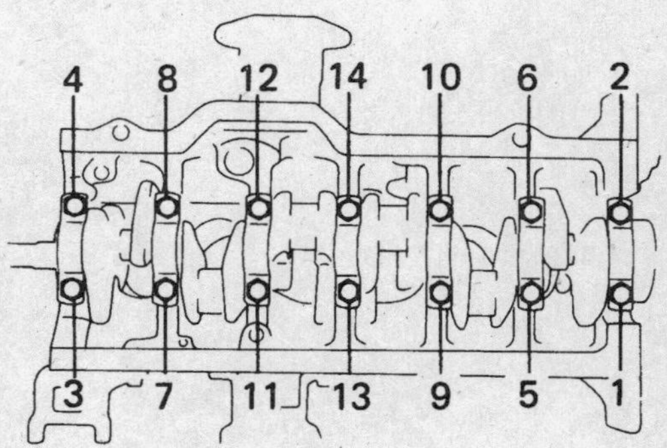

14.4c The main bearing cap bolts must be loosened and removed in the order shown here

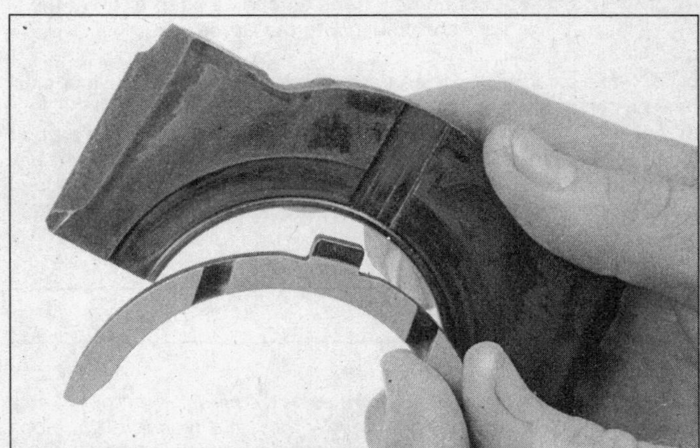
14.5 Make sure you keep the thrust washers with number four main bearing cap

14 Crankshaft - removal

Refer to illustrations 14.1, 14.4a, 14.4b, 14.4c and 14.5

Note: *The crankshaft can be removed only after the engine has been removed from the vehicle. It's assumed that the flywheel or driveplate, vibration damper, timing chain, oil pan, oil pump and piston/connecting rod assemblies have already been removed. The rear main oil seal housing must be unbolted and separated from the block before proceeding with crankshaft removal.*

1 Before the crankshaft is removed, check the endplay. Mount a dial indicator with the stem in line with the crankshaft and touching the nose of the crank **(see illustration)**.

2 Push the crankshaft all the way to the rear and zero the dial indicator. Next, pry the crankshaft to the front as far as possible and check the reading on the dial indicator. The distance that it moves is the endplay. If it's greater than the maximum endplay listed in this Chapter's Specifications, check the crankshaft thrust surfaces for wear. If no wear is evident, new main bearings should correct the endplay.

3 If a dial indicator isn't available, feeler gauges can be used. Gently pry or push the crankshaft all the way to the front of the engine. Slip feeler gauges between the crankshaft and the front face of the thrust main bearing to determine the clearance.

4 Check the main bearing caps to see if they're marked to indicate their locations. They should be numbered consecutively from the front of the engine to the rear. If they aren't, mark them with number stamping dies or a center-punch **(see illustrations)**. Main bearing caps generally have a cast-in arrow, which points to the front of the engine **(see illustration)**. Loosen the main bearing cap bolts 1/4-turn at a time each, until they can be removed by hand. Note if any stud bolts are used and make sure they're returned to their original locations when the crankshaft is reinstalled.

5 Gently tap the caps with a soft-face hammer, then separate them from the engine block. If necessary, use the bolts as levers to remove the caps. Try not to drop the bearing inserts if they come out with the

15.1 After knocking the core plugs sideways, pull them from the block with pliers

15.10 A large socket on an extension can be used to drive the new core plugs into the bores

caps. Make sure the thrust washers remain with the number four main bearing cap after removal **(see illustration)**.

6 Carefully lift the crankshaft out of the engine. It may be a good idea to have an assistant available, since the crankshaft is quite heavy. With the bearing inserts in place in the engine block and main bearing caps, return the caps to their respective locations on the engine block and tighten the bolts finger tight.

15 Engine block - cleaning

Refer to illustrations 15.1, 15.8 and 15.10

Caution: *The core plugs (also known as freeze plugs or soft plugs) may be difficult or impossible to retrieve if they're driven into the block coolant passages.*

1 Remove the core plugs from the engine block. To do this, knock one side of the plugs into the block with a hammer and punch, then grasp them with large pliers and pull them out **(see illustration)**.

2 Using a gasket scraper, remove all traces of gasket material from the engine block. Be very careful not to nick or gouge the gasket sealing surfaces.

3 Remove the main bearing caps and separate the bearing inserts from the caps and the engine block. Tag the bearings, indicating which cylinder they were removed from and whether they were in the cap or the block, then set them aside.

4 Remove all of the threaded oil gallery plugs from the block. The plugs are usually very tight - they may have to be drilled out and the holes retapped. Use new plugs when the engine is reassembled.

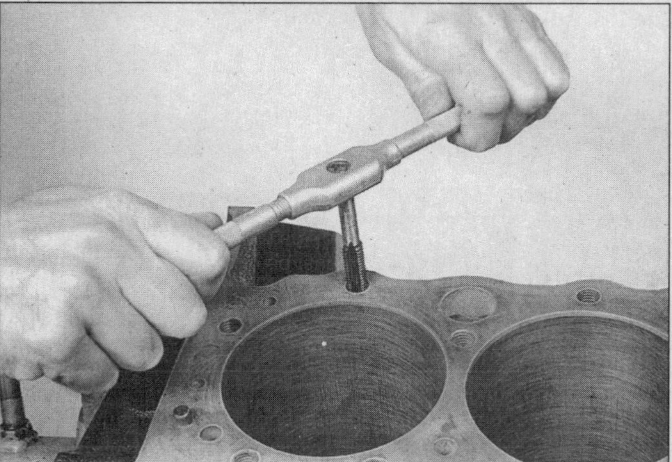

15.8 All bolt holes in the block - particularly the main bearing cap and head bolt holes - should be cleaned and restored with a tap (be sure to remove debris from the holes after this is done)

5 If the engine is extremely dirty it should be taken to an automotive machine shop to be steam cleaned or hot tanked.

6 After the block is returned, clean all oil holes and oil galleries one more time. Brushes specifically designed for this purpose are available at most auto parts stores. Flush the passages with warm water until the water runs clear, dry the block thoroughly and wipe all machined surfaces with a light, rust preventive oil. If you have access to compressed air, use it to speed the drying process and to blow out all the oil holes and galleries. **Warning:** *Wear eye protection when using compressed air!*

7 If the block isn't extremely dirty or sludged up, you can do an adequate cleaning job with hot soapy water and a stiff brush. Take plenty of time and do a thorough job. Regardless of the cleaning method used, be sure to clean all oil holes and galleries very thoroughly, dry the block completely and coat all machined surfaces with light oil.

8 The threaded holes in the block must be clean to ensure accurate torque readings during reassembly. Run the proper size tap into each of the holes to remove rust, corrosion, thread sealant or sludge and restore damaged threads **(see illustration)**. If possible, use compressed air to clear the holes of debris produced by this operation. Now is a good time to clean the threads on the head bolts and the main bearing cap bolts as well.

9 Reinstall the main bearing caps and tighten the bolts finger tight.

10 After coating the sealing surfaces of the new core plugs with Permatex no. 2 sealant, install them in the engine block **(see illustration)**. Make sure they're driven in straight and seated properly or leakage could result. Special tools are available for this purpose, but a large socket, with an outside diameter that will just slip into the core plug, a 1/2-inch drive extension and a hammer will work just as well.

11 Apply non-hardening sealant (such as Permatex no. 2 or Teflon pipe sealant) to the new oil gallery plugs and thread them into the holes in the block. Make sure they're tightened securely.

12 If the engine isn't going to be reassembled right away, cover it with a large plastic trash bag to keep it clean.

16 Engine block - inspection

Refer to illustrations 16.4a, 16.4b and 16.4c

1 Before the block is inspected, it should be cleaned (see Section 15).

2 Visually check the block for cracks, rust and corrosion. Look for stripped threads in the threaded holes. It's also a good idea to have the block checked for hidden cracks by an automotive machine shop that has the special equipment to do this type of work. If defects are

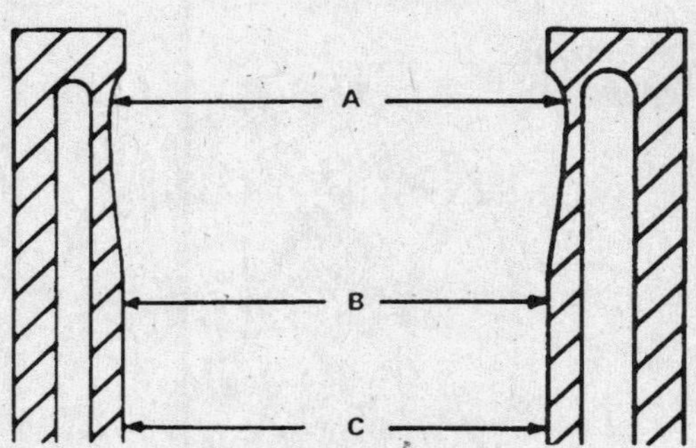

16.4a Measure the diameter of each cylinder just under the wear ride (A), at the center (B) and at the bottom (C)

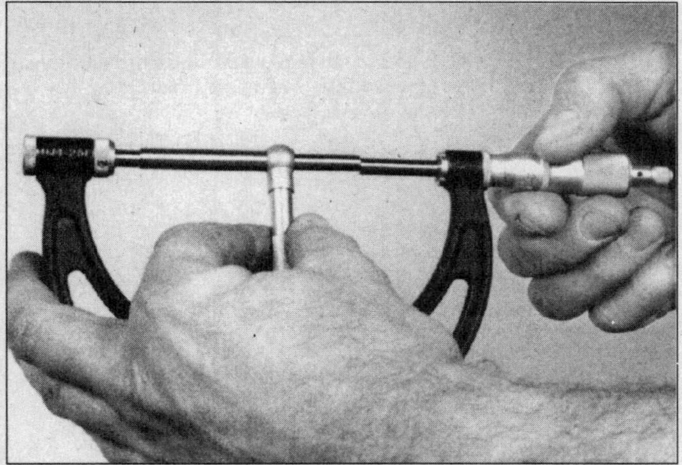

16.4c The gauge is then measured with a micrometer to determine the bore size

found, have the block repaired, if possible, or replaced.

3 Check the cylinder bores for scuffing and scoring.

4 Measure the diameter of each cylinder at the top (just under the ridge area), center and bottom of the cylinder bore, parallel to the crankshaft axis **(see illustrations)**.

5 Next, measure each cylinder's diameter at the same three locations across the crankshaft axis. Compare the results to this Chapter's Specifications.

6 If the required precision measuring tools aren't available, the piston-to-cylinder clearances can be obtained, though not quite as accurately, using feeler gauge stock. Feeler gauge stock comes in 12-inch lengths and various thicknesses and is generally available at auto parts stores.

7 To check the clearance, select a feeler gauge and slip it into the cylinder along with the matching piston. The piston must be positioned exactly as it normally would be. The feeler gauge must be between the piston and cylinder on one of the thrust faces (90-degrees to the piston pin bore).

8 The piston should slip through the cylinder (with the feeler gauge in place) with moderate pressure.

9 If it falls through or slides through easily, the clearance is excessive and a new piston will be required. If the piston binds at the lower end of the cylinder and is loose toward the top, the cylinder is tapered. If tight spots are encountered as the piston/feeler gauge is rotated in the cylinder, the cylinder is out-of-round.

10 Repeat the procedure for the remaining pistons and cylinders.

11 If the cylinder walls are badly scuffed or scored, or if they're out-of-round or tapered beyond the limits given in this Chapter's Specifications, have the engine block rebored and honed at an automotive machine shop. If a rebore is done, oversize pistons and rings will be required.

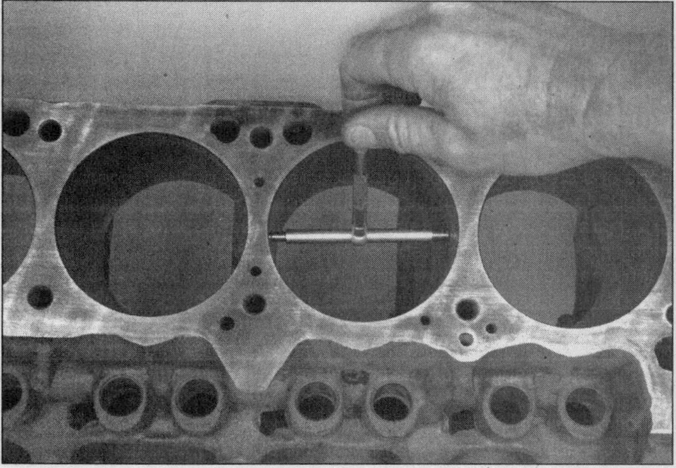

16.4b The ability to "feel" when the telescoping gauge is at the correct point will be developed over time, so work slowly and repeat the check until you're satisfied the bore measurement is accurate

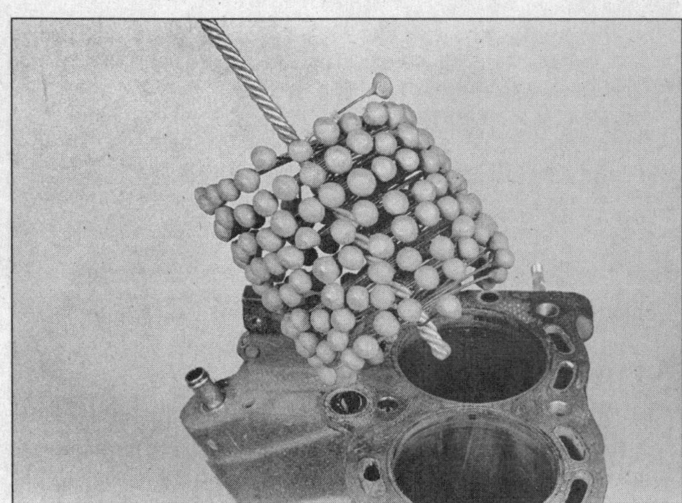

17.3a A "bottle brush" hone produces better results if you've never honed a cylinder before

12 If the cylinders are in reasonably good condition and not worn to the outside of the limits, and if the piston-to-cylinder clearances can be maintained properly, then they don't have to be rebored. Honing is all that's necessary (see Section 17).

17 Cylinder honing

Refer to illustrations 17.3a, 17.3b, 17.3c and 17.4

1 Prior to engine reassembly, the cylinder bores must be honed so the new piston rings will seat correctly and provide the best possible combustion chamber seal. **Note:** *If you don't have the tools or don't want to tackle the honing operation, most automotive machine shops will do it for a reasonable fee.*

2 Before honing the cylinders, install the main bearing caps and tighten the bolts to the torque listed in this Chapter's Specifications.

3 Two types of cylinder hones are commonly available - the flex hone or "bottle brush" type **(see illustration)** and the more traditional surfacing hone with spring-loaded stones. Both will do the job, but for the less experienced mechanic the "bottle brush" hone will probably be easier to use. You'll also need some kerosene or honing oil, rags and an electric drill motor. Proceed as follows:

17.3b A "bottle brush" hone will produce better results if you've never honed cylinders before

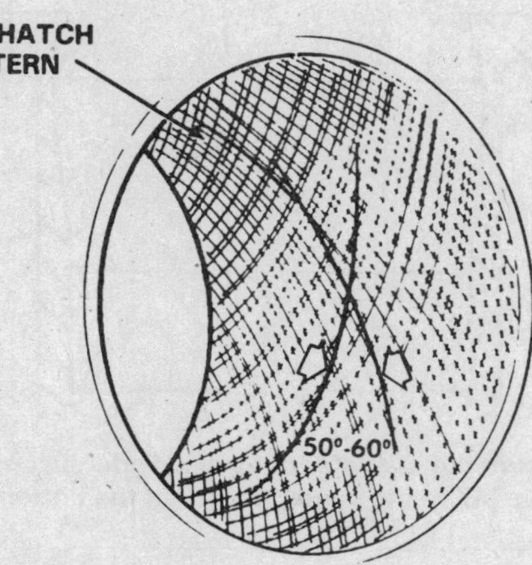

17.3c The cylinder hone should leave a smooth, crosshatch pattern with the lines intersecting at approximately a 60-degree angle

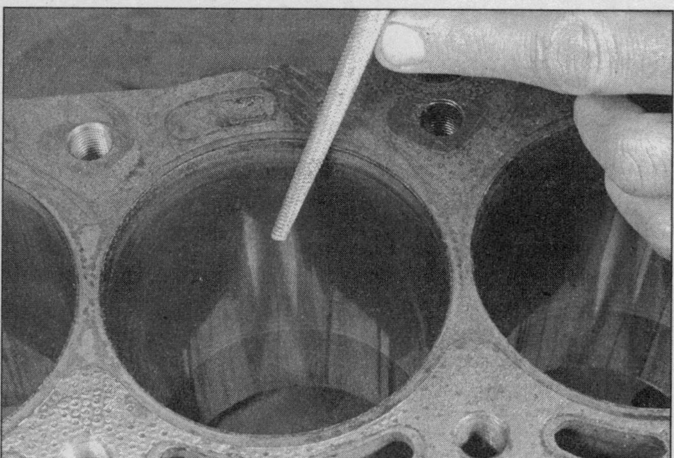

17.4 Use a small file to lightly chamfer the tops of the cylinders to keep the rings from catching when the pistons are installed - be very careful not to nick the cylinder walls with the end of the file

a) Mount the hone in the drill motor, compress the stones and slip it into the first cylinder **(see illustration)**. Be sure to wear safety goggles or a face shield!

b) Lubricate the cylinder with plenty of honing oil, turn on the drill and move the hone up-and-down in the cylinder at a pace that will produce a fine crosshatch pattern on the cylinder walls. Ideally, the crosshatch lines should intersect at approximately a 60-degree angle **(see illustration)**. Be sure to use plenty of lubricant and don't take off any more material than is absolutely necessary to produce the desired finish. **Note:** *Piston ring manufacturers may specify a smaller crosshatch angle than the traditional 60-degrees - read and follow any instructions included with the new rings.*

c) Don't withdraw the hone from the cylinder while it's running. Instead, shut off the drill and continue moving the hone up-and-down in the cylinder until it comes to a complete stop, then compress the stones and withdraw the hone. If you're using a "bottle brush" type hone, stop the drill motor, then turn the chuck in the normal direction of rotation while withdrawing the hone from the cylinder.

d) Wipe the oil out of the cylinder and repeat the procedure for the remaining cylinders.

4 After the honing job is complete, chamfer the top edges of the cylinder bores with a small file so the rings won't catch when the pistons are installed **(see illustration)**. Be very careful not to nick the cylinder walls with the end of the file.

5 The entire engine block must be washed again very thoroughly with warm, soapy water to remove all traces of the abrasive grit produced during the honing operation. **Note:** *The bores can be considered clean when a lint-free white cloth - dampened with clean engine oil - used to wipe them out doesn't pick up any more honing residue, which will show up as gray areas on the cloth. Be sure to run a brush through all oil holes and galleries and flush them with running water.*

6 After rinsing, dry the block and apply a coat of light rust preventive oil to all machined surfaces. Wrap the block in a plastic trash bag to keep it clean and set it aside until reassembly.

18 Pistons/connecting rods - inspection

Refer to illustrations 18.4a, 18.4b, 18.10 and 18.11

1 Before the inspection process can be carried out, the piston/connecting rod assemblies must be cleaned and the original piston rings removed from the pistons. **Note:** *Always use new piston rings when the engine is reassembled.*

2 Using a piston ring installation tool, carefully remove the rings from the pistons. Be careful not to nick or gouge the pistons in the process.

3 Scrape all traces of carbon from the top of the piston. A hand-held wire brush or a piece of fine emery cloth can be used once the majority of the deposits have been scraped away. Do not, under any circumstances, use a wire brush mounted in a drill motor to remove deposits from the pistons. The piston material is soft and may be eroded away by the wire brush.

4 Use a piston ring groove cleaning tool to remove carbon deposits from the ring grooves. If a tool isn't available, a piece broken off the old ring will do the job. Be very careful to remove only the carbon deposits - don't remove any metal and do not nick or scratch the sides of the ring grooves **(see illustrations)**.

5 Once the deposits have been removed, clean the piston/rod assemblies with solvent and dry them with compressed air (if available). Make sure the oil return holes in the back sides of the ring grooves are clear.

6 If the pistons and cylinder walls aren't damaged or worn excessively, and if the engine block is not rebored, new pistons won't be necessary. Normal piston wear appears as even vertical wear on the piston thrust surfaces and slight looseness of the top ring in its groove. New piston rings, however, should always be used when an engine is rebuilt.

18.4a The piston ring grooves can be cleaned with a special tool, as shown here, . . .

18.4b . . . or a section of a broken ring

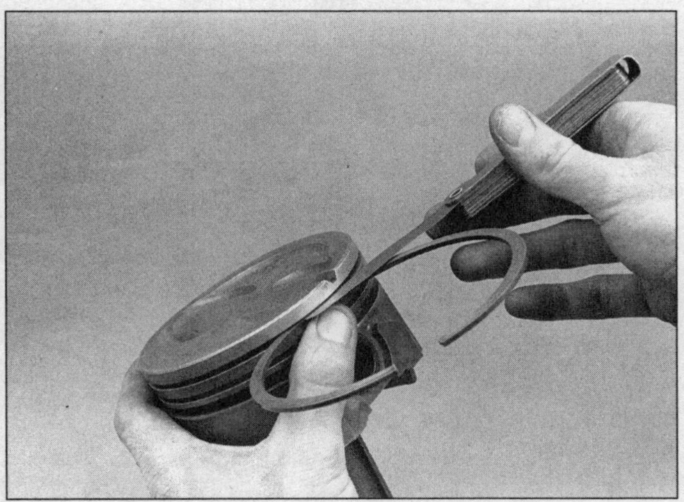

18.10 Check the ring side clearance with a feeler gauge at several points around the groove

18.11 Measure the piston diameter at a 90-degree angle to the piston pin and in line with it

7 Carefully inspect each piston for cracks around the skirt, at the pin bosses and at the ring lands.

8 Look for scoring and scuffing on the thrust faces of the skirt, holes in the piston crown and burned areas at the edge of the crown. If the skirt is scored or scuffed, the engine may have been suffering from overheating and/or abnormal combustion, which caused excessively high operating temperatures. The cooling and lubrication systems should be checked thoroughly. A hole in the piston crown is an indication that abnormal combustion (preignition) was occurring. Burned areas at the edge of the piston crown are usually evidence of spark knock (detonation). If any of the above problems exist, the causes must be corrected or the damage will occur again. The causes may include intake air leaks, incorrect fuel/air mixture, incorrect ignition timing and EGR system malfunctions.

9 Corrosion of the piston, in the form of small pits, indicates that coolant is leaking into the combustion chamber and/or the crankcase. Again, the cause must be corrected or the problem may persist in the rebuilt engine.

10 Measure the piston ring side clearance by laying a new piston ring in each ring groove and slipping a feeler gauge in beside it **(see illustration)**. Check the clearance at three or four locations around each groove. Be sure to use the correct ring for each groove - they are different. If the side clearance is greater than the figure listed in this Chapter's Specifications, new pistons will have to be used.

11 Check the piston-to-bore clearance by measuring the bore (see Section 16) and the piston diameter. Make sure the pistons and bores are correctly matched. Measure the piston across the skirt, at a 90-degree angle to and in line with the piston pin **(see illustration)**. Subtract the piston diameter from the bore diameter to obtain the clearance. If it's greater than specified, the block will have to be rebored and new pistons and rings installed.

12 Check the piston-to-rod clearance by twisting the piston and rod in opposite directions. Any noticeable play indicates excessive wear, which must be corrected. The piston/connecting rod assemblies should be taken to an automotive machine shop to have the pistons and rods resized and new pins installed.

13 If the pistons must be removed from the connecting rods for any reason, they should be taken to an automotive machine shop. While they are there have the connecting rods checked for bend and twist, since automotive machine shops have special equipment for this purpose. **Note:** *Unless new pistons and/or connecting rods must be installed, do not disassemble the pistons and connecting rods.*

14 Check the connecting rods for cracks and other damage. Temporarily remove the rod caps, lift out the old bearing inserts, wipe the rod and cap bearing surfaces clean and inspect them for nicks, gouges and scratches. After checking the rods, replace the old bearings, slip the caps into place and tighten the nuts finger tight. **Note:** *If the engine is being rebuilt because of a connecting rod knock, be sure to install new rods.*

19.1 The oil holes should be chamfered so sharp edges don't gouge or scratch the new bearings

19.2 Use a wire or stiff plastic bristle brush to clean the oil passages in the crankshaft

19.4 Rubbing a penny lengthwise on each journal will reveal its condition - if copper rubs off and is embedded in the crankshaft, the journals should be reground

19.6 Measure the diameter of each crankshaft journal at several points to detect taper and out-of-round conditions

19.8 If the seals have worn grooves in the crankshaft journals, or if the seal contact surfaces are nicked or scratched, the new seal will leak

19 Crankshaft - inspection

Refer to illustrations 19.1, 19.2, 19.4, 19.6 and 19.8

1 Remove all burrs from the crankshaft oil holes with a stone, file or scraper **(see illustration)**.

2 Clean the crankshaft with solvent and dry it with compressed air (if available). Be sure to clean the oil holes with a stiff brush **(see illustration)** and flush them with solvent.

3 Check the main and connecting rod bearing journals for uneven wear, scoring, pits and cracks.

4 Rub a penny across each journal several times **(see illustration)**. If a journal picks up copper from the penny, it's too rough and must be reground.

5 Check the rest of the crankshaft for cracks and other damage. It should be magnafluxed to reveal hidden cracks - an automotive machine shop will handle the procedure.

6 Using a micrometer, measure the diameter of the main and connecting rod journals and compare the results to this Chapter's Specifications **(see illustration)**. By measuring the diameter at a number of points around each journal's circumference, you'll be able to determine whether or not the journal is out-of-round. Take the measurement at each end of the journal, near the crank throws, to determine if the journal is tapered.

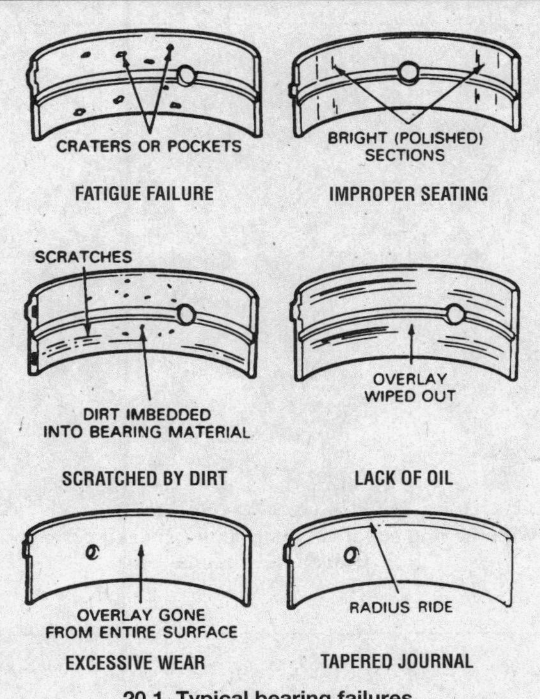

20.1 Typical bearing failures

7 If the crankshaft journals are damaged, tapered, out-of-round or worn beyond the limits given in the Specifications, have the crankshaft reground by an automotive machine shop. Be sure to use the correct size bearing inserts if the crankshaft is reconditioned.

8 Check the oil seal journals at each end of the crankshaft for wear and damage. If the seal has worn a groove in the journal, or if it's nicked or scratched **(see illustration)**, the new seal may leak when the engine is reassembled. In some cases, an automotive machine shop may be able to repair the journal by pressing on a thin sleeve.
If repair isn't feasible, a new or different crankshaft should be installed.

9 Examine the main and rod bearing inserts (see Section 20).

20 Main and connecting rod bearings - inspection

Refer to illustration 20.1

1 Even though the main and connecting rod bearings should be replaced with new ones during the engine overhaul, the old bearings should be retained for close examination, as they may reveal valuable information about the condition of the engine **(see illustration)**.

2 Bearing failure occurs because of lack of lubrication, the presence of dirt or other foreign particles, overloading the engine and corrosion. Regardless of the cause of bearing failure, it must be corrected before the engine is reassembled to prevent it from happening again.

3 When examining the bearings, remove them from the engine block,
the main bearing caps, the connecting rods and the rod caps and lay them out on a clean surface in the same general position as their location in the engine. This will enable you to match any bearing problems with the corresponding crankshaft journal.

4 Dirt and other foreign particles get into the engine in a variety of ways. It may be left in the engine during assembly, or it may pass through filters or the PCV system. It may get into the oil, and from there into the bearings. Metal chips from machining operations and normal engine wear are often present. Abrasives are sometimes left in engine components after reconditioning, especially when parts are not thoroughly cleaned using the proper cleaning methods. Whatever the source, these foreign objects often end up embedded in the soft bearing material and are easily recognized. Large particles will not embed in the bearing and will score or gouge the bearing and journal. The best prevention for this cause of bearing failure is to clean all parts thoroughly and keep everything spotlessly clean during engine assembly. Frequent and regular engine oil and filter changes are also recommended.

5 Lack of lubrication (or lubrication breakdown) has a number of interrelated causes. Excessive heat (which thins the oil),
overloading (which squeezes the oil from the bearing face) and oil leakage or throw off (from excessive bearing clearances, worn oil pump or high engine speeds) all contribute to lubrication breakdown. Blocked oil passages, which usually are the result of misaligned oil holes in a bearing shell, will also oil starve a bearing and destroy it. When lack of lubrication is the cause of bearing failure, the bearing material is wiped or extruded from the steel backing of the bearing. Temperatures may increase to the point where the steel backing turns blue from overheating.

6 Driving habits can have a definite effect on bearing life. Full throttle, low speed operation (lugging the engine) puts very high loads on bearings, which tends to squeeze out the oil film. These loads cause the bearings to flex, which produces fine cracks in the bearing face (fatigue failure). Eventually the bearing material will loosen in pieces and tear away from the steel backing. Short trip driving leads to corrosion of bearings because insufficient engine heat is produced to drive off the condensed water and corrosive gases. These products collect in the engine oil, forming acid and sludge. As the oil is carried to the engine bearings, the acid attacks and corrodes the bearing material.

7 Incorrect bearing installation during engine assembly will lead to bearing failure as well. Tight fitting bearings leave insufficient bearing oil clearance and will result in oil starvation. Dirt or foreign particles trapped behind a bearing insert result in high spots on the bearing which lead to failure.

21 Engine overhaul - reassembly sequence

1 Before beginning engine reassembly, make sure you have all the necessary new parts, gaskets and seals as well as the following items on hand:

Common hand tools
A torque wrench
Piston ring installation tool
Piston ring compressor
Vibration damper installation tool
Short lengths of rubber or plastic hose to fit over connecting rod bolts
Plastigage
Feeler gauges
A fine-tooth file
New engine oil
Engine assembly lube or moly-base grease
Gasket sealant
Thread locking compound

2 In order to save time and avoid problems, engine reassembly must be done in the following general order:

Piston rings
Crankshaft and main bearings
Piston/connecting rod assemblies
Oil pump
Oil pan
Cylinder head and valves
Camshaft (1979 through 1981 models)
Rocker arm assembly (1979 through 1981 models)
Lash adjusters and rocker arms (1982 through 1986 models)
Valve lifters and shims (1987 through 1992 models)
Camshafts and camshaft housings (1982 through 1986 models)
Camshafts (1987 through 1992 models)
Timing chain (1979 through 1981 models), or belt (1982 and later models), and sprockets
Timing cover
Intake and exhaust manifolds
Valve cover(s)
Engine rear plate
Flywheel/driveplate

22.3 When checking piston ring end gap, the ring must be square in the cylinder bore (this is done by pushing the ring down with the top of a piston as shown)

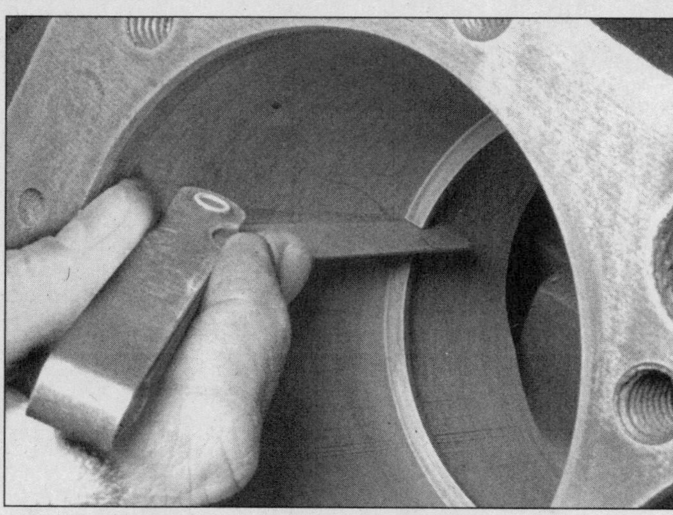

22.4 With the ring square in the cylinder, measure the end gap with a feeler gauge

22.5 If the end gap is too small, clamp a file in a vise and file the ring ends (from the outside in only) to enlarge the gap slightly

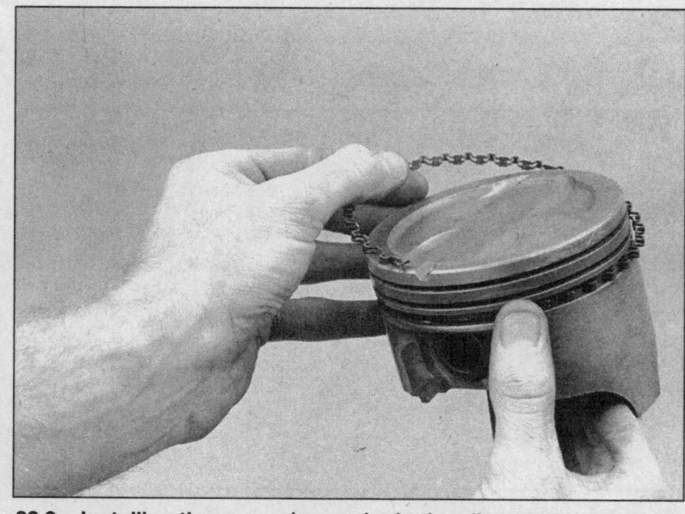

22.9a Installing the spacer/expander in the oil control ring groove

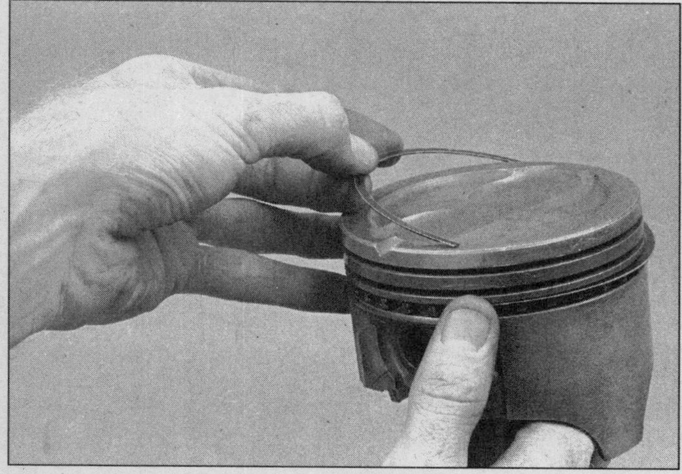

22.9b DO NOT use a piston ring installation tool when installing the oil ring side rails

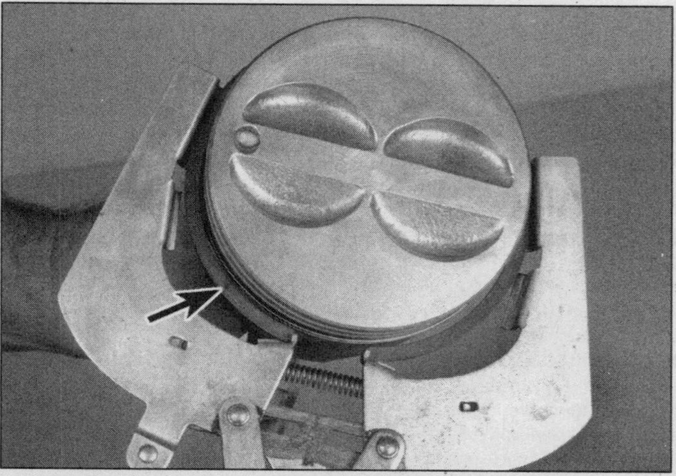

22.12 Installing the compression rings with a ring expander - the mark (arrow) must face up

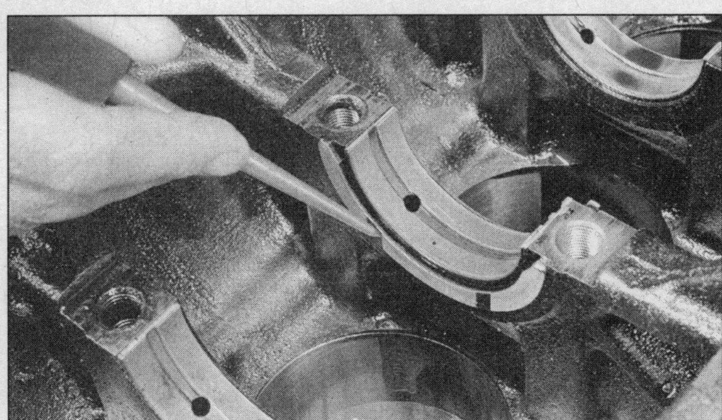

23.6 Apply grease to the thrust washers to hold them in place in the block as the crankshaft is installed

23.11 Lay the Plastigage strips (arrow) on the main bearing journals, parallel to the crankshaft centerline

22 Piston rings - installation

Refer to illustrations 22.3, 22.4, 22.5, 22.9a, 22.9b and 22.12

1 Before installing the new piston rings, the ring end gaps must be checked. It's assumed that the piston ring side clearance has been checked and verified correct (see Section 18).

2 Lay out the piston/connecting rod assemblies and the new ring sets so the ring sets will be matched with the same piston and cylinder during the end gap measurement and engine assembly.

3 Insert the top (number one) ring into the first cylinder and square it up with the cylinder walls by pushing it in with the top of the piston **(see illustration)**. The ring should be near the bottom of the cylinder, at the lower limit of ring travel.

4 To measure the end gap, slip feeler gauges between the ends of the ring until a gauge equal to the gap width is found **(see illustration)**. The feeler gauge should slide between the ring ends with a slight amount of drag. Compare the measurement to this Chapter's Specifications. If the gap is larger or smaller than specified, double-check to make sure you have the correct rings before proceeding.

5 If the gap is too small, it must be enlarged or the ring ends may come in contact with each other during engine operation, which can cause serious damage to the engine. The end gap can be increased by filing the ring ends very carefully with a fine file. Mount the file in a vise equipped with soft jaws, slip the ring over the file with the ends contacting the file face and slowly move the ring to remove material from the ends. When performing this operation, file only from the outside in **(see illustration)**.

6 Excess end gap isn't critical unless it's greater than 0.040-inch. Again, double-check to make sure you have the correct rings for your engine.

7 Repeat the procedure for each ring that will be installed in the first cylinder and for each ring in the remaining cylinders. Remember to keep rings, pistons and cylinders matched up.

8 Once the ring end gaps have been checked/corrected, the rings can be installed on the pistons.

9 The oil control ring (lowest one on the piston) is usually installed first. It's composed of three separate components. Slip the spacer/expander into the groove **(see illustration)**. If an anti-rotation tang is used, make sure it's inserted into the drilled hole in the ring groove. Next, install the lower side rail. Don't use a piston ring installation tool on the oil ring side rails, as they may be damaged. Instead, place one end of the side rail into the groove between the spacer/expander and the ring land, hold it firmly in place and slide a finger around the piston while pushing the rail into the groove **(see illustration)**. Next, install the upper side rail in the same manner.

10 After the three oil ring components have been installed, check to make sure that both the upper and lower side rails can be turned smoothly in the ring groove.

11 The number two (middle) ring is installed next. It's usually stamped with a mark which must face up, toward the top of the piston. **Note:** *Always follow the instructions printed on the ring package or box - different manufacturers may require different approaches. Do not mix up the top and middle rings, as they have different cross sections.*

12 Use a piston ring installation tool and make sure the identification mark is facing the top of the piston, then slip the ring into the middle groove on the piston **(see illustration)**. Don't expand the ring any more than necessary to slide it over the piston.

13 Install the number one (top) ring in the same manner. Make sure the mark is facing up. Be careful not to confuse the number one and number two rings.

14 Repeat the procedure for the remaining pistons and rings.

23 Crankshaft - installation and main bearing oil clearance check

1 Crankshaft installation is the first step in engine reassembly. It's assumed at this point that the engine block and crankshaft have been cleaned, inspected and repaired or reconditioned.

2 Position the engine with the bottom facing up.

3 Remove the main bearing cap bolts and lift out the caps. Lay them out in the proper order to ensure correct installation.

4 If they're still in place, remove the original bearing inserts from the block and the main bearing caps. Wipe the bearing surfaces of the block and caps with a clean, lint-free cloth. They must be kept spotlessly clean.

Main bearing oil clearance check

Refer to illustrations 23.6, 23.11, 23.13 and 23.15

5 Clean the back sides of the new main bearing inserts and lay one in each main bearing saddle in the block. If one of the bearing inserts from each set has a large groove in it, make sure the grooved insert is installed in the block. Lay the other bearing from each set in the corresponding main bearing cap. Make sure the tab on the bearing insert fits into the recess in the block or cap. **Caution:** *The oil holes in the block must line up with the oil holes in the bearing insert. Do not hammer the bearing into place and don't nick or gouge the bearing faces. No lubrication should be used at this time.*

6 The flanged thrust bearing must be installed in the No. 4 bearing saddle **(see illustration)**.

7 Clean the faces of the bearings in the block and the crankshaft main bearing journals with a clean, lint-free cloth.

8 Check or clean the oil holes in the crankshaft, as any dirt here can go only one way - straight through the new bearings.

9 Once you're certain the crankshaft is clean, carefully lay it in position in the main bearings.

10 Before the crankshaft can be permanently installed, the main bearing oil clearance must be checked.

11 Cut several pieces of the appropriate size Plastigage (they must be slightly shorter than the width of the main bearings) and place one piece on each crankshaft main bearing journal, parallel with the journal axis **(see illustration)**.

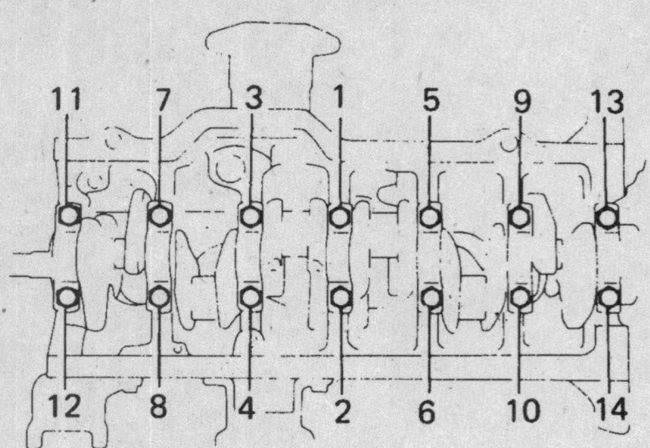

23.13 Tighten the main bearing cap bolts in the order shown here

12 Clean the faces of the bearings in the caps and install the caps in their respective positions (don't mix them up) with the arrows pointing toward the front of the engine. Don't disturb the Plastigage.

13 Starting with the center main and working out toward the ends, tighten the main bearing cap bolts, in three steps, to the torque listed in this Chapter's Specifications **(see illustration)**. Don't rotate the crankshaft at any time during this operation.

14 Remove the bolts and carefully lift off the main bearing caps. Keep them in order. Don't disturb the Plastigage or rotate the crankshaft. If any of the main bearing caps are difficult to remove, tap them gently from side-to-side with a soft-face hammer to loosen them.

15 Compare the width of the crushed Plastigage on each journal to the scale printed on the Plastigage envelope to obtain the main bearing oil clearance **(see illustration)**. Check the Specifications to make sure it's correct.

16 If the clearance is not as specified, the bearing inserts may be the wrong size (which means different ones will be required). Before deciding that different inserts are needed, make sure that no dirt or oil was between the bearing inserts and the caps or block when the clearance was measured. If the Plastigage was wider at one end than the other, the journal may be tapered (see Section 19).

17 Carefully scrape all traces of the Plastigage material off the main bearing journals and/or the bearing faces. Use your fingernail or the edge of a credit card - don't nick or scratch the bearing faces.

Final crankshaft installation

18 Carefully lift the crankshaft out of the engine.

19 Clean the bearing faces in the block, then apply a thin, uniform layer of moly-base grease or engine assembly lube to each of the bearing surfaces. Be sure to coat the thrust faces as well as the journal face of the thrust bearing.

20 Make sure the crankshaft journals are clean, then lay the crankshaft back in place in the block.

21 Clean the faces of the bearings in the caps, then apply lubricant to them.

22 Install the caps in their respective positions with the arrows pointing toward the front of the engine.

23 Install the bolts.

24 Tighten all except the thrust bearing cap bolts to the specified torque (work from the center out and approach the final torque in three steps).

25 Tighten the thrust bearing cap bolts to the torque listed in this Chapter's Specifications.

26 Tap the ends of the crankshaft forward and backward with a lead or brass hammer to line up the main bearing and crankshaft thrust surfaces.

27 Retighten all main bearing cap bolts to the specified torque, starting with the center main and working out toward the ends.

28 On manual transmission equipped models, install a new pilot bearing in the end of the crankshaft (see Chapter 8).

29 Rotate the crankshaft a number of times by hand to check for any obvious binding.

23.15 Compare the width of the crushed Plastigage to the scale on the container to determine the main bearing oil clearance (always take the measurement at the widest point of the Plastigage) - be sure to read the correct scale; standard and metric scales are included

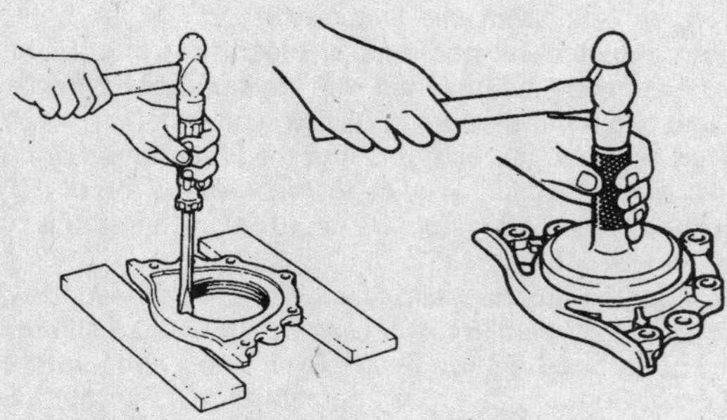

24.3 Tap the old seal out with a screwdriver and hammer, then install the new seal with a special tool or a piece of large diameter pipe

30 The final step is to check the crankshaft endplay with a feeler gauge or a dial indicator as described in Section 14. The endplay should be correct if the crankshaft thrust faces aren't worn or damaged and new bearings have been installed.

31 Install the new seal, then bolt the housing to the block (see Section 24).

24 Rear main oil seal installation

Refer to illustration 24.3

1 The crankshaft must be installed first and the main bearing caps bolted in place, then the new seal should be installed in the retainer and the retainer bolted to the block.

2 Before installing the crankshaft, check the seal contact surface very carefully for scratches and nicks that could damage the new seal lip and cause oil leaks. If the crankshaft is damaged, the only alternative is a new or different crankshaft.

3 The old seal can be removed from the housing with a hammer and punch by driving it out from the back side **(see illustration)**. Be sure to note how far it's recessed into the housing bore before removing it; the new seal will have to be recessed an equal amount. Be very careful not to scratch or otherwise damage the bore in the housing or oil leaks could develop.

4 Make sure the retainer is clean, then apply a thin coat of engine oil to the outer edge of the new seal. The seal must be pressed squarely into the housing bore, so hammering it into place is not rec-

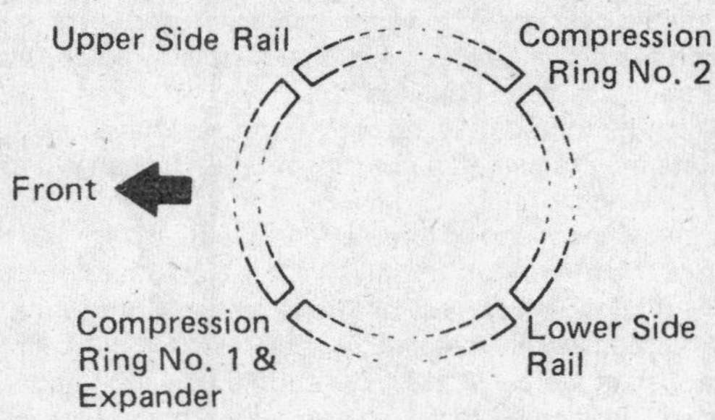

25.5 Position the ring gaps around the piston like this

ommended. If you don't have access to a press, sandwich the housing and seal between two smooth pieces of wood and press the seal into place with the jaws of a large vise. The pieces of wood must be thick enough to distribute the force evenly around the entire circumference of the seal. Work slowly and make sure the seal enters the bore squarely.

5 The seal lips must be lubricated with multi-purpose grease or clean engine oil before the seal/retainer is slipped over the crankshaft and bolted to the block. Use a new gasket - no sealant is required - and make sure the dowel pins are in place before installing the retainer.

6 Tighten the retainer nuts/screws a little at a time until they're all snug, then tighten them to the torque listed in this Chapter's Specifications.

25 Pistons/connecting rods - installation and rod bearing oil clearance check

Refer to illustrations 25.5, 25.11, 25.13 and 25.17

1 Before installing the piston/connecting rod assemblies, the cylinder walls must be perfectly clean, the top edge of each cylinder must be chamfered, and the crankshaft must be in place.

2 Remove the cap from the end of the number one connecting rod (refer to the marks made during removal). Remove the original bearing inserts and wipe the bearing surfaces of the connecting rod and cap with a clean, lint-free cloth. They must be kept spotlessly clean.

Connecting rod bearing oil clearance check

3 Clean the back side of the new upper bearing insert, then lay it in place in the connecting rod. Make sure the tab on the bearing fits into the recess in the rod. Don't hammer the bearing insert into place and be very careful not to nick or gouge the bearing face. Don't lubricate the bearing at this time.

4 Clean the back side of the other bearing insert and install it in the rod cap. Again, make sure the tab on the bearing fits into the recess in the cap, and don't apply any lubricant. It's critically important that the mating surfaces of the bearing and connecting rod are perfectly clean and oil free when they're assembled.

5 Position the piston ring gaps as shown **(see illustration)**.

6 Slip a section of plastic or rubber hose over each connecting rod cap bolt.

7 Lubricate the piston and rings with clean engine oil and attach a piston ring compressor to the piston. Leave the skirt protruding about 1/4-inch to guide the piston into the cylinder. The rings must be compressed until they're flush with the piston.

8 Rotate the crankshaft until the number one connecting rod journal is at BDC (bottom dead center) and apply a coat of engine oil to the cylinder walls.

9 With the mark or notch on top of the piston facing the front of the engine, gently insert the piston/connecting rod assembly into the number one cylinder bore and rest the bottom edge of the ring compressor on the engine block.

10 Tap the top edge of the ring compressor to make sure it's contacting the block around its entire circumference.

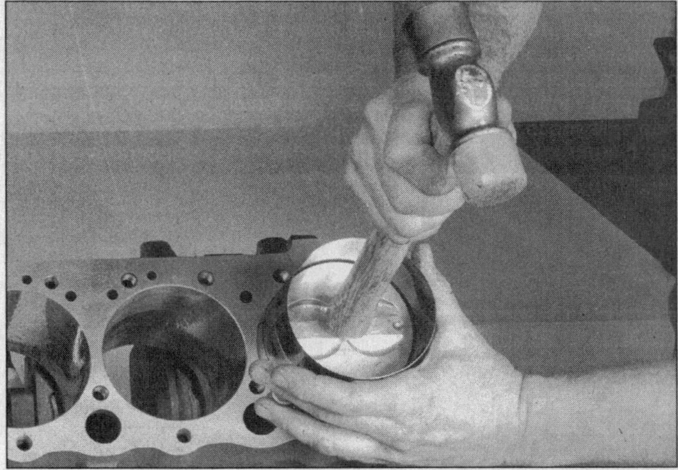

25.11 Drive the piston gently into the cylinder bore with the end of a wooden or plastic hammer handle

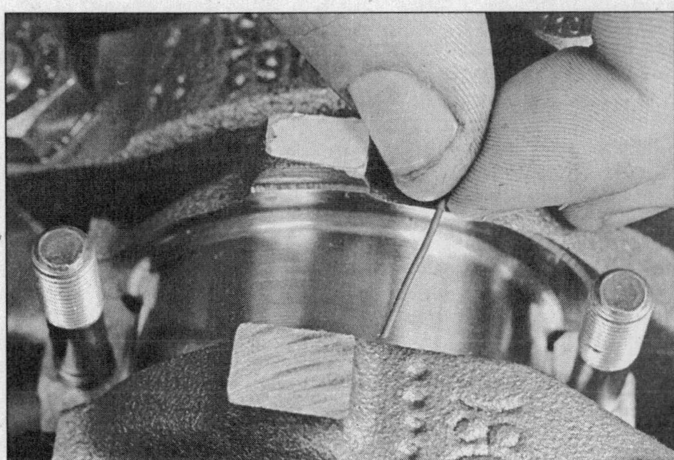

25.13 Lay the Plastigage strips on each rod bearing journal, parallel to the crankshaft centerline

11 Gently tap on the top of the piston with the end of a wooden hammer handle **(see illustration)** while guiding the end of the connecting rod into place on the crankshaft journal. The piston rings may try to pop out of the ring compressor just before entering the cylinder bore, so keep some downward pressure on the ring compressor. Work slowly, and if any resistance is felt as the piston enters the cylinder, stop immediately. Find out what's hanging up and fix it before proceeding. Do not, for any reason, force the piston into the cylinder - you might break a ring and/or the piston.

12 Once the piston/connecting rod assembly is installed, the connecting rod bearing oil clearance must be checked before the rod cap is permanently bolted in place.

13 Cut a piece of the appropriate size Plastigage slightly shorter than the width of the connecting rod bearing and lay it in place on the number one connecting rod journal, parallel with the journal axis **(see illustration)**.

14 Clean the connecting rod cap bearing face, remove the protective hoses from the connecting rod bolts and install the rod cap. Make sure the mating mark on the cap is on the same side as the mark on the connecting rod.

15 Install the nuts and tighten them to the torque listed in this Chapter's Specifications, working up to it in three steps. **Note:** *Use a thin-wall socket to avoid erroneous torque readings that can result if the socket is wedged between the rod cap and nut. If the socket tends to wedge itself between the nut and the cap, lift up on it slightly until it no longer contacts the cap. Do not rotate the crankshaft at any time during this operation.*

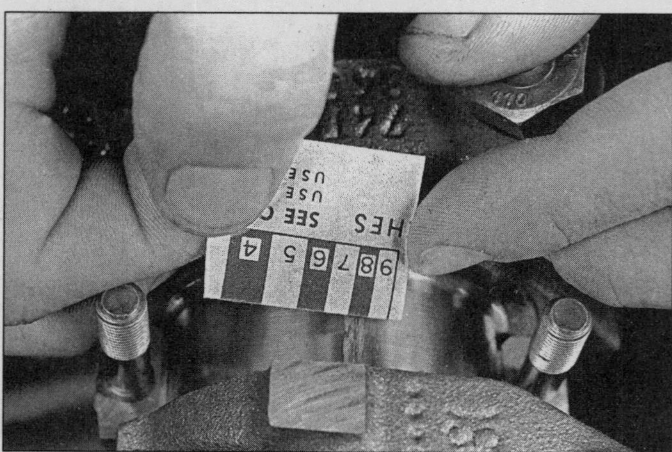

25.17 Measuring the width of the crushed Plastigage to determine the rod bearing oil clearance (be sure to use the correct scale - standard and metric ones are included)

16 Remove the nuts and detach the rod cap, being very careful not to disturb the Plastigage.

17 Compare the width of the crushed Plastigage to the scale printed on the Plastigage envelope to obtain the oil clearance **(see illustration)**. Compare it to the Specifications to make sure the clearance is correct.

18 If the clearance is not as specified, the bearing inserts may be the wrong size (which means different ones will be required). Before deciding that different inserts are needed, make sure that no dirt or oil was between the bearing inserts and the connecting rod or cap when the clearance was measured. Also, recheck the journal diameter. If the Plastigage was wider at one end than the other, the journal may be tapered (see Section 19).

Final connecting rod installation

19 Carefully scrape all traces of the Plastigage material off the rod journal and/or bearing face. Be very careful not to scratch the bearing - use your fingernail or the edge of a credit card.

20 Make sure the bearing faces are perfectly clean, then apply a uniform layer of clean moly-base grease or engine assembly lube to both of them. You'll have to push the piston into the cylinder to expose the face of the bearing insert in the connecting rod - be sure to slip the protective hoses over the rod bolts first.

21 Slide the connecting rod back into place on the journal, remove the protective hoses from the rod cap bolts, install the rod cap and tighten the nuts to the specified torque. Again, work up to the torque in three steps.

22 Repeat the entire procedure for the remaining pistons/connecting rods.

23 The important points to remember are:

a) Keep the back sides of the bearing inserts and the insides of the connecting rods and caps perfectly clean when assembling them.
b) Make sure you have the correct piston/rod assembly for each cylinder.
c) The notch or mark on the piston must face the front of the engine.
d) Lubricate the cylinder walls with clean oil.
e) Lubricate the bearing faces when installing the rod caps after the oil clearance has been checked.

24 After all the piston/connecting rod assemblies have been properly installed, rotate the crankshaft a number of times by hand to check for any obvious binding.

25 Check the connecting rod endplay (see Section 13).

26 Compare the measured endplay to the Specifications to make sure it's correct. If it was correct before disassembly and the original crankshaft and rods were reinstalled, it should still be right. If new rods or a new crankshaft were installed, the endplay may be inadequate. If so, the rods will have to be removed and taken to an automotive machine shop for resizing.

26 Oil pump driveshaft - installation

1 Apply clean engine oil to the bearing surfaces in the block.

2 While turning the oil pump driveshaft, slowly slide it into the block, taking care not to damage the driveshaft bearings.

3 Tighten the oil pump driveshaft retaining bolt to the torque listed in this Chapter's Specifications.

4 Install the timing belt case and tighten the bolts to the torque listed in this Chapter's Specifications.

27 Initial start-up and break-in after overhaul

Warning: *Have a fire extinguisher handy when starting the engine for the first time.*

1 Once the engine has been installed in the vehicle, double-check the engine oil and coolant levels.

2 With the spark plugs out of the engine and the ignition system disabled (see Section 3), crank the engine until oil pressure registers on the gauge or the light goes out.

3 Install the spark plugs, hook up the plug wires and restore the ignition system functions (see Section 3).

4 Start the engine. It may take a few moments for the fuel system to build up pressure, but the engine should start without a great deal of effort. **Note:** *If backfiring occurs through the carburetor or throttle body, recheck the valve timing and ignition timing.*

5 After the engine starts, it should be allowed to warm up to normal operating temperature. While the engine is warming up, make a thorough check for fuel, oil and coolant leaks.

6 Shut the engine off and recheck the engine oil and coolant levels.

7 Drive the vehicle to an area with minimum traffic, accelerate at full throttle from 30 to 50 mph, then allow the vehicle to slow to 30 mph with the throttle closed. Repeat the procedure 10 or 12 times. This will load the piston rings and cause them to seat properly against the cylinder walls. Check again for oil and coolant leaks.

8 Drive the vehicle gently for the first 500 miles (no sustained high speeds) and keep a constant check on the oil level. It is not unusual for an engine to use oil during the break-in period.

9 At approximately 500 to 600 miles, change the oil and filter.

10 For the next few hundred miles, drive the vehicle normally. Do not pamper it or abuse it.

11 After 2000 miles, change the oil and filter again and consider the engine broken in.

Chapter 3 Cooling, heating and air conditioning systems

Contents

3

Specifications

General

Radiator cap pressure rating	
Standard	10.7 to 14.9 psi
Minimum	8.5 psi
Thermostat rating	See Chapter 1
Starts to open	187 to 194 degrees F
Fully open	212 degrees F
Drivebelt tension	See Chapter 1
Refrigerant capacity	1.4 to 1.7 lbs.

1 General information

Engine cooling system

The models covered by this manual employ a pressurized engine cooling system with thermostatically controlled coolant circulation. An impeller type water pump mounted on the front of the block pumps coolant through the engine. The coolant flows around each cylinder and toward the rear of the engine. Cast-in coolant passages direct coolant around the intake and exhaust ports, near the spark plugs and in close proximity to the exhaust valve guides.

A wax pellet type thermostat is located in the front of the intake manifold. During warm up, the closed thermostat prevents coolant from circulating through the radiator. When the engine reaches normal operating temperature, the thermostat opens and allows hot coolant to travel through the radiator, where it is cooled before returning to the engine.

The cooling system is sealed by a pressure type radiator cap. This raises the boiling point of the coolant and the higher boiling point of the coolant increases the cooling efficiency of the radiator.

If the system pressure exceeds the cap pressure relief value, the excess pressure in the system forces the spring-loaded valve inside the cap off its seat and allows the coolant to escape through the overflow tube into a coolant recovery bottle. When the system cools the excess coolant is automatically drawn from the recovery bottle back into the radiator.

The coolant recovery bottle does double duty as both the point at which fresh coolant is added to the cooling system to maintain the proper fluid level and as a holding tank for overheated coolant. This type of cooling system is known as a closed design because coolant that escapes past the pressure cap is saved and reused.

3.8 Loosen the hose clamp (arrow) and remove the radiator hose from the thermostat housing (on 1982 through 1992 models, the thermostat housing is located above the water pump on the front of the engine, as shown; on 1979 through 1981 models, you'll find the thermostat housing above the intake manifold)

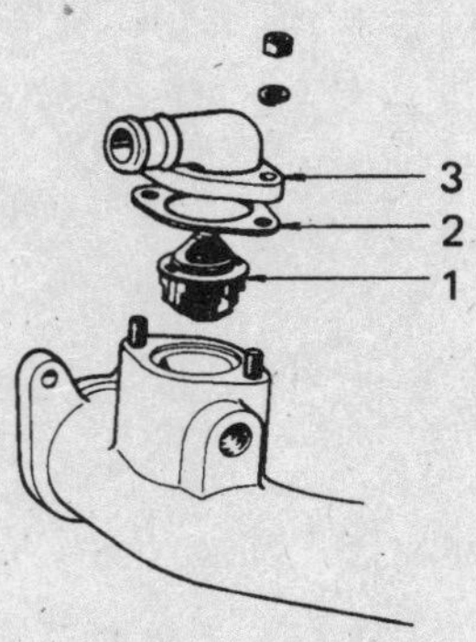

3.10a An exploded view of a typical thermostat assembly on 1979 through 1981 models

1 *Thermostat*
2 *Gasket*
3 *Housing cover*

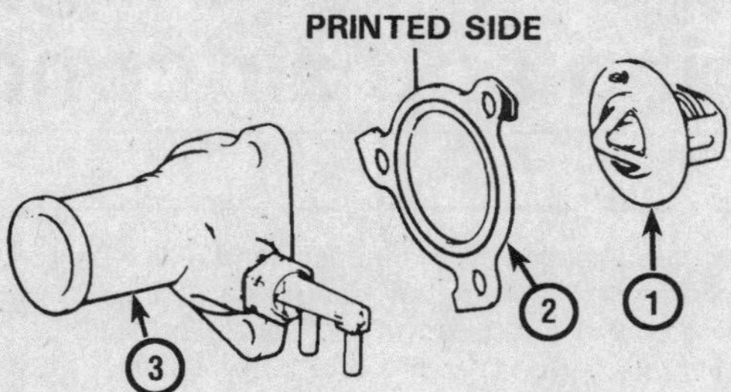

3.10b An exploded view of a typical thermostat assembly on 1982 through 1986 models - note that the printed side of the gasket faces forward

1 *Thermostat*
2 *Gasket*
3 *Housing cover*

Heating system

The heating system consists of a blower fan and heater core located under the dashboard, the inlet and outlet hoses connecting the heater core to the engine cooling system and the heater/air conditioning control assembly on the dashboard. Hot engine coolant is circulated through the heater core at all times. When the heater mode is activated, a flap door opens to expose the heater box to the passenger compartment. A fan switch on the control head activates the blower motor, which forces air through the core, heating the air.

Air conditioning system

The air conditioning system consists of a condenser mounted in front of the radiator, an evaporator mounted under the dash, a compressor mounted on the engine, a filter-drier (accumulator) which contains a high pressure relief valve and the plumbing connecting all of the above.

A blower fan forces the warmer air of the passenger compartment through the evaporator core (sort of a radiator-in-reverse), transferring the heat from the air to the refrigerant. The liquid refrigerant boils off into low pressure vapor, taking the heat with it when it leaves the evaporator.

2 Antifreeze - general information

Warning: *Do not allow antifreeze to come in contact with your skin or painted surfaces of the vehicle. Rinse off spills immediately with plenty of water. Antifreeze is highly toxic if ingested. Never leave antifreeze lying around in an open container or in puddles on the floor; children and pets are attracted by it's sweet smell and may drink it. Check with local authorities about disposing of used antifreeze. Many communities have collection centers which will see that antifreeze is disposed of safely.*

The cooling system should be filled with a water/ethylene glycol antifreeze solution which will prevent freezing down to at least -20 degrees F, or lower if local climate requires it. It also provides protection against corrosion and increases the coolant boiling point.

The cooling system should be drained, flushed and refilled at least every other year (see Chapter 1). The use of antifreeze solutions for periods of longer than two years is likely to cause damage and encourage the formation of rust and scale in the system. If your tap water is "hard," use distilled water with the antifreeze.

Before adding antifreeze to the system, check all hose connections, because antifreeze can leak through very minute openings. Engines don't normally consume coolant, if the level goes down, find the cause and correct it.

The exact mixture of antifreeze to water which you should use depends on the relative weather conditions. The mixture should contain at least 50 percent antifreeze, but should never contain more than 70 percent antifreeze. Consult the mixture ratio on the antifreeze container before adding coolant. Hydrometers are available at most auto parts stores to test the ratio of antifreeze to water. Use antifreeze which meets the vehicle manufacturer's specifications.

3 Thermostat - check and replacement

Warning: *Wait until the engine is completely cool before starting this procedure.*

Check

1 Before you assume the thermostat is causing a cooling system problem, check the coolant level (see Chapter 1), the drivebelt tension (see Chapter 1) and the temperature gauge (or light) operation.

2 If the engine takes a long time to warm up (as indicated by the temperature gauge or heater operation), the thermostat is probably stuck open. Replace the thermostat with a new one.

3 If the engine runs hot, use your hand to check the temperature of the upper radiator hose. If the hose isn't hot, but the engine is, the thermostat is probably stuck in the closed position, preventing the coolant inside the engine from escaping to the radiator. Replace the thermostat. **Caution:** *Don't drive the vehicle without a thermostat. The computer may stay in open loop and emissions and fuel economy will suffer.*

4 If the upper radiator hose is hot, it means that the coolant is flowing and the thermostat is open.

5 Consult the *Troubleshooting* section at the front of this manual for further diagnosis.

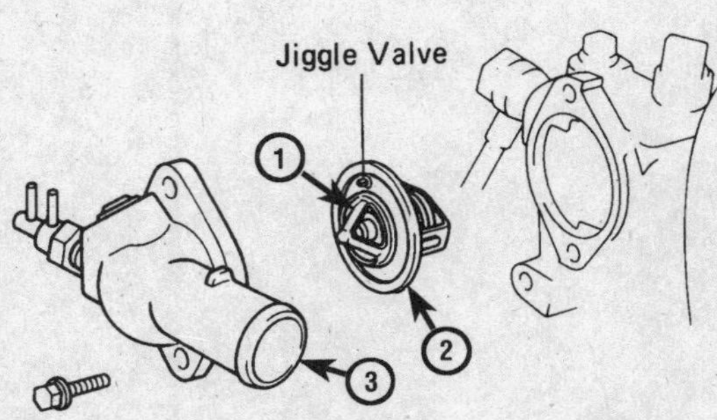

3.10c An exploded view of a typical thermostat assembly on 1987 through 1992 models - note that the jiggle valve on the thermostat faces up

1 *Thermostat*
2 *Gasket*
3 *Housing cover*

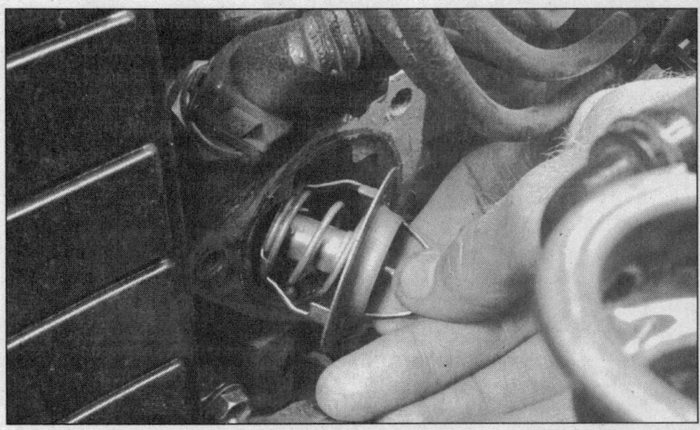

3.12 When you pull out the old thermostat, note its shape and position to ensure the new unit is correctly installed

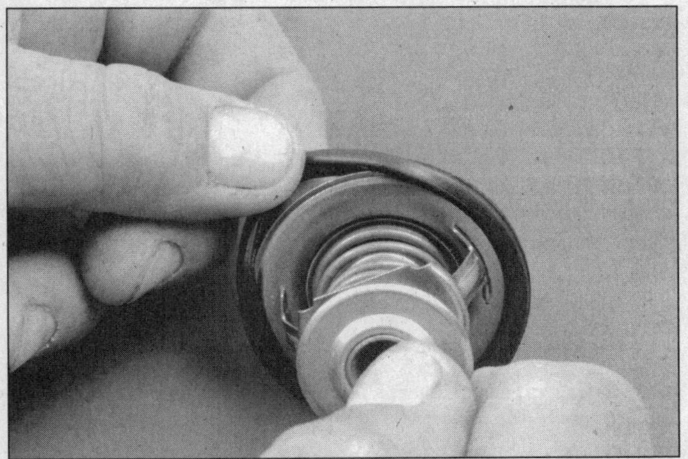

3.13 On 1987 and later models, replace the gasket that fits over the lip of the thermostat

4.9a To separate the upper half of the radiator shroud from the lower half on 1979 through 1981 models, remove the bolts (arrows) from the left side . . .

Replacement

Refer to illustrations 3.8, 3.10a, 3.10b, 3.10c, 3.12 and 3.13

6 Disconnect the cable from the negative terminal of the battery. **Caution:** *If the stereo in your vehicle is equipped with an anti-theft system, refer to the information on page 0-15 at the front of this manual before detaching the cable.*

7 Drain the coolant (see Chapter 1).

8 Disconnect the radiator hose from the thermostat housing **(see illustration)**.

9 On 1982 and later models, detach the two vacuum hoses from the vacuum switching valve.

10 Remove the thermostat housing bolts or nuts **(see illustrations)**.

11 Remove the thermostat housing.

12 Remove the thermostat **(see illustration)**. Note the shape of the top of the old thermostat to ensure that the new unit is installed with the correct side facing up.

13 Remove all traces of old gasket material and sealant from the mating surfaces of the thermostat housing. If so equipped, install a new gasket over the thermostat **(see illustration)**.

14 Place the new thermostat in position.

15 Install the thermostat housing, with the printed side of the gasket facing forward, and tighten the bolts or nuts securely.

16 Reattach the radiator hose to the thermostat housing and connect the vacuum hoses (if equipped) to the vacuum switch.

17 Fill the cooling system.

18 Connect the cable to the negative terminal of the battery.

19 Start the engine, bring the cooling system up to operating temperature and check the thermostat housing and hose for leaks.

4 Radiator - removal and installation

Refer to illustrations 4.9a, 4.9b, 4.9c, 4.10a and 4.10b

Warning: *The engine must be completely cool before this procedure is performed.*

Removal

1 Disconnect the cable from the negative terminal of the battery. **Caution:** *If the stereo in your vehicle is equipped with an anti-theft system, refer to the information on page 0-15 at the front of this manual before detaching the cable.*

2 Drain the coolant (see Chapter 1).

3 If the air cleaner housing is in the way, remove it (see Chapter 4).

4 On models with a fan motor for the air conditioning condenser, unplug the condenser fan motor connector.

5 On some models, you'll have to remove the lower shield to gain access to the lower hose clamps.

6 Disconnect the upper and lower radiator hoses and the overflow hose.

7 If the coolant reservoir hose is in the way, detach it from the reservoir. On some early models, it may be easier to simply detach the entire reservoir and remove it.

8 On models with automatic transmissions, wipe the area around the oil cooler pipe unions and then detach these pipes from the radiator. Plug the end to prevent dirt from entering the pipes and fluid loss.

9 On 1979 through 1981 models, remove the bolts that attach the upper radiator shroud to the lower half of the shroud **(see illustra-**

4.9b . . . and the right side (arrows) of the radiator shroud so the upper half of the shroud can come off with the radiator

4.10a On 1982 through 1986 models, remove the top two radiator retaining bolts (arrows)

tions). On 1982 through 1986 models, take off the small bottom portion of the fan shroud by undoing the two retaining clips **(see illustration)**.

10 Remove the upper radiator retaining bolts **(see illustrations)**.

11 Carefully lift the radiator, complete with the fan shroud, straight up and remove it. Take care not to damage the cooling fins, spill coolant on the on the vehicle or scratch the paint.

Installation

12 Installation is the reverse of the removal procedure.

13 After installation, fill the cooling system with the proper mixture of antifreeze and water (see Section 2 and Chapter 1).

14 Start the engine and check for leaks. Allow the engine to reach normal operating temperature, indicated by the upper radiator hose becoming hot. Recheck the coolant level and add more if required.

15 If you're working on an automatic transaxle equipped vehicle, check and add fluid as needed (see Chapter 1).

5 Fan/clutch assembly - check, removal and installation

Check

1 Check the fan carefully for cracks, especially around the base of each blade. If any cracks are evident, replace the fan.

4.9c On 1982 through 1986 models, release the retaining clips on the bottom portion of the fan shroud to remove it

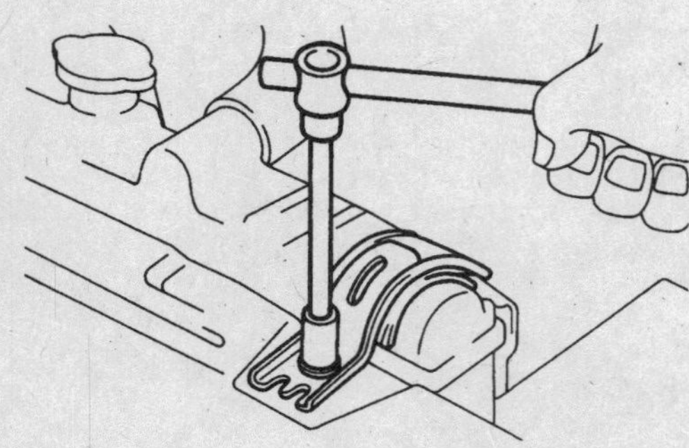

4.10b A pair of padded straps are bolted to the radiator support on 1987 and later models

5.9 To detach the fan clutch remove the nuts (arrows) behind the fan blades

2 Check the clutch for fluid leakage. If it's leaking, replace the clutch.

3 Try to move the fan blades in a front-to-rear direction. If they wobble, replace the fan clutch.

4 Spin the fan by hand. It should resist spinning (more when the engine is hot). If it spins freely, or won't spin at all, replace the fan clutch.

Removal and installation

Refer to illustrations 5.9 and 5.11

Warning: *The engine must be completely cool before this procedure is performed.*

5 Drain the cooling system (see Chapter 1).

5.11 Be careful not to damage the radiator cooling fins when withdrawing the fan clutch unit and the fan shroud

6.2 You should feel a pressure surge when the hose is released if the water pump is working properly

6 Disconnect the upper radiator hose and the overflow hose from the radiator.
7 Turn the air cleaner assembly up out of the way.
8 Loosen the alternator pivot and adjustment bolts (see Chapter 5), then pivot the alternator towards the engine so the drivebelt is slack.
9 Remove the nuts securing the fan clutch unit to the water pump pulley and drive flange **(see illustration)**.
10 Remove the fan shroud retaining bolts.
11 Withdraw the fan clutch unit together with the fan shroud **(see illustration)**, being careful not to damage the radiator cooling fins.
12 To separate the fan from the clutch, remove the four nuts that attach the two components.
13 Installation is the reverse of removal.

6 Water pump - check

Refer to illustration 6.2

1 Water pump failure can cause overheating and serious damage to the engine. There are three ways to check the operation of the water pump while it is installed on the engine. If any one of the three following quick checks cast suspicion on the water pump, it should be replaced immediately.
2 Start the engine and warm it up to normal operating temperature. Squeeze the upper radiator hose **(see illustration)**. If the water pump is working properly, you should feel a pressure surge as the hose is released.
3 A seal protects the water pump impeller shaft bearing from contamination by engine coolant. If this seal fails, weep holes in the top and bottom of the water pump snout will leak coolant when the vehicle is parked. If the weep hole is leaking, shaft bearing failure will follow. Replace the water pump immediately.
4 Besides contamination by coolant after a seal failure, the water pump impeller shaft bearing can also be prematurely worn out by an improperly tensioned drivebelt. When the bearing wears out, it emits a high pitched squealing sound. If such a noise is coming from the water pump during engine operation, the shaft bearing has failed. Replace the water pump immediately.
5 To identify excessive bearing wear before the bearing actually fails, grasp the water pump pulley and try to force it up and down or from side to side. If the pulley can be moved either horizontally or vertically, the bearing is nearing the end of its service life. Replace the water pump.

3

7 Water pump - removal and installation

Refer to illustrations 7.7a, 7.7b, 7.7c, 7.8a, 7.8b, 7.9 and 7.10

Warning: *The engine must be completely cool before this procedure is performed.*

1 Disconnect the cable from the negative terminal of the battery. **Caution:** *If the stereo in your vehicle is equipped with an anti-theft system, refer to the information on page 0-15 at the front of this manual before detaching the cable.*
2 Drain the coolant (see Chapter 1).
3 Loosen the alternator pivot nut and the power steering pump nut, then pivot the alternator and the power steering pump in towards the engine so that the drivebelts are slack (see Chapter 5).
4 Turn the air cleaner assembly housing up out of the way (see Chapter 4).
5 Disconnect the upper radiator hose.
6 Remove the four fan shroud bolts.
7 Remove the fan clutch unit (see Section 5). Also remove the water pump pulley and (if equipped) belt guide **(see illustrations)**.

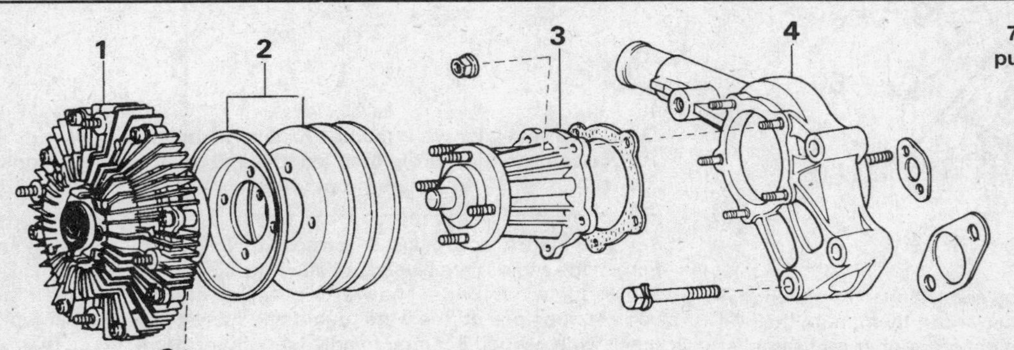

7.7a An exploded view of the water pump assembly used on 1979 through 1981 models

1 *Fan clutch*
2 *Water pump pulley belt guide (left) and pulley (right)*
3 *Water pump*
4 *Water pump body*

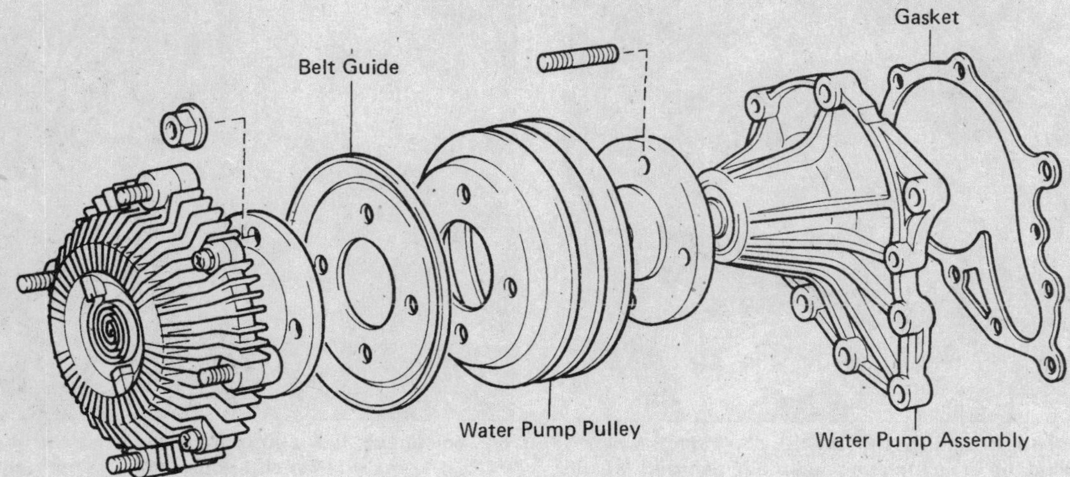

7.7b An exploded view of the water pump assembly used on 1982 through 1986 models

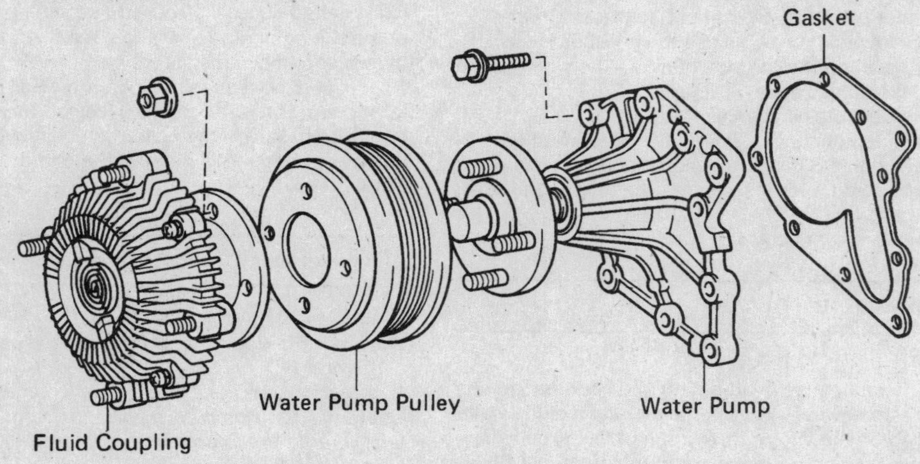

7.7c An exploded view of the water pump assembly used on 1987 and later models

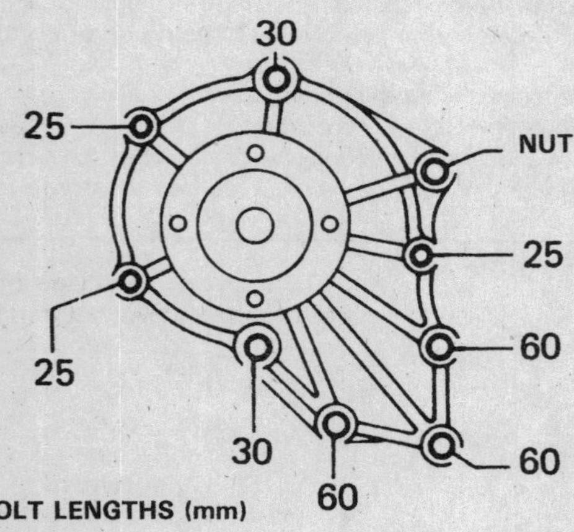

7.8a 1982 through 1986 water pumps are attached to the engine with eight bolts and a nut - as you remove them, note their lengths and respective locations to ensure proper reassembly

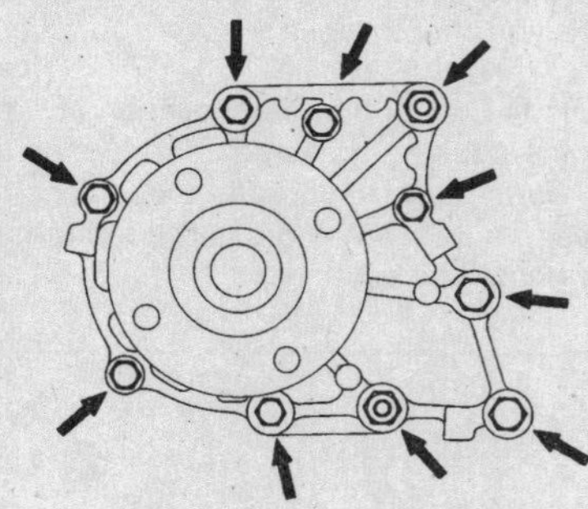

7.8b 1987 and later water pumps have eight bolts and two nuts - as you remove them, note their lengths and respective locations to ensure proper reassembly

8 Remove the bolts/nut(s) which secure the water pump unit to the front of the engine **(see illustrations)**.

9 Place a pan under the water pump to catch any remaining coolant, then pull off the water pump and gasket. If it's stuck, tap it gently with a wood hammer handle **(see illustration)**. If you plan to reuse the same pump, do NOT strike it with a metal object.

7.9 Tap the water pump lightly to break the gasket seal

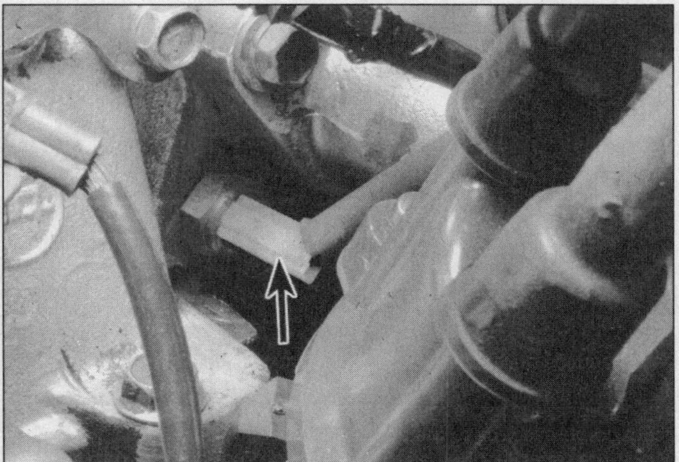
8.3a Coolant temperature sending unit (arrow) (1979 through 1981 models)

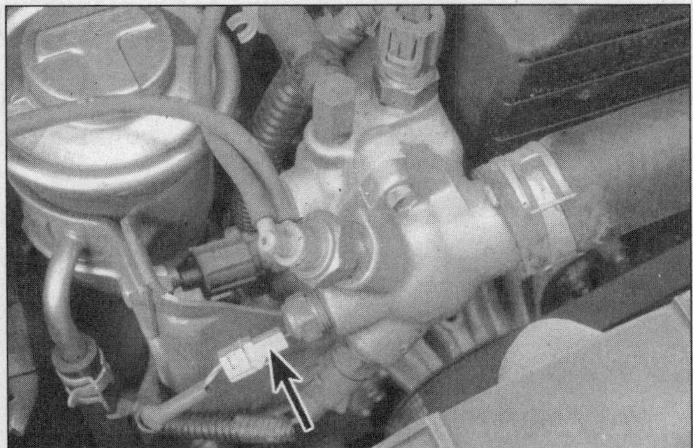
8.3c Coolant temperature sending unit (arrow) (1987 and later models) (switch on top is cold start injector time switch)

10 Remove all traces of old gasket material and sealant **(see illustration)**. The gasket mating faces of the pump and the pump body (1979 through 1981 models) or the engine block (1982 and later models) must be spotless or they'll leak.
11 Installation is the reverse of removal. Be sure to use a new gasket and tighten the bolts and nut(s) securely.
12 Adjust the drivebelt tension (see Chapter 1). If the belt is too tight, it will put a strain on the water pump and alternator bearings. If the belt

7.10 The gasket mating surfaces of the pump and block (or pump body on 1979 through 1981 models) must be free of old gasket material, or the pump may leak - but be careful not to gouge the mating surfaces when scraping off the old gasket material

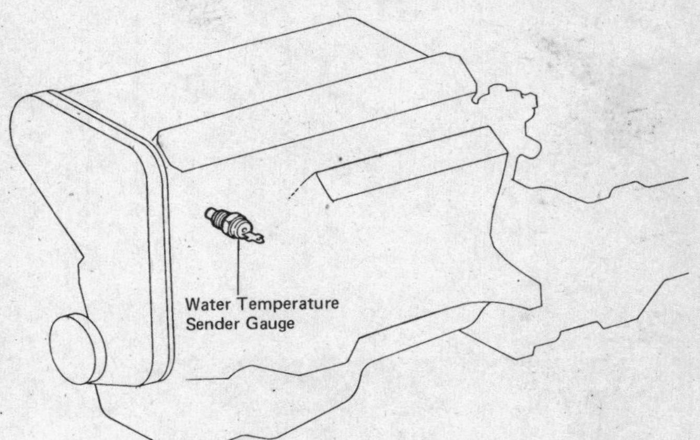

8.3b Coolant temperature sending unit (1982 through 1986 models)

is too loose, it will slip and wear rapidly, causing possible engine overheating and low alternator output.
13 Add coolant (see Chapter 1).
14 Connect the cable to the negative terminal of the battery.
15 Start the engine and check the water pump and hoses for leaks.

8 Coolant temperature sending unit - check and replacement

Warning: *Do not allow antifreeze to come in contact with your skin or painted surfaces of the vehicle. Rinse off spills immediately with plenty of water. Antifreeze is highly toxic if ingested. Never leave antifreeze lying around in an open container or in puddles on the floor; children and pets are attracted by it's sweet smell and may drink it. Check with local authorities about disposing of used antifreeze. Many communities have collection centers which will see that antifreeze is disposed of safely.*

Check

Refer to illustrations 8.3a, 8.3b and 8.3c

1 If the coolant temperature gauge is inoperative, check the fuses first (see Chapter 12).
2 If the temperature gauge indicates excessive temperature after running for a while, see the *Troubleshooting* section in the front of this manual.
3 If the temperature gauge indicates Hot as soon as the engine is started cold, disconnect the wire at the coolant temperature sending unit **(see illustrations)**. If the gauge reading drops, replace the send-

3

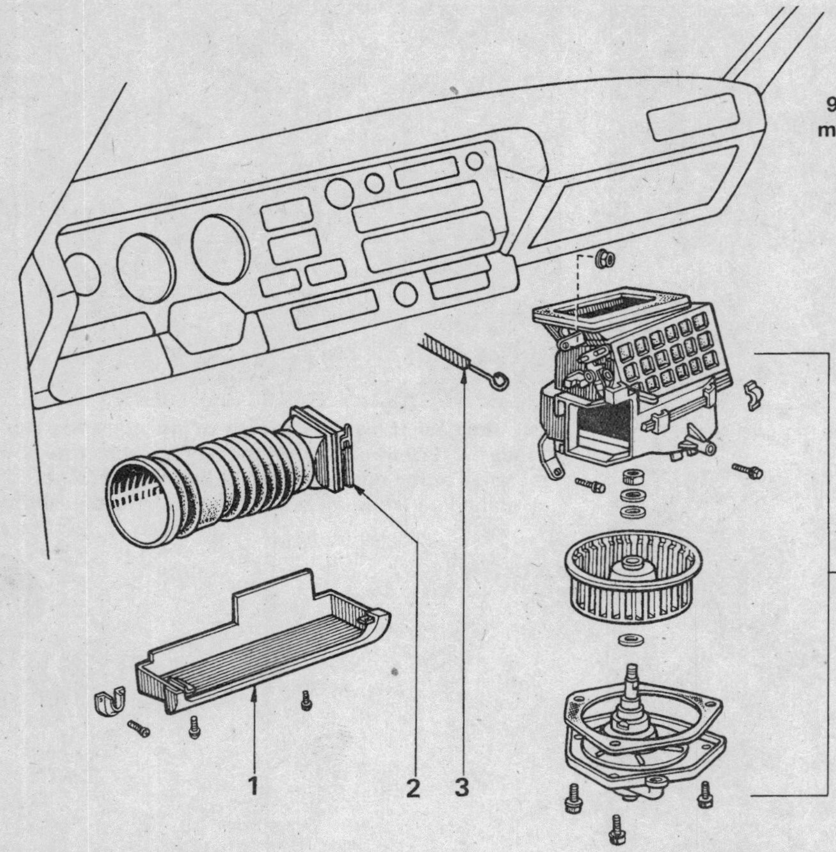

9.2 An exploded view of the heater blower motor assembly (1979 through 1981 models)

1. *Under tray*
2. *Side air duct*
3. *Heater control cable*
4. *Blower motor and fan assembly*

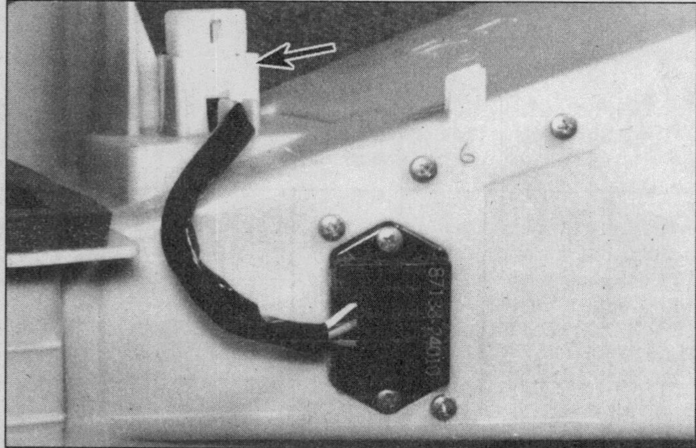

9.8 Detach the resistor electrical connector (arrow) (1982 through 1986 models)

ing unit. If the reading remains high, the wire to the gauge may be shorted to ground or the gauge is faulty.

4 If the coolant temperature gauge fails to show any indication after the engine has been warmed up (about 10 minutes), and the fuses check out okay, shut off the engine. Disconnect the wire at the sending unit and, using a jumper wire, connect it to a clean ground on the engine. Briefly turn on the ignition without starting the engine. If the gauge now indicates Hot, replace the sending unit.

5 If the gauge still doesn't work, the circuit may be open or the gauge itself may be faulty - see Chapter 12 for additional information.

Replacement

Warning: *The engine must be completely cool before this procedure is performed.*

6 Prepare the new sending unit for installation by applying thread sealant or Teflon tape to the threads.

7 Loosen the radiator cap, squeeze the upper radiator hose and then tighten the cap. This will create a slight vacuum in the cooling system which will reduce coolant loss.

8 Unplug the electrical connector and unscrew the switch. Immediately install the new switch and tighten it securely. Plug in the electrical connector.

9 Check the coolant level and add, if necessary, coolant (see Chapter 1). Start the engine and check for coolant leakage and gauge operation.

9 Heater blower motor - removal and installation

1 Disconnect the cable from the negative battery terminal. **Caution:** *If the stereo in your vehicle is equipped with an anti-theft system, refer to the information on page 0-15 at the front of this manual before detaching the cable.*

1979 through 1981 models

Refer to illustration 9.2

2 Remove the dashboard under tray screws and the tray **(see illustration)**.

3 Remove the side air duct.

4 Disconnect the heater control cable.

5 Unbolt and remove the heater blower motor unit.

6 Installation is the reverse of removal.

1982 through 1986 models

Refer to illustrations 9.8, 9.9 and 9.11

7 Remove the glovebox and the passenger side lower trim panel.

8 Remove the retaining screws and detach the center duct be-

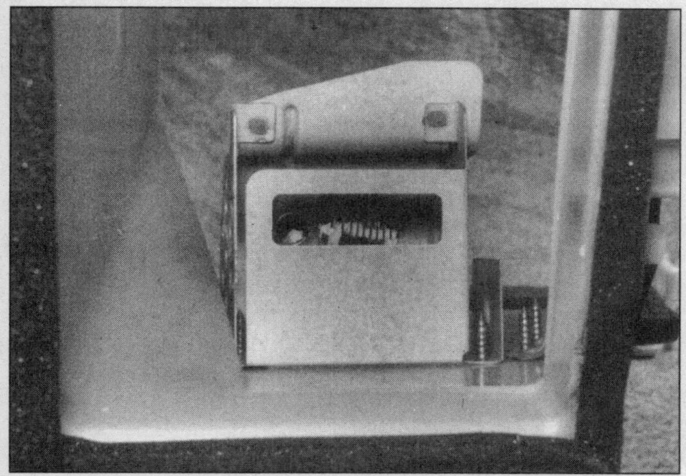

9.9 The resistor is mounted inside the duct (1982 through 1986 models)

9.11 Underside view of blower unit showing the motor retaining screws (arrows) (1982 through 1986 models)

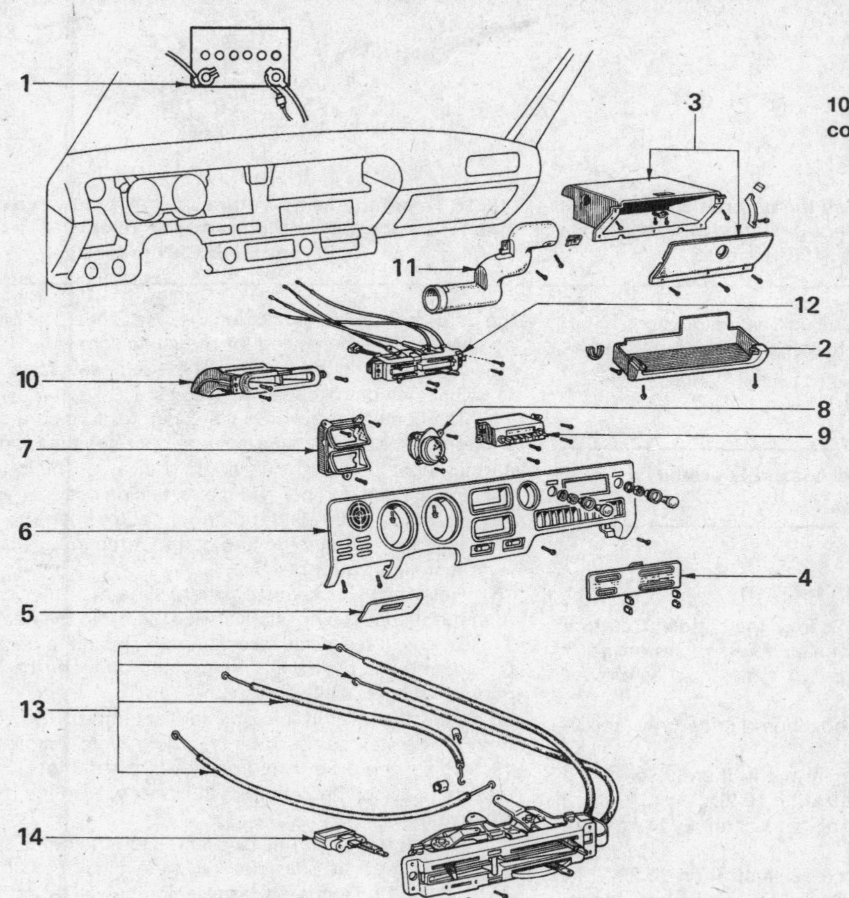

10.2 An exploded view of the heater control assembly components (1979 through 1981 models)

1 *Negative battery cable*
2 *Dashboard under tray*
3 *Glove box*
4 *Heater control panel*
5 *Fuse box cover*
6 *Instrument panel*
7 *Register*
8 *Clock*
9 *Radio*
10 *Angled air duct*
11 *Stepped air duct*
12 *Heater control assembly*
13 *Control cables*
14 *Blower motor switch*

3

tween the blower unit and the heater core. Disconnect the resistor electrical connector as it is withdrawn **(see illustration)**.

9 To separate the resistor from the duct, remove the retaining screws, detach the electrical connector from the bracket on top of the duct and remove the resistor unit **(see illustration)**.

10 To detach the motor unit, remove the three retaining screws from underneath, detach the electrical connector and the flap valve control cable. Withdraw the unit.

11 To separate the blower motor from the housing, detach the hose, remove the retaining bolts **(see illustration)** and withdraw the motor unit.

12 To separate the housing, remove the retaining screws, release the retaining clips and separate the housings.

13 Installation is the reverse of removal.

1987 and later models

14 Remove the glovebox and the passenger side lower trim panel.

15 Remove the cover from the blower motor housing (faces straight

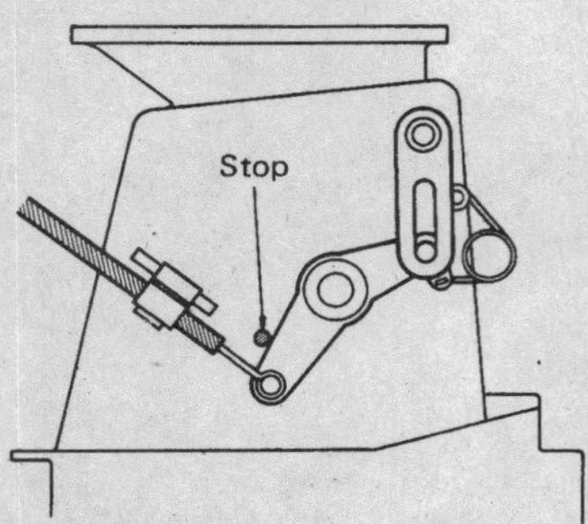

10.15 To adjust the air inlet damper cable, push the lever against its stop on the fresh air side and connect the inner wire to the damper lever (1979 through 1981 models)

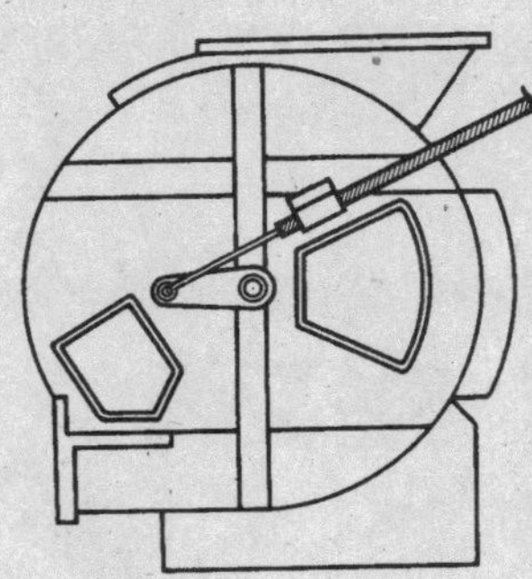

10.17 To adjust the Mode select damper cable, push the damper until its lever is horizontal (in the vent position) and connect the inner wire to the damper lever (1979 through 1981 models)

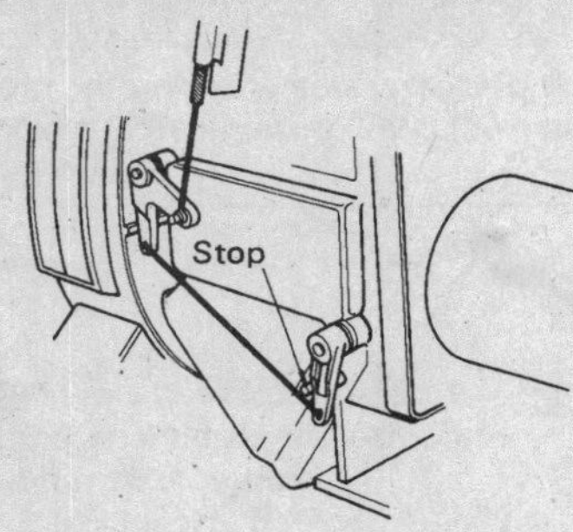

10.19 To set the Air mix damper, push the damper against its stop in the Cool position and connect the inner wire to the damper lever (1979 through 1981 models)

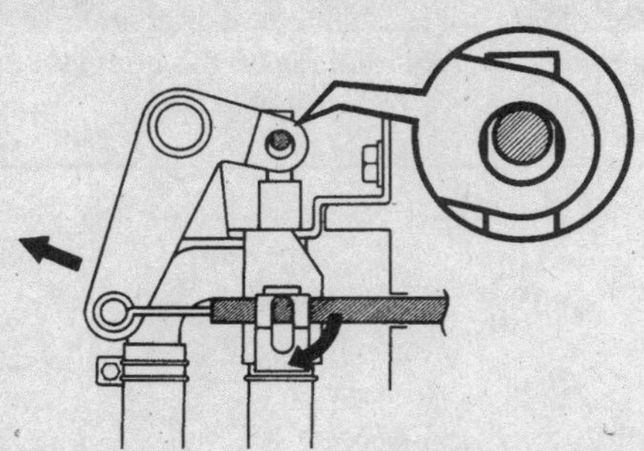

10.21 To set the Temperature valve, lift the valve control lever up as far as possible and connect the inner wire to the lever (1979 through 1981 models)

down at the far right end of the air conditioning/heating ducting).

16 Remove the blower motor from the housing and unplug the electrical connector.

17 Installation is the reverse of removal.

10 Heater and air conditioning control assembly - removal and installation

1979 through 1981 models

Refer to illustrations 10.2, 10.15, 10.17, 10.19, 10.21

1 Disconnect the negative battery cable from the battery. **Caution:** *If the stereo in your vehicle is equipped with an anti-theft system, refer to the information on page 0-15 at the front of this manual before detaching the cable.*

2 Remove the three screws from the dashboard under tray **(see illustration)** and remove the tray.

3 Remove the lid from the glove compartment, then unscrew the mounting screws and remove it **(see illustration 10.2)**.

4 Pull the knobs off the heater controls and carefully pry off the control panel with a screwdriver.

5 Remove the cover from the fuse box **(see illustration 10.2)**.

6 Remove the knobs from the radio and the six screws from the instrument panel. Pull the panel out from the bottom and remove it.

7 Disconnect and remove the instrument cluster and the clock.

8 Remove the four radio mounting screws, disconnect the aerial and speaker wires from the radio and remove the radio.

9 Remove the stepped air duct from the front of the heater assembly and the angled air duct from the top of the heater.

10 Disconnect the four heater control cables and disconnect the heater blower switch/wires.

11 Remove the four screws and withdraw the heater control assembly with the control cables attached **(see illustration 10.2)**.

12 The control panel may be dismantled by removing the clips from the outer cables and unhooking the inner ones. The blower switch may be taken off after removing the mounting screws.

13 Installation is the reversal of the removal procedure, but be sure to adjust the control cables as follows.

14 The heater control assembly operates four control cables, each of a different length. The shortest one operates the Mode select damper and the next longest the Temperature valve. The longest cable operates the Air inlet damper and the remaining one the Air mix damper.

15 To adjust the Air inlet damper cable, push the lever against its stop on the fresh air side and connect the inner wire to the damper lever **(see illustration)**.

16 Hold the lever in this position, slide the outer cable as far away from the damper as possible, then slide it into the cable clip.

17 To adjust the Mode select damper, push the damper until its lever is horizontal (in the vent position) and connect the inner wire to the damper lever **(see illustration)**.

18 Hold the lever in this position, slide the outer cable as far away from the damper as possible, then slide it into the cable clip.

19 To set the Air mix damper, push the damper against its stop in the Cool position and connect the inner wire to the damper lever **(see illustration)**.

20 Hold the lever in this position, slide the outer cable as far away from the damper as possible, then slide it into the cable clip.

21 To set the Temperature valve, lift the valve control lever up as far as possible and connect the inner wire to the lever **(see illustration)**.

22 Hold the lever in this position, slide the outer cable as far away from the lever as possible and slide the outer cable into the cable clip.

23 After connecting the cables, operate each of the control levers and make sure that they work smoothly over their full range of travel.

1982 through 1986 models

Refer to illustrations 10.26,10.27 and 10.32

24 Disconnect the negative battery cable from the battery. **Caution:** *If the stereo in your vehicle is equipped with an anti-theft system, refer to the information on page 0-15 at the front of this manual before detaching the cable.*

10.26 Remove the heater control panel (1982 through 1986 models)

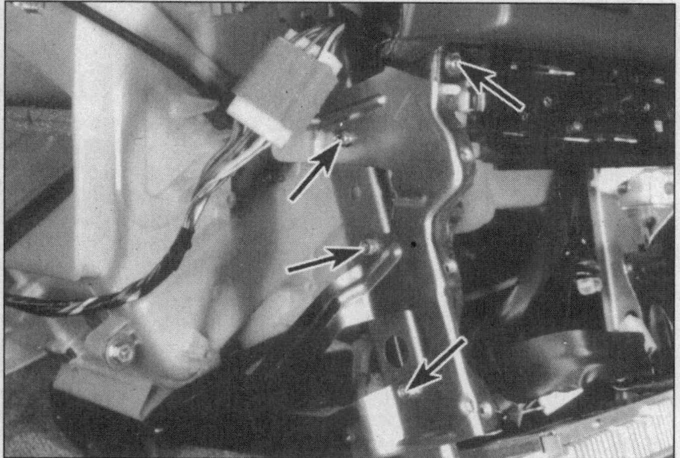

10.32 Metal side pillar support bracket (1982 through 1986 models)

25 Remove the control knobs by pulling the knobs free.

26 Undo the three panel securing screws and withdraw the panel **(see illustration)**.

27 Remove the upper console panel and the forward console **(see illustration)**.

28 Remove the ashtray and the lower retaining screws.

29 Remove the upper retaining screws, disconnect the lighter and ashtray light connectors and remove the panel.

30 Unclip and detach the gear lever boot for the console.

31 Remove the retaining screws on each side at the front and rear, pull the console forward and remove it. Disconnect any electrical connections.

32 Remove the screw and bolts and detach one of the metal side pillar support brackets **(see illustration)**.

33 Lower the control unit and disconnect the electrical connector and control cables.

34 Remove the heater and air conditioning control assembly.

35 Installation is the reverse of removal.

1987 and later models

Refer to illustrations 10.37, 10.38 and 10.39

36 Disconnect the negative battery cable from the battery. **Caution:** *If the stereo in your vehicle is equipped with an anti-theft system, refer to the information on page 0-15 at the front of this manual before detaching the cable.*

37 Remove the ash tray, then remove the two screws that attach the ash tray retainer to the dash **(see illustration)**.

38 On models with a manual transmission, remove the shift lever knob. Remove the three screws that attach the instrument cluster finish panel to the console **(see illustration)**.

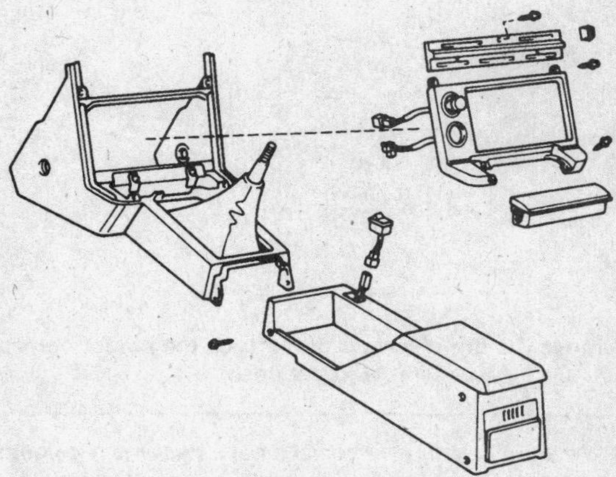

10.27 Location of the fasteners for the upper and forward consoles (1982 through 1986 models)

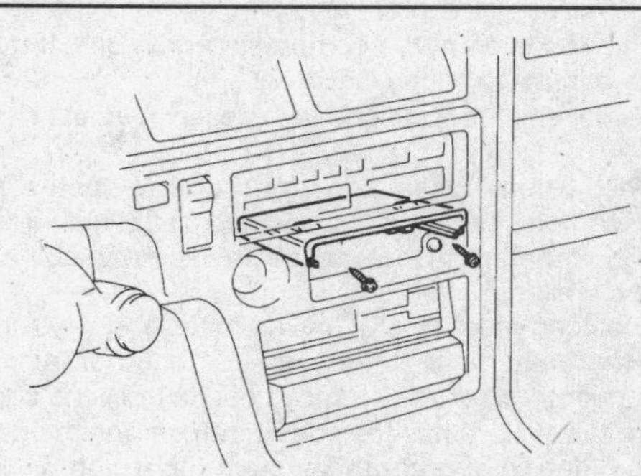

10.37 Remove the two screws that attach the ash tray retainer to the dash and remove the retainer (1987 and later models)

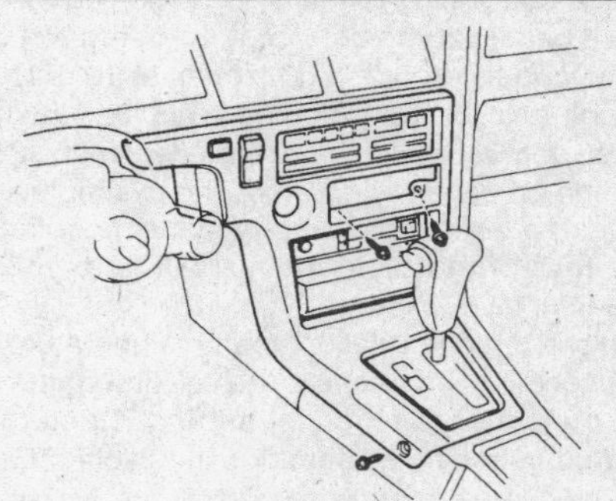

10.38 Remove the three screws that attach the instrument cluster finish panel to the console and remove the panel

39 Remove the three screws that attach the heater control assembly to the dash **(see illustration)**, pull out the control assembly, unplug all electrical connectors and remove the control assembly.

40 Installation is the reverse of removal.

11 Air conditioning and heating system - check and maintenance

Air conditioning system

Refer to illustration 11.7

Warning: *The air conditioning system is under high pressure. Do not loosen any fittings or remove any components until after the system has been discharged. Air conditioning refrigerant should be properly*

3

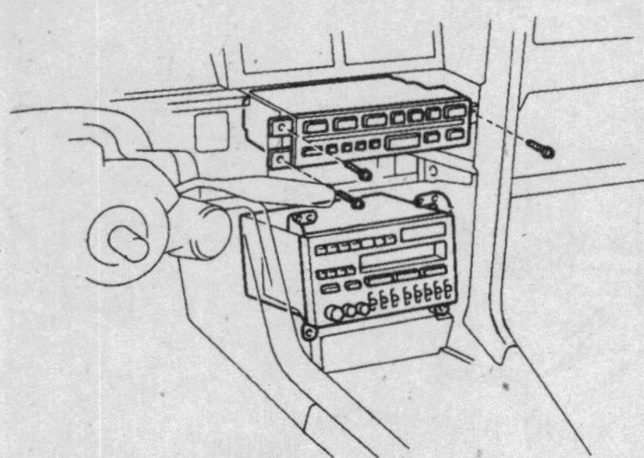

10.39 Remove the three screws that attach the heater control assembly to the dash

discharged into an EPA-approved container at a dealer service department or an automotive air conditioning repair facility. Always wear eye protection when disconnecting air conditioning system fittings.

1 The following maintenance checks should be performed on a regular basis to ensure that the air conditioner continues to operate at peak efficiency.

a) Inspect the condition of the compressor drivebelt. If it is worn or deteriorated, replace it (see Chapter 1).
b) Check the drivebelt tension and, if necessary, adjust it (see Chapter 1).
c) Inspect the system hoses. Look for cracks, bubbles, hardening and deterioration. Inspect the hoses and all fittings for oil bubbles or seepage. If there is any evidence of wear, damage or leakage, replace the hose(s).
d) Inspect the condenser fins for leaves, bugs and any other foreign material that may have embedded itself in the fins. Use a "fin comb" or compressed air to remove debris from the condenser.
e) Make sure the system has the correct refrigerant charge.

2 It's a good idea to operate the system for about ten minutes at least once a month. This is particularly important during the winter months because long term non-use can cause hardening, and subsequent failure, of the seals.

3 Because of the complexity of the air conditioning system and the special equipment necessary to service it, in-depth troubleshooting and repairs are beyond the scope of this manual (refer to the *Haynes Automotive Heating and Air Conditioning Manual*). However, simple component replacement procedures are provided in this Chapter.

4 The most common cause of poor cooling is simply a low system refrigerant charge. If a noticeable drop in system cooling ability occurs, one of the following quick checks will help you determine whether the refrigerant level is low.

5 Warm the engine up to normal operating temperature.

6 Place the air conditioning temperature selector at the coldest setting and put the blower at the highest setting. Open the doors (to make sure the air conditioning system doesn't cycle off as soon as it cools the passenger compartment).

7 With the compressor engaged - the clutch will make an audible click and the center of the clutch will rotate - inspect the sight glass, if equipped **(see illustration)**. If the refrigerant looks foamy, it's low. Charge the system as described later in this Section.

8 If there's no sight glass, feel the inlet and outlet pipes at the compressor. One side should be cold and one hot. If there's no perceptible difference between the two pipes, there's something wrong with the compressor or the system. It might be a low charge - it might be something else. Take the vehicle to a dealer service department or an automotive air conditioning shop. Refer to the *Haynes Automotive Heating and Air Conditioning Manual* or take the vehicle to a dealer service department or an automotive air conditioning shop.

Adding refrigerant

Note: *At the time this manual was written, the following procedure was still legal. However, new Federal regulations proposed by the Environmental Protection Agency (EPA) were expected to go into effect soon. Once these new regulations become law, the sale of 14-ounce cans of refrigerant will be prohibited; the only cans available will be the large size (usually 30 pounds). If you decide to add refrigerant from one of these larger cans, you will need a set of manifold gauges, all the necessary fittings, adapters and hoses to hook everything up and a copy of the* Haynes Automotive Heating and Air Conditioning Manual.

11.7 Inspect the sight glass (arrow) - if the refrigerant looks foamy, it's low, so you'll need to charge the system

9 Buy an automotive "charging kit" at an automotive parts store. A charging kit includes a 14-ounce can of refrigerant, a can tap valve and a short section of hose which can be attached between the tap valve and the system low side service valve. **Warning:** *Do not connect to the "high side" of the system!* Because one can of refrigerant may not be sufficient to bring the system charge up to its proper level, it's a good idea to buy an additional can. Make sure that one of the cans contains red refrigerant dye. If the system is leaking, the red dye will leak out with the refrigerant and help you pinpoint the location of the leak. **Warning:** *Wear eye protection while performing this Step and never add more than 1-1/2 14-ounce cans of refrigerant.*

10 Hook up the charging kit in accordance with the manufacturer's instructions.

11 Warm up the engine and turn the air conditioning system on. Keep the charging kit hose away from the fan and other moving parts.

12 Place a thermometer in the center dashboard vent and add refrigerant until the indicated temperature is around 40 to 45 degrees F.

Heating system

Refer to illustration 11.14

13 If the air coming out of the heater vents isn't hot, the problem could stem from any of the following causes:

a) The thermostat is stuck open, preventing the engine coolant from warming up enough to carry heat to the heater core. Replace the thermostat (see Section 3).
b) A heater hose is blocked, preventing the flow of coolant through the heater core. Feel both heater hoses at the firewall. They should be hot. If one of them is cold, there is an obstruction in one of the hoses or in the heater core, or the heater control valve is shut. Detach the hoses and back flush the heater core with a water hose. If the heater core is clear but circulation is impeded, remove the two hoses and flush them out with a water hose.
c) If flushing fails to remove the blockage from the heater core, the core must be replaced.

14 If the blower motor speed does not correspond to the setting selected on the blower switch, the problem could be a bad fuse, circuit, switch, blower motor resistor or motor.

a) Before checking the blower motor or circuit, always check the fuse first.
b) Using a test light or voltmeter, check the voltage at the motor.
c) Pull the heating/air conditioning control assembly (see Section 10) far enough from the dash to verify - with a test light or voltmeter - that current is reaching the blower switch on the control assembly. If the switch is not getting current, troubleshoot the circuit between the battery and the switch.

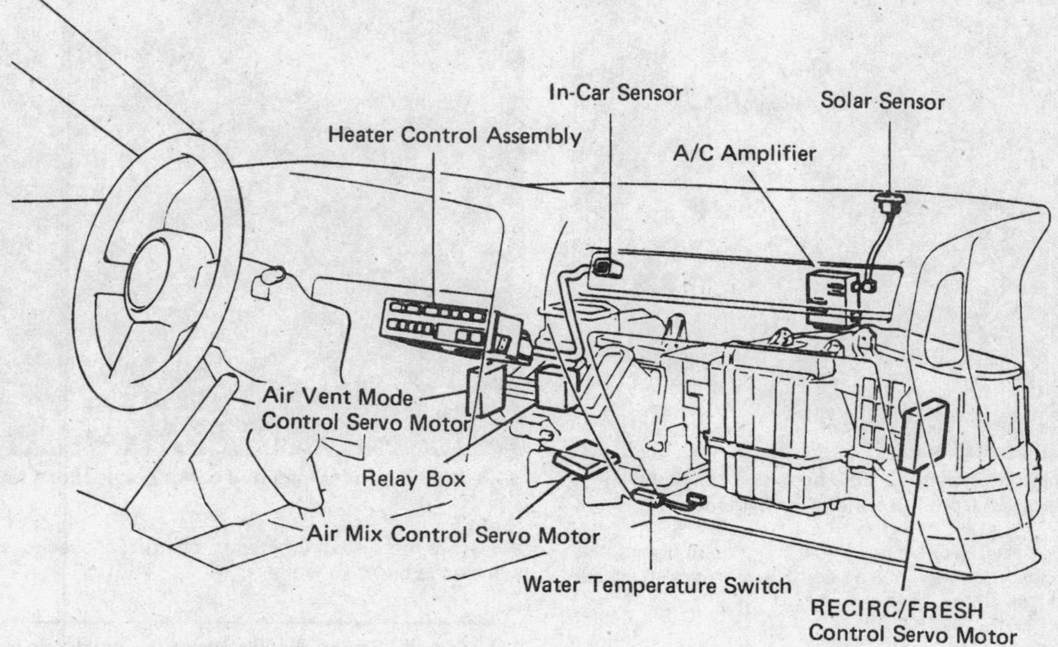

11.14 On 1987 and later models, the blower motor resistor is located under the dash, near the heater and air conditioning control assembly (on earlier models, you'll find it inside the center duct, as shown in illustration 9.9; on some models, it may be near the glovebox)

3

12.5 Compressor mounting bolt locations (arrows) (typical)

d) Locate the blower motor resistor: On most 1982 through 1986 models, it's inside the center duct **(see illustration 9.9)**; on most 1987 and later models, it's behind the heater control assembly **(see illustration)**. On some models, it may be located near the glove box. Check the resistor to make sure that it is getting current from the blower switch.
   1) If the resistor is not getting current, check the wire.
   2) If the wire is good, replace the switch (see Section 10).

e) Using a test light or voltmeter, verify that the blower motor is getting current. If the blower motor is not getting current, replace the resistor.

15 If there isn't any air coming out of the vents:

a) Turn the ignition ON and activate the fan control. Place your ear at the heating/air conditioning vent and listen. Most motors are audible. Can you hear the motor running?

b) If you can't (and have already verified that the blower switch and the blower motor resistor are good), the blower motor itself is probably bad (see Section 9). **Note:** *You can determine the motor's condition by hooking up a fused jumper wire directly between battery voltage and the blower motor.*

16 If the carpet under the heater core is damp, or if antifreeze vapor or steam is coming through the vents, the heater core is leaking. Remove it and install a new unit (most radiator shops will not repair a leaking heater core).

12 Air conditioning compressor - removal and installation

Refer to illustration 12.5

Warning: *The air conditioning system is under high pressure. Do not loosen any fittings or remove any components until after the system has been discharged. Air conditioning refrigerant should be properly discharged into an EPA-approved container at a dealer service department or an automotive air conditioning repair facility. Always wear eye protection when disconnecting air conditioning system fittings.*

1 Disconnect the cable from the negative terminal of the battery. **Caution:** *If the stereo in your vehicle is equipped with an anti-theft system, refer to the information on page 0-15 at the front of this manual before detaching the cable.*

2 Unplug the electrical connector from the compressor.

3 Detach the two flexible hoses from the compressor service valves. Cap the open fittings immediately to keep moisture out of the system.

4 Loosen the drivebelt (see Chapter 1).

5 Remove the compressor mounting bolts **(see illustration)**.

6 Remove the compressor. **Note:** *Keep the compressor level during handling and storage. If the compressor seized or you find metal particles in the refrigerant lines, the system must be flushed out by an air conditioning technician and the receiver/drier must be replaced* (see Section 14).

7 Installation is the reverse of the removal procedure. Make sure you tighten the compressor mounting bolts and the valve-to-hose fittings securely and adjust the drivebelt to the proper tension (see Chapter 1).

8 Connect the cable to the negative terminal of the battery.

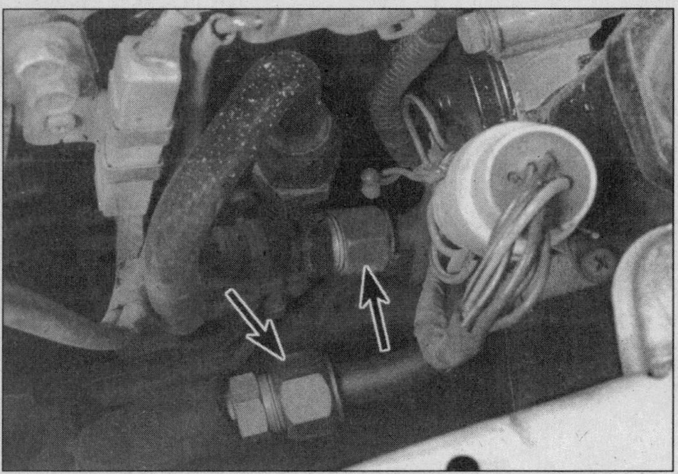

13.5 Disconnect the discharge flexible hose and the liquid line hose (arrows) from the condenser (typical)

9 Take the vehicle to a dealer service department or an automotive air conditioning specialist and have the air conditioning system evacuated, recharged and leak tested.

13 Air conditioning condenser - removal and installation

Refer to illustration 13.5

Warning: *The air conditioning system is under high pressure. Do not loosen any fittings or remove any components until after the system has been discharged. Air conditioning refrigerant should be properly discharged into an EPA-approved container at a dealer service department or an automotive air conditioning repair facility. Always wear eye protection when disconnecting air conditioning system fittings.*

1 Have the refrigerant discharged at a dealer service department or an automotive air conditioning repair facility.

2 Disconnect the cable from the negative terminal of the battery. **Caution:** *If the stereo in your vehicle is equipped with an anti-theft system, refer to the information on page 0-15 at the front of this manual before detaching the cable.*

3 Remove the hood lock brace.

4 Disconnect the discharge flexible hose from the condenser inlet fitting.

5 Disconnect the liquid line hose from the condenser outlet fitting **(see illustration)**. Be certain to cap the open fittings immediately to keep moisture out of the system.

6 Remove the four retaining screws and lift out the condenser. Store it upright to prevent oil loss.

7 Installation is the reverse of removal. However, make sure on installation that the liquid line hose and the discharge flexible hose to the condenser are tightened to the proper torque.

8 If a new condenser was installed add refrigerant oil to the system. On 1983 and earlier and 1987 and later models add 1.4 to 1.7 fl. oz. (40 to 50 cc), on 1984 and 1985 models add 0.8 to 1.0 fl. oz. (25 to 30 cc) and on 1986 models add 0.3 to 0.7 fl. oz. (10 to 20 cc).

14.3 Receiver/drier inlet and outlet connections (arrows) (typical)

9 Have the system evacuated, charged and leak tested by the shop that discharged it.

14 Air conditioning receiver/drier - removal and installation

Warning: *The air conditioning system is under high pressure. Do not loosen any fittings or remove any components until after the system has been discharged. Air conditioning refrigerant should be properly discharged into an EPA-approved container at a dealer service department or an automotive air conditioning repair facility. Always wear eye protection when disconnecting air conditioning system fittings.*

Removal

Refer to illustration 14.3

1 Have the refrigerant discharged at a dealer service department or an automotive air conditioning repair facility.

2 Disconnect the cable from the negative terminal of the battery. **Caution:** *If the stereo in your vehicle is equipped with an anti-theft system, refer to the information on page 0-15 at the front of this manual before detaching the cable.*

3 Disconnect the receiver/drier inlet and outlet connections **(see illustration)**. Cap or plug the open lines immediately.

4 Remove the receiver/drier from the receiver/drier holder.

Installation

5 Install the receiver/drier back into the holder. **Note:** *Do not remove the plugs from the fittings until ready for connection.*

6 Install the inlet and outlet connections, tighten the connections to the specified torque.

7 If the receiver/drier was replaced add 0.3 to 0.7 fl. oz. (10 to 20 cc) of compressor oil to the compressor.

8 Connect the cable to the negative terminal of the battery.

9 Have the air conditioning system evacuated and recharged by a dealer service department or an air conditioning specialist.

Chapter 4 Fuel and exhaust systems

Contents

4

Specifications

Fuel pressure

1979 through 1986	
Vacuum hose disconnected	33 to 38 psi
Vacuum hose connected	27 to 31 psi
1987 and 1988 (all) and 1989 and later turbo models	
Vacuum hose disconnected	33 to 40 psi
Vacuum hose connected	23 to 30 psi
1989 and later non-turbo models	
Vacuum hose disconnected	38 to 44 psi
Vacuum hose connected	33 to 37 psi

Resistance values

Cold start injector	
1979 through 1986	3 to 5 ohms
1987 through 1992 (non-turbo models only)	2 to 4 ohms
Air valve (1979 through 1981)	40 to 60 ohms
ISC valve	
B1 and S1 or B1 and S3	10 to 30 ohms
B2 and S2 or B2 and S4	10 to 30 ohms

Resistance values (continued)

Fuel injector	
1979 through 1986	1.5 to 3.0 ohms
1987	
Non-turbo	1.8 to 3.4 ohms
Turbo	2.0 to 3.8 ohms
1989 through 1992	
Non-turbo	Approximately 13.8 ohms
Turbo	2.0 to 3.8 ohms

Torque specifications

	Ft-lbs (unless otherwise indicated)
Air intake chamber bolts	14 to 22
Fuel rail mounting bolts	
1979 through 1986	108 to 132 in-lbs
1987 on	156 in-lbs
Pressure regulator locknut (1979 through 1986)	26 to 39
Fuel line-to-pressure regulator banjo bolt	18 to 25
Fuel delivery hose banjo bolt	19 to 25
Turbocharger outlet elbow nuts	32
Turbocharger-to-exhaust manifold nuts	33
Oil pipe-to-turbocharger	108 in-lbs
Water pipe-to-turbocharger	65 in-lbs
Turbocharger stay (brace)-to-turbocharger bolts	59

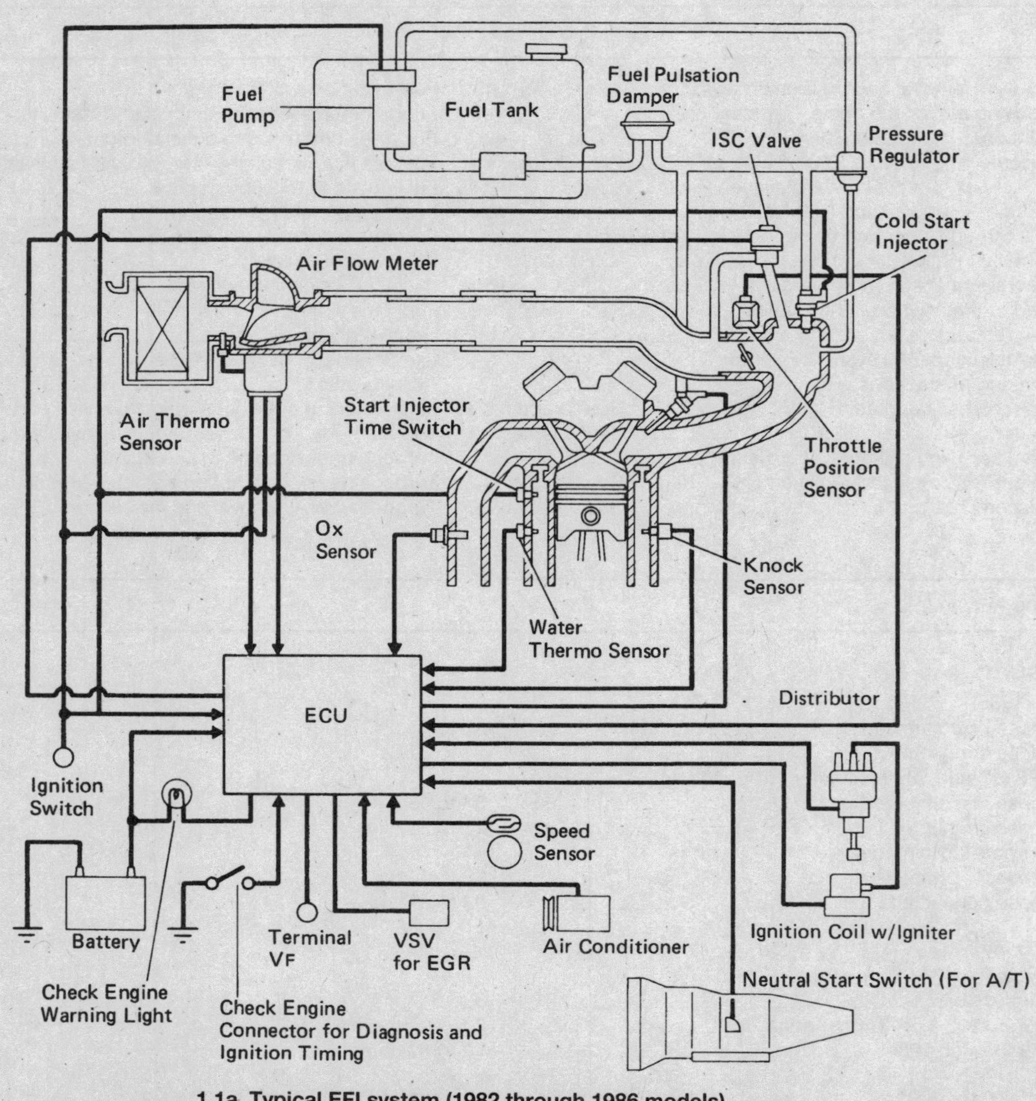

1.1a Typical EFI system (1982 through 1986 models)

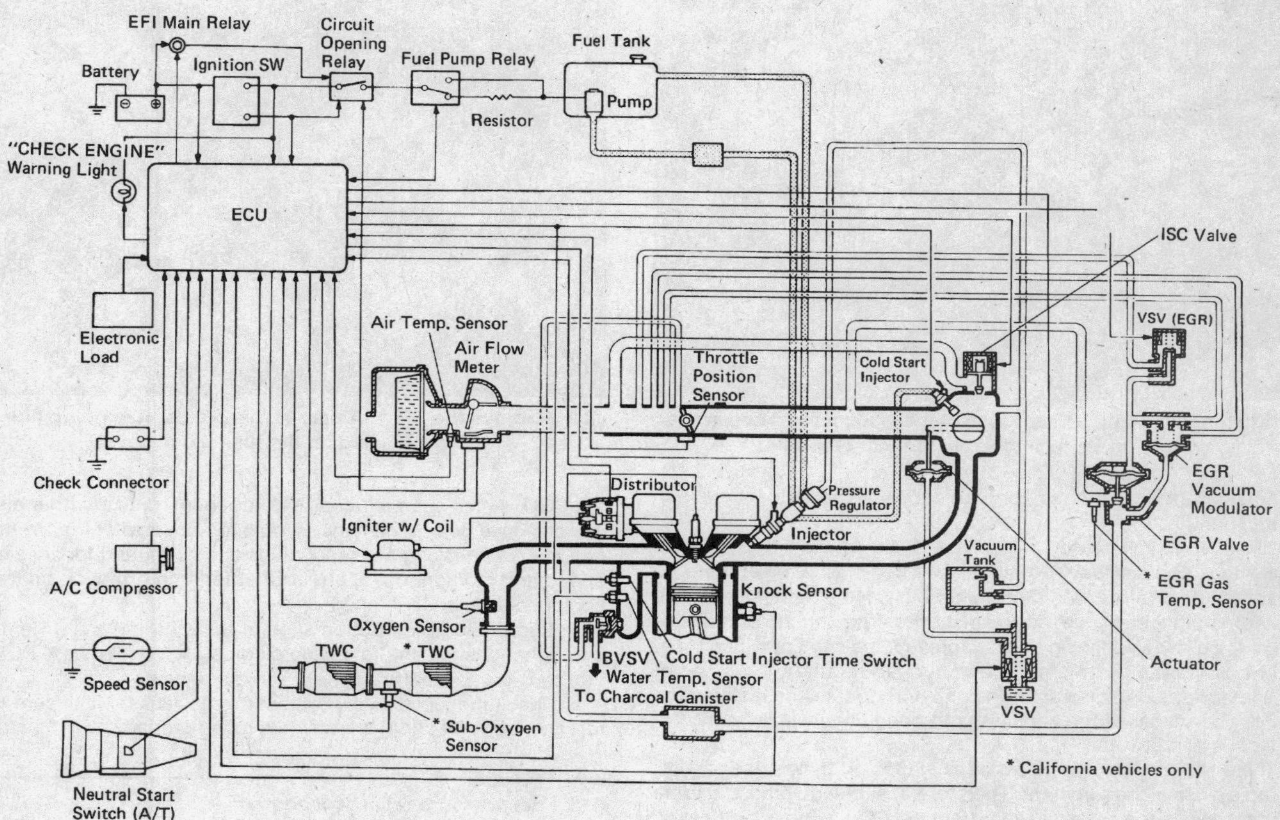

1.1b Typical EFI system (1987 and later non-turbo models)

4

1 Electronic Fuel Injection (EFI) system - general information and precautions

Electronic Fuel Injection (EFI) system

Refer to illustrations 1.1a and 1.1b

The Electronic Fuel Injection (EFI) system **(see illustrations)** consists of three basic subsystems: the fuel system, the air induction system and the electronic control system.

Fuel system

The fuel system consists of the fuel tank, an electrically-operated fuel pump (located in front of the fuel tank on 1979 through 1983 models and inside the tank on later models), a fuel injection system and the fuel supply and return lines between the tank and the fuel injection system.

The electric fuel pump provides fuel under constant pressure to the injectors, which inject a metered quantity of fuel into the intake manifold in accordance with signals from the Electronic Control Unit (ECU).

Air induction system

The air induction system filters the incoming air in the air cleaner housing and routes this filtered air to the throttle body by means of a system of ducting.

On 1979 through 1981 models, an air valve promotes a smoother idle during warm-ups by routing additional air into the air intake chamber during warm-ups; after the engine is warmed up, the air valve closes. On 1982 and later models, an idle speed control (ISC) valve does basically the same thing, except the ISC valve is controlled by the ECU as well as by engine coolant temperature.

Electronic control system

The electronic control system controls the injection duration (how long the injectors are open) by monitoring various operating conditions, such as intake air volume, intake air temperature, coolant temperature, engine rpm, acceleration and deceleration, the content of oxygen in the exhaust and other things. The ECU also alters the spark advance, the idle speed, recirculation of exhaust gases, the operation of the transmission and other operating variables. For more information about the electronic control system, see Chapter 6.

Exhaust system

The exhaust system consists of the exhaust manifold, the catalytic converter(s), the exhaust pipe and the muffler. The exhaust system is suspended from the floorpan with mounting brackets and rubber hangers. All 1979 through 1986 models, 1987 and 1988 non-turbo models and 1989 and later non-turbo Federal and Canadian models use a single three-way catalyst (TWC); 1987 and 1988 turbo models, 1989 and later non-turbo California models and all 1988 and later turbo models use two TWCs. The catalytic converter is an emission control device added to the exhaust system to reduce pollutants. For more information on the catalytic converter, refer to Chapter 6.

Precautions

Whenever it is necessary to work on the engine, the fuel injection system or associated components, certain special precautions must be observed:

a) When a tachometer is used to make adjustments to the engine, connect it to the ignition coil negative terminal or to the service connector.
b) Check the battery terminal connections and all ignition primary

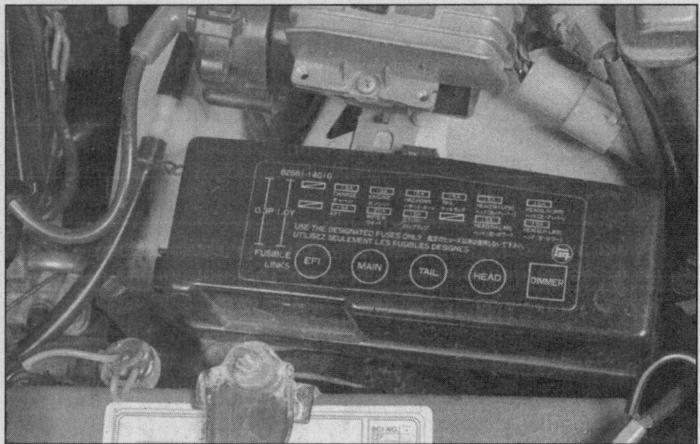

3.2 The engine compartment fuse block is located between the battery and the ignition coil on most models

3.3 Remove the EFI 15A fuse to disable the fuel pump (the fuses are labeled on the fuse block cover)

and secondary wiring connections to make sure they are clean and tight.

c) When working near the oxygen sensor, be careful not to strike or damage it in any way. Do not allow any gasoline, oil or water to come into contact with it or the rubber hose. The hose must be kept straight and must not be distorted. The connector must always be installed facing down to prevent the entry of water.

d) The air intake system must be checked regularly for signs of damaged, loose or cracked hoses and ducts. Any leaks in the system will cause the engine to run poorly and will generally affect its performance.

e) The performance of the ECU can be affected by the use of a CB radio or similar equipment. Therefore, if such equipment is to be used, install the antenna as far from the ECU as possible (that is, on the right side at the rear). The feeder and antenna must be properly adjusted and the feeder located at least eight inches from the ECU wiring.

f) The ECU must be handled with great care at all times. Do not remove its cover. Do not try to repair it and do not allow it to get wet. If defective, it must be replaced as a unit. When disconnecting the wiring from the ECU, make sure the ignition is off or the battery terminals are disconnected. **Caution:** *If the stereo in your vehicle is equipped with an anti-theft system, refer to the information on page 0-15 at the front of this manual before detaching the cable. Also, make sure that all electrical connections are clean and tight after reconnecting the wiring.*

2 General diagnosis

Warning: *Gasoline is extremely flammable, so take extra precautions when you work on any part of the fuel system. Don't smoke or allow open flames or bare light bulbs near the work area, and don't work in a garage where a natural gas-type appliance (such as a water heater or clothes dryer) with a pilot light is present. If you spill any fuel on your skin, rinse it off immediately with soap and water. When you perform any kind of work on the fuel system, wear safety glasses and have a Class B type fire extinguisher on hand.*

The EFI system is not usually the source of engine problems. Trouble is usually caused by a bad contact in the wiring connectors. Always make sure that all connections are secure by tapping or wiggling the connectors to see if the signal changes. Make sure that the connector terminals are not bent and that the connectors are pushed completely together and locked.

Before troubleshooting the EFI system, always check the condition of the ignition system. Make sure that the battery, all fuses, fusible links and grounds, the pick-up coil, the igniter, the ignition coil, the high tension wire, the distributor, the spark plug wires and the spark plugs are all in good condition, properly connected and functioning correctly. Check the idle speed and the ignition timing. Never replace the ECU, which is an expensive component, until all other electrical devices have been eliminated as possible sources of trouble (the procedures for checking the spark plugs and wires, and for adjusting idle speed and ignition timing are in Chapter 1; information on the other components is in Chapter 5).

Check the air induction system for vacuum leaks. Removal of components such as the engine oil dipstick, oil filler cap, PCV hose, etc. can also cause the engine to run out of tune.

Check the fuel delivery system for fuel leaks. Make sure that the fuel filter and fuel pump are both operating properly.

3 Fuel pressure relief procedure

Refer to illustrations 3.2 and 3.3

Warning: *Gasoline is extremely flammable, so take extra precautions when you work on any part of the fuel system. Don't smoke or allow open flames or bare light bulbs near the work area, and don't work in a garage where a natural gas-type appliance (such as a water heater or clothes dryer) with a pilot light is present. If you spill any fuel on your skin, rinse it off immediately with soap and water. When you perform any kind of work on the fuel system, wear safety glasses and have a Class B type fire extinguisher on hand.*

1 The fuel system remains under pressure even after the engine has been shut off for an extended time. Therefore you must relieve the pressure in the fuel system before any work is done on fuel injection components or lines.

2 Remove the cover from the engine compartment fuse block located just in front of the battery **(see illustration)**.

3 Pull the EFI fuse from the fuse block to disable the fuel pump. The EFI fuse is identified by the letters EFI 15A on the cover **(see illustration)**.

4 Start the engine and let it run until it dies from lack of fuel, then turn the engine over for several seconds with the starter to insure that all pressure has been eliminated from the system.

5 When disconnecting fuel line fittings or components, cover the fitting with a rag to absorb any fuel that may leak out.

6 Be sure to replace the EFI fuse when work is completed on the fuel system.

4 Fuel lines and fittings - general information

Refer to illustration 4.6

Warning: *Gasoline is extremely flammable, so take extra precautions when you work on any part of the fuel system. Don't smoke or allow open flames or bare light bulbs near the work area, and don't work in a garage where a natural gas-type appliance (such as a water heater or clothes dryer) with a pilot light is present. If you spill any fuel on your*

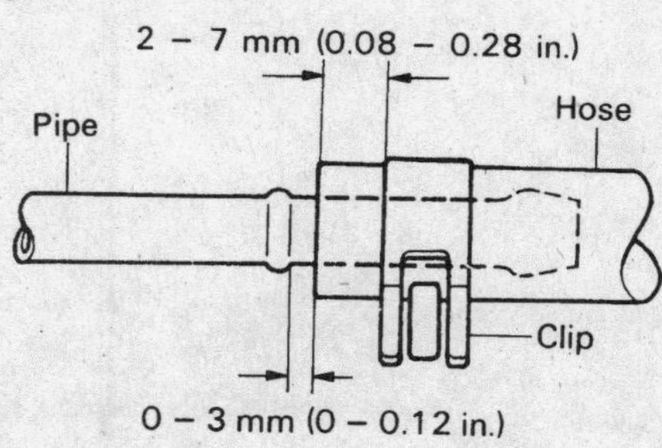

4.6 When attaching a section of rubber fuel hose to a metal fuel line, be sure to overlap the hose as shown and secure it to the line with a new hose clamp of the proper type

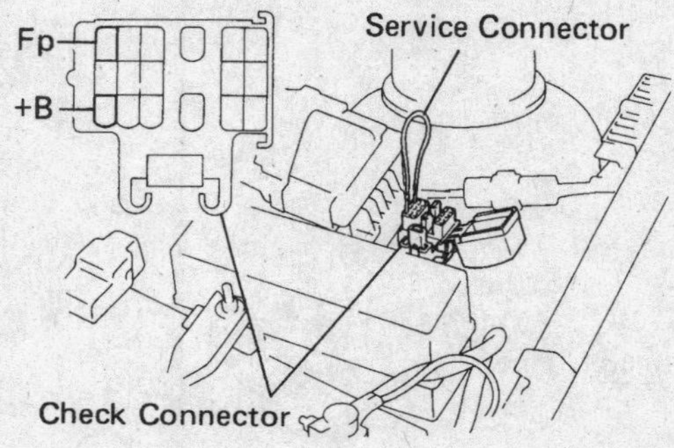

5.2b On 1987 and later models, bridge terminals +B and Fp of the fuel pump check connector

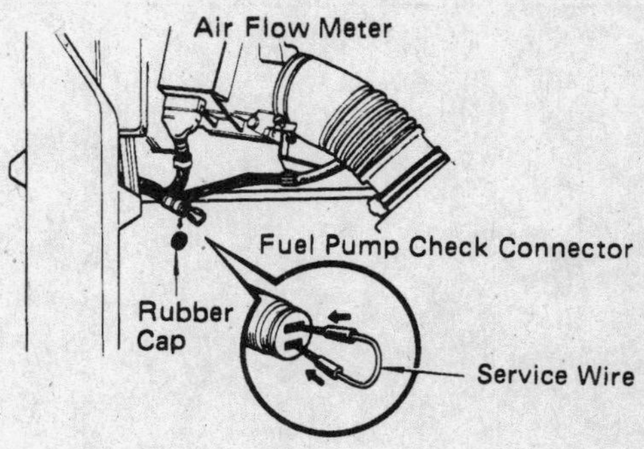

5.2a On 1979 through 1986 models, bridge both terminals of the fuel pump check connector with a jumper wire (1982 model shown, others similar)

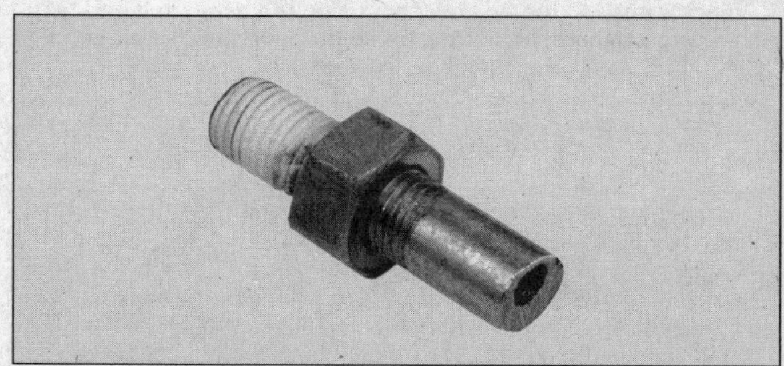

5.7 To make an adapter to fit in place of the cold start hose banjo bolt, take an 8.0 x 1.0 mm bolt, drill it out and install a nut and washer

skin, rinse it off immediately with soap and water. When you perform any kind of work on the fuel system, wear safety glasses and have a Class B type fire extinguisher on hand.

1 Check the fuel lines and all fittings and connections for cracks, leakage or deformation.

2 Check the fuel tank vapor vent system hoses and connections for looseness, sharp bends or damage.

3 Check the fuel tank for deformation, cracks, fuel leakage or tank band looseness.

4 Check the filler neck for damage or fuel leakage.

5 Repair or replace any damaged or deteriorated hoses or lines.

6 When attaching hoses to metal lines, overlap them as shown **(see illustration)**.

5 Fuel pump/fuel pressure - check

Warning: *Gasoline is extremely flammable, so take extra precautions when you work on any part of the fuel system. Don't smoke or allow open flames or bare light bulbs near the work area, and don't work in a garage where a natural gas-type appliance (such as a water heater or clothes dryer) with a pilot light is present. If you spill any fuel on your skin, rinse it off immediately with soap and water. When you perform any kind of work on the fuel system, wear safety glasses and have a Class B type fire extinguisher on hand.*

Fuel pump operation check

Refer to illustrations 5.2a and 5.2b

1 Turn on the ignition switch (but do not start the engine).

2 On 1979 through 1986 models, bridge both terminals of the fuel pump check connector with a jumper wire **(see illustration)**. On 1987 and later models, bridge terminals +B and Fp of the service connector **(see illustration)**.

3 Listen for fuel return noises from the fuel pressure regulator. On 1979 through 1986 models, verify that there's pressure in the hose to the cold start injector; on 1987 and later models, verify that there's pressure in the fuel inlet hose. And here's another test you can perform on any model (1984 and later) with an in-tank fuel pump: Remove the fuel filler neck cap, push the small "trap-door" in the mouth of the filler neck open with a pencil and place your ear close to the mouth of the neck. Have an assistant bridge the terminals of the fuel pump check connector. You should be able to hear a whirring sound as the pump is powered up (you can also perform this test on older models but the pump, which is under the vehicle, in front of the fuel tank, is more difficult to hear unless you're in a very quiet work space).

4 Remove the jumper wire. Close the cap on the service connector.

5 Turn off the ignition switch.

6 If the fuel pump isn't operating, inspect the following components: the EFI 15-amp fuse and the ignition 7.5-amp fuse and/or the EFI main relay (all located in the fuse panel next to the battery); the circuit opening relay (see *Electronic Control System* in Chapter 6); the fuel pump; and the wiring and electrical connectors (see the Wiring Diagrams at the end of the book).

Fuel pressure check

Refer to illustrations 5.7, 5.12, 5.13a, 5.13b and 5.18

7 A fuel pressure gauge equipped with an 8 mm banjo fitting on the end of the hose (Toyota SST 09268-45011) is required for the following procedure. There are a couple of alternatives to buying the special Toyota fuel pressure gauge setup:

a) Purchase an 8 mm banjo fitting and attach it to a fuel pressure gauge hose with a hose clamp.
b) If you can't find the correct size banjo fitting, buy an 8 mm bolt, cut the head off and drill it out. Add a nut with the same thread pitch and seal the threads with teflon tape **(see illustration)**.

8 Relieve the fuel pressure (see Section 3).

9 Verify that the battery voltage is 12 volts or more (see Chapter 5).

10 Detach the cable from the negative terminal of the battery. **Caution:** *If the stereo in your vehicle is equipped with an anti-theft system,*

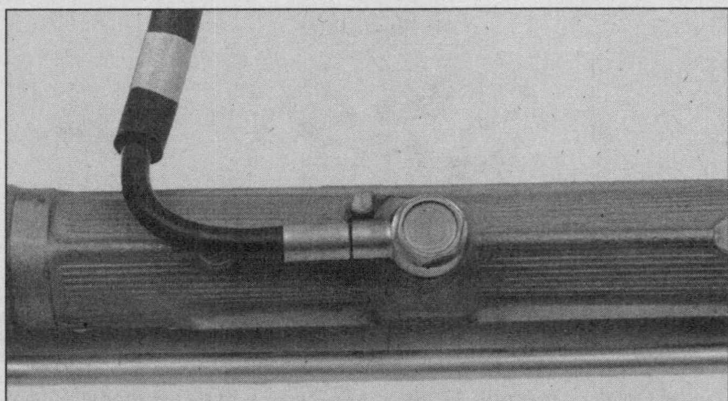

5.12 A typical Toyota fuel rail (removed from the vehicle for clarity): Remove the banjo bolt which connects the cold start injector hose to the fuel rail and, using the banjo bolt and two sealing washers, attach the banjo fitting of the fuel pressure gauge to the fuel rail

5.13a If you're using a makeshift adapter bolt, screw it into the fuel rail and tighten the nut . . .

5.13b . . . then attach the fuel pressure gauge hose with a hose clamp (fuel rail removed from engine for clarity)

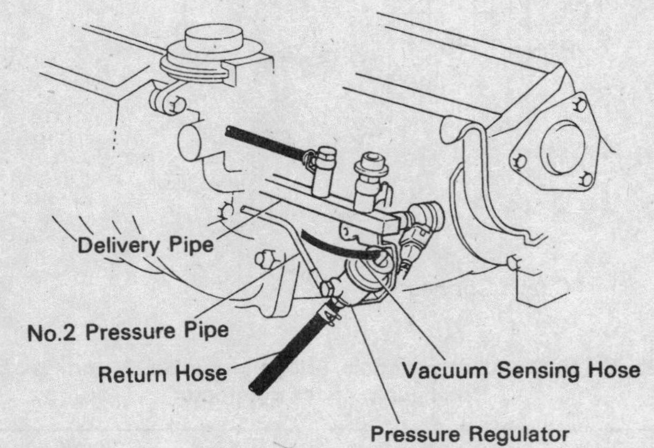

5.18 If the fuel pressure is too low, pinch the return hose - if the pressure goes up, the fuel pressure regulator is malfunctioning

refer to the information on page 0-15 at the front of this manual before detaching the cable.

11 Detach the electrical connector from the cold start injector.

12 Put a metal container or shop towel under the cold start injector pipe banjo bolt at the fuel rail **(see illustration)**, then remove the banjo bolt and detach the cold start injector pipe from the fuel rail.

13 To attach the fuel pressure gauge to the fuel rail:

a) If you are using the factory setup, or obtained an 8 mm banjo bolt for your pressure gauge kit, use the banjo bolt from the cold start injector pipe to attach the fuel pressure gauge to the fuel rail. Be sure to use sealing washers on both sides of the banjo fitting.

b) If you are using a drilled-out 8 mm bolt, attach the bolt to the fuel rail, tighten the locknut and attach the fuel pressure gauge hose with a hose clamp **(see illustrations)**.

14 Wipe off any gasoline that has leaked out of the fuel delivery pipe and attach the cable to the negative terminal of the battery.

15 Place the transaxle in Neutral (manual) or Park (automatic) and apply the parking brake.

16 If your vehicle is a 1979 through 1986 model, bridge both terminals of the fuel pump check connector **(see illustration 5.2a)**; if it's a 1987 or later model, bridge terminals +B and Fp of the check connector **(see illustration 5.2b)**. You should hear the fuel pump running and pressure should register on the gauge. If the fuel pump doesn't run, the fuel pump or control circuit is faulty. Remove the jumper wire.

17 Start the engine, detach the vacuum sensing hose from the pressure regulator and plug it.

18 Measure the fuel pressure at idle and compare it to the fuel pressure listed in this Chapter's Specifications.

a) If the pressure is high, check the fuel return line for an obstruction. If the line is clear, replace the fuel pressure regulator.

b) If the pressure is low, look for leaks in the fuel hoses, lines and fittings, in the fuel filter and in the vacuum sensing hose. If they all check out OK, pinch the fuel return hose **(see illustration)** and watch the gauge. If the fuel pressure rises, replace the fuel pressure regulator. If it is still low, the fuel pump is probably faulty.

19 Reattach the vacuum sensing hose to the pressure regulator, measure the fuel pressure at idle and compare your reading to the fuel pressure listed in this Chapter's Specifications. If the pressure didn't drop when the hose was connected, replace the fuel pressure regulator. Stop the engine. Verify that the fuel pressure remains at 21 psi or more for five minutes after the engine is turned off. If the pressure drops quickly, the fuel pump or pressure regulator may be defective or a fuel injector (or injectors) may be leaking.

20 Relieve the fuel pressure (see Section 3).

21 Detach the cable from the negative terminal of the battery.

22 Carefully remove the fuel pressure gauge.

23 Using new sealing washers, reattach the cold start injector pipe banjo fitting to the fuel rail.

24 Reattach the electrical connector to the cold start injector. Be sure to wipe up any spilled gasoline.

25 Attach the cable to the negative terminal of the battery.

26 Start the engine and check for leaks.

6 Fuel tank - removal and installation

Refer to illustrations 6.3, 6.4 and 6.5

Warning: *Gasoline is extremely flammable, so take extra precautions*

6.3 Unscrew the drain plug and drain any remaining fuel before removing the tank

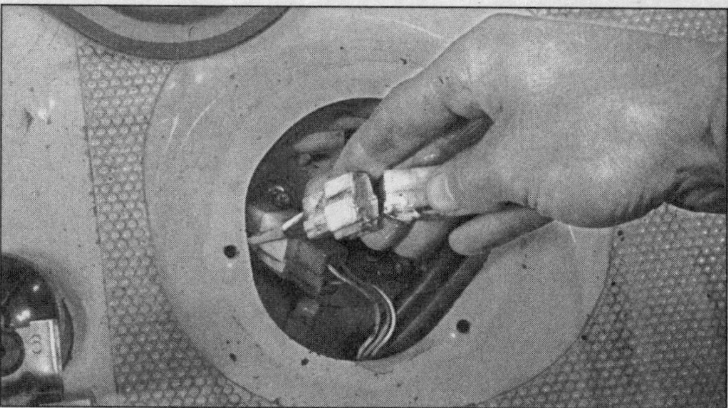

6.4 Remove the cover and disconnect the fuel tank sender unit wires before you lower the tank (or you'll break the wires!)

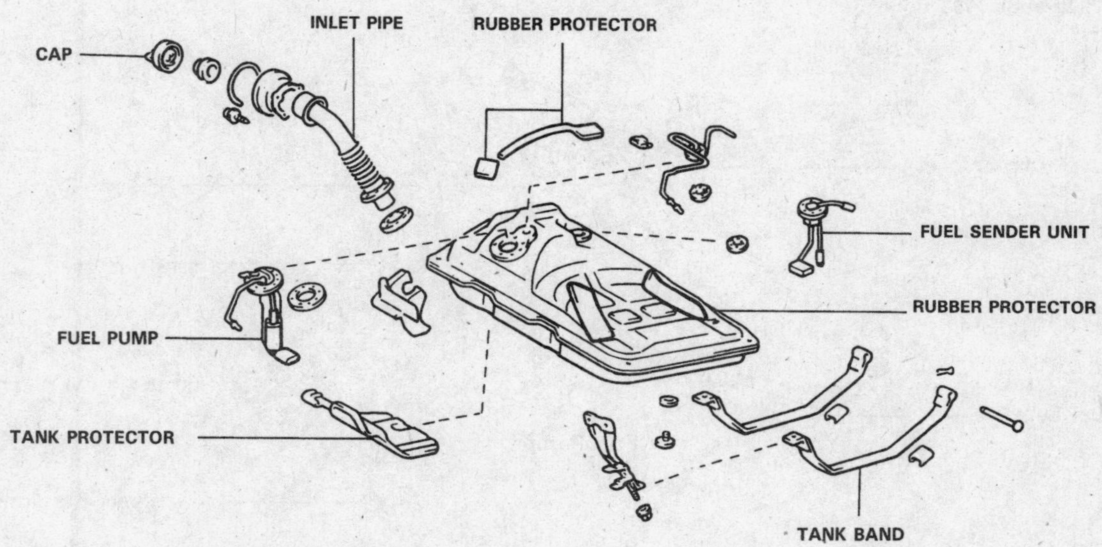

6.5 An exploded view of a typical fuel tank assembly

when you work on any part of the fuel system. Don't smoke or allow open flames or bare light bulbs near the work area, and don't work in a garage where a natural gas-type appliance (such as a water heater or clothes dryer) with a pilot light is present. If you spill any fuel on your skin, rinse it off immediately with soap and water. When you perform any kind of work on the fuel system, wear safety glasses and have a Class B type fire extinguisher on hand.

1 Relieve the pressure in the fuel system (see Section 3) and disconnect the cable from the negative terminal of the battery. **Caution:** *If the stereo in your vehicle is equipped with an anti-theft system, refer to the information on page 0-15 at the front of this manual before detaching the cable.*

2 To improve access when working underneath the vehicle, raise the rear end and support it securely on jackstands. Block the front wheels.

3 Unscrew the drain plug and empty any remaining fuel into an approved fuel container **(see illustration)**.

4 Pull back the carpet in the luggage compartment, remove the access cover for the fuel level sender unit and unplug the electrical connector **(see illustration)**.

5 Disconnect the fuel inlet (fuel filler) pipe flange from the fuel tank **(see illustration)**.

6 Clearly label, then disconnect, the fuel outlet, return and vapor recovery hoses (the outlet hose is the biggest in diameter, the return is smaller and the vapor recovery hose is the smallest).

7 Support the fuel tank with a transmission jack or a floor jack. Put a piece of wood between the jack pad and the tank to protect the tank. Disconnect the tank mounting bands and carefully lower the tank a few inches. Make sure you've disconnected all electrical connectors for the fuel level sender unit and/or the in-tank fuel pump (if equipped). Remove the tank from the vehicle.

8 Installation is the reverse of the removal procedure. Use a new seal gasket for the sender unit. Also use a new gasket when attaching the fuel filler pipe to the tank. Replace the rubber protectors on the top face of the tank and also those which are located between the tank and the bands.

9 Replace any defective or suspect hoses. The hose and pipe connections must be in good condition and secure.

10 Tighten the mounting band retaining nuts securely.

11 Reconnect the fuel level sender unit and fuel pump electrical connectors before reattaching the battery ground cable.

12 Refill the fuel tank and check for any signs of leaks from the tank or from the pipe/hose connections.

7 Fuel tank - cleaning and repair

Warning: *Gasoline is extremely flammable, so take extra precautions when you work on any part of the fuel system. Don't smoke or allow open flames or bare light bulbs near the work area, and don't work in a garage where a natural gas-type appliance (such as a water heater or*

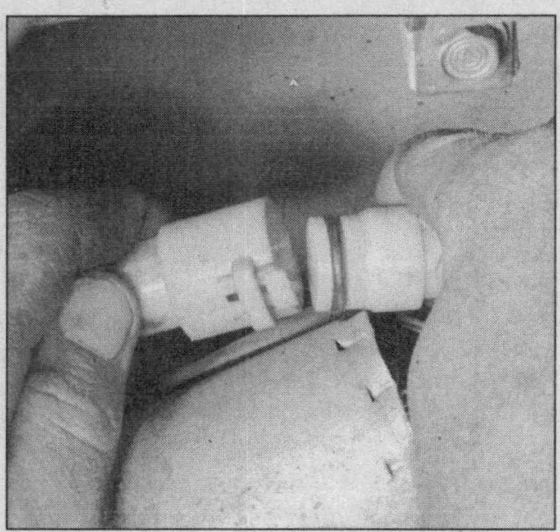
8.4 Unplug the electrical connector before proceeding with fuel pump removal (1979 through 1983 models)

8.6 Remove the fuel line outlet banjo fitting bolt (1979 through 1983 models)

8.7 Loosen the pump clamp bolt and nut and detach the pump from the bracket

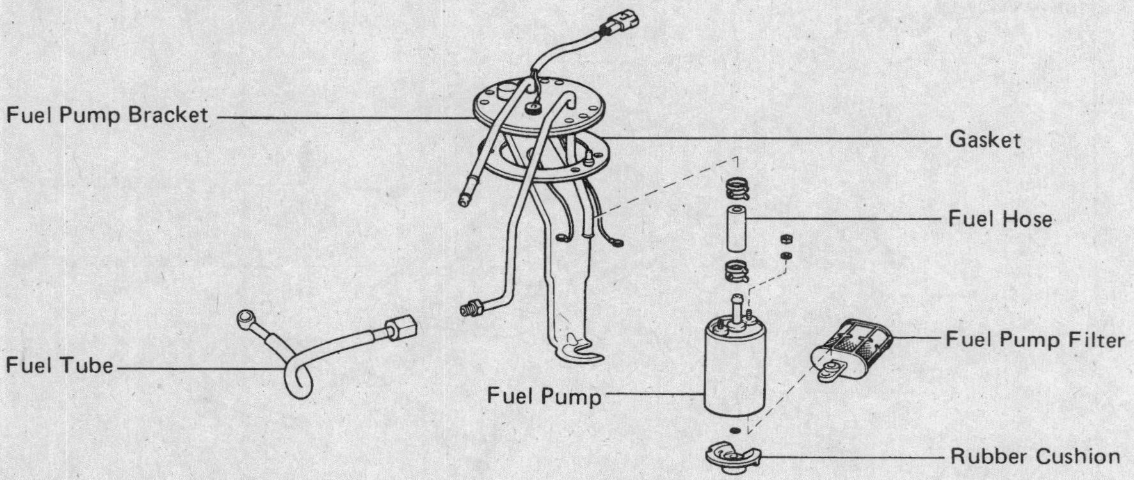

8.11 An exploded view of the fuel pump assembly used on 1987 and later models (1984 through 1986 models similar)

clothes dryer) with a pilot light is present. If you spill any fuel on your skin, rinse it off immediately with soap and water. When you perform any kind of work on the fuel system, wear safety glasses and have a Class B type fire extinguisher on hand.

1 Any repairs to the fuel tank or filler neck should be carried out by a professional who has experience in this critical and potentially dangerous work. Even after cleaning and flushing of the fuel system, explosive fumes can remain and ignite during repair of the tank.

2 If the fuel tank is removed from the vehicle, it should not be placed in an area where sparks or open flames could ignite the fumes coming out of the tank. Be especially careful inside garages where a natural gas appliance is located, because the pilot light could cause an explosion.

8 Fuel pump - removal and installation

Warning: *Gasoline is extremely flammable, so take extra precautions when you work on any part of the fuel system. Don't smoke or allow open flames or bare light bulbs near the work area, and don't work in a garage where a natural gas-type appliance (such as a water heater or clothes dryer) with a pilot light is present. If you spill any fuel on your skin, rinse it off immediately with soap and water. When you perform any kind of work on the fuel system, wear safety glasses and have a Class B type fire extinguisher on hand.*

1 Relieve the fuel pressure (see Section 3). Detach the cable from the negative terminal of the battery. **Caution:** *If the stereo in your vehicle is equipped with an anti-theft system, refer to the information on page 0-15 at the front of this manual before detaching the cable.*

2 Raise the vehicle and support it securely on jackstands.

1979 through 1983 models

Refer to illustrations 8.4, 8.6 and 8.7

3 The fuel pump is located just above the right inner CV joint, above the differential at the rear of the vehicle.

4 Unplug the fuel pump electrical connector **(see illustration)**.

5 Use vise grips or clamps to pinch the fuel line shut.

6 Remove the fuel line outlet banjo fitting bolt **(see illustration)**, then slide back the clamp and detach the hose from the inlet fitting.

7 Loosen the pump clamp bolt and nut, then slide the pump from the bracket **(see illustration)**.

8 Installation is the reverse of the removal procedure. Be sure to use new washers on the fuel line banjo bolts. Start the engine after installing the pump and check for leaks.

1984 and later models

Refer to illustrations 8.11, 8.13 and 8.14

9 The fuel pump on later models is located inside the fuel tank.

10 Remove the fuel tank (see Section 6).

11 Remove the fuel pump bracket bolts on top of the fuel tank and withdraw the pump unit from the fuel tank **(see illustration)**.

12 Disconnect the electrical wires from the fuel pump terminals.

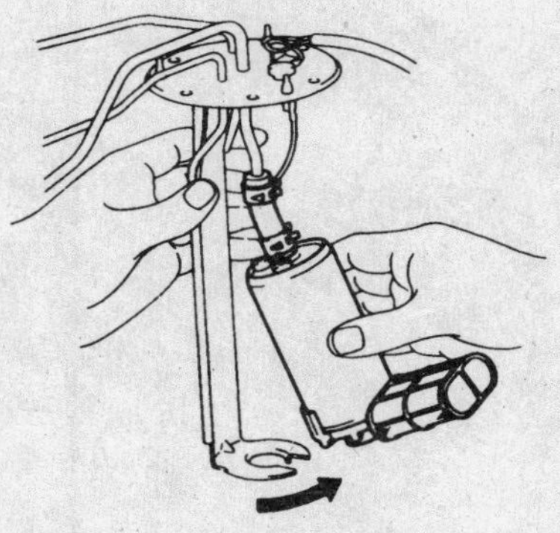

8.13 Swing the pump out from the bracket (1984 and later models)

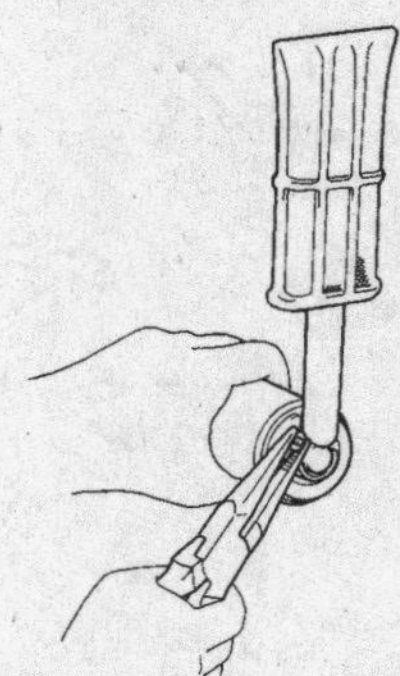

8.14 Detach the rubber cushion and hose clip to remove the pump filter (1984 and later models)

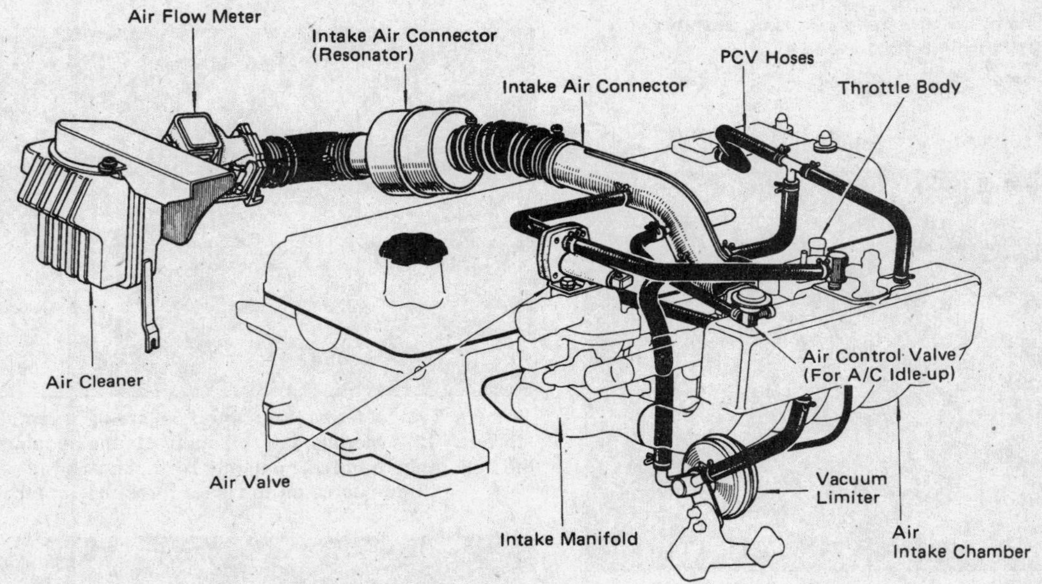

9.2 A typical air cleaner housing and intake duct assembly on 1979 through 1981 models

13 Swing the pump unit out from the bracket at the bottom end, loosen the upper hose clamp and pull the pump and short section of hose off the metal pump outlet line **(see illustration)**. When you install the new pump, replace this short section of hose with a new piece of hose (use only approved fuel hose).
14 To remove the fuel pump filter from the pump, detach the rubber cushion, remove the clip and withdraw the filter **(see illustration)**.
15 Installation is the reverse of the removal procedure. Replace the fuel filter, the outlet hose and the retaining clips as necessary. Always use a new gasket when installing the pump in the fuel tank and be sure that the mating surfaces are clean.
16 Start the engine and check for leaks at the hose and pipe connections.

9 Air cleaner housing and intake ducts - removal and installation

All models

1 Anytime you need to remove the valve cover, the throttle body, the air intake chamber, the intake or exhaust manifold or the engine itself, you'll need to remove the intake ducts. This is simply a matter of loosening the large hose clamps at either end of each section of duct you wish to remove. When you're done, make sure you reassemble the ducts exactly as shown in the accompanying illustrations and tighten the clamps securely. But make sure you don't tighten a clamp so tightly that it pinches or kinks the end of a duct, or you may get an air leak. Disconnected, loose or cracked ducts between the airflow meter and the throttle body will cause the engine to run lean.

1979 through 1981 models

Refer to illustrations 9.2, 9.3 and 9.5

Note: *The following procedure is for those models on which the nuts that attach the airflow meter to the air cleaner housing are inside the air cleaner housing; on some models, however, the nuts are on the outside of the housing, so no disassembly is necessary.*

2 The air cleaner assembly **(see illustration)** is attached to the body at the right front corner of the engine compartment.
3 The air cleaner inlet is attached to the top of the front half of the air cleaner housing with a couple of bolts **(see illustration)**. To separate the air cleaner inlet, remove these bolts and lift it off.
4 The front half of the air cleaner housing is attached to the body with three brackets. To detach it from the body, remove the bracket bolts.
5 The rear half of the air cleaner housing is attached to the airflow meter by four nuts. To reach these nuts, release the spring-type

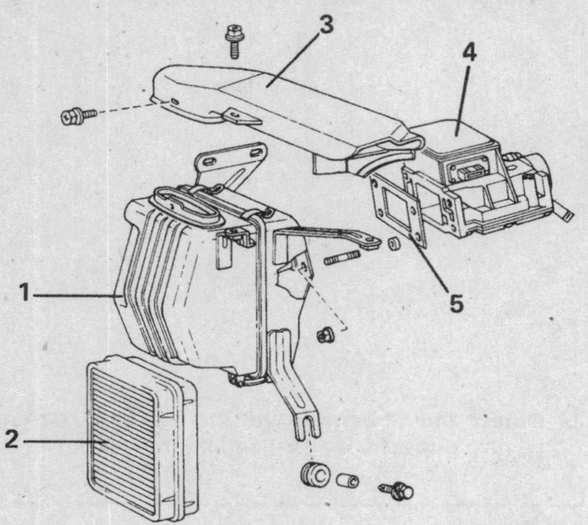

9.3 **An exploded view of the air cleaner housing assembly on 1979 through 1981 models**

1 Air cleaner housing
2 Air filter element
3 Air cleaner inlet
4 Airflow meter
5 Gasket

9.5 The air cleaner housing on 1979 through 1981 models is attached to the airflow meter with four nuts (arrows - upper left nut not visible in this photo)

9.7 On 1987 and later turbo models, separate the rear half of the air cleaner housing from the airflow meter by removing these four mounting nuts (arrows) from inside the housing

clamps, separate the front and rear halves of the housing and remove the filter element. Remove the nuts **(see illustration)** and detach the airflow meter from the air cleaner housing.

6 Reassembly is the reverse of disassembly.

1982 and later models

Refer to illustration 9.7

7 The air inlet and cylindrical air cleaner housing on these models are attached to the body with several fasteners. Individual sections of intake duct, or the entire duct assembly must be removed from these models for many operations. Removal is self-evident. Be sure to observe the precautions noted in Step 1 above. To detach the rear half of the air cleaner housing from the airflow meter, remove the four nuts inside **(see illustration)**.

10 Accelerator cable - removal and installation

Refer to illustrations 10.1, 10.2a and 10.2b

1 On 1979 through 1986 models, there is no accelerator cable; these models use a pair of rods, one between the accelerator pedal and a bellcrank assembly on the firewall (1979 through 1981 models) or the valve cover (1982 through 1986 models), and another between the firewall/valve cover bellcrank and the throttle linkage on the throttle body **(see illustration)**. To remove either rod, simply remove it from its clip. **Caution:** *Do NOT loosen the locknuts and turn the adjustment nuts on the end of either rod or you'll alter the idle setting.*

2 1987 and later models have an accelerator cable between the accelerator pedal and a bellcrank located on the valve cover **(see illustration)**, and a rod between the bellcrank and the throttle linkage on the throttle body **(see illustration)**. **Caution:** *Do NOT loosen the lock-*

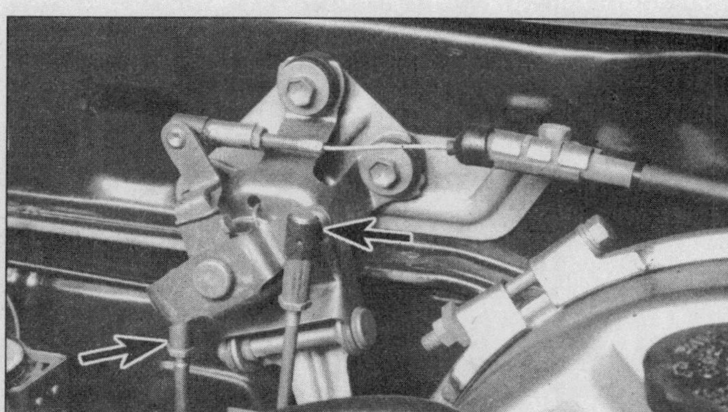

10.1 Typical firewall-mounted bellcrank assembly on 1979 through 1981 models: left rod connects the accelerator pedal to the bellcrank; right rod connects the bellcrank to the throttle body (the cable on top is for the cruise control)

10.2a Typical valve cover-mounted bellcrank assembly used on 1982 and later models (1992 turbo model shown) - to disconnect the accelerator cable, loosen the locknut and adjustment nut (right arrows), separate the cable from its mounting bracket and pry the cable end (middle arrow) loose from the bellcrank lever arm - to disconnect the rod from the bellcrank, pry it loose from its retaining clip (left arrow)

10.2b Typical throttle rod assembly used on 1982 and later models (1992 turbo model shown) - to disconnect the rod from the throttle linkage, pry it loose from its retaining clip (arrow)

nuts and turn the adjustment nuts on the end of the rod or you'll alter the idle setting.

3 To disconnect the accelerator cable from the bellcrank, loosen the locknut and adjustment nut at the cable bracket, then pry the cable end loose from the bellcrank lever.

4 Trace the throttle cable to the firewall, detaching it from all engine brackets as you go.

5 If the cable is secured to the firewall with mounting bolts, remove them from inside the vehicle.

6 Detach the accelerator cable from the accelerator pedal.

7 From inside the vehicle, pull the cable through the firewall.

8 Installation is the reverse of removal.

11 Fuel injection system - check

Refer to illustration 11.1

Warning: *Gasoline is extremely flammable, so take extra precautions when you work on any part of the fuel system. Don't smoke or allow open flames or bare light bulbs near the work area, and don't work in a garage where a natural gas-type appliance (such as a water heater or clothes dryer) with a pilot light is present. If you spill any fuel on your skin, rinse it off immediately with soap and water. When you perform any kind of work on the fuel system, wear safety glasses and have a Class B type fire extinguisher on hand.*

Note: *the following procedure is based on the assumption that the fuel pump and fuel pressure are normal (see Section 5).*

1 If the engine malfunctions, don't assume that the EFI system is the problem. Here are some simple checks you can perform before replacing any parts. First, check all wiring harness electrical connectors related to the system. Loose electrical connectors and poor grounds can cause many problems that resemble more serious malfunctions. Make sure all connections are clean, dry and tight. Pay particular attention to the following points:

a) Make sure no terminals are bent **(see illustration)**.
b) Make sure all electrical connectors are pushed together tightly and locked.
c) Shove the probe of a test light into the back of each electrical connector and ground it (or, if the circuit is open, use a self-powered continuity checker). Lightly tap and wiggle the electrical connector and verify that the light doesn't flicker.

2 Look for a blown fuse in the EFI circuit (see Chapter 12). If you find one, replace it and see if it blows again. If it does, search for a grounded wire in the EFI harness (the fuel pump circuit is always a likely suspect).

3 Verify that the battery is fully charged (see Chapter 5). The ECU must have an adequate - and accurate - voltage supply to control the EFI system.

4 Inspect the air filter element - a dirty or partially blocked filter will severely impede performance and economy (see Chapter 1).

11.1 Inspect all EFI-related electrical connectors for bent terminals, corrosion and moisture

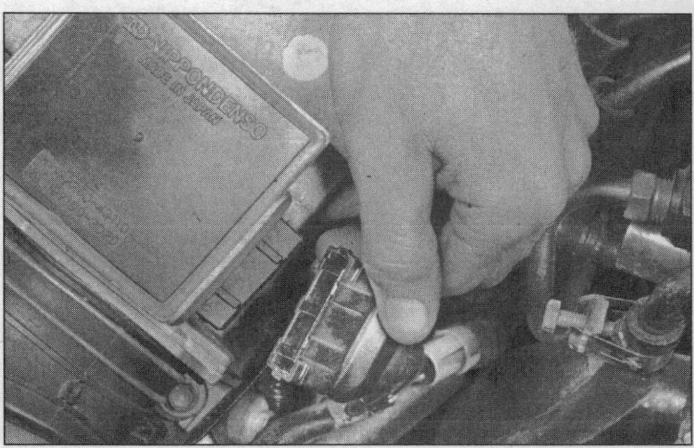

12.2a Unplug the airflow meter electrical connector, then connect the leads of an ohmmeter to the terminals indicated in the following illustrations and compare your measurements to the accompanying tables

5 Look for air leaks in the intake duct between the airflow meter and the intake manifold (they'll cause an excessively lean mixture). Also check the condition of the vacuum hoses connected to the intake manifold.

6 Detach the air intake duct from the throttle body and check for dirt, carbon or other residue build-up in the throttle body. If it's dirty, clean it with carburetor cleaner and a toothbrush.

7 With the engine idling, touch the tip of a screwdriver to each injector and listen through the handle for a clicking sound, indicating operation.

8 Verify that there's sufficient fuel in the tank and that the fuel pump is operational (see Section 5). When the ignition is switched On, you should feel pressure at the cold start injector fuel hose. If you don't, inspect the fuel line for cracks and loose connections, the electrical circuits involved, the fuel filter and the fuel regulator.

9 To find fuel leaks in the EFI system, pinch the pressure regulator return hose **(see illustration)**. Be careful not to damage the hose. This will increase the pressure in the line and any leaks within the system will be obvious.

12 Airflow meter - check, removal and installation

On-vehicle check (all models)

Refer to illustrations 12.2a through 12.2h

1 The airflow meter is located between the air cleaner housing and the air intake duct to the throttle body.

2 To test the airflow meter, unplug the electrical connector **(see il-**

4

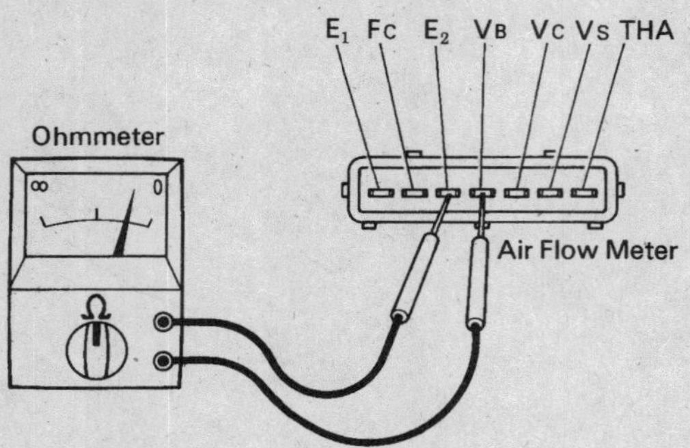

12.2b Airflow meter terminal guide for 1979 through 1983 models

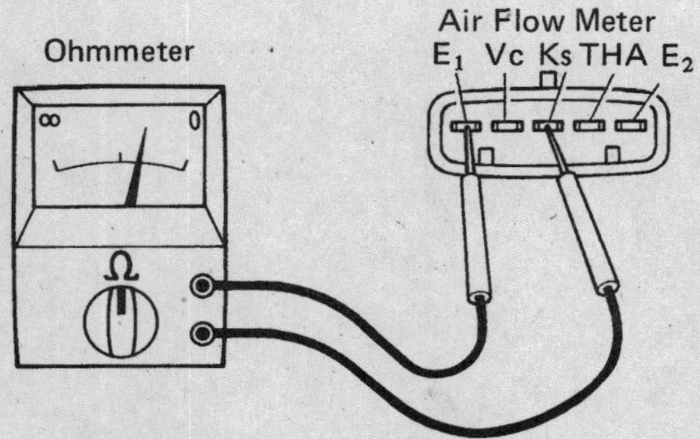

12.2d Airflow meter terminal guide for 1987 and later turbo models

Between terminals	Resistance	Temperature
E_2 – Vs	20 – 400 Ω (1984 through 1986 models) 20 – 600 Ω (1987 and later non-turbo models)	–
E_2 – Vc	200 – 400 Ω	–
E_2 – THA	10 – 20 KΩ 4 – 7 KΩ 2 – 3 KΩ 0.9 – 1.3 KΩ 0.4 – 0.7 KΩ	–20°C (4°F) 0°C (32°F) 20°C (68°F) 40°C (104°F) 60°C (140°F)
E_1 – Fc	Infinity	–

12.2f Airflow meter resistance table for 1984 and later non-turbo models

Terminals	Resistance (Ω)	Temp. °C (°F)
THA – E2	10,000 – 20, 000 4,000 – 7,000 2,000 – 3,000 900 – 1,300 400 – 700	–20 (–4) 0 (32) 20 (68) 40 (104) 60 (140)

12.2h Airflow meter resistance table for 1989 and later turbo models

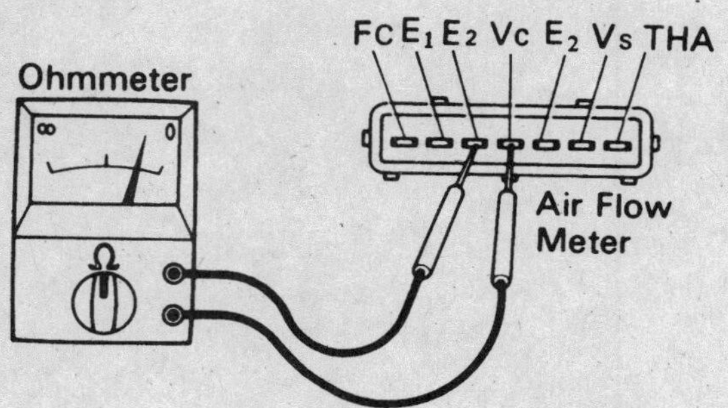

12.2c Airflow meter terminal guide for 1984 and later non-turbo models

Between terminals	Resistance	Temperature
E_2 – Vs	20 – 100 Ω	–
E_2 – Vc	100 – 300 Ω	–
E_2 – VB	200 – 400 Ω	–
E_2 – THA	10 – 20 KΩ 4 – 7 KΩ 2 – 3 KΩ 0.9 – 1.3 KΩ 0.4 – 0.7 KΩ	–20°C (4°F) 0°C (32°F) 20°C (68°F) 40°C (104°F) 60°C (140°F)
E_1 – Fc	Infinity	–

12.2e Airflow meter resistance table for 1979 through 1983 models

Terminals	Resistance	Temperature
Ks → E_1	∞ Ω	–
E_1 → Ks	5 – 10 kΩ	
Vc → E_1	10 – 15 kΩ	
E_1 → Vc	5 – 10 kΩ	
THA – E_2	10 – 20 kΩ 4 – 7 kΩ 2 – 3 kΩ 0.9 – 1.3 kΩ 0.4 – 0.7 kΩ	–20°C (4°F) 0°C (32°F) 20°C (68°F) 40°C (104°F) 60°C (140°F)

12.2g Airflow meter resistance table for 1987 and 1988 turbo models

lustration), then connect an ohmmeter to the terminals **(see illustration)**. Check that the resistance values are as given **(see illustrations)**. If any of the resistance values are outside those specified, the airflow meter must be replaced.

Removal

Non-turbo models

Refer to illustrations 12.5a and 12.5b

3 Unplug the electrical connector if you haven't already done so.

4 On 1979 through 1981 models, detach the airflow meter from the air cleaner housing (see Section 9), loosen the large hose clamp that

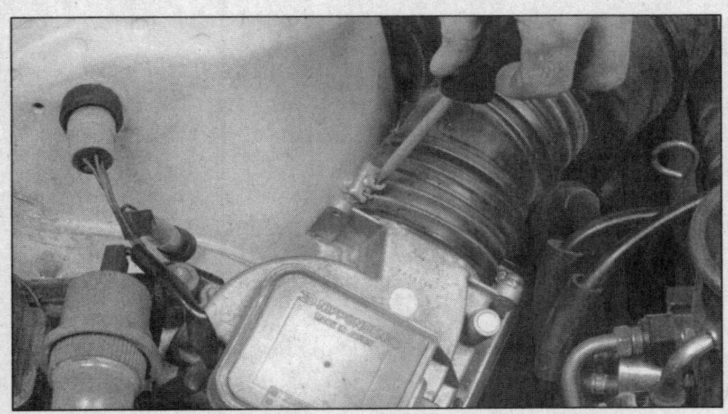

12.5a Loosen the large hose clamps and detach the air cleaner ducts from the airflow meter (1982 through 1986 models)

12.5b Remove the three retaining bolts (arrows) to remove the airflow meter unit

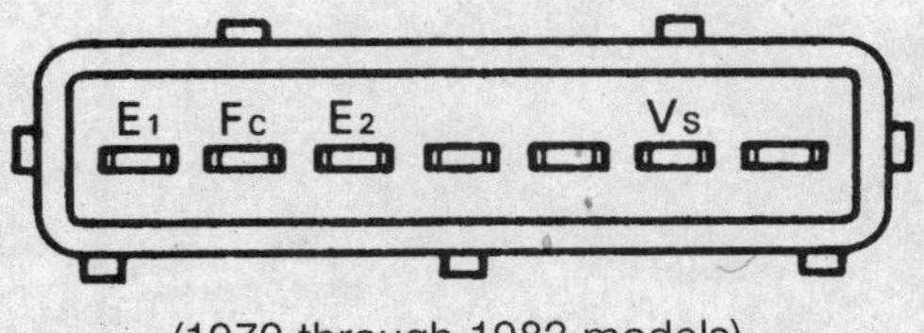

(1979 through 1983 models)

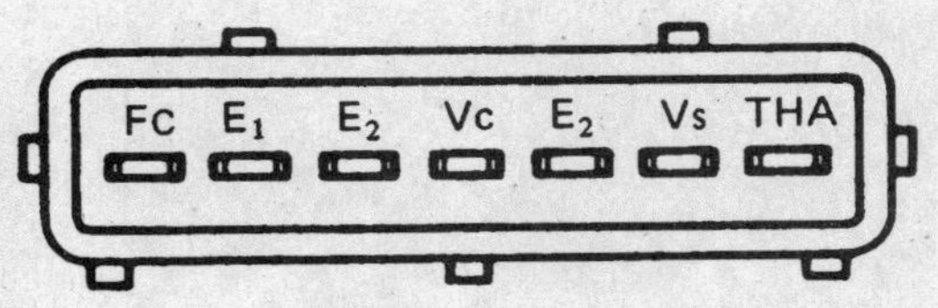

(1984 and later models)

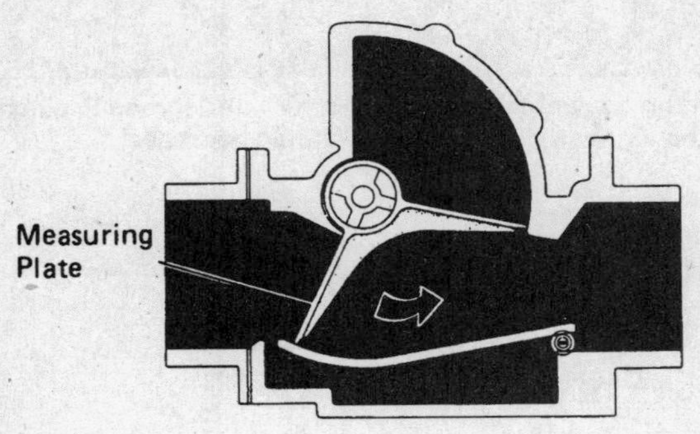

Between terminals	Resistance Ω	Measuring plate Opening
E_1 – Fc	Infinity	Fully closed
	Zero	Other than closed position
E_2 – Vs	20 - 100 (1979 through 1983 models) 20 - 400 (1984 through 1986 models) 20 - 600 (1987 and later models)	Fully closed
	20 - 1000	Fully closed to fully open position

12.7 Airflow meter resistance table for bench test (non-turbo models)

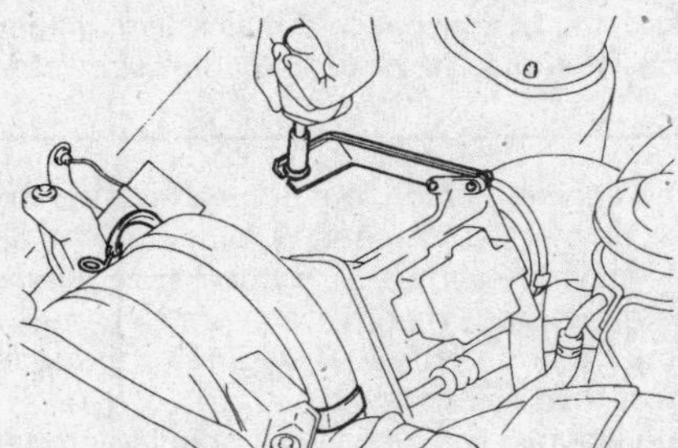

12.10a Release the three spring-type clamps and loosen the airflow meter bracket bolt (turbo models)

attaches the air intake duct to the airflow meter and remove the meter.

5 On 1982 through 1986 models, loosen the large hose clamps that secure the intake ducts to each end of the airflow meter **(see illustration)** and detach the ducts, then remove the three retaining bolts and detach the meter unit **(see illustration)**.

6 On 1987 and later models, loosen the large hose clamp for the No. 2 air cleaner hose and detach the hose, remove the two air cleaner cap bolts and the cap, remove the air filter element, pry off the lock plate, remove the four nuts that attach the airflow meter to the air cleaner and detach the airflow meter from the housing.

Bench check (non-turbo models only)

Refer to illustration 12.7

7 A further check can be made of the (non-turbo) airflow meter after it's removed. Connect an ohmmeter between the terminals indicated **(see illustrations)** and check the measuring plate openings. Note that the resistance between terminals E2 and Vs will change in accordance with the measuring plate opening.

Turbo models

Refer to illustrations 12.10a, 12.10b and 12.11

8 Remove the air cleaner ducts **(see illustration)**.

9 Unplug the electrical connector.

10 Release the three spring-type clamps and the airflow meter bracket bolt **(see illustration)**, loosen the large hose clamp **(see illustration)**, pull the duct off the meter and remove the airflow meter and air cleaner housing.

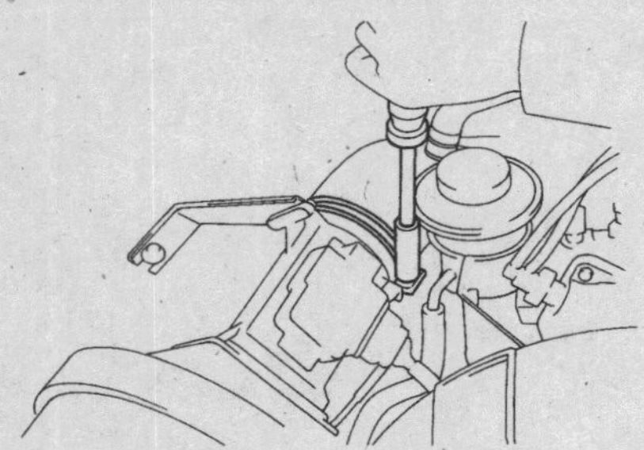

12.10b Loosen the large hose clamp, detach the duct from the airflow meter and remove the meter and air cleaner housing together (turbo models)

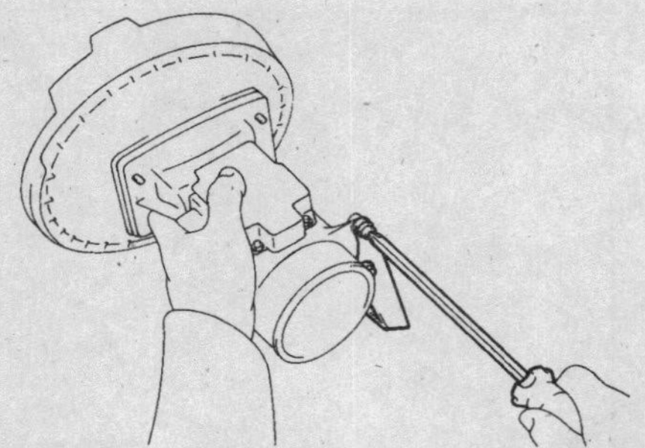

12.11 Remove the two screws and the bracket from the airflow meter (turbo models)

13.1a The air valve used on 1979 through 1981 models is located on the front of the intake manifold

13.1b With the coolant temperature below 140-degrees F, pinch the air hose - engine speed should decrease

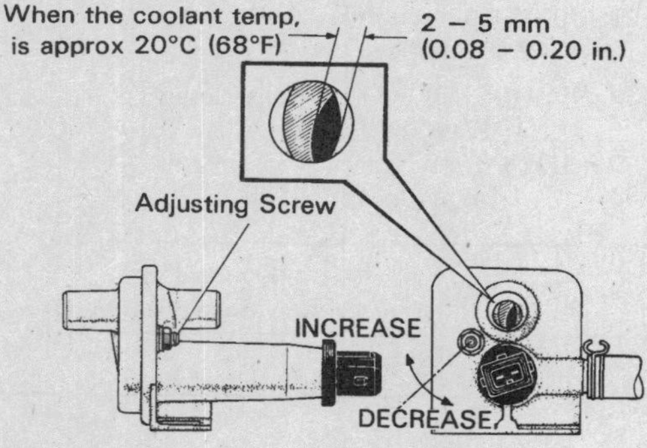

13.2 To determine whether the air valve is opening properly, detach the air hose and, when the coolant temperature at approximately 68 degrees F, note whether the valve starts to open as shown

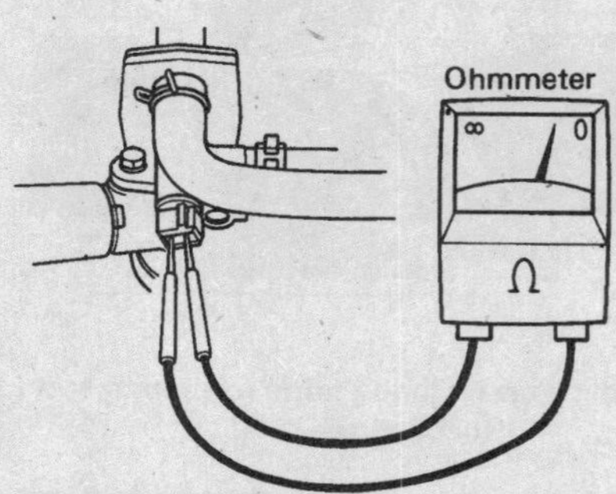

13.3 To check the heater coil in the air valve, measure its resistance - it should have 40 to 60 ohms resistance

11 Remove the two screws and the bracket **(see illustration)**, pry off the lock plate, remove the four nuts **(see illustration 9.7)**, remove the lock plates, the No. 1 air cleaner cover and the air cleaner cap.

Installation (all models)

12 Installation is the reverse of the removal procedure.

13 Air valve (1979 through 1981 and some 1982 models) - check, removal and installation

Check

Refer to illustrations 13.1a, 13.1b, 13.2 and 13.3

1 The air valve **(see illustration)** is located on the front of the intake manifold. With the engine running, but not warmed up (coolant temperature must be below 140-degrees F), pinch off the air hose between the air valve and the air intake chamber **(see illustration)** and verify that engine rpm drops. Then perform the same test again after the engine warms up and verify that engine rpm doesn't drop (it shouldn't drop more than 150 rpm).

2 To determine whether the air valve is opening properly, detach the air hose and, when the coolant temperature is at approximately 68-degrees F, note whether the valve starts to open as shown **(see illustration)**.

3 To check the heater coil in the air valve, measure its resistance **(see illustration)**. It should have 40 to 60 ohms resistance.

4 If the air valve fails any of the above three tests, replace it.

Removal and installation

5 Disconnect the cable from the negative terminal of the battery. **Caution:** *If the stereo in your vehicle is equipped with an anti-theft system, refer to the information on page 0-15 at the front of this manual*

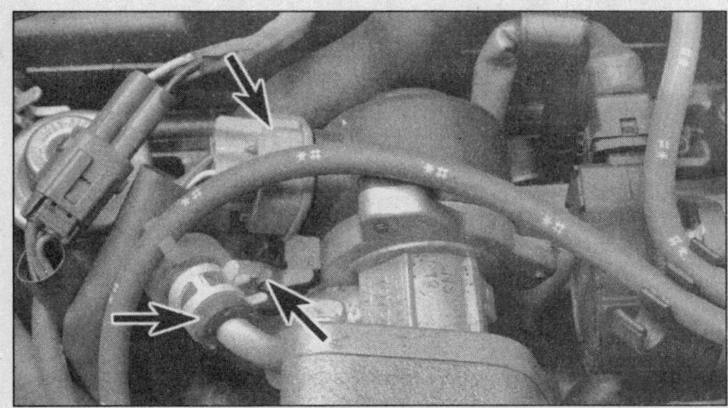

14.4 Unplug the ISC valve electrical connector (upper arrow), then detach the coolant by-pass hoses and the air hoses from the ISC valve (lower arrows - not all hoses visible in this photo)

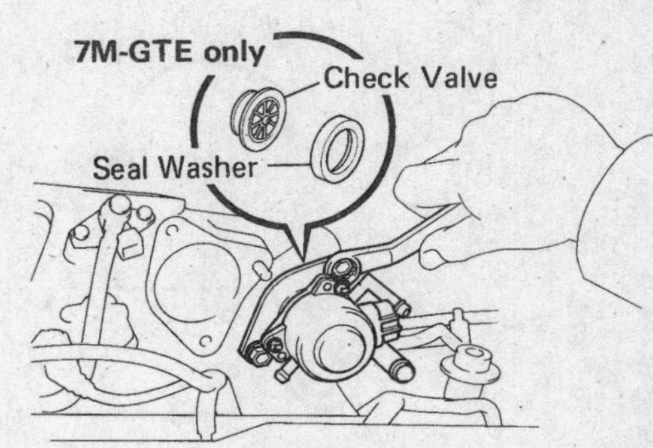

14.6 On turbo models, remove the seal washer and check valve from the air intake chamber

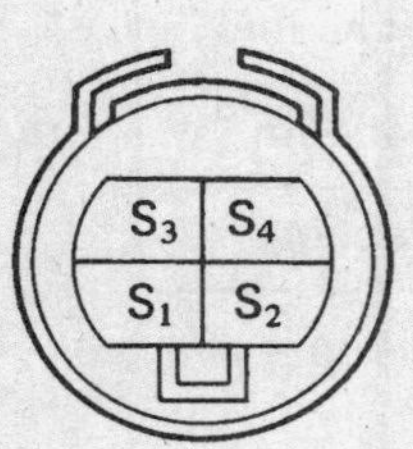

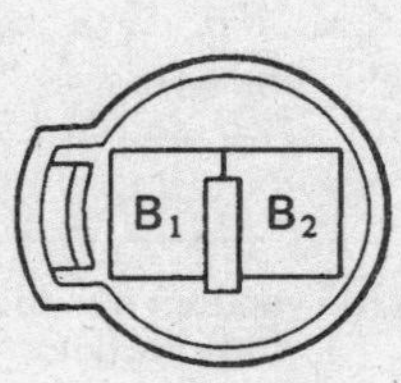

14.7a Measure the resistance between terminal B1 and S1 or S3, and between B2 and S2 or S4 (1982 through 1986 models)

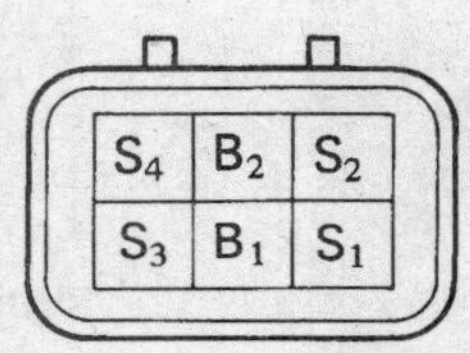

14.7b Measure the resistance between terminal B1 and S1 or S3, and between B2 and S2 or S4 (1987 and later models)

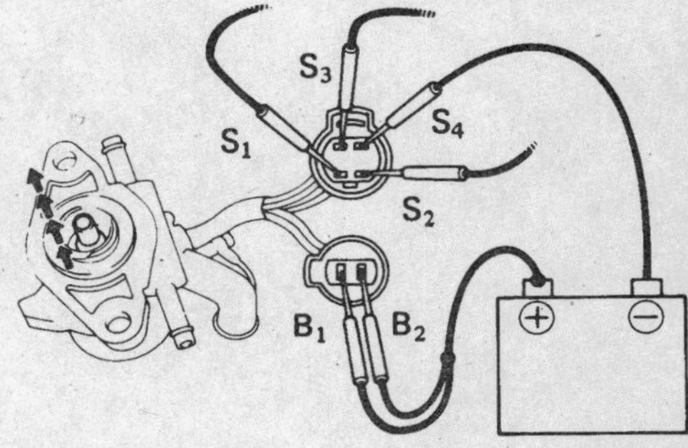

14.8a Apply battery voltage to terminals B1 and B2 and - while repeatedly grounding terminals S1, S2, S3, S4, S1, etc. in sequence - verify that the valve moves toward the closed position (1982 through 1986 models)

before detaching the cable.

6 Unplug the electrical connector from the air valve. Loosen the clamps and detach the coolant hoses from the valve and plug them if coolant begins to flow out.

7 Loosen the clamps and detach the air hoses from the valve. Remove the mounting bolts and detach the valve from the engine.

8 Installation is the reverse of removal. Check the coolant level and add, if necessary, to bring it to the desired level (see Chapter 1).

14 Idle Speed Control (ISC) valve - check, removal and installation

On-vehicle check

1 Start the engine, then turn it off. Verify that the ISC valve makes a clicking sound immediately after the engine is stopped.

2 If the valve doesn't make a clicking sound, remove it and bench test it.

Removal

Refer to illustrations 14.4 and 14.6

3 Disconnect the cable from the negative terminal of the battery. **Caution:** *If the stereo in your vehicle is equipped with an anti-theft system, refer to the information on page 0-15 at the front of this manual before detaching the cable.*

4 Unplug the ISC valve electrical connectors **(see illustration)**.

5 Detach the two coolant by-pass hoses and the air hoses from the ISC valve. Plug the coolant hoses if coolant begins to flow out.

6 Remove the ISC valve mounting bolts, the valve and the gasket.

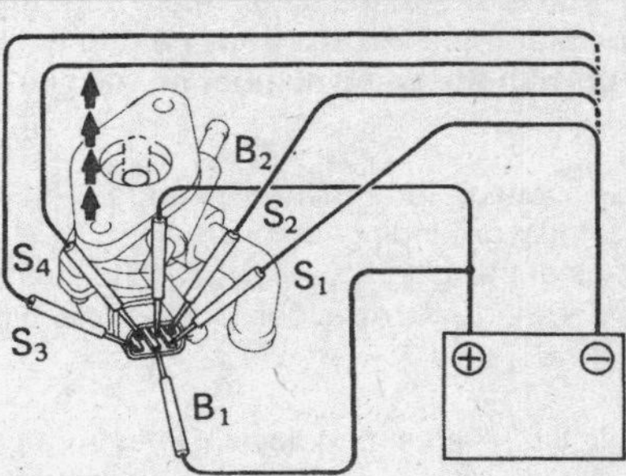

14.8b Apply battery voltage to terminals B1 and B2 and - while repeatedly grounding terminals S1, S2, S3, S4, S1, etc. in sequence - verify that the valve moves toward the closed position (1987 and later models)

On turbo models, remove the seal washer and check valve from the air intake chamber **(see illustration)**.

Bench test

Refer to illustrations 14.7a, 14.7b, 14.8a, 14.8b, 14.9a and 14.9b

7 Using an ohmmeter, measure the resistance between terminal B1 and S1 or S3, and between B2 and S2 or S4 **(see illustrations)**. Compare your measurements to the resistance values listed in this Chapter's Specifications. If the indicated resistance values are outside the specified resistance range, replace the ISC valve.

8 Apply battery voltage to terminals B1 and B2 **(see illustrations)** and - while repeatedly grounding terminals S1, S2, S3, S4, S1, etc. in sequence - verify that the valve moves toward the closed position.

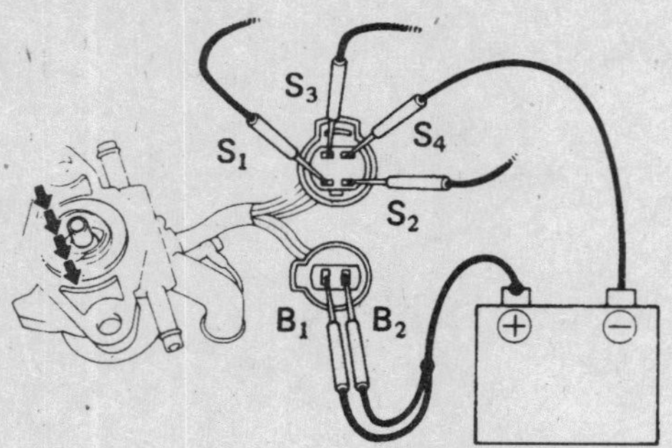

14.9a Apply battery voltage to terminals B1 and B2 and - while repeatedly grounding terminals S4, S3, S2, S1, S4, etc. in sequence - verify that the valve moves toward the open position (1982 through 1986 models)

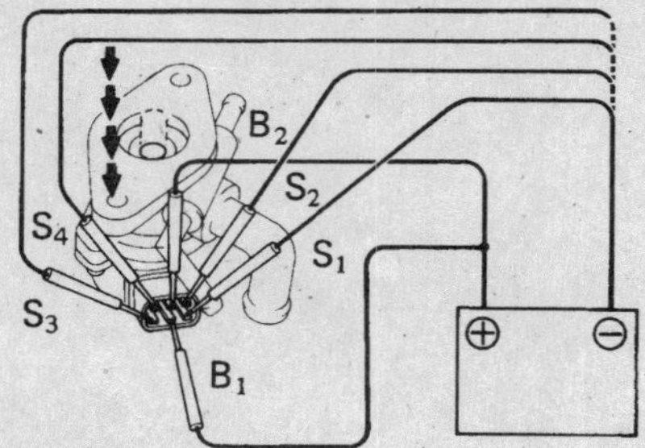

14.9b Apply battery voltage to terminals B1 and B2 and - while repeatedly grounding terminals S4, S3, S2, S1, S4, etc. in sequence - verify that the valve moves toward the open position (1987 and later models)

15.2a Throttle body vacuum lines (arrows) on 1979 through 1981 models - when you reattach the lines, make sure that the "8," "6" and "*" stamped onto the throttle body next to each port match up with the same number on the line

Part No.	At idling	Other than idling
8	Vacuum	No vacuum
6	No vacuum	Vacuum
*	No vacuum	Vacuum

15.2b Throttle body vacuum line table for 1979 through 1981 models

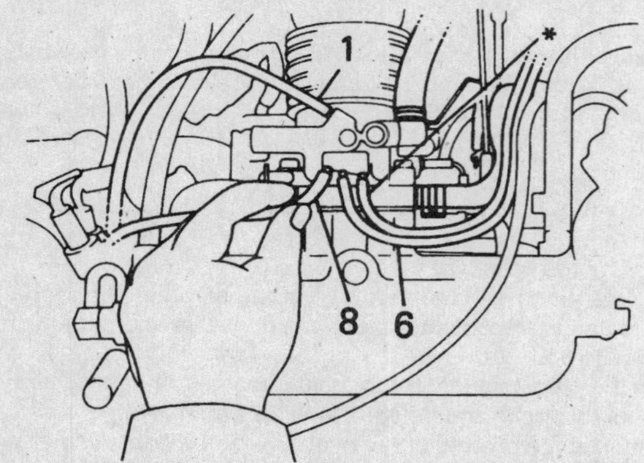

15.2c Throttle body vacuum lines on 1982 through 1986 models (1982 through 1984 models don't have line 6)

Part No.	At idling	Other than idling
8	No vacuum	Vacuum
*	No vacuum	Vacuum
1	No vacuum	No vacuum
6	No vacuum	Vacuum

15.2d Throttle body vacuum line table for 1982 through 1986 models

9 Apply battery voltage to terminals B1 and B2 **(see illustrations)** and - while repeatedly grounding terminals S4, S3, S2, S1, S4, etc. in sequence - verify that the valve moves toward the open position.

10 If the valve doesn't perform as described, replace it.

Installation

11 Installation is the reverse of removal. On turbo models, don't forget to install the check valve and seal washer in the air intake chamber first. And be sure to use a new gasket on all models.

12 Check the coolant level and add, if necessary, to bring it to the desired level (see Chapter 1).

15 Throttle body - check, removal and installation

Check

Refer to illustrations 15.2a through 15.2g

1 Verify that the throttle linkage moves freely.

2 Start the engine and allow it to idle. Detach each vacuum line from its respective port and note whether vacuum is present or not; open the throttle a little and note again whether there's vacuum present. Compare your observations to the accompanying tables **(see illustrations)**. If a line fails to indicate vacuum when it should, remove the throttle body, clean it thoroughly and re-check it. **Note:** *If the numbers on the vacuum lines aren't visible, mark them with pieces of numbered tape before detaching them.*

Removal and installation

Refer to illustration 15.8

3 Drain the cooling system and disconnect the battery ground cable. **Caution:** *If the stereo in your vehicle is equipped with an anti-theft system, refer to the information on page 0-15 at the front of this manual before detaching the cable.*

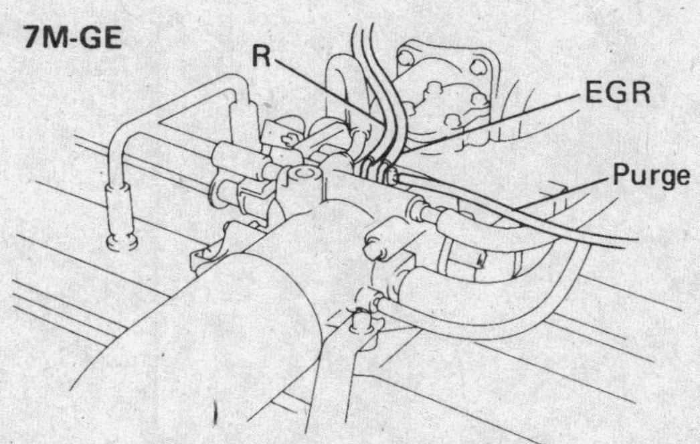

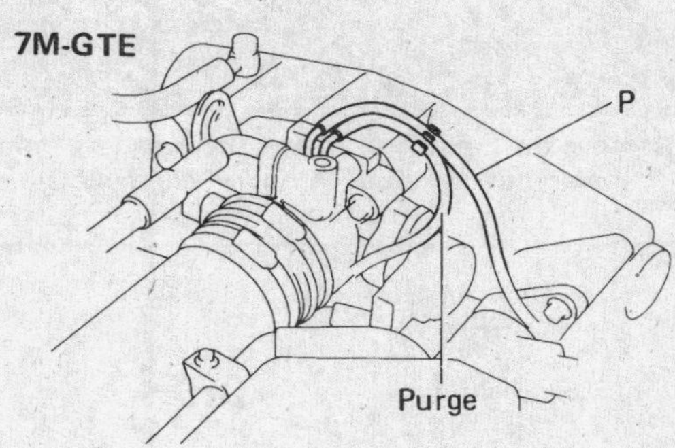

15.2e Throttle body vacuum lines on 1988, 1990 and later models - non-turbo model (upper), turbo model (lower)

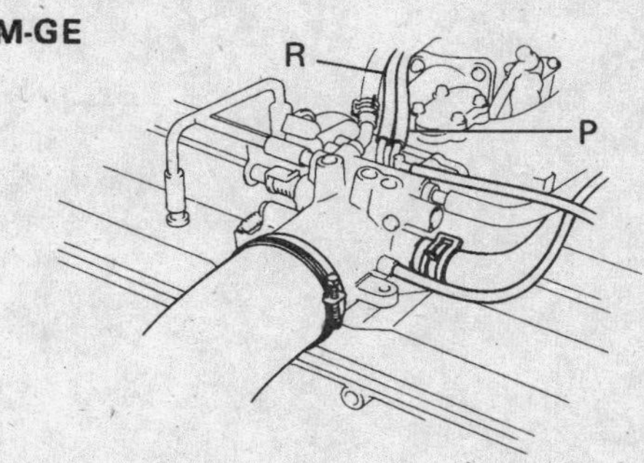

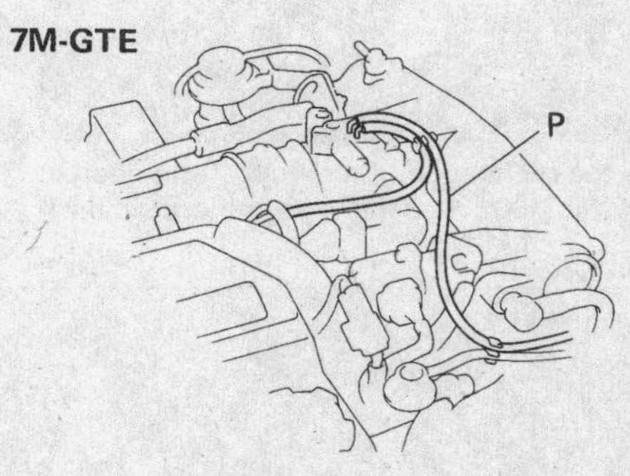

15.2f Throttle body vacuum lines on 1987 and 1989 models - non-turbo model (upper), turbo model (lower)

Port Name	At idling	Other than idling
Purge	No vacuum	Vacuum
EGR	No vacuum	Vacuum
R	No vacuum	No vacuum
P	No vacuum	Vacuum

15.2g Throttle body vacuum line table for 1987 through 1992 models (1987 and 1989 models don't have EGR and Purge lines; 1988 models don't have P line)

4 Clearly label, then disconnect all hoses from the intake duct. Remove the bolts from the bracket that attaches the duct to the valve cover. Loosen the large hose clamps and disconnect the intake air duct.

5 Detach the accelerator cable rod from the throttle linkage (see Section 10).

6 Disconnect the TV cable (automatic transmission only) (see Chapter 7B).

7 Clearly label, then detach, the coolant hoses and vacuum sensor hoses. Remove the four retaining bolts and detach the throttle body and gasket from the air intake chamber.

8 Clean the throttle bore and check for cracks in the body and obstructions in the ports. Check the throttle valve for smooth operation and the throttle valve shaft for excessive play. Verify that there's no clearance between the stop screw and throttle lever when the throttle valve is completely shut **(see illustration)**.

9 The throttle position sensor should be checked and adjusted (see Chapter 6).

10 Installation is the reverse of removal. Make sure all air, coolant and vacuum hose connections are tight. Refill the cooling system and check for leaks.

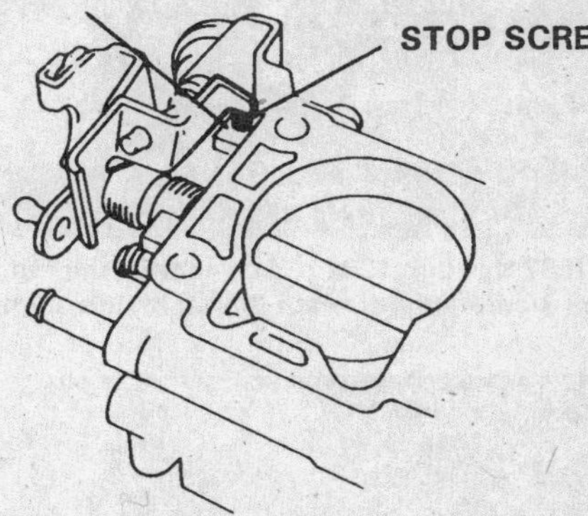

15.8 When the throttle valve is completely closed, there shouldn't be any clearance between the throttle stop screw and the th rottle lever

16 Cold start injector - check, removal and installation

Warning: *Gasoline is extremely flammable, so take extra precautions when you work on any part of the fuel system. Don't smoke or allow open flames or bare light bulbs near the work area, and don't work in a garage where a natural gas-type appliance (such as a water heater or clothes dryer) with a pilot light is present. If you spill any fuel on your skin, rinse it off immediately with soap and water. When you perform any kind of work on the fuel system, wear safety glasses and have a Class B type fire extinguisher on hand.*

Check

Refer to illustration 16.2

1 Unplug the electrical connector from the cold start injector.

2 Using an ohmmeter, measure the resistance of the cold start in-

16.2 Measure the resistance of the cold start injector with an ohmmeter (1981 model shown, others similar)

16.6a Remove the banjo bolt and sealing washers from the cold start injector (1982 through 1986 models)

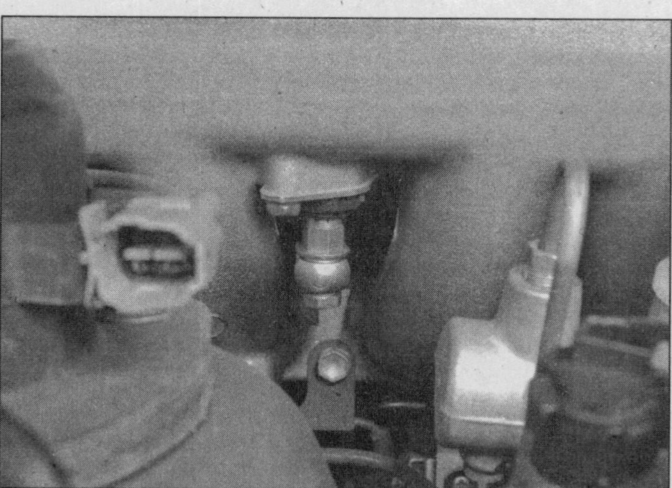

16.6b On 1987 through 1992 turbo models, the cold start injector is located underneath the air intake chamber

17.1 On 1982 through 1986 models, the cold start injector time switch (left arrow) is located to the left of the timing belt cover, near the thermostat housing, right next to the coolant temperature sensor (right arrow)

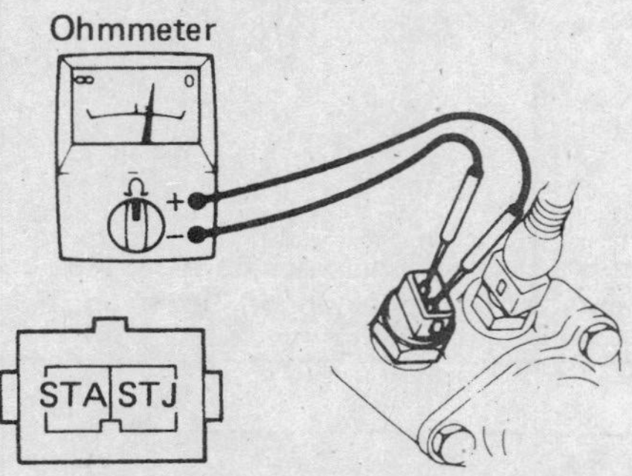

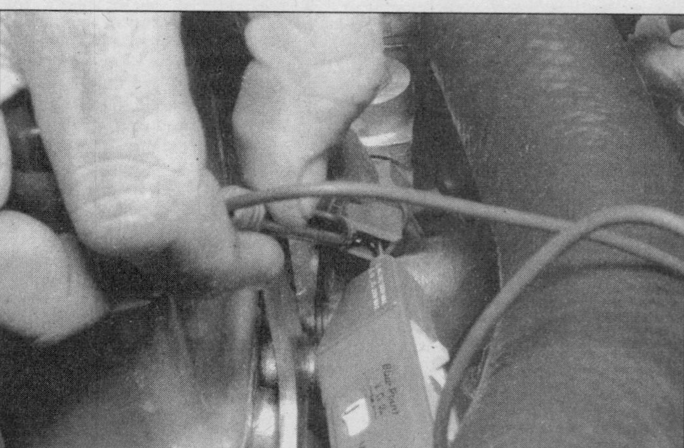

17.3a To measure the resistance of the cold start injector time switch, touch the probes of an ohmmeter to the terminals indicated in the accompanying tables (terminal guide applies to 1979 through 1986 models)

jector **(see illustration)** and compare your measurement to the resistance listed in this Chapter's Specifications. If the indicated resistance is outside the indicated range, replace the cold start injector.

Removal and installation

Refer to illustration 16.6a and 16.6b

3 Relieve the system fuel pressure (see Section 3).

4 Detach the cable from the negative battery terminal. **Caution:** *If the stereo in your vehicle is equipped with an anti-theft system, refer to the information on page 0-15 at the front of this manual before detaching the cable.*

Between terminals	Resistance (Ω)	Coolant temp.
STA – STJ	30 – 50	below 22°C (72°F)
	70 – 90	above 22°C (72°F)
STA – Ground	30 – 90	–

17.3b Resistance table for the cold start injector time switch used on 1979 through 1983 models

Between terminals	Resistance (Ω)	Coolant temp.
STA – STJ	20 – 40	below 30°C (86°F)
	40 – 60	above 40°C (104°F)
STA – Ground	20 – 80	—

17.3c Resistance table for the cold start injector time switch used on 1984 through 1986 models

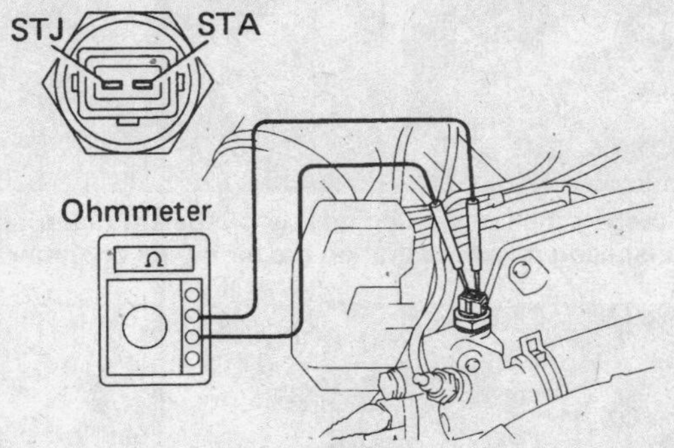

Terminals	Resistance (Ω)	Coolant temp.
STA – STJ	25 – 50	below 15°C (59°F)
	60 – 85	above 30°C (86°F)
STA – Ground	25 – 85	–

17.3d Resistance table and terminal guide for the cold start injector time switch used on 1987, 1988 and 1990 models

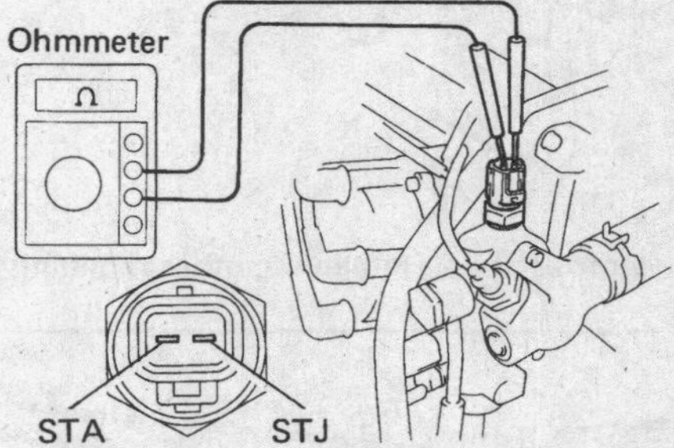

Terminals	Resistance	Coolant temp
STA – STJ	25 – 45 Ω 65 – 85 Ω	below 15°C (59°F) above 30°C (86°F)
STA – Ground	25 – 85 Ω	

17.3e Terminal guide and resistance table for the cold start injector time switch used on 1989, 1991 and 1992 models

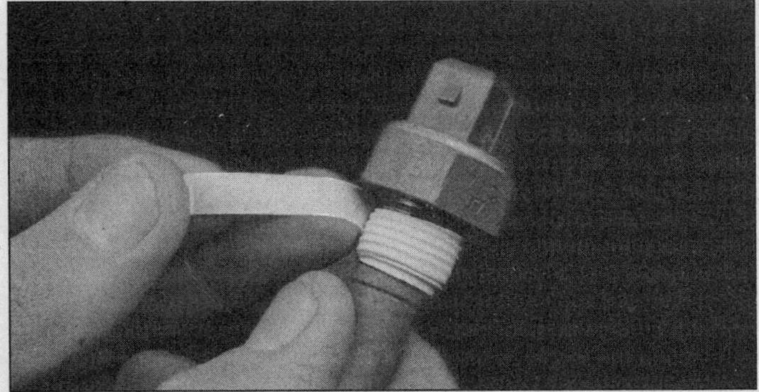

17.7 Be sure to apply Teflon tape or thread sealant to the threads before you install the new cold start injector time switch

5 On 1982 through 1986 models, remove the air intake chamber (see Section 18). The cold start injector is located in the underside of the air intake chamber, near the throttle body, on these models.
6 Remove the banjo bolt and sealing washers **(see illustrations)** and detach the fuel hose banjo fitting from the cold start injector.
7 Remove the cold start injector retaining bolts.
8 Remove the cold start injector and gasket from the air intake chamber.
9 Installation is the reverse of removal. Be sure to use a new flange gasket and new sealing washers at the fuel line banjo bolt. Tighten the banjo bolt to the torque listed in this Chapter's Specifications.

17 Cold start injector time switch - check and replacement

Check

Refer to illustrations 17.1 and 17.3a through 17.3e

1 On 1979 through 1981 models, the cold start injector time switch is located in the forward end of the intake manifold; on 1982 through 1986 models, it's to the left of the timing belt cover, near the thermostat housing, right next to the coolant temperature sensor **(see illustration)**; on 1987 and later models, it's also on the thermostat housing, next to the coolant temperature sensor, except the thermostat housing is to the right of the timing belt cover.
2 Unplug the electrical connector from the cold start injector time switch.
3 Using an ohmmeter, measure the resistance between the indicated terminals **(see illustrations)**. If any of the indicated resistance values are outside the specified ranges, replace the switch.

Replacement

Refer to illustration 17.7

4 Drain the coolant (or be prepared for some coolant to run out when you remove the switch).
5 Unplug the electrical connector, if you haven't already done so.
6 Unscrew and remove the switch.
7 Installation is the reverse of removal. Be sure to coat the threads of the new switch with Teflon tape **(see illustration)** or thread sealant to prevent coolant leaks.
8 Check the coolant level and add, if necessary, to bring it to the desired level (see Chapter 1).

18 Air intake chamber - removal and installation

Refer to illustrations 18.8, 18.10 and 18.11

1 Relieve the fuel pressure (see Section 3).
2 Detach the cable from the negative battery terminal. **Caution:** *If the stereo in your vehicle is equipped with an anti-theft system, refer to the information on page 0-15 at the front of this manual before detaching the cable.*
3 Drain the engine coolant (see Chapter 1).
4 Detach and remove the air intake duct from the throttle body.

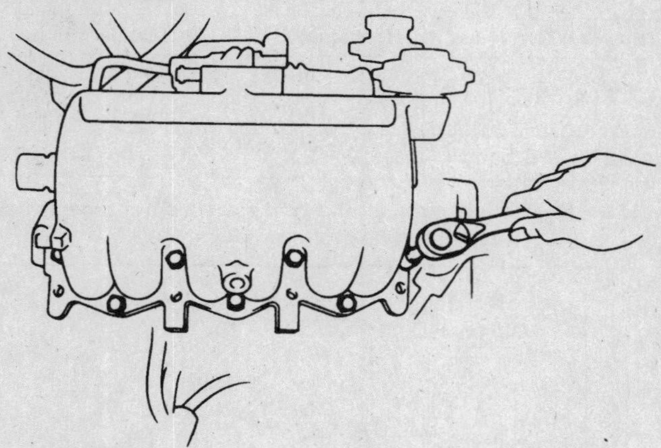

18.8 Remove the air intake chamber retaining bolts

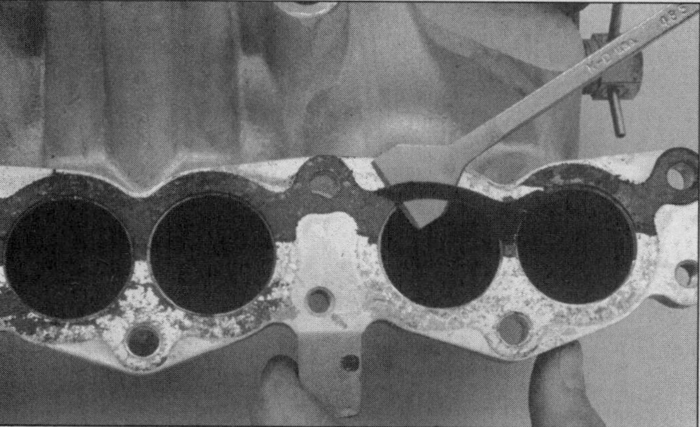

18.10 Scrape off all remaining gasket or sealant material before installing a new gasket on the air intake chamber

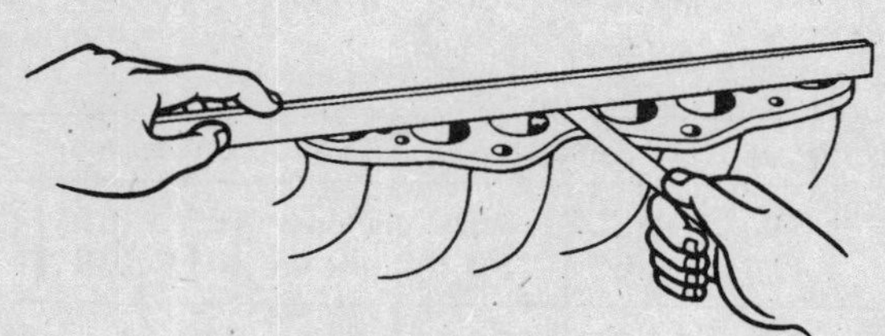

18.11 Check the intake manifold gasket surface of the air intake chamber for distortion with a straightedge and a feeler gauge

5 Disconnect the accelerator cable and, if equipped, the cruise control and/or TV cables, from the throttle body.
6 Clearly label, then disconnect, all coolant, fuel and vacuum hoses, electrical connectors and wiring harnesses. Note the routing of the various lines and wires.
7 If the air intake chamber has a support bracket, remove it.
8 Remove the air intake chamber retaining bolts **(see illustration)** and separate the chamber from the intake manifold.
9 If you're replacing the air intake chamber, remove the throttle body, cold start injector, etc. and transfer them to the new air intake chamber.
10 Clean the air intake chamber thoroughly. Scrape off all old gasket material from the intake manifold gasket mating surface and, if you've removed the throttle body, from the throttle body gasket mating surface **(see illustration)**.
11 Inspect the air intake chamber for cracks. Inspect the manifold gasket surface for distortion by laying a straightedge along the gasket surface and trying to slip a 0.010-inch feeler gauge under it at several places **(see illustration)**. If the feeler gauge slips under the straightedge, have the surface machined at an automotive machine shop.
12 Installation is the reverse of the removal. Be sure to use a new gasket and tighten the chamber bolts to the torque listed in this Chapter's Specifications.
13 Refill the cooling system (see Chapter 1), start the engine and check for leaks.
14 If the vehicle is equipped with an automatic transmission, adjust the TV cable (see Chapter 7B).

19 Fuel injectors - check, removal and installation

Warning: *Gasoline is extremely flammable, so take extra precautions when you work on any part of the fuel system. Don't smoke or allow open flames or bare light bulbs near the work area, and don't work in a garage where a natural gas-type appliance (such as a water heater or clothes dryer) with a pilot light is present. If you spill any fuel on your skin, rinse it off immediately with soap and water. When you perform any kind of work on the fuel system, wear safety glasses and have a Class B type fire extinguisher on hand.*

19.1 Using a mechanic's stethoscope, listen to each injector and verify that it sounds normal (it should make a steady, clicking sound)

Check

Refer to illustrations 19.1 and 19.3

1 If you suspect any of the injectors are malfunctioning, start the engine and touch each injector with a stethoscope or screwdriver (which will work like a stethoscope if you put your ear to it) **(see illustrations)**. Listen for a clicking sound proportional to engine speed; this indicates normal injector operation. If you hear no sound or an unusual sound from any injector, verify that the wiring connections are in good condition.
2 If you don't have a stethoscope, and you can't determine the condition of the injectors with a screwdriver, touch each injector with your finger and feel the injection pulses. You should feel a rhythmic clicking.
3 To measure the resistance of an injector, unplug the electrical connector and touch the probes of an ohmmeter to the connector terminals **(see illustration)** and compare your measurement to the resistance value listed in this Chapter's Specifications. If the indicated resistance of an injector is outside the specified range of resistance, replace the injector.

Removal

Refer to illustrations 19.9a, 19.9b, 19.12 and 19.13

4 Relieve the system fuel pressure (see Section 3).

19.3 . . . check the injector resistance with an ohmmeter and compare your measurements with the resistance listed in this Chapter's Specifications

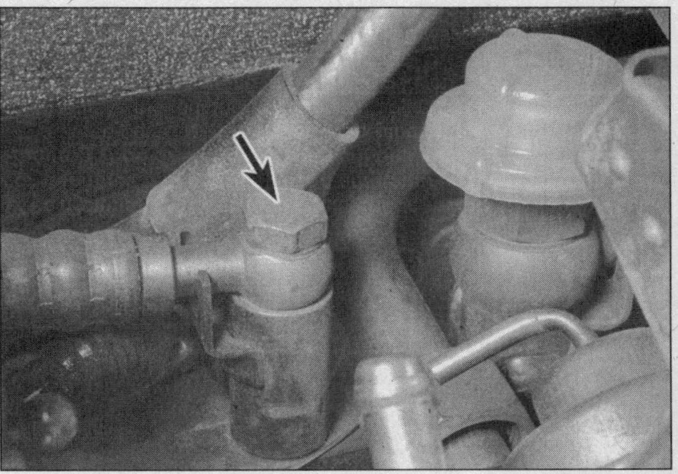

19.9b Remove the banjo bolt (arrow) securing the fuel delivery hose to the fuel rail and discard the sealing washers above and below the banjo fitting on the end of the hose (always use new sealing washers when you install the fuel delivery or return hose to the fuel rail)

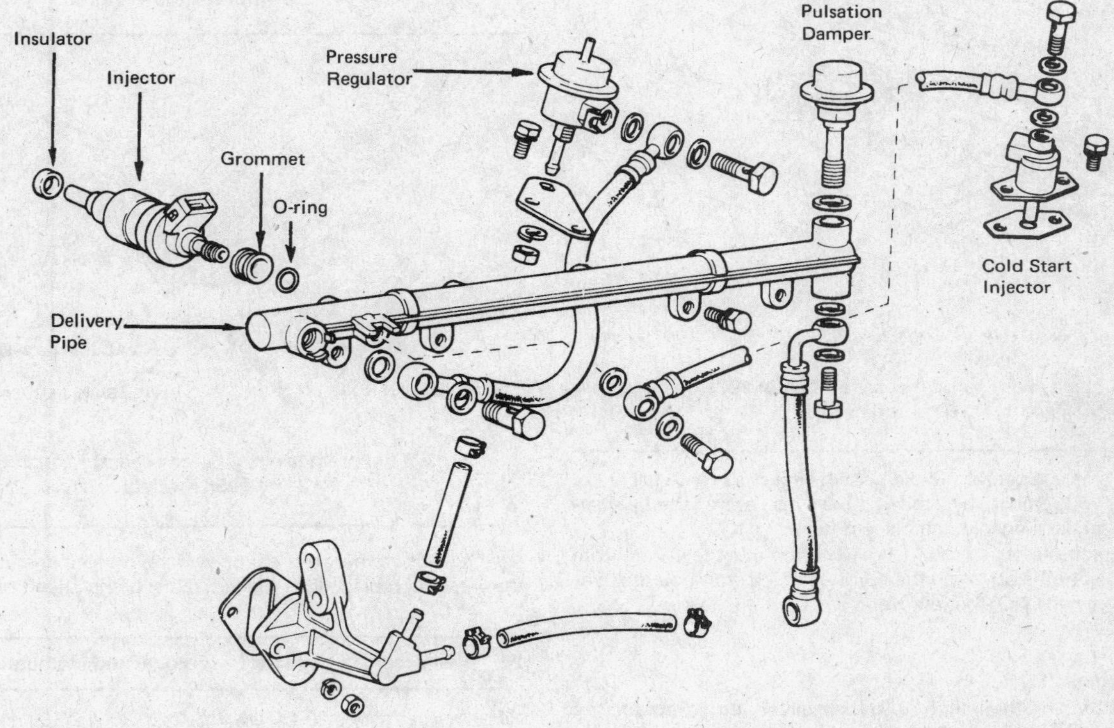

19.9a An exploded view of a typical fuel rail (1979 through 1981 models shown, others similar)

5 On 1979 through 1986 models, remove the air intake chamber (see Section 18); on 1987 and later models, you can remove the throttle body from the air intake chamber (see Section 15) and leave the air intake chamber attached.

5 On 1982 through 1986 models, remove the distributor (see Chapter 5).

6 On 1987 and later models, remove the ISC valve (see Section 14).

7 Unplug the electrical connectors from the injectors, if you haven't already done so, detach the fuel injector wiring harness from all retaining clips and set it aside.

8 On 1987 and later models, disconnect the cold start injector tube from the fuel rail.

9 On 1982 through 1986 models and 1987 and later turbo models, remove the pulsation damper which attaches the fuel delivery pipe to the fuel rail; on all other models, remove the banjo bolt which attaches the fuel delivery hose to the fuel rail **(see illustrations)**. Detach the hose and discard the old sealing washers.

10 Place a shop rag or a container under the pressure regulator to catch spilled fuel, then remove the banjo bolt from the fuel return hose, detach the hose and discard the old sealing washers.

11 If you're planning to replace the fuel pressure regulator, do it now, before you unbolt the fuel rail (see Section 20).

12 Remove the four fuel rail retaining bolts (1979 through 1986 models) or three bolts (1987 and later models) and remove the fuel rail and

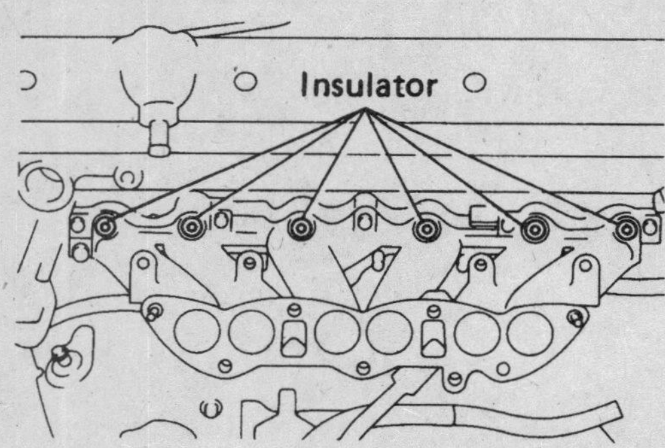

19.12 Remove all six insulators from their respective injector holes in the intake manifold and discard them (always use new insulators when reinstalling the injectors, whether you're using the old injectors or new units)

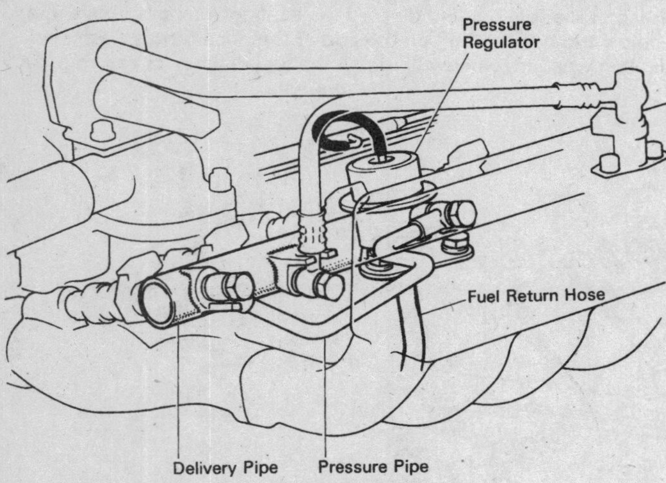

20.1a Fuel pressure regulator assembly on 1979 through 1981 models

19.13 DO NOT remove the cover from the injector tip

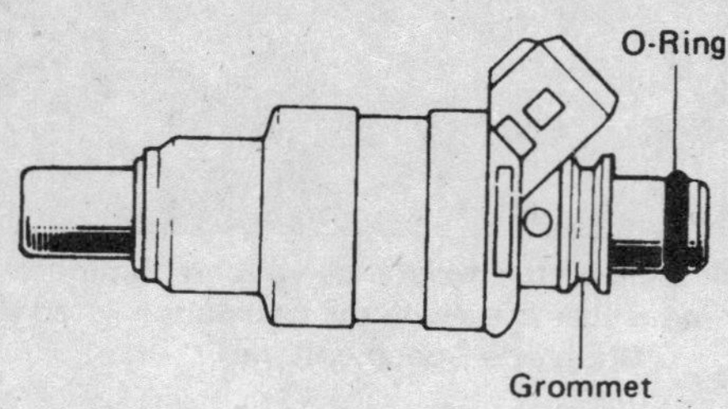

19.14 Even if you install the old injectors, always replace the grommets and O-rings

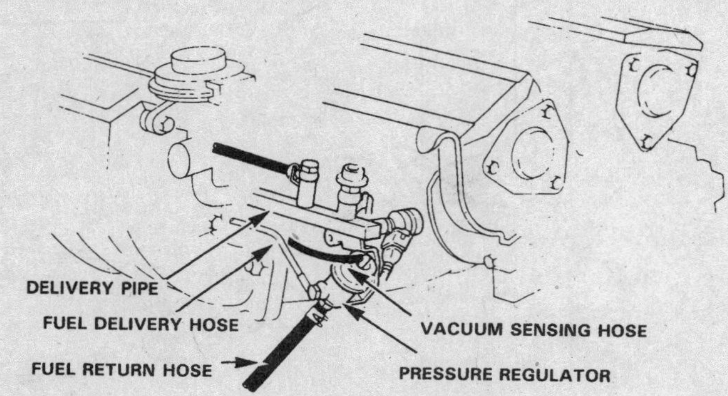

20.1b Fuel pressure regulator assembly on 1982 through 1986 models

injectors as a single assembly. Make sure the injectors don't fall out of the fuel rail as you remove it. Remove the six insulators **(see illustration)** from the intake manifold and discard them.

13 Pull the injectors out of the fuel rail and remove the O-ring from each injector. Note the cover on the tip of each injector **(see illustration)**. This cover must NOT be removed.

Installation

Refer to illustration 19.14

14 Before attaching the injectors to the delivery pipe, replace the grommet and O-ring on each injector **(see illustration)**.

15 Coat each O-ring with fuel before pushing the delivery pipe into position. Ensure that they are correctly aligned during assembly.

16 Insert six new insulators into position in the injector holes in the intake manifold, then install the injectors and the delivery pipe. Before installing the retaining bolts, ensure that the injectors rotate smoothly. If they do not, the O-rings are probably distorted. Remove the injector(s) and replace the O-ring(s). Align the injector retaining bolt holes, insert the bolts and tighten them to the torque listed in this Chapter's Specifications.

17 The rest of the installation is the reverse of the removal procedure.

18 When you're done, verify that there's no fuel leakage from the injectors and associated components: Remove the plug from the fuel pump check connector, bridge the terminals in the electrical connector with a jumper wire **(see illustration 5.2a or 5.2b)** and turn the ignition switch to On. If there's a leak anywhere, repair it immediately. Remove the wire and replace the plug in the fuel pump check connector.

20 Fuel pressure regulator - removal and installation

Refer to illustrations 20.1a, 20.1b, 20.1c, 20.7, 20.8a and 20.8b

Warning: *Gasoline is extremely flammable, so take extra precautions when you work on any part of the fuel system. Don't smoke or allow open flames or bare light bulbs near the work area, and don't work in a garage where a natural gas-type appliance (such as a water heater or clothes dryer) with a pilot light is present. If you spill any fuel on your skin, rinse it off immediately with soap and water. When you perform any kind of work on the fuel system, wear safety glasses and have a Class B type fire extinguisher on hand.*

1 The fuel pressure regulator is located between the fuel rail and the head on 1979 through 1981 models, below the rear end of the rail on 1982 through 1986 models and on top of the front end of the rail on 1987 and later models **(see illustrations)**. If you suspect a pressure regulator malfunction, check the system fuel pressure (see Section 5). If the fuel pressure test indicates a faulty regulator, replace it as follows.

2 Relieve the system fuel pressure (see Section 3).

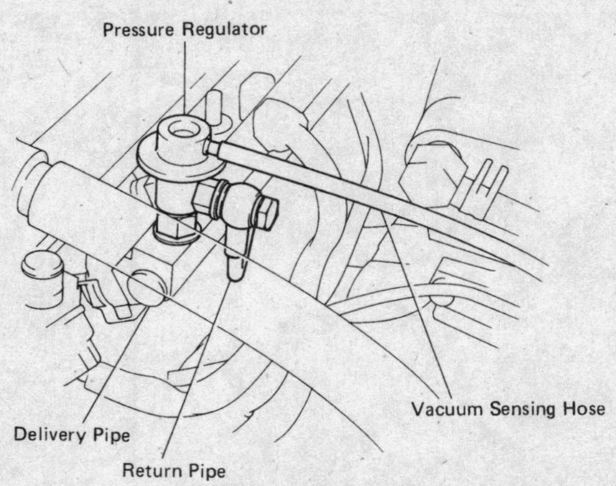

20.1c Fuel pressure regulator assembly on 1987 and later models

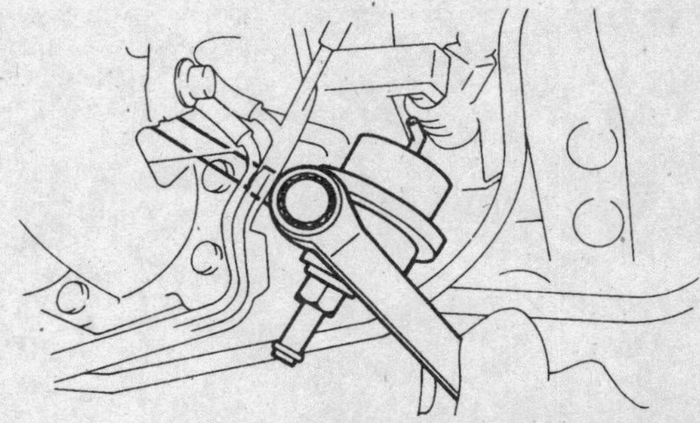

20.7 On 1982 through 1986 models, the fuel delivery hose is attached to the regulator with a banjo bolt and fitting (be sure to discard the old sealing washers and use new ones when you reattach the line)

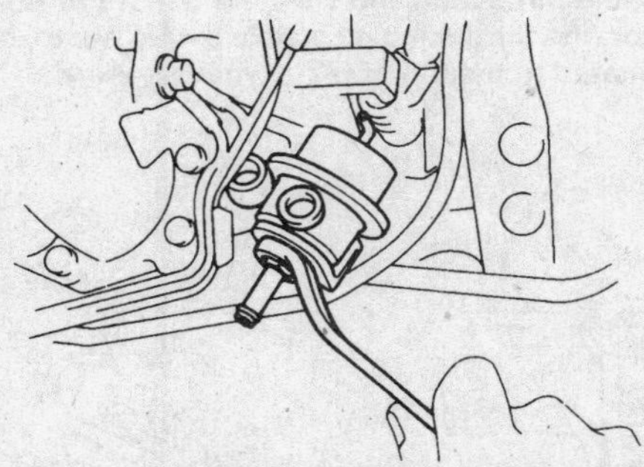

20.8a To remove the fuel pressure regulator from its mounting bracket on 1979 through 1986 models, remove the locknut underneath the bracket (1982 through 1986 model shown, earlier models similar)

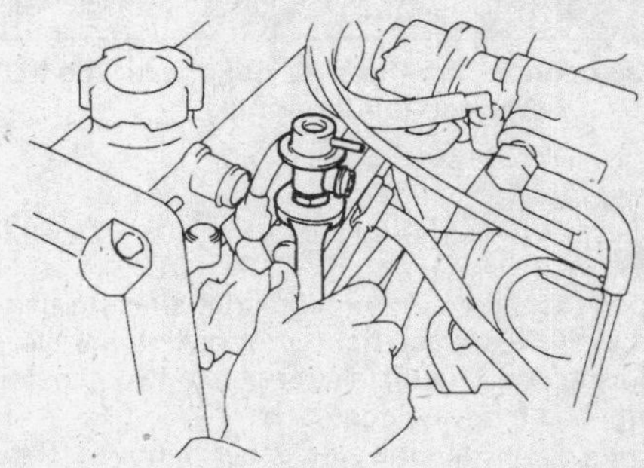

20.8b To remove the fuel pressure regulator from the fuel rail on 1987 and later models, remove this locknut

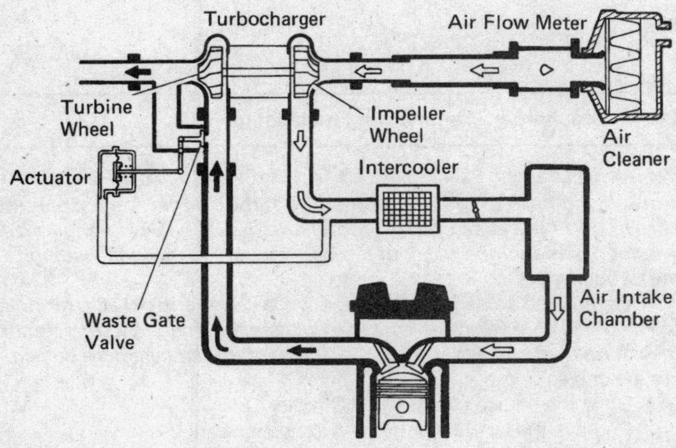

21.1 Schematic of the turbocharger system

3 Detach the cable from the negative terminal of the battery. **Caution:** *If the stereo in your vehicle is equipped with an anti-theft system, refer to the information on page 0-15 at the front of this manual before detaching the cable.*

4 On 1979 through 1981 models, remove the intake tube from the throttle body.

5 Detach the PCV hose if it's in the way. Detach the vacuum sensing hose from the fuel pressure regulator.

6 Place a shop rag or a container under the pressure regulator to catch spilled fuel, then detach the fuel return hose from the regulator. This hose is simply clamped onto 1979 through 1986 models; on 1987 and later models, it's connected with a banjo bolt similar to a fuel delivery hose fitting.

7 On 1982 through 1986 models, disconnect the fuel delivery line from the fuel pressure regulator **(see illustration)**. On 1987 and later models, there's no fuel delivery line fitting on the regulator - the fuel delivery line is connected to the fuel rail.

8 On 1979 through 1986 models, unscrew the locknut and detach the pressure regulator from its mounting bracket **(see illustration)**; on 1987 and later models, unscrew the locknut and remove the regulator from the fuel rail **(see illustration)**.

9 Installation is the reverse of the removal procedure. Make sure that the hose and vacuum connections are clean and tighten the regulator locknut and the banjo bolt to the torque listed in this Chapter's Specifications. Use new sealing washers when reconnecting the fuel return hose.

21 Turbocharger - description and precautions

Description

Refer to illustration 21.1

The turbocharger increases power by using an exhaust gas-driven turbine to pressurize the fuel/air mixture before it enters the combustion chambers **(see illustration)**. The amount of boost (intake manifold pressure) is controlled by the waste gate (exhaust bypass valve). The waste gate is operated by a spring-loaded actuator assembly which controls the maximum boost level by allowing some of the exhaust gas to bypass the turbine.

The turbocharger system uses an intercooler, located in front of the radiator, to reduce the temperature of the compressed intake air. Reducing the air temperature increases its density, which in turn increases engine output.

4

23.4 Disconnect the three air hoses and the PCV hose (underneath)

23.10 Remove the three nuts and washers and remove the turbo heat insulator (the third nut isn't visible in this photo, but it's located to the left of the oxygen sensor)

Precautions

Avoid sudden racing or acceleration right after starting a cold engine. Also don't stop the engine right after pulling a trailer, driving at high speed or driving uphill - let it idle for one to two minutes, depending on the severity of the driving condition.

Don't run the engine with the air cleaner removed. If foreign matter enters the intake system, it can damage the turbine and impeller wheels, which run at speeds of 20,000 to 110,000 rpm.

22 Turbocharger - check

1 While it is a relatively simple device, the turbocharger is also a precision component which can be severely damaged by an interrupted oil or coolant supply or loose or damaged ducts.

2 Due to the special techniques and equipment required, checking and diagnosis of suspected problems should be left to a dealer service department. The home mechanic can, however, check the connections and linkages for security, damage and other obvious problems.

3 Because each turbocharger has its own distinctive sound, a change in the noise level can be a sign of potential problems.

4 A high-pitched or whistling sound is a symptom of an inlet air or exhaust gas leak.

5 If an unusual sound comes from the vicinity of the turbine, the turbocharger can be removed and the turbine wheel inspected. **Caution:** *All checks must be made with the engine off and cool to the touch and the turbocharger stopped or personal injury could result. Operating the engine without all the turbocharger ducts and filters installed is also dangerous and can result in damage to the turbine wheel blades.*

6 With the engine turned off, reach inside the housing and turn the turbine wheel to make sure it spins freely. If it doesn't, it's possible the cooling oil has sludged or coked from overheating. Push in on the turbine wheel and check for binding. The turbine should rotate freely with no binding or rubbing on the housing. If it does the turbine bearing is worn out.

7 Check the exhaust manifold for cracks and loose connections.

8 Because the turbine wheel rotates at speeds up to 110,000 rpm, severe damage can result from the interruption of coolant or contamination of the oil supply to the turbine bearings. Check for leaks in the coolant and oil inlet lines and obstructions in the oil drain-back line, as this can cause severe oil loss through the turbocharger seals. Burned oil on the turbine housing is a sign of this. **Caution:** *Whenever a major engine bearing such as a main, connecting rod or camshaft bearing is replaced, the turbocharger should be flushed with clean oil.*

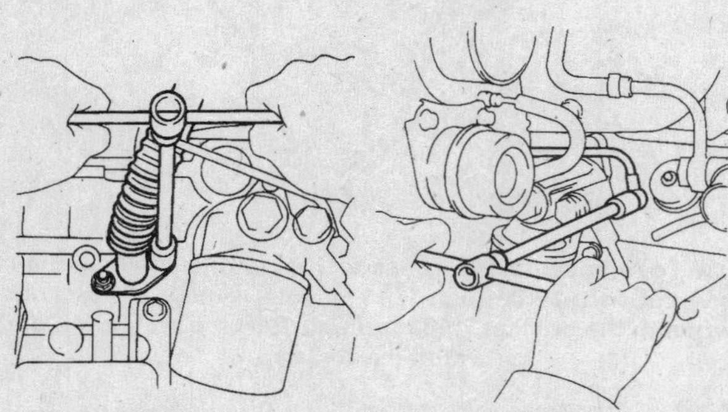

23.14 Remove the turbo oil pipe mounting nuts and bolt

23 Turbocharger - removal and installation

Refer to illustrations 23.4, 23.10, 23.14, 23.15, 23.18 and 23.19

Note: *If you have to replace a defective turbocharger, be absolutely sure to find the cause of the turbo failure first. Check the engine oil level and inspect the quality of the oil. Inspect the oil lines leading to the turbocharger.*

1 Detach the cable from the negative battery terminal. **Caution:** *If the stereo in your vehicle is equipped with an anti-theft system, refer to the information on page 0-15 at the front of this manual before detaching the cable.*

2 Drain the engine coolant (see Chapter 1).

3 Remove the air cleaner ducts and hoses, as necessary.

4 Disconnect the three air hoses and the PCV hose **(see illustration)**.

5 Unplug the airflow meter electrical connector.

6 Detach the power steering idle-up air hose.

7 Loosen the clamps and remove the bolt.

8 Remove the No. 7 air cleaner hose, the airflow meter and air cleaner housing cap as a single assembly.

9 Disconnect the oxygen sensor electrical connector.

10 Remove the three nuts and washers and remove the turbo heat insulator **(see illustration)**.

11 Remove the oil dipstick, remove the attaching bolt from the oil dipstick guide, remove the guide and remove the O-ring from the guide.

12 Loosen the hose clamps, unscrew the mounting bolt and detach

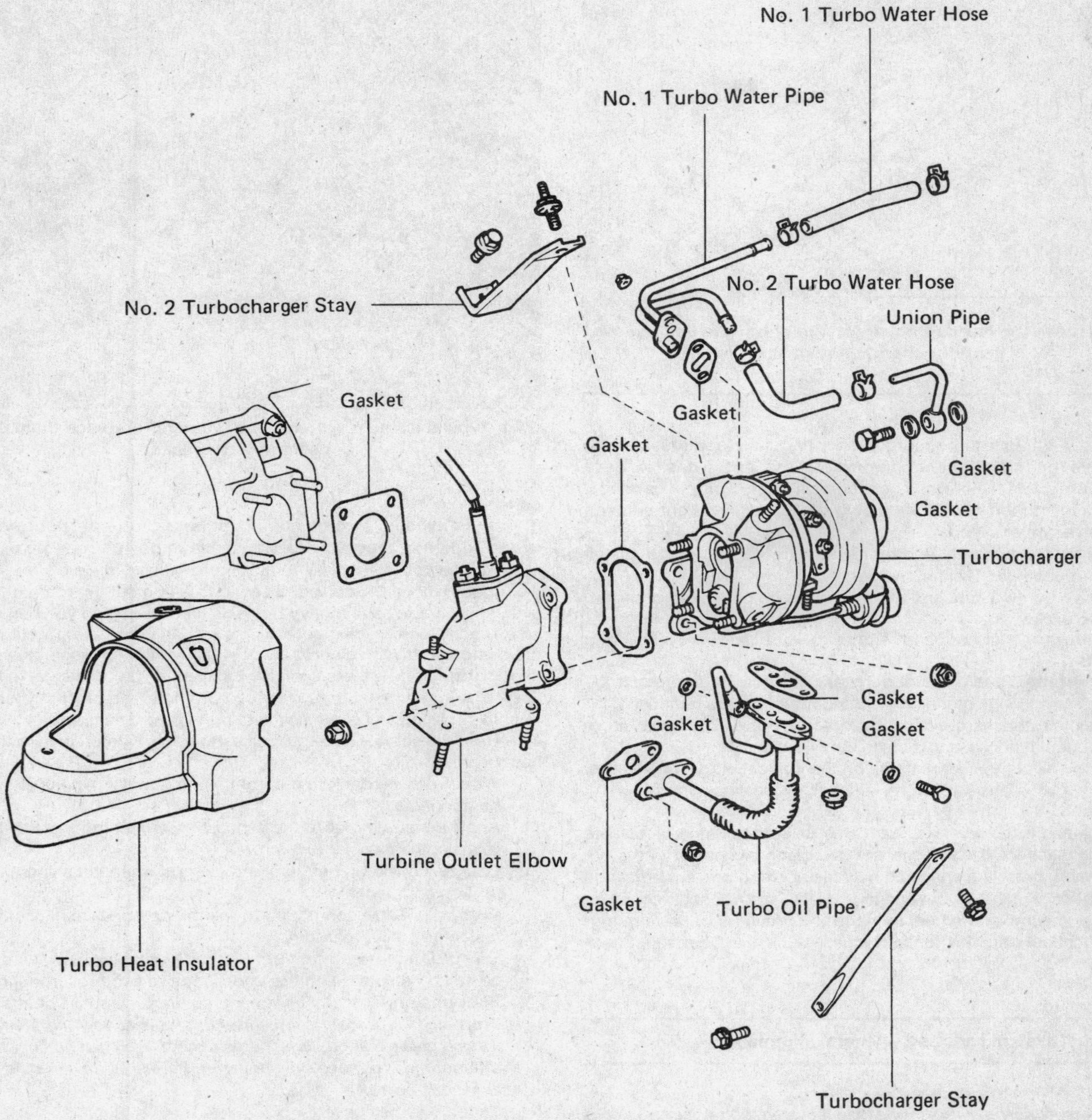

23.15 An exploded view of the turbocharger assembly and related components

23.18 Disconnect the banjo bolt and the sealing washers and detach the union pipe

the air cleaner pipe along with the air cleaner hose from the bottom of the turbo.

13 Remove the three nuts, loosen the clamp bolt and detach the exhaust pipe from the exhaust manifold. Remove and discard the old gasket.

14 Remove the turbo oil pipe mounting nuts and bolt **(see illustration)**.

15 Remove the turbocharger stay (brace) **(see illustration)**.

16 Remove the upper turbocharger stay (brace).

17 Loosen the hose clamps and detach the turbo coolant hose from the coolant outlet housing.

18 Disconnect the banjo bolt and the sealing washers and detach the union pipe **(see illustration)**. Discard the sealing washers.

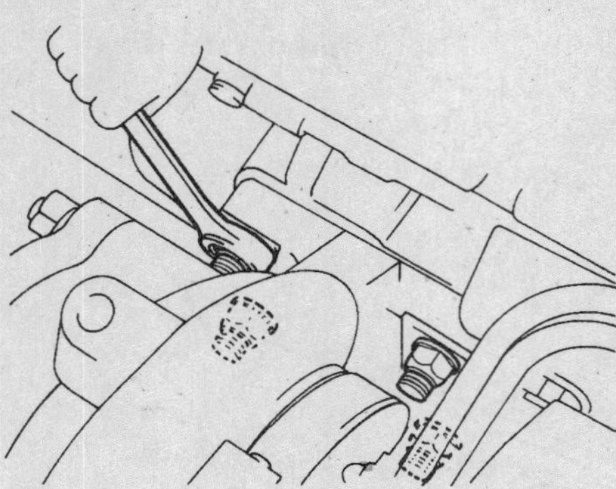

23.19 Remove the four turbocharger mounting nuts and remove the turbocharger and gasket

19 Remove the four turbocharger mounting nuts **(see illustration)** and remove the turbocharger and gasket. Discard the gasket. **Caution:** *Always handle the turbocharger carefully. Don't drop it or bang it against anything. And don't hold it by grasping easily deformed parts such as the actuator or rod.*
20 Unscrew the two nuts and remove the coolant pipe and gasket from the turbocharger. Discard the gasket.
21 Remove the two nuts and remove the turbo oil pipe and gasket. Discard the gasket.
22 Unscrew the four nuts and remove the turbine outlet elbow and the gasket.
23 Plug all intake and exhaust ports and the oil inlet to prevent the entry of dirt and foreign matter while the turbocharger is removed.
24 While the turbocharger is removed, inspect the oil lines for accumulated sludge. If necessary, replace the oil lines.
25 Remove all old gasket material on the lubrication oil pipe flange, the turbocharger oil flange and the outlet elbow sealing surfaces.

Installation

26 Installation is the reverse of removal. Be sure to use new gaskets and sealing washers. If it's necessary to replace any bolts or nuts, replace them only with the specified new fasteners to prevent breakage or deformation. Put 1/2-to-3/4 ounce of oil into the turbocharger oil inlet and turn the impeller wheel by hand to spread oil to the bearing. Tighten all critical fasteners to the torque listed in this Chapter's Specifications.

24 Exhaust system servicing - general information

Refer to illustrations 24.1, 24.5a and 24.5b

Warning: *Inspection and repair of exhaust system components should be done only after enough time has elapsed after driving the vehicle to allow the system components to cool completely. Also, when working under the vehicle, make sure it is securely supported on jackstands.*

1 The exhaust system consists of the exhaust manifold, catalytic converter(s), the muffler, the tailpipe and all connecting pipes, brackets, hangers and clamps. The exhaust system is attached to the body with mounting brackets and rubber hangers **(see illustration)**. If any of these parts are damaged or deteriorated, excessive noise and vibration will be transmitted to the body.

2 Regular inspections of the exhaust system will keep it safe and quiet. Look for any damaged or bent parts, open seams, holes, loose connections, excessive corrosion or other defects which could allow exhaust fumes to enter the vehicle. Deteriorated exhaust system components should not be repaired - they should be replaced with new

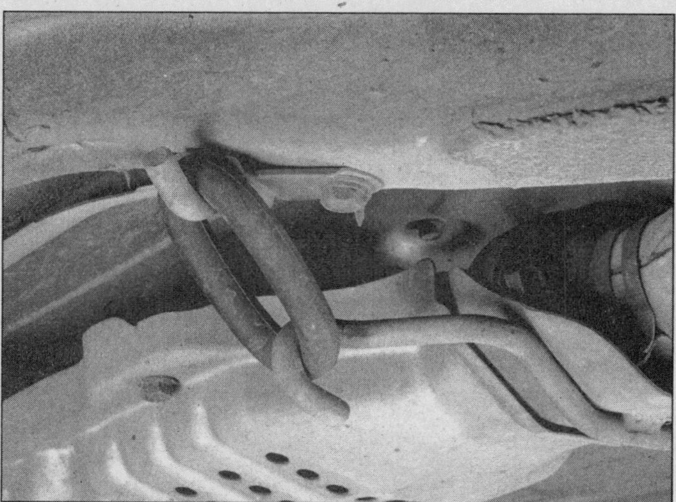

24.1 Typical exhaust system rubber hanger - replace them if they appear worn or cracked

parts.

3 If the exhaust system components are extremely corroded or rusted together, they will probably have to be cut from the exhaust system. The convenient way to accomplish this is to have a muffler repair shop remove the corroded sections with a cutting torch. If, however, you want to save money by doing it yourself (and you don't have an oxy/acetylene welding outfit with a cutting torch), simply cut off the old components with a hacksaw. If you have compressed air, special pneumatic cutting chisels can also be used. If you do decide to tackle the job at home, be sure to wear eye protection to protect your eyes from metal chips and work gloves to protect your hands.

4 Here are some simple guidelines to apply when repairing the exhaust system:

a) Work from the back to the front when removing exhaust system components.
b) Apply penetrating oil to the exhaust system component fasteners to make them easier to remove.
c) Use new gaskets, hangers and clamps when installing exhaust system components.
d) Apply anti-seize compound to the threads of all exhaust system fasteners during reassembly.
e) Be sure to allow sufficient clearance between newly installed parts and all points on the underbody to avoid overheating the floor pan and possibly catalytic converter and its heat shield. **Warning:** *The catalytic converter operates at very high temperatures and takes about 30 minutes to cool. Wait half an hour before attempting to remove the converter. Failure to do so could result in serious burns.*

5 To remove the converter:

a) Raise the vehicle and place it securely on jackstands.
b) Make sure that the converter is cool.
c) Apply penetrating oil to the flange bolts at the front and rear converter flanges.
d) Remove the flange bolts **(see illustrations)** from the front and the rear flanges of the converter.
e) Remove the converter and gaskets. Discard the gaskets.

6 Inspect the upper heat shield while the converter is removed. It should be firmly attached to the underside of the vehicle and there should be adequate clearance between the shield and the converter.

7 Installation is the reverse of removal. Use new gaskets and coat the threads of all bolts/studs with anti-seize compound. Tighten the bolts securely. Note: For further information regarding the catalytic converter, refer to Chapter 6.

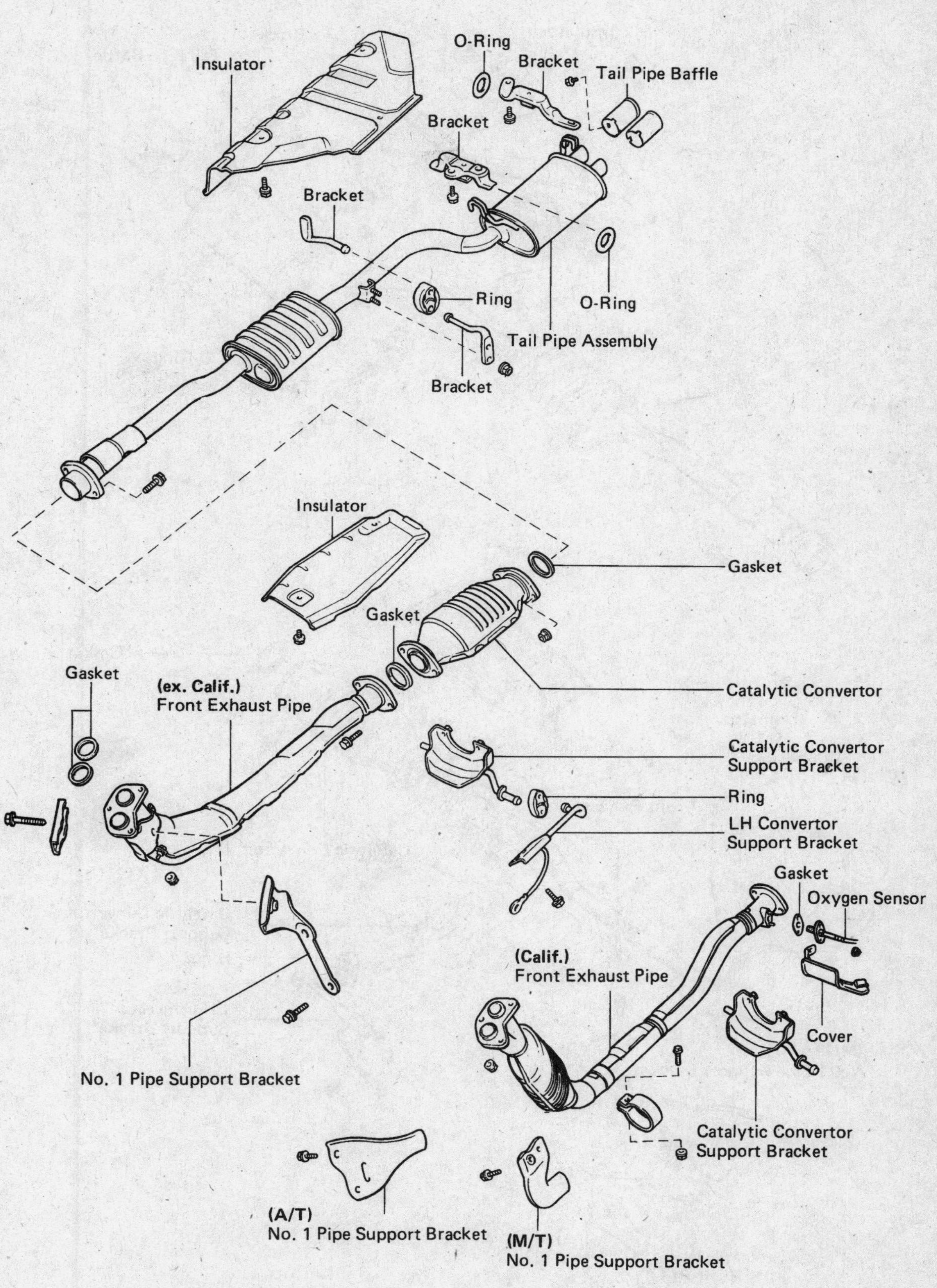

24.5a An exploded view of a typical late-model non-turbo exhaust system (earlier models similar)

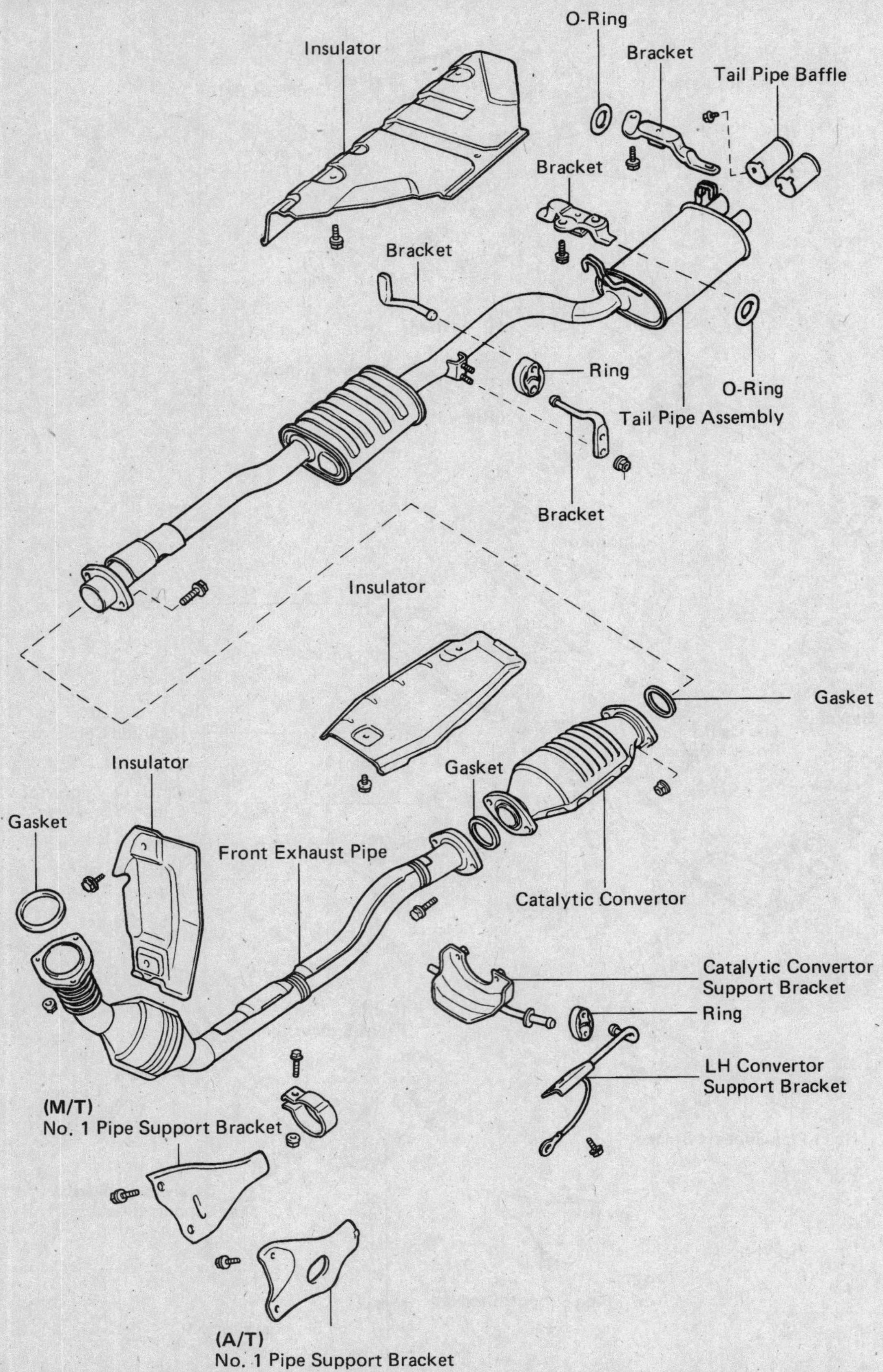

24.5b An exploded view of a typical late-model turbo exhaust system (earlier models similar)

Chapter 5 Engine electrical systems

Contents

5

Specifications

Ignition system

Type .... Transistorized (electronic)

Ignition coil

Coil primary resistance
- 1979 through 1982 .... 0.5 to 0.7 ohms
- 1983 through 1986 .... 0.4 to 0.5 ohms
- 1987 on
  - Non-turbo .... 0.2 to 0.3 ohms
  - Turbo
    - 1987 .... 0.3 to 0.6 ohms
    - 1988 through 1990 .... 0.3 to 0.5 ohms
    - 1991 .... 0.34 to 0.42 ohms
    - 1992 .... 0.3 to 0.6 ohms

Coil secondary resistance
- 1979 through 1982 .... 11.5 to 15.5 K-ohms
- 1983 through 1986 .... 8.5 to 11.5 K-ohms
- 1987 through 1991 .... 9 to 12.5 K-ohms*
- 1992 .... 8 to 13 K-ohms*

** Doesn't apply to turbo models*

Distributor

Pick-up coil resistance	
1979 through 1982	140 to 180 ohms
1983 through 1986	140 to 180 ohms (both pick-up coils have same resistance)
1987 and 1988 non-turbos	140 to 180 ohms (all three pick-up coils)
1987 through 1990 turbos	140 to 180 ohms (all three pick-up coils)
1989 through 1991 non-turbos	
G1 and G2 pick-up coils	140 to 180 ohms
Ne pick-up coil	180 to 220 ohms
1992 non-turbos	
G1 and G2 pick-up coils	125 to 190 ohms
Ne pick-up coil	155 to 240 ohms
1991 turbos	205 to 255 ohms (all three pick-up coils)
1992 turbos	185 to 265 ohms (all three pick-up coils)
Air gap (all models)	0.008 to 0.016 inch

Charging system

Alternator brushes	
Minimum exposed length	
1979 through 1983	0.217 inch
1984 through 1986	0.177 inch
1987 on	0.059 inch
Standard exposed length	
1979 through 1981	0.630 inch
1982 and 1983	0.492 inch
1984 on	0.413 inch

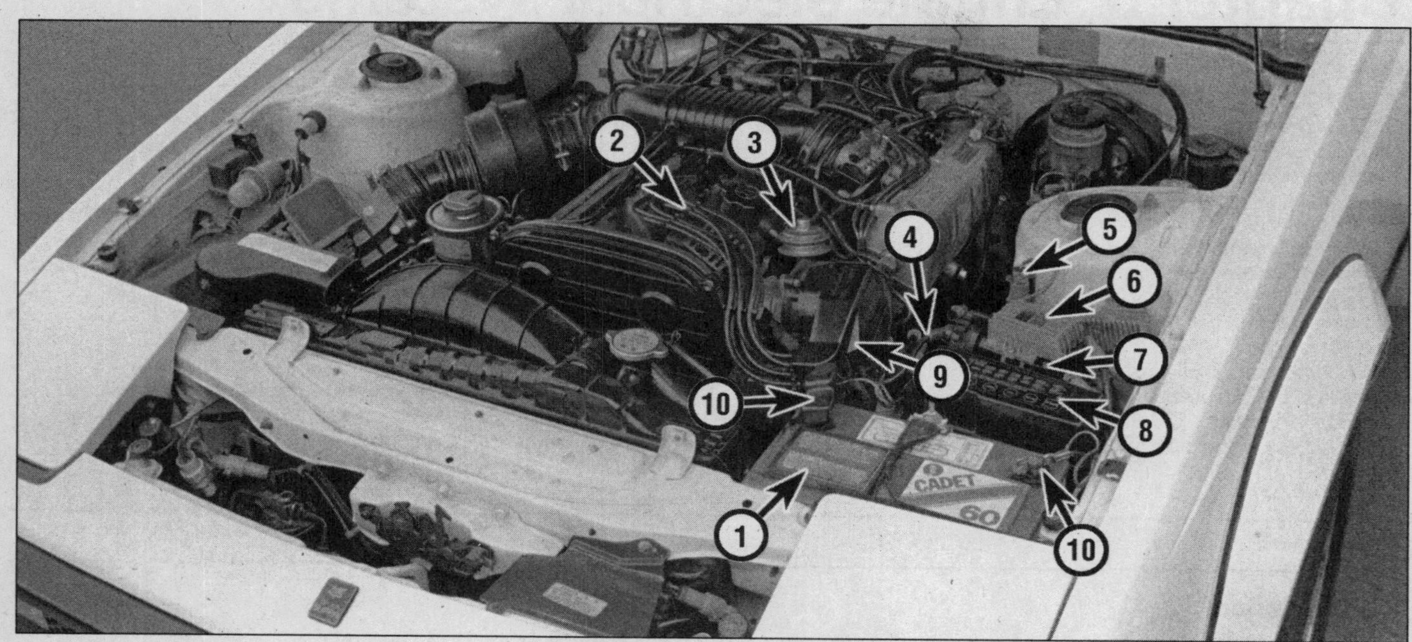

1.1a Typical ignition system components

1. *Battery*
2. *Spark plug wires*
3. *Vacuum advance unit (1982 models)*
4. *Coil high tension lead*
5. *Pick-up coil electrical connector*
6. *Igniter*
7. *Ignition coil*
8. *Fuse block*
9. *Distributor*
10. *Battery cables*

1 General information

Refer to illustrations 1.1a and 1.1b

The engine electrical system includes all ignition, charging and starting components **(see illustrations)**. Because of their engine-related functions, these components are considered separately from chassis electrical devices such as the lights, instruments, etc.

Safety-related information on the engine electrical systems can be found in *Safety first* near the front of this manual. It should be referred to before beginning any operation included in this Chapter.

2 Battery - removal and installation

Refer to illustration 2.3

1 The battery is located in the front (driver's side) corner of the engine compartment.

2 **Warning:** *Always disconnect the negative cable first and hook it up last or the battery may be shorted by the tool used to loosen up the cable clamps. Disconnect both cables from the battery terminals.* **Caution:** *If the stereo in your vehicle is equipped with an anti-theft system, refer to the information on page 0-15 at the front of this manual*

1.1b Typical starting and charging systems components - underside view

1 *Alternator* 2 *Starter motor*

before detaching the cable.

3 Unbolt the battery hold-down clamp **(see illustration)** and lift the battery from the battery support tray. **Warning:** *Do not tilt the battery when moving it.*

4 Installation is the reverse of the removal procedure. Be certain no nuts, bolts or tools are left in the support tray before installing the battery. Reattach the positive cable first, then the negative cable.

3 Battery - emergency jump starting

Refer to the *Booster battery (jump) starting* procedure at the front of this manual.

4 Battery cables - check and replacement

1 Periodically inspect the entire length of each battery cable for damage, cracked or burned insulation and corrosion. Poor battery cable connections can cause starting problems and decreased engine performance.

2 Check the cable-to-terminal connections at the ends of the cables for cracks, loose wire strands and corrosion. The presence of white, fluffy deposits under the insulation at the cable terminal connection is a sign that the cable is corroded and should be replaced. Check the terminals for distortion, missing mounting bolts and corrosion.

3 If only the positive cable is to be replaced, be sure to disconnect the negative cable from the battery first.

4 Disconnect and remove the cable. Make sure that the replacement cable is the same length and diameter. **Caution:** *If the stereo in your vehicle is equipped with an anti-theft system, refer to the information on page 0-15 at the front of this manual before detaching the cable.*

5 Clean the threads of the starter or ground connection with a wire brush to remove rust and corrosion. Apply a light coat of petroleum jelly to the threads to ease installation and prevent future corrosion.

6 Attach the cable to the starter or ground connection and tighten the mounting nut securely.

7 Before connecting the new cable to the battery, make sure it reaches the terminal without having to be stretched.

8 Connect the positive cable first, followed by the negative cable.

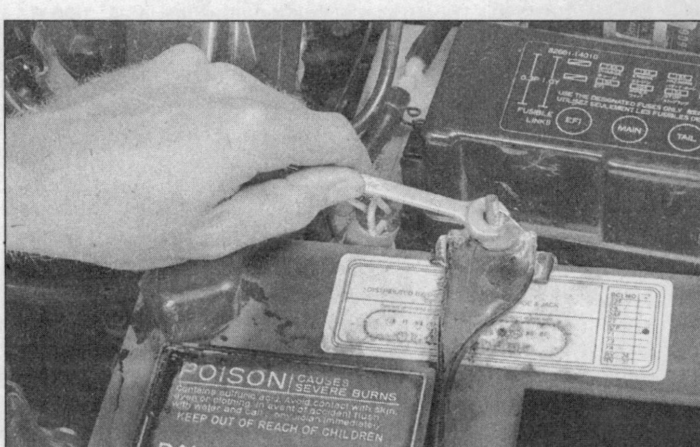

2.3 Remove the battery hold-down clamp to free the battery from the tray (when installing the battery, be careful not to overtighten the clamp)

6.2a If the engine turns over but won't start, disconnect the spark plug wire from any spark plug and attach it to a calibrated ignition tester (available at most auto parts stores), connect the clip on the tester to a bolt or metal bracket on the engine and see if you get a spark from the tester electrode to ground when the engine is cranked

6.2b If you don't have a calibrated ignition tester, hold the plug wire with an insulated tool about 1/4-inch from a good ground and have an assistant crank the engine - you should see bright, blue, well-defined sparks

5 Ignition system - general information and precautions

General information

The ignition system includes the ignition switch, the battery, the igniter, the coils, the primary (low voltage) and secondary (high voltage) wiring circuits, the distributor (non-turbo) or cam position sensor (turbo models) and the spark plugs. All models covered by this manual use an electronic ignition system instead of a conventional breaker-point system. An electronic ignition system functions similarly to a point-type system, but uses a signal generator, commonly known as a "pick-up coil" (non-turbo models) or cam position sensor (turbo models) and an ignition module, usually referred to by Toyota as an "igniter." Think of the pick-up coil or cam sensor as the "breaker points" of an electronic ignition system. For more information on the cam position sensor, refer to Chapter 6.

There are numerous advantages to an electronic ignition system: There are no moving parts that bear against each other, causing mechanical wear; dwell and timing don't change, even over thousands of miles of operation; electronic switching devices don't "bounce" at high rpm; there are no breaker points to adjust or maintain; low speed performance is improved; cold starting under adverse weather conditions is less likely to be affected.

On 1979 through 1982 models, ignition advance is handled by a combination of mechanical and vacuum operated components which respond to engine speed and load. These devices work exactly the same way as such components on a conventional point-type ignition system.

The ignition advance on 1983 and later models is controlled by an Electronic Spark Advance (ESA) system, which is located inside the Electronic Control Unit (ECU). In ESA systems, engine sensors monitor the varying engine operating conditions such as engine speed, load, coolant temperature and air intake, and send this information to the ECU. The ECU/ESA system adjusts ignition timing and advance in accordance with these changing operating conditions and loads, eliminating the need for centrifugal and vacuum advance devices on the distributor. For further information on the ECU, refer to Chapter 6.

Precautions

Certain precautions must be observed when working on a transistorized ignition system.

a) Do not disconnect the battery cables when the engine is running.
b) Make sure the igniter is always well grounded.
c) Keep water away from the igniter and distributor.
d) If a tachometer is to be connected to the engine, always connect the tachometer positive (+) terminal to the ignition coil negative terminal - never to the distributor.
e) Do not allow the coil terminals to be grounded, as the igniter or coil could be damaged.
f) Do not leave the ignition switch on for more than ten minutes if the engine isn't running or will not start.

6 Ignition system - check

Refer to illustration 6.2a, 6.2b and 6.6

Warning: *Because of the very high voltage generated by the ignition system, extreme care should be taken when this check is performed.*

1 If the engine turns over but won't start, disconnect the spark plug wire from any spark plug and attach it to a calibrated ignition tester (available at most auto parts stores).

2 Connect the clip on the tester to a bolt or metal bracket on the engine **(see illustration)**. If you're unable to obtain a calibrated ignition tester, remove the wire from one of the spark plugs and, using an insulated tool, hold the end of the wire about 1/4-inch from a good ground **(see illustration)**.

3 Crank the engine and watch the end of the tester or spark plug wire to see if bright blue, well-defined sparks occur. If you're not using a calibrated tester, have an assistant crank the engine for you. **Warning:** *Keep clear of drivebelts and other moving engine components that could injure you.*

4 If sparks occur, sufficient voltage is reaching the plug to fire it. Repeat this test on the rest of the plug wires to verify that the wires, distributor cap and rotor (on turbo models) or the other coils (turbo models) are okay. Also, the plugs themselves may be fouled - remove and check them (see Chapter 1). **Note:** *The following two Steps apply only to non-turbo models; if you have a turbo model, go to Step 7.*

5 If no sparks or intermittent sparks occur on non-turbo models, remove the distributor cap and check the cap and rotor (see Chapter 1). If moisture is present, dry out the cap and rotor, then reinstall the cap.

6 If there's still no spark on non-turbo models, detach the coil secondary (high tension) wire from the distributor cap and hook it up to the tester (reattach the plug wire to the spark plug), then repeat the spark check. Again, if you don't have a tester, hold the end of the wire about 1/4-inch from a good ground **(see illustration)**. If sparks occur now, the distributor cap, rotor or plug wire(s) may be defective.

7 If no sparks occur, check the wire connections at the coil to make sure they're clean and tight. Check for voltage to the coil. Make any necessary repairs, then repeat the check again.

8 On non-turbo models, if there's still no spark, the coil-to-cap wire

6.6 Check the coil high-tension wire in the same manner you checked the plug wires

may be bad (check the resistance with an ohmmeter - it should be 7000 ohms per foot or less). If a known good wire doesn't make any difference in the test results, the ignition module may be defective.

9 If there is still no spark, check the resistance of the spark plug and coil wires (see Chapter 1). If any of the wires are over 25 K-ohms, replace them.

10 If there is still no spark, check the power supply to the ignition coil (see Section 7). If there isn't battery voltage at the ignition coil positive terminal, troubleshoot the wiring between the ignition switch and the ignition coil (see the Wiring Diagrams at end of this book).

11 If there is still no spark, check the resistance of the ignition coil (see Section 7). If the resistance is not within specification, replace the ignition coil.

12 If there is still no spark, check the resistance of the signal generator or pick-up coil (see Section 10). If the resistance is not within the specified range, replace the pick-up coil (on 1979 through 1982 models) or the distributor (on 1983 and later models).

13 If there is still no spark on 1979 through 1982 and 1987 and later models, check the distributor air gap (see Section 11). If the air gap is not within specification, replace the distributor. **Note:** *Skip this Step if you've got a 1983 through 1986 model; there's no air gap specification for these models.*

14 If there is still no spark, the only other possibility besides the igniter is the wiring between the ECU and the distributor, or the ECU itself; however, checking the ECU multi-pin connector can be tricky and, if performed incorrectly, can damage the ECU circuitry. We recommend that you let a dealer service department or other repair shop handle problems with the ECU.

15 If the ECU is okay and the wiring and connectors between the ECU and the distributor are okay, check the igniter (see Section 8). **Note:** *On 1986 and later non-turbo models, there's no specific procedure for checking just the igniter, but if you've come this far, and everything else checks out, the igniter is probably defective.*

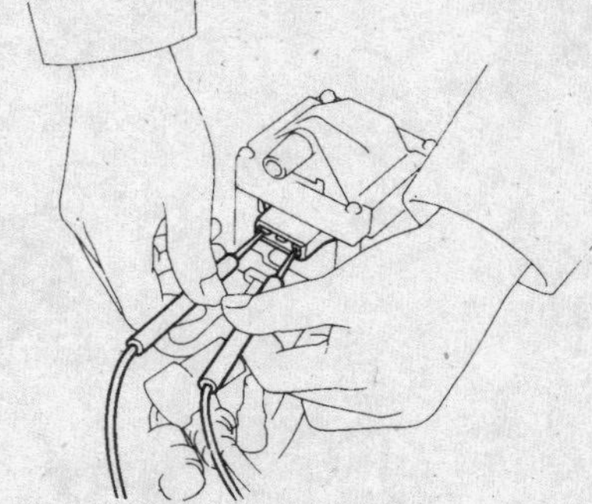

7.2b To measure the coil primary resistance on 1983 and later models, touch the leads of an ohmmeter to the primary terminals (the spade terminals inside the modular connector right below the high tension wire)

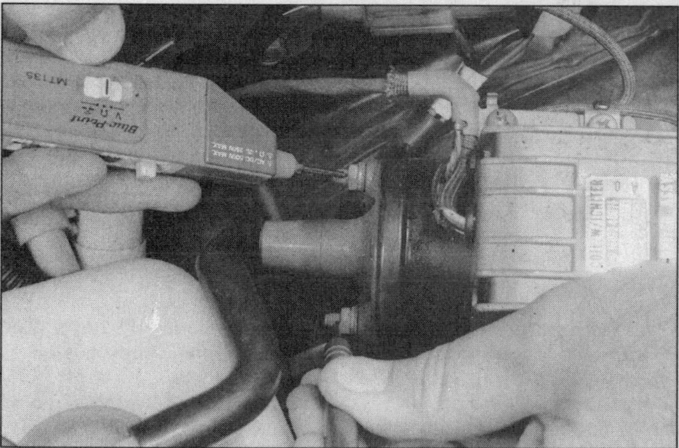

7.2a To measure the coil primary resistance on 1979 through 1982 models, touch the leads of an ohmmeter to the primary terminals (the two small studs protruding through the end of the coil, adjacent to the high tension wire)

7 Ignition coil - check and replacement

Check

Non-turbo models

Refer to illustrations 7.2a, 7.2b, 7.3a and 7.3b

1 Clean the coil primary terminals and check the coil tower terminal for corrosion. Clean it with a wire brush if any corrosion is found.

2 Measure the coil primary resistance by touching the leads of an ohmmeter to the primary terminals **(see illustrations)**. Compare your measurement to the coil primary resistance listed in this Chapter's Specifications.

3 Measure the coil secondary resistance by touching the leads of an ohmmeter to the positive primary terminal and the high tension terminal **(see illustrations)**. Compare your measurement to the coil secondary resistance listed in this Chapter's Specifications.

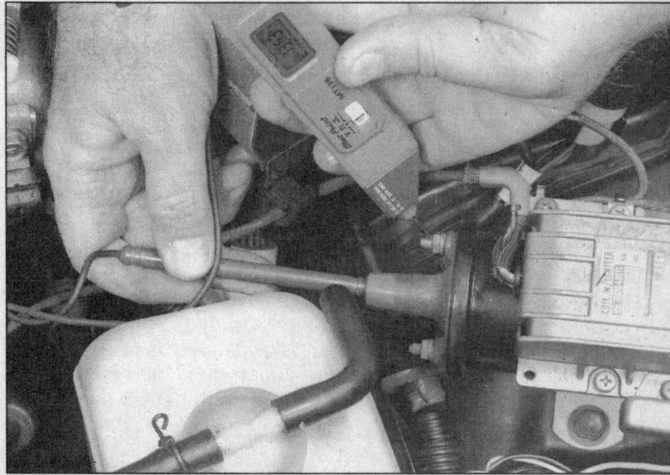

7.3a To measure the coil secondary resistance on 1979 through 1982 models, touch the leads of an ohmmeter to the positive primary terminal and the high tension terminal

5

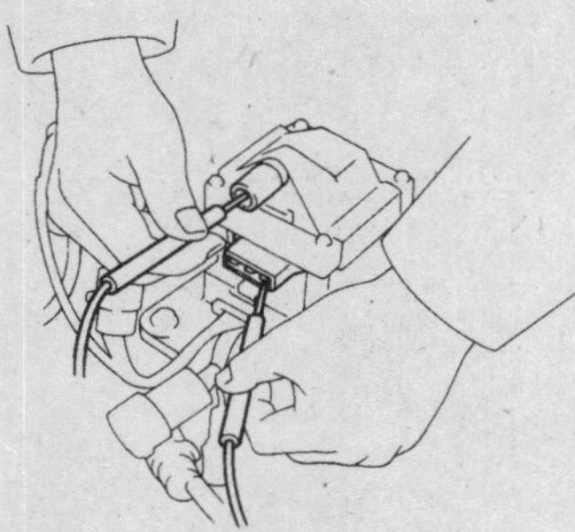

7.3b To measure the coil secondary resistance on 1983 and later models, touch the leads of an ohmmeter to the high tension terminal and the positive primary terminal (on 1983 through 1986 models, this is the brown side of the two primary terminals; on 1987 and later models, it's the terminal on the right, as shown in this illustration)

7.11a To check the power source line on turbo models, disconnect the spark plug wires from the ignition coil, . . .

4 If the indicated resistance values are outside specification, the coil is defective. Replace it. **Note:** *If you don't have an ohmmeter, have the coil checked by a dealer service department before assuming it's defective.*

Turbo models

Refer to illustrations 7.10, 7.11a, 7.11b, 7.11c, 7.12 and 7.13

5 Disconnect the No. 1 air cleaner hose (see Chapter 4).

6 Disconnect the cruise control cable and accelerator cable (see Chapter 4), and TV cable (see Chapter 7).

7 Remove the ISC pipe (see Chapter 4).

8 Remove the PCV pipe and hoses (see Chapter 6).

9 Remove the intake air connector (see Chapter 4).

10 Remove the ignition coil cover **(see illustration)**.

11 Check the power source line: Disconnect the spark plug wires from the ignition coil **(see illustration)**, unplug the electrical connectors from the ignition coil **(see illustration)**, turn the ignition switch to On and, using a voltmeter, measure the voltage between terminal 2 and body ground **(see illustration)**. It should indicate about 12 volts.

12 Measure the coil primary resistance: Using an ohmmeter, measure the resistance between the positive and negative terminals **(see illustration)**. Compare your measurement to the coil primary resistance listed in this Chapter's Specifications. **Note:** *There's no way to test the secondary resistance on the type of coils used on turbo models.*

13 Check the ignition coil ground: Using an ohmmeter, verify that there's no continuity between the ignition coil terminal and body ground **(see illustration)**.

14 Repeat these three Steps for each coil (there are three). If any coil fails any of the above three tests, replace it (see below).

7.10 To remove the coil cover on turbo models, remove the oil filler cap and all five cover retaining nuts (arrows) - you'll have to remove the pipe across the rear of the cover to get at the two rear cover nuts

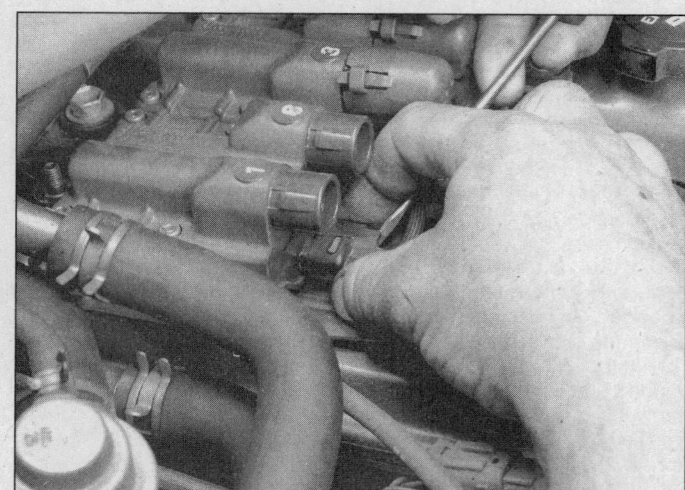

7.11b . . . unplug the electrical connectors from the ignition coil, . . .

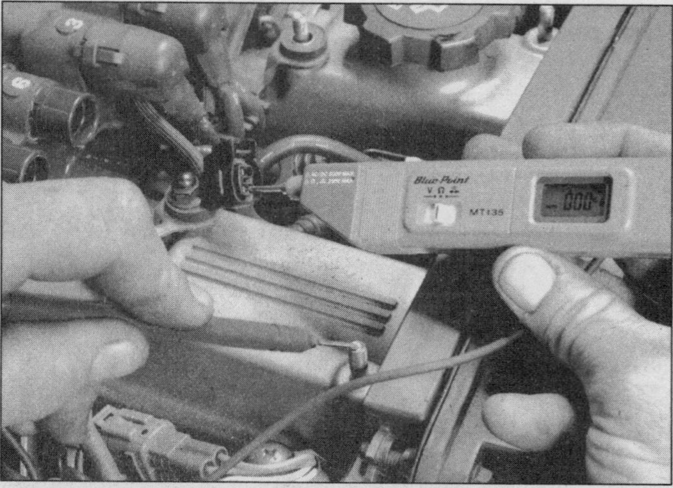

7.11c . . . turn the ignition switch to On and measure the voltage between terminal 2 and body ground with a voltmeter - it should be about 12 volts

7.12 To measure the coil primary resistance on turbo models, touch the probes of an ohmmeter to the positive and negative terminals of the primary connector and compare your measurement to the value listed in this Chapter's Specifications

7.13 Use an ohmmeter to verify that there's no continuity between the ignition coil terminal and body ground

7.16a To replace a coil on non-turbo models, simply detach the primary wires (1979 through 1982 models, as shown), or unplug the primary connector (1983 and later models), disconnect the coil wire and remove the mounting bracket bolts (arrows)

7.16b On turbo models, you'll need to use an Allen wrench to remove the coil bracket mounting screws

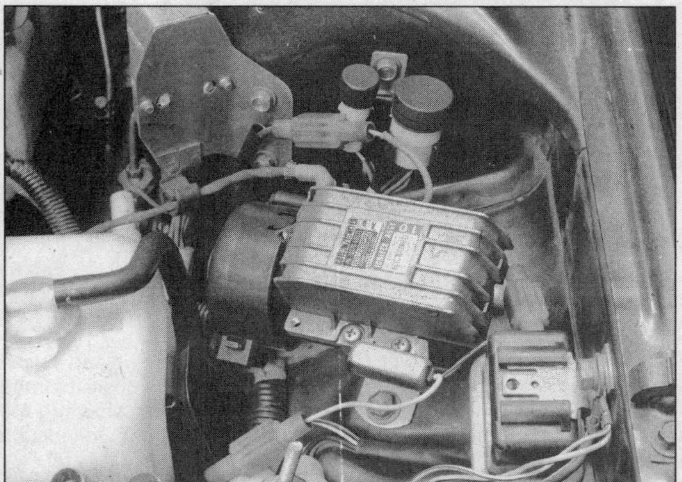

8.1 The igniter module on 1979 through 1982 models is located on top of the coil, right behind the battery

Replacement

Refer to illustrations 7.16a and 7.16b

15 Disconnect the coil high tension wire(s). Mark the wires and terminals with pieces of numbered tape, then detach the primary wires from the coil (1979 through 1982 models) or unplug the primary wire electrical connector(s) (1983 and later models).

16 Remove the coil mounting fasteners **(see illustrations)**, then remove the coil from its bracket. Clean the outer case and check it for cracks and other damage.

17 It is essential for proper ignition system operation that all coil terminals and wires be kept clean and dry.

18 Installation is the reverse of the removal procedure. On turbo models, refer to Steps 5 through 10 above.

8 Igniter - check and replacement

Check

1979 through 1982 models

Checking the power source line voltage

Refer to illustrations 8.1 and 8.2

1 The igniter is mounted on top of the ignition coil **(see illustration)**.

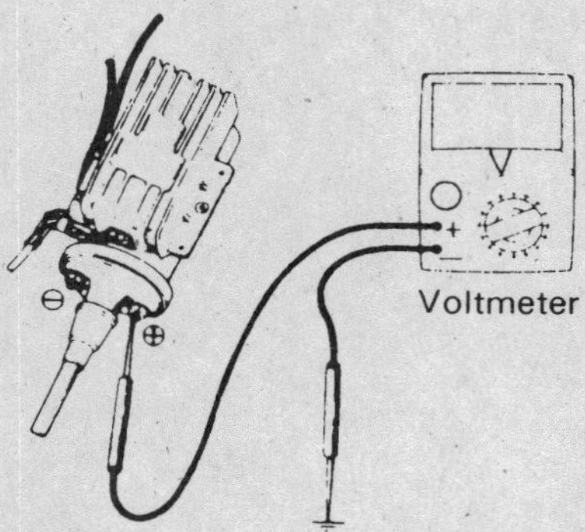

8.2 To check the power source line voltage to the igniter on 1979 through 1982 models, touch the positive probe of a voltmeter to the coil positive terminal and the negative probe to body ground - you should get about 12 volts

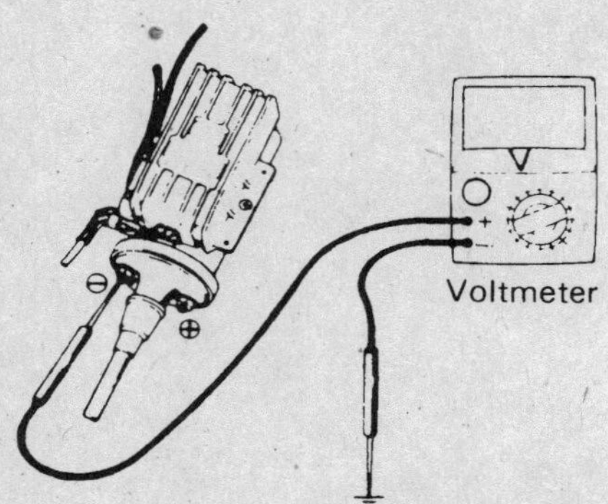

8.3 The first test of the power transistor in the igniter on 1979 through 1982 models: Touch the voltmeter positive probe to the coil negative terminal and the negative probe to body ground - again, you should get about 12 volts

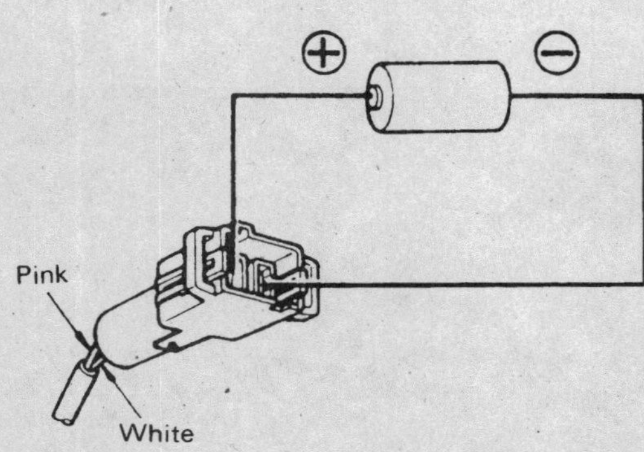

8.4 The second test of the power transistor in the igniter on 1979 through 1982 models: Turn the ignition switch to On, touch the positive probe of the voltmeter to the ignition coil negative terminal and the negative probe to body ground, then connect a 1.5-volt dry cell battery as shown (for no more than five seconds) - you should get about 7 volts

2 Turn the ignition switch to On and, using a voltmeter, touch the positive probe to the ignition coil positive terminal and the negative probe to body ground **(see illustration)**. It should indicate about 12 volts.

Checking the power transistor in the igniter

Refer to illustrations 8.3 and 8.4

3 Using a voltmeter, touch the positive probe to the ignition coil negative terminal and the negative probe to body ground **(see illustration)**. This should also be about 12 volts.

4 Unplug the electrical connector from the distributor. Using a dry cell 1.5 volt battery, touch the positive probe of the battery to the pink wire terminal and the negative probe to the white wire terminal **(see illustration)**. **Caution:** *Do NOT leave the battery hooked up for more than five seconds at a time, or the power transistor in the igniter will be destroyed. Instead, touch the jumper wire from the battery to the terminal only during the following test.*

5 With the ignition switch still turned to On, touch the positive probe of the voltmeter to the ignition coil negative terminal and the negative probe to body ground **(see illustration 8.3)** and simultaneously touch the jumper wire from the 1.5 volt battery to the pink wire terminal (remember: no longer than five seconds!). The voltmeter should indicate five volts LESS than battery voltage (or about 7 volts). If it doesn't, replace the igniter (see below).

6 Turn the ignition switch to Off, disconnect the test equipment and plug in the electrical connector for the distributor.

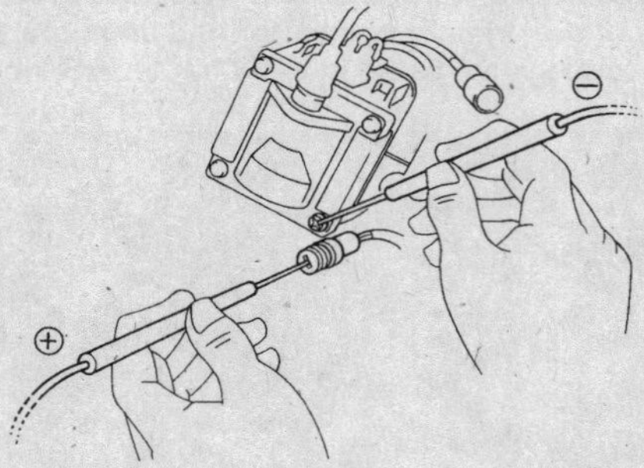

8.8 To check the power source line voltage to the igniter on 1983 through 1985 models, turn the ignition switch to On, unplug the brown and yellow wire electrical connector and connect a voltmeter as shown - you should get about 12 volts

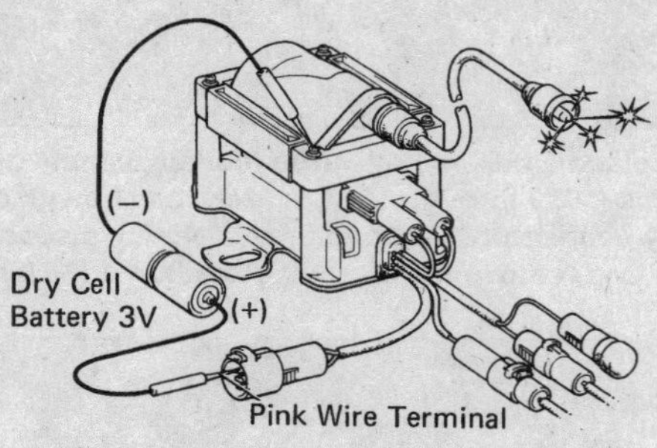

8.9 Electrical hookups for checking the power transistor in the igniter on 1983 through 1985 models (DON'T hook up the battery for more than five seconds or you'll destroy the diodes in the igniter)

1983 through 1985 models

Checking the power source line voltage

Refer to illustration 8.8

7 The igniter is below the coil.

8 Turn the ignition switch to On and unplug the brown and yellow wire electrical connector. Using a voltmeter, touch the positive probe to the brown electrical connector on the wire harness side and the negative probe to body ground **(see illustration)**. It should indicate about 12 volts.

Checking the power transistor in the igniter

Refer to illustration 8.9

9 Reattach the brown electrical connector, disconnect the coil wire

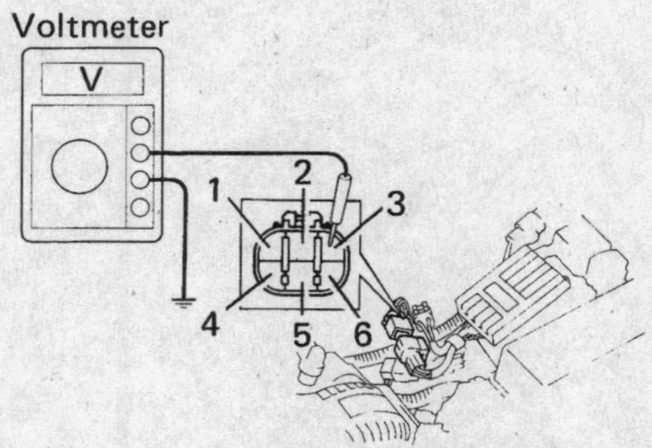

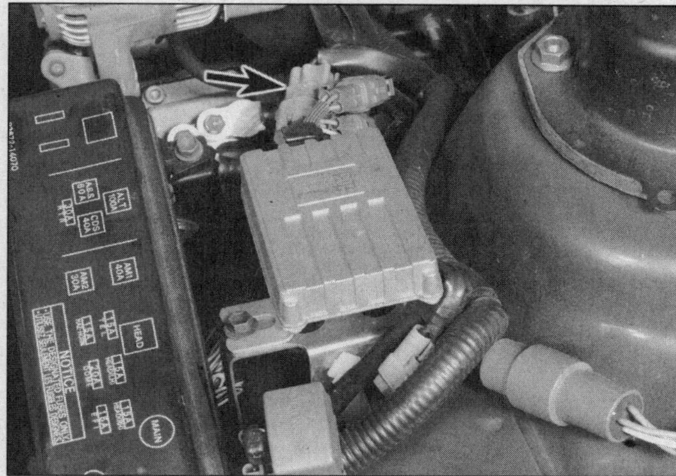

8.13 To check the power source line voltage on 1987 and later turbo models, unplug connector 6-P, turn the ignition switch to On and touch the positive probe of a voltmeter to terminal 3 of the harness side and the negative probe to body ground - the meter should indicate about 12 volts

from the distributor, place it near a good ground and unplug the pink and white electrical connector. Using a 1.5 volt dry cell battery and a pair of jumper wires, connect the positive pole of the battery to the pink wire terminal and the negative pole to body ground **(see illustration)**. **Caution:** *Do NOT leave the battery hooked up for more than five seconds at a time, or the diodes in the igniter will be destroyed. Instead, touch the jumper wire from the battery to the terminal only during the following test.*

10 Momentarily connect the positive pole of the 1.5 volt battery to the pink wire terminal. Verify that the high tension lead emits a a spark to ground in about one second. If it doesn't, replace the igniter (see below).

11 Turn the ignition switch to Off, disconnect the test apparatus and reattach the pink and white connector and the coil high tension lead.

1986 and later models

Non-turbo models

12 There is no specific procedure for checking the igniters on later models. If a check of the ignition system (see Section 6) rules out all other possible malfunctions, replace the igniter. Make sure, however, that you eliminate all other possibilities before buying a new unit.

Turbo models

Checking the power source line voltage

Refer to illustration 8.13

13 The igniter is located right behind the fuse panel at the left front corner of the engine compartment. Unplug connector 6-P, turn the ignition switch to On and, using a voltmeter, touch the positive probe to terminal 3 of the harness side and the negative probe to body ground **(see illustration)**. The meter should indicate about 12 volts. Reattach connector 6P.

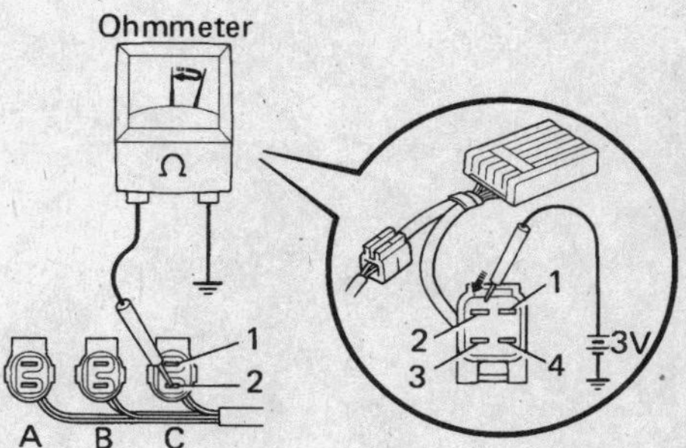

8.14 Electrical hookups for the first test of the power transistor in the igniter on 1987 and later turbo models (don't keep the battery connected for more than five seconds)

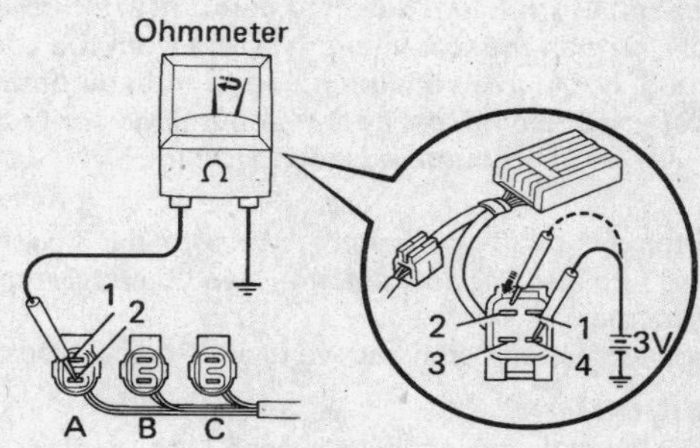

8.15 Electrical hookups for the second test of the power transistor in the igniter on 1987 and later turbo models (don't leave the battery connected for more than five seconds)

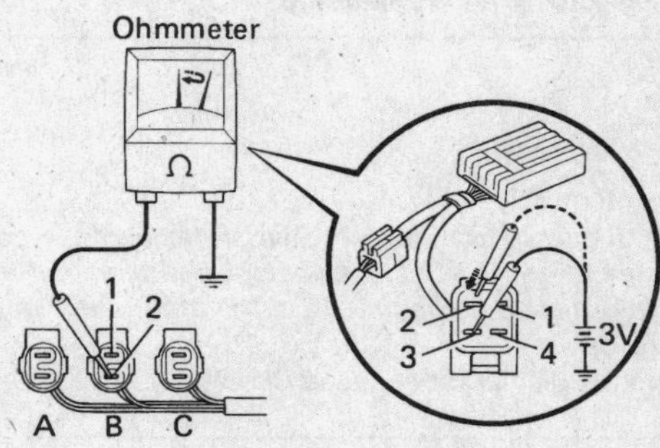

8.16 Electrical hookups for the third test of the power transistor in the igniter on 1987 and later turbo models (again, don't leave the battery connected for more than five seconds)

Checking the power transistor in the igniter

Refer to illustrations 8.14, 8.15 and 8.16

14 Unplug connector 4-P, unplug the electrical connector from each ignition coil and turn the ignition switch to On. Using an ohmmeter, touch the probes to terminal 2 of ignition coil C and body ground **(see illustration)**. Using a 3-volt dry cell battery (two 1.5-volt batteries in series), apply voltage to terminal 2 of connector 4-P. As you apply voltage, verify that there's momentary continuity.

15 Now, touch the ohmmeter probes to terminal 2 of ignition coil A and body ground **(see illustration)**. Apply voltage to terminal 4 of the 4-P connector with the 3-volt battery. With terminal 4 connected, apply voltage to terminal 2 of connector 4-P again. As you apply voltage, verify that there's momentary continuity.

16 Finally, touch the ohmmeter probes to terminal 2 of ignition coil B and body ground **(see illustration)**. Apply voltage to terminal 3 of the

9.3 To check the vacuum advance unit on 1979 through 1982 models, detach the two vacuum hoses from the vacuum advance unit, hook up a vacuum pump to both diaphragms with a T-fitting and two hoses, apply vacuum and verify that the vacuum advance works

4-P connector with the 3-volt battery. With terminal 3 connected, apply voltage to terminal 2 of connector 4-P. As you apply voltage, verify that there's momentary continuity.

17 If the igniter fails any of the above tests, replace it (see below).

Replacement

18 Clearly label, then disconnect all wiring to the igniter.

19 Unbolt the igniter from its mounting bracket.

20 Installation is the reverse of removal.

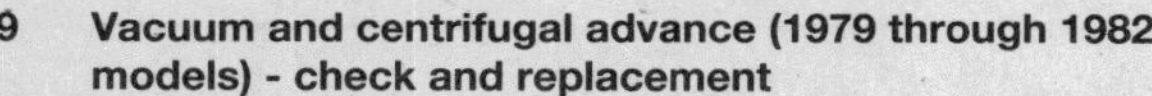

9 Vacuum and centrifugal advance (1979 through 1982 models) - check and replacement

Check

Vacuum advance

Refer to illustration 9.3

1 Detach the cable from the negative terminal of the battery. **Caution:** *If the stereo in your vehicle is equipped with an anti-theft system, refer to the information on page 0-15 at the front of this manual before detaching the cable.*

2 Remove the distributor cap (see Chapter 1).

9.13b . . . and the retaining screw, then pull out the vacuum advance unit

9.13a To replace the vacuum advance unit on 1979 through 1982 models, remove the E-clip . . .

3 Disconnect the two vacuum hoses from the vacuum advance unit and, using a T-fitting and two hoses, connect a vacuum pump to both diaphragms **(see illustration)**.

4 Apply vacuum and verify that the vacuum advancer link moves.

5 If the vacuum advancer doesn't work, replace it (see below).

Centrifugal advance

6 Turn the rotor clockwise, release it and verify that it returns slightly counterclockwise.

7 Verify that the rotor is not excessively loose.

8 If the centrifugal advance doesn't work as described, repair or replace it (see Section 13).

9 Install the distributor cap (see Chapter 1).

10 Attach the cable to the negative terminal of the battery.

Replacement

Refer to illustrations 9.13a and 9.13b

11 Detach the cable from the negative terminal of the battery. **Caution:** *If the stereo in your vehicle is equipped with an anti-theft system, refer to the information on page 0-15 at the front of this manual before detaching the cable.*

12 Remove the distributor cap (see Chapter 1).

13 Detach the two vacuum hoses from the vacuum advance unit, remove the E-clip and the retaining screw and detach the vacuum advance unit **(see illustrations)**.

14 Installation is the reverse of removal.

10.1 Unplug the electrical connector for the pick-up coil (1979 through 1982 models)

10.2 To check the pick-up coil on 1979 through 1982 models, touch the leads of an ohmmeter to each terminal in the distributor side of the pick-up coil connector

10 Pick-up coil - check and replacement

Check

1979 through 1982 models

Refer to illustrations 10.1 and 10.2

1 Unplug the electrical connector for the pick-up coil **(see illustration)**.

2 Touch the leads of an ohmmeter to each terminal in the distributor side of the pick-up coil connector **(see illustration)**. The resistance should be as listed in the Specifications. If it isn't, replace the pick-up coil (see below).

3 Plug in the connector.

1983 through 1986 models

Refer to illustration 10.5

4 Unplug the electrical connector for the pick-up coil.

5 Using an ohmmeter, check the resistance of each pick-up coil at the connector. To check the resistance of pick-up coil G, measure the resistance between negative terminal G (white wire) and positive terminal G (yellow wire); to check the resistance of pick-up coil Ne, measure the resistance between negative terminal G (white wire) and terminal Ne (red wire) **(see illustration)**. The indicated resistance for both coils should be within the range listed in this Chapter's Specifications. If either pick-up coil fails this test, replace it (see below).

6 Plug in the connector.

1987 and later models

Refer to illustration 10.8a and 10.8b

7 Unplug the electrical connector for the pick-up coil.

8 Using an ohmmeter, check the resistance of each pick-up coil at the connector. To check the resistance of pick-up coil G1, measure the resistance between terminal G1 and negative terminal G; then measure the resistance between terminal G2 and negative terminal G; finally, measure the resistance between terminal Ne and negative terminal G **(see illustrations)**. If any of the three pick-up coils fails this test, replace it (see below).

Replacement

Refer to illustrations 10.11 and 10.12

9 On 1979 through 1986 models, refer to the procedure that begins with the next Step; on 1987 through 1992 non-turbo models, replace the distributor (see Section 12); on 1987 through 1992 turbo models, replace the cam sensor assembly (see Chapter 6).

10 Remove the vacuum advance unit (see Section 9).

11 Remove the pick-up coil cover **(see illustration)**.

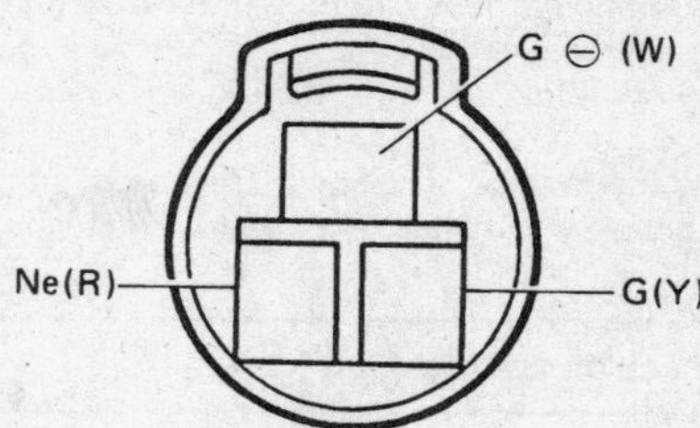

10.5 On 1983 through 1986 models, check the resistance of pick-up coil G by measuring the resistance between negative terminal G (white wire) and positive terminal G (yellow wire); to check the resistance of pick-up coil Ne, measure the resistance between negative terminal G (white wire) and terminal Ne (red wire)

10.8a On 1987 and 1988 non-turbo models and on 1987 through 1992 turbo models, check the resistance of pick-up coil G1 by measuring the resistance between terminal G1 and negative terminal G, then measure the resistance between terminal G2 and negative terminal G and, finally, the resistance between terminal Ne and negative terminal G

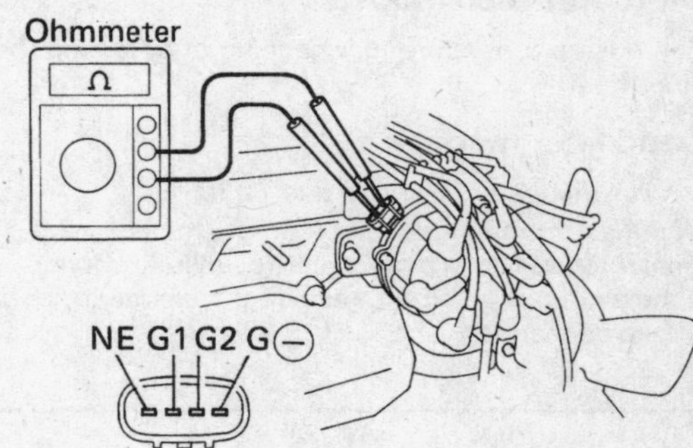

10.8b The connector and its terminals on 1989 through 1992 non-turbo models is different, but the test for the three pick-up coils is exactly the same as the test outlined in the previous illustration

10.11 To gain access to the pick-up coil, take off the cover

5

12 Remove the wiring harness clip **(see illustration)** and detach the harness.
13 Remove the two pick-up coil retaining screws and remove the pick-up coil.
14 Installation is the reverse of removal. Be sure to adjust the air gap (see Section 11) before you install the pick-up coil cover.

10.12 To detach the pick-up coil wiring harness from the distributor body, remove this clip retaining screw

All models

9 Install the pick-up coil cover.
10 Install the rotor and the distributor cap, or the dust cover on the cam position sensor.
11 Reattach the negative battery cable.

11 Air gap - check and adjustment

All models

Refer to illustration 11.2

1 Detach the cable from the negative battery terminal. **Caution:** *If the stereo in your vehicle is equipped with an anti-theft system, refer to the information on page 0-15 at the front of this manual before detaching the cable.*
2 On non-turbo models, remove the distributor cap and rotor (see Chapter 1); on turbo models, remove the cam position sensor dust cover **(see illustration)**.
3 Remove the pick-up coil cover, if equipped (see Section 10).

1979 through 1982 models

Refer to illustration 11.4

4 Using a non-magnetic feeler gauge, measure the gap between one of the teeth on the signal rotor and the "pole piece" (projection) on the pick-up coil **(see illustration)**. Compare your measurement to the air gap dimension listed in this Chapter's Specifications. If the gap is incorrect, adjust it as follows.
5 Loosen the two retaining screws and move the pick-up coil until the gap is correct. If you place the blade of a screwdriver between the two little posts and insert it into the slot in the pick-up coil base plate, turning the screwdriver will reposition the coil. Tighten the screws and recheck the gap.

1983 through 1986 models

6 There is no procedure for checking or adjusting the air gap on these models.

1987 and later models

Refer to illustrations 11.7a, 11.7b and 11.7c

7 Using a non-magnetic feeler gauge, measure the gap between the signal rotor and each pick-up coil **(see illustrations)**.
8 If the air gap is incorrect, replace the distributor or cam position sensor (see Section 12).

12 Distributor - removal and installation

Removal

Refer to illustrations 12.6 and 12.7

Note: *The following procedure also applies to the "cam position sensor" used in place of a distributor on turbo models. Although the cam position sensor has no spark plug wires, it must be removed and installed with the No. 1 piston at TDC on its compression stroke, just like a distributor. But because it has no rotor to align and mark, it's critical that you don't turn the engine over while the sensor is removed. Other than that, think of the cam position sensor,as a distributor without wires. Simply disregard those Steps which refer to the parts on a conventional distributor - looking for the No. 1 spark plug terminal, aligning and marking the position of the rotor, etc.*
1 Disconnect the cable from the negative terminal of the battery. **Caution:** *If the stereo in your vehicle is equipped with an anti-theft system, refer to the information on page 0-15 at the front of this manual*

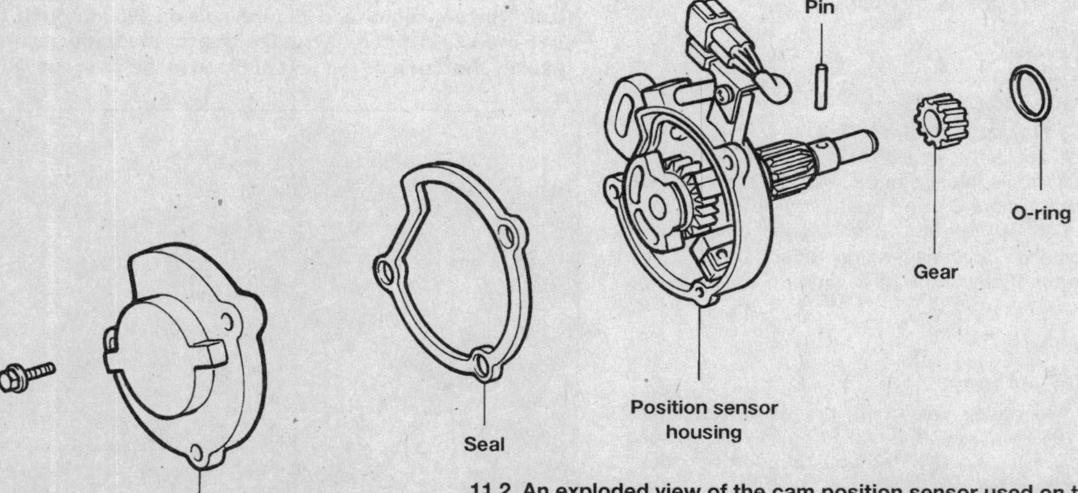

11.2 An exploded view of the cam position sensor used on turbo models

11.4 To adjust the air gap on 1979 through 1982 models, align one of the signal rotor teeth with the "pole piece" (projection) on each pick-up coil, insert a non-magnetic feeler gauge of the specified thickness into the gap as shown and move the pick-up coil adjustment plate by rotating a screwdriver tip in the adjustment slot until a slight drag is felt as the feeler gauge is withdrawn

before detaching the cable. Unplug the primary wires from the coil.

2 Unplug the electrical connector for the distributor or cam position sensor. Follow the wires as they exit the distributor/cam position sensor to find the electrical connector.

3 On 1979 through 1982 models, disconnect the hoses from the vacuum advance unit on the distributor.

4 Look for a raised "1" on the distributor cap. This marks the location for the number one cylinder spark plug wire terminal. If the cap does not have a mark for the number one terminal, locate the number one spark plug and trace the wire back to the terminal on the cap.

5 Remove the distributor cap (see Chapter 1) and turn the engine over until the rotor is pointing toward the number one spark plug terminal (*see locating TDC procedure in Chapter 2*).

6 Make a mark on the edge of the distributor base directly below the rotor tip and in line with it **(see illustration)**. Also, mark the distributor base and the engine block to ensure that the distributor is installed correctly.

7 Remove the distributor or cam position sensor hold-down bolt, then pull the distributor straight up (1979 through 1981 models) or out (1982 and later models) to remove it **(see illustration)**. Remove the old O-ring from the distributor/cam position sensor shaft and discard it. **Caution:** *DO NOT turn the crankshaft while the distributor/cam position sensor is out of the engine, or the alignment marks will be useless.*

11.7a To check the air gap on 1987 through 1988 non-turbo models, align one of the signal rotor teeth with the "pole piece" (projection) on each of the three pick-up coils, insert a non-magnetic feeler gauge of the specified thickness into the gap as shown and compare your measurement to the air gap listed in this Chapter's Specifications - if it's incorrect, replace the distributor

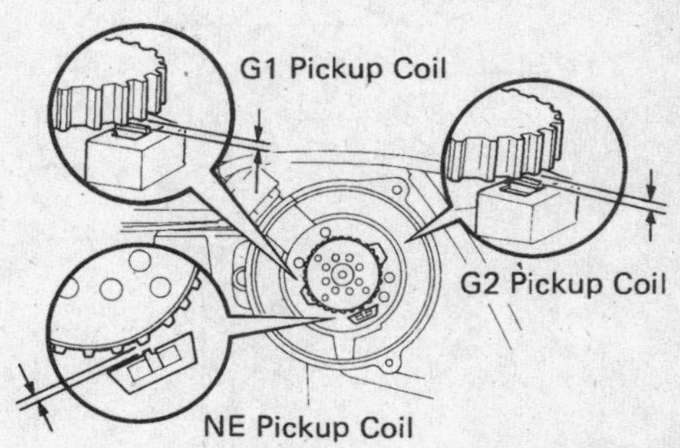

11.7b Checking the air gap on 1989 through 1992 non-turbo models is done the same way as in illustration 11.7a, except the three pick-up coils look a little different - again, if the air gap is incorrect, replace the distributor

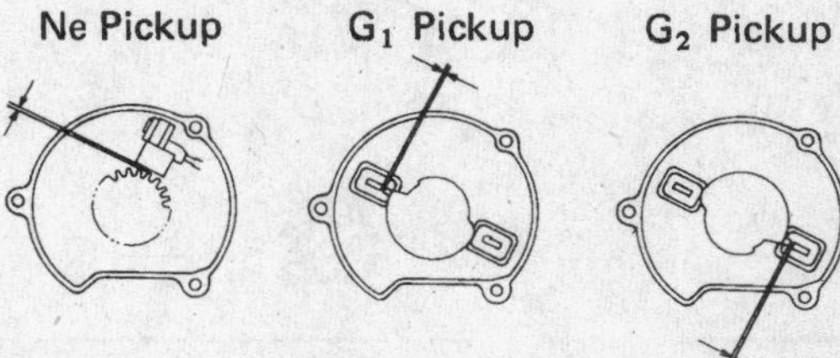

11.7c Checking the air gap on turbo models is also similar to the procedure outlined in illustration 11.7a - if the air gap is incorrect, replace the cam position sensor

5

12.6 Mark the distributor body in line with the rotor

12.7 Remove the distributor hold-down bolt and pull straight up (on 1979 through 1981 models) or straight out (on 1982 and later models, as shown)

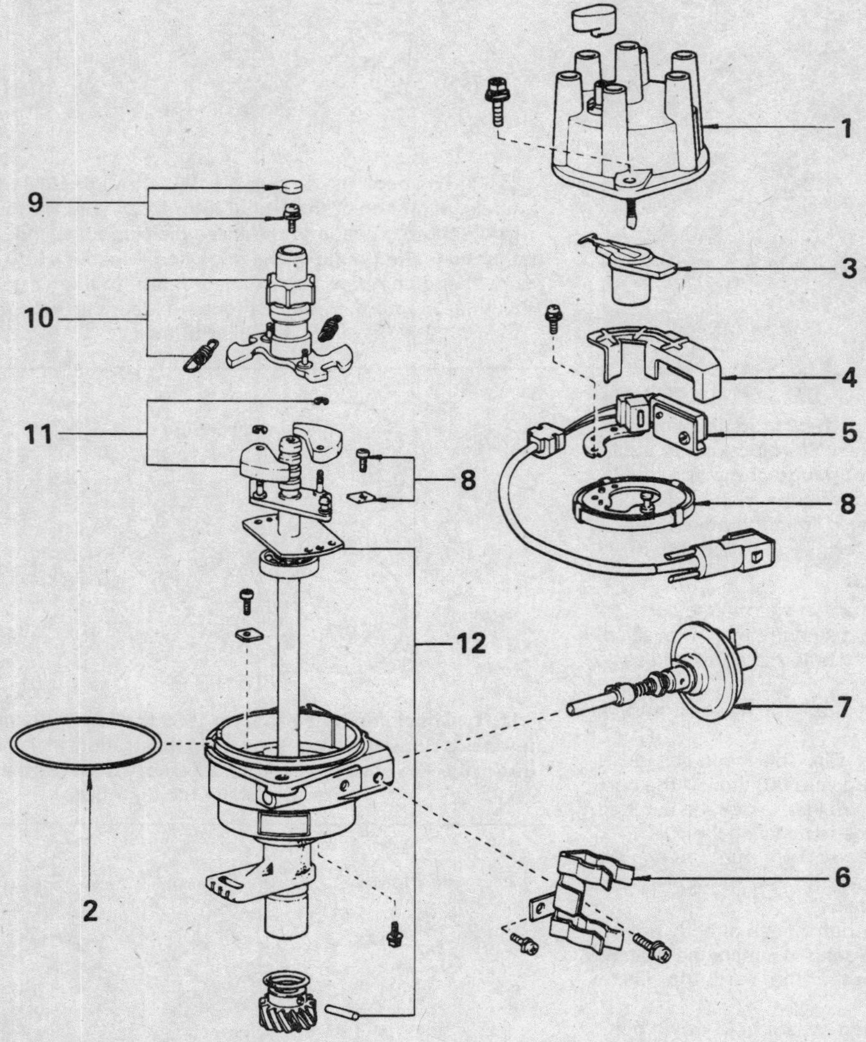

13.2 An exploded view of a typical distributor on 1979 through 1982 models

1 Distributor cap
2 O-ring
3 Rotor
4 Pick-up coil cover
5 Pick-up coil
6 Clamp
7 Vacuum advance unit
8 Breaker plate and screws
9 Grease stopper and screw
10 Signal rotor assembly
11 Centrifugal advance weights and E-clips
12 Shaft, gear and bearing

Installation

Note: *If the crankshaft has been moved while the distributor/cam position sensor is out, the number one piston must be repositioned at TDC. This can be done by feeling for compression pressure at the number one plug hole as the crankshaft is turned. Once compression is felt, align the ignition timing zero mark with the pointer.*

8 Install a new O-ring on the distributor/cam position sensor shaft. Insert the distributor/cam position sensor into the engine in exactly the same relationship to the block that it was in when removed.

9 To mesh the helical gears on the camshaft and the distributor/cam position sensor, it may be necessary to turn the rotor (or the signal rotor on the cam position sensor) slightly. Recheck the alignment marks between the distributor, or cam position sensor, base and the block to verify that the distributor/cam position sensor is in the same position it was in before removal. Also check the rotor to see if it's aligned with the mark you made on the edge of the distributor base.

10 Install the hold-down bolt finger tight.

11 Install the distributor cap.

12 Plug in the distributor/cam position sensor electrical connector.

13 Reattach the spark plug wires to the plugs (if removed).

14 Connect the cable to the negative terminal of the battery.

15 Check the ignition timing (see Chapter 1) and tighten the distributor/cam position sensor hold-down bolt securely.

13 Distributor - overhaul

1979 through 1982 models

Refer to illustration 13.2

1 Remove the distributor (see Section 12).

2 Remove the O-ring from the main body outer flange **(see illustration)**.

3 Detach the cover, then unscrew and remove the pick-up coil assembly.

4 Remove the clamp retaining screws and withdraw the clamp.

5 Detach and remove the vacuum advance unit from the main body. Remove the screws and lift out the breaker plate.

6 Pry the grease stopper out of the top of the signal rotor, then remove the screw from the top of the shaft.

7 Separate the rotor assembly and springs from the shaft, keeping the springs with their respective location pegs.

8 Remove the centrifugal advance weights after prying the E-clips off the pivot shafts.

9 Drill out the peened end of the pin, then drive the pin out of the gear and separate the gear from the shaft. Carefully pull the shaft out of the distributor body.

10 With the distributor disassembled, clean the metal components with solvent, dry them thoroughly and check the following items:

a) Check the cap for signs of hairline cracks and burned or corroded terminals.

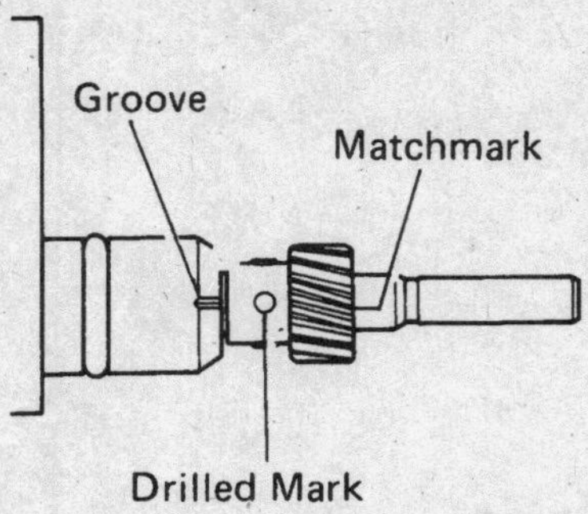

13.19 Before you remove the driven gear from a distributor on any 1983 through 1986 model, 1987 or 1988 non-turbo model or from a cam position sensor on any turbo model, align the drilled mark on the driven gear with the groove on the housing and make a matchmark on the distributor shaft that aligns with the groove of the housing

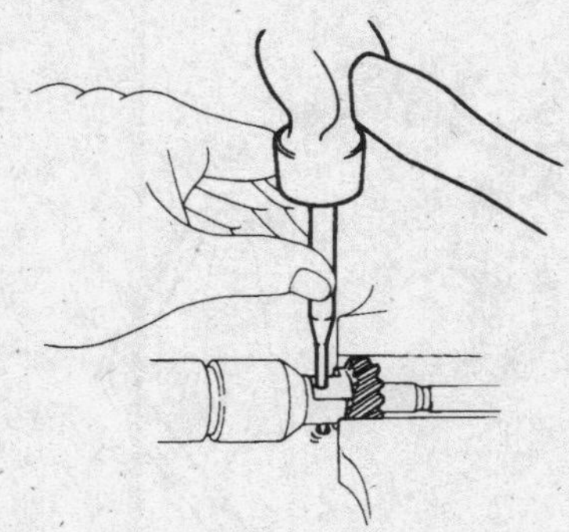

13.21 Using a hammer and punch, drive out the pin

b) Check the rotor for cracks and a burnt or corroded terminal section.
c) Check the breaker plate for smooth rotation.
d) Check the drive gear, shaft, bearing and housing for wear.
e) Check the signal rotor for smooth operation on the shaft, without excessive side play.
f) Check the centrifugal advance springs for cracks and sagging, and check the centrifugal weights for smooth operation.
g) Check the resistance of the pick-up coil with an ohmmeter and compare your measurements to the pick-up coil resistance listed in this Chapter's Specifications.

11 Replace worn, damaged or defective components as necessary.

12 Reassembly is the reverse of disassembly. Be sure to lubricate the shaft and bearing with oil prior to installation.

13 Align the locating mark and stopper, then install the signal rotor on the shaft.

14 With the centrifugal advance weights, breaker plate and rotor assembled, check the centrifugal advance operation by turning the rotor clockwise and releasing it. It should return immediately.

15 Adjust the air gap between the signal rotor and the signal generator, then tighten the signal generator mounting screws.

1983 and later models

Refer to illustrations 13.19, 13.20 and 13.21

16 The distributors on these models cannot be overhauled. On 1983 through 1988 non-turbo models and on all turbo models, the distributor driven gear can be replaced; on 1989 and later non-turbo units, nothing can be serviced. The following Steps outline the procedure for replacing a worn distributor (or cam position sensor) driven gear.

17 Remove the distributor/cam position sensor (see Section 12).

13.20 Using a grinding wheel, grind off the gear and pin

18 Mount the distributor/cam position sensor in a bench vise.

19 Align the drilled mark on the driven gear with the groove on the housing **(see illustration)**. Make a matchmark on the distributor/cam position sensor shaft that aligns with the groove of the housing.

20 Using a grinding wheel, grind off the gear and pin **(see illustration)**.

21 Using a hammer and punch, drive out the pin **(see illustration)**. Remove the old drive gear and discard it.

22 Align the matchmark on the shaft and the drilled mark on the new gear with the groove on the housing and, using a hammer and punch, install a new pin.

23 Install the distributor/cam position sensor (see Section 12).

14 Charging system - general information and precautions

The charging system includes the alternator, an internal rectifier and voltage regulator, a charge indicator, the battery, a fusible link and the wiring between all the components. The charging system supplies electrical power for the ignition system, the lights, the radio, etc. The alternator is driven by a drivebelt at the front of the engine.

The purpose of the voltage regulator is to limit the alternator's voltage to a preset value. This prevents power surges, circuit overloads, etc., during peak voltage output.

A fusible link is a short length of insulated wire integral with the engine compartment wiring harness. The link is usually about four wire gauges smaller in diameter than the circuit it protects, although because of its thick insulation it looks like a larger gauge wire. Production fusible links and their identification flags are identified by the flag color. See Chapter 12 for additional information regarding fusible links.

The charging system doesn't ordinarily require periodic maintenance. However, the drivebelt, battery and wires and connections should be inspected at the intervals outlined in Chapter 1.

The dashboard warning light should come on when the ignition key is turned to Start, then go off immediately. If it remains on, there is a malfunction in the charging system (see Section 15). Some vehicles are also equipped with a voltmeter. If the voltmeter indicates abnormally high or low voltage, check the charging system (see Section 15).

Be very careful when making electrical circuit connections to a vehicle equipped with an alternator and note the following:

a) When reconnecting wires to the alternator from the battery, be sure to note the polarity.
b) Before using arc welding equipment to repair any part of the vehicle, disconnect the wires from the alternator and the battery terminals.
c) Never start the engine with a battery charger connected.
d) Always disconnect both battery cables before using a battery charger. **Caution:** *If the stereo in your vehicle is equipped with an anti-theft system, refer to the information on page 0-15 at the front of this manual before detaching the cable.*
e) The alternator is turned by an engine drivebelt which could cause serious injury if your hands, hair or clothes become entangled in it with the engine running.
f) Because the alternator is connected directly to the battery, it could arc or cause a fire if overloaded or shorted out.
g) Wrap a plastic bag over the alternator and secure it with rubber bands before steam cleaning the engine.

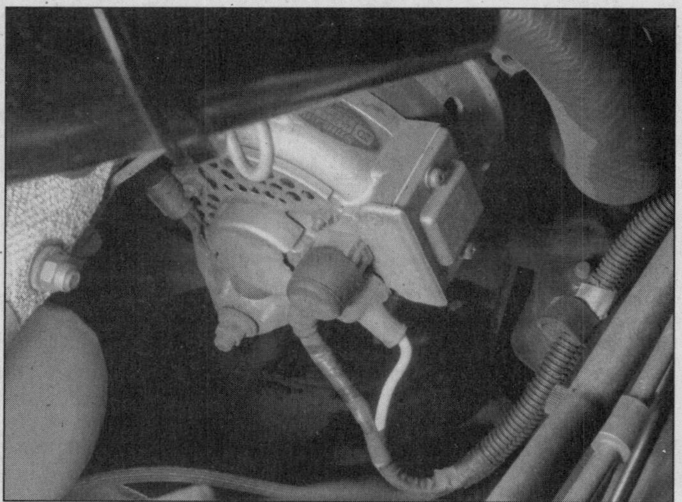

16.2a Typical alternator electrical connectors on 1979 through 1983 models - later models similar

16.2b Typical alternator electrical connectors on 1987 and later models

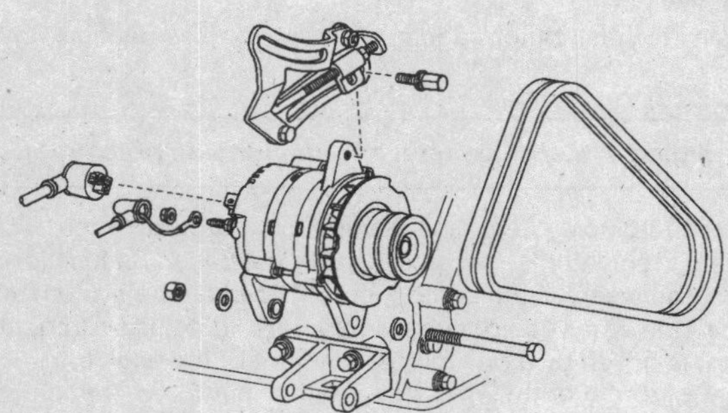

16.3a Typical alternator mounting brackets, adjustment bolt and pivot bolt on 1979 through 1983 models (1983 unit shown)

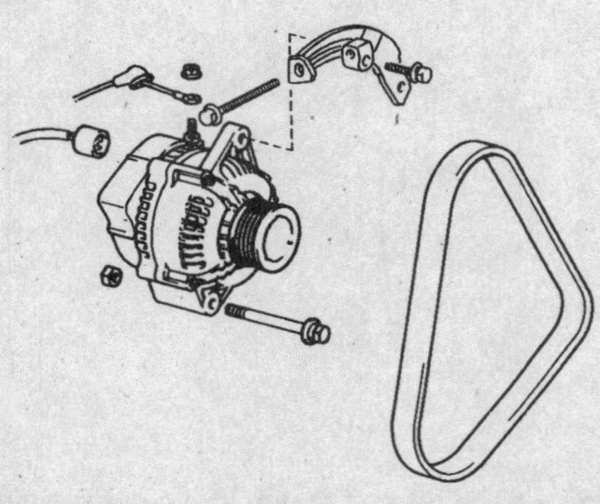

16.3b Typical alternator mounting brackets, adjustment bolt and pivot bolt on 1984 through 1986 models

15 Charging system - check

1 If a malfunction occurs in the charging circuit, don't automatically assume that the alternator is causing the problem. First check the following items:

a) Check the drivebelt tension and condition (see Chapter 1). Replace it if it's worn or deteriorated.
b) Make sure the alternator mounting and adjustment bolts are tight.
c) Inspect the alternator wiring harness and the electrical connectors at the alternator and voltage regulator. They must be in good condition and tight.
d) Check the main fusible link located in the wire between the battery positive terminal and the alternator. If it's burned, determine the cause, repair the circuit and replace the link (the vehicle won't start and/or the accessories won't work if the fusible link is blown). Sometimes a fusible link may look good, but still be bad. If in doubt, remove it and check for continuity.
e) Start the engine and check the alternator for abnormal noises (a shrieking or squealing sound indicates a bad bearing).
f) Check the specific gravity of the battery electrolyte. If it's low, charge the battery (doesn't apply to maintenance-free batteries).
g) Make sure the battery is fully charged (one bad cell in a battery can cause overcharging by the alternator).
h) Disconnect the battery cables (negative first, then positive). **Caution:** *If the stereo in your vehicle is equipped with an anti-theft system, refer to the information on page 0-15 at the front of this manual before detaching the cable.* Inspect the battery posts and the cable clamps for corrosion. Clean them thoroughly if necessary (see Chapter 1). Reconnect the cable to the positive terminal.
i) With the key off, connect a test light between the negative battery post and the disconnected negative cable clamp.
    1) If the test light does not come on, reattach the clamp and proceed to the next Step.
    2) If the test light comes on, there is a short (drain) in the electrical system of the vehicle. The short must be repaired before the charging system can be checked.
    3) Disconnect the alternator wiring harness.
        (a) If the light goes out, the alternator is bad.
        (b) If the light stays on, pull each fuse until the light goes out (this will tell you which component is shorted).

2 Using a voltmeter, check the battery voltage with the engine off. If should be approximately 12-volts.

3 Start the engine and check the battery voltage again. It should now be approximately 14-to-15 volts.

4 Turn on the headlights. The voltage should drop, and then come back up, if the charging system is working properly.

5 If the voltage reading is more than the specified charging voltage, replace the voltage regulator (see Section 18). If the voltage is less, the alternator diode(s), stator or rectifier may be bad or the voltage regulator may be malfunctioning.

16 Alternator - removal and installation

Refer to illustrations 16.2a, 16.2b, 16.3a, 16.3b, 16.3c and 16.3d

1 Detach the cable from the negative terminal of the battery. **Cau-**

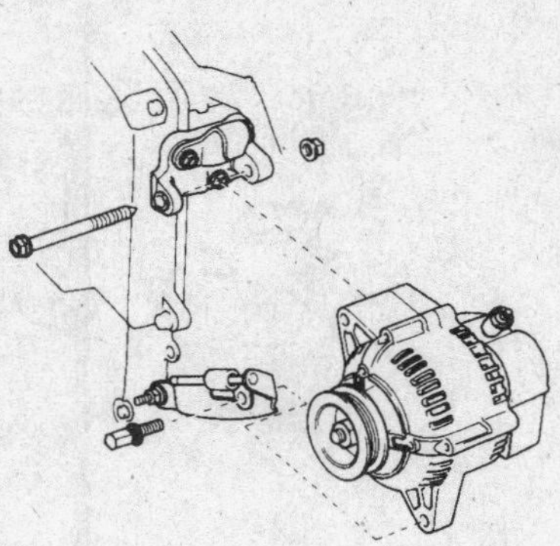
16.3c Typical alternator mounting brackets and bolts on 1987 and later models

16.3d The easiest way to get at the lower mounting bolt on early models is from underneath the vehicle (1982 model shown, others similar)

17.2 Mark the alternator case with paint or a scribe to ensure proper reassembly

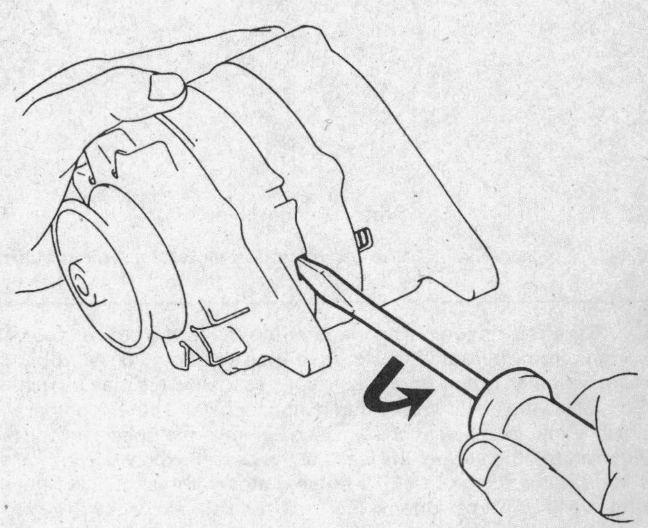
17.3 Use a screwdriver to pry the drive end frame from the stator (1979 through 1983 models)

tion: *If the stereo in your vehicle is equipped with an anti-theft system, refer to the information on page 0-15 at the front of this manual before detaching the cable.*

2 Detach the electrical connectors from the alternator **(see illustrations)**.

3 Loosen the alternator adjustment and pivot bolts and detach the drivebelt **(see illustrations)**.

4 Remove the adjustment and pivot bolts and separate the alternator from the engine.

5 If you are replacing the alternator, take the old one with you when purchasing a replacement unit. Make sure the new/rebuilt unit looks identical to the old alternator. Look at the terminals - they should be the same in number, size and location as the terminals on the old alternator. Finally, look at the identification numbers - they will be stamped into the housing or printed on a tag attached to the housing. Make sure the numbers are the same on both alternators.

6 Many new/rebuilt alternators DO NOT have a pulley installed, so you may have to switch the pulley from the old unit to the new/rebuilt one. When buying an alternator, find out the shop's policy regarding pulleys - some shops will perform this service free of charge.

7 Installation is the reverse of removal.

8 After the alternator is installed, adjust the drivebelt tension (see Chapter 1).

9 Check the charging voltage to verify proper operation of the alternator (see Section 15).

17 Alternator brushes - replacement

1 Remove the alternator (see Section 16).

1979 through 1983 models

Refer to illustrations 17.2, 17.3, 17.4, 17.5, 17.6 and 17.7.

Caution: *If you're not skilled at soldering, we don't recommend that you attempt the following procedure; instead, exchange your defective alternator for a rebuilt unit.*

2 Mark the alternator case to ensure correct reassembly **(see illustration)**.

3 Remove the three through-bolts and carefully separate the rectifier end frame and the stator from the drive-end frame and rotor. Insert a screwdriver into the slots in the drive-end frame and rotate the screwdriver to pry the stator free **(see illustration)**.

4 Remove all four nuts, the condenser and both terminal insulators from the rectifier end frame, then separate the rectifier end frame from the stator **(see illustration)**. Don't lose the insulator for the rectifier holder stud or the rubber cushion for the brush holder.

5

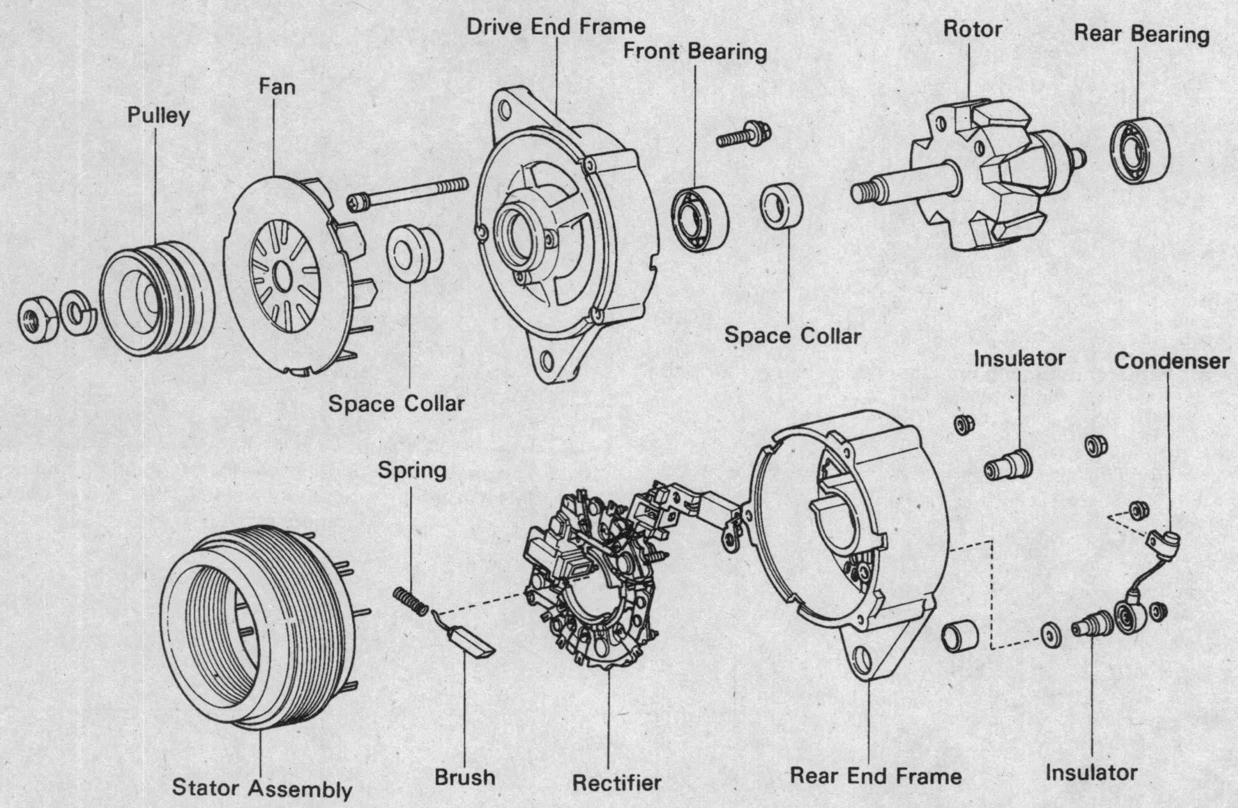

17.4 An exploded view of a typical alternator assembly used on 1979 through 1983 models

5 Carefully unsolder the leads and remove the old brushes and springs from the brush holder **(see illustration)**. Do not apply any more heat than is absolutely necessary, as the diodes may be ruined.

6 Install the new brushes and springs (one at a time), compare the brush length to the standard exposed length in the Specifications **(see illustration)**, then solder the leads at the proper exposed length. Make sure that the curvature of the brush matches the contour of the slip ring it will contact. Check the brushes to make sure they move smoothly in the holder, then cut off the excess portion of the lead.

7 Reassembly is the reverse of disassembly. However, here are a few important points to remember:

a) Again, *don't use any more heat than necessary for any longer than necessary* when soldering to prevent damage to delicate parts like diodes and rectifiers.
b) To aid in reassembly, push the brushes into the holder and insert a piece of wire through the access hole in the frame to hold the brushes in their retracted position **(see illustration)**.
c) The insulator goes on the *positive side* rectifier holder stud.
d) Don't forget to install the rubber cushion on the brush holder.

17.5 Carefully unsolder the leads to remove the old brushes - DO NOT apply any more heat than is necessary (1979 through 1983 models)

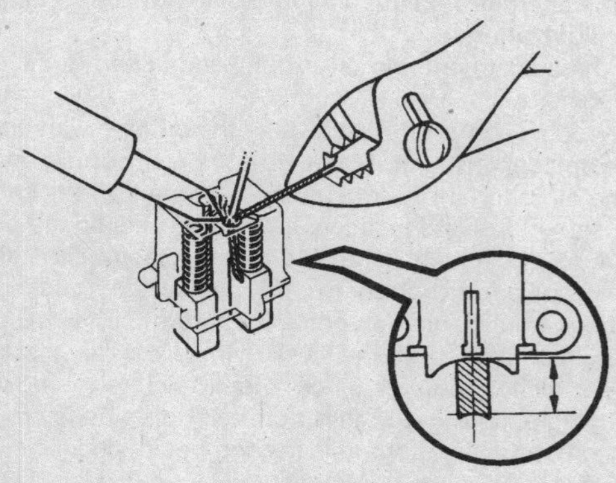

17.6 Measure the exposed brush length, compare it to the brush dimension listed in this Chapter's Specifications to get the proper length, then solder the leads (1979 through 1983 models)

17.7 To prevent damaging the brushes during installation of the rear end frame on 1979 through 1983 units, hold them in their retracted position with a paper clip until reassembly is complete (1979 through 1983 models)

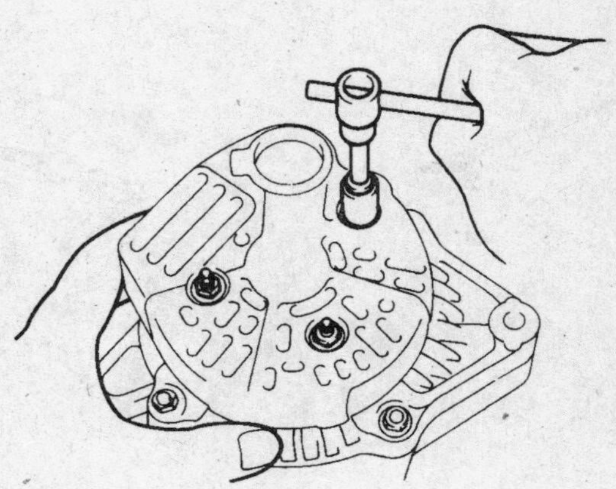

17.8a On 1984 and later models, remove the nut and terminal insulator, the three end cover retaining nuts and remove the rear end cover

e) When you install the rectifier end frame on the rectifier holder, make sure the wires aren't touching the case.
f) Place two insulators on the positive side studs.
g) Don't forget to install the condenser.

1984 and later models

Refer to illustration 17.8a, 17.8b, 17.8c, 17.9a, 17.9b, 17.10, 17.11, 17.13 and 17.14

8 Remove the three retaining nuts and insulators, then remove the alternator rear end cover **(see illustrations)**.

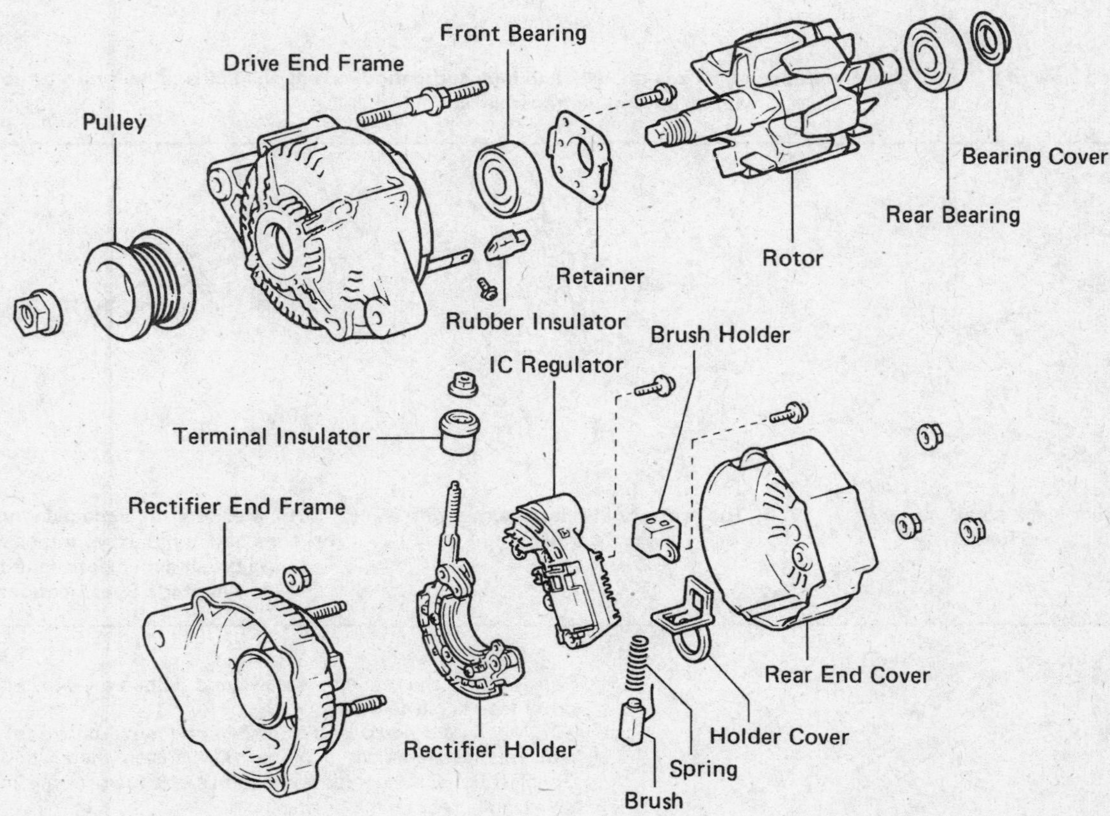

17.8b An exploded view of a typical alternator assembly used on 1984 through 1988 non-turbo models and on 1989 and later non-turbo models with a manual transmission

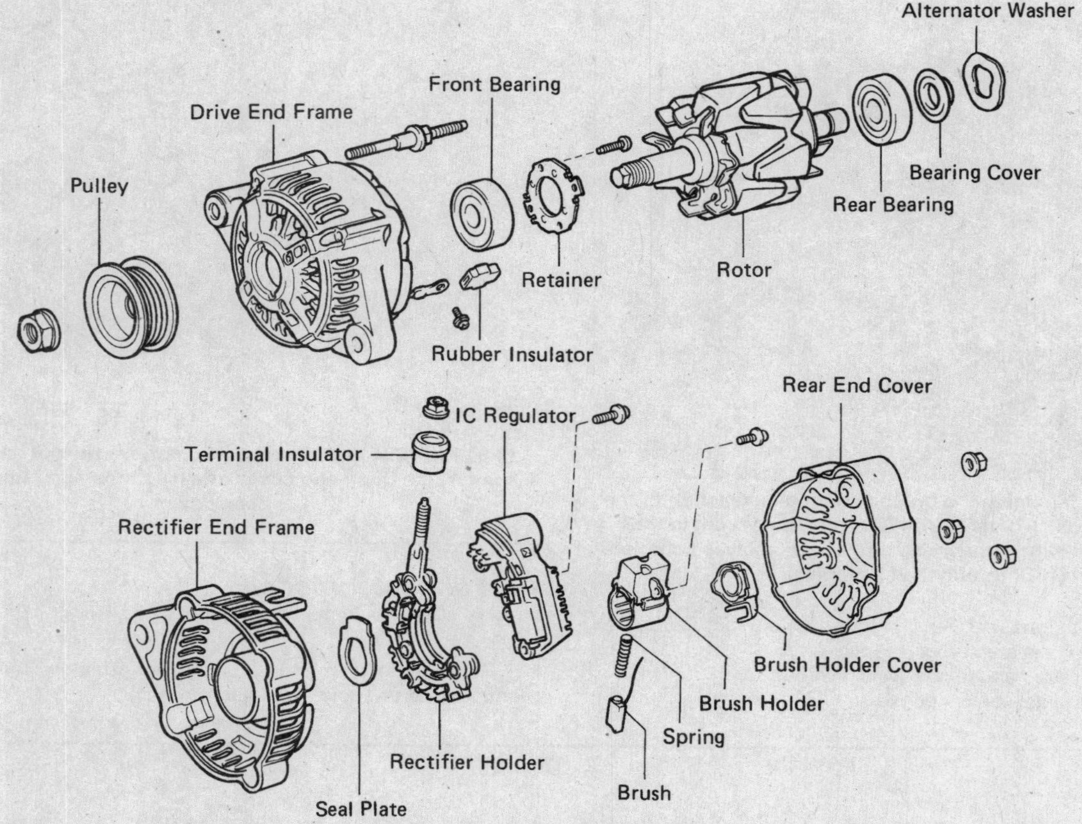

17.8c An exploded view of a typical alternator assembly used on 1987 and later turbo models and on 1989 and later non-turbo models with an automatic transmission

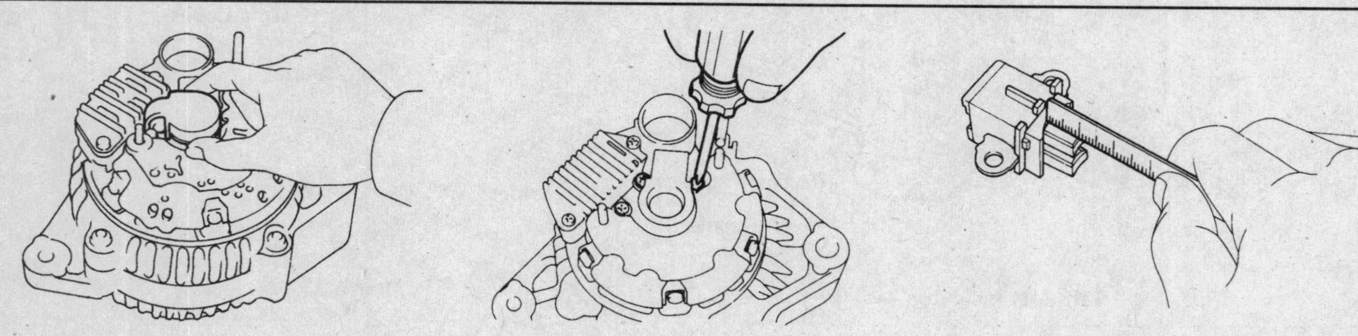

17.9a On most models, a small cover protects the brush holder

17.9b The brush holder is attached with a pair of screws

17.10 Measure the exposed length of the brushes and compare your measurements to the brush dimensions listed in this Chapter's Specifications

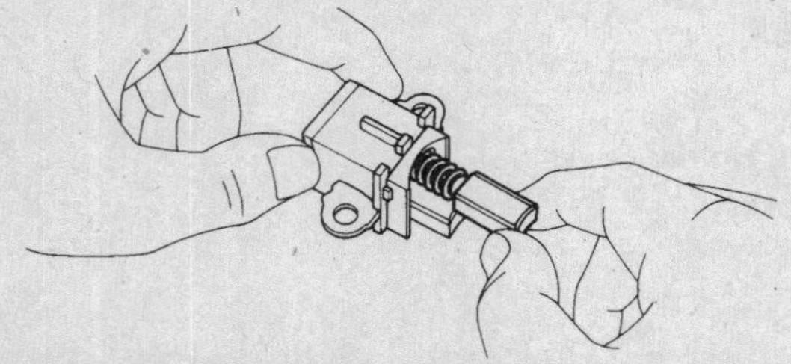

17.11 When you remove the old brushes, note how they're assembled so you'll put everything back together correctly

9 Remove the retaining screws and detach the brush holder and cover **(see illustrations)**.

10 Measure the exposed brush length **(see illustration)** and compare your measurement to the brush dimension listed in this Chapter's Specifications. If the exposed length is less than the minimum allowable length, replace the brushes.

11 Unsolder and remove the brush and spring **(see illustration)**.

12 Run the new brush lead through the hole in the brush holder, insert the spring and then the brush into the brush holder.

13 With the specified exposed length of brush protruding from the brush holder, solder each brush lead to the brush holder **(see illustra-**

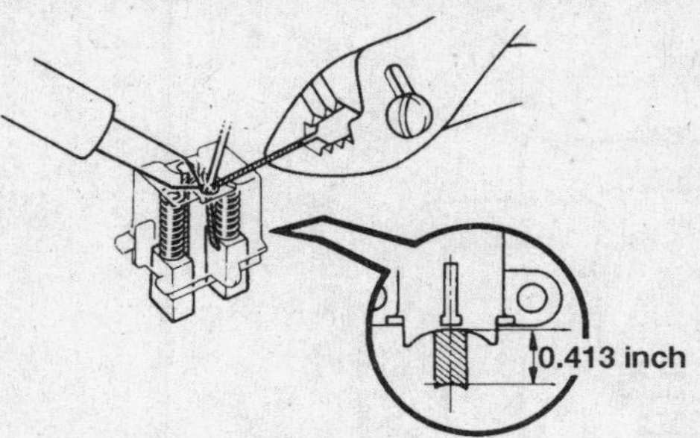

17.13 When soldering the leads to the new brushes to the brush holder, make sure the leads are long enough to allow the brushes to protrude the requisite length from the brush holder - but don't leave the leads any longer than necessary

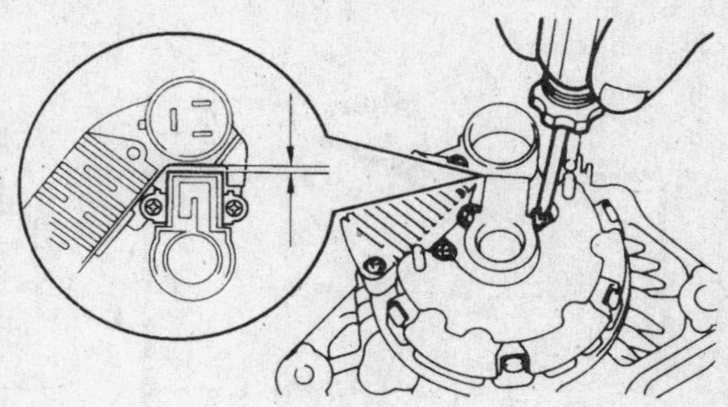

17.14 Tighten the cover screws until there's at least 0.04-inch clearance between the brush holder cover and the connector

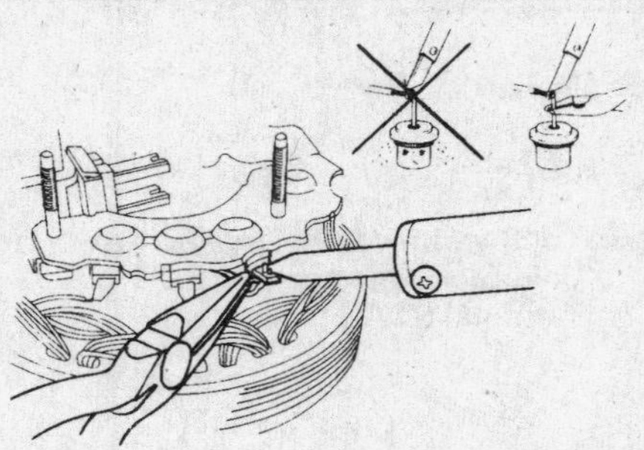

18.3 Hold the rectifier terminal with needle nose pliers and unsolder the stator leads from the rectifier holder - make sure you don't overheat the rectifiers (1979 through 1983 models)

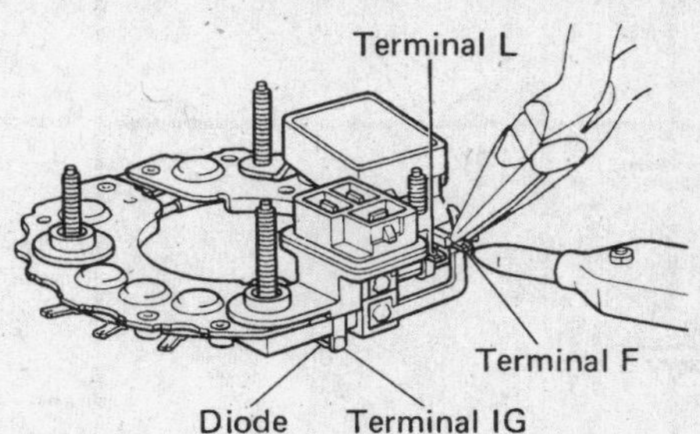

18.4 Holding each terminal with needle nose pliers, unsolder the regulator leads from terminals F, L and IG on the rectifier - make sure you don't overheat the diodes (1979 through 1983 models)

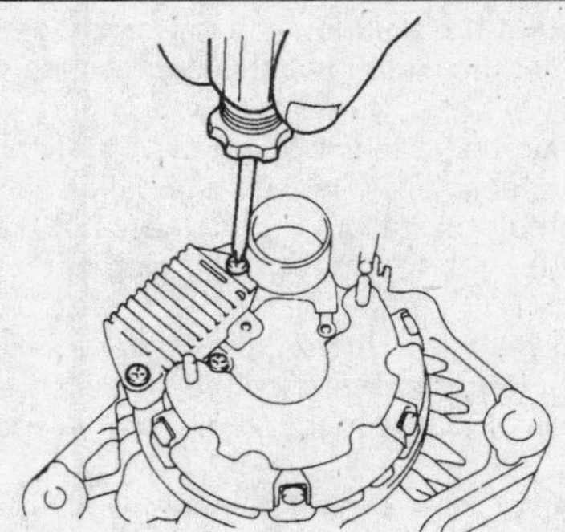

18.7 Remove all three regulator mounting screws and remove the regulator (1984 and later models)

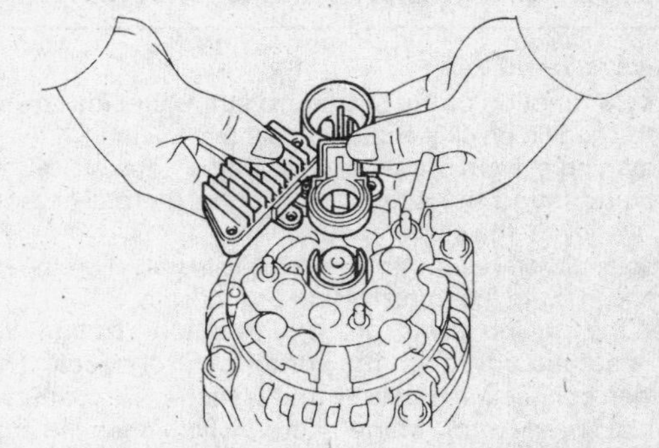

18.8 Holding the new regulator and the brush holder as shown, install them together (1984 and later models)

tion). Verify that the new brushes slide smoothly in and out of the brush holder. Cut off the excess wire. Apply insulation paint to the soldered point.

14 With the alternator sitting on a workbench, pulley side down, depress the brushes into the brush holder with your fingers and carefully install the brush holder and new brushes onto the rotor shaft. Tighten the cover screws until there's at least 0.04-inch clearance between the brush holder cover and the connector **(see illustration)**.

15 The remainder of reassembly is the reverse of disassembly.

18 Voltage regulator - replacement

1 Remove the alternator (see Section 16).

1979 through 1983 models

Refer to illustrations 18.3 and 18.4

Caution: *If you're not skilled at soldering, we don't recommend that you attempt the following procedure; instead, exchange your defective alternator for a rebuilt unit.*

2 Refer to Steps 2, 3 and 4 in Section 17.

3 Hold the rectifier terminal with needle-nose pliers and unsolder the stator leads from the rectifier holder **(see illustration)**. **Caution:** *Don't overheat the rectifiers.*

4 Holding each terminal with needle-nose pliers, unsolder the regulator leads from terminals F, L and IG on the rectifier **(see illustration)**. **Caution:** *Don't overheat the diodes.*

5 Reassembly is the reverse of disassembly. The points to remember during reassembly in Section 17, Step 7, also apply here.

1984 and later models

Refer to illustrations 18.7 and 18.8

6 Refer to Steps 8 and 9 in Section 17.

7 Remove all three regulator mounting screws **(see illustration)** and remove the regulator.

8 Holding the new regulator and the brush holder as shown **(see illustration)**, install them together. Installation is otherwise the reverse of removal. Refer to Steps 14 and 15 in Section 17.

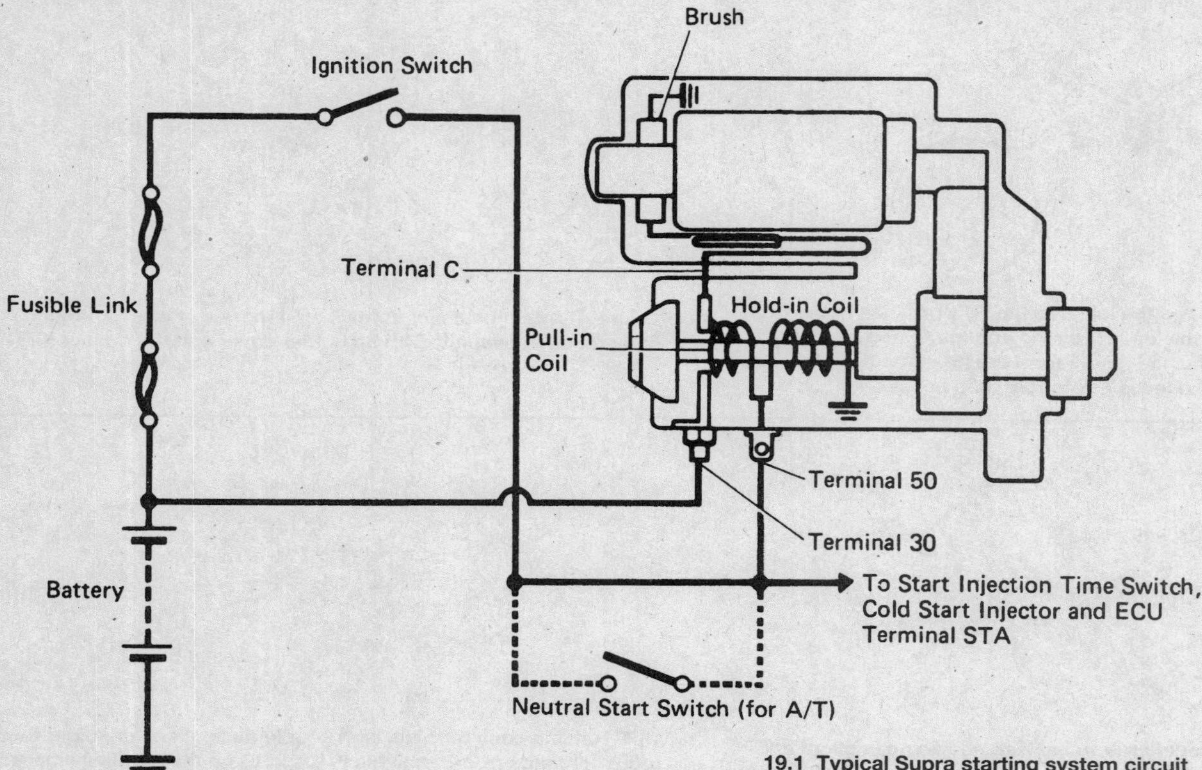

19.1 Typical Supra starting system circuit

19 Starting system - general information and precautions

Refer to illustration 19.1

The sole function of the starting system **(see illustration)** is to turn over the engine quickly enough to allow it to start.

The starting system consists of the battery, the starter motor, the starter solenoid and the wires connecting them. The solenoid is mounted directly on the starter motor.

The solenoid/starter motor assembly is installed on the lower part of the engine, next to the transmission bellhousing.

When the ignition key is turned to the Start position, the starter solenoid is actuated through the starter control circuit. The starter solenoid then connects the battery to the starter. The battery supplies the electrical energy to the starter motor, which does the actual work of cranking the engine.

The starter motor on a vehicle equipped with a manual transmission can only be operated when the clutch pedal is depressed; the starter on a vehicle equipped with an automatic transmission can only be operated when the transmission selector lever is in Park or Neutral.

Always observe the following precautions when working on the starting system:

a) Excessive cranking of the starter motor can overheat it and cause serious damage. Never operate the starter motor for more than 15 seconds at a time without pausing to allow it to cool for at least two minutes.
b) The starter is connected directly to the battery and could arc or cause a fire if mishandled, overloaded or shorted out.
c) Always detach the cable from the negative terminal of the battery before working on the starting system.

20 Starter motor - testing in vehicle

Note: *Before diagnosing starter problems, make sure the battery is fully charged.*

1 If the starter motor does not turn at all when the switch is operated, make sure that the shift lever is in Neutral or Park (automatic transmission) or that the clutch pedal is depressed (manual transmission).

2 Make sure that the battery is charged and that all cables, both at the battery and starter solenoid terminals, are clean and secure.

3 If the starter motor spins but the engine is not cranking, the overrunning clutch in the starter motor is slipping and the starter motor must be replaced.

4 If, when the switch is actuated, the starter motor does not operate at all but the solenoid clicks, then the problem lies with either the battery, the main solenoid contacts or the starter motor itself (or the engine is seized).

5 If the solenoid plunger cannot be heard when the switch is actuated, the battery is bad, the fusible link is burned (the circuit is open) or the solenoid itself is defective.

6 To check the solenoid, connect a jumper lead between the battery (+) and the ignition switch wire terminal (the small terminal) on the solenoid. If the starter motor now operates, the solenoid is OK and the problem is in the ignition switch, neutral start switch or the wiring.

7 If the starter motor still does not operate, remove the starter/solenoid assembly for disassembly, testing and repair.

8 If the starter motor cranks the engine at an abnormally slow speed, first make sure the battery is fully charged and that all terminal connections are tight. If the engine is partially seized or has the wrong viscosity oil in it (in cold weather), it will crank slowly. Also, verify the battery's Cold Cranking Amp (CCA) rating is sufficient for the engine (an auto parts store can usually tell you what the minimum should be).

9 Run the engine until normal operating temperature is reached, then disconnect the coil wire from the distributor cap and ground it on the engine.

10 Connect a voltmeter positive lead to the positive battery post and connect the negative lead to the negative post. A fully charged battery should read about 12.6 volts. If the reading is lower, charge the battery before proceeding.

11 Crank the engine and take the voltmeter readings as soon as a steady figure is indicated. Do not allow the starter motor to turn for more than 15 seconds at a time. A reading of 9 volts or more, with the

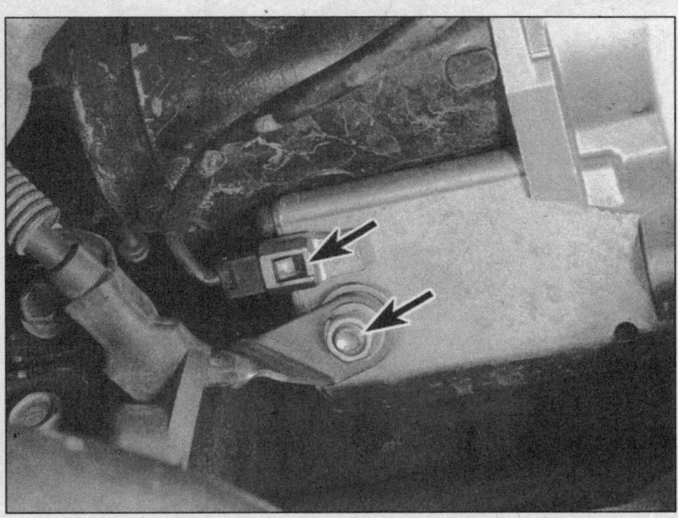
21.3 Disconnect the two wires from the terminals on the starter motor solenoid (arrows)

22.3 Disconnect the strap between the solenoid and the starter motor (left), then (on 1987 and later units) remove the pair of through-bolts that attach the starter motor to the starter housing (right)

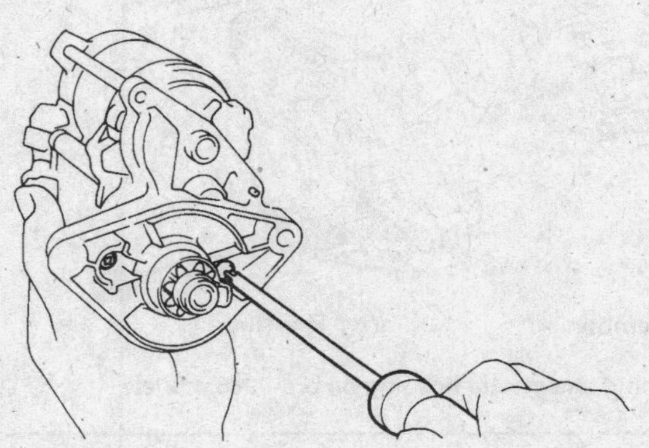
22.5a On 1987 and later units, remove the bolts that attach the solenoid to the starter housing

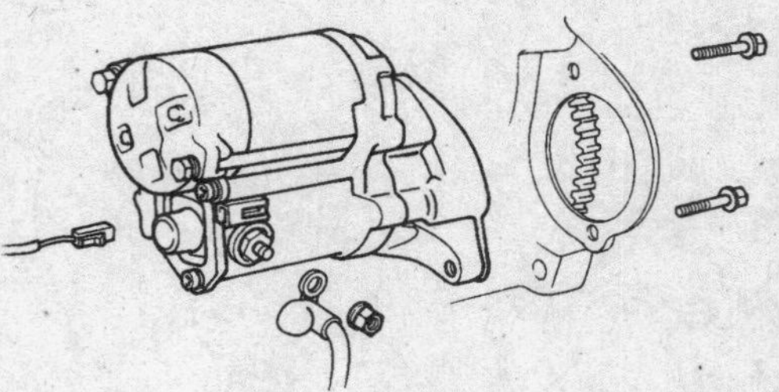
21.4 Typical starter motor installation details

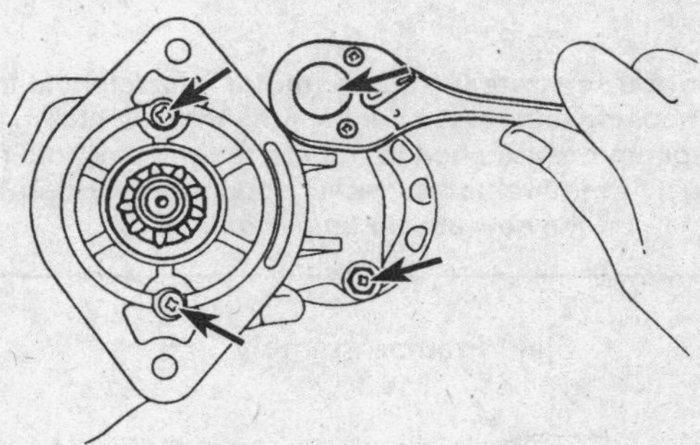
22.4 On pre-1987 units, the through bolts that attach the starter motor to the starter housing are on the right - the bolts on the left attach the solenoid to the housing

starter motor turning at normal cranking speed, is normal. If the reading is 9 volts or more but the cranking speed is slow, the solenoid contacts are burned, there is a bad connection or the starter motor is faulty. If the reading is less than 9 volts and the cranking speed is slow, the starter motor is bad or the battery is discharged.

21 Starter motor - removal and installation

Refer to illustrations 21.3 and 21.4

Note: *On some vehicles, it may be necessary to remove the exhaust pipe or frame crossmember to gain access to the starter motor. In extreme cases it may even be necessary to unbolt the mounts and raise the engine slightly to get the starter out.*

1 Detach the cable from the negative terminal of the battery. **Caution:** *If the stereo in your vehicle is equipped with an anti-theft system, refer to the information on page 0-15 at the front of this manual before detaching the cable.*

2 Raise the vehicle and support it securely on jackstands.

3 Clearly label, then disconnect the wires from the terminals on the starter motor solenoid **(see illustration)**.

4 Remove the mounting bolts **(see illustration)** and detach the starter.

5 If you're only replacing the starter - but intend to re-use the same solenoid - refer to the next Section and separate the starter motor from the solenoid.

6 Installation is the reverse of removal.

22 Starter solenoid - removal and installation

Refer to illustration 22.3, 22.4, 22.5a, 22.5b, 22.5c, 22.7a, 22.7b and 22.7c

1 Disconnect the cable from the negative terminal of the battery. **Caution:** *If the stereo in your vehicle is equipped with an anti-theft system, refer to the information on page 0-15 at the front of this manual before detaching the cable.*

2 Remove the starter motor (see Section 21).

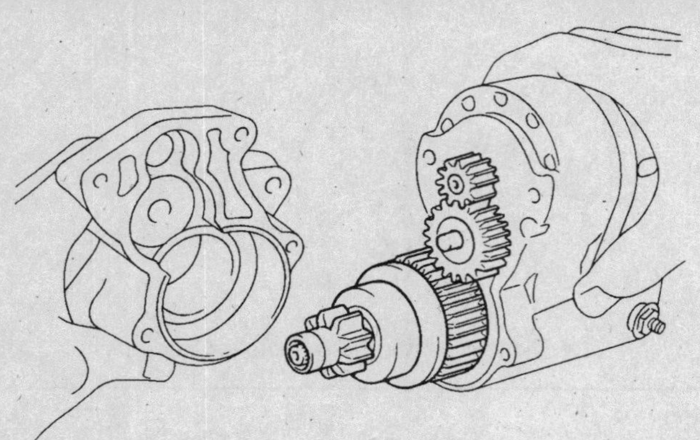

22.5b When you separate the starter motor and solenoid from the starter housing on pre-1987 units, note that the clutch and reduction gears are attached to the starter and solenoid (which means you'll have to remove, inspect, lubricate and install them on the new starter and/or solenoid)

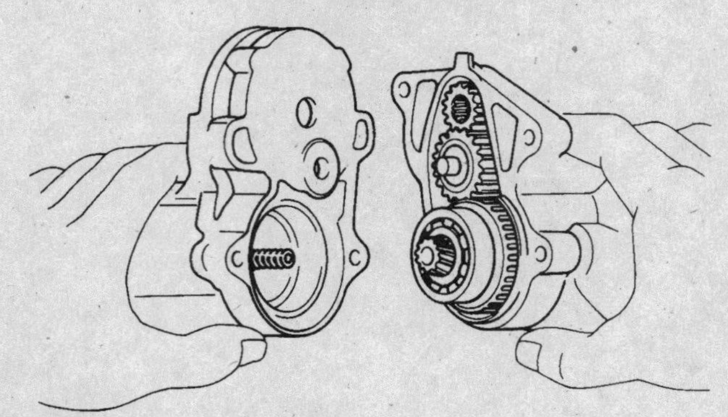

22.5c When you separate the solenoid from the starter housing on 1987 and later models, note that the clutch and reduction gears are part of the starter housing

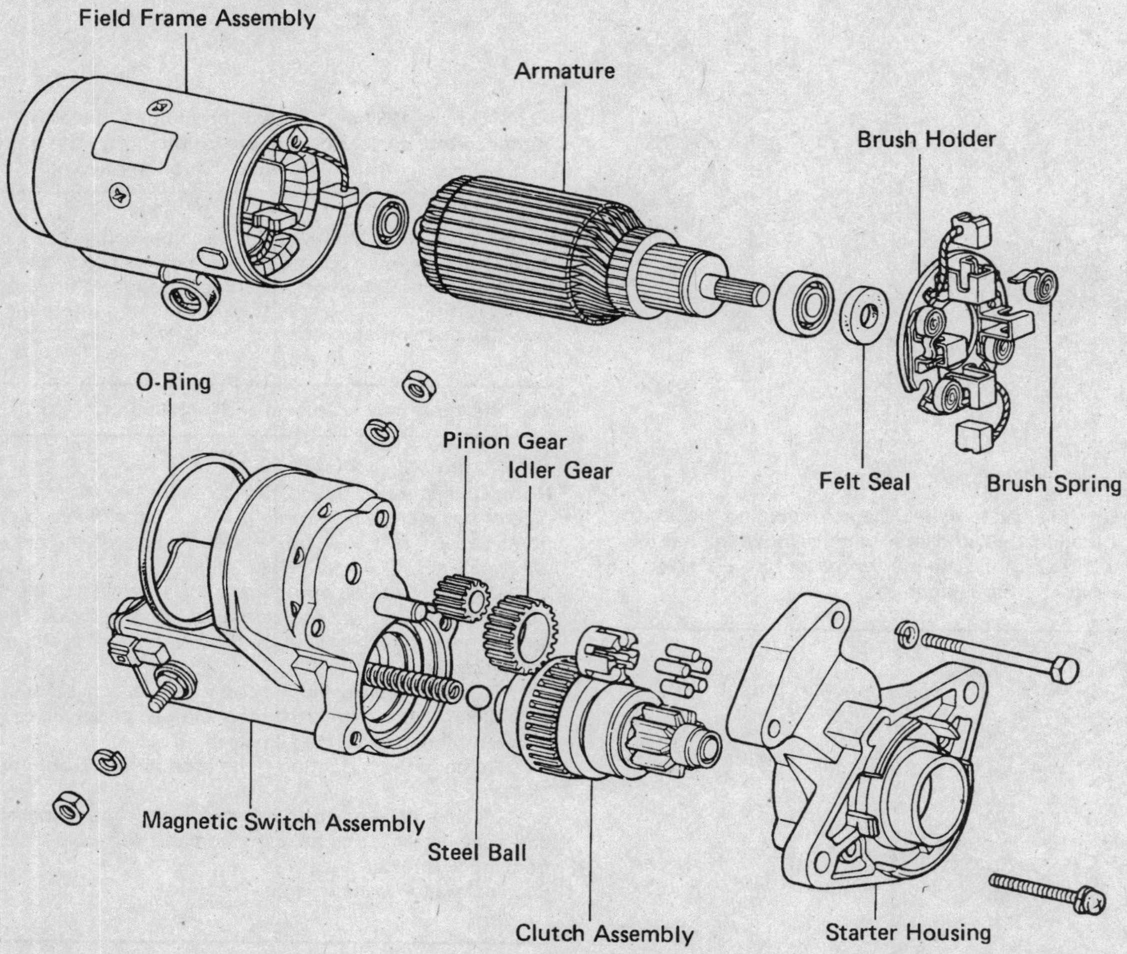

22.7a An exploded view of a typical starter motor, solenoid and starter housing on pre-1985 models

3 Disconnect the strap from the solenoid to the starter motor terminal **(see illustration)**.

4 Remove the two through-bolts that attach the starter motor to the starter housing (**see illustration**; also see previous illustration). Remove the starter motor and the felt seal and O-ring. Inspect the felt seal and the O-ring. If either of them is cracked, deteriorated or distorted, replace it.

5 Remove the bolts which attach the solenoid **(see illustration)** to the starter housing and separate the solenoid from the housing **(see illustrations)**.

6 If you're replacing the starter or solenoid on a pre-1987 unit, note how the clutch assembly on the solenoid and the pinion and idler

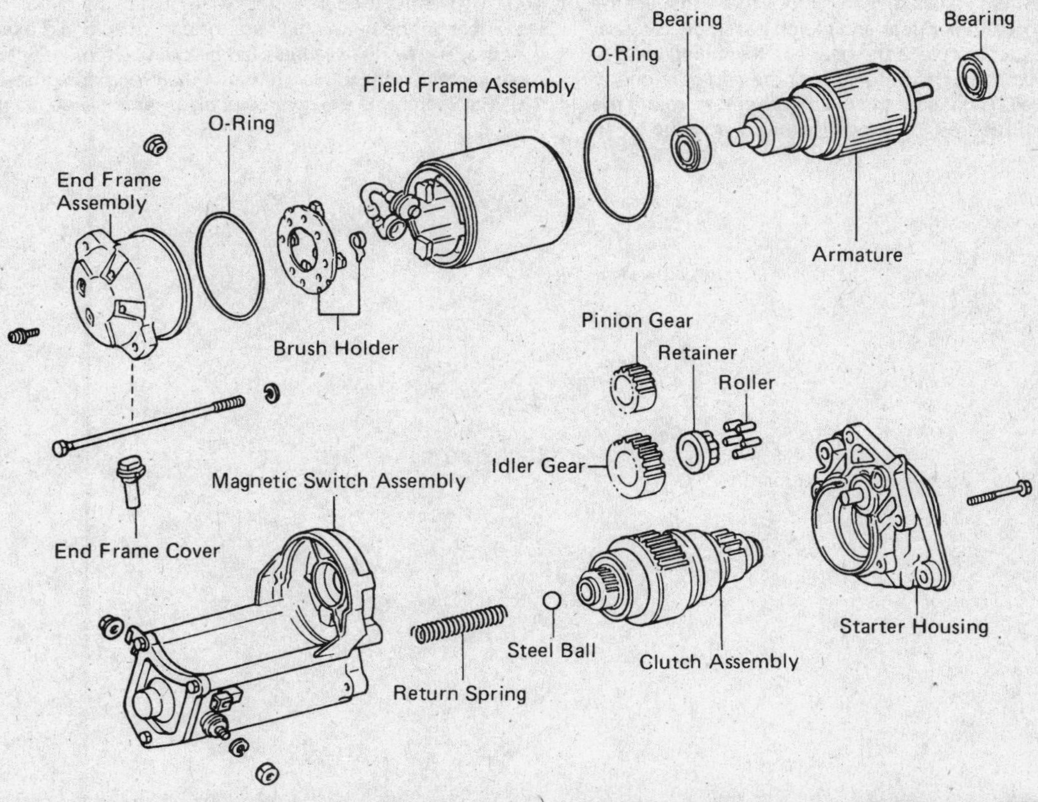

22.7b An exploded view of a typical starter motor, solenoid and starter housing on 1985 through 1990 models

5

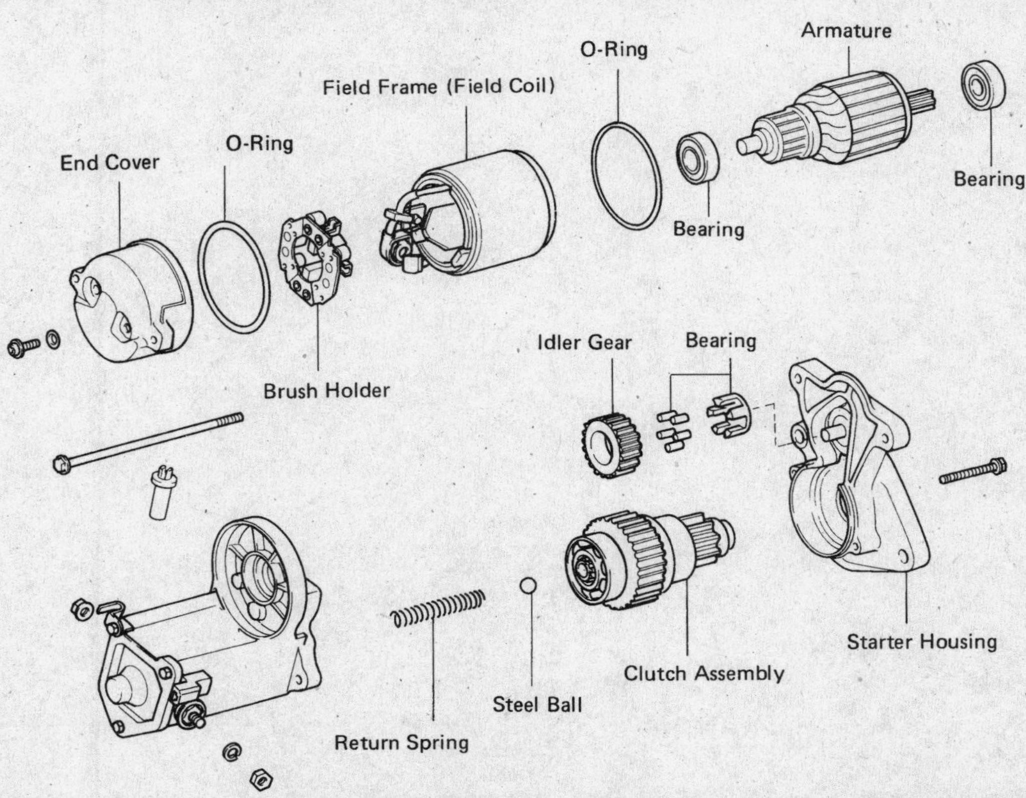

22.7c An exploded view of a typical starter motor, solenoid and starter housing on 1991 and later models

gears on the starter motor are installed, then remove them. Inspect the gear teeth on the pinion gear, idler gear and clutch assembly for wear or damage. If either is evident, replace the gear set. If you find wear or damage on the pinion, it's a good idea to inspect the ring gear on the flywheel/driveplate as well. To inspect the clutch assembly, rotate the pinion and verify that it turns freely. Also verify that it locks up when you try to rotate it counterclockwise. Install the clutch and idler gear assembly on the new/rebuilt starter and/or solenoid exactly the same way they were originally installed before you removed them. Lubricate them liberally with high temperature multi-purpose grease.

7 Reassembly is the reverse of disassembly **(see illustrations)**.

6

Chapter 6 Emissions control systems

Contents

1 General information

Refer to illustrations 1.1a through 1.1g, and 1.6

To minimize pollution of the atmosphere from incompletely burned and evaporating gases and to maintain good driveability and fuel economy, a number of emission control systems are used on this vehicle **(see illustrations)**. They include the:

Positive Crankcase Ventilation (PCV) system *- which reduces blowby gas (hydrocarbons)*

Evaporative Emission Control (EVAP) system *- which reduces evaporative hydrocarbons*

Dashpot system *- which reduces hydrocarbons and carbon monoxide*

Exhaust Gas Recirculation (EGR) system *- which reduces oxides of nitrogen*

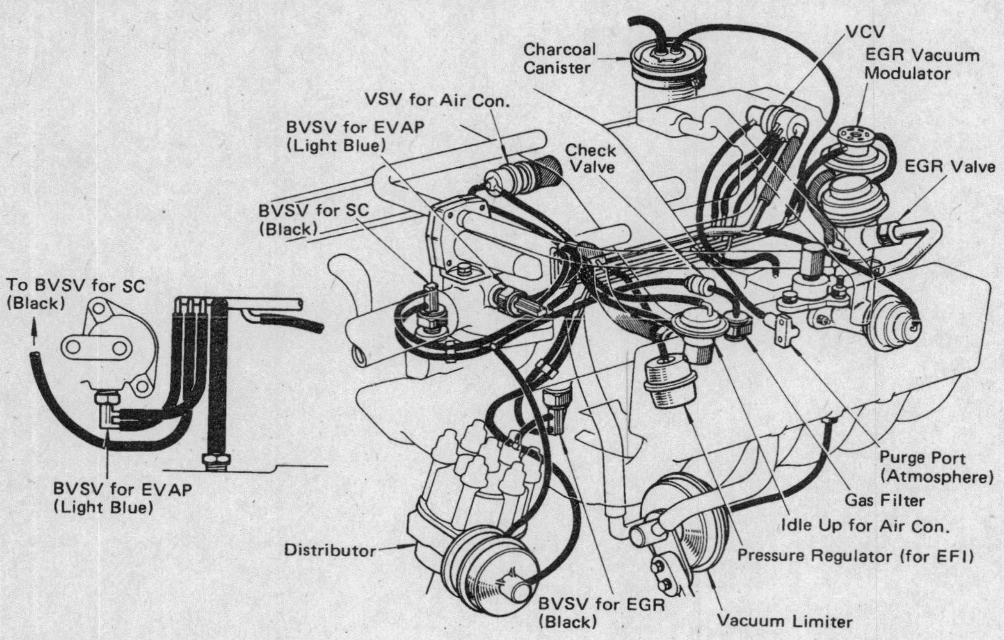

1.1a Component layout and vacuum hose routing for emissions control systems - 1979 models

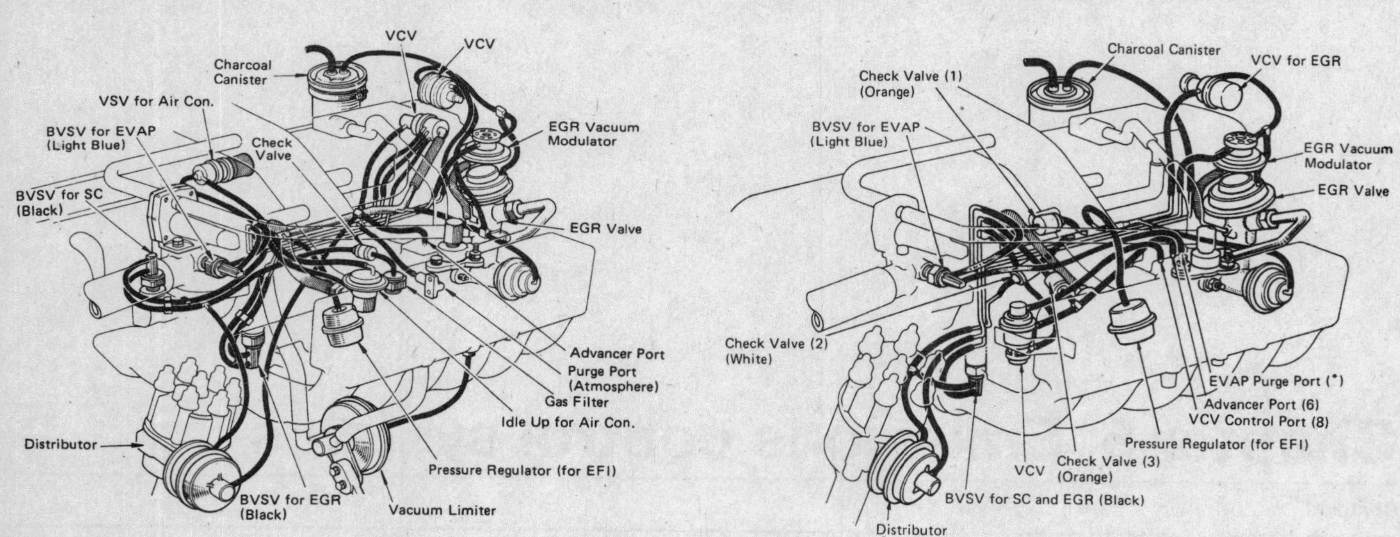

1.1b Component layout and vacuum hose routing for emissions control systems - 1980 models

1.1c Component layout and vacuum hose routing for emissions control systems - 1981 models

Three-way catalyst system *- which reduces hydrocarbons, carbon monoxide and oxides of nitrogen*

Electronic Fuel Injection (EFI) system *- which reduces all exhaust emissions by regulating the operating conditions of the engine (see Chapter 4 for further information on the EFI system).*

The sections in this chapter include general descriptions, checking procedures within the scope of the home mechanic and component replacement procedures (when possible) for each of the systems listed above.

Before assuming that an emissions control system is malfunctioning, check the fuel (see Chapter 4) and ignition (see Chapter 5) systems carefully. The diagnosis of some emission control devices requires specialized tools, equipment and training. If checking and servicing become too difficult or if a procedure is beyond the scope of your skills, consult your dealer service department.

This doesn't mean, however, that emission control systems are particularly difficult to maintain and repair. You can quickly and easily perform many checks and do most of the regular maintenance at home with common tune-up and hand tools. **Note:** *The most frequent cause of emissions problems is simply a loose or broken connector or vacuum hose, so always check the connectors and vacuum hoses first.*

Pay close attention to any special precautions outlined in this chapter. It should be noted that the illustrations of the various systems may not exactly match the system installed on your vehicle because of changes made by the manufacturer during production or from year-to-year.

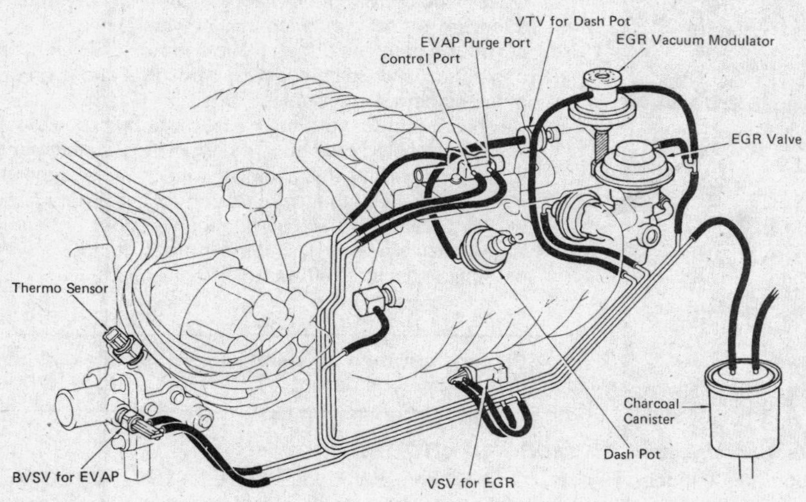

1.1d Component layout and vacuum hose routing for emissions control systems - 1982 through 1984 models

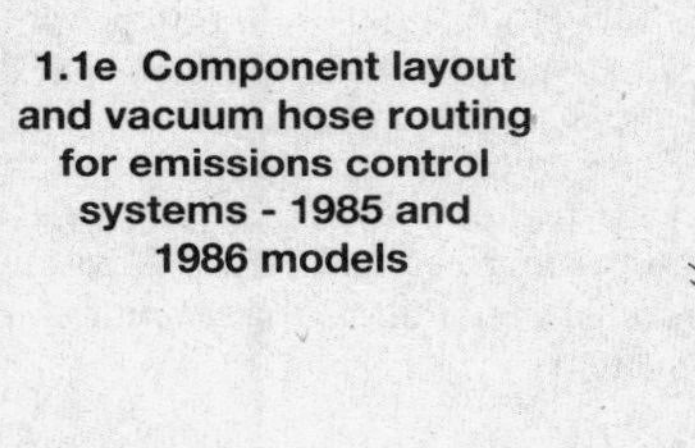
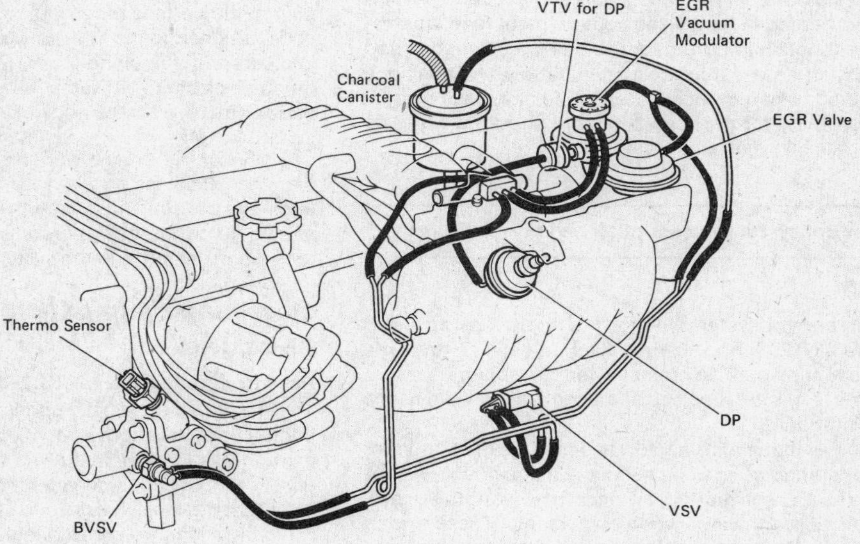

1.1e Component layout and vacuum hose routing for emissions control systems - 1985 and 1986 models

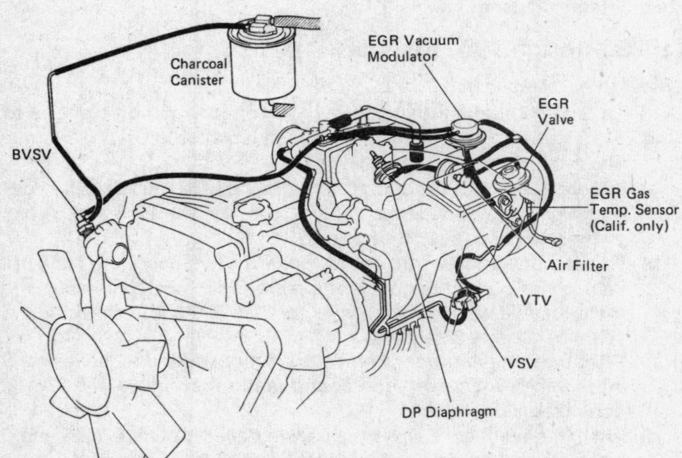

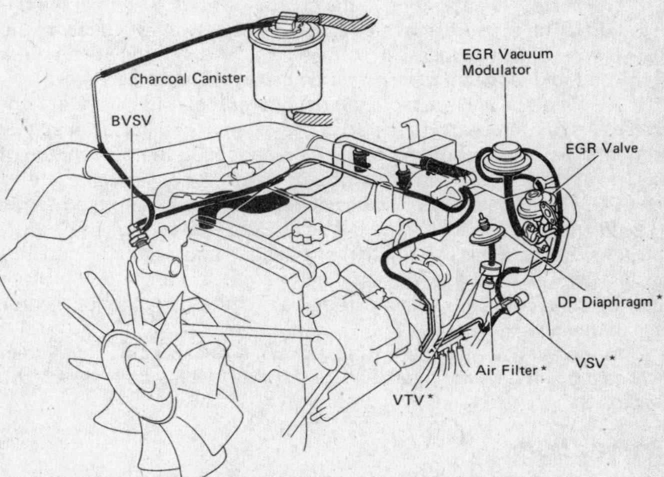

1.1f Component layout and vacuum hose routing for emissions control systems - 1987 through 1992 non-turbo models

1.1g Component layout and vacuum hose routing for emissions control systems - 1987 through 1992 turbo models (components marked with an asterisk used only on 1987 through 1990 models)

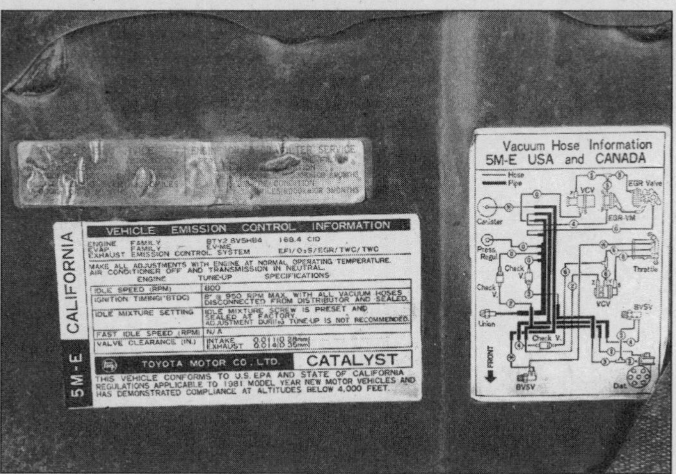

1.6 A typical Vehicle Emission Control Information (VECI) label - 1981 model shown

Vehicle Emissions Control Information label and Vacuum Hose Information labels are located in the engine compartment **(see illustrations)**. These labels contain important emissions specifications and setting procedures, and a vacuum hose schematic with emissions components identified. When servicing the engine or emissions systems, the VECI label in your particular vehicle should always be checked for up-to-date information.

2 Electronic control system - description and precautions

Description

The electronic control system (referred to as the Toyota Computer Control System (TCCS) on 1982 and later models) controls the fuel injection system, the spark advance system, the diagnosis system, the cooling fans, etc. by means of a microcomputer known as the Electronic Control Unit (ECU).

The ECU receives signals from various sensors which monitor changing engine operating conditions such as intake air volume, intake air temperature, coolant temperature, engine rpm, acceleration/deceleration, exhaust oxygen content, etc. These signals are utilized by the ECU to determine the correct injection duration and ignition timing.

The system is analogous to the central nervous system in the human body: The sensors (nerve endings) constantly relay signals to the ECU (brain), which processes the data and, if necessary, sends out a command to change the operating parameters of the engine (body).

Here's a specific example of how one portion of this system operates: An oxygen sensor, located in the exhaust manifold, constantly monitors the oxygen content of the exhaust gas. If the percentage of oxygen in the exhaust gas is incorrect, an electrical signal is sent to the ECU. The ECU takes this information, processes it and then sends a command to the fuel injection system, telling it to change the air/fuel mixture. This happens in a fraction of a second and it goes on continuously when the engine is running. The end result is an air/fuel mixture ratio which is constantly maintained at a predetermined ratio, regardless of driving conditions.

In the event of a sensor malfunction, a backup circuit will take over to provide driveability until the problem is identified and fixed (see Section 3).

Precautions

a) Always disconnect the power by either turning off the ignition switch or disconnecting the battery terminals before removing EFI wiring electrical connectors.
b) When installing a battery, be particularly careful to avoid reversing the positive and negative battery cables.
c) Do not subject EFI or emissions related components or the ECU to severe impact during removal or installation.
d) Do not be careless during troubleshooting. Even slight terminal contact can invalidate a testing procedure and even damage one of the numerous transistor circuits.
e) Never attempt to work on the ECU or open the ECU cover. The ECU is protected by a government mandated extended warranty that will be nullified if you tamper with or damage the ECU.
f) If you are inspecting electronic control system components during rainy weather, make sure that water does not enter any part. When washing the engine compartment, do not spray these parts or their connectors with water.

3 Diagnosis system - general information and obtaining diagnostic code output

General information

On 1982 and later models, the ECU contains a built-in self-diagnosis system which detects and identifies malfunctions occurring in the EFI system. When the ECU detects a problem, three things happen: the Check Engine light comes on, the trouble is identified and a diagnostic code is recorded and stored. The ECU stores the failure code assigned to the specific problem area until the diagnosis system is cleared by removing the STOP 15-amp fuse (1982 through 1986 models), or the EFI 15-amp fuse (1987 and later models), for 30 seconds or more, from the engine compartment fuse panel, with the ignition switch off.

The Check Engine warning light, which is located on the instrument panel, comes on when the ignition switch is turned to On and the engine is not running. When the engine is started, the warning light should go out. If the light remains on, the diagnosis system has detected a malfunction in the system.

Obtaining diagnostic code output

All models

Refer to illustrations 3.1, 3.3a, 3.3b and 3.3c

1 To obtain diagnostic codes **(see illustration)**, verify first that the battery voltage is above 11 volts, the throttle is fully closed, the transmission is in Park or Neutral, all accessory switches are off and the engine is at normal operating temperature.

2 Turn the ignition switch to On. Do not start the engine.

3 Use a jumper wire to bridge terminals T and E1 (all 1982 through 1987 models and 1988 non-California models) or TE1 and E1 (1988 California models and all 1989 and later models) of the service connector **(see illustrations)**.

1982 through 1984 models

Refer to illustrations 3.4, 3.5a and 3.5b

4 To "read" the diagnostic code, hook up an analog voltmeter to the EFI service connector as shown **(see illustration)**.

5 The procedure is as follows:

a) If there are no trouble codes stored in the ECU memory, the voltmeter needle will deflect back and forth between 2.5 and 5 volts every .6 second **(see illustration)**.
b) If the Check Engine light comes on and stays on during start-up, i.e. if there's a malfunction code stored in the ECU memory, the meter needle will indicate 5 volts for 2 seconds, then indicate 2.5 volts for another 2 seconds.
c) After that, the number of times the needle deflects between 2.5 volts and 5 volts every .6 second is the first figure of a 2-digit code **(see illustration)**.
d) Then, the number of times the needle deflects between 2.5 and 0 volts every .6 second is the second digit of the 2-digit code.
e) If there is more than one code stored in the ECU, the code with the lowest number will appear first, followed by another 2.5 volt indication for 2 seconds. Then the next code appears, in the same manner as described above, and so on.

Code	Probable cause
11	ECU power source (1982 through 1989 models only)
12	RPM signal (crank angle pulse)
13	RPM signal (crank angle pulse)
14	Ignition signal
21	Oxygen sensor signal
21	Oxygen sensor heater signal (1990 and later turbo models only)
22	Coolant temperature sensor signal
23	Intake air temperature signal (1982 through 1986 models only)
24	Intake air temperature signal (1987 and later models only)
25	Air-fuel ratio lean malfunction (1988 and later California models only)
26	Air-fuel ratio rich malfunction (1988 and later California models only)
27	Sub-oxygen sensor signal (1988 and later California models only)
27	Sub-oxygen sensor heater signal (1988 and later California models only)
31	Airflow meter signal
32	Airflow meter signal
32	High Altitude Compensation (HAC) sensor signal (1987 through 1989 turbo models only)
34	Turbocharger pressure signal
35	High Altitude Compensation (HAC) sensor signal (1990 and later turbo models only)
41	Throttle position sensor signal
42	Vehicle speed sensor signal
43	Starter signal
51	Air conditioner switch or neutral start switch signal
52	Knock sensor signal (1985 and later models only)
53	Knock control signal in ECU (1985 and later models only)
71	EGR system malfunction (1989 and later California models only)

3.1 Trouble code chart

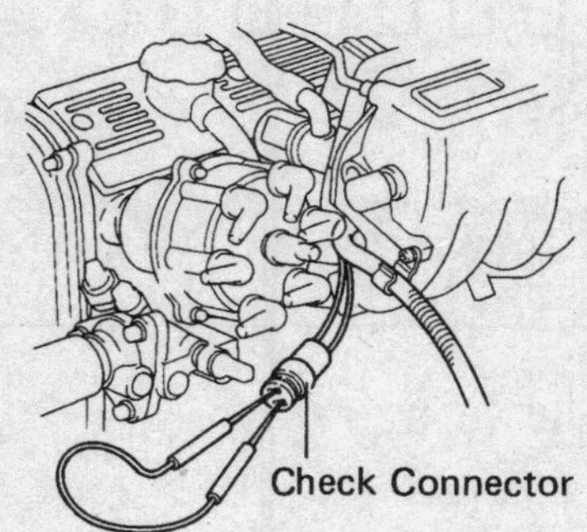

3.3a Use a jumper wire to bridge terminals T and E1 (1982 through 1984 models)

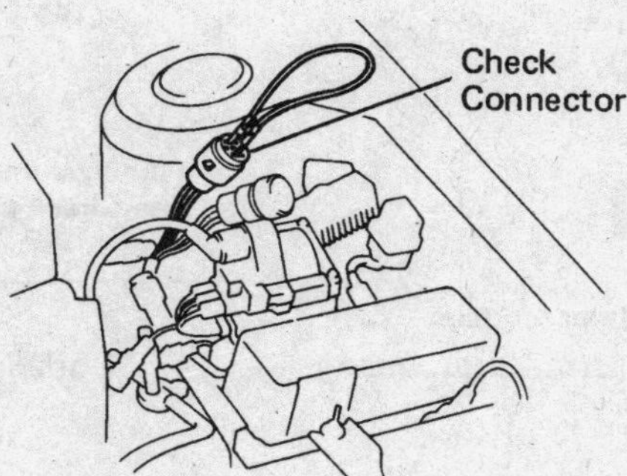

3.3b Use a jumper wire to bridge terminals T and E1 (all 1985 and 1986 models)

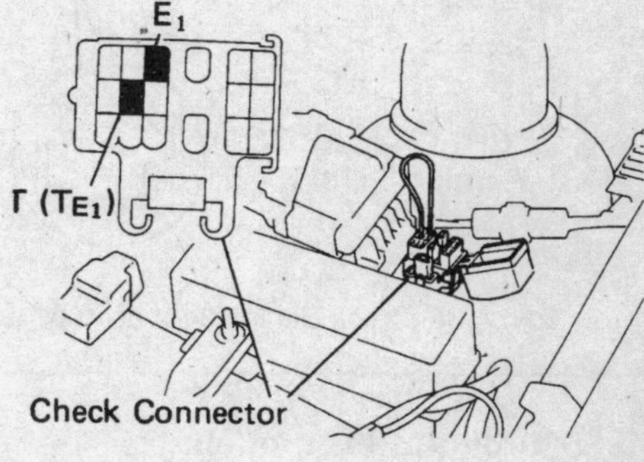

3.3c Use a jumper wire to bridge terminals T and E1 (1987 models and 1988 non-California models) or TE1 and E1 (1988 California models and all 1989 and later models) of the service connector

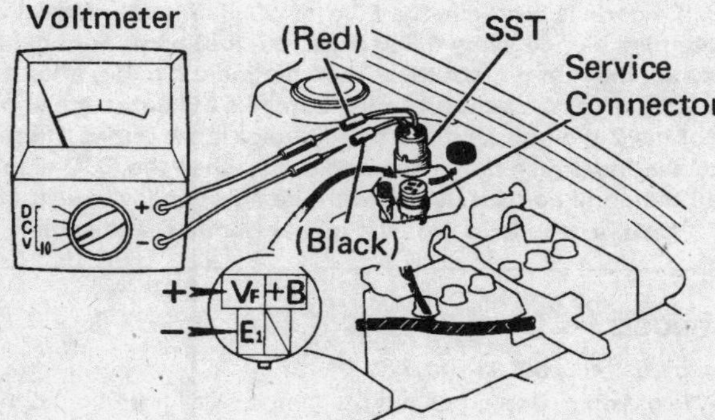

3.4 To "read" the diagnostic code on 1982 through 1984 models, hook up an analog voltmeter as shown (if you don't have access to the special adapter, just connect the positive probe of the meter to terminal VF and the negative probe to terminal E1)

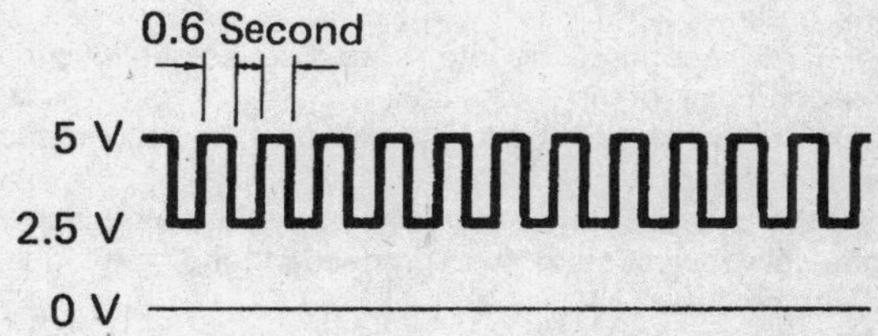

3.5a If there are no trouble codes stored in the ECU memory on 1982 through 1984 models, the voltmeter needle will deflect back and forth between 2.5 and 5 volts every .6 second

f) Once the ECU has displayed all its stored codes, in numerical order, from the lowest to the highest 2-digit number, it will repeat the same sequence again, and will continue to do so, as long as the service connector terminals are bridged.

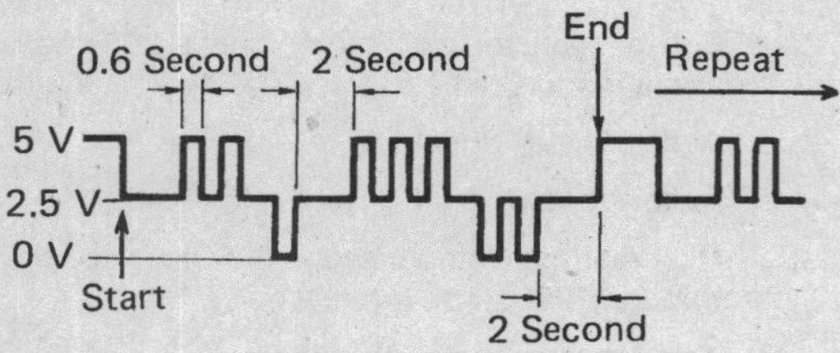

3.5b If a code is stored in ECU memory on 1982 through 1984 models, the meter needle indicates 5 volts for 2 seconds, then 2.5 volts for another 2 seconds; then it deflects back and forth between 2.5 and 5 volts every .6 second; the number of times it deflects is the first figure of a 2-digit code; then it deflects between 2.5 and 0 volts; again, the number of times it deflects is the second digit of the 2-digit code; if more than one code is stored, the code with the lowest number appears first, followed by a 2.5-volt indication for 2 seconds; then the next code appears, etc.

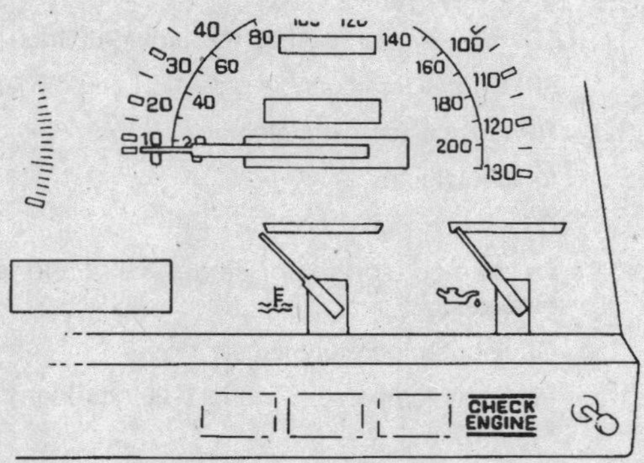

3.6a Location of the Check Engine light on 1982 through 1984 models (the light is in the same location on 1985 and 1986 models, but looks like the light in the next illustration)

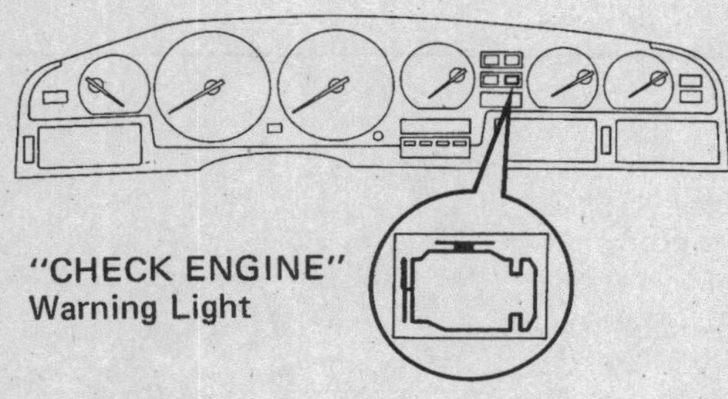

3.6b The Check Engine light on 1987 and later models

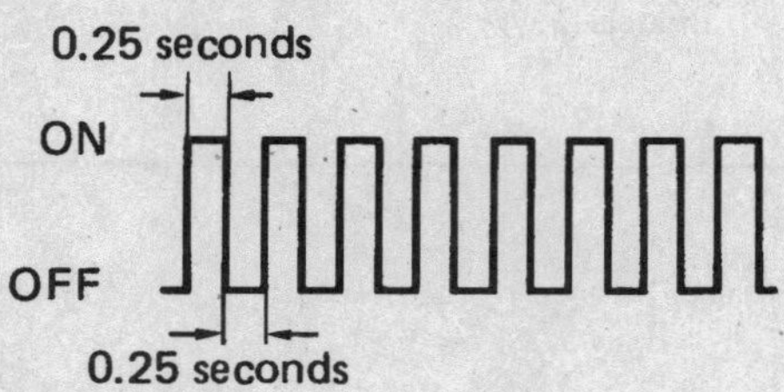

3.6c If the system is operating normally on 1985 and later models, the Check Engine light blinks once every 0.25 second

1985 through 1992 models

Refer to illustrations 3.6a, 3.6b, 3.6c and 3.6d

6 The Check Engine light **(see illustrations)** displays the stored trouble code(s) in a series of flashes. Here's how to read them:

a) If the system is operating normally, the Check Engine light blinks once every 0.25 second **(see illustration)**.
b) If a code has been stored in the ECU, the light blinks once every 0.5 second **(see illustration)**.
c) The first series of blinks indicates the first digit of the 2-digit diagnostic code.
d) After a 1.5-second pause, the second series of blinks indicates the second digit of the 2-digit code.
e) If there are two or more codes, there'll be a 2.5 second pause between each code.
f) When the ECU displays more than one code, it begins with the numerically lowest code, then proceeds to the next higher number, and so on.

Note: *The above procedure will work on all 1985 through 1992 models. On 1987 and 1988 models with the optional Super Monitor, you can also display the codes on the monitor screen: Turn the ignition switch to On, but don't start the engine. Simultaneously push and hold in the SELECT and INPUT M keys for at least three seconds - the letters DIAG will appear on the screen. After a short pause, hold in the SET key for at least three seconds. If the system is normal, an ENG-OK appears on the screen; if there's a problem, its code number appears on the screen. If there's more than one problem, the screen pauses three seconds, then displays the next code. After you've read out the stored code(s), turn off the ignition switch, or push any button except SET.*

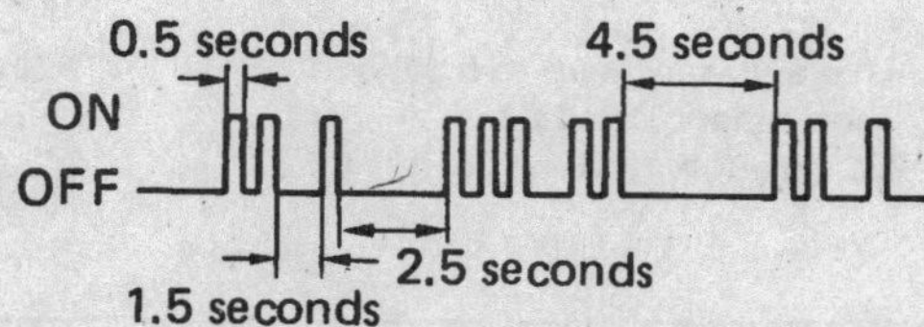

3.6d If a code is stored in the ECU on 1985 and later models, the light blinks once every 0.5 second; the first number of blinks indicates the first digit of the 2-digit diagnostic code; after a 1.5-second pause, the second series of blinks indicates the second digit of the 2-digit code; if there are two or more codes, there'll be a 2.5 second pause between each code; when the ECU displays more than one code, it begins with the numerically lowest code, then proceeds to the next higher number, and so on

All models

Refer to illustrations 3.8a and 3.8b

7 When you're done, pull out the jumper wire from the connector and install the rubber protective cap.

8 To remove the diagnostic code from memory, remove the STOP 15-amp fuse (1982 through 1986 models) or the EFI 15-amp fuse (1987 and later models) **(see illustrations)**, for at least 30 seconds (the lower the temperature, the longer the fuse must be removed), with the ignition switch off. You can also clear the codes by detaching the ca-

3.8a To remove the diagnostic code from memory on 1982 through 1986 models, remove the STOP 15-amp fuse in the engine compartment fuse panel, for at least 30 seconds with the ignition switch off

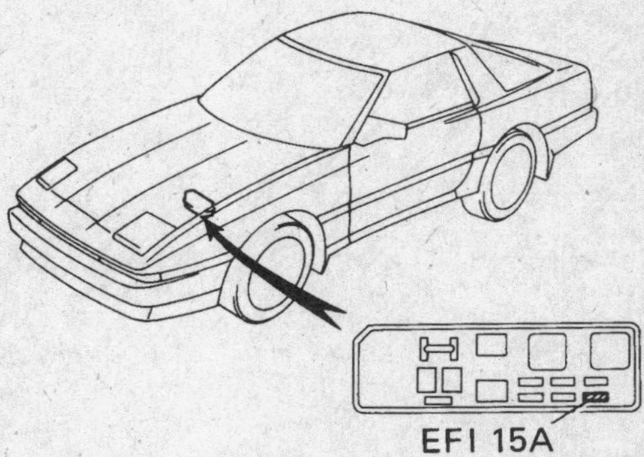

3.8b To remove the diagnostic code from memory on 1987 and later models, remove the EFI 15-amp fuse from the engine compartment fuse panel, for at least 30 seconds, with the ignition switch off

ble from the negative battery terminal, but you'll wipe out the memory in other accessories such as the radio and trip computer.

9 You must clear the stored code(s) when you're done servicing the faulty system/component, or the ECU will continue to store it, and will display it along with any other new code(s) in the event of future trouble.

10 Anytime you have to work on engine components requiring disconnection of the negative battery cable, make sure no codes are stored in the ECU, or you'll lose them when you disconnect the battery.

11 After canceling the code(s), perform a road test and verify that the voltmeter displays the "normal" pattern only; if the same trouble code appears, the fault is still present.

4 Electronic control system - component check and replacement

Note: *All of the components described in this section are protected by a Federally-mandated extended warranty. See your dealer for the details regarding your vehicle. It therefore makes little sense to either check or replace any of these parts yourself as long as they are still under warranty. However, once the warranty has expired, most of them can be checked (the oxygen sensor and the ECU are the exceptions) and all of them can be easily replaced.*

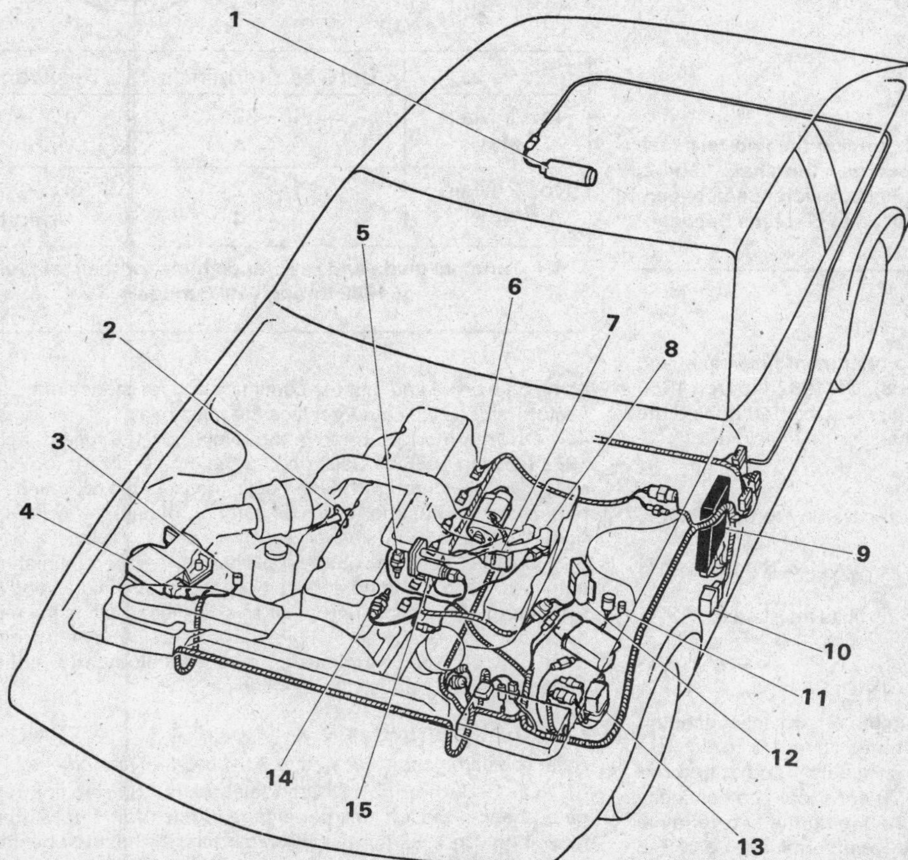

4.1a Component location for the electronic control system on 1979 through 1981 models

1 *Fuel pump*
2 *Oxygen sensor*
3 *Fuel pump check connector*
4 *Airflow meter*
5 *Coolant temperature sensor*
6 *Fuel injector*
7 *Throttle position sensor*
8 *Cold start injector*
9 *ECU*
10 *Circuit opening relay*
11 *Check connector*
12 *Solenoid resistor*
13 *EFI main relay*
14 *Cold start injector time switch*
15 *Air valve*

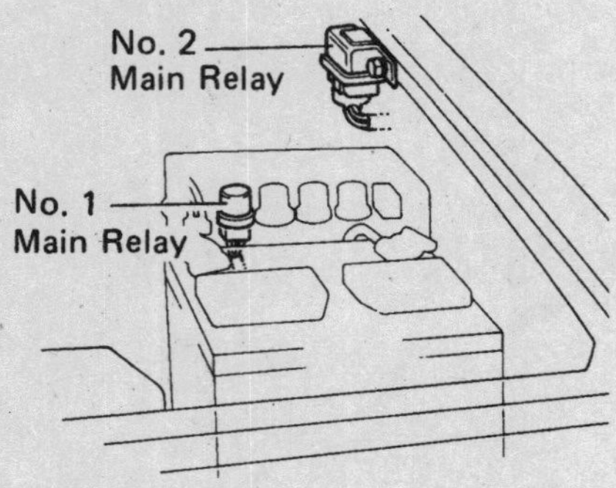

4.1b The No. 1 main relay on 1982 through 1986 models is located inside the main fuse panel, right behind the battery; the No. 2 main relay is located behind the fuse panel, on the fender

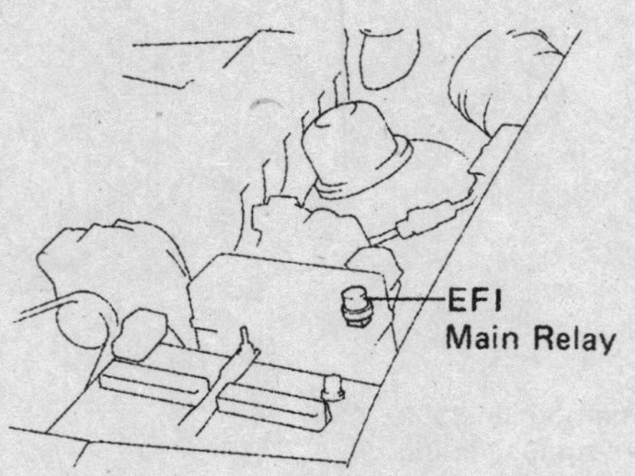

4.1c The EFI main relay on 1987 and later models is located inside the fuse panel, right behind the battery

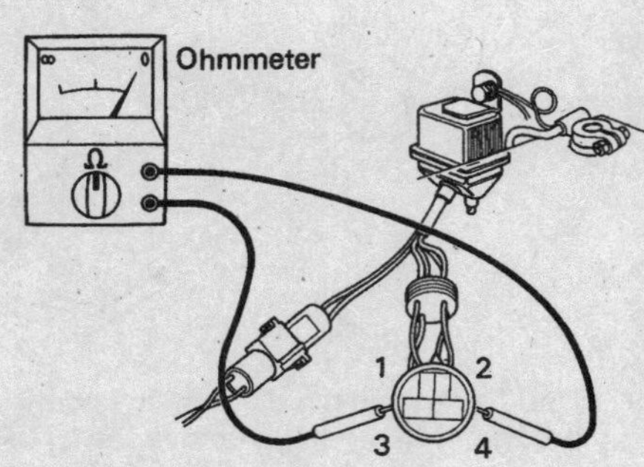

4.3a On 1979 through 1981 models, unplug the 4-terminal connector, turn on the ignition switch and note whether you hear the relay clicking, then check the continuity between terminals 1 and 2, and between terminals 3 and 4 - there should be continuity between both; . . .

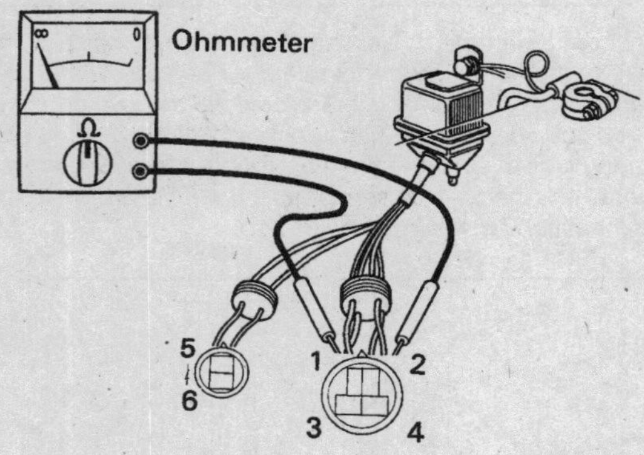

4.3b . . . then turn off the ignition switch, unplug the two-terminal connector and measure the resistance between terminals 1 and 2, 3 and 4, and 5 and 6 - there should be infinite resistance between terminals 1 and 2, and 3 and 4, and about 30 to 60 ohms between 5 and 6

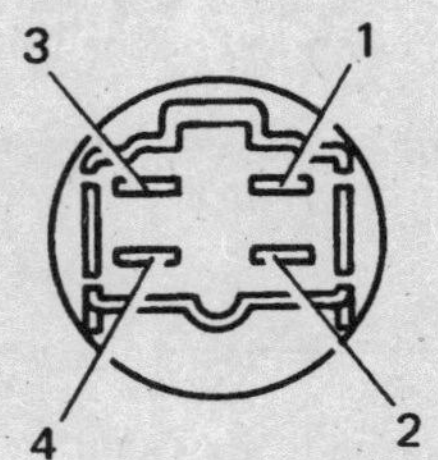

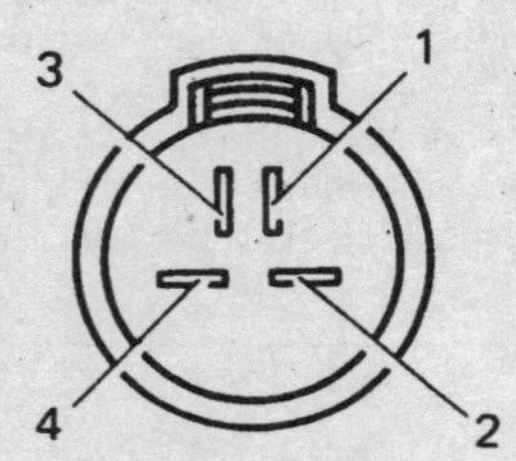

	Between terminals	Resistance Ω
No. 1 Main Relay	1 – 2 3 – 4	40 – 60 Infinity
No. 2 Main Relay	1 – 2 3 – 4	60 – 120 Infinity

4.4 Terminal guide and resistance table for the main relay on 1982 through 1986 models

EFI main relay

Refer to illustrations 4.1a, 4.1b and 4.1c

1 Remove the cover from the engine compartment fuse panel and locate the EFI main relay **(see illustrations)**. On 1982 through 1986 models, note that there is also a No. 2 main relay located behind the fuse panel, on the left fender. This relay must also be checked.

Operation check

2 Turn on the ignition switch and listen carefully to the relay(s), which should make a clicking noise.

a) If a relay clicks, it is probably operating correctly. The problem is most likely elsewhere.
b) If a relay doesn't click, remove it and check its resistance.

Resistance/continuity check

Refer to illustrations 4.3a, 4.3b, 4.4, 4.5a and 4.5b

3 On 1979 through 1981 models, unplug the 4-terminal connector, turn on the ignition switch and note whether you hear the relay clicking. Then check the continuity between terminals 1 and 2, and between terminals 3 and 4 **(see illustration)**. There should be continuity between both. Turn off the ignition switch, unplug the two-terminal connector and measure the resistance between terminals 1 and 2, 3 and 4, and 5 and 6 **(see illustration)**. There should be infinite resistance between terminals 1 and 2, and 3 and 4, and about 30 to 60 ohms between 5 and 6. If the continuity and resistance of the two connectors isn't as indicated, replace the main relay.

4 On later models, remove the relay from the fuse panel (and on 1982 through 1986 models, unplug the connector for the No. 2 main relay). On 1982 through 1986 models, measure the resistance between terminals 1 and 2, and terminals 3 and 4, of each relay **(see illustration)**. If either relay fails either resistance check, replace it.

5 On 1987 and later models, verify that there's continuity between terminals 1 and 3 and no continuity between terminals 2 and 4 **(see illustration)**. If the continuity is not as specified, replace the relay. Then apply battery voltage across terminals 1 and 3 and verify that there's continuity between terminals 2 and 4 **(see illustration)**. If the relay doesn't operate as described, replace it.

Circuit opening relay

Refer to illustrations 4.7a, 4.7b, 4.7c, 4.8a, 4.8b and 4.8c

6 On 1979 through 1981 models, the circuit opening relay is located behind the left kick panel **(see illustration 4.1a)** or behind the glove box. On 1982 through 1986 models, it's located behind the left kick panel. On 1987 and later models, it's located behind the right kick panel.

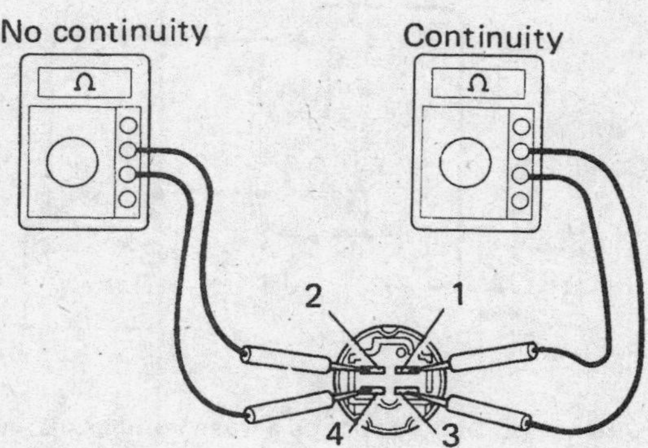

4.5a To test the EFI main relay on 1987 and later models, verify that there's continuity between terminals 1 and 3, but no continuity between terminals 2 and 4 . . .

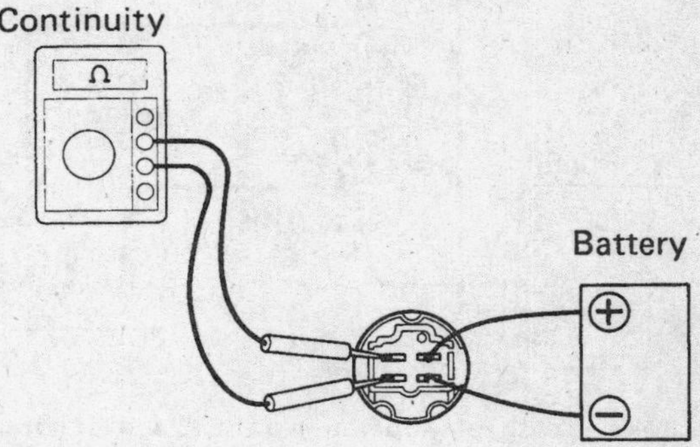

4.5b . . . then apply battery voltage across terminals 1 and 3 and verify that there's continuity between terminals 2 and 4

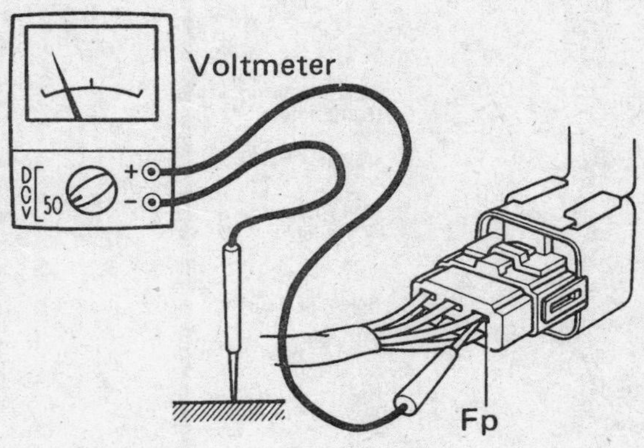

4.7a Circuit opening relay check (1979 through 1987 models) - there should be voltage at terminal Fp during cranking and starting

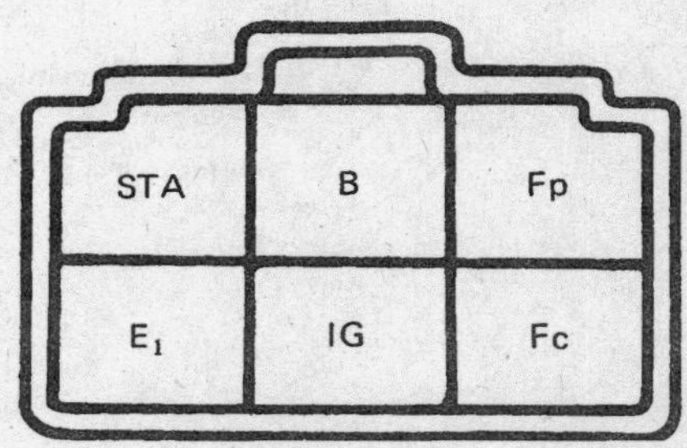

Between terminals	Resistance (Ω)
STA – E_1	30 – 60
IG – Fc	80 – 120
B – Fp	Infinity

4.7b Terminal guide and resistance table for the circuit opening relay on 1979 through 1984 models

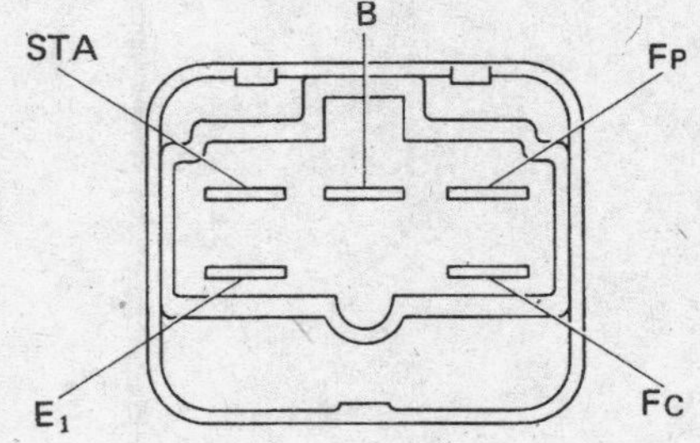

Between terminals	Resistance (Ω)
STA – E_1	17 – 25
B – Fc	88 – 132
B – Fp	Infinity

4.7c Terminal guide and resistance table for the circuit opening relay on 1985 through 1987 models

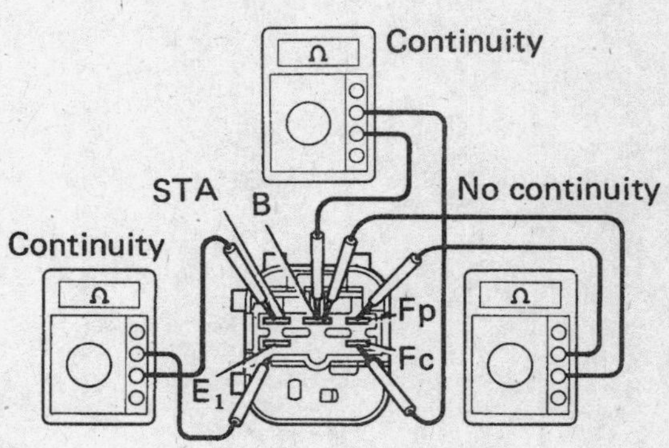

4.8a On 1988 and later models, verify that there's continuity between terminals STA and E1 and between terminals B and Fc, but no continuity between terminals B and Fp

7 On 1979 through 1987 models, check the operation of the relay first, then check its resistance: If necessary, remove the relay from its bracket so that the connector faces you. Don't unplug the connector. Crank, then start, the engine. Verify that there's voltage at terminal Fp during cranking and starting **(see illustration)**. Stop the engine. Unplug the connector and measure the resistance between the indicated terminals **(see illustrations)**. If the resistance isn't as specified between these terminals, replace the relay.

8 On 1988 and later models, check the continuity of the relay first, then its operation: Verify that there's continuity between terminals STA and E1 and between terminals B and Fc, but no continuity between terminals B and Fp **(see illustration)**. If the continuity isn't as specified, replace the relay. To check the relay operation, apply battery voltage across terminals STA and E1 and verify that there's continuity be-

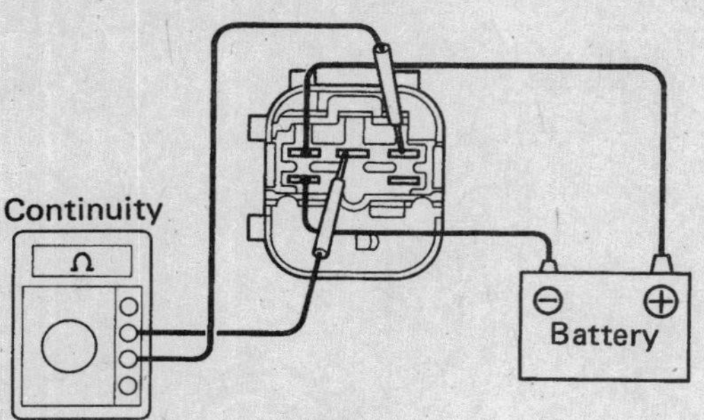

4.8b To check the relay operation on 1988 and later models, apply battery voltage across terminals STA and E1 and verify that there's continuity between terminals B and Fp, . . .

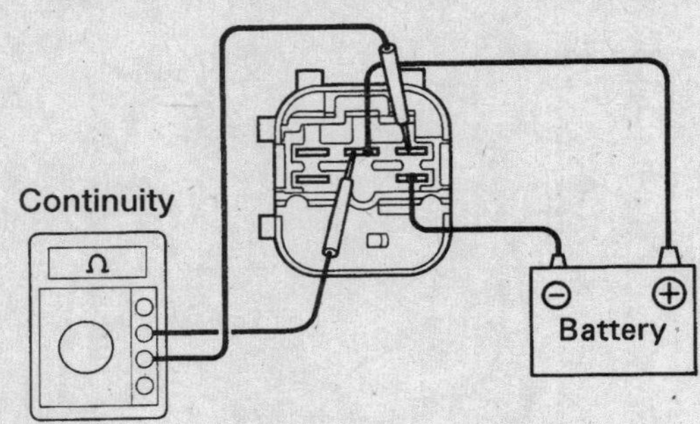

4.8c . . . then apply battery voltage across terminals B and Fc and verify that there's continuity between terminals B and Fp

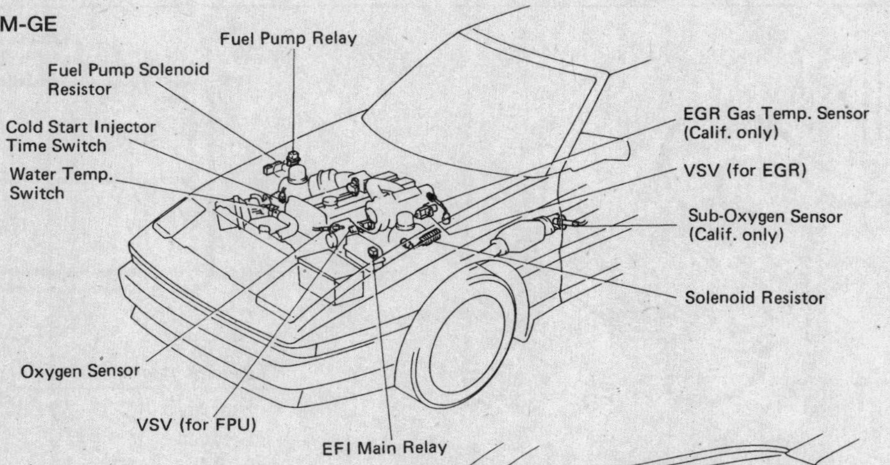

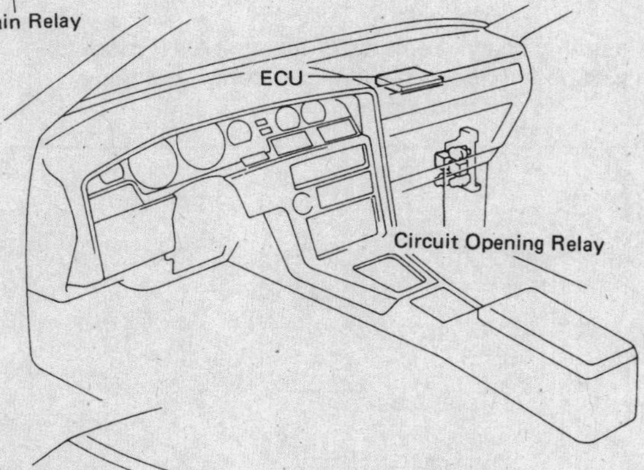

4.9a Component location on 1987 and later models - non-turbo models, above; turbo models, below (1988 model shown, others similar)

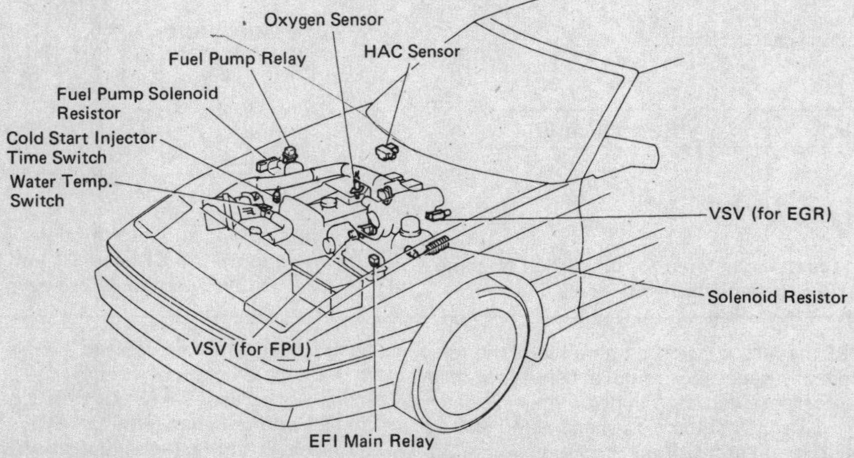

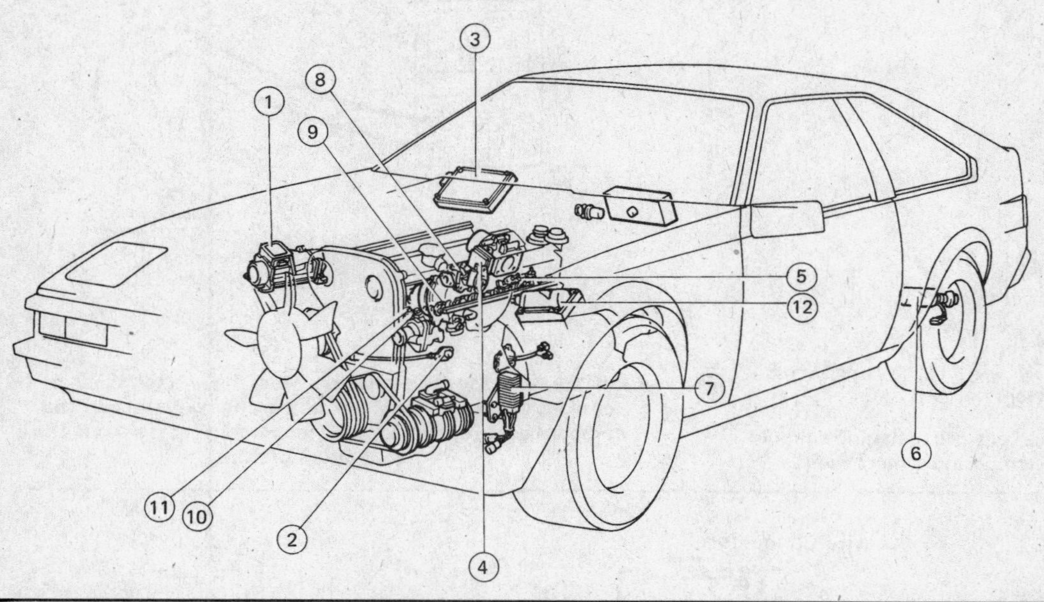

4.9b Component location on 1982 through 1986 electronic control system

1 *Airflow meter*
2 *Oxygen sensor*
3 *ECU*
4 *Throttle position sensor*
5 *Cold start injector*
6 *Fuel pump*
7 *Solenoid resistor*
8 *ISC valve*
9 *Fuel injectors (6)*
10 *Coolant temperature sensor*
11 *Cold start injector time switch*
12 *Igniter and ignition coil*

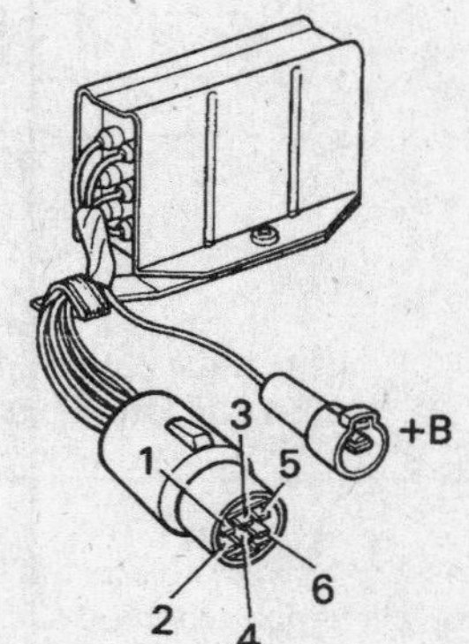

4.10a On 1979 through 1981 models, measure the resistance between terminal +B and the other terminals - each check should indicate 5 to 7 ohms resistance

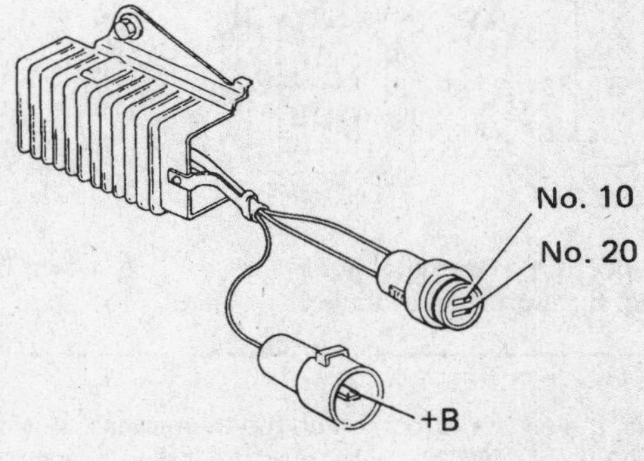

4.10b On 1982 through 1986 models, measure the resistance between terminal +B and the other terminals - each check should indicate 2 ohms resistance

tween terminals B and Fp **(see illustration)**. Then apply battery voltage across terminals B and Fc and verify that there's continuity between terminals B and Fp **(see illustration)**. If the relay doesn't operate as described, replace it.

Solenoid resistor

Refer to illustrations 4.9a, 4.9b, 4.10a, 4.10b and 4.10c

9 On 1979 through 1981 models, the solenoid resistor is located on the left shock tower **(see illustration 4.1a)**. On 1982 through 1986 models, it's located behind the headlight and below the coil and igniter **(see illustration)**. On 1987 and later models, it's located on the left side of the engine compartment, behind the main fuse panel **(see illustration)**.

10 Using an ohmmeter, measure the resistance between terminal +B and the other terminals **(see illustrations)**. There should be 5 to 7 ohms resistance (1979 through 1981 models), 2 ohms resistance (1982 through 1986 models) or 3 ohms resistance (1987 and later models) between +B and the other terminals. If there isn't, replace the resistor.

Cold start injector time switch

See Chapter 4.

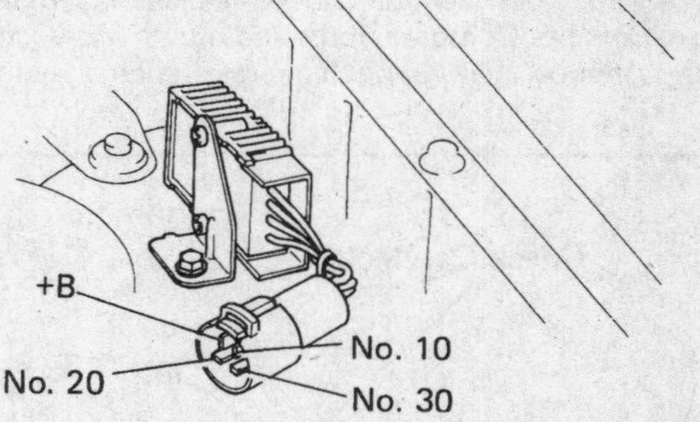

4.10c On 1987 and later models, measure the resistance between +B and the other terminals - each check should indicate 3 ohms resistance

Coolant temperature sensor

Refer to illustrations 4.12a and 4.12b

11 On 1979 through 1981 models, the coolant temperature sensor (sometimes called the water temperature switch) is located in the front part of the intake manifold **(see illustration 4.1a)**. On 1982 through

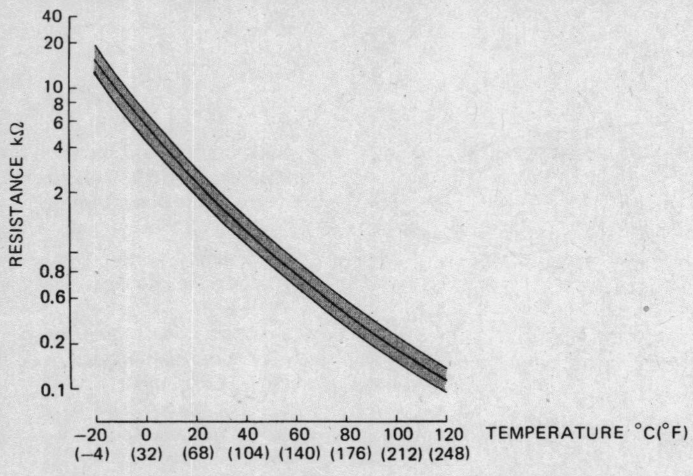

4.12a The coolant temperature sensor's resistance should decrease as the coolant temperature increases

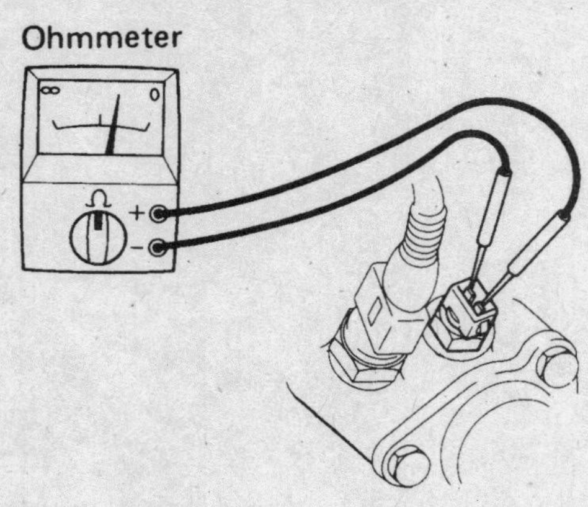

4.12b Measure the resistance between the two terminals of the coolant temperature sensor as the engine warms up and compare your readings to the accompanying resistance-to-temperature graph

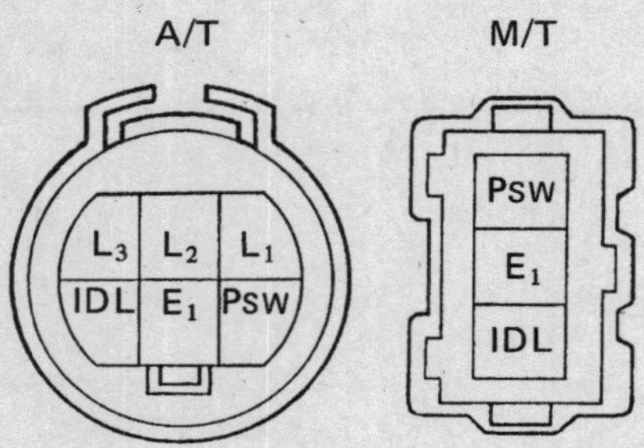

4.14a Fuel cut rpm terminal guide for 1982 through 1984 models

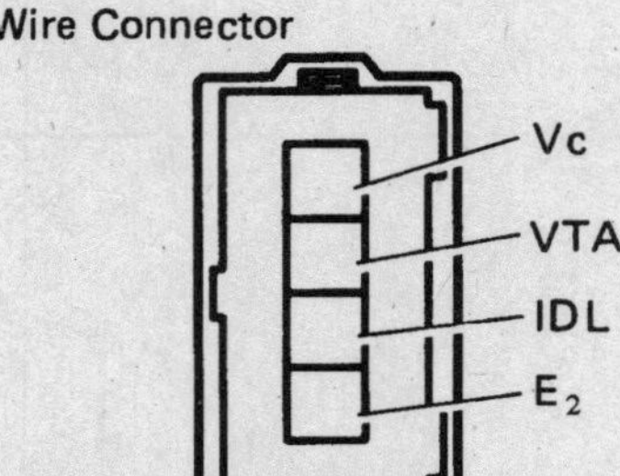

4.14b Fuel cut rpm terminal guide for 1985 and 1986 models

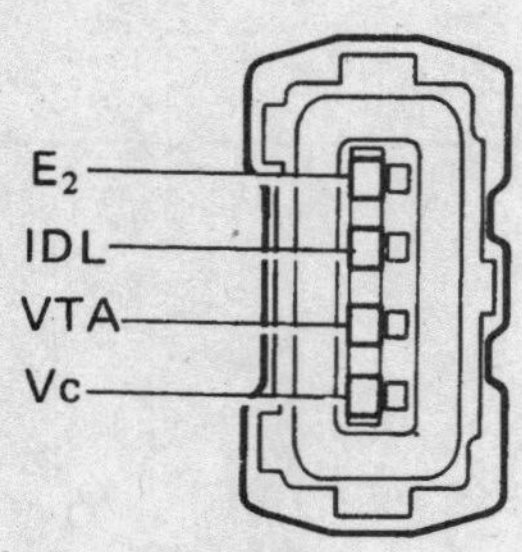

4.14c Fuel cut rpm terminal guide for 1987 and later (except 1991) models

1986 models, the sensor is located on the thermostat housing **(see illustration 4.9a)**; on 1987 and later models, it's also next to the cold start injector time switch, but they're to the right of the timing belt cover **(see illustration 4.9b)**.

12 The coolant temperature sensor's resistance should decrease as the coolant temperature increases as shown **(see illustration)**. To check the sensor, start the engine, unplug the connector and measure the resistance between the two terminals **(see illustration)** as the engine warms up. Compare your readings to the accompanying resistance-to-temperature graph. If the resistance doesn't decrease as the temperature increases as shown, replace the coolant temperature sensor. Be sure to use Teflon tape or thread sealant on the threads of the new switch to prevent leaks.

Fuel cut rpm (1982 and later models)

Refer to illustrations 4.14a, 4.14b, 4.14c, 4.15a and 4.15b

13 Start the engine and warm it up, then unplug the connector from the throttle position sensor.

14 On 1982 through 1990 models and on 1992 models, bridge terminals E1 and IDL (1982 through 1984 models) or E2 and IDL (1985 and

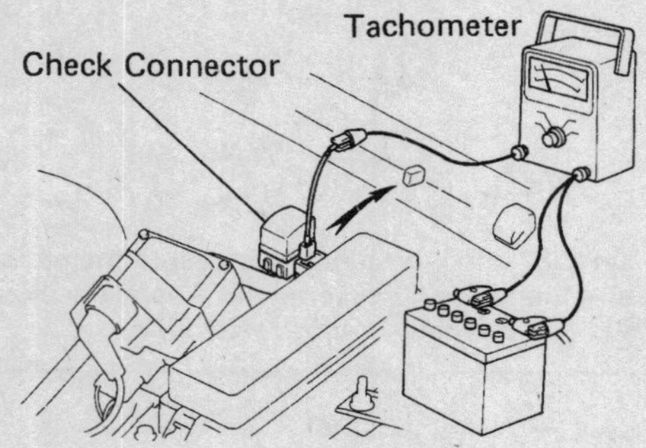

4.15a To check the fuel cut rpm on 1991 models, hook up a tachometer to the check connector

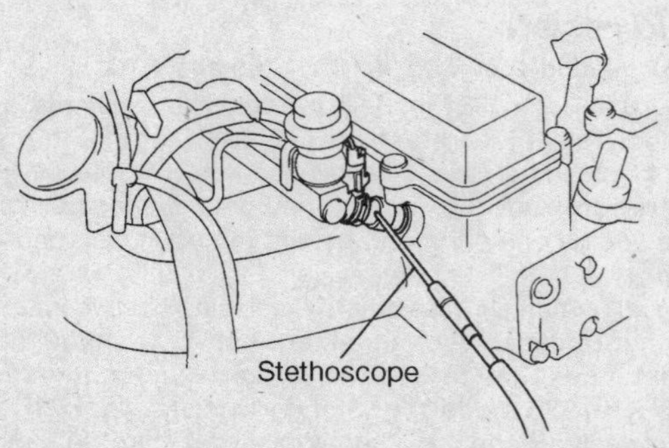

4.15b Using a stethoscope on 1991 models, you should be able to hear the injectors cut out at the specified rpm, then resume operation an instant later

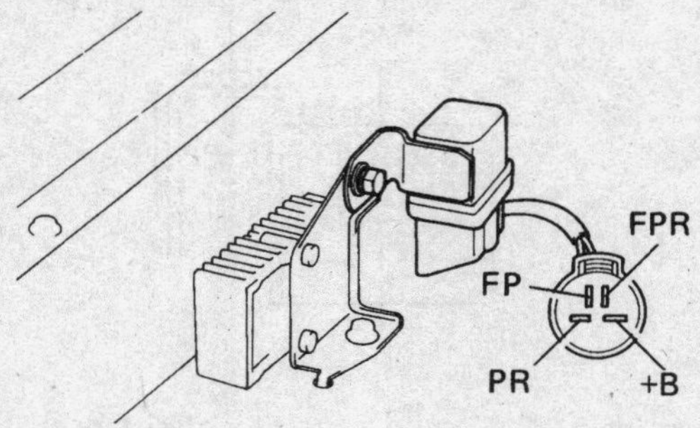

4.16 Terminal guide for the fuel pump relay, located on the right side of the engine compartment, used on 1987 and later models

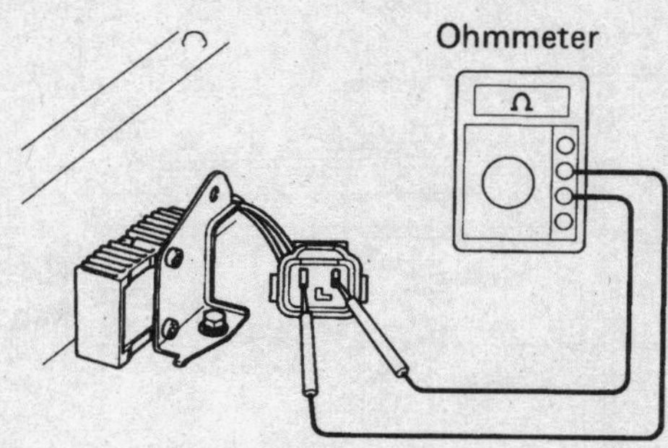

4.19 To check the fuel pump relay resistor, measure the resistance between both terminals - it should be about 0.7 ohms

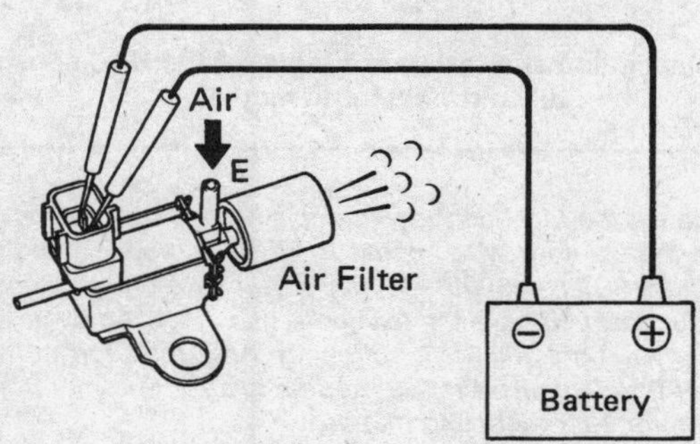

4.20a To check vacuum circuit continuity in the vacuum switching valve (VSV), connect the VSV terminals to the battery terminals, blow into pipe E and verify that air comes out of the air filter, . . .

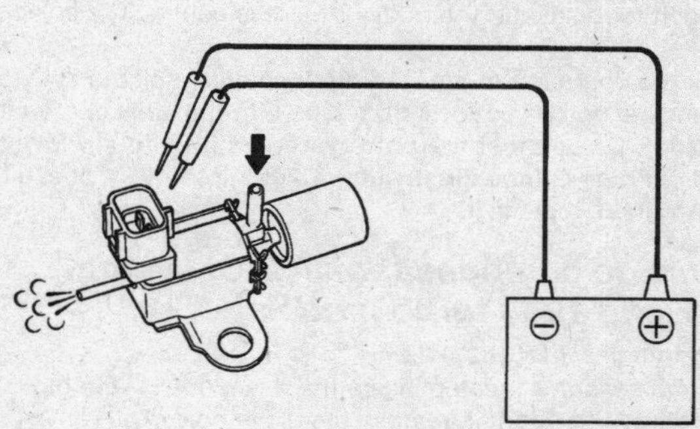

4.20b . . . then disconnect the battery, blow into pipe E and verify that air comes out of pipe G (high temperature line pressure-up check on 1987 and 1988 models)

later models) on the wiring harness side of the electrical connector **(see illustrations)**, gradually increase engine rpm and verify that there's fluctuation between the fuel cut and fuel return points. On 1982 through 1984 models with an automatic transmission, the fuel cut rpm is 1600 rpm and the fuel return rpm is 1400 rpm; on 1982 through 1984 models with a manual transmission, the fuel cut rpm is 2450 rpm and the fuel return rpm is 2250 rpm. On 1985 through 1987 models, the fuel cut rpm is 1800 rpm and the fuel return rpm is 1200 rpm for all models. On 1988 through 1990 non-turbo models, the fuel cut rpm is 1800 rpm and the fuel return rpm is 1200 rpm; on 1988 through 1990 turbo models, the fuel cut rpm is 1600 rpm and the fuel return rpm is 1200 rpm. On all 1992 models, the fuel cut rpm is 1800 rpm and the fuel return rpm is 1200 rpm.

15 To check the fuel cut rpm on 1991 models, insert the test probe of a tachometer into terminal IG of the check connector **(see illustration)**. **Caution:** *Don't allow the tach leads to touch ground - it could damage the igniter and/or the ignition coil. Also, some tachs may not be compatible with this system. Make sure you confirm compatibility before you hook up the tach.* Turn off the air conditioner, increase the engine speed to at least 2500 rpm, then abruptly release the throttle lever. Using a stethoscope, verify that injector operation noise ceases momentarily at 1200 rpm, then resumes **(see illustration)**.

Fuel pump relay and resistor (1987 and later models)

Refer to illustrations 4.16 and 4.19

16 The fuel pump relay **(see illustration)** is located on the right side of the engine compartment.

17 To check relay continuity, verify that there's continuity between terminals +B and FP, and between terminals +B and FPR, but no continuity between terminals +B and PR **(see illustration 4.16).** If the continuity isn't as specified, replace the relay.

18 To check relay operation, apply battery voltage across terminals +B and FPR **(see illustration 4.16)** and verify that there's continuity between terminals +B and PR, but no continuity between terminals +B and FP. If the relay doesn't operate as described, replace it.

19 To check the fuel pump resistor, measure the resistance between both terminals **(see illustration)**. It should be about 0.7 ohms. If it isn't, replace the resistor.

High temperature line pressure-up system (1987 and 1988 models)

Refer to illustrations 4.20a and 4.20b

20 First, check vacuum circuit continuity in the vacuum switching valve (VSV): Connect the VSV terminals to the battery terminals **(see illustration)**, blow into pipe E and verify that air comes out of the air filter. **Caution:** *Don't apply voltage to the VSV any longer than is necessary to perform the check.* Disconnect the battery, blow into pipe E and verify that air comes out of pipe G **(see illustration)**. If the VSV doesn't operate as described, replace it.

21 Using an ohmmeter, verify that there's no continuity between the terminal and the VSV body). If there is continuity, replace the VSV.

22 Finally, measure the resistance between the terminals of the VSV. There should be 30 to 50 ohms resistance. If the resistance isn't within this range, replace the VSV.

High temperature line pressure-up system (1989 turbo models)/fuel pressure control system (1990 and later turbo models)

23 Check the VSV for an open circuit: Verify that there's 30 to 50 ohms resistance between the terminals. If the resistance isn't within this range, replace the VSV.

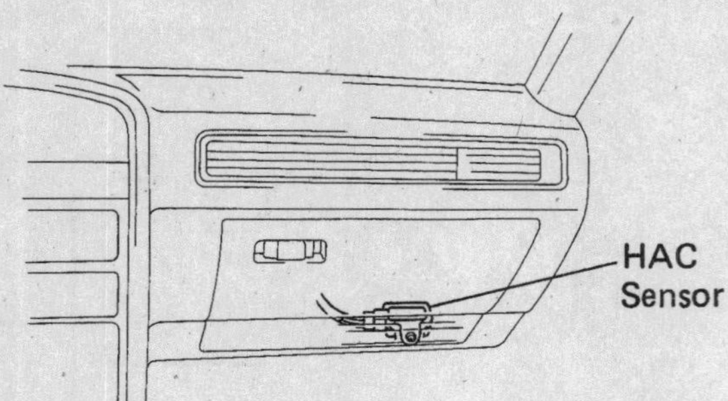

4.26 The HAC sensor on 1987 and 1988 turbo models is located inside the dash, behind the glove box

24 Check the VSV for a short circuit: Verify that there's no continuity between each terminal and the body. If there is continuity, replace the VSV.

25 Check the operation of the VSV: Apply battery voltage across the terminals and verify that air flows from pipe E to the air filter **(see illustration 4.20a).** Disconnect the battery and verify that air flows into pipe E and out pipe G **(see illustration 4.20b).** If the VSV doesn't operate as described, replace it.

High altitude compensation (HAC) system (1987 and 1988 turbo models)

Refer to illustrations 4.26 and 4.27

26 The HAC sensor is located inside the dash, behind the glove box **(see illustration)**. To get at it, remove the glove box.

27 Measure the resistance between each terminal and compare your measurements to the accompanying table **(see illustration)**. If the indicated resistance isn't as specified, replace the HAC sensor.

EGR gas temperature sensor (1988 and later California models only)

28 Remove the EGR gas temperature sensor **(see illustration 4.9b)** and immerse the sensor tip in a pot of hot water, along with a cooking thermometer. Measure the resistance between the terminals at 112-degrees F. It should be 69 to 89 k-ohms. If the resistance isn't as specified, replace the sensor. Be sure to coat the threads with anti-seize compound.

Oxygen sensor

Refer to illustrations 4.29a, 4.29b, 4.30a, 4.30b and 4.34

Note: *The following procedure won't work on 1979 through 1981 models, because the ECU on these models has no self-diagnosis capabilities, so there's no way to access the ECU without Toyota's special EFI checker (SST No. 09991-00100). If you have one of these early Supras, we suggest you have the oxygen sensor checked by an authorized dealer if you think it's malfunctioning. And don't forget that replacement of the sensor on these models is a routine maintenance item (see Chapter 1 for more information).*

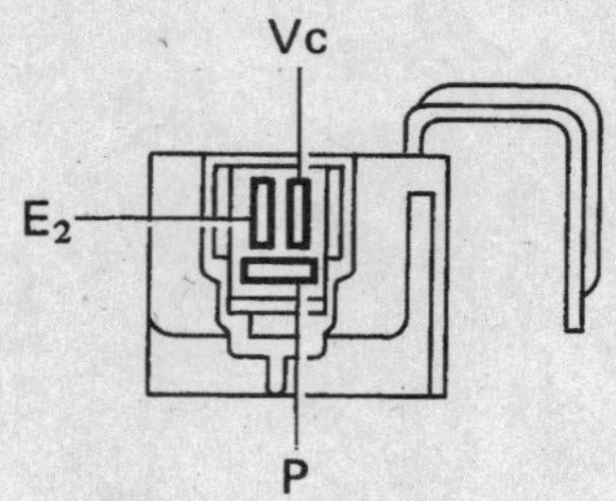

Terminals	Resistance
Vc – P	700 – 860 Ω
Vc – E_2	2.2 – 3.3 kΩ
P – E_2	2.9 – 4.2 kΩ

4.27 Terminal guide and resistance table for the HAC sensor on 1987 and 1988 turbo models

29 The oxygen sensor is located in the exhaust manifold **(see illustrations)**.

30 To check the oxygen sensor:

a) Warm up the engine to its normal operating temperature.
b) Insert the probes of a voltmeter into the terminal of the engine check connector on 1982 through 1986 models **(see illustration)**, or the positive probe into terminal VF (all 1987, some 1988 and all 1992 models) or VF1 (some 1988 and all 1989 through 1991 models), and the negative probe into terminal E1 (all 1987 and later models) of the check connector **(see illustration)**.
c) Warm up the oxygen sensor with the engine operating at 2500 rpm for about 90 seconds.
d) Bridge terminals T (all 1982 through 1987, some 1988 and all 1992 models), or TE1 (some 1988 and all 1989 through 1991 models), and E1 of the check connector **(see illustration 3.3c)**.
e) Note the number of times the voltmeter needle deflects in 10 seconds. If the needle deflects eight times or more, the oxygen sen-

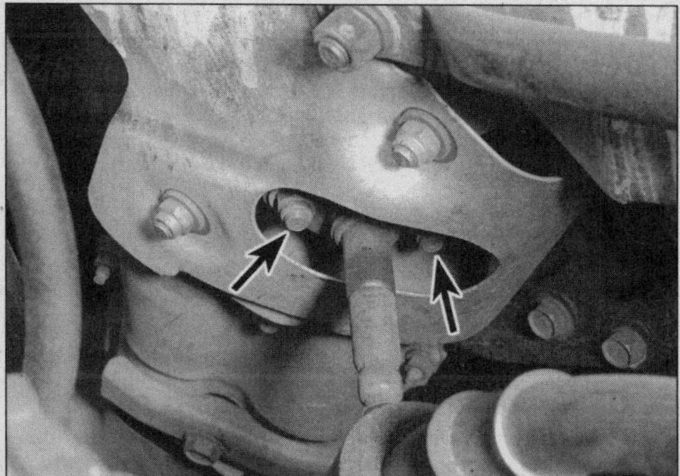

4.29a Typical oxygen sensor installation on a 1982 through 1986 model

4.29b Typical oxygen sensor installation on a 1987 through 1992 turbo model

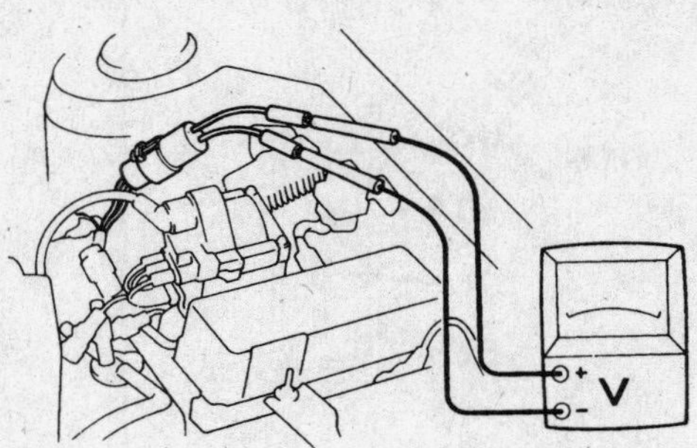

4.30a If you don't have Toyota's special adapter No. 09842-14010 shown here, alligator clips can be used to hook up a voltmeter to the check connector on 1982 through 1986 models (just be careful not to bridge the terminals together)

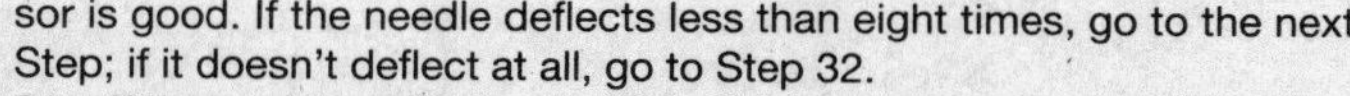

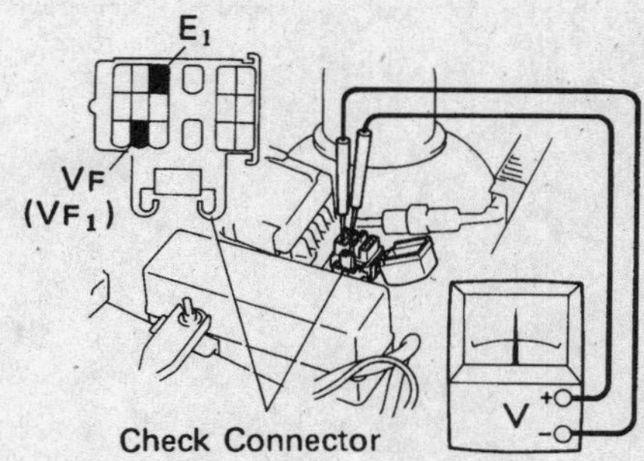

4.30b Terminal guide for the check connector used on all 1987 through 1992 models

sor is good. If the needle deflects less than eight times, go to the next Step; if it doesn't deflect at all, go to Step 32.

31 If the needle deflects less than eight times, try the above test one more time to make sure.

a) If the needle still deflects less than eight times, remove the jumper from terminals T or TE1 and E1 of the check connector and, with the engine still running at 2500 rpm, measure the voltage between terminals VF or VF1 and E1.

b) If the indicated voltage is more than zero volts, replace the oxygen sensor (see below).

c) If the indicated voltage is zero volts, output the stored trouble code(s) (see Section 3). If a Code 21 (oxygen sensor) is present, detach the PCV hose and measure the voltage between terminals VF or VF1 and E1 again. If the voltage is still zero, replace the oxygen sensor; if the voltage is more than zero, an excessively rich condition is being caused by the PCV system. Remove and clean the PCV components (see Section 5).

32 If the needle didn't deflect at all in Step 30, output the trouble code(s) (see Section 3). If you get a Code 21 (oxygen sensor) and either a Code 25 (lean air-fuel ratio) or Code 26 (rich air-fuel ratio), remove the jumper wire from terminals T or TE1 and E1 of the check connector and, with the engine still running at 2500 rpm, measure the voltage between terminals VF or VF1 and E1.

a) If you get five volts, disconnect the coolant temperature sensor connector and connect a resistor with 4 to 8 k-ohms resistance, or try another coolant temperature sensor (make sure it's the right unit for the model you're testing). Bridge terminals T or TE1 and E1 of the check connector, warm up the oxygen sensor with the engine at 2500 rpm for about 90 seconds and measure the voltage between terminals VF or VF1 and E1 while maintaining the engine rpm at 2500.

c) If you get zero volts, replace the oxygen sensor and retest.

d) If you get five volts, there's an excessively lean condition being caused by an air leak somewhere. Check the entire air intake system.

33 If you have to replace the oxygen sensor, always retest and make sure the sensor functions normally. If it still doesn't produce eight or more needle deflections, replace the ECU.

34 Finally, on 1988 through 1991 turbo models only, measure the resistance between terminals 2 and 3 of the oxygen sensor connector **(see illustration)**. It should be between 3.0 and 3.6 ohms. If it isn't, replace the oxygen sensor.

35 To replace the oxygen sensor, trace the electrical lead back to the connector and unplug it, remove the nuts or bolts and remove the sensor. Be sure to coat the threads of the new sensor with anti-seize compound, tighten it securely and reattach the connector.

Sub-oxygen sensor (1989 and later California non-turbo models only)

Refer to illustration 4.37

36 Check the sub-oxygen sensor only when Code No. 27 is displayed. Cancel the code (see Section 3), warm up the engine until it reaches its normal operating temperature and drive the vehicle as follows: On models with a manual transmission, drive for five minutes or more at less than 50 mph in fourth or fifth gear; on models with an automatic transmission, drive for five minutes or more at less than 50 mph in the D range. While doing so, press fully on the accelerator pedal for two seconds or more. Stop the vehicle and turn the ignition switch to Off. Repeat this test one more time. If Code 27 appears again, check the sub-oxygen sensor circuit (see the Wiring Diagrams at the end of Chapter 12). If the circuit appears to be normal, replace the sub-oxygen sensor.

37 Measure the resistance of terminals +B and HT of the sub-oxygen sensor heater **(see illustration)**. It should be about 5.1 to 6.3 ohms. If it isn't, replace the sub-oxygen sensor heater.

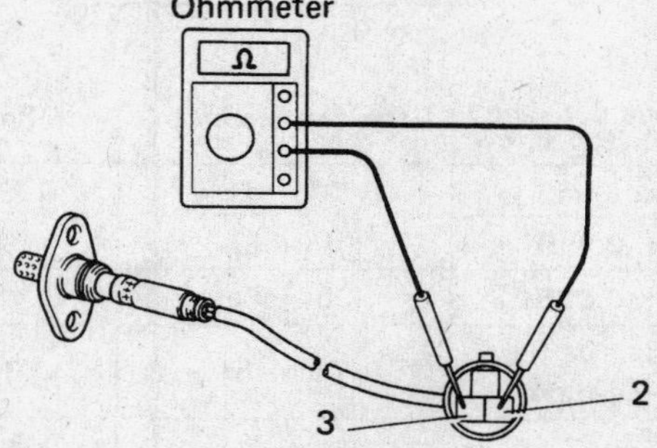

4.34 Terminal guide for checking the heater resistance of the oxygen sensor on 1988 through 1992 turbo models

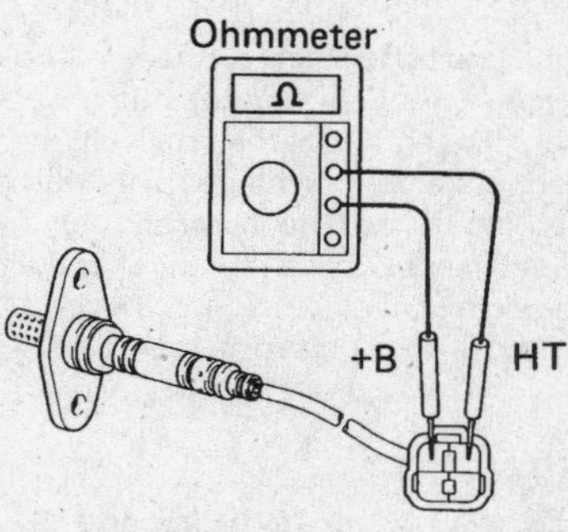

4.37 On 1989 and later California non-turbo models, measure the resistance of terminals +B and HT of the sub-oxygen sensor heater - it should be about 5.1 to 6.3 ohms

4.38a To release the throttle position sensor connector, pry the spring lock loose and pull (1982 model shown)

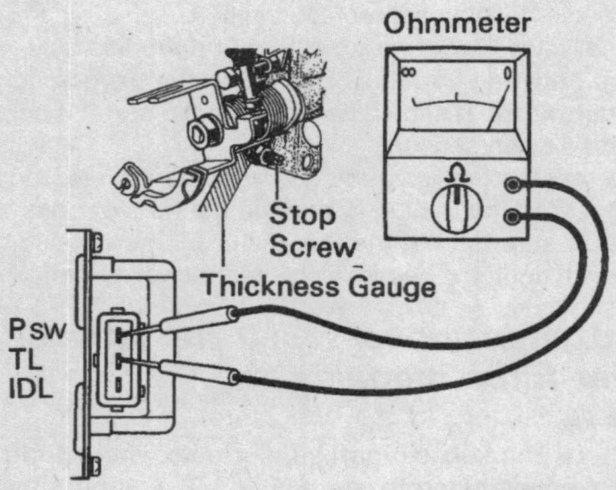

Clearance between lever and stop screw		Continuity of terminal		
		IDL – TL	PSW – TL	IDL – PSW
0.44 mm	(0.0173 in.)	Continuity	No continuity	No continuity
0.66 mm	(0.0260 in.)	No continuity	No continuity	No continuity
Throttle valve fully opened position		No continuity	Continuity	No continuity

4.39a Terminal guide and continuity table for checking the throttle position sensor on 1979 through 1981 models

Airflow meter

Refer to Chapter 4 for information on the airflow meter.

Throttle position sensor

On-vehicle check

Refer to illustrations 4.38a, 4.38b, 4.39a through 4.39d

38 Unplug the throttle position sensor connector **(see illustrations)**.

39 Insert a feeler gauge between the throttle stop screw and the stop lever. Using an ohmmeter, check the continuity between the indicated terminals and compare your measurements with the values provided in the accompanying tables **(see illustrations)**.

40 If the indicated resistance values are out of specification, try adjusting the sensor (see below), then retest it. If they're still out of specification, replace the throttle position sensor (see below).

Adjustment

Refer to illustration 4.43

Note: *No adjustment is provided for 1979 through 1981 models.*

41 Loosen the two sensor retaining screws at the sensor and insert a feeler gauge (0.0295-inch on 1982 through 1984 models, 0.0197-inch on 1985 and 1986 models, 0.0228-inch on 1987 and later non-turbo models, 0.0276-inch on 1987 and later turbo models) between the

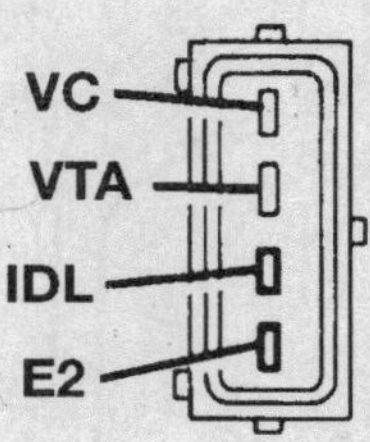

4.38b Typical late-model throttle position sensor connector (1992 turbo model shown)

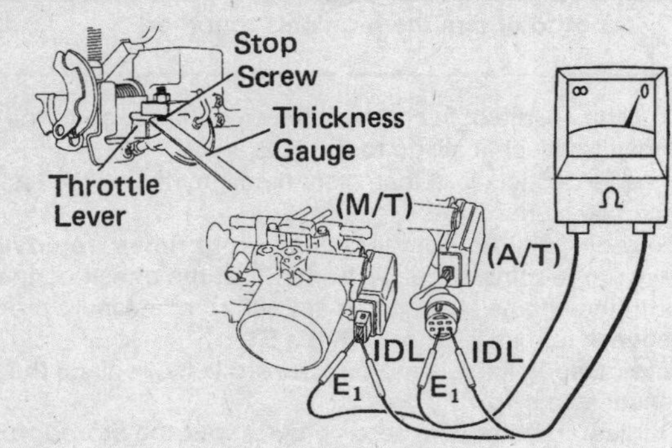

Clearance between lever and stop screw		Continuity of terminal		
		IDL – E_1	Psw – E_1	IDL – Psw
0.60 mm	(0.0236 in.)	Continuity	No continuity	No continuity
0.95 mm	(0.0374 in.)	No continuity	No continuity	No continuity
Throttle valve fully opened position		No continuity	Continuity	No continuity

4.39b Terminal guide and continuity table for checking the throttle position sensor on 1982 through 1984 models

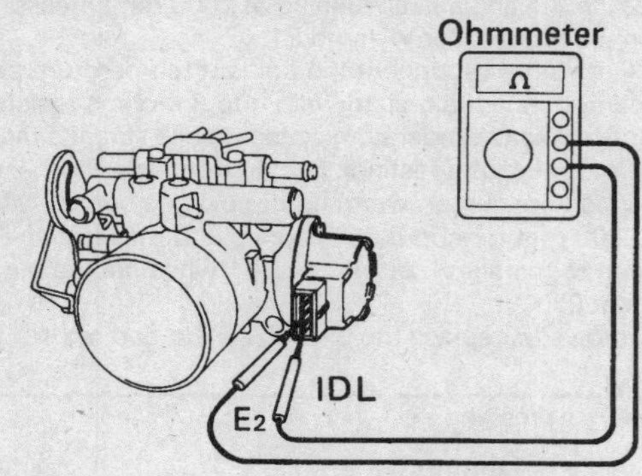

Clearance between lever and stop screw	Between terminals	Resistance
0 mm (0 in.)	VTA – E2	0.2 – 0.8 kΩ
0.50 mm (0.0197 in.)	IDL – E2	0 – 100 Ω
0.90 mm (0.0354 in.)	IDL – E2	Infinity
Throttle valve fully opened position	VTA – E2	3.3 – 10 kΩ
–	Vc – E2	3 – 7 kΩ

4.39c Terminal guide and resistance table for checking the throttle position sensor on 1985 and 1986 models

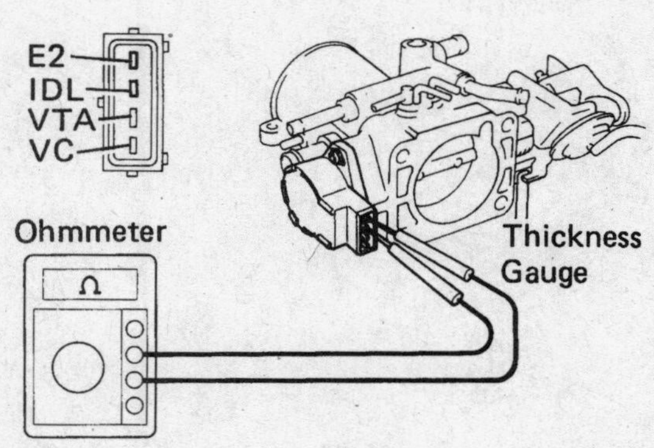

Clearance between lever and stop screw		Between terminals	Resistance
7M-GE	7M-GTE		
0 mm (0 in.)		VTA – E_2	0.3 – 6.3 kΩ (1987 - 1988) 0.2 – 1.2 kΩ (1989 on)
0.4 mm (0.0157 in.)	0.5 mm (0.0197 in.)	IDL – E_2	Less than 2.3 kΩ
0.75 mm (0.0295 in.)	0.9 mm (0.0354 in.)	IDL – E_2	∞
Throttle valve fully opened position		VTA – E_2	3.5 – 10.3 kΩ
–		Vc – E_2	4.25 – 8.25 kΩ

4.39d Terminal guide for checking throttle position sensor on 1987 and later models (non-turbo model shown, turbo models similar)

throttle lever stop screw and lever, and connect the ohmmeter to terminals IDL and E1 (1982 through 1984 models), IDL and E2 (1985 and later models) (see terminal guides in previous illustrations).

42 Gradually turn the sensor counterclockwise (1982 through 1984 models) or clockwise (1985 and later models) until the ohmmeter needle deflects, then tighten the sensor attaching screws.

43 Using a feeler gauge of the specified thickness, recheck the continuity between terminals IDL and E1, or IDL and E2 **(see illustration).** If it's incorrect, readjust the throttle position sensor until the continuity at each specified thickness matches that of the accompanying tables.

Replacement

44 Unplug the electrical connector.
45 Remove the retaining screws and remove the sensor.
46 Install the new sensor.
47 Adjust the sensor (see above).

Cam position sensor (turbo models)

See Chapter 5 for information on the cam position sensor.

Electronic Control Unit (ECU)

Note: *Because of the special tools necessary to check the ECU and the possibility of damage to the internal circuitry of the ECU if it is checked improperly, inspection is beyond the scope of the home mechanic. However, should a dealer service department determine that the ECU is faulty, you can replace it yourself.*

48 Detach the cable from the negative terminal of the battery.
49 Remove the glove box.
50 Remove the ECU mounting bracket bolts.
51 Carefully pull the ECU to the rear, unplug the electrical connectors and remove the ECU.
52 Installation is the reverse of removal.

Clearance between lever and stop screw	Continuity (IDL – E_1)
0.60 mm (0.0236 in.)	Continuity
0.95 mm (0.0374 in.)	No continuity

1982 through 1984 models

Clearance between lever and stop screw	Continuity (IDL – E_2)
0.50 mm (0.0197 in.)	Continuity
0.90 mm (0.0354 in.)	No continuity

1985 and 1986 models

Clearance between lever and stop screw		Continuity (IDL – E_2)
7M-GE	7M-GTE	
0.40 mm (0.0157 in.)	0.50 mm (0.0197 in.)	Continuity
0.75 mm (0.0295 in.)	0.90 mm (0.0354 in.)	No continuity

1987 and later models

4.43 Feeler gauge thickness and continuity table for adjusting the throttle position sensor

5 Positive Crankcase Ventilation (PCV) system

General description

Refer to illustration 5.1

1 The Positive Crankcase Ventilation (PCV) system **(see illustration)** is designed to reduce hydrocarbon emissions by routing blow-by

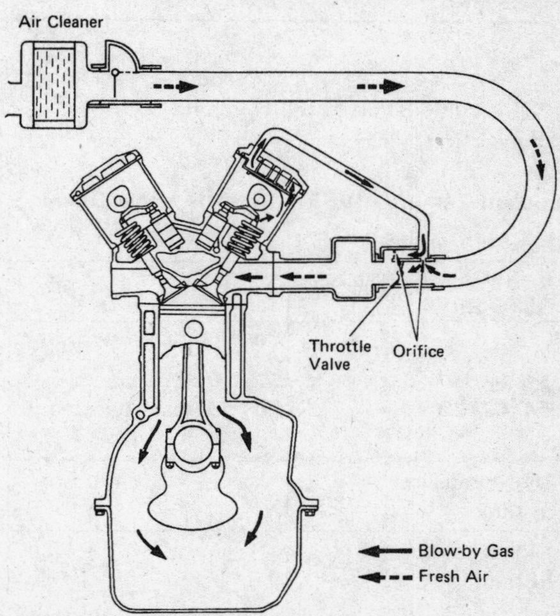

5.1 Typical PCV system (1983 model shown, others similar)

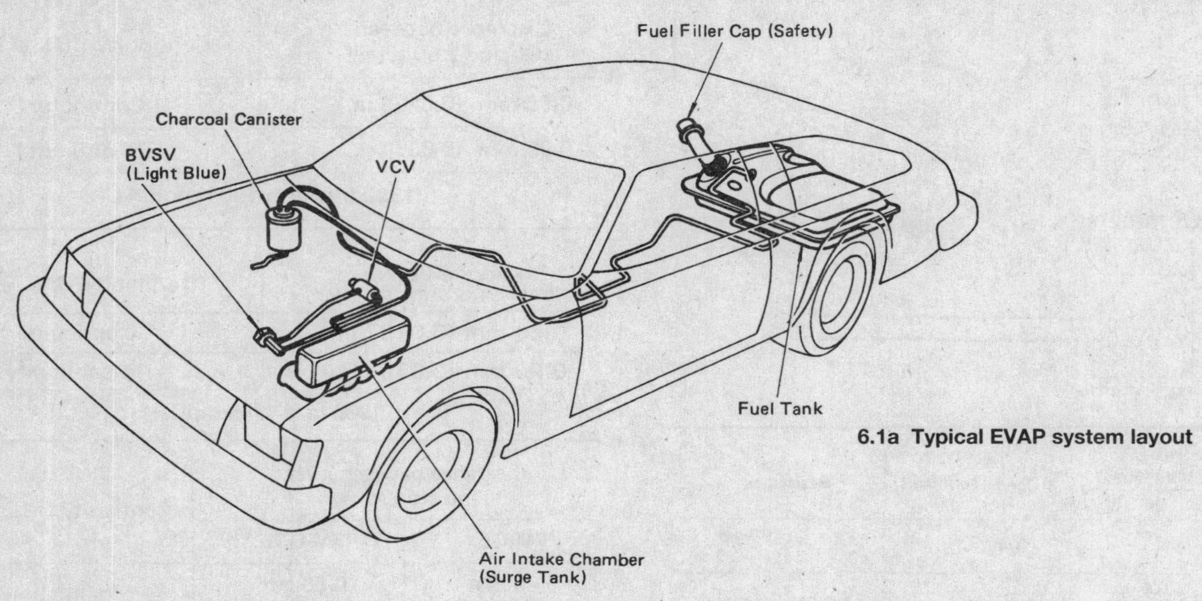

6.1a Typical EVAP system layout

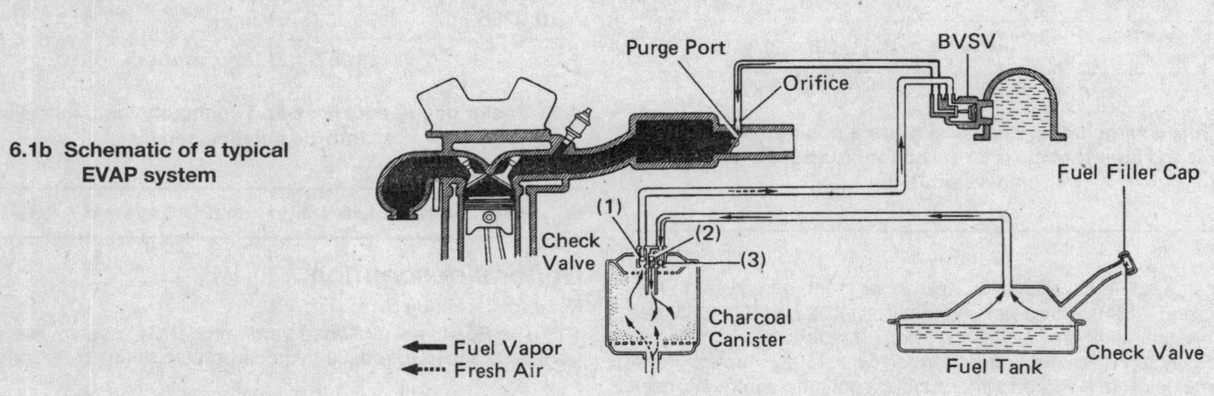

6.1b Schematic of a typical EVAP system

To reduce HC emission, evaporated fuel from the fuel tank is routed through the charcoal canister to the intake manifold for combustion in the cylinders

Coolant Temp.	BVSV	Throttle Valve Opening	Canister Check Valve			Check Valve in Cap	Evaporated Fuel (HC)
			(1)	(2)	(3)		
Below 35°C(95°F)	CLOSED	—	—	—	—	—	HC from tank is absorbed in the canister.
Above 54°C(129°F)	OPEN	Positioned below purge port	CLOSED	—	—	—	
		Positioned above purge port	OPEN	—	—	—	HC from canister is led into air intake chamber.
High pressure in tank	—	—	—	OPEN	CLOSED	CLOSED	HC from tank is absorbed in the canister.
High vacuum in tank	—	—	—	CLOSED	OPEN	OPEN	(Air is led into the fuel tank.)

6.3 Summary of system operation on all EVAP systems

6.5 The bi-metallic vacuum switching valve (BVSV) is located on the thermostat housing (follow the vacuum hose to make sure you are checking the proper valve or check the VECI label if you're still not sure)

gases (fuel/air mixture that escapes from the combustion chamber past the piston rings into the crankcase) and oil vapor from the crankcase to the intake manifold and combustion chamber, where they are burned during engine operation.

2 The system consists of rubber hoses and small, fixed orifices.

Checking and component replacement

3 Checking and cleaning the PCV system components is a routine maintenance procedure. Refer to Chapter 1 for details. Replacement of components is a very simple operation.

6 Fuel evaporative emission control (EVAP) system

General description

Refer to illustrations 6.1a, 6.1b and 6.3

1 The EVAP system **(see illustrations)** is designed to trap and store fuel that evaporates from the fuel tank, which would normally enter the atmosphere and contribute to hydrocarbon emissions.

2 The system consists of a charcoal filled canister, a bi-metallic vacuum switching valve (BVSV), check valves and connecting lines and hoses.

3 When the engine is off and a high pressure condition begins to build in the fuel tank (caused by fuel evaporation), the charcoal in the canister absorbs the fuel vapor. When the engine is started (cold), the charcoal continues to absorb and store fuel vapor. As the engine coolant warms up, the stored fuel vapors are routed to the intake manifold and combustion chambers where they are burned during normal engine operation. The check valve, which is mounted in the fuel tank filler cap, is calibrated to open when fuel tank vacuum reaches a certain level. This allows outside air to enter the fuel tank and relieve the vacuum **(see illustration)**.

Check

Canister, lines, hoses, fuel filler cap and check valve

4 Checking the canister, lines, hoses and fuel filler cap is a routine maintenance procedure. Refer to Chapter 1 for details.

BVSV

Refer to illustration 6.5

5 Locate the EVAP system bi-metallic vacuum switching valve on the thermostat housing **(see illustration)**. Follow the line from the canister to make sure you are checking the correct valve. Double-check by referring to the Vehicle Emission Control Information (VECI) label on the underside of the hood.

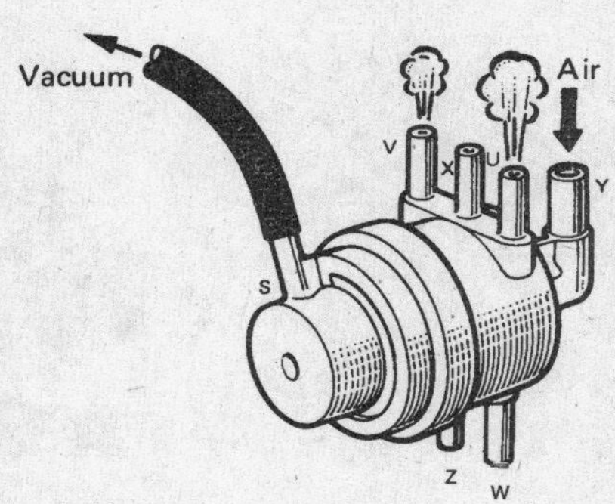

6.10 To check the VCV (1979 and 1980 models only), attach a section of vacuum hose to port S and apply a vacuum to the hose, then blow through port Y - the valve should be open (blowing through port Y should cause air to flow out ports V and U)

6 Disconnect the hoses from the BVSV and attach a separate section of vacuum hose to the upper port. With the engine cold, blow through the hose. No air should pass through the valve.

7 Start the engine and allow the coolant to reach normal operating temperature. Blow through the valve again. The valve should now be open and allow air to pass through. When the check is complete, be sure to reconnect the hoses.

8 If the BVSV does not check out as described, replace it with a new one.

VCV (1979 and 1980 models only)

Refer to illustration 6.10

9 Mark the positions of the hoses to simplify installation, then detach them from the ports.

10 Attach a separate section of vacuum hose to the port labeled S and apply a vacuum to the hose with a hand held vacuum pump **(see illustration)**. Blow through port Y - the valve should be open; blowing through port Y should cause air to flow out ports V and U.

11 Release the vacuum acting on port S and repeat the test. The valve should now be closed; blowing through port Y should produce no air flow through the other ports. If the VCV is faulty, replace it with a new one. Be sure to hook up the hoses correctly.

Component replacement

12 Replacement and maintenance of the charcoal canister, fuel filler cap gasket and lines are covered in Chapter 1.

13 If a new BVSV is required, remove the hoses, unscrew the old valve and install the new one in its place. Some of the coolant must be drained before removing the BVSV (see Chapter 1 for cooling system draining). Apply Teflon tape or thread sealant to the valve before installing it and be sure to hook up the hoses correctly.

14 To replace the VCV, disconnect the vacuum hoses from the faulty part and reconnect them to the new one. Remove and install one hose at a time to avoid mixing them up.

7 Vacuum limiter system (1979 and 1980 models)

General description

1 The vacuum limiter system allows outside (filtered) air to enter the air intake chamber during sudden deceleration (when the throttle valve is released and snaps shut). The result is a reduction in the emission levels of hydrocarbons (HC) and carbon monoxide (CO).

Check

Refer to illustrations 7.4 and 7.5

2 Check the system hoses for cracks, kinks, broken sections and proper connection.

3 Disconnect the vacuum limiter hose from the air connector, plug

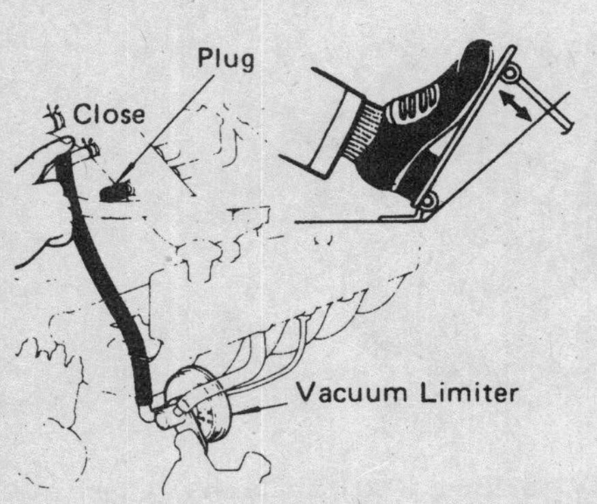

7.4 **To check the vacuum limiter on 1979 and 1980 models, place your finger over the end of the vacuum hose, then momentarily open and close the throttle - you should feel a vacuum at the hose**

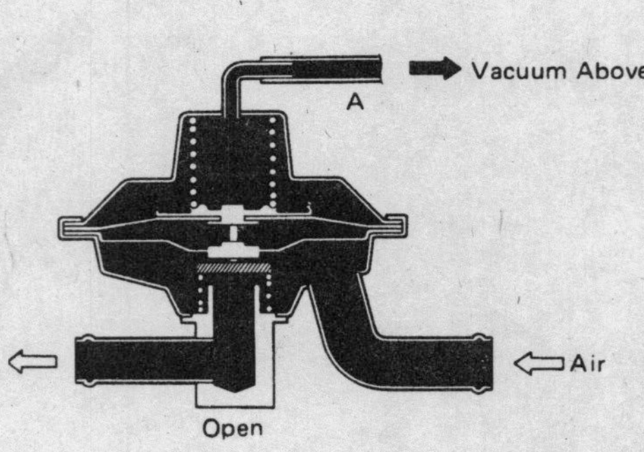

7.5 **Apply vacuum to port A with a hand-held vacuum pump and blow into one of the other ports - the limiter should be open (air should pass through it)**

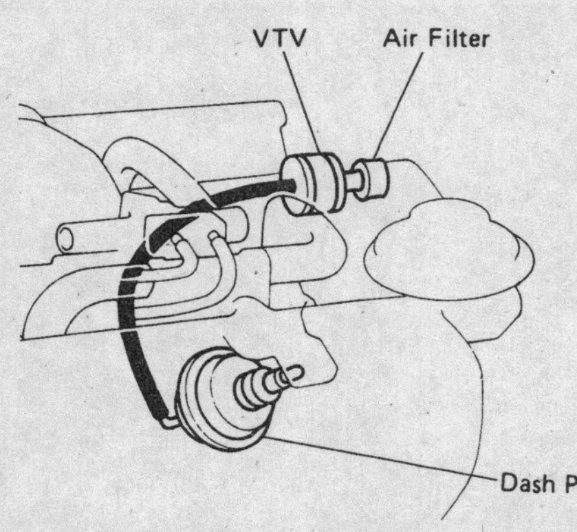

8.1a **Typical dashpot (DP) system (1982 through 1986 models)**

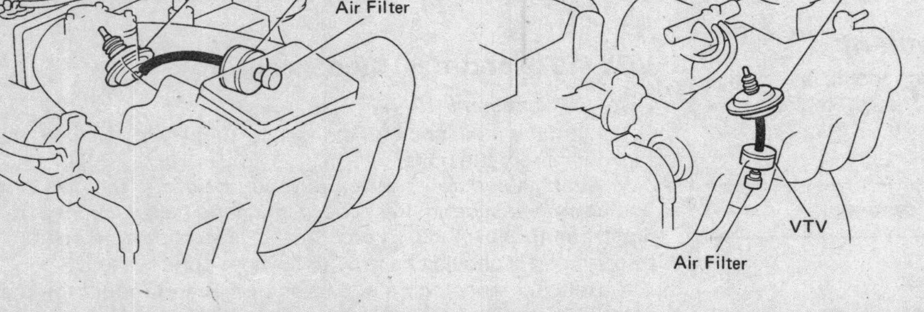
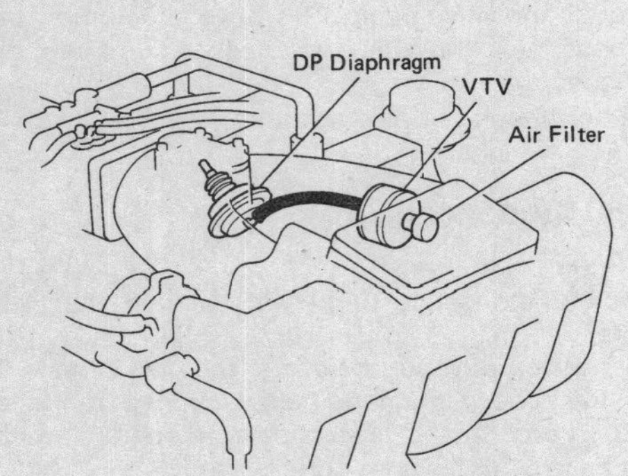

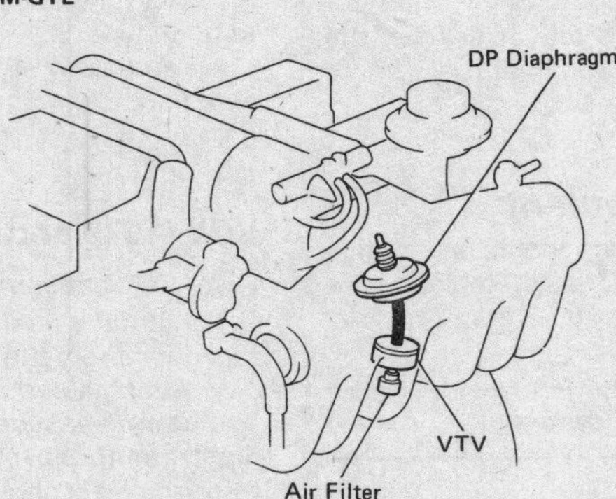

8.1b **Typical dashpot (DP) systems on 1987 through 1990 models (non-turbo model on left, turbo model on right)**

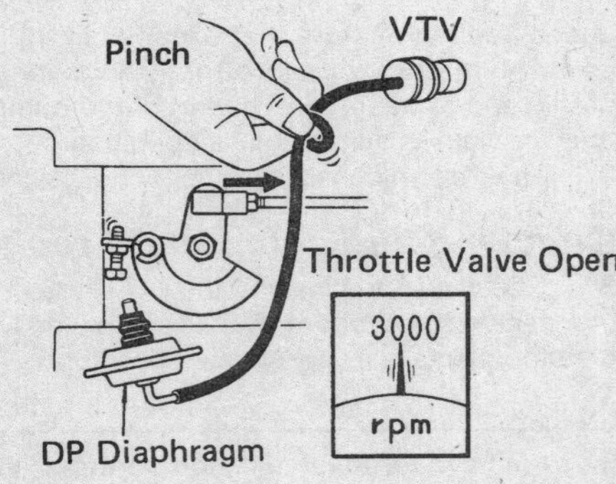

8.3a **With the engine speed at 3000 rpm, pinch the vacuum hose between the dashpot and the VTV, release the throttle and verify that the engine idle speed is 2000 rpm**

the hose fitting, then start the engine.

4 Place your finger over the end of the hose, then momentarily open and close the throttle **(see illustration)**. You should feel a vacuum at the hose. If not, remove the vacuum limiter and check it further before replacing it with a new one.

5 With the vacuum limiter removed from the vehicle, apply a vacuum to port A with a hand-held vacuum pump. Blow into one of the other ports. The limiter should be open; air should pass through it **(see illustration)**.

6 Release the vacuum and repeat the check. The limiter should now be closed; no air should pass through it. If the limiter fails this check, replace it with a new one.

Component replacement

7 Mark the hoses and disconnect them from the limiter ports. Remove the mounting bolt and detach the limiter. Attach the new valve to the bracket and tighten the mounting bolt, then connect the hoses. If the hoses are deteriorated or hardened, replace them with new ones.

8 Dashpot (DP) system (1982 through 1990 models)

General description

Refer to illustrations 8.1a and 8.1b

1 The dashpot (DP) system **(see illustrations)** is designed to ensure that the air/fuel mixture is completely burned during deceleration. To do this, it opens the throttle valve slightly more than when at idle position, then allows it to close slowly.

Check

Refer to illustrations 8.3a, 8.3b, 8.3c and 8.6

2 To check the system, connect a tachometer and run the engine until normal operating temperature is reached.

3 Increase the engine speed to 3000 rpm, then pinch the vacuum hose between the vacuum transmitting valve (VTV) and the dashpot **(see illustration)**. Release the throttle valve and check that the dashpot is set. The idle speed should now be 2000 rpm. To change the speed, turn the dashpot adjusting screw as necessary **(see illustrations)**.

4 With the dashpot speed set as described above, release the hose and check that the engine speed drops to normal idle speed within approximately one second.

5 If the idle speed does not drop, remove the filter from the valve by pulling it from the rubber housing. Clean the filter by blowing compressed air through it. Replace the filter if it is too contaminated to clean properly or is damaged.

6 Check the operation of the VTV by blowing through it from the B (black) side. Air should pass through the valve freely. Reverse the direction and check that when blowing from the A (white) side of the valve considerable resistance is felt **(see illustration)**. If the VTV is faulty it must be replaced.

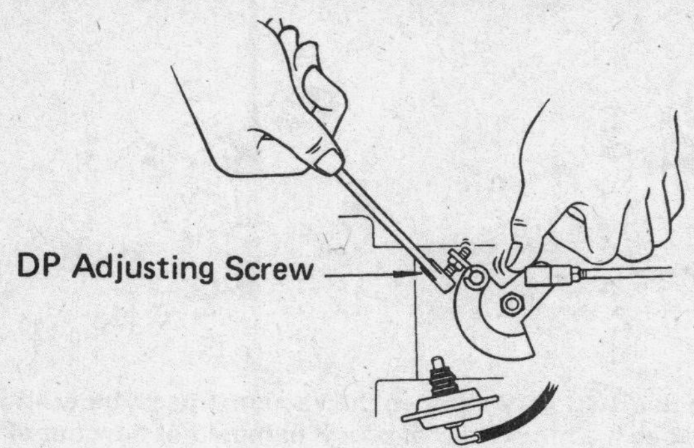

8.3b If the engine idle speed isn't correct, turn the dashpot adjusting screw to change it (1982 through 1986 models)

8.6 To check the VTV, verify that air flows without resistance from B to A, but with difficulty from A to B

Component replacement

7 Replacement of this component is a simple matter of removing the faulty valve and installing a new one. Be sure to mark the hoses before disconnecting them to ensure that they are correctly connected to the new component.

9 Spark control (SC) system (1979 through 1981 models)

General description

Refer to illustration 9.1

1 The spark control (SC) system **(see illustration)** is designed to reduce emission of hydrocarbons and oxides of nitrogen (NOX) emissions by advancing the ignition timing only when the engine is cold.

2 The system includes a distributor mounted vacuum unit, a BVSV, a VCV (except 1980 models), a check valve (or valves) and various hoses and fittings.

3 Depending on engine coolant temperature, altitude and the position of the throttle, vacuum is applied to either one or both of the diaphragms in the distributor vacuum unit and the ignition timing is changed to reduce emissions and improve cold engine driveability.

Check

Refer to illustration 9.4

4 The spark control system should be checked as follows:

a) The coolant temperature must be below 122-degrees F.
b) Hook up a vacuum gauge to the vacuum hose attached to the distributor sub-diaphragm with a T-fitting **(see illustration)**. On 1979 models, remove the hose from the sub-diaphragm and attach the vacuum gauge to the hose.
c) Start the engine and run it at idle.
d) The gauge should indicate a relatively high vacuum. If it doesn't,

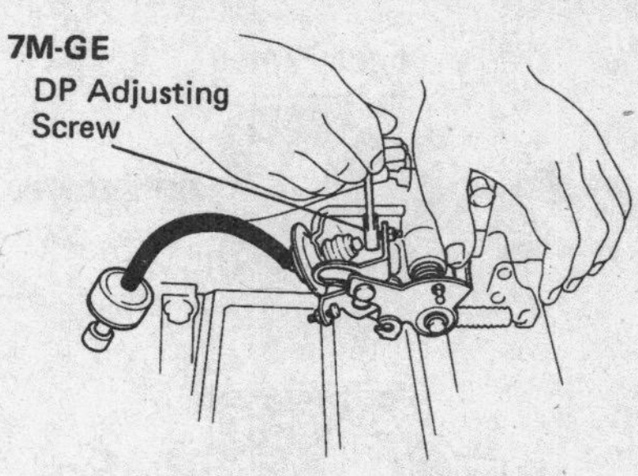

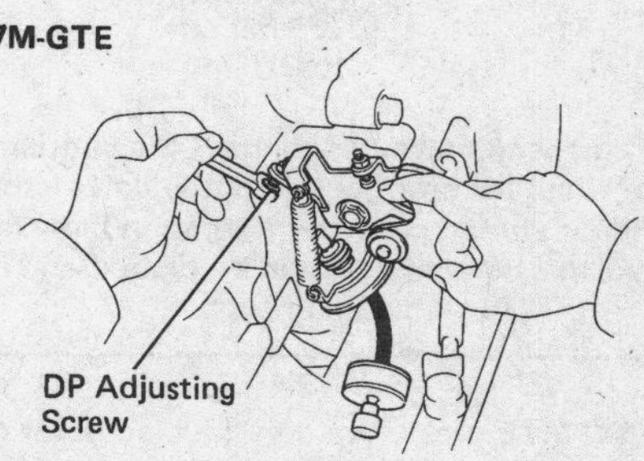

8.3c Dashpot adjusting screw location on 1987 through 1990 models (non-turbo model, above; turbo model, below)

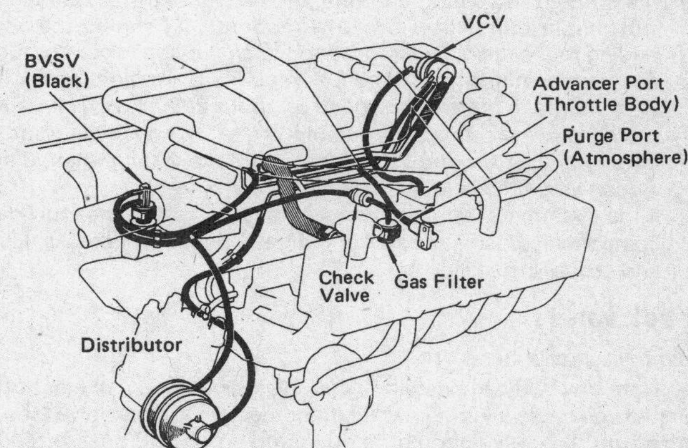

9.1 The spark control (SC) system is designed to reduce emission of hydrocarbons and oxides of nitrogen (NOX) emissions by advancing the ignition timing only when the engine is cold (1979 model shown)

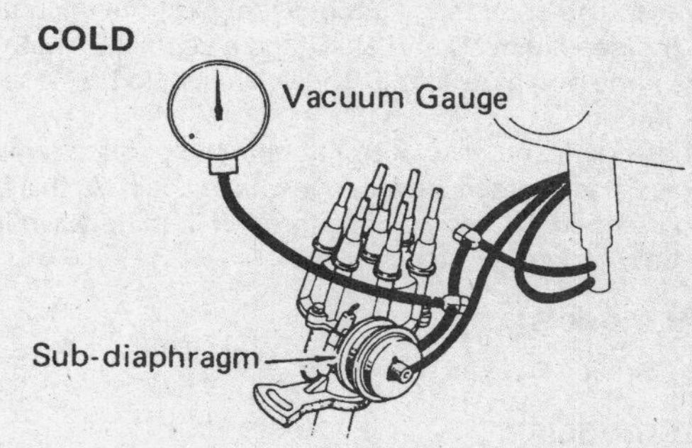

9.4 Hook up a vacuum gauge to the vacuum hose attached to the distributor sub-diaphragm with a T-fitting (on 1979 models, remove the hose from the sub-diaphragm and attach the vacuum gauge to the hose), start the engine and run it at idle - the gauge should indicate a relatively high vacuum

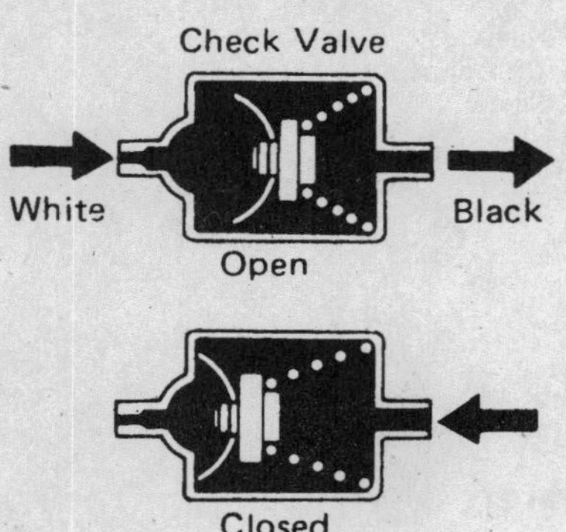

9.5 To test a check valve, disconnect the vacuum hoses and blow into the white (or orange) end of the valve - the valve should be open and air should pass through; then blow into the black end of the valve - the valve should be closed and no air should pass through

check the BVSV, the check valve and the distributor diaphragm (see below).

e) Allow the engine to reach normal operating temperature, then check the gauge again. It should indicate zero or very low vacuum at idle. If it doesn't, check the BVSV and the vacuum hoses.

f) Disconnect the vacuum gauge and reconnect the hose to the sub-diaphragm. **Note:** *On 1979 models, disconnect the hose leading to the main diaphragm and attach it to the vacuum gauge. The gauge should indicate a low vacuum. If it's high, check the VCV. Increase the engine speed to about 2000 rpm. The gauge should now indicate a high vacuum. If it's low, check the distributor diaphragm and the VCV. Disconnect the vacuum gauge and reconnect the hose to the main diaphragm.*

g) If the system doesn't perform as it should, check the individual components. Also, check all of the rubber hoses for cracks, kinks and proper installation.

Check valves

Refer to illustration 9.5

5 Note how they are installed, then disconnect the vacuum hoses from the valve. Blow into the white (or orange) end of the valve **(see illustration)**; the valve should be open and air should pass through. Next, blow into the black end of the valve; the valve should be closed and no air should pass through. If the valve is defective, replace it with a new one. Be sure to reconnect the vacuum hoses to the correct ports.

BVSV

6 With the engine completely cool, disconnect the vacuum hoses from the BVSV **(see illustration 9.1)**. Attach a separate length of hose to one of the ports and blow into it. The valve should be closed; no air should pass through it.

7 Start the engine and allow it to run until the coolant temperature reaches 147-degrees F, then blow into the hose again. At this point the valve should be open; air should pass through it. If the valve is defective, it must be replaced with a new one.

VCV (1979 models)

8 Refer to Section 6.

VCV (1981 models)

Refer to illustrations 9.9 and 9.11

9 Mark the vacuum hoses to simplify installation, then detach them from the VCV. Blow into port S and see if air flows out of port Z. It must not flow out of port Y **(see illustration)**.

10 Blow into port Y and make sure air does not flow out of the other ports.

9.9 To check a 1981 VCV, remove the vacuum hoses, blow into port S and see if air flows out of port Z (it must not flow out of port Y); then blow into port Y and make sure air does not flow out of the other ports

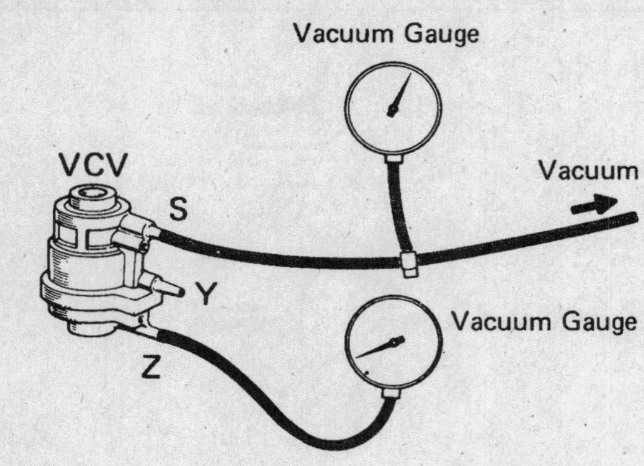

9.11 Checking the VCV with vacuum gauges

11 If the special tools required are available, perform the following checks. Connect a vacuum gauge to port Z and a vacuum gauge and pump to port S **(see illustration)**. Apply a 16-in Hg vacuum to port S. The gauge connected to port Z should indicate 9.65 to 12.60-in Hg.

12 Apply an 18-in Hg to port S. The gauge connected to port Z should indicate 2 to 4.5-in Hg. If the valve does not check out as described, replace it with a new one.

Distributor vacuum unit

See Chapter 5.

Component replacement

BVSV

13 The BVSV is threaded into a cooling system passage and its removal requires partial draining of the cooling system (see Chapter 1). Mark the hoses, to simplify installation, before disconnecting them. Apply thread sealant to the new valve before installing it and be sure to hook up the hoses correctly.

Check valve(s), VCV and hoses

14 Replacement of these components is a simple matter of removing the faulty component and installing a new one. Be sure to mark the hoses before disconnecting them to ensure that they are correctly connected to the new component(s).

Distributor vacuum unit

15 Since replacement of this component may require removal and partial disassembly of the distributor, refer to Chapter 5 for additional information.

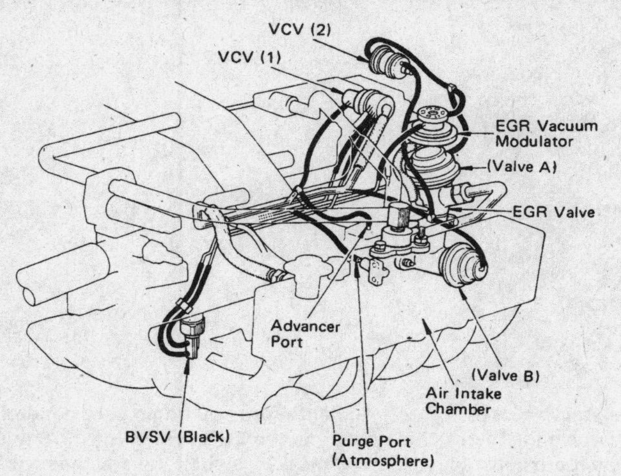

10.1a Typical 1979 and 1980 EGR system (1980 shown, 1979 similar)

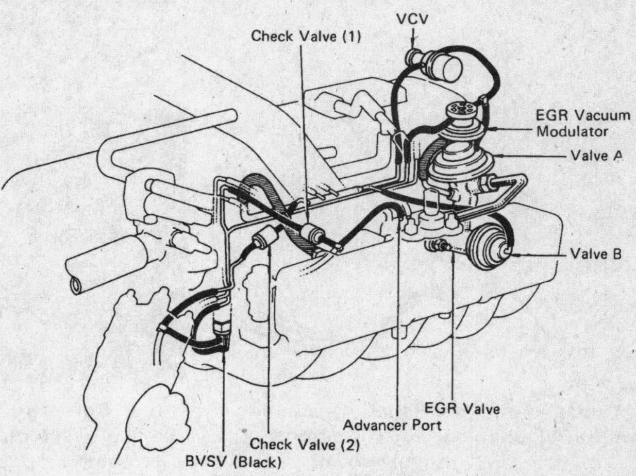

10.1b Typical 1981 EGR system

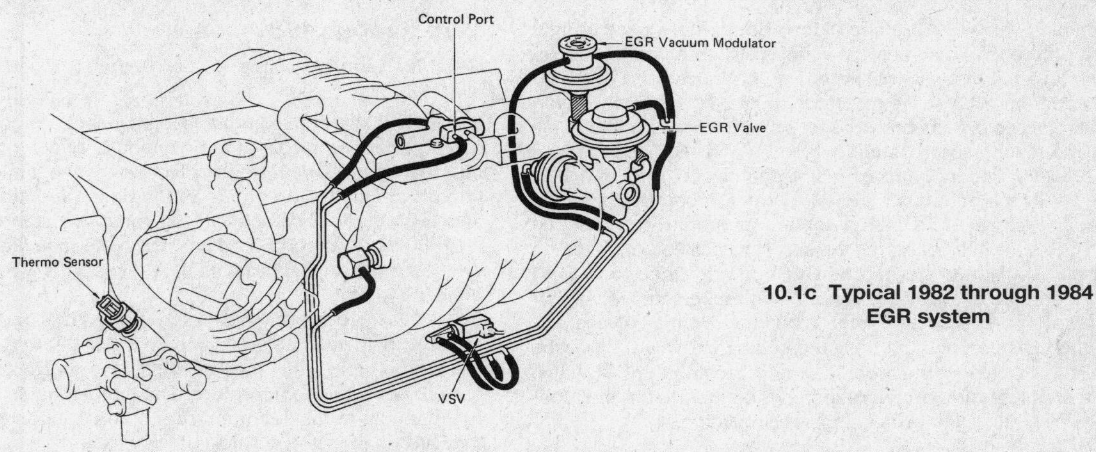

10.1c Typical 1982 through 1984 EGR system

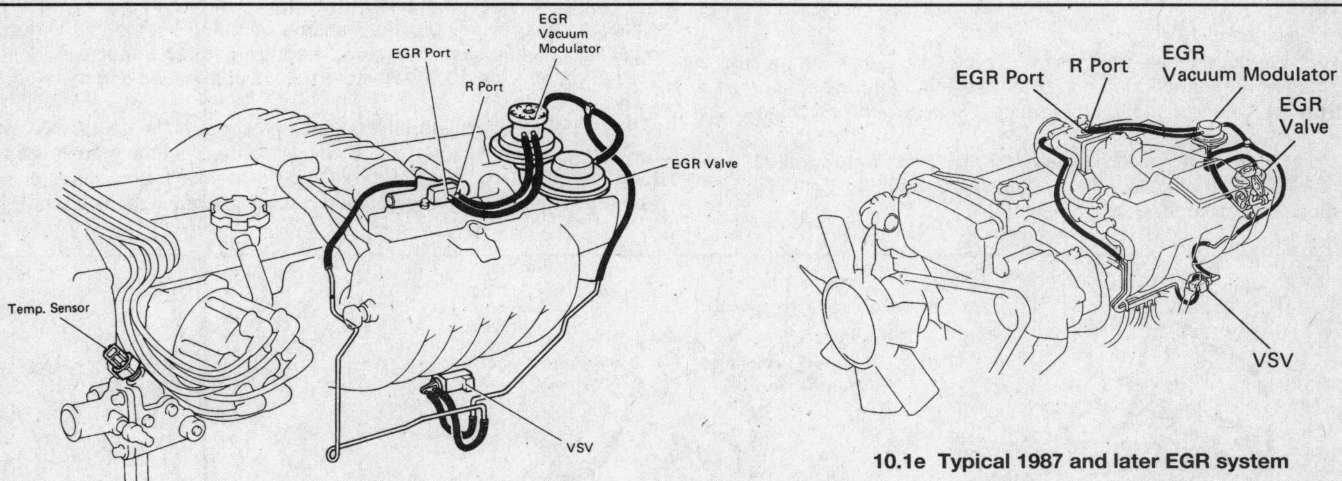

10.1d Typical 1985 and 1986 EGR system

10.1e Typical 1987 and later EGR system

10 Exhaust Gas Recirculation (EGR) system

General description

Refer to illustrations 10.1a through 10.1e and 10.2

1 The EGR system **(see illustrations)** recirculates a portion of the exhaust gases into the intake manifold in order to reduce the combustion temperatures and decrease the amount of oxides of nitrogen produced.

2 The main component in the system is the EGR valve. It is controlled by the EGR vacuum modulator, the vacuum control valve (VCV) (1979 through 1981 models) or vacuum switching valve (VSV) (1982 and later models) and, on 1979 through 1982 models, a bi-metallic

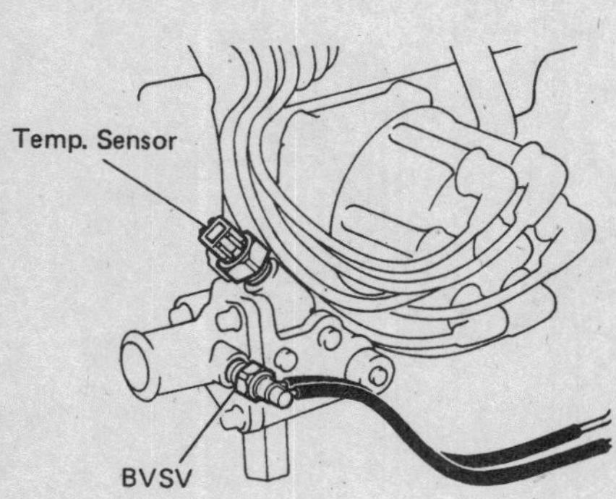

10.2 Typical bi-metallic vacuum switching valve (BVSV), used on 1979 through 1982 models (1982 model shown)

10.4 Before you check anything else in the EGR system, always remove the filter from the modulator, blow it out with compressed air and inspect it for cleanliness - if it's clogged, replace it

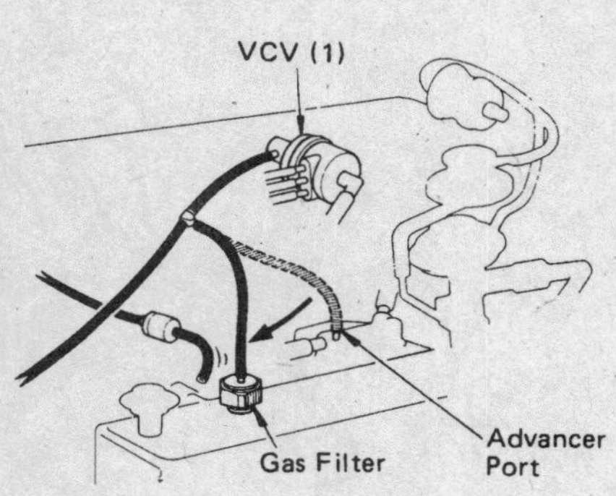

10.6a Before you begin your general check of the EGR system on 1979 and 1980 models, switch the advancer port hose to the intake manifold gas filter (1980 model shown)

vacuum switching valve (BVSV) **(see illustration)**. There are a couple of significant differences between the various systems used on these models. First, on 1980 models, there are two VCV valves and two EGR valves. The additional VCV valve responds to intake manifold vacuum changes and releases excess pressure to the atmosphere under alternating high and low pressure conditions. 1979 and 1981 models use only one VCV valve. Second, and more importantly, on 1983 and later models, the BVSV's function is handled by the EFI computer, which monitors coolant temperature via the coolant temperature sensor, although the EGR valve itself operates the same way as earlier units.

3 At low engine temperatures, the BVSV (if equipped) and EGR valve are shut and the exhaust gas is not being recirculated. At higher engine temperatures, the BVSV opens. When the throttle valve is pivoted above the EGR port and the pressure in the EGR valve is low, the pressure increases, closing the modulator and causing the EGR valve to open. The pressure then drops, reopening the modulator and closing the EGR valve, cutting off exhaust gas recirculation.

Check

Refer to illustration 10.4

4 Remove the filter element from the modulator, examine the filter for damage or contamination and clean it using compressed air **(see illustration)**. Check all hoses for cracks, kinks, broken sections and proper connection.

5 On 1979 through 1981 models, refer to Steps 6 through 21; on 1982 through 1986 models, refer to Steps 22 through 36; on 1987 and later models, refer to Steps 37 through 50.

1979 through 1981 models

Refer to illustrations 10.6a, 10.6b, 10.6c, 10.10, 10.11a, 10.11b and 10.12

6 On 1979 and 1980 models, disconnect the vacuum hose from the advance port on the throttle body and connect it to the gas filter **(see illustration)**. On all models, disconnect the hose from EGR valve A and attach a vacuum gauge to the hose **(see illustration)**. On 1980 and 1981 models, disconnect the vacuum hose from VCV (VCV No. 2 on 1980 models) port S and plug the hose **(see illustration)**.

7 Start the engine (from cold) and see if it will idle. If it won't, check the EGR valve.

8 With the coolant temperature below 122-degrees F, the vacuum gauge should indicate zero vacuum at 1500 rpm (1979 and 1980 models) or 2000 rpm (1981 models). Allow the engine to run until it reaches normal operating temperature. The gauge should now indicate manifold vacuum at the indicated rpm. If the gauge indicates zero, check the BVSV and the modulator.

9 On 1981 models, maintain the engine speed at 2000 rpm and make sure the gauge indicates manifold vacuum. Reconnect the hose to VCV port S and see if the gauge reads zero for 25 to 40 seconds. If it does not, check the VCV. Remove the vacuum gauge and reconnect the hoses.

10 On 1980 models, stop the engine and connect the check valve to the T-fitting as shown (white side closest to the T-fitting) **(see illustration)**. Reconnect the hose to the VCV port labeled S. Start the engine, race it once and see if the vacuum gauge indicates zero at idle. If it

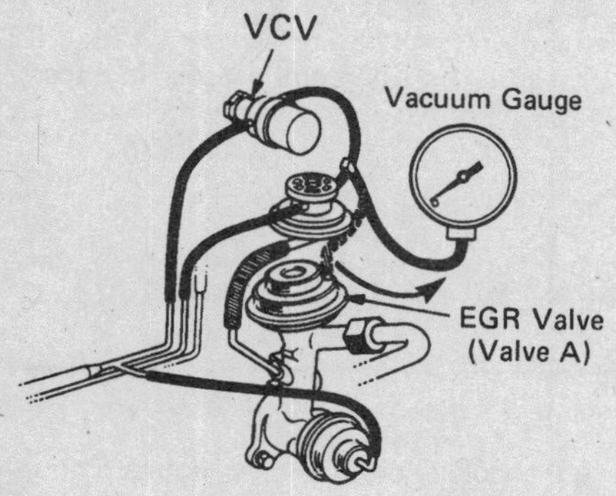

10.6b Vacuum gauge hook-up for EGR system general check (1981 model shown)

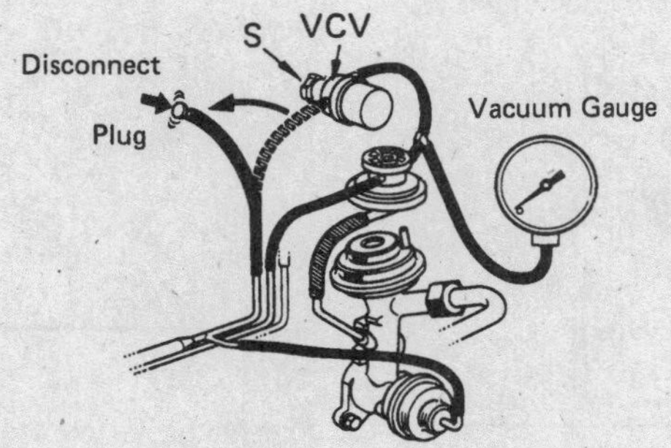

10.6c Before beginning the EGR system general check on 1980 and 1981 models, disconnect and plug the VCV input hose (port S)

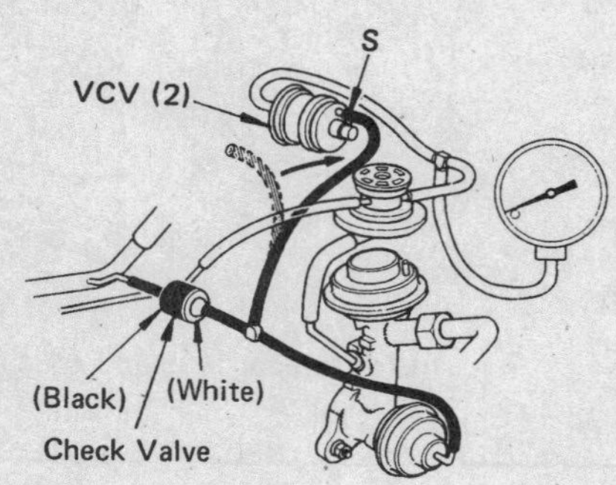

10.10 The check valve hook-up for the EGR system general check on 1980 models

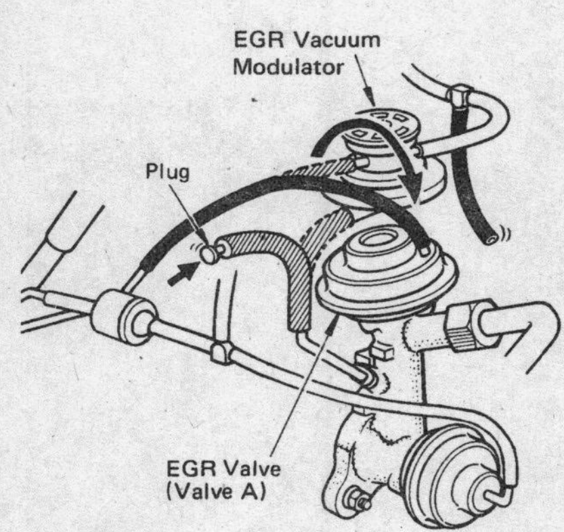

10.11a To check the operation of the EGR valve on a 1980 model, apply vacuum directly to the valve by unplugging the hose from the EGR vacuum modulator and connecting it to the EGR valve

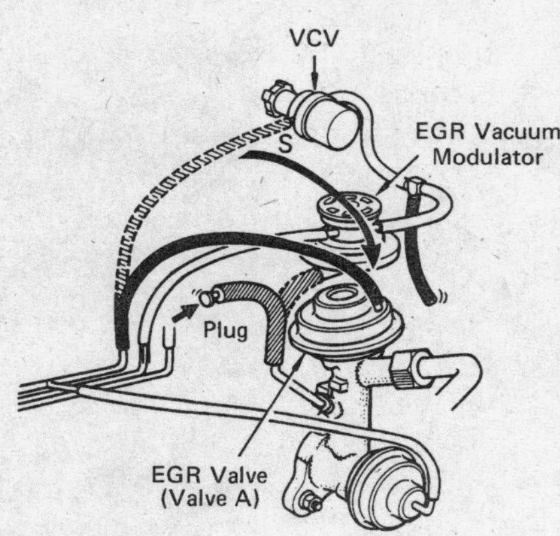

10.11b To check the operation of the EGR valve on a 1981 model, apply vacuum directly to the valve by unplugging the hose from the VCV and connecting it to the EGR valve

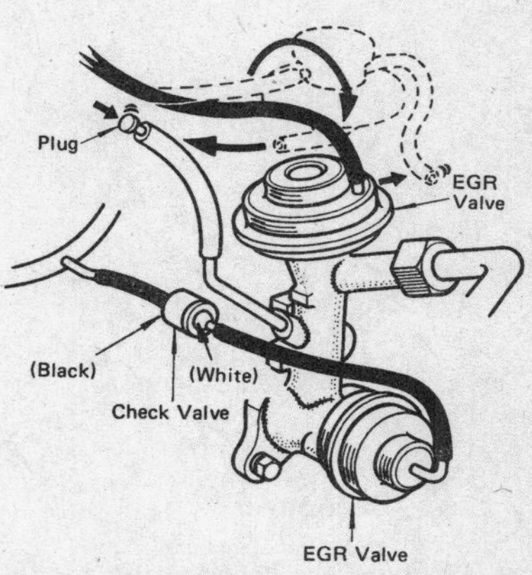

10.12 To check the operation of the EGR valve on a 1979 model, apply vacuum directly to the valve (valve A)

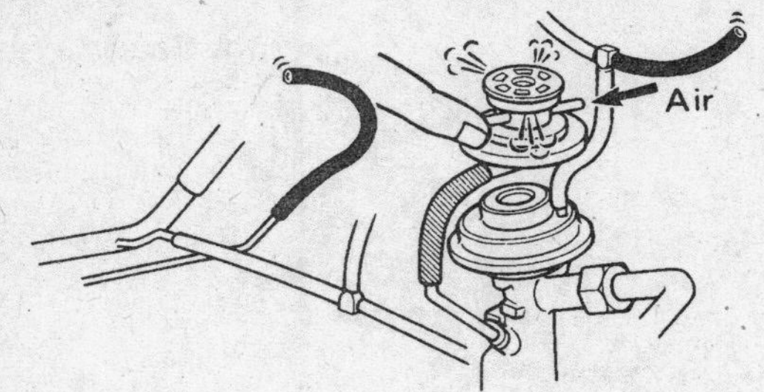

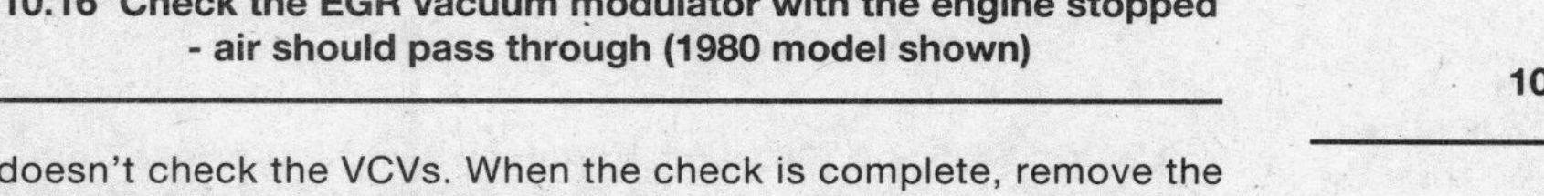

10.16 Check the EGR vacuum modulator with the engine stopped - air should pass through (1980 model shown)

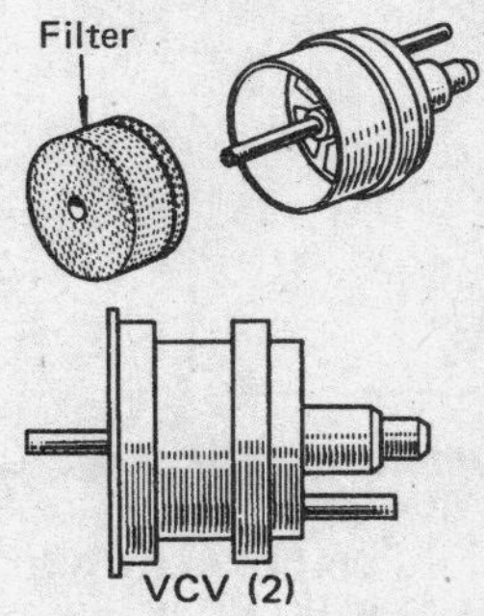

10.19a The filter for VCV No. 2 (1980 models)

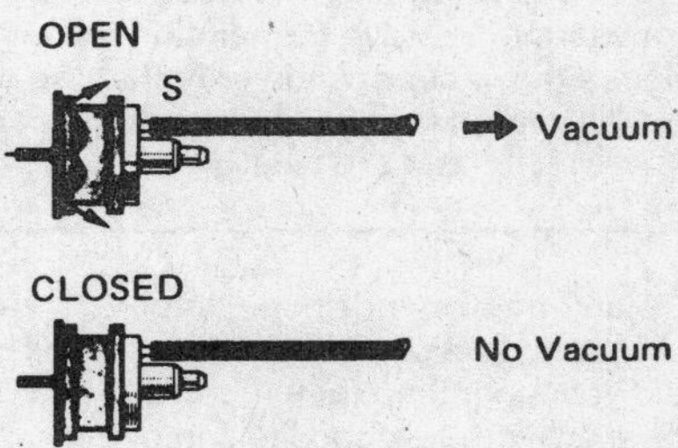

10.19b To check the VCV No. 2 on 1980 models, apply vacuum with a hand-held vacuum pump to port S and blow into the opposite end of the valve - it should be open and air should pass through it; release the vacuum and repeat the test - the valve should be closed (no air should pass through it)

doesn't check the VCVs. When the check is complete, remove the gauge and reconnect the hoses.

11 On 1980 and 1981 models, stop the engine, remove the EGR vacuum modulator and plug the exhaust gas hose **(see illustrations)**. Start the engine and race it once, then apply vacuum directly to the EGR valve A and see if the engine runs rough or stalls. If it does not, check the EGR valve and transfer pipe. Reinstall the vacuum modulator and reconnect all hoses.

12 On 1979 models, stop the engine, remove the EGR vacuum modulator and plug the exhaust gas hose **(see illustration)**. Connect the white side of the check valve **(see illustration 1.1a)** to EGR valve B as shown in the accompanying illustration. Start the engine and apply vacuum directly to EGR valve A. The engine should run smoothly without surging; if it doesn't, check EGR valve B. Disconnect the hose from the white side of the check valve and plug the valve. The engine should now run rough or stall; if it doesn't, check EGR valve A and the EGR gas passages. When the check is complete, reinstall the vacuum modulator, disconnect the check valve and reconnect all hoses.

13 If the preceding tests are positive, the EGR system is functioning properly. If they are negative, check the components as follows;

EGR valve check

14 Remove the EGR valve and transfer pipe and visually check for carbon deposits or a stuck valve. Replace the component with a new one if defects are noted.

BVSV check

15 Refer to Section 9, Steps 6 and 7, for the procedure to follow when checking this type of BVSV.

EGR vacuum modulator check

Refer to illustration 10.16

16 With the engine stopped, disconnect the hoses from the modulator. Block off one of the ports with your finger and blow into the other port **(see illustration)**; air should pass through the valve and exit the filter.

17 Start the engine and hold it at 2000 rpm, then repeat the check. There should now be strong resistance to air flow through the valve. If the valve fails the checks, replace it with a new one.

VCV check (1979 and 1980 models)

Refer to illustrations 10.19a and 10.19b

18 Refer to Section 6, Steps 9, 10 and 11 for the procedure to follow when checking the 1979 VCV and the 1980 VCV number 1.

19 To check the 1980 VCV number 2, unsnap the cover and check the filter **(see illustration)**. If it is clogged, clean it with compressed air

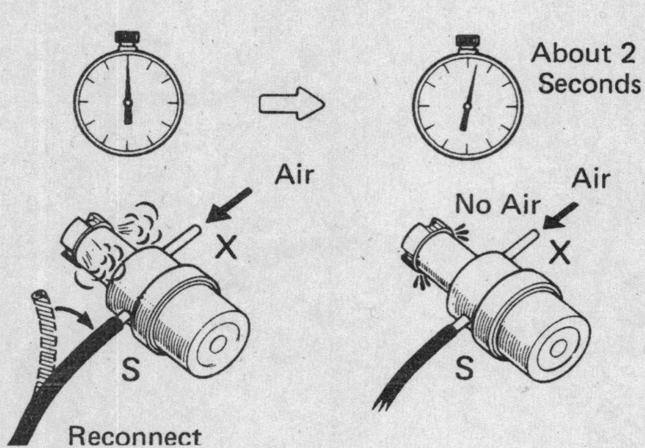

10.21 To check the VCV on 1981 models, apply vacuum with a hand-held vacuum pump to port S and blow into port X - air should pass through the valve for approximately two seconds, then it should close and the air flow should stop

10.22 With the coolant temperature below 135-degrees F, the vacuum gauge should indicate zero vacuum at 2500 rpm, which means no vacuum is acting on the EGR valve

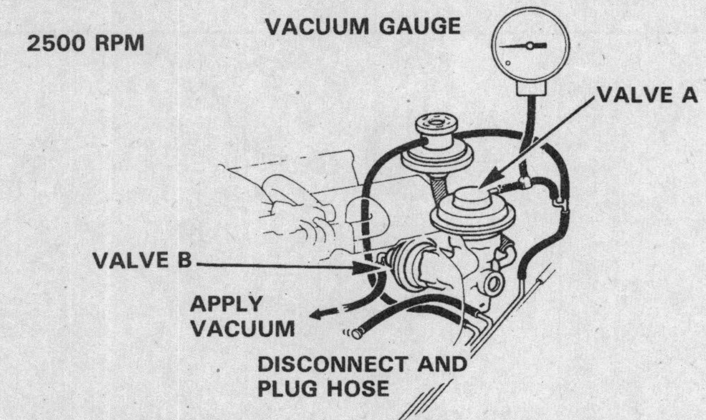

10.25 On 1982 through 1984 models, detach the vacuum hose from the EGR valve (valve B), plug the hose end, apply 600 mm Hg (23.62 in Hg) of vacuum to valve B, maintain the engine speed at 2500 rpm, release the vacuum and verify that the engine speed drops about 200 rpm - if it doesn't drop as indicated, replace the EGR valve

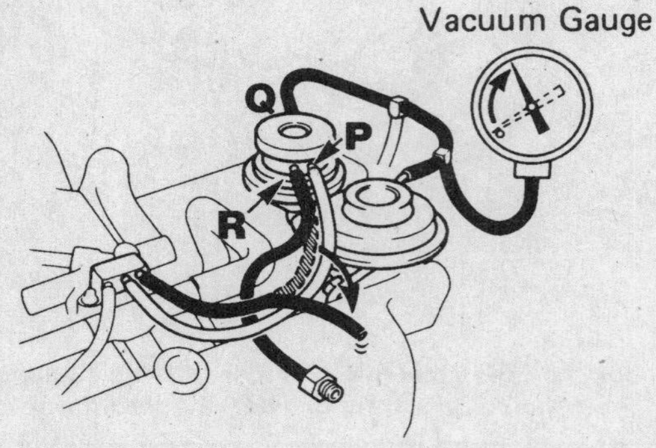

10.26 On 1985 and 1986 models, detach the vacuum hose from port R of the EGR vacuum modulator, connect port R directly to the intake manifold vacuum fitting with another hose and run the engine at 2500 rpm - the vacuum gauge should indicate a high reading

and reinstall it. Mark the hose positions, then remove them from the valve. Attach a separate section of hose to port S and apply a vacuum with a hand-held vacuum pump **(see illustration)**. With the vacuum acting on port S, blow into the opposite end of the valve; it should be open and air should pass through it. Release the vacuum and repeat the test; the valve should be closed (no air should pass through it).

VCV check (1981 models)

Refer to illustration 10.21

20 To check the VCV on this model engine, unsnap the cover and remove and check the filter. If it is clogged, clean it with compressed air and reinstall it.

21 Mark the hose positions, then remove them from the valve. Attach a separate section of hose to port S and apply a vacuum with your mouth or a hand type vacuum pump, then seal off the hose **(see illustration)**. With the vacuum acting on port S, blow into port X. Air should pass through the valve for approximately two seconds, then it should close and the air flow should stop.

1982 through 1986 models

Refer to illustrations 10.22, 10.25, 10.26, 10.27 and 10.28

22 Disconnect the vacuum hose from the EGR valve and attach a vacuum gauge to the hose **(see illustration)**.

23 Start the engine (from cold) and see if it will idle. If it won't, check the EGR valve to see if it is stuck open.

24 With the coolant temperature below 135-degrees F., the vacuum gauge should indicate zero vacuum at 2500 rpm. Allow the engine to warm up to normal operating temperature. The gauge should now indicate 70 mm Hg vacuum at 2500 rpm and zero vacuum at idle.

25 On 1982 through 1984 models, disconnect the vacuum hose from the EGR valve (valve B) and plug the hose end **(see illustration)**. Apply and maintain a 600 mm Hg (23.62 in Hg) of vacuum to valve B. Maintain the engine speed at 2500 rpm. Release the vacuum and check that the engine speed drops about 200 rpm. If it drops, disconnect the vacuum gauge and reconnect the vacuum hoses to the proper locations. If it does not drop as indicated, replace the EGR valve.

26 On 1985 and 1986 models, disconnect the vacuum hose from port R of the EGR vacuum modulator and connect port R directly to the intake manifold vacuum fitting with another hose **(see illustration)**. Run the engine at 2500 rpm. The vacuum gauge should indicate a high reading. **Note:** *As a large amount of EGR gas enters, the engine may misfire. When the check is complete, remove the gauge and reconnect the hoses.*

27 On 1985 and 1986 models, disconnect the vacuum hoses from ports P, Q and R of the EGR vacuum modulator **(see illustration)**. Block ports P and R with your finger. Blow air into port Q. Make sure that air passes through freely to the air filter side. Start the engine, maintain 2500 rpm and repeat the test. Check that there is now strong

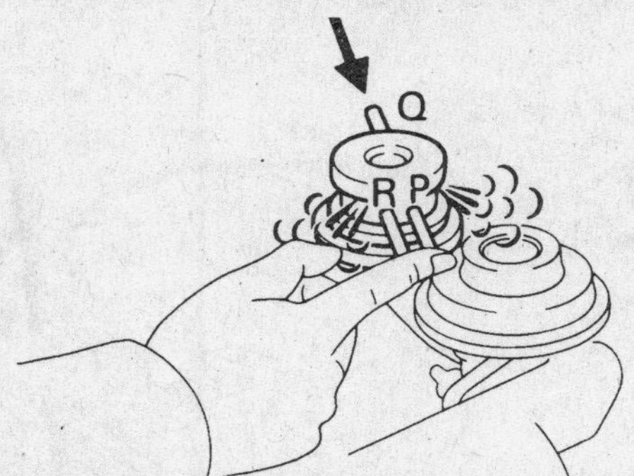

10.27 On 1985 and 1986 models, detach the vacuum hoses from ports P, Q and R of the EGR vacuum modulator, block ports P and R with your finger, blow air into port Q and make sure that air passes through freely to the air filter side; then start the engine, maintain 2500 rpm and repeat the test; verify that there's now strong resistance to air flow

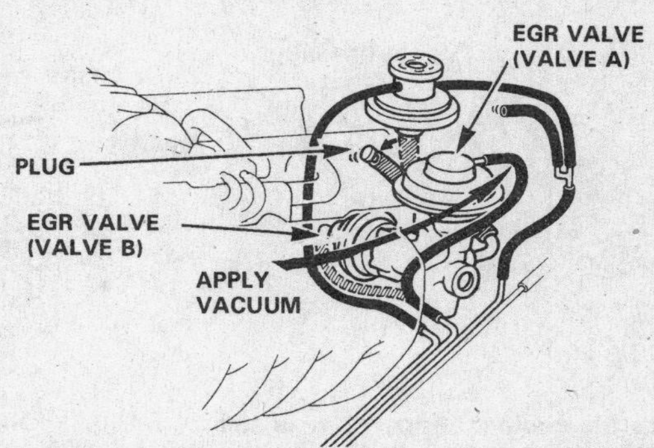

10.28 On 1982 through 1984 models, stop the engine, remove the EGR vacuum modulator exhaust gas hose, plug it, start the engine, race it once, then apply vacuum directly to the EGR valve and see if the engine runs rough or stalls - if it doesn't, check the EGR valve

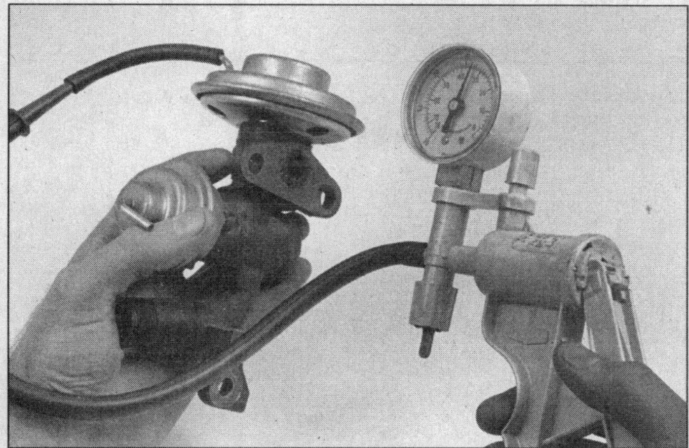

10.30 Remove the EGR valve and apply vacuum to check if the valve is sticking; also check for heavy carbon deposits - replace the component with a new one if defects are noted.

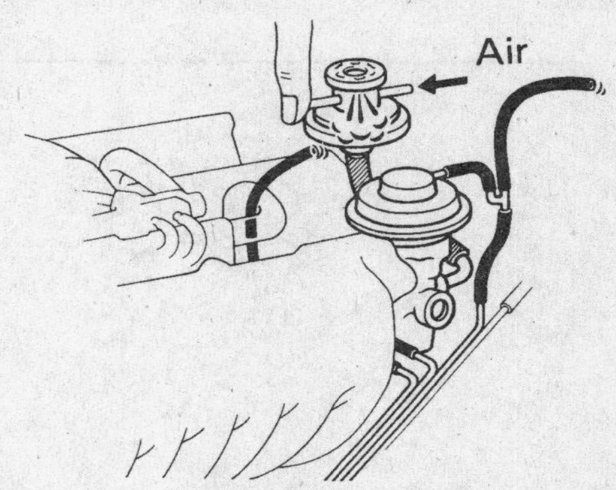

10.32 With the engine stopped, disconnect the hoses from the EGR modulator, block off one of the ports with your finger and blow into the other port - air should pass through the valve and exit the filter side (1982 through 1984 models only)

resistance to air flow. If a problem is found, replace the EGR vacuum modulator.

28 On 1982 through 1984 models, stop the engine, remove the EGR vacuum modulator exhaust gas hose and plug it **(see illustration)**. Start the engine and race it once, then apply vacuum directly to the EGR valve and see if the engine runs rough or stalls. If it does not, check the EGR valve. Reinstall the vacuum modulator and reconnect all hoses.

29 If the preceding tests are positive, the EGR system is functioning properly. If they are negative, check the components as follows:

EGR valve

Refer to illustration 10.30

30 Remove the EGR valve and apply vacuum to check if the valve is sticking **(see illustration)**. Also check for heavy carbon deposits. Replace the component with a new one if defects are noted.

BVSV

31 Refer to Section 3.

EGR vacuum modulator

Refer to illustration 10.32

32 With the engine stopped, disconnect the hoses from the modulator. Block off one of the ports with your finger and blow into the other port **(see illustration)**. Air should pass through the valve and exit the filter side (1982 through 1984 models only).

33 Start the engine and hold it at 2500 rpm, then repeat the check. There should now be strong resistance to air flow through the valve. If the valve fails the checks, replace it with a new one.

34 For 1985 and 1986 models, refer to Step 27.

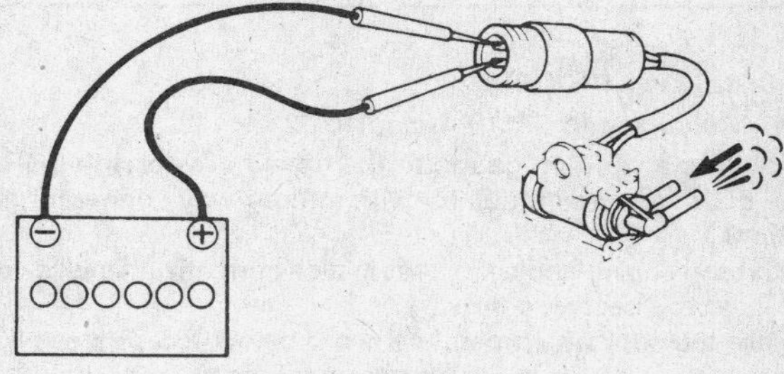

10.35 Mark the hose positions and remove them from the valve, connect the VSV terminals to the battery terminals and blow into one of the ports - the valve should be open

Vacuum Switching Valve (VSV)

Refer to illustration 10.35

35 Mark the hose positions and remove them from the valve. Using jumper wires, connect the VSV terminals to the battery terminals **(see illustration)**. Blow into one of the ports. The valve should be open.

36 Disconnect the battery from the VSV terminals and blow into the port again. The valve should now be closed. If the VSV fails either of these tests, replace it with a new one.

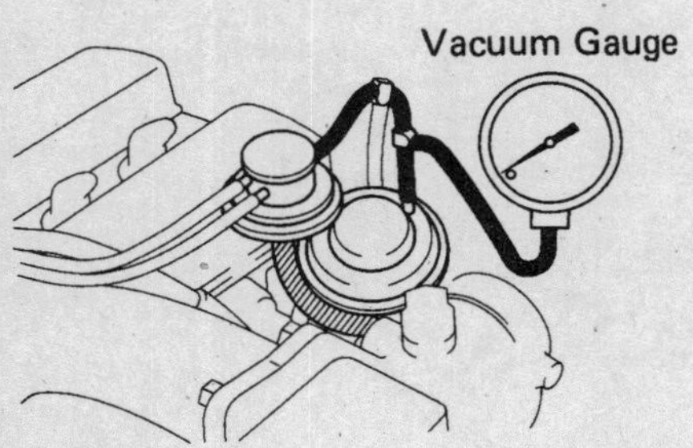

10.37 While the coolant temperature is still below 135-degrees F, verify that the vacuum gauge indicates zero vacuum at 2500 rpm (this tells you that the BVSV is operating correctly); once the engine warms up, verify that the gauge indicates zero vacuum at idle and about 2.76 in-Hg at 2500 rpm

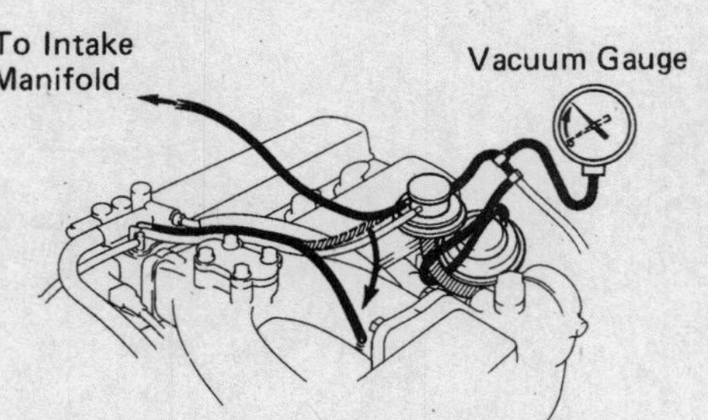

10.41 On non-turbo models, detach the vacuum hose from port R of the EGR vacuum modulator, connect the R port directly to the intake manifold with another hose and verify that the gauge indicates high vacuum at 2500 rpm (this tells you that the VSV and EGR vacuum modulator are operating correctly when the engine is warmed up)

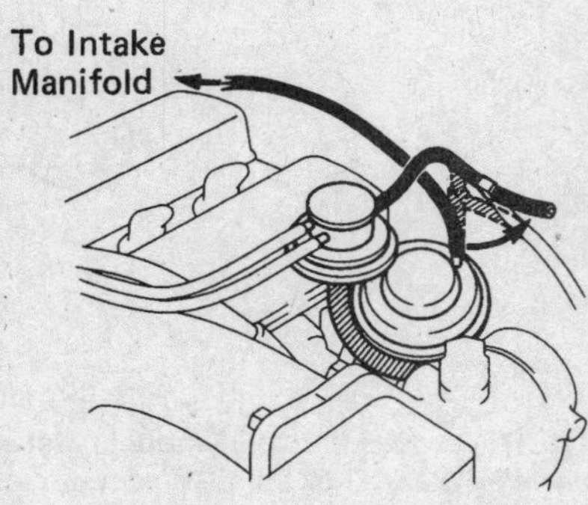

10.42 With the engine idling, apply vacuum directly to the EGR valve and verify that the engine runs roughly or dies

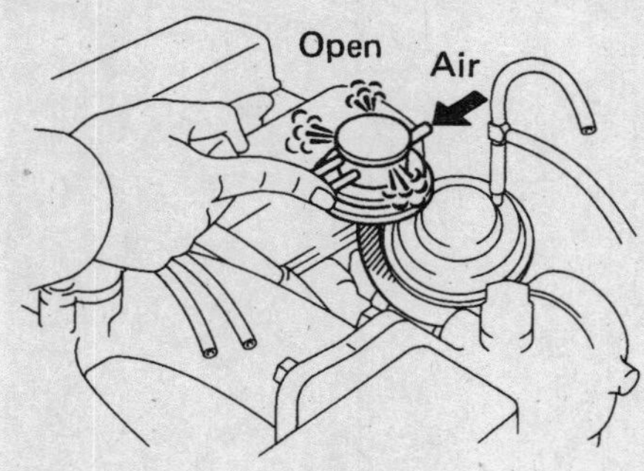

10.44 On non-turbo models, detach the vacuum hoses from ports P, Q and R at the EGR vacuum modulator, block ports P and R with your finger, blow air into port Q and verify that air passes through to the air filter - with the engine running, there should be strong resistance to air flow

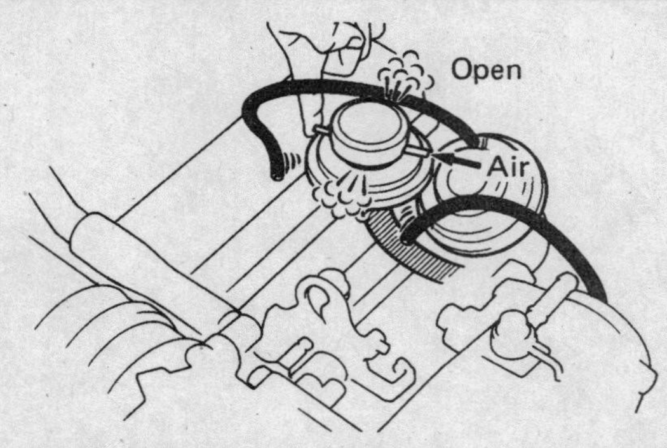

10.45 On turbo models, detach the vacuum hoses from the EGR vacuum modulator, block port P with your finger, blow air into the other pipe and verify that air passes through to the air filter - with the engine running, there should be a strong resistance to air flow

1987 and later models

Refer to illustrations 10.37, 10.41 and 10.42

37 Hook up a vacuum gauge to the hose between the EGR valve and the EGR vacuum modulator with a three-way connector **(see illustration)**.

38 Start the engine and verify that it idles correctly (this tells you that the EGR valve is seating correctly).

39 While the coolant temperature is still below 135-degrees F, verify that the vacuum gauge indicates zero vacuum at 2500 rpm (this tells you that the BVSV is operating correctly).

40 After the engine has warmed up, verify that the vacuum gauge indicates zero vacuum at idle and about 2.76 in-Hg at 2500 rpm.

41 On non-turbo models, detach the vacuum hose from port R of the EGR vacuum modulator, connect the R port directly to the intake manifold with another hose **(see illustration)** and verify that the gauge indicates high vacuum at 2500 rpm (this tells you that the VSV and EGR vacuum modulator are operating correctly when the engine is warmed up). **Note:** *As a large amount of EGR gas enters, the engine will misfire slightly. Detach the vacuum gauge and reattach the vacuum hoses to their respective ports.*

42 With the engine idling, apply vacuum directly to the EGR valve **(see illustration)** and verify that the engine runs roughly or dies. Reattach the vacuum hoses to their ports.

43 If everything operates as described up to this point, the EGR system is functioning correctly; if not, check each component.

EGR vacuum modulator

Refer to illustrations 10.44 and 10.45

44 On non-turbo models, detach the vacuum hoses from ports P, Q and R at the EGR vacuum modulator, block ports P and R with your finger, blow air into port Q and verify that air passes through to the air filter **(see illustration)**. Then start the engine, run it at 2500 rpm, repeat the above test and verify that there's a strong resistance to air flow. If the EGR vacuum modulator performs as described, reattach the hoses to their respective ports and go on to the next test; if it doesn't, replace it and retest the system.

45 On turbo models, detach the vacuum hoses from the EGR vacuum modulator, block port P with your finger, blow air into the other pipe and verify that air passes through to the air filter **(see illustration)**. Then start the engine, maintain a speed of 2500 rpm, repeat the above test and verify that there's a strong resistance to air flow. If the EGR vacuum modulator performs as described, reattach the hoses and go on to the next test; if it doesn't, replace it and retest the EGR system.

VSV

Non-turbo models

Refer to illustration 10.46

46 To verify vacuum circuit continuity in the VSV, connect the VSV terminals to the battery terminals, blow air into the indicated port and verify that the VSV is open **(see illustration)**. Then disconnect the battery, blow air into the same port and verify that the VSV is closed. Re-

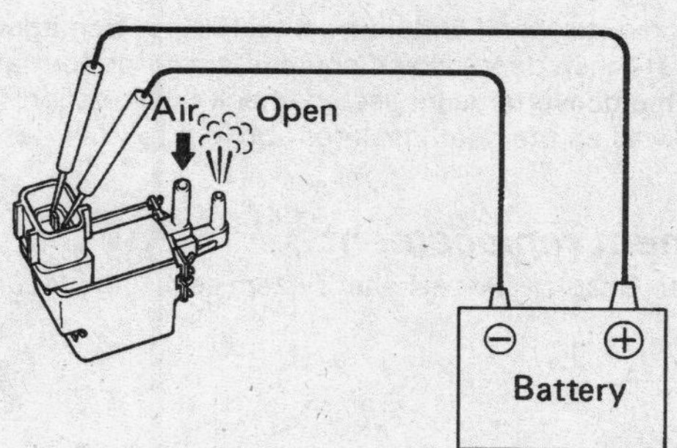

10.46 To check the VSV used on non-turbo models, connect the VSV terminals to the battery terminals, blow air into the indicated port and verify that the VSV is open, then disconnect the battery and verify that the valve is closed

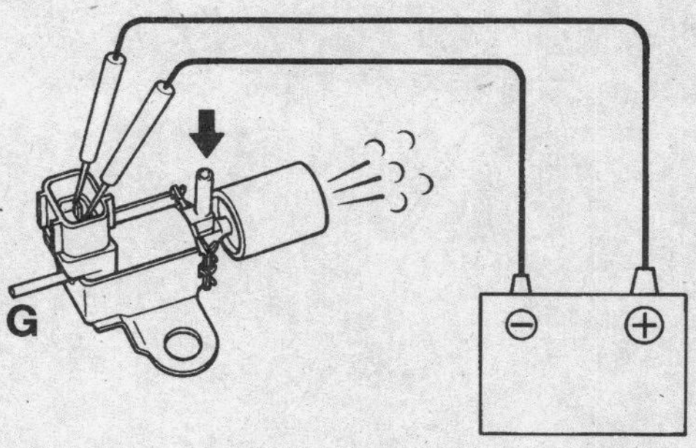

10.49 On 1989 and later turbo models, connect the VSV terminals to the battery terminals, blow into port E and verify that air comes out the filter, then disconnect the battery, blow into port E and verify that air comes out port G (on 1988 and earlier models, the VSV works just the opposite way)

place the VSV if it doesn't work as described.

47 To check for a short circuit in the VSV, verify that there's no continuity between the terminals and the VSV body. If there is, replace the VSV.

48 To check for an open in the VSV circuit, measure the resistance between the terminals. It should be about 38 to 44 ohms. If it isn't, replace the VSV.

Turbo models

Refer to illustration 10.49

49 On 1987 and 1988 models, connect the VSV terminals to the battery terminals, blow into port E and verify that air comes out pipe G. Then disconnect the battery, blow into port E and verify that air comes out the air filter. On 1989 and later models, the VSV works just the opposite way: when you blow into port E with the VSV hooked up to the battery, air comes out the filter **(see illustration)**; when you blow into port E with the battery disconnected, air comes out port G.

50 The checks for a short circuit and an open circuit in the VSV used on turbo models are the same as those for VSVs on non-turbo models (see Steps 47 and 48 above).

Component replacement

EGR valve

Warning: *Make sure the engine is cool before replacing the EGR valve.*

51 The EGR valve is bolted to the rear of the cylinder head and is easily removed. Be sure to mark the vacuum hoses before disconnecting them from the valve. Always use a new gasket when installing the valve and check for leaks when the job is complete.

BVSV, EGR vacuum modulator, VSV, hoses, etc.

52 Replacement of these components is self-evident. Some of them are held in place by small brackets and some are simply installed inline between two vacuum hoses. Remove the faulty part and install a new one. Be sure to mark the hoses before disconnecting them to ensure that they are correctly connected to the new component(s).

11 Catalytic converter(s)

General description

Refer to illustration 11.1

1 The catalytic converter used in the vehicles covered by this manual is a three-way catalyst design **(see illustration)** which reduces hydrocarbons (HC), carbon monoxide (CO) and oxides of nitrogen (NOX) in the exhaust. The system oxidizes these components and converts them to water, carbon dioxide and nitrogen. Some late model turbo and California models employ two converters.

Check

Refer to illustration 11.3

2 The catalytic converter requires little maintenance and servicing at regular intervals. However, the system should be inspected whenever the vehicle is raised on a lift or if the exhaust system is checked or serviced.

3 Check all connections in the exhaust pipe assembly for looseness and damage. Also check all the clamps for damage, cracks and

6

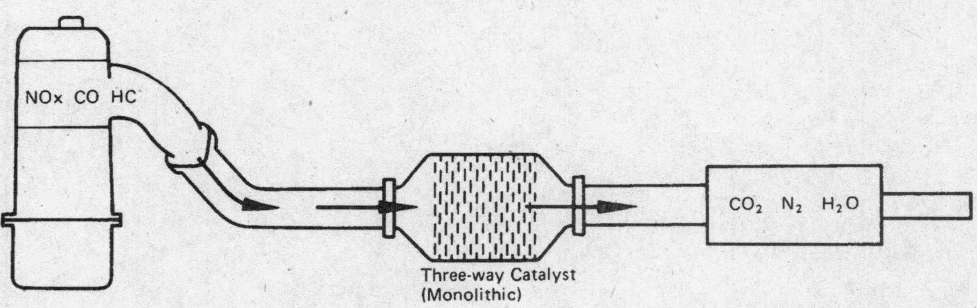

11.1 The catalytic converter used on the vehicles covered by this manual oxidizes, reduces and converts hydrocarbons, carbon monoxide and oxide of nitrogen emissions into nitrogen, carbon dioxide and water

11.3 With the metal protector plate removed, check the converter and the connections for looseness and damage - check for missing fasteners and inspect the rubber hangers for cracks (arrows)

missing fasteners **(see illustration)**. Check the rubber hangers for cracks.

4 The converter itself should be checked for damage and dents (maximum 3/4-inch deep) which could affect its performance. At the same time the converter is inspected check the metal protector plate under it as well as the heat insulator above it for damage and loose fasteners.

Component replacement

5 Refer to Chapter 4 for exhaust system servicing procedures.

Chapter 7 Part A Manual transmission

Contents

Specifications

Lubricant type and capacity	See Chapter 1
W50 transmission	
Gear thrust clearance	
First, Second and Third	
Standard	0.0039 to 0.0098 inch
Limit	0.012 inch
Fifth	
Standard	0.004 inch
Limit	0.010 inch
Gear oil clearance	
First and Fifth	
Standard	0.002 inch
Limit	0.008 inch
Second and Third	
Standard	0.0014 inch
Limit	0.0039 inch
Shift fork-to-hub sleeve clearance limit	0.040 inch
Synchronizer ring-to-gear clearance (maximum)	0.030 inch
W58 transmission	
Gear thrust clearance	
First, Second and Third	
Standard	0.0039 to 0.0098 inch
Limit	0.0118 inch
Counter Fifth	
Standard	0.0039 to 0.0161 inch
Limit	0.0181 inch
Gear oil clearance	
First and Second	
Standard	0.0004 to 0.0024 inch
Limit	0.0059 inch
Third	
Standard	0.0024 to 0.0041 inch
Limit	0.0079 inch
Counter Fifth	
Standard	0.0004 to 0.0024 inch
Limit	0.0059 inch
Shift fork-to-hub sleeve clearance limit	0.039 inch
Synchronizer ring-to-gear clearance	
Standard	0.028 to 0.067 inch
Limit	0.020 inch

R154 transmission

Gear thrust clearance	
First	
Standard	0.0039 to 0.0177 inch
Limit	0.0197 inch
Second and Third	
Standard	0.0039 to 0.0098 inch
Limit	0.0118 inch
Counter Fifth	
Standard	0.0039 to 0.0138 inch
Limit	0.0157 inch
Gear oil clearance	
First	
Standard	0.0008 to 0.0029 inch
Limit	0.0063 inch
Second and Third	
Standard	0.0006 to 0.0027 inch
Limit	0.0063 inch
Counter Fifth	
Standard	0.006 to 0.0027 inch
Limit	0.0063 inch
Shift fork-to-hub sleeve clearance limit	0.039 inch
Synchronizer ring-to-gear clearance	
Standard	0.031 to 0.063 inch
Limit	0.024 inch
Reverse idler gear-to-shift arm shoe	
Standard	0.020 to 0.098 inch
Limit	0.020 inch

Torque specifications

	Ft-lbs
Shift lever housing-to-shift and select lever	
W50, W58 transmissions	
1983 and earlier	22 to 28
1984 through 1992	28
R154 transmission	
1987 through 1992	29
Shift lever retainer-to-extension housing	
W50, W58 transmissions	
1983 and earlier	11 to 15
1984 through 1992	13
R154 transmission	
1987 through 1992	12
Drain and filler plugs	27 to 32
Bellhousing-to-transmission case	22 to 32
Transmission-to-engine bolts	47

1 General information

The manual transmission used in this vehicle is a five-speed. Early models are equipped with the W50 (1979 through 1981) or W58 (1982 and later) while later models (1987 through 1992) are equipped with either the W58 or the R154. The R154 is a larger and stronger unit installed on turbo models. The transmission is mounted at the rear of the engine and power is transmitted by a driveshaft to the rear axle. The transmission contains four sub-assemblies: the clutch housing, the main gear case, the intermediate plate with gear assemblies and the extension housing.

The reverse and fifth gear assemblies are positioned at the rear of the intermediate plate. The remaining forward gears are positioned on the front side. All forward gears have synchromesh. The intermediate plate also carries the selector rods. The main gear selector rod and change lever are carried in the extension housing.

2 Shifter - removal and installation

1 Remove the console box and radio trim panel (refer to Chapter 11).

2 Working from inside the vehicle, shift the transmission into Neutral, pull back on the flexible boot to remove the bracket retaining screws and remove the shift lever retainer and boot.

3 Remove the shifter retaining bolts and detach the shifter.

4 Installation is the reverse of the removal procedure.

3 Oil seal - replacement

Extension housing seal

Refer to illustrations 3.5, 3.6 and 3.7

1 Lubricant leaks can occur due to wear or damage of the exten-

3.5 Using a soft-faced hammer, gently tap the backside of the dust shield to remove it (W58 shown)

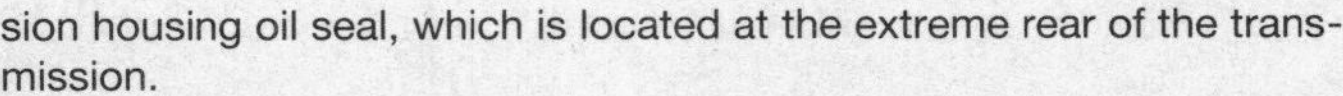

3.6 Being careful not to damage the splines on the transmission output shaft, pry out the extension housing oil seal (W58 shown)

sion housing oil seal, which is located at the extreme rear of the transmission.

2 Replacement of the seal can be done without removing the transmission from the vehicle.

3 If leakage at the seal is suspected, raise the rear of the vehicle and support it securely on jackstands. Be sure to block the front wheels to keep the vehicle from rolling. If the seal is leaking, transmission lubricant will be built up on the front of the driveshaft and may be dripping from the dust shield at the rear of the transmission.

4 Refer to Chapter 8 and remove the driveshaft.

5 Using a soft-faced hammer, carefully tap the dust shield from the rear and remove it from the transmission **(see illustration)**. Be careful not to distort it.

6 Using a screwdriver or pry bar, carefully pry the oil seal out of the rear of the transmission **(see illustration)**. Do not damage the splines on the transmission output shaft.

7 Using a large section of pipe or a large deep socket as a drift, install the new oil seal. Drive it into the bore squarely and make sure that it is completely seated **(see illustration)**.

8 Reinstall the dust shield by carefully tapping it into place. Lubricate the splines of the transmission output shaft and the outside of the driveshaft sleeve yoke with grease, then install the driveshaft. Be careful not to damage the lip of the new seal.

9 Check the transmission lubricant level and add the recommended lubricant (see Chapter 1) as necessary.

10 Lower the vehicle, test drive it and check for leaks.

Speedometer drive seal

11 Some of the transmissions are equipped with a speedometer drive seal that may require changing in the event of an oil leak.

12 Remove the bolt and bracket that retain the speedometer driven gear onto the transmission **(see illustrations 6.4a through 6.4g)**.

13 Use a thin screwdriver tip or pick and remove the O-ring from the gear housing.

14 Installation is the reverse of removal.

4 Transmission mount - check and replacement

1 Insert a large screwdriver or prybar into the space between the transmission extension housing and the crossmember. Try to pry the transmission up slightly.

2 The transmission should not move away from the transmission mount very much.

3 To replace the mount, remove the nuts attaching the mount to the crossmember and the bolts attaching the mount to the transmission.

3.7 Use a large socket or section of pipe to drive the new oil seal into the bore - make certain that the seal is completely seated (W58 shown)

7A

4 Raise the transmission slightly with a floor jack and remove the transmission mount. **Note:** *Be sure to remember to identify each mounting bolt and mark them with paint to aid in the proper reassembly.*

5 Installation is the reverse of removal. Be sure to tighten the nuts/bolts securely.

5 Transmission - removal and installation

Refer to illustrations 5.8, 5.9, 5.11, 5.12 and 5.14

1 The transmission can be removed from the vehicle leaving the engine in position.

2 Disconnect the negative cable from the battery. **Caution:** *If the stereo in your vehicle is equipped with an anti-theft system, refer to the information on page 0-15 at the front of this manual before detaching the cable.*

3 Drain enough coolant from the radiator to allow the upper hose to be removed (see Chapter 1).

4 Working inside the vehicle, remove the shifter (see Section 2).

5 Raise the front of the vehicle and support it with jackstands.

6 On 1982 and later models disconnect the steering shaft-to-pinion shaft universal joint and remove the steering gear housing (see Chapter 10).

5.8 A large socket, with the drive hole taped shut, can be used to plug the extension housing and prevent transmission fluid from leaking out (the socket should fit snugly in the seal) (W58 shown)

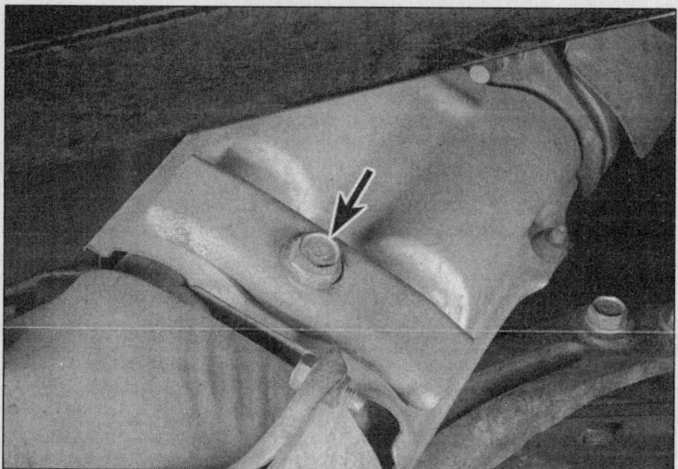

5.9 Remove the exhaust pipe clamp bolt (arrow) from the stiffener plate (W58 shown)

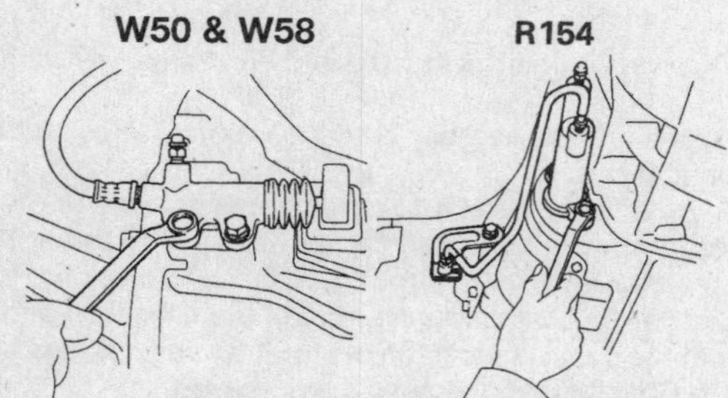

5.12 Remove the two retaining bolts from the clutch release/slave cylinder and suspend it out of the way

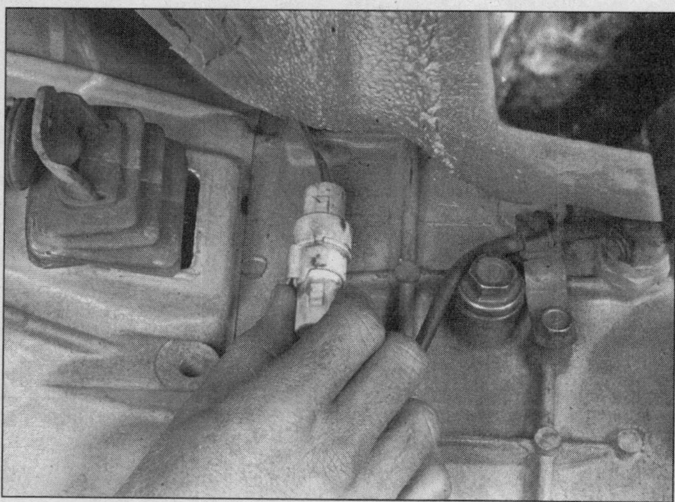

5.11 Unplug the back-up light switch connector (W58 shown)

5.14 After jacking up the transmission slightly, take out all eight retaining bolts and remove the rear crossmember (W58 shown)

7 Drain the transmission lubricant (see Chapter 1).

8 Take out the driveshaft (refer to Chapter 8). After removing the driveshaft, slip a large socket into the extension housing to prevent any residual transmission lubricant from leaking out **(see illustration)**.

9 Remove the exhaust pipe clamp bolt from the stiffener plate **(see illustration)**. On 1981 and earlier models, unbolt the exhaust pipe from the manifold.

10 Detach the speedometer cable.

11 Unplug the back-up light switch connector **(see illustration)**, then free it from the retaining clip. **Note:** *On vehicles equipped with the R154 transmission, disconnect the rear speed sensor also.*

12 Remove the clutch release/slave cylinder by removing the two retaining bolts **(see illustration)**, then suspend the cylinder up out of the way. DO NOT detach the fluid line from the slave cylinder.

13 Remove the starter (see Chapter 5).

14 Place a floor jack under the transmission and take its weight off the crossmember. Unbolt and remove the rear crossmember **(see illustration)**.

15 Remove the eight bolts which attach the bellhousing to the engine.

16 On models with the R154 transmission, remove the two clutch housing covers and remove the release fork through the left side cover hole. Scribe two marks on the flywheel and clutch cover and make sure on reinstallation that the marks match. Remove the clutch cover bolts through the housing cover and remove the transmission and clutch assembly as a unit.

17 Lower the jack carefully until the transmission can be withdrawn to the rear. Make sure that the engine does not damage components on the engine compartment firewall. If necessary, slip a block of wood between the engine oil pan and the crossmember or between the rear of the block and the firewall to keep the engine from tilting excessively.

18 Installation is the reverse of the removal procedure.

19 Refill the transmission with lubricant once the installation is complete.

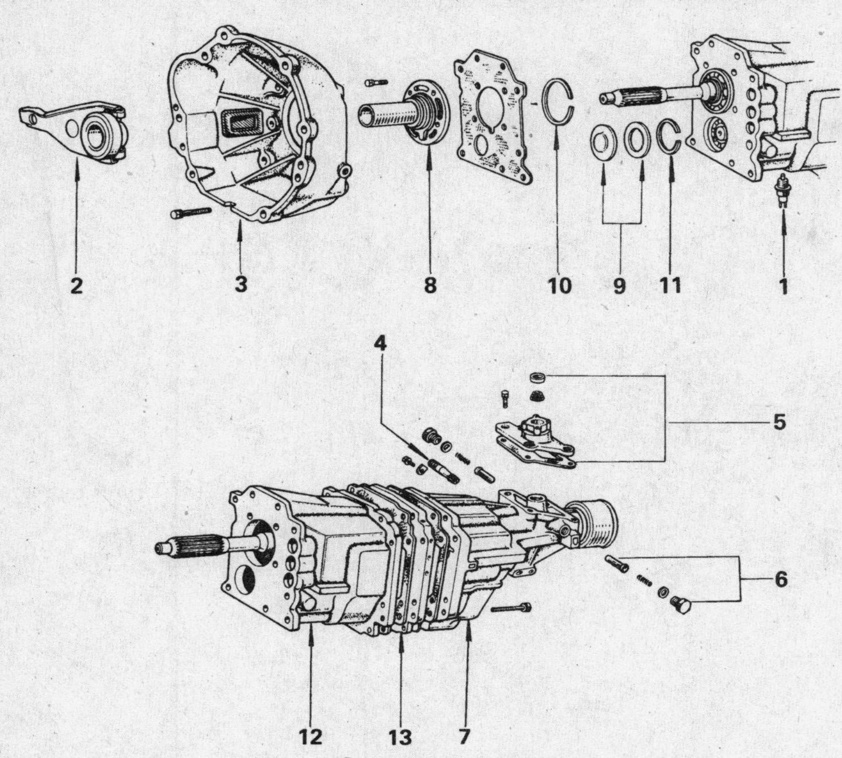

6.4a Transmission external components - exploded view (W50 transmission)

1 *Back-up light switch*
2 *Clutch release bearing and lever*
3 *Bellhousing*
4 *Speedometer driven gear*
5 *Shift lever turret*
6 *Restrictor pins, springs and plugs*
7 *Extension housing*
8 *Front bearing retainer*
9 *Countershaft cover and spacer*
10 *Circlip*
11 *Circlip*
12 *Transmission case*
13 *Intermediate plate*

6.4b Gear selector components - exploded view (W50 transmission)

14 *Detent balls, springs and plugs*
15 *Roll pins*
16 *Selector shafts (top - third/fourth; center - first/second; bottom - fifth/reverse)*
17 *Selector forks*

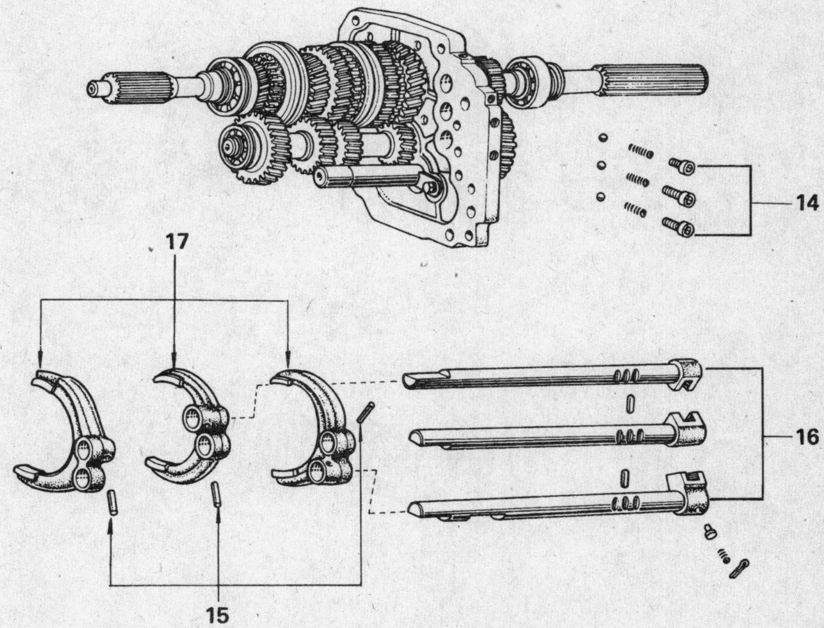

6 Transmission overhaul - general information

Refer to illustrations 6.4a through 6.4g

The overhaul of a manual transmission is a somewhat difficult job for the home mechanic. It involves the disassembly and reassembly of many small parts. Numerous clearances must be precisely measured and, if necessary, adjusted with selective fit spacers and snap-rings. For this reason, we strongly recommend that the home mechanic limit himself to the removal and installation of the transmission and leave overhaul to a transmission repair shop. Exchange transmissions are available at reasonable prices for this vehicle and the time and money involved in the at-home overhaul is almost sure to exceed the cost of a rebuilt unit.

Nevertheless, it's not impossible for the home mechanic to rebuild a transmission if the specialized tools are available, care is taken

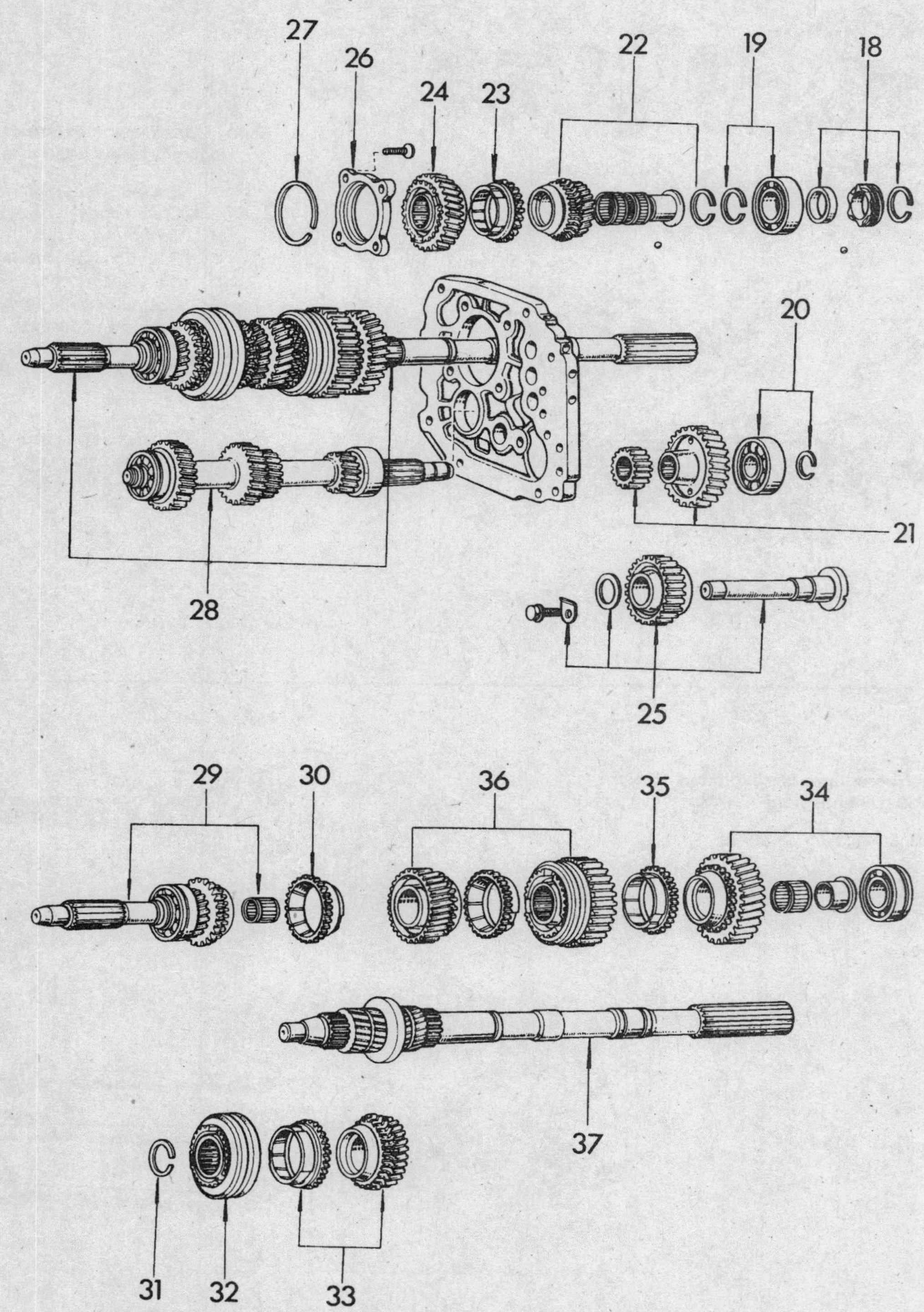

6.4c Mainshaft and countershaft components - exploded view (W50 transmission)

18 *Speedometer drive gear*
19 *Mainshaft rear bearing*
20 *Countershaft rear bearing*
21 *Countershaft Fifth and reverse gears*
22 *Mainshaft fifth gear and bearing*
23 *Synchro ring*
24 *Fifth/reverse gear synchro hub*
25 *Reverse idler gear*
26 *Bearing retainer*
27 *Circlip*
28 *Input shaft, mainshaft and countershaft assemblies*
29 *Input shaft and needle roller bearing*
30 *Synchro ring*
31 *Circlip*
32 *Third/fourth gear synchro hub*
33 *Synchro ring and third gear*
34 *Mainshaft bearing and first gear*
35 *Synchro ring*
36 *First/second gear synchro hub and second gear*
37 *Mainshaft*

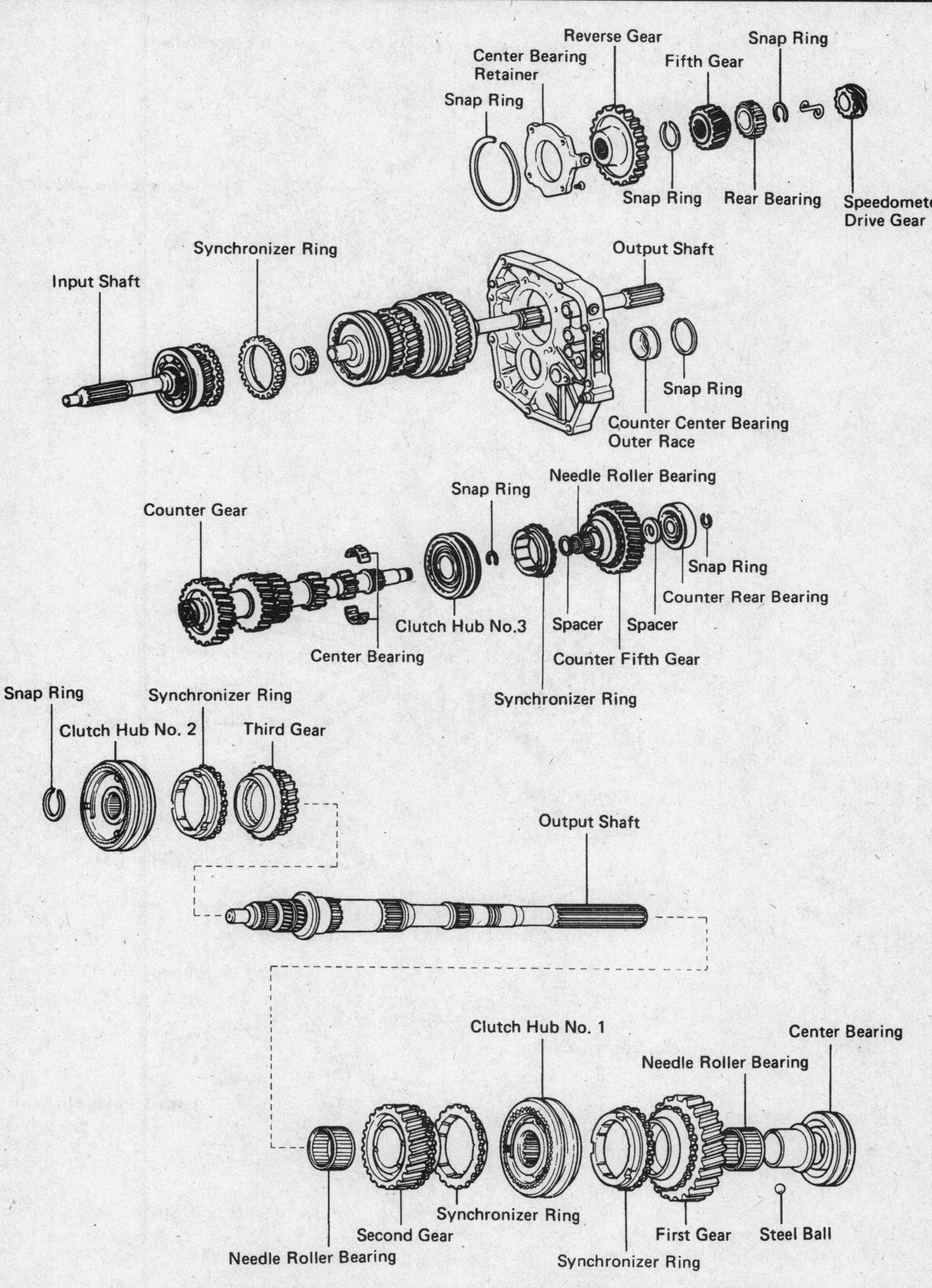

6.4d Manual transmission internal components - exploded view (W58 transmission)

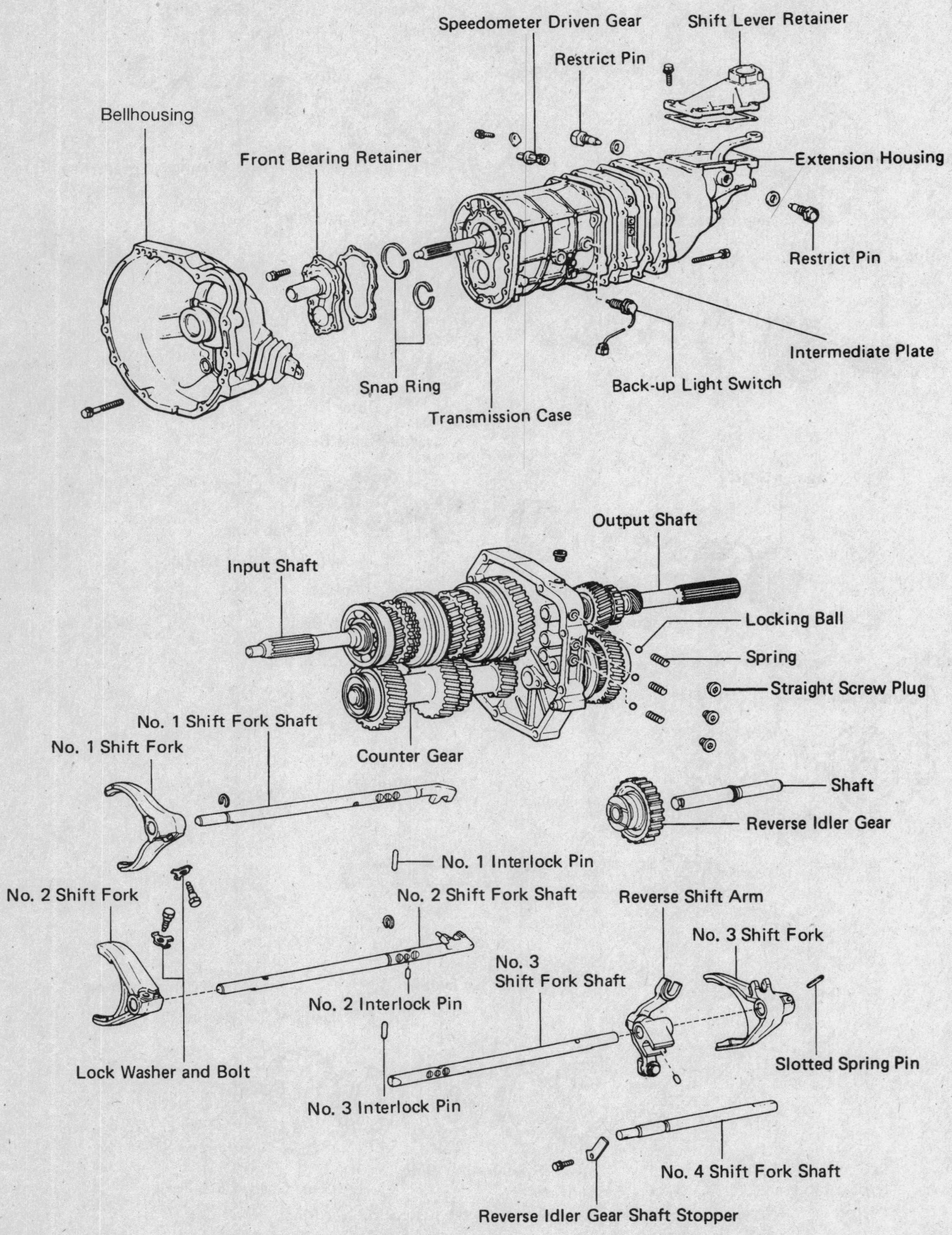

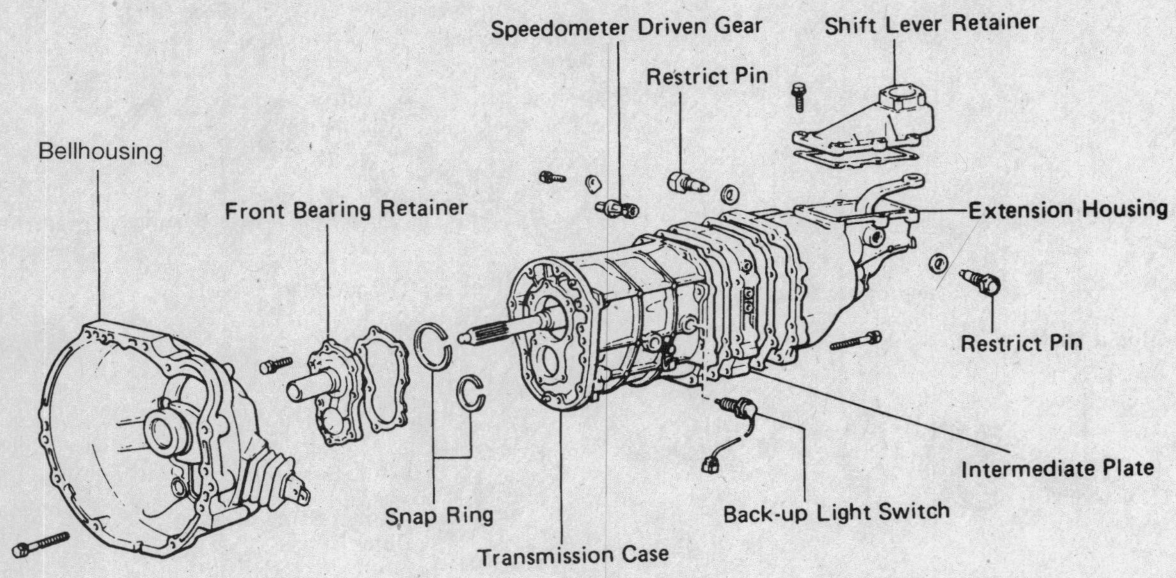

6.4e Manual transmission major components - exploded view (W58 transmission)

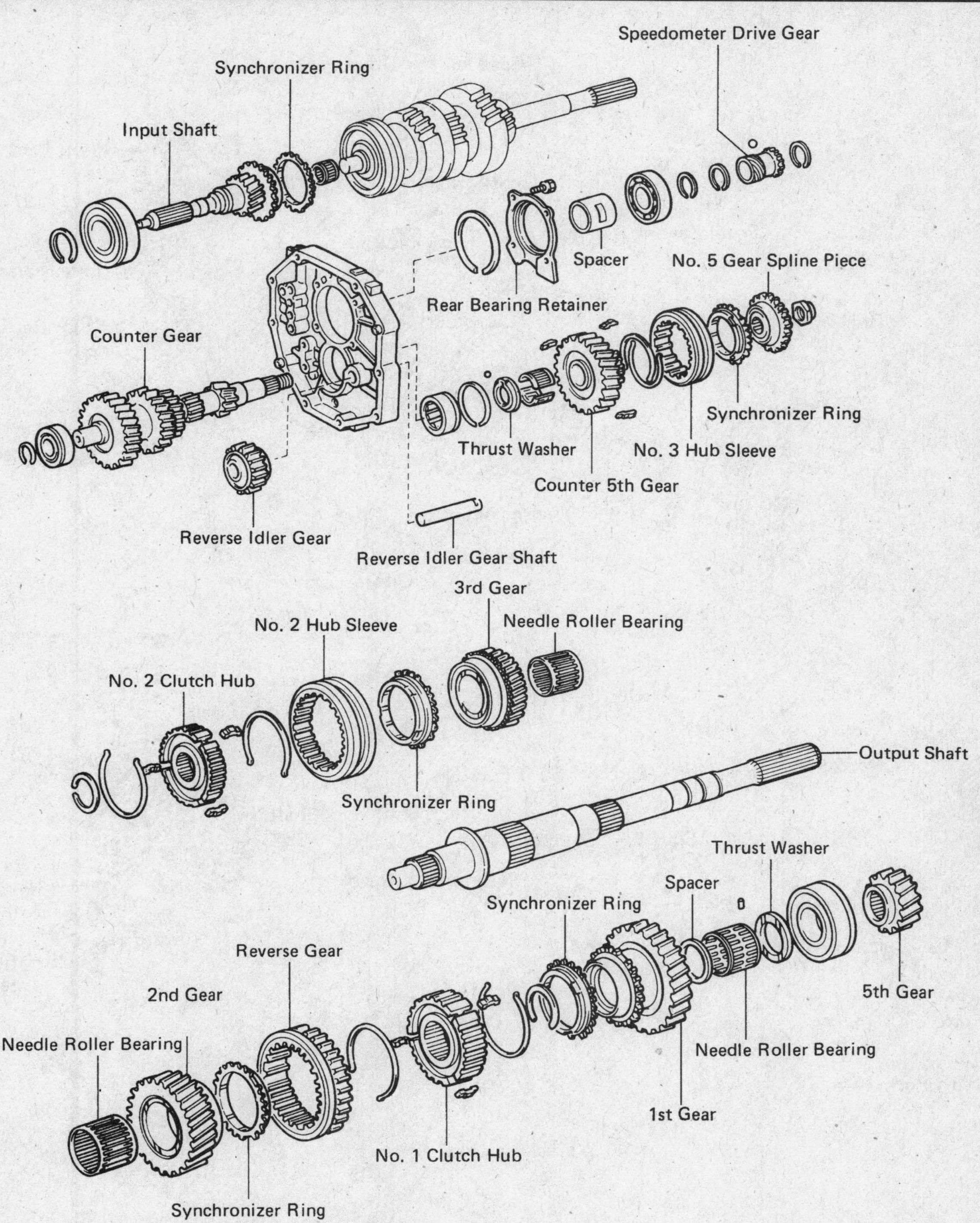

6.4f Manual transmission internal components - exploded view (R154 transmission)

to ensure that all the clearances are set to specification and the job is done in a deliberate step-by-step manner so that nothing is overlooked.

The essential tools necessary for the overhaul of this transmission include both internal and external snap-ring pliers, a bearing puller, a slide hammer, a set of various sized pin punches, a dial indicator and possibly a hydraulic press. In addition, a large, sturdy workbench and a vise or transmission stand will be required.

During disassembly of the transmission, make careful notes of how each piece comes off, where it fits in relation to other pieces and what holds it in place. Exploded views are included **(see illustrations)** to show where the parts go - but actually noting how they are installed when you remove the parts will make it much easier to get the transmission back together.

Before taking the transmission apart for repair, it will help if you have some idea of what area of the transmission may be malfunctioning. Certain problems can be closely tied to specific areas in the transmission, which can make component examination and replacement easier. Refer to the *Troubleshooting* section at the front of this manual for information regarding possible sources of trouble.

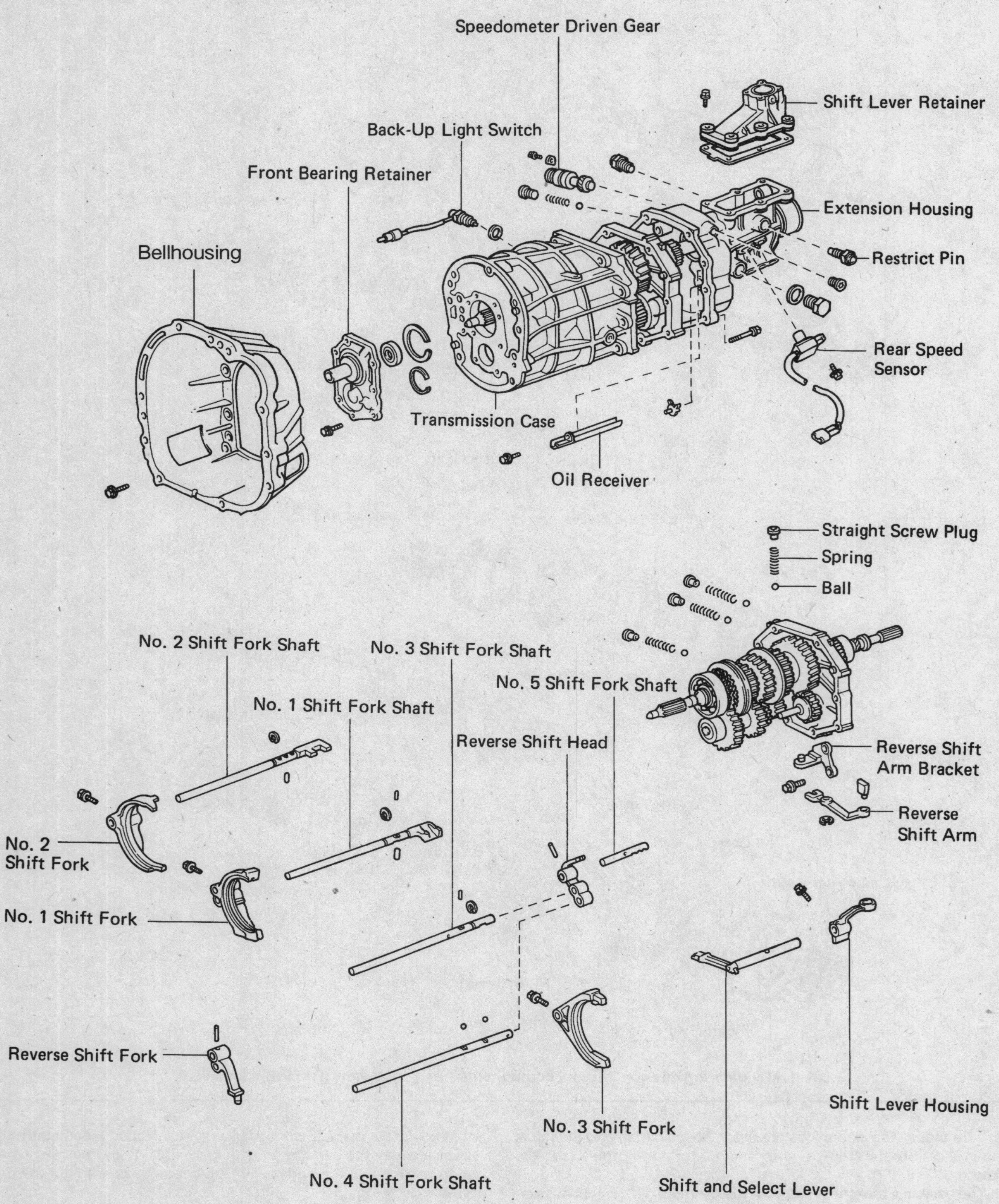

6.4g Manual transmission major components - exploded view (R154 transmission)

Chapter 7 Part B Automatic transmission

Contents

Specifications

Torque specifications	**Ft-lbs** (unless otherwise indicated)
Transmission-to-engine bolts	47
Transmission pan bolts	
1979 to 1986	39 in-lbs
1987 and later	65 in-lbs
Transmission strainer bolts	
1979 to 1986	48 in-lbs
1987 and later	84 in-lbs
Torque converter bolts	20

1 General information

These models are equipped with a four speed, automatic transmission. Later models (1983 through 1992) are also equipped with the lock-up torque converter and the Electronic Controlled Transmission (ECT). The transmissions installed from 1987 through 1992 are also equipped with a self diagnosis system that can be activated with the Overdrive button or by using the Super Monitor Display.

Because of the complexity of the clutch mechanisms and the hydraulic control systems, and because of the special tools and expertise needed to rebuild an automatic transmission, this work is usually beyond the scope of the home mechanic. The procedures in this Chapter are therefore limited to general diagnosis, routine maintenance, adjustments and transmission removal and installation.

Should the transmission require major repair work, take it to a dealer service department or a transmission repair shop. You can, however, save the expense of removing and installing the transmission by doing it yourself.

2 Diagnosis - general

General diagnostic procedures

1 Automatic transmission malfunctions may be caused by a number of conditions, such as poor engine performance, improper adjustments, hydraulic malfunctions and mechanical problems.

2 The first check should be of the transmission fluid level and condition. Refer to Chapter 1 for more information. Unless the fluid has been changed recently, drain the fluid and replace it.

3 Road test the vehicle and drive in all the various ranges, noting discrepancies in operation. Check as follows:

DRIVE range

While stopped, position the lever in the DRIVE range and accelerate. Check for a 1-2 shift, 2-3 shift and 3-OD shift. Also, the converter should lock-up in second, third or OD gear, depending on calibration. Check for part throttle downshift by depressing the accelerator 3/4 of

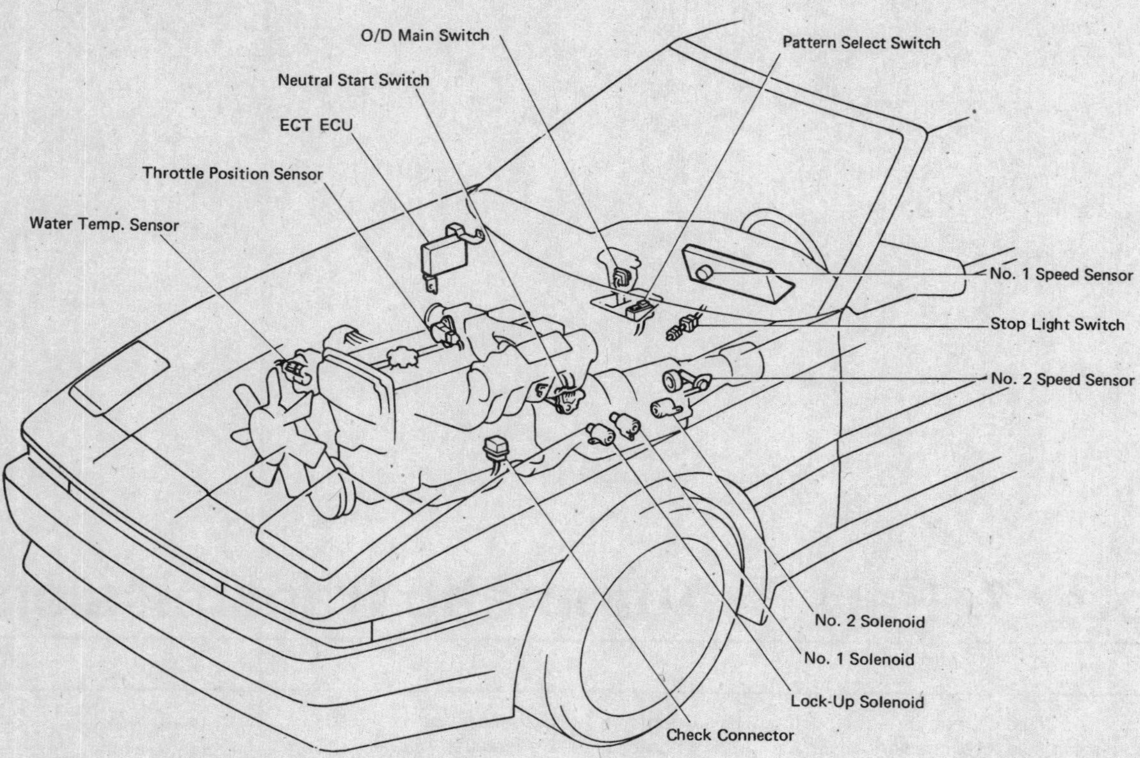

2.9a Component locations for the self diagnosis system on 1987 and later models

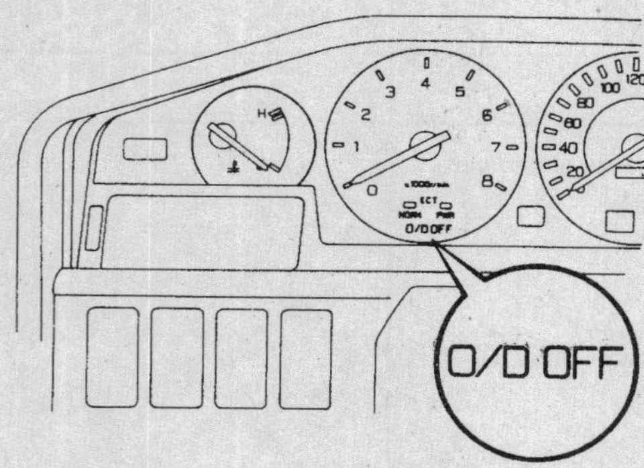

2.9b The O/D OFF warning light is located in the dashboard beneath the tachometer display

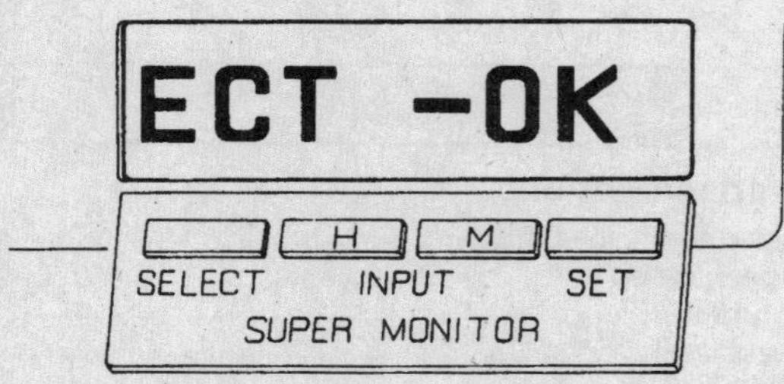

2.10 The Super Monitor Display allows easy code access and display for the automatic transmission codes

the way - the transmission should downshift. Check for full detent downshift by depressing the throttle all the way - the transmission should immediately downshift.

Range 2

At speed, shift the transmission to Range 2. The transmission should down shift immediately. It should not shift back to Overdrive. Also check for part throttle and full throttle downshifts in this range.

Low range

Position the lever in Low position and check the operation.

Overrun braking

This can be checked by manually shifting to a lower range. Engine rpm should increase and a braking effect should be noticed.

Reverse

Position the shifter in Reverse and check operation.

4 Verify that the engine is not at fault. If the engine has not received a tune-up recently, refer to Chapter 1 and make sure all engine components are functioning properly.

5 Check the adjustment of the throttle valve cable (see Section 3).

6 Check the condition of all vacuum and electrical lines and fittings at the transmission, or leading to it.

7 Check for proper adjustment of the shift linkage (see Section 4).

8 If at this point a problem remains, there is one final check before the transmission is removed for overhaul. The vehicle should be taken to a transmission specialist who will connect a special oil pressure gauge and check the line pressure in the transmission.

Self diagnosis system

Refer to illustrations 2.9a, 2.9b, 2.10, 2.11, 2.14a and 2.14b

9 A self diagnosis system is built into the electronic control system for the automatic transmission **(see illustration)**. A malfunction is indicated by the O/D OFF warning light **(see illustration)** on the dashboard (see Chapter 1).

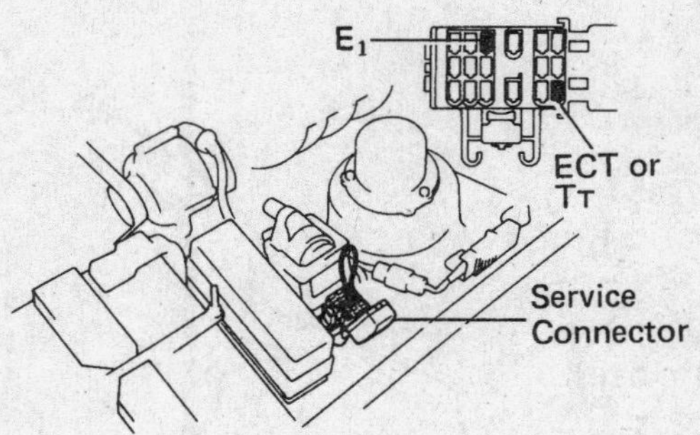

2.11 The service connector is located near the strut tower and the relay/fuse panel

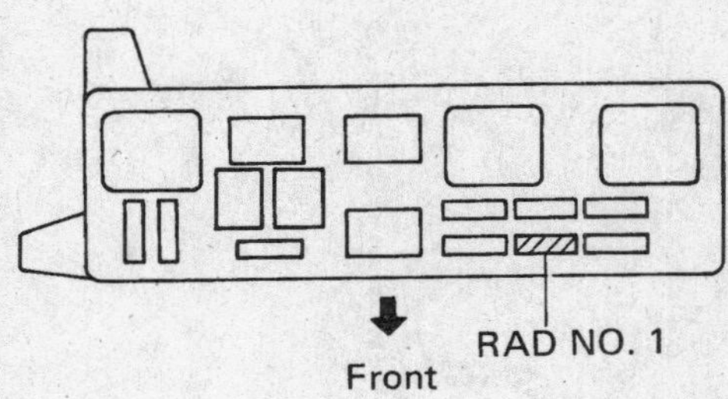

2.14a On 1987 through 1989 models, remove the RAD NO.1 fuse from the fuse panel to clear the codes from the ECU memory

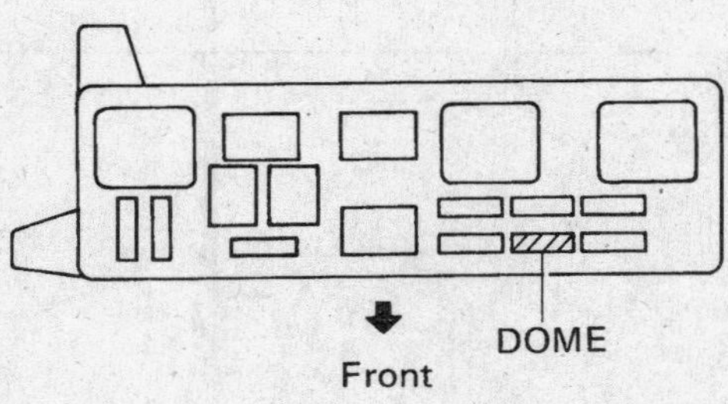

2.14b On 1990 and late rmodels, remove the DOME fuse from the fuse panel to clear the codes from the ECU memory

10 To access the self diagnosis codes for the automatic transmission, turn the ignition switch to ON (do not start the engine) and then press the O/D switch to ON. The O/D switch must be on or else the O/D OFF light will illuminate constantly. **Note:** *Some models are equipped with the Super Monitor Display located on the dashboard* **(see illustration).** *This allows the codes to be activated using a simple push-button system. Simultaneously push and hold in the SELECT and INPUT M keys for at least 3 seconds. The letters DIAG will appear on the screen. After a pause, hold in the SET key for at least 3 seconds. If the system is normal, a message ECT OK will flash on the screen. If there is a malfunction code stored, the screen will flash the digits: for example ECT 42.*

11 Use a jumper wire and connect the Tt and E1 terminals together **(see illustration)**. **Note:** *On earlier models, the pin connectors are designated E1 and ECT.*

12 Read the diagnostic codes directly from the O/D OFF light on the dashboard. If the system is operating correctly, the light will blink two times per second constantly. If there is a malfunction, the first digit of the code will blink followed by a pause of 1.5 seconds and then the second digit of the code will blink.

13 There are five codes with designated numbers and symptoms for diagnosing driveability problems with the automatic transmission.

Code 42 Defective number 1 speed sensor in the combination meter. Possible severed wire or short circuit.

Code 61 Defective number 2 speed sensor in the automatic transmission. Possible severed wire or short circuit.

Code 62 Defective number 1 solenoid or circuit. Possible severed wire or short circuit.

Code 63 Defective number 2 solenoid or circuit. Possible severed wire or short circuit.

Code 64 Defective lock-up solenoid or circuit. Possible severed wire or short circuit.

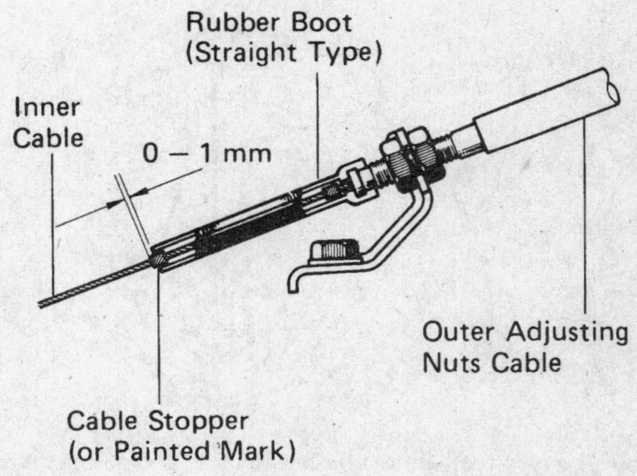

3.3 Check the distance between the end of the rubber boot and the stopper - adjust if necessary to attain the proper length

14 After the repair has been made, it is necessary to cancel the code from the memory by the ECU. Remove the RAD NO.1 fuse (1987 through 1989) or the dome fuse (1990 through 1992) (see Chapter 12) from the fuse panel for 10 seconds or more (see Chapter 12). **Note:** *It is possible to erase the codes from the ECU by simply detaching the negative terminal from the battery. Other memory systems (TCCS etc.) will be erased as well.* **Caution:** *If the stereo in your vehicle is equipped with an anti-theft system, refer to the information on page 0-15 at the front of this manual before detaching the cable.*

7B

3 Throttle Valve (TV) cable - adjustment

Refer to illustration 3.3

1 Make sure the throttle cable bracket is not bent or loose before attempting to make this adjustment. Also, the rubber boot must be seated properly on the adjuster.

2 Press the accelerator pedal all the way to the floor. **Note:** *The throttle valve in the throttle body must be completely open. Check and adjust it if necessary.*

3 Check the distance the stopper (or painted mark) on the cable extends from the boot **(see illustration)**. It must be 1.0 mm (0.040-inch).

4.4 Loosen the linkage nut, push the manual lever all the way forward to Park, then back three notches to Neutral; whole holding the selector slightly towards the Reverse range side, tighten the shift linkage nut

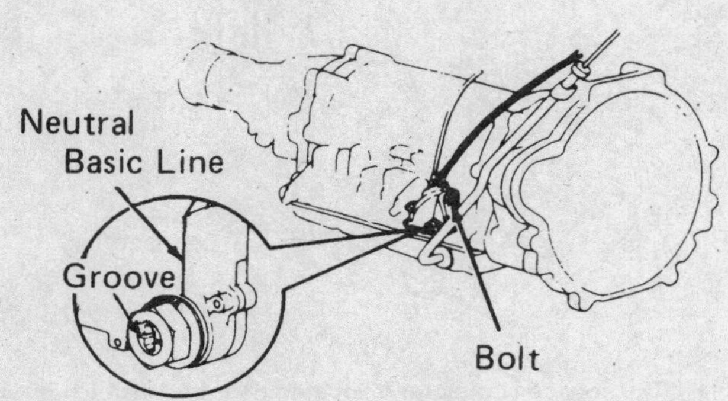

5.3 The groove in the end of the control shaft should be positioned vertically and directly in line with the neutral basic line on the switch

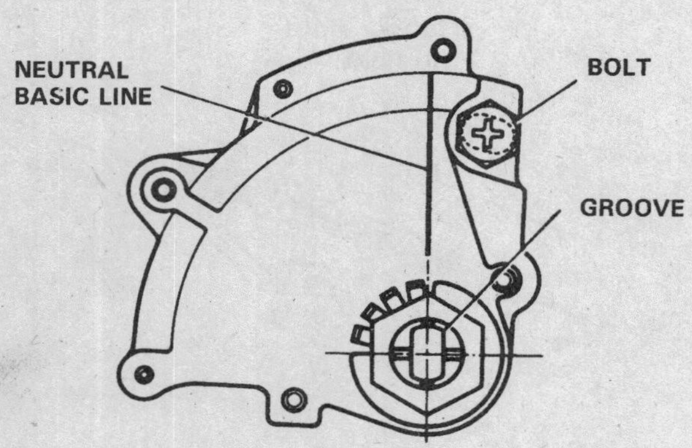

5.5 Loosen the neutral start switch bolt and adjust the switch until there is continuity between the terminals

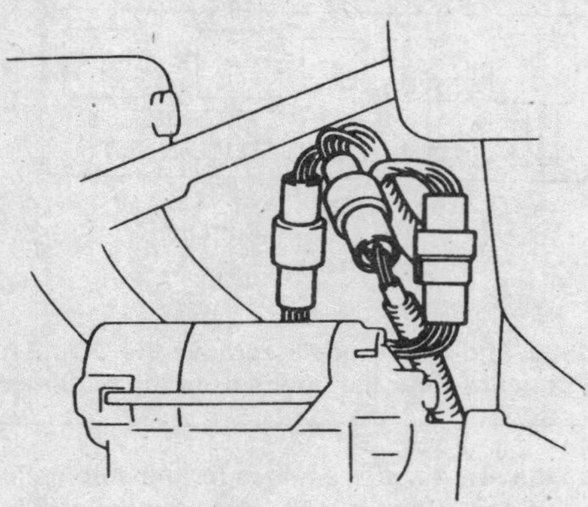

6.7 Unplug the three connectors located near the starter

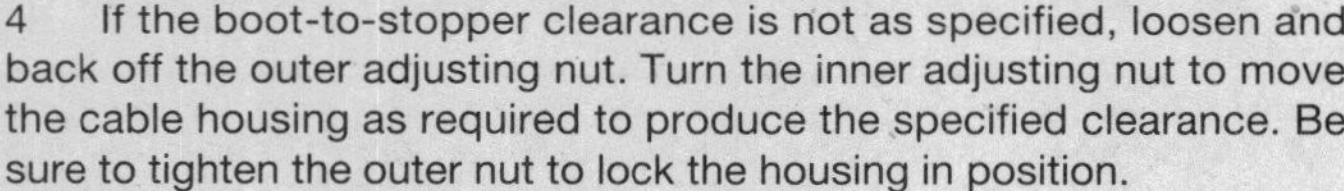

4 If the boot-to-stopper clearance is not as specified, loosen and back off the outer adjusting nut. Turn the inner adjusting nut to move the cable housing as required to produce the specified clearance. Be sure to tighten the outer nut to lock the housing in position.

4 Shift linkage - adjustment

Refer to illustration 4.4

1 This adjustment should not be considered routine and does not have to be done unless wear in the linkage or misalignment of the shift position indicator occurs.

2 Move the shift lever through the gear ranges and make sure the transmission responds accordingly. Position the lever in Neutral and see if the transmission shifts to Neutral. Check to see if the shift position indicator registers correctly with the lever in each detent position.

3 If adjustment is required, the vehicle must be raised and supported securely on jackstands.

4 Working under the vehicle, loosen the shift linkage nut **(see illustration)**. Move the selector lever all the way forward (to Park) then back three notches to the Neutral position.

5 With the shift selector in N, but held lightly towards R (reverse), tighten the shift linkage nut.

6 Lower the vehicle and drive it to check the operation of the linkage in each gear.

5 Neutral start switch - adjustment

Refer to illustrations 5.3 and 5.5

1 If the engine can be started with the shift lever in any position other than Park or Neutral, or if the back-up lights do not come on when the lever is moved to R, the neutral start switch should be checked and adjusted. The vehicle must be raised and supported on jackstands for this procedure.

1979 through 1984 models

2 Position the shift lever in Neutral, then loosen the switch bolt.

3 The groove in the end of the control shaft should be positioned vertically and directly in line with the neutral basic line on the switch **(see illustration)**. If it isn't, pivot the switch to align them, then tighten the bolt.

1985 and later models

4 Position the shift lever in Neutral, detach the electrical connector to the switch, then connect an ohmmeter between terminals N and B. **Note:** *The terminals are marked at the connector.*

5 Loosen the neutral start switch bolt and adjust the position of the switch until there is continuity between the N and B terminals **(see illustration)**. **Note:** *An alternate method is to align the groove in the shaft and the Neutral basic line and tighten the bolt.*

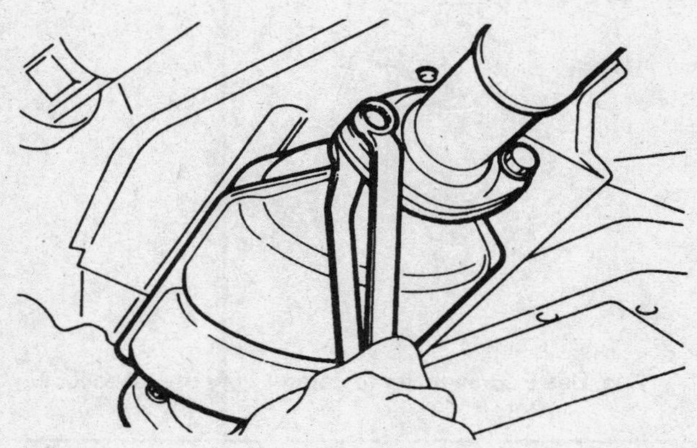

6.8 Using two wrenches, detach the exhaust pipe from the rear of the converter

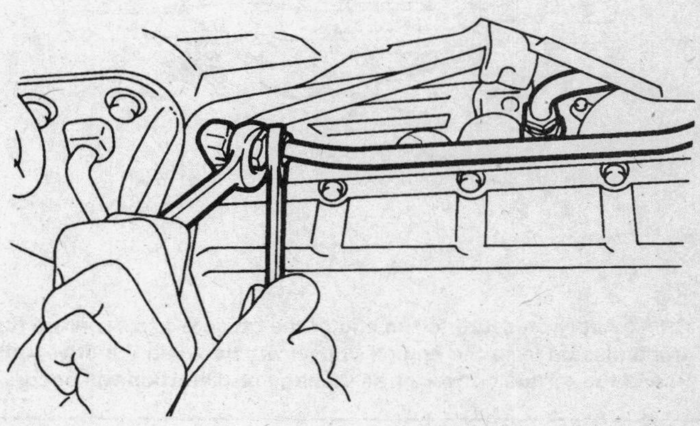

6.9 Disconnect the two oil cooler lines from the transmission case and plug them to prevent fluid loss

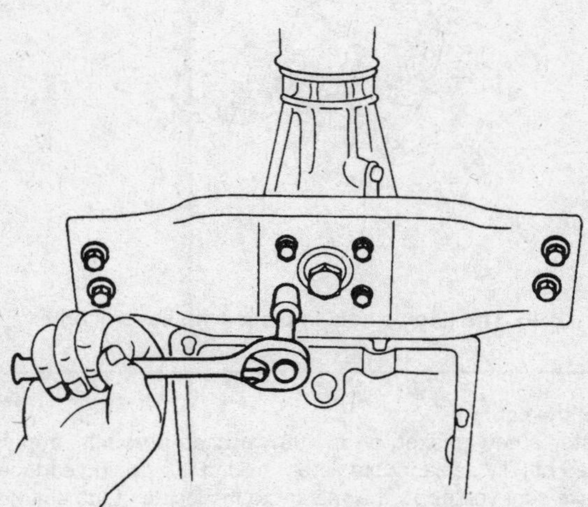

6.13 After supporting the transmission with a jack, take out the eight bolts and remove the rear support crossmember

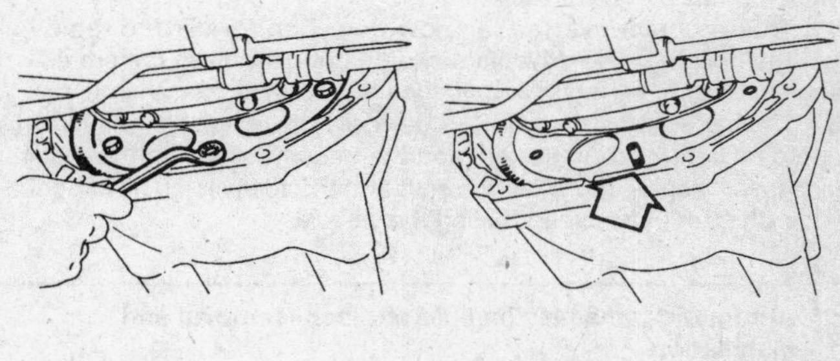

6.15 After removing the six torque converter mounting bolts, install the two guide pins (arrow)

6 Automatic transmission - removal and installation

Refer to illustrations 6.7, 6.8, 6.9, 6.13, 6.15 and 6.17

1 Disconnect the cable from the negative battery terminal. **Caution:** *If the stereo in your vehicle is equipped with an anti-theft system, refer to the information on page 0-15 at the front of this manual before detaching the cable.*

2 Refer to Chapter 1 and drain the coolant. Disconnect the upper radiator hose.

3 Disconnect the throttle linkage cable at the EFI throttle body and disconnect the air intake connector.

4 Raise the vehicle and support it on jackstands (if not already done).

5 Drain the fluid from the transmission (see Chapter 1).

6 Disconnect the driveshaft from the rear axle (see Chapter 8) and withdraw it from the transmission extension housing.

7 Unplug the three electrical connectors located near the starter **(see illustration)**, the neutral start switch and the back-up light switch.

8 Disconnect the exhaust pipe from the rear of the converter **(see illustration)** and remove the two rubber hangers. Remove the exhaust pipe retaining clamp from the transmission case.

9 Remove the oil cooler line clamp from the transmission case. Disconnect the two oil cooler lines from the transmission case and plug them **(see illustration)**.

10 Disconnect the speedometer drive cable.

11 Unbolt the two stiffener plates from the torque converter housing. Pull the fluid filler tube from the transmission and save the O-ring seals. Remove the driveplate cover.

12 Remove the sliding yoke from the power steering gear housing. Disconnect both tie-rod ends (see Chapter 10), then remove the fluid line clamps. Remove the four bolts, the two brackets and the rubber insulator, then remove the gear housing from the crossmember and suspend it with wire or a length of coat hanger.

13 Support the automatic transmission with a jack, then remove the rear support crossmember and mount **(see illustration)**.

14 Through the open lower half of the torque converter housing, remove the six bolts which join the driveplate and converter together. They can be removed one at a time by rotating the driveplate. To do this, turn the crankshaft with a wrench attached to the pulley bolt at the front of the engine.

15 Screw two guide pins (made from two old bolts of the correct size with the heads cut off) through opposite bolt holes in the front of the driveplate and into the torque converter, then rotate the engine until they are vertical **(see illustration)**. These pins will act as pivot points during removal of the transmission.

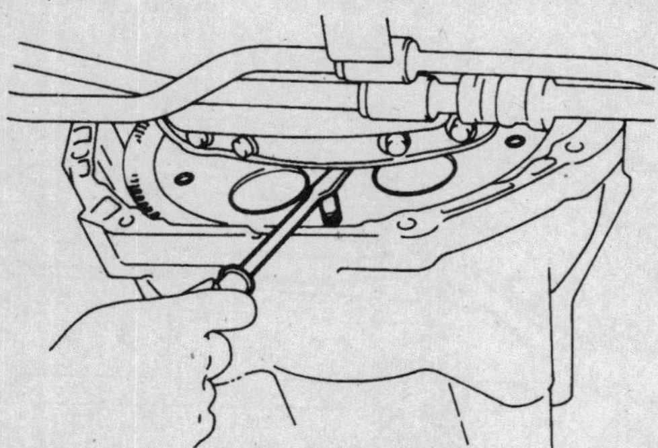

6.17 Apply pressure to the end of the guide pin to separate the transmission from the engine - never pry between the driveplate and the torque converter as damage or distortion will occur

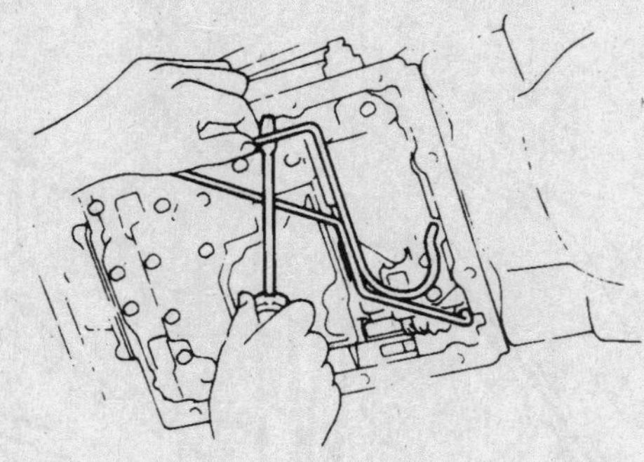

7.4a Use a screwdriver to carefully pry the tubes loose

16 Place a jack under the engine oil pan (use a block of wood to protect it), and remove the bolts which attach the torque converter housing to the engine.
17 Lower both jacks progressively until the transmission clears the lower edge of the firewall. Insert two levers or large screwdrivers between the engine rear plate and the guide pins and pry the transmission away from the engine **(see illustration)**. Catch the fluid which will run from the torque converter during this operation. **Caution**: *Never position the levers between the driveplate and the torque converter as damage or distortion will result*.
18 The torque converter can now be pulled forward to remove it from the housing. The driveplate can be unbolted from the crankshaft flange if it has to be replaced because of a worn starter ring gear.
19 The installation procedure is basically the reverse of removal. Be sure to refill the cooling system and the transmission with the required fluids (see Chapter 1). Adjust the shift and throttle linkage as described in this Chapter before road testing the vehicle.

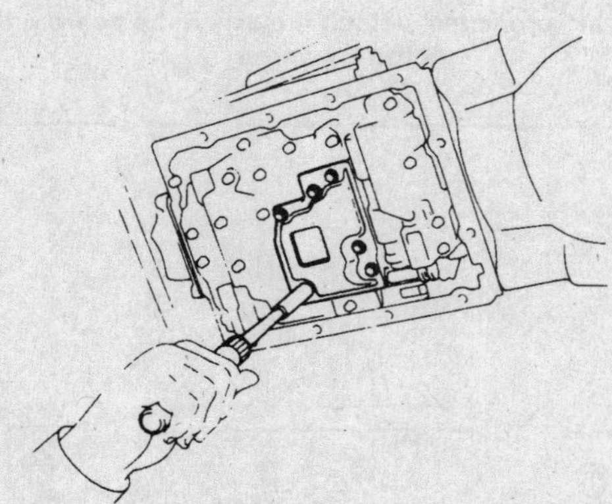

7.4b The filter is held in place with several bolts

7 Automatic transmission fluid strainer - removal and installation

Refer to illustrations 7.4a and 7.4b

1 Raise the vehicle and support it securely on jackstands.
2 Drain the transmission fluid (see Chapter 1). After it has drained completely, install the drain plug and tighten it securely.
3 Remove the bolts and the transmission pan.
4 Remove the bolts and the fluid strainer. On some models it will be necessary to remove the fluid tubes before you remove the strainer **(see illustrations)**.
5 Install a new strainer and tighten the bolts to the torque listed in this Chapter's Specifications. If removed, install the fluid tubes.
6 Clean the gasket sealing surface of the transmission and the pan. Remove all traces of old gasket material or sealant. Clean and dry the inside of the pan.
7 Install a new gasket, or on 1987 and later models, apply a 1/8-inch bead of RTV sealant completely around the sealing surface of the pan. Make sure you apply the sealant to the inside of the bolt holes.
8 Install the pan and tighten the bolts to the torque listed in this Chapter's Specifications.
9 Lower the vehicle and add the type and amount of fluid listed in Chapter 1 Specifications.
10 Place the transmission in Park, apply the parking brake and block the wheels. Start the engine and allow it to reach the normal operating temperature.
11 With the engine idling, move the transmission gear selector through each range and back to Park. Add more fluid as required (see Chapter 1) and check for leaks.

Chapter 8 Clutch and drivetrain

Contents

Specifications

Clutch

Fluid type .... Brake fluid conforming to DOT 3 specifications
Minimum rivet depth .... 0.012 inch

Rear axle

Drive pinion preload
used bearing .... 5.2 to 8.7 in-lb
new bearing .... 10.4 to 16.5 in-lb
Pinion oil seal installation depth .... 0.059 inch

Torque specifications

Torque specifications	Ft-lbs
Release fork support-to-clutch housing	29
Clutch master cylinder retaining nuts	18
Reservoir retaining bolt	18
Center bearing flange-to-universal joint flange yoke	31
Universal joint flange yoke-to-companion flange	31
Center bearing bracket-to-body	30
Center support bearing preload	134
Center support bearing nut	51
Rear axle bearing retainer	48
Driveaxle flange nuts	51

Differential pinion nut	
1979 through 1981 models	
initial	50
maximum	55
1982 through 1986 models	
initial	80
maximum	174
1987 through 1992 models	
initial	134
maximum	250
Pressure plate-to-flywheel bolts	13
Clutch housing-to-transmission case bolts	27
Flywheel-to-crankshaft bolts	54

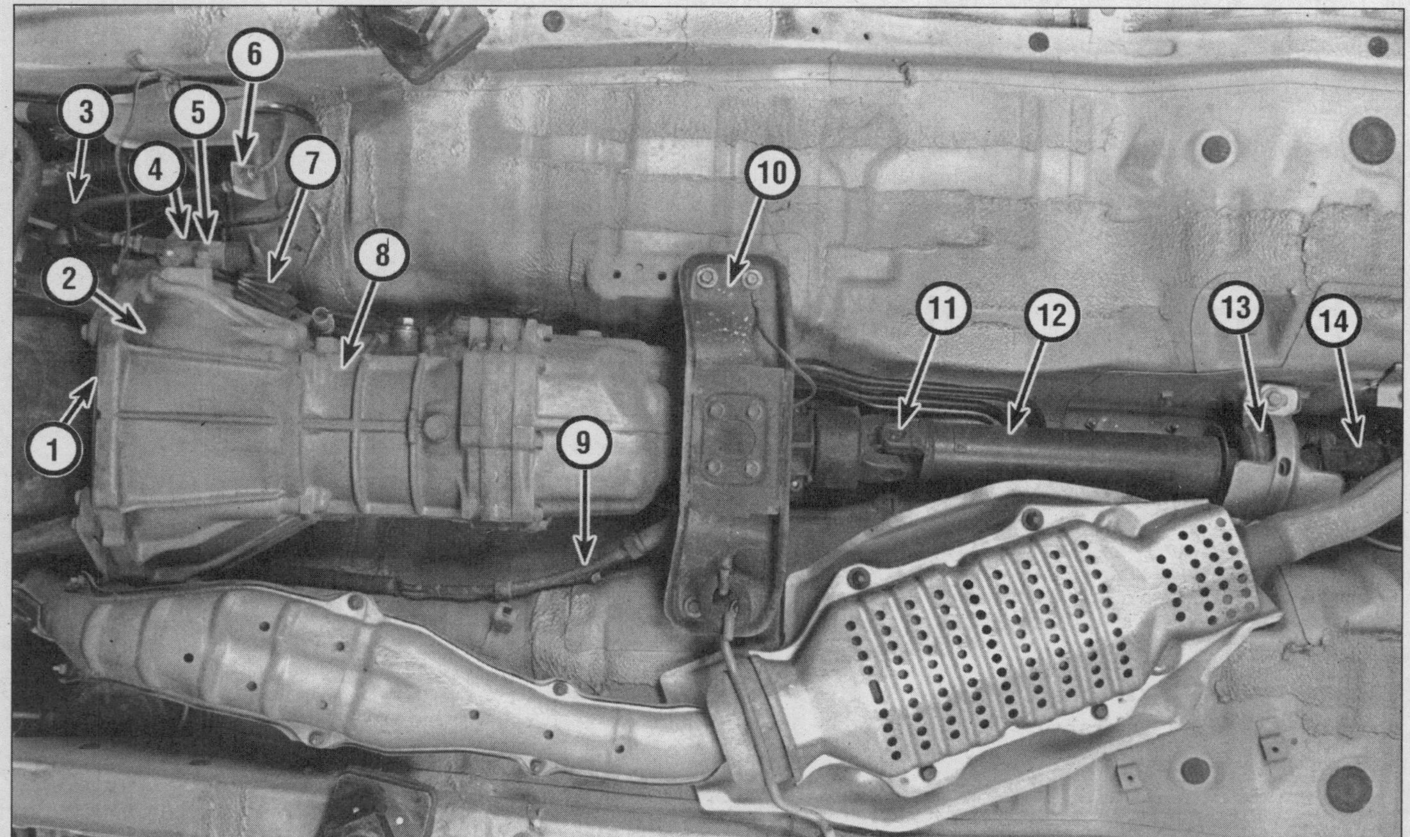

Typical transmission/drivetrain components viewed from underside of vehicle (1983 model shown)

1. *Flywheel inspection plate*
2. *Bellhousing*
3. *Clutch hydraulic system flexible hose*
4. *Slave cylinder bleeder screw*
5. *Clutch slave cylinder*
6. *Flexible hose-to-metal line union*
7. *Clutch release fork and boot*
8. *Transmission*
9. *Speedometer cable*
10. *Transmission support crossmember*
11. *U-joint*
12. *Intermediate driveshaft*
13. *Center bearing*
14. *U-joint*

1 General information

Manual transmission models are equipped with a conventional design clutch utilizing a hydraulically actuated release mechanism.

Power is transmitted from the transmission to the rear axle by a two piece driveshaft. Universal joints are located at the front, rear and center bearing to allow for vertical movement of the rear axle and slight movement of the engine and transmission. A slip joint is used to allow for fore-and-aft movement of the drivetrain.

The rear axle assemblies vary from year to year. Early models (1979 through 1981) are equipped with a solid rear axle. Middle years (1983 through 1986) are equipped with an independent rear suspension system, a differential support member, and axles pivoting through constant velocity (CV) joints. Late models (1987 through 1992) are equipped with an independent rear suspension with upper and lower control arms.

Most rear end component problems reveal themselves in the form of some sort of noise. The noise may be caused by gears or bearings (in the differential and the outer ends of the rear axle housing).

Gear noise is usually a high pitched whine, which may be more pronounced at certain speeds or when the vehicle is under load.

Bearing noise is generally a lower pitched, steady growl. It tends

Typical differential/drivetrain components viewed from the underside of vehicle (1983 model shown)

1 *Differential pinion oil seal*
2 *U-joint*
3 *Driveshaft*
4 *CV joint/boot*
5 *Axleshaft*
6 *Differential flange*
7 *Differential assembly*

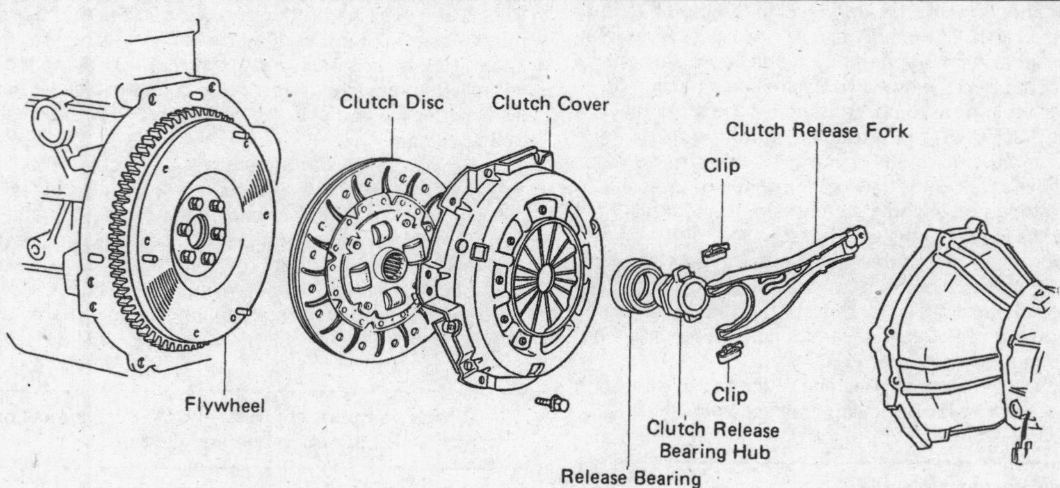

2.1 Typical clutch components (W50 and W58 transmissions) - exploded view

to get louder when accelerating under load. Swerving the vehicle from side-to-side on a flat, level road may help to pinpoint faulty wheel bearings. This practice throws additional side loads on the bearings, which should increase any noise coming from them. A bad bearing could show up in the differential assembly, although bearing failure in this area is much less likely than in the wheel bearings.

Major repair work on the differential (and other rear end components) requires many special tools and a high degree of expertise, and therefore should not be attempted by the home mechanic. If major repairs become necessary, we recommend that they be performed by a Toyota dealer service department or an independent repair shop.

2 Clutch - description and check

Refer to illustration 2.1

1 Models equipped with a manual transmission feature a single dry plate, diaphragm spring-type clutch **(see illustration)**. The actuation is through a hydraulic system.

2 When the clutch pedal is depressed, hydraulic fluid (under pressure from the clutch master cylinder) flows into the slave cylinder. Because the slave cylinder is connected to the clutch release fork, the fork moves the release bearing into contact with the clutch cover/pres-

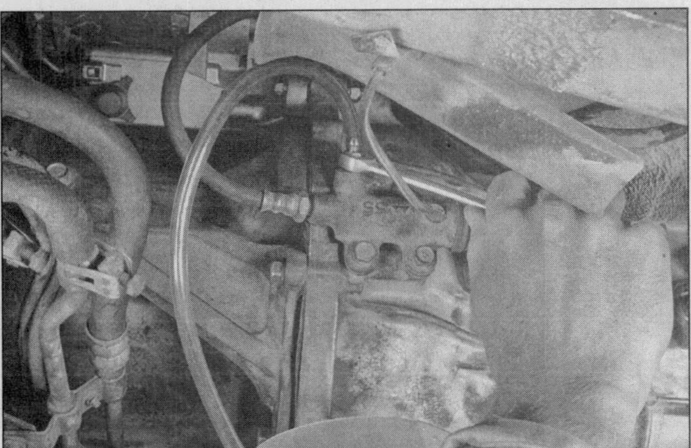

3.6 One end of the tube is attached to the bleeder screw fitting and the other end is submerged in a container of brake fluid - repeat the bleeding procedure until no air bubbles emerge from the cylinder

sure plate release fingers, disengaging the clutch disc.

3 The hydraulic system locates the clutch pedal and provides clutch adjustment automatically, so no adjustment of the linkage or pedal is required.

4 Terminology can be a problem regarding the clutch components because common names have in some cases changed from that used by the manufacturer. For example, the driven plate is also called the clutch plate or disc, the clutch release bearing is sometimes called a throwout bearing, the slave cylinder is sometimes called the operating or release cylinder.

5 Other than to replace components with obvious damage, some preliminary checks should be performed to diagnose a clutch system failure.

- a) The first check should be of the fluid level in the clutch master cylinder. If the fluid level is low, add fluid as necessary and retest. If the master cylinder runs dry, or if any of the hydraulic components are serviced, bleed the hydraulic system (see Section 3).
- b) To check "clutch spin down time," run the engine at normal idle speed with the transmission in Neutral (clutch pedal up - engaged). Disengage the clutch (pedal down), wait nine seconds and shift the transmission into Reverse. No grinding noise should be heard. A grinding noise would indicate component failure in the clutch cover assembly or the clutch disc.
- c) To check for complete clutch release, run the engine (with the brake on to prevent movement) and hold the clutch pedal approximately 1/2-inch from the floor mat. Shift the transmission between First gear and Reverse several times. If the shift is not smooth, component failure is indicated.
- d) Visually inspect the clutch pedal bushing at the top of the clutch pedal to make sure there is no sticking or excessive wear.

3 Clutch hydraulic system - bleeding

Refer to illustration 3.6

1 If air gets into the clutch release mechanism hydraulic system, the clutch may not release completely when the pedal is depressed. Air can enter the system whenever any part of it is dismantled or if the fluid level in the master cylinder reservoir runs low. Air can also leak into the system through a hole too small to allow fluid to leak out. In this case, it indicates that a general overhaul of the system is required.

2 To bleed the air out, you will need an assistant to pump the clutch pedal, a supply of new brake fluid of the recommended type, a clear plastic container, a section of clear, flexible plastic tubing which will fit over the bleeder screw and a wrench for the bleeder screw.

3 Check the fluid level in the master cylinder reservoir. Add fluid, if necessary, to bring the level up to the full mark. Use only the recommended brake fluid and do not mix different types. Never use fluid from a container that has been standing uncapped. You will have to check the fluid level in the master cylinder reservoir often during the bleeding procedure. If the level drops too far, air will enter the system through the master cylinder.

4.3 A metal rod or clutch alignment tool can be used to prevent the disc from dropping out as the pressure plate is removed

4 Raise the front of the vehicle and set it securely on jackstands. Apply the parking brake.

5 Remove the bleeder screw cap from the bleeder screw on the slave cylinder.

6 Attach one end of the plastic tube to the bleeder screw fitting and place the other end in the container, submerged in clean brake fluid **(see illustration)**.

7 Loosen the bleeder screw slightly, then tighten it to the point where it is snug yet easily loosened.

8 Have your assistant pump the pedal several times and hold it in the fully depressed position.

9 With pressure on the pedal, open the bleeder screw approximately one-half turn. As the fluid stops flowing through the tube and into the jar, tighten the bleeder screw. Again, pump the pedal, hold it in the fully depressed position and loosen the bleeder screw momentarily. Do not allow the pedal to be released with the bleeder screw in the open position.

10 Repeat the procedure until no air bubbles are visible in the fluid flowing through the tube. Be sure to check the fluid level in the master cylinder reservoir while performing the bleeding operation.

11 Tighten the bleeder screw completely, remove the tube and install the bleeder screw cap.

12 Check the clutch fluid level in the master cylinder to make sure it is adequate, then test drive the vehicle and check for proper clutch operation.

4 Clutch components (W50 and W58 transmissions only) - removal, inspection and installation

Refer to illustrations 4.3, 4.4, 4.5, 4.8, 4.9a, 4.9b, 4.10, 4.11, 4.12 and 4.16

Removal

Note: *On models with the R154 transmission the clutch cover, friction disc and release bearing are removed and installed as a unit and special tools are required for proper installation, see Chapter 7A for removal and installation of the transmission and clutch assembly.*

1 Access to the clutch components is normally accomplished by removing the transmission, leaving the engine in the vehicle. If, of course, the engine is being removed for major overhaul, then the opportunity should always be taken to check the clutch for wear and replace worn components as necessary. The following procedures will assume that the engine will stay in place.

2 Referring to Chapter 7, Part A, remove the transmission from the vehicle.

4.4 Be sure to mark the pressure plate and flywheel in order to insure proper alignment during installation

4.5 Loosen the pressure plate bolts (arrows) a little at a time until the spring tension is released

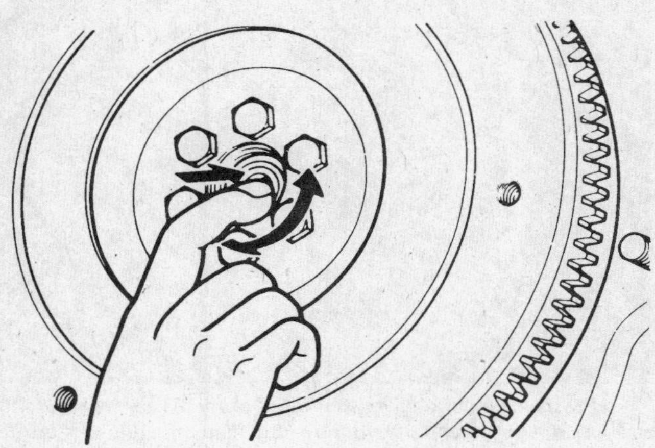

4.8 Turn the pilot bearing by hand while pressing in on it - if it is rough or noisy, a new one should be installed

4.9a Use a special pilot bearing puller (if available) or a regular slide hammer puller to remove the pilot bearing

4.9b Using a hammer and socket, carefully drive the new bearing into place

3 To support the clutch disc during removal, install a clutch alignment tool or a large metal rod through the middle of the clutch **(see illustration)**.

4 Carefully inspect the flywheel and pressure plate for indexing marks. If no marks are visible, use a center punch, scribe or paint to mark the pressure plate and flywheel so they can be reinstalled in the same relative positions **(see illustration)**.

5 Turning each bolt only one turn at a time, loosen the pressure plate-to-flywheel bolts. Work in a criss-cross pattern, until all spring pressure is relieved **(see illustration)**. Grasp the pressure plate and completely remove the bolts, then separate the pressure plate and clutch disc from the flywheel.

Inspection

6 Ordinarily, when a problem develops in the clutch, it can be attributed to wear of the clutch driven plate assembly (clutch disc). However, all components should be inspected at this time.

7 Inspect the flywheel (see Section 5).

8 Check the pilot bearing in the end of the crankshaft. Make sure that it turns smoothly and quietly **(see illustration)**. If the transmission input shaft contact surface is worn or damaged, replace the bearing with a new one.

9 Use a puller to remove the pilot bearing **(see illustration)**. Install a new bearing with a socket and hammer **(see illustration)**.

4.10 Once the clutch disc is removed, the rivet depth can be measured and compared to the Specifications

4.11 Take off the two spring clips and slide the release bearing off the transmission input shaft

4.12 Examine the pressure plate friction surface for score marks, cracks and evidence of overheating

4.16 Insert a clutch alignment tool or metal bar through the middle of the clutch and move the disc until it is centered

10 Inspect the lining on the clutch disc. Measure the rivet depth and compare it to the depth listed in this Chapter's Specifications **(see illustration)**. Check for loose rivets, distortion, cracks, broken springs and any other obvious damage. As mentioned above, the clutch disc is normally replaced each time it is removed, so if there is any doubt about its condition, install a new one.

11 Ordinarily, the release bearing is also replaced along with the clutch disc. Using a screwdriver, remove the upper and lower spring clips and pull the bearing off the input shaft **(see illustration)**. Reverse the procedure when replacing the bearing.

12 Check the machined surfaces of the pressure plate. If the surface is grooved or otherwise damaged it will have to be replaced. Also check for obvious damage, distortion and cracks **(see illustration)**. If a new pressure plate is indicated, new or factory rebuilt units are available.

Installation

13 Before installation, carefully clean the flywheel and pressure plate machined surfaces. Handle the parts only with clean hands. DO NOT get oil or grease on the clutch friction surfaces.

14 Position the clutch disc and pressure plate on the flywheel with the clutch disc held in place with the alignment tool. Make sure the disc is installed properly (most replacement discs will be marked "flywheel side" or something similar).

15 Tighten the pressure plate-to-flywheel bolts finger tight only, working around the pressure plate.

16 Insert an alignment tool, (if not already in place) through the middle of the clutch disc **(see illustration)**. Move the disc until it is exactly in the center so the transmission input shaft will pass easily through the disc and into the pilot bearing.

17 One turn at a time, tighten the pressure plate-to-flywheel bolts. Work in a diagonal pattern to prevent distorting the pressure plate as the bolts are tightened to the torque listed in this Chapter's Specifications.

18 Using a high melting point grease, lubricate the entire inner surface of the release bearing. Make sure the groove inside is completely filled. Also place grease on the ball socket and the fork fingers.

19 Install the transmission, slave cylinder and all components removed previously.

5 Flywheel - inspection, removal and installation

Refer to illustrations 5.2 and 5.3

1 The flywheel as used on manual transmission models is accessible only after removing the engine or the transmission.

2 Visually inspect the flywheel for cracks, hot spots and other obvious defects **(see illustration)**. If the imperfections are slight, a machine shop can machine the surface flat and smooth.

3 To detach the flywheel, remove the bolts which attach it to the engine **(see illustration)**. Be aware that it is fairly heavy and should be well supported as the final bolt is removed - do not drop it.

4 Upon installation, note that the flywheel fits over an alignment dowel so that it will go on only one way. Use thread locking compound

5.2 Check the flywheel for cracks, hot spots and other obvious defects (slight imperfections can be removed by a machine shop)

5.3 A large screwdriver can be used to jam the starter ring gear while loosening the flywheel mounting bolts

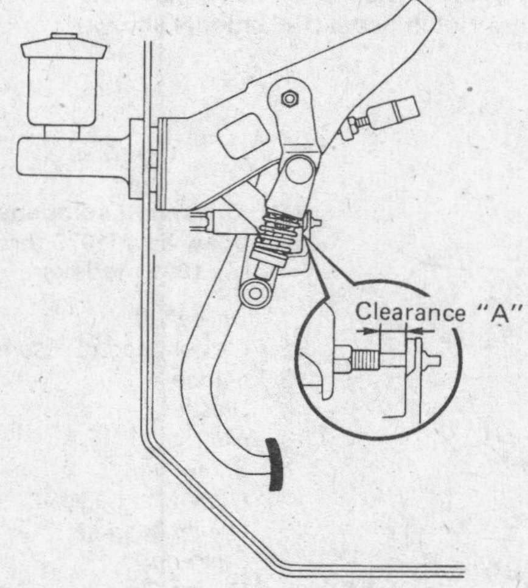

6.3 Clearance "A" is the actual length of the push rod as it sits inside the clutch start switch

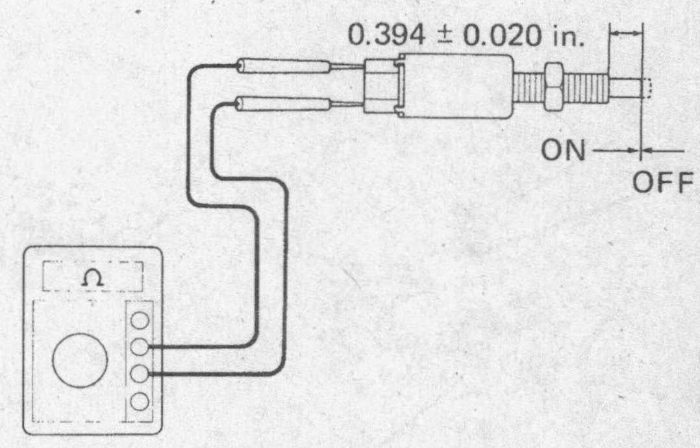

6.5 Check for the exact location (length) of the rod when the switch transfers from ON to OFF

on the bolts and tighten them in a criss-cross pattern to the torque listed in this Chapter's Specifications.

6 Clutch start switch - check and adjustment

Check

Refer to illustrations 6.3 and 6.5

1 Before checking the clutch start switch, make sure the pedal freeplay and pushrod play are correct (see Chapter 1).

2 Check that the engine does NOT start when the clutch pedal is NOT depressed.

3 Check that clearance "A" is greater than 0.04 inch (1.0 mm) when the clutch pedal is fully depressed **(see illustration)**.

4 If necessary, adjust the clutch start switch (see Steps 7 through 10).

5 Check that there is continuity between the terminals when the switch is ON **(see illustration)**.

6 Release the switch and check that there is NO continuity between the terminals. If the tests are not correct, replace the switch with a new one.

Adjustment

Refer to illustrations 6.7a and 6.7b

7 Measure the pedal stroke **(see illustration)** at different intervals according to the chart **(see illustration)**.

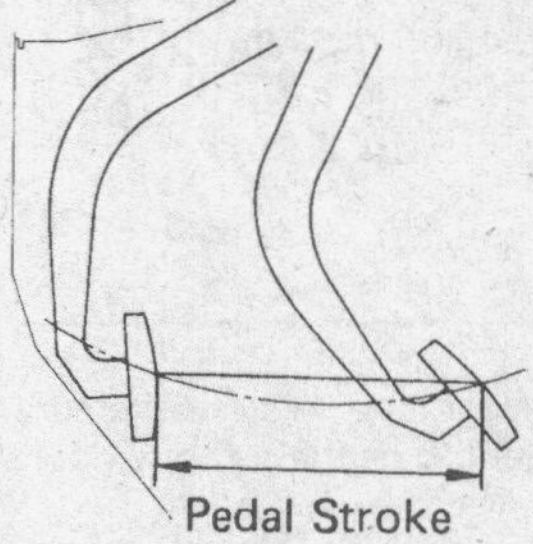

6.7a The pedal stroke is measured from complete rest (not depressed) to the end of the suggested travel length listed on the succeeding chart (6.102 inches)

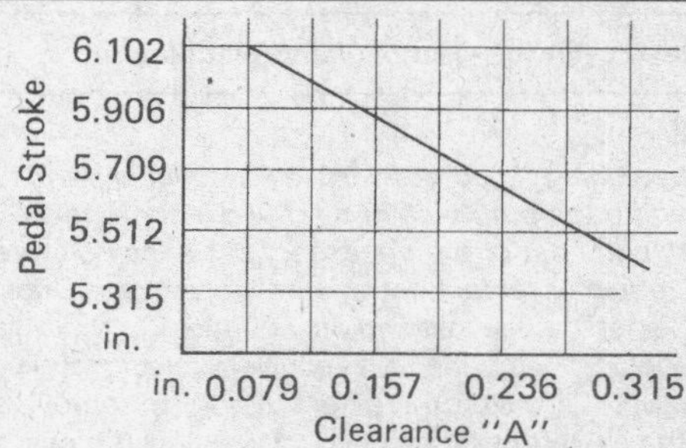

6.7b Start with the highest pedal stroke (6.102 inches) and slowly release the pedal to obtain the shorter clearance "A" readings

7.3 Slave cylinder on the R154 transmission (1992 Turbo model shown)

8.4 There are two nuts holding the master cylinder to the firewall, one next to the cylinder (visible) and one inside the vehicle above the clutch pedal (1983 model shown)

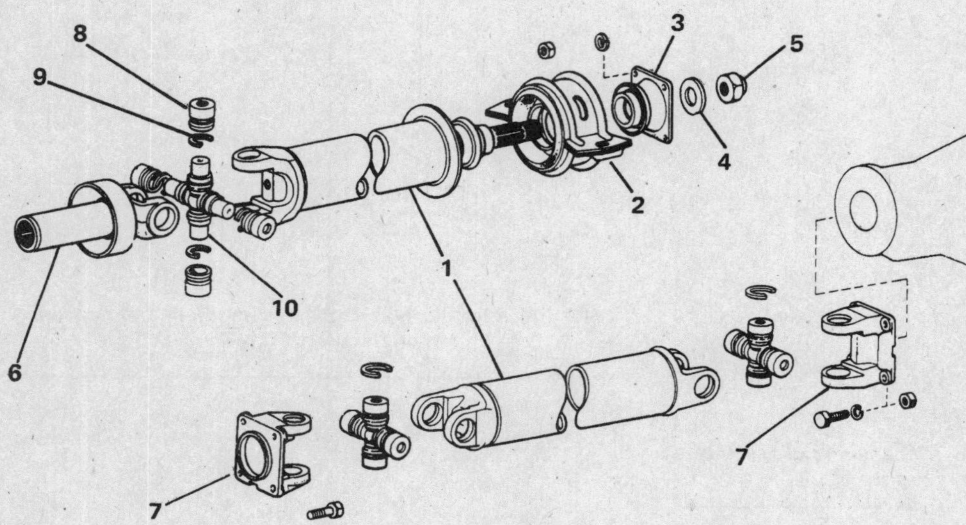

9.2a Driveshaft components - exploded view (1979 through 1981 models)

1 *Driveshaft*
2 *Center bearing assembly*
3 *Flange*
4 *Washer*
5 *Nut*
6 *Sleeve yoke*
7 *U-joint flange yoke*
8 *U-joint bearing*
9 *Snap-ring*
10 *Spider*

8 Carefully check clearance "A" to make sure the switch opens and closes at the correct length as the pedal is depressed **(see illustration 6.5)**.
9 Release the lock nut on the shaft and adjust the movement of the switch to coincide with the specifications listed in the chart in **illustration 6.7b**.
10 Tighten the locknut and recheck the system.

7 Clutch slave cylinder - removal and installation

Refer to illustration 7.3

Note: *Before beginning this procedure, contact local parts stores and dealers concerning the purchase of a rebuild kit or a new slave cylinder. Availability and cost of the necessary parts may dictate whether the cylinder is rebuilt or replaced with a new one. If it is decided to rebuild the cylinder, follow the instructions contained in the rebuild kit.*

1 Raise the vehicle and support it securely on jackstands.
2 Wipe the top of the clutch master cylinder to remove any loose dirt. Unscrew the cap and place a piece of plastic wrap over the top to create a partial vacuum and to stop fluid from siphoning out when the slave cylinder is removed. Replace the cap.
3 Wipe the area around the union on the slave cylinder **(see illustration)**. Using a flare nut wrench to avoid damaging the fitting, disconnect the flexible hydraulic hose from the rigid metal line. Plug or tape the end of the line to contain the remaining fluid in the line and to keep dirt out.
4 Remove the two cylinder retaining bolts, then withdraw the cylinder from the clutch housing, simultaneously disengaging the pushrod from the release arm.
5 Installation is the reverse of removal. Bleed the hydraulic system (see Section 3).

8 Clutch master cylinder - removal and installation

Refer to illustration 8.4

Note: *Before beginning this procedure, contact local parts stores and dealers concerning the purchase of a rebuild kit or a new master cylinder. Availability and cost of the necessary parts may dictate whether the cylinder is rebuilt or replaced with a new one. If it is decided to rebuild the cylinder, follow the instructions contained in the rebuild kit.*

Removal

1 Remove the under cover from the dash panel. This is required to gain access to the top of the clutch pedal.

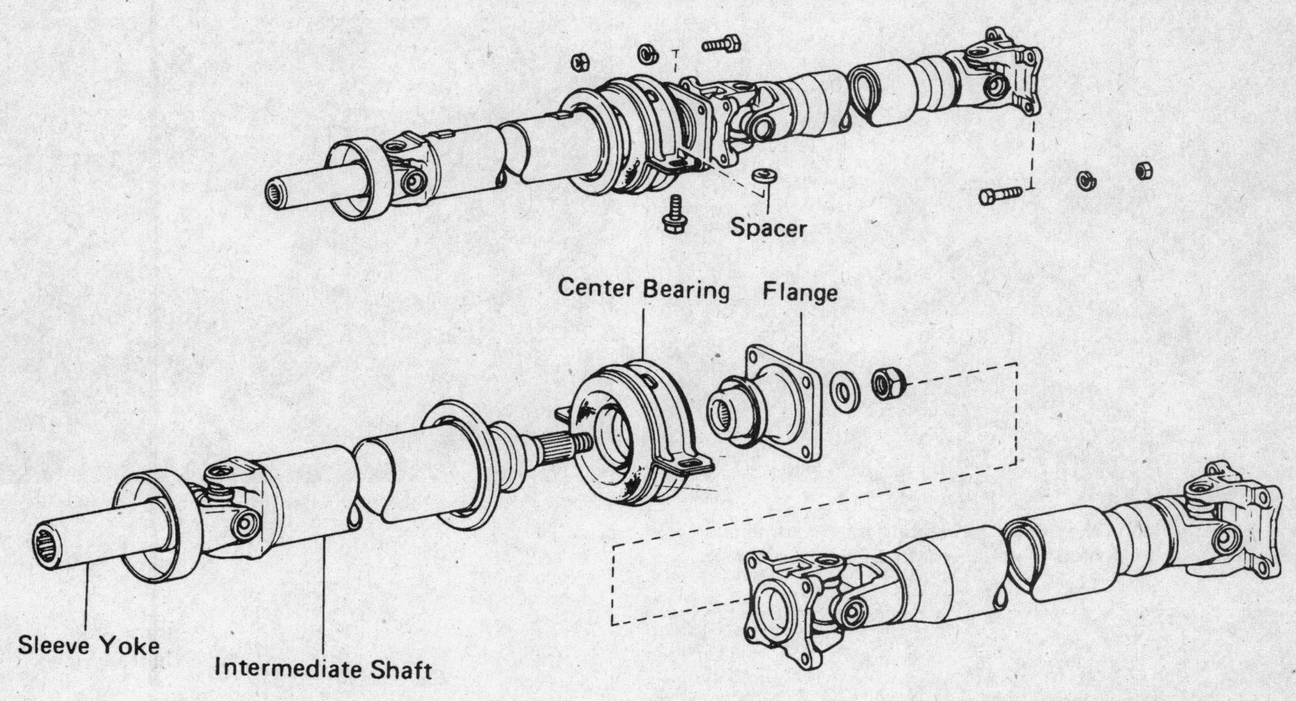

9.2b Driveshaft components - exploded view (1982 through 1986 models)

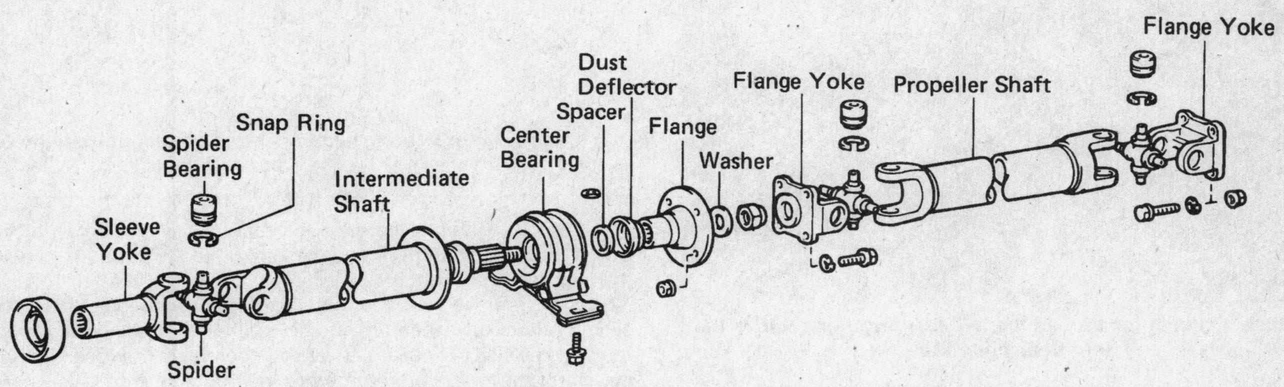

9.2c Driveshaft components - exploded view (1987 through 1992 models)

2 Working under the dash panel, disconnect the pushrod from the top of the clutch pedal. It is held in place with a clevis pin.

3 Disconnect the hydraulic line at the clutch master cylinder and seal the end to prevent the entry of dirt and loss of fluid. The master cylinder is located on the firewall, just to the right of the brake master cylinder. If available, use a flare nut wrench on the fitting, which will prevent the fitting from being rounded off. Have rags handy as some fluid will be lost as the line is removed. **Caution:** *Do not allow brake fluid to come into contact with paint as it will damage the finish.*

4 Remove the two nuts which secure the master cylinder to the engine firewall **(see illustration)**. One nut is located in the engine compartment and the other is inside the vehicle above the clutch pedal.

5 Remove the master cylinder, again being careful not to spill any of the fluid.

Installation

6 Position the master cylinder on the firewall, installing the two mounting nuts finger tight.

7 Connect the hydraulic line to the master cylinder, moving the cylinder slightly as necessary to thread the fitting properly. Do not crossthread the fitting as it is installed.

8 Tighten the two mounting nuts to the torque listed in this Chapter's Specifications.

9 Inside the vehicle, connect the pushrod to the clutch pedal and install the under cover.

10 Fill the clutch master cylinder reservoir with brake fluid conforming to DOT 3 specifications and bleed the clutch system (see Section 3).

9 Driveshaft - removal and installation

Refer to illustrations 9.2a, 9.2b, 9.2c, 9.3, 9.4, 9.5 and 9.6

1 Raise the rear of the vehicle and set it on jackstands. Block the front tires to keep the vehicle from rolling.

2 The driveshaft is made in two pieces; a front shaft from the transmission to the support bearing, and a rear shaft from the support bearing to the rear axle **(see illustrations)**.

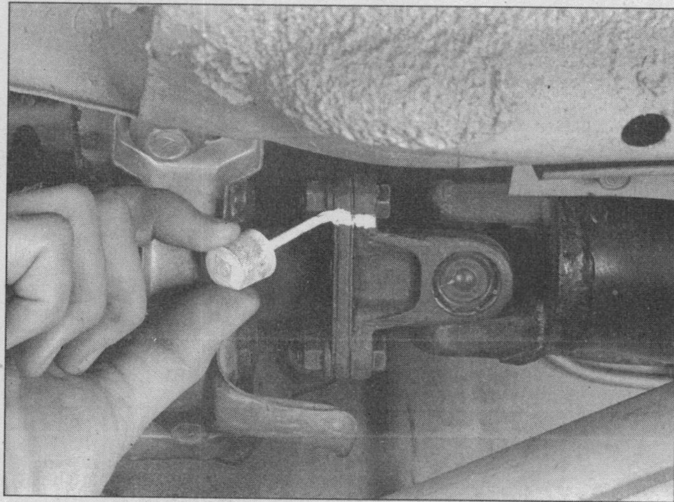
9.3 Place marks on the flange connecting the two driveshaft halves and remove the four bolts and nuts to separate the shafts

9.4 Remove the two center bearing mount bolts (arrow)

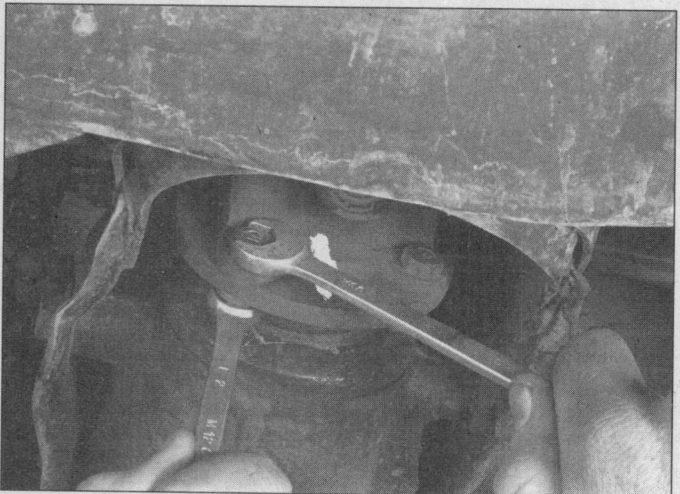
9.5 Place alignment marks on the two flanges, then remove the four bolts and nuts

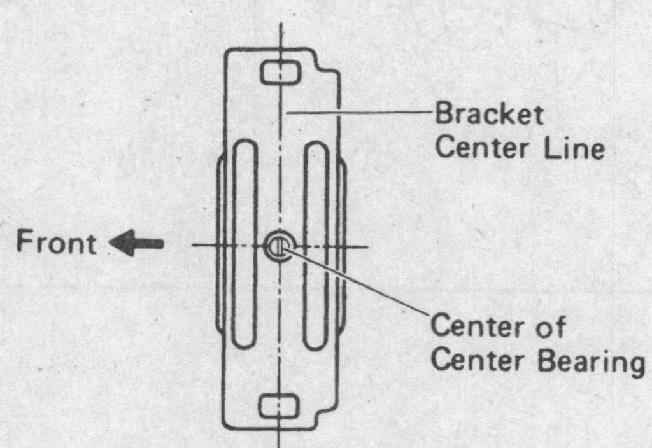

9.6 Check center bearing alignment and offset before tightening the bolts

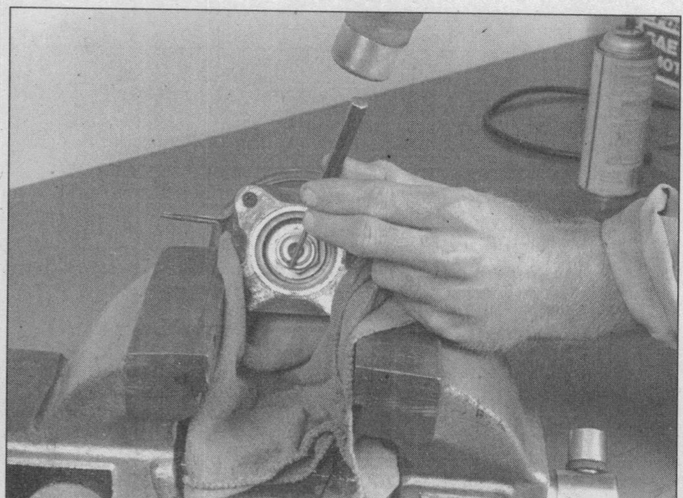
10.3 Line the vise with a rag to avoid damaging the flange; using a chisel or punch, bend back the staked part of the nut

3 Start by marking the driveshaft flanges with paint or a center punch **(see illustration)**, where they are bolted together, then remove the nuts and bolts from the flanges.

4 Next, remove the center bearing mount bolts **(see illustration)**, slide the front driveshaft forward, lower the rear end and pull it out of the transmission. If spacers are used under the center bearing mounting strap, they must be returned to their original locations when the bearing is bolted into place. Plug the rear of the transmission to avoid fluid loss.

5 Mark the rear ldriveshaft flange and the differential flange, then remove the nuts and bolts **(see illustration)**. Separate the rear driveshaft from the differential, lower the rear end and withdraw it toward the rear of the vehicle.

6 Installation of the driveshaft is basically the reverse of removal. However the following points should be noted: If originally installed, locate the height spacer between the center bearing support and the body. Hand tighten the bearing mounting bolts initially, then when the pinion joint is reconnected, check to make sure that the bearing support bracket is at a right angle to the driveshaft **(see illustration)**. After proper alignment, tighten the bolts to the torque listed in this Chapter's Specifications. Check the transmission oil level and add oil if necessary.

10 Center support bearing - check and replacement

Refer to illustrations 10.3, 10.4, 10.5, 10.6 and 10.7

1 Raise the vehicle and support it on jackstands.

2 Remove the driveshaft and separate it into two sections (see Section 9).

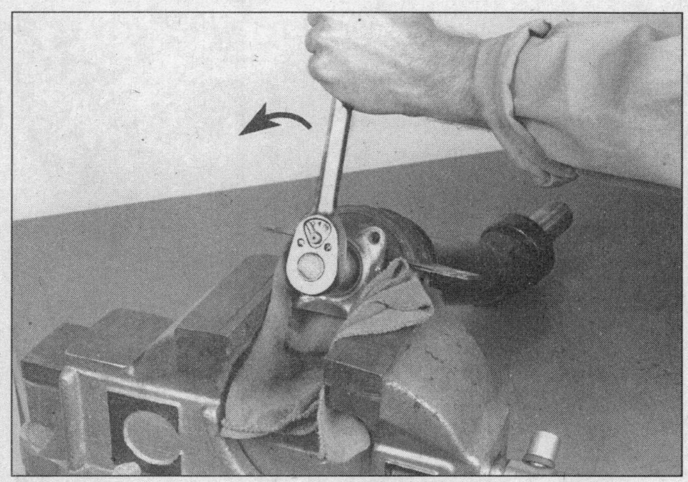

10.4 With the shaft flange held firmly in a vise, remove the nut

10.6 If the bearing doesn't turn freely or is worn or damaged, replace it

3 Hold the front driveshaft flange in a vise. Using a hammer and chisel, bend back the staked flange on the nut **(see illustration)**.

4 Remove the flange retaining nut **(see illustration)**.

5 Place alignment marks on the flange and shaft and pull the flange off **(see illustration)**. **Note:** *On later models, the shaft has a groove that will align with the matchmark on the flange.*

6 Inspect the center support bearing for wear and damage. Check that the bearing turns freely. If the bearing is damaged, worn or does not turn freely, replace it **(see illustration)**.

7 When replacing the center support bearing, install the bearing with the cutout toward the rear **(see illustration)**. Place a new nut on the shaft and tighten it to 134 ft-lbs to press the bearing into position, loosen the nut and then retighten it to 51 ft-lbs. Using a hammer and punch, stake the nut flange.

8 Reinstall the driveshaft by reversing the removal procedure (see Section 9).

11 Universal joints - check and replacement

Refer to illustrations 11.4, 11.6, 11.8a and 11.8b

Note: *The universal joints on 1982 through 1986 models are not serviceable. Therefore, when the joints become worn, the driveshaft and/or intermediate shaft must be replaced as a single unit.*

Check

1 Wear in the universal joints is characterized by vibration in the transmission, noise during acceleration, and in extreme cases of lack of lubrication, metallic squeaking and grating sounds as the bearings disintegrate.

10.5 After placing alignment marks on the flange and shaft, remove the flange

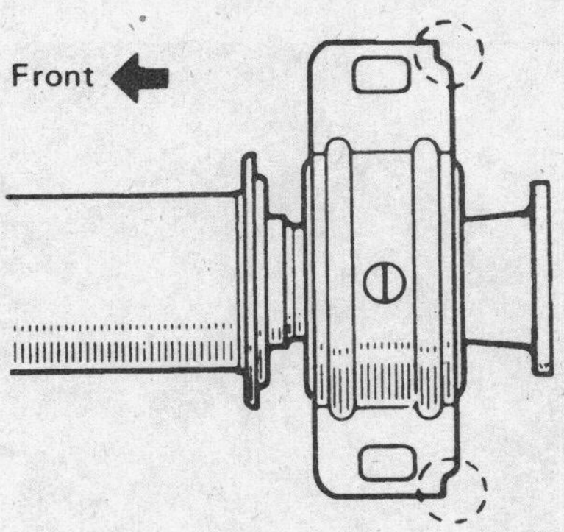

10.7 Install the support bearing with the cutout toward the rear of the vehicle

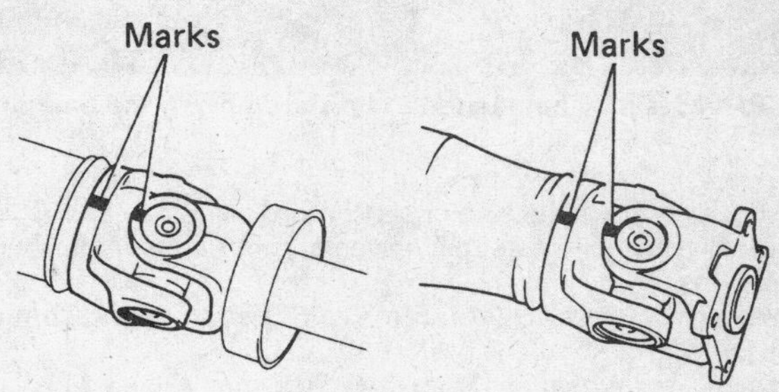

11.4 Mark the relationship of the driveshaft yoke and the flange yoke before disassembling the joint

8

2 It is easy to check if the needle bearings are worn with the driveshaft in position by trying to turn the shaft with one hand, the other hand holding the rear axle flange when the rear universal joint is being checked or the front-half coupling when the front universal joint is being checked. Any movement between the driveshaft and the front half couplings, and around the rear half couplings, is indicative of considerable wear.

3 With the driveshafts removed, the universal joints may be checked by holding the shaft in one hand and turning the yoke or flange with the other. If the axial movement is more than specified, replace the joints with new ones.

Replacement

4 Remove the driveshaft (see Section 9). Place alignment marks on each shaft yoke and flange yoke **(see illustration)**.

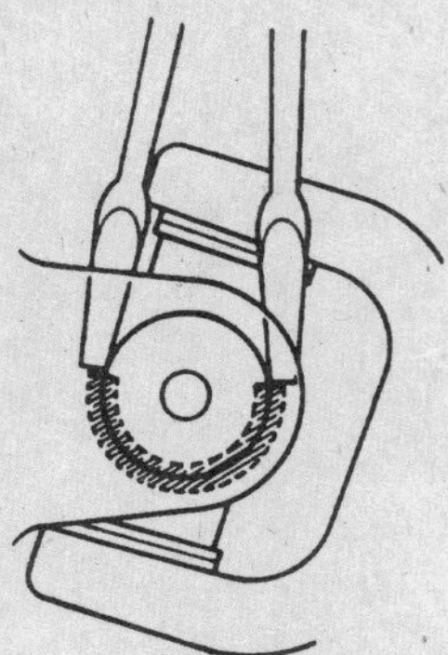

11.6 Push the snap-rings from the U-joint bearings with two small screwdrivers

11.8b Pliers may be needed to finish removing the bearing

5 Using a ratchet extension or similar tool and hammer, tap lightly on the bearing outer races of the universal joint to relieve pressure on the snap-rings.
6 Using two screwdrivers, remove the snap-rings from their grooves **(see illustration)**.
7 To remove the bearings from the yokes, you will need two sockets. One should be large enough to fit into the yoke where the snap-rings were installed and the other should have an inside diameter just large enough for the bearings to fit into when they are forced out of the yoke.
8 Mount the universal joint in a vise with the large socket on one side of the yoke and the small socket on the other side, pushing against the bearing. Carefully tighten the vise until the bearing is pushed out of the yoke and into the large socket **(see illustration)**. If it cannot be pushed all the way out, remove the universal joint from the vise and use pliers to finish removing the bearing **(see illustration)**.
9 Reverse the sockets and push out the bearing on the other side of the yoke. This time, the small socket will be pushing against the cross-shaped universal joint spider end.
10 Before pressing out the two remaining bearings, make sure the yokes are marked so they can be installed in the same relative position during reassembly.
11 The remaining universal joints can be disassembled following the same procedure. Be sure to mark all components for each universal joint so they can be kept together and reassembled in the proper position.
12 Check the spider journals for scoring, needle roller impressions, rust and pitting. Replace it if any of the above conditions exist.

11.8a Use a vise, a large socket (left) and a small socket (right) to press the bearing out of the universal joint

13 Check the sleeve yoke splines for wear and damage.
14 When reassembling the universal joints, replace all needle bearings, dust seals and snap-rings with new ones.
15 Before reassembly, pack each grease cavity in the spiders with a small amount of grease. Also, apply a thin coat of grease to the new needle bearing rollers and the roller contact areas on the spiders.
16 Apply a thin coat of grease to the dust seal lips and install the bearings and spider into the yoke using the vise and sockets that were used to remove the old bearings. Work slowly and be very careful not to damage the bearings as they are being pressed into the yokes.
17 Press the bearings in until the width of the snap-ring grooves is approximately 0.0020-inch (0.05 mm). Install snap-rings of the same thickness on each side (four sizes are available) and make sure there is no clearance between the bearing cups and the snap-rings. Tap the yoke with a hammer to move the cups slightly.
18 Make sure that the spider moves freely in the bearings, then check the axial play. If it is excessive, thicker snap-rings must be used to reduce the play.
19 Assemble the remaining universal joint(s) and rejoin the two driveshafts.

12 Pinion oil seal - replacement

Refer to illustration 12.1, 12.5, 12.8, 12.10 and 12.14

1 The pinion oil seal can be replaced without removing or disassembling the differential **(see illustration)**.
2 Raise the vehicle and set it on jackstands.
3 Remove the drain and fill plugs from the rear axle housing and allow the differential lubricant to drain into a container. When the draining is complete, loosely install the drain plug.
4 Separate the driveshaft from the differential by referring to Section 9. Be sure to tie the end of the driveshaft up, out of the way.
5 Using a punch or chisel, pry up the staked portion of the pinion shaft nut **(see illustration)**.
6 Using an inch-pound torque wrench, see how much torque is required to turn the pinion shaft within the range of gear backlash (if the axles and wheels turn, the backlash has been exceeded and the torque figure is incorrect). This figure is the drive pinion bearing preload. Record it before proceeding.
7 Set the parking brake to keep the rear wheels from turning and remove the nut and washer from the end of the pinion shaft.
8 Pull off the companion flange, using a gear puller, and the oil seal will be visible. Early models do not require a puller. After noting what the visible side of the oil seal looks like, carefully pry it out of the differential with a screwdriver or a prybar **(see illustration)**. Be careful not to damage the splines on the pinion shaft.

12.1 Typical pinion oil seal and related components - exploded view

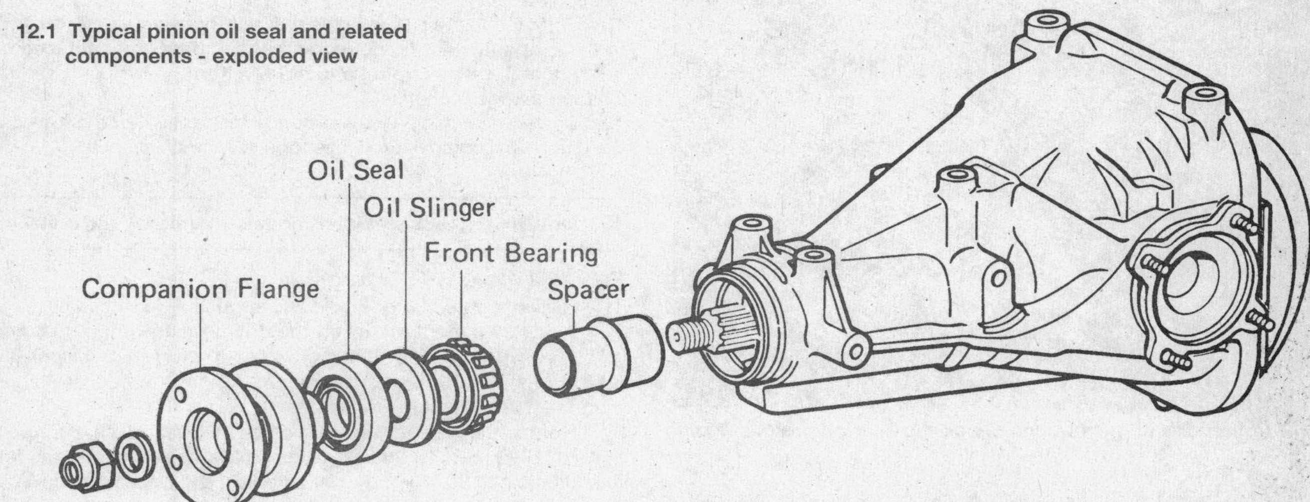

12.5 Use a punch to straighten the staked portion in the flange nut

12.8 Carefully position another screwdriver or similar tool under the larger screwdriver for the purpose of avoiding any damage on the flange area surrounding the seal

9 Clean the seal mounting area, the outside diameter of the seal and the pinion shaft with a clean rag.

10 Lubricate the new seal lip with multi-purpose grease and carefully install it in position in the differential. Tap the seal into place with a hammer and a block of wood or short section of pipe. Work around the entire circumference of the seal **(see illustration)**, a little at a time, until the face of the seal is at the specified drive in depth listed in this Chapter's Specifications. Work slowly and do not damage the rubber lip of the seal. DO NOT drive the seal beyond the depth listed in this Chapter's Specifications.

11 Clean the sealing lip contact surface of the companion flange. Apply a thin coat of multi-purpose grease to the seal contact surface and the shaft splines and carefully install the flange onto the end of the pinion shaft. You may have to rotate the flange slightly to line up the splines.

12 Use a soft-face hammer to tap the flange into place, then install the large washer and a new self-locking nut on the end of the pinion shaft.

13 Disengage the parking brake and snug up the nut as you let the flange rotate. This will help to seat the pinion shaft bearings properly as the nut is tightened.

12.10 Carefully tap the oil seal into the differential until it is flush with the flange, then proceed with a large socket

12.14 Tighten the flange nut and check the bearing preload again

14 Tighten the nut **(see illustration)** to the torque listed in this Chapter's Specifications, while holding the wheel to keep the pinion shaft from turning. This torque figure is very important, as it determines the preload on the pinion shaft bearings.
15 Turn the flange and pinion shaft several times in each direction to make sure that the bearings are seated, then check the preload as described in Step 6. If the torque required to start the shaft turning is excessive, the spacer on the pinion shaft must be replaced with a new one. This procedure should be done by a dealer service department or other repair shop to avoid damage to the internal parts of the differential.
16 If the preload is less than the figure recorded before disassembly, tighten the nut nine ft-lbs at a time and recheck the preload after each time. If the maximum torque specification for the nut is reached before the correct preload torque is attained, the spacer on the pinion shaft must be replaced with a new one (see Step 15). When the procedure is complete, stake the nut into the groove in the pinion shaft.
17 Fasten the rear of the driveshaft to the differential by referring to Section 9.
18 Tighten the drain plug in the rear axle housing and fill the housing to the proper level with the recommended gear lubricant (see Chapter 1). Install the filler plug and tighten it to the torque listed in this Chapter's Specifications.
19 Lower the vehicle to the ground. Test drive it and check around the differential companion flange for evidence of leakage.

13 Driveaxles (1982 and later models) - removal and installation

Refer to illustrations 13.2a and 13.2b

1 Raise the rear of the vehicle and support it on jackstands.
2 Place alignment marks on the driveaxle-to-differential and (on 1982 through 1986 models) the driveaxle-to-stub shaft flanges **(see illustrations)**. On 1987 and later models, remove the driveaxle/hub nut from the outer end of the driveaxle.
3 Remove the four (1982 through 1986 models) or six (1987 through 1992 models) retaining nuts on the inner joint and the four on the outer joint (1982 through 1986 models) and detach the driveaxle.
4 Installation is the reverse of removal. Be sure to line-up the matchmarks and tighten the fasteners to the torque values listed in this Chapter's Specifications.

14 Constant Velocity (CV) joints and boots - CV joint check and boot replacement

Note 1: *Some auto parts stores carry "split" type replacement boots, which can be installed without removing the driveaxle from the vehicle. This is a convenient alternative; however, it is recommended that the driveaxle be removed and the CV joint disassembled and cleaned to ensure that the joint is free from contaminants such as moisture and dirt, which will accelerate CV joint wear.*
Note 2: *If the CV joints exhibit signs of wear indicating need for an overhaul (usually due to torn boots), explore all options before begin-*

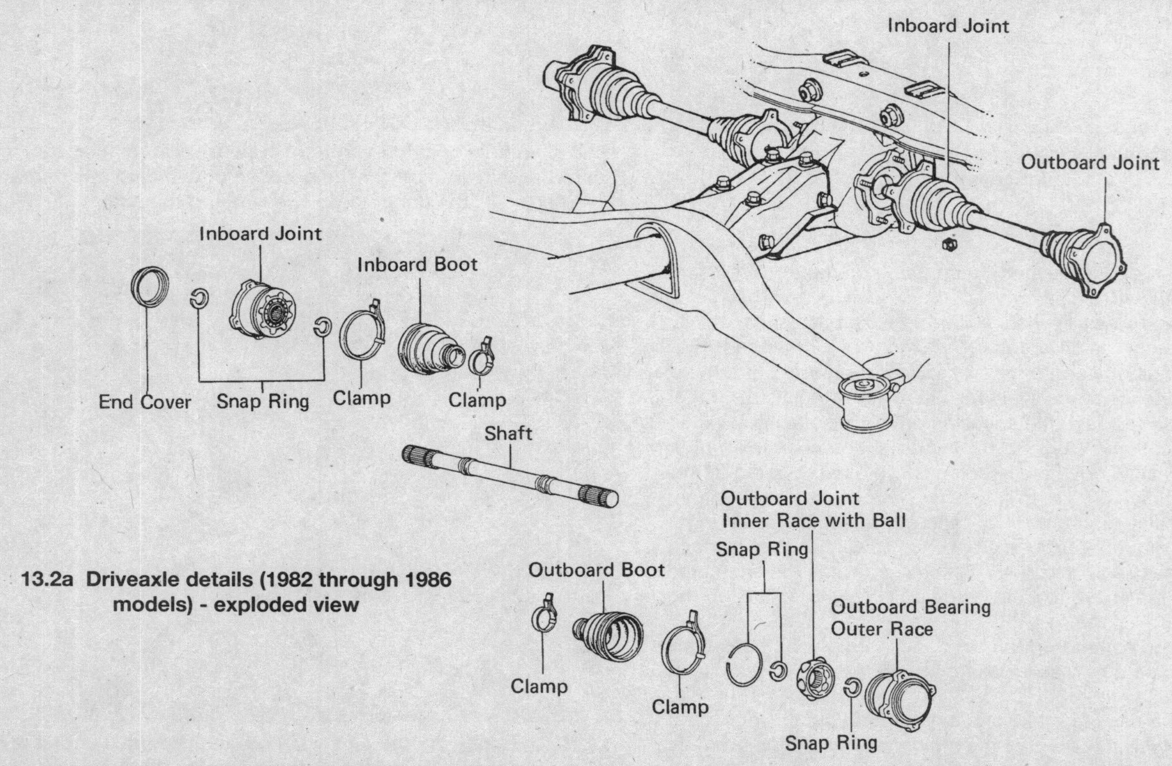

13.2a Driveaxle details (1982 through 1986 models) - exploded view

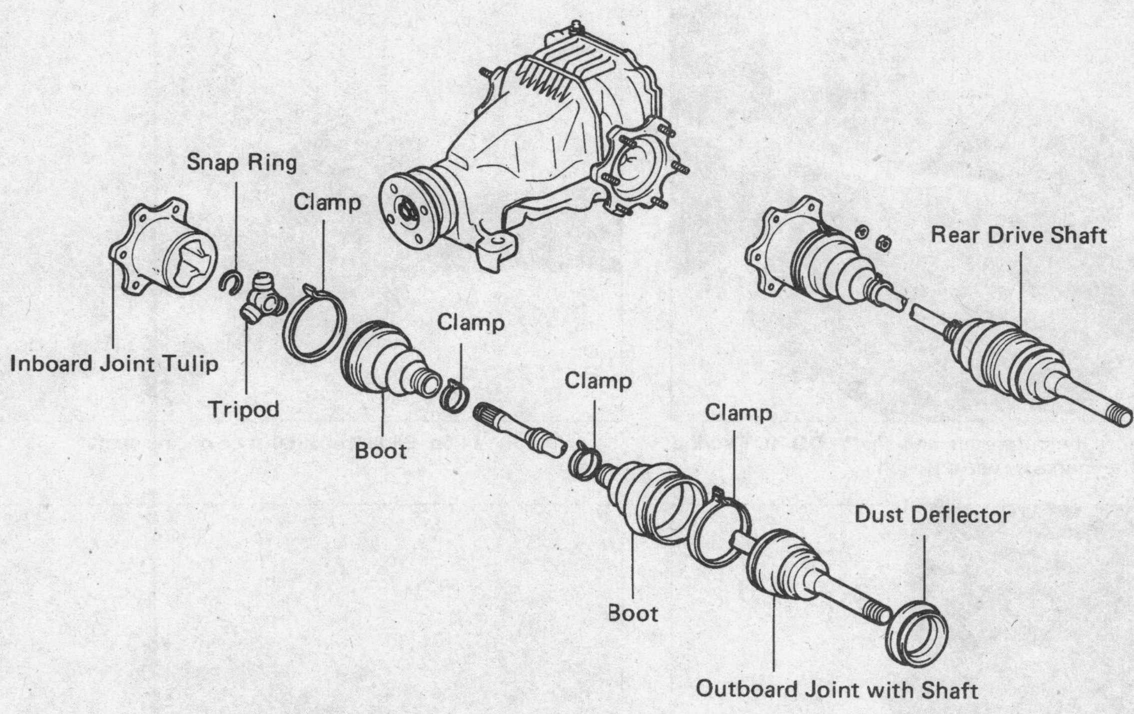

13.2b Exploded view of the driveaxles on 1987 and later models

ning the job. Complete rebuilt driveaxles are available on an exchange basis, which eliminates much time and work. Whichever route you choose to take, check on the cost and availability of parts before disassembling your vehicle.

Check

1 The CV joints and boots should be inspected periodically and whenever the vehicle is raised.

2 Raise the vehicle and support it securely on jackstands. Inspect the CV joint boots for cracks, leaks and broken retaining bands. If lubricant leaks out through a hole or crack in a boot, the CV joint will wear prematurely and require replacement. Replace any damaged boots immediately.

3 Grasp each driveaxle, rotate it in both directions and move it in and out to check for excessive movement, indicating worn splines or loose CV joints.

Boot replacement

1982 through 1986 models

Refer to illustrations 14.6, 14.7, 14.8a, 14.8b, 14.9a, 14.9b, 14.10a, 14.10b, 14.11, 14.12, 14.13, 14.17, 14.18a, 14.18b, 14.19a and 14.19b

Outer CV joint

4 Before beginning this procedure obtain a replacement boot kit.

5 Remove the driveaxles (see Section 13).

6 Cut off the boot retaining band **(see illustration)**, then slide the boot in towards the center of the axle.

7 Remove the spring clip from the outer race **(see illustration)**.

14.6 Using wire cutters, remove the boot retaining band, then slide the boot up the shaft . . .

14.7 . . . and remove the spring clip from the outer race

14.8a Use paint to mark the outer race and shaft - DO NOT scribe the marks or use a punch

14.8b Slide the outer race off the shaft

14.9a Paint alignment marks on the inner race and axleshaft, then . . .

14.9b . . . slide the snap-ring back

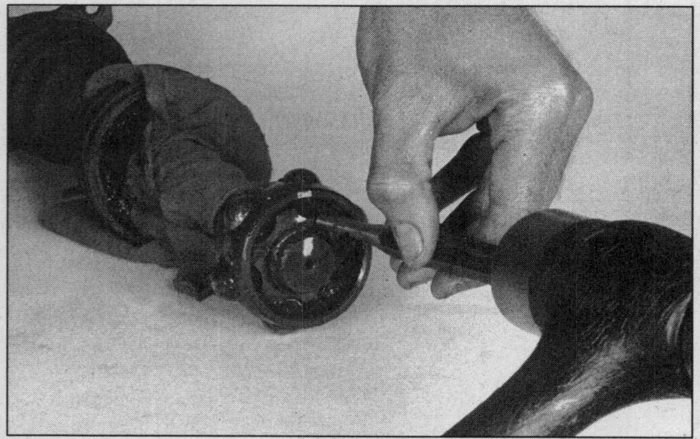
14.10a Use a hammer and punch to tap the inner race in far enough to gain access to the outer snap-ring . . .

14.10b . . . then, remove the outer snap-ring

8 Place alignment marks on the outer race and the driveaxle **(see illustration)**, then pull the outer race off **(see illustration)**.
9 Place marks on the inner race and driveaxle **(see illustration)**. Using snap-ring pliers, slide the inner snap-ring back **(see illustration)**.
10 Using a punch and hammer, tap the inner race in to gain access to the outer snap-ring, then remove the snap-ring **(see illustrations)**.
11 Use the hammer and punch to tap the inner race off the axle **(see illustration)**. Pull off the inner snap-ring and remove the boot.

Inner CV joint

12 Place the driveaxle in a vise. Using a chisel or screwdriver, pry the end plate from the inner CV joint **(see illustration)**.
13 Place alignment marks on the inner joint and axle. Remove the snap-ring **(see illustration)**.
14 Pull the joint assembly from the axle.
15 Remove the remaining snap-ring to pull the boot free from the axle.

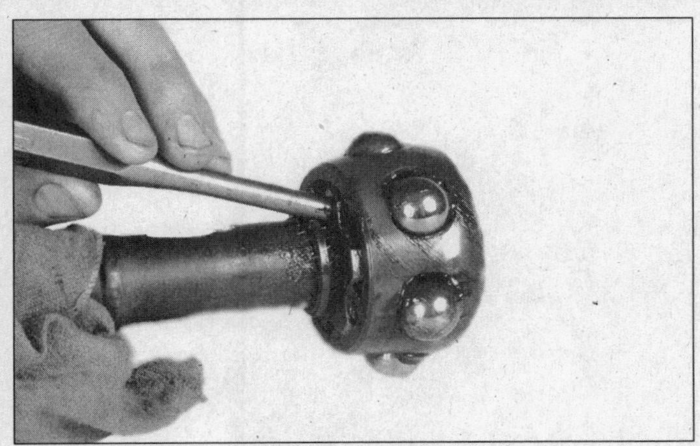
14.11 Using the punch and hammer, tap the inner race off the shaft

14.12 Hold the inner joint in a vise and pry out the end plate

14.13 After painting alignment marks on the inner joint and shaft, remove the snap-ring

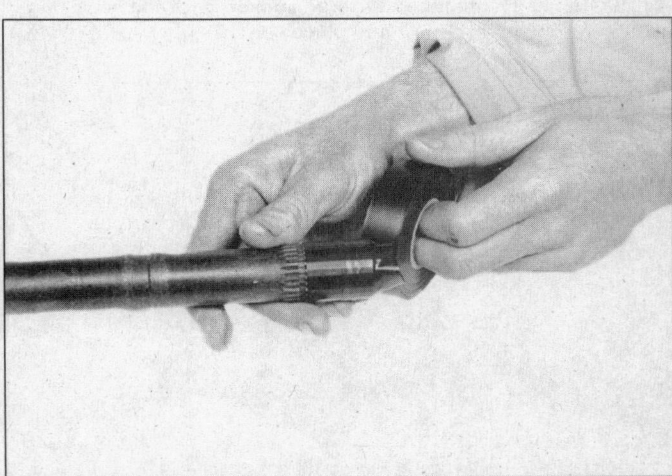
14.17 Before sliding the boot onto the shaft, tape the end of the shaft to protect the boot as it passes over the splines

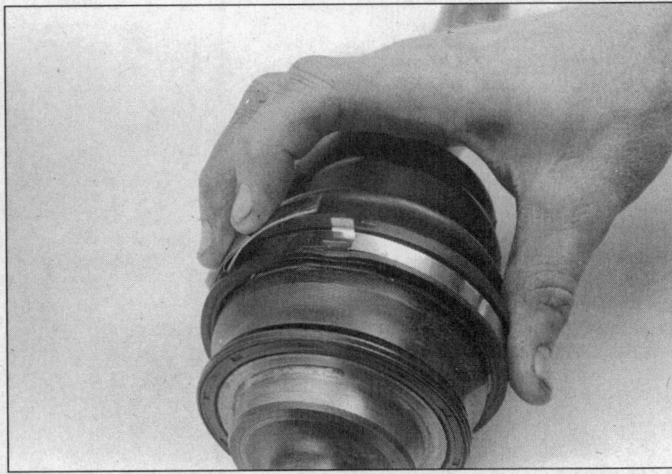
14.18a To install the new clamps, bend the tang down and . . .

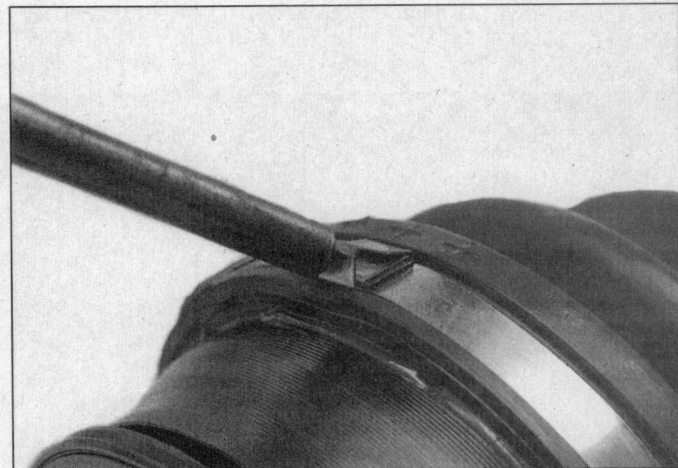
14.18b . . . tap the tabs over to hold it in place

Installation (outer and inner)

16 Reassembly is basically the reverse of disassembly, but keep the following points in mind.

17 Tape the ends of the axleshaft to protect the boots when sliding them on over the splines **(see illustration)**. Install the boot, followed by the inner snap-ring, inner race assembly and outer snap-ring.

18 Liberally apply the grease supplied with the kit to the CV joint. Install the outer race, then slide the boot into place. Install the new boot bands **(see illustrations)**.

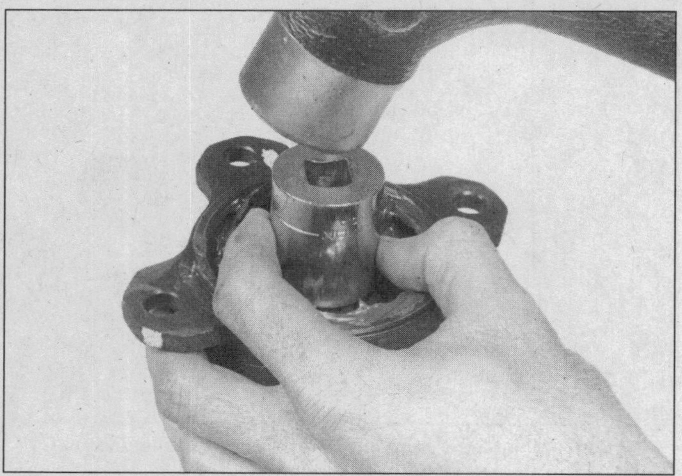
14.19a Using a hammer and a large socket, drive the snap-rings into place

14.19b A block of wood can be used to seat the end plate

14.21 Paint (do not punch) match marks on the inner joint tulip and the driveaxle

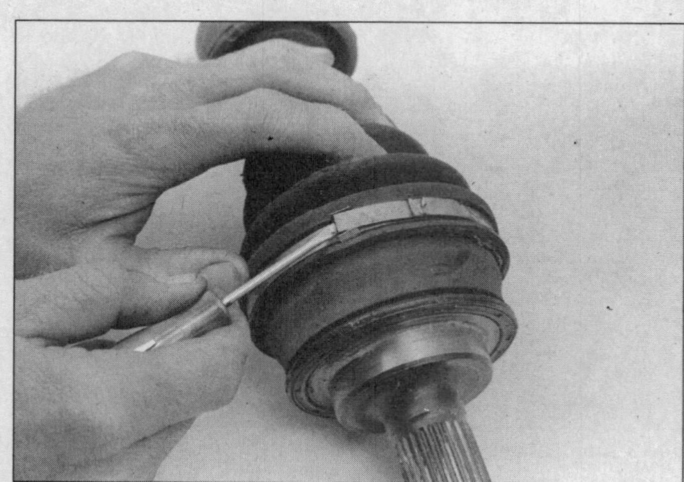
14.22 The large boot clamps can be pried open with a small screwdriver

14.24 Remove the snap-ring that retains the inner joint tripod with a pair of snap-ring pliers

14.25 Use a center-punch to place match marks (arrows) on the tripod and the driveaxle to ensure that they are reassembled properly

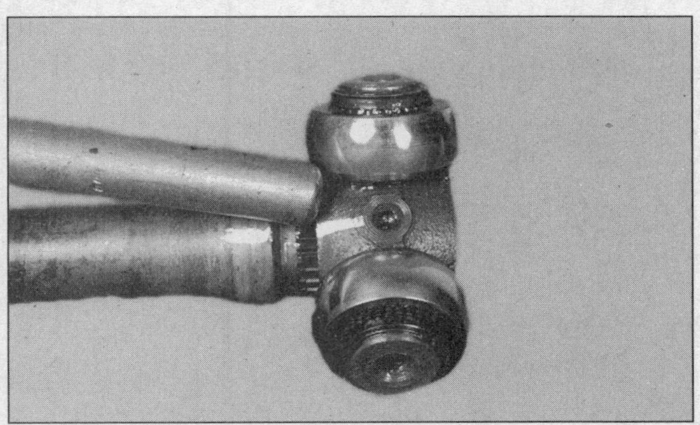

14.26 Drive the tripod joint from the driveaxle with a brass drift and hammer - be careful not to damage the bearing surfaces or the splines on the shaft

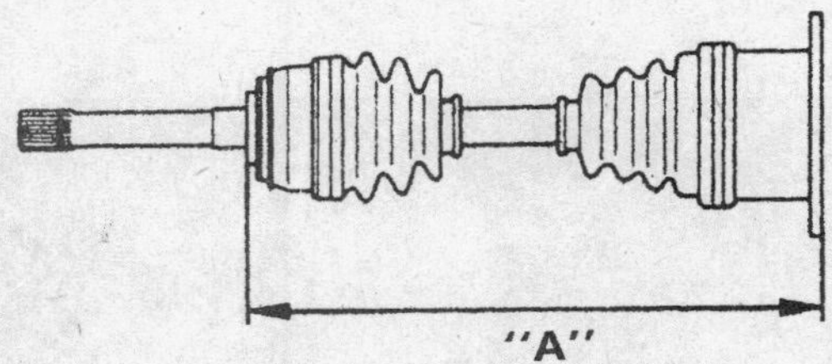

14.33 The driveaxle standard length (A) should be as specified, A = 21-23/32 to 21-27/32 inches

19 Use a large socket to replace the small snap-rings. Use a hammer and a block of wood to reseat the end plate **(see illustrations)**.

1987 through 1992 models

Refer to illustrations 14.21, 14.22, 14.24, 14.25, 14.26, 14.30 and 14.33

20 Remove the driveaxles (see Section 13).

21 Paint a pair of match marks on the joint tulip and the driveaxle **(see illustration)**.

22 Pry the outer (larger) clamps loose with a small screwdriver **(see illustration)** and slide them off the ends of the driveaxle. Cut the inner (smaller) clamps and the damper clamp with a pair of diagonal cutters and discard them.

23 Separate the inner joint tulip from the tripod joint.

24 Remove the tripod joint snap-ring with a pair of snap-ring pliers **(see illustration)**.

25 Punch match marks on the tripod and the driveaxle **(see illustration)**.

26 Using a hammer and brass punch, drive the tripod joint from the driveaxle **(see illustration)**.

27 Slide the inner joint boot and the outer joint boot off the driveaxle.

28 Thoroughly wash the inner and outer CV joints in clean solvent and blow dry with compressed air, if available. **Note:** *Because the outer joint cannot be disassembled, it is difficult to wash away all the old grease and to rid the bearing of solvent once it's clean. But it is imperative that the job be done thoroughly, so take your time and do it right.*

29 Inspect the inner tripod joint for signs of wear or damage. If the tripod is obviously worn or damaged, replace it, along with the tulip, as an assembly.

30 Bend the outer CV joint housing at an angle to the driveaxle to expose the bearings, inner race and cage **(see illustration)**. Inspect the bearing surfaces for signs of wear. If the bearings are damaged or worn, replace the driveaxle.

14.30 After the old grease has been rinsed away and the cleaning solvent has been blown out with compressed air, rotate the outer joint through its full range of motion and inspect the bearing surfaces for wear or damage - if any of the balls, the race or the cage look damaged, replace the driveaxle/outer joint assembly

15.3 A length of wire can be used to suspend the axle out of the way after it is separated from the differential flange (1983 model shown)

31 Slide the new outer boot onto the driveaxle. It's a good idea to wrap vinyl tape around the spline of the shaft to prevent damage to the boot. When the boot is in position, add the specified amount of grease (included in the boot replacement kit) to the outer joint and the boot (pack the joint with as much grease as it will hold and put the rest into the boot). Slide the boot on the rest of the way and install the new clamps **(see illustrations 14.18a and 14.18b)**.

32 Slide the inner boot onto the driveaxle. Align the match marks you made before removing the joint and, using a brass bar and hammer, tap the tripod onto the driveaxle. Install the snap-ring. Fill the inner joint tulip with grease and install it over the tripod joint. Slide the boot into place and equalize the pressure inside the boot by inserting a small screwdriver between the boot and joint.

33 Measure the driveaxle standard length and make sure that the boot is not stretched, contracted or distorted in any way **(see illustration)**. Tighten the boot clamps.

34 Install the driveaxle.

15 Differential housing side seals (1982 and later models) - replacement

Refer to illustrations 15.3, 15.4, 15.5 and 15.6

1 Raise the rear of the vehicle and support it on jackstands.

2 Drain the differential lubricant (see Chapter 1).

3 Separate the driveaxle from the differential (see Section 13) and suspend it out of the way **(see illustration)**.

15.4 Using a long punch, drive the differential flange out of the differential - be ready to catch the flange as it pops free

15.5 Pry the seal out of the differential with a large screwdriver

15.6 Use a large socket or section of pipe to drive the new seal into the differential

16.6 Working through the hole in the axleshaft flange, remove the bearing retainer nuts

4 Using a long punch and hammer, drive the differential flange gear out of the differential **(see illustration)**. Be ready to catch the flange as it comes out. **Note:** *On 1987 through 1992 models, it may be necessary to use a puller to remove the flange.*

5 Use a screwdriver to pry the seal out **(see illustration)**.

6 Use a large socket or section of pipe and a hammer to install the new seal **(see illustration)**. Be sure to apply grease to the lip of the seal before installing the differential flange. The rest of installation is the reverse of removal.

16 Rear axleshafts and oil seals (1979 through 1981 models) - removal and installation

Refer to illustrations 16.6, 16.12 and 16.16

Removal

1 The axleshafts can be removed without disturbing the differential assembly. They must be removed in order to replace the bearings and oil seals and when removing the differential carrier from the rear axle housing. **Note:** *Read the entire Section before starting work.*

2 Raise the rear of the vehicle and support it securely on jackstands. Block the front wheels to keep the vehicle from rolling.

3 Remove the rear wheels and release the parking brake, then remove the brake calipers and discs (see Chapter 9 for details).

4 Remove the drain plug and drain the differential oil into a suitable container. When the draining is complete, finger-tighten the drain plug.

5 Disconnect the brake line (see Chapter 9).

6 Remove the bearing retainer nuts **(see illustration)**.

7 The axleshaft can now be pulled out from the rear axle. If the axleshaft will not pull out by hand, a slide hammer can be attached to the wheel studs using an adapter plate.

8 Since the wheel bearing is press-fitted onto the axleshaft, its removal and installation will require the use of special tools and either a special puller or a hydraulic press. This operation should be left to a dealer service department or other suitably equipped shop.

9 Inspect the axleshaft for wear or damage.

10 Inspect the seal for wear or damage.

11 To replace the seal, remove it from the axle housing with a slide hammer puller.

Installation

12 Place the new seal in position, then use a seal driver or section of appropriately sized pipe and a hammer to drive in the new seal to a depth of 0.240-inch (6.0 mm) **(see illustration)**.

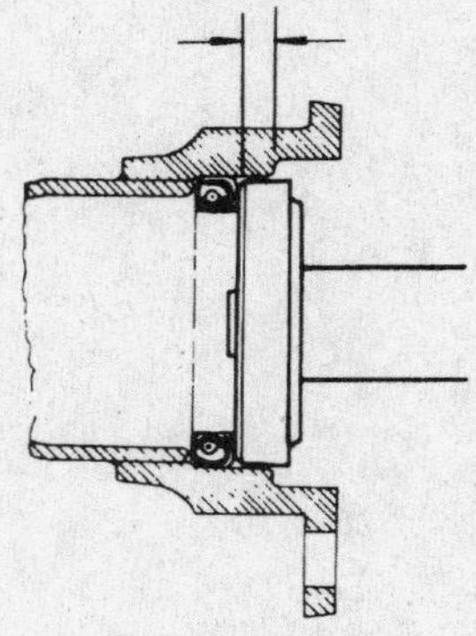

16.12 Press the new seal into the housing the specified distance

16.16 The notches in the gaskets must line up with the bulge in the bearing retainer (arrows)

13 To install the axleshaft, first apply multi-purpose grease to the lip of the oil seal.
14 Clean the contact surfaces of the axle housing and bearing retainer. Apply gasket sealant to both sides of the retainer gasket.
15 Place the end gasket in position on the axle housing with the notch facing down.
16 Place the backing plate and bearing retainer on the axleshaft. Install the axleshaft, aligning the gasket notches with the hole in the bearing retainer **(see illustration)**.
17 Attach the axle and bearing retainer to the axle housing and tighten the four retaining nuts to the torque listed in this Chapter's Specifications.
18 Following installation, tighten the drain plug and fill the differential with the proper grade and amount of lubricant as specified in Chapter 1.
19 Install the brake disc and caliper, bleed the brakes (see Chapter 9) and install the wheel. Tighten the lug nuts to the torque listed in the Chapter 1 Specifications.

17 Differential (1979 through 1981 models) - removal and installation

Removal

1 Raise the rear of the vehicle and support it securely on jackstands. Block the front wheels to keep the vehicle from rolling.
2 Remove the drain plug and drain the differential oil into a suitable container, then reinstall the drain plug finger-tight.
3 Remove the rear axleshafts (see Section 16).
4 Disconnect the driveshaft flange from the companion flange (see Section 9).
5 Remove the nuts from the differential carrier and pull out the differential assembly. The mounting nuts should be loosened in steps, following a criss-cross pattern.
6 The overhaul of the differential unit is not within the scope of the home mechanic, due to the specialized gauges and tools which are required. Where the unit requires servicing or repair, due to wear or excessive noise, it is most economical to exchange it for a factory reconditioned assembly.

Installation

7 Before reinstalling the rear differential, scrape all traces of old gasket from the mating surfaces of the axle housing. Position a new gasket on the housing (use RTV sealant).
8 Installation is the reverse of the removal procedure.
9 Following installation, fill the differential with the proper grade and quantity of lubricant (see Chapter 1).

18 Rear axle assembly (1979 through 1981 models) - removal and installation

Removal

1 Loosen the rear wheel lug nuts, raise the vehicle and support it securely on jackstands placed underneath the frame. Remove the wheels.
2 Support the rear axle assembly with a floor jack placed underneath the differential.
3 Remove the shock absorber lower mounting nuts and compress the shocks to get them out of the way (see Chapter 10).
4 Disconnect the driveshaft from the differential companion flange and hang it with a piece of wire from the underbody (see Section 9).
5 Unbolt the stabilizer bar from the stabilizer bar link, if so equipped (see Chapter 10).
6 Disconnect the parking brake cables.
7 Disconnect the flexible brake hose from the junction block on the rear axle housing. Plug the end of the hose or wrap a plastic bag tightly around it to prevent excessive fluid loss and contamination.
8 Disconnect the lateral control rod and the upper and lower suspension arms (see Chapter 10).
9 Slowly lower the axle to the floor with the jack while an assistant steadies it. Remove the axle from under the vehicle.

Installation

10 Installation is the reverse of the removal procedure. Be sure to tighten all suspension bolts and nuts (see Chapter 10) and the driveshaft companion flange bolts to the torque listed in this Chapter's Specifications.

NOTES

Chapter 9 Brakes

Contents

Specifications

General

Brake fluid type .... See Chapter 1
Brake pedal reserve distance (at 110 lbs of force)
- 1979 through 1981 .... more than 2-5/8 inches
- 1982 through 1986 .... more than 2-15/16 inches
- 1987 and later .... more than 3-1/8 inches

Power brake booster pushrod-to-master cylinder piston clearance
- 1979 through 1981 .... Not available
- 1982 through 1986 .... 0.004 to 0.020 inch
- 1987 and later .... 0.0 inch

Disc brakes

Minimum brake pad thickness .... See Chapter 1
Brake disc minimum (discard) thickness*
- 1979 through 1981
  - Front .... 0.450 inch
  - Rear .... 0.354 inch
- 1982 through 1986
  - Front .... 0.748 inch
  - Rear .... 0.669 inch
- 1987 on
  - Front .... 0.827 inch
  - Rear .... 0.669 inch

Disc brakes (continued)

Brake disc standard thickness	
1979 through 1981	
Front	Not available
Rear	Not available
1982 through 1986	
Front	0.787 inch
Rear	0.709 inch
1987 and later	
Front	0.866 inch
Rear	0.709 inch
Maximum disc runout	
1979 through 1986	0.0059 inch
1987 and later	0.0051 inch

** Refer to marks cast into the disc (they supersede information printed here)*

Parking brakes

Parking brake shoe lining thickness	
Standard	
1982 through 1986	0.079 inch
1987 and later	0.098 inch
Minimum	0.039 inch
Parking brake lever travel	5 to 8 clicks
Parking brake shoe-to-lever clearance	0.013 inch

Torque specifications

	Ft-lbs (unless otherwise indicated)
Front disc brake caliper mounting bolt(s)	
1982 through 1986	14
1987 and later	27
Front caliper torque plate (bracket)-to-steering knuckle bolts	
1979 through 1986	34
1987 and later	77
Rear disc brake caliper mounting bolt(s)	14
Rear caliper torque plate-to-axle assembly bolts	
1979 through 1981	48
1982 and later	34
Brake hose-to-caliper banjo fitting bolt	22
Master cylinder-to-brake booster nuts	9
Power brake booster mounting nuts	9
Wheel lug nuts	See Chapter 1

1 General information

The vehicles covered by this manual are equipped with hydraulically operated front and rear disc brake systems. Both the front and rear brakes are self adjusting. The disc brakes automatically compensate for pad wear.

Hydraulic system

The hydraulic system consists of two separate circuits. The master cylinder has separate reservoirs for the two circuits, and, in the event of a leak or failure in one hydraulic circuit, the other circuit will remain operative. Some later models are equipped with an anti-lock braking system (ABS).

Power brake booster

The power brake booster, utilizing engine manifold vacuum and atmospheric pressure to provide assistance to the hydraulically operated brakes, is mounted on the firewall in the engine compartment.

Parking brake

The parking brake operates the rear brakes only, through cable actuation. It's activated by a lever mounted in the center console. The parking brake assembly is either inside the caliper and not serviceable (1979 through 1981 models) or uses a shoe-type system that is located on the inside of the rear brake disc (1982 and later models).

Service

After completing any operation involving disassembly of any part of the brake system, always test drive the vehicle to check for proper braking performance before resuming normal driving. When testing the brakes, perform the tests on a clean, dry, flat surface. Conditions other than these can lead to inaccurate test results.

Test the brakes at various speeds with both light and heavy pedal pressure. The vehicle should stop evenly without pulling to one side or the other. Avoid locking the brakes, because this slides the tires and diminishes braking efficiency and control of the vehicle.

Tires, vehicle load and front-end alignment are factors which also affect braking performance.

2 Anti-lock brake system (ABS) - general information

The anti-lock brake system was introduced in 1987 and is designed to maintain vehicle steerability, directional stability and optimum deceleration under severe braking conditions and on most road surfaces. It does so by monitoring the rotational speed of each wheel and controlling the brake line pressure to each wheel during braking. This prevents the wheels from locking up.

Components

Refer to illustrations 2.2a and 2.2b

Actuator assembly

The actuator assembly consists of the master cylinder, an electric hydraulic pump and solenoid valves **(see illustrations)**. **Note:** *Early models equipped with ABS incorporate four solenoid valves while later*

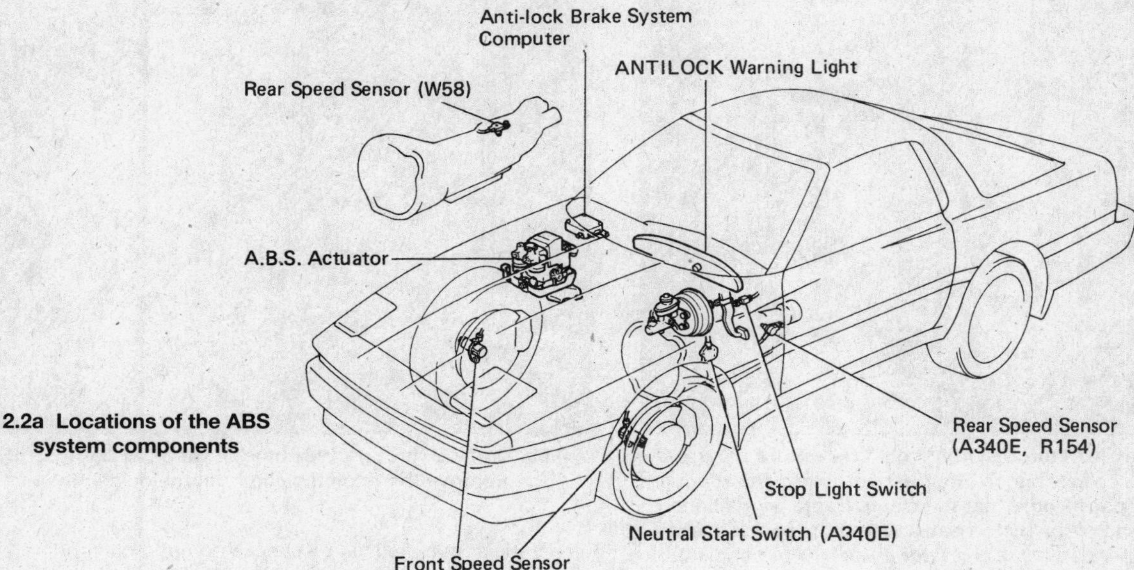

2.2a Locations of the ABS system components

models use only three.

a) The electric pump provides hydraulic pressure to charge the reservoirs in the actuator, which supply pressure to the braking system. The pump and reservoirs are housed in the actuator assembly.

b) The solenoid valves modulate brake line pressure during ABS operation.

Speed sensors

These sensors are located at each front wheel and at the rear of the transmission. Each generates small electrical pulsations when the toothed sensor rings are turning, sending a signal to the electronic controller indicating wheel rotational speed.

The front wheel sensors are mounted to the front spindles in close relationship to the toothed sensor rings, which are integral with the front hub assemblies.

The rear sensor is bolted to the tail section of the transmission. The sensor rings are built into the transmission gear assemblies.

ABS computer

The ABS computer is mounted inside the vehicle and is the "brain" for the ABS system. The function of the computer is to accept and process information received from the speed sensors to control the hydraulic line pressure, avoiding wheel lock up. The computer also constantly monitors the system, even under normal driving conditions, to find faults within the system.

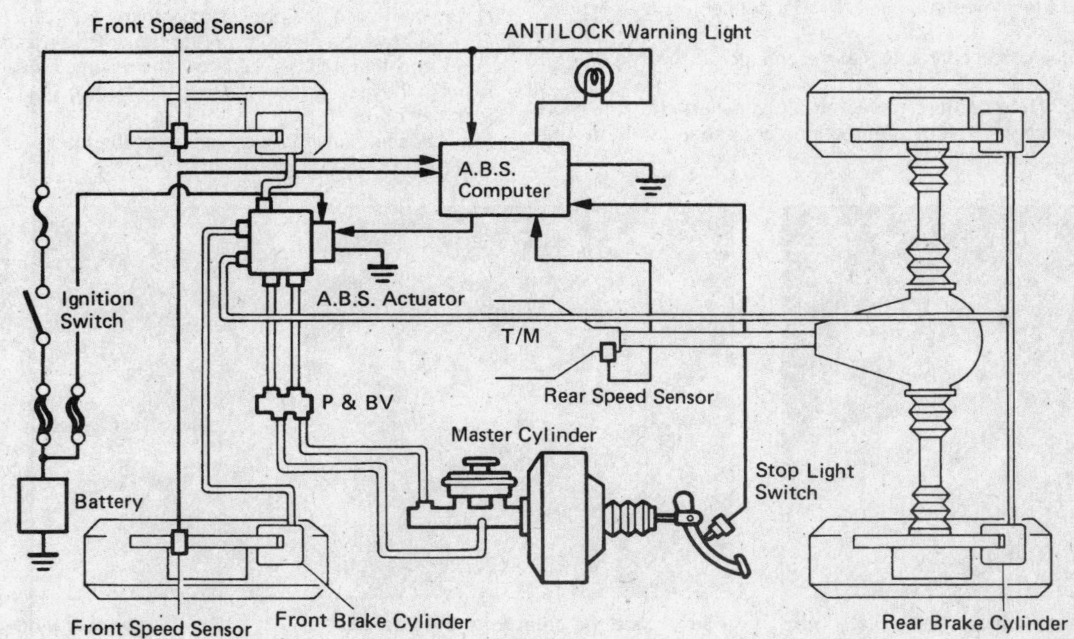

2.2b Hydraulic and electrical schematic of the ABS system

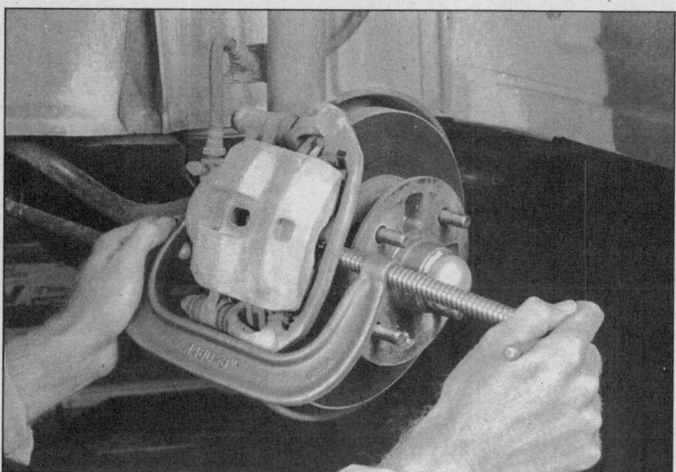

3.5a On all except 1979 through 1981 rear brakes, use a large C-clamp to push the caliper piston into the bore to provide room for the new, thicker pads - note that the clamp frame is positioned against the flat end of the piston housing and the screw pushes against the outer pad (1982 and later model caliper shown)

If a problem develops within the system, an "ANTILOCK" light (early models) or "ABS" light (later models) will glow on the dashboard. A diagnostic code will also be stored in the computer, which, when retrieved by a service technician, will indicate the problem area or component. Take your vehicle to a dealership service department for any additional diagnostics and repair.

Diagnosis and repair

If a dashboard warning light comes on and stays on while the vehicle is in operation, the ABS system requires attention. Although a special electronic ABS diagnostic tester is necessary to properly diagnose the system, the home mechanic can perform a few preliminary checks before taking the vehicle to a dealer service department which is equipped with this tester.

a) Check the brake fluid level in the reservoir.
b) Check that the computer master cylinder connectors are securely connected.
c) Check the electrical connectors at the actuator assembly.
d) Check the fuses.
e) Follow the wiring harness to each front wheel and transmission sensor and check that all connections are secure and that the wiring is not damaged.

3.5b On 1979 through 1981 models, use needle-nose pliers to remove the retaining clip from the guide plate. . .

If the above preliminary checks do not rectify the problem, the vehicle should be diagnosed by a dealer service department. Due to the complex nature of this system, all actual repair work must be done by a dealer service department.

3 Disc brake pads - replacement

Refer to illustrations 3.5a through 3.5j, 3.6, 3.7a and 3.7b

Warning: *Disc brake pads must be replaced on both front wheels or both rear wheels at the same time - never replace the pads on only one wheel. Also, the dust created by the brake system may contain asbestos, which is harmful to your health. Never blow it out with compressed air and don't inhale any of it. An approved filtering mask should be worn when working on the brakes. Do not, under any circumstances, use petroleum-based solvents to clean brake parts. Use brake cleaner or denatured alcohol only! When servicing the disc brakes, use only high quality, nationally recognized brand-name pads.*

Note: *This procedure applies to both the front and rear disc brakes.*

1 Remove the cap(s) from the brake fluid reservoir and siphon off about two-thirds of the fluid from the reservoir. Failing to do this could result in the reservoir overflowing when the caliper pistons are pressed into their bores.

2 Loosen the wheel lug nuts, raise the front of the vehicle and support it securely on jackstands.

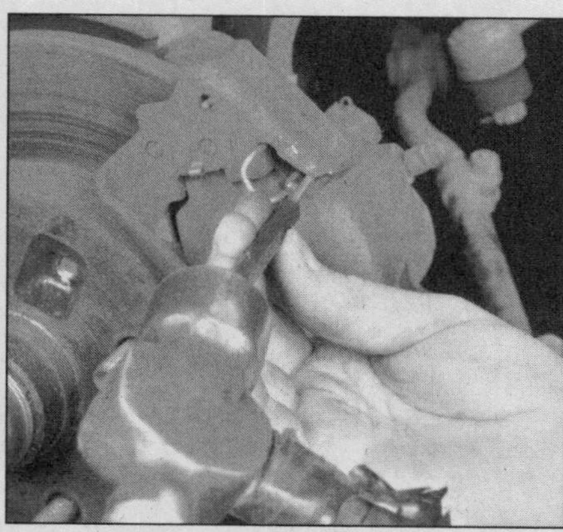

3.5c . . . then tap out the guide plate with a punch and hammer and remove it. . .

3.5d . . .and the shim from the backside of the caliper, . . .

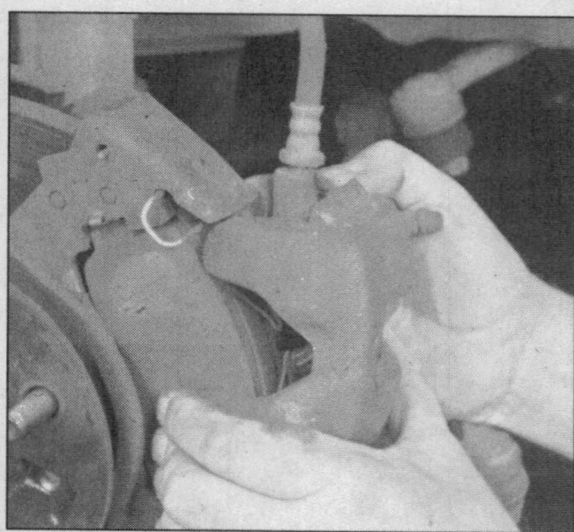

3.5e . . .then pivot the caliper out of the mounting bracket - suspend the caliper from the underbody with a piece of wire so you don't put strain on the brake hose. . .

3.5f . . . and remove the anti-squeal springs (if equipped). . .

3.5g . . . and pads - note the number and locations of the anti-squeal shims and other hardware so it can be returned to where it originally was - coat the guide plates with high-temperature brake caliper grease before reassembly

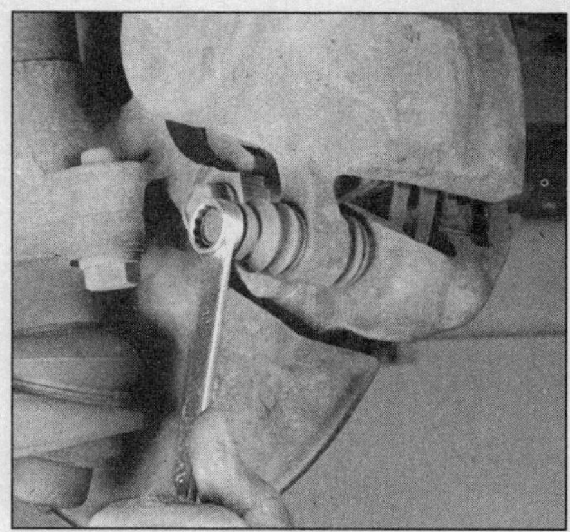
3.5h On 1982 and later models, remove the caliper bolt (some models may have two bolts - one at the top and one at the bottom), . . .

3 Remove the front wheels. Work on one brake assembly at a time, using the assembled brake for reference if necessary.

4 Inspect the brake disc carefully as outlined in Section 5. If machining is necessary, follow the information in that Section to remove the disc, at which time the pads can be removed from the calipers as well.

5 Follow the accompanying photos, beginning with illustration 3.5a, for the actual pad replacement procedure. Be sure to stay in order and read the caption under each illustration. **Note 1:** *Two different types of calipers are used on these models. Illustrations 3.5b through 3.5g are for calipers on 1981 and earlier models. Illustrations 3.5h through 3.5J are for 1982 and later models.* **Note 2:** *Some models have different numbers and designs of anti-squeal shims and other hardware than what is shown in this Chapter. It's best to note how the hardware is installed on the vehicle before disassembly so you can duplicate it on reassembly.*

6 Be sure to transfer any wear indicators from the old pads to the new ones **(see illustration)**.

7 Rear brakes on 1979 through 1981 models require a special tool to retract the caliper piston **(see illustrations)**. Do this before reinstalling the pads.

8 When reinstalling the caliper, be sure to tighten the mounting bolt(s) (if equipped) to the torque listed in this Chapter's Specifications. On 1981 and earlier models, coat the caliper guide plates with high-temperature caliper grease before reassembly.

9 After the job is completed, firmly depress the brake pedal a few times to bring the pads into contact with the discs. The pedal should be at normal height above the floorpan and firm. Check the level of the brake fluid, adding some if necessary. Check carefully for leaks and check the operation of the brakes before placing the vehicle into normal service.

4 Disc brake caliper - removal, overhaul and installation

Refer to illustrations 4.3, 4.4a, 4.4b, 4.5, 4.7, 4.8a and 4.8b

Warning: *Dust created by the brake system may contain asbestos, which is harmful to your health. Never blow it out with compressed air and don't inhale any of it. An approved filtering mask should be worn when working on the brakes. Do not, under any circumstances, use petroleum-based solvents to clean brake parts. Use brake cleaner or denatured alcohol only!.*

Note 1: *If an overhaul is indicated (usually because of fluid leakage), explore all options before beginning the job. New and factory rebuilt calipers are available on an exchange basis, which makes this job quite*

3.5i . . . then pivot the caliper up so you can remove the pads. . .

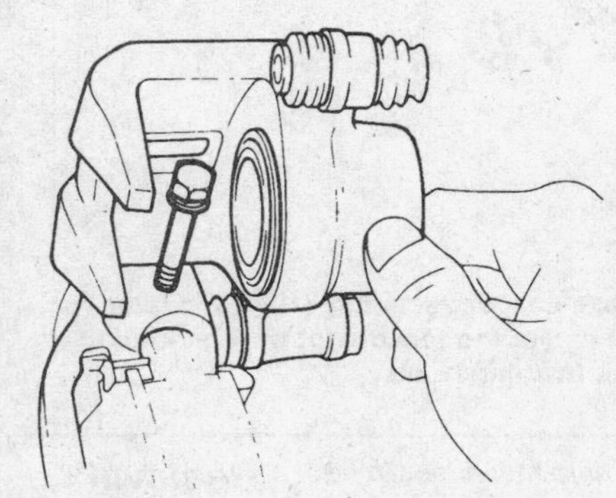
3.5j . . . and insert a long bolt into the bracket hole to keep the caliper up while you replace the pads - on models with two bolts, remove the caliper completely and suspend it from the underbody with a piece of wire

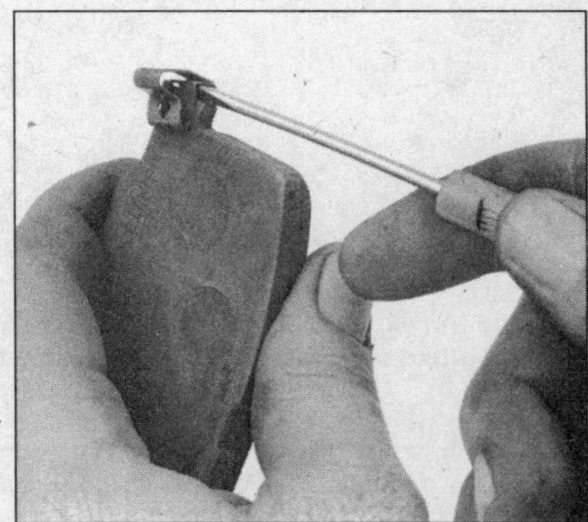
3.6 Pry the wear indicators (if equipped) off the brake pads and transfer them to the new pads - if they are worn or bent, replace them (the remainder of the brake pad replacement procedure is the reverse of removal)

3.7a On 1979 through 1981 rear brakes, the caliper piston must be retracted to make room for the new, thicker pads. Remove the brake disc and reinstall the caliper, then engage the piston notches (arrow). . .

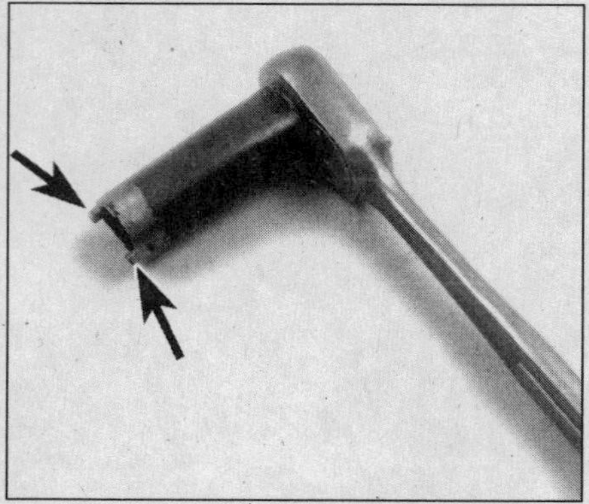

3.7b . . . with the protrusions (arrows) in a special tool such as this one which is fabricated from an old socket (you can buy special tools from auto parts stores and tool suppliers - needle-nose pliers may also work if you're careful). With the tool engaged in the notches, press in and rotate the piston clockwise until it's bottomed

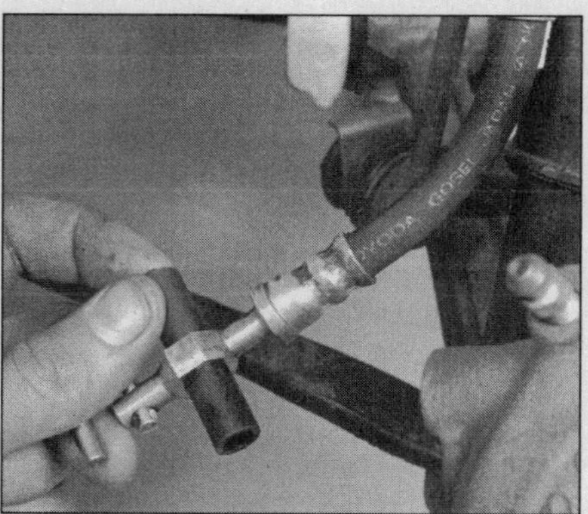

4.3 On models with banjo-type brake hose fittings, use a piece of rubber hose of the appropriate size to plug the brake line

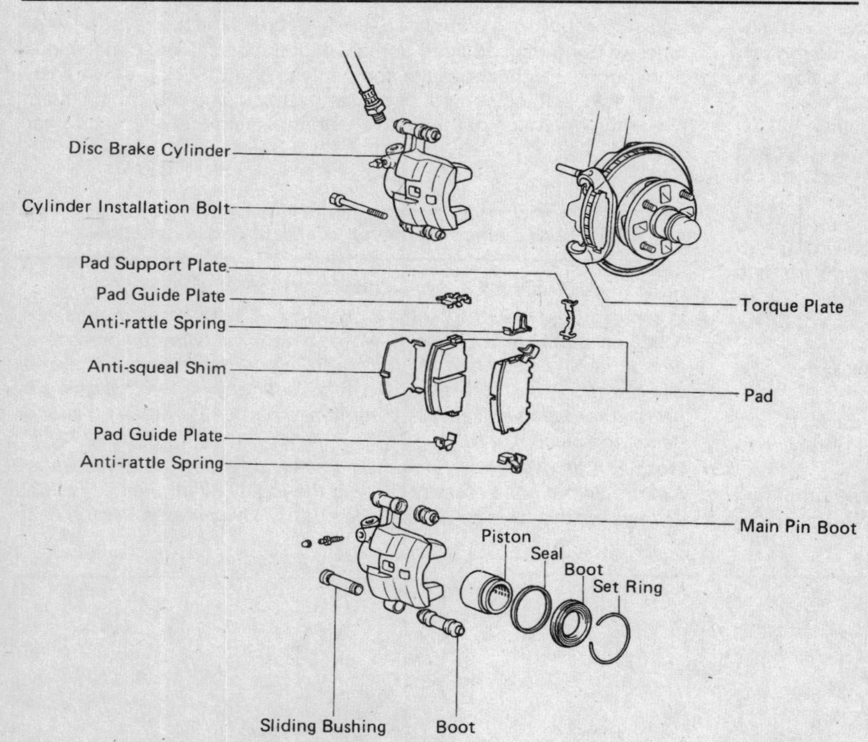

4.4a An exploded view of a typical disc brake caliper assembly (1982 and later front brake shown, others similar - note that earlier models do not have mounting bolts, sliding bushings or bushing boots)

4.4b Using a screwdriver, remove the boot set ring

4.5 With the caliper padded to catch the piston, use compressed air to force the piston out of its bore. Make sure your hands or fingers are not between the piston and caliper

easy. If it's decided to rebuild the calipers, make sure that a rebuild kit is available before proceeding. Always rebuild the calipers in pairs - never rebuild just one of them.

Note 2: *Do not attempt to overhaul the rear calipers on 1979 through 1981 models. This job requires special tools to remove the piston from the caliper body. Remove the caliper assembly and exchange it for a new or rebuilt part from a dealer service department or auto parts store.*

Removal

1 On 1979 through 1981 rear calipers, disconnect the parking brake cable from the caliper by removing the cotter pin and clevis pin.

2 Refer to Section 3 for either front or rear caliper removal procedure - it's part of the brake pad replacement procedure. **Warning:** *If the vehicle is equipped with anti-lock brakes, turn the ignition key to OFF and apply the brake pedal firmly at least 20 times to release residual pressure in the system.*

4.7 The piston seal should be removed with a plastic or wooden tool to avoid damage to the bore and seal groove. A pencil will do the job

4.8a On models so equipped, push the sliding bushing up through the boot and pull it free, then remove the dust boots

4.8b Push the bushing sleeve, if equipped, out of the caliper

3 Disconnect the brake line from the caliper and plug it to keep contaminants out of the brake system and to prevent losing any more brake fluid than is necessary **(see illustration)**.

Overhaul

4 To overhaul the caliper, remove the rubber boot set ring and the rubber boot **(see illustrations)**. Before you remove the piston, place a wood block between the piston and caliper to prevent damage as it is removed.

5 To remove the piston from the caliper, apply compressed air to the brake fluid hose connection on the caliper body **(see illustration)**. Use only enough pressure to ease the piston out of its bore. **Warning:** *Be careful not to place your fingers between the piston and the caliper as the piston may come out with some force.*

6 Inspect the mating surfaces of the piston and caliper bore wall. If there is any scoring, rust, pitting or bright areas, replace the complete caliper unit with a new one.

7 If these components are in good condition, remove the rubber seal from the caliper bore using a wooden or plastic tool **(see illustration)**. Metal tools may damage the cylinder bore.

8 On 1982 and later models, push the sliding bushings out of the caliper ears **(see illustration)** and remove the rubber boots from both ends. Slide the bushing sleeves (if equipped) out of the caliper ears **(see illustration)**.

9 Wash all the components in clean brake fluid or alcohol.

10 Using the correct rebuild kit for your vehicle, reassemble the caliper as follows **Note:** *During reassembly, apply silicone-based grease (supplied with the rebuild kit) between the sliding bushing and the bushing sleeve.*

11 Submerge the new rubber seal and the piston in brake fluid and install them into the caliper bore. Do not force the piston into the bore, but make sure that it is squarely in place, then apply firm (but not excessive) pressure to install it.

12 Install the new rubber boot and retaining ring.

13 Lubricate the sliding bushings and sleeves with silicone-based grease (supplied in the kit) and push them into the caliper ears. Install the dust boots.

Installation

14 Install the caliper by reversing the removal procedure. If the caliper has a banjo-type hose connection, remember to replace the copper sealing washer on the brake line union bolt (comes with the rebuild kit).

15 Bleed the brake circuit according to the procedure in Section 13.

5 Brake disc - inspection, removal and installation

Note: *This procedure applies to both the front and rear brake discs.*

Inspection

Refer to illustrations 5.2, 5.3, 5.4a, 5.4b, 5.5a and 5.5b

1 Loosen the wheel lug nuts, raise the vehicle and support it securely on jackstands. Remove the wheel and install three lug nuts to hold the disc in place. If the rear brake disc is being worked on, release the parking brake.

2 Remove the brake caliper as outlined in Section 4. It is not necessary to disconnect the brake hose. After removing the caliper bolts, suspend the caliper out of the way with a piece of wire. Remove the two bolts **(see illustration)** and remove the torque plate (bracket).

3 Visually inspect the disc surface for scoring or damage. Light scratches and shallow grooves are normal after use and may not al-

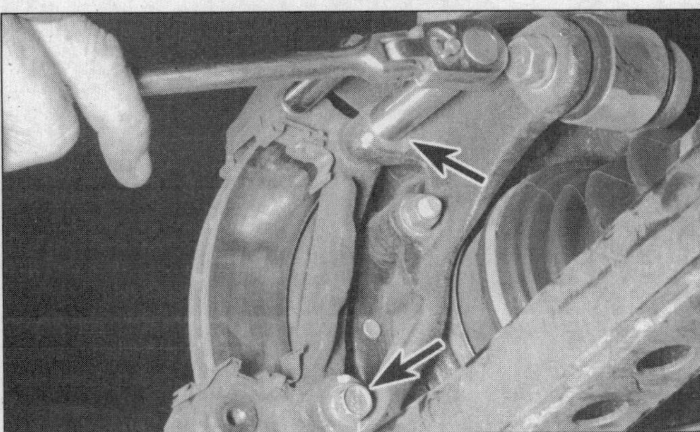

5.2 The torque plate (caliper mounting bracket) is secured to the steering knuckle with two bolts (arrows)

5.3 The brake pads on this vehicle were obviously neglected, as they wore down to the rivets and cut deep grooves into the disc - wear this severe will require replacement of the disc

5.4a Use a dial indicator to check disc runout - if the reading exceeds the maximum allowable runout limit, the disc will have to be machined or replaced

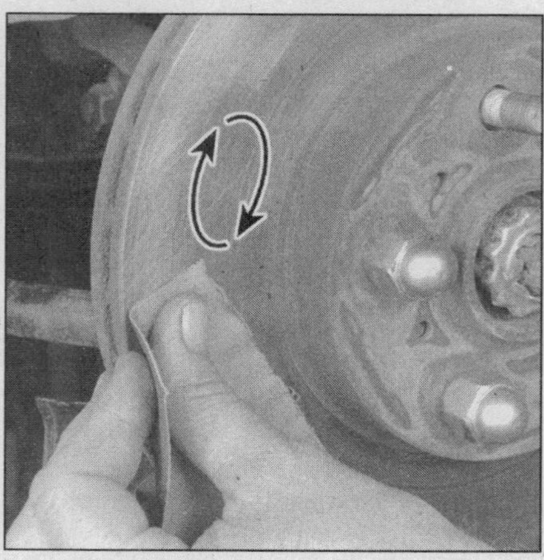
5.4b Using a swirling motion, remove the glaze from the disc surface with sandpaper or emery cloth

5.5a The minimum wear dimension is cast into the backside of the disc

ways be detrimental to brake operation, but deep scoring - over 0.015 inch - requires disc removal and refinishing by an automotive machine shop. Be sure to check both sides of the disc **(see illustration)**. If pulsating has been noticed during application of the brakes, suspect disc runout.

4 To check disc runout, place a dial indicator at a point about 1/2-inch from the outer edge of the disc **(see illustration)**. Set the indicator to zero and turn the disc. The indicator reading should not exceed the specified allowable runout limit. If it does, the disc should be refinished by an automotive machine shop. **Note:** *It is recommended that the discs be resurfaced regardless of the dial indicator reading, as this will impart a smooth finish and ensure a perfectly flat surface, eliminating any brake pedal pulsation or other undesirable symptoms related to questionable discs. At the very least, if you elect not to have the discs resurfaced, remove the glazing from the surface with emery cloth or sandpaper using a swirling motion* **(see illustration)**.

5 It is absolutely critical that the disc not be machined to a thickness under the specified minimum allowable thickness. The minimum wear (or discard) thickness is cast into the inside of the disc **(see illustration)**. The disc thickness can be checked with a micrometer **(see illustration)**.

Removal

Refer to illustrations 5.6a and 5.6b

6 Remove the two lug nuts which were put on to hold the disc in place and remove the disc from the hub. If the disc is stuck to the hub and won't come off on 1982 and later models, rotate the disc until the adjuster hole is at the bottom, remove the plug from the hole and use a brake adjusting tool or thin, flat-bladed screwdriver to rotate the star wheel on the parking brake adjusting screw to contract the parking brake shoes **(see illustration)**. On all models, if the disc is still stuck, thread three bolts into the holes provided **(see illustration)** and tighten them. Alternate between the bolts, turning them a couple of turns at a time, until the disc is free.

Installation

Refer to illustration 5.7

7 Place the disc in position over the threaded studs **(see illustration)** and install the torque plate and caliper. Tighten the bolts to the torque listed in this Chapter's Specifications.

8 Install the wheel, then lower the vehicle to the ground. Depress the brake pedal a few times to bring the brake pads into contact with

5.5b Use a micrometer to measure disc thickness

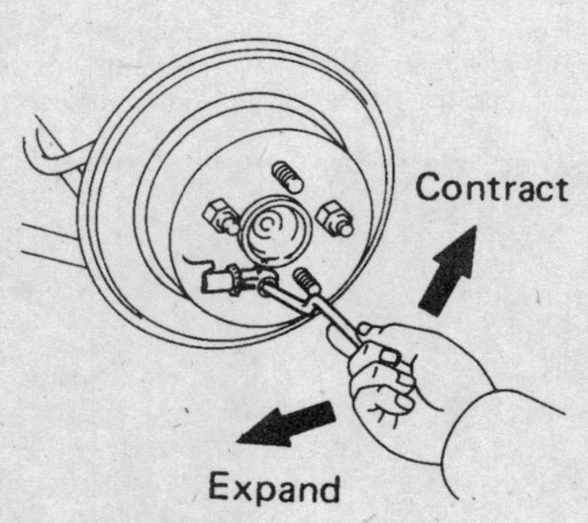

5.6a Once the plug is removed, insert a brake adjusting tool or long screwdriver through the hole and turn the star wheel on the adjusting screw to adjust the parking brake shoes - contracting the shoes may help the disc to be removed more easily (1982 and later models)

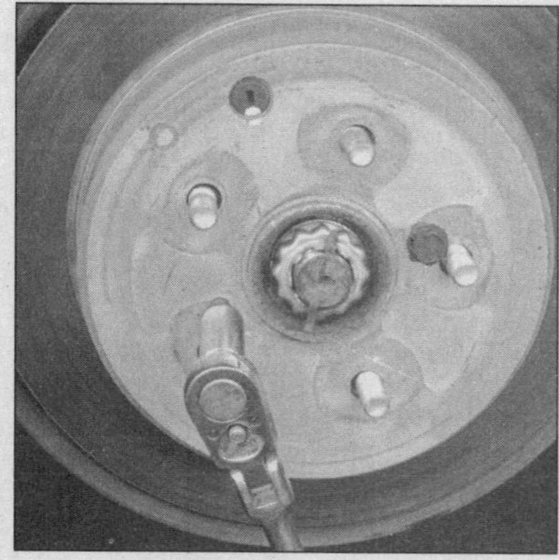
5.6b To help free the disc, thread bolts of the appropriate size into the two holes provided in the disc. Alternate between the bolts, turning them a little at a time, until the disc is free

the disc. Bleeding of the system will not be necessary unless the fluid hose was disconnected from the caliper. Check the operation of the brakes carefully before placing the vehicle into normal service.

6 Master cylinder - removal, overhaul and installation

Refer to illustrations 6.1a, 6.1b, 6.4, 6.8a, 6.8b, 6.9, 6.10, 6.11a, 6.11b and 6.26

Note: *Before deciding to overhaul the master cylinder, check on the availability and cost of a new or factory rebuilt unit and also the availability of a rebuild kit.*

Removal

1 The master cylinder is connected to the brake booster and both are attached to the firewall, located on the driver's side of the engine compartment **(see illustrations)**.

2 Remove as much fluid as you can from the reservoir with a syringe. **Warning:** *If the vehicle is equipped with anti-lock brakes, turn the ignition key to OFF and apply the brake pedal firmly at least 20 times to release residual pressure in the system.*

3 Place rags under the line fittings and prepare caps or plastic bags to cover the ends of the lines once they are disconnected. **Caution:** *Brake fluid will damage paint. Cover all body parts and be careful not to spill fluid during this procedure.*

4 Loosen the tube nuts at the ends of the brake lines where they enter the master cylinder. To prevent rounding off the flats on these nuts, a flare-nut wrench, which wraps around the nut, should be used **(see illustration)**.

5 Pull the brake lines away from the master cylinder slightly and plug the ends to prevent contamination.

6 Disconnect the electrical connector at the master cylinder, then remove the four nuts attaching the master cylinder to the power booster. Pull the master cylinder off the studs and lift it out of the engine compartment. Again, be careful not to spill fluid as this is done.

5.7 Be sure to align the access hole with the adjuster cutout (arrows) when installing the rotor over the parking brake assembly (1982 and later models)

Overhaul

7 Before attempting to overhaul the master cylinder, obtain the proper rebuild kit, which will contain the necessary replacement parts and also any instructions which may be specific to your model.

8 Inspect the reservoir grommet for indications of leakage near the base of the reservoir. Remove the reservoir **(see illustrations)**. **Note:**

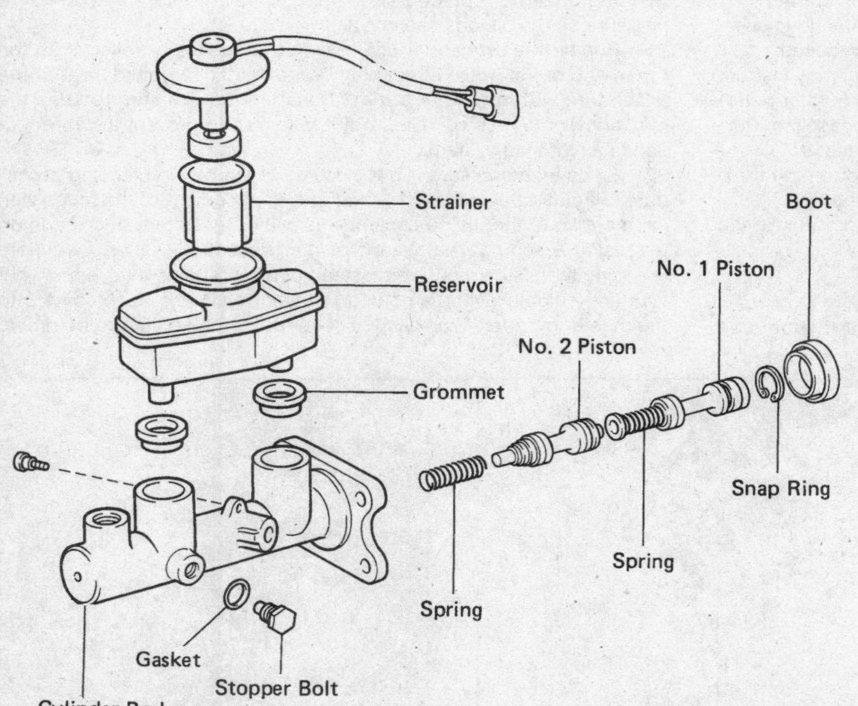

6.1a An exploded view of a typical master cylinder. Note that the stopper bolt on some master cylinders is in a different location

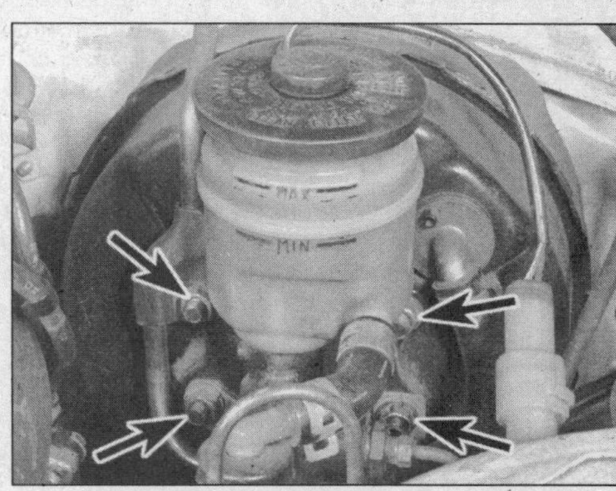

6.1b The master cylinder is attached to the brake booster (note the four mounting nuts [arrows]) (1983 model shown)

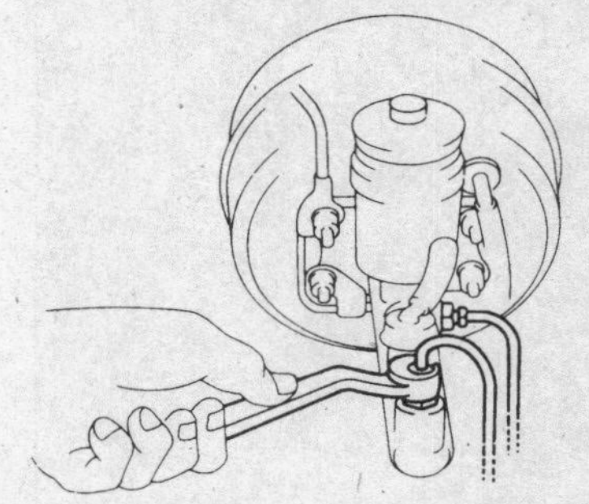

6.4 To prevent rounding off the flats on the fittings, use a flare-nut wrench to loosen the brake lines

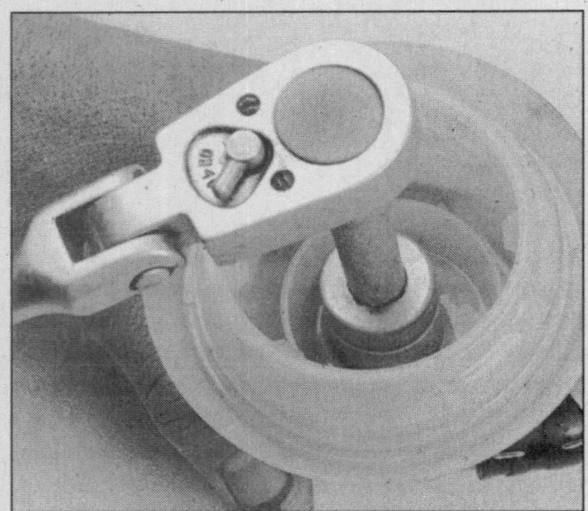
6.8a Most models have nut(s) inside the reservoir(s), . . .

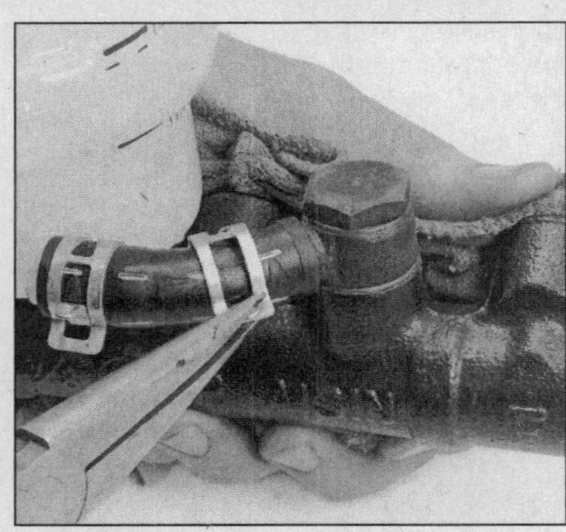
6.8b . . . and, on some models, you'll have to disconnect the reservoir hose before you can pull off the reservoir

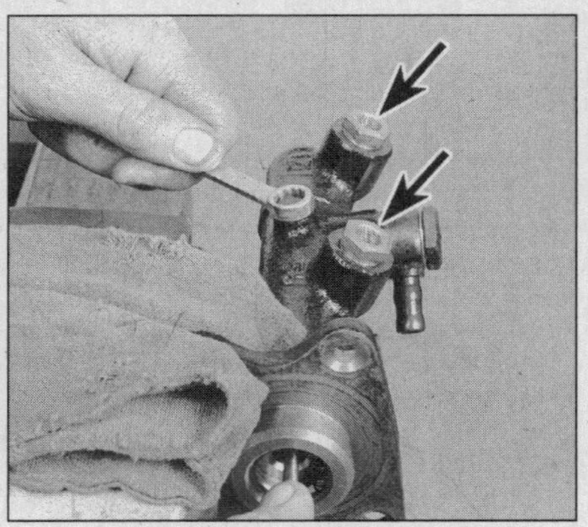
6.9 Push the pistons in all the way and remove the piston stopper bolt and the copper gasket (also remove the two outlet plugs - if equipped - [arrows] and gaskets)

The illustrations shown cover most models from 1982 through 1986. Earlier models have two reservoirs and no hose (nuts inside the reservoirs secure them). Later models have a single reservoir like the one shown in illustration 6.1a that is secured by an external screw.

9 Place the cylinder in a vise and use a wooden dowel to depress the pistons until they bottom against the other end of the master cylinder. Hold the pistons in this position and remove the stop bolt on the side of the master cylinder. Remove the two outlet plugs and the copper gaskets - if equipped - **(see illustration)**.

10 Carefully remove the snap-ring at the end of the master cylinder **(see illustration)**.

11 The internal components can now be removed from the cylinder bore **(see illustrations)**. Make note of the installed order of the components so they can be returned to their original locations. **Note:** *The two springs are different, so pay particular attention to their order*.

12 Carefully inspect the bore of the master cylinder. Any deep scoring or other damage will mean a new master cylinder is required.

13 Replace all parts included in the rebuild kit, following any instructions in the kit. Clean all reused parts with clean brake fluid or denatured alcohol. Do not use petroleum-based solvents or gasoline. During assembly, lubricate all parts liberally with clean brake fluid.

14 Push the assembled components into the bore, bottoming them against the end of the master cylinder, then install the stop bolt.

15 Install the new snap-ring, making sure it is seated properly in the groove.

Bench bleeding procedure

16 Before installing a new or rebuilt master cylinder it should be bench bled. Because it will be necessary to apply pressure to the master cylinder piston and, at the same time, control flow from the brake line outlets, it is recommended that the master cylinder be mounted in a vise. Use caution not to clamp the vise too tightly, or the master cylinder body might crack.

17 Insert threaded plugs into the brake line outlet holes and snug them down so that there will be no air leakage past them, but not so tight that they cannot be easily loosened.

18 Fill the reservoir with brake fluid of the recommended type (see *Recommended lubricants and fluids* in Chapter 1).

19 Remove one plug and push the piston assembly into the master cylinder bore to expel the air from the master cylinder. A large Phillips screwdriver can be used to push on the piston assembly.

20 To prevent air from being drawn back into the master cylinder, the plug must be replaced and snugged down before releasing the pressure on the piston assembly.

21 Repeat the procedure until only brake fluid is expelled from the brake line outlet hole. When only brake fluid is expelled, repeat the procedure with the other outlet hole and plug. Be sure to keep the master cylinder reservoir filled with brake fluid to prevent the introduction of air into the system.

22 Since high pressure is not involved in the bench bleeding procedure, an alternative to the removal and replacement of the plugs with each stroke of the piston assembly is available. Before pushing in on the piston assembly, remove the plug as described in Step 19. Before releasing the piston, however, instead of replacing the plug, simply put your finger tightly over the hole to keep air from being drawn back into the master cylinder. Wait several seconds for brake fluid to be drawn

6.10 Push the pistons in and use snap-ring pliers to remove the snap-ring

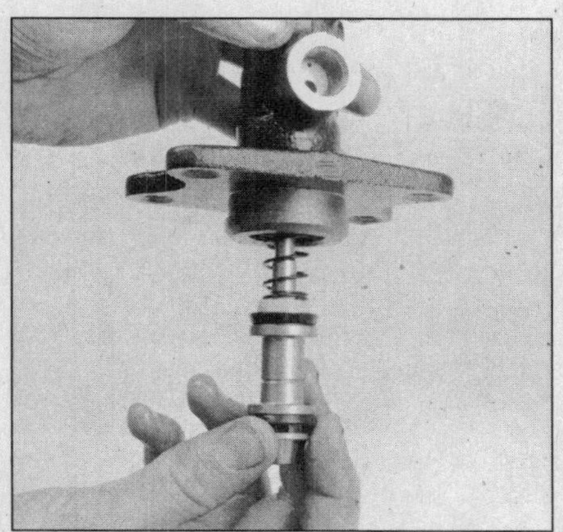
6.11a Tilt the cylinder and remove the No. 1 piston and spring

6.11b To free the No. 2 piston and spring, tap the cylinder sharply on a block of wood

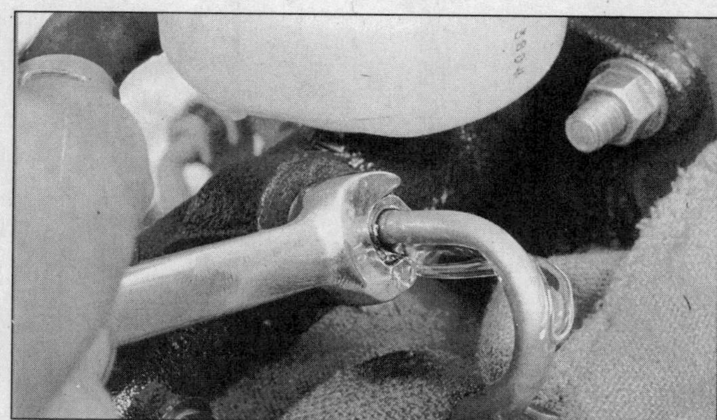

6.26 After the master cylinder is installed, it can be bled by loosening the fittings (one at a time) and applying the brakes

from the reservoir into the piston bore, then depress the piston again, removing your finger as brake fluid is expelled. Be sure to put your finger back over the hole each time before releasing the piston, and when the bleeding procedure is complete for that outlet, replace the plug and snug it up before going on to the other port.

Installation

23 Install the master cylinder over the studs on the power brake booster and tighten the mounting nuts only finger tight at this time.

24 Thread the brake line fittings into the master cylinder. Since the master cylinder is still a bit loose, it can be moved slightly in order for the fittings to thread in easily. Do not strip the threads as the fittings are tightened.

25 Completely tighten the brake fittings and the mounting nuts.

26 Fill the master cylinder reservoir with fluid, then bleed the master cylinder (only if the cylinder has not been bench bled) and the brake system as described in Section 13. To bleed the cylinder on the vehicle, have an assistant pump the brake pedal several times and then hold the pedal to the floor. Loosen the fitting nut to allow air and fluid to escape, then tighten the nut. Repeat this procedure on both fittings until the fluid is clear of air bubbles **(see illustration)**. Test the operation of the brake system carefully before placing the vehicle into normal service.

7 Brake booster - check, removal and installation

Operating check

1 Depress the brake pedal several times with the engine off and make sure there is no change in the pedal reserve distance.

2 Depress the pedal and start the engine. If the pedal goes down slightly, operation is normal.

Air tightness check

3 Start the engine and turn it off after one or two minutes. Depress the brake pedal several times slowly. If the pedal goes down further the first time but gradually rises after the second or third depression, the booster is air tight.

4 Depress the brake pedal while the engine is running, then stop the engine with the pedal depressed. If there is no change in the pedal reserve travel after holding the pedal for 30 seconds, the booster is air tight.

Removal and installation

Refer to illustrations 7.10 and 7.11

5 Dismantling of the power booster requires special tools and cannot be performed by the home mechanic. If a problem develops, it is recommended that a new or factory rebuilt unit be installed.

6 Remove the master cylinder as described in Section 6.

7.10 The four brake booster mounting nuts (arrows) can be reached from under the dashboard

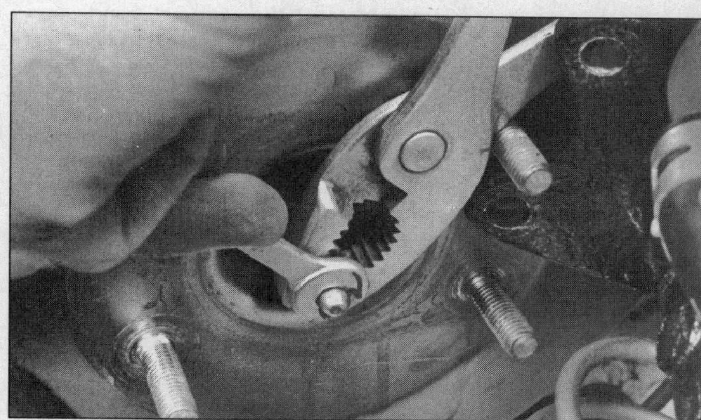

7.11 Turn the adjusting nut on the end of the brake pushrod to change the clearance - hold the pushrod with pliers to keep it from turning

7 Disconnect the vacuum hose where it attaches to the brake booster.

8 Working in the passenger compartment, remove the lower finish panel (below the steering column) and air duct.

9 Disconnect the brake pedal return spring, then remove the clip and clevis pin to disconnect the push rod from the brake pedal **(see illustration 11.5)**.

10 Remove the four mounting nuts and withdraw the booster unit from the engine compartment **(see illustration)**.

11 Installation is the reverse of the removal procedure, but before mating the master cylinder to the booster, check the clearance between the back of the piston and the brake pushrod. Using a depth micrometer or vernier caliper, measure the distance from the bottom of the piston bore to the master cylinder mounting flange. Measure the distance from the end of the brake pushrod to the surface on the booster assembly that the master cylinder mounting flange is in contact with when installed. Subtract the two measurements to get the clearance. If the clearance is more or less than specified, turn the adjusting nut on the end of the brake pushrod until the clearance is within the specified limit **(see illustration)**.

12 Upon installation, place the booster in position and install the retaining nuts. Connect the brake pedal.

13 Install the master cylinder and vacuum hose.

14 Carefully test the operation of the brakes before placing the vehicle in normal operation.

8 Parking brake cable - replacement

Refer to illustrations 8.4, 8.5 and 8.8

1 Refer to Chapter 1 for a general inspection of the parking brake.

8.4 After removing the cable from the parking brake shoe lever, use a pair of pliers to squeeze the cable retaining clip and push it out through the opening in the backing plate (1982 and later models)

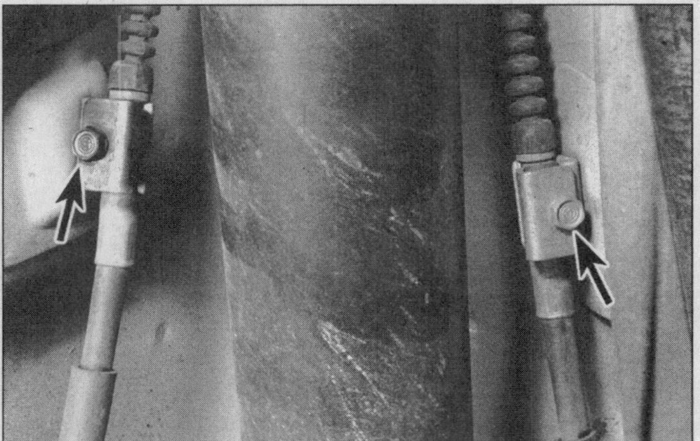

8.5 Remove the two retaining bolts to release the cable brackets

Equalizer-to-parking brake cable

2 Raise the vehicle and support it securely on jackstands.
3 On 1982 and later models, remove the rear wheels and the brake discs (rotors) (refer to Section 5).
4 Disconnect the cable from the caliper or brake backing plate **(see illustration)**.
5 Remove the two cable brackets **(see illustration)**.
6 Disconnect the cable at the equalizer and pull the cable free.

Equalizer-to-brake lever cable

7 Remove the console and/or trim around the parking brake lever.
8 With the lever in the down (off) position, remove the locknut and the adjustment nut and detach the cable from the lever **(see illustration)**.
9 From underneath the vehicle, pull the cable out and through the cable guide, then disconnect it from the equalizer.
10 Installation is the reverse of removal. Apply a thin coat of grease to the portion of the cable that contacts the equalizer.

9 Parking brake cable - adjustment

Refer to illustration 9.1

1 Pull the parking brake lever all the way up and count the number of notches the lever travels **(see illustration)**. Compare it to the Specifications. If incorrect, adjust the parking brake.

8.8 Remove the lock and adjusting nuts to free the cable from the lever

2 Before adjusting the parking brake, be certain that the rear brake shoe clearance has been adjusted (refer to Section 10).
3 Remove the console and/or trim around the parking brake lever.
4 Loosen the locknut and turn the adjusting nut until the travel is correct **(see illustration 8.8)**.
5 Tighten the locknut and replace the console and/or trim.

10 Parking brake assembly - check, removal and installation

Refer to illustrations 10.4a, 10.4b, 10.5, 10.6, 10.7, 10.8a, 10.8b, 10.9 and 10.10

Warning: *Some of the parking brake components are made of asbestos, which may cause serious harm if inhaled. When servicing these components, do not create dust by grinding or sanding the linings or by using compressed air to blow away dust. Use a water dampened cloth to wipe away the residue.*
Note: *This procedure applies to 1982 and later models only.*

Check

1 The parking brake system should be checked as a normal part of driving. With the vehicle parked on a hill, apply the brake, place the transmission in Neutral and check that the parking brake alone will hold the vehicle. However, every 24 months (or whenever a fault is suspected), the assembly itself should be visually inspected.
2 With the vehicle raised and supported on jackstands, remove the rear wheels.
3 Remove the rear rotors (discs) as outlined in Section 5. Support the caliper assemblies with a coat hanger or heavy wire and do not disconnect the brake line from the caliper.
4 With the rotor removed, the parking brake components are visible

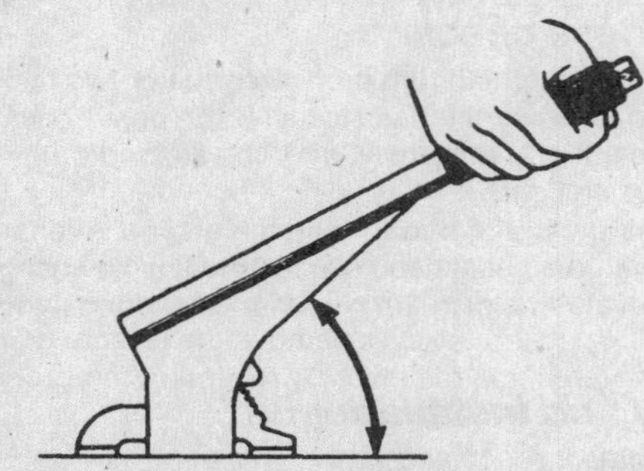

9.1 Pull the lever all the way up, count the number of clicks until the lever stops and compare it to the Specifications

Shoe Strut and Spring
Rear Shoe with Lever
Shoe Return Spring
Pin
Pin
Spring
Front Shoe
Shoe Adjusting Screw Set
Shoe Hold-Down Spring

10.4a Typical parking brake components - exploded view

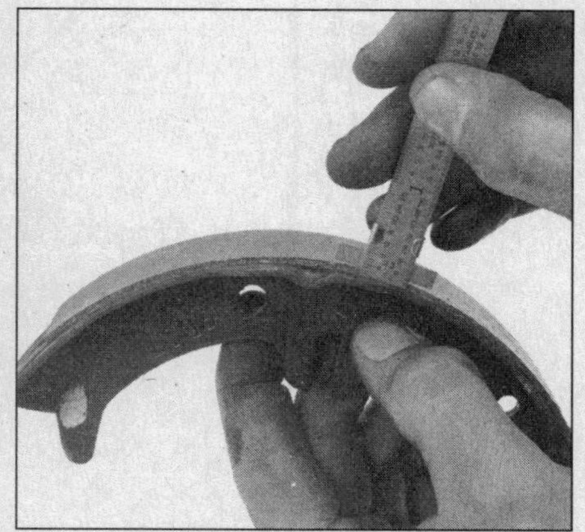

10.4b If the shoe lining measures less than the specified minimum, replace the parking brake shoes

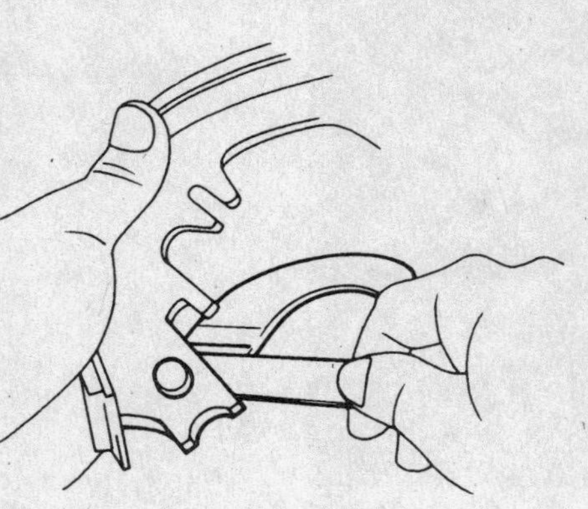

10.5 Place a feeler gauge between the brake lever and the shoe, compare the measurement to the Specifications and adjust if necessary

10.6 Using needle-nose pliers, pull the shoe return spring up and out to release it

and can be inspected for wear and damage **(see illustration)**. Most critical are the linings, which can wear after a time, especially if the parking brake system has been improperly adjusted. Measure the brake shoe lining thickness **(see illustration)** and compare it to the Specifications. Replace the shoes if necessary. Also check the springs and adjuster mechanism for damage. Inspect the drum for deep scratches and other damage.

5 Using a feeler gauge, measure the brake shoe clearance. Place the feeler gauge between the brake shoe and the lever **(see illustration)**. Compare your measurement to the Specifications. If the clearance is not as specified, remove the shoes (see below) and replace the shim with one of the correct size. Use a screwdriver to release the retaining clip from the brake lever, remove the lever and install the correct size shim. Replace the lever by reversing the procedure. Use a pair of pliers to reinstall the retaining clip.

Removal

6 Using needle-nose pliers, remove the shoe return springs **(see illustration)**.

7 Pull out the shoe strut with the spring **(see illustration)**.

10.7 Turn and lift out the shoe strut and spring

10.8a Pull the adjusting screw back and out to remove it

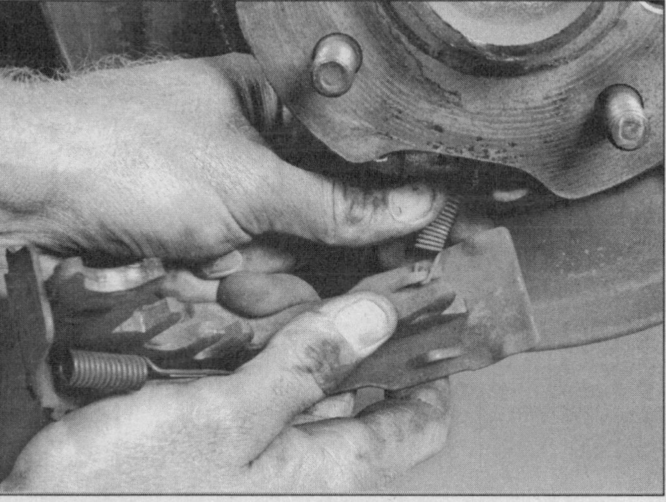

10.8b Twist the shoe and remove the tension spring

10.9 Pull the cable out and up to free it from the lever on the rear shoe

8 Slide out the front shoe and remove the shoe adjusting screw set **(see illustration)**. Turn the shoe out and remove the tension spring and the front shoe **(see illustration)**.

9 To remove the rear shoe, disconnect the parking brake cable from the lever **(see illustration)**.

Installation

10 Apply high-temperature brake grease to the backing plate and to the shoe adjusting screw set **(see illustration)**.

11 Reassemble the parking brake components.

12 After replacing the rotor, adjust the parking brake shoes. Temporarily install two lug nuts, turn the adjuster and expand the shoes until the rotor locks, then back off the adjuster eight notches **(see illustration 5.6)**.

13 Inspect and adjust the parking brake lever as necessary.

11 Brake light switch - removal, installation and adjustment

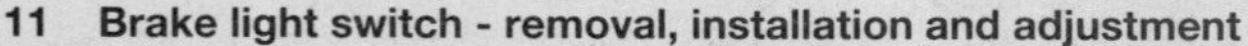

Removal and installation

1 The brake light switch is located on a bracket at the top of the brake pedal. The switch activates the brake lights at the rear of the vehicle whenever the pedal is depressed.

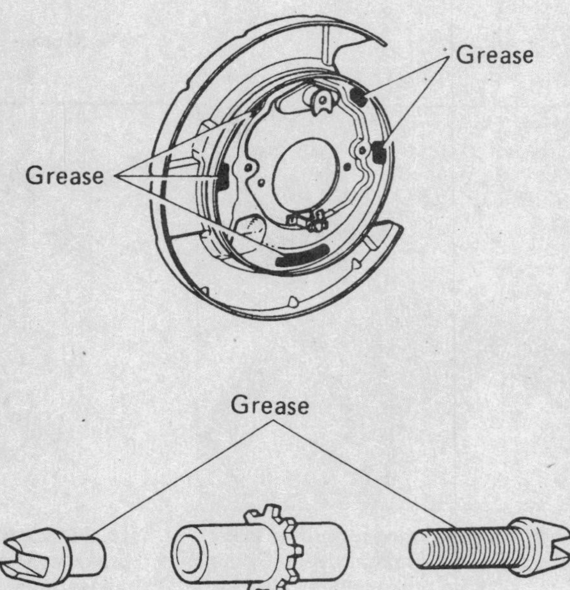

10.10 Apply high-temperature brake grease to the backing plate and the adjusting screw set

2 Disconnect the negative battery cable and secure it out of the way so that it cannot come into contact with the battery post. **Caution:** *If the stereo in your vehicle is equipped with an anti-theft system, refer to the information on page 0-15 at the front of this manual before detaching the cable.*

3 Disconnect the wiring harness at the brake light switch.

4 Loosen the locknut and unscrew the switch from the pedal bracket. Install the new switch in the reverse order.

Adjustment

Refer to illustration 11.5

5 Loosen the locknut **(see illustration)**, adjust the switch so that the threaded portion lightly contacts the pedal stopper, then tighten the locknut.

6 Connect the wiring at the switch and the battery. With an assistant, check that the rear brake lights are functioning properly.

12 Brake hoses and lines - inspection and replacement

Inspection

1 About every six months, with the vehicle raised and placed securely on jackstands, the flexible hoses which connect the steel brake lines with the front and rear brake assemblies should be inspected for cracks, chafing of the outer cover, leaks, blisters and other damage. These are important and vulnerable parts of the brake system and inspection should be complete. A light and mirror will prove helpful for a thorough check. If a hose exhibits any of the above conditions, replace it with a new one.

Flexible (rubber) hose replacement

Warning: *If the vehicle is equipped with anti-lock brakes, turn the ignition key to OFF and apply the brake pedal firmly at least 20 times to release residual pressure in the system.*

2 Clean all dirt away from the ends of the hose.

3 To disconnect the hose at the frame end, hold the nut on the flexible hose steady, loosen the other union nut and disconnect the hose from the line. If necessary, soak the connections with penetrating oil. After the hose is disconnected from the metal line, detach the hose from the frame bracket (usually this involves removing a clip with a pair of pliers).

4 Detach the hose from the caliper by unscrewing it or removing the banjo bolt and copper crush washers. Warning: Always replace the crush washers with new ones on reassembly.

5 Installation is the reverse of the removal procedure, but carefully check that all the brackets are in good condition and that the locknuts are tight. Install a new hose clip.

6 Carefully check to make sure the suspension and steering components do not make contact with the hoses. Have an assistant push on the vehicle and also turn the steering wheel from lock-to-lock during inspection.

7 Bleed the brake system as described in Section 13.

Metal brake line replacement

Warning: *If the vehicle is equipped with anti-lock brakes, turn the ignition key to OFF and apply the brake pedal firmly at least 20 times to release residual pressure in the system.*

8 When replacing brake lines, use the proper parts only. Do not use copper line for any brake system connections. Purchase steel brake lines from a dealer or auto parts store.

9 Prefabricated brake line, with the tube ends already flared and fittings installed, is available at auto parts stores and dealers. These lines are also bent to the proper shapes. Do not, under any circumstances, use anything other than the steel line recommended for brakes on these vehicles.

10 If prefabricated lines are not available, obtain the recommended steel tubing and fittings to match the line to be replaced. Determine the correct length by measuring the old brake line (a piece of string can usually be used for this) and cut the new tubing to length, allowing about 1/2-inch extra for flaring the ends.

11 Install the fitting over the cut tubing and flare the ends of the line with an ISO flaring tool.

12 If necessary, carefully bend the line to the proper shape. A tube bender is recommended for this. **Warning:** *Do not crimp or damage the line.*

13 When installing the new line, make sure it is well supported in the brackets and the routing matches the original. Be sure there is plenty of clearance between moving or hot components.

14 After installation, check the master cylinder fluid level and add fluid as necessary. Bleed the brake system as outlined in Section 13 and test the brakes carefully before driving the vehicle. Be sure there are no leaks.

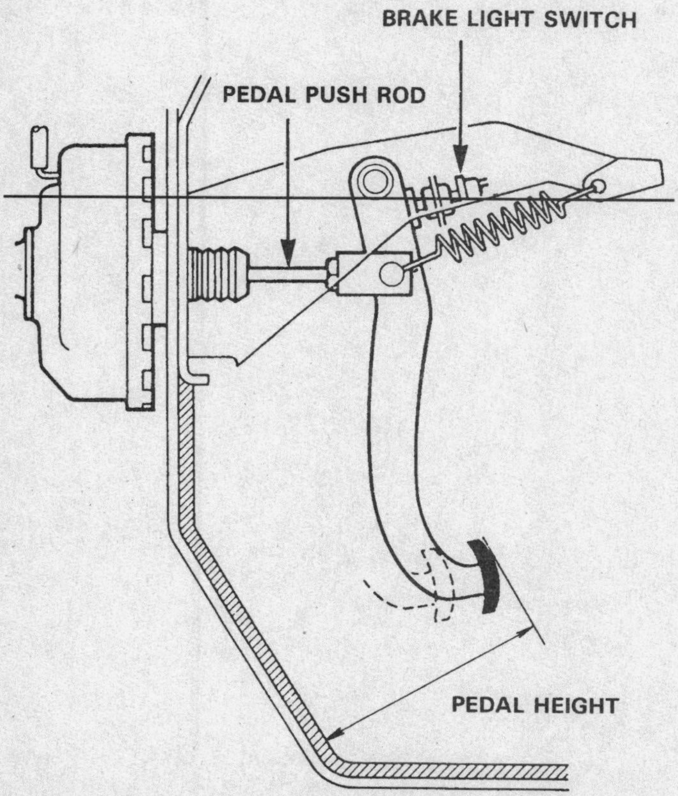

11.5 A diagram of the brake light switch and pedal assembly

13 Brake hydraulic system bleeding

Refer to illustration 13.9

Warning: *Wear eye protection when bleeding the brake system. If the fluid comes in contact with your eyes, immediately rinse them with water and seek medical attention.*

Note: *Bleeding the hydraulic system is necessary to remove any air which has entered the system during removal and installation of a hose, line, caliper or master cylinder.*

1 It will probably be necessary to bleed the system at all four brakes if air has entered the system due to low fluid level or if the brake lines have been disconnected at the master cylinder.

2 If a brake line was disconnected at only one wheel, then only that caliper must be bled.

3 If a brake line is disconnected at a fitting located between the master cylinder and any of the brakes, that part of the system served by the disconnected line must be bled.

4 Bleed the right rear, the left rear, the right front and the left front caliper, in that order, when the entire system is involved.

5 Remove any residual vacuum from the power brake booster and anti-lock brake system (if equipped) by applying the brake about 30 times with the engine off.

6 Remove the master cylinder reservoir cover and fill the reservoir with brake fluid. Reinstall the cover. **Note:** *Check the fluid level often during the bleeding operation and add fluid as necessary to prevent the fluid level from falling low enough to allow air into the master cylinder.*

7 Have an assistant on hand, as well as a supply of new brake fluid, an empty clear plastic container, a length of 3/16-inch clear plastic or vinyl tubing to fit over the bleeder screws and a wrench to open and close the bleeder screws.

8 Beginning at the right rear wheel, loosen the bleeder screw slightly, then tighten it to a point where it is snug but can still be loosened quickly and easily.

9 Place one end of the tubing over the bleeder valve and submerge the other end in brake fluid in the container **(see illustration)**.

10 Have the assistant pump the brakes a few times to get pressure in the system, then hold the pedal firmly depressed.

11 While the pedal is held depressed, open the bleeder screw just enough to allow a flow of fluid to leave the caliper. Watch for air bubbles to exit the submerged end of the tube. When the fluid flow slows after a couple of seconds, close the screw and have your assistant release the pedal.

12 Repeat Steps 10 and 11 until no more air is seen leaving the tube, then tighten the bleeder screw and proceed to the left rear wheel, the right front wheel and the left front wheel, in that order, and perform the same procedure. Be sure to check the fluid in the master cylinder reservoir frequently.

13 Never reuse old brake fluid. It contains moisture which will deteriorate the brake system components.

14 Refill the master cylinder with fluid at the end of the operation.

15 Check the operation of the brakes. The pedal should feel solid when depressed, with no sponginess. If necessary, repeat the entire process. **Warning:** *Do not operate the vehicle if you are in doubt about the effectiveness of the brake system.*

16 If any difficulty is experienced in bleeding the hydraulic system, or if an assistant is not available, a pressure bleeding kit is a worthwhile investment. If connected in accordance with the instructions, each bleeder screw can be opened in turn to allow the fluid to be pressure ejected until it is clear of air bubbles without the need to replenish the master cylinder reservoir during the process.

13.9 When bleeding the brakes, a clear piece of tubing is attached to the bleeder screw fitting and submerged in brake fluid - air bubbles can be easily seen in the tube and container (when no more bubbles appear, the air has been purged from the caliper)

Chapter 10
Suspension and steering systems

Contents

Specifications

General

Strut bar (front) installed length **(see illustration 4.3b)**

1979 through 1981	14.900 inches
1982 through 1986	14.531 inches
Front hub axial play	0.002 inch
Power steering fluid type	See Chapter 1
Manual steering gear lubricant type	See Chapter 1

Torque specifications

	Ft-lbs
Front suspension	
Shock absorber damper rod-to-suspension support nut	
1979 through 1981	Not available
1982 through 1986	34
1987 on	22
Lower control arm-to-crossmember bolt/nut	
1979 through 1981	58
1982 through 1986	80
1987 on	177
Upper control arm-to-suspension member bolt/nut (1987 on)	121
Balljoint-to-steering knuckle nut	
1979 through 1981	58
1982 through 1986	58
1987 on	92
Balljoint-to-lower control arm bolts (1987 on)	94
Strut bar-to-bracket nut (1979 through 1986)	76
Strut bar-to-control arm nuts (1979 through 1986)	48
Strut bar bracket-to-body bolts (1979 through 1986)	34
Tie-rod end-to-steering knuckle nut	43
Stabilizer bar-to-lower arm (1979 through 1986)	13
Stabilizer bar-to-link (1987 on)	47
Stabilizer bar bracket-to-strut bar bracket bolts (1979 through 1986)	9
Strut-to-steering knuckle bolts (1979 through 1986)	72
Strut-to-body nuts (1986 and earlier models)	27
Shock absorber/coil spring assembly-to-lower control arm nut (1987 on)	106
Shock absorber/coil spring assembly-to-body nuts (1987 and later models)	26
Suspension member (crossmember)-to-body bolts	80
Rear suspension	
Shock absorber-to-body	18
Shock absorber-to-axle (1979 through 1981)	30
Shock absorber-to-lower suspension arm	
1982 through 1986	27
1987 on	101
Upper suspension arm-to-body	
1979 through 1981	100
1987 on	121
Upper suspension arm-to-rear axle (1979 through 1981)	90
Upper suspension arm-to-hub assembly (1987 on)	80
Lower suspension arm-to-differential support member (1982 through 1986)	
Inside	96
Outside	85
Lower suspension arm-to-axle (1979 through 1981)	90
Lower suspension arm-to-hub assembly (1987 on)	
Number 1	43
Number 2	121
Lower suspension arm-to-body (1987 on)	
Number 1	136
Number 2	136
Lateral control rod-to-axle housing (1979 through 1981)	30
Lateral control rod-to-body (1979 through 1981)	58
Strut rod-to-hub assembly (1987 on)	121
Strut rod-to-body (1987 on)	121
Steering system	
Steering wheel-to-steering shaft nut	25
Intermediate shaft pinch bolt	25
Rack-and-pinion steering gear bracket bolts	56
Steering gearbox-to-frame bolts	50
Tie-rod clamp bolt	13
Tie-rod end-to-steering knuckle nut	43
Relay rod-to-Pitman arm (1979 through 1981)	45
Idler arm-to-frame (1979 through 1981)	45
Idler arm-to-relay rod (1979 through 1981)	45
Tie-rod-to-relay rod (1979 through 1981)	45

1.1 Front suspension and steering components - 1982 through 1986 models (1983 model shown, 1981 and earlier models similar)

1. *Tie-rod*
2. *Tie-rod-to-steering knuckle balljoint*
3. *MacPherson strut*
4. *Steering knuckle-to-control arm balljoint*
5. *Control arm*
6. *Strut bar*
7. *Stabilizer bar bracket*
8. *Strut bar bracket*
9. *Stabilizer bar*
10. *Rack-and-pinion steering gear*
11. *Power steering lines*

1.2 Front suspension and steering components - 1987 and later models (1992 model shown)

1. *Steering knuckle-to-control arm balljoint*
2. *Stabilizer link*
3. *Lower control arm*
4. *Stabilizer bar*
5. *Power steering lines*
6. *Rack-and-pinion steering gear*
7. *Stabilizer bar bracket*
8. *Upper control arm*
9. *Shock absorber*
10. *Tie-rod*
11. *Tie-rod end*

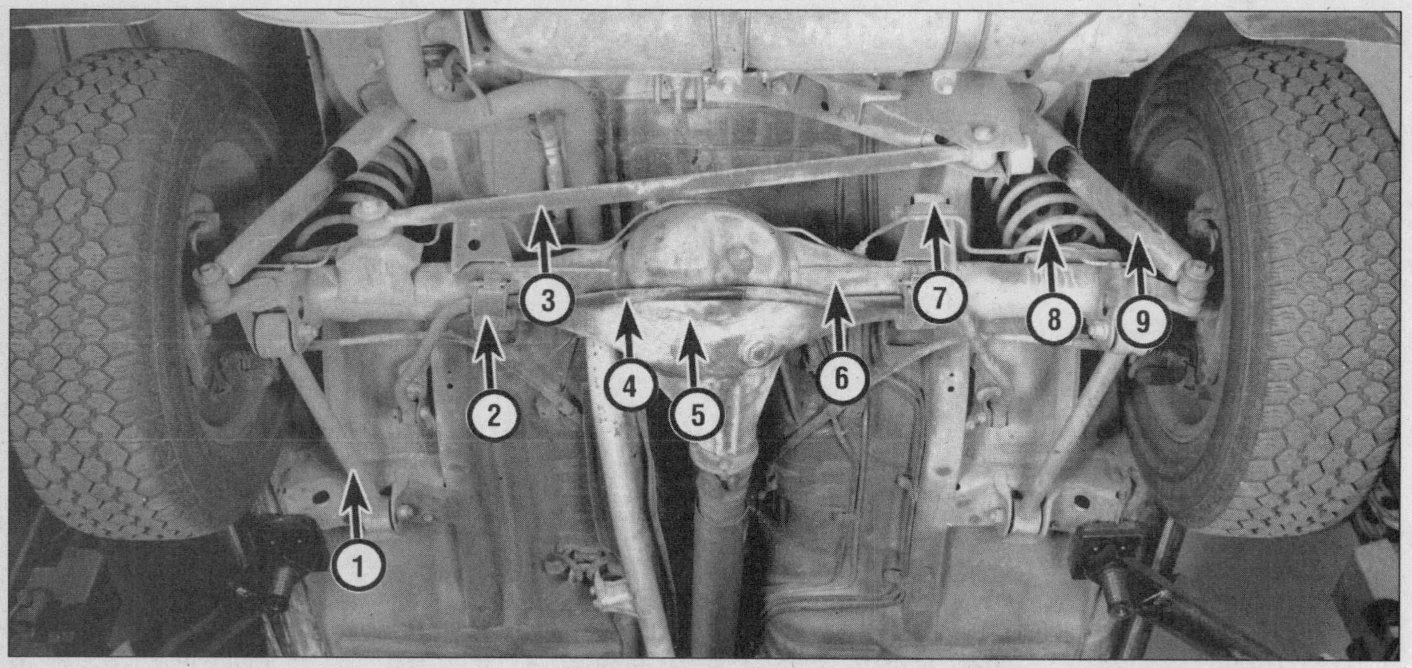

1.3 Rear suspension components - 1979 through 1981 models (1981 model shown)

1. *Lower control arm*
2. *Stabilizer bar bracket*
3. *Lateral rod*
4. *Stabilizer bar*
5. *Differential*
6. *Rear axle housing*
7. *Upper control arm*
8. *Coil spring*
9. *Shock absorber*

1.4 Rear suspension components - 1982 through 1986 models (1983 model shown)

1. *Rear suspension arm*
2. *Stabilizer bar-to-suspension arm link*
3. *Coil spring*
4. *Stub axle*
5. *Shock absorber*
6. *Axleshaft*
7. *Stabilizer bar bracket*
8. *Differential*
9. *Stabilizer bar*

1.5 Rear suspension components - 1987 and later models (1992 model shown)

1 *Strut rod*
2 *Coil spring and shock absorber assembly*
3 *Number 2 control arm*
4 *Number 1 control arm*
5 *Differential*
6 *Stabilizer bar*
7 *Stabilizer bar bracket*
8 *Axleshaft*
9 *Upper control arm*
10 *Stabilizer bar link*

1 General information

Refer to illustrations 1.1, 1.2, 1.3, 1.4 and 1.5

Warning: *Whenever any of the suspension or steering fasteners are loosened or removed, they must be inspected and if necessary, replaced with new ones of the same part number or of original equipment quality and design. Torque specifications must be followed for proper reassembly and component retention. Never attempt to heat, straighten or weld any suspension or steering component. Instead, replace any bent or damaged part with a new one.*

The front suspension on 1979 through 1986 models is a MacPherson strut type. The struts are secured at the upper ends to reinforced areas under the fenders and at the lower ends to the steering knuckle **(see illustration).** A strut bar is installed between the lower control arm and the frame and a stabilizer bar is also used to ensure good handling characteristics.

The front suspension on 1987 and later models uses upper and lower control arms, a steering knuckle and a shock absorber/coil spring assembly positioned vertically between the lower control arm and frame **(see illustration)**. Body side roll is controlled by a stabilizer bar.

1979 through 1981 models use a solid rear axle, coil springs, telescopic shock absorbers and a stabilizer bar. The rear axle housing is attached to the frame with control arms and a lateral control rod **(see illustration)**.

The independent rear suspension system on 1982 through 1986 models features coil springs and telescopic shock absorbers mounted on semi-trailing arms. A stabilizer bar is included to improve handling **(see illustration)**.

The independent rear suspension system on late models (1987 and later) consists of coil springs, shock absorbers, a stabilizer bar, two lower control arms and a single upper control arm **(see illustrations)**.

The steering system consists of the steering wheel, steering column, an articulated intermediate shaft, the steering gear, power steering pump and the tie-rods, which connect the steering gear to the spindles.

Some models are equipped with the TEMS or Toyota Electronic Modulated Suspension system. This feature automatically adjusts the suspension to suit road conditions and driving style.

2 Toyota Electronic Modulated Suspension (TEMS) system - general information

Refer to illustration 2.1

The Toyota Electronic Modulated Suspension (TEMS) system **(see illustration)**, available as an option on later models, automatically changes the shock absorber valving to firm up the suspension to suit road conditions and driving style. The system incorporates a switch

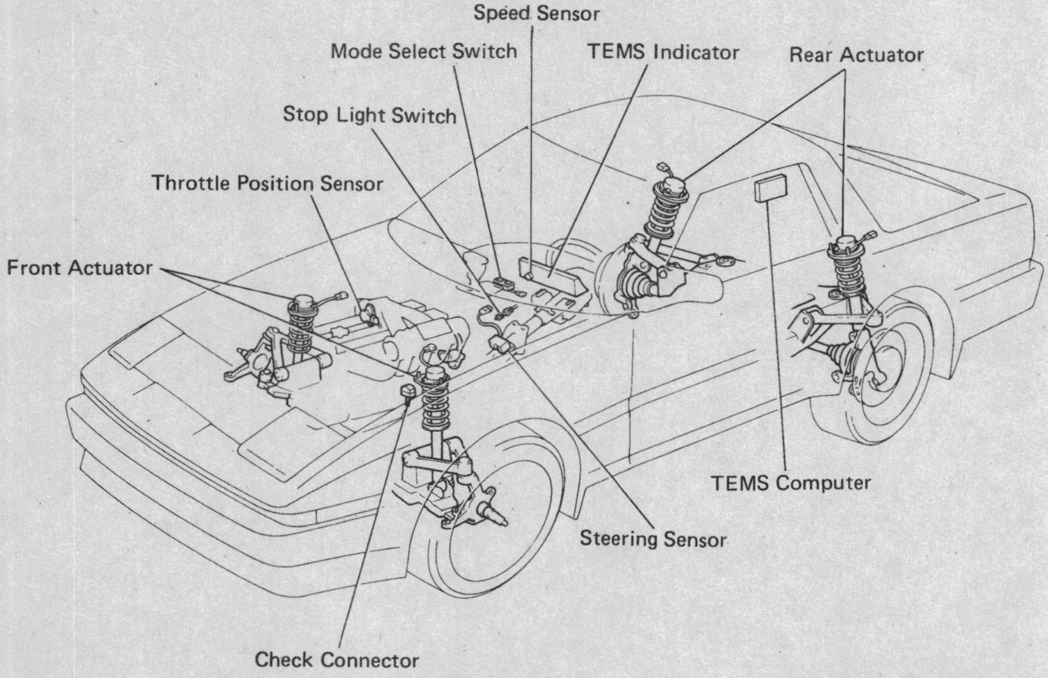

2.1 Component layout of the TEMS system

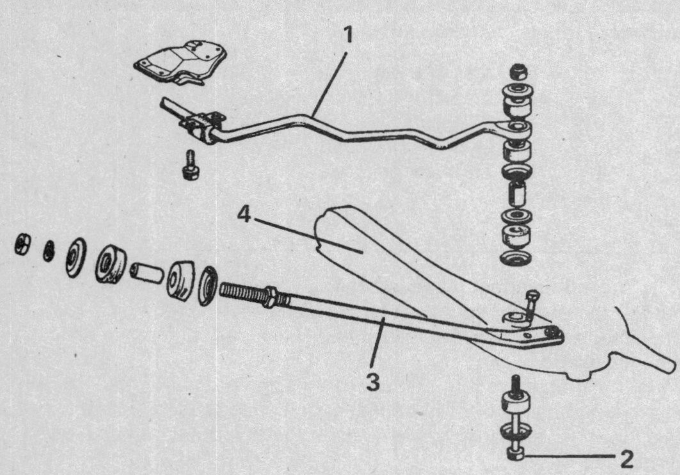

3.3a Front stabilizer bar and strut bar components (1979 through 1981 models) - exploded view

1 *Stabilizer bar*
2 *Link*
3 *Strut bar*
4 *Control arm*

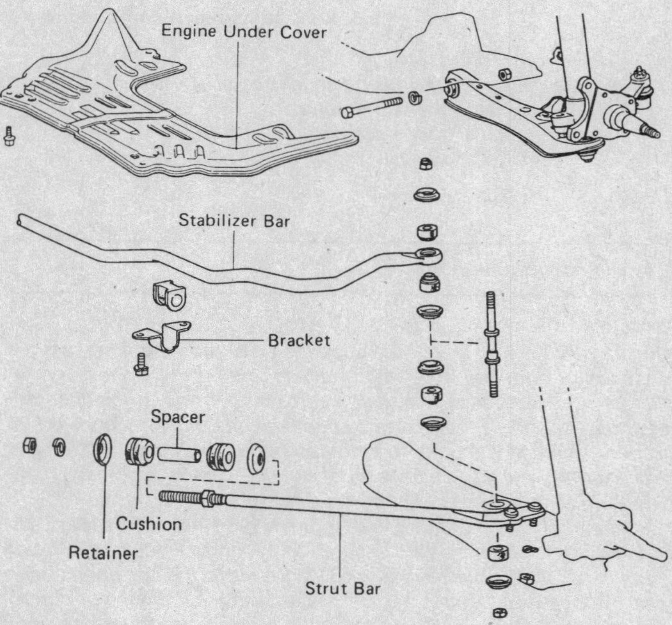

3.3b Front suspension stabilizer bar and strut bar components (1982 through 1986 models) - exploded view

mounted on the center console which allows the driver to select SPORT mode or NORMAL mode. With the mode select in NORMAL, the suspension will maintain a smooth, soft ride during normal driving conditions until the system's computer detects harsh or abnormal cornering, hard braking, rapid acceleration or high speed. Now the computer adjusts the suspension for a much firmer response from the shock absorbers. With the mode select in SPORT, the shock damping will always be firm no matter what driving conditions are present.

All diagnosis and repair of the TEMS system should be left to a dealer service department or other repair shop.

3 Front stabilizer bar - removal and installation

Refer to illustrations 3.3a, 3.3b, 3.3c and 3.4

1 Raise the front of the vehicle and support it securely on jackstands.

2 Remove the engine under-cover.

Upper control arm with Upper Ball Joint
Upper Suspension Arm Shaft
Adjusting Cam
Lower control arm
Stabilizer Bar
Cushion
Bracket
Lower Ball Joint
Stabilizer Link
Engine Under Cover

3.3c Front suspension stabilizer bar and components (1987 and later models) - exploded view

3.4 Remove the stabilizer bar bracket bolts (arrows), then (on 1982 through 1986 models only) unbolt the strut bar bracket from the body

4.2 Remove the two mounting nuts (arrows) and separate the strut bar from the lower arm, . . .

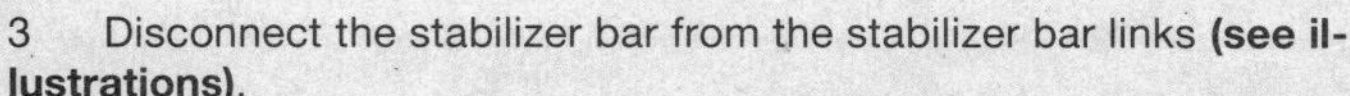

3 Disconnect the stabilizer bar from the stabilizer bar links **(see illustrations)**.

4 Remove the bolts from the stabilizer bar brackets. On 1982 through 1986 models, detach the strut bar (on one side only) from the control arm and unbolt the strut bar bracket from the body **(see illustration)**.

5 Remove the stabilizer bar from the vehicle. On 1982 through 1986 models, separate the stabilizer bar from the strut bar bracket.

6 Installation is the reverse of the removal procedure. Be sure to tighten all fasteners to the torque listed in this Chapter's Specifications.

4 Front strut bar (1979 through 1986 models) - removal and installation

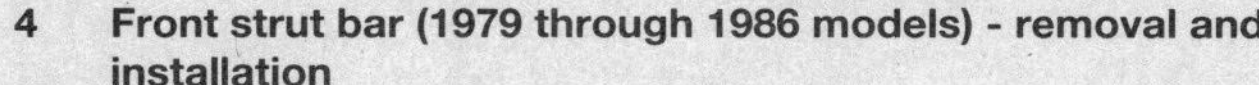

Refer to illustrations 4.2, 4.3a and 4.3b

1 Raise the front of the vehicle and support it on jackstands.

2 Unbolt the bar from the lower arm **(see illustration)**.

3 Remove the nut from the strut bar and separate the bar from the bracket **(see illustration)**. The backing nut at the bracket is staked in

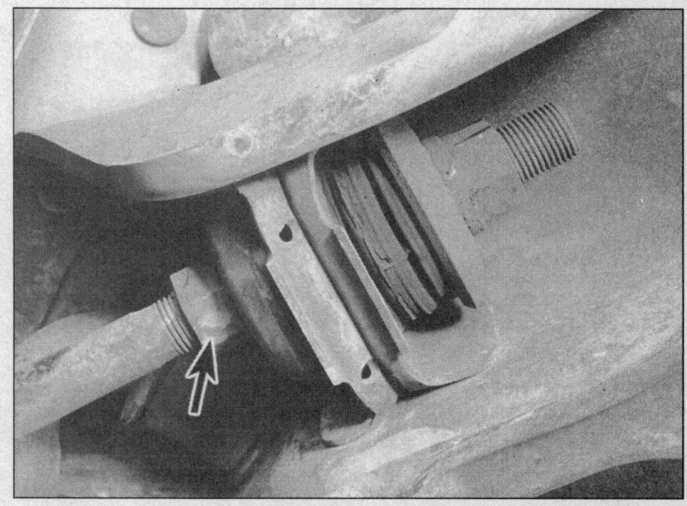

4.3a . . . then remove the outside nut and detach the strut bar from the bracket - DO NOT remove the inside staked nut (arrow)

10

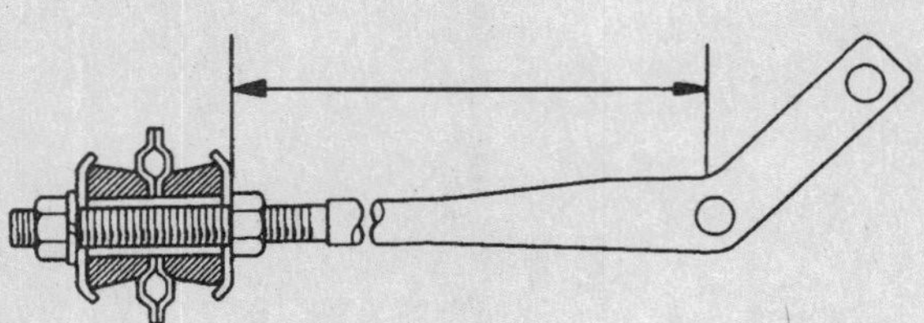

4.3b If the strut bar is being replaced with a new one or the staked nut must be moved for any reason, be sure to set the distance between the nut and the center of the bolt hole to the proper distance

position and should not be removed or the caster angle will be altered. However, if a new bar is installed, check the distance between the staked nut and the center of the bolt hole. Compare it to the Specifications and adjust it as necessary **(see illustrations)**.

4 Installation is the reverse of removal.

5 When finished, drive the vehicle to a dealer service department or alignment shop and have the alignment checked, and if necessary, adjusted.

5 Front strut and coil spring assembly (1979 through 1986 models) - removal and installation

Refer to illustrations 5.6, 5.7, 5.8a, 5.8b and 5.9

Note: *Although strut assemblies don't always fail or wear out simultaneously, replace both left and right struts at the same time to prevent handling peculiarities and abnormal ride quality.*

Removal

1 Loosen but do not remove the front wheel lug nuts.

2 Raise the front of the vehicle and support it on jackstands.

3 Remove the front wheel.

4 Remove the brake caliper and bracket (see Chapter 9).

5 Take off the front hub (see Section 11).

6 Using a flare nut wrench and an open end wrench, disconnect the brake line from the flexible hose **(see illustration)**. To prevent excess fluid leakage from the brake line, seal off the reservoir with a sheet of clean plastic wrap stretched across the filler neck and secured with a rubber band. Plug the exposed line ends to prevent dirt from entering.

7 Remove the three mounting nuts at the top of the strut, located inside the engine compartment **(see illustration).**

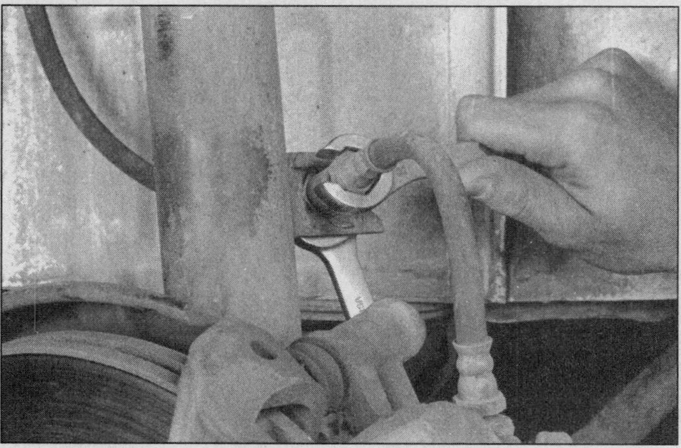

5.6 To avoid rounding-off the fitting, use a flare nut wrench when separating the brake lines

8 Remove the two bolts securing the strut to the steering knuckle **(see illustrations)**.

9 The strut can now be removed. Push down on the suspension arm so the strut clears the collars which protrude from the knuckle bolt holes **(see illustration)**.

Installation

10 To install the strut and coil spring assembly, reverse the removal procedure.

11 After connecting the brake hose, top up the brake reservoir and bleed the brakes (see Chapter 9).

12 If the strut has been replaced with a new one, drive the vehicle to a dealer service department or an alignment shop and have the alignment checked, and if necessary, adjusted.

6 Front shock absorber and coil spring assembly (1987 and later models) - removal and installation

Note: *Although shock absorbers don't always fail or wear out simultaneously, replace both front shocks at the same time to prevent handling peculiarities and abnormal ride quality.*

Removal

Refer to illustrations 6.6a, 6.6b and 6.8

1 Loosen the front wheel lug nuts, raise the vehicle and support it securely on jackstands.

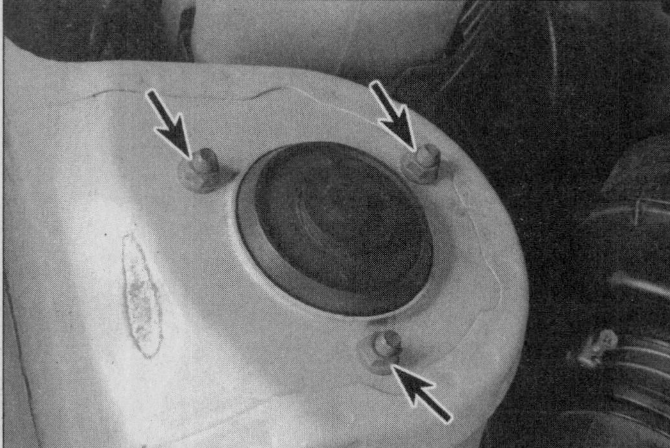

5.7 The three mounting nuts (arrows) securing the top of the strut are located in the engine compartment

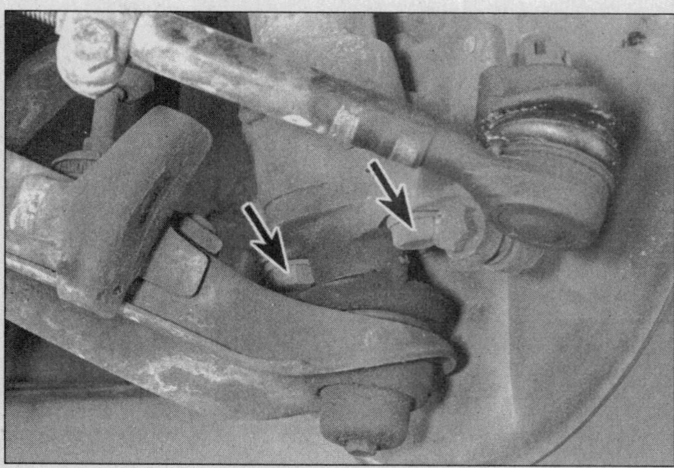

5.8a The bolts (arrows) securing the bottom of the strut are located at the bottom of the steering knuckle

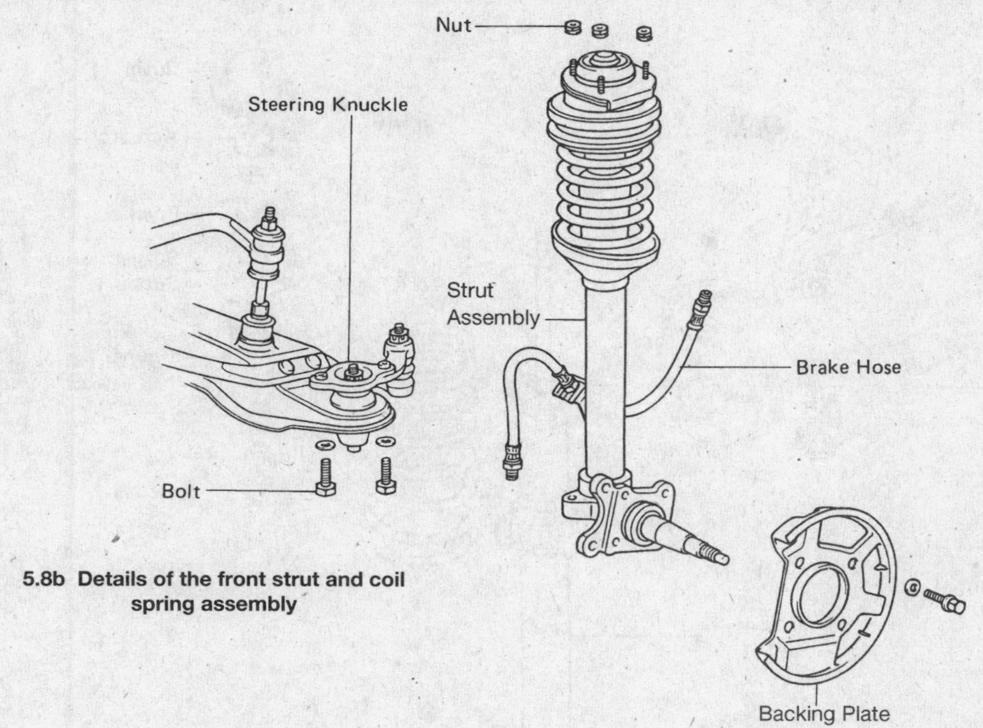

5.8b Details of the front strut and coil spring assembly

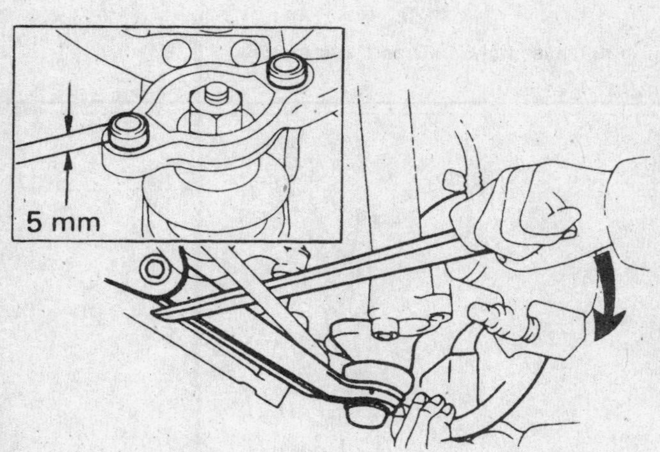

5.9 The collars extend into the steering knuckle bolt holes about 5.0 mm (0.20-inch) - push the suspension arm down to remove the front strut assembly

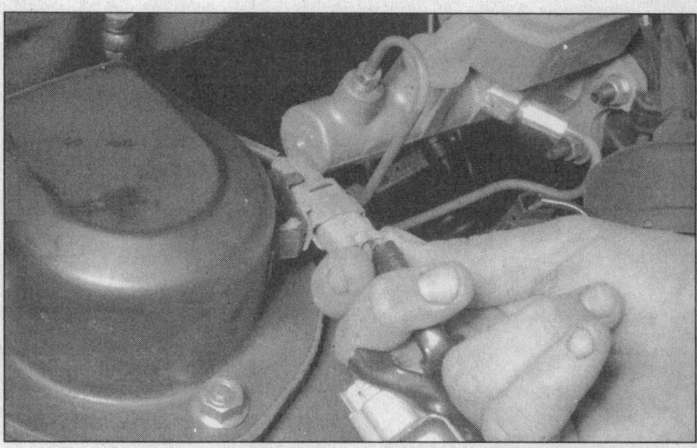

6.6a Disconnect the electrical connector from the TEMS actuator assembly.

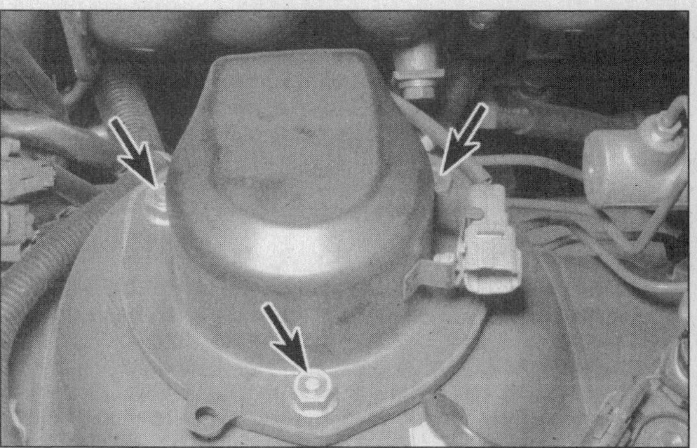

6.6b Remove the bolts and lift the actuator assembly from the shock tower

2 Remove the wheel.
3 Place a floor jack under the lower control arm.
4 Remove the upper control arm (see Section 10).
5 Remove the stabilizer link mounting nut and separate the stabilizer bar from the link.
6 On models equipped with Toyota Electronic Modulated Suspension (TEMS), select the SPORT mode on the switch, remove the actuator cover retaining screws and lift the actuator from its mounting bracket **(see illustrations)**.
7 Loosen the three upper mount-to-shock tower retaining nuts but do not remove them completely. If the upper mount is to be removed from the shock absorber/coil spring assembly, also loosen (but do not remove) the center nut at this time.

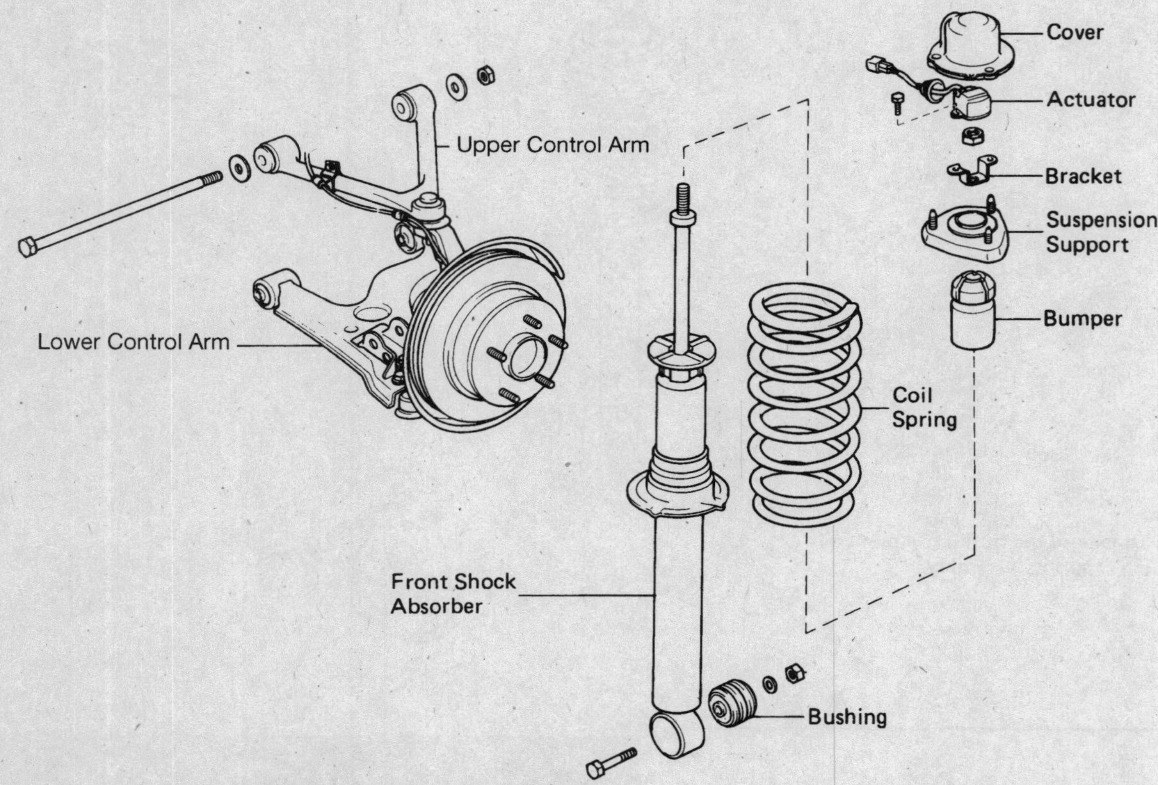

6.8 Exploded view of the front shock absorber/coil spring assembly (1987 and later models)

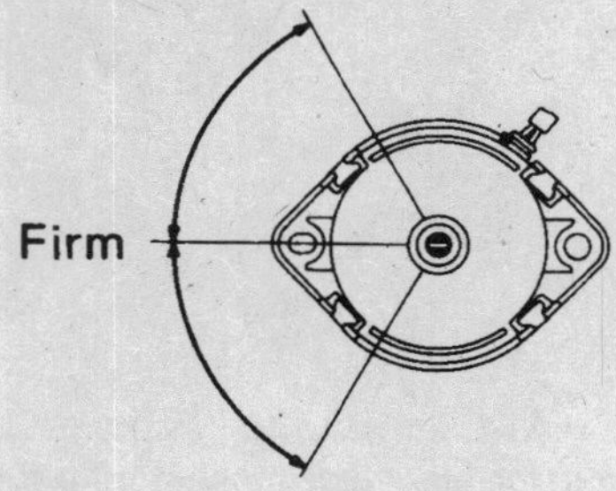

6.17a Check the actuator position is FIRM or horizontal to the alignment holes

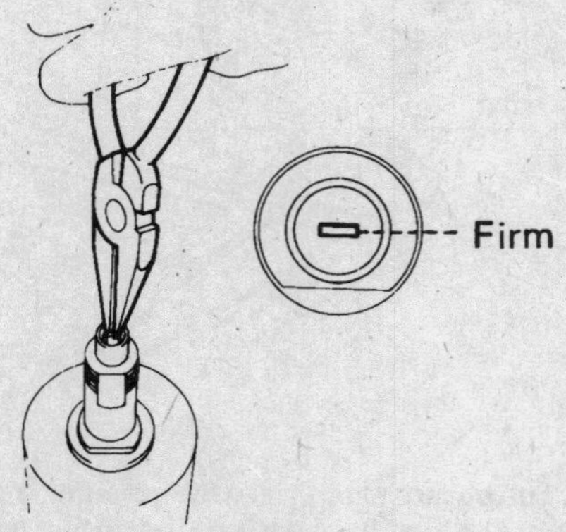

6.17b Next, use a needle-nose pliers and set the shock absorber to FIRM (horizontal to the recess)7.3 Install the spring compressor according to the tool manufacturer's instructions and compress the spring until all pressure is relieved from the upper spring seat

8 Remove the shock-to-lower control arm nut and bolt **(see illustration)**.

9 Separate the shock absorber/coil spring assembly from the lower control arm.

10 Remove the shock tower-to-upper mount nuts and remove the shock absorber/coil spring assembly from the vehicle.

Installation

Refer to illustrations 6.17a and 6.17b

11 If the upper mount was removed, place it over the top of the new shock absorber/coil spring assembly and install the nut.

12 Guide the assembly into position in the wheel well, pushing the upper mount studs through the holes in the shock tower. Install the three nuts and tighten them to the torque listed in this Chapter's Specifications.

13 Attach the shock absorber/coil spring assembly to the lower control arm, tightening the nut securely.

14 Install the upper control arm (see Section 10).

15 Connect the stabilizer link to the spindle.

16 Tighten the upper mount nut to the torque listed in this Chapter's Specifications (if removed). Also tighten the three upper mounting nuts to the torque listed in this Chapter's Specifications.

17 On models equipped with Toyota Electronic Modulated Suspension (TEMS), attach the actuator to the mounting bracket, aligning the flats on the actuator rod with the slot in the shock absorber **(see illustrations)**.

7.3 Install the spring compressor according to the tool manufacturer's instructions and compress the spring until all pressure is relieved from the upper spring seat

7.4 Remove the damper rod nut

18 Remove the jack from under the lower control arm. Install the wheel, lower the vehicle and tighten the lug nuts to the torque listed in the Chapter 1 Specifications.

7 Front shock absorber/strut or coil spring - replacement

Refer to illustrations 7.3, 7.4, 7.5, 7.6, 7.7, 7.12, 7.13a and 7.13b

1 If the shock absorbers/struts or coil springs exhibit the telltale signs of wear (leaking fluid, loss of damping capability, chipped, sagging or cracked coil springs) explore all options before beginning any work. The strut/shock absorber assemblies are not serviceable (the damping units can't be rebuilt) and must be replaced if a problem develops. However, strut assemblies complete with springs may be available on an exchange basis, which eliminates much time and work. Whichever route you choose to take, check on the cost and availability of parts before disassembling your vehicle. **Warning:** *Disassembling a strut assembly is a potentially dangerous undertaking and utmost attention must be directed to the job at hand, or serious bodily injury may result. Use only a high quality spring compressor and carefully follow the manufacturer's instructions furnished with the tool. After removing the coil spring from the strut assembly, set it aside in a safe, isolated area (a steel cabinet is preferred).*

2 Remove the shock absorber or strut and spring assembly following the procedure described in Section 5 or 6. Mount the assembly in a vise. Line the vise jaws with wood or rags to prevent damage to the unit and don't tighten the vise excessively.

3 Following the tool manufacturer's instructions, install the spring compressor (which can be obtained at most auto parts stores or equipment yards on a daily rental basis) on the spring and compress it sufficiently to relieve all pressure from the suspension support **(see illustration)**. This can be verified by wiggling the spring.

4 Loosen the damper rod nut with a socket wrench **(see illustration)**. To prevent the suspension support and damper rod from turning, wedge a screwdriver or prybar between one of the upper mounting studs and the socket.

5 Remove the nut and suspension support **(see illustration)**. Inspect the bearing in the suspension support for smooth operation. If it doesn't turn smoothly, replace the suspension support. Check the rubber portion of the suspension support for cracking and general deterioration. If there is any separation of the rubber, replace it.

6 Lift the spring seat and upper insulator from the damper shaft **(see illustration)**. Check the rubber spring seat for cracking and hardness, replacing it if necessary.

7.5 Lift the suspension support off the damper rod

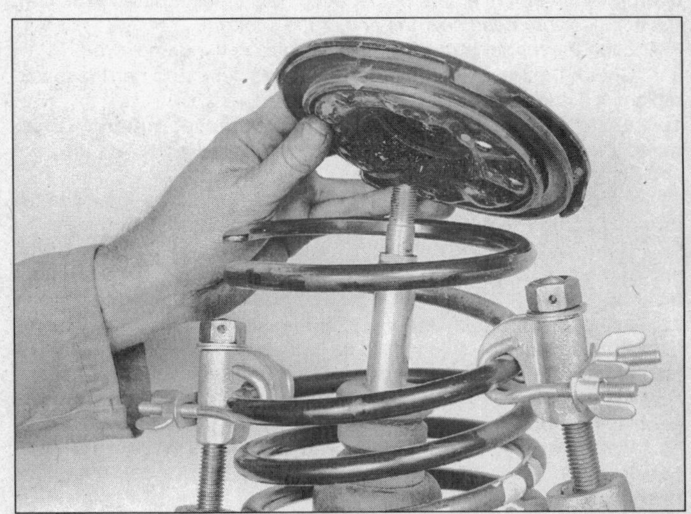

7.6 Remove the spring seat from the damper rod

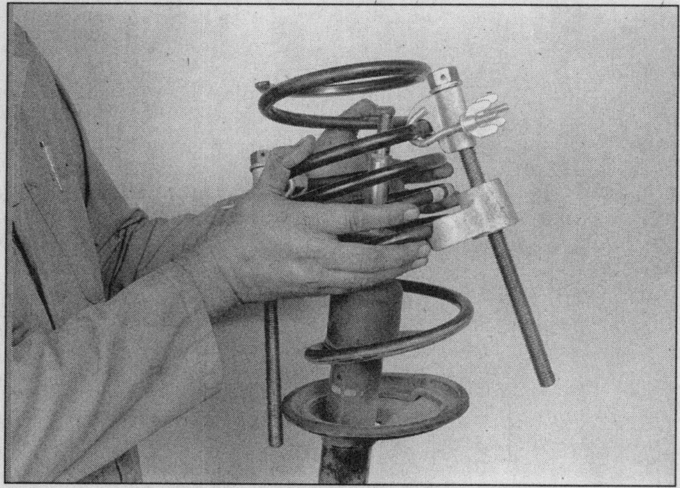

7.7 Remove the compressed spring assembly - use extreme caution whenever handling the spring

7.12 When installing the spring, make sure that the lower end of the spring fits into the recessed portion of the lower seat (arrow)

7.13a The flats on the damper rod (arrow) must match up with the flats in the spring seat

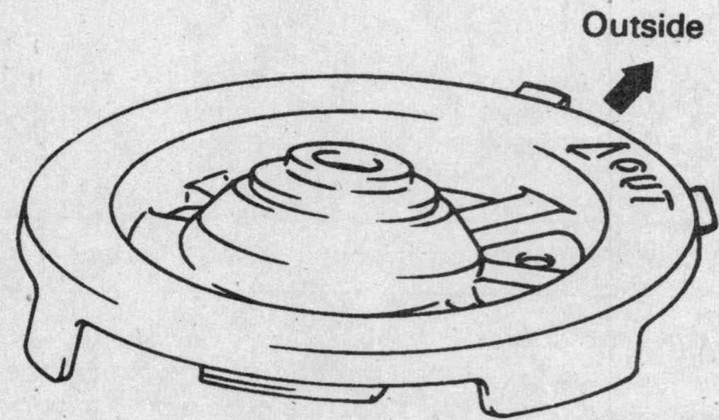

7.13b The "OUT" marking on the spring seat must face towards the strut bracket opening

7 Carefully lift the compressed spring from the assembly **(see illustration)** and set it in a safe place, such as a steel cabinet. **Warning:** *Never place your head near the end of the spring!*
8 Slide the rubber bumper and dust boot off the damper rod.
9 Check the lower insulator for wear, cracking and hardness and replace it if necessary.
10 Assemble the strut beginning with the dust boot and rubber bumper - extend the damper rod as far as it will go and slide the boot and bumper down to the strut body.
11 If the lower insulator is being replaced, set it into position with the dropped portion seated in the lowest part of the seat.
12 Carefully place the coil spring onto the lower insulator, with the end of the spring resting in the lowest part of the insulator **(see illustration)**.
13 Install the upper insulator and spring seat, making sure that the flats in the hole in the seat match up with the flats on the damper rod **(see illustration)**. Also make sure that the "out" marking on the spring seat faces toward the lower bracket, where the steering knuckle fits **(see illustration)**.
14 Install the dust seal and suspension support to the damper rod.
15 Install the nut and tighten it to the torque listed in this Chapter's Specifications.
16 Install the strut or shock absorber and coil spring assembly following the procedure outlined in Section 5 or 6.

8 Balljoints - check and replacement

Refer to illustrations 8.3 and 8.8

Note: *The lower control arm balljoints on 1979 through 1986 models and the upper control arm balljoints on 1987 and later models cannot be replaced individually. If these balljoints become worn and need to be changed, replace the entire control arm (the lower control arm balljoints on 1987 and later models are replaceable).*

Check

1 Raise the vehicle and support it securely on jackstands.
2 Visually inspect the rubber boot for cuts, tears or leaking grease. If any of these conditions are noticed, the balljoint should be replaced.
3 Place a large prybar under the balljoint and attempt to push the balljoint up. Next, position the prybar between the steering knuckle and the lower arm and apply pressure **(see illustration)**. If any movement is seen or felt during either of these checks, a worn out balljoint is indicated.
4 Have an assistant grasp the tire at the top and bottom and shake the top of the tire with an in-and-out motion. Touch the balljoint stud nut. If any looseness is felt, suspect a worn out balljoint stud or a widened hole in the steering knuckle boss. If the latter problem exists, the steering knuckle should be replaced as well as the balljoint.

Replacement (1987 and later model lower balljoint only)

5 Loosen the wheel lug nuts, raise the vehicle and support it securely on jackstands.
6 Remove the circlip from the balljoint stud and loosen the castle

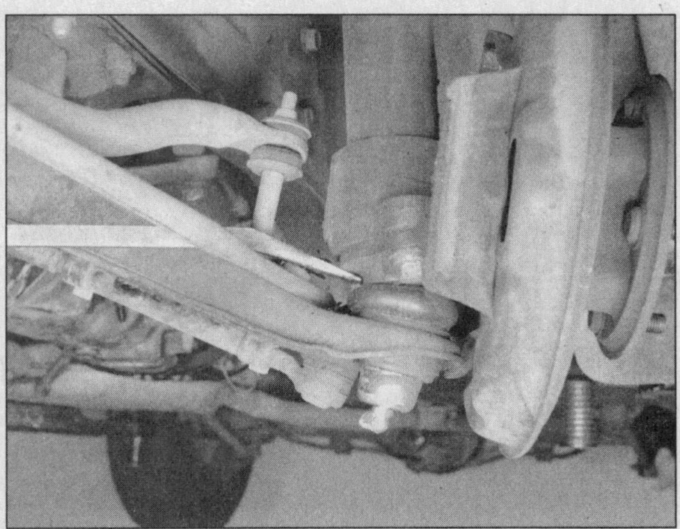

8.3 Check for any excessive vertical or lateral movement of the balljoint while applying pressure

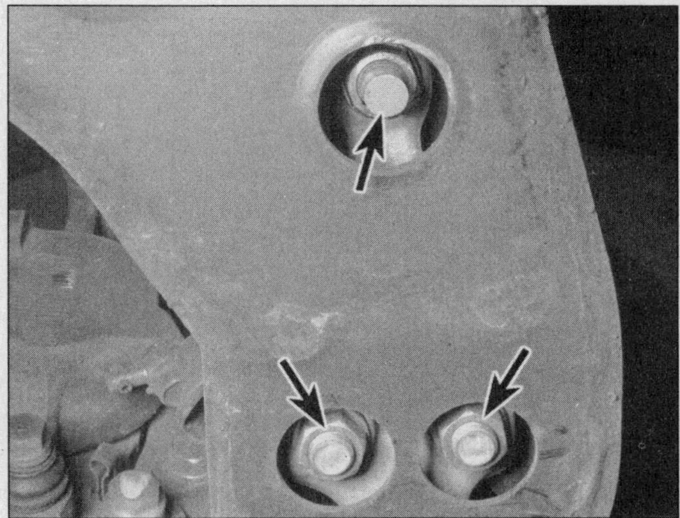

8.8 Remove the three bolts from under the lower control arm and remove the balljoint assembly

nut a couple of turns.

7 Separate the balljoint from the steering knuckle with a balljoint separator, then remove the nut.

8 Remove the three bolts that retain the balljoint to the lower control arm and slide the balljoint out **(see illustration)**.

9 To install the balljoint, position it on the lower arm and install the bolts, but don't tighten them yet.

10 Insert the balljoint stud into the steering knuckle and install the nut, tightening it to the torque listed in this Chapter's Specifications.

11 Tighten the balljoint-to-lower arm bolts to the torque listed in this Chapter's Specifications.

12 Install the wheel and lug nuts. Lower the vehicle and tighten the lug nuts to the torque listed in the Chapter 1 Specifications.

9 Front control arm (1979 through 1986 models) - removal and installation

Refer to illustrations 9.7, 9.8a, 9.8b, 9.10a, 9.10b, 9.12 and 9.13

Removal

1 Loosen but do not remove the lug nuts.

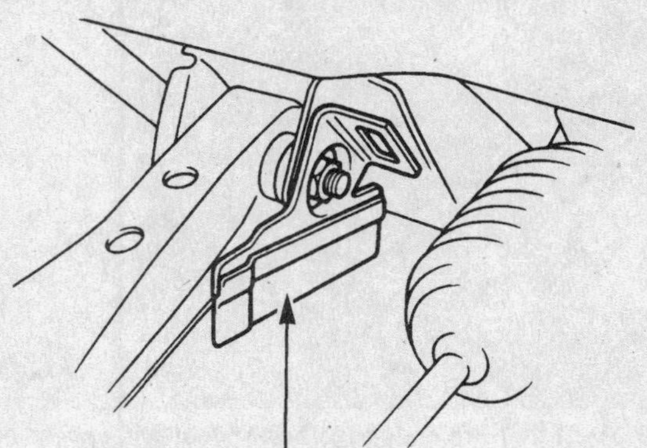

9.7 Take out the pivot bolt holding the control arm to the crossmember, then remove the arm, along with the rack boot protector

2 Raise the front of the vehicle and support it on jackstands. Remove the lug nuts and the front wheel.

3 Remove the two bolts securing the steering knuckle to the bottom of the strut assembly **(see illustrations 5.8a and 5.8b)**. Press down on the control arm to disengage the strut assembly from the knuckle.

4 Disconnect the tie-rod end from the steering knuckle (see Section 25).

5 Disconnect the stabilizer bar from the control arm (see Section 3).

6 Disconnect the strut bar from the control arm (see Section 4).

7 Remove the nut from the pivot bolt at the inner end of the control arm. Support the weight of the control arm, withdraw the pivot bolt and remove the arm, along with the rack boot protector, from the crossmember **(see illustration)**.

8 If the bushings are worn at the inner end of the arm, they can be removed and new ones installed using a press or a vise, socket and piece of pipe **(see illustrations)**.

9.8a To remove the bushing, use a large socket and a piece of pipe with a diameter large enough to allow the bushing to pass through - tighten the vise jaws to press out the bushing

9.8b To install the new bushing, use two sockets; one to hold the bushing and another to press it into place

9.10a After taking out the cotter pin, loosen the nut securing the steering knuckle to the balljoint a couple of turns, but don't remove it

9.10b Tighten the puller and, if necessary, tap the puller as illustrated to drive the stud through the knuckle arm

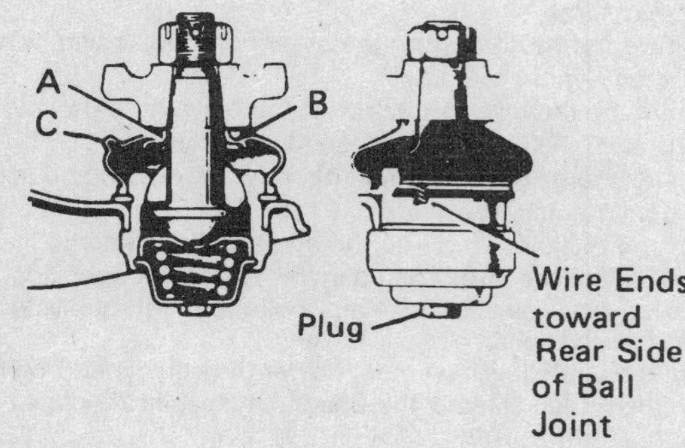

9.12 Apply grease to areas A and B of the new dust cover and install the dust cover with the escape valve (C) facing the rear of the vehicle

9 If the control arm balljoint is worn excessively, the control arm must be replaced as a complete assembly. The balljoint dust cover, however, can be replaced. To do so, separate the knuckle from the control arm as follows.

10 Remove the cotter pin and loosen the nut securing the steering knuckle to the balljoint **(see illustration)**. With the knuckle supported in a vise, use a press or steering wheel puller and hammer to drive or press the balljoint stud down through the knuckle arm. Take care not to damage the stud threads **(see illustration)**.

11 Use a screwdriver to pry off the dust cover set ring and the cover.

12 Clean the stud and the cover seat on the balljoint. Lubricate the new cover with grease where indicated **(see illustration)**, then install the dust cover over the stud and onto the joint seat so that the escape valve (C) is facing the rear of the vehicle.

13 Wind the new retaining wire two full turns around the dust cover, with the ends meeting at the front. Twist the ends of the wire together to secure it **(see illustration)**. Trim off the excess wire ends and bend the wire knot down.

14 Remove the plug from the base of the balljoint, insert a grease fitting and lubricate the joint with moly-base grease. Remove the fitting and install the plug.

Installation

15 Attach the steering knuckle to the control arm balljoint, tighten the nut to the torque listed in this Chapter's Specifications and insert the new cotter pin.

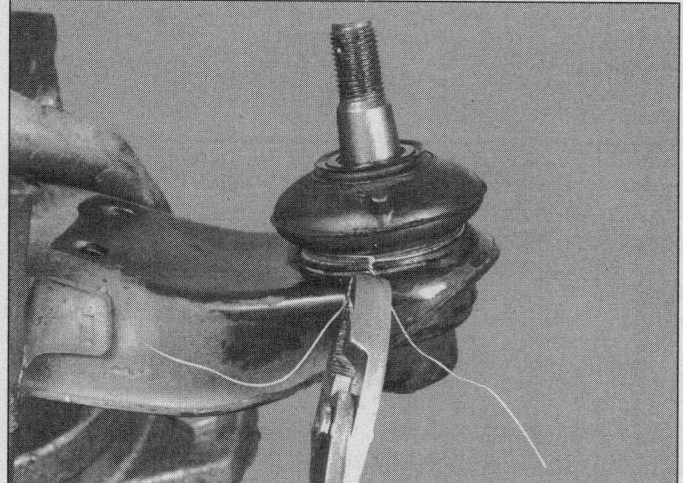
9.13 Twist the wire ends together, trim off the excess and bend the wire knot down

16 To install the control arm, align it with the pivot bolt holes in the crossmember on the inner end, insert the pivot bolt (front-to-rear) and

10.5 Mark the position of the camber adjustment cam to the chassis

hand tighten the nut.

17 Reconnect the stabilizer bar and strut bar to the control arm and tighten the fasteners to the torque listed in this Chapter's Specifications.

18 Attach the tie-rod end to the steering knuckle, tighten the nut and install a new cotter pin.

19 Reconnect the steering knuckle to the bottom of the strut assembly and tighten the two bolts to the torque listed in this Chapter's Specifications.

20 Install the wheels and lug nuts. Lower the vehicle and tighten the lug nuts to the torque listed in the Chapter 1 Specifications.

21 Bounce the front end of the vehicle up and down a few times to ensure that the suspension is settled, then tighten the control arm pivot bolt and nut to the torque listed in this Chapter's Specifications.

22 When finished, have the front wheel alignment checked by an alignment shop or a dealer service department.

10 Front control arms (1987 and later models) - removal and installation

Removal

1 Loosen the wheel lug nuts, raise the vehicle and support it securely on jackstands. Remove the wheel.

Upper control arm

2 Remove the upper balljoint-to-steering knuckle bolt and nut **(see illustration 12.5)**. Separate the steering knuckle from the upper control arm. Support the steering knuckle with a piece of wire or rope.

3 Remove the upper control arm bolts and remove the control arm. **Note:** *Use a six-point socket to avoid rounding off the head of the bolt.* If the pivot bushings appear to be worn out or deteriorated, take the control arm to a dealer service department or other repair shop to have the old bushings pressed out and new ones pressed in. Since the bolt is very long, it may be necessary to remove the inner fenderwell plastic cover for extra clearance.

Lower control arm

Refer to illustration 10.5

4 Loosen (but do not remove) the balljoint retaining nut **(see illustration 12.5)**, then separate the lower control arm from the spindle. Use a special balljoint separator tool (available at most auto parts stores). Also, it is a good idea to support the spindle so the upper control arm does not sag excessively.

5 Mark the position of the camber adjustment cams to the chassis **(see illustration)**. **Note:** *Be sure to mark all four cams.*

6 Remove the nut that attaches the stabilizer link to the control arm (see Section 3).

7 Remove the shock absorber lower mounting bolt and nut.

8 Remove the pivot bolt and nut, then detach the control arm. If the pivot bushing appears to be worn out or deteriorated, take the control arm to a dealer service department or other repair shop to have the old bushings pressed out and new ones pressed in.

Installation

9 Installation is the reverse of the removal procedure, but don't tighten the pivot fasteners until the suspension is at normal ride height. This can be accomplished by positioning a floor jack under the lower control arm balljoint and raising it until the vehicle just raises off the jackstand. Be sure to tighten all of the fasteners to the torque values listed in this Chapter's Specifications.

10 Have the front end alignment checked at a dealer service department or alignment shop.

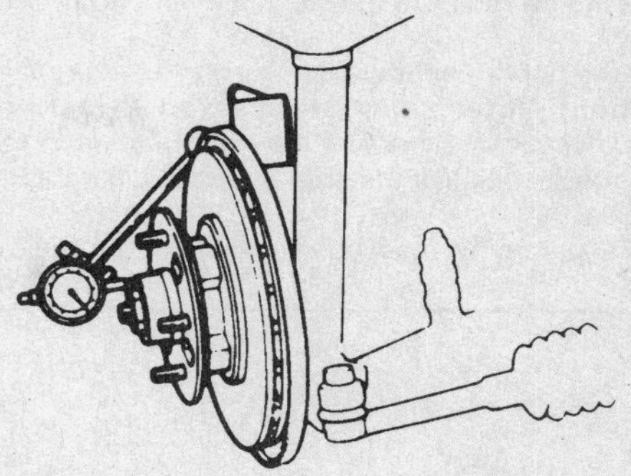

11.2 Use a dial indicator to measure the hub axial (in-and-out) play on the spindle

11 Front hub and wheel bearing assembly (1979 through 1986 models) - check, removal and installation

Refer to illustration 11.2

Note: *The front hub and bearing assembly on 1987 through 1992 models is a sealed bearing that requires a special press and jig in order to safely remove the bearing from the steering knuckle. In the event of front bearing problems, have a dealer service department or other repair shop install the new bearings.*

1 Front hub removal is required to service the front wheel bearings, which is a routine maintenance procedure. See Chapter 1, *Wheel bearing check, repack and adjustment* for the procedure.

2 If a wheel bearing problem is suspected, check the hub axial play with a dial indicator **(see illustration)**. If the play is excessive, service the wheel bearings and adjust the bearing preload as described in Chapter 1. After the hub has been disassembled, wear in the bearings and races will be obvious and new parts can be installed if required.

12 Steering knuckle (1987 and later models) - removal and installation

Removal

Refer to illustrations 12.5, 12.8 and 12.9

1 Loosen the wheel lug nuts, raise the vehicle and support it securely on jackstands. Remove the wheel.

2 Remove the brake caliper and support it with a piece of wire as described in Chapter 9. Separate the brake disc from the hub.

3 Support the lower control arm with a floor jack and loosen the shock absorber-to-lower control arm bolts (see Section 6).

4 Separate the tie-rod from the steering knuckle arm as outlined in Section 25.

5 Remove the upper and lower balljoint-to-steering knuckle bolts **(see illustration)**. **Note:** *It may be necessary to remove the lower shock bolt and nut to make room for the balljoint removal tool.*

6 Install a special balljoint removal tool and separate the balljoints from the knuckle.

7 Carefully separate the steering knuckle from the vehicle.

8 Remove the hub bearing cap located on the backside of the steering knuckle assembly with a flat-bladed screwdriver **(see illustration)**.

9 Clamp the axle assembly in a soft jawed vise and remove the hub nut. **Note:** *First, straighten out the stake mark in the indented portion of the hub bolt* **(see illustration)**.

10 Have the inner bearing and race pressed out by an automotive machine shop.

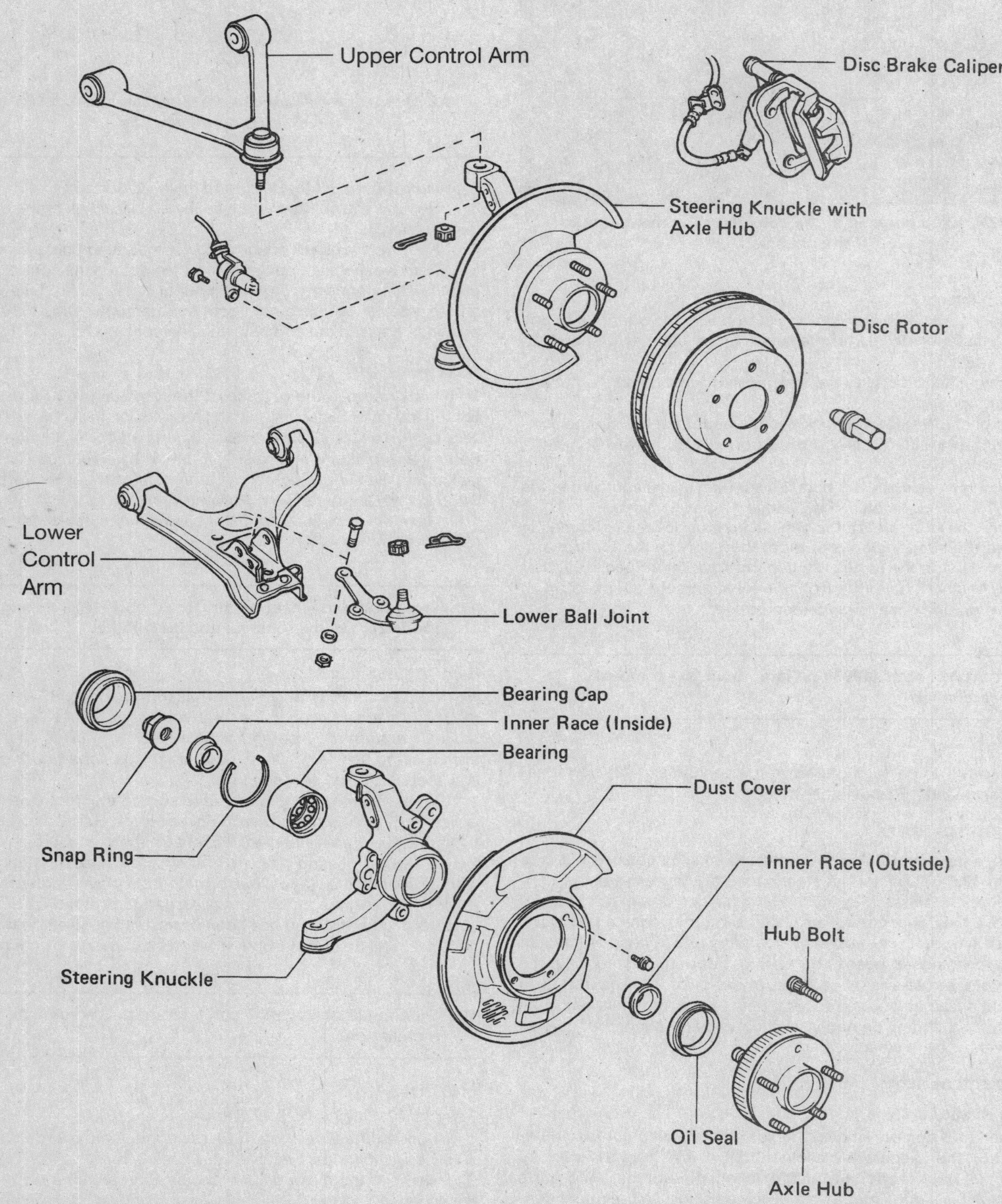

12.5 Exploded view of the steering knuckle, control arms and related components (1987 and later models)

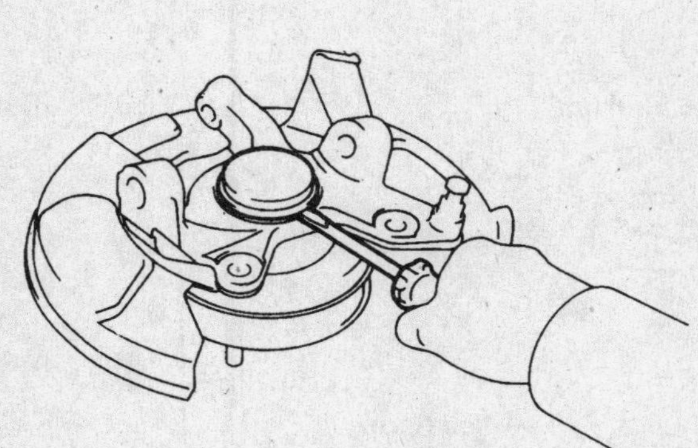
12.8 Pry the cap off the backside of the steering knuckle

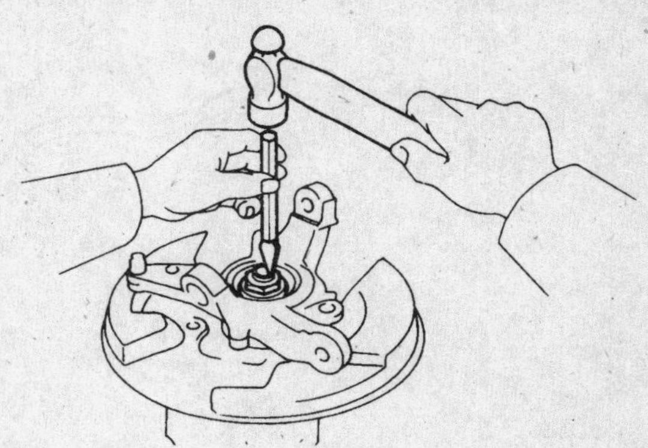
12.9 Use a chisel to straighten the stake mark in the hub

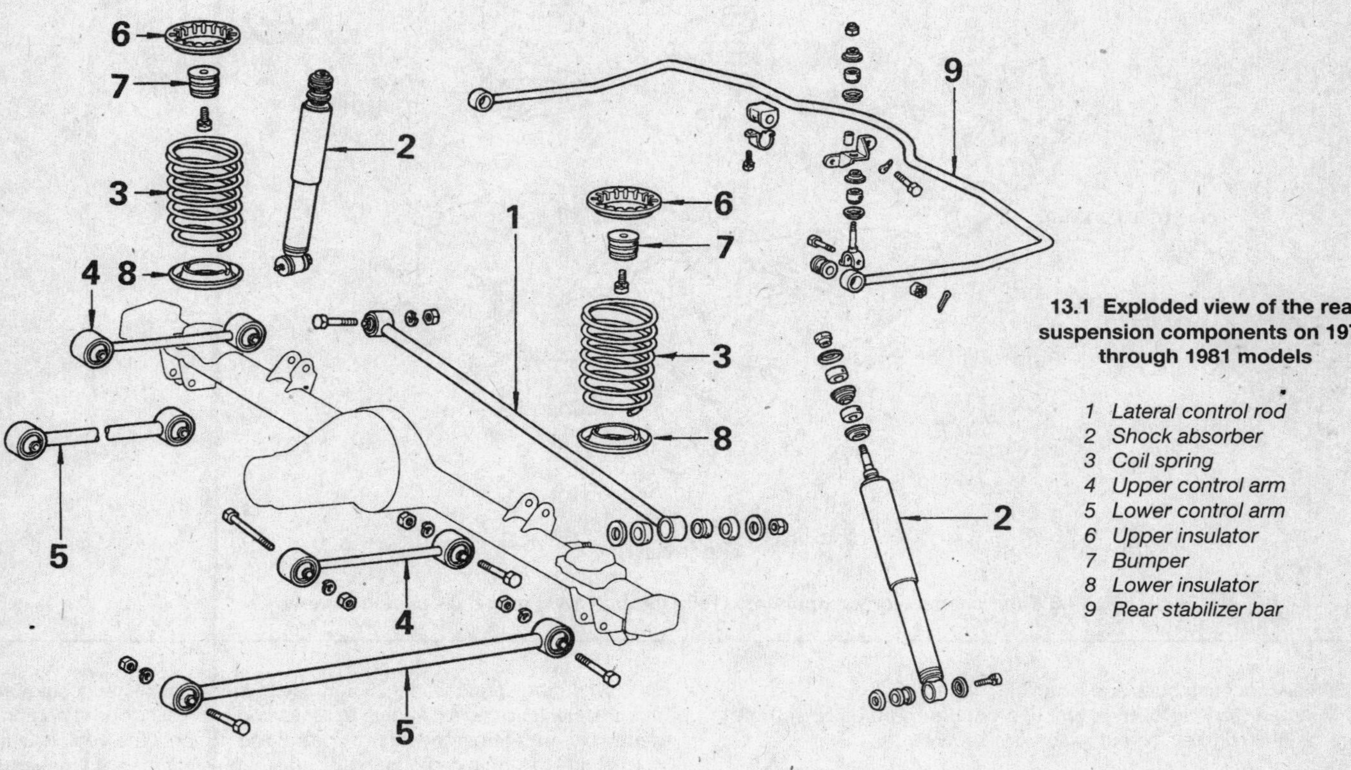

13.1 Exploded view of the rear suspension components on 1979 through 1981 models

1. *Lateral control rod*
2. *Shock absorber*
3. *Coil spring*
4. *Upper control arm*
5. *Lower control arm*
6. *Upper insulator*
7. *Bumper*
8. *Lower insulator*
9. *Rear stabilizer bar*

Installation

11 Installation is the reverse of removal. Have the new bearings pressed into place by an automotive machine shop.

12 Guide the knuckle and hub assembly into position.

13 Push the knuckle into the upper balljoint and install the nut, but don't tighten it yet.

14 Pry down on the lower control arm then set the bottom of the steering knuckle on the balljoint. Install the nut (don't tighten it yet).

15 Attach the tie-rod to the steering knuckle arm as described in Section 25. Tighten the shock absorber nuts, the balljoint nuts and the tie-rod nut to the torque values listed in this Chapter's Specifications.

16 Place the brake disc on the hub and install the caliper as outlined in Chapter 9.

17 Install the wheel and lug nuts.

18 Lower the vehicle and tighten the lug nuts to the torque listed in this Chapter's Specifications.

13 Rear shock absorbers and coil springs (1979 through 1981 models) - removal and installation

Shock absorber

Refer to illustration 13.1

1 If a shock absorber is to be replaced with a new one, it is recommended that both shocks on the rear of the vehicle be replaced at the same time **(see illustration)**.

2 Raise the rear of the vehicle and support it securely on jackstands placed under the rear axle housing.

3 Remove the shock absorber lower mounting bolt.

4 Remove the upper mounting nuts and remove the shock absorber.

5 If the unit is defective, it must be replaced with a new one. Replace worn rubber bushings with new ones.

6 Install the shocks in the reverse order of removal, but don't

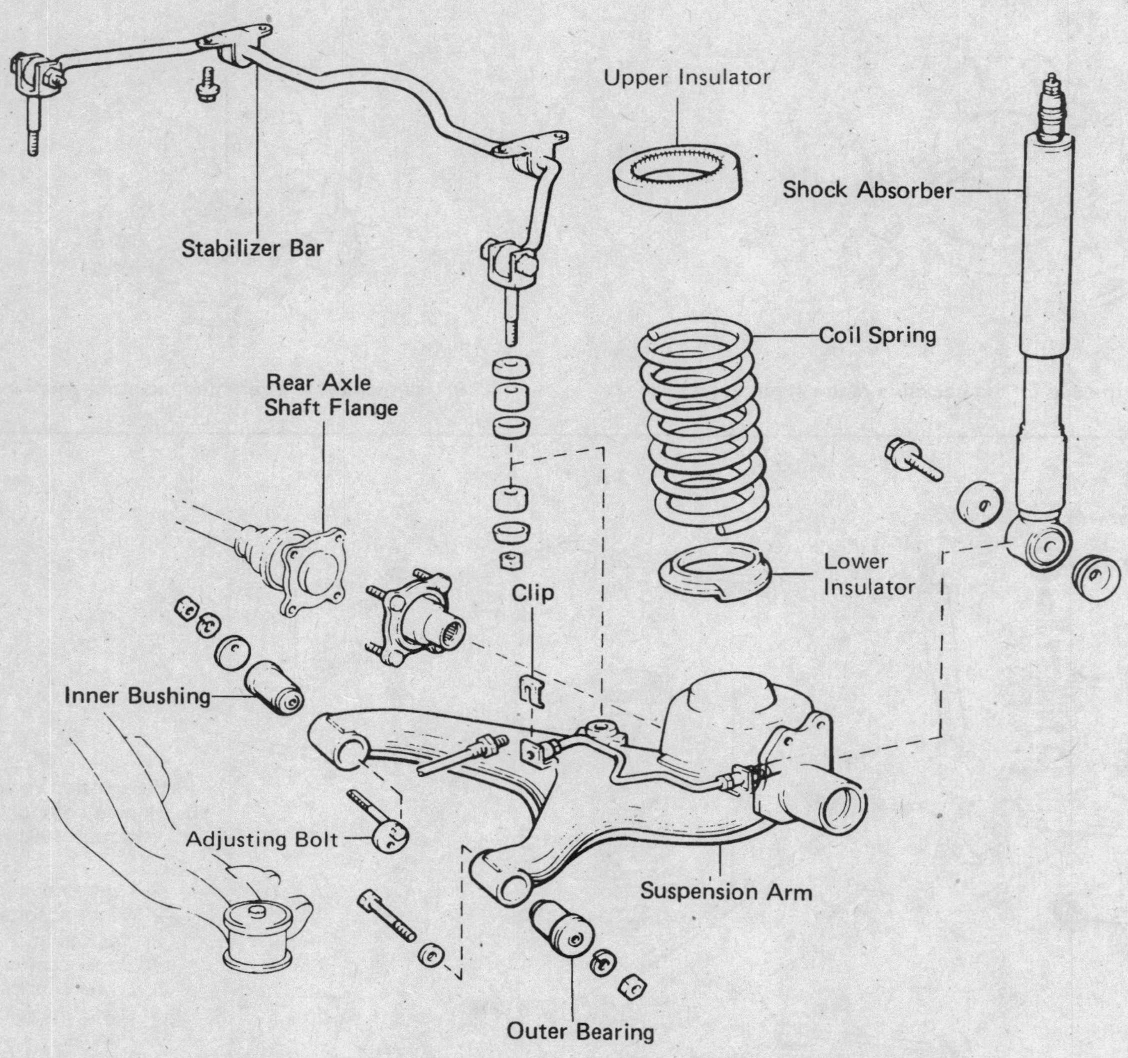

14.3 Rear suspension components (1982 through 1986 models) - exploded view

tighten the mounting bolts and nuts yet.

7 Bounce the rear of the vehicle a couple of times to settle the bushings, then tighten the nuts and bolts securely.

Coil spring

8 Loosen the wheel lug nuts. Raise the rear of the vehicle and support it securely on jackstands placed under the frame (not under the rear axle housing. Make sure that the stands will not interfere with the axle when it is lowered and raised during this procedure.

9 Remove the wheels. Support the rear axle housing with a floor jack placed underneath the differential. If you have two floor jacks, place one under each axle tube. Unbolt the lower ends of the shock absorbers.

10 Disconnect the lateral control rod from the axle housing.

11 Carefully lower the axle housing until the coil springs are extended completely. Make sure that the rear brake lines and parking brake cable are not stretched or distorted.

12 Remove the coil springs and related parts. Again, avoid damaging the brake lines and cables.

13 Installation is the reverse of the removal procedure. Don't interchange the left and right-side springs. Be sure to position the upper insulation ring on the top of the spring before installing it. The lower insulator fits on the axle housing before you install the spring.

14 When the spring is installed, make sure it is correctly positioned and then jack up the axle again to reassemble the associated components. Do not tighten the lateral control rod nut until the vehicle is at normal ride height and can be bounced a couple of times at the rear to settle the bushings.

15 Install the wheel and tighten the lug nuts to the torque listed in the Chapter 1 Specifications. Tighten the lateral control rod nut to the torque listed in this Chapter's Specifications.

14 Rear shock absorbers and coil springs (1982 through 1986 models) - removal and installation

Refer to illustrations 14.3, 14.5, 14.7, 14.8 and 14.9

Note: *Although shock absorbers and coil springs don't always wear out simultaneously, replace both left and right shocks at the same time to prevent handling peculiarities and abnormal ride quality.*

Removal

1 Loosen the wheel lug nuts, raise the vehicle and support it securely on jackstands. Remove the wheels.

2 Remove the brake hoses from the brackets by releasing the re-

14.5 Using a block of wood and a jack, support the suspension arm

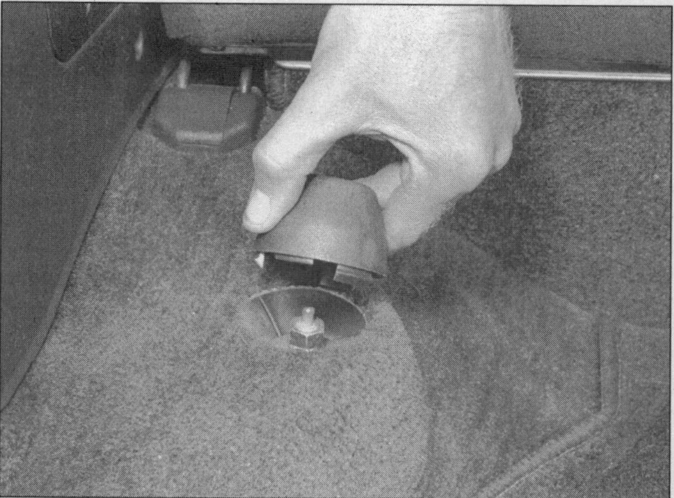

14.7 Lift up the trim cover to expose the upper shock absorber mounting nut

14.8 Lower the suspension arm just far enough to remove the coil spring

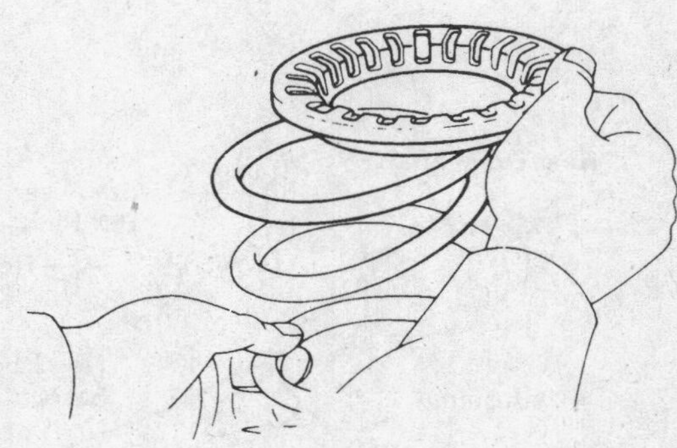

14.9 Put the upper insulator on the coil spring and install them as a unit

taining clips on the suspension arm. Don't separate the brake hose from the metal line.

3 Remove the nut, cushion and retainer and detach the stabilizer bar link from the suspension arm **(see illustration)**.

4 Remove the nuts and separate the driveaxle from the stub axle flange (see Chapter 8).

5 Position a jack under the suspension arm to support it **(see illustration)**.

6 Remove the bolt holding the shock absorber to the suspension arm and disconnect the shock absorber.

7 If the shock absorber is being replaced, remove the trim cover in the luggage compartment for access to the top mounting nut, remove the nut, and withdraw the shock absorber **(see illustration)**.

8 Lower the jack under the suspension arm, being careful not to allow the brake line and parking brake cable to stretch. Lower the suspension arm to the point where the coil spring can be removed, together with the upper and lower insulators **(see illustration)**. DO NOT allow the suspension arm to be lowered any further.

Installation

9 Install the coil spring by first placing the lower insulator on the suspension arm, then position the spring with the top insulator attached to it **(see illustration)**.

10 Raise the jack under the suspension arm and check that the lower insulator is correctly positioned. If not, lower the jack and reposition the insulator.

11 Reconnect the driveaxle (see Chapter 8).

12 Install the shock absorbers in the reverse order of removal. Tighten the fasteners securely.

13 Reconnect the stabilizer bar to the rear suspension arm. Tighten the nut securely.

14 Reconnect the brake hoses to the brackets and install the retaining clips.

15 Install the wheels and lug nuts, lower the vehicle and tighten the lug nuts to the torque listed in the Chapter 1 Specifications.

15 Rear shock absorber and coil spring assembly (1987 and later models) - removal and installation

Removal

Refer to illustrations 15.4 and 15.6

1 Raise the rear of the vehicle and support it securely on jackstands.

2 Support the lower suspension arm with a floor jack to prevent it from dropping when the shock absorber is disconnected. The jack must remain in this position throughout the entire procedure.

3 Open the rear compartment and remove the side trim panel.

4 On models equipped with TEMS (Toyota Electronic Modulated Suspension), remove the cover, disconnect the TEMS actuator electri-

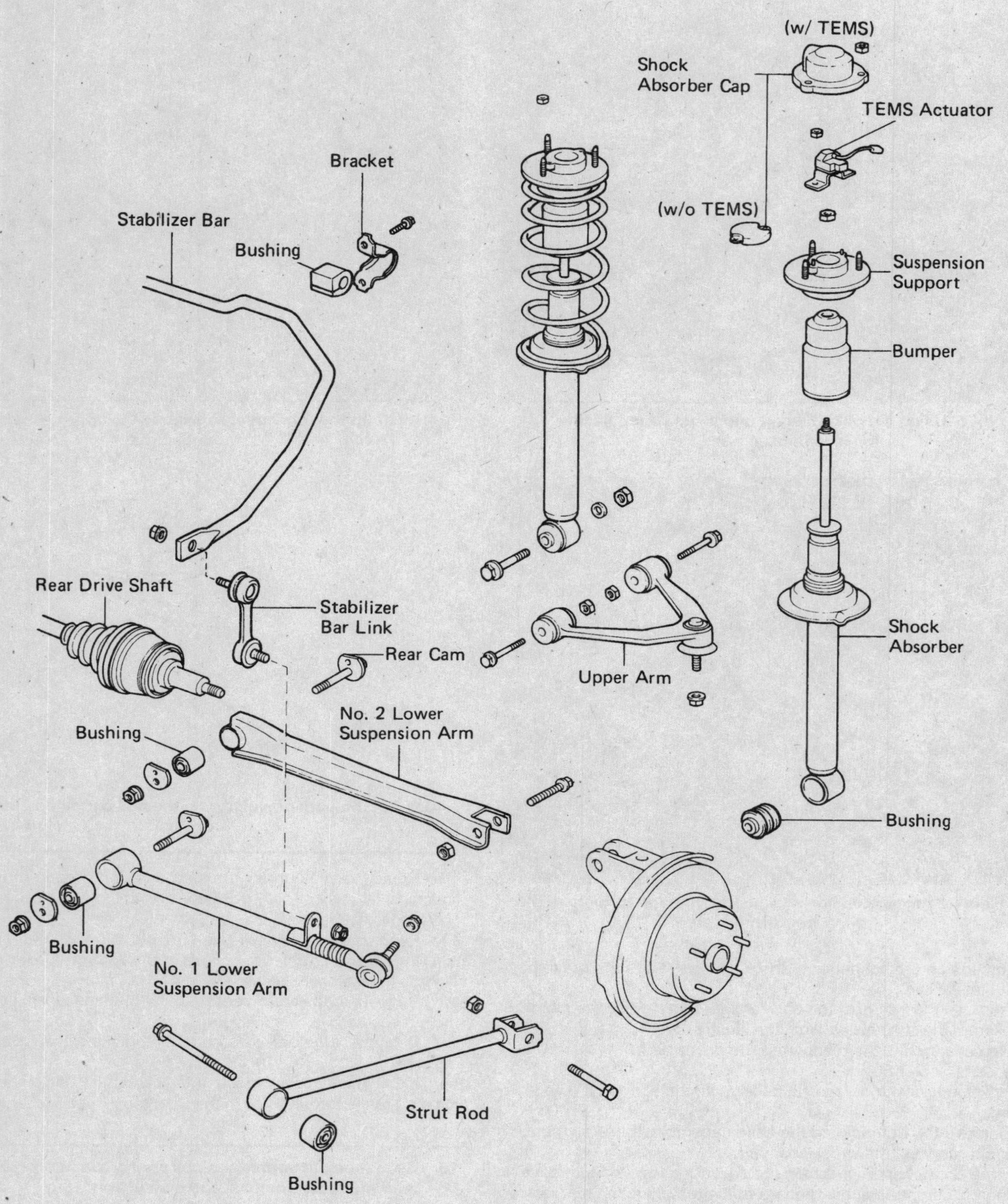

15.4 Exploded view of the rear suspension on 1987 and later models

cal connector and lift the actuator from the top of the shock absorber **(see illustration)**.

5 Remove the upper mounting nuts from the shock absorber assembly **(see illustration 15.4)**. It may be necessary to prevent the rod from turning by holding it with a wrench or locking pliers.

6 Remove the lower mounting bolt and nut **(see illustration)**, pull the bottom of the shock absorber assembly out of the mounting bracket and remove it from the vehicle.

Installation

7 Place the inner washer and rubber insulator on the shock rod and insert the rod through the upper mounting hole. Push up on the shock

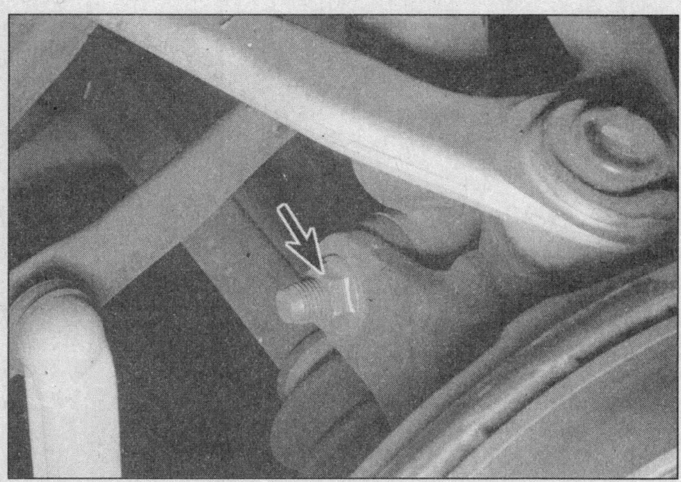

15.6 Remove the nut (arrow) from the shock absorber and the hub assembly

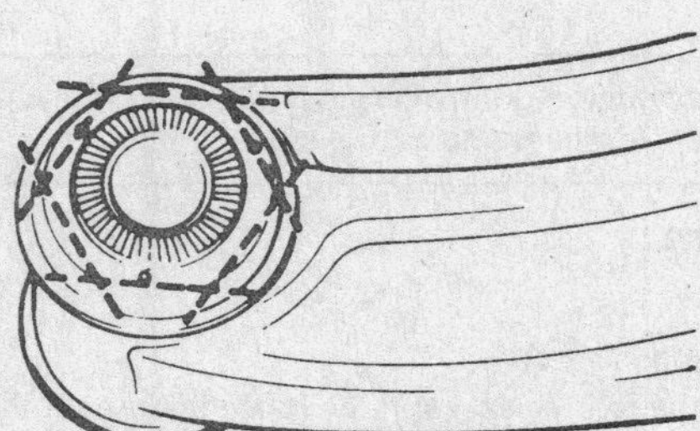

17.8a Cut off the bushing flange tips with a hacksaw

absorber to align the lower shock eye in the mounting bracket and install the bolt and nut, tightening them securely.

8 Install the upper mounting rubber insulator and the dished washer on the shock rod. Install the nut and tighten it securely.

9 On models equipped with TEMS, install the TEMS actuator and reconnect the electrical connector. **Note:** *Follow the installation details for the actuator in illustrations 6.17a and 6.17b.*

10 Install the side trim panel inside the trunk.

16 Rear suspension control arms (1979 through 1981 models) - removal and installation

1 Loosen the wheel lug nuts, raise the rear of the vehicle and support it securely on jackstands. Remove the wheel(s).

2 Support the axle housing with a floor jack.

3 Both upper and lower suspension arms are assembled in a similar fashion **(see illustration 13.1)**. Unscrew the bolt at the axle housing and body mounting side, then remove the arm from the vehicle .

4 Installation is the reverse of the removal procedure, but do not completely tighten the retaining bolts until the vehicle has been lowered and is free standing. It can then be rocked a couple of times to settle the bushings before tightening the bolts to the torque listed in this Chapter's Specifications.

17 Rear suspension control arm (1982 through 1986 models) - removal and installation

Refer to illustrations 17.5, 17.8a and 17.8b

Note: *The following procedure describes the removal and installation of the rear suspension arm, complete with the rear brake assembly, leaving the stub axle assembly in position. If it is necessary to remove*

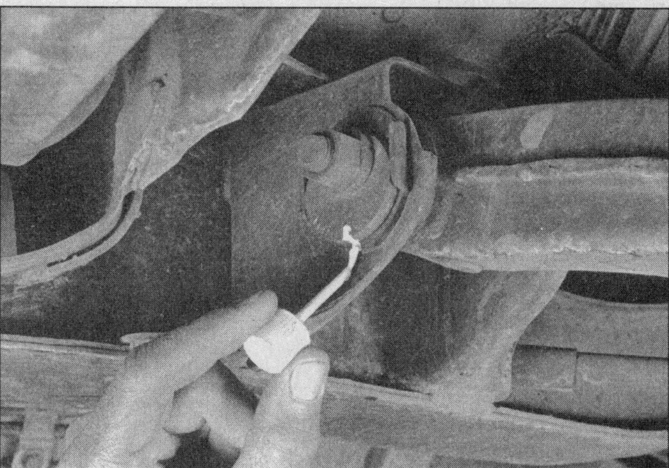

17.5 Before removing the inner pivot bolt, place alignment marks on the toe-in adjusting cam and the bracket

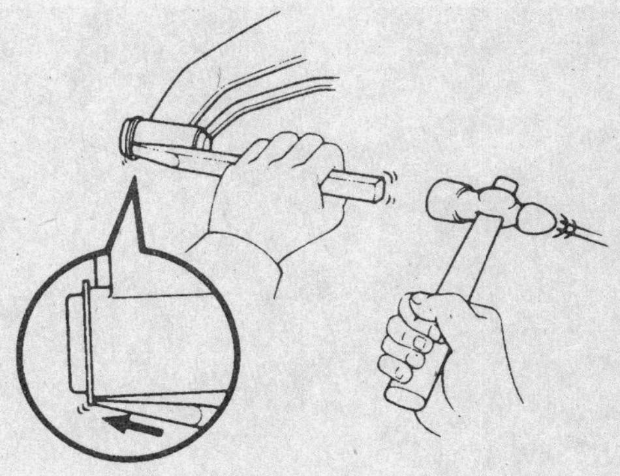

17.8b Bend the remaining portions of the flange out with a chisel and hammer

the stub axle from the suspension arm, it is recommended that the entire assembly be taken to a Toyota dealer. A number of special tools and techniques are required, taking this procedure out of the scope of the home mechanic.

Removal

1 Disconnect the rear stabilizer bar from the suspension arm (refer to Section 19).

2 Disconnect the driveaxle from the stub axle (see Chapter 8).

3 Disconnect the brake hydraulic line and the parking brake cable from the rear brake assembly (see Chapter 9).

4 Remove the shock absorber and the coil spring (see Section 14).

5 With the weight of the suspension arm supported by a jack, remove the pivot bolt retaining nuts. Note that the inner pivot bolt incorporates a toe-in adjusting cam. Mark the position of the cam **(see illustration)**. Remove the pivot bolts and adjusting cam, then lower and withdraw the suspension arm.

6 If the suspension arm pivot bushings are excessively worn, cracked or in generally poor condition they must be replaced.

7 If the suspension arm is distorted, cracked or damaged in any way it must be replaced.

8 To install new bushings, cut the exposed end flange tips off the bushings **(see illustration)**, then bend the remaining sections out using a chisel and hammer **(see illustration)**. Be careful not to damage the flange.

9 Pull the flange off. The remaining flange section must be bent so that it does not interfere with the press or socket used to drive the bushing out.

18.4 Remove the pivot bolts and nuts from the upper suspension arm

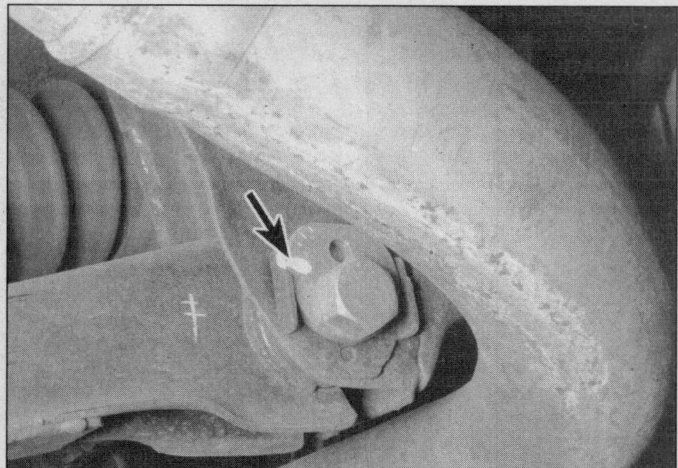

18.9 Be sure to mark the relationship of the adjustment cams to the subframe before removing the pivot bolts and nuts from the lower suspension arms

18.11 Remove the stabilizer link nut (arrow) from the Number 1 lower suspension arm

10 Support the inner flange face of the suspension bushing eye on a steel tube with an inside diameter large enough to allow the bushing to pass through it and slightly longer than the bushing in length.

11 Drive the bushing through the eye and into the support tube using a large socket and a hammer. The outer and inner arm bushings are removed in a similar manner.

Installation

12 Installation of the bushings is the reverse of removal. Do not lubricate the bushings with oil or grease. Press or drive the bushings in from the opposing outer faces of the arm. When installed, make sure that the flanges are in contact with the faces of the suspension arm eyes.

13 Installation of the suspension arm is basically the reverse of removal, but note the following:

a) When installing the inner pivot bolt, align the index and toe-in cam alignment marks made during removal. Do not completely tighten the pivot bolts and nuts at this stage.
b) Install the coil spring and shock absorber (see Section 14), but do not tighten the shock absorber lower mounting bolt at this point.
c) With the wheels installed, lower the vehicle and bounce it several times to settle the suspension, then tighten the suspension arm pivot bolts and the shock absorber lower mounting bolt to the torque listed in this Chapter's Specifications.
d) Bleed the brake hydraulic system (see Chapter 9).
e) When finished, have the rear wheel alignment checked by a Toyota dealer service department or an alignment shop.

18 Rear suspension control arms (1987 and later models) - removal and installation

Upper arm

Removal

Refer to illustration 18.4

1 Loosen the rear wheel lug nuts. Raise the rear of the vehicle and support it securely on jackstands placed beneath the frame rails. Block the front wheels and remove the rear wheel.

2 Support the knuckle and hub assembly with wire so it can't swing out when it's disconnected from the upper suspension arm. Support the lower arm with a floor jack. It must remain in this position throughout the entire procedure.

3 Remove the upper suspension arm-to-hub carrier bolt and nut. Separate the upper arm from the hub carrier with a balljoint separator tool.

4 Remove the upper arm pivot bolts and nuts **(see illustration)** and remove the upper suspension arm from the vehicle.

Installation

5 Position the arm in its mounting bosses and install the pivot bolts and nuts, but don't tighten them completely yet. Connect the balljoint to the hub carrier and install the nut, tightening it to the torque listed in this Chapter's Specifications.

6 Raise the floor jack until the vehicle just raises off the jackstand. Tighten the pivot bolt nuts to the torque listed in this Chapter's Specifications.

7 Install the wheel and tighten the lug nuts to the torque listed in the Chapter 1 Specifications.

Lower arm(s)

Removal

Refer to illustrations 18.9, 18.11 and 18.12

8 Loosen the wheel lug nuts, raise the rear of the vehicle and support it securely on jackstands placed under the frame rails. Block the front wheels and remove the rear wheel. Support the hub carrier with a floor jack.

9 Mark the position of the adjusting cam(s) to the subframe **(see illustration)**.

10 Remove the bolts and nuts that secure the Number 1 and Number 2 rear suspension arms to the hub carrier assembly (see illustration 15.4).

11 Disconnect the stabilizer link from the Number 1 suspension arm **(see illustration)**.

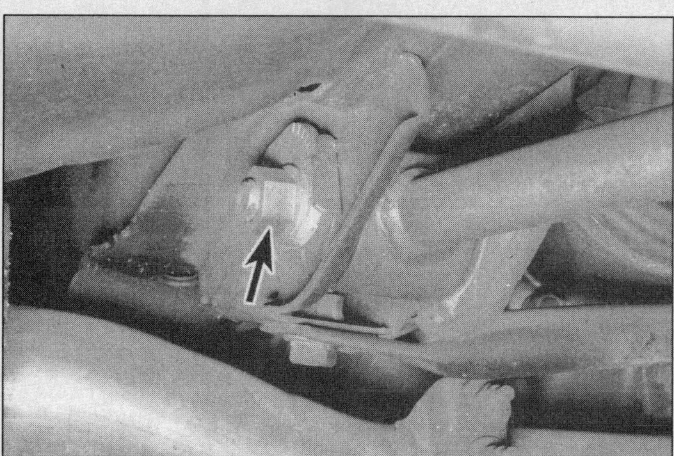

18.12 After marking all the adjustment cams, the pivot nuts and bolts can be removed

19.2 Remove the stabilizer bar bracket bolts (arrows) and detach the brackets (1982 through 1986 models shown)

12 Remove the lower arm-to-frame pivot bolts and nuts **(see illustration)**, then remove the arm(s) from the vehicle.

Installation

13 Install the lower suspension arm(s) but do not tighten the nuts completely at this time. Align the matchmarks made on the adjustment cam(s) and subframe.
14 Install the stabilizer link to the Number 1 suspension arm.
15 Position a floor jack under the lower arm and raise it until the vehicle just barely lifts off the jackstand, then tighten the nuts to the torque values listed in this Chapter's Specifications.
16 Install the wheel and lug nuts. Lower the vehicle and tighten the lug nuts to the torque listed in the Chapter 1 Specifications.
17 Have the alignment checked at a dealer service department or an alignment shop.

19 Rear stabilizer bar - removal and installation

Refer to illustrations 19.2 and 19.3

Note: *The rear stabilizer bar is mounted basically the same way on all models. Follow these general removal and installation procedures keeping in mind any variations. See illustrations 13.1, 14.3 and 15.4 for exploded views of the different suspension systems.*

1 Raise the rear of the vehicle and support it securely on jackstands. Block the front wheels to keep the vehicle from rolling.
2 Remove the stabilizer bar bracket bolts **(see illustration)**.
3 Remove the nut, cushions and stabilizer link at each end of the stabilizer bar **(see illustration)** and detach the stabilizer bar.
4 Inspect and, if necessary, replace any worn or defective bushings, cushions or links.
5 Installation is the reverse of removal. Tighten all fasteners securely.

20 Lateral control rod (1979 through 1981 models) - removal and installation

1 Raise the rear of the vehicle and support it securely on jackstands placed under the frame (not under the rear axle housing).
2 Remove the nut and bolt from the upper mount and the nut from the lower (axle) mount, then remove the lateral control rod **(see illustration 13.1)**.
3 Press or cut out the old bushings if they are to be replaced with new ones. Press the new ones into position.
4 Installation is the reverse of the removal procedure. Don't forget to install the spacer between the two bushings on the one end. Do not completely tighten the retaining nuts until the vehicle is lowered and free standing when it can be bounced to center the bushings. Tighten the retaining nuts to the torque listed in this Chapter's Specifications.

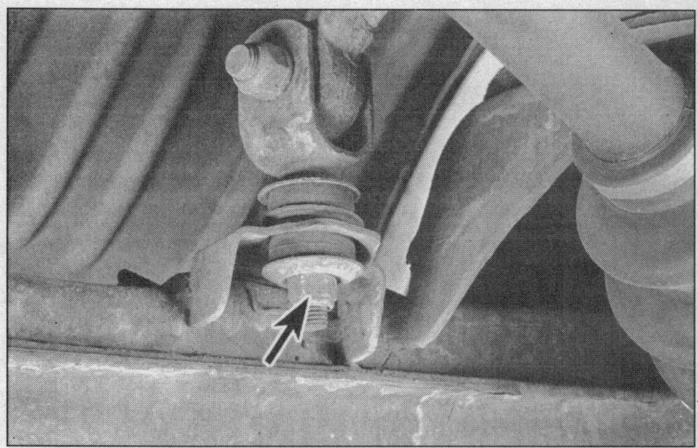

19.3 Remove the retaining nut, cushion and retainer and disconnect the stabilizer link from the rear suspension arm (1982 through 1986 models shown)

21 Steering system - general information

These vehicles are equipped with a conventional steering box (1979 through 1981 models) or with a power assisted rack and pinion steering system (1982 and later models).

On rack-and-pinion steering systems, when the steering wheel is turned the motion is transferred by the steering column to the intermediate shaft and finally to the pinion gear. The pinion gear teeth mesh with the gear teeth of the rack, so the rack moves right or left in the housing when the pinion is turned. The movement of the rack is transmitted through the inner and outer tie-rods to the steering knuckles, which turn the wheels.

The steering column also houses the ignition switch lock, key warning buzzer and the flashing hazard light switch. The ignition and steering wheel can both be locked to prevent theft when the vehicle is parked.

22 Power steering pump - removal and installation

Refer to illustrations 22.2a, 22.2b and 22.2c

1 If you're working on a 1987 or later model, raise the vehicle and support it securely on jackstands. Remove the engine under-cover.

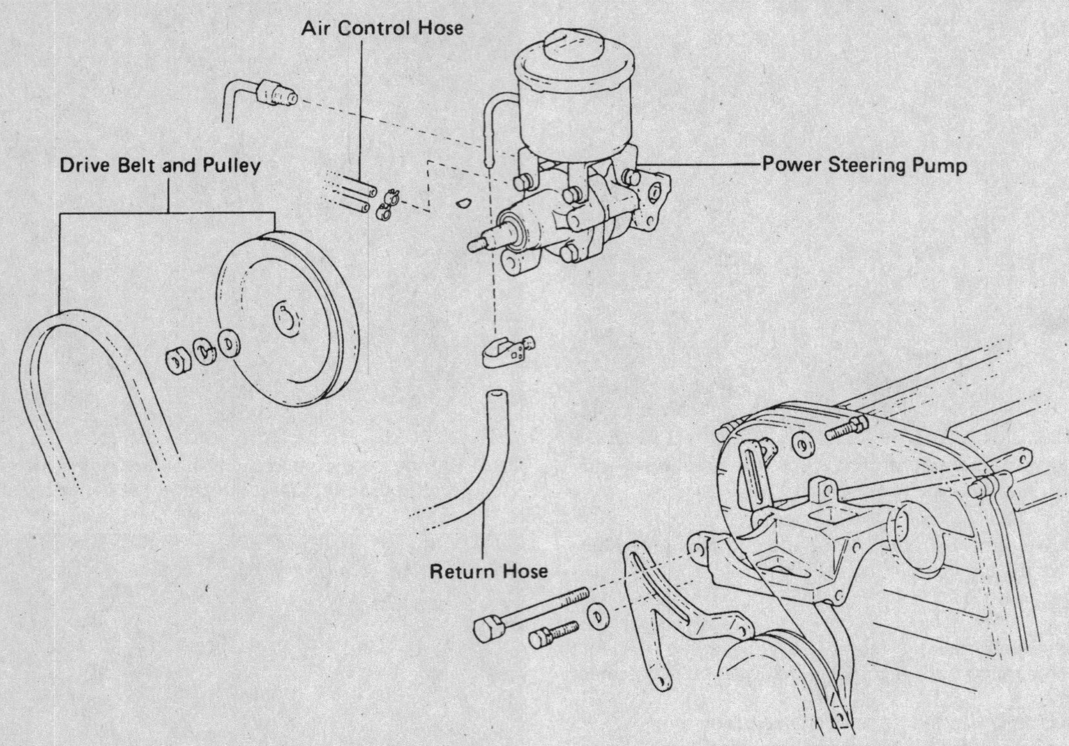

22.2a Power steering pump mounting details - 1982 through 1986 models

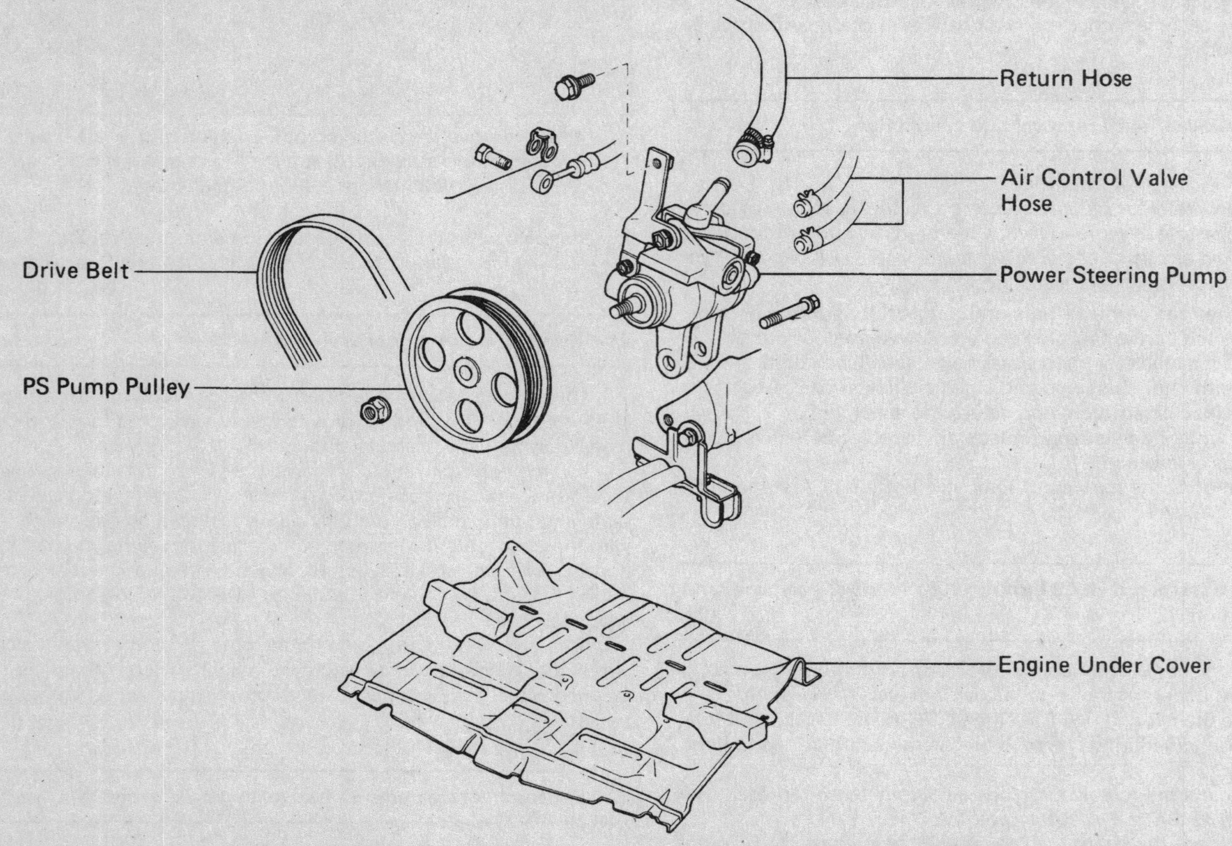

22.2b Power steering pump mounting details - 1987 and later non-turbo models

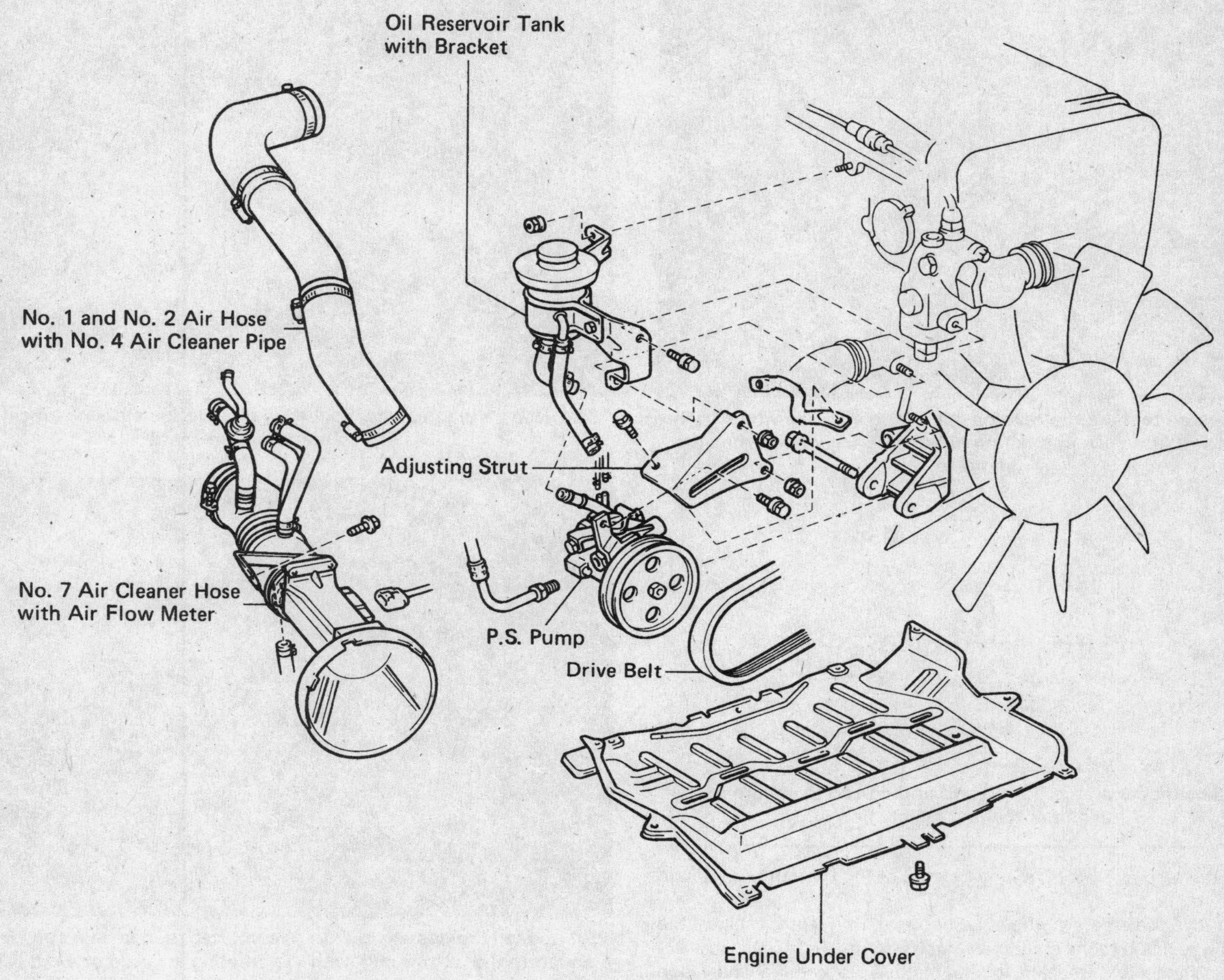

22.2c Power steering pump mounting details - 1987 and later turbo models

2 Loosen the clamps and detach the air control valve hoses (if equipped) from the pump **(see illustrations)**.
3 Disconnect the fluid return hose from the reservoir tank and drain the power steering fluid from the reservoir into a clean container.
4 Disconnect the pressure line from the pump.
5 Push on the power steering pump drivebelt by hand to increase the tension, then unscrew the pulley nut.
6 Loosen the drivebelt adjuster bolt and remove the drivebelt.
7 Remove the mounting bolts and detach the power steering pump unit.
8 Installation is the reverse of removal. Tighten the fasteners securely. Adjust the drivebelt tension (see Chapter 1).
9 Top up the fluid level in the reservoir and bleed the system (see Chapter 1 and Chapter 10).

23 Power steering system - bleeding

1 To bleed the power steering system, begin by checking the power steering fluid level and adding fluid if necessary (see Chapter 1).
2 Raise and support the front of the vehicle on jackstands.
3 Turn the steering wheel from lock-to-lock several times and recheck the fluid level.
4 Start the engine and run it at 1000 rpm or less. Turn the steering wheel from lock-to-lock again (three or four times) and recheck the fluid level one more time.
5 Lower the front of the vehicle to the ground. Run the engine and again turn the wheels from lock-to-lock several more times. Recheck the fluid level. Position the wheels straight ahead.
6 Bleeding is complete if the fluid level did not rise from the FULL mark more than 3/16-inch and if no foaming is observed in the fluid when the engine is stopped.

24 Steering wheel - removal and installation

Refer to illustrations 24.3 and 24.4

Warning: *If the vehicle is equipped with an airbag, do not attempt to remove the steering wheel. Have it removed by a dealer service department or other qualified repair shop.*

1 Disconnect the negative battery cable. **Caution:** *If the stereo in your vehicle is equipped with an anti-theft system, refer to the information on page 0-15 at the front of this manual before detaching the cable.*
2 On 1982 and 1983 models, remove the steering wheel trim plate by pulling out on the bottom portion of the plate. On all other models,

24.3 Be sure to mark the relationship of the steering wheel to the shaft to ensure correct position of the steering wheel when it's installed

24.4 Use a steering wheel puller to remove the steering wheel - DO NOT hammer on the shaft!

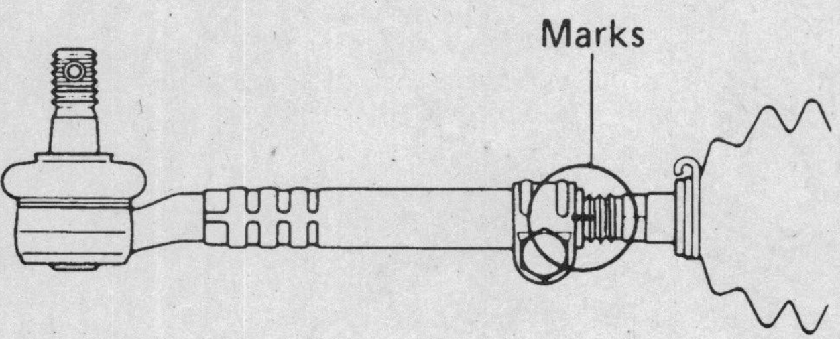

25.4 Place marks on the tie-rod end and tie-rod to ensure proper alignment during installation

remove the single retaining screw located at the bottom of the plate first.

3 Remove the steering wheel nut and mark the relationship of the steering wheel hub to the shaft **(see illustration)**.

4 Install a steering wheel puller and remove the steering wheel **(see illustration)**.

5 To install the steering wheel reverse the removal procedure. Be sure to align the match marks applied in Step 3.

6 Install the nut and tighten it to the torque listed in this Chapter's Specifications.

7 Install the steering wheel trim plate and reconnect the negative battery cable.

25 Tie-rod ends - removal and installation

Refer to illustrations 25.4 and 25.6

1 Loosen but do not remove the wheel lug nuts.

2 Raise the front of the vehicle and secure it on jackstands.

3 Remove the front wheel.

4 Loosen the clamp bolt that locks the tie-rod end to the tie-rod, then apply an alignment mark on the threads to ensure the tie-rod end is installed in the same position **(see illustration)**.

5 Remove the cotter pin, then loosen the castellated nut on the tie-rod end stud.

6 Install a puller and disconnect the tie-rod end from the steering knuckle arm **(see illustration)**, then unscrew the tie-rod end from the tie-rod.

7 Thread the tie-rod end onto the steering rack until it reaches the alignment mark. Tighten the clamp bolt securely.

8 Install the tie-rod end stud through the steering knuckle arm and tighten the castellated nut to the torque listed in this Chapter's Specifications. Install a new cotter pin.

25.6 Loosen the castellated nut a few turns, then install a puller to separate the tie-rod end from the steering knuckle (the nut will prevent the components from separating violently)

9 It is a good idea to have the toe-in adjusted at a dealer service department or alignment shop after the tie-rod end is installed.

26 Rack-and-pinion steering gear (1982 and later models) - removal and installation

Refer to illustration 26.4

Removal

1 Loosen but do not remove the wheel lug nuts.

2 Raise the vehicle and support it securely on jackstands.

3 Remove the front wheels. Remove the bolts and detach the engine under cover.

4 Remove the intermediate shaft lower clamp bolt **(see illustration)**.

5 Disconnect the tie-rod ends from the steering knuckle arms (see Section 25).

6 Use a flare nut wrench to disconnect the power steering pressure and return lines from the steering gear. Place a container under the lines to catch spilled fluid. Plug the lines to prevent excessive fluid loss and contamination.

7 Remove the bolts from the steering gear mounting brackets **(see illustration 26.4)**.

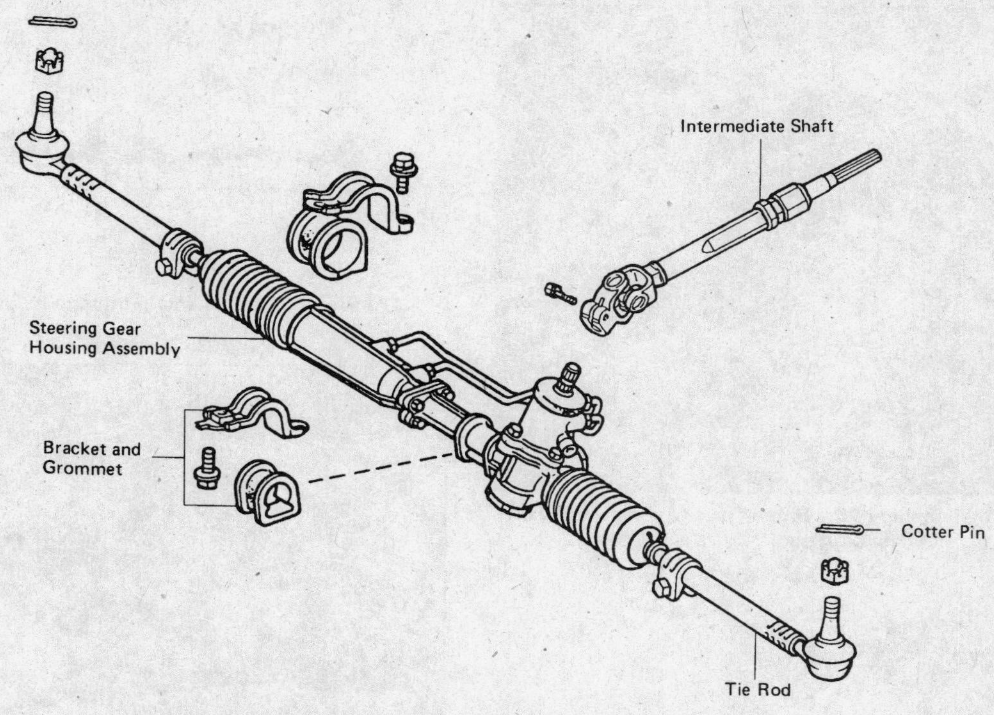

26.4 Typical rack-and-pinion steering gear components

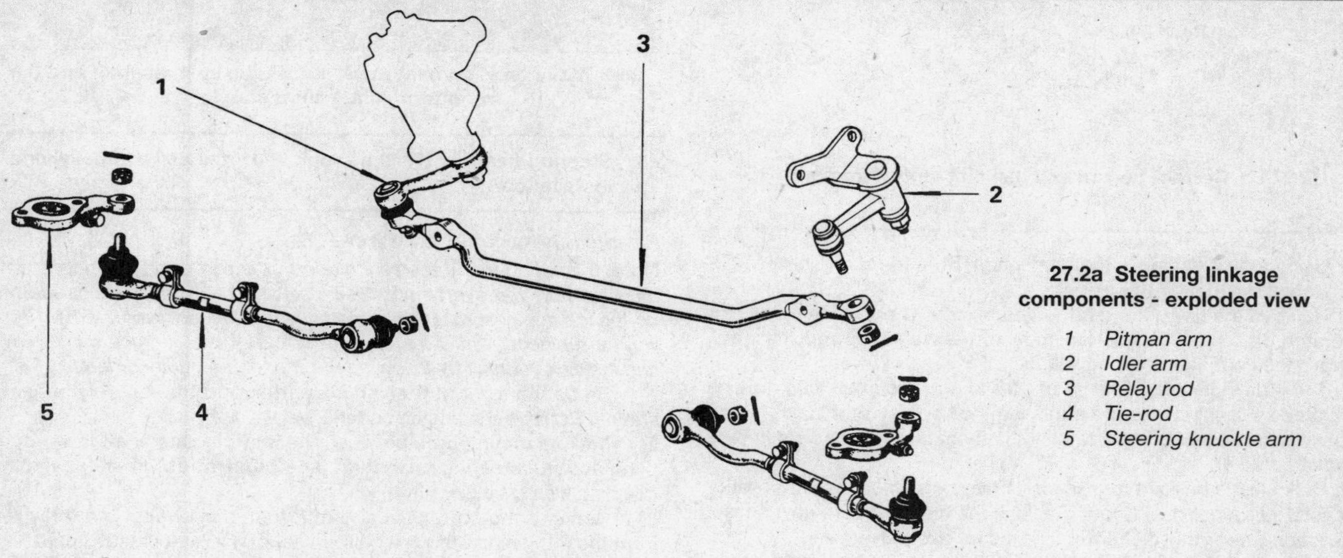

27.2a Steering linkage components - exploded view

1 *Pitman arm*
2 *Idler arm*
3 *Relay rod*
4 *Tie-rod*
5 *Steering knuckle arm*

8 Withdraw the assembly from beneath the vehicle. Take care not to damage the rack boots.

Installation

9 To install the assembly, reverse the removal procedure. Tighten the mounting bolts, the tie-rod end nuts and the intermediate shaft clamp bolts to the torque values listed in this Chapter's Specifications.
10 Install the front wheels. Tighten the wheel lug nuts finger tight.
11 Fill the reservoir with the recommended fluid (see Chapter 1).
12 Bleed the steering system (refer to Section 23).
13 Lower the vehicle and tighten the wheel lug nuts to the torque listed in the Chapter 1 Specifications.
14 It is a good idea to have the front wheels aligned by a dealer service department or alignment shop after reassembly.

27 Steering linkage (1979 through 1981 models) - removal and installation

Refer to illustrations 27.2a, 27.2b, 27.9a and 27.9b

1 Before dismantling the steering linkage, obtain a balljoint separator. This may be a screw type puller or a wedge-type tool (although the wedge-type tends to tear the balljoint boots). It is possible to jar the balljoint taper pin free from its eye by striking opposite sides of the eye simultaneously with two large hammers, but the space available to do this is very limited.
2 Unscrew and remove the Pitman arm retaining nut **(see illustrations)**. Before separating the joint, look for match marks between the steering shaft and arm, If none are present, scribe a mark across the bottom face of both parts.

27.2b Mark the relationship of the Pitman arm to the steering box (sector) shaft

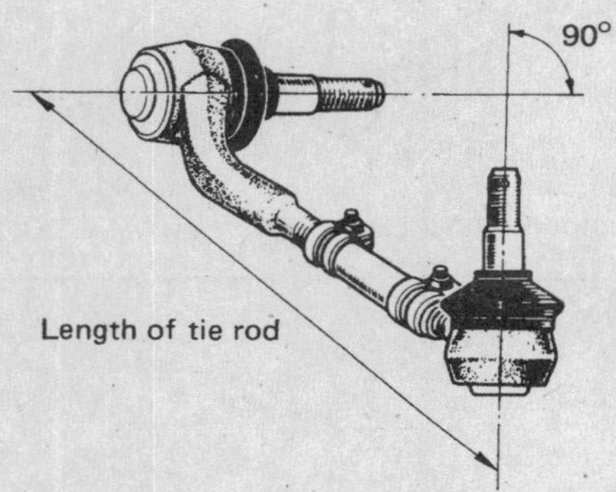

27.9b Correct tie-rod and balljoint stud alignment

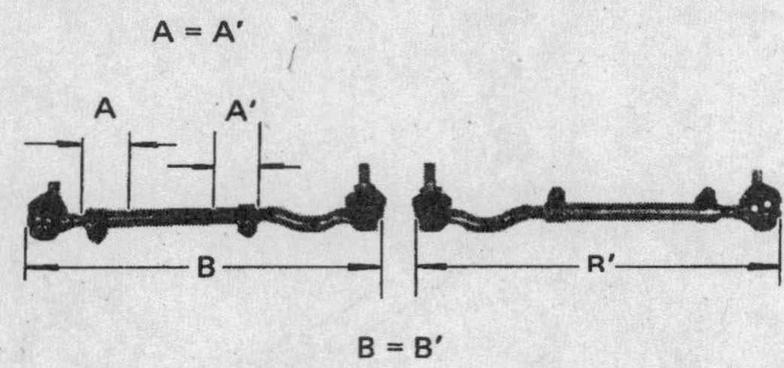

27.9a Check the tie-rod lengths to be sure they are equal

28.2 Make an alignment mark across the splined shaft and the intermediate shaft coupler

3 Using a puller, remove the Pitman arm from the shaft splines.

4 Unbolt the idler arm bracket.

5 Remove the tie-rod end nut on each side. Then, using a balljoint separator, disconnect the tie-rod ends from the steering knuckle arms. Remove the complete steering linkage.

6 The individual components of the linkage assembly can now be separated as required. Before removing the tie-rod clamps, mark their respective positions as a guide to adjustment during reassembly **(see illustration 25.4)**.

7 Check each balljoint for excessive play or stiffness and for split or deteriorated rubber dust boots. Replace the balljoints with new ones if necessary. Check the idler arm bushings for excessive wear.

8 When installing a balljoint dust boot, pack the interior with moly-base grease.

9 Reassembly is the reverse of the disassembly procedure, but observe the following points:

a) When installing the tie-rod ends, position them so that the match marks made during disassembly are aligned and make sure they are equally spaced on each side **(see illustration)**.
b) Position the tie-rod end balljoint studs at an angle of 90-degrees to each other **(see illustration)**.
c) Make sure that the right and left tie-rod ends are equal in length when they are installed.
d) Tighten all retaining bolts to the torque listed in this Chapter's Specifications.
e) Realign the match marks of the Pitman arm and the steering shaft when reassembling them.
f) When reassembly of the linkage is complete, have the front wheel alignment checked, and if necessary, adjusted.

28 Steering gearbox (1979 through 1981 models) - removal and installation

Refer to illustrations 28.2, 28.3 and 28.8

Note: *If you find that the steering gearbox is defective, it is not recommended that you overhaul it. Because of the special tools needed to do the job it is best to let your dealer service department overhaul it for you (or replace it with a factory rebuilt unit). However, you can remove and install it yourself by following the procedure outlined here:*

1 Raise the front of the vehicle and support it securely on jackstands. Remove the engine under cover.

2 Make a match mark between the intermediate shaft lower coupling and the steering gear shaft **(see illustration)**, then loosen the coupling clamp bolt.

3 Remove the cotter pin and nut, then disconnect the relay rod from the Pitman arm using a balljoint separator **(see illustration)**.

4 If you're working on a model with power steering, disconnect the pressure and return lines from the steering box. Plug the ends of the lines to prevent fluid loss and contamination.

5 Remove the three steering box retaining bolts, separate the box from the steering column lower coupling and remove it from the vehicle.

6 If it's necessary to detach the Pitman arm from the gearbox sector shaft, make a match mark across the two for correct reassembly **(see illustration)**. Remove the Pitman arm retaining nut and washer. Use a puller to withdraw the arm if necessary.

8 Install the Pitman arm by aligning the match marks made during removal, then tighten the nut to the torque listed in this Chapter's Specifications.

9 When installed, the Pitman arm must not have any measurable endplay within 100 degrees from the neutral position. If play exists, have the following parts checked:

a) Sector shaft and bearings (for wear)

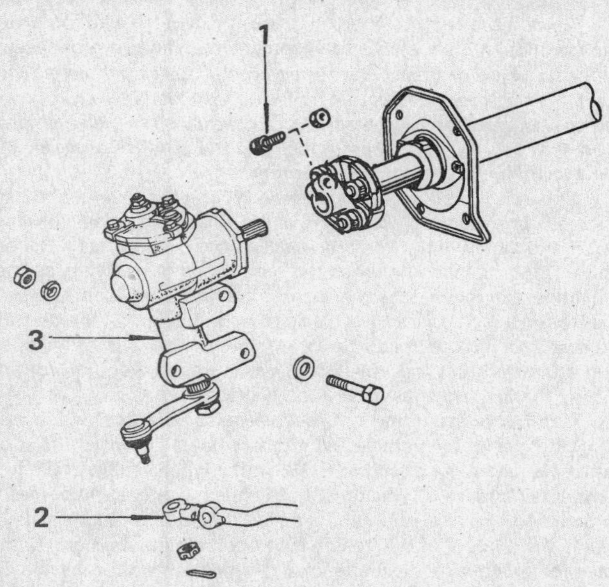

28.3 Steering gearbox installation details (manual steering gear shown, power steering gear similar)

1 Coupling clamp bolt
2 Relay rod
3 Gearbox

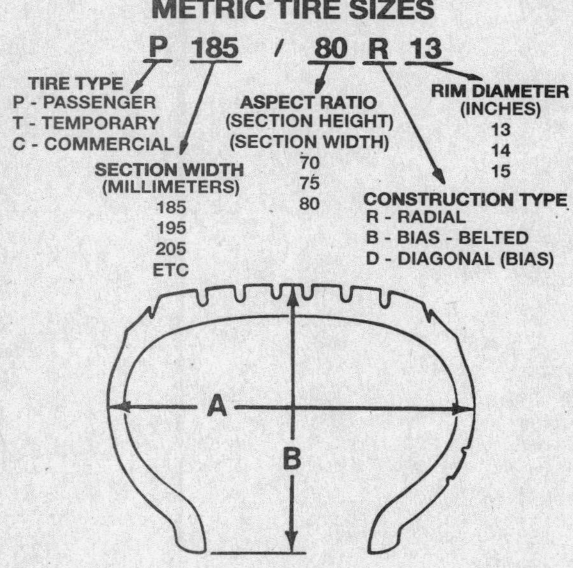

29.1 Metric tire size code

b) Thrust washer and adjuster bolt head (for wear)

c) Ball nut and worm shaft (for wear)

10 Raise the steering gearbox into position. Align the mark on the steering gear shaft with the mark on the intermediate shaft and tighten the steering gear retaining bolts and the coupling bolt to the torque values listed in this Chapter's Specifications.

11 If you're working on a model without power steering, fill the steering box to the proper level with the recommended lubricant (see Chapter 1) and install the filler plug **(see illustration)**.

12 If you're working on a model with power steering, connect the lines to the steering box and tighten the fittings securely. Make sure the hoses are clear of the inner fenderwell when installed. Refer to Chapter 1 and fill the power steering reservoir with the recommended fluid, then bleed the system as described in Section 23. Check for leakage from the lines and connections.

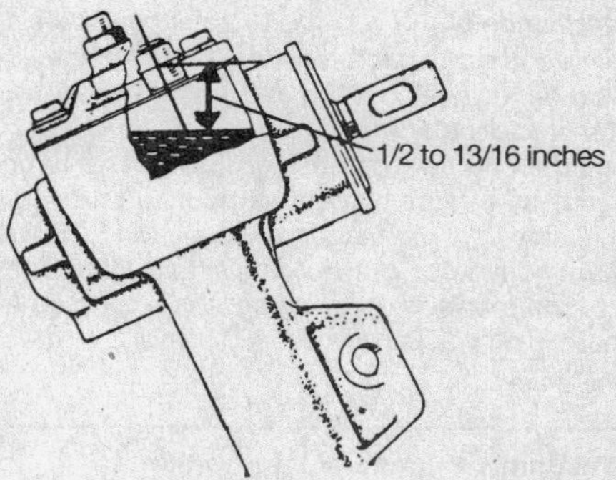

28.11 Manual steering gearbox oil level

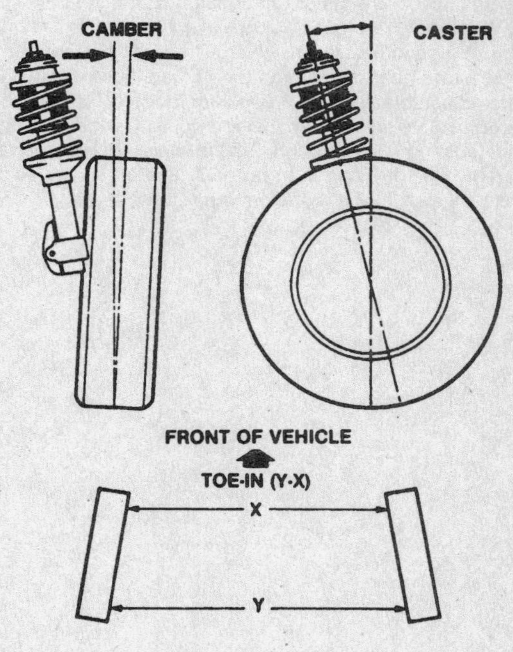

30.1 Camber, caster and toe-in angles

29 Wheels and tires - general information

Refer to illustration 29.1

1 All vehicles covered by this manual are equipped with metric-sized fiberglass or steel belted radial tires **(see illustration)**. Use of other size or type of tires may affect the ride and handling of the vehicle. Don't mix different types of tires, such as radials and bias belted, on the same vehicle as handling may be seriously affected. It's recommended that tires be replaced in pairs on the same axle, but if only one tire is being replaced, be sure it's the same size, structure and tread design as the other.

2 Because tire pressure has a substantial effect on handling and wear, the pressure on all tires should be checked at least once a month or before any extended trips (see Chapter 1).

3 Wheels must be replaced if they are bent, dented, leak air, have elongated bolt holes, are heavily rusted, out of vertical symmetry or if the lug nuts won't stay tight. Wheel repairs that use welding or peening are not recommended.

4 Tire and wheel balance is important in the overall handling, braking and performance of the vehicle. Unbalanced wheels can adversely affect handling and ride characteristics as well as tire life. Whenever a tire is installed on a wheel, the tire and wheel should be balanced by a shop with the proper equipment.

5 Because the compact spare is designed as a temporary replacement for an out-of-service standard wheel and tire, it should be used on the vehicle only until the standard wheel and tire can be repaired or replaced. Continuous use of the compact spare at speeds of over 50 mph is not recommended. In addition, the expected tread life of the compact spare is only 3000 miles.

30 Wheel alignment - general information

Refer to illustration 30.1

A wheel alignment refers to the adjustments made to the wheels so they are in proper angular relationship to the suspension and the ground. Wheels that are out of proper alignment not only affect vehicle control, but also increase tire wear. The front end angles normally measured are camber, caster and toe-in **(see illustration)**. Caster and toe-in are adjustable on 1986 and earlier models. Camber, caster and toe-in is adjustable on 1987 and later models. On the rear wheels, toe-in is adjustable on 1982 through 1986 models, and camber and toe-in is adjustable on 1987 and later models. The other angles should be measured to check for bent or worn suspension parts.

Getting the proper wheel alignment is a very exacting process, one in which complicated and expensive machines are necessary to perform the job properly. Because of this, you should have a technician with the proper equipment perform these tasks. We will, however, use this space to give you a basic idea of what is involved with a wheel alignment so you can better understand the process and deal intelligently with the shop that does the work.

Toe-in is the turning in of the wheels. The purpose of a toe specification is to ensure parallel rolling of the wheels. In a vehicle with zero toe-in, the distance between the front edges of the wheels will be the same as the distance between the rear edges of the wheels. The actual amount of toe-in is normally only a fraction of an inch. On the front end, toe-in is controlled by the tie-rod end position on the tie-rod. On the rear end, it's controlled by a cam on the inner end of the suspension arm. Incorrect toe-in will cause the tires to wear improperly by making them scrub against the road surface.

Camber is the tilting of the wheels from vertical when viewed from one end of the vehicle. When the wheels tilt out at the top, the camber is said to be positive (+). When the wheels tilt in at the top the camber is negative (-). The amount of tilt is measured in degrees from vertical and this measurement is called the camber angle. This angle affects the amount of tire tread which contacts the road and compensates for changes in the suspension geometry when the vehicle is cornering or travelling over an undulating surface.

Caster is the tilting of the front steering axis from the vertical. A tilt toward the rear is positive caster and a tilt toward the front is negative caster.

Chapter 11 Body

Contents

1 General information

These models feature a "unibody" layout, using a floor pan with front and rear frame side rails which support the body components, front and rear suspension systems and other mechanical components.

Certain components are particularly vulnerable to accident damage and can be unbolted and repaired or replaced. Among these parts are the body moldings, bumpers, hood and back door (hatchback) and all glass.

Only general body maintenance practices and body panel repair procedures within the scope of the do-it-yourselfer are included in this Chapter.

2 Body - maintenance

1 The condition of your vehicle's body is very important, because the resale value depends a great deal on it. It's much more difficult to repair a neglected or damaged body than it is to repair mechanical components. The hidden areas of the body, such as the wheel wells, the frame and the engine compartment, are equally important, although they don't require as frequent attention as the rest of the body.

2 Once a year, or every 12,000 miles, it's a good idea to have the underside of the body steam cleaned. All traces of dirt and oil will be removed and the area can then be inspected carefully for rust, damaged brake lines, frayed electrical wires, damaged cables and other problems. The front suspension components on early models (1979 through 1981) should be greased after completion of this job.

3 At the same time, clean the engine and the engine compartment with a steam cleaner or water soluble degreaser.

4 The wheel wells should be given close attention, since undercoating can peel away and stones and dirt thrown up by the tires can cause the paint to chip and flake, allowing rust to set in. If rust is found, clean down to the bare metal and apply an anti-rust paint.

5 The body should be washed about once a week. Wet the vehicle thoroughly to soften the dirt, then wash it down with a soft sponge and plenty of clean soapy water. If the surplus dirt is not washed off very

These photos illustrate a method of repairing simple dents. They are intended to supplement *Body repair - minor damage* in this Chapter and should not be used as the sole instructions for body repair on these vehicles.

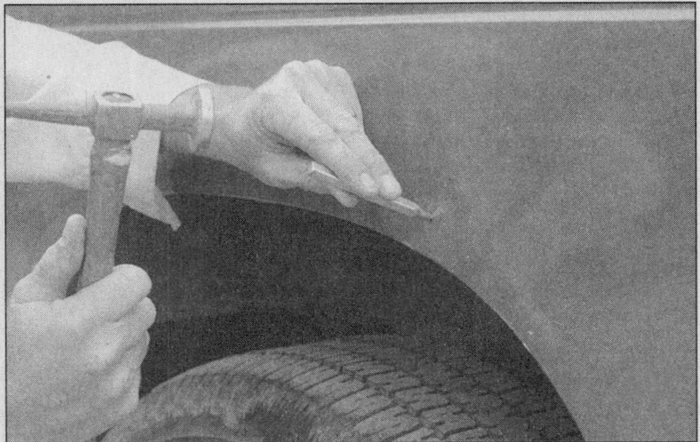

1 If you can't access the backside of the body panel to hammer out the dent, pull it out with a slide-hammer-type dent puller. In the deepest portion of the dent or along the crease line, drill or punch hole(s) at least one inch apart . . .

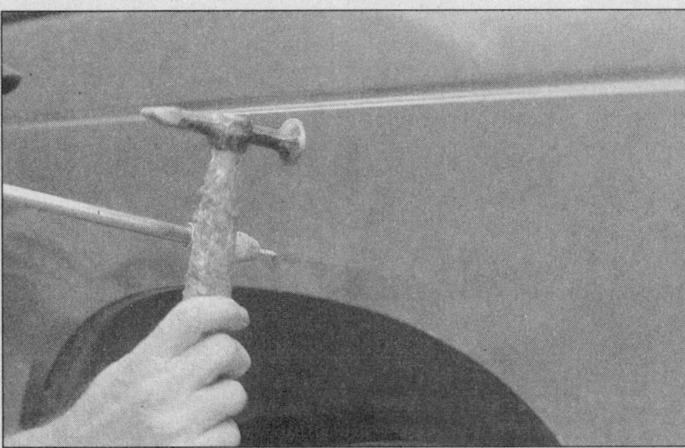

2 . . . then screw the slide-hammer into the hole and operate it. Tap with a hammer near the edge of the dent to help 'pop' the metal back to its original shape. When you're finished, the dent area should be close to its original contour and about 1/8-inch below the surface of the surrounding metal

3 Using coarse-grit sandpaper, remove the paint down to the bare metal. Hand sanding works fine, but the disc sander shown here makes the job faster. Use finer (about 320-grit) sandpaper to feather-edge the paint at least one inch around the dent area

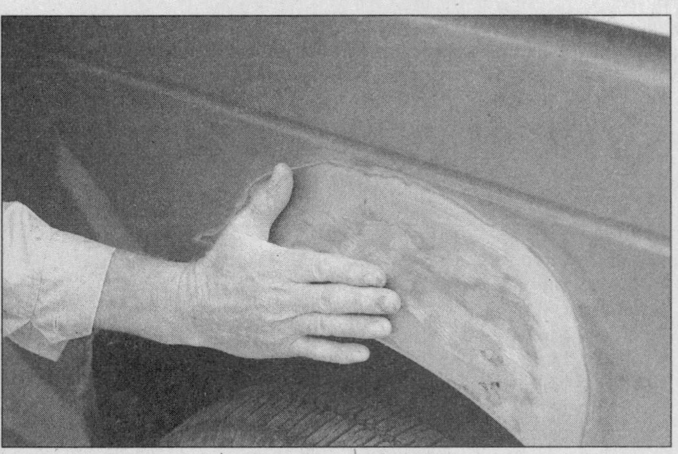

4 When the paint is removed, touch will probably be more helpful than sight for telling if the metal is straight. Hammer down the high spots or raise the low spots as necessary. Clean the repair area with wax/silicone remover

5 Following label instructions, mix up a batch of plastic filler and hardener. The ratio of filler to hardener is critical, and, if you mix it incorrectly, it will either not cure properly or cure too quickly (you won't have time to file and sand it into shape)

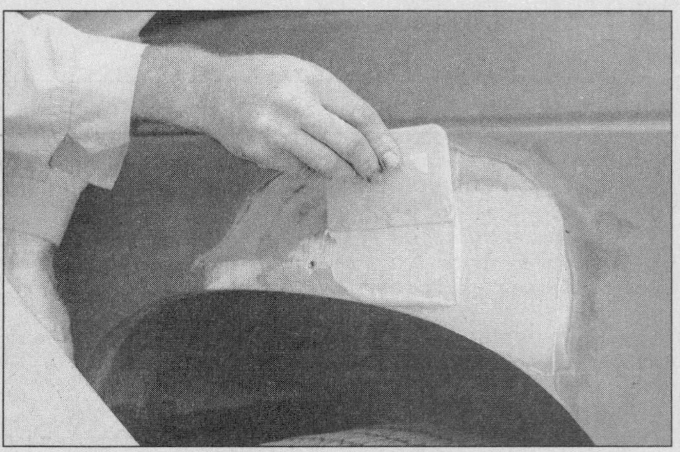

6 Working quickly so the filler doesn't harden, use a plastic applicator to press the body filler firmly into the metal, assuring it bonds completely. Work the filler until it matches the original contour and is slightly above the surrounding metal

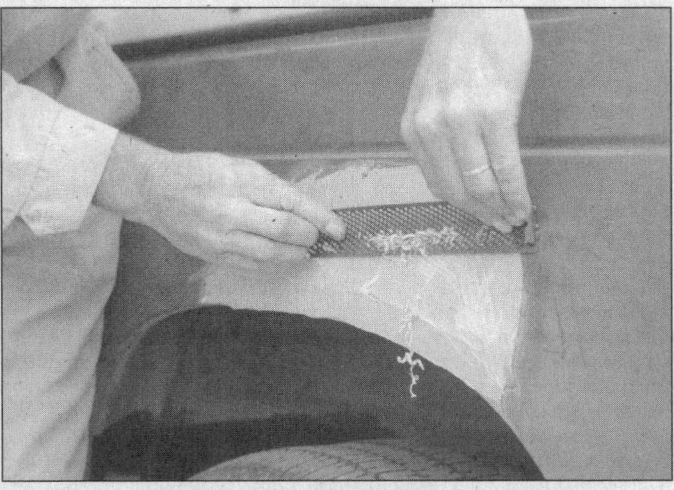

7 Let the filler harden until you can just dent it with your fingernail. Use a body file or Surform tool (shown here) to rough-shape the filler

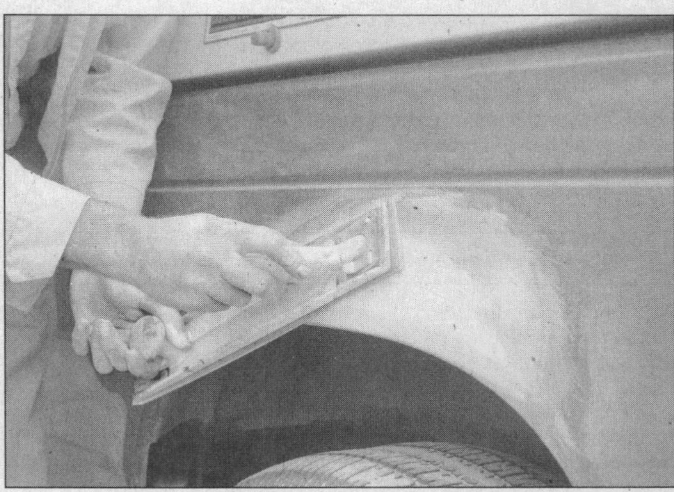

8 Use coarse-grit sandpaper and a sanding board or block to work the filler down until it's smooth and even. Work down to finer grits of sandpaper - always using a board or block - ending up with 360 or 400 grit

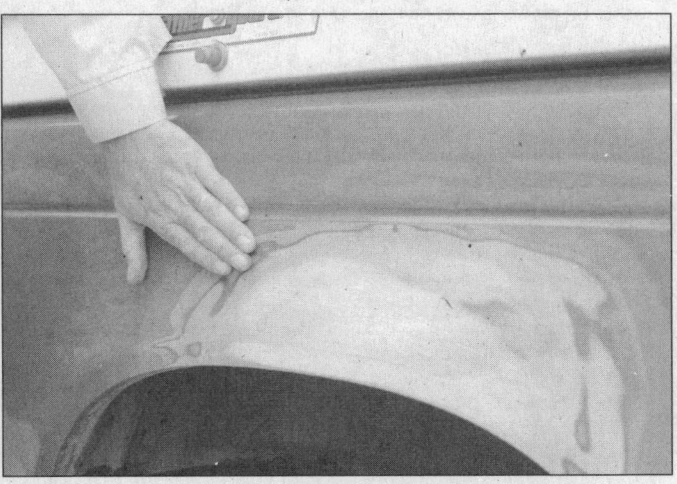

9 You shouldn't be able to feel any ridge at the transition from the filler to the bare metal or from the bare metal to the old paint. As soon as the repair is flat and uniform, remove the dust and mask off the adjacent panels or trim pieces

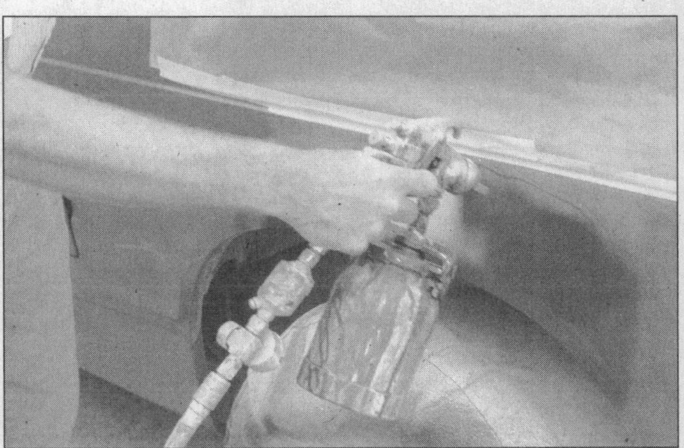

10 Apply several layers of primer to the area. Don't spray the primer on too heavy, so it sags or runs, and make sure each coat is dry before you spray on the next one. A professional-type spray gun is being used here, but aerosol spray primer is available inexpensively from auto parts stores

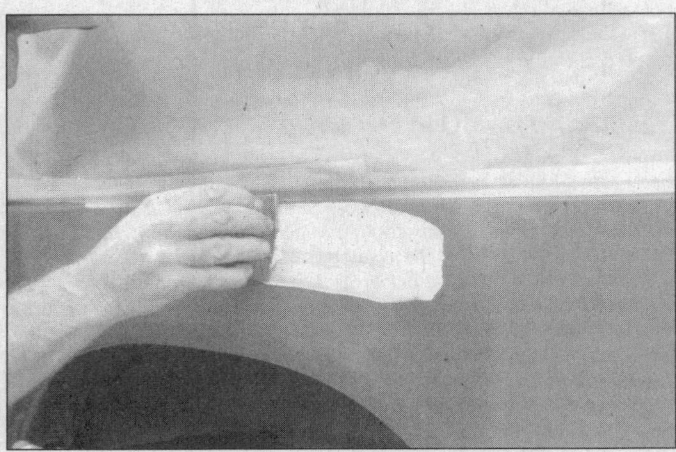

11 The primer will help reveal imperfections or scratches. Fill these with glazing compound. Follow the label instructions and sand it with 360 or 400-grit sandpaper until it's smooth. Repeat the glazing, sanding and respraying until the primer reveals a perfectly smooth surface

12 Finish sand the primer with very fine sandpaper (400 or 600-grit) to remove the primer overspray. Clean the area with water and allow it to dry. Use a tack rag to remove any dust, then apply the finish coat. Don't attempt to rub out or wax the repair area until the paint has dried completely (at least two weeks)

carefully, it can wear down the paint.

6 Spots of tar or asphalt thrown up from the road should be removed with a cloth soaked in solvent.

7 Once every six months, wax the body and chrome trim. If a chrome cleaner is used to remove rust from any of the vehicle's plated parts, remember that the cleaner also removes part of the chrome, so use it sparingly.

3 Vinyl trim - maintenance

Don't clean vinyl trim with detergents, caustic soap or petroleum-based cleaners. Plain soap and water works just fine, with a soft brush to clean dirt that may be ingrained. Wash the vinyl as frequently as the rest of the vehicle.

After cleaning, application of a high quality rubber and vinyl protectant will help prevent oxidation and cracks. The protectant can also be applied to weatherstripping, vacuum lines and rubber hoses, which often fail as a result of chemical degradation, and to the tires.

4 Upholstery and carpets - maintenance

1 Every three months remove the carpets or mats and clean the interior of the vehicle (more frequently if necessary). Vacuum the upholstery and carpets to remove loose dirt and dust.

2 Leather upholstery requires special care. Stains should be removed with warm water and a very mild soap solution. Use a clean, damp cloth to remove the soap, then wipe again with a dry cloth. Never use alcohol, gasoline, nail polish remover or thinner to clean leather upholstery.

3 After cleaning, regularly treat leather upholstery with a leather wax. Never use car wax on leather upholstery.

4 In areas where the interior of the vehicle is subject to bright sunlight, cover leather seats with a sheet if the vehicle is to be left out for any length of time.

5 Body repair - minor damage

See photo sequence

Repair of minor scratches

1 If the scratch is superficial and does not penetrate to the metal of the body, repair is very simple. Lightly rub the scratched area with a fine rubbing compound to remove loose paint and built-up wax. Rinse the area with clean water.

2 Apply touch-up paint to the scratch, using a small brush. Continue to apply thin layers of paint until the surface of the paint in the scratch is level with the surrounding paint. Allow the new paint at least two weeks to harden, then blend it into the surrounding paint by rubbing with a very fine rubbing compound. Finally, apply a coat of wax to the scratch area.

3 If the scratch has penetrated the paint and exposed the metal of the body, causing the metal to rust, a different repair technique is required. Remove all loose rust from the bottom of the scratch with a pocket knife, then apply rust inhibiting paint to prevent the formation of rust in the future. Using a rubber or nylon applicator, coat the scratched area with glaze-type filler. If required, the filler can be mixed with thinner to provide a very thin paste, which is ideal for filling narrow scratches. Before the glaze filler in the scratch hardens, wrap a piece of smooth cotton cloth around the tip of a finger. Dip the cloth in thinner and then quickly wipe it along the surface of the scratch. This will ensure that the surface of the filler is slightly hollow. The scratch can now be painted over as described earlier in this section.

Repair of dents

4 When repairing dents, the first job is to pull the dent out until the affected area is as close as possible to its original shape. There is no point in trying to restore the original shape completely as the metal in the damaged area will have stretched on impact and cannot be restored to its original contours. It is better to bring the level of the dent up to a point which is about 1/8-inch below the level of the surrounding metal. In cases where the dent is very shallow, it is not worth trying to pull it out at all.

5 If the back side of the dent is accessible, it can be hammered out gently from behind using a soft-face hammer. While doing this, hold a block of wood firmly against the opposite side of the metal to absorb the hammer blows and prevent the metal from being stretched.

6 If the dent is in a section of the body which has double layers, or some other factor makes it inaccessible from behind, a different technique is required. Drill several small holes through the metal inside the damaged area, particularly in the deeper sections. Screw long, selftapping screws into the holes just enough for them to get a good grip in the metal. Now the dent can be pulled out by pulling on the protruding heads of the screws with locking pliers.

7 The next stage of repair is the removal of paint from the damaged area and from an inch or so of the surrounding metal. This is done with a wire brush or sanding disk in a drill motor, although it can be done just as effectively by hand with sandpaper. To complete the preparation for filling, score the surface of the bare metal with a screwdriver or the tang of a file, or drill small holes in the affected area. This will provide a good grip for the filler material. To complete the repair, see the subsection on filling and painting later in this Section.

Repair of rust holes or gashes

8 Remove all paint from the affected area and from an inch or so of the surrounding metal using a sanding disk or wire brush mounted in a drill motor. If these are not available, a few sheets of sandpaper will do the job just as effectively.

9 With the paint removed, you will be able to determine the severity of the corrosion and decide whether to replace the whole panel, if possible, or repair the affected area. New body panels are not as expensive as most people think and it is often quicker to install a new panel than to repair large areas of rust.

10 Remove all trim pieces from the affected area except those which will act as a guide to the original shape of the damaged body, such as headlight shells, etc. Using metal snips or a hacksaw blade, remove all loose metal and any other metal that is badly affected by rust. Hammer the edges of the hole inner to create a slight depression for the filler material.

11 Wire brush the affected area to remove the powdery rust from the surface of the metal. If the back of the rusted area is accessible, treat it with rust inhibiting paint.

12 Before filling is done, block the hole in some way. This can be done with sheet metal riveted or screwed into place, or by stuffing the hole with wire mesh.

13 Once the hole is blocked off, the affected area can be filled and painted. See the following subsection on filling and painting.

Filling and painting

14 Many types of body fillers are available, but generally speaking, body repair kits which contain filler paste and a tube of resin hardener are best for this type of repair work. A wide, flexible plastic or nylon applicator will be necessary for imparting a smooth and contoured finish to the surface of the filler material. Mix up a small amount of filler on a clean piece of wood or cardboard (use the hardener sparingly). Follow the manufacturer's instructions on the package, otherwise the filler will set incorrectly.

15 Using the applicator, apply the filler paste to the prepared area. Draw the applicator across the surface of the filler to achieve the desired contour and to level the filler surface. As soon as a contour that approximates the original one is achieved, stop working the paste. If you continue, the paste will begin to stick to the applicator. Continue to add thin layers of paste at 20-minute intervals until the level of the filler is just above the surrounding metal.

16 Once the filler has hardened, the excess can be removed with a body file. From then on, progressively finer grades of sandpaper

8.2 Take out the two retaining screws (arrows) to remove the kick panel (1983 model shown)

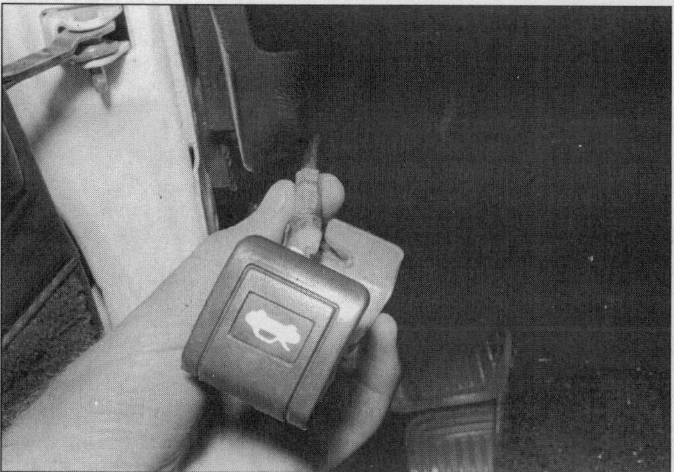

8.3 With the release lever off, pull the cable end out of the release lever (1983 model shown)

should be used, starting with a 180-grit paper and finishing with 600-grit wet-or-dry paper. Always wrap the sandpaper around a flat rubber or wooden block, otherwise the surface of the filler will not be completely flat. During the sanding of the filler surface, the wet-or-dry paper should be periodically rinsed in water. This will ensure that a very smooth finish is produced in the final stage.

17 At this point, the repair area should be surrounded by a ring of bare metal, which in turn should be encircled by the finely feathered edge of good paint. Rinse the repair area with clean water until all of the dust produced by the sanding operation is gone.

18 Spray the entire area with a light coat of primer. This will reveal any imperfections in the surface of the filler. Repair the imperfections with fresh filler paste or glaze filler and once more smooth the surface with sandpaper. Repeat this spray-and-repair procedure until you are satisfied that the surface of the filler and the feathered edge of the paint are perfect. Rinse the area with clean water and allow it to dry completely.

19 The repair area is now ready for painting. Spray painting must be carried out in a warm, dry, windless and dust free atmosphere. These conditions can be created if you have access to a large indoor work area, but if you are forced to work in the open, you will have to pick the day very carefully. If you are working indoors, dousing the floor in the work area with water will help settle the dust which would otherwise be in the air. If the repair area is confined to one body panel, mask off the surrounding panels. This will help minimize the effects of a slight mismatch in paint color. Trim pieces such as chrome strips, door handles, etc., will also need to be masked off or removed. Use masking tape and several thicknesses of newspaper for the masking operations.

20 Before spraying, shake the paint can thoroughly, then spray a test area until the spray painting technique is mastered. Cover the repair area with a thick coat of primer. The thickness should be built up using several thin layers of primer rather than one thick one. Using 600-grit wet-or-dry sandpaper, rub down the surface of the primer until it is very smooth. While doing this, the work area should be thoroughly rinsed with water and the wet-or-dry sandpaper periodically rinsed as well. Allow the primer to dry before spraying additional coats.

21 Spray on the top coat, again building up the thickness by using several thin layers of paint. Begin spraying in the center of the repair area and then, using a circular motion, work out until the whole repair area and about two inches of the surrounding original paint is covered. Remove all masking material 10 to 15 minutes after spraying on the final coat of paint. Allow the new paint at least two weeks to harden, then use a very fine rubbing compound to blend the edges of the new paint into the existing paint. Finally, apply a coat of wax.

6 Body repair - major damage

1 Major damage must be repaired by an auto body shop specifically equipped to perform unibody repairs. These shops have the specialized equipment required to do the job properly.

2 If the damage is extensive, the body must be checked for proper alignment or the vehicle's handling characteristics may be adversely affected and other components may wear at an accelerated rate.

3 Due to the fact that all of the major body components (hood, fenders, etc.) are separate and replaceable units, any seriously damaged components should be replaced rather than repaired. Sometimes the components can be found in a wrecking yard that specializes in used vehicle components, often at considerable savings over the cost of new parts.

7 Hinges and locks - maintenance

Once every 3000 miles, or every three months, the hinges and latch assemblies on the doors, hood and back door (hatchback) should be given a few drops of light oil or lock lubricant. The door latch strikers should also be lubricated with a thin coat of grease to reduce wear and ensure free movement. Lubricate the front doors and back door locks with spray-on graphite lubricant.

8 Hood and liftgate latch and cable - removal, installation and adjustment

Refer to illustrations 8.2, 8.3, 8.4, 8.6 and 8.9

Warning: *On airbag-equipped models, always disconnect the negative battery cable when working in the vicinity of the impact sensors to avoid the possibility of accidental deployment of the airbag, which could cause personal injury.*

Caution: *If the stereo in your vehicle is equipped with an anti-theft system, refer to the information on page 0-15 at the front of this manual before detaching the cable.*

Hood

1 Remove the dashboard left under cover by taking out the three retaining screws.

2 Pull off the outer fuse box cover, then remove the two retaining screws and detach the kick panel **(see illustration)**.

3 To remove the cable, pull up the release lever and take out the retaining screws. Withdraw the release lever and detach the cable from it **(see illustration)**.

8.4 The cable (arrow) is accessible with the inner fender panel removed (1983 model shown)

8.6 Loosen the latch bolts, move the latch assembly into the proper position and tighten the bolts

8.9 Remove the bolt (arrow) to withdraw the release lever assembly (1983 model shown)

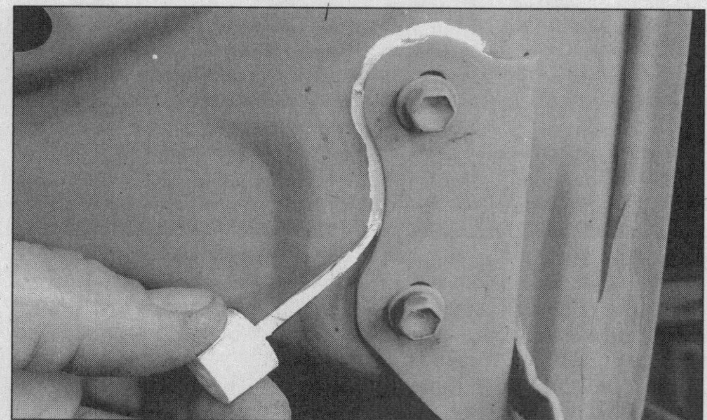
9.2 Mark the relationship of the hood hinge to the hood

4 Remove the left front inner fender panel, exposing the cable route **(see illustration)**.

5 To remove the hood latch at this time, take out the three mounting bolts and detach the cable. With the cable now free, withdraw both ends through the wheel well.

6 Installing the cable and latch is the reverse of removal. Before closing the hood, check that the latch release mechanism operates in a satisfactory manner, that the safety catch engages (the auxiliary catch release tab needs to be lifted before the hood can be opened) and that, when fully closed, the hood is securely held. Adjust the hood latch by loosening the mounting bolts and moving the latch in the desired direction **(see illustration)**.

Liftgate

7 Remove the rear and left side luggage compartment trim panels by lifting them up and out.

8 Take out the driver's seat, then remove the sill plate and pull back the carpet to expose the cable and release lever.

9 Disconnect the cable from the latch. Remove the bolt holding the release lever and disconnect the cable from the lever **(see illustration)**. Tape the end of the new cable to the old cable and pull both cables through from the release lever side. Pry off the top of the left rear armrest cover and begin pulling from there.

10 Detach the rear latch by removing the three mounting bolts and disconnecting the light connector.

11 Installation is the reverse of removal.

9 Hood - removal, installation and adjustment

Note: *The hood is heavy and somewhat awkward to remove and install - at least two people should perform this procedure.*

Removal and installation

Refer to illustrations 9.2

1 Use blankets or pads to cover the cowl area of the body and fenders. This will protect the body and paint as the hood is lifted free.

2 Scribe or paint alignment marks around the hood hinges to ensure proper alignment upon installation **(see illustration)**.

3 Disconnect any cables or electrical connectors which will interfere with removal.

4 Have an assistant support the weight of the hood. Remove the hinge-to-hood screws or bolts.

5 Lift off the hood.

6 Installation is the reverse of removal.

Adjustment

Refer to illustration 9.11

7 Fore-and-aft and side-to-side adjustment of the hood is made by moving the hinge plate slot after loosening the bolts or nuts.

8 Scribe a line around the entire hinge plate so you can judge the amount of movement **(see illustration 9.2)**.

9 Loosen the bolts or nuts and move the hood into correct alignment. Move the hood only a little at a time. Tighten the hinge bolts or nuts and carefully lower the hood to check the position.

10 If necessary after installation, the entire hood latch assembly can be adjusted up-and-down as well as side-to-side on the radiator support so the hood closes securely. Refer to the adjustment procedure (see Section 8). Following adjustment, retighten the mounting bolts.

11 Finally, if the vehicle is equipped with hood bumpers, adjust them on the radiator support so that the hood, when closed, is flush with the fenders **(see illustration)**.

12 The hood latch assembly, as well as the hinges, should be periodically lubricated with white lithium base grease to prevent sticking or jamming.

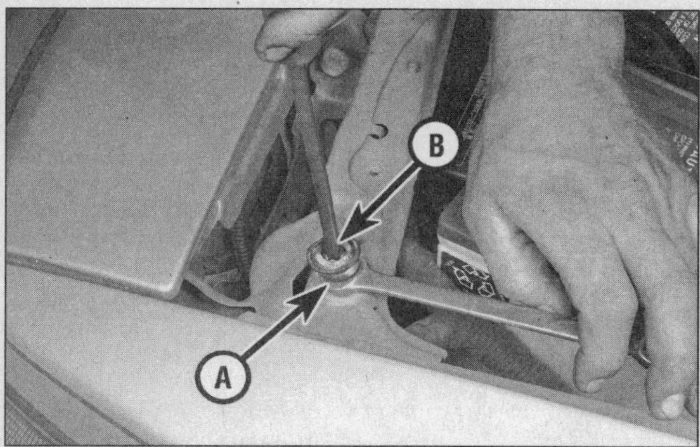

9.11 To adjust the hood bumpers, loosen the locking nut (A) and prevent it from tightening while adjusting the screw (B)

10 Door trim panel - removal and installation

Refer to illustrations 10.2a, 10.2b, 10.2c, 10.3, 10.4 and 10.9

1 Disconnect the negative cable from the battery. **Caution:** *If the stereo in your vehicle is equipped with an anti-theft system, refer to the*

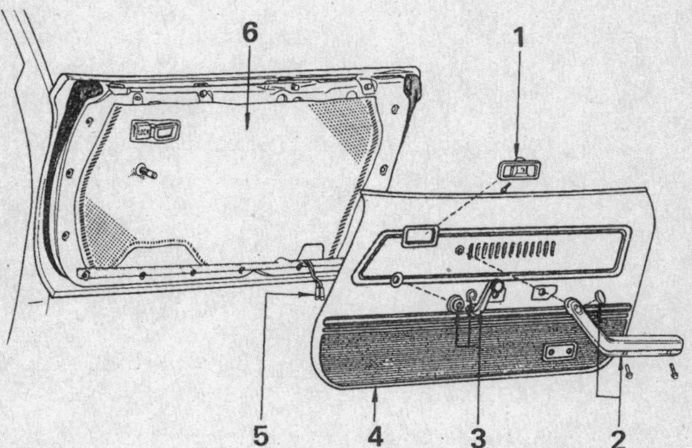

10.2a Door trim panel components on 1979 through 1981 models

1 *Inside handle cover*
2 *Arm rest*
3 *Window crank and snap ring*
4 *Trim panel*
5 *Courtesy light wiring connectors*
6 *Service hole weather-proof cover*

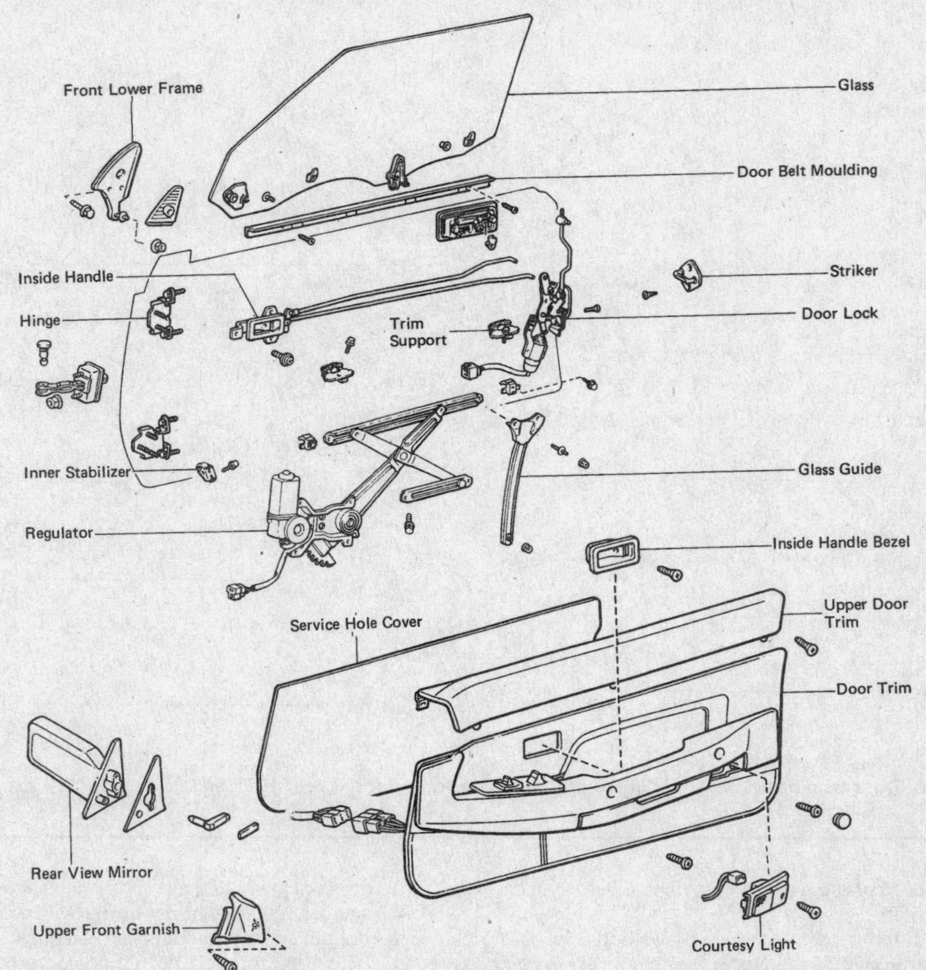

10.2b Door trim panel, window glass and regulator components on 1982 through 1986 models - exploded view

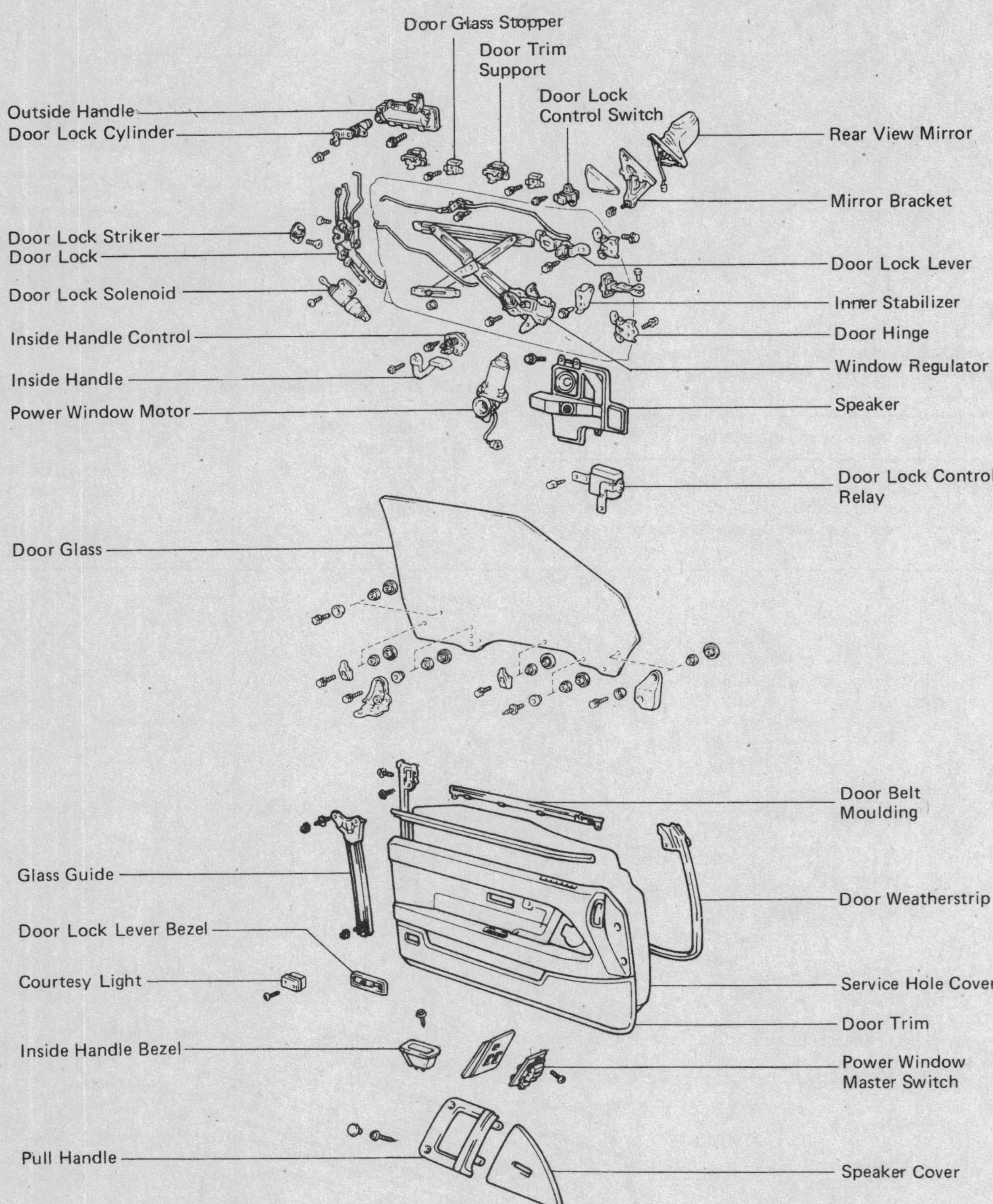

10.2c Door trim panel, window glass and regulator components on 1987 and later models - exploded view

information on page 0-15 at the front of this manual before detaching the cable.

2 Remove any door trim panel retaining screws and door pull/armrest assemblies **(see illustrations)**. **Note:** *Some armrest assemblies use a plug to cover the access hole for the screws. Pry the plugs out with a small screwdriver.*

3 On manual window regulator equipped models, remove the window crank by working a small piece of wire or a small, angled pick into the snap-ring **(see illustration)**. On power regulator models, pry off the control switch assembly and unplug it.

4 On 1982 through 1986 models, remove the retaining screw and withdraw the courtesy light and lens from the trim panel **(see illustration)**.

5 Insert a large putty knife or a thin pry bar between the trim panel

10.3 **Removing the window crank snap ring on an early model (1979 through 1981)**

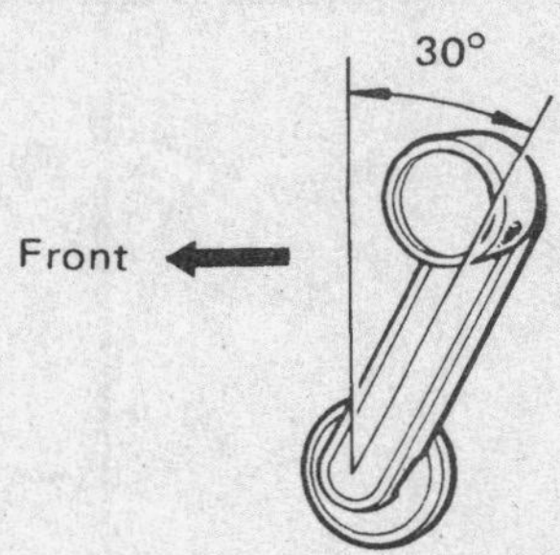

10.9 **Correct installed position of the window crank handle with the window fully raised**

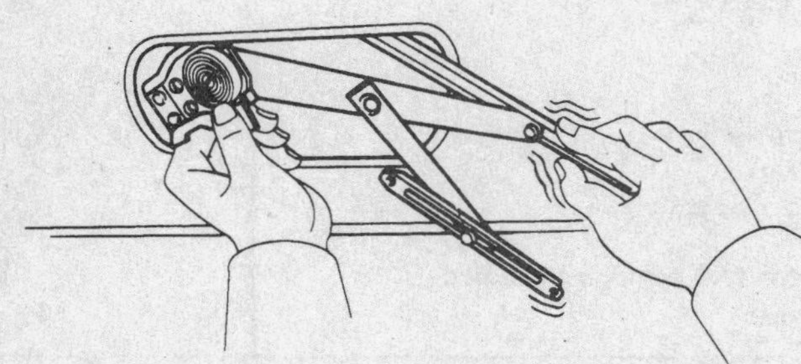

11.7 **After taking out the regulator mounting bolts, withdraw the regulator and the power window motor through the service hole**

and the door and disengage the retaining clips, working around the outer edge until the panel is free of the door.

6 Once all of the clips are disengaged, detach the trim panel, lift it away, unplug any electrical connectors and remove the trim panel from the vehicle.

7 For access to the inner door, peel back the plastic service hole cover, taking care not to tear it. To install, place the service hole cover in position and press it in place.

8 Prior to installation of the door panel, make sure to reinstall any clips in the panel which may have come out during the removal procedure and remain in the door itself.

9 Plug in any electrical connectors and place the panel in position in the door. Press the door panel into place until the clips are seated and install any retaining screws and armrest/door pulls. Install the manual regulator window crank **(see illustration)** or power switch assembly.

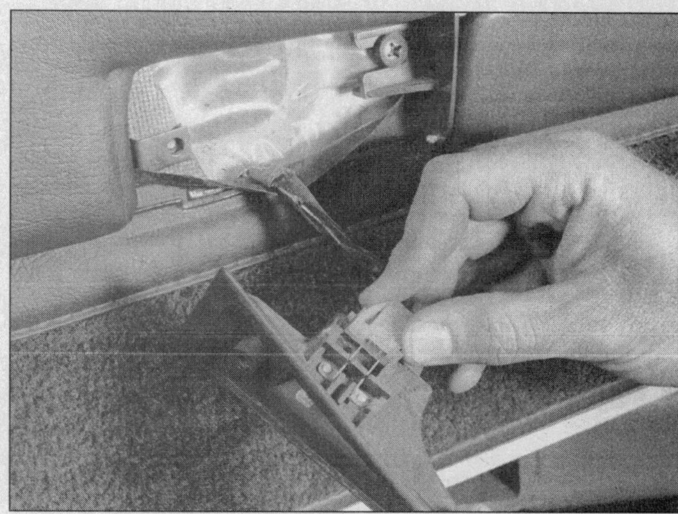

10.4 **Press down the tab on the connector and pull the connector free from the door courtesy light**

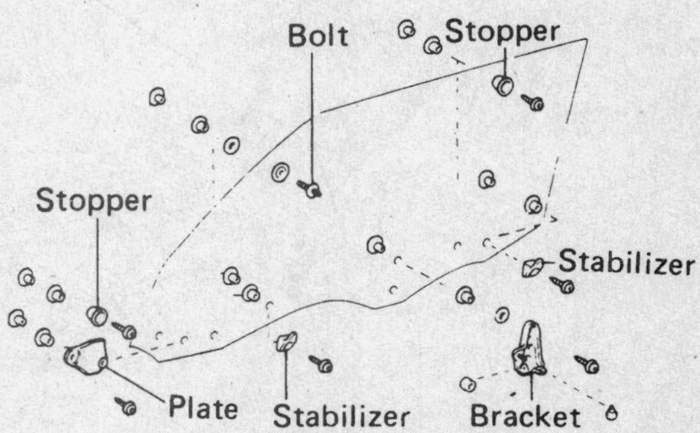

11.5 **Typical door glass and fittings - exploded view**

11 Door window glass and regulator - removal, installation and adjustment

Refer to illustrations 11.5, 11.7, 11.8, 11.11a and 11.11b

Removal

1 Remove the door trim panel and service hole cover (Section 10).

2 Lower the window glass. **Note:** *On 1982 through 1986 models, remove the upper door trim panel* **(see illustration 10.2b)**.

3 Remove the door mirror (see Section 22).

4 Scribe or paint marks on the two window-to-glass channel nuts and remove them.

5 Take out the retaining screws and remove the upper stopper, the trim support and the inner stabilizer **(see illustration)**.

6 Remove the window glass by tilting it to detach the glass from the glass channel studs and then sliding the glass up and out of the door.

7 If necessary, remove the regulator retaining bolts and then slide the regulator out of the opening in the door **(see illustration)**.

Installation

8 Before installing the regulator and the glass, coat the sliding surfaces of the regulator and the spring and gears with multi-purpose

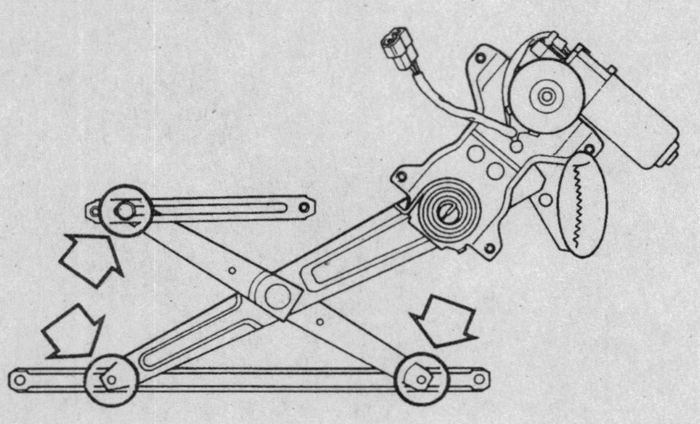

11.8 Before installing the regulator, apply multi-purpose grease to the areas indicated

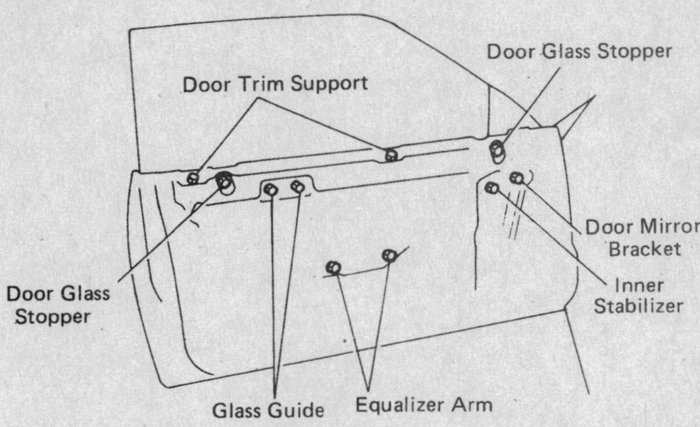

11.11a Door glass adjustment diagram for 1982 through 1986 models

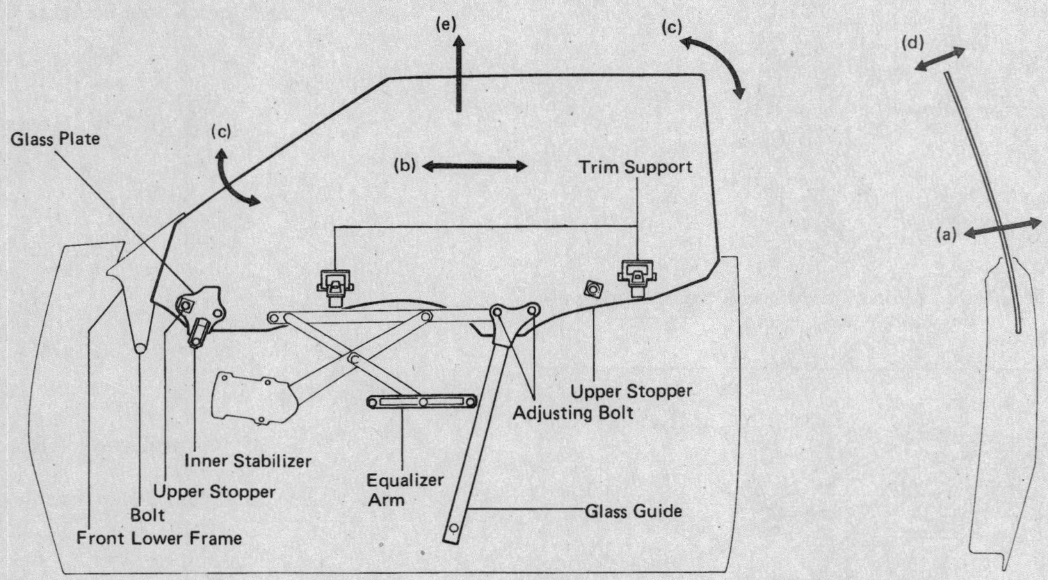

11.11b Door glass adjustment bolt locations for 1987 through 1992 models

grease **(see illustration)**.

9 Installation is the reverse of removal. When installing the belt molding, tap it down carefully by hand.

10 Before installing the trim panel, check the door glass for satisfactory operation and if necessary adjust it as follows:

Adjustment

11 Prior to making any adjustments, first check that the door to body alignment and installed position is satisfactory. Check the glass-to-belt molding contact. If necessary adjust by repositioning the trim supports as required (a) **(see illustrations)**.

12 Move the glass backwards and forwards and if necessary, adjust the position of the upper glass guide tip (b).

13 The tilt angle of the glass can be adjusted by repositioning the equalizer (c).

14 The upper glass contact can be adjusted by setting the two glass guide tip adjuster bolts as required (d).

15 Move the front and rear upper stoppers as required to adjust the upper position of the glass (e).

16 When completely raised, the roller of the inner stabilizer should make light contact with the glass.

12 Door lock, lock cylinder and handle - removal, installation and adjustment

1 Remove the door trim panel and service hole cover (see Section 10).

2 Remove the door window glass (see Section 11).

Door lock

Refer to illustrations 12.3, 12.4 and 12.6

3 Reach in through the door service hole and disconnect the control link from the lock **(see illustration)**.

4 Remove the door lock retaining screws from inside of the door **(see illustration)**. Remove the door lock and (if equipped) solenoid.

5 Installation is the reverse of removal.

6 When connecting the outside door handle control link to the lock on 1982 through 1986 models, raise the link 0.020 to 0.039 inch (0.5 to 1.0 mm) and insert the pin into the lock hole by turning the adjuster **(see illustration)**.

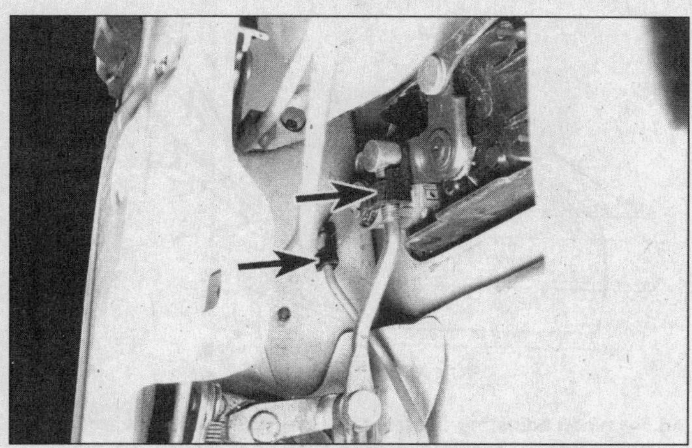

12.3 Pop off the nylon clips (arrows), which secure the connecting rods to the handle and lock cylinder, then disconnect the rods (1982 through 1986 models shown)

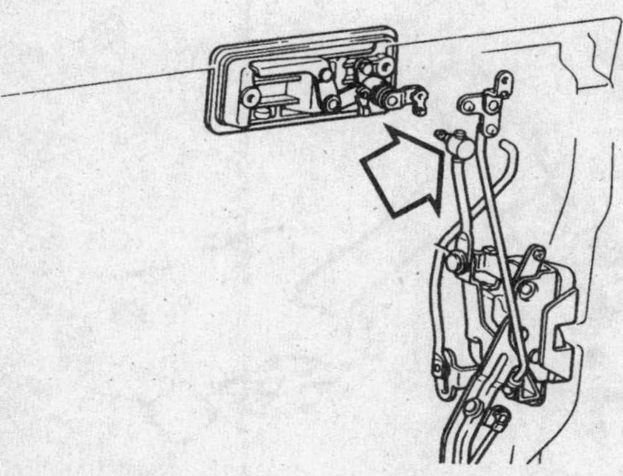

12.6 Lift the outside door handle, then fit the pin into the hole by turning the adjuster (arrow)

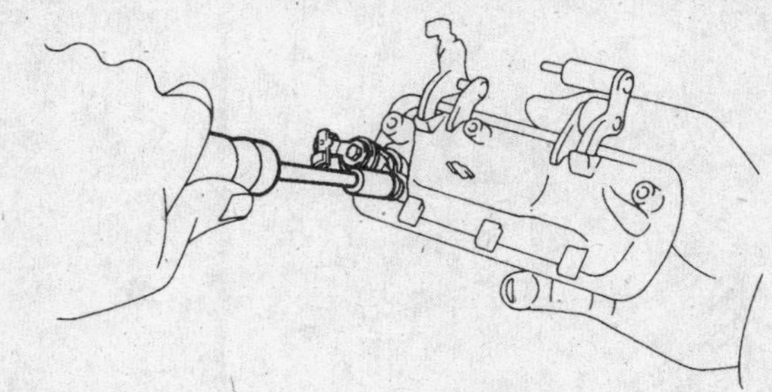

12.8b Remove the bolt to separate the lock cylinder from the handle (1987 through 1992 model shown)

Lock cylinder

Refer to illustrations 12.8a and 12.8b

7 Disconnect the control link and electrical connector (if equipped) from the lock cylinder.

8 Remove the bolt that retains the lock cylinder to the lock **(see illustrations)**.

9 Installation is the reverse of removal.

Handle

10 Remove the retaining screw(s).

11 Rotate the handle away and detach it from the door.

12 Installation is the reverse of removal.

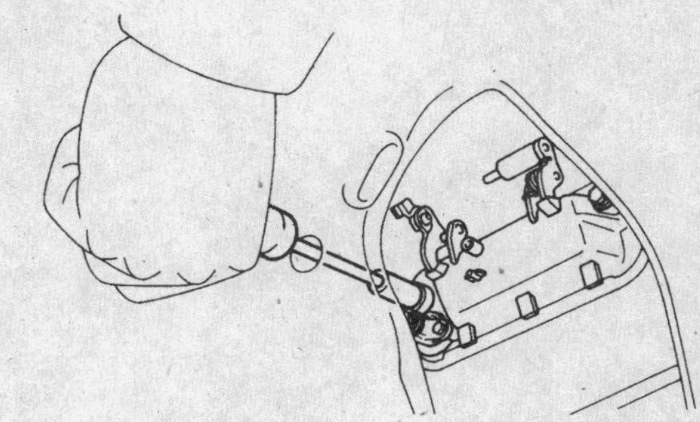

12.4 Remove the bolts from the inside of the door (1987 through 1992 models shown)

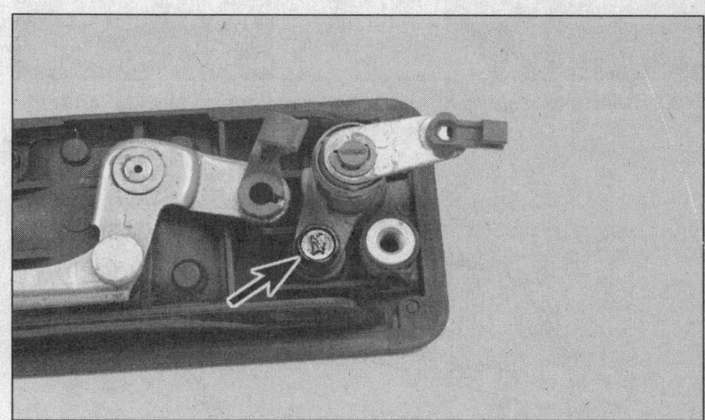

12.8a Remove the bolt (arrow) to separate the lock cylinder from the handle (1982 through 1987 model shown)

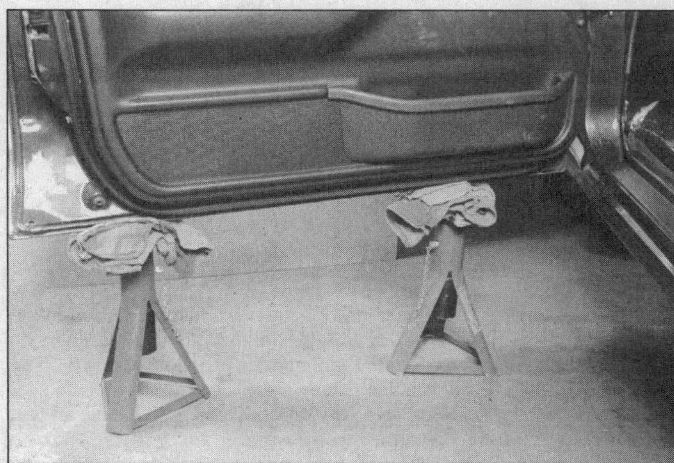

13.2 Use two jackstands padded with rags (to protect the paint) to support the door during the removal and installation procedures

13 Door - removal, installation and adjustment

Refer to illustrations 13.2, 13.3, 13.5a, 13.5b and 13.5c

1 Remove the door trim panel. Disconnect any electrical connectors and push them through the door opening so they won't interfere with door removal.

2 Either place a jack or stand under the door or have an assistant on hand to support it when the hinge bolts are removed **(see illustration)**. **Note:** *If a jack or stand is being used, place a rag between it and the door to protect the door's painted surfaces.*

13.3 Before loosening or removing them, scribe or paint around the door bolts

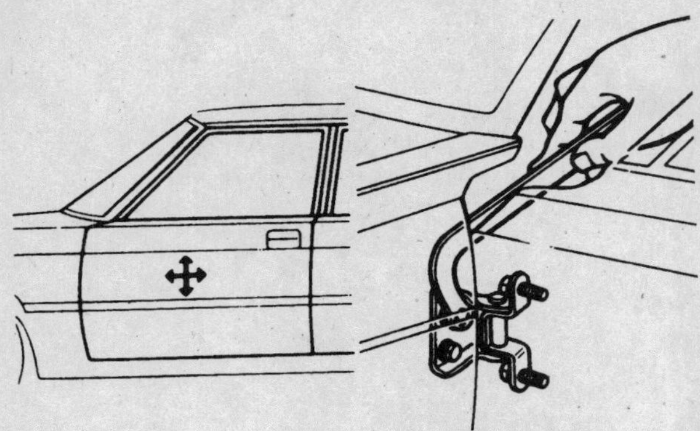

13.5a When adjusting the front door forward or backward, up or down, a special cranked wrench such as this one (SST-09812-00010, available from your dealer) or equivalent will make the job easier

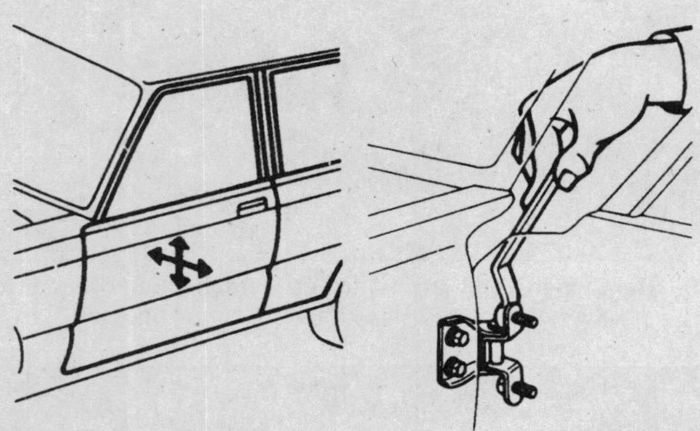

13.5b Adjust the front door up and down or in and out after loosening the hinge to door bolts with a box end wrench

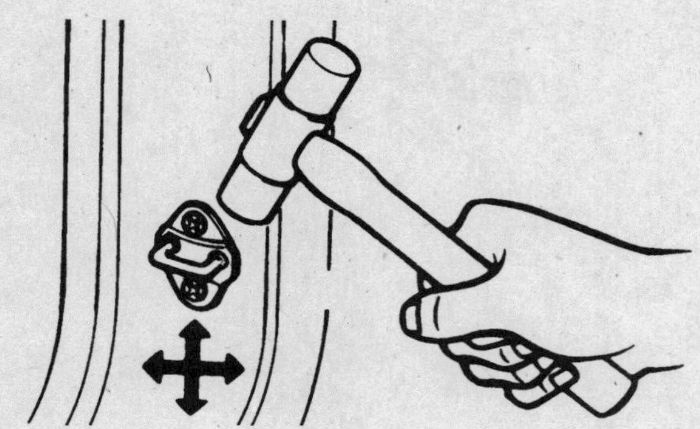

13.5c Adjust the door lock striker by loosening the retaining screws and tapping the striker in the desired direction

3 Scribe around the door bolts **(see illustration)**.

4 Remove the hinge-to-door bolts and carefully lift off the door. Installation is the reverse of removal.

5 Following installation of the door, check that it is in proper alignment and adjust it if necessary as follows:

a) Up-and-down and forward-and-backward adjustments are made by loosening the hinge-to-body bolts and moving the door, as necessary. A special cranked tool may be required to reach some of the bolts (see illustrations).
b) The door lock striker can also be adjusted both up-and-down and sideways to provide a positive engagement with the locking mechanism. This is done by loosening the screws and moving the striker, as necessary **(see illustration)**.

14 Front bumper - removal and installation

Refer to illustration 14.4

Warning: *On airbag-equipped models, always disconnect the negative battery cable when working in the vicinity of the impact sensors to avoid the possibility of accidental deployment of the airbag, which could cause personal injury.*

Caution: *If the stereo in your vehicle is equipped with an anti-theft system, refer to the information on page 0-15 at the front of this manual before detaching the cable.*

1 Remove the radiator grille (see Section 16).

2 Remove the turn signal/fog light (see Chapter 12).

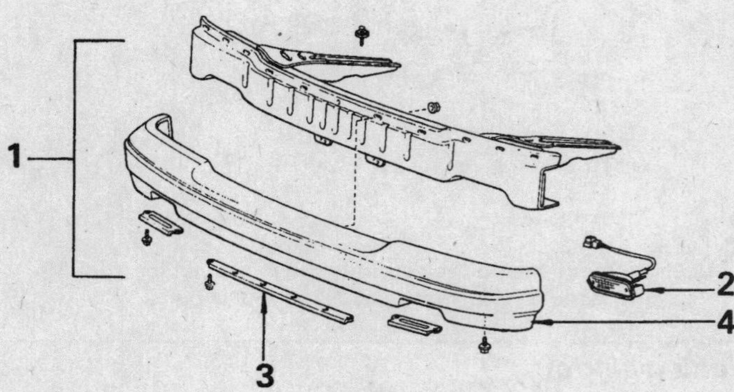

14.4 Front bumper components on 1979 through 1981 models

1 *Bumper assembly*
2 *Turn signal light*
3 *Retainer*
4 *Bumper absorber*

3 Take off the bumper cover fasteners.

4 To remove the bumper, take out the mounting bolts **(see illustration)** located on either end of the bumper.

5 Installation is the reverse of the removal procedure.

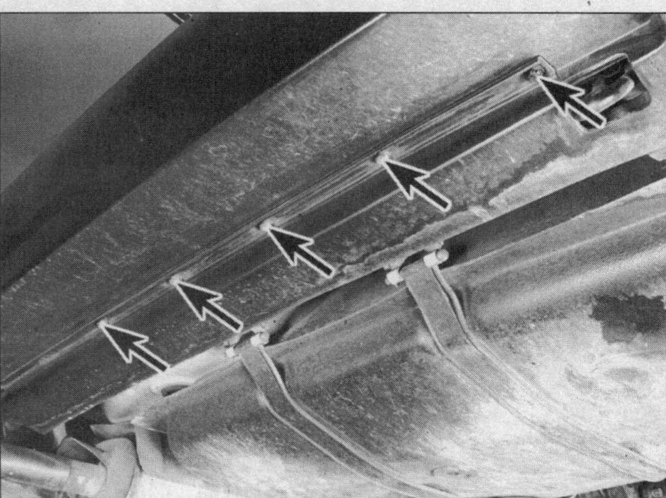

15.2 Remove the securing bolts and the reinforcement bar along the bottom of the bumper (1983 model shown)

17.8 To adjust the door lock, loosen the retaining bolts and move the lock in the desired direction and then tighten the bolts

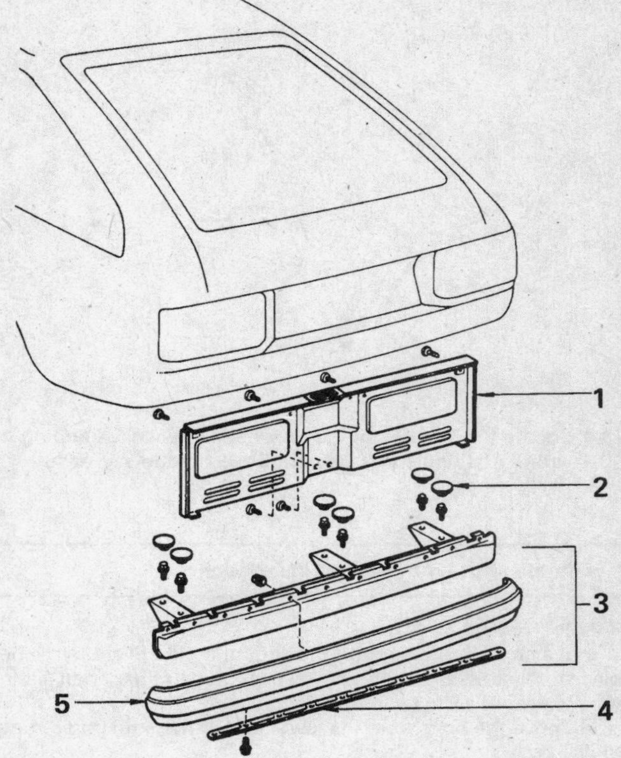

15.3 Rear bumper components on the 1979 through 1981 models

1 *Rear trim cover*
2 *Bolt hole plugs*
3 *Bumper assembly*
4 *Retainer*
5 *Bumper absorber*

15 Rear bumper - removal and installation

Refer to illustrations 15.2 and 15.3

1 From inside the luggage compartment, remove the left, right and rear trim panels by lifting them out.
2 Take off the bumper cover by removing the fasteners. There is a row of bolts inside the luggage compartment behind the panels that were removed and a row along the bottom of the bumper **(see illustration)**.
3 Lift up the carpet in the luggage compartment, pry out the plastic bolt caps and remove the bumper bolts **(see illustration)**.
4 Installation is the reverse of removal.

16 Grille - removal and installation

Warning: *On airbag-equipped models, always disconnect the negative battery cable when working in the vicinity of the impact sensors to avoid the possibility of accidental deployment of the airbag, which could cause personal injury.*
Caution: *If the stereo in your vehicle is equipped with an anti-theft system, refer to the information on page 0-15 at the front of this manual before detaching the cable.*

1 Remove the single retaining screw located in the middle of the grille.
2 Compress the four recessed securing clips at the ends of the grille to release them and detach the grille.
3 Installation is the reverse of removal.

17 Liftgate - removal, installation and adjustment

Refer to illustration 17.8

Removal and installation

1 Open the liftgate and cover the upper body area around the opening with pads or cloths to protect the painted surfaces when the liftgate is removed.
2 Disconnect any cables, hoses or electrical connectors which would interfere with removal of the liftgate.
3 Paint or scribe around the mounting bolts.
4 While an assistant supports the liftgate, detach the support struts (see Section 18).
5 Remove the hinge bolts and detach the liftgate from the vehicle.
6 Installation is the reverse of removal.

Adjustment

7 After installation, close the liftgate and check that the door is in proper alignment with the surrounding panels. Adjustments to the liftgate are made by moving the position of the hinge bolts in their slots. To adjust, loosen the hinge bolts and reposition them either side-to-side or fore-and-aft the desired amount and retighten the bolts.
8 The engagement of the liftgate can be adjusted by loosening the door lock bolts, repositioning the door lock and tightening the bolts **(see illustration)**. See Section 19 for additional information.

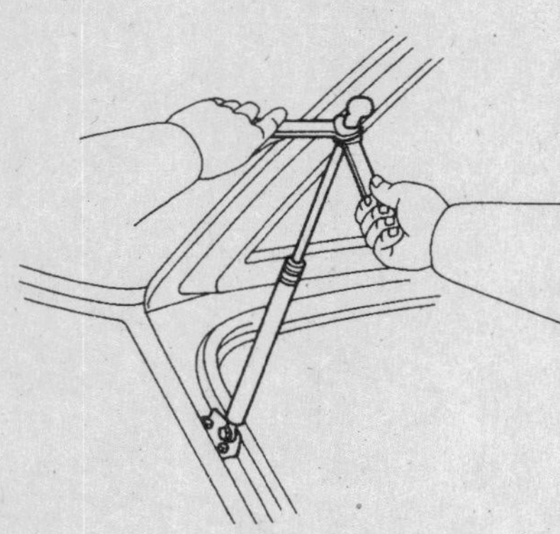

18.4 Locate the two hex nuts and loosen one while keeping the other stationary (1987 through 1992 models shown)

18 Liftgate strut - removal and installation

Refer to illustration 18.4

1 Have an assistant support the liftgate while the struts are being replaced. If necessary, use a special hood support bar or an alternate device to keep the liftgate from falling.

2 Remove the bolts from the lower end of the strut and remove it from the body.

3 If necessary, remove the inner side garnish from the liftgate.

4 On 1987 and later models, use two open end wrenches and disconnect the upper end of the strut **(see illustration)**. Remove the strut from the liftgate.

5 Installation is the reverse of removal.

19 Liftgate lock cylinder - removal, installation and adjustment

Refer to illustrations 19.1, 19.2 and 19.3

1 Remove the liftgate lower trim panel by removing the four retaining screws, then work around the edges of the panel pulling the panel free from the pop fasteners. Lower the panel and disconnect the liftgate light wire harness **(see illustration)**.

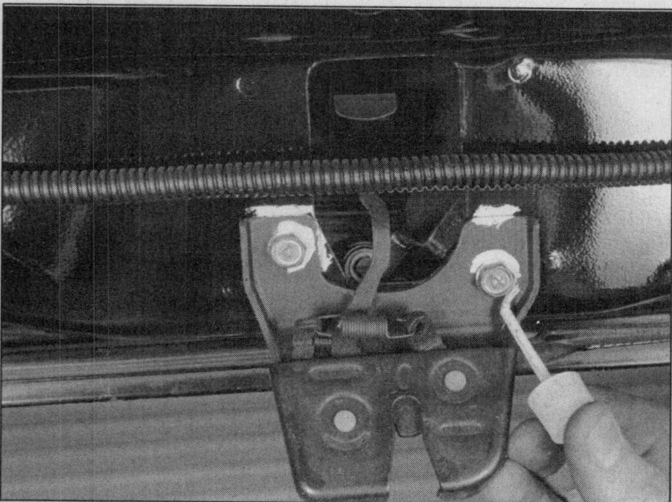

19.2 Paint alignment marks around the latch and the bolt heads, then remove the bolts (1983 model shown)

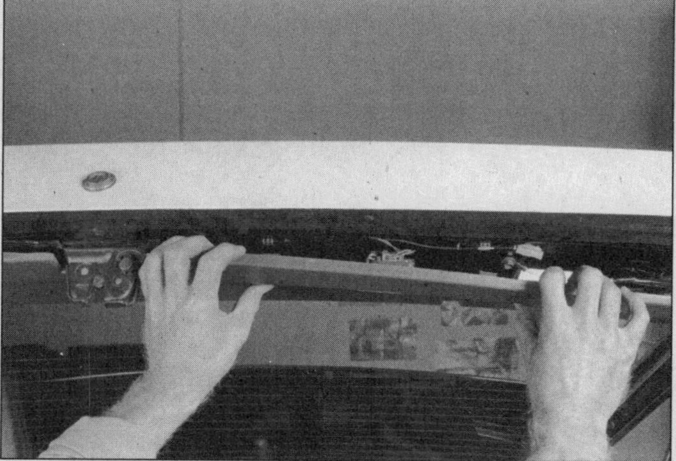

19.1 Work around the edges of the panel, pulling down as you go, to separate the panel from the pop fasteners (1983 model shown)

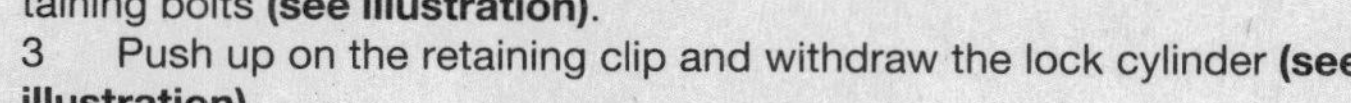

2 Make alignment marks around the latch, then remove the two retaining bolts **(see illustration)**.

3 Push up on the retaining clip and withdraw the lock cylinder **(see illustration)**.

4 Installation is the reverse of removal.

20 Interior trim components - removal and installation

Refer to illustrations 20.5a, 20.5b, 20.5c, 20.7, 20.11 and 20.12

Console

1 Disconnect the cable from the negative battery terminal. **Caution:** *If the stereo in your vehicle is equipped with an anti-theft system, refer to the information on page 0-15 at the front of this manual before detaching the cable.*

2 Remove the shift lever knob (manual transmission only).

3 Lift out the ashtray.

4 Remove the five heater control knobs. Remove the retaining screws and detach the heater control panel.

5 Take out the console screws, unplug the electrical connectors

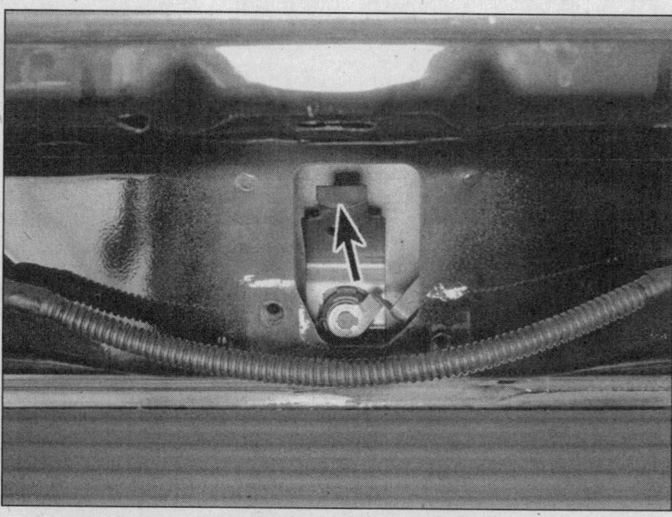

19.3 Push up on the retaining clip and remove it (arrow) - the liftgate lock cylinder can then be removed from the outside of the liftgate (1983 model shown)

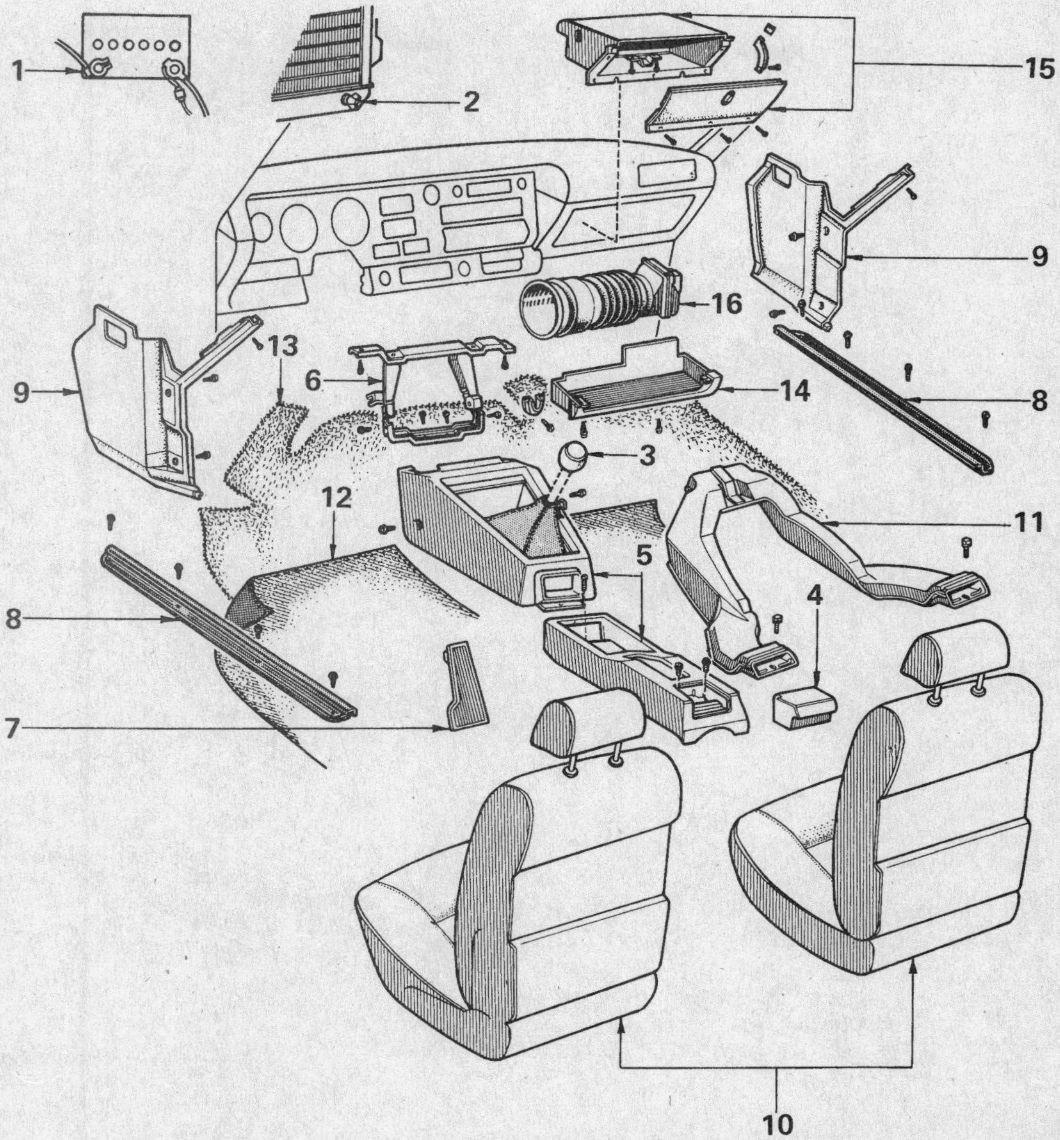

20.5a Interior trim components on 1979 through 1981 models

1. *Negative battery cable*
2. *Radiator drain*
3. *Gearshift lever knob*
4. *Rear ashtray*
5. *Console*
6. *Console support bracket*
7. *Accelerator pedal*
8. *Scarf plates*
9. *Cowl side trim*
10. *Front seats*
11. *Heater rear duct*
12. *Front carpet*
13. *Sound deadener*
14. *Dashboard under tray*
15. *Glove compartment*
16. *Blower duct*

and lift out the console assembly **(see illustrations)**.

6 Remove the upper panel screws, unplug any electrical connectors and detach the console upper panel.

Glove compartment, dash panel and under cover

7 Take out the under cover securing screws and lower the panel **(see illustration)**.

8 Detach the glove compartment door check arm by removing the two retaining screws. Remove the glove compartment door. Remove the door lock striker, lower the glove compartment, disconnect the two connectors and detach the glove compartment.

Instrument cluster finish panel and steering column cover

9 Take off the steering wheel (see Chapter 10).

10 Remove the retaining screws located at the bottom of the steering column cover and take off the cover.

11 Using a screwdriver, pry the driver's side speaker panel loose and remove it **(see illustration)**.

12 Remove the retaining screws and the clamps and detach the driver's side under cover **(see illustration)**.

13 Remove the retaining screws, unplug the connectors and remove the driver's side lower finish panel.

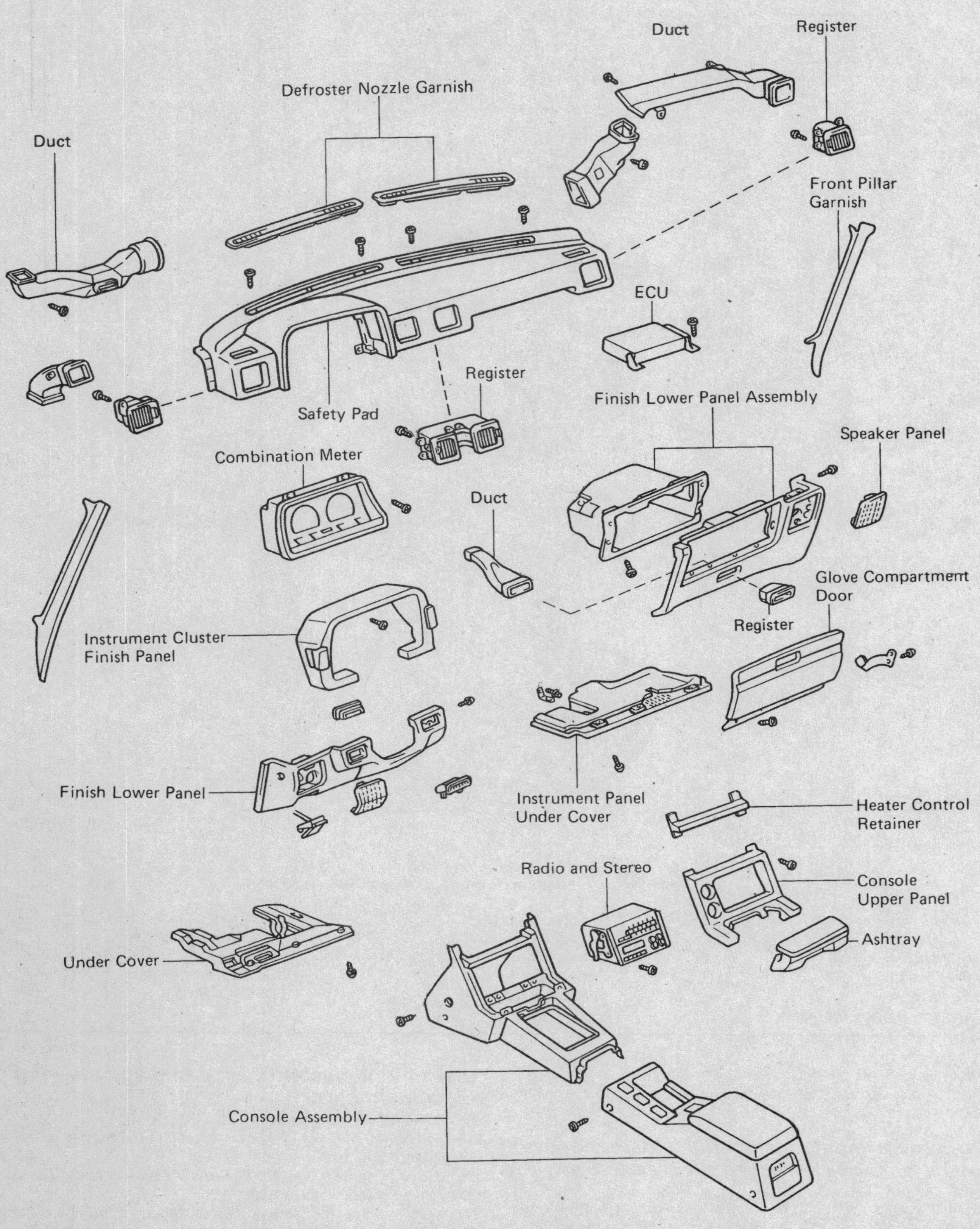

20.5b Dash and console components on 1982 through 1986 models

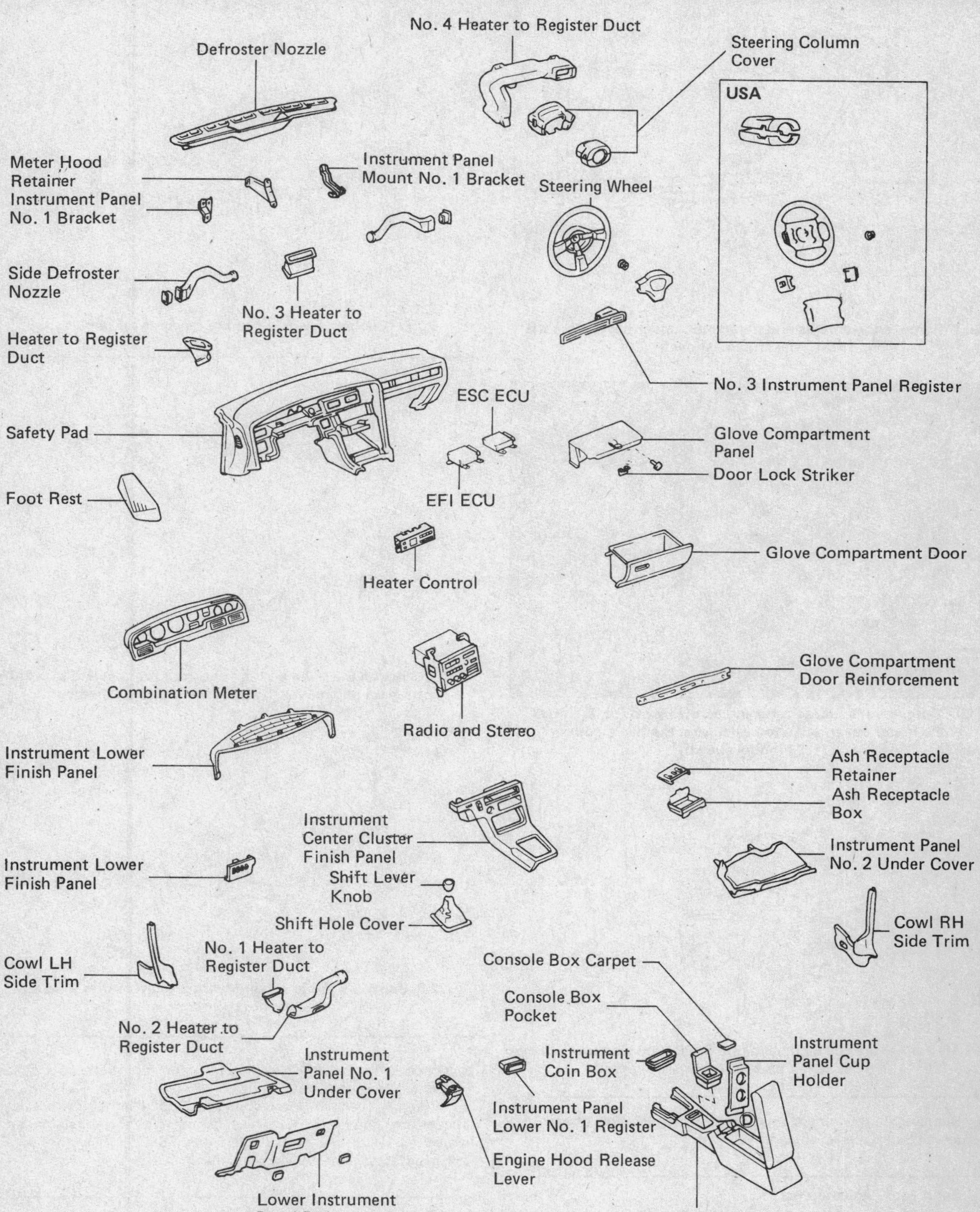

20.5c Dash and console components on 1987 and later models

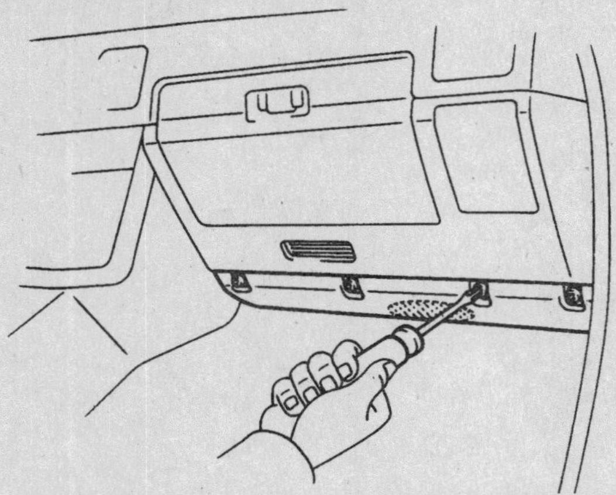

20.7 Remove the screws and detach the under cover from the dash (1983 model shown)

20.12 Remove the three retaining screws (arrows), then pull the under cover down to free it from the two clamps (1983 model shown)

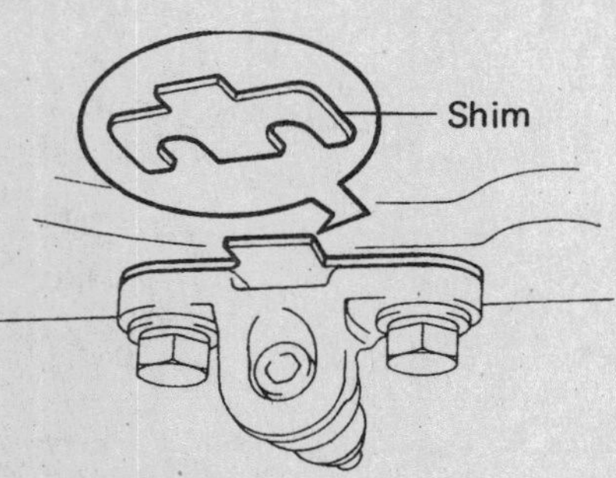

21.3 Use either a 0.039 inch shim or a 0.079-inch shim available at a dealer parts department

14 Remove the retaining screws, unplug the electrical connectors and detach the cluster finish panel.

21 Sport roof - adjustment

Refer to illustrations 21.2 and 21.3

1 Remove the sport roof headliner and the rear roof headliner.

2 Adjust the sport roof bracket and rear bracket **(see illustration)**

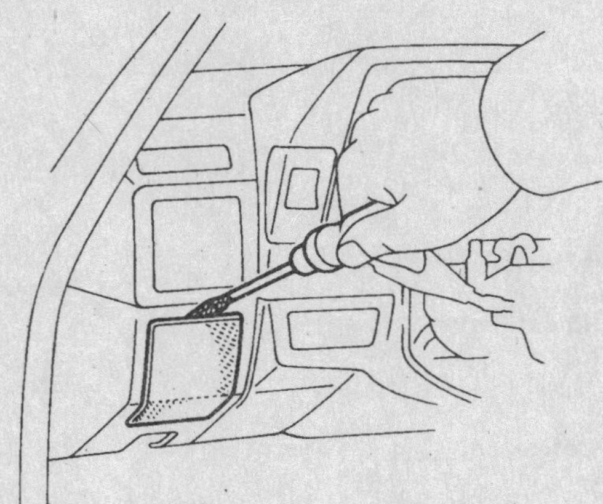

20.11 Use a screwdriver to pry the speaker panel loose

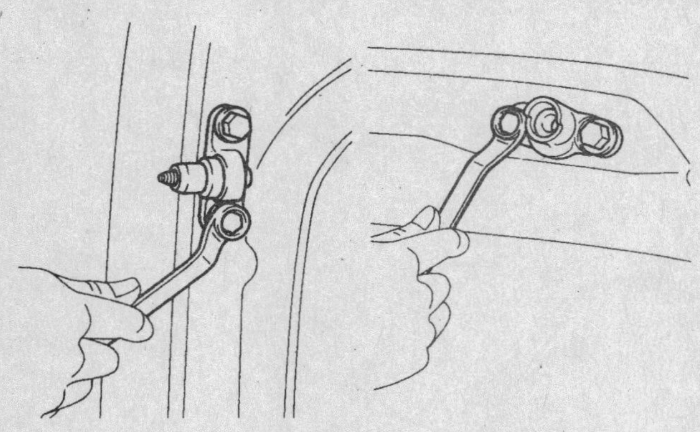

21.2 Loosen the bolts on the sport roof bracket and the rear bracket and move them into the correct adjustment

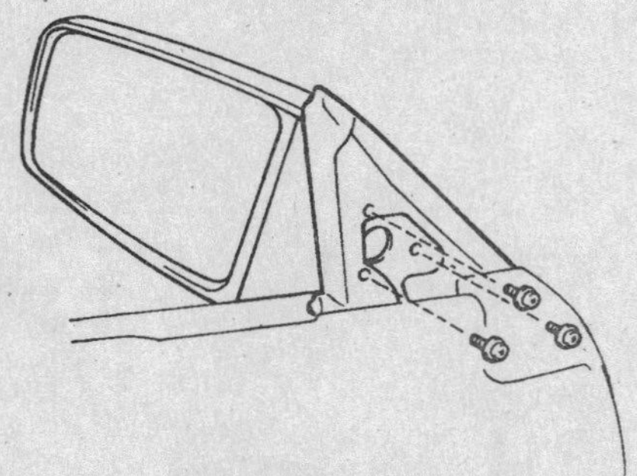

22.3 Use a magnetic screwdriver tip to avoid dropping any screws into the door panel

by loosening the bolts and moving the sport roof to the front or rear. Tighten the bracket bolts.

3 Carefully check the level of the sport roof and the rear roof panel. If necessary, change the level by substituting a different shim **(see illustration)**.

4 Installation is the reverse of removal.

22 Outside mirror - removal and installation

Refer to illustration 22.3

1 Use a screwdriver to pry off the trim cover.

23.1 Headlight door emergency operation crank assembly (1983 model shown)

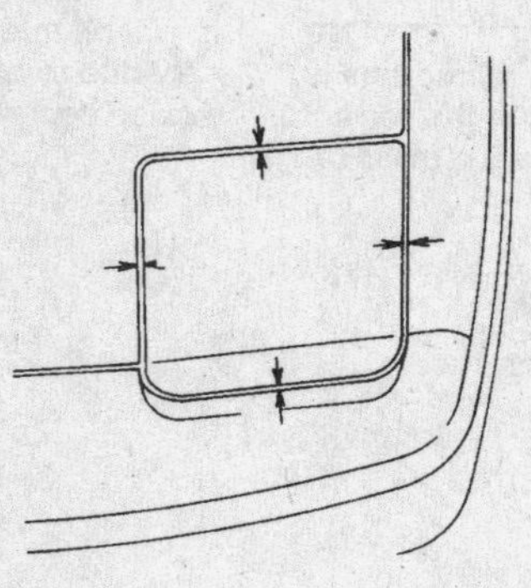

24.1a The headlight door can be moved in all directions evenly

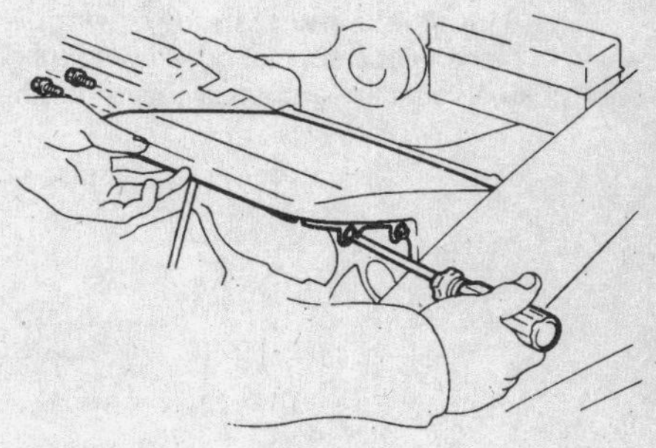

24.1b Location of the set screws on the headlight door

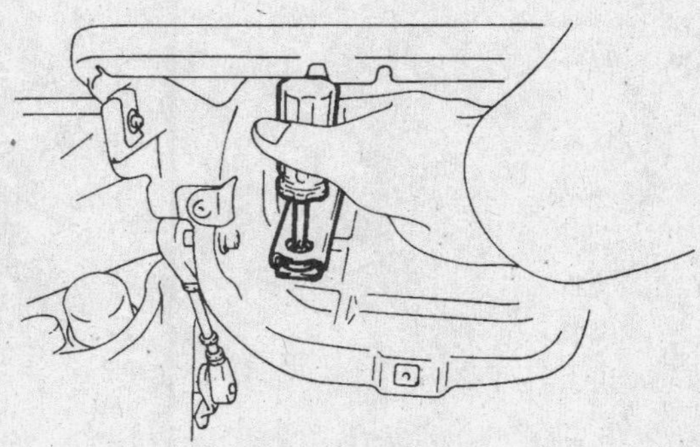

24.2a Use a Phillips screwdriver and a back-up wrench to adjust the stopper lock-nut and bolt

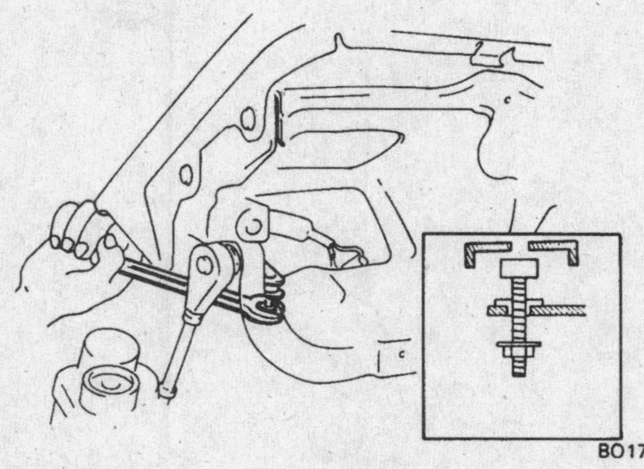

24.3 Turn the stopper until it touches the headlight bracket and then an extra 4/5 of a turn counterclockwise

2 On power mirrors unplug the electrical connector.
3 Remove the three retaining screws and lift off the mirror **(see illustration)**.
4 Installation is the reverse of removal.

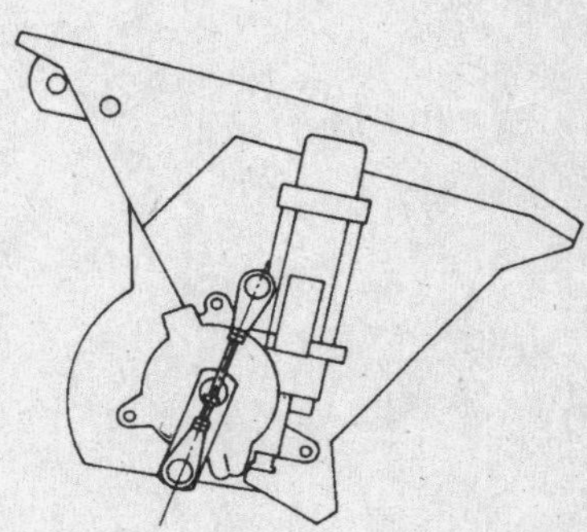

24.2b Align the rod and the motor link

23 Headlight door - emergency (manual) operation

Refer to illustration 23.1

If the headlight door fails to open when the headlights are turned on, a manually operated crank assembly, located next to the headlight assembly, can be used to raise the door **(see illustration)**.

24 Headlight door - adjustment

Refer to illustrations 24.1a, 24.1b, 24.2a, 24.2b and 24.3

Warning: *Before adjusting each section, raise or lower the headlight with the headlight control switch. When adjusting each section, be sure to remove the headlight fuse (see Chapter 12 for the location) from the fuse panel.*

1 Adjust the headlight door to the front, rear or side-to-side by loosening the set screws **(see illustrations)**.

2 Adjust the slant of the door:
First, loosen the stopper lock nut (see illustration)
Second, lower the headlight
Third, turn the manual operation knob (see Section 23) to align the rod and motor link (see illustration).
Fourth, change the length of the rod to adjust the headlight slant

3 Adjust the headlight stopper position:
First, raise the headlight
Second, turn the stopper counterclockwise (see illustration) until it touches the headlight bracket, then turn it another 4/5 of a turn counterclockwise
Third, tighten the stopper lock nut

11

25 Windshield and stationary glass - replacement

The windshield and stationary window glass on all models is sealed in place with a special butyl compound. Removal of the sealant requires an electric knife specially made for the operation and glass replacement is a complex operation.

In view of this, it is not recommended that stationary glass removal be attempted by the home mechanic. If replacement is necessary due to breakage or leakage, the work should be left to a dealer service department or a qualified glass or body shop.

Chapter 12 Chassis electrical system

Contents

1 General information

The electrical system is a 12-volt, negative ground type. Power for the lights and all electrical accessories is supplied by a lead/acid-type battery which is charged by the alternator.

This Chapter covers repair and service procedures for the various electrical components not associated with the engine. Information on the battery, alternator, distributor and starter motor can be found in Chapter 5.

It should be noted that when portions of the electrical system are serviced, the cable should be disconnected from the negative battery terminal to prevent electrical shorts and/or fires. **Caution:** *If the stereo in your vehicle is equipped with an anti-theft system, refer to the information on page 0-15 at the front of this manual before detaching the cable.*

2 Electrical troubleshooting - general information

A typical electrical circuit consists of an electrical component, any switches, relays, motors, fuses, fusible links or circuit breakers related to that component and the electrical wiring and connectors that link the component to both the battery and the chassis. To help you pinpoint an electrical circuit problem, wiring diagrams are included at the end of this book.

Before tackling any troublesome electrical circuit, first study the appropriate wiring diagrams to get a complete understanding of what makes up that individual circuit. Trouble spots, for instance, can often be narrowed down by noting if other components related to the circuit are operating properly. If several components or circuits fail at one time, chances are the problem is in a fuse or ground connection, because several circuits are often routed through the same fuse and ground connections.

Electrical problems usually stem from simple causes, such as loose or corroded connections, a blown fuse, a melted fusible link or a bad relay. Visually inspect the condition of all fuses, wires and connections in a problem circuit before troubleshooting it.

If testing instruments are going to be utilized, use the diagrams to plan ahead of time where you will make the necessary connections in order to accurately pinpoint the trouble spot.

The basic tools needed for electrical troubleshooting include a circuit tester or voltmeter (a 12-volt bulb with a set of test leads can also be used), a continuity tester, which includes a bulb, battery and set of test leads, and a jumper wire, preferably with a circuit breaker incorporated, which can be used to bypass electrical components. Before attempting to locate a problem with test instruments, use the wiring diagram(s) to decide where to make the connections.

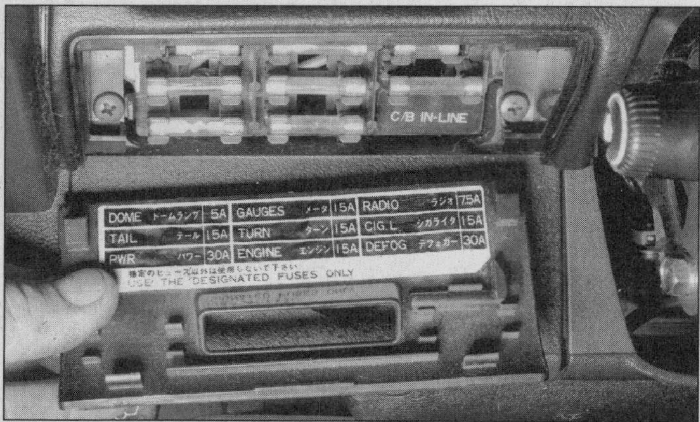

3.1a The fuses are located under a panel on the left side of the dash on 1982 through 1986 models

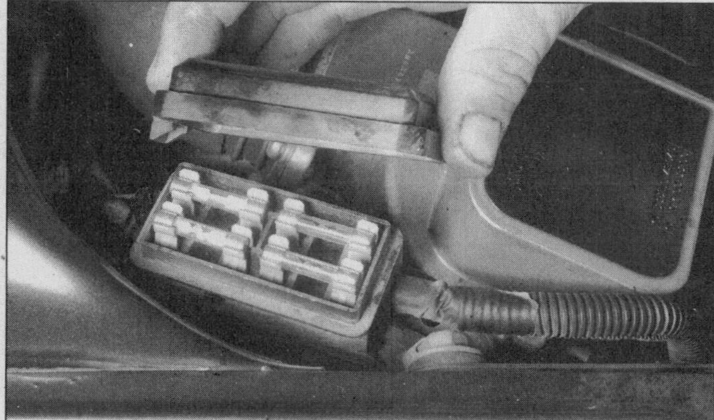

3.1b Also on 1982 through 1986 models, there is a specialty fuse panel located next to the air flow meter

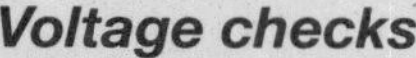

Voltage checks

Voltage checks should be performed if a circuit is not functioning properly. Connect one lead of a circuit tester to either the negative battery terminal or a known good ground. Connect the other lead to an electrical connector in the circuit being tested, preferably nearest to the battery or fuse. If the bulb of the tester lights, voltage is present, which means that the part of the circuit between the connector and the battery is problem free. Continue checking the rest of the circuit in the same fashion. When you reach a point at which no voltage is present, the problem lies between that point and the last test point with voltage. Most of the time the problem can be traced to a loose connection. **Note:** *Keep in mind that some circuits receive voltage only when the ignition key is in the Accessory or Run position.*

Finding a short

One method of finding shorts in a circuit is to remove the fuse and connect a test light or voltmeter in its place to the fuse terminals. There should be no voltage present in the circuit. Move the electrical wiring harness from side to side while watching the test light. If the bulb goes on, there is a short to ground somewhere in that area, probably where the insulation has rubbed through. The same test can be performed on each component in the circuit, even a switch.

Ground check

Perform a ground test to check whether a component is properly grounded. Disconnect the battery and connect one lead of a self-powered test light, known as a continuity tester, to a known good ground. **Caution:** *If the stereo in your vehicle is equipped with an anti-theft system, refer to the information on page 0-15 at the front of this manual before detaching the cable.*

Connect the other lead to the wire or ground connection being tested. If the bulb goes on, the ground is good. If the bulb does not go on, the ground is not good.

Continuity check

A continuity check is done to determine if there are any breaks in a circuit - if it is passing electricity properly. With the circuit off (no power in the circuit), a self-powered continuity tester can be used to check the circuit. Connect the test leads to both ends of the circuit (or to the "power" end and a good ground), and if the test light comes on the circuit is passing current properly. If the light doesn't come on, there is a break somewhere in the circuit. The same procedure can be used to test a switch, by connecting the continuity tester to the power in and power out sides of the switch. With the switch turned On, the test light should come on.

Finding an open circuit

When diagnosing for possible open circuits, it is often difficult to locate them by sight because oxidation or terminal misalignment are hidden by the electrical connectors. Merely wiggling a connector on a sensor or in the electrical wiring harness may correct the open circuit condition. Remember this when an open circuit is indicated when troubleshooting a circuit. Intermittent problems may also be caused by oxidized or loose connections.

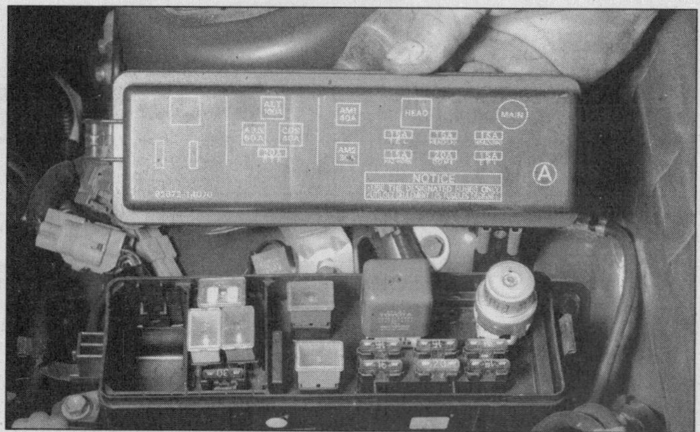

3.1c The fuse and relay panel is located under the hood

Electrical troubleshooting is simple if you keep in mind that all electrical circuits are basically electricity running from the battery, through the wires, switches, relays, fuses and fusible links to each electrical component (light bulb, motor, etc.) and to ground, from which it is passed back to the battery. Any electrical problem is an interruption in the flow of electricity to and from the battery.

3 Fuses - general information

Refer to illustrations 3.1a, 3.1b, 3.1c and 3.3

The electrical circuits of the vehicle are protected by a combination of fuses, circuit breakers and fusible links. The fuse blocks are located under left side of the dashboard, behind the driver's side kick panel, behind the passenger side kick panel and next to the battery in the engine compartment **(see illustrations)**.

Each of the fuses is designed to protect a specific circuit, and the various circuits are identified on the fuse panel itself.

Miniaturized fuses are employed in the fuse block. These compact fuses, with blade terminal design, allow fingertip removal and replacement. If an electrical component fails, always check the fuse first. A blown fuse is easily identified through the clear plastic body. Visually inspect the element for evidence of damage **(see illustration)**. If a continuity check is called for, the blade terminal tips are exposed in the fuse body.

Be sure to replace blown fuses with the correct type. Fuses of different ratings are physically interchangeable, but only fuses of the proper rating should be used. Replacing a fuse with one of a higher or

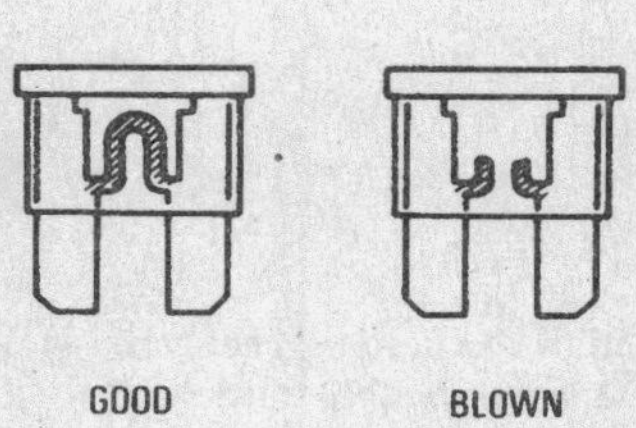

3.3 The fuses used on these models can be checked visually to determine if they are blown

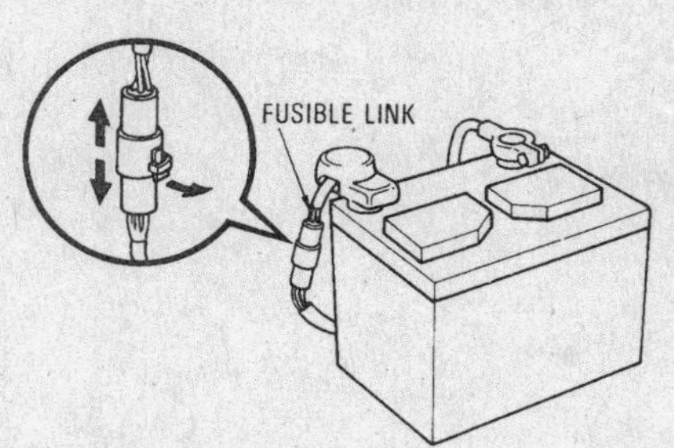

4.2 Fusible links can be checked visually to determine if they are melted

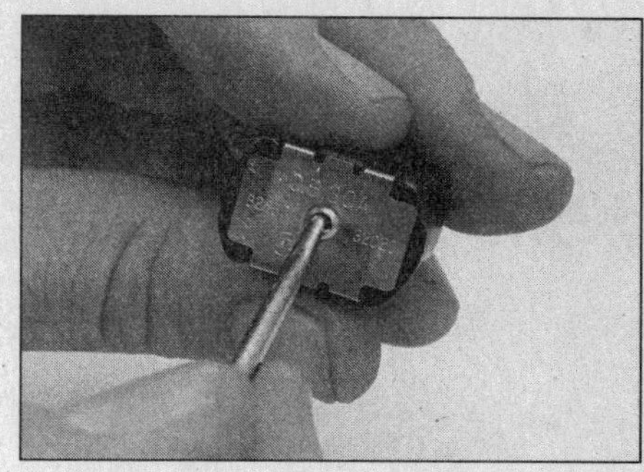

5.3 Insert a pin or paper clip into the circuit breaker reset hole and push in to reset it

lower value than specified is not recommended. Each electrical circuit needs a specific amount of protection. The amperage value of each fuse is molded into the fuse body.

If the replacement fuse immediately fails, don't replace it again until the cause of the problem is isolated and corrected. In most cases, this will be a short circuit in the electrical wiring caused by a broken or deteriorated wire.

4 Fusible links - general information

Refer to illustration 4.2

Some circuits are protected by fusible links. The links are used in circuits which are not ordinarily fused, such as the ignition circuit.

The fusible links on these models are similar to fuses in that they can be visually checked to determine if they are melted **(see illustration)**.

To replace a fusible link, first disconnect the negative cable from the battery. **Caution:** *If the stereo in your vehicle is equipped with an anti-theft system, refer to the information on page 0-15 at the front of this manual before detaching the cable.* Unplug the burned out link and replace it with a new one (available from your dealer). Always determine the cause for the overload which melted the fusible link before installing a new one.

5 Circuit breakers - general information

Refer to illustration 5.3

Note: *For the location of the circuit breakers, refer to illustrations 6.2a through 6.2j*

Circuit breakers protect components such as power windows, power door locks and headlights. Some circuit breakers are located in the fuse box.

Because on some models the circuit breaker resets itself automatically, an electrical overload in a circuit breaker protected system will cause the circuit to fail momentarily, then come back on. If the circuit does not come back on, check it immediately. Note, however, that some circuit breakers must be reset manually. Once the condition is corrected, the circuit breaker will resume its normal function.

To reset a manual circuit breaker, first disconnect the cable from the negative battery terminal. Remove the circuit breaker, insert a pin into the reset hole and push in **(see illustration)**. Reinstall the circuit breaker. **Caution:** *If the stereo in your vehicle is equipped with an anti-theft system, refer to the information on page 0-15 at the front of this manual before detaching the cable.*

6 Relays - general information

Refer to illustrations 6.2a through 6.2k

Several electrical accessories in the vehicle use relays to transmit the electrical signal to the component. If the relay is defective, that component will not operate properly.

The various relays are grouped together in several locations under the dash and in various locations around the chassis for convenience in the event of needed replacement **(see illustrations)**.

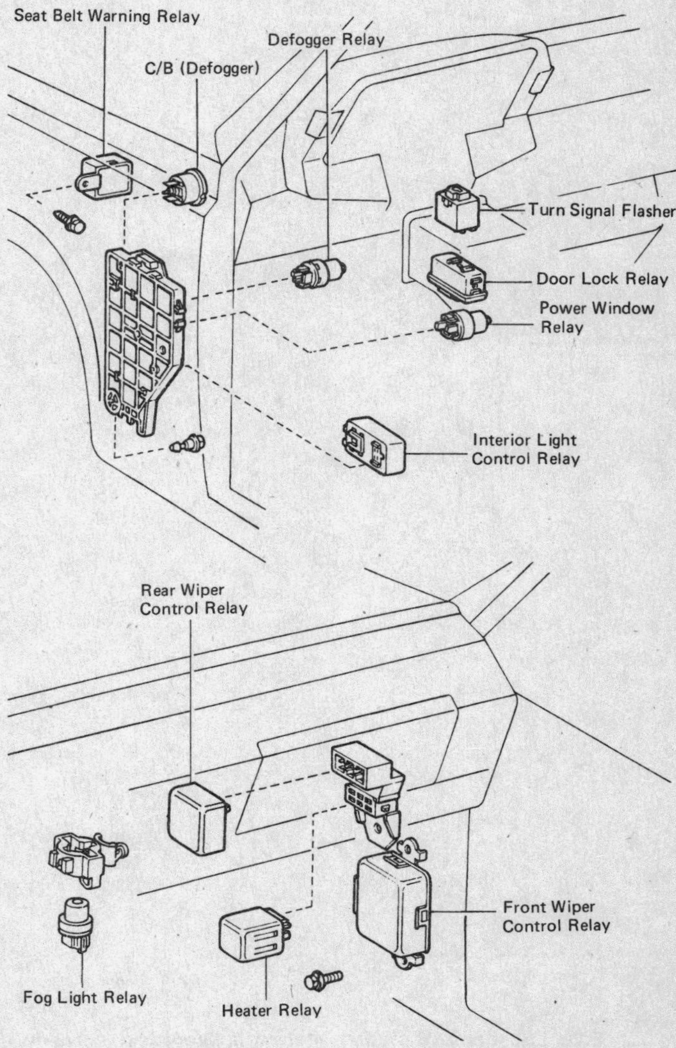

6.2a Location of the relays on 1982 through 1986 models

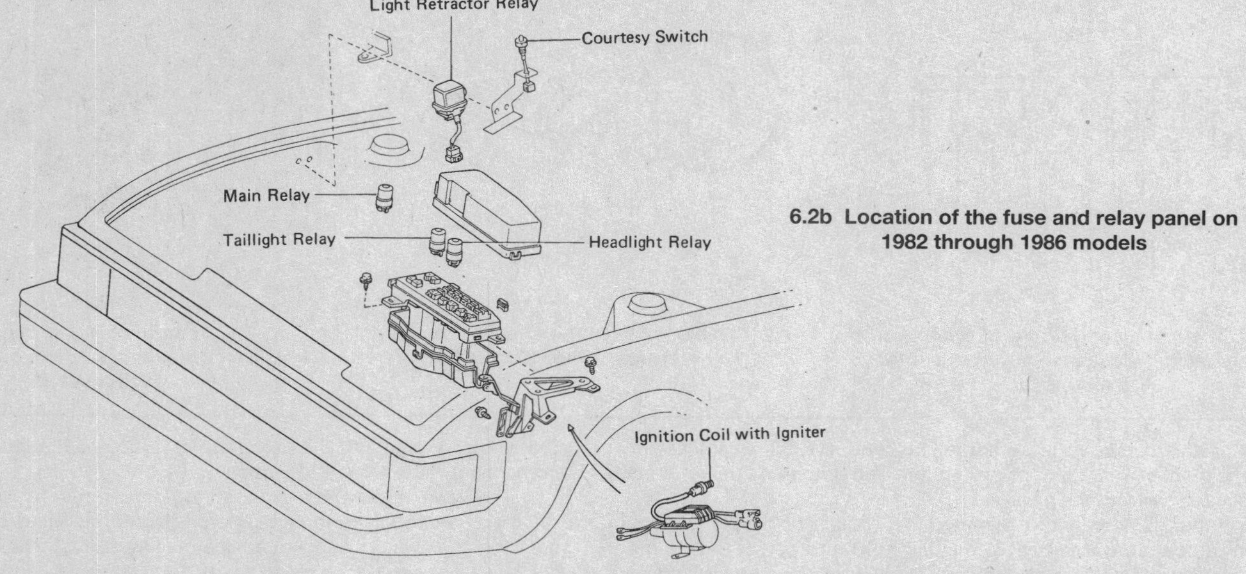

6.2b Location of the fuse and relay panel on 1982 through 1986 models

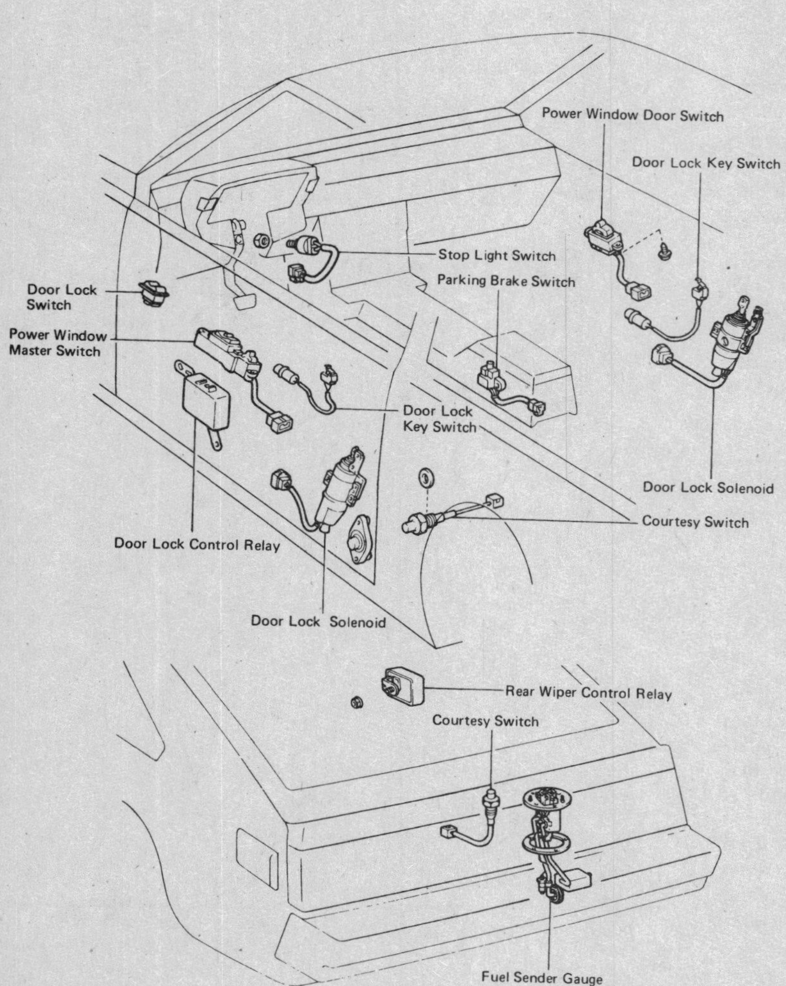

6.2c Location of various switches, flashers and relays on 1982 through 1986 models

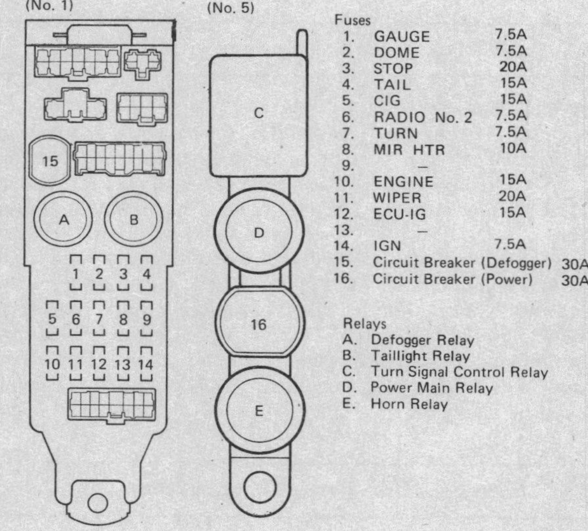

6.2d Fuse and relay designations for Junction Block No. 1 and Relay Block No. 5 on 1987 models only

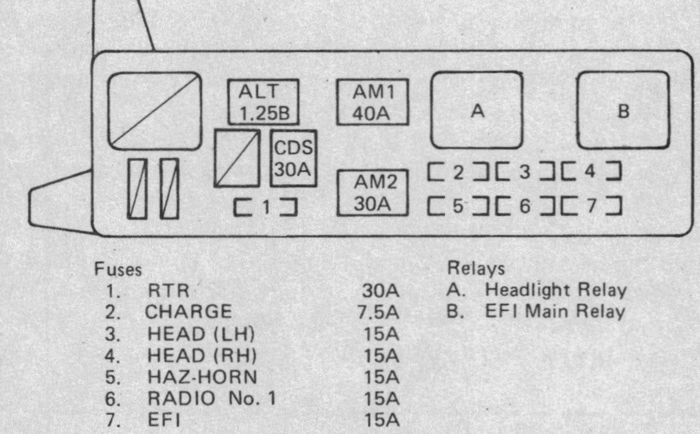

6.2e Fuse and relay designations for Junction Block No.2 on 1987 models only

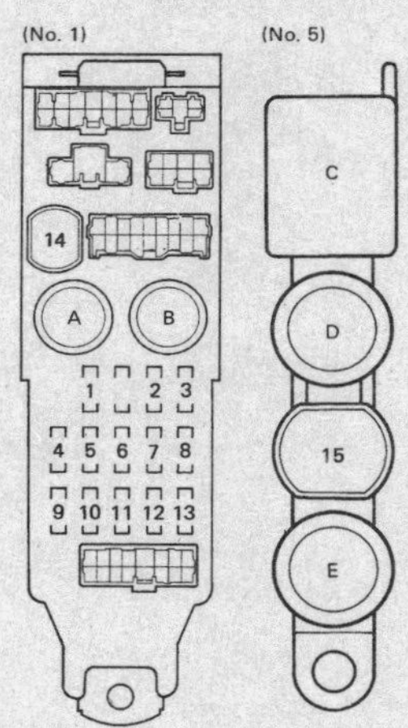

Fuses		
1.	GAUGE	7.5A
2.	STOP	20A
3.	TAIL	15A
4.	CIG	15A
5.	RADIO No. 2	7.5A
6.	TURN	7.5A
7.	MIR HTR	10A
8.	–	
9.	ENGINE	15A
10.	WIPER	20A
11.	ECU-IG	15A
12.	–	
13.	IGN	7.5A
14.	Circuit Breaker (Defogger)	30A
15.	Circuit Breaker (Power)	30A

Relays
A. Defogger Relay
B. Taillight Relay
C. Turn Signal Control Relay
D. Power Main Relay
E. Horn Relay

6.2f Fuse and relay designations for Junction Block No.1 and Relay Block No. 5 on 1988 models only

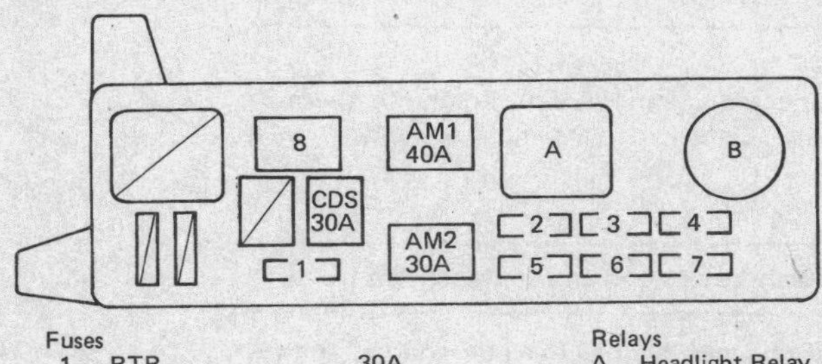

6.2g Fuse and relay designations for Junction Block No.2 on 1988 models only

Fuses		
1.	RTR	30A
2.	CHARGE	7.5A
3.	HEAD (LH)	15A
4.	HEAD (RH)	15A
5.	HAZ-HORN	15A
6.	RADIO No. 1	20A
7.	EFI	15A
8.	ALT	1.25B (7M-GE E/G)
	ALT	100A (7M-GTE E/G)

Relays
A. Headlight Relay
B. EFI Main Relay

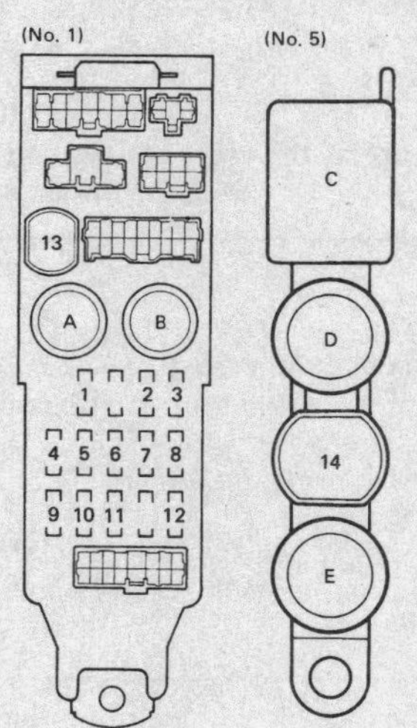

Fuses		
1.	GAUGE	7.5A
2.	STOP	20A
3.	TAIL	15A
4.	CIG	15A
5.	RADIO	7.5A
6.	TURN	7.5A
7.	MIR-HTR	10A
8.	–	
9.	ENGINE	15A
10.	WIPER	20A
11.	ECU-IG	15A
12.	IGN	7.5A
13.	Circuit Breaker (Defogger)	30A
14.	Circuit Breaker (Power)	30A

Relays
A. Defogger Relay
B. Taillight Relay
C. Turn Signal Control Relay
D. Power Main Relay
E. Horn Relay

6.2h Fuse and relay designations for Junction Block No.1 and Relay Block No. 5 on 1989 and later models

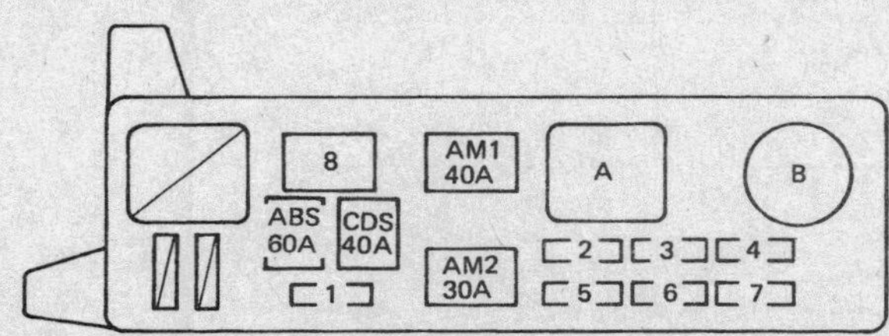

Fuses		
1.	RTR	30A
2.	–	
3.	HEAD (LH)	15A
4.	HEAD (RH)	15A
5.	HAZ-HORN	15A
6.	DOME	20A
7.	EFI	15A
8.	ALT (H-Fuse)	100A

Relays
A. Headlight Relay
B. EFI Main Relay

6.2i Fuse and relay designations for Junction Block No.2 on 1989 and later models

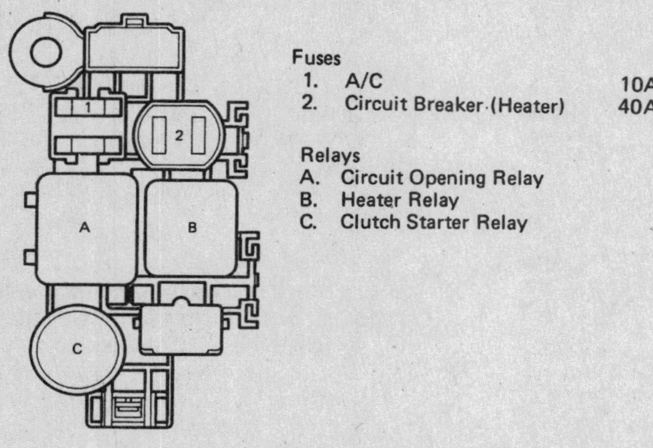

6.2j Fuse and relay designations for Junction Block No.4 on 1989 and later models

If a faulty relay is suspected, it can be removed and tested by a dealer or other qualified shop. Defective relays must be replaced as a unit.

7 Turn signal/hazard flashers - check and replacement

1 The turn signal/hazard flasher, a small canister shaped unit located under the dash or in Relay Block No.5 **(see illustrations 6.2a through 6.2k)**, flashes the turn signals.

2 When the flasher unit is functioning properly, and audible click can be heard during its operation. If the turn signals fail on one side or the other and the flasher unit does not make its characteristic clicking sound, a faulty turn signal bulb is indicated.

3 If both turn signals fail to blink, the problem may be due to a blown fuse, a faulty flasher unit, a broken switch or a loose or open connection. If a quick check of the fuse box indicates that the turn signal fuse has blown, check the electrical wiring for a short before installing a new fuse.

4 To replace the flasher, simply pull it out of the fuse block or electrical wiring harness.

5 Make sure that the replacement unit is identical to the original. Compare the old one to the new one before installing it.

6 Installation is the reverse of removal.

8 Ignition switch and lock cylinder - check and replacement

Warning: *On airbag-equipped models, always disconnect the negative battery cable when working in the vicinity of the instrument panel or steering column to avoid the possibility of accidental deployment of the airbag, which could cause personal injury.*

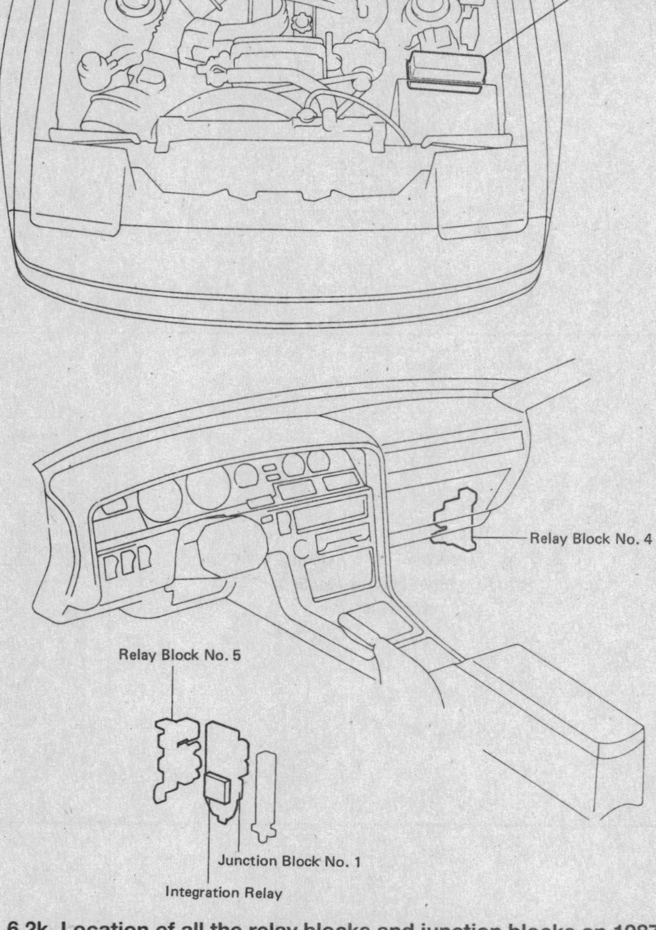

6.2k Location of all the relay blocks and junction blocks on 1987 and later models

Check

Refer to illustrations 8.3a, 8.3b, 8.3c and 8.3d

1 Disconnect the cable from the negative terminal of the battery. **Caution:** *If the stereo in your vehicle is equipped with an anti-theft system, refer to the information on page 0-15 at the front of this manual before detaching the cable.*

2 Locate the large plastic electrical connector adjacent to the turn signal/hazard flasher/dimmer switch electrical connector at the bottom

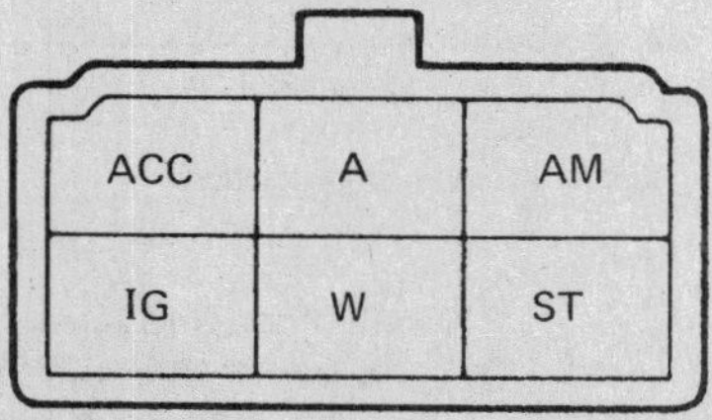

Switch position \ Terminal (Wire color)	AM (B-R)	ACC (L-R)	IG (B-Y)	ST (B-W)	W (G-W)	A (G-W or B)
LOCK					○	○
ACC	○	○			○	○
ON	○	○	○			
START	○		○	○		

8.3a Ignition switch and warning buzzer terminal locations with continuity chart (1982 through 1984 models)

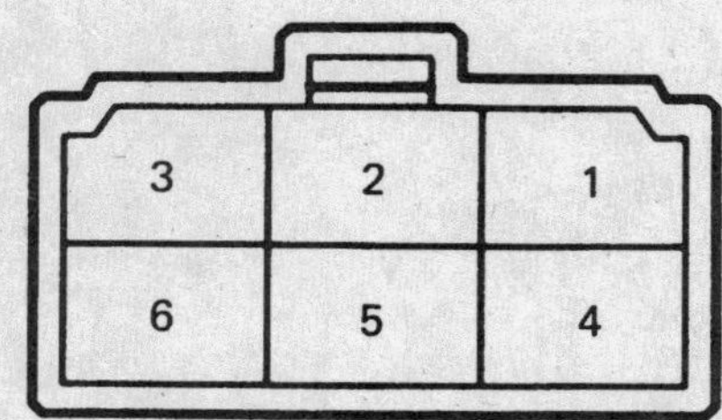

Continuity chart for 1985 models

Switch position \ Terminal	1	3	6	4	2	5
LOCK					○	○
ACC	○	○			○	○
ON	○	○	○			
START	○		○	○		

Continuity chart for 1986 models

Switch position \ Terminal		1	3	6	4	2	5
LOCK							
ACC		○	○				
ON		○	○	○			
START		○		○	○		
Warning	Normal						
	Push					○	○

8.3b Ignition switch and warning buzzer terminal locations with continuity chart (1985 and 1986 models)

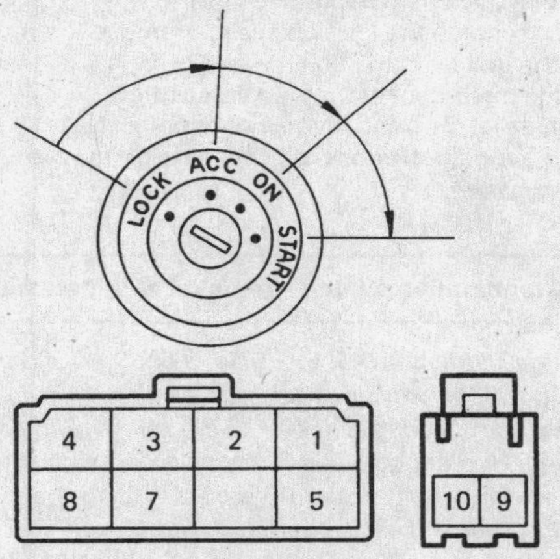

Switch Position \ Terminal		1	2	3	4	5	7	8	9	10
LOCK										
ACC				○	○					
ON			○	○	○		○	○		
START		○	○		○	○	○	○		
Warning	Normal									
	Push								○	○

8.3c Ignition switch and warning buzzer terminal locations with continuity chart (1987 through 1990 models)

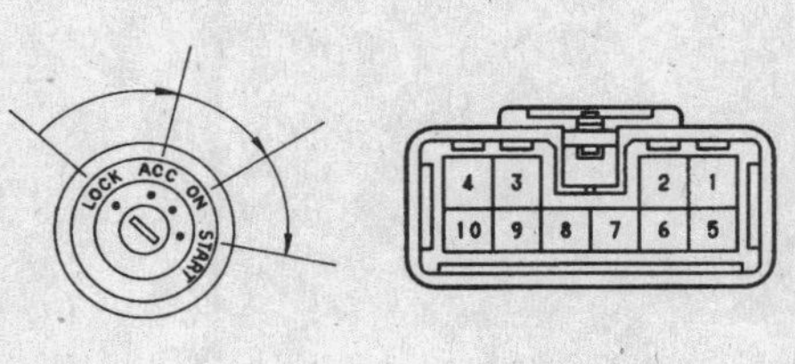

Switch position \ Terminal	2 IG1	3 ACC	4 AM1	6 ST2	7 ST1	9 IG2	10 AM2
LOCK							
ACC		○	○				
ON	○	○	○			○	○
START	○		○		○		
				○		○	○

8.3d Ignition switch and warning buzzer terminal locations with continuity chart (1991 and later models)

of the steering column assembly. Remove the steering column cover first **(see illustration 9.3)**.

3 To check the ignition switch and the warning buzzer, use an ohmmeter to check for continuity between the indicated terminals in the electrical connectors **(see illustrations)**. If the continuity of the ignition switch or the buzzer is not as specified, replace the ignition switch.

Replacement

Refer to illustrations 8.5, 8.7, 8.8 and 8.9

4 Disconnect the negative cable from the battery. **Caution:** *If the stereo in your vehicle is equipped with an anti-theft system, refer to the information on page 0-15 at the front of this manual before detaching the cable.*

12

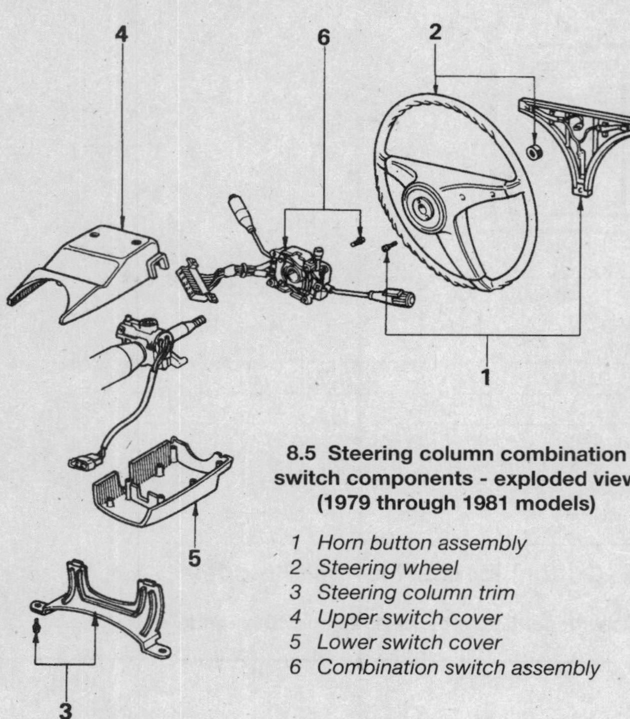

8.5 Steering column combination switch components - exploded view (1979 through 1981 models)

1. *Horn button assembly*
2. *Steering wheel*
3. *Steering column trim*
4. *Upper switch cover*
5. *Lower switch cover*
6. *Combination switch assembly*

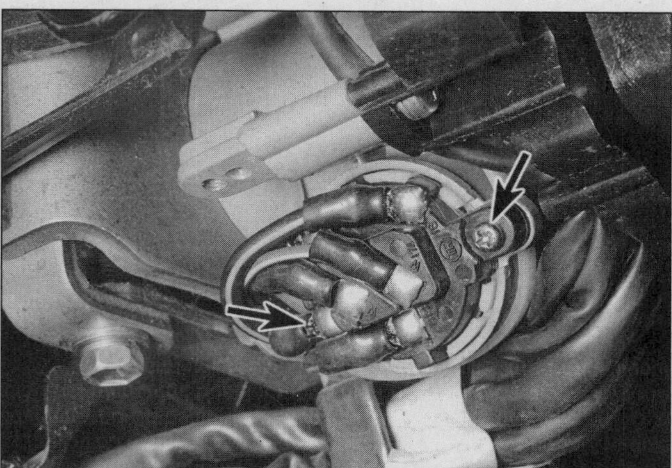

8.8 Take out the two ignition switch retaining screws (arrows), lower the switch and disconnect it from the multi-connector

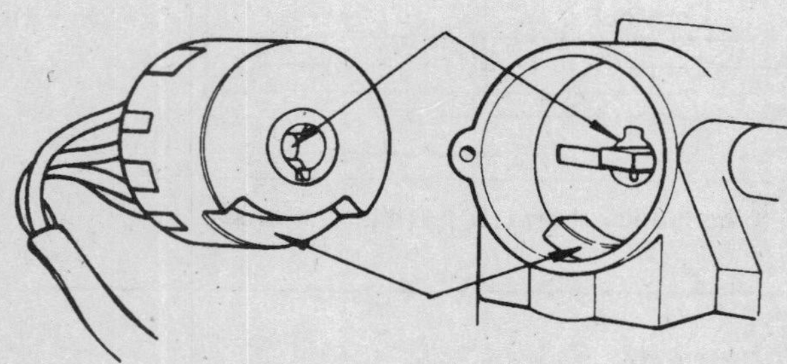

8.9 On early models (1979 through 1981 models), be sure to align the tab in the bracket with the recess in the ignition switch before installing it

8.7 Turn the key to the ACC position and depress the retaining pin while at the same time pulling out the lock cylinder

5 Remove the steering column cover **(see illustration)**.

6 Remove the two screws and detach the bezel along with the illumination bulb holder.

7 Set the key in the ACC position, then depress the inset retaining pin in the side of the unit and simultaneously pull on the key to withdraw the lock unit **(see illustration)**.

8 To remove the ignition switch, remove the retaining screws, withdraw the unit from the column and detach the electrical wiring harness from the multi-connector **(see illustration)**.

9 Installation is the reverse of removal. **Note:** *If the ignition switch is slotted* **(see illustration)***, be sure to align the tab with the recess in the ignition switch.*

9 Combination switch - removal and installation

Refer to illustrations 9.3, 9.4, 9.5a, 9.5b, 9.5c and 9.5d

Warning: *If the vehicle is equipped with an airbag DO NOT attempt to remove the steering wheel. Have it removed by a dealer service department or other qualified repair shop.*

1 Disconnect the negative cable at the battery. **Caution:** *If the stereo in your vehicle is equipped with an anti-theft system, refer to the information on page 0-15 at the front of this manual before detaching the cable.*

2 Remove the steering wheel (see Chapter 10).

3 Remove the lower finish panel **(see illustration)** and steering column cover.

9.3 Remove the lower steering column cover set screws

4 Remove the retaining screws **(see illustration)**.

5 Trace the electrical wiring harness down the steering column to the connector. Release the electrical wiring retainer clamp (if equipped), unplug the connector and slide the switch up off the column **(see illustrations)**.

6 Installation is the reverse of removal.

10 Steering column switches and relays - check and replacement

Warning: *On airbag-equipped models, always disconnect the negative battery cable when working in the vicinity of the instrument panel or steering column to avoid the possibility of accidental deployment of the airbag, which could cause personal injury.*

9.4 Remove the screws (arrows) that retain the combination switch to the steering column

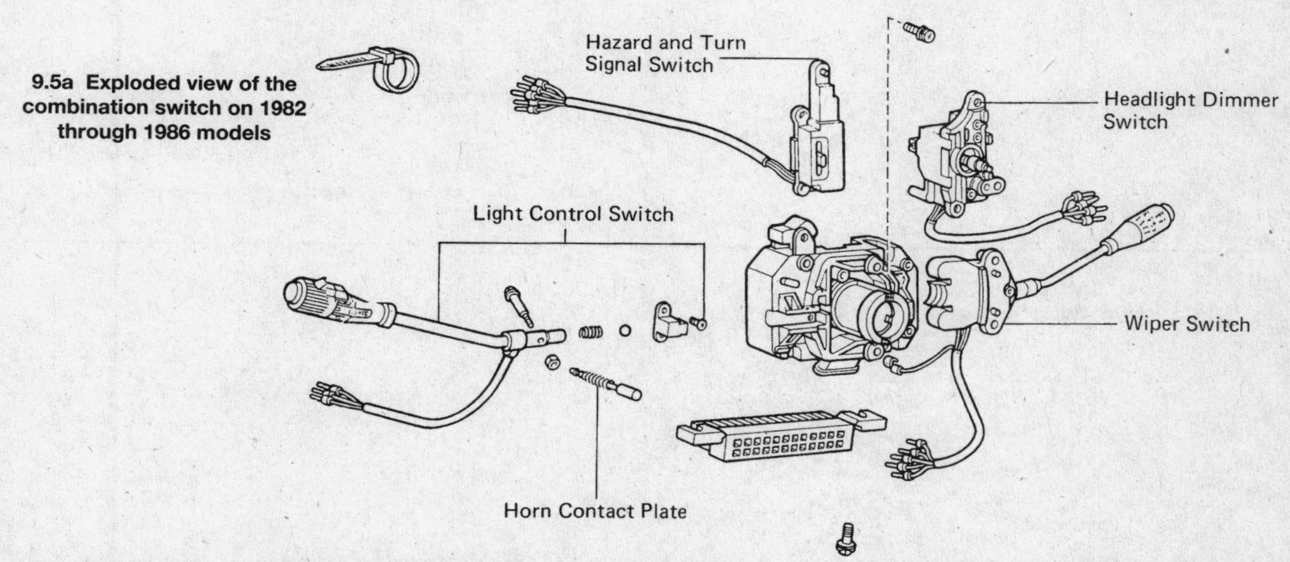

9.5a Exploded view of the combination switch on 1982 through 1986 models

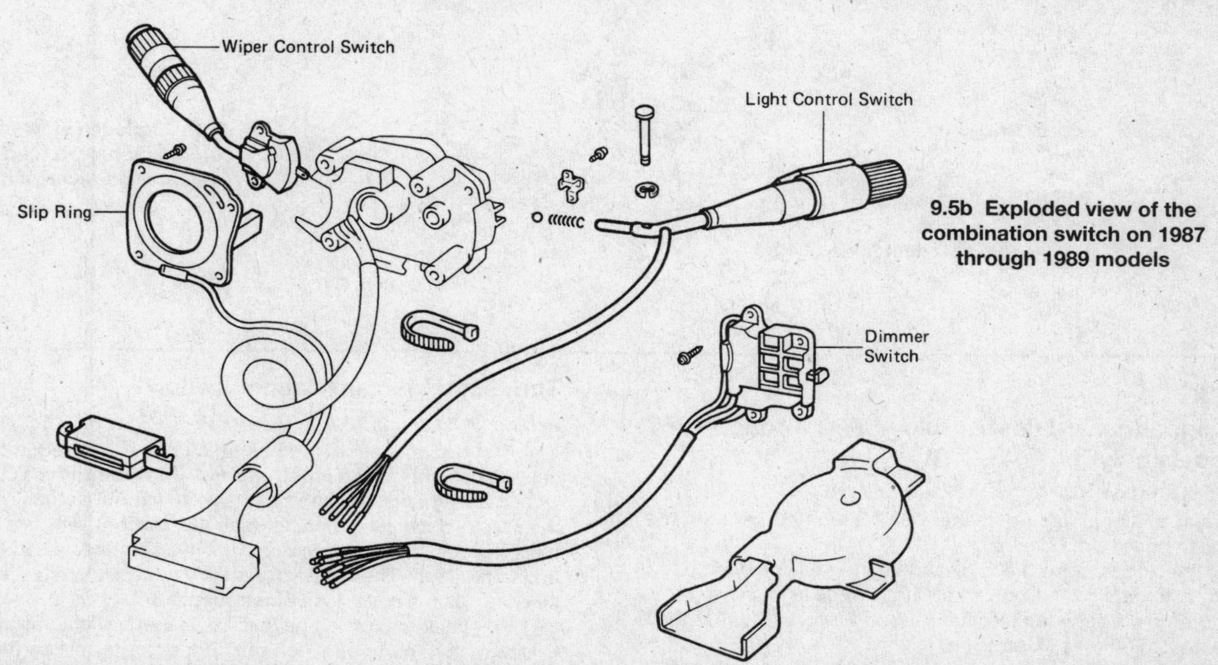

9.5b Exploded view of the combination switch on 1987 through 1989 models

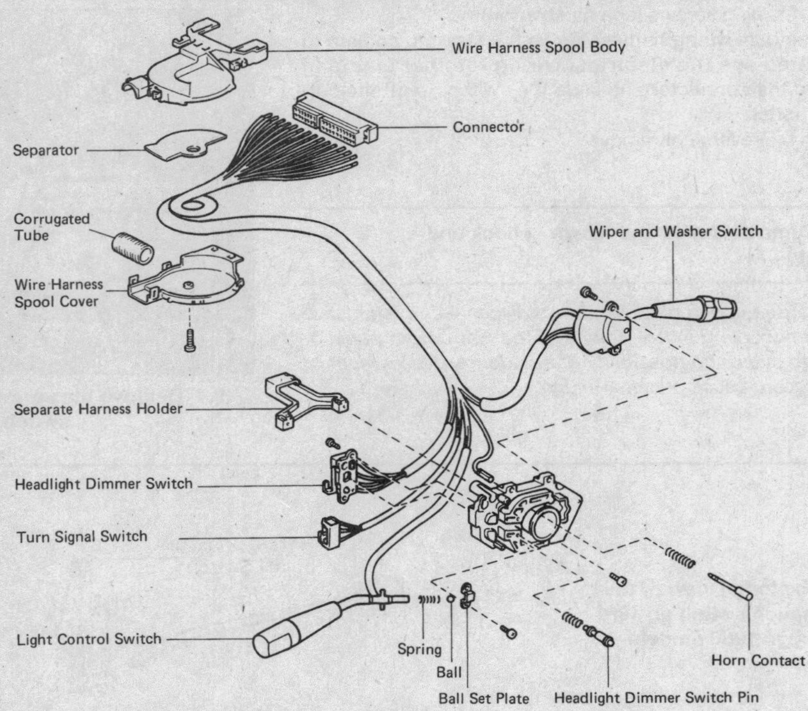

9.5c Exploded view of the combination switch on 1990 and later USA models

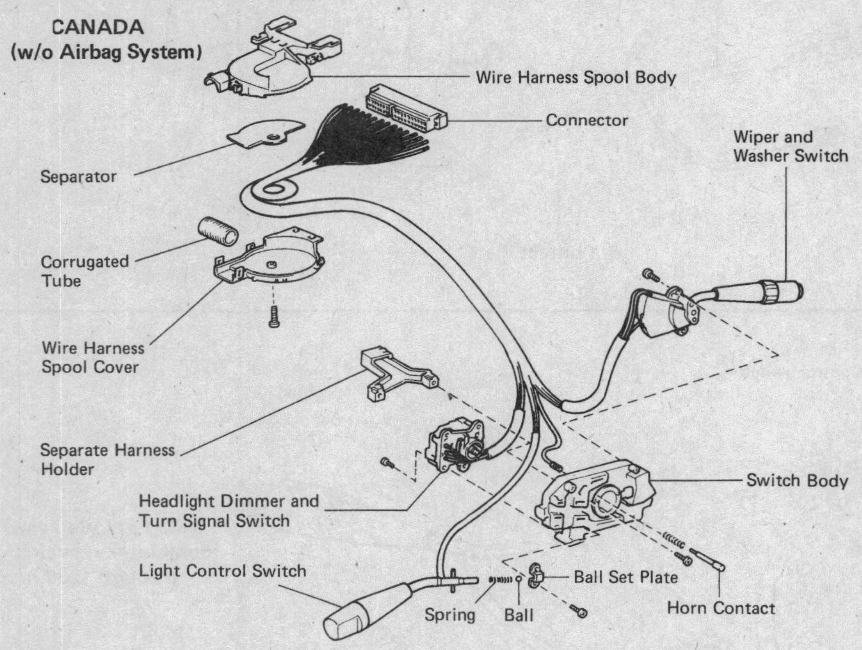

9.5d Exploded view of the combination switch on 1990 and later Canadian models

Check

Turn signal/hazard flasher relay (1982 through 1986 models only)

Refer to illustration 10.2

1 The turn signal/hazard flasher relay is located beneath the left lower dash panel.

2 To check it, remove the relay and connect the positive lead from the battery to terminal 3. Connect the negative lead to terminal 2. Connect a 55W bulb between terminals 1 and 2 and verify that the bulb flashes on and off **(see illustration)**.

3 If the flasher relay does not operate as described, replace it.

Turn signal/hazard flasher switch

Refer to illustrations 10.4, 10.5a, 10.5b, 10.5c and 10.5d

4 The turn signal/hazard flasher switch is located in the steering column assembly **(see illustrations 9.5a through 9.5d)**. Though the switch assembly itself can be checked without actually removing it, the switch electrical connector **(see illustration)**, which is mounted at the lower end of the steering column, must be unscrewed (two screws) and unplugged. The connector is only accessible after removing the steering column cover **(see illustration 9.3)**.

5 To check the turn signal/hazard flasher switch, use an ohmmeter to check continuity between the connector terminals **(see illustrations)**. If continuity is not as specified, replace the flasher switch.

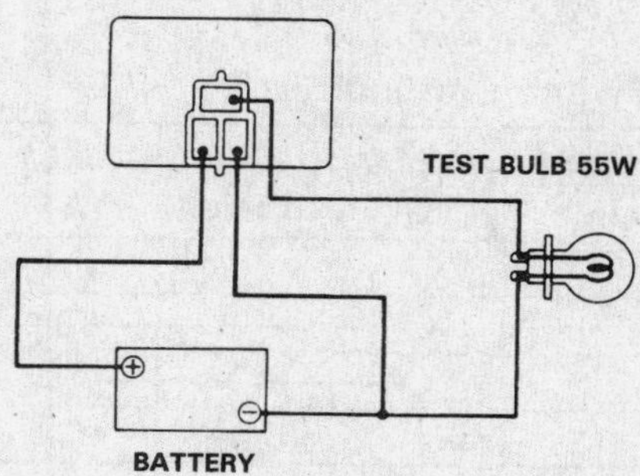

10.2 To test the turn signal/hazard flasher relay, attach the negative terminal of the battery to terminal 2 of the flasher electrical connector and the positive terminal to terminal 3, hook up a 55W light bulb between terminals 1 and 2 and apply battery voltage - the light should flash on and off

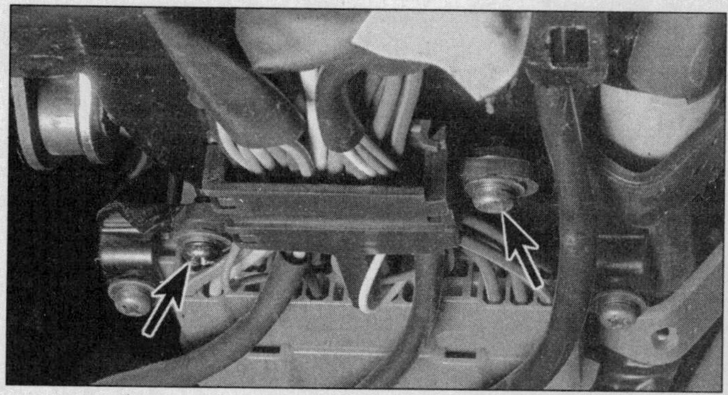

10.4 The turn signal/dimmer/hazard flasher electrical connector is located at the base of the steering column - remove the two screws (arrows) from the connector guide to disconnect it (1982 through 1986 models)

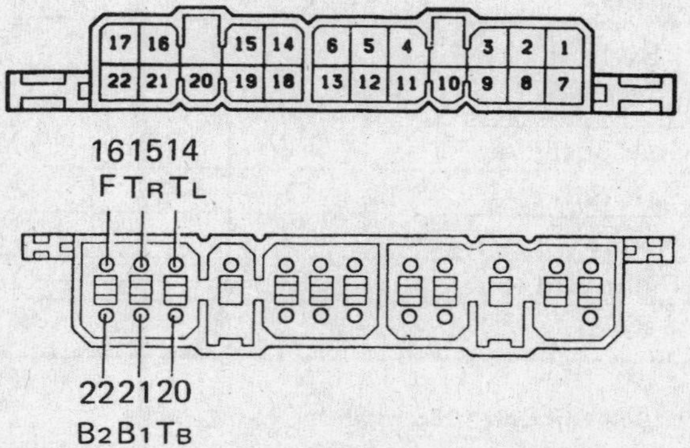

10.5a Refer to this terminal number guide when checking the continuity of the turn signal/hazard flasher switch or the dimmer switch at the large electrical connector at the bottom of the steering column (1982 through 1986 models)

Switch position		Terminal (Wire color): 9 TL (G-B)	3 TB (G-W)	8 TR (G-Y)	2 B1 (G-L)	7 F (G)	1 B2 (G-O)
Turn Signal	L	O	O		O	O	
	N				O	O	
	R		O	O	O	O	
Hazard	ON	O	O	O		O	O

Switch position		Terminal (Wire color): 14 TL (G-B)	20 TB (G-W)	15 TR (G-Y)	21 B (G-L)	16 F (G)	22 B2 (G-O)
Turn signal	L	O	O		O	O	
	N				O	O	
	R		O	O	O	O	
Hazard	ON	O	O	O		O	O

10.5b Use this table to check continuity between the terminals of the turn signal/hazard flasher switch (1982 through 1986 models)

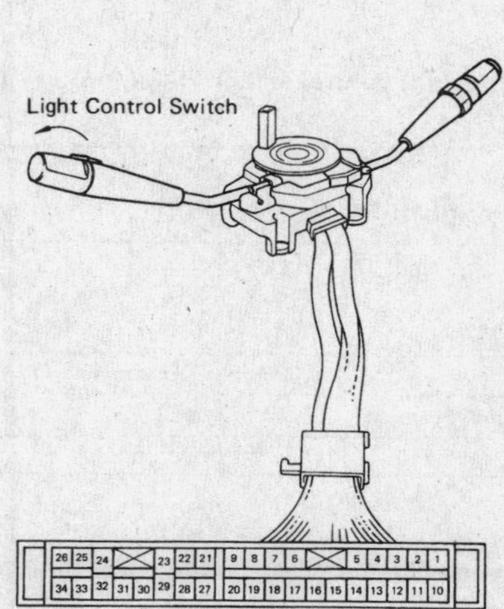

10.5c Use this table to check continuity between the terminals of the turn signal/hazard flasher switch (1987 through 1989 models)

Light control switch

Switch Position \ Terminal (Wire color)	20 U (G)	22 T (Clear)	31 EL (W)	33 H (R)
OFF				
UP	O		O	
TAIL	O	O	O	
HEAD		O	O	O

Headlight dimmer switch

Switch Position \ Terminal (Wire color)	23 HL (R-G)	29 ED (W-B)	32 HU (R-Y)	34 HF (R-W)
Flash		O	O	O
Low Beam	O	O		
High Beam		O	O	

Turn signal switch

Switch Position \ Terminal (Wire color)	21 TB (G-W)	25 TL (G-B)	28 TR (G-Y)
Left Turn	O	O	
Neutral			
Right Turn	O		O

Reference:

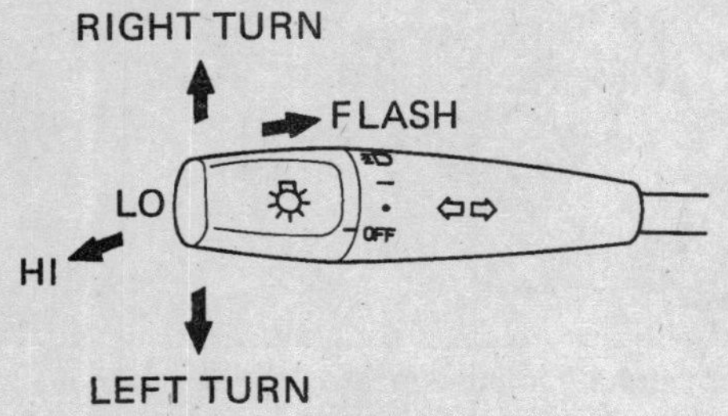

10.5d Use this table to check continuity between the terminals of the turn signal/hazard flasher switch (1990 and later models)

(Light Control Switch/Continuity)

Terminal (Wire color) / Switch position	20/20 (G)	2/14 (Clear)	11/14 (W)	13/14 (R)
OFF				
UP	O	—	O	
TAIL	O	O	O	
HEAD		O	O	O

Headlight Dimmer Switch

Terminal (Color) / Switch position	3/14 (R-G)	9/14 (W-B)	12/14 (R-Y)	14/14 (R-W)
Flash		O	O	O
Low beam	O	O		
High beam		O	O	

Turn Signal Switch

Terminal (Color) / Switch position	1/14 (G-W)	5/14 (G-B)	8/14 (G-Y)
Left turn	O	O	
Neutral			
Right turn	O	—	O

1982 and 1983 models

Terminal (Wire color) / Switch position	13EL (W)	12T (Y)	19H (R)	23D (BR)	26U (G)
OFF	O	—	—	O	
UP	O	—	—	—	O
TAIL	O	O	—	—	O
HEAD	O	O	O		

1984 through 1986 models

Terminal (Wire color) / Switch position	10 EL (W)	11 T (Y)	4 H (R)	26 U (LG-B)
OFF				
UP	O	—	—	O
TAIL	O	O	—	O
HEAD	O	O	O	

10.7a Use this table to check for continuity between the terminals of the light control switch (1982 through 1986 models)

1982 and 1983 models

Terminal (Wire color) / Switch position	10ED (W-B)	18HU (R-Y)	11HF (R-W)
Headlight F	O	O	O
Headlight L			
Headlight U	O	O	

1984 through 1986 models

Terminal (Wire color) / Switch position	13 ED (W-B)	6 HL (R-G)	5 HU (R-Y)	12 HF (R-W)
Flash	O	—	O	O
Low Beam	O	O		
High Beam	O	—	O	

10.7b Use this table to check for continuity between the terminals of the headlight dimmer switch (1982 through 1986 models)

Light control switch and headlight dimmer switch

Refer to illustrations 10.7a and 10.7b

6 The light control and headlight dimmer switches are also located inside the steering column assembly, right next to the turn signal/hazard flasher switch.

7 To check the light control switch and the dimmer switch, use an ohmmeter to check for continuity between the switch terminals **(see illustrations)**. **Note:** *Refer to illustrations 10.5c and 10.5d for the 1987 and later continuity charts.*

8 If continuity is not as specified, replace the switch.

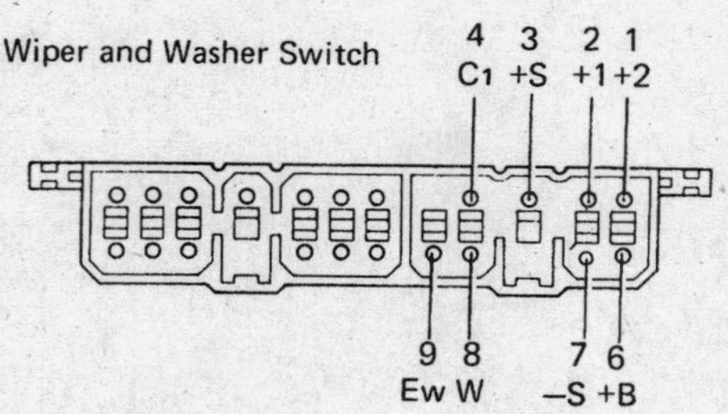

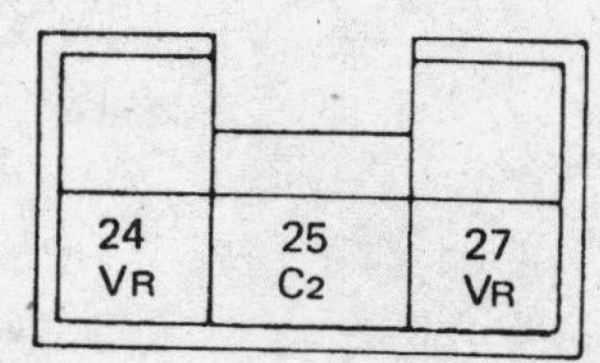

Switch	Switch position	8 W (L)	4 C_1 (LG-R)	9 Ew (B)	7 –S (LG)	3 +S (L-R)	25 C_2 (LG-B)	2 +1 (L-B)	6 +B (L-W)	1 +2 (L-O)	24 VR (Y)	27 VR (Y)
Wiper	OFF			O	O	O	O					
	INT	O	O				O	O				
	LO							O	O			
	HI								O	O		
Washer	OFF											
	ON	O		O								
INT Time control	SLOW	50 kΩ									O	O
	•	34.25 kΩ									O	O
	●	15.75 kΩ									O	O
	FAST	0 KΩ									O	O

10.11a Terminal locations and continuity chart for the windshield wiper and washer switch (1982 and 1983 models)

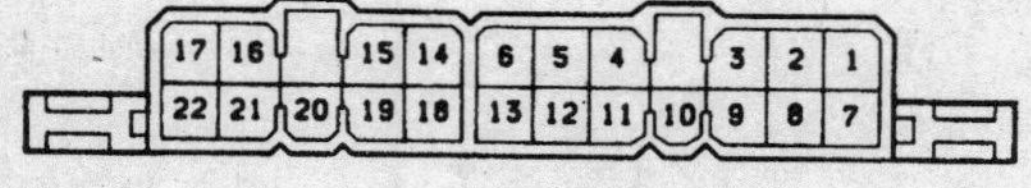

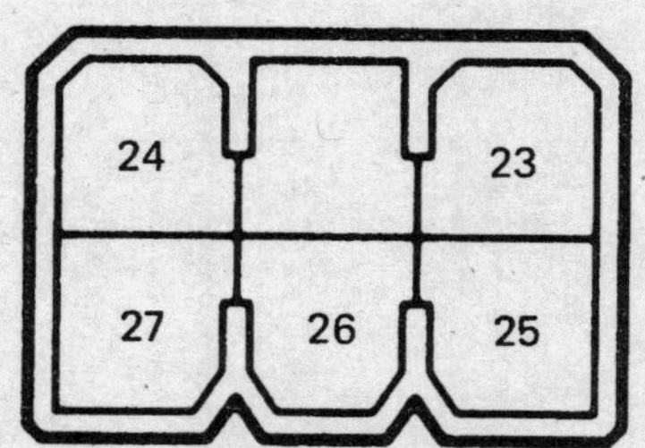

Switch	Switch position	15 W (L)	19 C_1 (LG-R)	14 Ew (B)	16 -S (LG)	20 +S (L-R)	26 C_2 (LG-B)	21 + 1 (L-B)	17 +B (L-W)	22 + 2 (L-O)	25 VR_1 (Y)	27 VR_2 (Y)
Wiper	OFF			O	O	O	O					
	INT		O	O			O	O				
	LO							O	O			
	HI								O	O		
Washer	OFF											
	ON	O		O								
INT Time Control	SLOW	50 kΩ									O	O
	•	34.75 kΩ									O	O
	●	15.75 kΩ									O	O
	FAST	0 kΩ									O	O

10.11b Terminal locations and continuity chart for the windshield wiper and washer switch (1984 through 1986 models)

Windshield wiper/washer switch

Refer to illustrations 10.11a through 10.11f

9 The windshield wiper and washer switch is located on the right side of the steering column. You must first remove the steering wheel (see Chapter 10) and column cover to gain access to the switch electrical connector.

10 To check the windshield wiper and washer switch, unplug the electrical connector from the bottom of the steering column.

11 Using an ohmmeter, check for continuity between the terminals **(see illustrations)**. If continuity is not as specified, replace the switch.

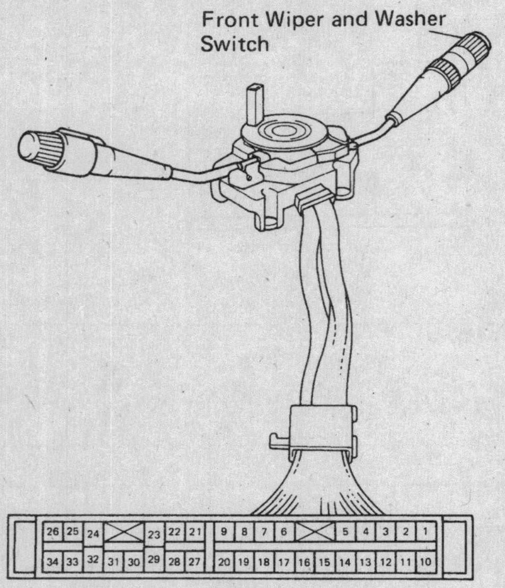

Switch	Terminal (Wire color) / Switch Position	4 +S (L-R)	7 +1 (L-B)	8 W (L)	12 C_1 (Y-B)	13 +2 (L-O)	16 Ew (B)	18 +B (L-W)
Wiper	OFF	O	O					
	INT	O	O		O		O	
	LO		O					O
	HI					O		O
Washer	OFF							
	ON			O			O	

10.11c Terminal locations and continuity chart for the front windshield wiper and washer switch (1987 through 1989 models)

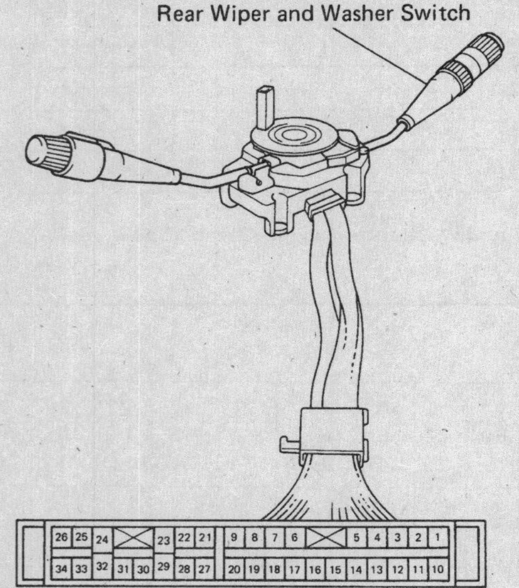

Terminal (Wire color) / Switch Position	1 +1R (GR)	2 WR (V)	10 C_1 R (O)	16 Ew (B)
Washer I		O		O
OFF				
INT			O	O
ON	O			O
Washer II	O	O		O

10.11d Terminal locations and continuity chart for the rear windshield wiper and washer switch (1987 through 1989 models)

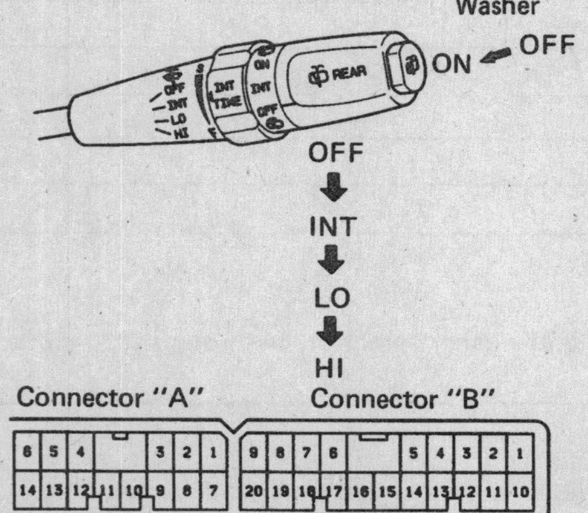

Switch	Terminal (Wire color) / Switch position	B4 +S	B7 +1	B8 WF	B12 C_1	B13 +2	B16 Ew	B18 +B	B6 VR_1	B14 VR_2
Wiper	OFF	O	O							
	INT	O	O		O		O			
	LO		O					O		
	HI					O		O		
Washer	OFF									
	ON			O			O			
INT Time Control	SLOW	Approx. 50 kΩ							O (variable resistor)	O
	FAST								O (variable resistor)	O

10.11e Terminal locations and continuity chart for the front windshield wiper and washer switch (1990 and later models)

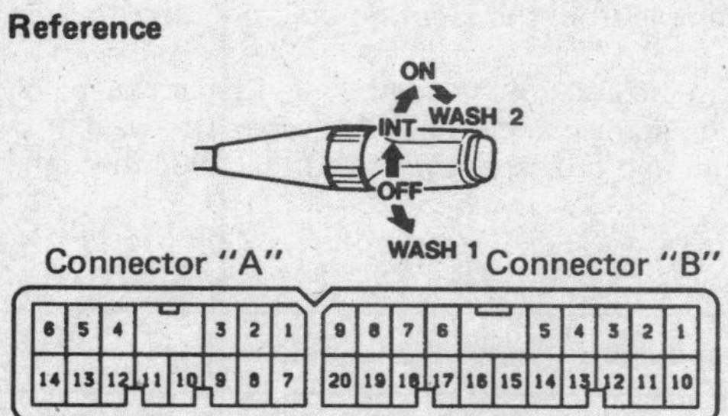

Terminal (Wire color) / Switch Position	B1	B2	B10	B16
Washer I		O		O
OFF				
INT			O	O
ON	O			O
Washer II	O	O		O

10.11f Terminal locations and continuity chart for the rear windshield wiper and washer switch (1990 and later models)

Replacement

Turn signal/hazard flasher, light control switch or headlight dimmer switch

Refer to illustrations 10.16, 10.17, 10.18, 10.20a and 10.20b

12 Remove the steering wheel (see Chapter 10).

13 Remove the steering column cover (see Chapter 11).

14 Remove the turn signal/hazard flasher, light control switch and dimmer switch wire harness electrical connector guide retaining screws if you have not already done so.

15 Unplug the wire harness electrical connector.

16 From the open side of the connector, insert a miniature screwdriver between the locking lug and terminal you intend to remove **(see illustration)**.

17 Pry up the locking lug with the screwdriver **(see illustration)** and pull the terminal out from the rear.

18 Remove the four turn signal/hazard flasher and dimmer switch assembly mounting screws **(see illustration)**. Detach the switch assembly from the steering column.

19 Flip the switch assembly over so that you are looking at its back. Remove the mounting screws from the problem switch and detach the switch.

20 Installation is basically the reverse of removal. Install the headlight dimmer switch. Attach the spring to the lever and install the lever with the pin and E-ring **(see illustration)**. Place the ball on the spring, place the lever in the HIGH position and install the retaining plate **(see illustration)**.

21 Be sure to push in the terminals of the electrical wire harness for the switch you are replacing until each one is securely locked in the connector. Pull on each wire to verify that it is locked.

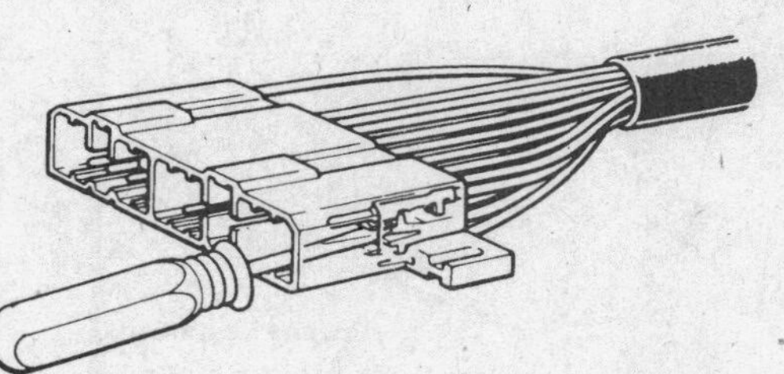

10.16 From the open end of the electrical connector, insert a miniature screwdriver between the locking lug and the terminal of each wire you are disconnecting, ...

10.18 Remove the four mounting screws (arrows) and remove the turn signal/hazard flasher and headlight dimmer switch assembly (combination switch) (1982 through 1986 model shown)

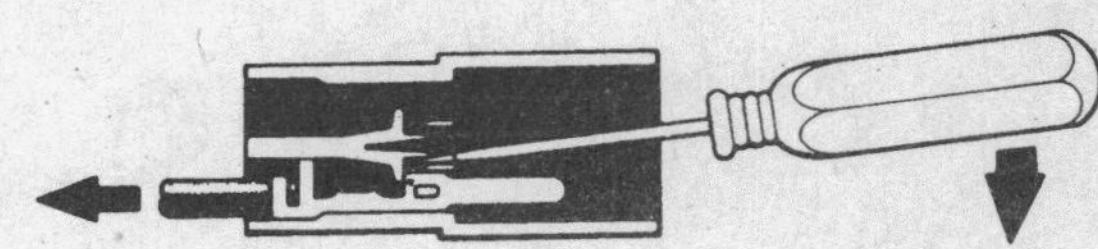

10.17 ... pry up the locking lug with the screwdriver and pull the terminal out from the rear

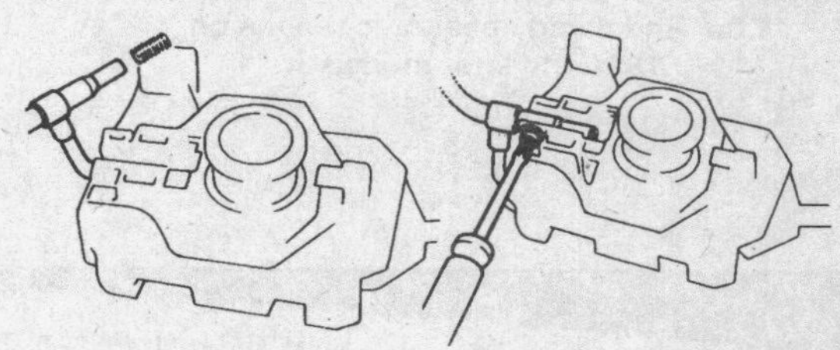

10.20a Place the spring on the lever, then install the lever on the assembly with the pin and E-ring

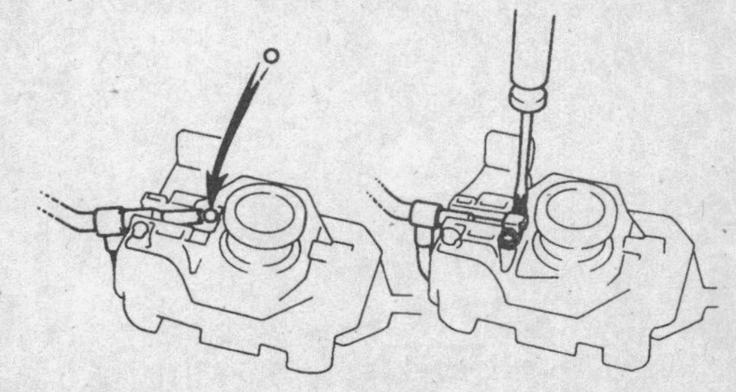

10.20b Insert the ball into the spring, turn the switch to the HIGH setting and install the retaining plate

11.3a Radio/tape player/amplifier retaining screw locations (arrows) (1983 model shown)

Windshield wiper/washer switch

22 To replace the wiper switch you must first remove the combination switch assembly from the steering column (refer to Steps 12 through 18).

23 Working from the back of the combination switch assembly, remove the retaining screws and detach the wiper and washer switch (the wiper, washer and cruise control switch on 1984 through 1986 models).

24 Installation is the reverse of removal.

11 Radio and speakers - removal and installation

1 Disconnect the negative cable at the battery. **Caution:** *If the stereo in your vehicle is equipped with an anti-theft system, refer to the information on page 0-15 at the front of this manual before detaching the cable.*

Radio

Refer to illustration 11.3a and 11.3b

2 Remove the instrument panel center upper finish panel (see Chapter 11).

3 Remove the radio mounting screws or bolts **(see illustrations)**.

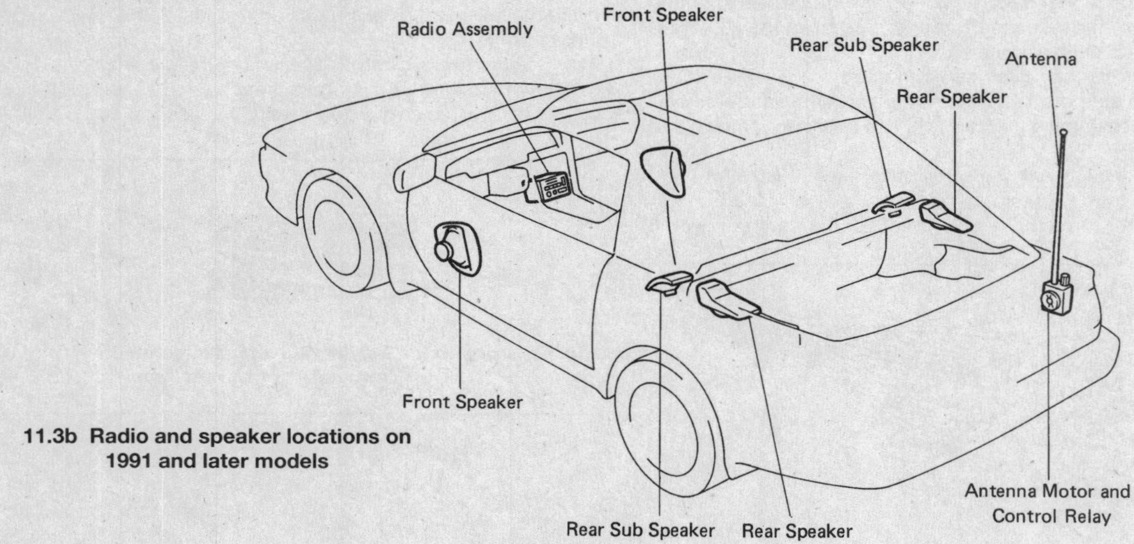

11.3b Radio and speaker locations on 1991 and later models

12.3a Take out the four headlight retaining ring screws (arrows) and withdraw the ring (1983 model shown)

12.3b Remove the retaining ring screws (arrows) (1981 model shown)

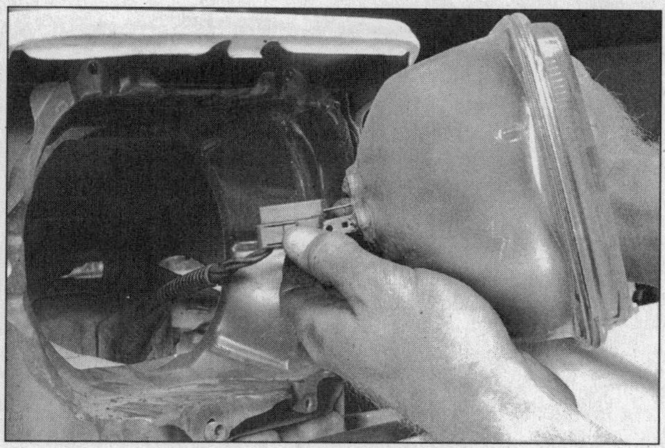

12.4 Pull out the headlight and unplug the electrical connector

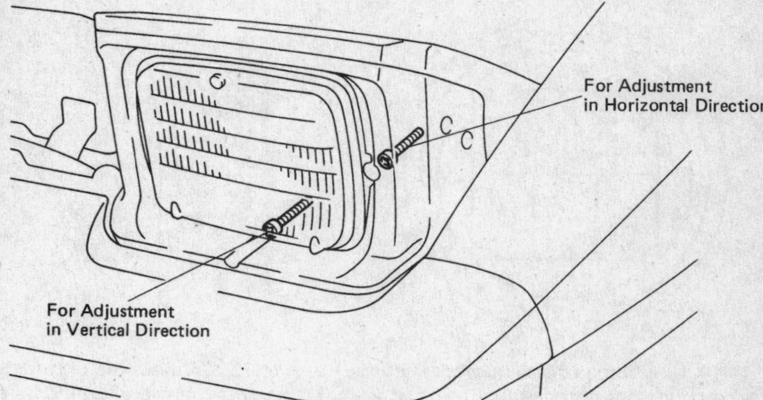

13.6 Location of the headlight adjustment screws

4 Pull the radio out, reach behind it and unplug the electrical connector and the antenna lead.
5 Lift the radio from the instrument panel.
6 Installation is the reverse of removal.

Speakers

7 Remove the speaker cover(s) (see Chapter 11).
8 Remove the retaining screws or bolts, unplug the electrical connector and lower the speaker from the instrument panel.
9 Installation is the reverse of removal.

12 Headlights - removal and installation

Refer to illustrations 12.3a, 12.3b and 12.4

1 On 1982 and later models, raise the headlights, then disconnect the negative cable from the battery. The headlights will remain up. **Caution:** *If the stereo in your vehicle is equipped with an anti-theft system, refer to the information on page 0-15 at the front of this manual before detaching the cable.*
2 Remove the four screws from the headlight bezel and lift off the bezel.
3 Remove the four screws from the headlight retaining ring and take off the ring **(see illustrations)**.
4 Pull out the headlight far enough to unplug the electrical connector and remove the headlight **(see illustration)**.
5 Be certain to adjust the headlights after installation (Section 13).

13 Headlights - adjustment

Refer to illustration 13.6

Note: *It is important that the headlights be aimed correctly. If adjusted incorrectly they could blind the driver of an oncoming vehicle and cause a serious accident or seriously reduce your ability to see the road. The headlights should be checked for proper aim every 12 months and any time a new headlight is installed or front end body work is performed. It should be emphasized that the following procedure is only an interim step which will provide temporary adjustment until the headlights can be adjusted by a properly equipped shop.*

1 Headlights have two adjusting screws, one on the top controlling up and down movement and one on the side controlling left and right movement.
2 There are several methods of adjusting the headlights. The simplest method requires a blank wall 25 feet in front of the vehicle and a level floor.
3 Position masking tape vertically on the wall in reference to the vehicle centerline and the centerlines of both headlights.
4 Position a horizontal tape line in reference to the centerline of all the headlights. **Note:** *It may be easier to position the tape on the wall with the vehicle parked only a few inches away.*
5 Adjustment should be made with the vehicle sitting level, the gas tank half-full and no unusually heavy load in the vehicle.
6 Starting with the low beam adjustment, position the high intensity zone so it is two inches below the horizontal line and two inches to the right of the headlight vertical line. Adjustment on sealed beam equipped models is made by turning the top adjusting screw clockwise to raise the beam and counterclockwise to lower the beam **(see illustration)**. The adjusting screw on the side should be used in the same manner to move the beam left or right. On bulb-type headlights, the top adjusting screw moves the headlight assembly right or left and the lower one moves it up and down.
7 With the high beams on, the high intensity zone should be vertically centered with the exact center just below the horizontal line. **Note:** *It may not be possible to position the headlight aim exactly for both high and low beams. If a compromise must be made, keep in mind that the low beams are the most used and have the greatest effect on driver safety.*
8 Have the headlights adjusted by a dealer service department at the earliest opportunity.

14 Headlight retractor motor - check and replacement

Check

Refer to illustrations 14.2, 14.10, 14.12, 14.18, 14.20 and 14.21

1982 and 1983 models

1 Connect a test light between terminal 3 and body ground. There should be power present.
2 Raise the headlights, then unplug the electrical connector from the retractor motor. Connect an ohmmeter between terminals 3 and 4 **(see illustration)**. There should be continuity. If the motor fails either of these tests, replace it.

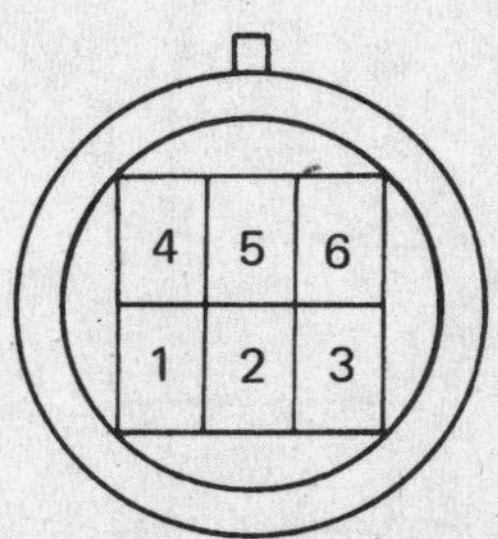

14.2 Use this terminal number guide when checking the headlight retractor motor (1982 and 1983 models)

12

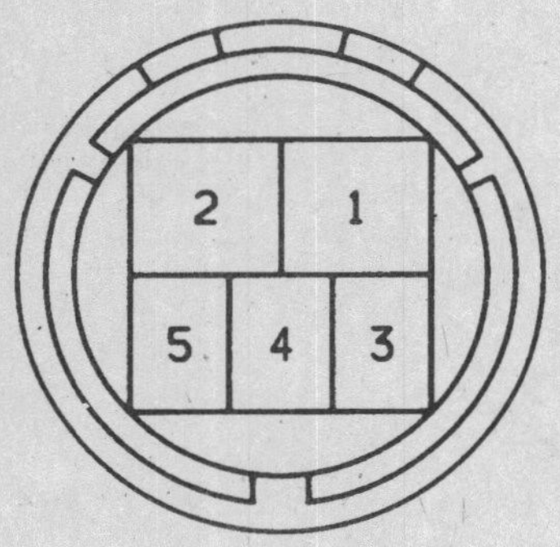

14.10 **Use this terminal number guide when checking the headlight retractor motor (1984 through 1988 models)**

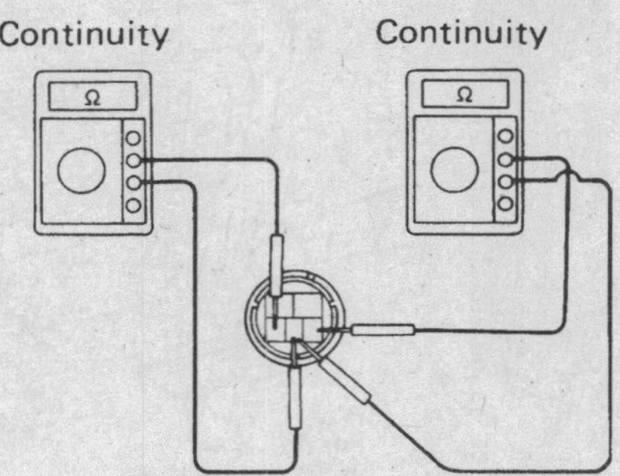

14.12 Connect the ohmmeter test leads as shown - there should be continuity for both checks

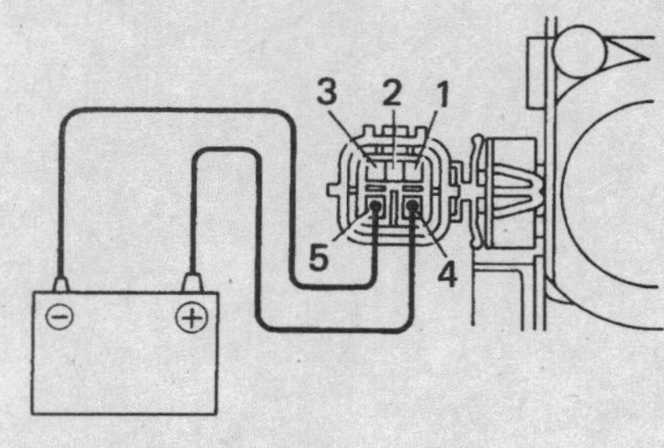

14.18 Use this terminal number guide when checking the headlight retractor motor (1989 through 1992 models)

3 To check diode continuity of the motor, move the headlights to any position except the upper or lower positions. Connect the ohmmeter positive lead to terminal 6 and the negative lead to terminal 3. There should be continuity. Connect the ohmmeter positive lead to terminal 2 and the negative lead to terminal 6. There should be continuity. If there is no continuity, replace the motor assembly.

4 Reverse the test leads of the ohmmeter and repeat the above two checks. There should be no continuity for either check. If there is, replace the motor assembly.

1984 through 1988 models

5 Turn the headlights on.

6 Remove the headlight retractor control relay. The relay is located under the dash panel, above the steering column.

7 Turn the headlights off.

8 Remove the headlight trim piece.

9 Unplug the electrical connector from the retractor motor.

10 The retractor motor is difficult to check when it is installed in the vehicle, but the second of the two following checks must be done with the motor installed because it can't be done any other way. Refer to the accompanying terminal number guide and make sure that you are probing the correct terminals **(see illustration)**.

11 To check motor operation, connect the positive lead from the battery to terminal 2 and connect the negative lead to terminal 1. Verify that the motor runs. If it doesn't, replace it.

12 To check diode continuity of the motor, move the headlights to any position except the upper or lower positions. Connect the ohmmeter positive lead to terminal 4 and the negative lead to terminal 5 **(see illustration)**. There should be continuity. Connect the ohmmeter positive lead to terminal 4 and the negative lead to terminal 3. There should be continuity. If there is no continuity, replace the motor assembly.

13 Reverse the test leads of the ohmmeter and repeat the above two checks. There should be no continuity for either check. If there is, replace the motor assembly.

1989 and later models

14 Turn the headlights on.

15 Remove the headlight retractor control relay. The relay is located in the engine compartment in Junction Block Number 2.

16 Turn the headlights off.

17 Unplug the electrical connector from the retractor motor.

18 The retractor motor is difficult to check when it is installed in the vehicle, but the second of the two following checks must be done with the motor installed because it can't be done any other way. Refer to the accompanying terminal number guide and make sure that you are probing the correct terminals **(see illustration)**.

19 To check motor operation, connect the positive lead from the battery to terminal 4 and connect the negative lead to terminal 5. Verify that the motor runs. If it doesn't, replace it **(see illustration 14.18)**.

20 To check diode continuity of the motor, move the headlights to any position except the upper or lower positions. Connect the ohmmeter positive lead to terminal 1 and the negative lead to terminal 2. There should be no continuity. Connect the ohmmeter positive lead to terminal 3 and the negative lead to terminal 2. There should be no continuity. If there is continuity, replace the motor assembly **(see illustration)**.

21 Reverse the test leads of the ohmmeter and repeat the above two checks **(see illustration)**. There should be continuity for either check. If there is none, replace the motor assembly.

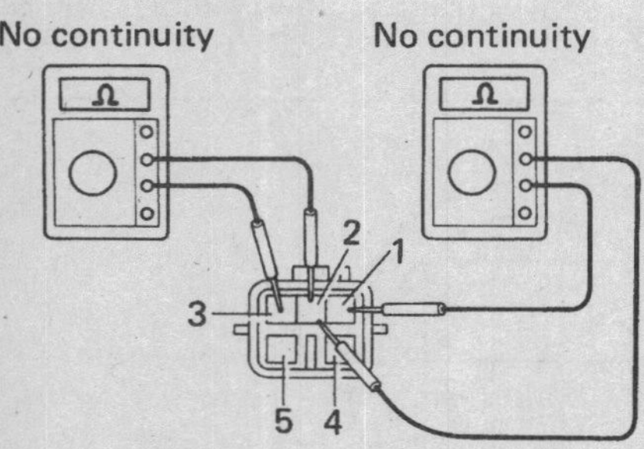

14.20 First check the terminals with the ohmeter positive (+) lead to terminal 1 and the negative (-) lead to terminal 2

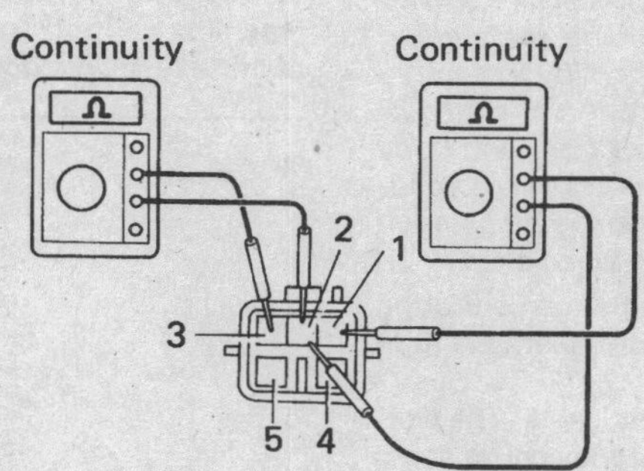

14.21 Reverse the ohmmeter test leads and repeat the two tests - this time there should be continuity for both checks

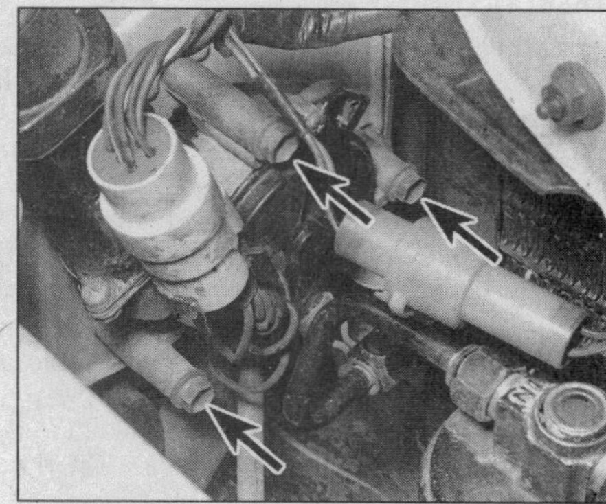

14.26 To remove the headlight retractor motor, take out the three mounting bolts (arrows) and unplug the electrical connector (1983 model shown)

15.2 After the retaining screw has been removed, carefully pry the lens housing from the frame

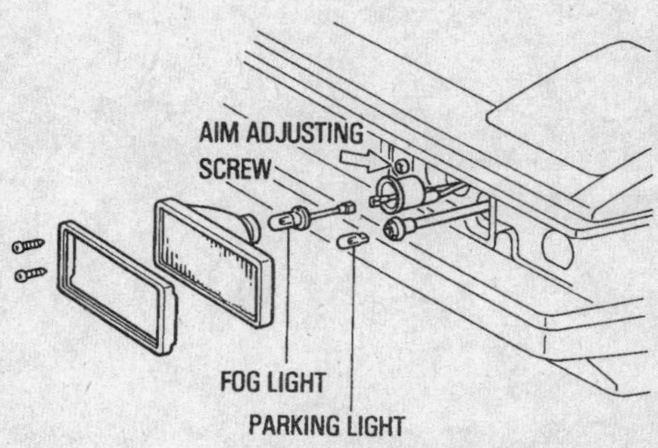

15.3 The fog light and parking light is removed as an assembly

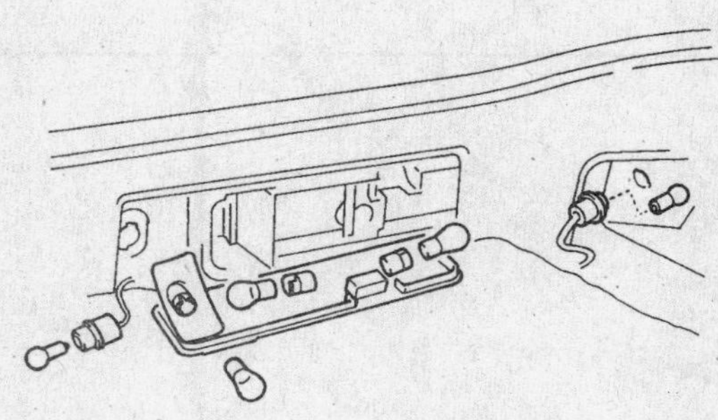

15.5 Rear turn signal, stop and tail, back-up, and license plate lights

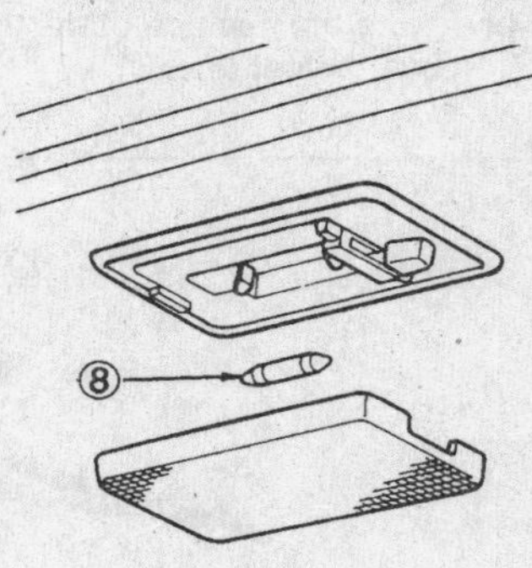

15.7 Dome light assembly

Replacement

Refer to illustration 14.26

22 Raise the headlights and disconnect the negative cable from the battery. **Caution:** *If the stereo in your vehicle is equipped with an anti-theft system, refer to the information on page 0-15 at the front of this manual before detaching the cable.*

23 Remove the battery or the air filter housing depending on which side you're working on (see Chapter 5 and Chapter 4).

24 Using a screwdriver, pry apart the headlight motor-to-headlight retractor linkage.

25 Take out the two nuts and the two bolts from the rear of the assembly.

26 Remove the three motor mounting bolts, unplug the electrical connector and pull out the motor **(see illustration)**.

27 With the motor out, the last headlight assembly retaining bolt is accessible. Remove it.

28 Lift up the headlight assembly, unplug the headlight electrical connector and withdraw the assembly.

29 Installation is the reverse of the removal procedure.

15 Bulb replacement

Refer to illustrations 15.2, 15.3, 15.5, 15.7 and 15.11

Caution: *If the stereo in your vehicle is equipped with an anti-theft system, refer to the information on page 0-15 at the front of this manual before detaching the cable.* **Note:** *Whenever any bulbs are replaced, the same type bulb with the same wattage rating must be used.*

Removal

Turn signals/fog lights

1 Remove the radiator grille (see Chapter 11).

2 To replace the turn signals, remove the lens retaining screws and pry the lens housing free **(see illustration)**. Turn the bulb holder and pull it out from the rear of the housing to replace the bulb.

3 The fog lights are replaced by removing the retaining screws from the frame and pulling the housing out **(see illustration)**. Unplug the electrical connector from the back of the light and replace it.

Front side marker lights

4 Take out the retaining screws, remove the lens and pull out the bulb.

Rear side marker and rear turn signal lights

5 Work from inside the luggage compartment. On the right side, remove the storage compartment cover, then place your finger through the hole in the small inside panel and pull the panel free. The bulb holders will now be visible. Turn the holder counterclockwise and remove it from the side marker assembly **(see illustration)**. Pull the bulb straight out of the bulb holder.

6 On the left side, remove the panel from the tool/jack storage compartment to gain access to the bulb holder.

Dome light

7 Pry the plastic lens cover off with a small screwdriver. Remove the bulb from the dome light assembly **(see illustration)**.

Instrument panel lights

8 To remove an instrument panel bulb, you must first remove the instrument cluster (see Section 17) and remove the appropriate bulb carrier from the printed circuit board by twisting it counterclockwise.

Rear combination light

9 Open the liftgate.

10 For either the right or left side, remove the panel covering the back of the combination light assembly.

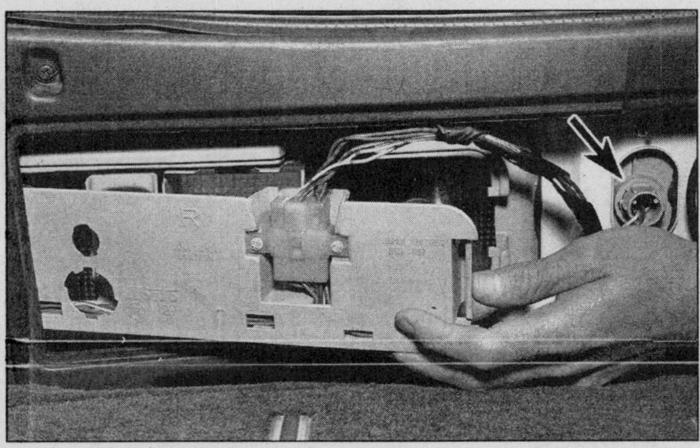

15.11 Press in on the tab and lift out the rear combination light bulb carrier assembly - note the position of the license plate light bulb holder (arrow)

16.5a The windshield wiper motor is fastened to the firewall with four bolts (arrows) - note that the upper left bolt secures a ground lead (1982 model shown)

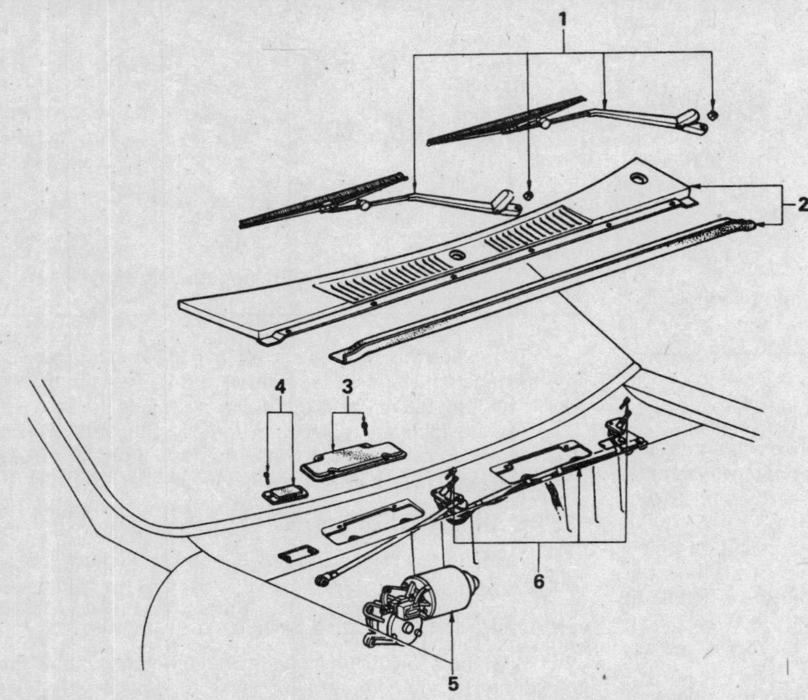

16.5b Front windshield wiper components on 1979 through 1981 models - exploded view

1 *Wiper arms*
2 *Louvered panel*
3 *Cover panel*
4 *Cover panel*
5 *Wiper motor*
6 *Wiper linkage*

11 Push in the on the tab on the light assembly and pull it out **(see illustration)**. Replace the burned out bulb and install the assembly.

License plate light

12 Remove the panel covering as described in Step 10. The bulb holder will be visible. Turn it counterclockwise to remove it. Remove the bulb from the holder by pulling it straight out.

Installation

13 In all instances, installation is the reverse of removal. When finished, check the lights for satisfactory operation.

16 Windshield wiper motor - check, removal and installation

1 The front windshield wiper motor is located, facing the engine compartment, in the left corner against the firewall. The rear windshield wiper motor is located in the rear door. If the motor does not work at both speeds or does not park properly, and the wiper switch(es) checks okay, the wiper motor will have to be replaced. See Section 10 for all the checks on the windshield wiper switch.

Front

Refer to illustration 16.5a, 16.5b and 16.6

2 Disconnect the negative cable at the battery. **Caution:** *If the stereo in your vehicle is equipped with an anti-theft system, refer to the information on page 0-15 at the front of this manual before detaching the cable.*

3 Remove the windshield washer reservoir by pulling it straight up.

4 Disconnect the wiring from the motor.

5 Take out the four mounting bolts **(see illustrations)**. Note that one bolt secures a ground lead.

6 Using a screwdriver, pry the linkage arm from the motor, then withdraw the motor **(see illustration)**.

7 Installation is the reverse of removal. Lubricate the linkage pivots before assembly. Place a screwdriver behind the linkage arm and push it back into place on the motor crank arm.

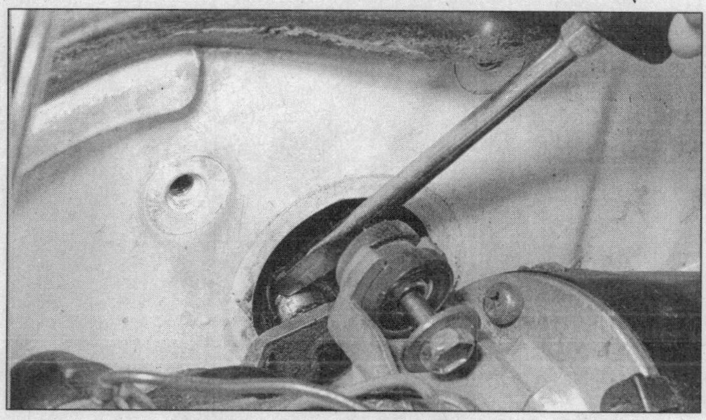

16.6 Using a screwdriver, separate the wiper motor from the linkage arm (1982 model shown)

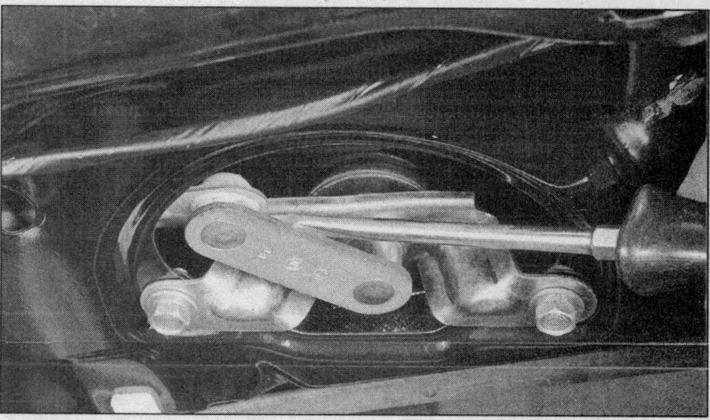

16.10 The link and crank arm can be separated with a screwdriver

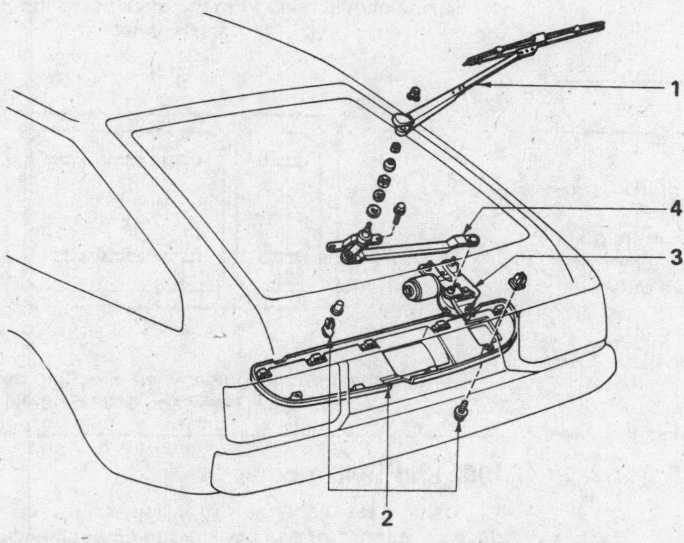

16.11a Rear windshield wiper components on 1979 through 1981 models - exploded view

1. *Wiper arms*
2. *Rear door trim*
3. *Wiper motor and bracket*
4. *Link and drive spindle*

Rear

Refer to illustrations 16.10, 16.11a, 16.11b and 16.12

8 Disconnect the negative cable from the battery. **Caution:** *If the stereo in your vehicle is equipped with an anti-theft system, refer to the information on page 0-15 at the front of this manual before detaching the cable.*

9 Remove the rear trim panel from the liftgate (see Chapter 11).

10 Using a screwdriver, pop the link off the crank arm **(see illustration)**.

11 Disconnect the electrical connector from the motor, remove the three mounting bolts and withdraw the motor **(see illustrations)**.

12 To remove the wiper arm and blade, take off the wiper arm retaining nut **(see illustration)**.

13 Installation is the reverse of removal.

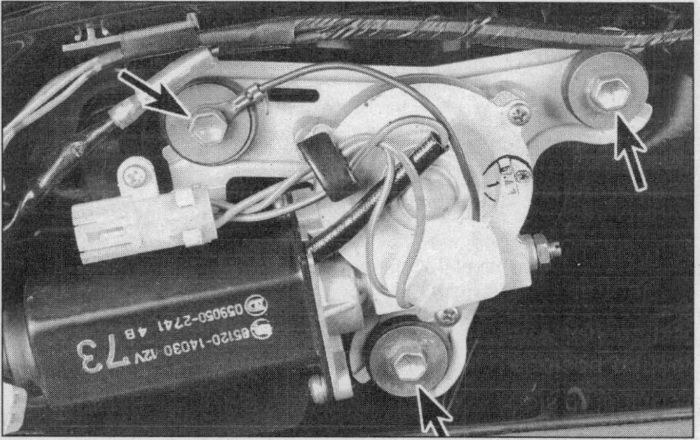

16.11b To remove the rear wiper motor, take out the three mounting bolts (arrows) and disconnect the electrical wiring harness

16.12 Lift up the cap and take off the retaining nut to remove the rear wiper arm and blade

17.5 To remove the instrument cluster, remove the four retaining screws (arrows) (1983 model shown)

19.3 To remove the rear window defogger switch, take out the two retaining screws from the back of the instrument cluster finish panel

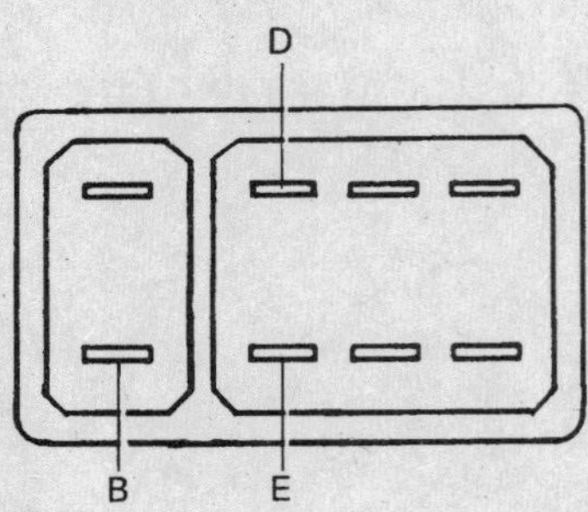

19.4 Use this terminal guide when checking the rear window defogger (1982 and 1983 models)

17 Instrument cluster - removal and installation

Refer to illustration 17.5

Note: *Refer to Chapter 11 for additional exploded views of the instrument trim panels.*

1 Disconnect the negative cable from the battery. **Caution:** *If the stereo in your vehicle is equipped with an anti-theft system, refer to the information on page 0-15 at the front of this manual before detaching the cable.*

2 Remove the steering column covers **(see illustration 9.3)**.

3 Remove the screws holding the cluster finish panel in place, then remove the finish panel (see Chapter 11).

4 Disconnect the speedometer cable.

5 Remove the retaining screws, then pull out the instrument cluster and disconnect the electrical connectors **(see illustration)**.

6 To replace any faulty components within the cluster, simply unbolt or unscrew them and replace them with new units.

7 Installation is the reverse of removal.

18 Radio antenna - removal and installation

1 Disconnect the negative battery cable from the battery. **Caution:** *If the stereo in your vehicle is equipped with an anti-theft system, refer to the information on page 0-15 at the front of this manual before detaching the cable.*

2 Remove the antenna set nut.

3 Remove the inner trim panel for access to the antenna motor unit.

4 Take out the retaining bolts, disconnect the electrical connector and antenna lead, then remove the antenna unit, complete with the relay.

5 Installation is the reverse of removal.

19 Rear window defogger and switch - check and repair

Refer to illustrations 19.3, 19.4, 19.5, 19.8, 19.10, 19.13, 19.14 and 19.15

Defogger switch

1 The rear window defogger switch is located on the left side of the instrument cluster finish panel.

2 To check the switch, you must first remove the instrument cluster finish panel (see Chapter 11).

3 Remove the two retaining screws and withdraw the defogger switch **(see illustration)**.

1982 and 1983 models

4 Using a test light, check for power between terminal B of the electrical connector and body ground **(see illustration)**. Check between terminal E and body ground. There should not be any power.

5 Check for continuity between the terminals using the accompanying chart **(see illustration)**.

6 If the switch fails any of these checks, replace it. To remove the switch from the housing, remove the three retaining screws, detach the wire securing clip and withdraw the switch.

7 Installation is the reverse of removal.

1984 through 1986 models

8 To check the switch, unplug the electrical connector from the switch, connect a positive lead from the battery to terminal 5 and a negative lead to terminal 6. Connect a test light between terminals 2 and 5 **(see illustration)**.

9 Turn the switch on. The test light should come on and remain on for between 10 and 20 minutes. If it does not, replace the switch.

1987 and later models

10 To check the switch, unplug the electrical connector from the switch, connect a positive lead from the battery to terminal 3 and a negative lead to terminal 4. Connect a test light (3.4W) between terminals 3 and 5 **(see illustration)**.

11 Turn the switch on. The test light should come on and remain on for between 12 and 18 minutes. If it does not, replace the switch.

Rear window defogger

Caution: *Use a soft, dry cloth when cleaning the glass and wipe it in the direction of the wire. Take care not to damage the wires. Do not use detergents or glass cleaners with abrasive ingredients.*

12 Turn the ignition and defogger switches to ON.

Switch Position \ Terminal (Wire color)	E (W-B)	D (R-W)	B (R)
OFF		○	○
ON	○	○	○

19.5 Refer to this chart when checking continuity in the rear window defogger switch (1982 and 1983 models)

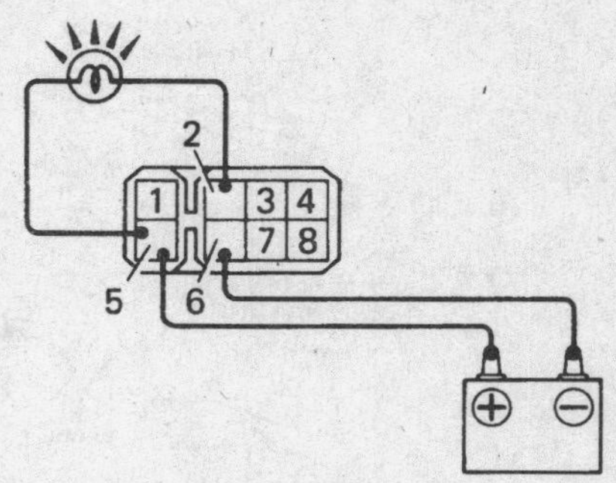

19.8 Use this terminal number guide when checking the rear window defogger switch (1984 through 1986 models)

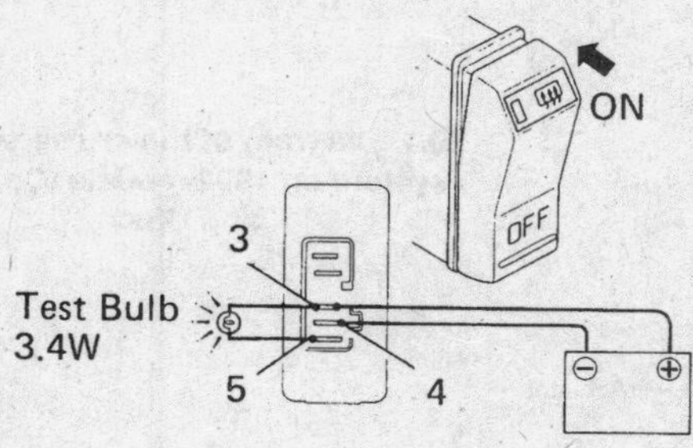

19.10 Use this terminal number guide when checking the rear window defogger switch (1987 and later models)

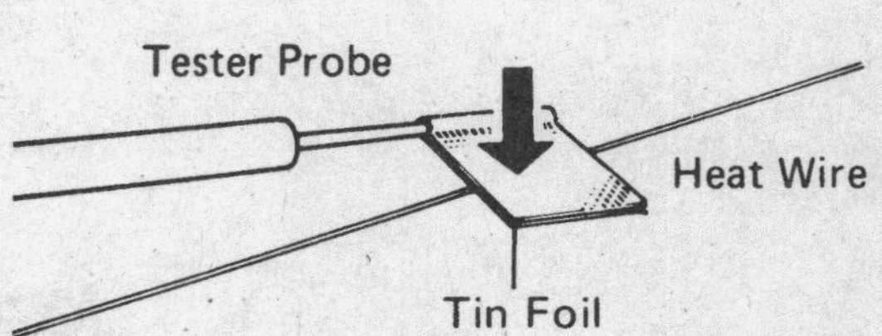

19.13 When measuring the voltage at the rear window defogger grid, wind a piece of aluminum foil around the negative probe of the voltmeter and press the foil against the wire with your finger

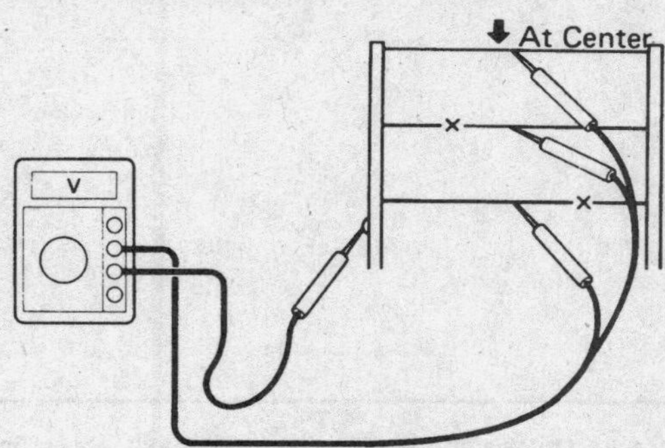

19.14 To determine if a wire has broken, check the voltage at the center of each wire - if the voltage is 5-volts, the wire is unbroken; if the voltage is 10-volts, the wire is broken between the center of the wire and the positive end; if the voltage is 0-volts, the wire is broken between the center of the wire and ground

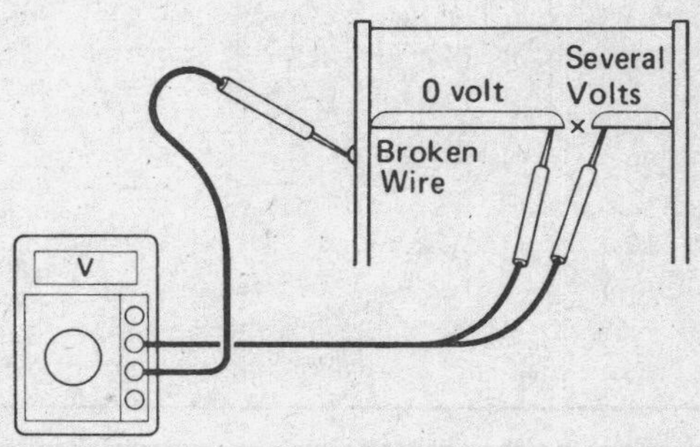

19.15 To find the break, place the voltmeter positive lead against the defogger positive terminal, place the voltmeter negative lead with the foil strip against the heat wire at the positive terminal end and slide it toward the negative terminal end - the point where the voltmeter deflects from zero to several volts is the point at which the wire is broken

13 When measuring voltage during the next two tests, wind a piece of aluminum foil around the tip of the voltmeter negative probe and press the foil against the wire with your finger **(see illustration)**.

14 Check the voltage at the center of each heat wire **(see illustration)**. If the voltage is 5-volts, the wire is okay (there is no break). If the voltage is 10-volts, the wire is broken between the center of the wire and the positive end of the wire. If there is no voltage reading, the wire is broken between the center of the wire and ground.

15 To find the break, place the voltmeter positive lead against the defogger positive terminal. Place the voltmeter negative lead with the foil strip against the heat wire at the positive terminal end and slide it toward the negative terminal end. The point where the voltmeter deflects from zero to several volts is the point at which the heat wire is broken **(see illustration)**. **Note:** *If the heat wire is not broken, the voltmeter will indicate no voltage at the positive end of the heat wire but gradually increase to about 12-volts as the meter probe is moved to the other end.*

Rear window defogger repair

16 Clean the broken wire tips with denatured alcohol.

17 Place masking tape along both sides of the wire to be repaired.

18 Thoroughly mix the repair agent (Dupont paste No. 4817, available at your Toyota dealer or other auto parts stores).

19 Using a fine tip brush, apply a small amount to the wire.

20 After a few minutes, remove the masking tape.

21 Allow the repair to cure for at least 24 hours.

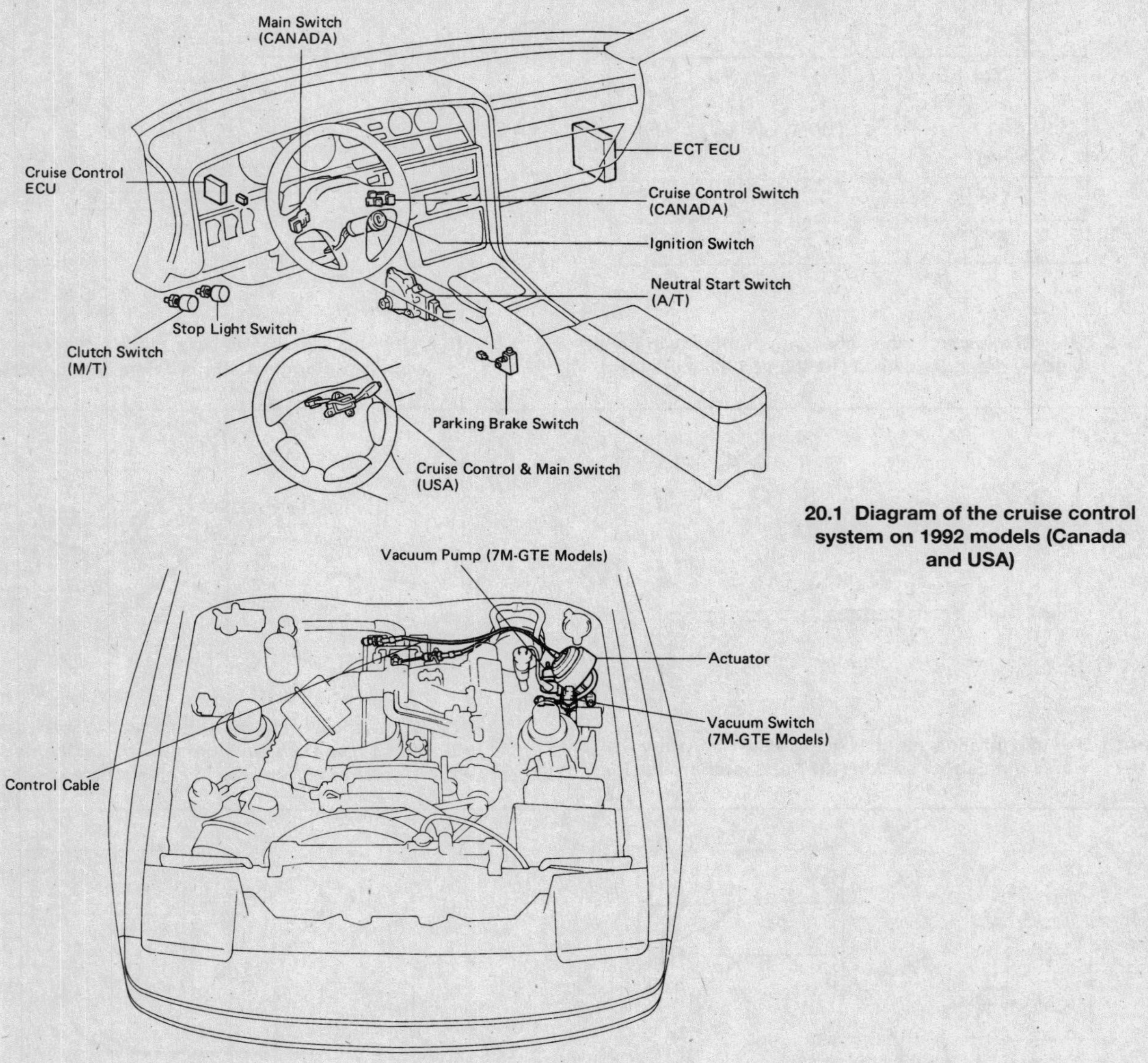

20.1 Diagram of the cruise control system on 1992 models (Canada and USA)

20 Cruise control system - general information

Refer to illustration 20.1

The cruise control system **(see illustration)** maintains vehicle speed by means of a vacuum actuated servo motor located in the engine compartment which is connected to the throttle linkage by a cable. The system consists of the ECU, servo motor, clutch switch, stoplight switch, control switches, a relay and associated vacuum hoses.

Newer models are equipped with a computer to analyze all the working parameters of the cruise control system for purposes of smoother transition from normal driving and greater control of the various driving ranges. Also, the newer systems are equipped with a self diagnosis system built into the computer to aid in the diagnosis of any problems with the cruise control system. The codes are accessed by the SET/COAST switch and the ignition switch.

Because of the complexity of the cruise control system, diagnosis and repair should be left to a dealer or properly equipped shop. However, it is possible for the home mechanic to make simple checks of the wiring and vacuum connections for minor faults which can be easily repaired. These include:

a) Checking the cruise control fuse.
b) Checking the hoses in the engine compartment for tight connections, cracked hoses and obvious vacuum leaks. The cruise control system is operated by a vacuum so it is critical that all vacuum switches, hoses and connections be secure.
c) Inspecting the cruise control actuating switches and electrical wiring for broken wires or loose connections.

21 Airbag system - general information

Refer to illustration 21.1

Warning: *On airbag-equipped models, always disconnect the negative battery cable when working in the vicinity of the impact sensors to avoid the possibility of accidental deployment of the airbag, which could cause personal injury.* **Caution:** *If the stereo in your vehicle is equipped with an anti-theft system, refer to the information on page 0-15 at the front of this manual before detaching the cable.*

Later models are equipped with a Supplemental Restraint System (SRS) **(see illustration)**, more commonly called an airbag system. This system is designed to protect the driver from serious injury in the event of a head-on or frontal collision. It consists of an airbag housing in the center of the steering wheel, two crash sensors mounted at the front of the vehicle and a diagnostic module located inside the passenger compartment.

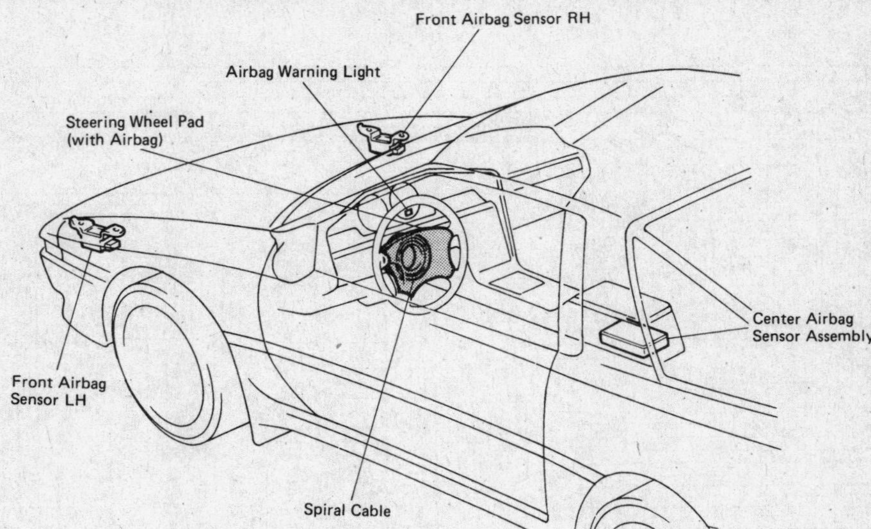

21.1 Diagram of the airbag system

Airbag module

The airbag module contains a housing incorporating the cushion (airbag) and the inflator unit. The inflator assembly is mounted on the back of the housing over a hole through which gas is expelled, inflating the bag almost instantaneously when an electrical signal is sent from the system. A spiral cable which is specially wound so it can transmit an electrical signal regardless of steering wheel position is used to carry this signal to the module.

Sensors

The system has three sensors: two crash sensors mounted at the front of the vehicle and sensor located in the center airbag sensor assembly located in the passenger compartment.

The front crash sensors are pressure-sensitive switches that complete an electrical circuit during an impact of sufficient force. The electrical signal from the sensors is sent to the center airbag sensor assembly which then completes the circuit and inflates the airbag.

Self diagnosis system

The airbag system is also equipped with a self diagnosis system that aids in the diagnosis of any airbag problems or electrical malfunctions. The driver is warned by a constant AIRBAG light on the dashboard (see Chapter 1). If there is a fault in the system, the light will go on and stay on and fault codes indicating the nature of the fault will be stored. If the AIRBAG light does go on and stays on, the vehicle should be taken to your dealer immediately for service. Because of the complexity of the airbag system and the special tools and techniques required for diagnosis and repair, this should be left to a dealership service department or properly equipped shop.

22 Power door lock system - general information

The power door lock system operates the door lock actuators mounted in each door. The system consists of the switches, actuators and associated electrical wiring. Diagnosis can usually be limited to simple checks of the wiring connections and actuators for minor faults which can be easily repaired. These include:

a) Checking the system fuse and/or circuit breaker.
b) Checking the switch wiring for damage or loose connections.
c) Checking the switches for continuity.
d) Removing the door panel(s) and checking the actuator electrical connections for looseness or damage. Inspect the actuator rods (if equipped) to make sure they are not bent, damaged or binding. The actuator can be checked by applying battery power momentarily. A solid click indicates the solenoid is operating properly.

23 Power window system - general information

The power window system operates the electric motors mounted in the doors which lower and raise the windows. The system consists of the control switches, the motors (regulators), glass mechanisms and associated wiring.

Diagnosis can usually be limited to simple checks of the electrical connections and motors for minor faults which can be easily repaired. These include:

a) Inspecting the power window actuating switches and electrical wiring for broken wires or loose connections.
b) Checking the power window fuse and/or circuit breaker.
c) Removing the door panel(s) and checking the power window motor electrical wiring connections for looseness and damage, and inspecting the glass mechanisms for damage which could cause binding.

24 Wiring diagrams - general information

Refer to illustration 24.4

Since it isn't possible to include all electrical wiring diagrams for every year covered by this manual, the following diagrams are those that are typical and most commonly needed.

Prior to troubleshooting any circuits, check the fuse and circuit breakers (if equipped) to make sure they are in good condition. Make sure the battery is properly charged and has clean, tight cable connections (see Chapter 1).

When checking the electrical system, make sure all connectors are clean, with no broken or loose pins. When unplugging a connector, do not pull on the wires, only on the connector housings themselves.

Refer to the accompanying illustration for the wire color codes applicable to your vehicle **(see illustration)**.

Wire colors are indicated by an alphabetical code.

B = Black	L = Light Blue	R = Red
BR = Brown	LG = Light Green	V = Violet
G = Green	O = Orange	W = White
GR = Gray	P = Pink	Y = Yellow

The first letter indicates the basic wire color and the second letter indicates the color of the stripe.

24.4 Wiring diagram color code chart

12

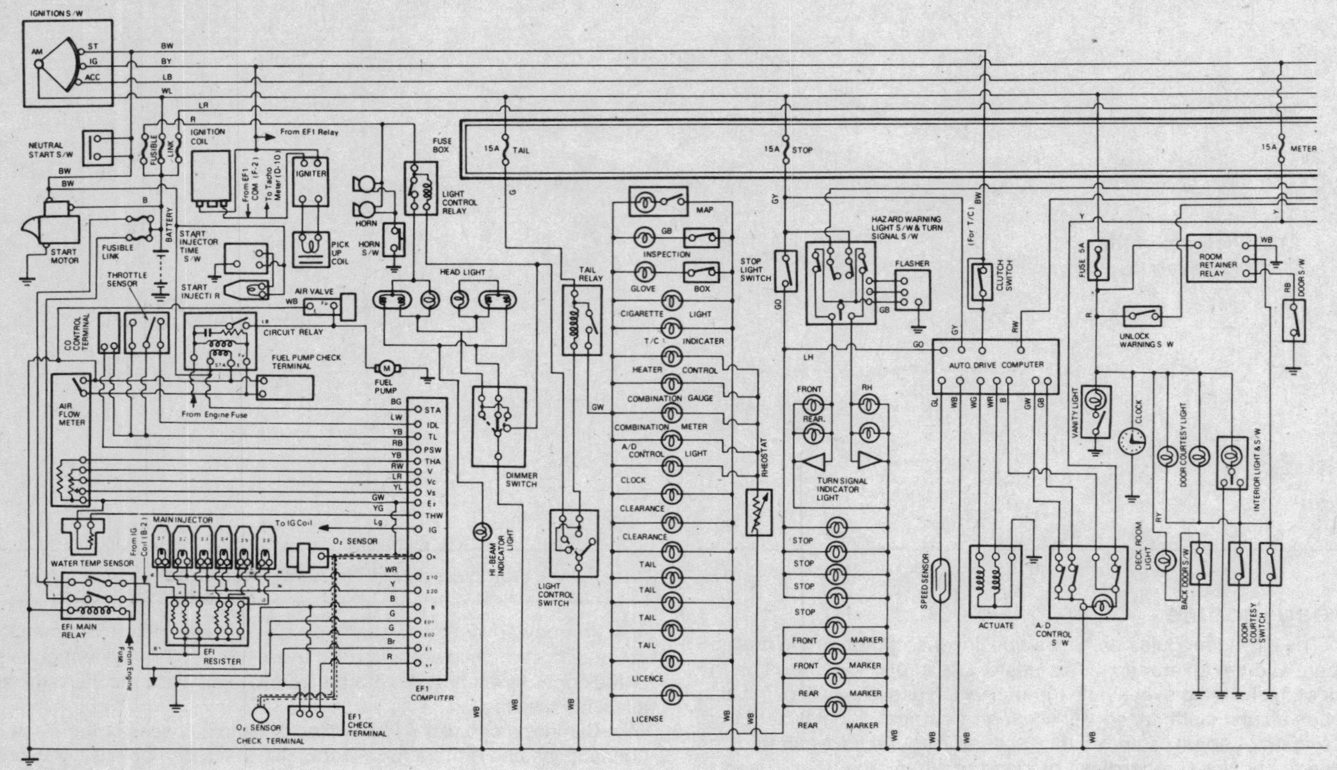

Wiring diagram - 1979 models (1 of 2)

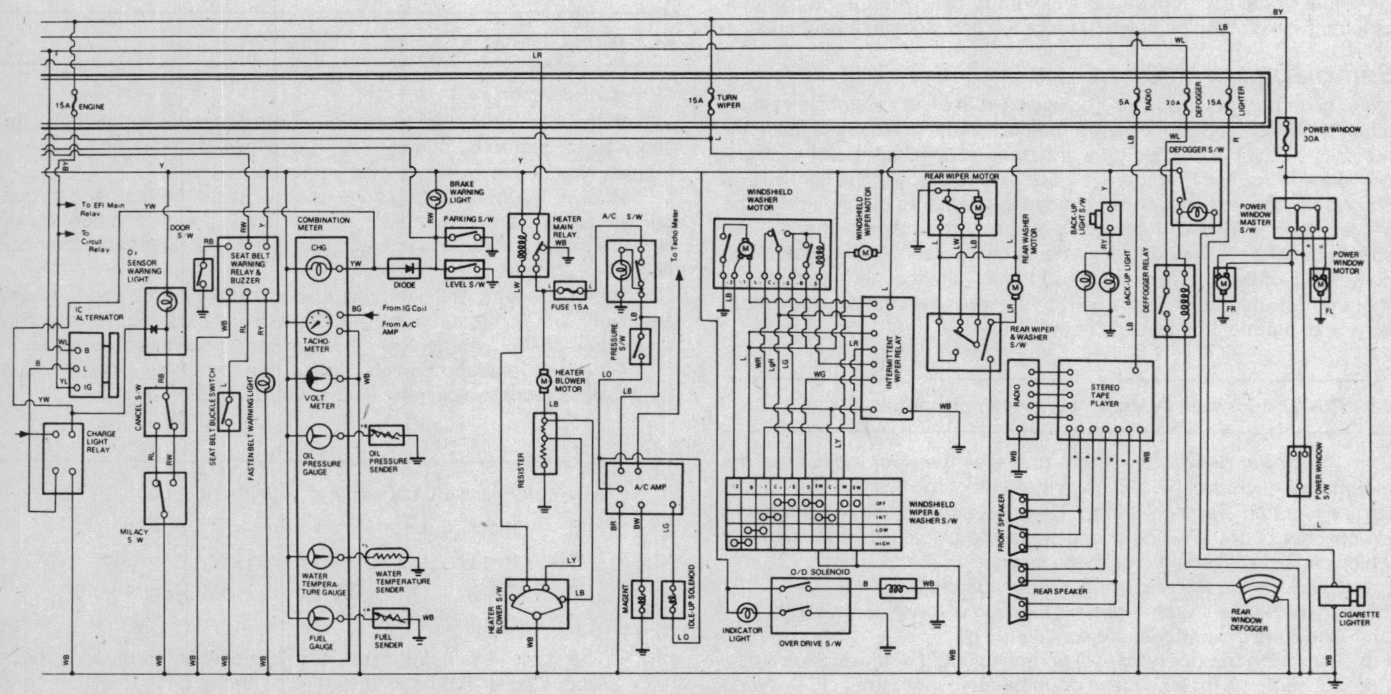

Wiring diagram - 1979 models (2 of 2)

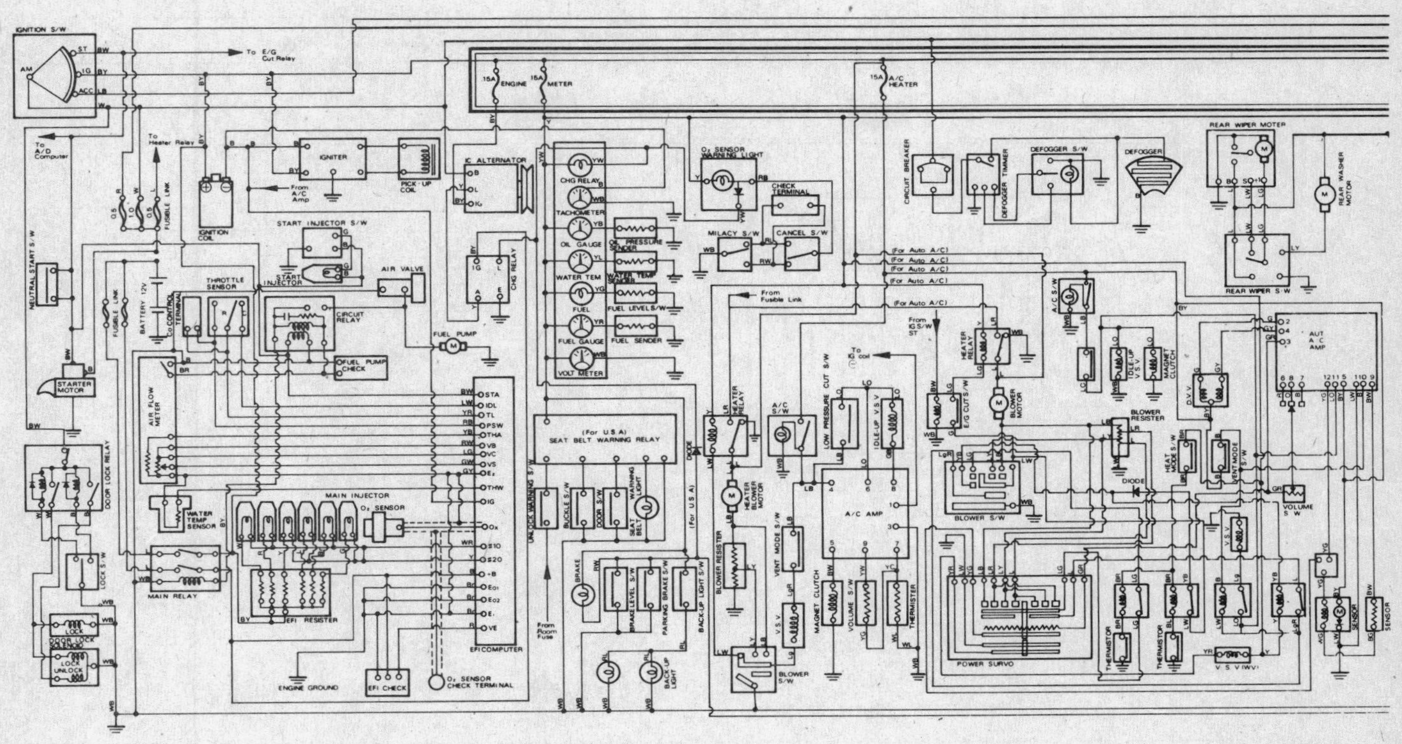

Wiring diagram - 1980 models (1 of 2)

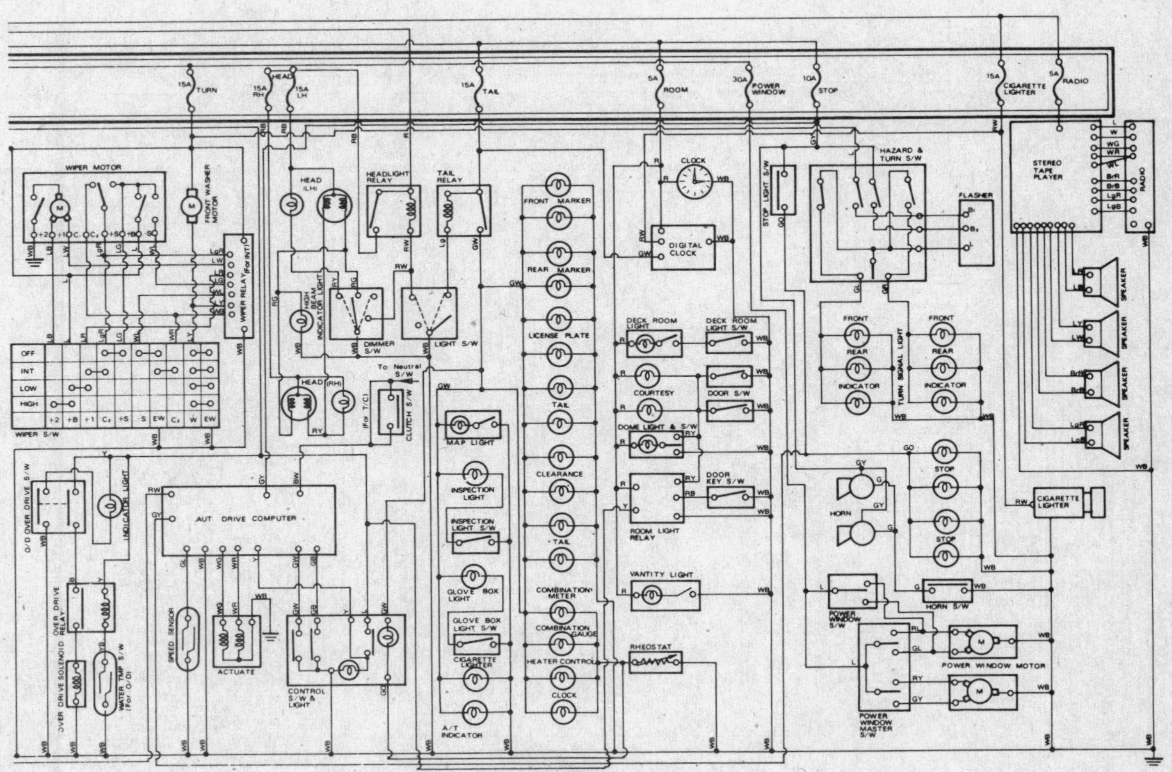

Wiring diagram - 1980 models (2 of 2)

12

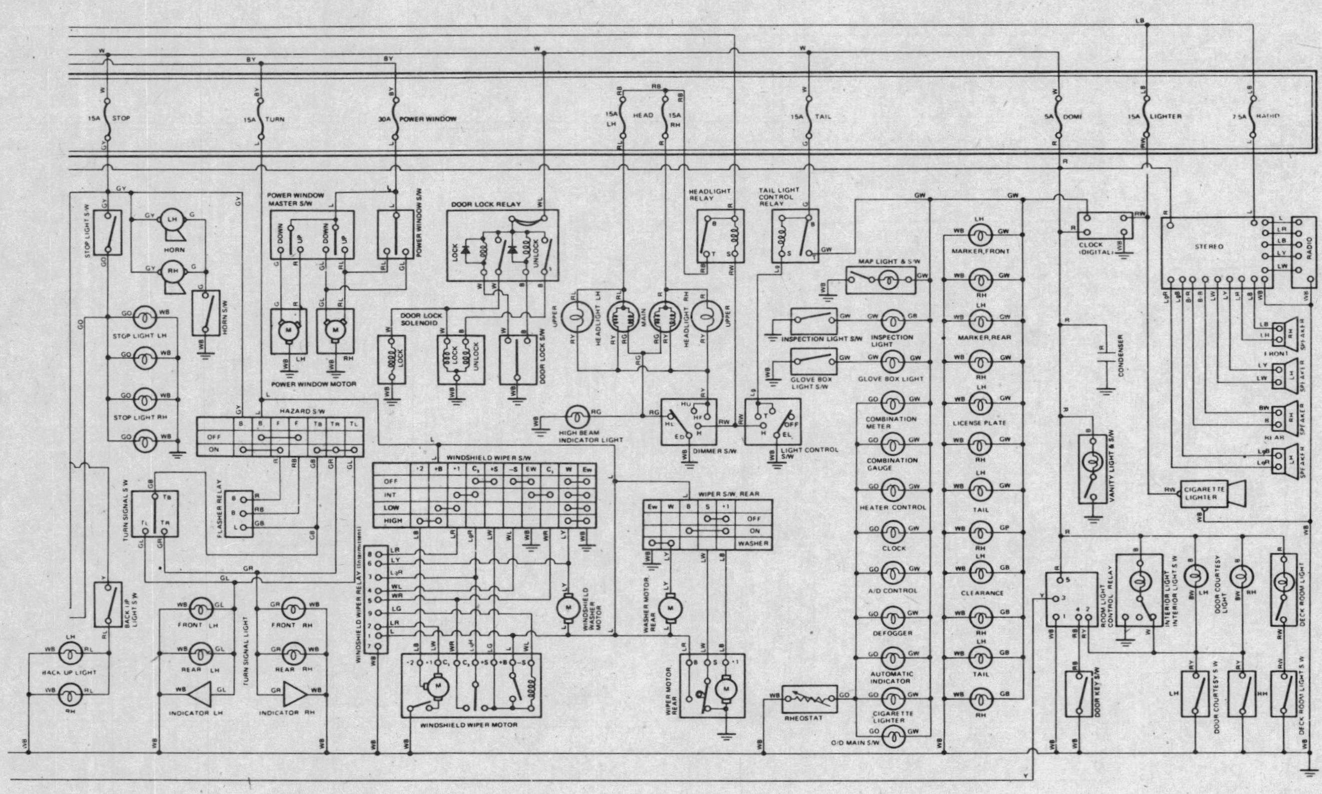

Wiring diagram - 1981 models (1 of 2)

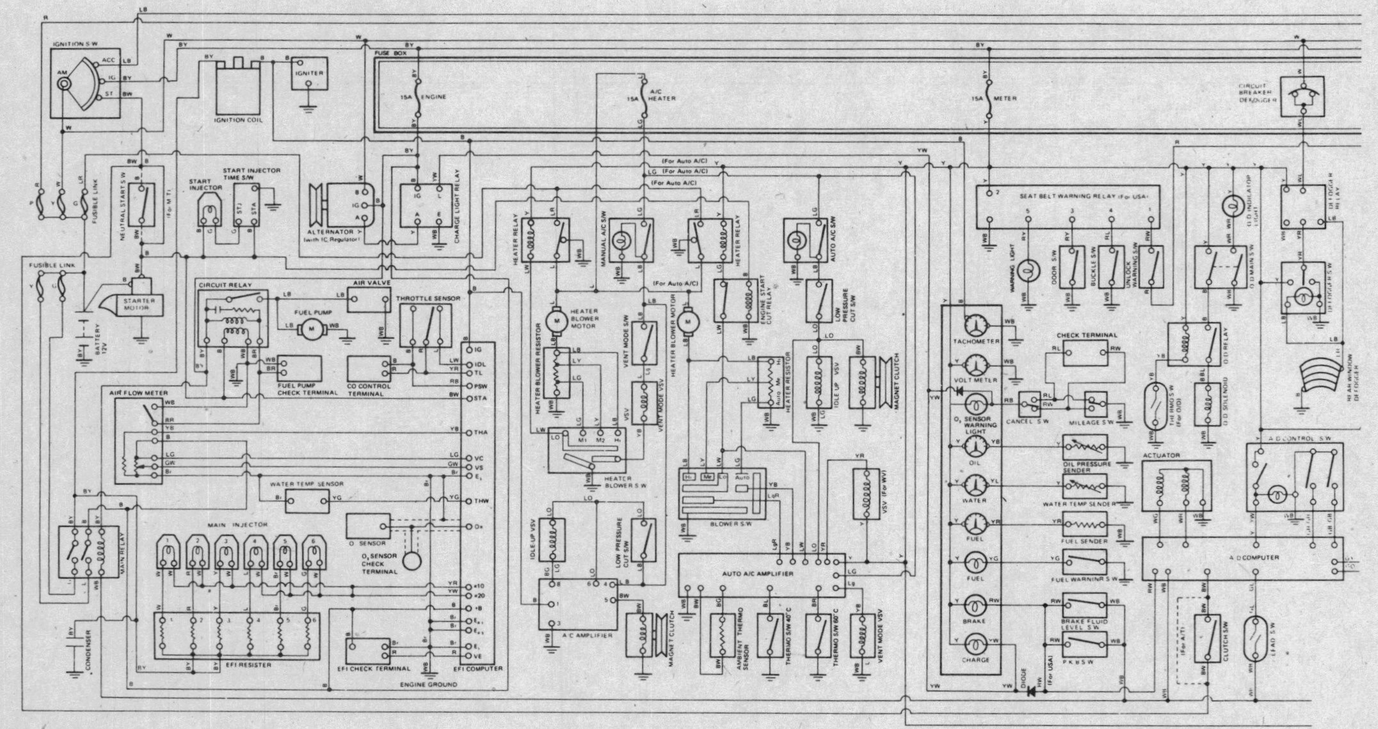

Wiring diagram - 1981 models (2 of 2)

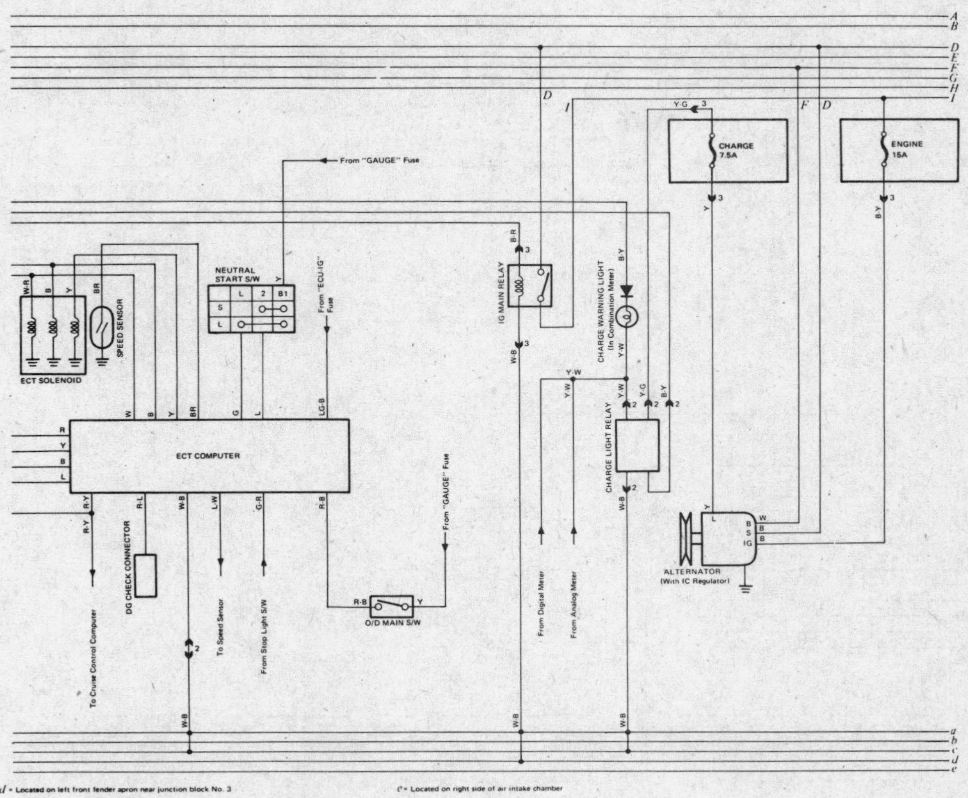

ECT and charging system - 1982 and 1983 models

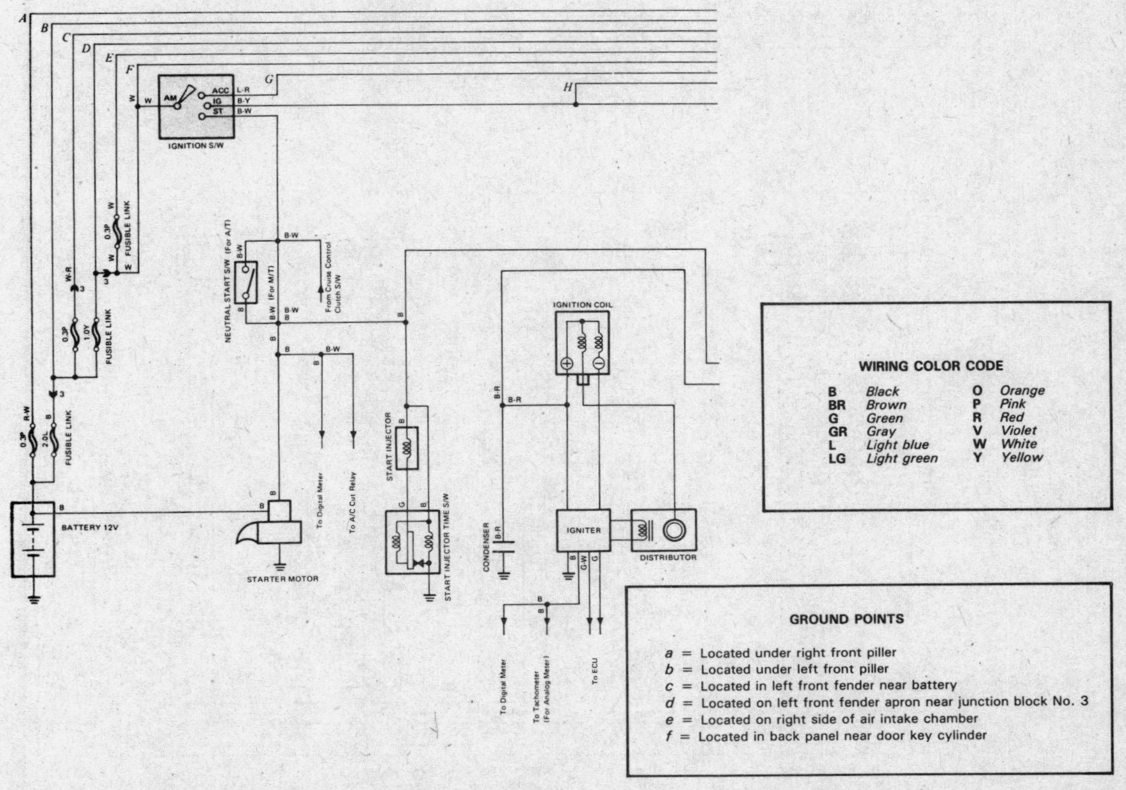

Power distribution, starting and ignition systems - 1982 and 1983 models

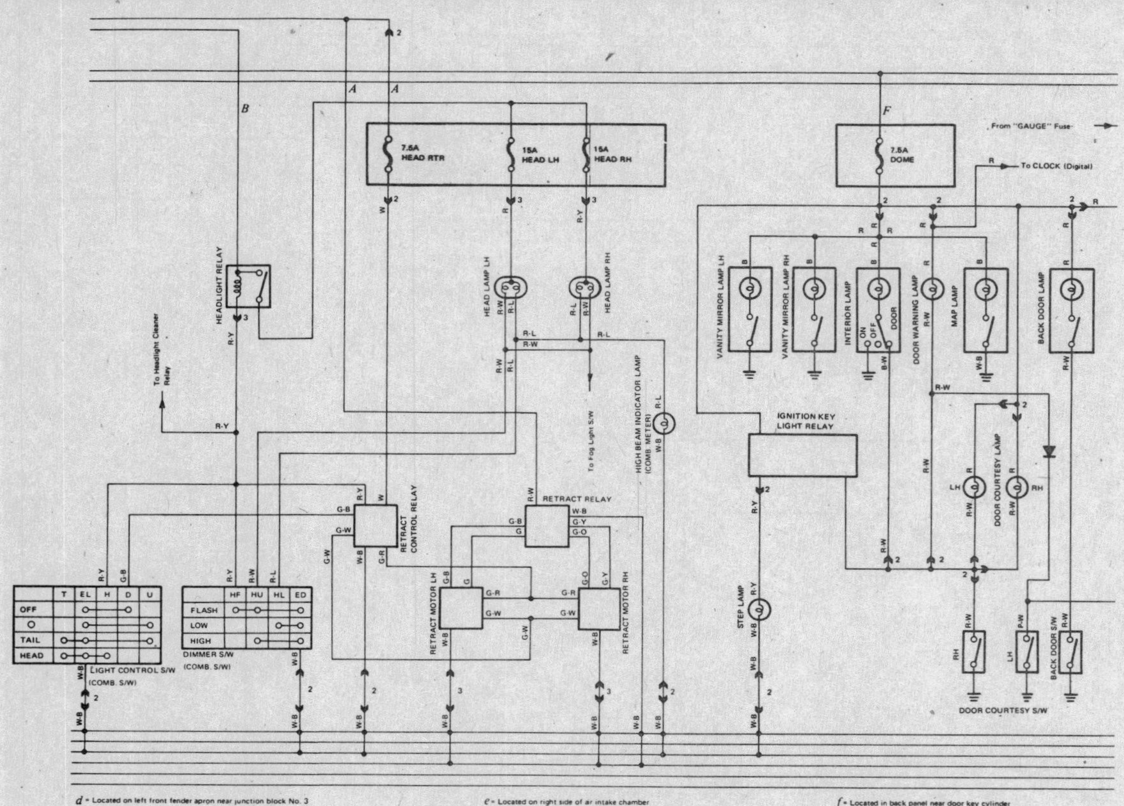

Headlights and interior lights - 1982 through 1984 models

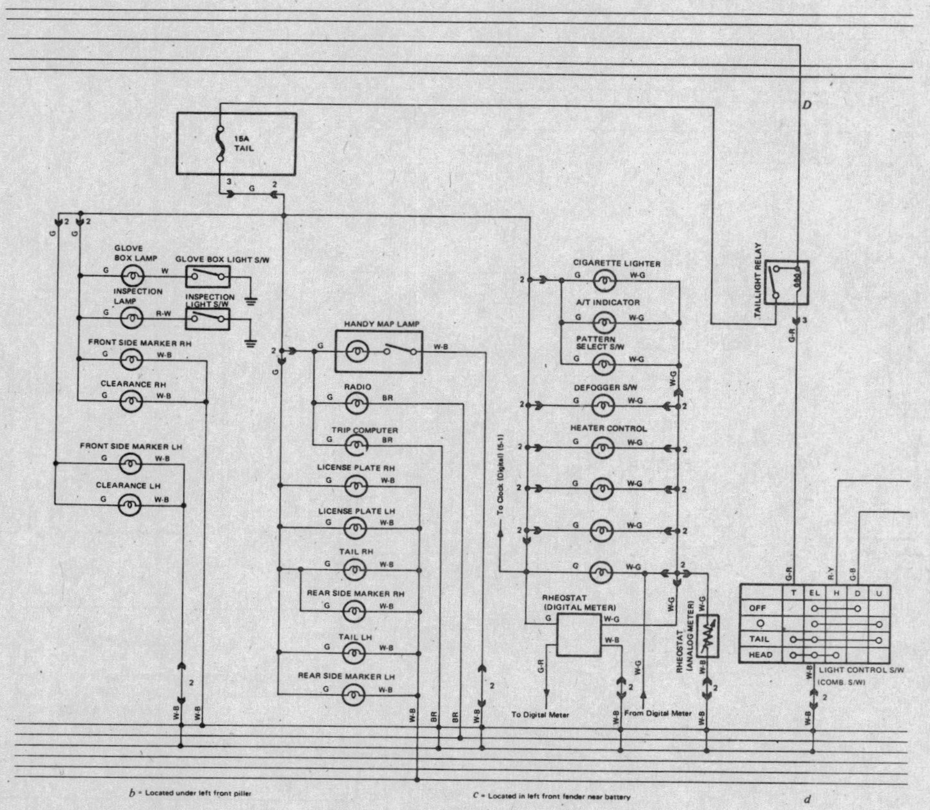

Tail lights and interior lights - 1982 through 1984 models

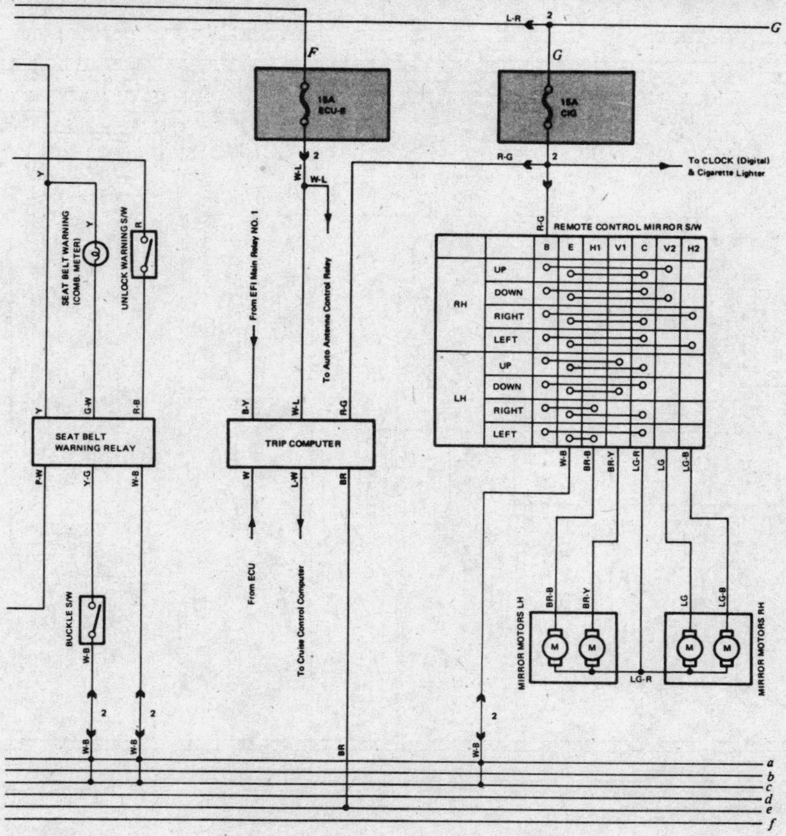

Seatbelts, trip computer and rear view mirror - 1982 through 1984 models

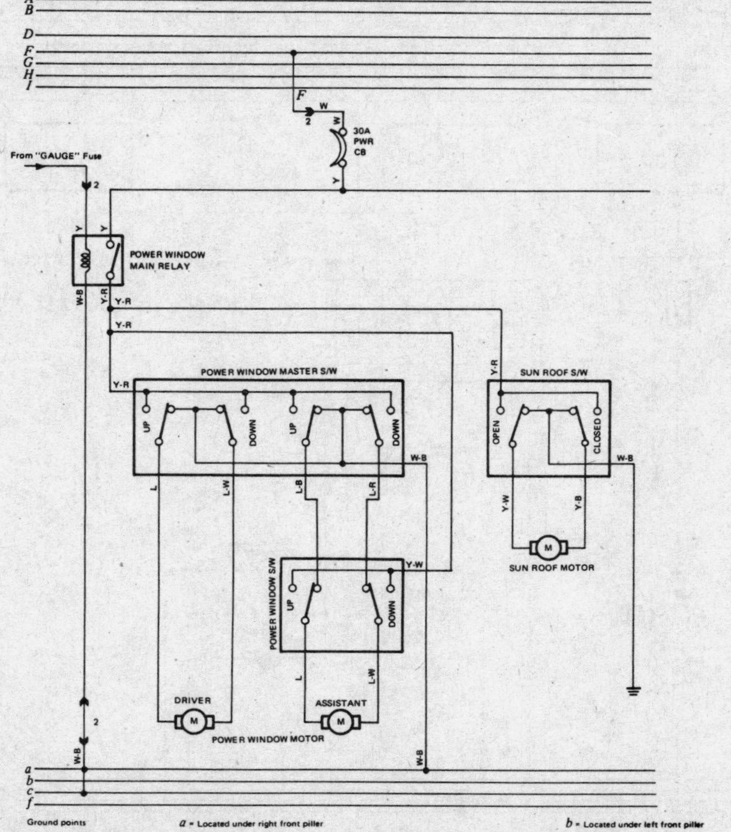

Power windows and sunroof - 1982 through 1984 models

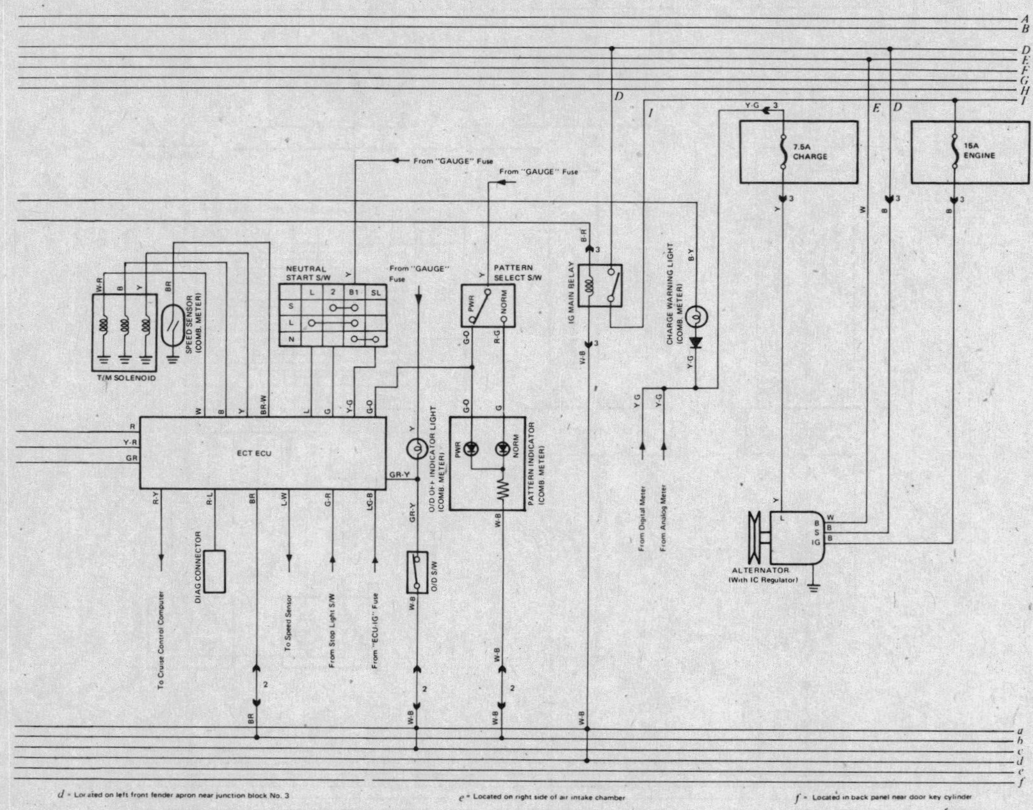

ECT and charging system - 1984 and 1985 models

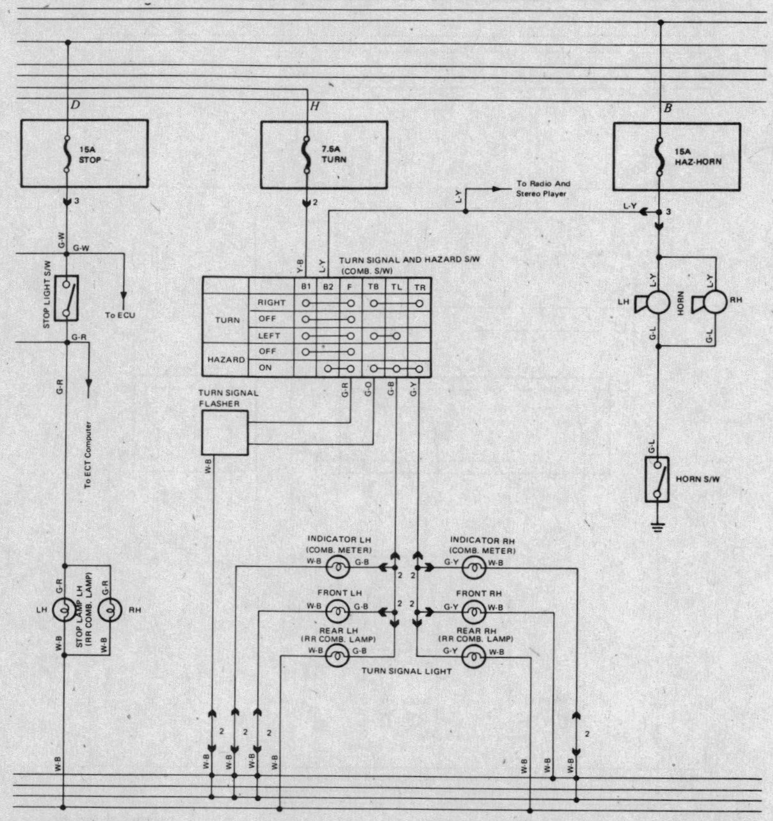

Brake lights, turn signals and horn - 1982 through 1984 models

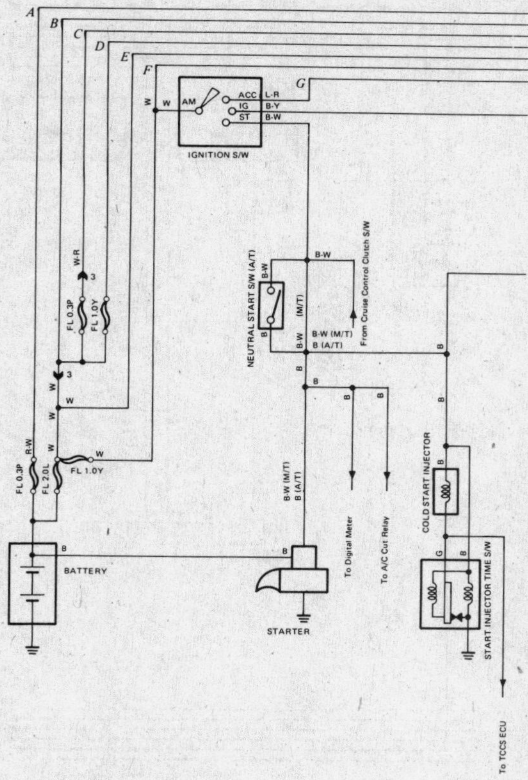

Power distribution and starting system - 1986 models

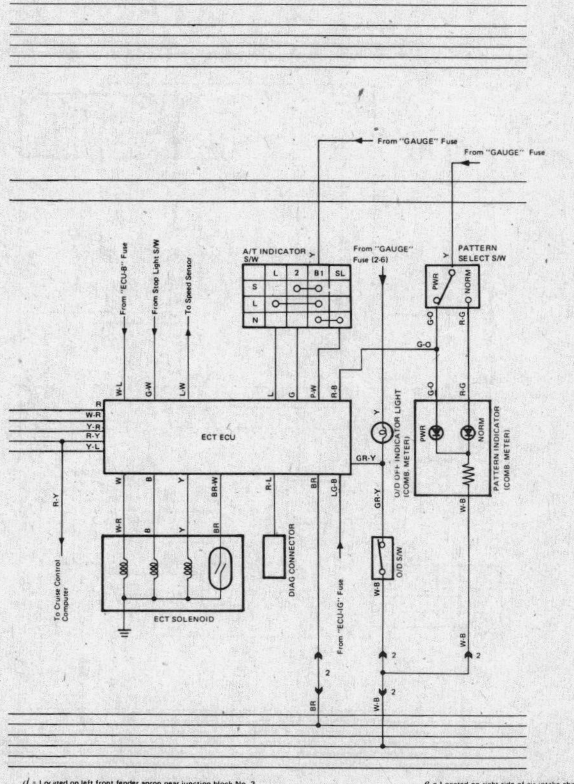

ECT - 1986 models

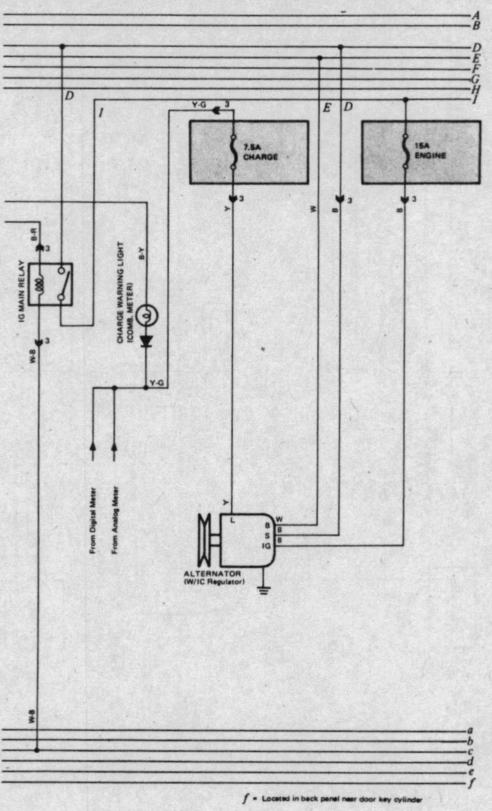

Charging system - 1986 models

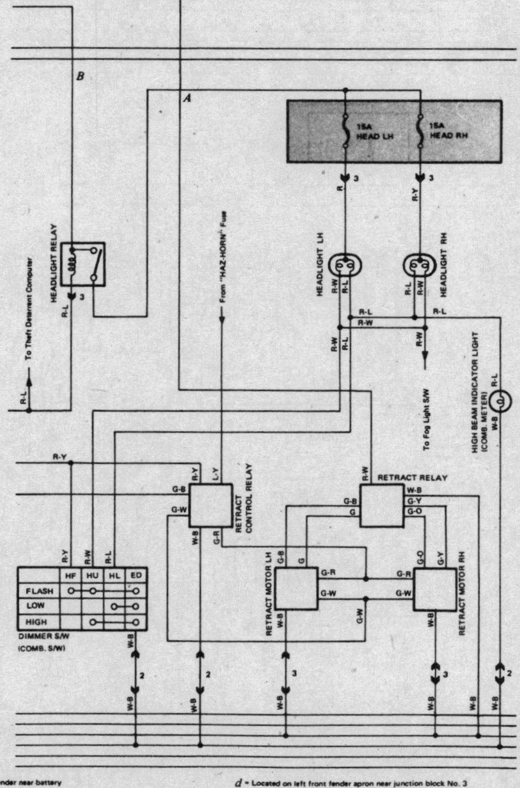

Headlights - 1985 and 1986 models

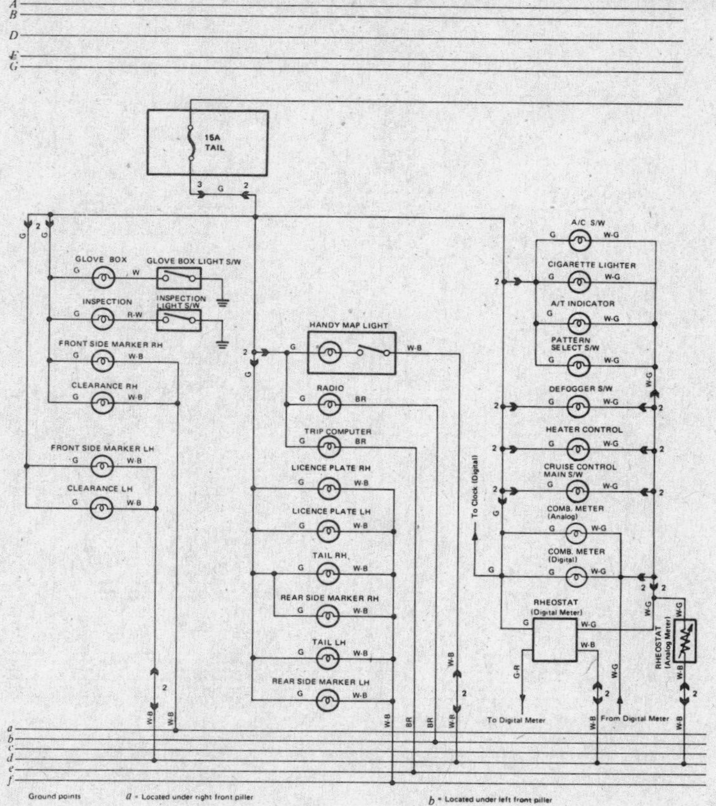

Tail lights and interior lights - 1985 and 1986 models

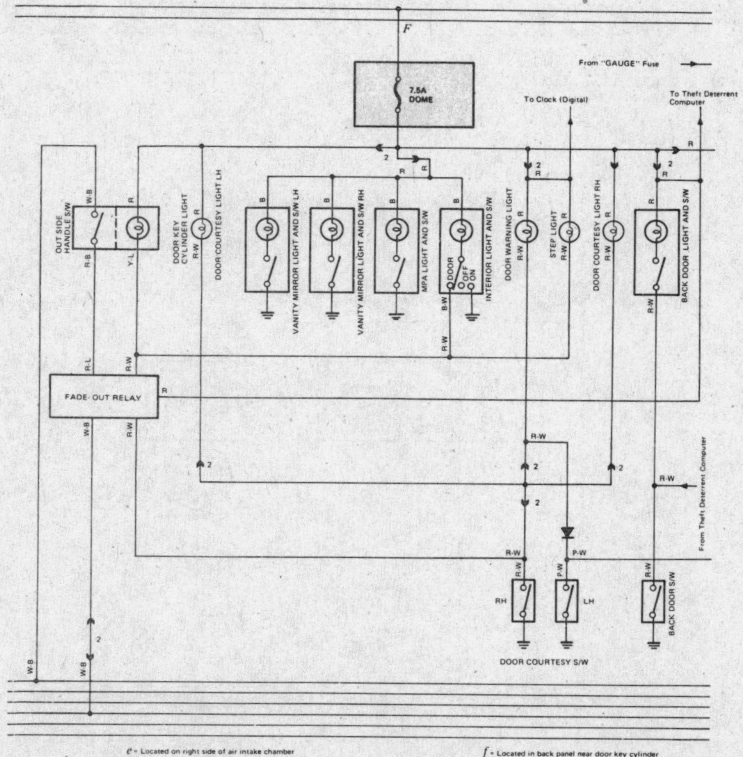

Interior lights - 1985 and 1986 models

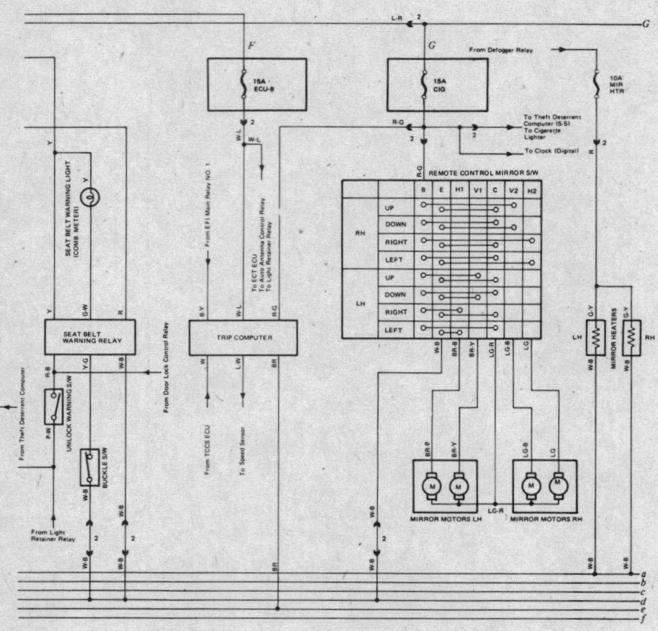

Seatbelts, trip computer and rear view mirror - 1985 and 1986 models

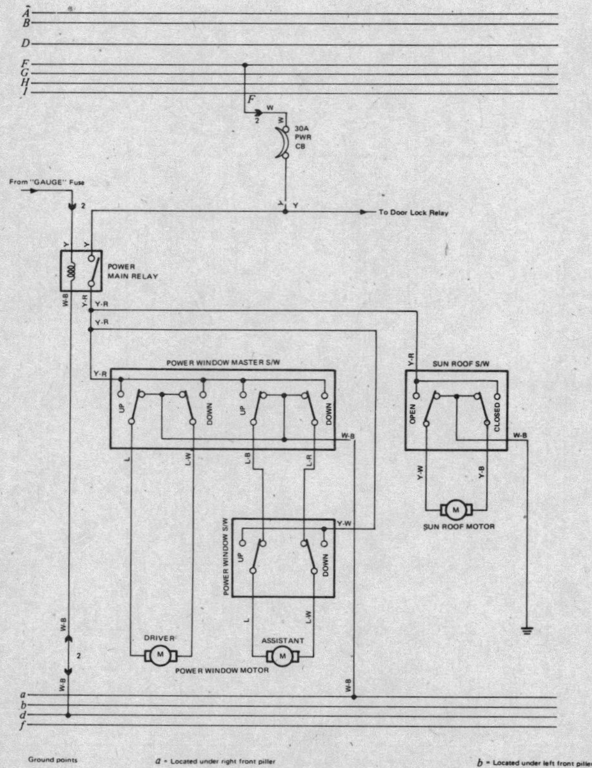

Power windows and sunroof - 1985 and 1986 models

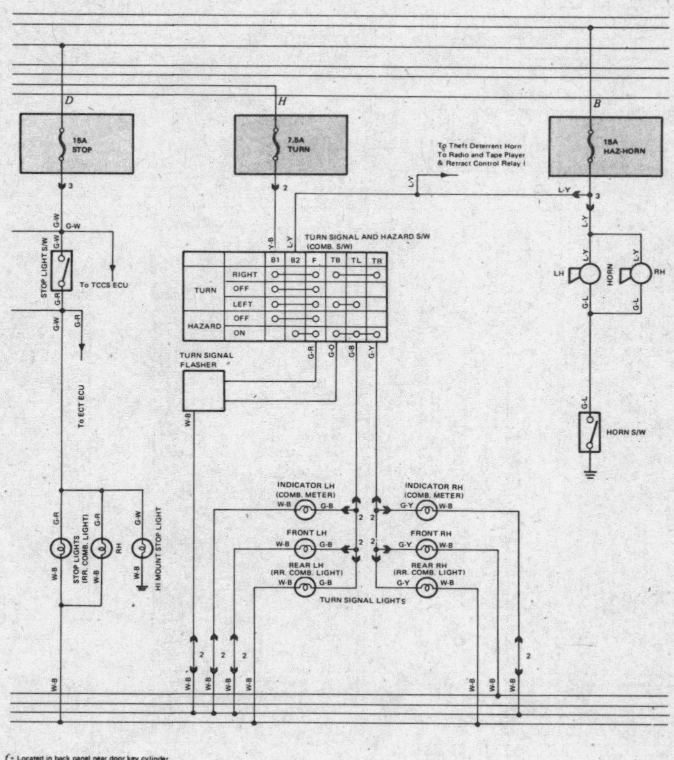

Brake lights, turn signals and horn - 1985 and 1986 models

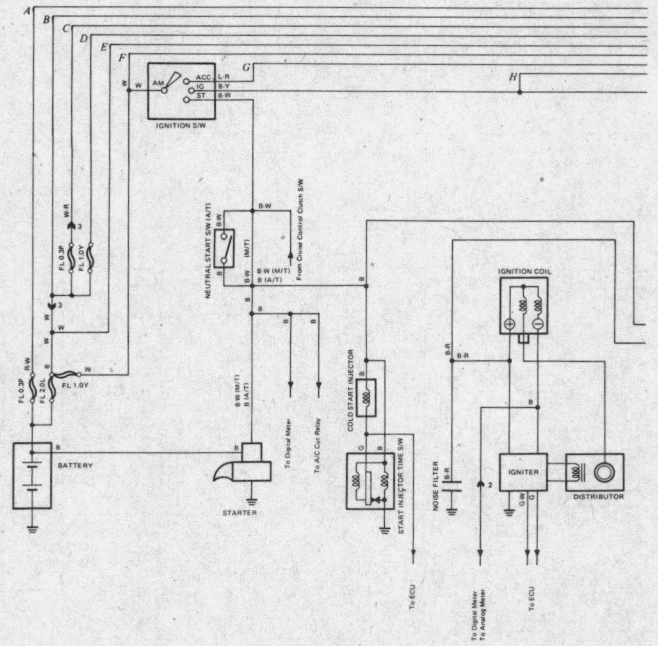

Typical ignition system - 1983 through 1986 models

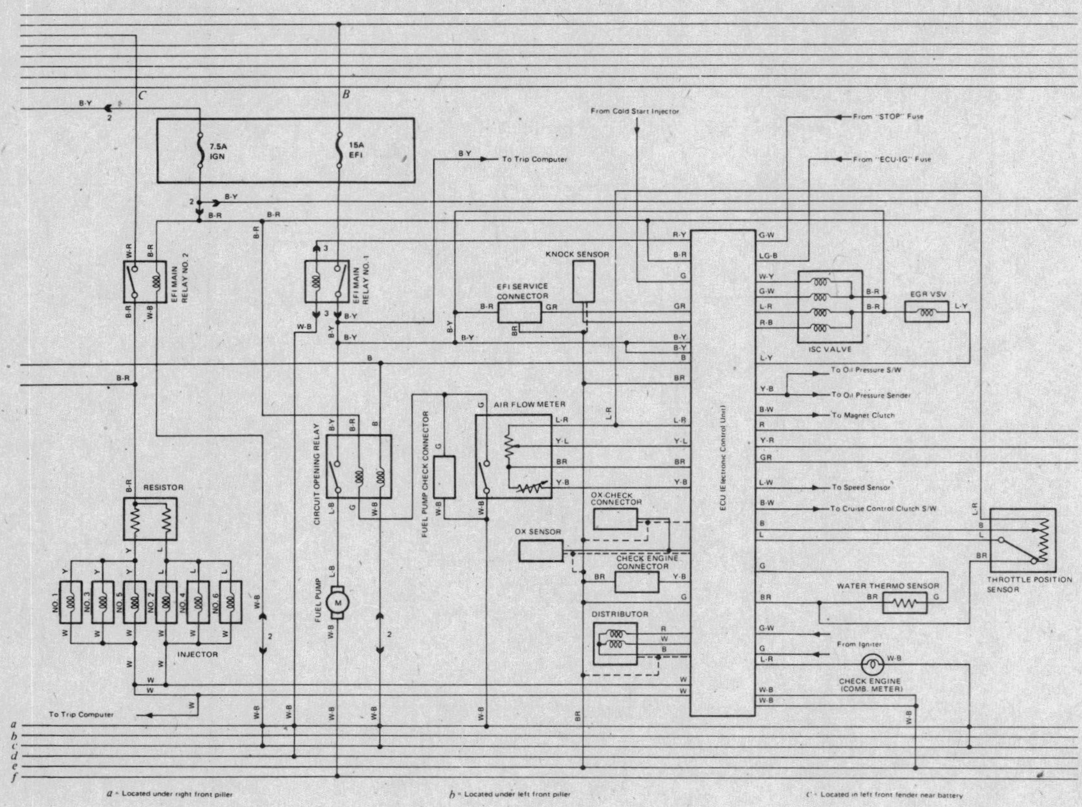

EFI system - 1982 through 1986 models

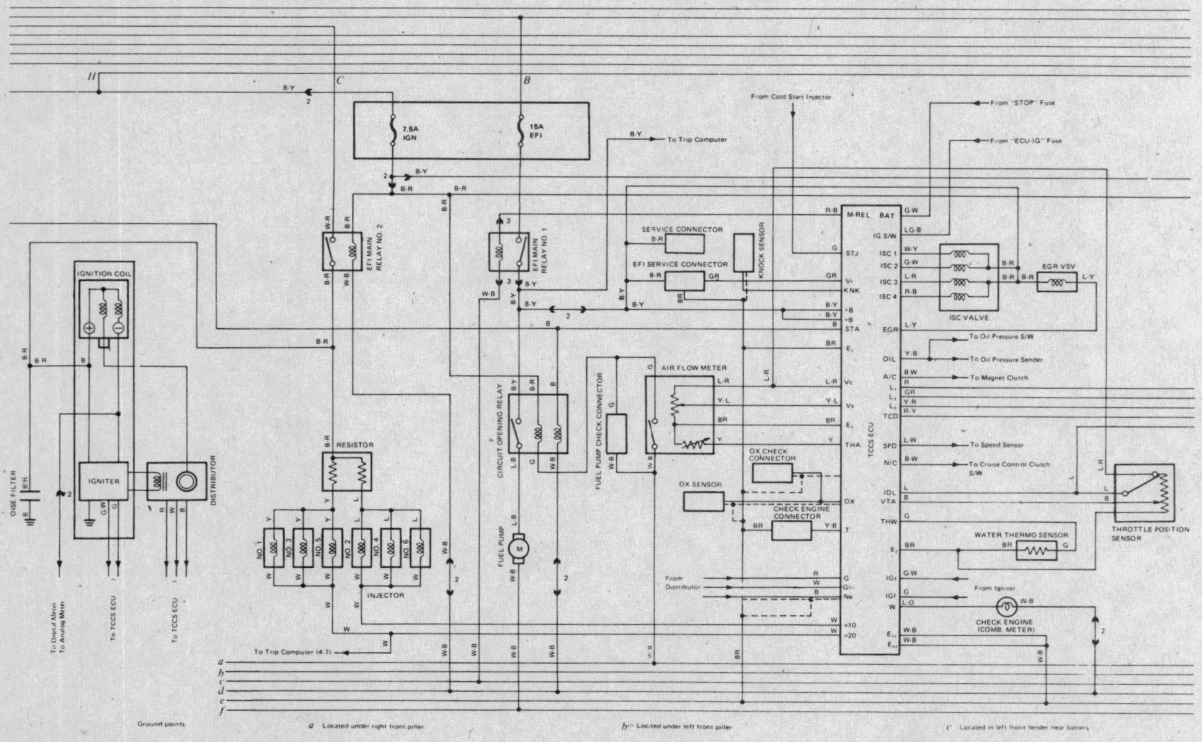

TCCS system - 1982 through 1986 models

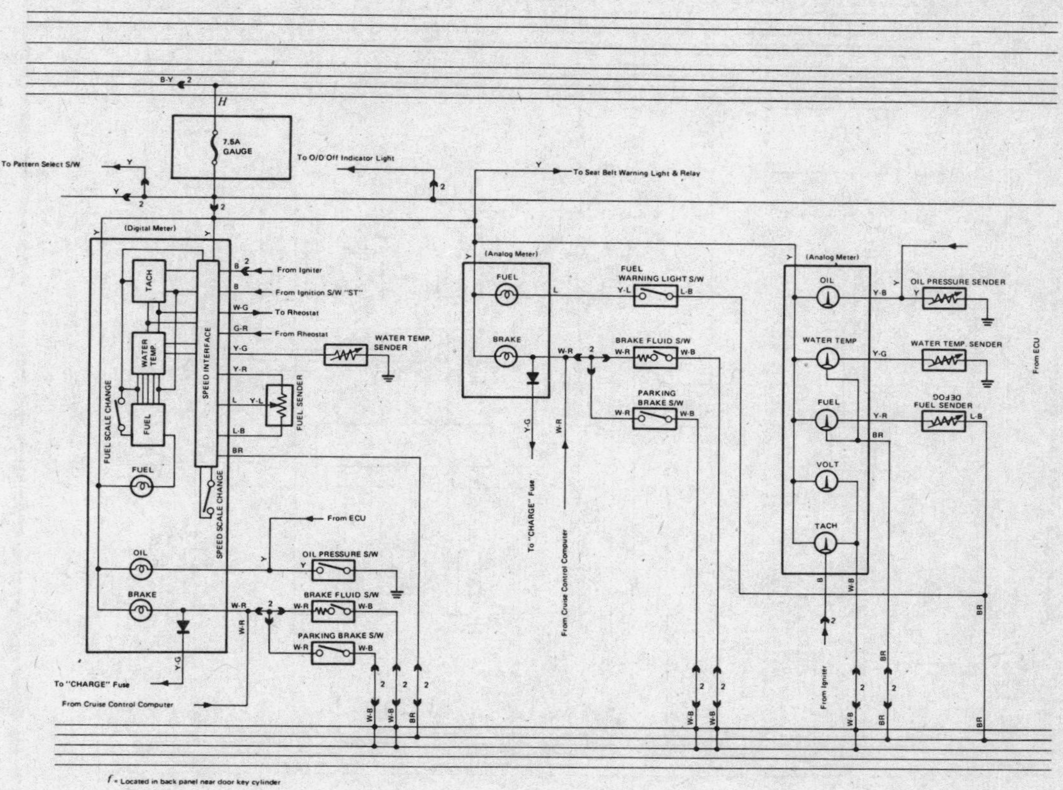

Combination meter - 1982 through 1986 models

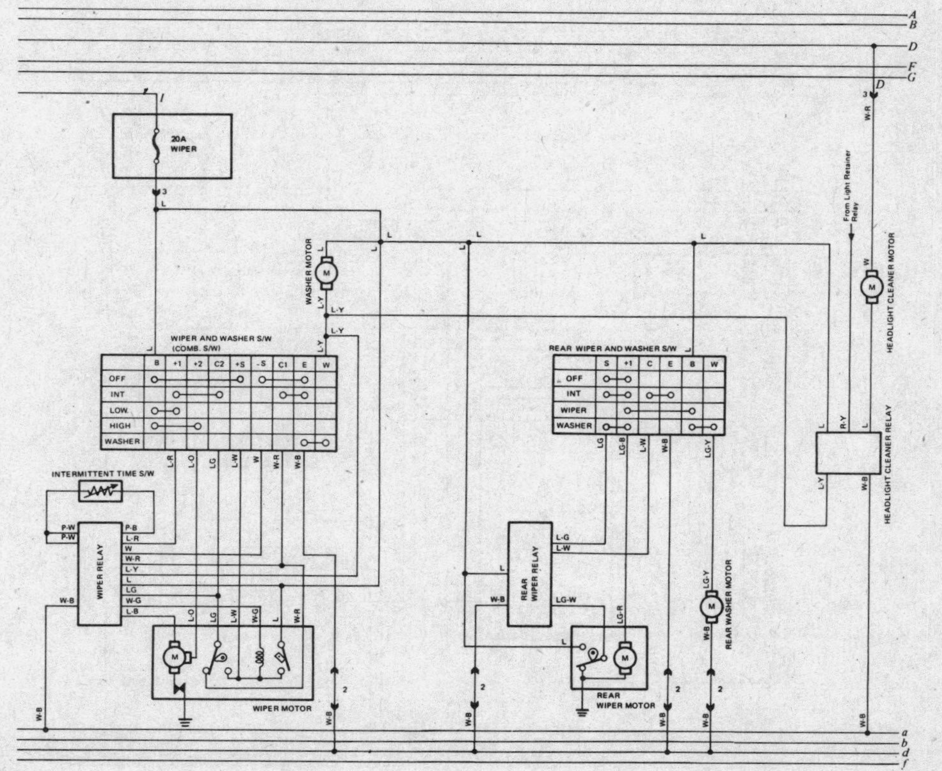

Front and rear windshield wiper/washer and headlight cleaner circuits - 1982 through 1986 models

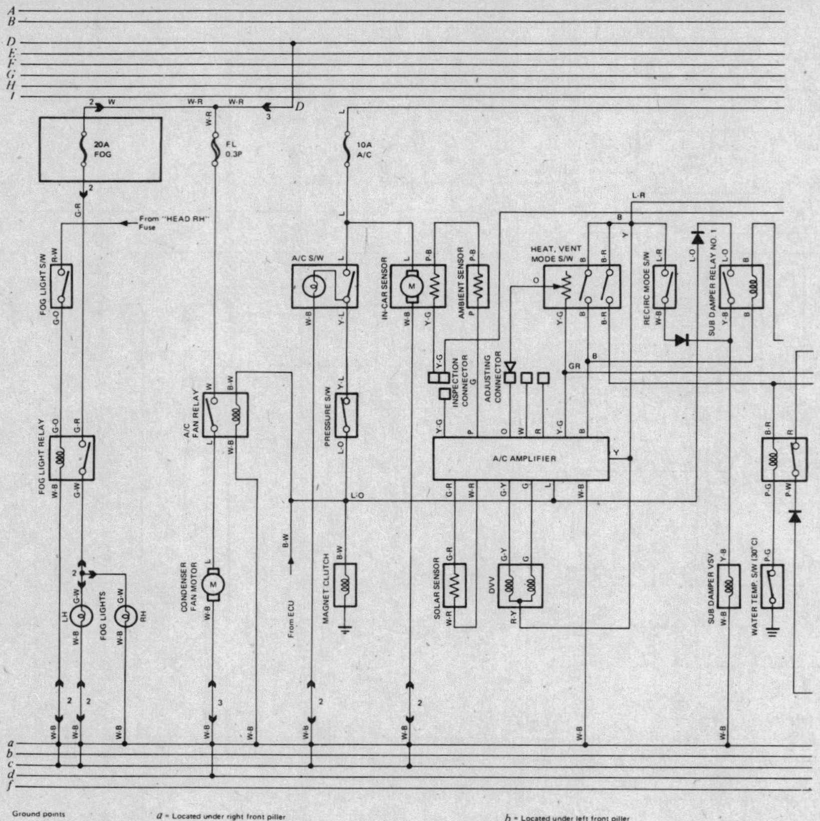

Fog lights and air conditioning system - 1982 through 1986 models

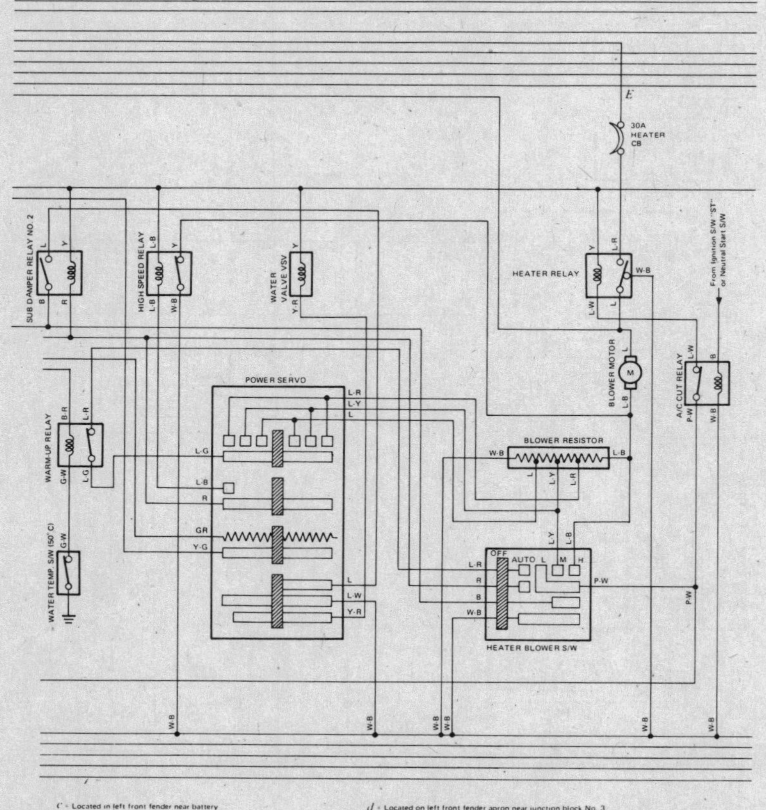

Heater - 1982 through 1986 models

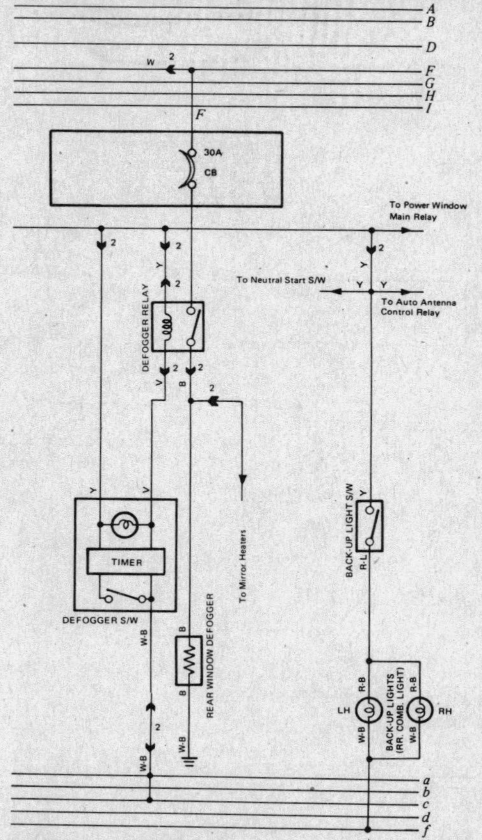

Rear defogger and back-up lights - 1982 through 1986 models

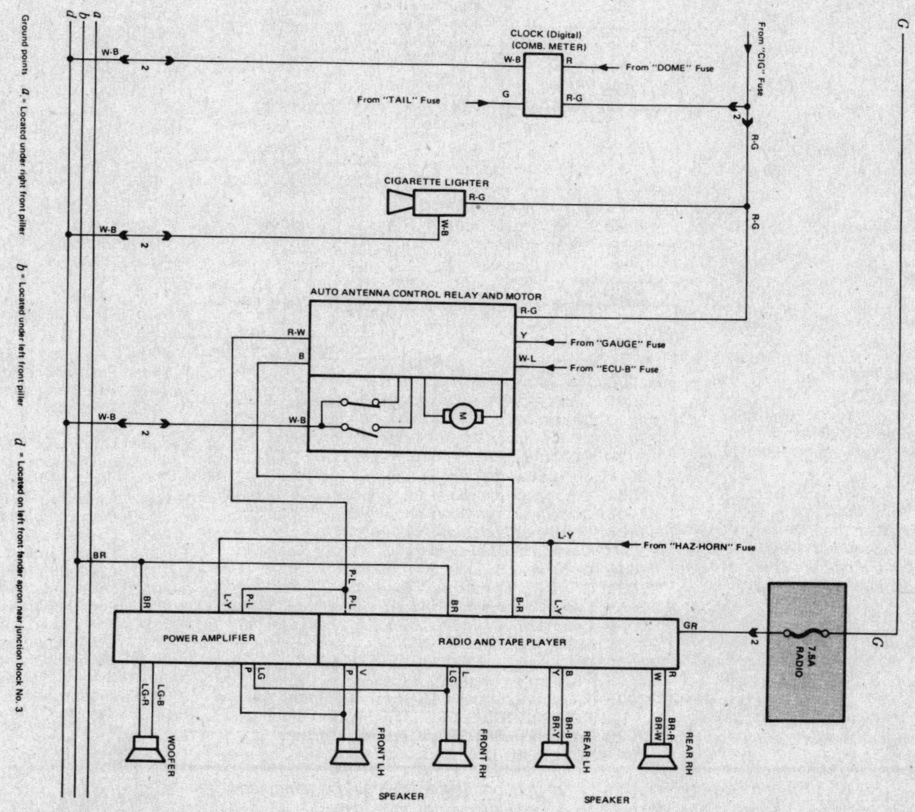

Clock, cigarette lighter, antenna and radio - 1982 through 1986 models

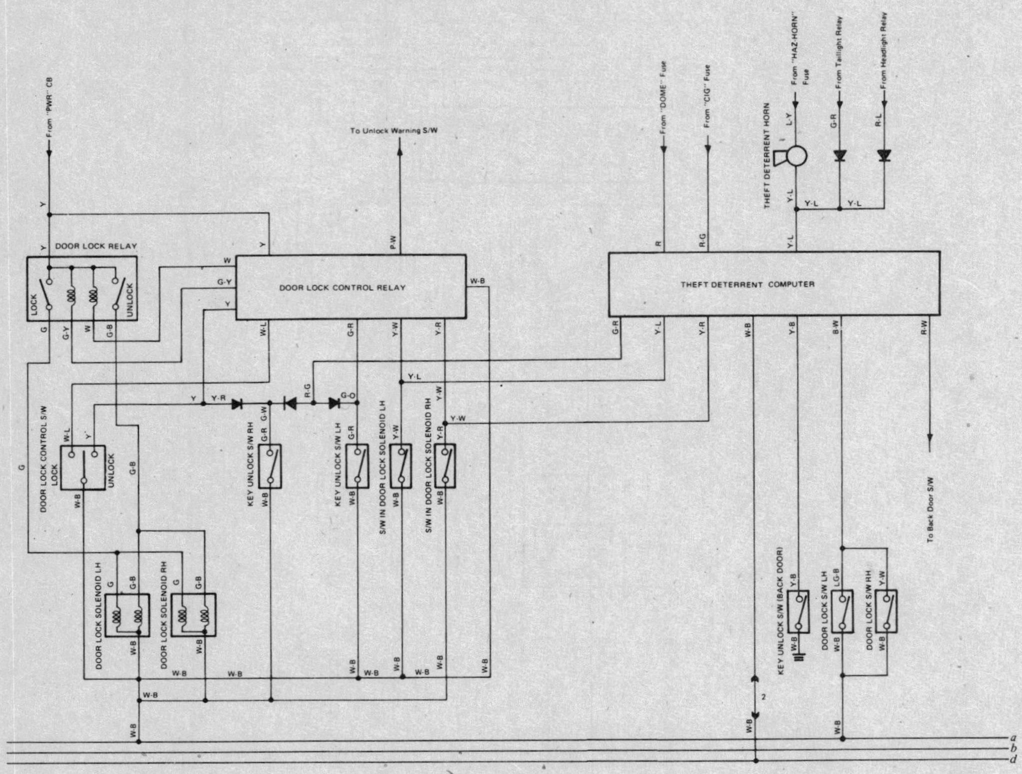

Door locks and theft protection system - 1982 through 1986 models

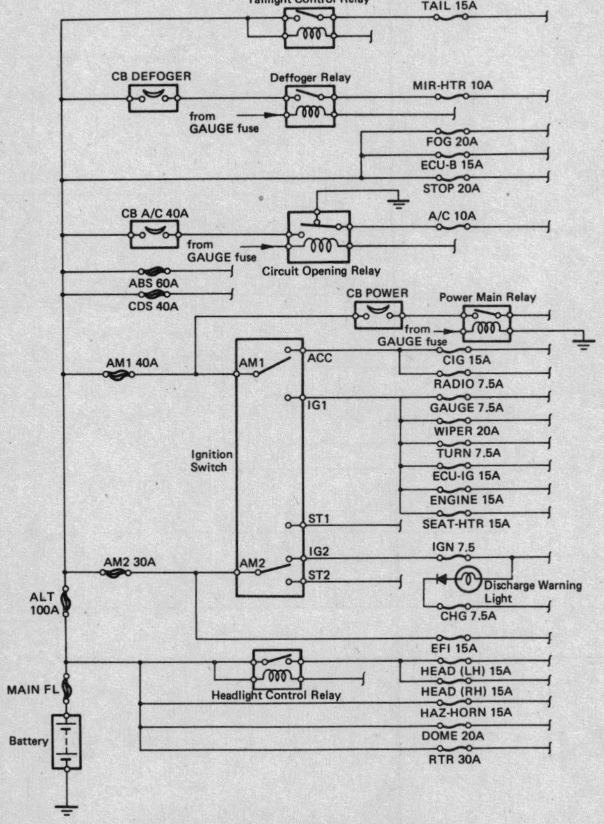

Power distribution - 1991 and 1992 models

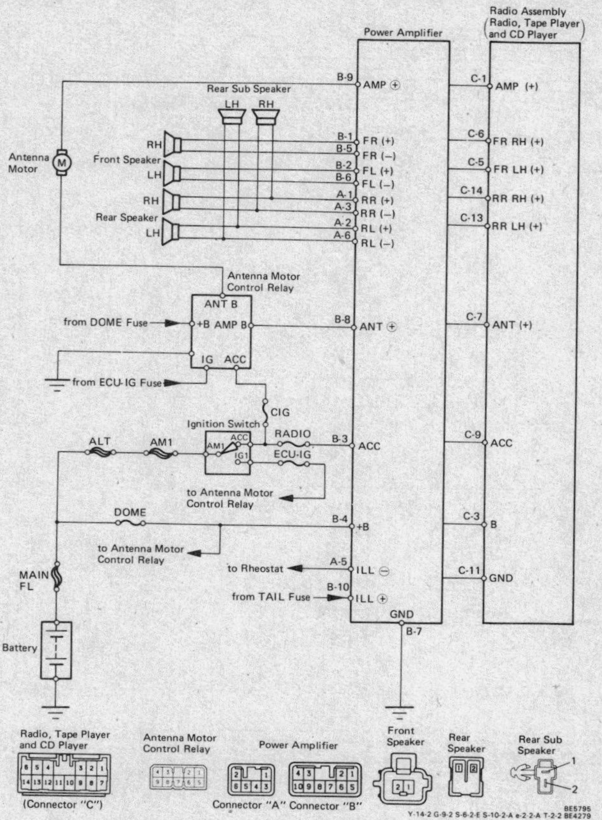

Radio, tape player and CD unit - 1991 and 1992 models

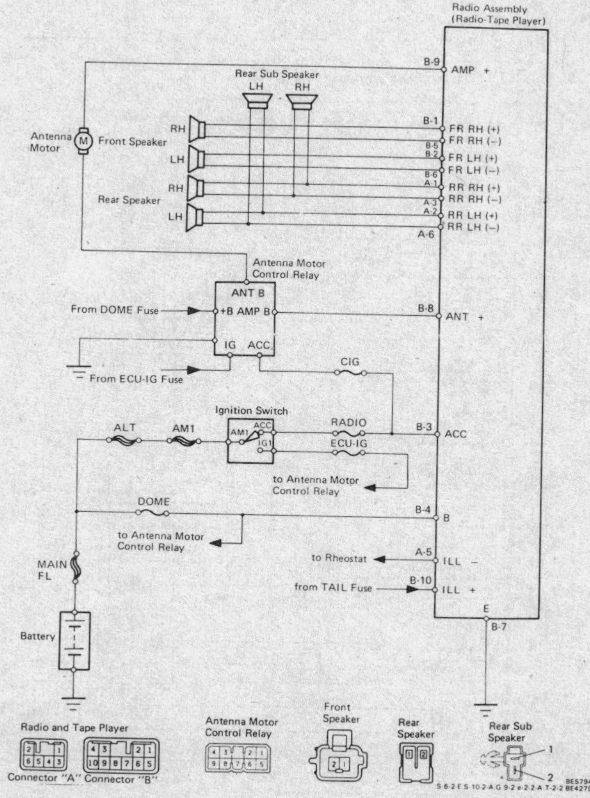

Radio, tape player unit - 1991 and 1992 models

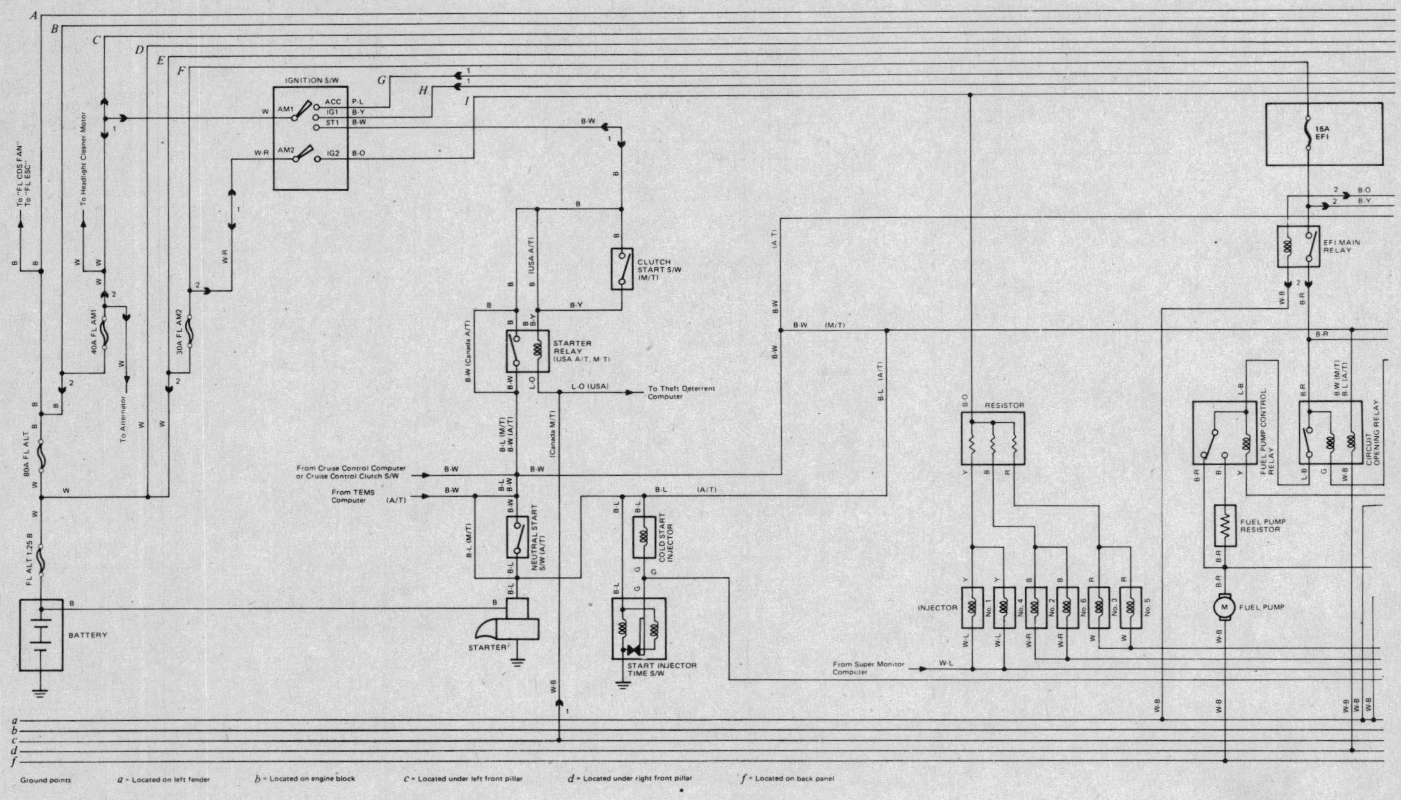

Power distribution, starting and engine control - 1987 models (1 of 2)

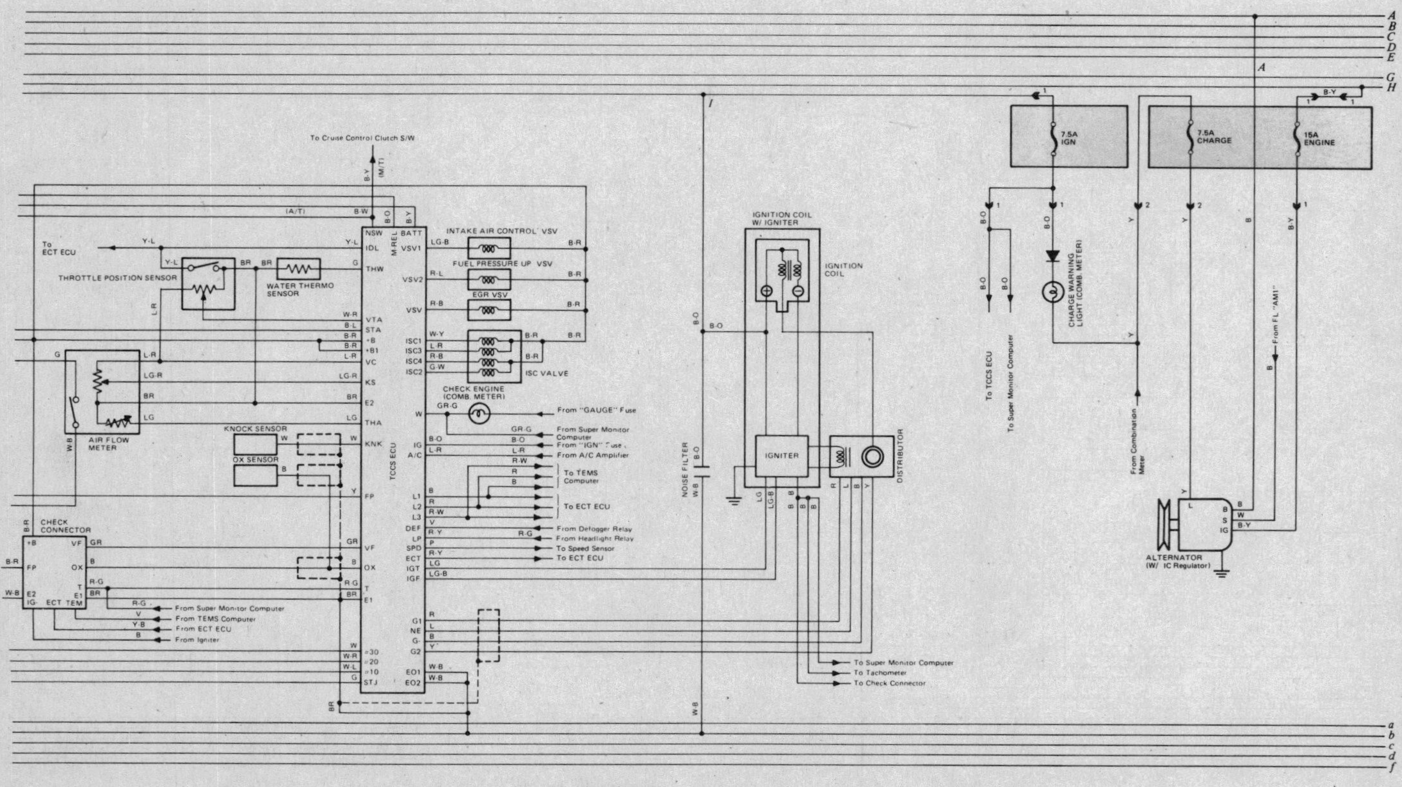

Power distribution, starting and engine control - 1987 models (2 of 2)

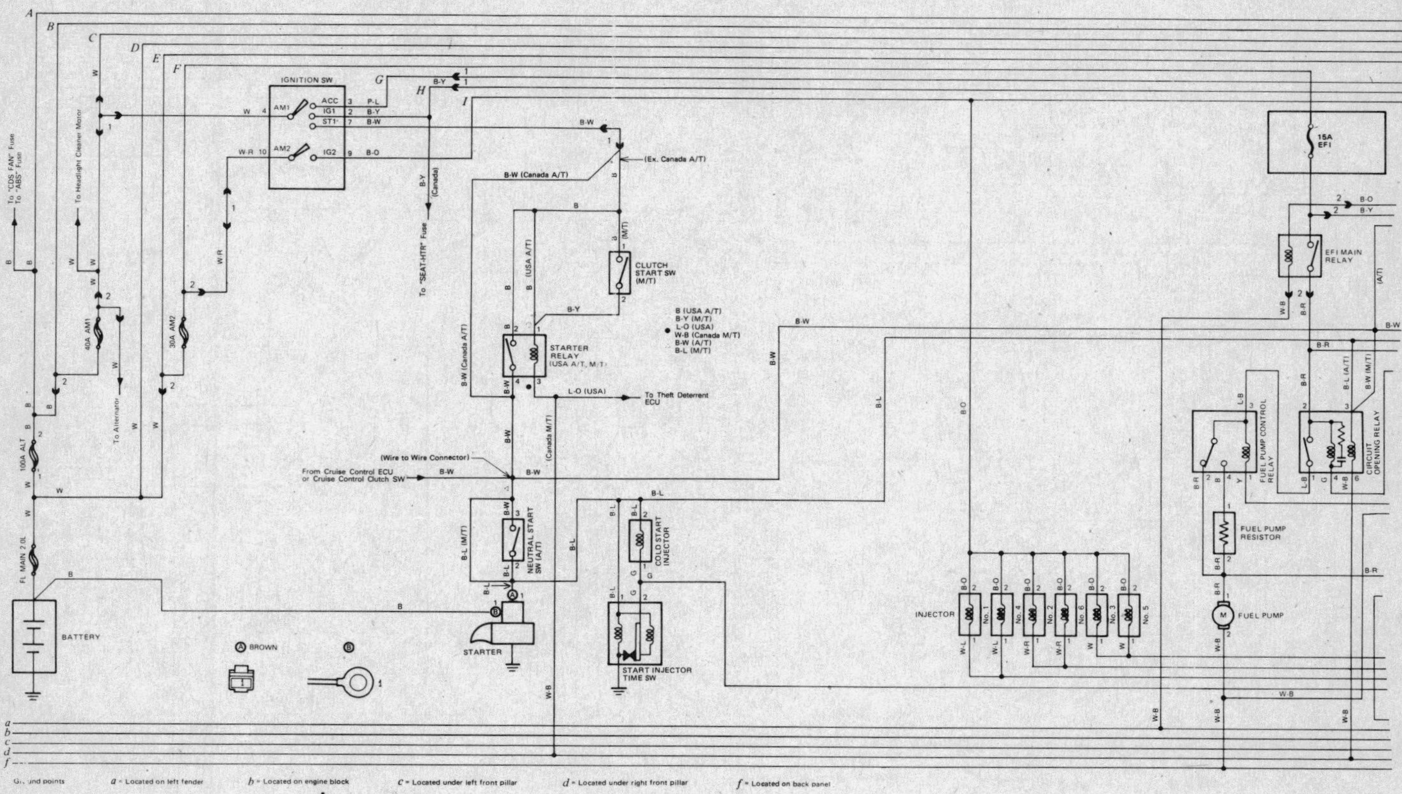

Power distribution, starting and engine control - 1992 models (1 of 2)

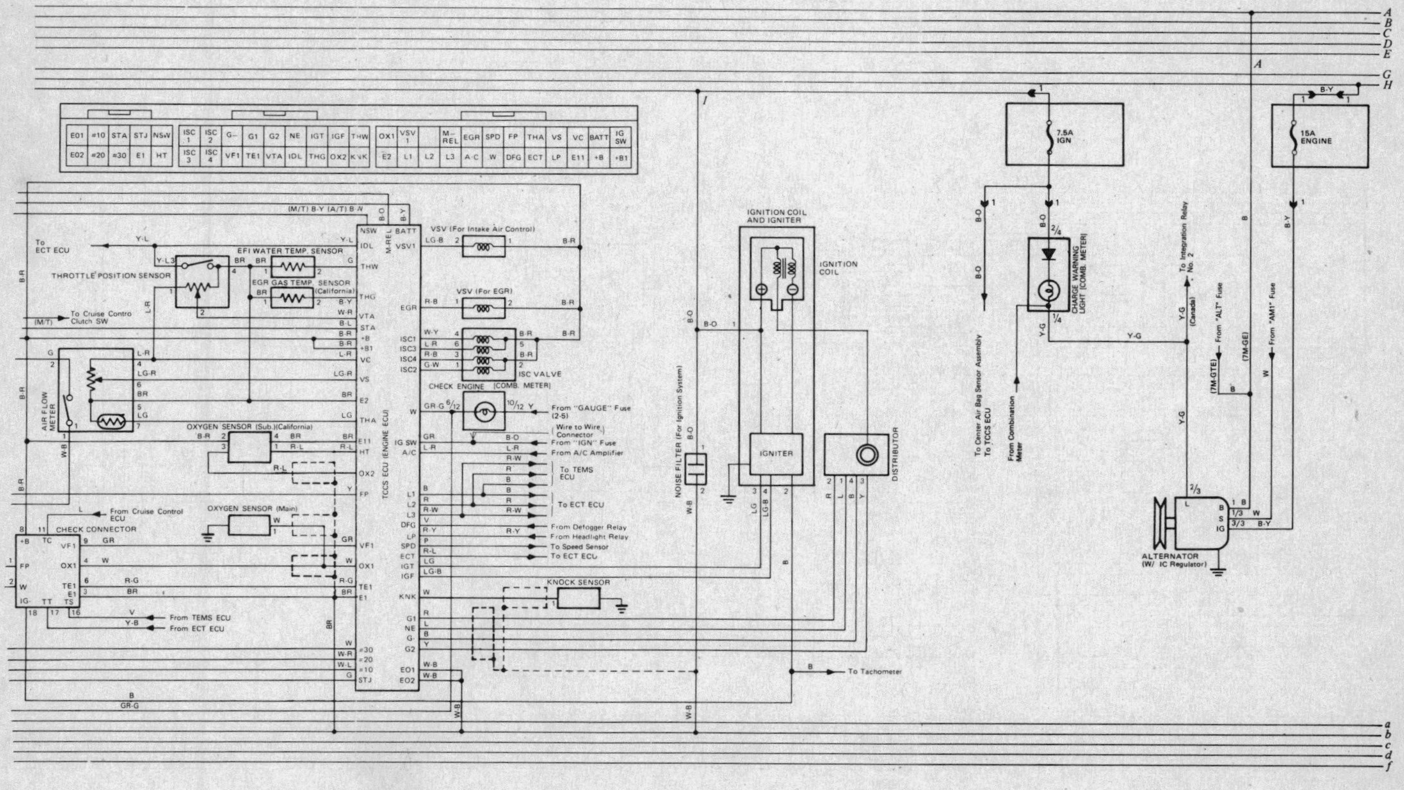

E01	#10	STA	STJ	NSW	ISC 1	ISC 2	G–	G1	G2	NE	IGT	IGF	THW	OX1	VSV 1		M–REL	EGR	SPD	FP	THA	VS	VC	BATT	IG SW
E02	#20	#30	E1	HT	ISC 3	ISC 4	VF1	TE1	VTA	IDL	THG	OX2	KNK	E2	L1	L2	L3	A·C	W	DFG	ECT	LP	E11	+B	+B1

Power distribution, starting and engine control - 1992 models (2 of 2)

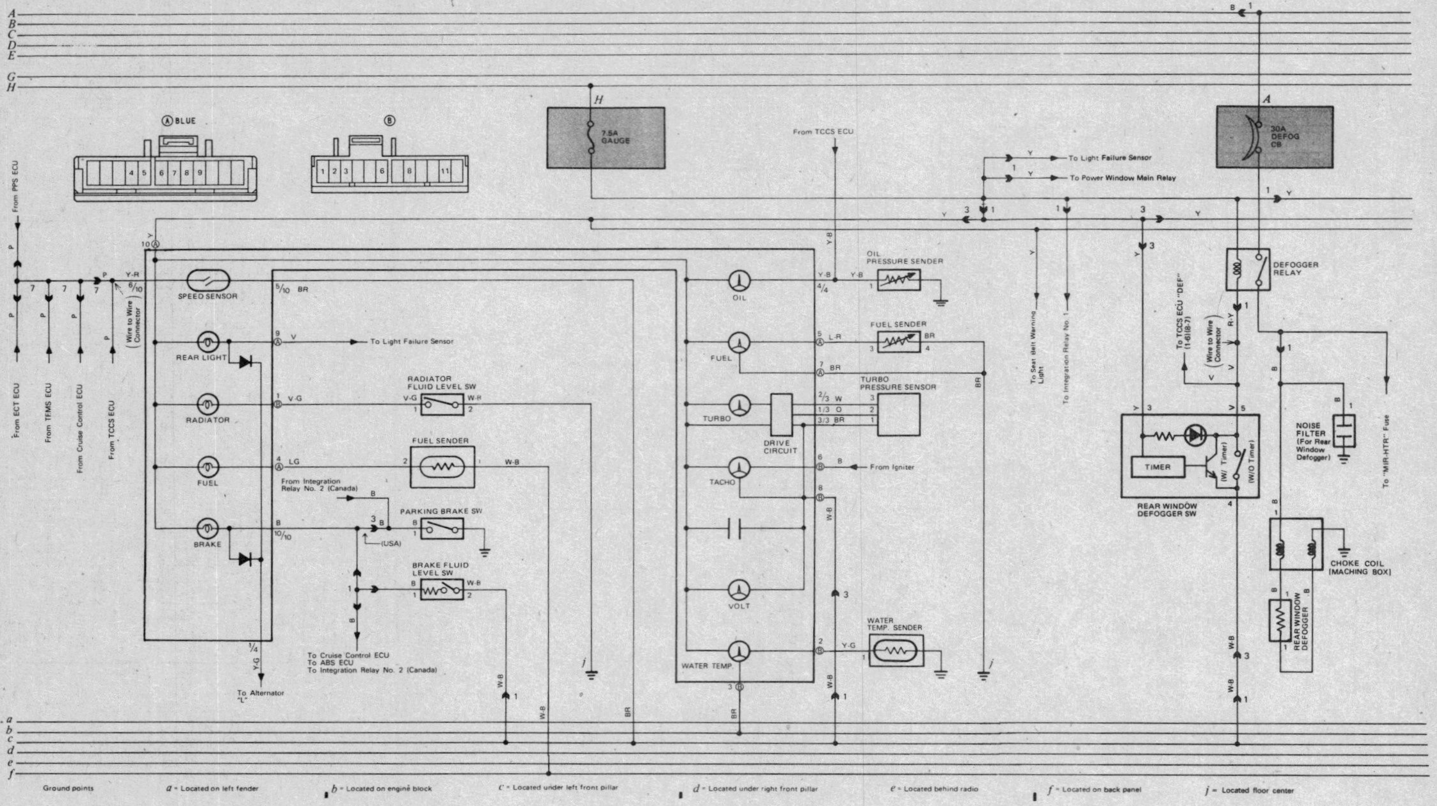

Combination meter, back-up light, rear window defogger and ECT system - 1992 models (1 of 2)

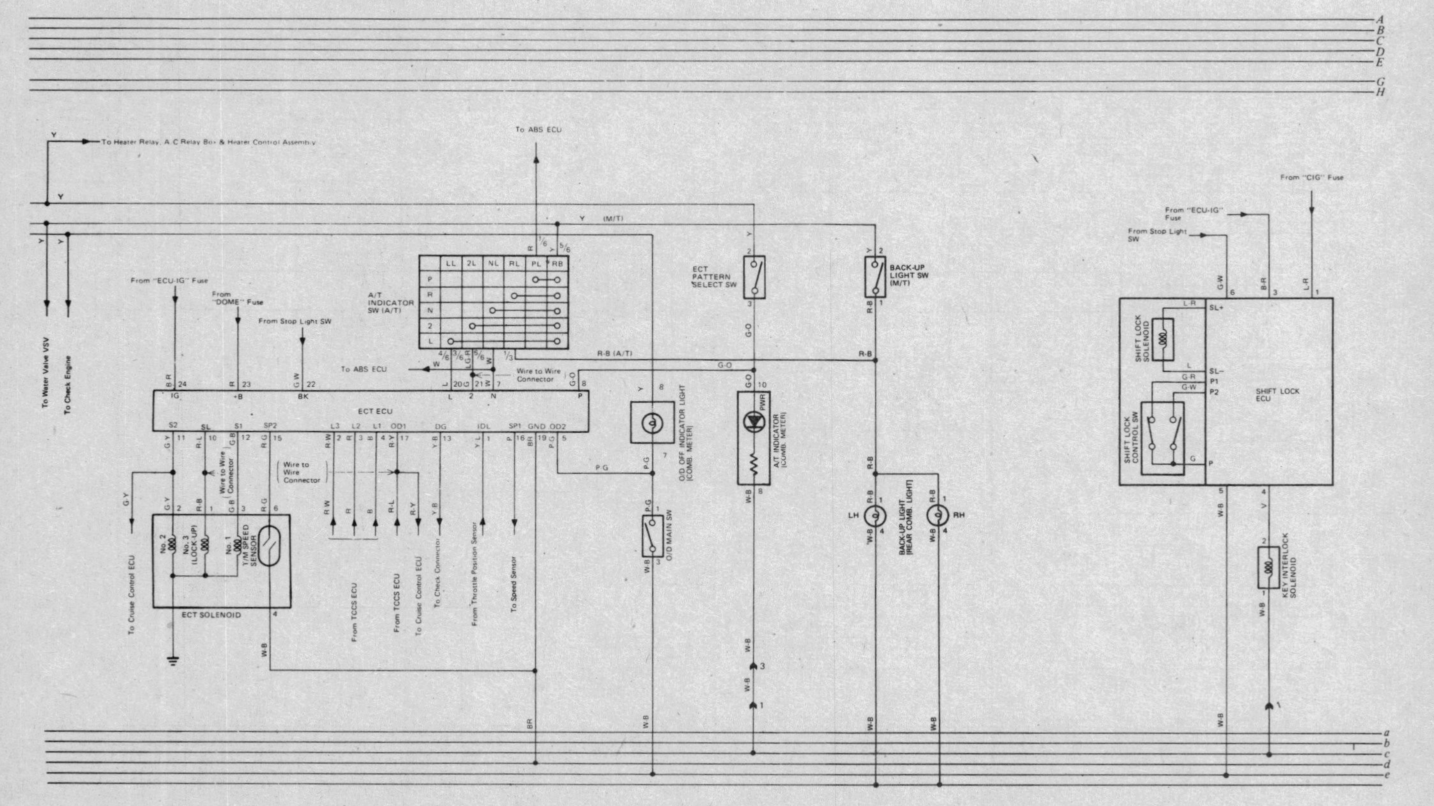

Combination meter, back-up light, rear window defogger and ECT system - 1992 models (2 of 2)

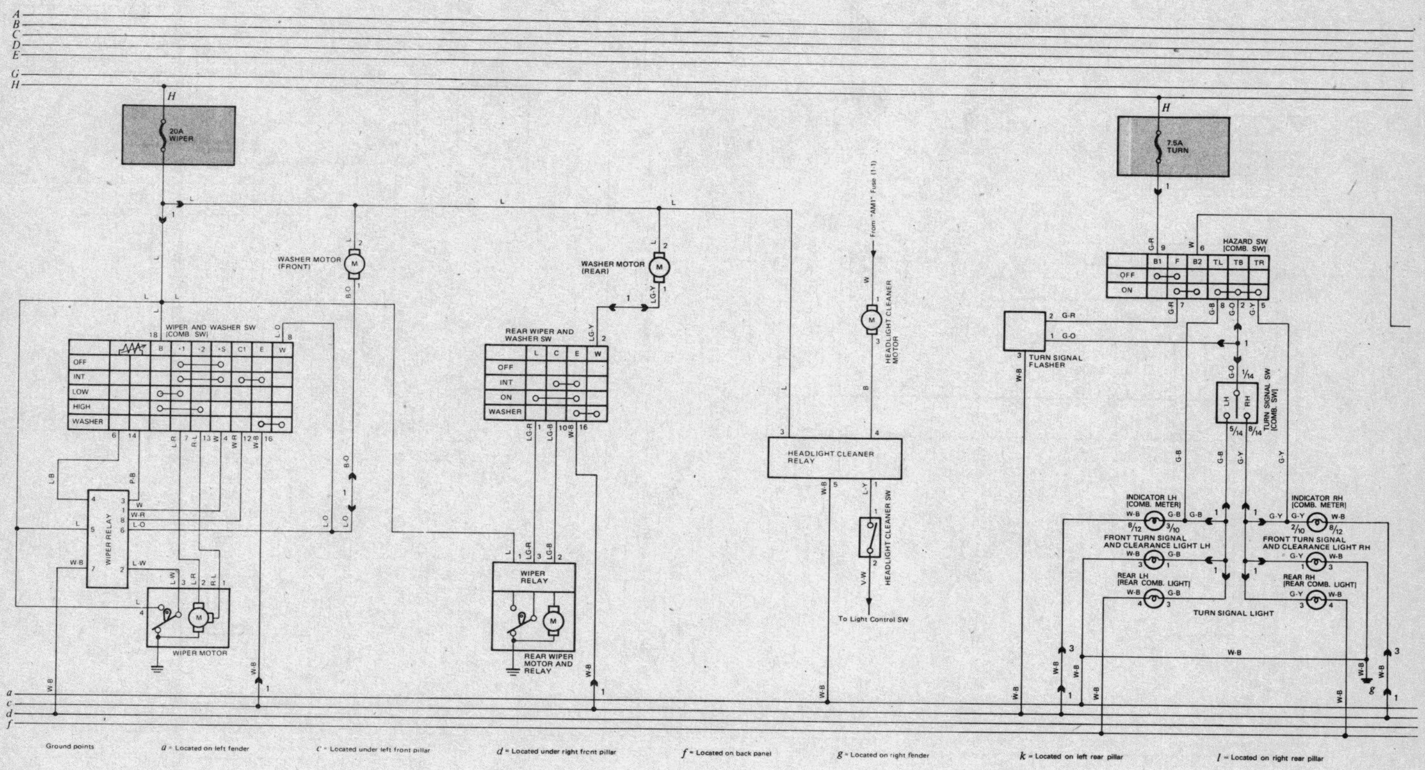

Front and rear wiper, horn, turn signal and hazard, headlight cleaner and TEMS system 1992 models (1 of 2)

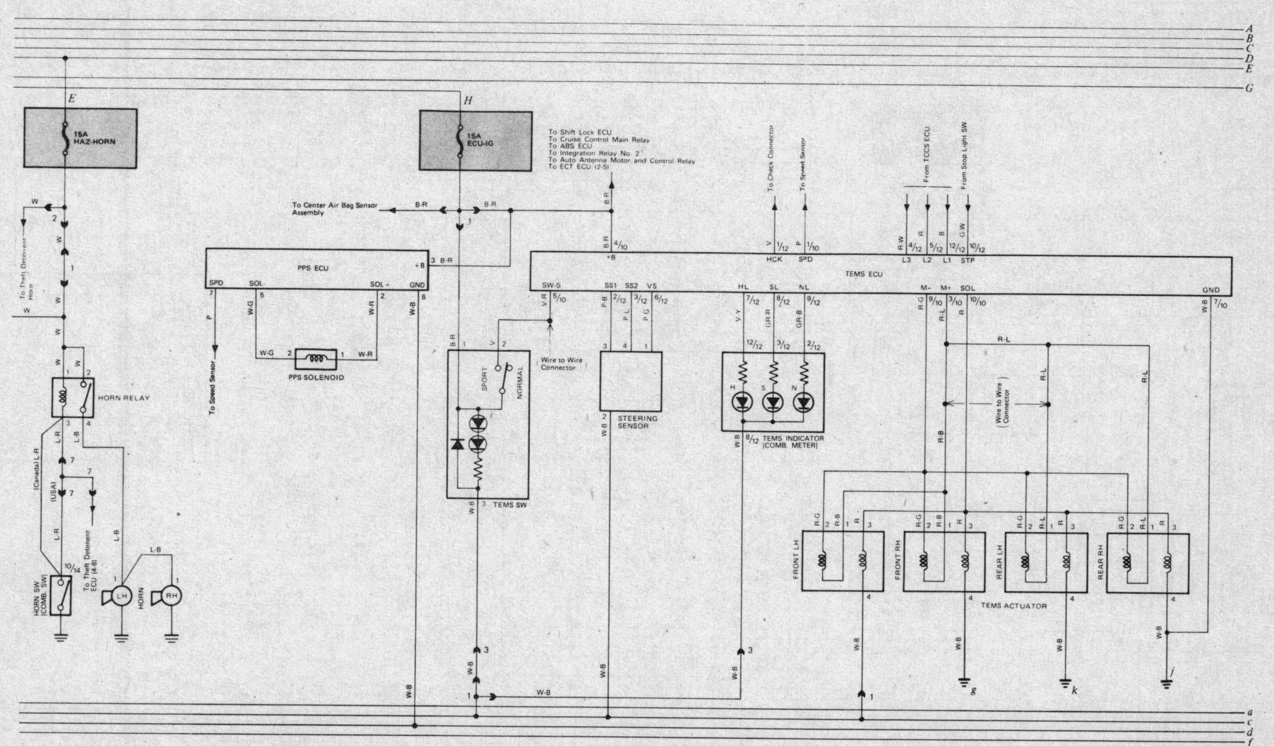

Front and rear wiper, horn, turn signal and hazard, headlight cleaner and TEMS system 1992 models (2 of 2)

12

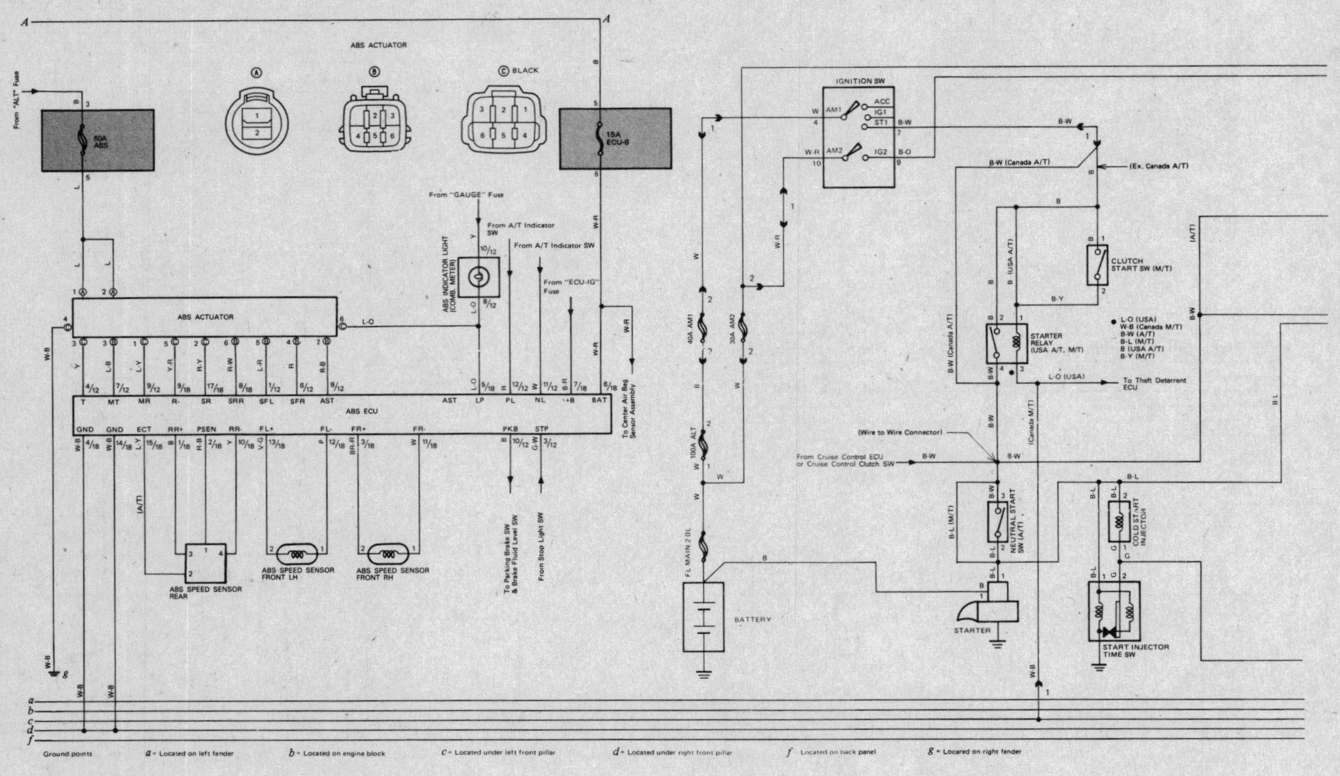

Power distribution, ABS, starting and engine control - 1992 turbo models (1 of 2)

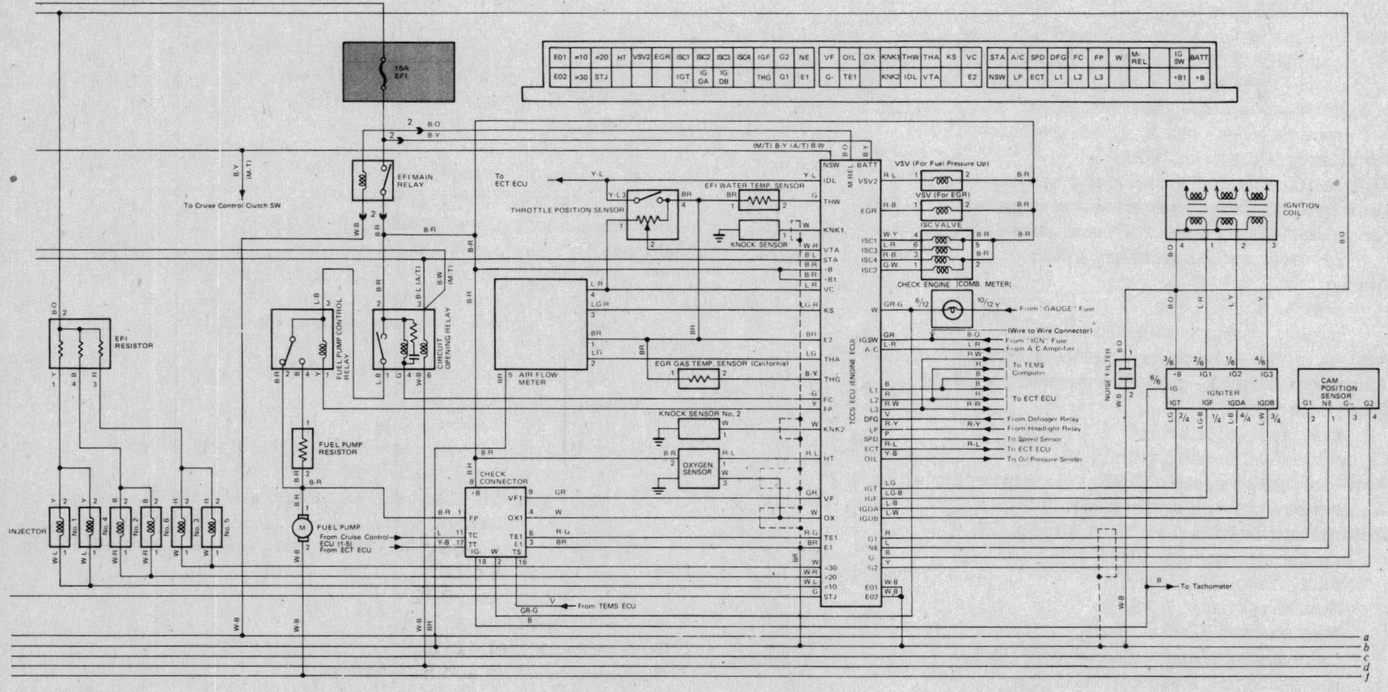

Power distribution, ABS, starting and engine control - 1992 turbo models (2 of 2)

Index

A

B

C

D

E

F

G

H

(6??) 437 7647 ?064

R

S

T

Haynes Automotive Manuals

NOTE: New manuals are added to this list on a periodic basis. If you do not see a listing for your vehicle, consult your local Haynes dealer for the latest product information.

ACURA
12020 **Integra** '86 thru '89 **& Legend** '86 thru '90
12021 **Integra** '90 thru '93 **& Legend** '91 thru '95

AMC
Jeep CJ - *see JEEP (50020)*
14020 **Mid-size models** '70 thru '83
14025 **(Renault) Alliance & Encore** '83 thru '87

AUDI
15020 **4000** all models '80 thru '87
15025 **5000** all models '77 thru '83
15026 **5000** all models '84 thru '88

AUSTIN-HEALEY
Sprite - *see MG Midget (66015)*

BMW
*18020 **3/5 Series** not including diesel or all-wheel drive models '82 thru '92
18021 **3-Series** incl. Z3 models '92 thru '98
18025 **320i** all 4 cyl models '75 thru '83
18050 **1500 thru 2002** except Turbo '59 thru '77

BUICK
*19010 **Buick Century** '97 thru '02
Century (front-wheel drive) - *see GM (38005)*
*19020 **Buick, Oldsmobile & Pontiac Full-size (Front-wheel drive)** '85 thru '02
Buick Electra, LeSabre and Park Avenue; **Oldsmobile** Delta 88 Royale, Ninety Eight and Regency; **Pontiac** Bonneville
19025 **Buick Oldsmobile & Pontiac Full-size (Rear wheel drive)**
Buick Estate '70 thru '90, Electra'70 thru '84, LeSabre '70 thru '85, Limited '74 thru '79
Oldsmobile Custom Cruiser '70 thru '90, Delta 88 '70 thru '85,Ninety-eight '70 thru '84
Pontiac Bonneville '70 thru '81, Catalina '70 thru '81, Grandville '70 thru '75, Parisienne '83 thru '86
19030 **Mid-size Regal & Century** all rear-drive models with V6, V8 and Turbo '74 thru '87
Regal - *see GENERAL MOTORS (38010)*
Riviera - *see GENERAL MOTORS (38030)*
Roadmaster - *see CHEVROLET (24046)*
Skyhawk - *see GENERAL MOTORS (38015)*
Skylark - *see GM (38020, 38025)*
Somerset - *see GENERAL MOTORS (38025)*

CADILLAC
21030 **Cadillac Rear Wheel Drive** all gasoline models '70 thru '93
Cimarron - *see GENERAL MOTORS (38015)*
DeVille - *see GM (38031 & 38032)*
Eldorado - *see GM (38030 & 38031)*
Fleetwood - *see GM (38031)*
Seville - *see GM (38030, 38031 & 38032)*

CHEVROLET
*24010 **Astro & GMC Safari Mini-vans** '85 thru '02
24015 **Camaro V8** all models '70 thru '81
24016 **Camaro** all models '82 thru '92
24017 **Camaro & Firebird** '93 thru '00
Cavalier - *see GENERAL MOTORS (38016)*
Celebrity - *see GENERAL MOTORS (38005)*
24020 **Chevelle, Malibu & El Camino** '69 thru '87
24024 **Chevette & Pontiac T1000** '76 thru '87
Citation - *see GENERAL MOTORS (38020)*
24032 **Corsica/Beretta** all models '87 thru '96
24040 **Corvette** all V8 models '68 thru '82
24041 **Corvette** all models '84 thru '96
10305 **Chevrolet Engine Overhaul Manual**
24045 **Full-size Sedans** Caprice, Impala, Biscayne, Bel Air & Wagons '69 thru '90
24046 **Impala SS & Caprice and Buick Roadmaster** '91 thru '96
Impala - *see LUMINA (24048)*
Lumina '90 thru '94 - *see GM (38010)*
*24048 **Lumina & Monte Carlo** '95 thru '01
Lumina APV - *see GM (38035)*
24050 **Luv Pick-up** all 2WD & 4WD '72 thru '82
Malibu '97 thru '00 - *see GM (38026)*
24055 **Monte Carlo** all models '70 thru '88
Monte Carlo '95 thru '01 - *see LUMINA (24048)*
24059 **Nova** all V8 models '69 thru '79
24060 **Nova and Geo Prizm** '85 thru '92
24064 **Pick-ups '67 thru '87** - Chevrolet & GMC, all V8 & in-line 6 cyl, 2WD & 4WD '67 thru '87; Suburbans, Blazers & Jimmys '67 thru '91
24065 **Pick-ups '88 thru '98** - Chevrolet & GMC, full-size pick-ups '88 thru '98, C/K Classic '99 & '00, Blazer & Jimmy '92 thru '94; Suburban '92 thru '99; Tahoe & Yukon '95 thru '99
*24066 **Pick-ups '99 thru '01** - Chevrolet Silverado & GMC Sierra full-size pick-ups '99 thru '01, Suburban/Tahoe/Yukon/Yukon XL '00 thru '01
24070 **S-10 & S-15 Pick-ups** '82 thru '93, **Blazer & Jimmy** '83 thru '94,
*24071 **S-10 & S-15 Pick-ups** '94 thru '01, **Blazer & Jimmy** '95 thru '01, **Hombre** '96 thru '01
24075 **Sprint** '85 thru '88 **& Geo Metro** '89 thru '01
24080 **Vans - Chevrolet & GMC** '68 thru '96

CHRYSLER
25015 **Chrysler Cirrus, Dodge Stratus, Plymouth Breeze** '95 thru '00
10310 **Chrysler Engine Overhaul Manual**
25020 **Full-size Front-Wheel Drive** '88 thru '93
K-Cars - *see DODGE Aries (30008)*
Laser - *see DODGE Daytona (30030)*
25025 **Chrysler LHS, Concorde, New Yorker, Dodge** Intrepid, **Eagle** Vision, '93 thru '97
*25026 **Chrysler LHS, Concorde, 300M, Dodge** Intrepid, '98 thru '03
25030 **Chrysler & Plymouth Mid-size** front wheel drive '82 thru '95
Rear-wheel Drive - *see Dodge (30050)*
*25035 **PT Cruiser** all models '01 thru '03
*25040 **Chrysler** Sebring, **Dodge** Avenger '95 thru '02

DATSUN
28005 **200SX** all models '80 thru '83
28007 **B-210** all models '73 thru '78
28009 **210** all models '79 thru '82
28012 **240Z, 260Z & 280Z** Coupe '70 thru '78
28014 **280ZX** Coupe & 2+2 '79 thru '83
300ZX - *see NISSAN (72010)*
28016 **310** all models '78 thru '82
28018 **510 & PL521 Pick-up** '68 thru '73
28020 **510** all models '78 thru '81
28022 **620 Series Pick-up** all models '73 thru '79
720 Series Pick-up - *see NISSAN (72030)*
28025 **810/Maxima** all gasoline models, '77 thru '84

DODGE
400 & 600 - *see CHRYSLER (25030)*
30008 **Aries & Plymouth Reliant** '81 thru '89
30010 **Caravan & Plymouth Voyager** '84 thru '95
*30011 **Caravan & Plymouth Voyager** '96 thru '02
30012 **Challenger/Plymouth Saporro** '78 thru '83
30016 **Colt & Plymouth Champ** '78 thru '87
30020 **Dakota Pick-ups** all models '87 thru '96
*30021 **Durango** '98 & '99, **Dakota** '97 thru '99
30025 **Dart, Demon, Plymouth Barracuda, Duster & Valiant** 6 cyl models '67 thru '76
30030 **Daytona & Chrysler Laser** '84 thru '89
Intrepid - *see CHRYSLER (25025, 25026)*
*30034 **Neon** all models '95 thru '99
30035 **Omni & Plymouth Horizon** '78 thru '90
30040 **Pick-ups** all full-size models '74 thru '93
*30041 **Pick-ups** all full-size models '94 thru '01
30045 **Ram 50/D50 Pick-ups & Raider and Plymouth Arrow Pick-ups** '79 thru '93
30050 **Dodge/Plymouth/Chrysler** RWD '71 thru '89
30055 **Shadow & Plymouth Sundance** '87 thru '94
30060 **Spirit & Plymouth Acclaim** '89 thru '95
*30065 **Vans - Dodge & Plymouth** '71 thru '03

EAGLE
Talon - *see MITSUBISHI (68030, 68031)*
Vision - *see CHRYSLER (25025)*

FIAT
34010 **124 Sport Coupe & Spider** '68 thru '78
34025 **X1/9** all models '74 thru '80

FORD
10355 **Ford Automatic Transmission Overhaul**
36004 **Aerostar Mini-vans** all models '86 thru '97
36006 **Contour & Mercury Mystique** '95 thru '00
36008 **Courier Pick-up** all models '72 thru '82
*36012 **Crown Victoria & Mercury Grand Marquis** '88 thru '00
10320 **Ford Engine Overhaul Manual**
36016 **Escort/Mercury Lynx** all models '81 thru '90
36020 **Escort/Mercury Tracer** '91 thru '00
36024 **Explorer & Mazda Navajo** '91 thru '01
36028 **Fairmont & Mercury Zephyr** '78 thru '83
36030 **Festiva & Aspire** '88 thru '97
36032 **Fiesta** all models '77 thru '80
*36034 **Focus** all models '00 and '01
36036 **Ford & Mercury Full-size** '75 thru '87
36040 **Granada & Mercury Monarch** '75 thru '80
36044 **Ford & Mercury Mid-size** '75 thru '86
36048 **Mustang V8** all models '64-1/2 thru '73
36049 **Mustang II** 4 cyl, V6 & V8 models '74 thru '78
36050 **Mustang & Mercury Capri** all models Mustang, '79 thru '93; Capri, '79 thru '86
*36051 **Mustang** all models '94 thru '03
36054 **Pick-ups & Bronco** '73 thru '79
36058 **Pick-ups & Bronco** '80 thru '96
*36059 **F-150 & Expedition** '97 thru '02, **F-250** '97 thru '99 **& Lincoln Navigator** '98 thru '02
*36060 **Super Duty Pick-ups, Excursion** '97 thru '02
36062 **Pinto & Mercury Bobcat** '75 thru '80
36066 **Probe** all models '89 thru '92
36070 **Ranger/Bronco II** gasoline models '83 thru '92
*36071 **Ranger** '93 thru '00 & **Mazda Pick-ups** '94 thru '00
36074 **Taurus & Mercury Sable** '86 thru '95
*36075 **Taurus & Mercury Sable** '96 thru '01
36078 **Tempo & Mercury Topaz** '84 thru '94
36082 **Thunderbird/Mercury Cougar** '83 thru '88
36086 **Thunderbird/Mercury Cougar** '89 and '97
36090 **Vans** all V8 Econoline models '69 thru '91
*36094 **Vans** full size '92 thru '01
*36097 **Windstar Mini-van** '95 thru '03

GENERAL MOTORS
10360 **GM Automatic Transmission Overhaul**
38005 **Buick Century, Chevrolet Celebrity, Oldsmobile Cutlass Ciera & Pontiac 6000** all models '82 thru '96
*38010 **Buick Regal, Chevrolet Lumina, Oldsmobile Cutlass Supreme & Pontiac Grand Prix** (FWD) '88 thru '02
38015 **Buick Skyhawk, Cadillac Cimarron, Chevrolet Cavalier, Oldsmobile Firenza & Pontiac J-2000 & Sunbird** '82 thru '94
*38016 **Chevrolet Cavalier & Pontiac Sunfire** '95 thru '01
38020 **Buick Skylark, Chevrolet Citation, Olds Omega, Pontiac Phoenix** '80 thru '85
38025 **Buick Skylark & Somerset, Oldsmobile Achieva & Calais and Pontiac Grand Am** all models '85 thru '98
*38026 **Chevrolet Malibu, Olds Alero & Cutlass, Pontiac Grand Am** '97 thru '00
38030 **Cadillac Eldorado** '71 thru '85, **Seville** '80 thru '85, **Oldsmobile** Toronado '71 thru '85, **Buick Riviera** '79 thru '85
*38031 **Cadillac Eldorado & Seville** '86 thru '91, **DeVille** '86 thru '93, **Fleetwood & Olds** Toronado '86 thru '92, **Buick Riviera** '86 thru '93
38032 **Cadillac DeVille** '94 thru '02 **& Seville** - '92 thru '02
38035 **Chevrolet Lumina APV, Olds Silhouette & Pontiac Trans Sport** all models '90 thru '96
*38036 **Chevrolet Venture, Olds Silhouette, Pontiac Trans Sport & Montana** '97 thru '01
General Motors Full-size Rear-wheel Drive - see BUICK (19025)

GEO
Metro - *see CHEVROLET Sprint (24075)*
Prizm - *'85 thru '92 see CHEVY (24060), '93 thru '02 see TOYOTA Corolla (92036)*

(Continued on other side)

** Listings shown with an asterisk (*) indicate model coverage as of this printing. These titles will be periodically updated to include later model years - consult your Haynes dealer for more information.*

Haynes North America, Inc., 861 Lawrence Drive, Newbury Park, CA 91320-1514 • (805) 498-6703

Haynes Automotive Manuals (continued)

NOTE: New manuals are added to this list on a periodic basis. If you do not see a listing for your vehicle, consult your local Haynes dealer for the latest product information.

40030 **Storm** all models '90 thru '93
Tracker - *see SUZUKI Samurai (90010)*

GMC

Vans & Pick-ups - *see CHEVROLET*

HONDA

42010 **Accord CVCC** all models '76 thru '83
42011 **Accord** all models '84 thru '89
42012 **Accord** all models '90 thru '93
42013 **Accord** all models '94 thru '97
*42014 **Accord** all models '98 and '99
42020 **Civic 1200** all models '73 thru '79
42021 **Civic 1300 & 1500 CVCC** '80 thru '83
42022 **Civic 1500 CVCC** all models '75 thru '79
42023 **Civic** all models '84 thru '91
42024 **Civic & del Sol** '92 thru '95
*42025 **Civic** '96 thru '00, **CR-V** '97 thru '00, **Acura Integra** '94 thru '00
42040 **Prelude CVCC** all models '79 thru '89

HYUNDAI

*43010 **Elantra** all models '96 thru '01
43015 **Excel & Accent** all models '86 thru '98

ISUZU

Hombre - *see CHEVROLET S-10 (24071)*
*47017 **Rodeo** '91 thru '02; **Amigo** '89 thru '94 and '98 thru '02; **Honda Passport** '95 thru '02
47020 **Trooper & Pick-up** '81 thru '93

JAGUAR

49010 **XJ6** all 6 cyl models '68 thru '86
49011 **XJ6** all models '88 thru '94
49015 **XJ12 & XJS** all 12 cyl models '72 thru '85

JEEP

50010 **Cherokee, Comanche & Wagoneer Limited** all models '84 thru '00
50020 **CJ** all models '49 thru '86
*50025 **Grand Cherokee** all models '93 thru '00
50029 **Grand Wagoneer & Pick-up** '72 thru '91 Grand Wagoneer '84 thru '91, Cherokee & Wagoneer '72 thru '83, Pick-up '72 thru '88
*50030 **Wrangler** all models '87 thru '00

LEXUS

ES 300 - *see TOYOTA Camry (92007)*

LINCOLN

Navigator - *see FORD Pick-up (36059)*
*59010 **Rear-Wheel Drive** all models '70 thru '01

MAZDA

61010 **GLC Hatchback (rear-wheel drive)** '77 thru '83
61011 **GLC (front-wheel drive)** '81 thru '85
61015 **323 & Protogé** '90 thru '00
*61016 **MX-5 Miata** '90 thru '97
61020 **MPV** all models '89 thru '94
Navajo - *see Ford Explorer (36024)*
61030 **Pick-ups** '72 thru '93
Pick-ups '94 thru '00 - *see Ford Ranger (36071)*
61035 **RX-7** all models '79 thru '85
61036 **RX-7** all models '86 thru '91
61040 **626** (rear-wheel drive) all models '79 thru '82
61041 **626/MX-6 (front-wheel drive)** '83 thru '91
61042 **626** '93 thru '01, **MX-6/Ford Probe** '93 thru '97

MERCEDES-BENZ

63012 **123 Series Diesel** '76 thru '85
63015 **190 Series** four-cyl gas models, '84 thru '88
63020 **230/250/280** 6 cyl sohc models '68 thru '72
63025 **280 123 Series** gasoline models '77 thru '81
63030 **350 & 450** all models '71 thru '80

MERCURY

64200 **Villager & Nissan Quest** '93 thru '01
All other titles, see FORD Listing.

MG

66010 **MGB** Roadster & GT Coupe '62 thru '80
66015 **MG Midget, Austin Healey Sprite** '58 thru '80

MITSUBISHI

68020 **Cordia, Tredia, Galant, Precis & Mirage** '83 thru '93
68030 **Eclipse, Eagle Talon & Ply. Laser** '90 thru '94
*68031 **Eclipse** '95 thru '01, **Eagle Talon** '95 thru '98
68040 **Pick-up** '83 thru '96 **& Montero** '83 thru '93

NISSAN

72010 **300ZX** all models including Turbo '84 thru '89
72015 **Altima** all models '93 thru '01
72020 **Maxima** all models '85 thru '92
*72021 **Maxima** all models '93 thru '01
72030 **Pick-ups** '80 thru '97 **Pathfinder** '87 thru '95
*72031 **Frontier Pick-up** '98 thru '01, **Xterra** '00 & '01, **Pathfinder** '96 thru '01
72040 **Pulsar** all models '83 thru '86
Quest - *see MERCURY Villager (64200)*
72050 **Sentra** all models '82 thru '94
72051 **Sentra & 200SX** all models '95 thru '99
72060 **Stanza** all models '82 thru '90

OLDSMOBILE

73015 **Cutlass** V6 & V8 gas models '74 thru '88
For other OLDSMOBILE titles, see BUICK, CHEVROLET or GENERAL MOTORS listing.

PLYMOUTH

For PLYMOUTH titles, see DODGE listing.

PONTIAC

79008 **Fiero** all models '84 thru '88
79018 **Firebird** V8 models except Turbo '70 thru '81
79019 **Firebird** all models '82 thru '92
79040 **Mid-size Rear-wheel Drive** '70 thru '87
For other PONTIAC titles, see BUICK, CHEVROLET or GENERAL MOTORS listing.

PORSCHE

80020 **911** except Turbo & Carrera 4 '65 thru '89
80025 **914** all 4 cyl models '69 thru '76
80030 **924** all models including Turbo '76 thru '82
80035 **944** all models including Turbo '83 thru '89

RENAULT

Alliance & Encore - *see AMC (14020)*

SAAB

*84010 **900** all models including Turbo '79 thru '88

SATURN

*87010 **Saturn** all models '91 thru '02

SUBARU

89002 **1100, 1300, 1400 & 1600** '71 thru '79
89003 **1600 & 1800** 2WD & 4WD '80 thru '94

SUZUKI

90010 **Samurai/Sidekick & Geo Tracker** '86 thru '01

TOYOTA

92005 **Camry** all models '83 thru '91
92006 **Camry** all models '92 thru '96
*92007 **Camry, Avalon, Solara, Lexus ES 300** '97 thru '01
92015 **Celica Rear Wheel Drive** '71 thru '85
92020 **Celica Front Wheel Drive** '86 thru '99
92025 **Celica Supra** all models '79 thru '92
92030 **Corolla** all models '75 thru '79
92032 **Corolla** all rear wheel drive models '80 thru '87
92035 **Corolla** all front wheel drive models '84 thru '92
92036 **Corolla & Geo Prizm** '93 thru '02
92040 **Corolla Tercel** all models '80 thru '82
92045 **Corona** all models '74 thru '82
92050 **Cressida** all models '78 thru '82
92055 **Land Cruiser** FJ40, 43, 45, 55 '68 thru '82
92056 **Land Cruiser** FJ60, 62, 80, FZJ80 '80 thru '96
92065 **MR2** all models '85 thru '87
92070 **Pick-up** all models '69 thru '78
92075 **Pick-up** all models '79 thru '95
*92076 **Tacoma** '95 thru '00, **4Runner** '96 thru '00, **& T100** '93 thru '98
*92078 **Tundra** '00 thru '02 **& Sequoia** '01 thru '02
92080 **Previa** all models '91 thru '95
*92082 **RAV4** all models '96 thru '02
92085 **Tercel** all models '87 thru '94

TRIUMPH

94007 **Spitfire** all models '62 thru '81
94010 **TR7** all models '75 thru '81

VW

96008 **Beetle & Karmann Ghia** '54 thru '79
*96009 **New Beetle** '98 thru '00
96016 **Rabbit, Jetta, Scirocco & Pick-up** gas models '74 thru '91 & Convertible '80 thru '92
96017 **Golf, GTI & Jetta** '93 thru '98 **& Cabrio** '95 thru '98
*96018 **Golf, GTI, Jetta & Cabrio** '99 thru '02
96020 **Rabbit, Jetta & Pick-up** diesel '77 thru '84
96023 **Passat** '98 thru '01, **Audi A4** '96 thru '01
96030 **Transporter 1600** all models '68 thru '79
96035 **Transporter 1700, 1800 & 2000** '72 thru '79
96040 **Type 3 1500 & 1600** all models '63 thru '73
96045 **Vanagon** all air-cooled models '80 thru '83

VOLVO

97010 **120, 130 Series & 1800 Sports** '61 thru '73
97015 **140 Series** all models '66 thru '74
97020 **240 Series** all models '76 thru '93
97040 **740 & 760 Series** all models '82 thru '88
97050 **850 Series** all models '93 thru '97

TECHBOOK MANUALS

10205 **Automotive Computer Codes**
10210 **Automotive Emissions Control Manual**
10215 **Fuel Injection Manual, 1978 thru 1985**
10220 **Fuel Injection Manual, 1986 thru 1999**
10225 **Holley Carburetor Manual**
10230 **Rochester Carburetor Manual**
10240 **Weber/Zenith/Stromberg/SU Carburetors**
10305 **Chevrolet Engine Overhaul Manual**
10310 **Chrysler Engine Overhaul Manual**
10320 **Ford Engine Overhaul Manual**
10330 **GM and Ford Diesel Engine Repair Manual**
10340 **Small Engine Repair Manual,** 5 HP & Less
10341 **Small Engine Repair Manual,** 5.5 - 20 HP
10345 **Suspension, Steering & Driveline Manual**
10355 **Ford Automatic Transmission Overhaul**
10360 **GM Automatic Transmission Overhaul**
10405 **Automotive Body Repair & Painting**
10410 **Automotive Brake Manual**
10411 **Automotive Anti-lock Brake (ABS) Systems**
10415 **Automotive Detaiing Manual**
10420 **Automotive Eelectrical Manual**
10425 **Automotive Heating & Air Conditioning**
10430 **Automotive Reference Manual & Dictionary**
10435 **Automotive Tools Manual**
10440 **Used Car Buying Guide**
10445 **Welding Manual**
10450 **ATV Basics**

SPANISH MANUALS

98903 **Reparación de Carrocería & Pintura**
98905 **Códigos Automotrices de la Computadora**
98910 **Frenos Automotriz**
98915 **Inyección de Combustible 1986 al 1999**
99040 **Chevrolet & GMC Camionetas** '67 al '87 Incluye Suburban, Blazer & Jimmy '67 al '91
99041 **Chevrolet & GMC Camionetas** '88 al '98 Incluye Suburban '92 al '98, Blazer & Jimmy '92 al '94, Tahoe y Yukon '95 al '98
99042 **Chevrolet & GMC Camionetas Cerradas** '68 al '95
99055 **Dodge Caravan & Plymouth Voyager** '84 al '95
99075 **Ford Camionetas y Bronco** '80 al '94
99077 **Ford Camionetas Cerradas** '69 al '91
99083 **Ford Modelos de Tamaño Grande** '75 al '87
99088 **Ford Modelos de Tamaño Mediano** '75 al '86
99091 **Ford Taurus & Mercury Sable** '86 al '95
99095 **GM Modelos de Tamaño Grande** '70 al '90
99100 **GM Modelos de Tamaño Mediano** '70 al '88
99110 **Nissan Camioneta** '80 al '96, **Pathfinder** '87 al '95
99118 **Nissan Sentra** '82 al '94
99125 **Toyota Camionetas y 4Runner** '79 al '95

** Listings shown with an asterisk (*) indicate model coverage as of this printing. These titles will be periodically updated to include later model years - consult your Haynes dealer for more information.*

Over 100 Haynes motorcycle manuals also available

8-03

Haynes North America, Inc., 861 Lawrence Drive, Newbury Park, CA 91320-1514 • (805) 498-6703